University of
Hertfordshire

and Information Services

ning Resources Centre

HTML:
The Complete Reference

Third Edition

About the Author...

Thomas A. Powell has been professionally involved in the Internet community for more than 10 years. His career began at UCLA's PICnet, followed by several years at CERFnet, one of the first Internet service providers in the country. In 1994, he founded the Internet consultancy that eventually became PINT, Inc.,(www.pint.com), a well-known Web design and development firm headquartered in San Diego, California.

Beyond his various business interests, Powell is the author of numerous books on Web technology, including *Web Design: The Complete Reference*, *Web Site Engineering*, and *HTML Programmers Reference*. He has also written extensively on the subject for *Network World*, *IT World*, *NetGuide*, *Internet Week*, and *Interactive Age*.

Mr. Powell teaches Web publishing classes through the Information Technologies program at University of California San Diego, Extension and also is an instructor the UCSD Computer Science and Engineering Department. He holds a B.S. from UCLA and an M.S. in computer science from UCSD.

HTML:
The Complete Reference

Third Edition

Thomas A. Powell

Osborne/**McGraw-Hill**

Berkeley   New York   St. Louis   San Francisco
Auckland   Bogotá   Hamburg   London   Madrid
Mexico City   Milan   Montreal   New Delhi   Panama City
Paris   São Paulo   Singapore   Sydney
Tokyo   Toronto

Osborne/**McGraw-Hill**
2600 Tenth Street
Berkeley, California 94710
U.S.A.

For information on translations or book distributors outside the U.S.A., or to arrange bulk purchase discounts for sales promotions, premiums, or fund-raisers, please contact Osborne/**McGraw-Hill** at the above address.

HTML: The Complete Reference, Third Edition

1234567890 DOC DOC 01987654321

ISBN 0-07-212951-4

Publisher
  Brandon A. Nordin

Copy Editor
  Rachel Lopez

Vice President & Associate Publisher
  Scott Rogers

Proofreader
  Sossity Smith

Acquisitions Editor
  Megg Bonar

Indexer
  David Heiret

Project Editor
  Pamela Woolf

Computer Designers and Illustrators
  Black Hole Publishing

Acquisitions Coordinator
  Tim Madrid

Series Design
  Peter Hancik

Technical Editor
  Fritz Schneider

This book was composed with Corel VENTURA™ Publisher.

Contents

Part II

Core HTML

Part III

Presentation and Layout

Part IV

Programming and HTML

Part V

Site Delivery and Management

Part VI

Advanced Topics

Acknowledgments

The third edition of this book represents a significant rewrite of the content from previous editions. Many of the changes are because of the introduction of new technologies such as XHTML, but numerous fixes and improvements are directly due to the wonderful feedback from the many students I have had the pleasure of instructing at University of California, San Diego over the years, and from readers from all over the world who have sent me e-mail encouragement. You deserve my greatest appreciation.

I would also like to thank the many staff members at PINT (www.pint.com) who have helped me with my various projects over the years. PINT's HTML expert in residence, Dan Whitworth, once again was indispensable in getting this edition put together. The technical editor Fritz Schneider also deserves a great deal of credit helping me keep things straight on a variety of Web-related subjects. After reading this much about HTML I'm sure he wishes he never was my graduate teaching assistant now.

I also had plenty of help PINT staff members. Special thanks to Rob McFarlane who did many of the illustrations, as well as Anh Tran and Jason Zimmerman who helped with numerous scripting examples. PINT staffers Maria Defante, Eric Raether, Jimmy Tam, David Snow, Meredith Hodge, Cathleen Ryan, Cory Ducker, Reuben Poon, Kim Smith, Patrick Fischer, Peter Larson, Vergil Pascual, Matt Plotner, Michele Bedard,

Nigel Paxton and many others kept things in line while I was working. Special thanks as well goes to our summer intern Kate Grantham, who helped with much of the legwork required to update the massive appendix, and Daisy Bhonsle, who always made sure to find the hard to find errors.

All the folks at Osborne have been especially nice to work with. Megg Bonar in particular always tried to give me the motivation necessary to finish this, while Timothy Madrid, Cindy Wathen, and Pamela Woolf kept the editing and production running smoothly.

Finally, family and friends deserve special thanks for always being there for me. That especially means you, Sylvia and Diana. After five books, many with numerous editions and updates, they must start to think I never stop writing. They must be getting tired of all the chilidog deliveries and other requests from pesky writers. I just hope they won't get too grumpy if I take on another one.

Thomas A. Powell
tpowell@pint.com
November 2000

The Complete Reference

Part I

Introduction

Chapter 1

Introduction to HTML and XHTML

ypertext Markup Language (HTML) is the text markup language currently used on the World Wide Web. If you have ever written a school report or business memo, you have encountered text markup. Your documents probably came back to you covered in red ink, courtesy of your teacher or boss. The symbols and acronyms used in those editorial markups suggested changes for you to interpret or implement. In that scenario, markup is separate from the actual content of your document. When you create a document with a word processing program such as Microsoft Word or WordPerfect, the program uses markup language to indicate the structure and formatting of that electronic document. What you see on your screen looks like a page of formatted text; the rest is done "behind the scenes." HTML is the not-so-behind-the-scenes markup language that is used to tell Web browsers how to structure and display Web pages.

First Look at HTML

In the case of HTML, markup commands directed to your Web-based content relay the structure of the document to the browser software and, where appropriate, indicate how you want the content to be displayed. For example, if you want to display a section of text in boldface, you surround the corresponding text with the boldface markup tags, **** and ****, as shown here:

```
<b>This is important text</b>
```

When the browser reads a document that has HTML markup in it, it determines how to render it onscreen by considering the HTML elements embedded within the document (see Figure 1-1). Be aware that browsers don't always render things in the way that you think they will. This is due partially to the design of HTML and partially to the differences in the variety of Web browsers currently in use.

An HTML document is simply a text file that contains the information you want to publish. It also contains embedded instructions, called *elements*, which indicate how a Web browser should structure or present the document. An element is made up of a start tag such as ****, and also might include an end tag, which is indicated by a slash within the tag such as ****. The tag pair should fully enclose any content to be affected by the element including text and other HTML markup. However, some HTML elements have optional close tags because their closure can be inferred. Other HTML elements, called *empty elements*, do not enclose any content, thus need no close tags at all. For example, to insert a line break we would use the **
** element, which is an empty element as it doesn't enclose any content and has no corresponding close tag.

The start tag of an HTML element might contain attributes that modify the meaning of the tag. The inclusion of the **noshade** attribute in the **<hr>** element shown here:

```
<hr noshade>
```

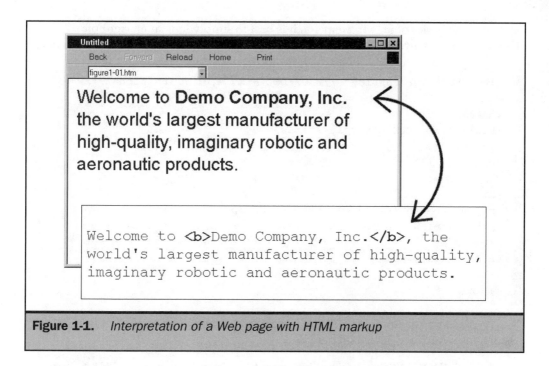

Figure 1-1.   *Interpretation of a Web page with HTML markup*

indicates that there should be no shading applied to the horizontal rule element. Most attributes require values that are set with an equal sign; these values should be enclosed within double or single quotes. For example,

```
<img src="logo.gif" alt="Demo Company" height="100" width="100">
```

specifies four attributes for the **<img>** element that are used to provide more information about the use of the included image. A complete overview of the structure of HTML elements is shown here:

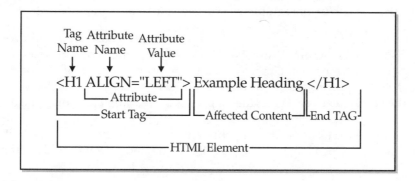

Given the basics of HTML elements it is best to simply look at an example document to see how they are used. Our first complete HTML example is shown here:

```
<!DOCTYPE HTML PUBLIC "-//W3C//DTD HTML 4.01 Transitional//EN">
<html>
<head>
<title>First HTML Example</title>
</head>
<body>
<h1>Welcome to the World of HTML</h1>
<hr>
<p>HTML <b>really</b> isn't so hard!</p>
<p>You can put in lots of text if you want to. In fact, you
could keep on typing and make up more sentences and continue
on and on.</p>
</body>
</html>
```

The preceding example uses some of the most common elements used in HTML documents, which are described here:

- The **<!DOCTYPE>** comment indicates the particular version of HTML being used in the document.

- The **<html>**, **<head>**, and **<body>** tag pairs are used to specify the general structure of the document.

- The **<title>** and **</title>** tag pair specifies the title of the document that generally appears in the title bar of the Web browser.

- The **<h1>** and **</h1>** header tag pair creates a headline indicating some important information.

- The **<hr>** element, which has no end tag, inserts a horizontal rule, or bar, across the screen.

- The **<p>** and **</p>** paragraph tag pair indicates a paragraph of text.

If you are using a text editor, you could type in the previous listing and save it with a filename such as "firstexample.htm" or "firstexample.html." For a browser to read your file properly, it must end either in the .htm or .html extension. If you don't save your file with the appropriate extension, the browser probably won't attempt to interpret the HTML markup. When this happens, the markup elements appear in the browser window as shown in Figure 1-2.

After you save the example file on your system, use your browser to open it by using the "Open," "Open Page," or "Open File" command which should be found on

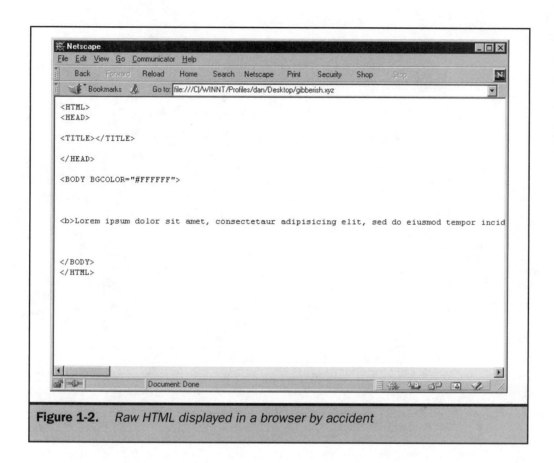

Figure 1-2.   *Raw HTML displayed in a browser by accident*

the browser's File menu. After your browser reads the file, it should render a page like the one shown in Figure 1-3.

If your page does not display properly, review your file to make sure that you typed the page correctly. If you find a mistake and make a change to the file, save the file, go back to your browser, and click the "Reload" or "Refresh" button. Sometimes the browser will still reload the page from its memory cache; if a page does not update correctly on reload, hold down the shift key while clicking the reload button, and the browser should re-fetch the page. Keeping the browser and text editor open simultaneously is a good idea, to avoid constantly reopening one or the other. Once you get the hang of HTML design, you'll see that, at this raw level, it is much like the edit, compile, and run cycle so familiar to programmers. This manual process probably isn't the way that you want to develop Web pages, because it can be tedious, error prone, and inefficient when thinking of visual design. For our current illustrative purposes, however, it works fine. Better approaches to HTML document creation will be discussed in Chapter 2.

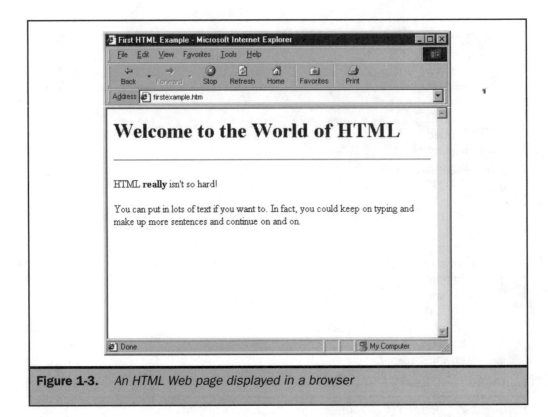

Figure 1-3.   *An HTML Web page displayed in a browser*

Based on the simple example just presented, you might surmise that learning HTML is merely a matter of learning the multitude of markup tags, such as **<b>**, that specify the format and structure of documents to browsers. While this certainly is an important first step, it trivializes the role HTML plays on the Web, and would be similar to trying to learn print publishing by understanding only the various commands available in Microsoft Word, while disregarding page layout, document structure, and output formats. Similarly on the Web, in addition to learning the various markup tags, you need to consider screen layout and visual design, programming facilities, navigation and interface design, and the method by which Web pages are actually delivered. These topics are discussed only to a limited degree in this book. Interested readers are encouraged to see *Web Design: The Complete Reference* (ISBN 007212297-8), which presents these topics and many others required for site creation. However, for now let's concern ourselves with understanding basic HTML syntax.

HTML: A Structured Language

HTML has a very well-defined syntax; all HTML documents should follow a formal structure. The *World Wide Web Consortium* (W3C) is the primary organization that attempts to standardize HTML (as well as many other technologies used on the Web). To provide a standard, the W3C must carefully specify all aspects of the technology. In the case of HTML, this means precisely defining the elements in the language. The W3C has defined HTML as an application of the *Standard Generalized Markup Language* (SGML). In short, SGML is a language used to define other languages by specifying the allowed document structure in the form of a *document type definition (DTD)*, which indicates the syntax that can be used for the various elements of a language such as HTML.

Note *In 1999 the W3C rewrote HTML as an application of XML (Extensible Markup Language) and renamed it XHTML. XML serves the same purpose as SGML: a language in which to write the rules of a language. For now we are going to only concern ourselves with traditional HTML, rather than XHTML. However, all discussions of markup will take into consideration the eventual migration toward XHTML, which is discussed later in this chapter.*

From the HTML 4.01 DTD, a basic template can be derived for a basic HTML document as shown here:

```
<!DOCTYPE HTML PUBLIC "-//W3C//DTD HTML 4.01 Transitional//EN">
<html>
<head>
<title>Document Title Goes Here</title>

...Head information describing the document and providing
supplementary information goes here....
</head>
<body>
...Document content and markup go here....

</body>
</html>
```

The first line of the template is the **<!DOCTYPE>** indicator, which shows the particular dialect of HTML being used. Within the **<html>** element, the basic structure of a document reveals two primary sections: the "head" and the "body." The head of the document, as indicated by the **<head>** element, contains various information describing the document such as its title. The body of the document, as indicated by the **<body>** element, contains the document itself with associated markup required for structure or presentation.

Alternatively, an HTML document might replace the **<body>** element with the **<frameset>** element, which encloses potentially numerous **<frame>** elements corresponding to individual portions of the browser window, termed *frames*. Each frame in turn would reference another HTML document containing either a standard document complete with **<html>**, **<head>**, and **<body>**, or perhaps another framed document. The **<frameset>** element also should include the **<noframes>** element that provides a version of the page for browsers that do not support frames. Within this element occurs the **<body>** tag for non-frame–supporting browsers. An example template for a frameset document is shown here. Note that the DTD for a framed document is different from that of a normal document.

```
<!DOCTYPE HTML PUBLIC "-//W3C//DTD HTML 4.01 Frameset//EN">
<html>
<head>
<title>Document Title Goes Here</title>

...Head information describing the frameset and providing
supplementary information goes here...
</head>
<frameset>
...numerous <frame> elements here...
<noframes>
  <body>
...Alternative content for non-frame aware browsers...
  </body>
</noframes>
</frameset>
</html>
```

Framed documents are discussed in greater depth in Chapter 8. For now let's concentrate on a typical document template of **<!DOCTYPE>**, **<html>**, **<head>**, and **<body>** and examine each piece more in depth.

Document Types

HTML follows the SGML notation for defining structured documents. From SGML, HTML inherits the requirement that all documents begin with a **<!DOCTYPE>** declaration. In an HTML context, this identifies the HTML "dialect" used in a document by referring to an external document type definition, or *DTD*. A DTD defines the actual elements, attributes, and element relationships that are valid in the document. The **<!DOCTYPE>** declaration allows validation software to identify the HTML DTD being followed in a document, and verify that the document is syntactically correct—in other words, that all tags used are part of a particular specification and are being used correctly. The process of validation is discussed in greater depth in Chapter 2.

There are numerous HTML DTDs that can be used, corresponding to the various standard as well as proprietary versions of HTML in existence. At the time of this edition, the most likely **<!DOCTYPE>** being used would either be the HTML 4.0 transitional form as shown here:

```
<!DOCTYPE HTML PUBLIC "-//W3C//DTD HTML 4.0 Transitional//EN">
```

or the HTML 4.01 transitional specification indicated by

```
<!DOCTYPE HTML PUBLIC "-//W3C//DTD HTML 4.01 Transitional//EN">
```

Over the course of time the stricter form of HTML—XHTML— probably will be adopted. It will be indicated by

```
<!DOCTYPE html PUBLIC "-//W3C//DTD XHTML 1.0 Transitional//EN">
```

There are numerous document type identifiers that could be used at the start of the document as shown in Table 1-1.

HTML Version	<!DOCTYPE> Declaration
2.0	<!DOCTYPE HTML PUBLIC "-//IETF//DTD HTML//EN">
3.2	<!DOCTYPE HTML PUBLIC "-//W3C//DTD HTML 3.2 Final//EN">
4.0 Transitional	<!DOCTYPE HTML PUBLIC "-//W3C//DTD HTML 4.0 Transitional//EN">
4.0 Frameset	<!DOCTYPE HTML PUBLIC "-//W3C//DTD HTML 4.0 Frameset//EN">
4.0 Strict	<!DOCTYPE HTML PUBLIC "-//W3C//DTD HTML 4.0//EN">
4.01 Transitional	<!DOCTYPE HTML PUBLIC "-//W3C//DTD HTML 4.01 Transitional//EN">

Table 1-1.   *Common HTML DOCTYPE Declarations*

HTML Version	<!DOCTYPE> Declaration
4.01 Frameset	<!DOCTYPE HTML PUBLIC "-//W3C//DTD HTML 4.01 Frameset//EN">
4.01 Strict	<!DOCTYPE HTML PUBLIC "-//W3C//DTD HTML 4.01//EN">
XHTML 1.0 Transitional	<!DOCTYPE html PUBLIC "-//W3C//DTD XHTML 1.0 Transitional//EN">
XHTML 1.0 Strict	<!DOCTYPE html PUBLIC "-//W3C//DTD XHTML 1.0 Strict//EN">
XHTML 1.0 Frameset	<!DOCTYPE html PUBLIC "-//W3C//DTD XHTML 1.0 Frameset//EN">

Table 1-1.   *Common HTML DOCTYPE Declarations* (continued)

Note   *On occasion you might see other HTML document type indicators, notably one for the 3.0 standard that was never really adopted in the Web community.*

While XHTML is almost certainly the future of HTML, the fact of the matter is there will be multiple forms of HTML in use on the Web for a long time. Document authors should be familiar with the many forms of HTML. A brief explanation of each version of HTML is given in Table 1-2.

HTML Version	Description
2.0	Classic HTML dialect supported by browsers such as Mosaic. This form of HTML supports core HTML elements and features such as tables and forms but does not consider any of the browser innovations of advanced features such as style sheets, scripting, or frames.
3.0	The proposed replacement for HTML 2.0 that was never widely adopted, most likely due to the heavy use of browser-specific markup.

Table 1-2.   *Description of Common HTML Versions*

HTML Version	Description
3.2	An HTML finalized by the W3C in early 1997 that standardized most of the HTML features introduced in browsers such as Netscape 3. This version of HTML supports many presentation elements such as <font> as well as early support for some scripting features.
4.0 Transitional	The 4.0 transitional form finalized by the W3C in December of 1997 preserves most of the presentational elements of HTML 3.2. It provides a basis of transition to CSS as well as a base set of elements and attributes for multiple language support, accessibility, and scripting.
4.0 Strict	The strict version of HTML 4.0 removes most of the presentation elements from the HTML specification such as <font> in favor of using Cascading Style Sheets (CSS) for page formatting.
4.0 Frameset	The frameset specification provides a rigorous syntax for framed documents that was lacking in previous versions of HTML.
4.01 Transitional/ Strict/Frameset	A minor update to the 4.0 standard that corrects some of the errors in the original specification.
XHTML 1.0 Transitional	A reformulation of HTML as an XML application. The transitional form preserves many of the basic presentation features of HTML 4.0 transitional but applies the strict syntax rules of XML to HTML.
XHTML 1.0 Strict	A reformation of HTML 4.0 Strict using XML. This language is rule enforcing and leaves all presentation duties to technologies like Cascading Style Sheets.

Table 1-2.   *Description of Common HTML Versions*

The browser vendors also have provided their own various extensions to HTML. While many of the elements introduced should not be used, some of the innovations made by browser vendors eventually were adopted as part of the standard. Web page authors also should be aware of the primary contributions of each browser as well as the core version of HTML supported. Table 1-3 lists a few of the major browser versions and summarizes some of their element introductions.

Browser	Features Introduced	Standards Support
Netscape 2.x	Java, JavaScript, Frames, Plug-ins,	2.0 and Netscape extensions, many of which became 3.2 standard
Netscape 3.x	A few proprietary elements like <spacer> and <multicol>	3.2 with Netscape extensions
Netscape 4.x	Basic CSS support and the proprietary HTML element <layer>	3.2, part of 4.0, part of CSS1, and Netscape extensions
Netscape 6.x	Heavy standards support	4.0, CSS1, much of CSS2, good portion of Document Object Model
Internet Explorer 3.0	Frames and Inline Frames, Jscript, ActiveX controls, VBScript, some proprietary HTML elements like <marquee> and <bgsound>	3.2 with some Microsoft extensions and a limited amount of CSS1
Internet Explorer 4.0	Significant JavaScript access to page elements	Most of 4.0 with Microsoft extensions, most of CSS1
Internet Explorer 5.0/5.5	Native XML support, close to full Document Object Model Level 1	4.0 with Microsoft extensions, most of CSS1, most of the Document Object Model
WebTV	Proprietary tags useful for television screen layout and integration with television viewing.	3.2 with WebTV extensions. Support for many Netscape and Microsoft extensions.

Table 1-3.   *Summary of Browser Innovations and Standard Support*

Knowing the various versions of **<!DOCTYPE>** declarations, as well as extensions made by the browser vendors, is very important for document authors. When checking syntax, it is important to contend with the fact that strict adherence to W3C specifications is not currently a reasonable goal, given the lack of browser support and widespread use of HTML extensions. Hopefully, as promised by XHTML, someday correct document construction will require us only to follow the specifications as written. For now, page designers should be able to find the common ground among their browser population and try to stick to what is standard as best as possible.

The <html> Element

The **<html>** element delimits the beginning and the end of an HTML document. It contains only the **<head>** element, the **<body>** element, and potentially the **<frameset>** element instead of the **<body>** element. The HTML document template, shown earlier in the chapter, shows the **<html>** element's typical use in a document, as a container for all other elements.

The <head> Element

The information in the head of an HTML document is very important because it is used to describe or augment the content of the document. The head of an HTML document is like the front matter or cover page of a document. In many cases, the information contained within the **<head>** element is information about the information of the page, which generally is referred to as *meta-information*. This is a very important and often overlooked aspect of HTML documents. Search engines use meta-information to index Web pages. Aside from meta-information, the **<head>** element can include author contact information, scripts, style sheets, comments—and, most importantly, a page title.

The <title> Element

The most important head element is the **<title>** element, which most browsers display in a title bar at the top of the browser window. The document title is required under current HTML specifications and should occur as the first element within the **<head>** element. The **<title>** element must be used in every HTML document. It gives an HTML document a title by which it is known to browsers and indexing robots. Browsers display the document title while the document is being viewed, and might also use the title in bookmark lists.

Note   *Most browsers attempt to deduce a title for a document that is missing the **<title>** element. The browser often uses the URL of the document being viewed, which might indicate nothing about the document's content. However, this behavior isn't guaranteed. For example, Classic WebTV simply lists the document as "untitled document."*

A document title might contain standard text as well as character entities (for example, **©**), which are discussed later in the chapter. However, HTML markup isn't permitted in the **<title>** element and doesn't produce the expected result. So, according to the rules of the **<title>** element,

```
<title><b>Home Page</b></title>
```

is not valid, whereas

```
<title>The Demo Company Story &copy; 2000</title>
```

is valid. However, a well-formed title is not necessarily a meaningful title. Remember that a user sees a title in his or her bookmark list if the page is bookmarked. Search engines that index the Web often place special meaning on the contents of the **<title>** element when determining what a page is about. Because of this, a title should indicate the contents of a page without ambiguity. Titles such as "My Page" or "Home Page" don't make much sense; "John Smith's Home Page" and "Demo Company, Inc." do. A well-formed title actually can add navigational value to a site by showing an implicit hierarchy among a group of pages. Although "Widget X-103 Datasheet" seems to be a reasonable title, "Demo Company: Products: Trainer Robot " is a better title. It not only indicates the company the product is related to, but implies a hierarchy in the site.

Note *Initially, using characters such as colon (:), slash (/), or backslash (\) in titles was a problem. An operating system might have a problem with these titles if the document is saved to the local system. For example, the colon isn't allowed within Macintosh filenames, and slashes generally aren't allowed within filenames, because they indicate directories. Although this appears to be a problem, most browsers remove the suspect characters and reduce them to spaces during the Save process. To be on the safe side, dashes can be used to delimit sections in the title.*

While titles should be descriptive, they should also be concise. Authors should limit title length to a reasonable number of characters. Netscape and Internet Explorer display around 20–30 characters of a title in their bookmark lists. One way to limit the length of titles is to remove words such as "a," "an," and "the," which provide little extra value.

Tip *Browsers are very sensitive to the **<title>** element. Even before the rise of XHTML, according to the HTML 3.2 and 4.0 specifications, the **<title>** element is mandatory, while the **<body>**, **<head>**, and **<html>** elements are not. In some versions of Navigator, omitting the **<title>** element causes a document to not display. So, if you get a bunch of junk on your screen (see Figure 1-4), check the **<title>** element right away.*

According to the HTML 4.01 specification, only one **<title>** element should appear in every document. The title should appear in the head of the document. Under very old browser versions multiple **<title>** elements often were used within documents to create an animated title. This was a bug and modern browsers don't support this capability, thus it shouldn't be used.

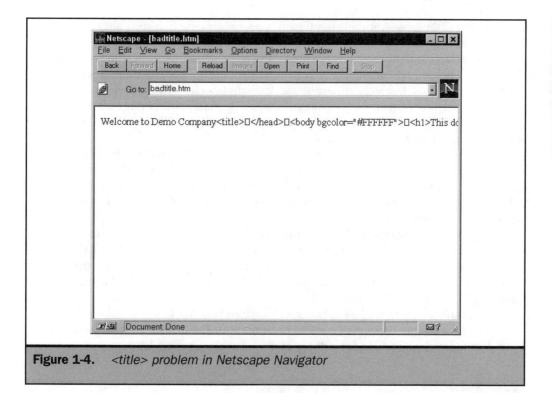

Figure 1-4.   *<title> problem in Netscape Navigator*

Other <head> Elements

In addition to the **<title>** element under the HTML 4.01 transitional DTD, the elements allowed within the **<head>** element include **<base>**, **<isindex>**, **<link>**, **<meta>**, **<object>**, **<script>**, and **<style>**, which has already been discussed. A brief discussion of the other head elements follows. Complete information is available in the cross-referenced chapters and reference section.

The **<base>** element specifies an absolute URL address that is used to provide server and directory information for partially specified URL addresses used within the document. Known as *relative links*, they are discussed in Chapter 4, which covers linking.

The **<isindex>** element indicates that the document contains a searchable index. It causes the browser to display a query prompt and a field for entering a query. This element usually is used with simple site searching mechanisms, but is rarely used today, having been mostly replaced by forms. Under the HTML 4.0 strict definition, **<isindex>** is deprecated. The element is discussed solely in Appendix A, as its use is discouraged.

The **<link>** element specifies a special relationship between the current document and another document. One use concerns hypertext navigational relationships. This is discussed in Chapter 4. Another use, which concerns linking to a style sheet, is discussed in Chapter 10.

The **<meta>** element uses name/value pairs to provide meta-information about a document. The **<meta>** element often provides descriptive information targeted by Web search engines. In a very different use, the **<meta>** element can define an HTTP request header that causes one page to automatically load another page after a specified time interval. These and other uses are discussed in Chapter 16, which covers site maintenance and related elements.

The **<object>** element allows programs and other binary objects to be directly embedded in a Web page. The most popular current approaches use Java applets, plug-ins, or ActiveX controls. This approach to making Web pages more interactive is known as *client-side programming*. The **<object>** element and associated usage is discussed in Chapter 14.

The **<script>** element allows programs written in a scripting language to be directly embedded in a Web page. The most popular scripting languages is ECMAScript, generally called JavaScript. The **<script>** element and associated usage of scripts, often called *Dynamic HTML* (DHTML), should simply be considered a form of client-side scripting; it is discussed in Chapter14.

The **<style>** element encloses style specifications relating to fonts, colors, positioning, and other aspects of content presentation. These styles can be associated with document elements. Use of **<style>** is discussed in Chapter 10.

The <body> Element

After the head section, as previously shown in the HTML document template, the body of a document is delimited by **<body>** and **</body>**. Under the HTML 4.01 specification and many browsers, the **<body>** element is optional, but should always be included, particularly as it is required in XHTML. Only one **<body>** element can appear per document. Because the **<body>** element delimits the document itself, its attributes are primarily used to effect change across the entire document, such as setting background images, background colors, and link and text color. These attributes will be discussed in depth in Chapter 6. The rest of the chapter introduces the basic types of HTML elements that might be found in a document's body and leaves the discussion of their specific syntax for later chapters.

Element and Characters

Within the body of a Web document is a variety of types of elements. For example, *block-level elements* define structural content blocks such as paragraphs **<p>** or headings **<h1>**. Block-level elements generally introduce line breaks visually. Within blocks occur *inline elements* such as bold (**<b>**), strong (**<strong>**), and numerous others. These types of elements do not introduce any returns. Other types of elements include those that reference other objects such as images (**<img>**) or programs (**<object>**). Other hard-to-characterize elements also could be grouped and defined, but generally these are related to browser-specific elements such as **<marquee>**. Each of these types of elements will be introduced in subsequent chapters, with the core elements being discussed in Chapter 3.

Finally, within the elements in the body, regular text can be typed in, as well as special characters inserted as character entities occur. Occasionally it might be necessary to put special characters within a document, such as accented letters, copyright symbols, or even the angle brackets used to enclose HTML elements. To use such characters in an HTML document, they must be "escaped" by using a special code. All character codes take the form *&code;*, in which code is a word or numeric code indicating the actual character that you want to put onscreen. For example, when adding a less than symbol, <, you could use **<** or **<** Character entities also are discussed in Chapter 3; a complete list of the character entities is presented in Appendix C.

The Rules of HTML

HTML does have some rules, even in its standard form. Unfortunately, these "rules" really aren't rules, but more like suggestions. Most browsers pretty much let just about anything render. However, under XHTML these rules will be enforced, and incorrect documents will not be allowed to render. Most HTML, whether created by hand or a tool, generally lies somewhere between strict conformance and no conformance to the specification. Let's take a brief tour of some of the more important aspects of HTML syntax.

HTML Is Not Case Sensitive

These markup examples

```
<B>Go boldly</B>
<B>Go boldly</b>
<b>Go boldly</B>
<b>Go boldly</b>
```

are all equivalent under traditional HTML. Developers are highly opinionated on how to case elements. Some designers point to the ease of typing lowercase tags as well as the upcoming favor of XHTML for lowercase elements as reasons to go all lowercase.

Other designers point out that, statistically, lowercase letters are more common than upper; keeping tags in all uppercase makes them easier to pick out in a document, thus making its structure more clear to someone doing hand markup. Of course, if tools correctly generated all HTML markup, nobody would care, but for now the key is consistency. In general you might consider choosing either upper or lowercase, and stick to it. Fortunately, if you change your mind most HTML editors and maintenance tools can instantly change case. However, if you have to pick one style over another, choose lowercase given XHTML's preference for this style.

 With the rise of XHTML, lowercasing will become the published style. If hand coding continues it might be difficult to push this, but if XHTML does come to pass, designers should be consistent in using lowercase.

One interesting aspect of HTML's case sensitivity is that although HTML element names and attribute names are not case sensitive, this doesn't mean everything is case insensitive. For example, consider **<img SRC="test.gif">** and **<img src="test.gif">**. These are equivalent because the **<img>** element and the **SRC** attribute are not case sensitive. However, attribute values may be case sensitive, particularly where URLs are concerned. So **<img src="test.gif">** and **<img src="TEST.GIF">** are not necessarily referencing the same image. When referenced from a UNIX system where filenames are case sensitive, test.gif and TEST.GIF would be two different files, while on an NT system where filenames are not case sensitive they would be the same file. This is a common problem and will keep a site from easily being transported from one server to another.

HTML Is Sensitive to a Single White Space Character

Browsers will collapse white space between characters down to a single element. This includes all tabs, line breaks, and carriage returns.

Consider the markup

```
<b>T e s t o f s p a c e s</b><br>
<b>T    e    s    t    of    s p a c e s </b><br>
<b>T
e s
t o f s p              a c e s</b><BR>
```

As shown here, all the spaces, tabs, and returns are collapsed to a single element.

T e s t o f s p a c e s
T e s t o f s p a c e s
T e s t o f s p a c e s

Note that in some situations, HTML does treat white space characters differently. In the case of the **<pre>** element, which defines a preformatted block of text, white space is not ignored. Also white space is preserved within the **<textarea>** element when setting default text for a multi-line text entry field.

Because browsers will ignore most white space, HTML authors often format their HTML documents for readability. However, the reality is that browsers really don't care one way or another. Because of this, some sites have adopted an idea called "HTML crunching," which is discussed in Chapter 2.

Subtle errors tend to creep into HTML files where white space is concerned; be especially careful with spacing around **<img>** and **<a>** elements. For example, consider the markup here:

```
<a href="http://www.democompany.com">
<img src="democompany.gif" width="221" height="64"
border="0" alt="Demo Company">
</a>
```

Notice the line return after the **<img>** element, just before the **</a>** tag that closes the link. Under some browsers this will result in a small "tail" to the image, often termed a tick, as shown here:

Gap in HTML code can cause a "tick" around linked images

Some browsers will fix the tick problem; others won't. What's interesting is that the browsers showing the tick actually are interpreting the HTML specification properly.

The last aspect of spacing to consider is the use of the non-breaking space entity, or ** **. Some might consider this the duct tape of the Web—useful in a bind when a little bit of formatting is needed or an element has to be kept open. While the ** ** entity can be used in many useful ways, such as keeping empty table cells from collapsing, designers should avoid relying on it for significant formatting. While it is true that markup such as

```
      Look, I'm spaced!
```

would space in some text, the question is, exactly how far? In print, using spaces to format is dangerous and things rarely line up. It is no different on the Web.

HTML Supports a Content Model

HTML supports a strict content model that says that certain elements are supposed to only occur within other elements. For example, markup like this:

```
<ul>
    <p>It's simple to break the content model!</p>
</ul>
```

which often is used for simple indentation, actually doesn't strictly follow the HTML content model. The **<ul>** element is supposed to contain **<li>** elements. The **<p>** element is not really appropriate in this context. Even worse, some elements only belong within other elements. An **<input>** element can only live inside a **<form>** element; an **<option>** element can only be found within a **<select>** element. HTML elements and text content should follow a structured content model.

HTML Elements Should Close Unless Empty

Some HTML elements have optional close tags. For example, both of the paragraphs here are allowed, although the second one is better:

```
<p>This isn't closed
<p>This is</p>
```

A few tags like the horizontal rule **<hr>** or line break **
** do not have close tags because they do not enclose any content. These are considered empty elements and can be used as is. However, for elements with optional close tags some confusion can arise. Consider

```
<p><p><p>
```

Does this produce numerous blank lines? No, since the browser minimizes the empty **<p>** elements. Some HTML editors output markup such as

```
<p> </p><p> </p><p> </p>
```

to deal with this. This is a misuse of HTML. Multiple **
** elements should have been used instead to achieve line breaks.

HTML Elements Should Nest

A simple rule states that HTML should nest, not cross, thus

```
<b><i>is in error as tags cross</b></i>
```

whereas

```
<b><i>is not since tags nest</i></b>.
```

Breaking this rule seems harmless enough, but it does introduce some ambiguity if tags are automatically manipulated using a program. Under XHTML, proper nesting is mandatory.

HTML Attributes Should Be Quoted

Although it is true that simple attribute values do not need to be quoted, not doing so can lead to trouble with scripting. For example,

```
<img src=bozo.gif height=10 width=10>
```

would work fine in most browsers. Not quoting the **src** attribute is troublesome but should work. But what would happen if the **src** attribute where manipulated by JavaScript and changed to "bozo 2.gif" complete with a space? This could cause a problem. Furthermore, XHTML does enforce quoting, so all attributes should be quoted like so:

```
<img src="bozo.gif" height="10" width="10">
```

Although it doesn't matter if single or double quotes are used, be consistent. Also, be particularly careful when mixing JavaScript with your HTML code.

Browsers Ignore Unknown Attributes and Elements

For better or worse, browsers will ignore unknown elements and attributes, so

```
<bogus>this text will display on screen</bogus>
```

and an element such as

```
<p id="myPara" obviouslybad="TRUE">will also render fine.</p>
```

This last idea results in browser software making best guesses at structuring malformed content, and ignoring code that obviously is wrong. The permissive nature of browsers has resulted in so much poorly formatted markup that automatic exchange of HTML documents is very difficult; the language serves as a shaky foundation, at best, on which to build presentation and later, interactivity. The introduction of XHTML brings some hope for stability and structure on the Web.

XHTML: The Rules Enforced

The new version of HTML called XHTML became a W3C Recommendation in January 2000. XHTML is a reformulation of HTML using XML that attempts to change the direction and use of HTML to the way it ought to be. So what does that mean? In short, rules now matter. In the past you could feed your browser just about anything and it would render. XHTML ends all that. Now if you make a mistake it matters significantly. The page won't render at all. The rules are fortunately pretty simple; they were already pretty well covered in the previous sections. Briefly, they include things such as:

- You must have a doctype indicator and conform to its rules. **<!DOCTYPE html PUBLIC "-//W3C//DTD XHTML 1.0 Transitional//EN" "http://www.w3.org/TR/ xhtml1/DTD/xhtml1-transitional.dtd">**.

- You must have **<html>**, **<head>**, and **<body>** (or a **<frameset>** containing a **<body>** inside of a **<noframes>**).

- **<title>** must come first in the **<head>** element.

- You have to quote ALL your attributes, even simple ones like **<p align=left>**.

- You must nest your tags properly, so ****is ok****, but **** is not ****.

- You cannot omit optional close tags, so **<p>** cannot stand alone; you must have **<p>** and **</p>**.

- Empty tags must close, so tags such as **<hr>** become **<hr />**.

- You have to lowercase everything.

There's more, but this is most of them. Except for a few changes in syntax, such as the empty tag changes and the forced lowercase, just do your HTML correctly (as you should have done before). A typical XHTML document wouldn't look that dissimilar to an HTML one, as shown here:

```
<?xml version="1.0" encoding="UTF-8"?>
<!DOCTYPE html PUBLIC "-//W3C//DTD XHTML 1.0 Strict//EN"
"DTD/xhtml1-strict.dtd">
<html xmlns="http://www.w3.org/1999/xhtml" xml:lang="en" lang="en">
<head>
<title>Title here</title>
</head>
<body>
Content here
</body>
</html>
```

Although XHTML doesn't appear to be a big deal, it is. Enforcing rules is going to cause problems, and most pages will have to be restructured somewhat. So the big question then rears its head: Will this really come to pass? If it does, XHTML will probably not sweep the Web in a short period of time. In some sense the technology should be a big deal because the payoff of well-formed HTML, actually XHTML, is huge: easier document conversion, improved editors that can generate clean markup, a continued movement toward the separation of Web page presentation from structure, and even automated extraction of content because pages can be precisely parsed. Yet what will happen when the first XHTML enforcing browser is released and it doesn't render 99% of the pages on the net? Most likely, browsers will include some old markup compatibility mode. Designers aren't getting away from old HTML anytime soon. You might call HTML the DOS of the Web, always lurking around some place. However, moving to XHTML is not difficult and the benefit is great. With careful formatting, normal Web pages can be written to conform to XHTML. Tools like HTML Tidy (http://www.w3.org/People/Raggett/tidy/) and XHTML-aware editors should make easier the job of both creating new documents and migrating old ones.

Logical and Physical HTML

No introduction to HTML would be complete without a discussion of the logical versus physical markup battle at the heart of HTML. *Physical HTML* refers to using HTML to make pages look a particular way; *logical HTML* refers to using HTML to specify the structure of a document while using another technology, such as Cascading Style Sheets (see Chapter 10), to designate the look of the page.

Most people are already very familiar with physical document design, because they normally use WYSIWYG (*what you see is what you get*) text editors, such as Microsoft

Word. When Word users want to make something bold, they simply select the appropriate button, and the text is made bold. In HTML, you can make something bold simply by enclosing it within the **<b>** and **</b>** tags, as shown here:

```
<b>This is important.</b>
```

This can easily lead people to believe that HTML is nothing more than a simple formatting language. WYSIWYG HTML editors (such as Microsoft FrontPage) also reinforce this view. But as page designers try to use HTML in this simplistic fashion, they sooner or later must face the fact that HTML is *not* a physical page-description language. Page authors can't seem to make the pages look exactly the way they want, and even when they can, doing so often requires heavy use of **<table>** tags, giant images, and even trick HTML. Other technologies, such as style sheets, might provide a better solution for formatting text than a slew of inconsistently supported tricks and proprietary HTML elements.

According to many experts, HTML was not designed to provide most of the document layout features people have come to expect, and it shouldn't be used for that purpose. Instead, HTML should be used as a logical, or generalized, markup language that defines a document's structure, not its appearance. For example, instead of defining the introduction of a document with a particular margin, font, and size, HTML just labels it as an introduction section and lets another system, such as Cascading Style Sheets, determine the appropriate presentation. In the case of HTML, the browser or a style sheet has the final say on how a document looks.

HTML already contains many logical elements. An example of a logical element is **<strong>**, which indicates something of importance, as shown here:

```
<strong>This is important.</strong>
```

The **<strong>** element says nothing about how the phrase "This is important" will actually appear, although it probably will be rendered in bold. Although most of the logical elements are relatively underutilized, others, such as headings (**<h1>** through **<h6>**) and paragraphs **<p>**, are used regularly.

The benefits of logical elements might not be obvious to those comfortable with physical markup. To understand the benefits, it's important to realize that on the Web, many browsers render things differently. In addition, predicting what the viewing environment will be is difficult. What browser does the user have? What is his or her monitor's screen resolution? Does the user even have a screen? Considering the extreme of the user having no screen at all, how would a speaking browser render the **<bold>** element? What about the **<strong>** elements? Text tagged with **<strong>** might be read in a firm voice, but boldfaced text might not have a meaning outside the visual realm.

Many realistic examples exist of the power of logical elements. Consider the multinational or multilingual aspects of the Web. In some countries, the date is written with the day first, followed by the month and year. In the United States, the date generally is written with the month first, and then the day and year. A **<date>** element, if it existed, could tag the information and enable the browser to localize it for the appropriate viewing environment. Another example is the problem of screen sizes which, theoretically, could be reduced by logical structuring concepts. For example, logical elements could allow for different renderings based on the screen size of the computer running the browser. This would allow the creation of documents that look good on laptop screens as well as on large workstation monitors. In short, separation of the logical structure from the physical presentation allows multiple physical displays to be applied to the same content. This is a powerful idea which, unfortunately, is rarely taken advantage of. We'll take a look at this approach to page design in Chapter 10 when we cover HTML's intersection with style sheets.

Whether you subscribe to the physical (specific) or logical (general) viewpoint, traditional HTML is not purely a physical *or* logical language—yet. In other words, currently used HTML elements come in both flavors: physical and logical. Elements that specify fonts, type sizes, type styles, and so on are physical. Elements that specify content or importance, such as **<cite>** and **<h1>**, and let the browser decide how to do things are logical. A quick look at Web pages across the Internet suggests that logical elements and style sheets often go unused, because Web developers want more layout control than raw HTML provides, and style sheets are relatively new and still buggy. Furthermore, many designers just don't think in the manner required for logical markup, and WYSIWYG page editors generally don't encourage such thinking. Of course, XHTML will change all this, returning the language to a primarily logical formatting language.

So, like it or not, to achieve the look that they want, page designers probably will continue to abuse elements, such as **<table>** and **<frame>**, and use tricks to implement layouts in the way that they want them. This is the struggle that currently exists between what people want out of HTML and what HTML actually provides. With the rise of HTML 4, XHTML, and Cascading Style Sheets, this struggle might eventually go away, but the uptake is still slow, and millions of documents will continue to be authored with no concept of logical structuring. Web page development continues to provide an interesting study of the difference between what theorists say and what people want.

Myths about HTML and XHTML

HTML is a powerful technology, but many misconceptions exist about it. Understanding what HTML is *not* will certainly help page developers avoid common mistakes.

Myth: HTML Is a WYSIWYG Design Language

HTML isn't a specific, screen- or printer-precise formatting language like PostScript. Many people struggle with HTML on a daily basis, trying to create perfect layouts by using HTML elements inappropriately or by using images to make up for HTML's lack of screen and font-handling features. Other technologies, such as Cascading Style Sheets (CSS), are far better than HTML for handling presentation issues; their use returns HTML back to its structural roots.

Myth: HTML Is a Programming Language

Many people think that making HTML pages is similar to programming. However, HTML is unlike programming in that it does not specify logic. It specifies the structure and often the layout of a document. With the introduction of scripting languages such as JavaScript, however, the concept of dynamic HTML (DHTML) is becoming more and more popular and is used to create highly interactive Web pages. Simply put, DHTML provides scripting languages with the capability to modify HTML elements and their content before, and possibly after, the page has been loaded.

DHTML blurs the lines between HTML as a layout language and HTML as a programming environment. However, the line should be distinct, because HTML is not a programming language. Heavily intermixing code with HTML markup in the ad-hoc manner that many DHTML authors do is far worse than trying to use HTML as a WYSIWYG markup language. Programming logic can be cleanly separated in HTML in the form of script code, as discussed in Chapter 13. Unfortunately, if this separation isn't heeded, the page maintenance nightmare that results from tightly binding programming logic to content will dwarf the problems caused by misuse of HTML code for presentation purposes.

Myth: HTML Is Complete

HTML is not finished. The language does not provide all the facilities it should, even as a logical markup language. However, work is presently focused on implementing the current HTML standards under a new language, called *eXtensible Markup Language* (XML). Future versions of HTML will almost certainly be defined as a subset of XML. Theoretically, this is a wise decision, but the ubiquitous nature of HTML and its huge installed base suggest that considering how to extend HTML or fill in its small gaps is an incredibly important task. The W3C's current HTML *Activity Statement* can be found on its Web site (http://www.w3.org/MarkUp/Activity.html).

Myth: HTML Is Completely Standardized

Although the W3C defines the HTML specification, in practical terms browser vendors and users often define their own de facto standards, or decide what aspects of the standards they support. While this might sound like heresy, it is true. Up until recently, when a new browser supporting a new feature was released, many companies and individuals would rush to use it, regardless of whether the feature was included in the

W3C HTML standard. Today a major goal of browser vendors is to bring standard conformance to the Web, which cannot happen too soon. However, for the time being designers have to respect the past forms of markup, problems and all.

Myth: Traditional HTML Is Going Away

HTML is the foundation of the Web; with literally billions of pages in existence, not every document is going to be upgraded anytime soon. The "legacy" Web will continue for years, and HTML will always be lurking around underneath even the most advanced Web page years from now.

Myth: XHTML Will Take the Public Web By Storm

Wishful thinking, but having taught HTML for years and noticing how both editors and people build Web pages, it is very unlikely that XHTML will be the norm before the end of the year 2000, or probably even for years well beyond that. The problem is that if browsers suddenly enforced XHTML rules, few of today's existing Web documents would render at all; remember that although HTML has had rules for years, people have not really bothered much of the time to follow them. Many people learn HTML simply through imitation by viewing the source of existing pages, which are not always written correctly, and going from there. Like learning a spoken language, it is the occasional, loosely enforced rules that have allowed many document authors to quickly get involved with HTML. Like the English language, HTML is well understood and used in lots of places, but not often used perfectly. Rigor will come to the Web, but don't expect it to happen all at once.

Myth: Hand-Coding of HTML Will Continue for Decades

Although some will continue to craft pages like mechanical typesetting, as the Web editors improve and standards take root, the requirement to hand-tweak HTML layouts will diminish. Hopefully, designers will realize that knowledge of the "invisible pixel" trick is not a bankable resume bullet and instead focus on development of their talents along with a firm understanding of HTML markup.

Myth: HTML Is All You Need to Know to Create Good Web Pages

Whereas HTML is the basis for Web pages, you need to know a lot more than HTML to build useful Web pages (unless the page is very simple). Document design, graphic design, and even programming often are necessary to create sophisticated Web pages. HTML serves as the foundation environment for all of these tasks, and a complete understanding of HTML technology can only aid document authors. A brief discussion of some of the other aspects of Web design is presented in the next chapter.

Summary

HTML is the markup language for building Web pages and traditionally has combined physical and logical structuring ideas. Elements—in the form of tags such as **** and ****—are embedded within text documents to indicate to browsers how to render pages. The rules for HTML are fairly simple. Unfortunately, these rules have not been enforced by browsers in the past. Because of this looseness, there has been a great deal of misunderstanding about the purpose of HTML, and a good portion of the documents on the Web do not conform to any particular "official" specification of HTML. The introduction of XHTML attempts to return HTML to its roots as a structural language, leaving presentational duties to other technologies such as Cascading Style Sheets. The newest version of HTML also attempts to introduce the required rigor and enforcement of syntax that will make HTML a solid foundation on which to build tomorrow's Web applications. While heavy use of strict XHTML has yet to occur on the Web, document authors following the rules presented, even using classic HTML, should be well suited to make the transition to perfectly formed documents. Before plunging in to the core elements of HTML, we'll take a look at Web development practices and project planning useful to aspiring HTML document authors.

The preceding is only a brief introduction to some of the "rules" that HTML documents tend to follow. Unfortunately, the benefit of following the rules isn't always apparent to new Web developers, because most browsers don't strictly enforce the standards. For example, although the nesting rule agrees with the formal definition of HTML, most browsers have no problem with crossed tags, or even with tags being used totally improperly. The reason for the browsers' laxity in enforcement is actually very logical: A browser would display nonstop error messages if it displayed a message every time that it encountered a slightly miscoded Web page! Nevertheless, don't use the browsers' laxity in enforcing HTML's "rules" as an excuse to misuse HTML or sloppily code a page. Standards impose specific structural requirements on documents, and as the Web becomes increasingly more complicated and technologies such as the eXtensible Markup Language (XML) are adopted, following the standards will become much more important.

Unfortunately, many document authors are unfamiliar with standards. Thus, they might not pay attention to the structure because they don't understand the philosophy of HTML; or, they might think of HTML as a physical page–description language, such as PostScript, rather than a logical, structure-oriented markup language. Browsers don't discourage this view, and might even encourage the physical view.

Chapter 2

Web Development Overview

One of the problems with discussing the creation of Web pages is that mastery of HTML often is confused with understanding the process of Web development. HTML is only one part of the process. Graphic design and programming-oriented technologies also are important aspects of that Web development process. Web publishing or Web development are more appropriate terms to describe the overall process of planning and putting together a Web site, particularly when some degrees of forethought, skill, and artistry are employed. Knowledge of HTML alone does not provide all the facilities required to make appealing, usable Web sites. Before you get too caught up in the details of markup tags, you need to understand the Web process and how HTML works in that process. This chapter provides a brief overview of some of the development ideas presented in the companion book, *Web Design: The Complete Reference* (ISBN 007212297-8), with a special focus on the HTML aspects of a Web site project.

The Need for Careful Web Development

Today a crisis similar to the "software crisis" of the late 1960s exists in Web development. A few years ago most Web sites were little more than digital brochures, and often were termed "brochureware." Creating such a site didn't require a great deal of planning—often, simply developing an interface and then populating the site with content worked adequately. Today sites are becoming much larger and more complex. With the introduction of e-commerce and dynamic pages, sites clearly have moved away from brochureware to full-fledged software applications. However, many developers have yet to adopt a robust site building methodology and often continue to rely on ad hoc methods.

Note *The "software crisis" refers to a time in the software development field when increasing hardware capabilities allowed for significantly more complex programs to be built. However, building and maintaining the new programs was challenging because little methodology had been used in the past, thus resulting in experts stating a crisis was occurring because of numerous project failures. Methodology such as structured or top-down design was introduced to combat this crisis.*

Evidence of the crisis in Web development practices is everywhere. Unlike the in-house software projects of the past, the dirty laundry of many failed Web projects often is aired for all to see. The number of pages that seem to be forever under construction or coming soon suggests how poorly planned many Web sites are. Unfortunately, the yellow and black construction signs and animated jackhammers rarely are removed. Some sites have been in a state of construction for years judging by their content or date of last modification. Like some form of online ghost town, these half-dead sites are cluttered with old content, old-style HTML, dated technologies, broken links, and malfunctioning scripts. Don't discount some of these problems as mere typos or slight oversights. A broken link is a catastrophic failure. Imagine if a software program had menus that just didn't go anywhere!

The reason that sites might exhibit problems certainly varies. Some sites might deteriorate simply because the site's builders got bored or moved on. Other sites might fall apart because the site wasn't considered useful or funding was withdrawn. Still other sites probably just couldn't be completed because the site's complexity overwhelmed the developer. Sometimes the developer just might not have understood the tools he or she was working with, or was not well versed in medium restrictions. Even when designers do understand the medium they might end up trying to do the project too quickly or not planning enough before implementing the site. Often the process for building the Web site is so fast that the process almost boils down to two steps: implement and then release. Notice that many Web design tools encourage this design-on-the-fly approach. Some tools encourage the developer to immediately begin mocking up an interface and later use wizards to add functionality, whereas others can create huge amounts of code but consider adding interface later on. There is no doubt that the speedy approach to development, given the time demands of the Web, is important. However, releasing a shoddy, poorly thought-out site could backfire when the user becomes frustrated with the site's problems. The reason for development project failure varies, but the numerous dead sites on the Web suggest that Web development projects are risky and often fail. We should strive to provide a method to approach site building in a structured manner to reduce risk.

Basic Web Process Model

To help reduce the difficulty in constructing sites, we should adopt a *process model* that describes the various phases involved in Web site development. Each step then can be carefully performed by the developer, using guidelines and documentation along the way that tell the developer how to do things and ensure that each step is carried out properly. An ideal process model for the Web would help the developer address the complexity of the site, minimize the risk of project failure, deal with the near certainty of change during the project, and deliver the site quickly with adequate feedback for management during the process. Of course, the ideal process model also would have to be easy to learn and execute. This is a pretty tall order, and it is unlikely that any single process model is always going to fit the particular requirements of a project.

The most basic process model used in Web site development should be familiar to most people—at least in spirit, as it is deductive or more simply "top-down." The basic Web project process starts with the big picture and narrows down to the specific steps necessary to complete the site. The model starts first with a planning stage, then a design phase, then implementation and testing, and ends with a maintenance phase. The phases might appear to be distinct steps, but the progress from one stage to another might not always be obvious. Furthermore, progress isn't always toward a conclusion, and occasionally previous steps might need to be revisited if the project encounters unforeseen changes. The actual number of steps and their names varies from person to person, but a general idea of the procedure is shown in Figure 2-1.

 In software engineering this model often is called the waterfall model, or sometimes the software lifecycle model, because it describes the phases in the lifetime of software. Each stage in the waterfall model proceeds one after another until conclusion.

The good thing about this site development approach is that it makes developers plan everything up front. That also is its biggest weakness. In a Web project there often is a great deal of uncertainty in what is required to accomplish a project, particularly if the developer has not had a great deal of Web development experience. Another problem with this development model is that each step is supposed to be distinct, but the reality is that in Web development, like software, steps tend to overlap, influence previous and future steps, and often have to be repeated. Unfortunately, the basic Web site development approach can be fairly rigid and might require the developer to stop

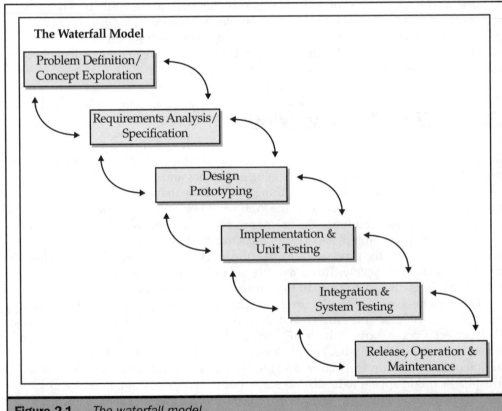

Figure 2-1. *The waterfall model*

the project and redo many steps if too many changes occur. In short, the process doesn't deal well with change. However, this simple model for site design continues to be very popular because it is both easy to understand and easy to follow. Furthermore, the distinct steps in the process appeal to management as they can easily be monitored and serve as project milestones.

In theory, Web site development process models make sense, but do they work in practice? The answer is a resounding yes. However, site development rarely works in a consistent manner because of the newness of the field, the significant time constraints, and the ever-changing nature of Web projects. Developers should always proceed with caution. The next few sections guide the reader through the typical steps that should be taken to build a Web site.

Goals and Problems

Many Web site projects ultimately fail because they lack clear goals. In the first few years of Web design, many corporate sites were built purely to show that the firm had a site. Somehow, without a site the firm would not be progressive or a market leader, and competitors with sites were somehow a threat. Many times, the resulting site provided little benefit because it was only designed to provide a presence for the company. As familiarity with the Web has grown, the reasons for having Web sites have become clearer. Today, site goals have become important and usually are clearly articulated up front. However, don't assume that logic rules the Web—a great number of site development projects continue to be driven by pure fancy, and often react more to perceived threats than to solve real problems.

Coming up with a goal for a Web site isn't difficult; the problem is refining it. Be wary of vague goals like "provide better customer service" or "make more money by opening up an online market." This might serve as a good sound bite or mission statement for a project, but details are required. Good goal statements might include something such as one of the following:

- Build a customer support site that will improve customer satisfaction by providing 24/7 access to common questions and result in a 25 percent decrease in telephone support.

- Create an online toy store that will sell at least $10,000/month of product directly to the consumer.

- Develop a Japanese food restaurant site that will inform potential customers of critical information such as hours, menu, atmosphere, and prices and encourage them to order by phone or visit the location.

Notice that two of the three goal statements had measurable goals. This is very important as it provides a way to easily determine success or failure as well as assign a realistic budget to the project. The third goal statement did not provide an obviously measurable goal. This can be dangerous because it is difficult to convince others that the site is successful, or even to place a value on the site. In the case of the restaurant informational site, a goal for number of viewers of the site or a way to measure customer visits using a coupon or something would help. Consider a revised goal statement such as:

- Develop a Japanese food restaurant site that will inform 300 potential customers per month of critical information such as hours, menu, atmosphere, and prices and encourage them to order by phone or visit the location.

The simple addition of a particular number of visitors makes the goal statement work. By stating a number of desired visitors, the restaurant owner could compare the cost of placing advertisements in print or on the radio versus the cost of running the site to provide the same effective inquiry rate.

Brainstorming for Site Purpose

Generally, coming up with a goal statement is fairly straightforward. The largest problem is keeping the statement concise and realistic. In many Web projects there is a desire to include everything in the site. Remember, the site can't be everything to everyone; there must be a specific audience and set of tasks in mind. To determine goals, a brainstorming session often is required. The purpose of a brainstorming session is simply to bring out as many ideas about the site as possible. A white board is useful during a brainstorming session to quickly write down or modify any possible ideas for the site.

Oftentimes, brainstorming sessions get off track because participants jump ahead or bring too much philosophy about site design to the table. In such a case, it is best to focus the group by talking about site issues they should all agree on. Attempt to find a common design philosophy by having people discuss what they don't want to see in the site. Getting meeting participants to agree they don't want the site to be slow, difficult to use, and so on usually is easy. Once you obtain a sense of a common goal in the group, even if it is just that they all believe that the site shouldn't be slow, future exploration and statements of what the site should do seem to go smoother.

| Note | *When conducting a project to redo a site, be careful to not run brainstorm meetings by berating the existing site unless no participant in the project has any ownership stake in the site. A surefire way to derail a site overhaul project is to get the original designers on the defensive because of criticism of their work. Remember, people have to build sites, so building a positive team is very important.* |

Narrowing the Wish List

During the brainstorming session, all ideas are great. The point of the session is to develop what might be called the *wish list*. A wish list is a document that describes all possible ideas for inclusion in a site regardless of price, feasibility, or applicability. It is important to avoid stifling any ideas during brainstorming lest it take away the creative aspect of site development. However, eventually the wish list will have to be narrowed down to what is reasonable and appropriate for the site. This can be a significant challenge for a site with many possible goals. Consider, for example, a corporate site that contains product information, investor information, press releases, job postings, and technical support sections. Each person with ownership stakes in a particular section will think their section is most important. Everyone literally wants a big link to his or her section to be on the home page. Getting compromise with so many stakeholders can be challenging!

One possibility for narrowing the goal is to use small sheets of paper or a deck of 3 × 5 cards. Have each one of the ideas written on a card and put them in a large pile. Now go around the room and have each person pull out one card at a time and suggest where to include the item in the site based upon importance. Of course, make sure to limit the number of cards pulled from the pile. Hopefully, performing a procedure like this will allow the most important ideas to surface. Unfortunately, depending on the group, this exercise might fail—particularly if the participants place a great deal of ownership in their respective areas.

Hopefully, out of the brainstorming process the goals will be further refined and expanded upon. For most sites there probably will be a variety of goals for the project and all should be accounted for and well documented. Although the brainstorming process is useful for project participants to identify the purpose of a Web site, it represents only half of the equation. What a site builder wants isn't necessarily what a site visitor wants. To come up with a good site plan you must always take into account the needs of the site's audience early on.

Audience

The best way to narrow a goal is to make sure that the audience is always considered. What a brainstorming group wants compared to what a user wants doesn't always correspond. The first thing to do is to accurately describe the site's audience and their reason for visiting the site. However, don't look for a generic "Joe" or "Jane Enduser" with AOL and a 56K modem who happened on your site by chance. It is unlikely such a user could be identified for most sites, and most users probably will have a particular goal in mind. Consider first what kind of people your end users are. Consider asking some basic questions about the site's users, such as:

- Where are they located?
- How old are they?
- What is their gender?
- What language do they speak?

- How technically proficient are they?
- What kind of connection would they have to the Internet?
- What kind of computer would they use?
- What kind of browser would they probably use?

Next, consider what the users are doing at the site:

- How did they get to the site?
- What do the users want to accomplish at the site?
- When will they visit the site?
- How long will they stay during a particular visit?
- On what page(s) will they leave the site?
- When will they return to the site, if ever?

Although you might be able to describe the user from these questions, you should quickly determine that your site probably would not have one single type of user with a single goal. For most sites, there are many types of users, each with different characteristics and goals.

User Profiling

The best way to understand users is to actually talk to them. If at all possible, you should interview users directly to verify any guess you might have about their wants and characteristics. A survey also might be appropriate, but live interviews provide the possibility to explore ideas beyond predetermined questions. Unfortunately, interviewing or even surveying users can be very time-consuming and it is not possible to account for every single type of user characteristic or desire. From user interviews, surveys, or even just thinking about users generically, you should attempt to create stereotypical but detailed profiles of common users. Consider developing at least three named users. For most sites, consider that the three stereotypical users should correspond roughly to an inexperienced user, a user who has Web experience but doesn't visit your site often, and a power user who understands the Web and might visit the site frequently. Most sites will have these classes of users, with the intermediate infrequent visitor most often being the largest group. Make sure to assign percentages to each of the generic groups so that you account for each with appropriate weight. Now name each person. You might want to name each after a particular, real user you interviewed, or use generic names such as Bob Beginner, Irene Intermediate, and Paul Poweruser. Now work up very specific profiles for each stereotypical user using the questions from the previous section. Try to make sure that the answers correspond roughly to the average answers for each group. So, if there were a few intermediate users interviewed who had fast connections, but most have slow connections, assume the more common case.

Once your profiles for each generic site visitor are complete, you should begin to create visit scenarios. What exactly would Bob Beginner do when he visits your site? What are the tasks he wishes to perform? What is his goal? Scenario planning should help you focus on what each user actually will want to do. From this exercise, you might find that your goal statements are not in line with what the users probably are interested in doing. If so, you are still in the risk analysis phase. Return to the initial step and modify your goal statements based on your new information.

Requirements

Based on the goals of the site and what the audience is like, the site's requirements should begin to present themselves. The requirements of a Web project should fall into four primary categories: content, visual, technology, and delivery. For example, what kind of content will be required? What kind of look should the site have? What types of programs will have to be built? How many servers will be required to service the site's visitors? What kind of restrictions will users place on the site bandwidthwise, screen-sizewise, browserwise, and so on? Requirements will begin to show site costs and potential implementation problems. The requirements will suggest how many developers are required and show what content is lacking. If the requirements seem excessive relative to the potential gain, it is time to revisit the goal stage or question whether the audience was accurately defined. The first three steps of the Web development process could be repeated numerous times until a site plan or specification finally is determined.

The Site Plan

Once a goal, audience, and site requirements have been discussed and documented, a formal site plan should be drawn up. The site plan should contain the following sections:

- **Project Overview**   This section would contain a brief discussion to explain the overall purpose of the site and its basic success measurements.

- **Project and Goal Discussion**   This section would discuss the site's goals in detail and provide measurable goals to verify the benefit of the site.

- **Audience Analysis**   This section would profile the users who would visit the site. The section would describe both audience characteristics as well as the tasks the audience would try to accomplish at the site.

- **Requirements**   This section would provide the requirements necessary to meet the goals presented early and would contain four subsections.

  - **Content requirements**   The content requirements section should provide a laundry list of all text, images, and other media required in the site. A matrix showing the required content, form, existence, and potential owner or creator is useful as it shows how much content might be outstanding. A simple matrix is shown in Table 2-1.

- **Technical requirements**   This section should provide an overview of the types of technology the site will employ, such as HTML, JavaScript, CGI, ColdFusion, Java applets, plug-ins, and so on. The technology requirements should directly relate to the user's as well as developer's capabilities.

- **Visual requirements**   The visual requirements section should outline basic considerations for interface design. The section should indicate in broad strokes how the site should relate to any existing marketing materials and provide an indication of user constraints for graphic and multimedia use such as screen size, color depth, bandwidth, and so on. The section could outline some specifics such as font or color use, but many of the details of the site's visuals will be determined later in the development process.

Content Name	Description	Content Type	Content Format	Exists?	Owner
Butler Robot Press Release	Press release for new Butler 7 series robot that ran in *Robot's Today*	Text	Microsoft Word	Yes	Jennifer Tuggle
Software Agreement Form	Brief description of legal liability of using trial robot personality software	Text	Paper	Yes	John P. Lawyer
Handheld Supercomputer Screen Shot	Picture of the new Demo Company Cray-9000 handheld palm size computer	Image	GIF	No	Pascal Wirth
Welcome from President Message	Brief introduction letter from President to welcome user to site	Text	Microsoft Word	No	President's Executive Assistant

Table 2-1.   *Content Matrix*

- **Delivery requirements** This section should indicate the delivery requirements, particularly any hosting considerations. A basic discussion of how many users will visit the site, how many pages will be consumed on a typical page, and the size of a typical page should be included in this section. Even if these are just guesses, it is then possible to provide a brief analysis of required server and bandwidth to deliver the site.

- **Site Architecture** This section should provide a site structure or flow diagram detailing the various sections within a site. Appropriate labels for sections and general ideas for each section should be developed based on the various user scenarios explored in earlier project phases. Organization of the various sections of the site is important and might have to be refined over time. Building a site architecture can be complex but, in general, a site diagram will look something like the one shown in Figure 2-2.

- **Logistics** Although it probably won't be labeled this way the final section of the site plan should present the real world details that are required to build the site. How many people will it take? How long will the project run? And possibly most important, how much will it cost? For a commercial Web

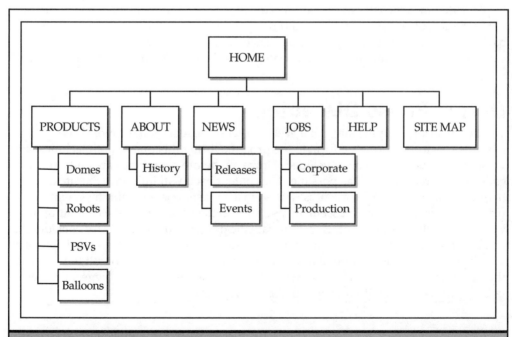

Figure 2-2. *Typical site diagram*

development plan all sorts of legal information also could be provided in the final portion of a site plan.

- **Staffing** This section should detail the resources required to execute the site. Measurements can be in simple man-hours and should relate to each of the four staffing areas: content, technology, visual design, and management.

- **Timeline** The timeline should show how the project would proceed using the staffing estimates from the preceding section combined with the typical building process outlined earlier in the chapter.

- **Budget** A budget is primarily determined from the staffing requirements and the delivery requirements. However, marketing costs or other issues such as content licensing could be addressed in the budget.

This simply is a suggested organization for a Web site plan. The actual organization and content of the site plan really is up to the developer. Remember, the purpose of the plan is to communicate the site's goals to the various people working on the project and help guide the project toward a positive conclusion. Don't skip writing the plan even though it might seem daunting, as without such a document you can only develop a project in an ad hoc, trial-and-error manner. Furthermore, it will be nearly impossible to obtain any realistic bids from outside vendors on a Web site without a specification. However, a finished plan doesn't allow you to immediately proceed to implementation. Once the specification is developed, it should be questioned one last time. The completed specification could reveal unrealistic estimates that will throw you back into questioning initial goals or audience. If not, it might be time to actually continue the process and fall over the waterfall into the design and prototyping stage.

Design Phase Dissected

The design or prototyping stage of a Web project is the most fun for most Web designers, as it starts to bring form to the project. During this phase, both technical and visual prototypes should be developed. However, before prototypes are built, consider collecting as much content as possible. The content itself will influence the site and help guide its form. If the content is written in a very serious tone but the visuals are fun and carefree, the site will seem very strange to the user. Seeing the content up front would avoid the designer failing to integrate the design and content. Also consider that content collection can be one of the slowest aspects of site design. Many participants in a Web project are quick to attend brainstorming meetings but are difficult to find once their content contributions are required. Lack of content is by far the biggest problem in Web projects. Deal with this potential problem early.

Block Comps

Design should proceed top-down. Consider first how the user will enter the site and conclude with how they will leave. In most cases, this means designing the home page first, followed by subsection pages, and finally form or content pages. First consider creating page mockups on paper in a block form, as shown in Figure 2-3.

The block comps allow designers to focus on the types of objects and their organization in the page without worrying too much about precise placement and detail. The block sectioning approach also will help the designer to consider making templates for pages, which will make it easier to implement them later on. Make sure to create your block comps within the constraints of a Web browser window. The influence of the browser's borders can be a significant factor. Once the home page

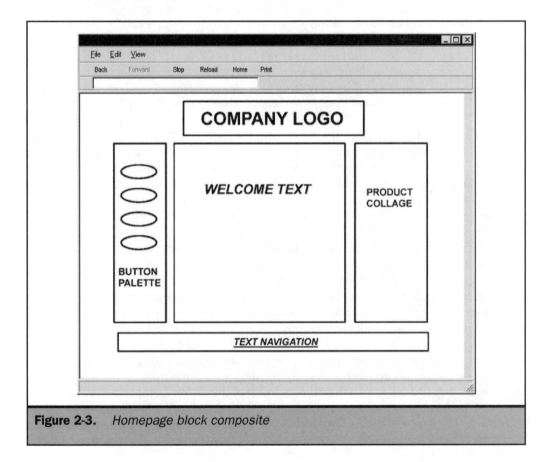

Figure 2-3. *Homepage block composite*

block comp has been built, flesh out the other types of pages in the site in a similar fashion. Once a complete scenario has been detailed in this abstract sense, make sure that the path through the blocked screen is logical. If so, move on to the next phase.

Screen and Paper Comps

The next phase of design is the paper or screen prototyping phase. In this phase, the designer can either sketch or create a digital composite that shows a much more detailed example of a typical page in the site. Make sure that, whether you do the composite on paper or screen, a browser window is assumed and that screen dimensions are considered. A piece of paper with a browser window outline as used in the block comp stage can be used for sketches.

Sketch the various buttons, headings, and features within the page. Make sure to provide some indication of text in the page—either a form of "greeked" text or real content, if possible.

Note	*Many designers appear to use only lorem ipsum or greeked text within screen composites. Although this approach does bring focus to the designed page elements, if real content is available use it, as it more closely simulates what the final result will be like.*

The comping stage provides the most room for creativity, but designers are warned to be creative within the constraints of what is possible on the Web and what visual requirements were presented in the design specification. Thinking about file size, color support, and HTML layout capabilities might seem limiting, but it avoids the designer coming up with a page that looks visually stunning but is nearly impossible to implement. Resist the urge to become so artistic as to reinvent an organization's look in a Web site. Remember, the site plan will have spelled out visual requirements, including marketing constraints. The difficult balance between site form, function, purpose, and content should become readily apparent as designers grapple with satisfying their creative urges within the constraints of Web technology, user capabilities, and site requirements. A typical paper comp is shown in Figure 2-4.

In the case of a digital prototype, create a single image that shows the entire intended screen, including all buttons, images, and text. Save the image as a GIF or JPEG and load it into the Web browser to test how it would look within a typical environment. At this stage, resist the urge to fully implement your page design with HTML. You might end up having to scrap the design, and it would be wasteful to implement. Figure 2-5 shows a digital composite of the Demo Company site as one large GIF image.

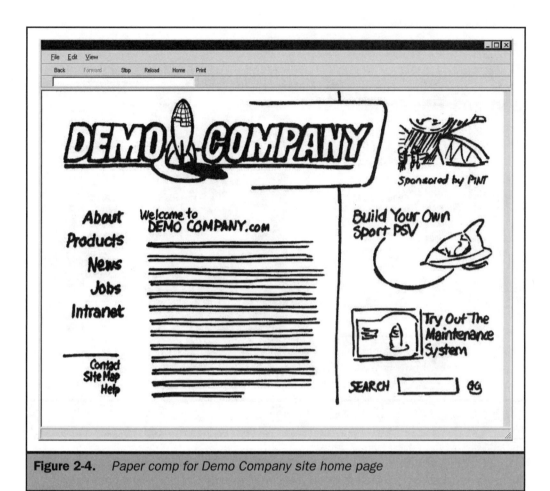

Figure 2-4. *Paper comp for Demo Company site home page*

Once your paper or digital prototype is complete, it should be tested with users. Ask a few users to indicate which sections on the screen are clickable and what buttons they would select in order to accomplish a particular task. Make sure to show the prototype to more than one user, as individual taste might be a significant factor in prototype acceptance. If the user has too many negative comments about the page, consider going completely back to the drawing board. During prototyping, you can't get too attached your children, so to speak. If you do, the site will no longer be user

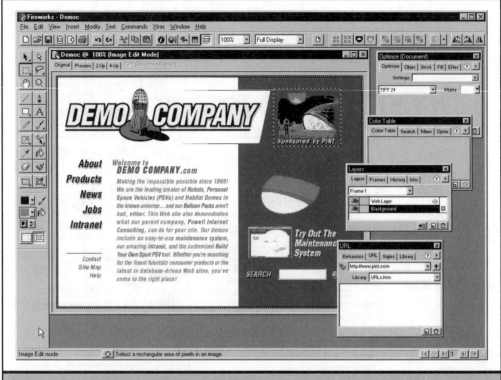

Figure 2-5.   *Digital comp for Demo Company*

focused, but developer focused. Once you come up with an acceptable home page design, continue the process with subpages and content pages. A typical subpage composite is shown in Figure 2-6.

In highly interactive sites, you might have to develop prototype pages for each step within a particular task such as purchasing or download. Prototype pages for such pages might have to be more fully fleshed out and include form field labels and other details to be truly useful. A sample paper comp for an interactive page is shown in Figure 2-7.

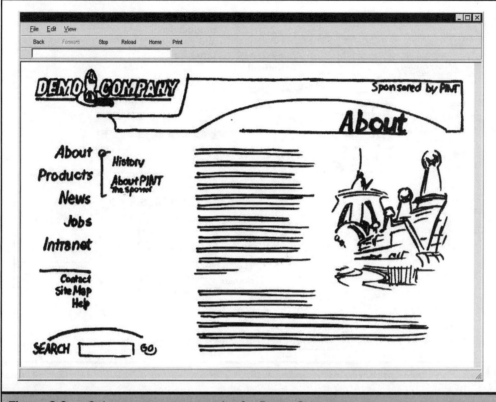

Figure 2-6. *Subpage paper composite for Demo Company*

Although not all sites will require technical prototypes, highly interactive sites should consider developing not only interface prototypes but working proof of concept prototypes that show how technological aspects such as database query, personalization, e-commerce, and so on work. Unfortunately, what tends to happen is that technical prototypes are not built until a nearly complete interface is put in place, which might result in heavy rework.

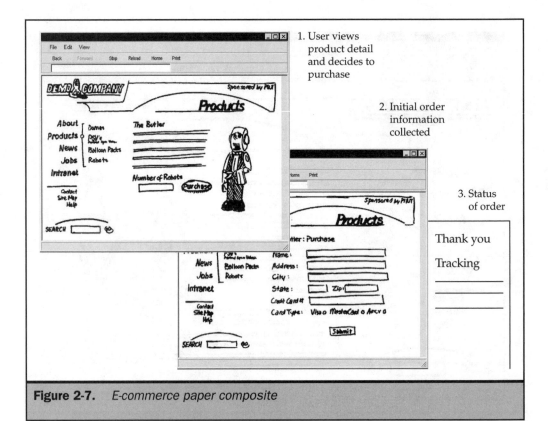

Figure 2-7.   *E-commerce paper composite*

Creating the Mock Site

After all design prototypes have been finalized, it is time to create what might be called the mock or alpha site. Implementation of the mock site starts by cutting a digital comp into its pieces and assembling the pages using HTML and, potentially, cascading style sheets. Try assembling the site in templates so that the entire site can be quickly assembled. However, do not put the content in place during this phase. Many of today's modern publishing tools aid in the assembly of sample pages from screen composites. For example, consider the digital home page composite of the Demo Company site shown in Figure 2-5. We then can use a tool such as Macromedia Fireworks (www.macromedia.com/software/fireworks) to "slice" the sample layout into its appropriate pieces as shown in Figure 2-8.

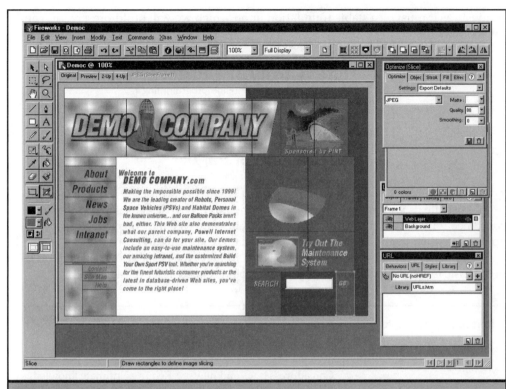

Figure 2-8. *Slicing comps and building templates*

Designers should be cautious when using the HTML produced by slice and save features of tools such as Fireworks or Adobe ImageReady. These tools often produce very complex or difficult-to-maintain HTML markup.

With the various pieces that make up the home page and the various subpages of a site a Web designer can use HTML tools to assemble the components into fully working pages lacking real content.

Producing the HTML

While visuals and technical elements are very important to Web design, the heart of nearly every modern Web page is still HTML. Creation of HTML should be taken very seriously as it must be a stable foundation upon which we will build presentation and interactivity.

```
┌─────────────────────────────────────────────────┐
│           Interactivity of a Page:              │
│    Built with server- and client-side programming │
└─────────────────────────────────────────────────┘
┌─────────────────────────────────────────────────┐
│            Presentation of Page:                │
│    Built with HTML, CSS, Flash, and Media Elements │
└─────────────────────────────────────────────────┘
┌─────────────────────────────────────────────────┐
│               Structure of Page:                │
│              Built in HTML/XHTML                 │
└─────────────────────────────────────────────────┘
```

Yet despite its importance as the page's foundation, Web designers often are more concerned with how they create HTML rather than how well they do it, or how appropriate their method of creation is. In truth, there are pros and cons to every method of HTML page creation, from hand editing of markup to the latest WYSIYWG editor. Each of the basic methods and some of its pros and cons are presented in Table 2-2.

Method	Example	Pros	Cons
By hand	Coding pages with Notepad	Great deal of control over the HTML Can address bugs and new HTML elements or CSS properties immediately	Slow Error prone Requires intimate knowledge of HTML elements and CSS properties No direct visual representation
Translation	"Save as HTML" from another tool like Microsoft Word	Quick Simplifies conversion of existing documents	Produced HTML often is problematic Still requires editing to add links and clean up problems
Tagging Editor	Using HomeSite	Great deal of control Faster than hand editing Provides help addressing errors and writing structured HTML or correct CSS	Slow Requires intimate knowledge of HTML and CSS
WYSIWYG Editor	Using FrontPage or Dreamweaver	Works on visual representation of page Requires no significant knowledge of HTML or CSS	Might generate incorrect HTML or CSS Precise control of layout often requires direct markup editing

Table 2-2.   *Methods of HTML Production*

The reality of creating HTML documents is that there are occasions to use nearly every approach. For example, making a quick change of a single tag often is fastest in a pure text editor, saving out large existing print documents might make sense using a translator, precision coding of an HTML template might best performed within a tagging editor, and building a modest site in a visual manner is easily done using a WYSIYWG editor. Always consider the applicability of the tool to the job before marrying it.

The tools change all the time but at the time this edition was written the HTML tools mentioned in Table 2-3 are popular. Certainly many tools exist—all with their own features and benefits—but given their use at large-scale Web firms the combination of Dreamweaver and HomeSite is suggested for professional developers.

Product	Platform(s)	URL	Comments
Dreamweaver	Windows Macintosh	http://www.macromedia.com/	A good visual design tool that balances WYSIWYG design capabilities with code editing. Strong CSS and DHTML support.
HomeSite	Windows	http://www.allaire.com/ homesite	A top-notch text editor for HTML professionals. Poor visual support but incredible code and markup handling. Its sister product, Cold Fusion Studio, adds even greater support for dynamic site building technologies.
GoLive	Macintosh Windows	http://www.adobe.com/ products/golive/	Very popular among the Macintosh set, this tool has a visual designers–oriented interface. Some generated markup problems have limited its popularity with strict standards developers.
FrontPage	Windows	http://www.microsoft.com/ frontpage	Popular with the small developer and internal corporate development crowds. It has improved greatly, but still has a reputation for generating bad or too Microsoft-specific pages.

Table 2-3. *A Selection of Popular HTML Development Tools*

WYSIWYG Promises

Given the HTML creation approaches previously mentioned, many people will wonder why anyone would bother with anything other than the *WYSIWYG* (What You See Is What You Get) variety of tool such as FrontPage or Dreamweaver. Consider the difference between direct markup editing and visual editing shown in Figure 2-9.

At first glance, it would be pretty hard to convince any pragmatic individual that direct editing of HTML markup is the way to go. While WYSIWYG page creation tools certainly hide the complexity of HTML from the designer, they also don't always deliver on their promises. The reality is that these tools really are somewhat misnamed and instead ought to be called WYSIWYMG (What You See is What You *Might* Get) editors. Remember that the browser is the final display environment for HTML, so what a visual editor shows you might not accurately reflect what the eventual presentation might be, as shown in Figure 2-10.

Even worse than the not-quite WYWIWYG issue, many visual Web page editors have a difficult time dealing with all the various browser extensions. They often seem to introduce their own special ways of using HTML. Often visual editors simply produce bad or extremely bulky HTML.

Yet while the ultimate promise of visual Web page editing hasn't quite panned out yet, few pundits would suggest that hand production of HTML is the wave of the future. Once HTML becomes more rigorous in the form of XHTML, and CSS becomes

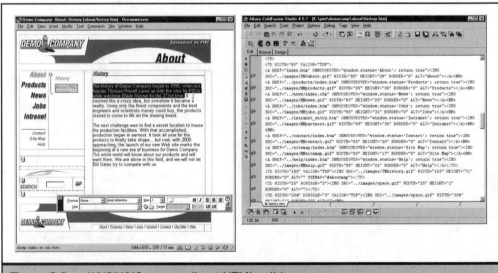

Figure 2-9.   *WYSIWYG versus direct HTML editing*

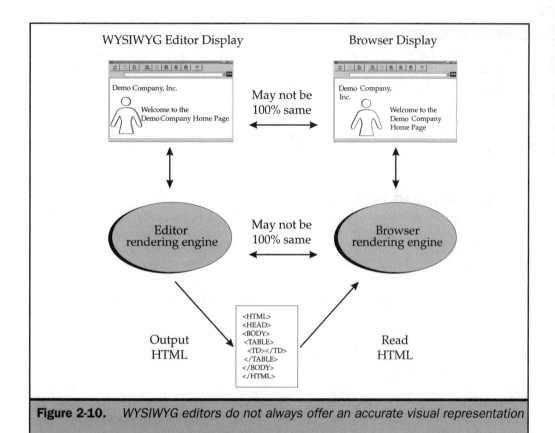

Figure 2-10. *WYSIWYG editors do not always offer an accurate visual representation*

better supported, editors will find it far easier to produce quality markup. Hand editing of markup eventually will go the way of mechanical typesetting. For now though, page designers had better know HTML backward and forward to make sure that pages render correctly.

HTML Production Tips

Regardless of how HTML documents are constructed, special care should be taken when producing markup. Standards should be followed and a style adopted. In this book it is always suggested to utilize most, if not all, of the XHTML rules briefly introduced in Chapter 1 in order to make your markup as future-proof as possible. This section will summarize this approach as well as present some other tips that should lead to better HTML production.

Use Lowercase

Although stylistically it might be easier to pick out uppercase tags when viewing HTML documents, as mentioned in the previous edition of this book, it is best to use lowercase given that XHTML requires this.

Use Quotes

Just because you can write markup like **<p align=right>** under traditional HTML, doesn't mean you should. Quote *all* attributes so that the document is closer to XHTML compliance: **<p align="right">**.

Use Well-Formed Markup

Remember, HTML is based on a well-defined specification. Just because a browser lets you get away with bad markup doesn't mean you should. In general make sure that all HTML is well formed—tags closed, nested, and properly used. Always specify a DTD line such as

```
<!DOCTYPE HTML PUBLIC "-//W3C//DTD HTML 4.01 Transitional//EN">
```

at the top of your document to indicate what form of HTML you are using and try to follow the rules indicated by that specification. Of course, mistakes do happen—so make sure to validate, which is discussed next.

Validate

The benefit of validation cannot be overstated. No matter how HTML documents are created, they should always be validated. Validation involves checking an HTML file to ensure that it meets the HTML specification and rules previously discussed. Few tools actually create HTML markup completely correctly, and when building HTML files by hand it is easy to make mistakes. Many popular Web editors offer built-in validation. Online validation also is possible using a site such as http://validator.w3.org. The CSE Validator (www.htmlvalidator.com) is probably the best standalone HTML validator available. To understand the benefits of validation consider the HTML shown here. This example has numerous errors including proprietary attribute usage, missing quotes, bad nesting, tags used in inappropriate ways and tags that aren't closed.

```
<html>
<head>
<title>Messed <b>Up!</b></title>
</head>
<body bgproperties="fixed">
<h1 align="center">Broken HTML
```

```
<hr>
<ul>
<p>Is this <b><i>correct</b></i>?<br>
<a href=HTTP://WWW.DEMOCOMPANY.COM>
Visit DemoCompany</a>
<pre>
      Should we do <b>this?</b>
      How about entities &copy; ?
</pre>
</ul>
</body>
<html>
```

Running the page through a validator catches all the errors as shown in Figure 2-11.

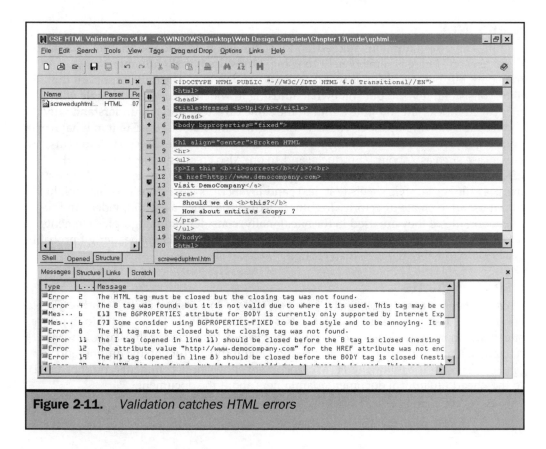

Figure 2-11. *Validation catches HTML errors*

Don't Mix Script, Style, and Structure

Designers should always try to keep HTML files as simple as possible. With the inclusion of style sheet information and JavaScript an HTML file can get pretty huge and very complicated. Rather than intermix presentation described in CSS into a page directly, designers should link to an external style using markup like

```
<link rel="stylesheet" href="styles/pagestyle1.css">
```

as discussed in Chapter 10. For JavaScript, files should be linked using syntax like this:

```
<script src="scripts/validate.js" type="javascript"></script>
```

as discussed in Chapter 13 to isolate potentially complex code rather than including it in the HTML directly. By cleanly separating look and interactivity to other files it is far easier to make changes to a page.

Name Well

Naming can be a continuous suggestion for some designers—to use an .htm or .html file extension? There is some benefit to using .htm since it is slightly more transportable, but the reality is that it really doesn't matter. The only important thing is to be consistent. It is sad but somewhat amusing to watch developers struggle with files called index.htm and index.html in the same directory and not understand why changes are showing up. Save yourself the aggravation and be consistent in whatever you choose. Also consider making sure to use common, simple directory names in lower case such as /about, /products, and so on. Also create simple, well-named directories for common site elements. In particular you should create a directory for images (/images), style sheets (/styles) , and JavaScripts (/scripts). You also might find it useful to create directories for other media types such as sound, video, and animation files if they are used in the site. Finally, consider naming graphic elements and other site components in an easy-to-understand manner. Homeheader.gif probably is a better name for an image than r1c1.gif.

Use Comments

Recall that comments can be inserted into an HTML document using <!-- and -->. Use a comment to describe difficult sections, insertions, or simply to leave a note for a future site maintainer. In particular, you might want to put comments at the start of HTML documents indicating important information about the document, the author, and so on. For example, the following HTML document shows how comments could be used in the **<head>** to inform document maintainers about the document.

```
<!DOCTYPE HTML PUBLIC "-//W3C//DTD HTML 4.01 Transitional//EN">
<html>
<head>
<title>Demo Company Announces Butler 1.0</title>
<!--
    Document Name: Butler Robot Press Release

    Description: The press release announcing the newest Robot
                 Butler in the Demo Company family.

    Author: Thomas A. Powell (tpowell@democompany.com)

    Creation Date: 9/15/00
    Last Updated: 9/25/00
    Comments: Used SuperDuperEdit 7.0 to build the page.
-->
</head>
<body>
...
</body>
</html>
```

Use Templates

One of the best things to consider when authoring HTML pages is not pages, but templates. Why make ten different press releases, when a single press release template can be created and modified? Unfortunately, many tools and design books alike tend to take a one-page-at-a-time approach. Avoid this and create generic templates. Using a template will speed up development and make resulting pages more consistent in style and structure. Some designers are hesitant to use templates thinking that it limits design possibilities. Templates don't take the creativity out of design. In fact, using templates takes much of the tedium out of building sites, leaving the designer more time to design. In most cases, if a designer is following the rules of consistency and usability, there really are no restrictions imposed by templates.

Format

When producing HTML by hand, it is a good idea to format the document in a consistent manner. For example, consider matching tags up on tab stops, using white space to separate sections of a document and ordering attributes within tags alphabetically. Following simple formatting really can make it easier to come back later on and make changes.

On the opposite end of the spectrum, if you end up using a visual HTML editor of some sort and never plan on looking at or editing the underlying HTML markup, you might want to go all the way and "crunch" the page as shown in Figure 2-12. The idea of crunching is to remove all spaces and other non-required elements such as comments from the final page. This will make the page smaller and thus faster to deliver to the user. If you don't plan on ever editing the document outside a visual tool, crunching HTML is okay, but be careful. Once HTML is crunched it can be difficult to go back to something easily readable, so keep a spare copy of your pages around just in case.

The previous few section discussed some of the design and production issues required to build a simple mock or alpha site. The mock or alpha site is like the frame of a house. There is much more to fill in. You still might have to add technical "plumbing and wiring" and finally populate your site with real content before you can release a site.

Beta Site Implementation

Once the mock site is produced and deemed acceptable, it is time to actually implement the beta site. Real content should be placed in pages, and back-end components and interactive elements should be integrated with the final visual design.

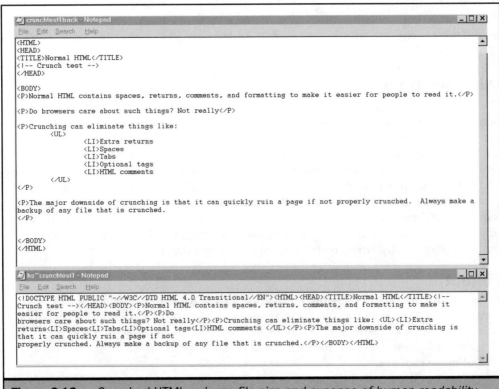

Figure 2-12. *Crunched HTML reduces file size and expense of human readability*

Although implementation would seem to be the most time-consuming aspect of a project, in reality, if all the components have been collected and prototypes built prior to this stage, the actual site implementation might occur relatively rapidly.

Testing

For most developers, testing is probably the least favorite aspect of the Web development process. After all the hard work of specification, design, and implementation, most people are ready to just launch the site. Resist the urge. Testing is key to a positive user takeaway value. Don't force your users to test your site after its release. If they encounter bugs with what is considered a production site, they won't be forgiving. Unfortunately, testing on the Web generally is relegated to a quick look at the site using a few browsers and maybe checking the links in the site. Bugs will exist in Web sites, no matter what. Unfortunately, most developers consider that if the site looks right, it is right. Yet Web design doesn't just include visual design: You must test all the other aspects of site design as well. The basic aspects of Web testing are overviewed here.

Visual Acceptance Testing

Visual acceptance testing ensures that the site looks the way it was intended. View each of the pages in the site and make sure that they are consistent in layout, color, and style. Look at the site under different browsers, resolutions, and viewing environments equivalent to those of a real user. Browse the site very quickly and see if the layouts jump slightly. Consider looking at the pages while squinting to notice abstract irregularities in layout. Visual acceptance testing also might require each page to be printed. Remember to avoid focusing on print testing pages that are designed solely for online consumption.

Functionality Testing

Functionality testing and visual testing do overlap in the sense that the most basic function of a page is to simply render onscreen. However, most sites contain at least basic functions such as navigation. Make sure to check every link in a site and rectify any broken links. Broken links should be considered catastrophic functional errors. Make sure to test all interactive elements such as forms or shopping carts. Use both realistic test situations as well as extreme cases. Try to break your forms by providing obviously bad data. Remember: Users won't think as you do, so prepare for the unexpected.

Content Proofing

The content details of a site are very important. Make sure content is all in place and that grammar and word usage is consistent and correct. Check details such as product names, copyright dates, and trademarks. And always remember to check the spelling! Clients and users often will regard an entire site as being poor just on the basis of one small typo; the importance of this cannot be stressed enough. The best way to perform this test is to print each page and literally read every single line for accuracy.

System and Browser Compatibility Testing

Hopefully, system and browser restrictions have been respected during development, but this must be verified during testing. Make sure to browse the site with the same types of systems and browsers the site's users will have. Unfortunately it often seems that designers check compatibility on systems far more powerful than the typical user. The project plan should have detailed browser requirements, so make sure the site works under the specified browsers.

Delivery Testing

Check to make sure the site is delivered adequately. Try browsing the site under real user conditions. If the site was designed for AOL modem users, set up an AOL account and a modem to test delivery speed. To simulate site traffic, consider using testing software to create virtual users clicking on the site. This will simulate how the site will react under real conditions. Make sure that you test the site on the actual production server to be used or a system equivalent to it. Be careful to not underestimate delivery influences. The whole project might be derailed if this was not adequately thought about during specification. For further information on delivery issues such as hosting, see Chapter 15.

User Acceptance Testing

User acceptance testing should be performed after the site appears to work correctly. In software, this form of testing often is called *beta* testing. Let the users actually try the working site and comment on it one last time. Do not perform this type of testing until the more obvious bugs have been rectified. User testing is the most important form of testing because it most closely simulates real use. If problems are uncovered during this phase of testing, you might not be able to correct them right away. If the problems are not dramatic, you can still release the site and correct the problems later. However, if any significant issues are uncovered, it is wise to delay release until they can be corrected.

Release and Beyond

Once the site is ready to be released, don't relax—you are not done. In fact, your work has just begun. It is time now to observe the site in action. Does the site meet user expectations? Were the site development goals satisfied? Are any small corrections required? The bottom line is that the site must live on. New features will be required. Upgrades to deal with technology changes are inevitable. Visual changes to meet marketing demands are very likely. The initial development signifies the start of a continual development process most call *maintenance*. Web development is a process; once you are done it might be time to go back to the beginning of the design process to assess the goals and whether or not they were met and try again—plan, design, develop, release, repeat.

Welcome to the Real World

Although the site development process appears to be a very straightforward cycle, it doesn't always go so smoothly. There are just too many variables to account for in the real world. For example, consider the effects of building a site for another person such as boss or client. If someone else is paying for a site to be built, you might still need to indulge their desires regardless of whether the requests conform to what the user wants. Make sure you attempt to persuade others that decisions should always be made with the user in mind. Try to show the benefits of design theories rather than preaching rules. Be prepared to show examples of your ideas that are fully fleshed out. However, accept that they often might be shot down.

Note *Experienced designers often will create a variety of site comps to guide discussion, similar to a book of haircuts for customers who can't verbalize what they want.*

Most Web projects tend to have political problems. Don't expect everyone to agree. Departments in a company will wrestle for control, often with battle lines being drawn between the marketing department and the technology groups. To stir up even more trouble, there might be numerous self-proclaimed Web experts nearby who are ready to give advice. Don't be surprised when someone's brother's friend turns out to be a Web "expert" who claims you can build the whole site with Microsoft FrontPage wizards in one hour. The only way to combat political problems is to be patient and attempt to educate. Not everyone will understand the purpose of the site; without a clear specification in place, developers might find themselves in a precarious position open to attack from all sides.

Always remember that the purpose of following a process model such as the one discussed in this chapter is to minimize the problems that occur during a Web project. However, a process model won't account for every real-world problem, particularly people issues. Experience is the only teacher for dealing with many problems. Developers lacking experience in Web projects are always encouraged to roll with the punches and consider all obstacles as learning experiences.

Summary

Building a modern Web site can be challenging, so site builders should adopt a methodology or process model to guide the development process and hopefully minimize risk, manage complexity, and generally improve the end result. Software engineering process models such as the waterfall easily can be applied to most Web projects. However, occasionally because of a lack of project management experience or clear goal statements, a prototype-driven or joint application process should be employed.

Although a prototype-based approach would seem to easily fit with the organic nature of many sites, it can produce needless risk and result in building the wrong site numerous times, before building the right one. Planning during the early stages of a site's development minimizes risk and should improve the end result. A design document that usually includes site goals, audience and task analysis, content requirements, site structure, technical requirements, and management considerations should always be developed. The design document guides the production of the Web site. During the design phase of site production, use block diagrams, paper mock-ups, storyboards, and even mock sites to reduce the likelihood of having to redesign the site later on.

If a plan is well thought out and the design phase prototypes built, implementation ranging from HTML to JavaScript should proceed rapidly and require little rework. However, once finished, be careful to not rush the site online—adequate testing is required and HTML quality should be treated very seriously. If a poorly crafted site is released, maintenance might immediately be required.

The Complete Reference

Part II

Core HTML

The
Complete
Reference

Chapter 3

Core Elements

This chapter introduces the basic HTML elements common to nearly every browser, as defined by the HTML 4.0 transitional specification. These elements fall into three distinct groups: block-level elements, text-level elements, and character entities. The elements are presented for the most part from top-down; from larger, block-oriented structures (such as paragraphs), to smaller units (such as the actual character entities). First, however, the core attributes that are common to all HTML elements are presented.

Core HTML Attributes

To accommodate new technologies such as style sheets and scripting languages, some important changes have been made to HTML. A set of four core attributes has been added that nearly all HTML elements support. At this stage, the purpose of these attributes might not be obvious, but it is important to address their existence before discussing the various HTML elements. HTML 4.0's core attributes are **id**, **class**, **style**, and **title**. Most HTML elements will have these attributes associated with them.

id Attribute

The **id** attribute is used to set a unique name for a tag in a document. For example, using **id** with the paragraph element, **<p>**,

```
<p id="FirstParagraph">
This is the first paragraph of text.
</p>
```

names the bound tag **"FirstParagraph"**. Naming a tag is useful for manipulating the enclosed contents with a style sheet. For example, a style sheet rule such as

```
<style type="text/css">
<!--
#FirstParagraph {color: red;}
-->
</style>
```

could be put in the **<head>** of a document. This style rule says to make an element named "FirstParagraph" red. Naming is key to associating style or interactivity to particular elements. Of course, document authors must make sure objects are named uniquely, as having elements with the same **id** attribute value might cause significant bugs. The uses of the **id** attribute for style sheets and scripting are discussed in Chapter 10 and Chapter 13, respectively.

class Attribute

The **class** attribute is used to indicate the class or classes that a tag might belong to. Like **id**, **class** is used to associate a tag with a name, so

```
<p id="FirstParagraph" class="important">
   This is the first paragraph of text.
</p>
```

not only names the paragraph uniquely as **FirstParagraph**, but also indicates that this paragraph belongs to a class grouping called **important**. Class names don't have to be unique to a document. The main use of the **class** attribute is to relate a group of elements to various style sheet rules. For example, a style sheet rule such as

```
<style>
<!--
.important {background-color: yellow;}
-->
</style>
```

would give all elements with the **class** attribute set to **important** a yellow background. More examples of the use of **class** and **id** with style sheets can be found in Chapter 10.

style Attribute

The **style** attribute is used to add style sheet information directly to a tag. For example,

```
<p style="font-size: 18pt">
   This is the first paragraph of text.
</p>
```

sets the font size of the paragraph to be 18 point. Although the **style** attribute allows CSS rules to easily be added to an element, it is preferable to use **id** or **class** to relate a document-wide or linked style sheet. The use of CSS is discussed in Chapter 10.

title Attribute

The **title** is used to provide advisory text about a tag or its contents. In the case of

```
<p title="Introductory paragraph">
This is the first paragraph of text.
</p>
```

the **title** attribute is set to indicate that this particular paragraph is the introductory paragraph. Browsers can display this advisory text in the form of a tool tip, which might be useful to provide context-sensitive help, extra information, or other advice to the user, as shown here:

> This is the first paragraph of text.
> Introductory paragraph

The core attributes might not make a great deal of sense at this time, because generally they are most useful with scripting and style sheets, but keep in mind that these four attributes are assumed with every tag that is introduced for the rest of this chapter.

Core Language Attributes

One major goal of HTML 4.0 is to provide better support for languages other than English. The use of other languages might require that text direction be changed from left to right across the screen to right to left. Nearly all HTML elements now support the **dir** attribute, which can be used to indicate text direction as either **ltr** (left to right) or **rtl** (right to left). For example,

```
<p dir="rtl">
This is a right to left paragraph.
</p>
```

Furthermore, mixed-language documents might become more common after support for non-ASCII-based languages is improved within browsers. The use of the **lang** attribute enables document authors to indicate, down to the tag level, the language being used. For example,

```
<p lang="fr">
    C'est Francais.
</p>

<p lang="en">
    This is English.
</p>
```

Although the language attributes should be considered part of nearly every HTML element, in reality, these attributes are poorly supported by currently available browsers.

Core Events

The last major change made in HTML 4.0 was to improve the possibility of adding scripting to HTML documents. In preparation for a more dynamic Web, a set of core events has been associated with nearly every HTML element. Most of these events are associated with a user doing something. For example, the user clicking an object is associated with an **onclick** event attribute. So,

```
<p onclick="alert('Ouch!')">
Press this paragraph
</p>
```

would associate a small bit of scripting code with the paragraph event, which would be triggered when the user clicks the paragraph. In reality, the event model is not fully supported by all browsers for all tags, so the previous example might not do much of anything. A much more complete discussion of events is presented in Chapter 13, as well as in Appendix A. For now, just remember that any tag can have a multitude of events associated with it, paving the way for a much more dynamic Web experience.

Now that the core attributes have been covered we can avoid mentioning them for every element presented, and turn to the most common elements used in HTML. The next section begins the discussion with some of the most common block-level elements found in a document—headings.

Headings

The heading elements are used to create "headlines" in documents. Six different levels of headings are supported: **<h1>**, **<h2>**, **<h3>**, **<h4>**, **<h5>**, and **<h6>**. These range in importance from **<h1>**, the most important, to **<h6>**, the least important. Most browsers display headings in larger and/or bolder font than normal text. This causes many HTML authors to think erroneously of heading elements as formatting that makes text bigger or bolder. Actually, heading elements (such as headings themselves) convey logical meaning about a document's structure. Sizing and weight are relative to the importance of the heading, so **<h1>** level headings are larger than **<h3>** headings. As headings, included text is displayed in an alternative style (bigger and/or bold) and on a line of its own. In addition, as a block element returns generally are inserted after the heading. The following example markup demonstrates the heading elements:

```
<!DOCTYPE HTML PUBLIC "-//W3C//DTD HTML 4.01 Transitional//EN">
<html>
<head>
<title>Heading Example</title>
</head>
```

```
<body>
        <h1>Heading 1</h1>
        <h2>Heading 2</h2>
        <h3>Heading 3</h3>
        <h4>Heading 4</h4>
        <h5>Heading 5</h5>
        <h6>Heading 6</h6>
</body>
</html>
```

A sample rendering of this heading example is shown in Figure 3-1.

  The Lynx text browser renders headings very differently from commercial graphical browsers. Lynx can't display larger fonts, so it might attempt to bold them or align them. <h1> headings are aligned in the center, and each lower-level heading is indented more than the next-highest level heading.

   An attribute that aligns the text left, right, or center can be added to the heading elements. By default, headings usually are left-aligned, but by setting the **align** attribute of the various heading elements, the text can be aligned to the right, left, or

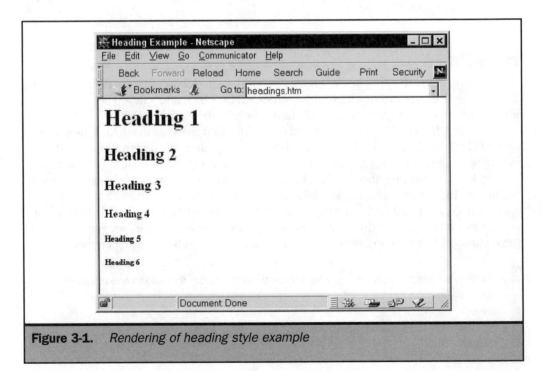

Figure 3-1.   *Rendering of heading style example*

center of the screen. The following example markup show the usage of the **align** attribute for headings:

```
<!DOCTYPE HTML PUBLIC "-//W3C//DTD HTML 4.01 Transitional//EN">
<html>
<head>
<title>Heading Alignment Example</title>
</head>
<body>
<h1 align="left">Aligned Left</h1>
<h1 align="center">Aligned Center</h1>
<h1 align="right">Aligned Right</h1>
</body>
</html>
```

Under the strict version of HTML 4.01, as well as under XHTML, the **align** attribute has been deprecated in favor of using style sheets.

HTML authors often use headings to make text large. As with all HTML elements, size is a relative concept, not an absolute concept. The actual size of the heading depends on the browser, the browser's setting, and the platform on which it is running. The size of an **<h1>** header under Navigator on a UNIX system appears different from the same **<h1>** header on a Windows machine running Internet Explorer. The headlines are relatively bigger, but the exact size is unknown, making consistent layout difficult. Furthermore, headlines have an implied logical meaning, and typically do more than to simply make something big.

 *A quick survey of heading use on the Web should reveal that headings beyond **<h3>** rarely are used. Why? Partially because people use headings in a visual fashion. The effects of **<h4>**, **<h5>**, and **<h6>** can be achieved with other elements. Furthermore, it is unusual for documents to have sections nested more than three levels deep.*

Paragraphs and Breaks

Unlike documents in word processors, HTML documents ignore multiple spaces, tabs, and carriage returns. Word wrapping can occur at any point in your source file, and multiple spaces are collapsed into a single space. To preserve some semblance of text formatting, elements are introduced to sectionalize the document. One of the most important structuring elements is the paragraph element. Surrounding text with the **<p>** and **</p>** tags indicates that the text is a logical paragraph unit. Normally, the browser places a blank line or two before the paragraph, but the exact rendering of the text depends on the browser and any applied style sheet. Text within the **<p>** normally is rendered flush left, with a ragged right margin. The **align** attribute makes it possible to specify a left, right, or center alignment. Under HTML 4.01, you also can set an **align** value of **justify**, to justify all text in the paragraph. Due to the poor quality of justification in some browsers and lack of support, this value seems to be used only rarely. The following example shows four paragraphs with alignment, the rendering of which is shown in Figure 3-2:

```
<!DOCTYPE HTML PUBLIC "-//W3C//DTD HTML 4.01 Transitional//EN">
<html>
<head>
<title>Paragraph Example</title>
</head>
<body>

<p>This is the first paragraph in the example about the P tag.
There really isn't much to say here.</p>

<p align="center">This is the second paragraph. Again, more of the
same. This time the paragraph is aligned in the center. This might
not be such a good idea as it makes the text hard to read.</p>

<p align="right">Here the paragraph is aligned to the right. Right
aligned text is also troublesome to read. The rest of the text of this
paragraph is of little importance.</p>

<p align="justify">Under HTML 4.0 compliant browsers, you are
able to justify text. As you may notice, the way browsers tend to
justify text is sometimes imprecise. Furthermore, not all browsers
support this attribute value.</p>

</body>
</html>
```

Because the **<p>** element generally causes a blank line, some HTML authors attempt to insert blank lines into a document by using multiple **<p>** elements. This rarely results in the desired outcome. The browser collapses empty **<p>** elements, because they represent logical text units, not physical formatting.

Note   *Many WYSIWYG HTML editors and some page authors try to get around the collapsing paragraph "problem" by using a non-breaking space character within a paragraph, to keep the element from collapsing, as shown here:* **<p> </p>**. *This approach isn't recommended, because it doesn't reduce markup used and further obscures the meaning of the document.*

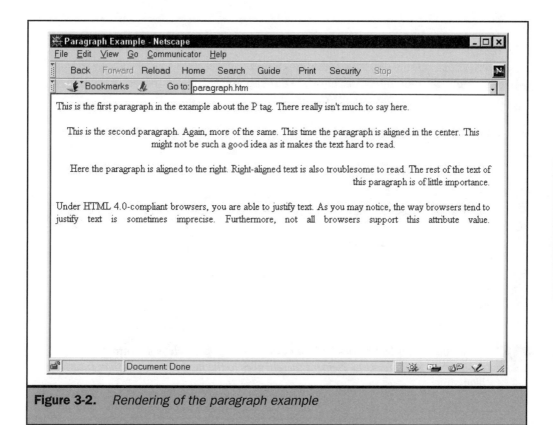

Figure 3-2.   *Rendering of the paragraph example*

To insert returns or blank lines in a document, the **
** element must be used. The **
** element is a text-level element that inserts a single carriage return or break into a document. It contains no content and has no end tag. It is an empty element—thus, no close tag. Because of this, under XHTML you would use **
** instead of just plain **
**. (See Chapters 1 and 17 for more about XHTML.) The one attribute commonly used with **
** is **clear**. This attribute allows **
** to affect how text flows around images or embedded objects. The use of **
** in this fashion is discussed in Chapter 5.

The following code fragment shows the basic uses of **<p>** and **
**, and also shows that the two elements are not equivalent, despite their physical rendering similarities (a screen rendering appears in Figure 3-3):

```
<!DOCTYPE HTML PUBLIC "-//W3C//DTD HTML 4.01 Transitional//EN">
<html>
<head>
<title>Break and Paragraph Example</title>
```

```
</head>
<body>
<p>This is the first paragraph.<br>
Not much to say here, either. You can use
breaks within a paragraph<br><br>
like so.
</p>

<p><p><p>

<p>This is the second paragraph. Notice that the three P
tags are treated as empty paragraphs and ignored.</p>

<p>If you use breaks</p>
<br><br><br><br>
<p>you'll get the desired result.</p>
</body>
</html>
```

Tip *Users looking for blank lines have to insert multiple **
** elements into their documents. A single **
** element merely goes to the next line rather than inserting a blank line.*

Divisions and Centering

The **<div>** element is used to structure HTML documents into unique sections or divisions. The **<div>** element is a logical block element that has no predefined meaning. Under traditional HTML the only major value of the **<div>** element is to align sections of content by setting the **align** attribute to left, right, or center. By default, content within the **<div>** element is left-aligned. Divisions are more significantly useful when used in conjunction with style sheets (see Chapter 10).

Aside from using the **<div>** element to align blocks of text, it is possible to center text using a difficult-to-characterize element: **<center>**. Under HTML 2.0-based browsers, centering text was impossible. One of the major additions introduced by Netscape was the **<center>** element. HTML 3.2 adopted this element because of its widespread use. To center text or embedded objects (such as images), simply enclose the content within **<center>** and **</center>**. In this sense, **<center>** appears to be a text-formatting style element, but under the HTML 3.2 and transitional 4.0 specification (and beyond), **<center>** is defined as an alias for a block-level structuring element and eventually will be deprecated under strict versions of HTML. Under the HTML 4.01 DTD, **<center>** simply is an alias for **<div align="center">** and is treated exactly the same way. The **<center>** element is unlikely to go away, considering its simplicity and

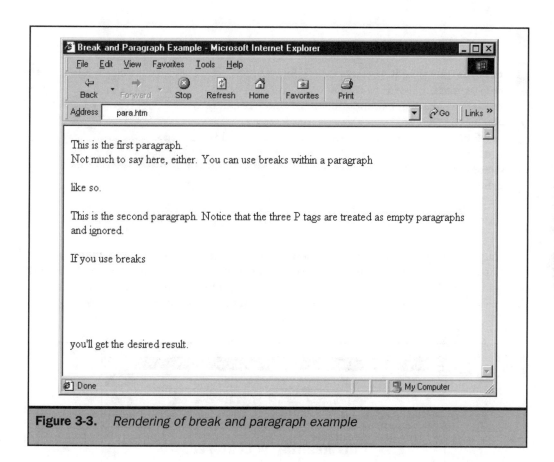

Figure 3-3. *Rendering of break and paragraph example*

widespread use. But according to specifications, there are two preferred ways to center content: the **<div>** element with a **center** alignment attribute, or the **align** attribute used in conjunction with **<img>** and possibly other elements. The following example shows the use of **<center>** and **<div>**. (Figure 3-4 shows their screen rendering.)

```
<!DOCTYPE HTML PUBLIC "-//W3C//DTD HTML 4.01 Transitional//EN">
<html>
<head>
<title>Center and Division Example</title>
</head>
<body>
<center>
<h1>This heading is centered</h1>
<p>This paragraph is also centered.</p>
</center>
```

```
<br><br>

<div align="right">
<h1>Division Heading</h1>
<p>Many paragraphs and other block elements
can be affected by a DIV at once</p>
<p>Notice all the paragraphs are right aligned</p>
</div>
</body>
</html>
```

Spans

Although the **<div>** element can be used to group large sections of a document for later application of a style sheet or various other formatting, it is not appropriate to put everything within a division. Consider that **<div>** is a block element; therefore, it will induce a return. If you want to group text without using a block element, use the

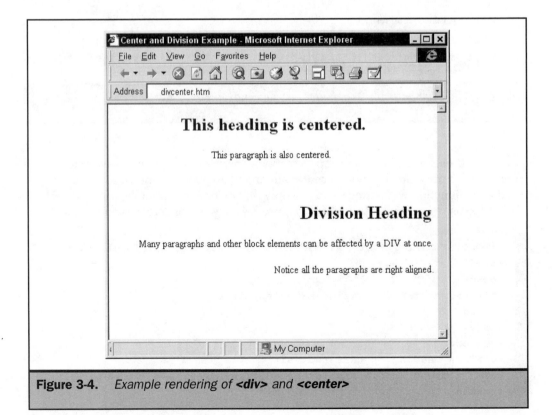

Figure 3-4.   *Example rendering of **<div>** and **<center>***

<span> element, as it provides logical grouping inline with no predefined look. Consider the following markup:

```
<p>In this sentence <span class="important">some of the text is
important!</span></p>
```

In this markup fragment, the **<span>** element wouldn't necessarily cause any particular presentation under plain HTML. However, as shown, using the **class** attribute it could be related to a style sheet to make the enclosed text look different, while at the same time providing no particular logical meaning. At this point the use of **<div>** and **<span>** elements might not make a great deal of sense, but they are some of the most useful of the core elements of HTML. Their use with style sheets will be discussed in Chapter 10.

Quotations

Occasionally, you might want to quote a large body of text to make it stand out from the other text. The **<blockquote>** element provides a facility to enclose large block quotations from other works within a document. Although the element is logical in nature, enclosing text within **<blockquote>** and **</blockquote>** usually indents the blocked information from both the left and right. Inline with its meaning, the **<blockquote>** element supports the cite attribute, which can be set to the Web address of the document or site from which the quotation was pulled, or a brief message describing the quote or its source.

Whereas a **<blockquote>** element will cause a return like other block elements, it is possible to create an inline quotation using the **<q>** element. The quote element (**<q>**) should put quotation marks around the quoted elements following the language being used in the page. This also includes following the rules for switching quotes within quotes. Older browsers do not support the **<q>** element, but it is part of the HTML 4.0/4.01 specifications. Like the **<blockquote>** element, **<q>** also supports a cite attribute. The following shows an example of **<blockquote>** and **<q>** (rendered in Figure 3-5):

```
<!DOCTYPE HTML PUBLIC "-//W3C//DTD HTML 4.01 Transitional//EN">
<html>
<head>
<title>Quotation Example</title>
</head>
<body>
<h1 align="center">Demo Company Quotes</h1>

<p>See the comments the press has about DemoCompany's
futuristic products.</p>
```

```
<q>My friend's friend said, <q cite="sounds fishy">My mother's
uncle's cousin thinks that the Demo Company robot is the
greatest invention ever!</q></q>
<br>--George P. Somolovich, Ordinary Citizen

<blockquote cite="http://www.democompany.com">
Demo Company's products are by far the best fictitious products
ever produced! Gadget lovers and haters alike will marvel at the
sheer uselessness of Demo Company gadgets. It's a true shame that
their products are limited only to HTML examples!
</blockquote>

--Matthew J. Foley, Useless Products Magazine

<p>With kudos like this, you need to make sure to buy your
Demo Company products today!</p>
</body>
</html>
```

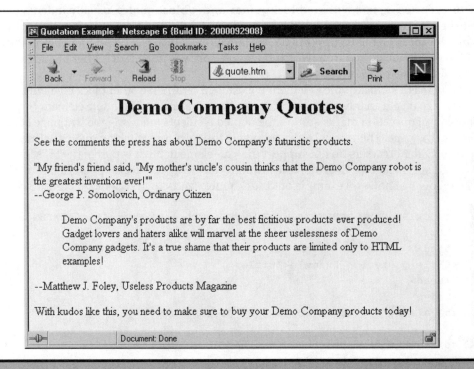

Figure 3-5. *Rendering of quotations example*

Note   *The first Web browsers did not provide any indentation or tab facility in regular text. Many HTML authors use **<blockquote>** to provide indentation. Text within **<blockquote>** can be indented on both sides of a page; it also can render in an alternative style (for example, italics). For this reason, the list elements, particularly the unordered list, are common workarounds to provide indentation in Web pages. In fact, many HTML editors insert these elements to create indentation. Until style sheets become more common, these workarounds will continue*

Preformatted Text

Occasionally, spacing, tabs, and returns are so important in text that HTML's default behavior of disregarding them would ruin the text's meaning. In such cases, you might want to preserve the intended formatting by specifying the text to be preformatted. Imagine that programming source code or poetry needs to be inserted into a Web page. In both cases, the spacing, returns, and tabs in the document must be preserved to ensure proper meaning. This situation requires an HTML directive that indicates the preservation of format. The **<pre>** and **</pre>** tags can be used to surround text that shouldn't be formatted by the browser. The text enclosed within the **<pre>** tags retains all spacing and returns, and doesn't reflow when the browser is resized. Scrollbars and horizontal scrolling are required if the lines are longer than the width of the window. The browser generally renders the preformatted text in a monospaced font, usually Courier. Some text formatting, such as bold, italics, or links, can be used within the **<pre>** tags. The following sample, displayed in Figure 3-6, uses the **<pre>** element and compares it to regular paragraph text:

```
<!DOCTYPE HTML PUBLIC "-//W3C//DTD HTML 4.01 Transitional//EN">
<html>
<head>
<title>PRE Example</title>
</head>
<body>
<pre>
This is P   R   E   F   O   R   M   A   T   T   E   D


    T

        E

          X

            T


SPACES       are ok!   So are


    RETURNS!
```

```
</pre>
<br><br>
<p>

This is NOT P   R   E   F   O   R   M   A   T   T   E   D

    T
      E
        X
          T

SPACES      and
RETURNS are lost.
</p>
</body>
</html>
```

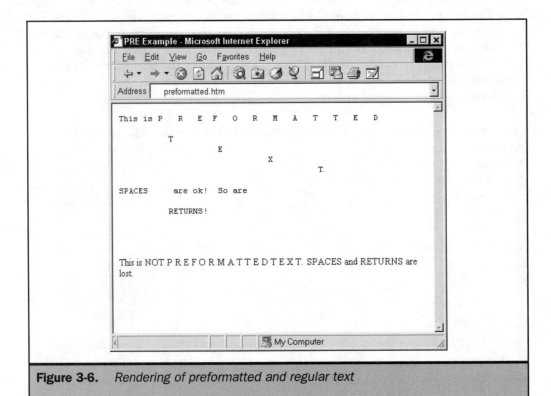

Figure 3-6. *Rendering of preformatted and regular text*

Note   *According to the HTML 4.0 specification, other HTML elements are allowed within the*
<pre> element, but some elements, such as <img>, are excluded. Most browsers allow
any elements, even those beyond the stated specification, to appear within the <pre>
elements, and render these as expected. Authors should not, however, rely on this.

Authors should be careful about using the **<pre>** element to create simple tables or
preserve spacing. Unpredictable differences in browser window sizes could introduce
horizontal scrolling for wide preformatted content. In these cases, other elements might
provide better formatting control.

Lists

Modern HTML has three basic forms of lists: ordered lists (**<ol>**), unordered lists
(**<ul>**), and definition lists (**<dl>**). Two other rarely used list elements, **<menu>** and
<dir>, are sparsely supported and usually are treated as unordered lists. Lists are
block-level, although they can be nested, and their items can contain other block-level
structures, such as paragraphs.

Ordered Lists

An ordered list, as enclosed by **<ol>** and **</ol>**, defines a list in which order matters.
Ordering typically is rendered by a numbering scheme, using Arabic numbers, letters,
or Roman numerals. Ordered lists are suitable for creating simple outlines or
step-by-step instructions, because the list items are numbered automatically by the
browser. List items in ordered and other lists are defined by using the list item element,
<li>, which doesn't require an end tag. For XHTML compliance, however, use of the
closing **</li>** tag is recommended. List items usually are indented by the browser.
Numbering starts from one. A generic ordered list looks like this:

```
<ol>
   <li>Item 1</li>
   <li>Item 2</li>
      . . .
   <li>Item n</li>
</ol>
```

In many browsers, the **<li>** element has some meaning outside a list. It often
renders as nonindented bullet. Some books recommend using **<li>** in this way, but it
isn't correct practice given the HTML content model. Although many browsers assume
an unordered bullet list, this use of **<li>** is undefined outside of a list structure.

The **<ol>** element has three basic attributes, none of which are required: **compact**,
start, and **type**. The **compact** attribute requires no value. It simply suggests that the
browser attempt to compact the list, to use less space onscreen. In reality, most
browsers ignore the **compact** attribute.

The **type** attribute of **<ol>** can be set to **a** for lowercase letters, **A** for uppercase letters, **i** for lowercase roman numerals, **I** for uppercase Roman numerals, or **1** for regular numerals. The numeral **1** is the default value. Remember that the **type** attribute within the **<ol>** element sets the numbering scheme for the whole list, unless it is overridden by a **type** value in an **<li>** element. Each **<li>** element can have a local **type** attribute set to **a, A, i, I,** or **1**. Once an **<li>** element is set with a new type, it overrides the numbering style for the rest of the list, unless another **<li>** sets the **type** attribute.

The **<ol>** element also has a **start** attribute that takes a numeric value to begin the list numbering. Whether the **type** attribute is a letter or a numeral, the **start** value must be a number. To start ordering from the letter *j*, **<ol type="a" start="10">** would be used, because *j* is the tenth letter. An **<li>** element within an ordered list can override the current numbering with the **value** attribute, which also is set to a numeric value. Numbering of the list should continue from the value set.

Note   *Numbering lists to count backward from 10 to 1 or to count by twos or other values is not directly possible in HTML. The author's opinion is that a single addition of a step attribute could address this, but it appears that the few remaining holes in HTML have been left unfilled.*

The use of ordered lists and their attributes is shown next, the rendering of which is shown in Figure 3-7:

```
<!DOCTYPE HTML PUBLIC "-//W3C//DTD HTML 4.01 Transitional//EN">
<html>
<head>
<title>Ordered List Example</title>
</head>
<body>

<p>Ordered lists can be very simple.</p>

<ol>
     <li>Item 1
     <li>Item 2
     <li>Item 3
</ol>

<p>Ordered lists can have a variety of types.</p>

<ol>
     <li type="a">Lowercase letters
     <li type="A">Uppercase letters
     <li type="i">Lowercase Roman numerals
     <li type="I">Uppercase Roman numerals
```

```
      <li type="1">Arabic numerals
</ol>

<p>Ordered lists can start at different values
and with different types.</p>

<ol start="10" type="a">
<li>This should be j
<li value="3">This should be c
   <ol>
      <li>Lists can nest
         <ol>
            <li>Nesting depth is unlimited
         </ol>
   </ol>
</ol>
</body>
</html>
```

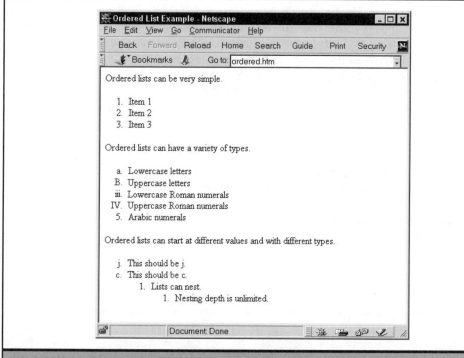

Figure 3-7.   *Rendering of ordered list example*

When dealing with extremes, numbering should be used with caution. Negative values or very large values produce unpredictable results. Whereas Navigator ignores negative numbers, Internet Explorer numbers up toward zero. Browsers can allocate a fixed width to the left of a list item to display its number. Under Navigator, a list not embedded in another block structure can accommodate only about four digits; larger numbers can overwrite list elements. A list indented by nesting in another block structure could have more space. Numbering in both Navigator and Internet Explorer loses meaning with large integer values, most likely because of limitations within the operating environment.

Unordered Lists

An unordered list, signified by **<ul>** and **</ul>**, is used for lists of items in which the ordering is not specific. This can be useful in a list of features and benefits for a product. A browser typically adds a bullet of some sort (a filled circle, a square, or an empty circle) for each item and indents the list.

Unordered lists can be nested. Each level of nesting indents the list farther, and the bullet changes accordingly. Generally, a filled circle or solid round bullet is used on the first level of lists. An empty circle is used for the second-level list. Third-level nested lists generally use a square. These renderings for bullets are common to browsers, but shouldn't be counted on. The **type** attribute can be used to set the bullet type for a list. The **type** attribute can appear within the **<ul>** element and set the type for the whole list, or it can appear within each **<li>**. A **type** specification in an **<li>** element overrides the value for the rest of the list, unless it is overridden by another **type** specification. The allowed values for **type**, as suggested by the default actions, are **disc**, **circle**, or **square**. This change isn't consistently supported across browsers. In the case of WebTV, a triangle bullet type also is available, because on a television a circle and square generally look the same due to limited resolution. For the greatest level of cross-browser compatibility, authors are encouraged to set the bullet type only for the list as a whole.

*Internet Explorer 3.0–level browsers under Windows don't render **type** settings for unordered lists. This has been fixed under Internet Explorer 4.0.*

The following is an example of unordered lists, various renderings of which are shown in Figure 3-8:

```
<!DOCTYPE HTML PUBLIC "-//W3C//DTD HTML 4.01 Transitional//EN">
<html>
<head>
<title>Unordered List Example</title>
</head>
<body>

<ul>
    <li>Unordered lists
        <ul>
            <li>can be nested.
                <ul>
                    <li>Bullet changes on nesting.
                </ul>
        </ul>
</ul>

<p>Bullets can be controlled with the TYPE attribute.
Type can be set for the list as a whole or item by item.</p>

<ul type="square">
    <li>First item bullet shape set by UL
    <li type="disc">Disc item
    <li type="circle">Circle item
    <li type="square">Square item
</ul>

</body>
</html>
```

Definition List

A definition list is a list of terms paired with associated definitions—in other words, a glossary. Definition lists are enclosed within **<dl>** and **</dl>**. Each term being defined is indicated by a **<dt>** element, which is derived for "definition term." Each definition itself is defined by **<dd>**. Neither the **<dt>** nor the **<dd>** element requires a close tag,

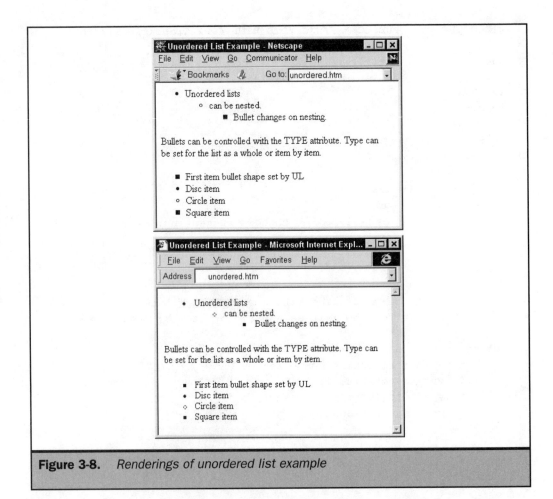

Figure 3-8. *Renderings of unordered list example*

but for long definitions and conformance to XHTML in the future, it is suggested. The following is a basic example using **<dl>**, the rendering of which is shown in Figure 3-9:

```
<!DOCTYPE HTML PUBLIC "-//W3C//DTD HTML 4.01 Transitional//EN">
<html>
<head>
<title>Definition List Example</title>
</head>
<body>
<h1 align="center">Definitions</h1>
<dl>
```

```
<dt>Gadget</dt>
<dd>A useless device used in many HTML examples.</dd>

<dt>Gizmo</dt>
<dd>Another useless device used in a few HTML examples.</dd>
</dl>
</body>
</html>
```

Vestigial Lists: <dir> and <menu>

Beyond basic ordered, unordered, and definition lists, two other lists are specified in HTML: **<menu>** and **<dir>**. These rarely used elements generally appear as unordered lists in most browsers. These elements are presented for completeness. HTML authors are warned to avoid using them, because they have been dropped from the strict version of HTML 4.0.

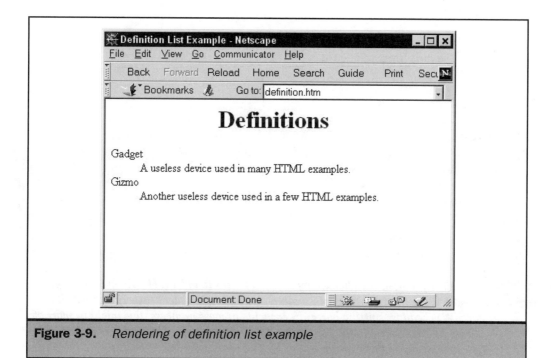

Figure 3-9.   *Rendering of definition list example*

Using Lists for Presentation

Because definition lists don't add numbering or bullets, many HTML writers have used this element to indent text. Although functionally this is the most appropriate way to achieve some rudimentary indentation, the unordered list often is used instead. Looking at the use of **<ul>** and the output of HTML tools suggests that the use of **<ul>** instead of **<dl>** to indent text quickly is very common. The reason for this preference for **<ul>** is that it requires fewer elements to achieve indentation. Remember that lists can be nested, so a varying degree of indentation can be achieved. Users desiring a fine degree of control should avoid using lists to move things around. How far something is moved away from the left margin isn't precise, and might depend on the font size of the browser. A simple example of indenting with lists is shown next, with its rendering shown in Figure 3-10:

```
<!DOCTYPE HTML PUBLIC "-//W3C//DTD HTML 4.01 Transitional//EN">
<html>
<head>
<title>List Indent Example</title>
</head>
<body>

<dl><dd><p>This paragraph is indented. Watch out for
the left edge. Get too close and you'll hurt yourself!</p>
</dl>

<br><br>

<ul><ul>
<p>This paragraph is even further indented. Most HTML authors
and authoring tools tend to use this style to indent because
it takes fewer tags.</p>
</ul></ul>

</body>
</html>
```

Note   *Some HTML purists are offended by the use of **<ul>** to indent. HTML authors might consider using the definition list, or tables, if possible, to indent text. However, with WYSIWYG editors spitting out **<ul>** elements in mass numbers, this might be more of a fine point than a real issue. The rise of style sheets and other technologies should, in time, put an end to this question.*

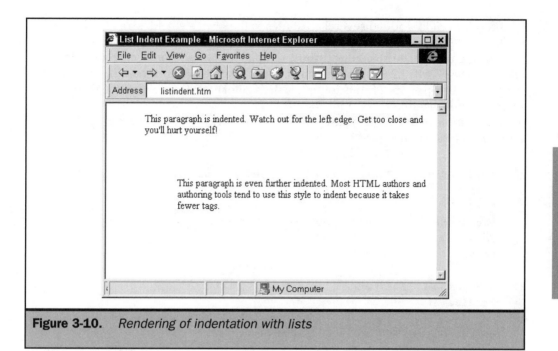

Figure 3-10.   *Rendering of indentation with lists*

Horizontal Rules

As sections are added to an HTML document, breaking up the document into visually distinct regions often is useful. A horizontal rule, indicated by the **<hr>** element, is a block-level element that serves this purpose. Under HTML 2.0, horizontal rules generally were rendered as an etched bar or line across a browser window. With HTML 3.2 and beyond, more control over the horizontal rule's look and size was added. Under strict HTML 4.0 and XHTML, the various presentation attributes for the horizontal rule have been removed leaving the exact look of the line to the browser rendering the page.

Note   *Although it looks like a physical element, **<hr>** can have some logical meaning as a section break. For example, under an alternative browser, such as a speech-based browser, a horizontal rule theoretically could be interpreted as a pause. A handheld browser with limited resolution might use it as a device to limit scrolling of the text.*

The **<hr>** element is an empty element, because it has no close tag and encloses no data. Adding an **<hr>** element between two paragraphs provides a simple way to put a horizontal rule between two sections.

Browser vendors added several attributes to the **<hr>** element. **size** sets the bar's thickness (height). The **width** attribute sets the bar's width. The **align** attribute sets its vertical alignment. The **noshade** attribute renders the bar without a surrounding shadow. The HTML 3.2 and transitional 4.0 specification support these basic attributes. Additional, browser-specific attributes (such as **color**) are described in the element reference in Appendix A.

An example of horizontal rules and their basic attributes is shown next. A browser rendering is shown in Figure 3-11:

```
<!DOCTYPE HTML PUBLIC "-//W3C//DTD HTML 4.01 Transitional//EN">
<html>
<head>
<title>Horizontal Rule Example</title>
</head>
<body>

<p>HR size of 10</p>
<hr size="10">

<p>HR width of 50% and no shading</p>
<hr width="50%" noshade>

<p>HR with width of 200 pixels, size of 3 pixels, and no shade</p>
<hr width="200" size="3" noshade>

<p>HR with width of 100, aligned right</p>
<hr align="right" width="100">

<p>HR with width of 100, aligned left</p>
<hr align="left" width="100">

<p>HR with width of 100, aligned center</p>
<hr align="center" width="100">

</body>
</html>
```

Other Block-Level Elements

HTML has many other block-level elements, most notably tables and forms. Many other elements are available under Navigator and Internet Explorer, including frames, layers, and a variety of other formatting and structuring features. These elements could be introduced in this chapter, but because of their complexity, it makes more sense to

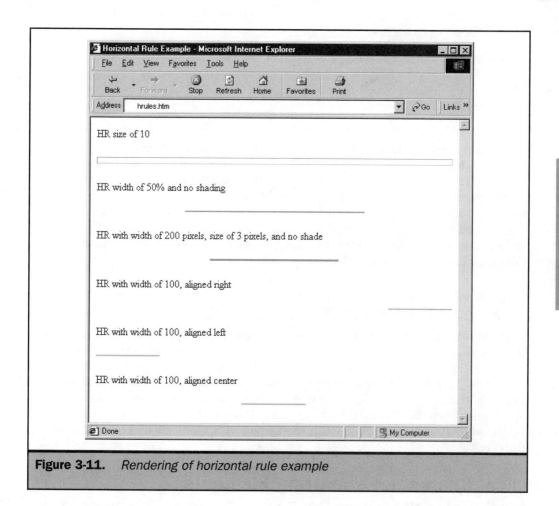

Figure 3-11.   *Rendering of horizontal rule example*

discuss them in later chapters. Tables are discussed in depth in Chapter 7, and forms
are discussed in Chapter 11. Before moving on to inline elements, let's cover one
element that's somewhat difficult to characterize: **<address>.**

address

The **<address>** element is used to surround information, such as the signature of the
person who created the page, or the address of the organization the page is about.
For example,

```
<address>
Demo Company, Inc.<br>
```

```
1122 Fake Street<br>
San Diego, CA 92109<br>
619.555.2086<br>
info@democompany.com<br>
</address>
```

can be inserted toward the bottom of every page throughout a Web site.

The **<address>** element tends to act like a logical formatting element and results, typically, in italicized text. The HTML specification treats **<address>** as an idiosyncratic block-level element. Like other block-level elements, it inserts a blank before and after the block. It can enclose many lines of text, formatting elements to change the font characteristics and even images. According to the specification, it isn't supposed to enclose other block-level elements such as **<ul>**. Browsers generally allow this, particularly with the **<p>** element.

Text-Level Elements

Text-level elements in HTML come in two basic flavors: physical and logical. *Physical elements*, such as **<b>** for bold and **<i>** for italic, are used to specify how text should be rendered. *Logical elements*, such as **<strong>** and **<em>**, indicate what text is, but not necessarily how it should look. Although common renderings exist for logical text elements, the ambiguity of these elements and the limited knowledge of this type of document structuring have reduced their use. However, the rise of style sheets and the growing diversity of user agents mean using logical elements makes more sense than ever.

Physical Character-Formatting Elements

Sometimes you might want to use bold, italics, or other font attributes to set off certain text, such as computer code. Common HTML supports various elements that can be used to influence physical formatting. The elements have no meaning other than to make text render in a particular way. Any other meaning is assigned by the reader. The common physical elements are listed in Table 3-1.

The following example code shows the basic use of the physical text-formatting elements:

```
<!DOCTYPE HTML PUBLIC "-//W3C//DTD HTML 4.01 Transitional//EN">
<html>
<head>
<title>Physical Text Elements</title>
</head>
```

```
<body>

<h1 align="center">Physical Text Elements</h1>
<hr>

This is <b>Bold</b>                                      <br>
This is <i>Italic</i>                                    <br>
This is <tt>Monospaced</tt>                              <br>
This is <u>Underlined</u>                                <br>
This is <strike>Strike-through</strike>                  <br>
This is also <s>Strike-through</s>                       <br>
This is <big>Big</big>                                   <br>
This is even <big><big>Bigger</big></big>               <br>
This is <small>Small</small>                             <br>
This is even <small><small>Smaller</small></small>      <br>
This is <sup>Superscript</sup>                           <br>
This is <sub>Subscript</sub>                             <br>

</body>
</html>
```

Element	Element Type
<i> ... </i>	Italics
<b> ... </b>	Bold
<tt> ... </tt>	Typewriter (monospaced)
<u> ... </u>	Underline
<strike> ... </strike>	Strikethrough
<s> ... </s>	Alternative element form of strikethrough (non-standard but common)
_{...}	Subscript
^{...}	Superscript
<big> ... </big>	Bigger font (one font size bigger)
<small> ... </small>	Smaller font (one font size smaller)

Table 3-1.   *Table of Common Physical Text-Formatting Elements*

Physical elements can be combined in arbitrary ways. However, just because text *can* be made monospaced, bold, italic, and superscript doesn't mean that various types of formatting *should* be applied to text. Figure 3-12 shows the rendering of the physical text elements under popular browsers.

Several physical text formatting elements—particularly **<u>**, **<big>**, and **<small>**—present certain problems that warrant extra discussion.

Confusion Caused by Underlining

Most browsers support the **<u>** element, which underlines text. It was not initially defined under HTML 2.0, and for good reason. The meaning of underlined text can be unclear to people who use the Web. In most graphical browsers, clickable hypertext links are represented as blue underlined text. (Link color might vary.) Users instinctively think of underlined text as something that can be clicked. Some feel that the link color sufficiently distinguishes links from text that is underlined purely for

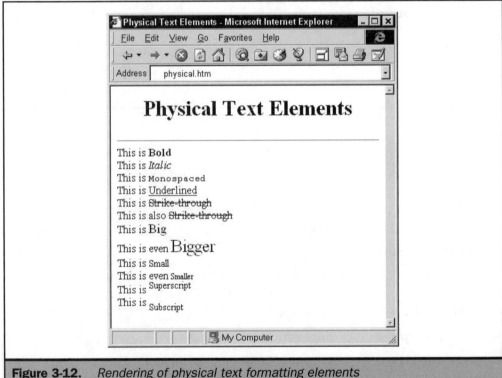

Figure 3-12.   *Rendering of physical text formatting elements*

stylistic purposes. However, this doesn't take into consideration monochrome monitors or people who are colorblind. Because the underline element could introduce more trouble than it is worth, it should be avoided.

Using <big> and <small>

What do the **<big>** and **<small>** elements actually do? On the face of it, putting the **<big>** element around something makes it bigger. Putting the **<small>** element around something makes it smaller. What about when multiple **<big>** and **<small>** elements are nested? HTML has relative fonts ranging from size 1, very small, to size 7, very large. Every application of **<big>** generally bumps up the font one notch to the next level. The default font for a document usually is relative size 3, so two applications of **<big>** would raise the font size to 5. Multiple occurrences of **<small>** do the opposite—they make things one size smaller. HTML authors familiar with the **<font>** element discussed in Chapter 6 should note that **<big>** is equivalent to **<font size="+1">** and **<small>** equivalent to **<font size="-1">**.

Logical Elements

Logical elements indicate the type of content that they enclose. The browser is relatively free to determine the presentation of that content, although there are expected renderings for these elements that are followed by nearly all browsers. Although this practice conforms to the design of HTML, there are issues about perception. Will a designer think **<strong>** or **<b>**? As mentioned previously, HTML purists push for **<strong>**, because a browser for the blind could read strong text properly. For the majority of people coding Web pages, however, HTML is used as a visual language, despite its design intentions. Furthermore, how do you indicate something is **<strong>** in a WYSIWYG editor?

Seasoned experts know the beauty and intentions behind logical elements, and hopefully, with style sheets logical elements will catch on more. For now, a quick survey of sites will show that logical text elements are relatively rare. In fact, many HTML editors make it downright difficult to add logical elements to a page, which only furthers the reasons why most logical elements are rarely used. When style sheets become more commonplace, HTML authors should reexamine their use of these elements. Table 3-2 illustrates the logical text-formatting elements generally supported by browsers.

The following example uses all the logical elements in a test document (shown in Figure 3-13 under common browsers):

```
<!DOCTYPE HTML PUBLIC "-//W3C//DTD HTML 4.01 Transitional//EN">
<html>
<head>
```

```
<title>Logical Text Elements</title>
</head>
<body>

<h1 align="center">Logical Text Elements</h1>
<hr>
<acronym>WWW</acronym> is an acronym <br>
<abbr>WWW</abbr> is an abbreviation  <br>
This is <em>Emphasis</em>            <br>
This is <strong>Strong</strong>      <br>
This is <cite>Citation</cite>        <br>
This is <code>Code</code>            <br>
This is <dfn>Definition</dfn>        <br>
This is <kbd>Keyboard</kbd>          <br>
This is <samp>Sample</samp>          <br>
This is <var>Variable</var>          <br>

</body>
</html>
```

Element	Element Type
< acronym> ... </acronym>	Acronym
<abbr> ... </abbr>	Abbreviation
<cite> ... </cite>	Citation
<code> ... </code>	Source code
<dfn> ... </dfn>	Definition
<em> ... <em>	Emphasis
<kbd> ... </kbd>	Keystrokes
<samp> ... </samp>	Sample (example information)
<strong> ... </strong>	Strong emphasis
<var> ... </var>	Programming variable

Table 3-2. *Table of Logical Text Formatting Elements*

CORE HTML

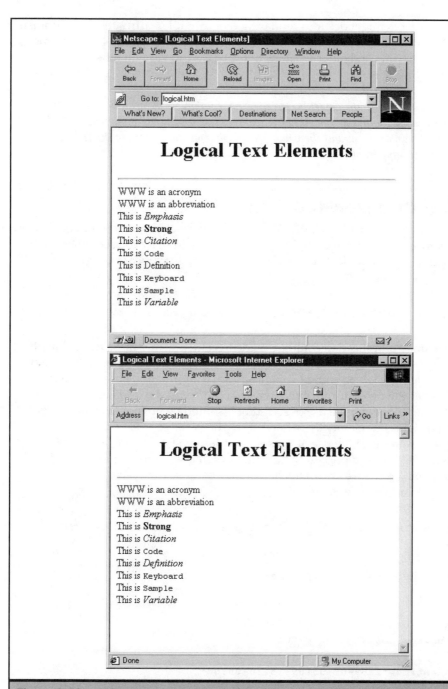

Figure 3-13. *Rendering of logical text formatting elements under Navigator and Internet Explorer*

Subtle differences might occur in rendering. For example, **<dfn>** results in Roman text under Netscape, but yields italicized text under Internet Explorer 4. There is no guarantee of rendering, and older versions of browsers can vary on other logical elements, including **<em>**.

 *The **abbr** and **acronym** elements currently have no practical meaning unless the **title** attribute is used with them; no browser changes text display for either element—but those that support them will show a tooltip display for the content of the **title** attribute. For browser support of these elements, see Appendix A.*

Inserted and Deleted Text

HTML 4.01 provides elements to indicate inserted and deleted text. The **<ins>** element is used to show inserted text and might appear underlined in a browser, whereas the **<del>** element is used to indicate deleted text and generally appears as struck text. For example the markup here

```
<p>There are <del>6</del><ins>5</ins> robot models</p>
```

shows how a small modification could be made to content using these two elements. It is possible to provide more information about the insert or delete through the use of the core attribute **title**, which could provide advisory information about the text change as well as the **datetime** attribute, which could be used to indicate when the change happened. Through the use of scripting it should be possible to hide various revisions made with this element.

A complete example of the use of **<ins>** and **<del>** is shown here; a rendering is given in Figure 3-14. It is important to note that in some sense these elements, like the **<center>** element, are very difficult to characterize because they can contain any amount of block or inline elements.

```
<!DOCTYPE HTML PUBLIC "-//W3C//DTD HTML 4.01 Transitional//EN">
<html>
<head>
<title>Insert and Delete</title>
</head>
<body>
<del><h1>Old Heading</h1></del>
<ins><h2>New Heading</h2></ins>
<p>This paragraph needs some changes.
<ins datetime="1999-01-05T09:15:30-05:00"
```

```
           title="New info inserted by TAP.">
This is a new sentence.</ins>
Here is some more text.</p>
</body>
</html>
```

Character Entities

After covering most of the block elements and the basic inline text formatting elements, you might think that nothing remains to talk about—but there is one more level to HTML documents: the characters themselves.

Sometimes, you need to put special characters within a document, such as accented letters, copyright symbols, or even the angle brackets used to enclose HTML elements. To use such characters in an HTML document, they must be "escaped" by using a special code. All character codes take the form &*code*;, in which *code* is a word or numeric code indicating the actual character that you want to put onscreen. Some of the more commonly used characters are shown in Table 3-3.

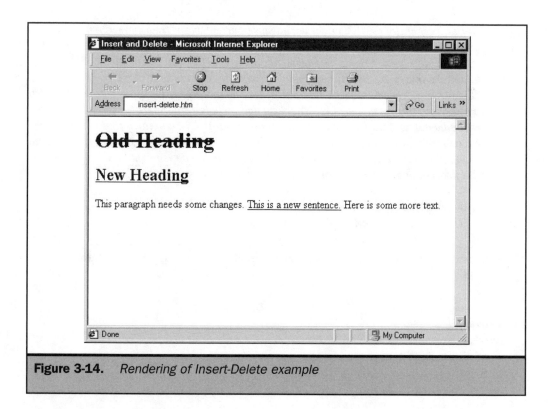

Figure 3-14.   *Rendering of Insert-Delete example*

Numeric Value	Named Value	Symbol	Description
&#034;	&quot;	"	Quotation mark
&#038;	&amp;	&	Ampersand
&#060;	&lt;	<	Less than
&#062;	&gt;	>	Greater than
&#153;	N/A	™	Trademark
			Non-breaking space
&#169;	&copy;	©	Copyright symbol
&#174;	&reg;	®	Registered trademark

Table 3-3.   *A Few Common Character Entities*

Note
The character entity ™ might not always be acceptable as trademark. On many UNIX platforms, and potentially on Macs or Windows systems using various "other" character sets, this entity doesn't render as trademark. Because &153; can be undefined, HTML authors should try to avoid it, even though it tends to coincide with ™ on the default Windows platform and some character sets. Trademarks are important legally, so they often are needed. A future version of HTML likely will include a trademark element, but for now, the commonly used workaround is to use ^{<small>TM</small>}. This code creates a superscript trademark symbol (™) in a slightly smaller font. Because it's standard HTML, it works on nearly every platform. Older Unix browsers might have some problems with this, but more recent Unix browsers might render this as [TM].

The following example shows some basic uses of HTML character entities; Figure 3-15 shows how the example might render:

```
<!DOCTYPE HTML PUBLIC "-//W3C//DTD HTML 4.01 Transitional//EN">
<html>
<head>
<title>Character Entities Example</title>
</head>
<body>
```

```
<h1 align="center">Demo Company Inc.'s Tagging Products</h1>
<hr>
<p>Character entities like &amp;copy; allow users to insert
special characters like &copy;.

<p>One entity that is both useful and abused is the
non-breaking space.</p>

<br><br>

Inserting spaces is easy with  <br>
Look:   S       P      
A       C       E
      S.<br>

<hr>
<address>
Contents of this page &copy; 1999 Demo Company, Inc.<br>
The <b>Wonder Tag</b> &lt;P&gt; &#153; is a registered
trademark of Demo Company, Inc.
</address>

</body>
</html>
```

 The use of the non-breaking space to push text or elements around the screen is an overused crutch. Many HTML editors overuse this technique in an attempt to preserve look and feel. This entity is discussed further in Chapter 6.

Note *Excessive use of character entities can make HTML source documents difficult to read if the character entities aren't well spaced.*

The character set currently supported by HTML is the ISO Latin-1 character set. Many of its characters, such as accents and special symbols, cannot be typed on all keyboards. They must be entered into HTML documents by using the appropriate code. Even if the character in question is supported on the keyboard (for example, the copyright symbol), simply typing in the symbol probably will not produce the correct encoding. Of course, many HTML editors make the appropriate insertion for you. A complete list of the character entities is presented in Appendix C.

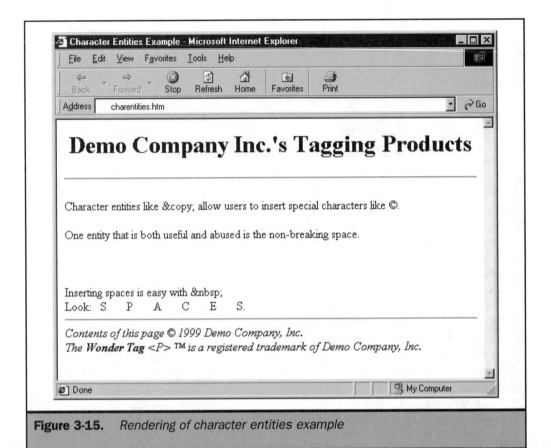

Figure 3-15. Rendering of character entities example

HTML is capable of representing the standard ASCII characters and all the extended characters defined by the ISO Latin-1 character set. However, for non-Western characters, such as Japanese, Russian, or Arabic alphabets, special encoding and a special browser are needed.

Comments

The last topic that should be considered a core aspect of HTML is the use of comments in an HTML document. The contents of HTML comments are not displayed within a browser window. Comments are denoted by a start value of **<!--** and an end value of **-->**. Comments can be many lines long. For example,

```
<!--

Document Name: Sample HTML Document
Author: Thomas A. Powell
Creation Date: 1/5/00

(c) 2000 Demo Company, Inc.
  -->
```

is a valid comment. Be careful to avoid putting spaces between the dashes or any additional exclamation points in the comment. Comments are useful in the **<head>** of a document to describe information about a document as shown above. Comments might also be useful when trying to explain complex HTML markup.

Comments also can include HTML elements. This is very useful in hiding new HTML elements from older browsers, and is commonly used with **<style>** and **<script>** elements, discussed in Chapters 10 and 13, respectively. For example, consider trying to hide a style sheet's contents from an older browser. The **<style>** element might occur in the **<head>** of the document and contain various style rules as shown here.

```
<style type="text/css">
H1    {font-size: 48pt; color: red;}
</style>
```

In the case of a non-style-sheet–aware browser the **<style>** tag would be skipped and the actual style rule might even be printed out on the screen. A simple use of an HTML comment would help solve this problem like so:

```
<style type="text/css">
<!--
H1    {font-size: 48pt; color: red;}
-->
</style>
```

In this case, style sheet–aware browsers are smart enough to know to look within a comment found directly inside the **<style>** element, whereas older browsers would just skip over the comment, and nothing would happen. Unfortunately, the comment-out trick does have some problems; aside from not being XHTML appropriate, older browsers might have problems when commenting out HTML tags. For more information about comments, see Appendix A.

Summary

The HTML elements presented so far are common across nearly all systems. Whether or not they are used, they are simple and widely understood. Yet, despite their simplicity, many of these basic elements are still abused to achieve a particular look within a document, which continues the struggle between the logical and physical nature of HTML. Despite some manipulation, these elements generally are used in a reasonable manner. More complex formatting elements and programming elements are introduced in later chapters. The simplicity of this chapter should provide you with some assurance that HTML rests on a stable core.

A great number of elements have been left out of this discussion. No mention was made of layout-oriented elements, and graphics have been completely avoided. These topics and others are covered in upcoming chapters. First, we'll deal with the "H" in HTML, namely hypertext, and present the concept of linking documents and objects in the next chapter.

The
Complete
Reference

Chapter 4

Links and Addressing

Previous chapters show how HTML can be used as a document formatting and structuring language, but little has been said about the hypertext aspect of the language. HTML makes it possible to define hyperlinks to other information items located all over the world, thus allowing documents to join the global information space known as the World Wide Web. Linking is possible because every document on the Web has a unique address, known as a *uniform resource locator* (URL). The explosive growth of documents on the Web has created a tangled mess, even when document locations are named consistently. The disorganized nature of the Web often leaves users lost in cyberspace. Finding information online can feel like trying to find the proverbial needle in a worldwide haystack. However, things don't have to be this way if designers pay attention to site structure.

Linking Basics

In HTML, the main way to define hyperlinks is with the anchor element, **<a>**. A *link* is simply a unidirectional pointer from the source document that contains the link to some destination. In hypertext, the end points of a link typically are called *anchors*, thus the use of the anchor nomenclature in HTML documentation.

For linking purposes, the **<a>** element requires one attribute: **href**. The **href** attribute is set to the URL of the target resource, which basically is the address of the document to link to, such as http://www.democompany.com. The text enclosed by the **<a>** elements specifies a "hot spot" to activate the hyperlink. Anchor content can include text, images, or a mixture of the two. A general link takes the form **<a href="url">**Visit our site**</a>**. The text "Visit our site" is the link. The URL specified by the **href** attribute is the destination if the link is activated. The following is an example of simple **<a>** element usage:

```
<!DOCTYPE HTML PUBLIC "-//W3C//DTD HTML 4.01 Transitional//EN">
<html>
<head>
<title>Simple Link Example</title>
</head>
<body>
<h1 align="center">Lots of links</h1>
<hr>
<ul>
   <li>Visit <a href="http://www.yahoo.com">Yahoo!</a></li>
   <li>Just a <a href="http://www.democompany.com">Demo Company</a></li>
   <li>Go to the <a href="http://www.w3.org">W3C</a></li>
</ul>
</body>
</html>
```

When the preceding example is loaded into a Web browser, the links generally are indicated by underlined text, typically in a different color—usually blue or purple, depending on whether the link object has been viewed before. Link objects are displayed in a different color after you visit the linked page, so that you know in the future which links you have already followed. Status information in the browser might change when a mouse is positioned over a link. The pointer also might change, as well as other indicators showing that the information is a link. Examples of link feedback in various browsers is shown in Figure 4-1. Note that the cursor over the Demo Company link in the upper-left corner now looks like a pointing finger, and the URL for the Demo Company home page appears in the status area in the lower-left corner of the browser frame.

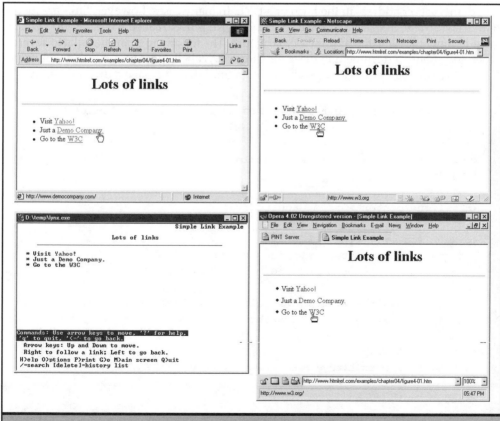

Figure 4-1.   *Example rendering and link feedback in various browsers*

Under some browsers, link underlining can be turned off. This might cause usability problems for some users, but many find pages rendered in this way more aesthetically pleasing.

The actual rendering of links depends on the browser or other user agent. If you are using HTML style sheets, the links that you create might have different decoration. For example, a color might change for a link that has been visited previously.

Note *You can underline any text in an HTML document by tagging it with the underline element, <u>. This practice might lead to confusion between hyperlinks and text that is underlined for stylistic purposes only. This is particularly evident if the link is viewed in a black-and-white environment or by a color-blind individual. Therefore, for non-linked items use the <u> element with caution to avoid confusion.*

In the simplest example, all the <a> elements refer to an address that contains only an external server address in the form of a URL. In many cases, however, links are made within a Web site. In this situation, a shortened URL is used, called a *relative URL*, which includes only the filename or directory structure. The following example links to several other documents: a document in the same directory, called specs.htm; a document in the "extras" subdirectory, called access.htm; and a link back to a page a directory above:

```
<!DOCTYPE HTML PUBLIC "-//W3C//DTD HTML 4.01 Transitional//EN">
<html>
<head>
<title>Simple Link Example 2</title>
</head>
<body>
<h1 align="center">Green Gadgets</h1>
<hr>
<p>Here you will find
information about the mysterious green
gadget--the wonder tool of the millennium.</p>
<ul>
    <li><a href="specs.htm">specifications</a></li>
    <li><a href="extras/access.htm">accessories</a></li>
</ul>
<p align="center">
<a href="../index.htm">Back to Demo Company Home</a>
</p>
</body>
</html>
```

These basic examples show that the use of links, at least within text, is simple. Specifying the destination URL might not be so obvious. HTML authors often are tempted to use only very simple relative URLs, such as a filename; or they use fully qualified URLs, but without a sense of what URLs really can provide. Later in this chapter, the discussion returns to the HTML syntax for forming links. First, take a closer look at URLs, because a thorough understanding of URLs is quite important for forming links.

What Are URLs?

A URL is a uniform way to refer to objects and services on the Internet. Even novice users should be familiar with typing a URL, such as http://www.democompany.com/, in a browser dialog box, to get to a Web site. Internet users use URLs to invoke other Internet services, such as transferring files via FTP or sending e-mail. HTML authors use URLs in their documents, to define hyperlinks to other Web documents. Despite its potentially confusing collection of slashes and colons, the URL syntax is designed to provide a clear, simple notation that people can easily understand. The following concepts will help you to understand the major components of a URL address.

CORE HTML

Note *Some people call URLs "universal resource locators." Except for a historical reference to "universal resource locators" in documentation from a few years ago, the current standard wording is "uniform resource locator."*

Basic Concepts

To locate any arbitrary object on the Internet, you need to find out the following information:

1. First, you need to locate and access the machine on the Internet (or intranet) on which the object resides. Locating the site might be a matter of specifying its domain name or IP address, whereas accessing the machine might be a matter of providing a username and password.

2. After you access the machine, you need determine the name of the desired file, where the file is located, and what protocol will be used to retrieve the information or access the object.

The URL describes where something is and how it will be retrieved. The *how* is specified by the protocol (for example, HTTP). The *where* is specified by the machine name, the directory name, and the filename. Slashes and other characters are used to separate the parts of the address into machine-readable pieces. The basic structure of the URL is shown here:

```
protocol://site address/directory/filename
```

The next several sections look at the individual pieces of a URL in closer detail.

Site Address

Every Web document exists on some server computer somewhere on the global Internet or within a private intranet. The first step in finding a document is to identify its server. The most convenient way to do this on a TCP/IP-based network is with a symbolic name, called a *domain name*. On the Internet at large, a fully qualified domain name (FQDN) typically consists of a machine name, followed by a domain name. For example, www.microsoft.com specifies a machine named *www* in the microsoft.com domain. On an intranet, however, things might be a little different, because you can avoid using a domain name. For example, a machine name of *hr-server* might be all that you need to access the human resources server within your company's intranet.

> **Note**
>
> *A machine name indicates the local, intra-organizational name for the actual server. A machine name can be just about any name, because machine naming has no mandated rules. Conventions exist, however, for identifying servers that provide common Internet resources. Servers for Web documents usually begin with the www prefix. However, many local machines have names similar to the user's own name (for example, jsmith), his or her favorite cartoon character (for example, homer), or even an esoteric machine name (for example, dell-p6-200-a12). Machine naming conventions are important because they allow users to form URLs without explicitly spelling them out. A user who understands domain names and machine naming conventions should be able to guess that Toyota's Web server is http://www.toyota.com/.*

The other part of most site addresses—the domain name—is fairly regular. Within the United States, a domain name consists of the actual domain or organization name, followed by a period, and then a domain type. An example is sun.com. The domain itself is sun, which represents Sun Microsystems. The sun domain exists within the commercial zone, because of Sun's corporate status, so it ends with the domain type of *com*. In the United States, most domain identifiers currently use a three-character code that indicates the type of organization that owns the server. The most common codes are *com* for commercial, *gov* for government, *org* for nonprofit organizations, *edu* for educational institutions, *net* for networks, and *mil* for military. Recently, some debate has ensued regarding the extent of the domain name space. Soon, a variety of new domain endings might be added. At the time of this book's second edition, many names were claimed to be right around the corner. With the writing of the third edition the wait continues, but hopefully a variety of new, generic, top-level domains will be available soon. Table 4-1 sets forth a basic listing of U.S. domain types.

Domain space beyond the United States is somewhat more complicated. An FQDN, including a country code, generally is written as follows:

```
machine name. domain name . domain type . country code
```

Zone identifiers outside the U.S. use a two-character code to indicate the country hosting the server. These include *ca* for Canada, *mx* for Mexico, and *jp* for Japan. Within each country, the local naming authorities might create domain types at their own

Domain Type	Domain Description	Example
Com	Commercial entities and individuals	apple.com
Net	Networks and network providers	cerf.net
Org	Nonprofits and other organizations	greenpeace.org
Edu	Four-year colleges and universities	ucla.edu
Gov	United States federal government agencies	whitehouse.gov
Mil	United States federal government military entities	nosc.mil
Us	Used for a variety of organizations and individuals, including K through 12 education, libraries, and city and county governments	co.san-diego.ca.us

Table 4-1. *Domain Types in the United States, circa Fall 2000*

discretion, but these domain types can't correspond to American extensions. For example, www.sony.co.jp specifies a Web server for Sony in the *co* zone of Japan. In this case, co, rather than com, indicates a commercial venture. In the United Kingdom, the educational domain space has a different name, *ac*. Oxford University's Web server is www.ox.ac.uk, whereby ac indicates *academic,* compared to the U.S. edu extension for *education*. Despite a flattening of geographical name use for large, multinational companies (such as Sony), regional naming differences are very much alive. Web page authors linking to non-native domains are encouraged to first understand the naming conventions of those environments. One special top-level domain, *int*, is reserved for organizations established by international treaties between governments, such as the European Union (eu.int). Top-level domains, such as *com*, *net*, and any upcoming new domains, will not necessarily correspond to a particular geographic area.

Note *Symbolic names make it convenient for people to refer to Internet servers. A server's real address is its Internet Protocol (IP) numeric address. Every accessible server on the Internet has a unique IP address by which it can be located using the TCP/IP protocol. An IP address is a numeric string that consists of four numbers between 0 and 255 and is separated by periods (for example, 213.6.17.34). This number then might correspond to a domain name, such as www.democompany.com. Note that a server's symbolic name must be translated, or resolved, into an IP address before it can be used to locate a server. An Internet service known as Domain Name Service (DNS) automatically performs this translation. You can use an IP address instead of a symbolic name to specify an Internet server, but doing so gives up mnemonic convenience. In some cases, using an IP address might be necessary because although every server has an IP address, not all servers have symbolic names.*

Investigating all aspects of the domain name structure is beyond the scope of this book. However, it should be noted that domain name formats and the domain name lookup service are very critical to the operation of the Web. If the domain name server is unavailable, it is impossible to access a Web server. To learn more about machine and domain names, explore the following Web sites:

- http://rs.internic.net/
- http://www.iana.org/
- http://www.gtld-mou.org/

Note
Domain names are not case-sensitive. Addresses can be written as www.Democompany. com or www.DEMOCOMPANY.com. A browser should handle both properly. Case typically is changed for marketing or branding purposes. Directory values following the domain name might be case-sensitive, depending on the operating system the Web server is running on. For example, UNIX systems are case-sensitive, whereas Windows machines are not. Trouble can arise if casing is used randomly. As a rule of thumb, keep everything in lowercase, or consistently use uppercase for just the first letters in directory or file names.

After you specify the machine, either by its domain name or its IP address, you might need to specify the particular directory on the particular machine, as described next.

Directory

Servers might contain hundreds, if not thousands, of files. For practical use, files need to be organized into manageable units, analogous to the manila folders traditionally used to organize paper documents. This unit is known as a *file directory*. After you have determined the server on which a document resides, the next step toward identifying its location is to specify the directory that contains the file. Just as one manila folder can contain other folders; directories can contain other directories. Directories contain other directories in a nested, hierarchical structure that resembles the branches of a tree. The directory that contains all others is known as the *root directory*. Taken together, all the directories and files form a file tree, or *file system*. A file is located in a file system by specifying its *directory path*. This is the nested list of all directories that contain the file, from the most general—the root directory—to the most specific. Similar to the UNIX operating system, directories hosted on Web servers are separated by forward slashes (/) rather than backslashes (\), as in DOS. Figure 4-2 shows a sample file tree for a Web site.

Figure 4-2 shows how directories are organized within (or above and below) one another. For example, the directory called **special** is within the **products** directory, which is within the root directory, as indicated by the forward slash. The full path should be written as /products/special/ to indicate that **special** is an actual directory, not a file in the **products** directory. When linking to other files, you might need to refer to a directory above the current directory, or to the current directory itself. In the scheme presented, ./ means the current directory, whereas ../ means one directory up

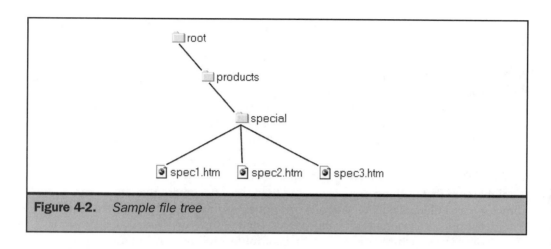

Figure 4-2.   *Sample file tree*

in the hierarchy. A document in the **special** directory with a link path of ../ will link up to the **products** directory.

   Directory names might follow conventions specific to an operating system, including being case-sensitive. Authors are cautioned to look carefully at directory casing. Furthermore, directories might follow popular usage conventions (for example, tmp), or they can be arbitrary. Usually, directory names reflect aspects of their content such as media types, subject matter, or access privileges. For example, a directory called "images" might be the name of a directory containing images.

Filename

After you specify the server and directory path for a document, the next step toward locating it is to specify its filename. This step typically has two parts: a filename, followed by a standard file extension. Filenames can be any names that are applicable under the server's operating system. Special characters such as spaces, colons, and slashes can play havoc if used in names of Web-available files. A file named test:1.htm would present problems on a Macintosh system, whereas test/1.htm might be legal on a Macintosh but problematic on a PC or UNIX machine.

A dot separates the filename and the *extension*, which is a code, usually composed of three letters, that identifies the type of information contained in the file. For example, HTML source files have an .htm or .html extension. JPEG images have a .jpg extension. A file's extension is critically important for Web applications, because it usually is the only indication of the information type that a file contains. A Web server reads a file extension and uses it to determine which headers, in the form of a MIME type (discussed in Chapter 15), to attach to a file when delivering it to a browser. If file extensions are omitted or misused, the file could be interpreted incorrectly. When browsers read files directly, they also look at file extensions to determine how to render the file. If the extension is missing or incorrect, a file will not be properly displayed in a Web browser.

Note	*Although many operating systems support four or more letters for file extensions, using a three-letter extension (.htm) versus a four-letter extension (.html) ensures that cross-platform incompatibilities are minimized. Spaces, uppercasing, and special characters also should be avoided to provide the greatest flexibility. Authors and users particularly should be aware of case sensitivity in filenames and directory names.*

Protocol

It might seem that nothing more is needed to locate a document than its server, directory, and filename. However, one component is missing—the protocol. The Internet supports a standard set of resources, each with its own associated protocol. A *protocol* is the structured discussion that computers follow to negotiate resource-specific services. For example, the protocol that makes the Web possible is the Hypertext Transfer Protocol (HTTP). When you click a hyperlink in a Web document, your browser uses the HTTP protocol to contact a Web server and retrieve the appropriate document.

Note	*Although HTTP stands for Hypertext Transfer Protocol, it doesn't specify how a file is transported from a server to a browser, only how the discussion between the server and browser will take place to get the file. The actual transport of files usually is the responsibility of a lower-layer network protocol, such as the Transmission Control Protocol (TCP). On the Internet, the combination of TCP and IP makes raw communication possible. Although a subtle point, many Internet professionals are unaware of lower-level protocols below application protocols such as HTTP, which are part of URLs.*

Although less frequently used than HTTP and TCP/IP, several other protocols are important to HTML authors, because they can be invoked by hyperlinks. The following table lists some examples:

Protocol	Description
File	Enables a hyperlink to access a file on the local file system
File Transfer Protocol (FTP)	Enables a hyperlink to download files from remote systems
Gopher	Enables a hyperlink to access a Gopher server
mailto	Calls the *Simple Mail Transfer Protocol* (SMTP), which is the Internet mail protocol, and enables a hyperlink to send an addressed e-mail message

Protocol	Description
Network News Transport Protocol (NNTP)	Enables a hyperlink to access a USENET news article
News	Enables a hyperlink to access a USENET newsgroup
telnet	Enables a hyperlink to open a telnet session on a remote host

These are the common protocols, but a variety of new protocols and URL forms are being debated all the time. Someday, such things as LDAP (Lightweight Directory Access Protocol), IRC (Internet Relay Chat), phone, fax, and even TV might be used to reference how data should be accessed. More about the future of URLs and other naming ideas are discussed toward the end of this chapter.

Beyond the protocol, server address, directory, and filename, URLs often include a username and password, port number, and sometimes a fragment identifier. Some URLs, such as mailto, might even contain a different form of information altogether, such as an e-mail address rather than a server or filename.

User and Password

FTP and telnet are protocols for *authenticated services*. Authenticated services can assume access by authorized users, and the protocols can require a username and password as parameters. A username and password precede a server name, like this: *username:password@server-address*. The password could be optional or unspecified in the URL, making the form simply *username@server-address*.

 HTML authors are warned to avoid including password information in URLs, because the information may be readily viewable in a Web page or within the browser's URL box.

Port

Although the situation is rare, the communication port number used in a URL also can be specified. Browsers speaking a particular protocol communicate with servers through entry points, known as *ports*, which generally are identified by numeric addresses. Associated with each protocol is a default port number. For example, an HTTP request defaults to port number 80. A server administrator can configure a server to handle protocol requests at ports other than the default numbers. Usually this occurs for experimental or secure applications. In these cases, the intended port must be explicitly addressed in a URL. To specify a port number, place it after the server address, separated by a colon; for example, *site-address*:8080. Web administrators are forewarned to avoid changing port numbers arbitrarily, because it confuses users and might result in difficulty accessing a site, particularly if access comes from behind a firewall. In short, users coming from sites with well-defined security policies might not be set up to access sites running on nonstandard port numbers.

Some Web development systems might require users to log in on nonstandard ports. A common example is an administrator who needs to access a nonstandard port to configure a Web server using a Web browser.

Fragment

After a user specifies a file, the user might want to go directly to a particular point within the file. Because you can set up named links under HTML, you can provide links directly to different points within a file. To jump to a particular named link, the URL must include the link name, preceded by a hash symbol (#), which indicates that the value is a fragment identifier. To specify a point called "contents" in a file called test.htm, you would use test.htm#contents. Elsewhere in the file, the fragment name would be set using a named anchor, such as **<a name="contents"></a>**. This is discussed later in this chapter in the section "Using the **name** Attribute."

Encoding

When writing the components of a URL, take care that they are written using only the displayable characters in the US-ASCII character set. Even when using characters within this basic keyboard character range, you will find certain unsafe characters. You also might find reserved characters that could have special meaning within the context of a URL or the operating system on which the resource is found. If any unsafe, reserved, or nonprintable characters occur in a URL, they must be encoded in a special form. Failure to encode these characters might lead to errors.

The form of encoding consists of a percent sign and two hexadecimal digits corresponding to the value of the character in the ASCII character set. Within many intranet environments, filenames often include user-friendly names, such as "first quarter earnings 1999.doc." Such names contain unsafe characters. If this file were to live on a departmental Web server, it would have a URL with a file portion of first%20quarter%20earnings%201999.doc. Notice how the spaces have been mapped to **%20** values—the hex value of the space character in ASCII. Other characters that will be troublesome in URLs include the slash character (/), which encodes as **%2F**, the question mark, which maps to **%3F**, and the percent itself, which encodes as **%25**. Only alphanumeric values and some special characters ($ - _ . + ! * '), including parentheses, may be used in a URL; other characters should be encoded. In general, special characters such as accents, spaces, and some punctuation marks have to be encoded. HTML authors are encouraged to name files with encoding in mind, so that encoding can be avoided whenever possible. Table 4-2 shows the reserved and potentially dangerous characters for URLs.

Many of the characters in Table 4-2 don't have to be encoded, but encoding a character never causes problems, so when in doubt, encode it.

With this brief discussion of the various components coming to a close, the next section presents a formula for creating URLs, as well as some examples.

Character	Encoding Value	Character	Encoding Value
Space	%20	{	%7B
/	%2F	}	%7D
?	%3F	[	%5B
:	%3A	]	%5D
;	%3B	"	%22
&	%26	`	%27
@	%40	'	%60
=	%3D	^^	%5E
#	%23	~	%7E
%	%25	\	%5C
>	%3E	|	%7C
<	%3C		

Table 4-2.   *Common Character Encoding Values*

CORE HTML

Formula for a URL

All URLs share the same basic syntax: a protocol name, followed by a colon, followed by a protocol-specific resource description:

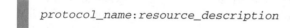

```
protocol_name:resource_description
```

Beyond this basic syntax, enough variation exists between protocol specifics for a few of the more common ones to warrant a more in-depth discussion.

HTTP

A minimal HTTP URL simply gives a server name. It provides no directory or file information.

- ■ **Formula**   http://*server*/ (with or without trailing /)
- ■ **Example**   http://www.democompany.com/

A minimal HTTP URL implicitly requests the home directory of a Web site. Even when a trailing slash isn't used, it is assumed and added either by the user agent or the Web server, so that an address such as http://www.democompany.com becomes http://www.democompany.com/. By default, requesting a directory often results in the server returning a default file from the directory, termed the *index file*. Usually, index files are named index.htm or default.htm (or index.html and default.html, respectively), depending on the server software being used. This is only a convention; Web administrators are free to name default index files whatever they like. Interestingly, many people put special importance on the minimal HTTP URL form when, like all other file-retrieval URLs, this form simply specifies a particular directory or default index file to return, although this isn't always explicitly written out.

> **Note**   *Some sites now are renaming their systems so that the use of www is optional. For example, http://pint.com/ is the same as http://www.pint.com. Although browsers often provide similar shorthand functionality, users should be careful to not assume such forms are valid. For example, in some browsers, typing democompany by itself might resolve to http://www.democompany.com. This is a browser usability improvement and can't be used as a URL in an HTML document. Because of misunderstandings with URLs, site managers are encouraged to add as many variable forms as possible, so that the site works regardless of browser improvements or slight mistakes in linking.*

Making the HTTP URL example slightly more complex, a formula is presented to retrieve a specific HTML file that is assumed to exist in the default directory for the server:

- **Formula**   http://*server*/*file*
- **Example**   http://www.democompany.com/hello.htm

An alternate, incremental extension adds directory information without specifying a file. Although the final slash should be provided, servers imply its existence if it is omitted, and look for a "home" document in the given directory. In practice, the final slash is optional, but recommended:

- **Formula**   http://*server*/*directory*/
- **Example**   http://www.democompany.com/products/

An HTTP URL can specify both a directory and a file:

- **Formula**   http://*server*/*directory*/*file*
- **Example**   http://www.democompany.com/products/greeting.htm

On some systems, special shorthand conventions might be available for directory use. For example, a UNIX-based Web server might support many directories, each owned by a specific user. Rather than spelling out the full path to a user's root directory, the user directory can be abbreviated by using the tilde character (~), followed by the user's account, followed by a slash. Any directory or file information that follows this point will be relative to the user's root directory:

- **Formula** http://*server*/*~user*/
- **Example** http://www.bigisp.com/~jsmith/

User directories indicated by the tilde are somewhat similar to the convention used on the UNIX operating system, although other Web servers on different operating systems might provide similar shortcut support.

A URL can refer to a named location inside an HTML document, which is called a *marker*, or *named link*. How markers are created is discussed later in this chapter in the section "Using the **name** Attribute," but for now, to refer to a document marker, follow the target document's filename with the pound character, (#), and then with the marker name:

- **Formula** http://*server*/*directory*/*file#marker*
- **Example** http://www.democompany.com/profile.htm#introduction

In addition to referring to HTML documents, an HTTP URL can request any type of file. For example, http://www.democompany.com/images/logo.gif would retrieve from a server a GIF image rather than an HTML file. Authors should be aware that the flexibility of Web servers and URLs often is overlooked due to the common belief that a Web-based document must be in the HTML format for it to be linked to.

To the contrary, even an HTTP URL can reference and execute a server program. These server-side programs typically are termed *Common Gateway Interface* (CGI) programs, referring to the interface standard that describes how to pass data in and out of a program. CGI and similar server-side programming facilities are discussed in Chapter 12. Quite often, server-side programs are used to access databases and then generate HTML documents in response to user-entered queries. Parameters for such programs can be directly included in a URL by appending a question mark, followed by the actual parameter string. Because the user might type special characters in a query, characters that normally are not allowed within a URL are encoded. Remember that the formula for special-character encoding is a percent sign, followed by two hex numbers representing the character's ASCII value. For example, a space can be represented by **%20**.

- **Formula** http://*server/directory/file?parameters*
- **Example** http://www.democompany.com/products/search.cgi?cost=400.00 &name=Super%20Part

Forming complex URLs with encoding and query strings looks very difficult. In reality, this rarely is done manually. Typically, the browser generates such a string on the fly based on data provided through a form. A more detailed discussion of HTML interaction with programming facilities appears in Chapters 12–14.

Finally, any HTTP request can be directed to a port other than the default port value of 80 by following the server identification with a colon and the intended port number:

- **Formula** http://*server:port/directory/file*
- **Example** http://www.democompany.com:8080/products/greetings.htm

In the preceding example, the URL references a Web server running on port 8080. Although any unreserved port number is valid, using nonstandard port numbers on servers is not good practice. To access the address in the example, a user would need to include the port number in the URL. If it is omitted, accessing the server will be impossible.

One case of HTTP exists that is, in a sense, a different protocol: secured Web transactions using the Secure Sockets Layer (SSL). In this case, the protocol is referenced as https, and the port value is assumed to be 443. An example formula for Secure HTTP is shown here; other than the cosmetic difference of the *s* and the different port value, it is identical to other HTTP URLs:

- **Formula** https://*server:port/directory/file*
- **Example** https://www.welllsfargo.com

An HTTP URL for a Web page probably is the most common URL, but users might find files or similar types of URLs growing in popularity due to the rise of intranets.

file

The file protocol specifies a file residing somewhere on a computer or locally accessible computer network. It does not specify an access protocol and has limited value except for one important case: It enables a browser to access files residing on a user's local computer, an important capability for Web page development. In this usage, the server name is omitted or replaced by the keyword *localhost*, which is followed by the local directory and file specification:

- **Formula** file://drive or network path/*directory/file*
- **Example** file:///dev/web/testpage.html

In some environments, the actual drive name and path to the file are specified. On a Macintosh, a URL might be the following:

```
file:///Macintosh %20HD/Desktop%20Folder/Bookmarks.html
```

A file URL such as the following might exist to access a file on the C drive of a PC on the local network, pc1:

```
file://\\pc1\C\Netlog.txt
```

Depending on browser complexity, file URLs might not be required, as with Internet Explorer 4, in which the operating system is tightly coupled with the user agent.

Interestingly, in the case of intranets, many drives might be mapped or file systems mounted so that no server is required to deliver files. In this "Web-serverless" environment, accessing network drives with a file URL might be possible. This idea demonstrates how simple a Web server is. In fact, to some people, a Web server merely is a very inefficient, though open, file server. This realization regarding file transfer leads logically to the idea of the FTP URL, discussed next.

FTP

The File Transfer Protocol, which predates the browser-oriented HTTP protocol, transfers files to and from a server. It generally is geared toward transferring files that are to be locally stored rather than immediately viewed. A browser might allow files to be viewed immediately. Today, because of its efficiency, FTP most commonly is used to download large files such as complete applications. These URLs share with HTTP the formula for indicating a server, port, directory, and file:

- **Formula**   ftp://server:port/directory/file
- **Example**   ftp://ftp.democompany.com:9978/info/somefile.exe

A minimal FTP URL specifies a server and then lists the following directory: ftp://ftp.democompany.com. Generally, however, FTP URLs are used to access by name and directory a particular file in an archive, as shown in this formula:

- **Formula**   ftp://*server*/*directory path*/*file*
- **Example**   ftp://ftp.democompany.com/info/somefile.exe

FTP is an *authenticated* protocol, which means that every valid FTP request requires a defined user account on the server downloading the files. In practice, many FTP resources are intended for general access, and defining a unique account for every potential user is impractical. Therefore, an FTP convention known as *anonymous FTP* handles this common situation. The username "anonymous" or "ftp" allows general access to any public FTP resource supported by a server. As in the previous example, the anonymous user account is implicit in any FTP URL that does not explicitly provide account information.

An FTP URL can specify the name and password for a user account. If included, they precede the server declaration, according to the following formula.

- **Formula**   ftp://*user:password@server/directory/file*
- **Example**   ftp://jsmith:harmony@ftp.democompany.com/products/list

This formula shows the password embedded within the URL. Including an account password in a public document (such as an HTML file) is a dangerous proposition because it is transmitted in plain text and viewable both in the HTML source and browser address bar. Only public passwords should be embedded in any URL for an authenticated service. Furthermore, if you omit the password, the user agent typically prompts you to enter one if a password is required. Thus, it is more appropriate to provide a link to the service and *then* require the user to enter a name and password, or just provide the user ID and have the user agent prompt for a password, as happens in this example:

- **Formula**   ftp://*user@server/directory/file*
- **Example**   ftp://jsmith@ftp.democompany.com/products/sales

The FTP protocol assumes that a downloaded file contains binary information. You can override this default assumption by appending a type code to an FTP URL. The following are three common values for type codes:

- An **a** code indicates that the file is an ASCII text file.
- The **i** code, which also is the default, indicates that the file is an image/binary file.
- A **d** code causes the URL to return a directory listing of the specified path instead of a file.

An example formula is presented here for completeness:

- **Formula**   ftp://*server/directory/file*;type=*code*
- **Example**   ftp://ftp.democompany.com/products;type=d

In reality, the type codes rarely are encountered, because the binary transfer format generally does not harm text files, and the user agent usually is smart enough to handle FTP URLs without type codes. Like many other URLs, the port accessed can be changed to something other than the default port of 21, but this is not recommended.

mailto

Atypically, the mailto protocol does not locate and retrieve an Internet resource. Instead, it opens a window for editing and sending a mail message to a particular user address:

- **Formula**   mailto:*user@server*
- **Example**   mailto:president@whitehouse.gov

This rather simple formula shows standard Internet mail addressing; other, more complex addresses might be just as valid. Using mailto URLs is very popular in Web sites, to provide a basic feedback mechanism. Note that if the user's browser hasn't been set up properly to send e-mail, this type of URL might produce error messages when used in a link, prompting the user to set up mailing preferences. Because of this problem, page authors are warned to not rely solely on mailto-based URL links to collect user feedback.

> **Note** *Some browsers have introduced proprietary extensions to the mailto protocol, such as the ? subject extension. These extensions currently aren't standard and will cause other browsers to be unable to send e-mail using the link. Work is underway to standardize extensions to the mailto protocol, but for now, use of the proprietary extensions is discouraged.*

telnet

The telnet protocol allows a user to open an interactive terminal session on a remote host computer. A minimal telnet URL, shown next, simply gives the remote system's name. After a connection is made, the system prompts for an account name and password.

- ■ **Formula**   telnet://*server*
- ■ **Example**   telnet://host.democompany.com

As an authenticated protocol, telnet generally requires a defined user account on the remote system. When this is unspecified, the user agent or helper application handling telnet prompts for such information. Like FTP, a telnet URL also can contain an account name and password as parameters. But, as with FTP URLs, be careful about including passwords in public access documents such as HTML files on the Web. Because of the risk of password interception, the password is optional in the formula:

- ■ **Formula**   telnet://*user:password@server*
- ■ **Example**   telnet://jsmith:harmony@host.democompany.com
- ■ **Example**   telnet://jsmith@host.democompany.com

Finally, any telnet URL can direct a request to a specific port by appending the port address to the server name:

- ■ **Formula**   telnet://*server:port*
- ■ **Example**   telnet://host.democompany.com:94

Some telnet information sources can be configured to run on a particular port other than port 23, the standard telnet port. Consequently, use of the port within a telnet URL is more common than with other URLs.

Other Protocols

A wide variety of other protocols can be used including Gopher, NNTP, news, and so on. Modern browsers should support many of these URL forms. However, some protocols, such as the wais protocol, have little more than historical value. Little evidence suggests that people actually use this protocol much on the Web, despite its presence in books that are only one or two years old. Beyond old protocols like wais, other protocols include operating system–biased protocols, such as finger, and esoteric protocols for things like VEMMI video text services. New protocols are being added all the time. In fact, dozens of proposed or even implemented protocols exist that can be referenced with some form of nonstandard URL. If you are interested in other URL forms, visit http://www.w3.org/pub/WWW/Addressing/schemes or http://www.ics.uci.edu/pub/ietf/uri/ for more information.

Relative URLs

Up to this point, the discussion has focused on a specific form of URL, typically termed an absolute URL. Absolute URLs completely spell out the protocol, host, directory, and filename. Providing such detail can be tedious and unnecessary, which is where a shortened form of URL, termed a *relative URL*, comes in to use. With relative URLs, the various parts of the address—the site, directory, and protocol—can be inferred by the URL of the current document, or through the **<base>** element. The best way to illustrate the idea of relative URLs is by example.

If a Web site has an address of www.democompany.com, a user can access the home page with a URL such as http://www.democompany.com/. A link to this page from an outside system also would contain the address http://www.democompany.com/. Once at the site, however, there is no reason to continue spelling out the full address of the site. A fully qualified link from the home page to a staff page in the root directory called staff.html would be http://www.democompany.com/staff.html. The protocol, address, and directory name can be inferred, so all that is needed is the address staff.html. This relative scheme works because http://www.democompany.com/ is inferred as the base of all future links, thus allowing for the shorthand relative notation. The relative notation can be used with filenames and directories, as shown by the examples in Table 4-3.

When relative URLs are used within a Web site, the site becomes transportable. By not spelling out the server name in every link, you can develop a Web site on one server and move it to another. Contrarily, if you use absolute URLs, all links have to be changed if a server changes names or the files are moved to another site.

Of course, using relative URLs also has a potential downside: They can become confusing in a large site, particularly if centralized directories are used for things such as images. Imagine having URLs such as ../../../images/logo.gif in files deep in a site structure. Some users might be tempted to simply copy files to avoid such problems, but then updating and caching issues arise. One solution is to use the **<base>** element. Another solution is to use symbolic links on the Web server to reference one copy of

Current Page Address	Destination Address	Relative URL
http://www.democompany.com/ index.htm	http://www.democompany.com/ staff.htm	staff.htm
http://www.democompany.com/ index.htm	http://www.democompany.com/ products/gadget1.htm	products/ gadget1.htm
http://www.democompany.com/ products/gadget1.htm	http://www.democompany.com/ index.htm	../index.htm

Table 4-3.   *Relative URL Formation Examples*

the file from multiple locations. However, because HTML is the subject here, the focus is the former solution, using the **<base>** element.

The **<base>** element defines the base for all relative URLs within a document. Setting the **href** attribute of this element to a fully qualified URL enables all other relative references to use the defined base. For example, if **<base>** is set as **<base href="http://www.democompany.com/">**, then all the anchors in the document that aren't fully qualified will prefix http:// www.democompany.com / to the destination URL. Because **<base>** is an empty element it would have to be written as **<base href="http://www.democompany.com/" />** to be XHTML compliant.

The **<base>** element can occur only once in an HTML document—within its head—so creating sections of a document with different base URL values is impossible. Such a feature might someday be added to a sectioning element, but until then, HTML authors have to deal with shorthand notation being useful only in some places. See Appendix A for more information on the **<base>** element.

Linking in HTML

The discussion thus far has focused solely on the forms of URLs. Little has been said about how to link objects together on the Web. Later in this chapter, the discussion becomes more theoretical and discusses the relationship between URLs, URIs, URCs, and URNs.

The Anchor Element

Using a URL enables you to specify the location of many types of information resources, both on the Internet and within a local area network. But how, exactly, is HTML used to specify a hyperlink that links one document to another? The most common way to define hyperlinks is with the anchor element, **<a>**. In its most basic form, this element needs two pieces of information: the URL of the target resource, and the document content needed to activate the hyperlink. Assigning a URL value to an **<a>** element's **href** attribute specifies the target resource. Most defined hyperlinks probably use an HTTP URL to link one HTML document to another. Remember, however, that URLs to other information resources also are possible.

The **<a>** element's content specifies a document's "hot spot" for activating the hyperlink. Anchor content can include text, images, or a mixture of the two. By enclosing some text or other content within the **<a>** and **</a>** tags, you make the item into a link that, when selected, requests a new object to be accessed. In the following code fragment, the text "Linked content" will load the URL referenced by the **href** attribute when it's selected:

```
<a href="URL">Linked content</a>
```

 An <a> element may not enclose another <a> element. The code <a href="URL1">Linked<a href="URL2">More linked</a></a> makes no sense.

The simplest hyperlink combines an **<a>** element with a URL that contains only a Web server address. Implicitly, the referenced document is the server's home page, which is the default document returned from the Web server's root directory. Many, more complex examples of links also are possible. The following are various examples of HTTP links, each of which is followed by a short description:

```
<a href="http://www.whitehouse.gov/">Visit the President</a>
```

Adding a link to the home page of a Web site with a basic HTTP URL references the home page of the Web site.

```
<a href="http://www.democompany.com/about/">About Demo Company</a>
```

Adding a directory path to the URL references the default document in a specific directory.

```
<a href="http://www.democompany.com/products/domes.htm">D.C.
Domes</a>
```

Adding a filename to a URL fully describes the document location.

```
<a href="http://www.democompany.com/products/domes.htm#top">Go to
top</a>
```

Adding a fragment to a filename describes a particular location within a document.

```
<a href="products/robots.htm">Robots</a>
```

Anchors may use relative URLs.

```
<a href="../../index.htm">Back to home</a>
```

Relative URLs can be complex.

```
<a href="ftp://ftp.democompany.com">Access FTP archive</a>
```

Anchors are not limited to HTTP URLs.

```
<a href="mailto:info@democompany.com">More information?</a>
```

Beyond retrieving files, anchors can trigger sending an e-mail or even run programs.

Note   *Be careful when using mailto URLs; they often do not work because a browser is not configured to send mail or does not support this URL form properly.*

The following example shows a complete example of relative and absolute URLs and their use within an HTML document:

```
<!DOCTYPE HTML PUBLIC "-//W3C//DTD HTML 4.01 Transitional//EN">
<html>
<head>
<title>Link Example 3</title>
</head>
<body>
<h1 align="center">Green Gadgets</h1>
<hr>
<p>Here you will find information about the mysterious green
gadget--the wonder tool of the millennium.</p>
<ul>
<li><a href="specs.htm">Specifications</a></li>
<li><a href="extras/access.htm">Accessories</a></li>
<li><a href="http://www.democompany.com">Distributors</a></li>
<li><a href="ftp://ftp.democompany.com/pdfs/order.pdf">
    Download order form</a></li>
</ul>
```

```
<div align="center">
<a href="../index.htm">Back to Demo Company Home </a>
</div>
<hr>
<address>
Questions?
<a href="mailto:info@democompany.com">info@democompany.com</a>
</address>
</body>
</html>
```

Renderings of the link examples are shown in Figure 4-3.

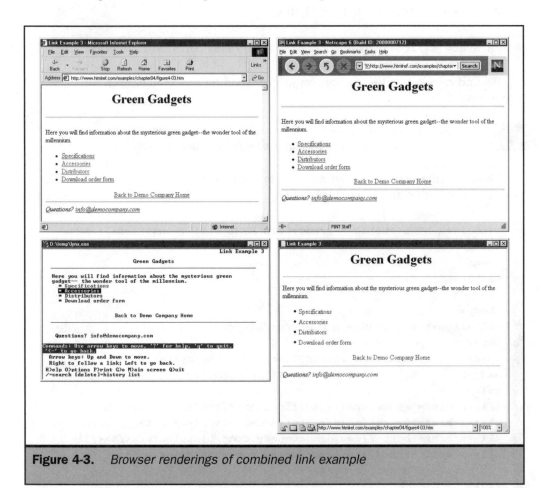

Figure 4-3.   *Browser renderings of combined link example*

Link Renderings

In most browsers, text links are indicated by underlined text. Coloring the text—blue if the destination has never been visited, purple if it has been visited—is another common convention. If a link includes an image, the border of the image also will be blue or purple, unless the border attribute has been set to zero. HTML authors can override these default link colors with changes to the **link**, **alink**, and **vlink** attributes of the **<body>** element. The **link** attribute changes the color of all unvisited links; the **vlink** attribute changes all visited links. The **alink** attribute changes the color of the active link, which is the brief flash that appears when a link is pressed. By using an HTML style sheet, authors also can change the decoration of links to turn off underlining, change the style in hover mode or even display all links in completely different fashion. These presentation changes are shown in the following example markup:

```
<!DOCTYPE HTML PUBLIC "-//W3C//DTD HTML 4.01 Transitional//EN">
<html>
<head>
<title>Link Style Changes</title>
<style type="text/css">
<!--
A        {text-decoration: none;}
A:hover {color: red; text-decoration: underline;}
-->
</style>
</head>
<body link="blue" alink="red" vlink="red">
<a href="http://www.yahoo.com">Test Link to Yahoo!</a>
</body>
</html>
```

Aesthetically, changing link colors or removing underlining might seem to make sense—but it also can confuse readers who have come to expect a standard color scheme for links. Occasionally, authors can try to encourage return visits by changing the setting for visited links to remain blue, or might reverse colors for layout consistency. Such changes can significantly impair the usability of the site by thwarting user expectations.

Like it or not, the standard Web experience has taught users to click underlined text that is blue or purple. Such user habits suggest that underlining for emphasis be used sparingly, if at all, in HTML documents. Furthermore, HTML text probably shouldn't be colored blue or purple, unless it obviously isn't a link. Controlling link colors is very important, but it is only one of many aspects of anchors that can be controlled.

Anchor Attributes

The **<a>** element has many possible attributes that are specific to it, besides **href**, as shown in Table 4-4. The more important attributes are discussed in the sections to follow, along with the concepts of binding scripts to anchors, using anchors with images, and creating a special type of image link called an *image map*. Refer to the element reference (Appendix A) to see a complete listing of all possible attributes for the **<a>** element.

Attribute Name	Possible Value	Description
href	URL	Sets the URL of the destination object for the anchor
name	Text	Names the anchor so that it can be a target of another anchor
id	Text	Identifies the anchor for target by another anchor, style sheet access, and scripting exposure
target	A frame name	Defines the frame or window destination of the link.
title	Text	Sets the hint text for the link
accesskey	A character	Sets the key for keyboard access to the link
tabindex	A numeric value	Sets the order in the tabbing index for using the TAB key to move through links in a page
rel	Text	Defines the relationship of the object being linked to
rev	Text	Defines the relationship of the current object to the object being linked to

Table 4-4. *Common Anchor Attributes*

> **Note** *In HTML 4, the <a> element also can support the **shape** and **coords** attributes, which can be used with the <object> element to create a generalized form of image maps. These extensions to <a> are discussed in the element reference in Appendix A, as well as in Chapter 5, which discusses the <object> element in relation to images. Today, however, these attributes of <a> are not widely supported. HTML authors are encouraged to use client-side image maps, which are discussed later in this chapter in the section "Image Maps."*

Using the name Attribute

The **<a>** element usually defines a hyperlink's source location: where the link goes, and what you click to go there. One possible destination for a hyperlink is a named location inside an HTML document. The **<a>** element also is used to define these locations in a special usage known as *setting a fragment*, although the term *marker* might make more sense. To set a marker, the **name** attribute replaces the **href** attribute. The value of the **name** attribute is an arbitrary, symbolic name for the marker location that must be unique within the document. Wherever the marker is placed within an HTML document becomes a named candidate destination for hyperlinks. For example, the HTML markup **<a name="marker">**This is a marker**</a>** sets the text "This is a marker" to be associated with the fragment identifier **#marker**.

> **Note** *Unlike hyperlink anchors, a marker location is not underlined or in any way visually distinguished.*

In practice, when an **<a>** element is used solely as a marker, it often doesn't enclose any text, although this doesn't suggest that the close tag should be omitted, as it often is. Setting a marker such as **<a name="top">** is accepted by most browsers, but **<a name="top"></a>** is the valid form.

An **<a>** element can serve as both a destination and a link at the same time. For example,

```
<a name="yahoolink" href="http://www.yahoo.com/">Yahoo!</A>
```

creates a link to a site and names the anchor so that it can be referenced by other links. The dual use of the **<a>** element might cause some confusion, but it is valid HTML.

Note *As discussed in Chapter 3, under the current version of HTML, the **id** attribute also is available for nearly every element. It also can be used to set a marker. The preceding example could have been written **<a id="yahoolink" href="http://www.yahoo.com">**Yahoo!**</a>**, thus exposing the anchor for targeted linking, style sheets, and dynamic manipulation via a scripting language. For backward compatibility, the **name** attribute also should be used, because many browsers do not support **id** fully.*

The need for named anchors isn't always obvious. There main purpose is to name a location within a document to jump to; for example, the common "back to top" links found at the bottom of long pages. Such link usage can be accomplished by using **<a name="top"></a>** to define named locations and then reference them with links containing fragment identifiers such as **<a href="#top">**Top of the document**</a>**. Be careful to always use the # symbol with marker names. Otherwise, the user agent probably will interpret the link as referencing a file rather than a marker.

In the more general case, a marked location in any HTML document can be referenced by placing # and a marker name after its normal URL. For example,

```
<a href="http://www.democompany.com/products/robots.htm#specs">
    Robot Specs</a>
```

will link to a named marker called "specs" in the robots.htm file. A complete example of linking within a file and to markers outside the file is shown here:

```
<!DOCTYPE HTML PUBLIC "-//W3C//DTD HTML 4.01 Transitional//EN">
<html>
<head>
<title>Name Attribute Example</title>
</head>
<body>
<a name="top"></a>
Go to the <a href="#bottom">bottom</a> of this document.<br>
Link right to a
<a href="../examples/chapter4/testfile.htm#marker1">marker</a>
in another document.

<p>To make this work we need to simulate the document being very
long by
using many breaks.</p>
<br><br><br><br><br><br><br><br><br>
<br><br><br><br><br><br><br><br><br>
<strong id="middle">the middle</strong>
<br><br><br><br><br><br><br><br><br>
```

```
<br><br><br><br><br><br><br><br><br>
<hr>
<a name="bottom" href="#top">return to top</a>
<a href="#middle">go to middle</a>

</body>
</html>
```

 *Named values must be unique, whether they are set using the **name** attribute or the **id** attribute.*

Title Attributes for Anchors

As discussed in Chapter 3, normally the **title** attribute will not seem terribly helpful to a user because it provides only basic advisory information about the use of a particular element. In the case of anchors, however, **title** is very useful because it can be used to provide tool tip information or help balloons for the link. In browsers such as Internet Explorer, if a user holds the mouse over the link long enough, a tool tip showing the information specified by the **title** attribute will be displayed. The following code fragment provides some helpful information for the link:

```
<a href="staff/index.htm"
   title="Resumes and information about our staff">Staff</a>
```

If the **title** attribute is not used, the destination URL generally is displayed. Figure 4-4 shows a tool tip for a link under Internet Explorer 4.

Note *Although the **title** attribute is usable in nearly every HTML element under Internet Explorer, using it makes sense mainly for links, images, binary objects, and forms.*

The **title** attribute serves another purpose: It provides the title information for a bookmark when a link is bookmarked before the destination page is visited. Although this might not be intuitive, with many browsers, you can right-click a link to access a menu that enables you to bookmark the link before it is visited. Then, when the page is visited, the information enclosed within the <**title**> element of the destination page is used in the bookmark instead of the information in the **title** attribute of the anchor that loaded the page. (Note that the **title** attribute and the <**title**> element are two entirely different things.)

Accelerator Keys

The HTML 4 proposed specification adds the **accesskey** to the <**a**> element, as well as to various form elements as discussed in Chapter 11. With this attribute, you can set a

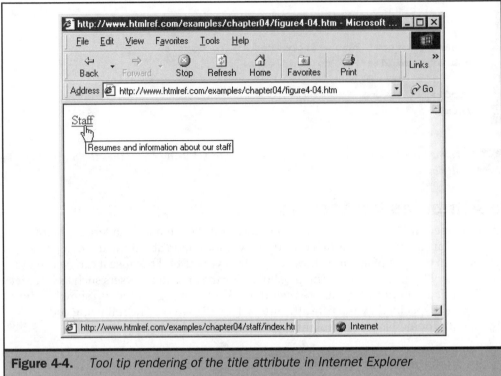

Figure 4-4.   *Tool tip rendering of the title attribute in Internet Explorer*

key to invoke an anchor without requiring a pointing device to select the link. The link is activated with the combination of the accelerator key, usually ALT, and the key specified by the attribute. So,

```
<a href="http://www.yahoo.com/" accesskey="Y">Yahoo!</a>
```

makes a link to Yahoo!, which can be activated by pressing ALT+Y. So far, many browsers do not appear to fully support this upgrade to link access.

Although adding keyboard access to a Web page seemingly would be a dramatic improvement, HTML authors are cautioned to be aware of access key bindings in the browsing environment. Under Internet Explorer 4 and higher, eight keys are already reserved for browser functions. Netscape's Communicator 4 and higher differs in one accelerator key. Assuming that both browsers eventually will support this function (Netscape doesn't at the time of this update), authors are cautioned to stay away from accelerators that use the keys in Table 4-5.

One other problem with accelerator keys is how to show them in the page. In most software, underlining indicates the letter of the accelerator key. Links generally are

Key	Mapping	Notes
F	File menu	
E	Edit menu	
C	Communicator menu	Netscape Communicator only
V	View menu	
G	Go menu	
A	Favorites menu	Internet Explorer only
H	Help	
LEFT ARROW	Back in history	
RIGHT ARROW	Forward in history	

Table 4-5. *Reserved Browser Key Bindings*

CORE HTML

underlined in browsers, so this approach isn't feasible. Style sheets can be used to change link direction, so underlining the first letter is possible, but then the user might be disoriented, expecting links to be fully underlined. Another approach to indicating the accelerator keys might be to set the access key letter of a text link in bold or a slightly larger size.

tabindex Attribute

The **tabindex** attribute of the **<a>** element defines the order in which links will be tabbed through in a browser that supports keyboard navigation. The value of **tabindex** usually is a positive number. Browsers tab through links in order of increasing **tabindex** values, but generally skip over those with negative values. So, **<a href="about.htm" tabindex="1">** sets this anchor to be the first thing tabbed to by a browser. If the **tabindex** attribute is undefined, the browser tends to tab through links in the order in which they are found within an HTML document.

*WebTV supports a usability improvement similar to **tabindex**: the **selected** attribute. When you add the word **selected** as an attribute to an anchor, the WebTV browser preselects the anchor with the yellow highlight rectangle. If two or more anchors are selected in a page, the last one appearing in the document will be selected. Although it seems that the browser would scroll to the first item selected if it did not appear in the first screen, in practice, the WebTV browser does not do this.*

target Attribute

The **target** attribute is used in conjunction with frames, which are discussed in Chapter 8. The attribute also is part of the HTML 4 specification. To target a link so that the result loads in a particular frame or window, the **target** attribute is added to the **<a>** element. Generally, a frame has a name, so setting the **target** equal to the frame name results in the link loading in the frame named in the attribute. For example, when selected, a link such as

```
<a href="http://www.yahoo.com/" target="display_frame">
```

loads the object referenced by the URL into the frame named **"display_frame"**. If the **target** attribute is left out, the current window or frame the document is in is used. Aside from author-named frames, the following are several reserved names for frames that, when used with the **target** attribute, have special meaning: **_blank**, **_self**, **_parent**, and **_top**. For more information about frames, as well as instructions on how to use the **<a>** element with frames and the various reserved frame names, refer to the element reference (Appendix A) and Chapter 8.

Anchors and Link Relationships

The **<a>** element has the following two attributes whose meanings often are misunderstood. These attributes are not widely supported by browsers:

- **rel**   Used to describe the relationship between the document and the destination document referenced by the anchor's **href** attribute. For example, if the destination of the link specifies the glossary associated with a document, the anchor might read:

  ```
  <a href="words.htm" rel="glossary">
  ```

- **rev**   Defines the reverse relationship of what **rel** defines; in this case, what the relationship is from the destination document's perspective. An example is a linear set of documents in which the **rel** attribute is set to **"next"** and the **rev** attribute is set to **"prev"**, as shown in the following code fragment:

  ```
  <a href="page2.htm" rel="next" rev="prev">Page 2</a>
  ```

Although the **rel** and **rev** attributes might seem very useful, few, if any, browsers support them. Currently, the only major use of these attributes is to document the relationship of links with the **<a>** elements themselves. The **<link>** element (discussed later in this chapter), which has semantic-link purposes similar to the **rel** and **rev** attributes, actually is supported in a limited manner by some browsers. A list of many of the proposed values for the **rel** and **rev** attributes can be found in this chapter's upcoming section about link relationships.

Scripting and Anchors

Adding logic to anchors is possible through the use of client-side scripting languages such as JavaScript. Under HTML 4, core event attributes have been added to the **<a>** element and include **onclick, onmouseover, onmouseout**, and other attributes, which can be bound to scripting events. The events named correspond to an anchor being clicked (**onclick**), a pointer being positioned on a link (**onmouseover**), and a pointer leaving a link (**onmouseout**). One obvious use of such events is to animate links so that when a mouse passes over the link, the text changes color, and when the link is clicked, the system issues a click sound. Generically, this is the idea of a *rollover button*. Aside from the basic events that might be useful to create rollover links or trigger programming logic, event models from Microsoft and Netscape can include a variety of other events such as the assigned Help key on the keyboard (generally F1) being pressed or other keys on the keyboard being pressed or released. HTML authors interested in scripting anchor activities should consult Chapter 13. Combined with images, anchor-oriented scripting additions can be used to create very persuasive Web pages.

Images and Anchors

As mentioned earlier, **<a>** elements can enclose text and other content, including images. When an anchor encloses an image, the image becomes *hot*. A hot image can activate the link and provide a basic mechanism for a graphic button. Normally, a browser shows an image to be part of an anchor by putting a colored border around the image; generally, the same color as the colored link text, either blue or purple. The browser also can indicate that the image is a link by changing the pointer to a different shape (such as a finger) when the pointer is positioned over an image link. If combined with scripting, the anchor also can modify the size or content of the image, creating a form of animated button. The following HTML markup code shows how an anchor can be combined with the **<img>** element, as discussed in Chapter 5, to create a button:

```
<!DOCTYPE HTML PUBLIC "-//W3C//DTD HTML 4.01 Transitional//EN">
<html>
<head>
<title>Anchors and Images</title>
</head>
<body>
<b>Button with a border</b><br>
<a href="about.htm">
<img src="about.gif" alt="About Button" height="55" width="55">
</a>
<br><br>
<b>Same button without a border</b><br>
```

```
<a href="about.htm">
<img src="about.gif" alt="About Button" border="0" height="55"
     width="55">
</a>
</body>
</html>
```

Notice how the **border** attribute is set to **"0"** to turn off the image's border. Further, note that the code contains a small but significant error. When a space exists between the close of an **<img>** element and the closing **</a>** element, a small blue or purple line, or "tick," might occur, as shown in Figure 4-5. To remove a tick, make sure that no space is between the **<img>** element and the closing **</a>** tag.

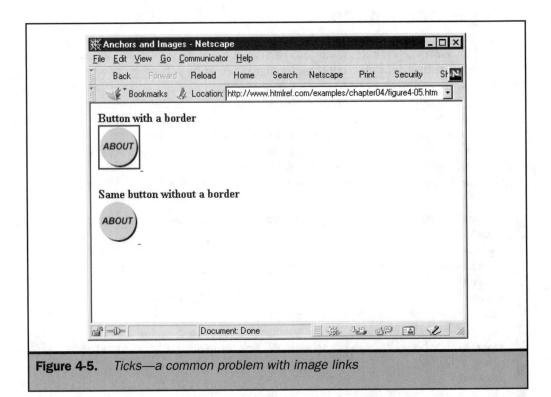

Figure 4-5.   *Ticks—a common problem with image links*

> **Note** *Although ticks aren't the worst offense on the Web, they indicate a lack of attention to detail in Web page coding. In print literature, spelling errors or small nicks or ticks on an image would be cause for serious alarm. Eventually, the same level of standards will be applied to Web pages, so HTML authors should begin to look for such small mistakes. Be careful when looking for ticks, though. Some browsers such as Internet Explorer might actually try to fix such small spacing problems for you, leading you to believe there isn't a tick if you look at it under only one browser. Testing in many browsers and validation of HTML markup should help catch subtle errors such as ticks.*

All the examples given so far show images with only one destination. Wherever a user clicks on the image link, the destination remains the same. In another class of image links, called *image maps*, different regions of the image can be made hot links for different destinations.

Image Maps

An image map is an image that contains numerous hot spots that might result in a different URL being loaded, depending on where the user clicks. The two basic types of image maps are *server-side image maps* and *client-side image maps*. In the server-side image map, the following process is followed:

1. The user clicks somewhere within the image.

2. The browser sends a request to the Web server, asking for the URL of the document associated with the area clicked. The coordinates clicked are sent to a program on the server, usually called Imagemap, which decodes the information.

3. After consulting a file that shows which coordinates map to which URL, the server sends back the requested information.

4. After receiving the response, the browser requests the new URL.

The concept of server-side image maps has some major downsides and, fortunately, rarely is used today. Regardless, it will be covered in this edition to further convince users to not consider this older format. The first downside of server-side image maps is that users really don't have a sense, URL-wise, of where a particular click will take them. All that users see as they run a mouse over the image is a set of coordinates showing the current x, y value. The second—and more significant—major problem is that the server must be consulted to go to the next page. This can be a major bottleneck that slows down the process of moving between pages. The slow speed of decoding, combined with the possibility that a user will click an unmapped hot spot and have nothing happen, makes client-side image maps preferable to server-side maps.

With client-side image maps, all the map information—which regions map to which URLs—can be specified in the same HTML file that contains the image.

Including the map data with the image and letting the browser decode it has several advantages, including,

- A server doesn't need to be visited to determine the destination, so links are resolved faster.
- Destination URLs can be shown as the user's pointer moves over the image.
- Image maps can be created and tested locally without requiring a server or system administration support.

Although this discussion makes it obvious that client-side image maps are far superior to their server-side cousins, very old browsers might not support this feature. This doesn't have to be a problem, however, because you can include simultaneous support for both types of image maps.

Server-Side Image Maps

To specify a server-side image map, you use the **<a>** element to enclose a specially marked **<img>** element. The **<a>** element **href** attribute should be set to the URL of a program or map file to decode the image map. The **<img>** element must contain the attribute **ismap** so that the browser can decode the image appropriately.

Note *Depending on the Web server being used, support for server-side image maps might or might not be built in. If image maps are supported directly, the <a> element simply must directly point to the URL of the map file and it will be decoded. This is shown in the example in Figure 4-6. On some older servers, however, the anchor might have to point to an image map program in that server's cgi-bin directory.*

As with all linked images, turning off the image borders might be desirable; you can do this by setting the **<img>** element's **border** attribute equal to 0. A simple example showing the syntax of a server-side image map is shown here; a rendering is shown in Figure 4-6:

```
<!DOCTYPE HTML PUBLIC "-//W3C//DTD HTML 4.01 Transitional//EN">
<html>
<head>
<title>Server-side Image Map Example</title>
</head>
<body>
<h1 align="center">Server-side Imagemap Test</h1>
<div align="center">
<a href="http://www.htmlref.com/examples/chapter4/shapes.map">
<img src="shapes.gif" ismap border="0" width="400"
```

```
height="200"></a>
</div>
</body>
</html>
```

As previously mentioned, server-side image maps do not provide adequate feedback to the user and could incur performance penalties. Figure 4-6 shows that the browser provides image coordinate information rather than a destination URL with a server-side image map.

HTML authors are encouraged to favor client-side image maps and to use server-side image maps only as needed to support very old browsers.

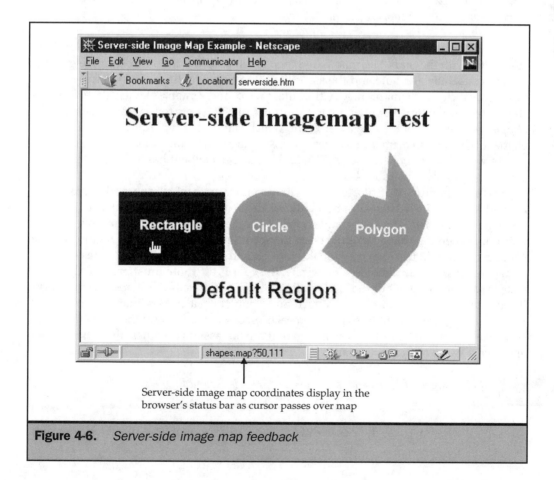

Figure 4-6.   *Server-side image map feedback*

Client-Side Image Maps

The key to using a client-side image map is to add the **usemap** attribute to the **<img>** element and have it reference a **<map>** element that defines the image map's active areas. An example of the **<img>** element syntax is **<img src="controlbar.gif" usemap="#controlmap">**. Note that unlike server-side image maps, the image will be indicated as a link regardless of the lack of the **<a>** element surrounding the **<img>**. The **border** attribute should be set to zero, if necessary.

The **<map>** element generally occurs within the same document, although support for it might exist outside of the current document. This is similar, in a sense, to the way server-side maps work. The **<map>** element can occur anywhere within the body of an HTML document, although usually it is found at the end.

> **Note** Theoretically, a client-side image map file can exist within another file, but most browsers do not support such a feature.

The **<map>** element has one attribute, **name**, which is used to specify the identifier associated with the map. The map name then is referenced within the **<img>** element, using the **usemap** attribute and the associated fragment identifier. The **<map>** element must have a closing **</map>** tag. Within the **<map>** and **</map>** elements are defined shapes that are mapped onto an image, defining the hot spots for the image map. Shapes are defined by the **<area>** element, which is found only within the **<map>** element. The **<area>** element requires no closing tag under traditional HTML, but of course would require one under XHTML. The **<area>** element has a variety of attributes, as shown in Table 4-6.

The most important attributes of an **<area>** entity are **href**, **shape**, and **coords**. The **href** attribute defines the destination URL for the browser if that particular region of the image is selected. The **shape** and **coords** attributes define the particular region in question. When the **shape** attribute is set to **rect**, it defines a rectangular region, and the coordinates should be set to provide the top-left and bottom-right coordinates of the image. If the **shape** attribute is set to **circle**, the **coords** attribute must provide the x, y coordinates of the center of the circle, followed by its radius. If the shape is set to **poly**, it indicates that the area defined is an irregular polygon; each coordinate makes up a point in the polygon, with lines between each successive point, and the last point connected to the first. Areas of the image that are not assigned values might be assigned a value of **shape="default"**.

> **Note** If the **shape** attribute is not set or omitted, **rect** is assumed.

Table 4-7 summarizes the possibilities for the **area** element, and provides examples.

CORE HTML

Attribute Name	Possible Values	Description
shape	rect, circle, and poly	Sets the type of shape
coords	x, y coordinate pairs	Sets the points that define the shape
href	A URL	Defines the destination of the link
id	Text	Identifies the anchor for target by another anchor, style sheet access, and scripting exposure
target	A frame name	Defines the frame or window destination of the link
nohref	N/A	Indicates that the region has no destination
alt	Text	Defines the alternative text for the shape
title	Text	Sets the hint text for a shape
tabindex	A number	Sets numeric order in tabbing sequence
onclick	A script	Relates the click event of a link with a script
onmouseover	A script	Relates mouse over event with a script
onmouseout	A script	Relates mouse out event with a script

Table 4-6.   *Attributes for <area>*

Shape	Coordinate Format	Example
rect	left-x, top-y, right-x, bottom-y	<area shape="rect" coords="0,0,100,50" href="about.htm">
circle	center-x, center-y, radius	<area shape="circle" coords="25,25,10" href="products.htm">
poly	x1, y1, x2, y2, x3, y3,...	<area shape="poly" coords="255,122,306,53,334,62,255,122" href="contact.htm">

Table 4-7.   *Shape Format and Examples*

*Under some browsers, the **shape** attribute also supports **rectangle**, **circ**, and **polygon**. HTML authors are encouraged to use only **rect**, **circle**, and **poly**, because they are defined by the standard.*

The various x and y coordinates are measured in pixels from the top-left corner (0,0) of the mapped image. Percentage values of the image's height and width also might be used. For example, **<area shape="rect" coords="0,0,50%,50%">** defines a rectangular region from the upper-left corner to a point halfway up and down and halfway across. Although percentage-style notation can allow the image to resize, it generally isn't useful for any but the most basic image maps. The biggest difficulty with image maps is how to determine the coordinates for the individual shapes within the image. Rather than measuring these values by hand, HTML authors are encouraged to use an image-mapping tool. Many HTML editing systems such as Allaire's Homesite (http://www.allaire.com) and Macromedia Dreamweaver (http://www.macromedia.com) include image-mapping facilities as shown in Figure 4-7.

Mapedit (http://www.boutell.com/mapedit) for Windows and UNIX, and MapMaker (http://www.kickinit.net/mapmaker/) for Macintosh also provide rudimentary mapping facilities.

Note

*Using any **height** and **width** values other than the actual sizes for a mapped image isn't recommended. Once a map has been mapped, resizing will ruin it.*

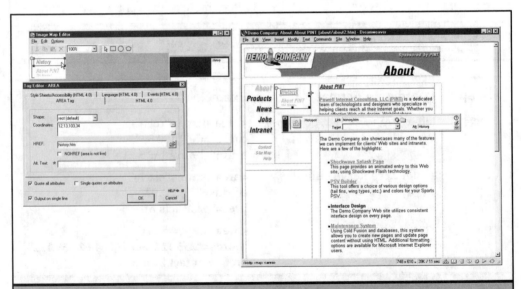

Figure 4-7. *Image Mapping made easy in an editor*

The following is an example of a client-side image map, the results of which are rendered in Figure 4-8:

```
<!DOCTYPE HTML PUBLIC "-//W3C//DTD HTML 4.01 Transitional//EN">
<html>
<head>
<title>Client-side Image Map Example</title>
</head>
<body>
<h1 align="center">Client-side Imagemap Test</h1>
<div align="center">
<img src="shapes.gif" usemap="#shapes" border="0" width="400"
     height="200">
</div>
<!-- start of client side image map -->

<map name="shapes">
<area shape="rect" coords="6,50,140,143" href="rectangle.htm"
      alt="rectangle">
<area shape="circle" coords="195,100,50" href="circle.htm"
alt="circle">
<area shape="poly"
coords="255,122,306,53,334,62,338,0,388,77,374,116,323,171,255,122"
      href="polygon.htm" alt="polygon">
<area shape="default" href="defaultreg.htm">
</map>
</body>
</html>
```

You can combine support for both server-side and client-side image maps into one file. The browser typically overrides the server-side support with the improved client-side style. This approach guarantees backward compatibility with older browsers. To support both image maps, use the **ismap** and **usemap** attributes in conjunction with an embedded map and a remote map, as shown by the following code fragment:

```
<a href="shapes.map">
<img src="shapes.gif" usemap="#shapes" border="0" ismap width="400"
     height="200"></a>
```

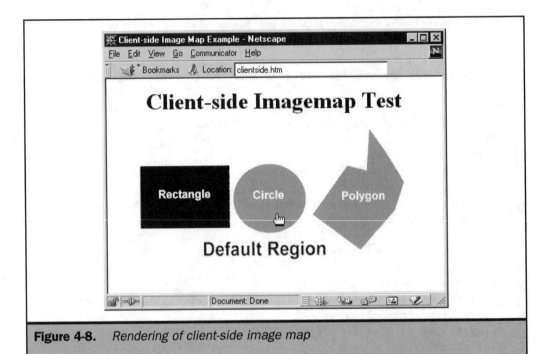

Figure 4-8.   *Rendering of client-side image map*

Image Map Attributes

Client-side image maps have a variety of attributes that can be used with the **<area>**
element. Server-side image maps have no attributes other than those normally
associated with the **<img>** element, such as **border**. The important attributes are
discussed here, as well as the issues of adding scripting facilities to image maps.

target

The **<area>** element for client-side image maps has been extended to support a **target**
attribute, much like the addition to the **<a>** element. The **target** value should be set to
the name of a frame or window. Generally, a frame has a name, so setting **target** to the
frame name results in the link loading in the frame named in the attribute. When
selected, a link such as

```
<area shape="rect" coords="0,0,50%, 50%"
     href="http://www.yahoo.com"
     target="display_frame">
```

loads the page referenced by the URL set by **href** into the frame named
"display_frame". If the **target** attribute is omitted, the current window or frame that
the document is in is used. In addition to author-named frames, the following are
several reserved names for frames that, when used with the **target** attribute, have
special meaning: **_blank**, **_self**, **_parent**, and **_top**. For more information about frames,
as well as instructions for how the **<area>** element is used with frames and the various
reserved frame names, refer to the element reference (Appendix A) and Chapter 8.

nohref

The **nohref** attribute appears to have little use, but it can be used to set a region in the
map that does nothing when clicked. This might be useful when attempting to cut a
hole in something. For example, an image of a donut might make a great image map,
particularly if the hole in the middle of the donut isn't an active, clickable area. The
nohref attribute makes this simple. Just define a large click region for the whole image
and then declare the middle of the image nonclickable with the **nohref** attribute. An
example of this is shown here:

```
<!DOCTYPE HTML PUBLIC "-//W3C//DTD HTML 4.01 Transitional//EN">
<html>
<head>
<title>Nohref Example</title>
</head>
<body>
<img src="donut.gif" width="300" height="300" border="0"
    alt="donut widget" usemap="#donut">

<map name="donut">
  <area shape="circle" coords="150,150,81" nohref>
  <area shape="circle" coords="150,150,146" href="donut.htm">
  <area shape="default" nohref>
</map>

</body>
</html>
```

Note   *Under XHTML you would have to set **nohref** to a value; for example, <area
shape="circle" coords="150,150,81" nohref="nohref" />.*

When this code is rendered under Netscape, the hand cursor, indicating a clickable
area, disappears when it passes over the nonclickable area; under Internet Explorer, the
cursor appears the same, but the area still isn't clickable.

Given that **nohref** creates an inactive region that sits on top of another, what happens when one region overlaps another? According to the specification, if two or more regions overlap, the region defined first within the **<map>** element takes precedence over subsequent regions. This rule implies that **<area>** elements with the **nohref** attribute should be placed before **<area>** elements that are active, so that clicking the **<area>** element with the **nohref** attribute doesn't take the user to a new URL as a result of a previously placed, overlapping active **<area>** element.

alt and title

Image maps have some major drawbacks, even in their client-side aspect, with text-based browsers. The **alt** attribute can be used, as shown in the previous examples, and should provide text labels that are displayed in the status line when the pointer passes over the hot spots. Although the **title** attribute can be added to all elements, and can provide a function somewhat similar to **alt** in graphical browsers, in practice, browsers seem to pick up **alt** before **title**. To be on the safe side, you can use both attributes simultaneously. One unfortunate problem with the **alt** attribute and client-side image maps is that non-graphical browsers don't always pick up the **alt** attributes and build meaningful renderings. Instead of a set of links, the viewer might only see a cryptic message, as shown in Figure 4-9.

HTML authors are encouraged to provide secondary navigation that mirrors the choices available in the image map. This secondary navigation should consist of text links located below the image, which makes the site accessible for non-graphical user agents and might improve the site's usability. Users on slow connections can opt to select text links before the image is completely downloaded. An example of text links in conjunction with an image map is shown in Figure 4-10. Also, when using server-side image maps, you can make the inactive or default area link to a new page that contains a text menu of the choices provided through the image map. In this way, a user who selects the **ismap** provided by an older browser receives the menu, not the map.

Discussion of the design and navigation issues surrounding image maps is left to books that focus on site design. Where possible, HTML authors should avoid relying too heavily on single-image–style image maps for navigation purposes.

tabindex

Under the HTML 4 proposed specification, you can use the **tabindex** attribute of the **<area>** element to define the order in which hot spots in a client-side image map are tabbed through in a browser that supports keyboard navigation. The value of **tabindex** typically is a positive number. A browser tabs through links in order of increasing **tabindex** values, but generally skips over those with negative values. So, the following line sets this anchor to be the first thing tabbed to:

```
<area shape="rect" coords="0,0,50%,50%"
      href="http://www.yahoo.com/"
      tabindex="1">
```

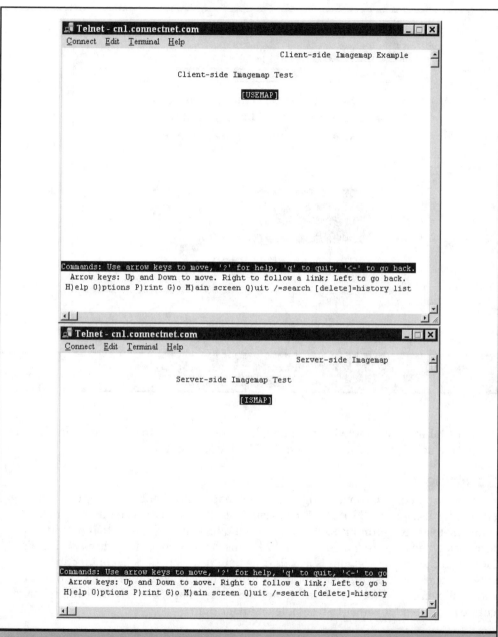

Figure 4-9.   *Non-meaningful image map renderings*

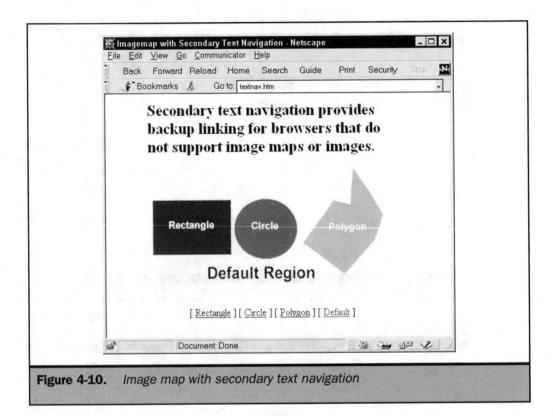

Figure 4-10.   *Image map with secondary text navigation*

If the **tabindex** attribute is undefined, the browser tends to tab though links in the order in which they are found within an HTML document.

Scripting

As already noted, you can add logic to image maps with client-side scripting languages such as JavaScript or VBScript. Three extensions to the **<area>** element—**onclick**, **onmouseover**, and **onmouseout**—can be bound to scripting events that provide feedback when a mouse passes over a link. This is the rollover idea discussed earlier. However, the **<area>** element is less flexible than using anchors in conjunction with single images, because replacing only a portion of the image on the fly is impossible. Most rollover-style Web interfaces do not use image maps, but rely instead on images cut up and pieced together to resemble an image map.

Semantic Linking with the <link> Element

Syntactically, a link to another document created by an anchor says nothing about the relationship between the current document and the object being pointed to. You can use the **title** attribute to provide a hint or advisory information about the link, so that the viewer of a page can associate meaning with a link. The linked image or text also might give some clue about what happens when the link is selected, but in HTML itself, links lack any semantic meaning. The **<link>** element, however, does provide a way to define the relationship between linked objects. The concept of the **<link>** element is that a document might have predefined relationships that can be specified, and that some of these relationships might be useful to a browser when offering navigation choices, rendering a page, or preparing a page to be printed. Although **<link>** has been around for several years, until recently, few browsers have supported **<link>** in any way. With the rise of style sheets, scripting, and proprietary extensions, **<link>** finally is being supported by browsers, at least in a limited manner.

The **<link>** element is found in the head of an HTML document, where it might occur more than once. The two most important attributes of the element are **href** and **rel**. Like the **href** attribute for the **<a>** element, the **href** attribute for **<link>** specifies the URL of another document, whereas **rel** specifies the relationship with that document. The value of **rel** often is called the *link type*. The basic syntax of the **<link>** element is **<link href="url" rel="relationship">**. Under HTML 4, **<link>** also supports a reverse semantic relationship, indicated by the **rev** attribute, as well as the **title** attribute, which can be used to set advisory information for the link. The most mysterious aspect of the **<link>** element is the value of the **rel** and **rev** attributes.

Link Relationships in Detail

Like the **rel** attribute for the **<a>** element, the **rel** attribute for **link** defines the relationship between the current document and the linked object. The value of the **rel** attribute is simply a text value, which can be anything the author desires. However, a browser can interpret standardized relationships in a particular way. For example, a browser might provide special icons or navigation features when the meaning of a link is understood. Currently, no standard set of document relationship values exists, but the HTML 4 specification lists some proposed relationship values, as shown in Table 4-8. Note that these values are not case-sensitive.

Beyond the HTML 4 proposed relationships, various other relationships are being discussed. In fact, HTML authors can make up their own relationships if they desire, but should be careful to avoid using **prev** or **next** as **rel** or **rev** values, because they tend to hold special meaning for browsers.

WebTV Support for <link>

The only fairly common browser to support **<link>** is WebTV. In the WebTV environment, **<link>** is used to improve performance. If the **rel** attribute is set with the

CORE HTML

Relationship Value	Explanation	Example
alternate	The link references an alternate version of the document that the link is in. This can be a translated version of the document, as suggested by the **lang** attribute.	`<link href="frenchintro.htm" rel="alternate" lang="fr">`
appendix	The link references a document that serves as an appendix for a document or site.	`<link href="intro.htm" rel="appendix">`
bookmark	The link references a document that serves as a bookmark; the **title** attribute can be used to name the bookmark.	`<link href="index.htm" rel="bookmark" title="homepage">`
chapter	The link references a document that is a chapter in a site or collection of documents.	`<link href="ch01.htm" rel="chapter">`
contents	The link references a document that serves as a table of contents, most likely for the site, although it might be for the document. The meaning is unclear.	`<link href="toc.htm" rel="contents">`
index	The link references a page that provides an index for the current document.	`<link href="docindex.htm" rel="index">`
glossary	The link references a document that provides a glossary of terms for the current document.	`<link href="glossary.htm" rel="glossary">`
copyright	The link references a page that contains a copyright statement for the current document.	`<link href="copyright.htm" rel="copyright">`
next	The link references the next document to visit in a linear collection of documents. It can be used, for example, to "pre-fetch" the next page, as in the WebTV browsers.	`<link href="page2.htm" rel="next">`

Table 4-8.   *rel Values Proposed for HTML*

Relationship Value	Explanation	Example
prev	The link references the previous document in a linear collection of documents.	`<link href="page1.htm" rel="previous">`
section	The link references a document that is a section in a site or collection of documents.	`<link href="sect07.htm" rel="section">`
start	The link references the first document in a set of documents.	`<link href="begin.htm" rel="start">`
stylesheet	The link references an external style sheet.	`<link href="style.css" rel="stylesheet">`
subsection	The link references a document that is a subsection in a collection of documents.	`<link href="sect07a.htm" rel="subsection">`
help	The link references a help document for the current document or site.	`<link href="help.htm" rel="help">`

Table 4-8. *rel Values Proposed for HTML* (continued)

value of **next** and an **href** is specified, the browser will "pre-fetch" the page in question. If the content of the next page is stored in a memory cache, the page loads much faster than if the page has to be requested from the server. If a WebTV user is being presented with a brief set of pages in a linear fashion, such as a slide-show or tour, the next page could be preloaded with the **<link>** element. For example, **<link rel="next" href="second.htm">** loads the next page, called second.htm, in advance. This technique assumes that the user is going to a predictable next page. This might not be easy to determine for all possible Web site organizations.

Note *HTML authors not using WebTV who are interested in pre-fetching pages can use Microsoft's preloader ActiveX control. Images also can be pre-fetched by setting both their height and width attributes to 1: <img src="image_on_nextpage.gif" height="1" width="1">. This technique loads an image into the page, but the image appears as a barely perceptible dot. Then, when the next page loads, the image will have been pre-cached by the browser. Combined with a scripting language, the loading of images can be handled after the current page has loaded, by using the onload event for the document.*

`<link>` and Style Sheets

A variety of attributes are defined for the **`<link>`** element including **type**, **media**, and **target**. These new attributes are already supported for handling style sheets in browsers such as Internet Explorer and Netscape. The **`<link>`** element allows a style sheet for a document to be referenced from a separate file. If the markup code **`<link rel="stylesheet" href="corpstyle.css">`** is inserted in the head of an HTML document, it associates the style sheet corpstyle.css with the current document. The **rel** value of **stylesheet** indicates the relationship.

The **alternate stylesheet** relationship, which would allow users to pick from a variety of styles, also has been suggested. To define several alternative styles, the **title** attribute must be set to group elements belonging to the same style. All members of the same style must have exactly the same value for **title**. For example, the following fragment defines a standard style called basestyle.css, and two alternative styles, titled 640 x 480 and 1024 x 768, have been added; these refer to style sheets to improve layout at various screen resolutions:

```
<link rel="alternate stylesheet" title="640by480"
href="small-1.css">
<link rel="alternate stylesheet" title="640by480"
href="small-2.css">
<link rel="alternate stylesheet" title="1024by768" href="big.css">
<link rel="stylesheet" href="basestyle.css">
```

A Web browser should provide a method for users to view and pick from the list of alternative styles, where the **title** attribute can be used to name each choice. Currently, this alternative choice for style sheets is not supported by any popular browser.

Because the potential exists for many different kinds of linked objects, the **type** attribute was added to the **`<link>`** element, to indicate the data type of the related object. **type** can be especially helpful when used to indicate the type of style sheet being used, because many varied style sheet technologies currently exist. **type** is used by browsers to indicate the type of the linked style, as in this example:

```
<link rel="stylesheet" href="corpstyle.css" type="text/css">
```

For style sheets, **type** usually takes a MIME type, which indicates the format of the style sheet being linked to.

The **media** attribute is another new attribute for the **`<link>`** element, but it isn't widely supported. For style sheets, this attribute would indicate what type of media the style sheet should be used with; the same document could thus reference one style sheet when viewed on a computer screen, and a different style sheet when being printed. The browser then is responsible for filtering out those style sheets that aren't appropriate for the current environment. The following code fragment shows an example of this idea:

```
<link rel="stylesheet" media="print" href="corp-print.css">
<link rel="stylesheet" media="screen" href="corp-screen.css">
```

A variety of values have been proposed for the **media** attribute including **print**, **projection**, **screen**, **braille**, **aural**, **tv**, and **all**. When not specified, **all** would be the default type, suggesting that the style should be used in all output environments.

Before concluding the chapter, let's consider some of the practical and theoretical limitations of linking on today's Internet.

Beyond Location

An amazing wealth of information is available on the Web. Although many people complain of information overload, the real problem isn't volume. It's relevance. How can a particular piece of information be located quickly and easily? If the Web were ideal, it would be like the computer on *Star Trek*™, which always seems to deliver in a matter of seconds any information a user requests. On the Internet, a request to a search tool often yields an overwhelming list of tens of thousands of entries. Some of these entries might be outdated, the documents to which others refer might have moved, or the server that specifies an entry might be unreachable. Although the Web isn't science fiction, many of the computer and information systems presented in science fiction represent valid goals for the Web. The key problem with building a more organized Web is URL-based addressing.

Problems with URLs

The primary problem with URLs is that they define location rather than meaning. URLs specify where something is located on the Web, not what it is or what it's about. URLs specify where to go, not what to get. URLs blur the line between what a document is and where it actually is located. This might not seem to be a big deal, but it is. This issue becomes obvious when the problems with URLs are enumerated:

- *URLs aren't persistent.* Documents move around, servers change names, and documents might eventually be deleted. This is the nature of the Web, and the reason why the **404 Not Found** message is so common. When users hit a broken link, they might be at a loss to determine what happened to the document and how to locate its new home. Wouldn't it be nice if, no matter what happened, a unique identifier indicated where to get a copy of the information?

- *URLs tend to be long and confusing.* People often have to transcribe addresses. For example, the following is quite a lot to write on a piece of literature:

  http://pint.com/about

Marketing firms already are scrambling for short domain names and site structures that use short URLs, such as http://www.democompany.com/prod1. Advertisers often omit http:// in their promotional material. Although most browsers fill in http://, omitting it could cause problems with older browsers that require complete URLs.

■ *URLs create an artificial bottleneck and extreme reliance on DNS services by specifying location rather than meaning.* For example, the text of the HTML 4 specification is a useful document and certainly has an address at the W3C Web site. But does it live in other places on the Internet? It probably is mirrored in a variety of locations, but what happens if the W3C server is unreachable, or DNS services fail to resolve the host? In this case, the resource is unreachable. URLs create a point source for information. Rather than trying to find a particular document, wherever it might be on the Internet, Web users try to go to a particular location. Rather than talking about where something is, Web users should try to talk about *what* that something is.

URNs, URCs, and URIs

Talking about what a document is rather than where it is makes sense when you consider how information is organized outside the Internet. Nobody talks about which library carries a particular book, or what shelf it is on. The relevant information is the title of the book, its author, and perhaps some other information. But what happens if two or more books have the same title, or two authors have the same name? This actually is quite common. Generally, a book should have a unique identifier such as an ISBN number that, when combined with other descriptive information, such as the author, publisher, and publication date, uniquely describes the book. This naming scheme enables people to specify a particular book and then hunt it down.

The Web, however, isn't as ordered as a library. On the Web, people name their documents whatever they like, and search robots organize their indexes however they like. Categorizing things is difficult. The only unique item for documents is the URL, which simply says where the document lives. But how many URLs does the HTML 4 specification have? A document might exist in many places. Even worse than a document with multiple locations, what happens when the content at the location changes? Perhaps a particular URL address points to information about dogs one day and cats the next. This is how the Web really is. However, a great deal of research is being done to address some of the shortcomings of the Web and its addressing schemes.

URN

A new set of addressing ideas, including URNs, URCs, and URIs, are emerging to remedy some of the Web's shortcomings. A *uniform resource name* (URN) can locate a resource by giving it a unique symbolic name rather than a unique address. Network services analogous to the current DNS services will transparently translate a URN into the URL (server IP address, directory path, and filename) needed to actually locate a resource. This translation could be used to select the closest server, to improve document delivery speed, or to try various backup servers in case a server is unavailable. The benefit of the abstraction provided by URNs should be obvious from this simple idea alone.

To better understand the idea behind URNs, consider the idea of domain names, such as www.democompany.com. These names are already translated into numeric IP addresses, such as 192.102.249.3, all the time. This mapping provides the ability to change a machine's numeric address or location without seriously disrupting access to it, because the name stays the same. Furthermore, numeric addresses provide no meaning to a user, whereas domain names provide some indication of the entity in question. Obviously, the level of abstraction provided by a system such as DNS would make sense on the Web. Rather than typing some unwieldy URL, a URN would be issued that would be translated to an underlying URL. Some experts worry that using a resolving system to translate URNs to URLs is an inherently flawed idea that will not scale well. Because the DNS system is fairly fragile, some truth might lie behind this concern. Another problem with this idea is that, in reality, URNs probably won't be something easy to remember, such as urn: *booktitle*, but instead be something more difficult, such as urn:isbn: 0-12-518408-5.

URC

A *uniform resource characteristic* (URC), also known as a *uniform resource citation*, describes a set of attribute/value pairs that defines some aspect of an information resource. URCs are somewhat like the **<meta>** data items or the PICS labels associated with a Web document. The form of a URC is still under discussion, but many of the ideas of URCs are already in use.

Combined, a URL, URN, and a collection of URCs describe an information resource. For example, the document "Demo Company Corporate Summary" might have a unique URN such as urn://corpid:55127.

The syntax of the preceding URN is fictional. It simply shows that URNs probably won't have easily remembered names and that many naming schemes can be used, such as ISBN numbers or corporate IDs.

The "Demo Company Corporate Summary" also would have a set of URCs that describes the rating of the file, the author, the publisher, and so on. In addition, the document would have a location(s) on the Web where the document lives, such as one of the following:

```
http://www.democompany.com/about/corp.htm
http://www.democompany.co.jp/about/corp.htm.
```

CORE HTML

URI

Taken all together, a particular information resource has been identified. The collection of information, which is used to identify this document specifically, is termed a *uniform resource identifier* (URI).

> **Note**   *Occasionally, URI is used interchangeably with URL. Although this is acceptable, research into the theories behind the names suggests that URI is more generic than URLs, and serves to encompass the ideal of an information resource. Currently, a URL is the only common way to identify an information resource on the Internet. Although technically a URL could be considered a URI, this confuses the issue and obscures the ultimate goal of trying to talk about information more generally than in terms of a network location.*

Although many of the ideas covered here are still being discussed, some systems, such as Persistent URLs, or PURLs (www.purl.org), and Handles (www.handle.net), already implement many of the features of URNs and URCs. Furthermore, many browser vendors and large Web sites are implementing special keyword navigation schemes that mimic many of the ideas of URNs and URCs. Unfortunately, as of the writing of this book, none of these approaches are widely implemented or accepted. Although any of these approaches probably can be considered as true URIs when compared to the URLs used today, for the near future, URLs are likely to remain the most common way to describe information on the Web. Therefore, the system has to be extended to deal with new types of information and access methods.

New URL Forms

URLs are here to stay, but as new ideas are added to the Internet, URLs will evolve into new forms. For example, as telephones and televisions are joined with desktop computers and the Internet, addressing schemes for telephone numbers and TV channels will become necessary. WebTV, video game consoles, and cellular phone browsers already demonstrate that the Web is reaching users beyond the personal computer or workstation. On these devices, some of the URL schemes described early in the chapter are inappropriate. Many of these devices lack local storage, so the file protocol discussed earlier in the chapter is of little use. On the other hand, many of these devices usually have access to other sources of information, such as television channels and telephone services. A television channel URL form might look like tv://*channel*, whereby *channel* is either an alpha-numeric name (such as nbc or nbc7-39) or a numeric channel number. Similar to the news URL form, differentiating between nbc in one area and another would be unnecessary because the system would be configured to get the information locally. Similarly, a phone URL might look like phone://*phone-number*, with a numeric value for the phone number and any extra digit information required, such as the country code or calling card information. For example, phone://+1-555-270-2086 might

CORE HTML

dial a phone number in the United States. An instruction to send a fax could be written in a similar way, except with fax://*phone-number*.

New content types and URL schemes bring new challenges; particularly in the way links and fragment identifiers are used within HTML documents. For example, how will a particular scene in a video stream be addressed? Random access to large audio and video files is very useful, particularly considering the download requirements for such data. Subsections or "clips" of a data stream must be addressable through URLs that describe a time range. How can a URL describe the idea of accessing an audio file called mozart.audio and playing a ten-second clip starting at time 2:05? Once into clips, particularly video clips, some mechanism will be needed to link from the data stream to other data streams or objects on the Web. Some experimental systems already show video with hot spots that work like image maps. Given that video certainly will be an important media form on the Web of tomorrow and that other media forms also will have to be added as well, it should be obvious that current URL schemes are far from complete. Many new schemes are being proposed all the time. A variety of esoteric schemes are out there already. If you are interested in new URL schemes, take a look at the W3 area on addressing (www.w3.org/Addressing/) for more information.

Summary

Linking documents on the Web requires a consistent naming scheme. URLs provide the basic information necessary to locate an object on the Internet by including the host name, directory, filename, and access protocol. URLs are written in a regular format, so that an address can be written for any object. A common shorthand notation, relative URLs, is particularly useful when creating links within a Web site. If a document's URL can be determined, whether it's relative or fully spelled out, it can be specified in the **<a>** element to create an anchor from one document to another. Links within HTML documents can be made with text or with images. A special type of clickable image, called an *image map*, allows areas of an image to be defined as "hot."

Simply linking documents together is the most basic form of hypertext. By using the **<link>** element, as well as the **rel** and **rev** attributes of the **<a>** element, you can create relationships between documents. So far, the **<link>** element primarily is used with style sheets.

Even if Web authors master all aspects of linking, a bigger picture remains to worry about. Chapter 16 covers various topics related to linking including link management, **<meta>** information, and filtering, but theoretical limitations still exist. The Web is a chaotic environment, and navigating among documents and linking documents presents serious challenges to the HTML author. In the future, some of these problems might be solved by URNs, URCs, and improved URLs, which, taken together, make up the uniform resource identifier (URI). However, until URNs or similar technologies are more readily available, HTML authors should be cautious about linking, and should consistently check links in their sites.

The Complete Reference

Part III

Presentation and Layout

Chapter 5

HTML and Images

A great Web site isn't just about correct HTML. Site organization, navigation, interactivity, content, delivery, and a multitude of other issues affect a user's perception of a site. However, images probably are the most obvious part of a great Web site. Carefully used imagery can add to both the appeal and usability of a Web site. Creation of Web-ready images certainly is beyond the scope of this book, but HTML authors should at minimum be aware of the basics of Web image formats such as GIF and JPEG and know when they are being used appropriately. Although the basic HTML syntax of adding images to a page using the **<img>** element is relatively straightforward, creation of an aesthetically pleasing page is truly more art than it is science. Tools can make Web image creation easier, but readers should be realistic and consider both their own artistic limitations as well as the download considerations of the Web before going overboard with images.

Image Preliminaries

Before discussing image use in HTML, it is important to discuss what image formats are supported on the Web today. In general, Web-based images come in two basic flavors: GIF (Graphics Interchange Format) as designated by the .gif extension and JPEG (Joint Photographic Experts Group) as indicated by the .jpg or .jpeg file extension. A third format PNG (Portable Network Graphics) as indicated by the .png file extension is slowly gaining ground as a Web format. Table 5-1 details the supported image types found in most, but for now page authors should only use GIF or JPEG images.

Note *Internet Explorer also supports the bitmap (BMP) file type popular with Windows users. This format has not been widely adopted on the Web.*

File Type	File Extension
GIF (Graphics Interchange Format)	.gif
JPEG (Joint Photographic Experts Group)	.jpg or .jpeg
XBM (X Bitmaps)	.xbm
XPM (X Pixelmaps)	.xpm
PNG (Portable Network Graphics)	.png

Table 5-1. *Selected Web Image File Types*

Choosing the correct image for the job is an important part of Web design. In general, GIF images tend to be good for illustrations such as logos or cartoons whereas JPEG images usually are the choice for complex imagery such as photographs. The main concern for site designers when considering an image format is the size of the file itself and the quality of the reproduction. Table 5-2 provides a concise summary of the qualities of each format.

Note *An obscure fact is that according to the GIF specification, layering can be used to create a GIF image that supports more than 256 colors. However, not all browsers support this little-known feature. Layering also allows for an interesting form of color interlacing, which can bring in one set of colors before another.*

Subsequent sections will explain each of these basic features of the two main image formats in slightly more detail.

GIF Images

The main consideration for most designers when choosing image formats is, of course, file size versus image quality. The run-length encoding compression scheme used by GIF works well with large areas of continuous color, so GIF is very efficient in

Format	Compression Scheme	Color Depth Supported	Progressive or Interlaced Rendering	Transparency	Animation
GIF	Lossless (preserves file size for minimal compression of continuous horizontal regions of color)	8-bit (256 colors)*	Interlaced	Yes (1 degree)	Yes
JPEG	Lossy (trade image quality for file size)	24-bit (millions of colors	Progressive	No	No

Table 5-2. *Web Image Format Overview*

compression of flat-style illustration. Notice here that a GIF image with vertical bars is larger file size–wise than one with horizontal bars. This is just the same image rotated.

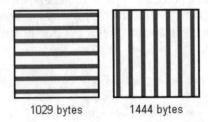

1029 bytes   1444 bytes

GIF also supports only 8-bit color for a maximum of 256 colors in the image. Consequently, some degree of loss is inevitable when representing true-color images such as photographs. Typically, when an image is remapped from a large number of colors to a smaller color palette, *dithering* occurs. Dithering attempts to imitate colors by placing similar colors near each other. It also produces a speckling or banding effect that might cause images to appear rough or fuzzy. Web authors should be careful to use GIF images appropriately. Netscape and Microsoft currently use a so-called "browser-safe" color palette of 216 colors that are common across systems such as Macintosh or Windows. If a GIF image using a color outside this color palette is displayed on an 8-bit system, dithering will occur as illustrated here.

Non-dithered colors

Dithered colors

GIF images also support a concept called *transparency*. One bit of transparency is allowed, which means that one color can be set to be transparent. Transparency allows the background that an image is placed upon to show through, making a variety of complex effects possible.

Without
Transparency

With
Transparency

GIF transparency is far from ideal, as it can result in a halo effect in certain situations. For example, in order to smooth images, a technique called *anti-aliasing* is used. Anti-aliased images appear smooth because the image progressively is made light to fade into the background as shown in this comparison of aliased and anti-aliased imagery.

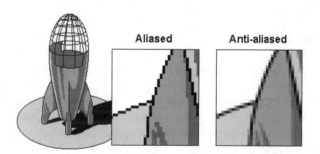

However, because only one color of transparency can be set in an image, the anti-aliasing colors might show up as a halo or residue around the image.

GIF images also support a feature called *interlacing*. Interlacing allows an image to load in a venetian-blind fashion rather than from top to bottom, a line at a time. The interlacing effect allows a user to get an idea of what an image looks like before the entire image has downloaded. The idea of interlacing is shown in Figure 5-1. Notice as the image is loaded that more and more of its shows. At first the user can only see an indistinct, highly pixelated image. Once the image is completely loaded, it will present a clear image of an office building; at this point in its progress, however, it already gives the user a good idea of what is being downloaded. The previsualization benefit of interlacing is very useful on the Web, where download speed often is an issue. Although interlacing a GIF image generally is a good idea, occasionally it comes with a downside. First, interlaced images might be slightly larger than noninterlaced images. Second, an interlaced image might not always provide its intended previsualization

PRESENTATION AND
LAYOUT

Figure 5-1. *Example of GIF interlacing*

benefit. For example, if the GIF image is of graphic text, the text probably will not be readable until the image is fully loaded.

Starting with the GIF89a format, which was supported first by Netscape 2, animation has been possible on the Web. The GIF89a format supports a series of GIF images that act as the individual frames of animation. The animation can be set up so one image is displayed after another, similar to a little flipbook. The animation extension also allows timing and looping information to be added to the image. Today, animated GIFs are one of the most popular ways to add simple animation to a Web page because nearly every browser supports them. Browsers that do not support the animated GIF format generally display the first frame of the animation in its place. Even though plug-ins or other browser facilities are not required, authors should not rush out to use animation on their pages. Excessive animation can be distracting as well as inefficient to download, particularly when frames are not used efficiently. One approach to combating file bloat is to replace only the moving parts of an individual animation frame. This might result in a dramatic saving of file size, as shown in Figure 5-2.

In summary, because of their compression scheme and support for 8-bit color, GIF images tend to be best suited for illustrations. GIF images do support interlacing, which can provide previsualization for Web-based imagery. Because of the nature of their image compression, GIF images might not be suitable for photographic-style imagery, which is probably better left to the JPEG format discussed in the next section. In their favor, GIF images are the most widely supported image format, and do have advanced features such as transparency and animation. Probably the only controversial aspect of the image format, aside from its compression issues, is its pronunciation with either a hard "g" or a "j" sound. The author prefers the hard "g" as the other pronunciation sounds like a popular brand of peanut butter, but this sticky issue probably will never be settled.

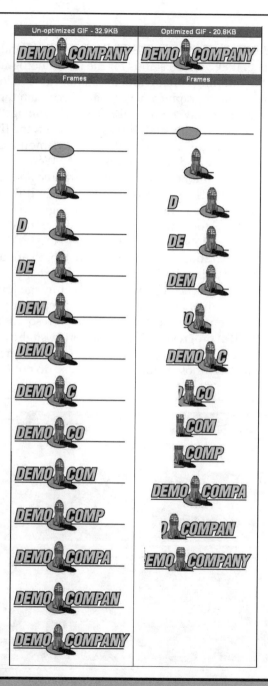

Figure 5-2.   *Example of animated GIF frames and optimization*

JPEG Images

The other common Web image format is JPEG, which usually is indicated by a filename ending with .jpg or .jpeg. JPEG, which stands for the Joint Photographic Experts Group—the name of the committee that wrote the standard—is a lossy image format designed for compressing photographic images that can contain thousands, or even millions, of colors or shades of gray. Because JPEG is a lossy image format, there is some trade-off between image quality and file size. However, the JPEG format stores high-quality, 24-bit color images in a significantly smaller amount of space than GIF, thus saving precious disk space or download time on the Web.

Although the JPEG format might compress photographic images well, it is not well suited to line drawings or text. The degree of compression in JPEG images, which shows how the format favors photographs, is shown in Figure 5-3. Note that when illustrations are saved in JPEG format, they might acquire extraneous information, often in the form of unwanted dots or other residue. Because JPEG is so well suited to photographs and GIF to illustrations, it's no wonder that both are used on the Web. JPEG images do not support animation, nor do they support any form of transparency. Web designers needing such effects must turn to another image format, such as GIF. JPEG images do support a form of interlacing in a format called *progressive JPEG*. Progressive JPEGs fade in from a low resolution to a high resolution, going from fuzzy to clear. Like interlaced GIFs, progressive JPEG images are slightly larger than their nonprogressive counterparts. One very minor problem with progressive JPEGs is that very old browsers, particularly those before Netscape 2.x, do not support them.

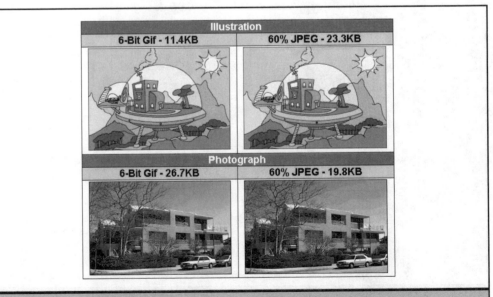

Figure 5-3. *Comparison between GIF and JPEG formats*

PNG Images

The Portable Network Graphics (PNG) format has all of the features of GIF89a in addition to several other features. Notable features include greater color depth support, color and gamma correction, and 8-bit transparency. In addition, the compression algorithm for PNG is nonproprietary, making PNG a likely successor of GIF. Internet Explorer 4 supports inline PNG images in a limited way. Some versions of Netscape Communicator require a plug-in, and later versions provide limited support. No 4.x or even 5.x generation browser supports PNG well enough to rely on the format, so Web designers are warned to avoid using the format unless browser sensing is utilized so as to guarantee images will render properly.

Other Image Formats

There are many image formats beyond GIF, JPEG, and PNG that can be used on the Web. Vector formats such as Flash (with the file extension .swf) or Scalable Vector Graphics (SVG) files, might use exotic compression technology such as fractal or wavelet compression. Most of the less common image formats might require a helper application or plug-in to allow the image to be displayed. Unless you have a specific need, you probably should avoid special image types requiring browser add-ons; users might become frustrated by the work involved in obtaining the extra software.

For now it will be assumed that a page designer simply has a Web-compatible image that needs to be placed into a Web page and requires the appropriate HTML syntax to do so.

HTML Image Basics

To insert an image into a Web page, use the **<img>** element and set the **src** attribute of the element equal to the URL of the image. As discussed in Chapter 4, the form of the URL can be either an absolute URL or a relative URL. Most likely, the image element will use a relative URL to an image found locally. To insert a GIF image called logo.gif residing in the same directory as the current document, use

```
<img src="logo.gif">
```

Of course, an absolute URL also could be used to reference an image on another server, for example

```
<img src="http://www.democompany.com/images/logo.gif">
```

Using an external URL is not advised, because images could move, or cause the page to load at an uneven pace.

*The **src** attribute must be included. Otherwise, browsers that support images might
display a placeholder or broken image icon.*

To set up a simple example, first create a directory to hold your images. It usually is
a good idea to store all your image media in a directory named "images." This will
help you keep your site contents organized as you build the Web site. Now place a GIF
format image named "robot.gif" in that directory. To retrieve an image from the
Internet, you can simply right-click with your mouse on an image and save the file to
your directory. Macintosh users will have to hold the mouse button down on an image
to access the menu for saving the image. Once you have a GIF image, you should be
able to use a short piece of HTML markup to experiment with the use of **<img>**, as
shown in the following:

```
<!DOCTYPE HTML PUBLIC "-//W3C//DTD HTML 4.01 Transitional//EN">
<html>
<head>
<title>Image Example</title>
</head>
<body>
<h2 align="center">Image Example</h2>
<img src="images/robot.gif" width="234" height="150" border="0">
</body>
</html>
```

*The name of the image, its path, its width, and height all are made up for this example.
Your particular attribute values might be different.*

A possible rendering of the image example is shown in Figure 5-4.

Under the original HTML 2 specification, aside from **src**, there were only three
other attributes to the **<img>** element: **ismap**, **align**, and **alt**. Later on, Netscape and
Microsoft added numerous attributes, many of which have been incorporated into the
HTML 4 specification that currently is in progress. The next few sections will cover the
basic attributes. A more complete rundown of the image options available will follow.

Alternative Text Using the alt Attribute

The **alt** attribute was set to provide alternative text for user agents that did not display
images, or for graphical browsers in which the user has turned image rendering off as
shown in Figure 5-5. The **alt** attribute's value can display in place of the image or be used
as a tool tip or placeholder information in image-based browsers. Today with the rise of
the **title** attribute, the **alt** value really should show only as an alternative rendering when
the image is unavailable and the advisory text specified by the **title** attribute should be
used as a tool tip. Of course there is no guarantee that browsers will interpret the meaning
of **alt** and **title** properly, thus it might make sense to set them to the same value.

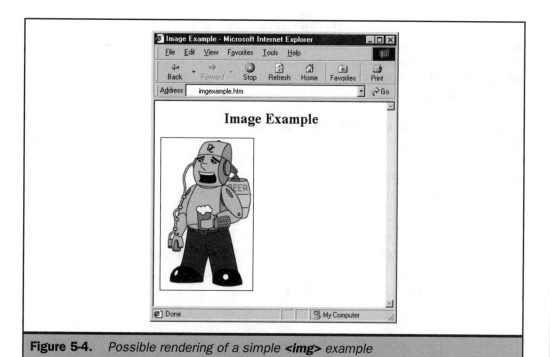

Figure 5-4.   *Possible rendering of a simple* **<img>** *example*

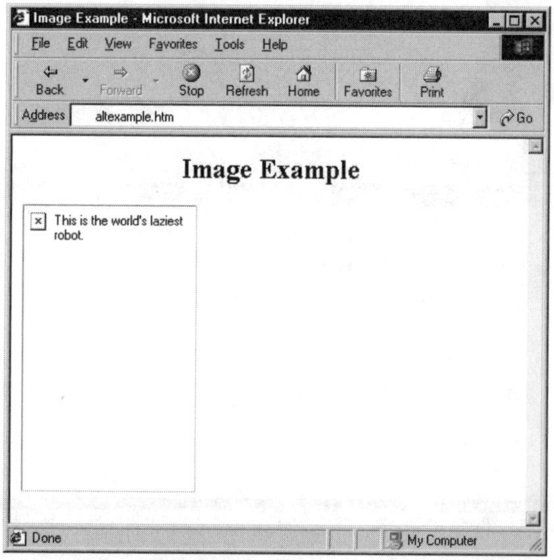

Figure 5-5.   *Alternative text rendering*

While some sources suggest that **alt** text be limited to 1,024 characters, there is no limit to the text that might theoretically be used. However, anything more than a few hundred characters might become unwieldy. Furthermore, some browsers, including some versions of Netscape 4, do not handle long tool tips properly and might not wrap the descriptive text.

The Importance of Alternative Text

It is easy to forget that many different types of browsers can be used to access the Web. Whereas much of the world might access a page using Netscape or Microsoft products, what about everyone else out there? There are people who have access to the Web from a text-only environment. Figure 5-6 shows the same page two ways: under Netscape with the image turned on and as rendered under Lynx.

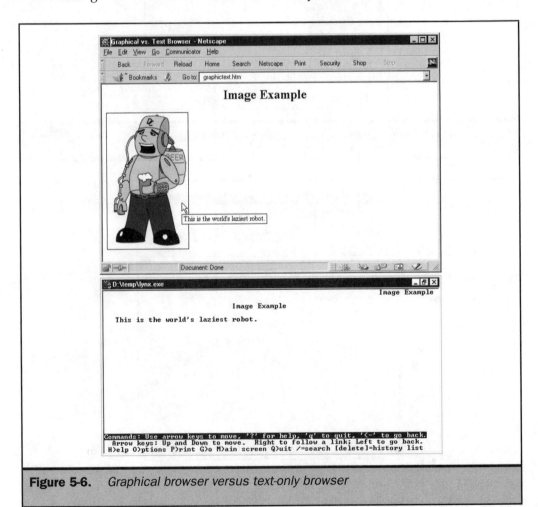

Figure 5-6.   *Graphical browser versus text-only browser*

In addition to those who choose to access the Web through a text-only environment, some visually impaired people might require a different type of browser. Blind people might access the Web using a text mode browser fed into a speaking machine or using a browser such as pwWebSpeak (www.issound.com), which can integrate with a voice synthesizer. Other users might access the Web using a telephone or other automated system just for ease of use or quick information. Already, systems can be used to provide automated phone access to Web sites. Imagine a situation where an automated telephone system to access the Web read, "Press 1 for corporate information, press 2 for product information." Finally, what about robots that come through and index a Web site for relevant information? The contents of images provide no information to index. In all of these cases—the text mode browser, the automated Web access system, and the site indexing robots—images don't mean much. In these cases, the **alt** attribute can be very valuable.

Setting the **alt** attribute to provide alternative information for an image can solve many accessibility problems, but simply setting alternative text is not adequate. The biggest problem with alternative text is that it often does not really provide any benefit. Imagine a company logo on a page for a company called Demo Company. Should the **alt** text be set to something like "Logo of Demo Company, Inc."? Imagine a person hearing this read out loud. Does just "Demo Company, Inc." make more sense?

alt text for pictures of things can prove even more cryptic. A picture of the corporate office with **alt** text set to read "Picture of Corporate Office" is not terribly explanatory. A more detailed description such as "A picture of the exterior of the Demo Company Corporate office—a three-story building with beach-flavored architecture surrounded by large trees" is much more useful. In this case, there is some added value even for the sighted user. A general rule is that if an image conveys information, the **alt** text should convey the same information, and if an image is simply decoration, you can set the **alt** text to nothing: **alt=" "**.

Last is the famous case of the bulleted item. Many users add small red or blue circles or bullets to their pages. In many cases, the **alt** text for these objects is set to be "bullet." Now think about the aggravation of seeing the word "bullet" over and over again on a page, not to mention hearing it read aloud. Maybe putting an asterisk would be more appropriate for **alt** text in this instance.

Although a lot of people might argue that the Web wasn't popular until graphics were integrated or that the Web inherently is a visual medium, the value of textual content on the Web is indisputable. Consequently, it should be made as accessible as possible. There is no arguing that a picture might be worth a thousand words; but if that is the case, why not provide a few words in exchange?

Image Alignment

Probably the first thing a user wants to do after he is able to put an image in a Web page is to figure out how to position it on the page. Under the HTML 2 standard, there was very little that allowed the user to format image layout on a page. Initially, the **align** attribute could be set to a value of **top**, **bottom**, or **middle**. When an image was included within a block structure of text, the next line of text would be aligned either to the top, middle, or bottom of the image depending on the value of the **align** attribute. If the attribute wasn't set, it would default to the bottom. The example below illustrates basic image alignment as first defined in HTML 2. The rendering of the image alignment example is shown in Figure 5-7.

```
<!DOCTYPE HTML PUBLIC "-//W3C//DTD HTML 4.01 Transitional//EN">
<html>
<head>
<title>Basic Image Alignment</title>
</head>
<body>

<p><img src="images/aligntest1.gif" align="top" border="1">
This text should be aligned to the top of the image.</p>

<p><img src="images/aligntest1.gif" align="middle" border="1">
This text should be aligned to the middle of the image.</p>

<p><img src="images/aligntest1.gif" align="bottom" border="1">
This text should be aligned to the bottom of the image.</p>

</body>
</html>
```

One of the problems with initial image alignment in early HTML was that the text really didn't flow around the image. In fact, only one line of text was aligned next to the image, which meant the inline images had to be very small or the layout looked somewhat strange, as shown in Figure 5-8.

Netscape introduced the **left** and **right** values for **align**, which allowed text to flow around the image. When setting an image element such as **<img src="logo.gif" align="left">**, the image is aligned to the left and the text flows around to the right. Correspondingly, when you are using markup such as **<img src="logo.gif" align="right">**, the image is aligned to the right and the text flows around to the left. It is even possible to flow the text between two objects if things are done carefully. The HTML presented here shows how the **align** attribute would be used to flow text around images. The rendering of this example is shown in Figure 5-9.

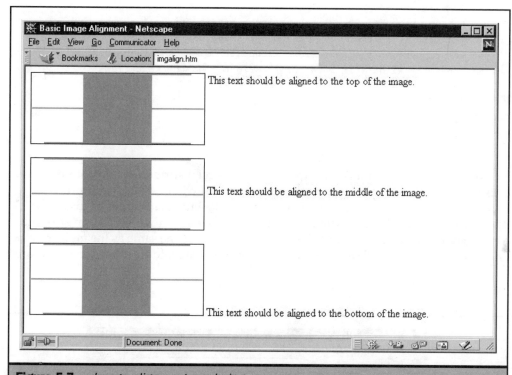

Figure 5-7.   *Image alignment rendering*

```
<!DOCTYPE HTML PUBLIC "-//W3C//DTD HTML 4.01 Transitional//EN">
<html>
<head>
<title>Improved Text Flow</title>
</head>
<body>

<img src="images/redsquare.gif" align="left">
The top image has its align attribute set to "left," so the text flows
around it to the right. The top image has its align attribute set to
"left," so the text flows around it to the right. The top image has its
align attribute set to "left," so the text flows around it to the right.

<br clear="left"><br><br>

<img src="images/redsquare.gif" align="right">
```

```
The bottom image has its align attribute set to "right," so the text
flows around it to the left. The bottom image has its align attribute
set to "right," so the text flows around it to the left. The bottom
image has its align attribute set to "right," so the text flows
around it to the left.

</body>
</html>
```

Notice in the previous example that there is a special attribute to the **
** element. This is necessary to force the text to flow properly and will be discussed shortly. However, there are still some aspects of the **align** attribute that should be discussed. There is some confusion regarding the use of the value **center** with the **align** attribute for the **<img>** element. Typically, this attribute value acts the same as the **middle** value and should be avoided. To actually center an image in the middle of the screen requires

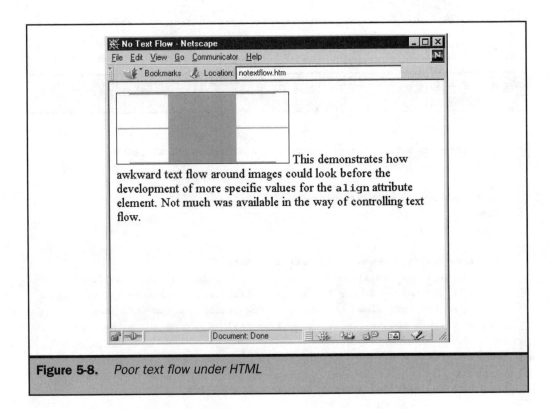

Figure 5-8.   *Poor text flow under HTML*

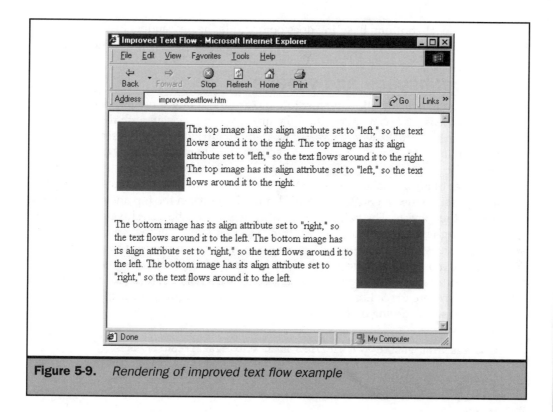

Figure 5-9.   *Rendering of improved text flow example*

enclosing the image within **<p align="center">**, **<div align="center">**, or a plain **<center>** element.

Netscape and Microsoft also support four other values for **align: textop, baseline, absmiddle**, and **absbottom**. All these attributes should be avoided in most cases, because they might not be supported identically across browsers and are not yet part of any standards. Positioning is handled more precisely by technologies such as style sheets, to be discussed in Chapter 10. The basic meaning of these attribute values is discussed here.

Setting the **align** attribute to **texttop** aligns the top of an image with the top of the tallest character in the current line; this attribute works erratically under various browsers. The **baseline** value aligns the bottom of an image with the baseline of the text in the current line. (The baseline is the unseen line that all the characters sit on.) **absmiddle** aligns the middle of an image with the middle of the text in the current line, which means in the actual middle of the characters themselves. The **absbottom** value aligns the bottom of an image with the bottom of the lowest item in the current line of text, including descender characters, such as lowercase "y" and "g," that go below the baseline. Unlike **absbottom**, **baseline** does not include the descenders in a character. For example, in a lowercase "g," the lower half of the letter will sit below the baseline.

Buffer Space: hspace and vspace

Just floating an image and allowing text to wrap around it might not be adequate. There also is the issue of how to position the image more precisely with the text and make sure that text breaks where it ought to. Initially introduced by Netscape and made official in HTML 3.2, the **hspace** and **vspace** attributes can be used to introduce "runaround" or buffer space around an inline image. The **hspace** attribute is used to insert a buffer of horizontal space on the left and right of an image, whereas the **vspace** attribute is used to insert a buffer of vertical space in between the top and bottom of the image and other objects. The value of both attributes should be a positive number of pixels. Although under some browsers it might be possible to set the attribute values to percentage values, this is inadvisable, as very high values can produce strange results. However, the most problematic aspect of the **hspace** and **vspace** attributes is the amount of buffer space that occurs on both sides of the image. Take a look at the HTML markup shown here to see how **hspace** and **vspace** work. Figure 5-10 displays a possible browser rendering of the example code.

```
<!DOCTYPE HTML PUBLIC "-//W3C//DTD HTML 4.01 Transitional//EN">
<html>
<head>
<title>HSPACE and VSPACE Example</title>
</head>
<body>

<p>The image below has its <tt><b>&lt;HSPACE&gt;</b></tt> and
<tt><b>&lt;VSPACE&gt;</b></tt> attributes set to 50 pixels, so the
text will flow around it at a distance of 50 pixels. The rest of
this text is dummy text. If it said anything interesting you would
certainly be the first to know.

<img src="images/redsquare.gif" align="left" hspace="50" vspace="50">
This is dummy text. If it said anything interesting you would certainly
be the first to know. There's really no point in reading the rest of it.
This is dummy text. If it said anything interesting you would certainly
be the first to know. There's really no point in reading the rest of it.
This is dummy text. If it said anything interesting you would certainly
be the first to know. There's really no point in reading the rest of it.
This is dummy text. If it said anything interesting you would certainly
be the first to know. There's really no point in reading the rest of it.
This is dummy text. If it said anything interesting you would certainly
```

```
be the first to know. There's really no point in reading the rest of it.
This is dummy text. If it said anything interesting you would certainly
be the first to know. There's really no point in reading the rest of it.
</p>

</body>
</html>
```

It turns out that in the future, by using style sheets (discussed in Chapter 10), it might be possible to avoid these somewhat imprecise layout features altogether. The **hspace** and **vspace** attributes have been very useful, albeit occasionally abused by Web designers. How these attributes can be used in conjunction with the so-called *invisible pixel gif* to force layouts will be discussed in Chapter 6.

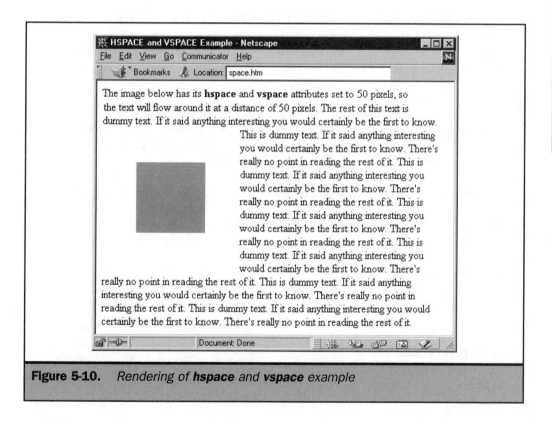

Figure 5-10.   *Rendering of **hspace** and **vspace** example*

Extensions to

In flowing text around an image, there might be a situation in which the designer wants to clear the text flow around the image. For example, creating an image with a caption like the one shown in Figure 5-11 could be problematic because the text might reflow.

To deal with such problems, a new attribute called **clear** was added to the **
** element; this extension now is part of the HTML standard. The **clear** attribute can be set to **left**, **right**, **all**, or **none** and will clear the gutter around an inline object like an image. For example, imagine the fragment **<img src="photo. gif" align="left">** with text wrapping around it. If **<br clear="left">** is included in the text and the wrapped text is still wrapping around the image, the text will be cleared to pass the image. The **clear="right"** attribute to **
** works for text flowing around right-aligned images. Of course, setting the attribute to **none** makes the element act as it normally would and is implied when using the **
** by itself. An example of the use of this attribute is shown here; a rendering appears in Figure 5-12.

```
<!DOCTYPE HTML PUBLIC "-//W3C//DTD HTML 4.01 Transitional//EN">
<html>
<head>
<title>Break and Clear Example</title>
</head>
<body>

<img src="images/building.jpg" width="234" height="150" border="2"
    alt="Outside of the DemoCompany corporate headquarters"
    align="left"  hspace="20" vspace="10">

<b>Photo:</b> Demo Company, Inc Corporate Headquarters<br><br>

<b>Description:</b> This building is a fine example of the <i>Miami
Vice</i> influence on mid-80s southern California architecture.

<br><br>

The next paragraph should appear under the photo, not next to it,
thanks to the <tt>&lt;br clear=&quot;left&quot;;</tt>.

<br clear="left">
<i>Photo copyright &copy; 1999 by Demo Company, Inc.</i>
</body>
</html>
```

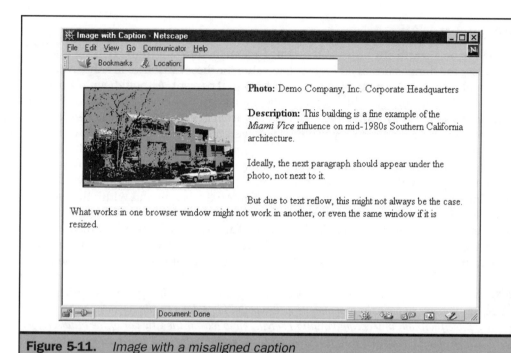

Figure 5-11.   *Image with a misaligned caption*

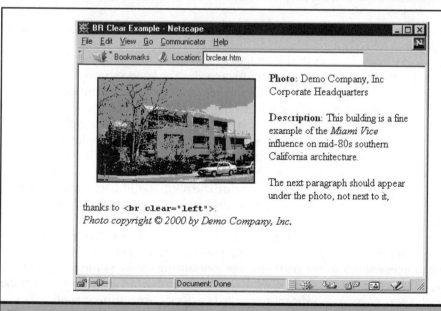

Figure 5-12.   *Rendering of <br clear> example*

height and width

The **height** and **width** attributes to the **<img>** element, introduced in HTML 3.2, are used to set the dimensions of an image. The value for these attributes is either a positive pixel value or a percentage value from 1–100 percent. Although an image can be stretched or shrunk with this attribute, the main purpose actually is to reserve space for images that are being downloaded. As pages are requested by a browser, each individual image is requested separately. However, the browser can't lay out parts of the page, including text, until the space that the image takes up is determined. This might mean waiting for the image to download completely. By telling the browser the height and width of the image, the browser can go ahead and reserve space with a bounding box into which the image will load. Setting the height and width thus allows a browser to download and lay out text quickly while the images are still loading. For an image called test.gif that has a height of 10 and width of 150, use **<img src="test.gif" height="10" width="150">**. The usability improvement of using **height** and **width** attributes for images is significant, and they should always be included.

> **Note**   *Many people wonder what the measurements of a particular image are. Using Netscape, it is possible to view the dimensions quite easily. First, load the image into the browser by itself without any accompanying HTML. Now look at the title bar of the browser, which should display the dimensions. Also, using the option to view document information for the image within the browser should reveal the dimensions. Most Web editors also can automatically show the dimensions of an image.*

Beyond the prelayout advantages, the **height** and **width** attributes can also be used to size images. This is rarely a good idea, as the image might end up being distorted. One way to avoid distortion is to shrink images in a proportional manner. However, if the image is to be made smaller, it is a better idea to size the image appropriately in a graphics program. Shrinking the image with the **height** and **width** attributes does not affect the file size, whereas resizing the image beforehand will shrink the file, hence reducing the download time. Another use of **height** and **width** sizing might be to increase the size of a simple image. For example, imagine an image of a single green pixel, and set the height and width alike: **<img src="greenpixel.gif" height="100" width="100">**. The resulting image is a large green box with very little download penalty. A few sites even use the **height** and **width** attributes with percentage values such as 100 percent to create interesting effects such as full-screen images or vertical or horizontal color bars.

One other interesting use of the **height** and **width** attributes would be to help preload images. With the desire for fast-loading pages, preloading can be used to create the illusion of a quick download. Imagine that during the idle time on a page, the images on the next page are being downloaded so that they are precached when the user goes to the next page. A significant perceived performance improvement is achieved. One way to perform this prefetching is by putting an image that will appear later on the current page with **height** and **width** both set to **1**. In this case, the image won't really be visible but will be fully loaded into the browser's cache. Once the user visits the next page, the image can be fetched from the local disk and displayed quickly.

One potential problem with this approach is that the browser doesn't load images at the same rate or in the same order. Because of this, some logic should be added to the page so that the image to preload only loads after the page has finished. Another issue occurs if the user chooses a page that doesn't use the prefetched image. Because of these potential problems, a linear order of pages probably is the only structure that can benefit from this trick.

Low Source Images

Another potential speed improvement introduced by Netscape and still not part of the HTML 4 standard is the **lowsrc** attribute. The **lowsrc** attribute should be set to the URL of an image to load in first, before the so-called high source image indicated by the **src** attribute. In this sense, the attribute can be set to the address of a low-resolution or black-and-white file, which can be downloaded first and then followed by a high-resolution file. For example,

```
<img src="hi-res-photo.gif" lowsrc="bw-photo.gif" height="100"
width="100"alt="Outside of building photograph">
```

The **lowsrc** attribute can provide significant usability improvement when large full-screen images must be used.

One interesting aspect of the **lowsrc** attribute is that the browser tends to use the image dimensions of the **lowsrc** file to reserve space within the Web page if the **height** and **width** attributes are not set. Because of this, some strange distortion could happen if the high-resolution image is not the same size as the low-resolution image. This problem actually occurs under versions of Netscape.

Another interesting aspect of the **lowsrc** attribute is the possibility for simple animation. For example, the **lowsrc** attribute could be set to a picture of a closed book and the regular **src** attribute set to a picture of an open book. When loaded, it appears as a small, two-frame animation. However, this method of animation is very simplistic and lacks timing; so although it might look good on a relatively slow connection, the effect might be lost over a T1 connection where the images load rapidly. For animation, an animated GIF should be used as discussed earlier in the chapter. Animated GIFs require no special syntax and can be used for either **src** or **lowsrc**. If more complex animation is required, using an **<embed>** or **<object>** element to reference a Flash file might be called for, as discussed in Chapter 9.

These are only the most basic attributes for the **<img>** element. A more complete listing of **<img>** element attributes can be found in the element reference in Appendix A.

Images as Buttons

One of the most important aspects of images, as previously discussed in Chapter 4, is how they can be combined with the **<a>** element to create buttons. To make an image "pressable," simply enclose it within an anchor.

```
<a href="http://www.democompany.com"><img src="logo.gif"></a>
```

When the page is rendered in the browser, clicking on the image will take the user to the anchor destination specified. Generally, to indicate that an image is pressable, the browser will put a border around the image, as well as provide some feedback to the user when the cursor or pointing device is over the hot area, such as turning the pointer to a finger or highlighting the text. For some basic feedback types, note the example in Figure 5-13, which shows a border, finger pointer, and URL destination—all indicating that the image is pressable.

One issue that might be troublesome for page designers is the border that appears around the image when it is made pressable. It is possible to turn this border off by setting the **border** attribute of the image equal to **0**. For example,

```
<a href="http://www.democompany.com"><img src="logo.gif" border="0"></a>
```

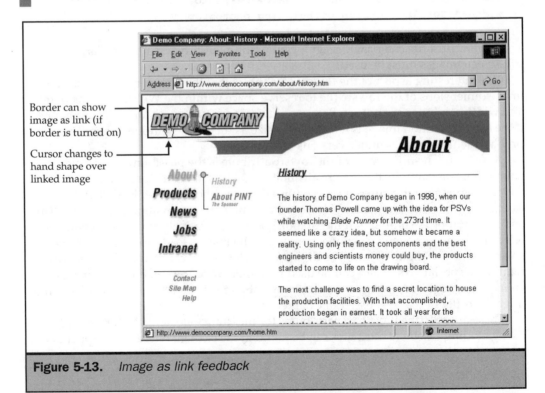

Figure 5-13.   *Image as link feedback*

Of course, without the border it might be difficult to determine which images on a page are links and which are not. This can cause users to play a little game of finding the active click region by running their mouse all over the screen. One way to avoid such usability problems is to provide visual cues in images that are made pressable. These might include embossing, beveling, or drop shadows. Examples of such buttons are shown in Figure 5-14.

Although from a design perspective some of these effects, particularly drop shadows, are a little overused, there are tangible benefits to adding feedback information to button graphics. Another approach to providing feedback about what images are clickable is to animate the buttons. Using a very simple piece of JavaScript, it is possible to animate a button so that when a mouse passes over an image it comes alive. A brief discussion about how HTML pages can be made more dynamic using a scripting language such as JavaScript can be found in Chapter 13.

One non–button-oriented use of the **border** attribute is to put a simple stroke around an image. Many times people will use a graphics tool to create a frame on an image, but the **border** attribute is a bandwidth-cheap way to get much of the same effect. Try setting the **border** attribute equal to a positive value on a nonclickable image—for example, **<img src="portrait.gif" border="5">**. This little change provides an easy way to frame an image and might even lend itself to interesting design ideas.

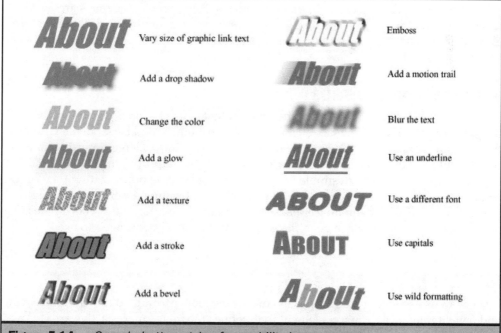

Figure 5-14.   *Sample button styles for usability improvement*

Image Maps

Another form of clickable images, discussed previously in Chapter 4, is the idea of an image map. An image map is a large image that contains numerous hot spots that can be selected, sending the user to a different anchor destination. Recall from the previous chapter that there are two basic forms of image maps: *server side* and *client side*. In the server-side image map, the user clicks on an image but the server must decode where the user clicked before the destination page (if any) is loaded. With client-side image maps, all of the map information—which regions map to which URLs—can be specified in the same HTML file that contains the image. Including the map data with the image and letting the browser decode it has several advantages, including the following:

- There is no need to visit a server to determine the destination, so links are resolved faster.

- Destination URLs can be shown in the status box as the user's pointer moves over the image.

- Image maps can be created and tested locally, without requiring a server or system administration support.

- Client-side image maps can be created so that they present an alternate text menu to users of text-only browsers.

Although this discussion makes it obvious that client-side image maps are far superior to their server-side cousins, very old browsers might not support this feature. This does not have to be a problem, as it is possible to include support for both types of image maps at once.

Server-Side Image Maps

To specify a server-side image map, the **<a>** element is used to enclose a specially marked **<img>** element. The **<a>** element's **href** attribute should be set to the URL of the program or map file to decode the image map. The **<img>** element must contain the attribute **ismap** so the browser can decode the image appropriately. As with all linked images, it might be desirable to turn the image borders off by setting the **<img>** element's **border** attribute equal to **0**. As mentioned in Chapter 4, server-side image maps do not provide adequate feedback to the user because they show coordinates, and might incur performance penalties. HTML authors are encouraged to use client-side image maps.

Client-Side Image Maps

The key to using a client-side map is to add the **usemap** attribute to the **<img>** element and have it reference a **<map>** element that defines the image map's active areas. An example of the **<img>** element syntax is **<img src="controlbar.gif" usemap="#controlmap">**. Note that, like server-side image maps, the image will be indicated as a link regardless of the lack of the **<a>** element surrounding the **<img>**. The **border** attribute should be set to **0** if necessary. The **<map>** element generally occurs within the same document, although support for it outside of the current document is sparse at best. This is similar, in a sense, to the way server-side maps work. The **<map>** element can occur anywhere within the body of an HTML document, although it usually is found at the end of HTML documents.

The **<map>** element has one attribute, **name**, which is used to specify the identifier associated with the map. The map name then is referenced within the **<img>** element using the **usemap** attribute and the associated fragment identifier. The **<map>** element must have a closing **</map>** element. Within the **<map>** and **</map>** tags are defined "shapes" that are mapped onto an image and define the hot spots for the image map. Shapes are defined by the **<area>** element, which is found only within the **<map>** element. The format of the mapping tags is discussed in Chapter 4. However, memorizing or creating client- or server-side image maps by hand is not advised. Page designers should find that most Web page editors like Macromedia Dreamweaver or Allaire HomeSite automate the creation of image hot spots. However, a popular standalone tool for doing this is MapEdit, which can be retrieved from www.boutell.com/mapedit if image maps are to be developed from scratch.

It is possible to combine support for both server-side and client-side image maps into one file. The browser will override the server-side support with the improved client-side style. This approach will guarantee backward compatibility with older browsers. To support both, use the **ismap** and **usemap** attributes in conjunction with an embedded map and a remote map as shown in the following code fragment:

```
<a href="shapes.map">
<img src="shapes.gif" usemap="#shapes" border="0" ismap width="400"
height="200"></a>
```

Client-side image maps have a variety of attributes that can be used with the **<area>** element. Server-side image maps really have no attributes other than those normally associated with the **<img>** element, such as **border**. The important attributes supported for image maps are discussed in Chapter 4, as well as in the element reference in Appendix A.

Advanced Image Considerations: Scripting, Style, and <object>

Although most of the basic uses of images have been discussed, there are some issues that should be mentioned for later discussion. First, because an image can be referenced by a style sheet or by a scripting environment, it might be very important to provide a name or identifier for it. The **class**, **id**, and **name** attributes can be used to provide names for images so they can be referenced and manipulated by scripting or style information that usually is found in the head of the document. Names should be unique and in the proper HTML form.

It is possible to include inline scripting or style information directly with an image. For example, setting the **style** attribute allows an inline style to bind to the particular **<img>** element. Style sheets are discussed in Chapter 10. Furthermore, it is possible to have images bound to a particular event using an event attribute such as **onmouseover** and tying it to a script. A very simple but motivating use of tying an event with an image is to have the image change state depending on the user's action. The most basic use would be to create animated buttons or buttons that make a sound when clicked, but the possibilities are endless. A more detailed discussion and examples of how to bind JavaScript to create animated buttons are presented in Chapter 13.

The last advanced comment to make about the **<img>** element is that under HTML 4 it is supposed to be possible to include images using the **<object>** element. For example,

```
<object data="images/logo.gif">Picture of the Demo Company
building</object>
```

Similar to the **<img>** tag, the **data** attribute is set to the URL of the included image while the alternative rendering is placed within the **<object>** element. Although this new syntax might create some interesting possibilities, the reality is that browsers currently don't support this form of image inclusion. Whereas this generic **<object>** tag for image support makes sense given that an image is no different from any other included binary object, the fact is that until browser vendors implement it properly, it should be avoided. A more complete discussion of this element can be found in Appendix A, which provides the full syntax of the **<object>** element.

Tips on Image Use

Many readers find Web page creation frustrating because it always seems that other sites just look better or load faster. Although this book is very focused on HTML, a few points about image use should be considered at this point. A much deeper discussion of image considerations can be found in *Web Design: The Complete Reference* (http://www.webdesignref.com).

Image Use

The first thing to consider is that the quality of the image being used certainly will affect the outcome of the page layout. Even when armed with a scanner, digital camera, or appropriate software such as Adobe Photoshop, Adobe Illustrator or Macromedia

Fireworks, you might be a long way from being able to produce aesthetically pleasing Web pages. Don't fret—you would never consider that just owning a copy of a word processor would help you produce a great novel; it takes skill, patience, and years of practice.

Although this certainly is not a book on Web design, a simple tip on Web design is to aim for a minimal design. Straight lines, basic colors, and modest use of imagery should produce a relatively clean and uncluttered design. Furthermore, the simple design probably will load very fast! When you decide to use imagery on your site, whether for pure decoration or information, don't skimp on quality. If you use clip art from some free Web site your site will reflect this. Fortunately, there are many sites that sell professional quality clip-illustrations and photographs such as EyeWire (www.eyewire.com) relatively cheaply. While this might cost money, don't simply right-click your way to a nice new image free of charge. Web users are sophisticated enough to know when they're having a cheap site foisted on them.

Legal Issues with Images

Unfortunately the expense of licensing images and the ease with which images can be copied have convinced many people that they can simply appropriate whatever images they need. Unfortunately, this is stealing the work of others. Although there are stiff penalties for copyright infringement, it can be difficult to enforce these laws. Also, some page designers tend to bend the rules thanks to the legal concept called *fair use*, which allows the use of someone else's copyrighted work under certain circumstances.

There are four basic questions used to define the fair-use concept:

■ **First, is the work in question being appropriated for a nonprofit or profit use?**
The fair use defense is less likely to stand up if the "borrowed" work has been used to make money for someone other than its copyright holder.

■ **Second, is the work creative or factual?**
A creative work could be a speculative essay on the impact of a recent congressional debate; a factual work would be a straightforward description of the debate without commentary. "Fair use" would cover use of the factual work more than use of the creative one.

■ **Third, how much of the copyrighted work has been used?**
It is possible to use someone else's images if it is changed substantially from the original. The problem is determining what constitutes enough change in the image to make it a new work. Simply using a photo-editing tool to flip an image or change its colors is not enough. There is a fine line between using portions of another person's work and outright stealing. Even if you don't plan on using uncleared images, be careful of using images from free Internet clip art libraries. These so-called free images might have been submitted with the belief that they are free, but some of them might have been appropriated from a commercial clip art library somewhere down the line. Be particularly careful

with high-quality images of famous individuals and commercial products. Although such groups often might appreciate people using their images, the usage generally is limited to noncommercial purposes.

■ **The third fair use question leads to the fourth: What impact does the image have on the economic value of the work?**
 Although unauthorized use of a single *Star Trek*–related image might not substantially affect the money earned by Paramount Pictures in a given fiscal year, Paramount's lawyers take a dim view of such use. In fact, some entertainment organizations have taken steps to make it very difficult for Web page designers to use such images.

■ **One could, perhaps, add a fifth question to the list: Who owns the original work, and how vigorously will the owner defend it?**
 This whole discussion begs many legal questions that are far beyond the scope of this book. Suffice it to say that in the long run, it's always safer to create original work, license images, or use material in the public domain. Just because many Web designers skirt the law doesn't mean you should.

Images and Download Speed

Even if it is filled with wonderful imagery, few people want to wait literally minutes for your beautifully designed page to load. Page designers should always consider download time when adding images to their pages. Never assume that everyone has the latest high-speed cable connection or that high bandwidth is right around the corner. This section presents a few tips for improving download time of pages.

■ Make sure to use the correct format for the job

Recall that GIF images are good for illustrations whereas JPEG images are good for photographs. If you break this rule of thumb you might find that your images are unnecessarily big byte-wise and will take longer to download.

■ Reduce colors if possible

When using GIF images, reducing the number of colors in the image (the bit-depth) can substantially reduce the file size. If your company logo only has 30 colors in it, why use an 8-bit GIF image when you can use a 5-bit image that supports 32 colors? Tools such as Macromedia Fireworks or Adobe Photoshop make color reduction easy to do.

■ Reduce the number of images in the page

The number of individual images in a page can substantially affect the load speed regardless of the total number of bytes transferred. Consider that each individual request does have some overhead and that the network might not be quite as effectively utilized compared to a few larger image downloads. Remember, time counts—not bytes delivered—so wherever possible try to reduce the number of individual image pieces used.

■ Use the browser's cache

Once an image has been downloaded once it should stay in the browser's cache. If the same file is used later on the browser should be able to reuse the one from the cache. If you can use scripting it might even be possible to download images ahead of time to the browser cache using the idea of precaching or preloading. However, reliance on the cache only works if the complete file names are the same. This means a single image directory probably is better than copying the files to individual image directories all over your site.

■ Give a preview

If it is going to take a while to download give the user something to look at. Interlacing a GIF image or making a JPEG progressive results in images that load incrementally. The user might get the gist of an image long before it completely downloads. Thumbnails of images also are a useful way to let a user take a look at the general idea of image before committing to a long download. If a long download is required it is a good idea to warn the user as well.

■ Do the HTML correctly

Making sure to use **alt**, **height**, and **width** attributes can do a lot to improve page rendering. The alternative text will give the user something to read as an image loads in. Setting the **height** and **width** values properly will allow the browser to specify the page layout, quickly allowing the text to flow in right away.

If you have to resort to large file sizes on your Web site, hopefully the ends justify the means. A big wait for a huge logo or heavily designed page with little content will result in frustrated users who might never want to come back again. Could this be why the largest sites like Amazon and Yahoo! use relatively simple visuals that download quickly? Almost certainly this is the case. In short, always remember when using images to make sure they add something to the overall experience of the user whether it be to make the site more pleasing visually or provide information.

Summary

Like them or not, inline images are what helped popularize the Web. However, just because images can be used to improve the look and feel of a Web page doesn't mean that they should be used without concern. Although presentation is important to the Web, it is still fundamentally about the communication of information, some of which does well in image form and some of which does not. Adding images to a Web page is accomplished using the **<img>** element, which has numerous attributes. Many of the attributes of the **<img>** element—including **alt, height, width,** and **lowsrc**—are useful in improving the accessibility and usability of Web pages.

As always, the eternal struggle between nice-looking pages and download time continues, and knowledge of HTML features is helpful to combat excessive wait time. Many of the other attributes for the **<img>** element were developed with layout in mind, particularly **align**. Images can be used in conjunction with colors to create motivating layouts, including tiled backgrounds. This will be discussed in the next chapter. In the future, style sheets and the **<object>** element could take over many of the duties of the **<img>** element and its attributes; for the moment, the use of the latter is very important.

The Complete Reference

Chapter 6

Basic Layout: Text, Colors, and Backgrounds

Web page designers strive to create attractive Web pages, but it hasn't always been easy. HTML really was not created with design features in mind. Even a simple layout technique such as centering text has been possible only for a few years. Browser vendors have added many HTML elements and attributes to provide page developers with more control over the look and feel of their pages. Standardized elements such as **<ul>** were pressed into service as structuring and layout tools. New font facilities also have provided more design capabilities in HTML. Ultimately the presentation duties of HTML will be alleviated by Cascading Style Sheets, as discussed in Chapter 10. Despite ongoing improvements in browser support of CSS, HTML tricks and workarounds are still occasionally required to create visually appealing pages that work in older browsers. Although in theory it would be best to avoid these nonstandard techniques, they often are the grim reality of page design—at least until technologies such as style sheets become better supported.

Design Requirements

In the best of all possible Web worlds, what would the designer want? The Web was created for a cross-platform environment with little support for screen presentation, but today's Web requires better positioning control. The ability to design for every platform is the ideal situation, but the reality of designing for a particular audience is becoming more accepted. By understanding a user's environment, the designer has more control over presentation. Designers also want more control over font use. Initially, there was no way to specify what font to use in a document, whether or not the user actually had the font. Other complex layout features common to electronic composition, such as true color control and positioned objects also are desirable. Ultimately, perfect pixel-level control and font selection are necessary to bring the Web closer to a level equal with print design.

Simply providing features to allow pixel-level placement of objects and text on the screen doesn't make Web design a straightforward process, any more than font selection does. It is still difficult to understand exactly what kind of display environment the end user has. Web displays range from small liquid crystal screens on cellular phones and pocket organizers to 20-inch monitors—or larger. Each display might have different types of color support, ranging from four shades of gray on a typical handheld machine to millions of colors on a high-end graphic designer's system. There might not even be a screen at all, as in the case of voice-based browsers. If a guess is made about what screen configuration the user might have, or some programming facilities are provided to determine the same, a better layout could be provided.

The challenges of designing for the Web are significant. In the past they have only been exacerbated by the lack of technology and tools, not to mention problems associated with bandwidth or usability.

HTML Approach to Web Design

While HTML was not designed with layout in mind, it has been abused and extended to support layout as best it can. Today there are many elements, both standard and nonstandard, that can provide layout control. These include the various **align** values for elements, browser-specific proprietary elements such as **<spacer>** and **<multicol>**, and tables. This section covers some of the basic HTML elements, both standard and proprietary, that are used to control text and screen layout. Readers are reminded that the use of such approaches is best suited to environments that must deal with older browsers—those that do not support technologies such as Cascading Style Sheets. Ultimately the role of HTML will not be for presentation, but for structure.

Text Alignment with HTML Elements

The first thing to consider in the HTML approach to layout is all the elements and attributes used to position text and objects on a page. Web page designers have long tended to assume the default presentation of an element such as **<ul>** to attempt to move text around the page, as shown in the example here:

```
<!DOCTYPE HTML PUBLIC "-//W3C//DTD HTML 4.01 Transitional//EN">
<html>
<head>
<title>Unordered List Layout</title>
</head>
<body>

<ul>
This is indented text
</ul>

<ul><ul>
This text is indented more.
</ul></ul>

<ul><ul><ul><ul><ul><ul><ul><ul><ul><ul><ul><ul><ul><ul><ul><ul>
This is indented heavily, but may not produce the effect you expect.

</ul></ul></ul></ul></ul></ul></ul></ul>
</ul></ul></ul></ul></ul></ul></ul></ul>

</body>
</html>
```

A rendering of formatting using the unordered list element is shown in Figure 6-1; this code also can be viewed online at http://www.htmlref.com/examples/chapter06/ulindentation.htm.

Many HTML page development tools still use this tag or the **<blockquote>** to move things around the screen. If you are unconvinced, just try using the indent feature in a WYSIWYG editor; then view the generated HTML. Consider that while this does not really use the meaning of these tags properly, there also really is no guarantee of exactly how far things will be indented per application of the element. This can vary from browser to browser.

Another HTML-based approach to control text layout is the use of the **<pre>** tag. As discussed in Chapter 3, any text enclosed by **<pre>** preserves returns, tabs, and spaces. Using **<pre>**, it is possible to force text to lay out the way the page author requires, even forcing the browser to scroll to the right to read text. Generally speaking, the browser changes the typeface of any preformatted text to a fixed-width font such as Courier. This font change might not be desired.

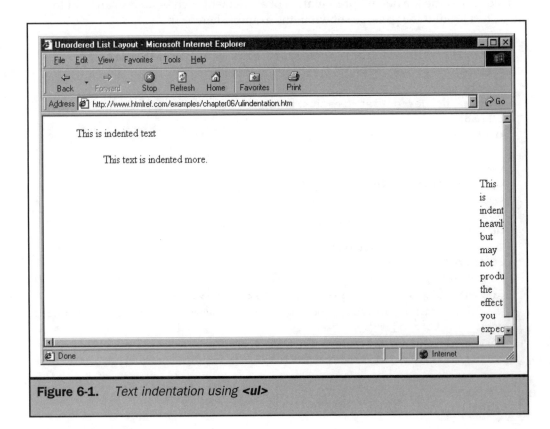

Figure 6-1.   *Text indentation using* **<ul>**

Non-Breaking Spaces

Web browsers are supposed to minimize all forms of white space to a single white space character; this includes spaces, tabs, and returns. Page authors might be frustrated when attempting to put two spaces between words unless they resort to using the **<pre>** element. However, using the character entity ** ** or ** ** should insert a non-breaking space that will not be collapsed by the browser. To enter three spaces between words, use **   **. This leads many people to force text layout like so:

```
          
Now we are ten spaces from the left!
```

Although use of this non-breaking space often is a convenient crutch, it won't work properly in all situations. This should make sense to you, particularly if you have tried to align columns of text in a word processor using the spacebar. Things just never quite seem to line up this way. This problem has to do with the proportional nature of fonts versus the size of the space character. Why would this work any differently on the Web?

Although not perfect for forcing layout flawlessly, the ** ** entity can be considered the "duct tape" of the Web. Anyone who has performed a little home repair knows a little duct can go a long way; so can the ** ** on the Web! Consider for example the fact that browsers often will minimize elements that do not appear to be needed or used because there is no content within them. A single character within the element would keep this minimization from happening, but do you want that character to appear on the screen? Probably not, so in comes the ** ** entity. Although useful with table tags and such, this approach unfortunately is often abused, particularly by WYSIWYG editors. Consider the markup

```
<p> </p>
```

that often is created by a WYSIWG web editor after a simple press of the return key. This particular markup says we have an empty paragraph, but does that really make sense? Maybe what you are really looking for is something more like

```
<br><br>
```

Another time you might see the non-breaking space is when playing with lists. Consider the markup

```
<ul>
  <li>Item 1</li>
  <li>Item 2</li>
  <li>Item 3</li>
</ul>
```

This will render a bullet list, like this:

- Item 1
- Item 2
- Item 3

This rendering might be too tight; so a designer might put returns in the list items to space things out,

```
<ul>
    <li>Item 1<br><br></li>
    <li>Item 2<br><br></li>
    <li>Item 3<br><br></li>
</ul>
```

but they might find this spacing to be too much.

- Item 1

- Item 2

- Item 3

Finally, resorting to the non-breaking space in conjunction with a subscript element, the list elements are nudged apart. The markup here

```
<ul>
  <li>Item 1<sub> </sub></li>
  <li>Item 2<sub> </sub ></li>
  <li>Item 3<sub> </sub ></li>
</ul>
```

produces a slightly better rendering on most browsers:

- Item 1
- Item 2
- Item 3

These kinds of tricks seem appealing, but they are just tricks. They rely significantly on how browsers tend to render things and make HTML markup much more complicated than it should be. However, for now a little knowledge of how to apply the ** ** element can go a long way toward fixing troublesome Web problems.

The <center> Element

In the early days of the Web it was difficult, if not impossible, to control screen layout. Netscape eventually introduced a few elements and attribute changes useful for positioning, including the **<center>** element.

The **<center>** element can enclose any form of content, which then is centered in the browser window. In early HTML, text could be centered using the following code:

```
<center>Welcome to Demo Company!</center>
```

The **<center>** element can be used around an arbitrary amount of content in many different forms, including images and text. Use of the **<center>** element is common on the Web, and it has been included in the HTML 4.0 standard. However, the element is shorthand for **<div align="center">**. Later, the **align** attribute (discussed in the next few paragraphs) was added to many elements.

Alignment Attributes

Beyond **<center>**, there are many elements under HTML 3.2 and 4.0 that support the **align** attribute. The **<div>** element, which is used to create a division in a document, might have the **align** attribute set to **left**, **center**, **right**; or, under 4.0, **justify**. If the **align** attribute is not set, text generally is aligned to the left when language direction is set to **ltr** (left to right) and to the right when the language direction is set to **rtl** (right to left). Until recently, the **justify** attribute did not work in most browsers; now it is supported by the latest versions of the two major browsers. The **<p>** paragraph element; the **<table>** element; and the headings **<h1>**, **<h2>**, **<h3>**, **<h4>**, **<h5>**, and **<h6>** also support the **align** attribute, with the same basic values and meaning. Note that, as discussed in Chapter 5, the **align** attribute on the **<img>** element serves a different purpose.

Note   *Under strict HTML 4 and XHTML the use of alignment attributes and the **<center>*** *element are deprecated.*

Word Hinting with <nobr> and <wbr>

Under many browsers, it is possible to control text layout beyond simple alignment. Because font size and browser widths might be different, word wrapping can occur in strange ways. Microsoft and Netscape, as well as many other browsers, support the **<nobr>** and **<wbr>** elements as a way to provide browser with hints for text layout.

The **<nobr>** element makes sure that a line of text does not wrap to the next line, regardless of browser width. This element is useful for words or phrases that must be kept together on one line. If the line of text is long, it might extend beyond the browser window, obliging the user to scroll in order to view the unbroken text. A simple example of using the **<nobr>** element is shown here:

```
<nobr>This is a very important long line of text, so it should not
be allowed to break across two lines.</nobr>
```

It is possible to use the **<nobr>** element in conjunction with images, but the browser window might need to be scrolled for all the images to be seen.

In some cases, the browser might attempt to rescale the images in order to fit them all on one line. In the case of WebTV, the browser will scale down to 80 percent of the image's original size before moving the image to the next line. **<nobr>** acts differently under WebTV because WebTV does not allow for any horizontal scrolling.

In contrast to the **<nobr>** element, which is quite firm in its word wrapping, the **<wbr>** element allows the page designer to suggest a soft break within text enclosed by the **<nobr>** element. (**<wbr>** is not part of the HTML standard, but many browsers support it.) In essence, the **<wbr>** element marks a spot where a line break can take place. The element is an advisory one, unlike **
** and **<nobr>**, which force layout. Depending on the situation, the browser may choose to ignore the **<wbr>** element because there is no need for it. The **<wbr>** element is an empty element that does not require a closing tag. Here's a simple example showing how **<wbr>** works:

```
<nobr>This is a very important long line of text that should not
break across two lines. If the line must be split, it should
happen here <wbr> and nowhere else.</nobr>
```

The **<wbr>** element should exist only within a **<nobr>** element, although it might work outside of it. This element does not have any major attributes. The basic point—and a very useful one—of this element simply is to suggest a line break point.

Alignment with Images

As discussed in Chapter 5, under HTML 2.0 the **<img>** element specified the **align** attribute with allowed values of **top**, **bottom**, or **middle**. When an image was included within a block structure of text, the next line of text would be aligned to the top, middle, or bottom of the image, depending on the value of the **align** attribute. If the attribute were not set, it would default to the bottom.

One problem with image alignment in early HTML was that the text didn't flow around the image. Only one line of text was aligned next to the image. Netscape introduced the **left** and **right** values for **align**, which allowed text to flow around the image. When setting an image element like **<img src="logo.gif" align="left">**, the image is aligned to the left and the text flows around to the right. Correspondingly, when using code such as **<img src="logo.gif" align="right">**, the image is aligned to the right and the text flows around to the left. An easy way to think of this is to consider an image a rock in a river with the text flowing around it. Align the image to the left and the text flows around to the right. Align the image to the right and text flows to the left.

Whereas the basic alignment values became standard HTML, Netscape and Microsoft also support four other values for **align: textop**, **baseline**, **absmiddle**, and **absbottom**. Avoid these attributes in most cases, since they might not be supported identically across browsers, and are not yet part of any standards. For more information on these attributes, see Chapter 5 as well as the element reference (see Appendix A).

Because text might flow in undesirable ways around images, an extension to the **
** element was developed. The **
** element now takes a **clear** attribute, which can be set to **left**, **right**, **all**, or **none**. By default, the **clear** attribute is set to **none**, which makes the element produce a carriage return. When an image is aligned to the **left**, it might be useful to return past the image to start a new section of text. Placing another object using **<br clear="left">** causes the browser to go all the way down a column until the left side of the window is clear. **<br clear='right'>** does the same thing with right-aligned images. When trying to pass multiple images that might be aligned both on the **left** and **right**, use **<br clear="all">**.

Although the **align** attribute and the extensions to **
** provide some degree of page layout control, technologies such as style sheets handle positioning with greater precision. Until style sheets become more common, there are certain instances in which the **<img>** element and its attributes (including **hspace**, **vspace**, and **align**) can be used to create interesting page layouts.

Invisible Images and Layout

Another way to push text around in a layout is by using an image. This approach is well known to users of the desktop publishing program QuarkXPress. With this program, users can create invisible regions and run text around them to achieve specific layout effects. This can be done under HTML by using an invisible image in combination with the **align**, **hspace**, and **vspace** attributes. Given a transparent 1-pixel image or, if you like, "invisible pixel," the designer can perform a variety of interesting tricks. For example, take a clear pixel and set the **width** to **10**. Now put this at the front of a paragraph, as shown here:

```
<p><img src="pixel.gif" width="10" align="left">This is the start
of the paragraph.</p>
```

Given this fragment, the first line of the paragraph is indented 10 pixels. The illustration here shows this basic trick with a border on the image turned on and off to show where the invisible pixel is.

This is the start of the paragraph.

☐ This is the start of the paragraph.

> **Note**   *While it certainly is very easy to make a transparent pixel, you can have one of your own free of charge from http://www.htmlref.com/examples/chapter06/ pixel.gif. If you find it difficult to save, try http://www.htmlref.com/examples/ chapter06/pixel.htm, which provides explicit instructions on how to grab one of these images.*

Aside from indentation, you could format text in a variety of manners and with careful use of **hspace** and **vspace** attributes you could even space out lines without using style sheets. Of course it is so much easier in CSS that this really should never be done. Much larger regions also can be created with an invisible pixel by setting the **height** and **width** attributes of the **<img>** element and using **align** to flow text around the invisible region. For example, **<img src="pixel.gif" height="100" width="50" align="left">** could create a large invisible block to run text around.

The pixel trick can be a useful workaround. However, the trick has its failings. Consider what happens when the page is viewed with the images turned off, or the stop button is pressed before the pixel.gif image is loaded? The resulting page might look like the one in Figure 6-2.

Despite its problems, image layout tricks are still very common on the Web. They are considered so useful that Netscape introduced a special element called **<spacer>** that mimics much of the functionality of invisible images.

The <spacer> Element

The proprietary **<spacer>** element, introduced with Netscape 3.0, enables users to create invisible regions to push text and other objects around the browser screen. In many ways, this element is a response to the invisible, single-pixel GIF trick discussed in the previous section. Although **<spacer>** does an adequate job of reproducing this

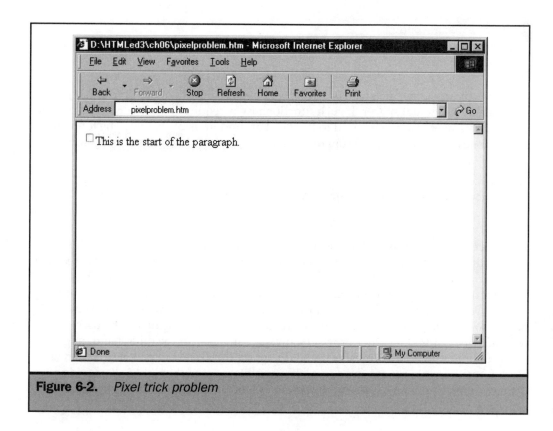

Figure 6-2.   *Pixel trick problem*

hack for screen design, its lack of cross-platform support suggests that using the single-pixel image or a style sheet is more appropriate.

The **<spacer>** element is an empty element and is used to insert an invisible region to force layout. Its main attribute is **type**, which specifies the form of the invisible region as **horizontal**, **vertical**, or **block**. The other attributes are used to set the size of the spacer. Example code to create a horizontal space of 75 pixels between words in a sentence is shown here:

```
This is the start of the sentence <spacer align="left"
type="horizontal" size="75"> and this is the end.
```

As with invisible pixels, it is possible to push lines apart. In the next example, the **<spacer>** element is set to create a vertical region of 24 pixels to give the appearance of double spacing. Notice how the vertical spacer induces line breaks.

```
This is line one.
<spacer align="left" type="vertical" size="24">
This is line two
```

The **<spacer>** element can be only one type at a time. It is not possible to have a vertical and horizontal spacer. If such functionality is required, use the **block** type. The **<spacer>** element also can be used to flow text around invisible blocks. The following HTML code creates an invisible runaround region 150 pixels high and 100 pixels across.

```
... text...
<spacer type="block" height="150" width="100" align="left">
... text...
```

Notice how the **align** attribute is used just as it would be with an image, with a default alignment value of **bottom** and so on. The element also could be combined with **<br clear="left">** to avoid the spacing element affecting text that might follow.

Be careful that layouts don't rely on **<spacer>**, as it is a somewhat all-or-nothing element which is completely unsupported beyond Netscape browsers. If it is just hinting, or providing browser tips, page layout such as line spacing can be used and will safely be ignored by other browsers. Invisible images, on the other hand, might show up under text-only browsers if you do not set the **alt** text to no value. When using block forms to create runaround space, the invisible pixel trick might still provide a better workaround than **<spacer>**, because it will be picked up by most graphical browsers.

*Some WYWIYG editors seem to like to use **<spacer>** in conjunction with table-based layouts. As the tag probably will be deprecated over time designers should avoid its use in all instances!*

The <multicol> Element

Like **<spacer>**, the **<multicol>** element is unique to Netscape browsers starting with Navigator 3.0. This element allows page designers to specify text in multiple columns, which are rendered with equal width. The element is not supported in previous versions of Netscape or Internet Explorer; it will not degrade gracefully if layout depends on it. In short it should never be used unless the page using it is viewed in a Netscape-only environment. The presentation of the tag is presented primarily as an example to explain why page designers should avoid the use of proprietary HTML elements when designing pages.

The most important attribute of the **<multicol>** element is **cols**, which is set to the number of text columns to display. The browser should attempt to flow the text evenly across columns and make the columns the same height, except for the last column, which might be shorter depending on the amount of text in the columns. The element also supports the attribute **gutter**, which is used to specify the gutter space between columns in pixels. By default, the gutter width (if unspecified) is 10 pixels. The last attribute supported by **<multicol>** is **width**, which specifies the width of each column in pixels. All columns are the same width; there is no way to directly adjust a particular column's width. If the **width** attribute is not set, its value is determined by subtracting from the display width the number of pixels that constitute the gutter and then dividing by the number of columns set in the **cols** attribute. The syntax is summarized here:

```
<multicol
    cols="number of columns"
    gutter="gutter width in pixels or percentage"
    width="column width in pixels or percentage">

Text to put in column form

</multicol>
```

An example showing how **<multicol>** can be used is shown here, and online at http://www.htmlref.com/examples/chapter06/multicol.htm; renderings of the example are shown in Figure 6-3. Notice that the layout is not preserved in Internet Explorer.

```
<!DOCTYPE HTML PUBLIC "-//W3C//DTD HTML 4.01 Transitional//EN">
<html>
<head>
<title>MULTICOL Example</title>
</head>
<body>

<multicol cols="2" gutter="50" width="80%">
This only works in Netscape, so don't try this at home!
The rain in Spain falls mainly on the plain. Now is the time
for all good men to come to the aid of the country. There's
no business like show business. The rain in Spain falls
mainly on the plain. Now is the time for all good men to
come to the aid of the country. There's no business like
show business. The rain in Spain falls mainly on the plain.
Now is the time for all good men to come to the aid of the
country. There's no business like show business. The rain
in Spain falls mainly on the plain.  Now is the time for all
good men to come to the aid of the country. There's no business
like show business. The rain in Spain falls mainly on the plain.
The rain in Spain falls mainly on the plain.
```

```
</multicol>

</body>
</html>
```

When including other objects within the **<multicol>** element, particularly tables and images with alignment information, the element will be unpredictable, as shown in Figure 6-4.

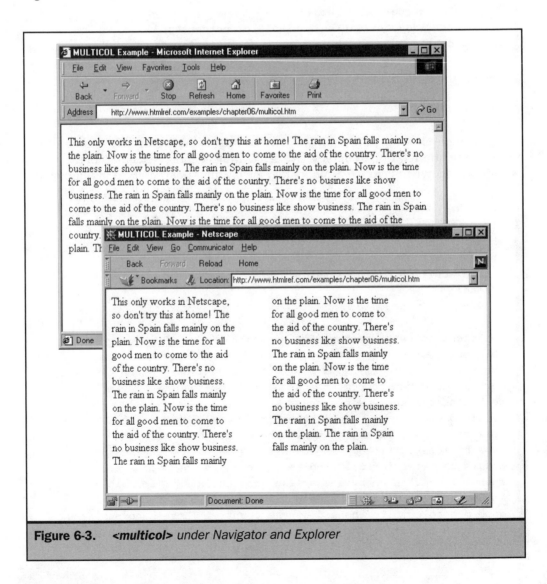

Figure 6-3. *<multicol> under Navigator and Explorer*

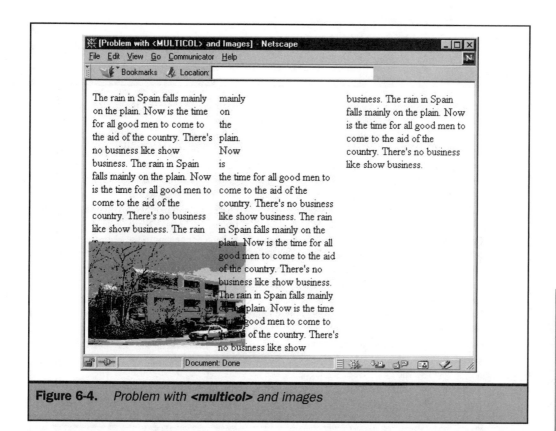

Figure 6-4.   *Problem with* ***<multicol>*** *and images*

Because browsers generally are unable to set hyphenation, page authors might need to manually insert **<wbr>** elements between words that might overrun column size. Another problem with **<multicol>** is that it will degrade when too many columns are set, so try to keep the value for **cols** around six or less. An example showing how the problem of too many columns and how **<wbr>** can help is shown in Figure 6-5.

Remember if this tag is to be used at all it should only be used in an all-Netscape environment. Like other browser-specific elements such as **<blink>**, **<marquee>**, and **<bgsound>**, **<multicol>** really should never be used. The problems presented both in cross-browser compatibility, as well as rendering issues, should convince readers that the proprietary HTML approach is not the appropriate one. In fact the basic facility provided by the tag can be accomplished with tables as discussed in Chapter 7 or style sheets as discussed in Chapter 10. For now let's move away from the limited layout capabilities of HTML and turn our attention to fonts; then colors and backgrounds.

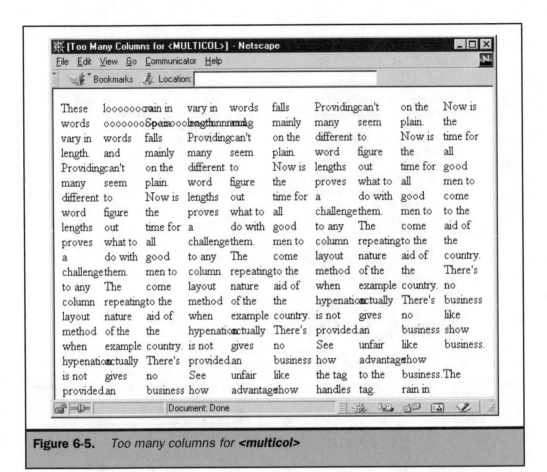

Figure 6-5. *Too many columns for <multicol>*

Fonts

Aside from better support for layout, Web page designers have long desired to be able to specify fonts in their documents. HTML 2.0 only supported two fonts, a proportional font and a fixed-width font. Under browsers such as Netscape and Internet Explorer, the proportional font usually was Times or Times New Roman, whereas the fixed-width font was Courier. To set text into Courier, page authors would use an element such as <tt>. Otherwise, all text on the page generally was in the proportional font unless it was preformatted with the <pre> element. There also was little control over the size of the font, even in relative terms. The font size of the browser generally was 12 point for the variable-width font and 10 point for the fixed-width font, but end users were free to change font size as they pleased.

There wasn't much control over typography in early browsers. In fact, the only way to use a new font or control the precise layout of text was to make it a graphic. To this day, many page designers still embed a great deal of text as graphics in order to precisely control spacing and to use fonts that the user might not have. Because of download and accessibility issues, this should not be the *de facto* approach to dealing with fonts.

With Netscape Navigator 1.1, it became possible to control fonts a little more. Netscape introduced the **<font>** element, which was used to specify the size and, starting with Navigator 2.0, color of text using the **size** and **color** attributes. Microsoft later added an attribute called **face** to indicate which font type should be used. Both **size** and **color** were introduced to the standard in HTML 3.2. Today all of these attributes are considered part of the HTML 4.0 transitional standard. However, like many layout facilities, the use of this HTML element should be phased out in the future in favor of style sheets.

Under HTML 4.0, it is possible to color a certain portion of text a particular color by enclosing it within the **<font>** element and setting the **color** attribute equal to a valid color name like "red" or an equivalent value such as #FF0000. RGB hexadecimal equivalent codes will be discussed later in this chapter and also are presented in Appendix E. So the code

```
<font color="red">This is important</font>
```

sets the text "This is important" in red. The **<font>** element can contain a great deal of text or very little, so it is possible to control the colors of individual letters, although the resulting rainbow effects might be hard on the eyes.

It also is possible to set the relative size of type by setting the **size** attribute of the **<font>** element. In a Web page, there are seven relative sizes for text numbered from 1–7, where **1** is the smallest text in a document and **7** is the largest. To set some text into the largest size, use **<font size="7">This is big</font>**. By default, the typical size of text is **3**; this can be overridden with the **<basefont>** element discussed later in this chapter. If the font size is not known but the text should be made just one size bigger, the author can use an alternative sizing value such as **<font size="+1">** instead of specifying the size directly. The + and - nomenclature makes it possible to bring the font size up or down a specified number of settings. The values for this form of the **size** attribute should range from **+1–+6** and **-1–-6**. It is not possible to specify **<font size="+10">** because there are only seven sizes. If the increase or decrease goes beyond acceptable sizes, the font generally defaults at the largest or smallest size, respectively.

Microsoft introduced the **face** attribute to the **<font>** element that has come to be supported by nearly all browsers, as well as the HTML 4 specification. The **face** attribute can be set to the name of the font to render the text. So, a page designer who wants to render a particular phrase in Britannic Bold could use the following code:

```
<font face="Britannic Bold">This is important</font>
```

The browser then would read this HTML fragment and render the text in the different font—but only for users who have the font installed on their systems. This raises an interesting problem: What happens if a user doesn't have the font specified? Using the **face** attribute, it is possible to specify a comma-delimited list of fonts to attempt one by one before defaulting to the normal proportional or fixed-width font. The fragment shown here would first try Arial, then Helvetica, and finally Sans Serif before giving up and using whatever the current browser font is.

```
<font face="Arial, Helvetica, Sans-serif">This should be in a
different font</font>
```

Although it is impossible to know what fonts users might have on their systems, the previous example shows how a little guesswork can be applied to take advantage of the **face** attribute. Most Macintosh, Windows, and Unix users have a standard set of fonts. If equivalent fonts are specified, it might be possible to provide similar page renderings across platforms. Table 6-1 shows some of the fonts that can be found on Macintosh, Windows, and Unix systems.

Windows	Macintosh	Unix*
Arial	Chicago	Charter
Comic Sans MS	Courier	Clean
Courier New	Geneva	Courier
Impact	Helvetica	Fixed
Times New Roman	Monaco	Helvetica
Symbol	New York	Lucida
Verdana	Palatino	Sans Serif
Wingding	Symbol	Serif
	Times	Symbol
		Times
		Utopia

*Unix fonts vary; this is just meant to show most of the common fonts under a standard X Window environment.

Table 6-1.   *Sample System Fonts by Platform Type*

Given the similarity of these fonts it generally is safe to use the following combinations of font faces as shown in this code fragment and achieve approximately the same results across platforms.

```
<font face="Arial,Helvetica,sans-serif">A sans-serif font</font>
<br>
<font face="Verdana, Arial, Helvetica, sans-serif">
A sans-serif font 2</font>
<br>
<font face="'Times New Roman', Times, serif">A serif font</font>
<br>
<font face="Georgia, Times New Roman, Times, serif">A serif font 2</font>
<br>
<font face="'Courier New',Courier,monospace">A mono spaced font</font>
```

A rendering of these fonts on Windows system and a Macintosh system is shown in Figure 6-6 as a comparison.

Users might have many other fonts beyond the ones shown in the previous example. Users of Microsoft Office also probably will have access to fonts such as Algerian, Book Antiqua, Bookman Old Style, Britannic Bold, Desdemona, Garamond, Century Gothic, Haettenschweiller, and many others. The various browsers also are trying to make new fonts available. For example under Internet Explorer 4.0, Microsoft has introduced a new font called WebDings, which provides many common icons for use on the page. Some of these icons would be useful for navigation, like arrows, whereas others look like audio or video symbols that could provide an indication of link contents before selection. Just using font sizing, colors, and simple layout, it is possible to make interesting but very browser-specific layouts with WebDings as shown in Figure 6-7.

Fonts on a PC	*Fonts on a Macintosh*
A sans-serif font A sans-serif font 2 A serif font A serif font 2 A mono spaced font	A sans-serif font A sans-serif font 2 A serif font A serif font 2 A mono spaced font

Figure 6-6.   *Common fonts across platforms*

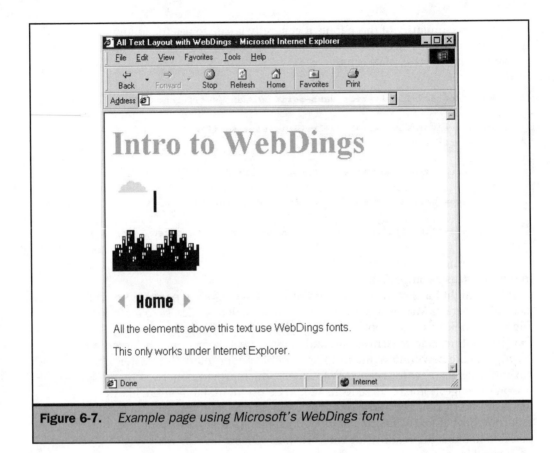

Figure 6-7. *Example page using Microsoft's WebDings font*

A common set of icons for the Web actually is not a new idea. The W3C at one point had a working draft covering a predefined set of icon-like symbols, although this does not appear to be gaining any support in the industry. The Microsoft font actually includes many of these symbols, but does not use the same naming convention. It might eventually be possible to include **&audio;** to add an audio icon to a Web page, but for now setting the WebDings value or inserting a GIF is the best choice.

A complete example demonstrating all the **<font>** element attributes and their use is presented in the following code. A rendering is shown in Figure 6-8.

```
<!DOCTYPE HTML PUBLIC "-//W3C//DTD HTML 4.01 Transitional//EN">
<html>
<head>
<title>Font Element Demo</title>
</head>
<body>
```

```
<h2 align="center">Font Sizing</h2>

<font size="1">Font size 1</font><br>
<font size="2">Font size 2</font><br>
<font size="3">Font size 3</font><br>
<font size="4">Font size 4</font><br>
<font size="5">Font size 5</font><br>
<font size="6">Font size 6</font><br>
<font size="7">Font size 7</font><br>
This is <font size="+2">+2 from the base size.</font>
Now it is <font size="-1">-1 from base size.</font>

<h2 align="center">Font Color</h2>

<font color="red">Red Text</font><br>
<font color="#ffcc66">Hex #ffcc66 color</font>

<h2 align="center">Font Face</h2>

<font face="Arial">Set font to common fonts like Arial</font><br>
<font face="'Viner Hand ITC'">Take a chance on an unusual
font</font><br>
Even set text to dingbat characters
<font face="Webdings">f3khilqm </font><br>

<h2 align="center">Common Font Face Combinations</h2>

<font face="Arial,Helvetica,sans-serif">
Arial,Helvetica,sans-serif</font><br>

<font face="Verdana, Arial, Helvetica, sans-serif">
Verdana, Arial, Helvetica, sans-serif</font><br>

<font face="'Times New Roman',Times,serif">
Times New Roman,Times,serif</font><br>

<font face="Georgia, 'Times New Roman', Times, serif">
Georgia, Times New Roman, Times, serif</font><br>

<font face="'Courier New', Courier, monospace">
Courier New, Courier, monospace</font><br>

<h2 align="center">Combination</h2>

You can <font size="+2" color="red" face="Arial">set all font
attributes at once!</font>

</body>
</html>
```

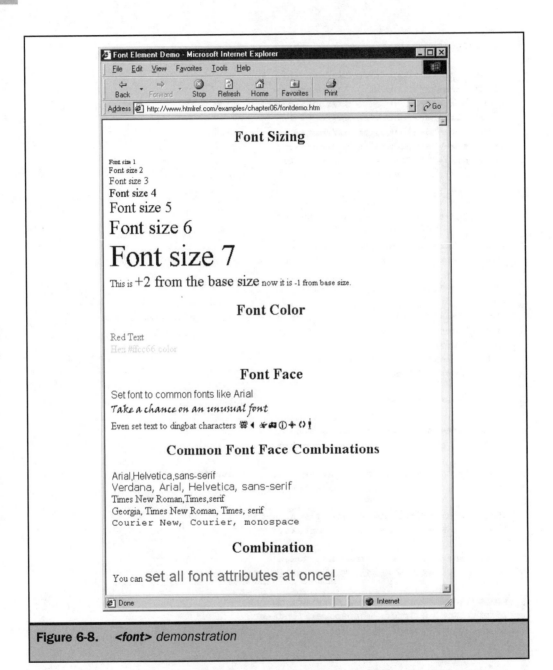

Figure 6-8. *<font>* demonstration

The <font> element is deprecated under strict HTML 4 and XHTML in favor of style sheets. However, its use is common and probably will continue for some time.

Document-Wide Font Settings

In some cases, it might be appropriate to change the font size, color, or face document width. To do this, use the **<basefont>** element in the **<head>** of the document. The **<basefont>** should occur only once in the document and includes major attributes such as **color**, **face**, and **size**. Like the **<font>** element, **color** should be set to an RGB hexadecimal equivalent value or color name. **face** should be set to a font name or comma-delimited list of fonts. **size** should be set to a size value between **1** and **7**. Relative sizing for the **size** attribute generally does not make any sense. To set the font of the document in red Arial or Helvetica with a relative size of 6 use **<basefont color="red" face="Arial, Helvetica" size="6">** within the **<head>** element of the document. More information on **<basefont>** can be found in Appendix A.

> **Note**   *Recall that because this element is empty, in order to be XHTML compliant it would need a self-identifying close; for example, <basefont color="red" face="Arial, Helvetica" size="6" />*

Downloadable Fonts

Although one Microsoft solution to type on the Web attempts to promote a common set of faces, it isn't a very flexible approach outside the Windows world. Although many Windows, Macintosh, and Unix systems have similar fonts, what about the situation in which the page author wants to use a customized font? In this case, the page author is forced to create a static image of the font. This could take a great deal of time to download, and gives up the ability to easily index the text, let alone copy and paste it.

The best solution for fonts on the Web would be to come up with some cross-platform form of font that could be downloaded to the browser on the fly. Although this sounds easy enough, the problem with downloadable fonts is that they must be highly compact. Page viewers must not be able to steal the font from the page and install it on their own machines. Both of the major browser vendors have been working on downloadable fonts. Microsoft's solution for Web type is called OpenType (www.microsoft.com/typography). Netscape's solution, called Dynamic Fonts, is based on BitStream's TrueDoc (www.truedoc.com). Currently, only Netscape 4.0 and Internet Explorer 4.0 and above support downloadable fonts, so be careful to not rely too heavily on the font being available or your page layout might fall apart.

Netscape's Dynamic Fonts

To use a dynamic font under Netscape, the page author simply uses the face attribute of the **<font>** element, or a style sheet attribute as discussed in Chapter 10, to set the font face. If the user does not have the font installed on the system, a downloadable font linked to the page can be fetched and used to render the page. To include a link to a Netscape font definition file in Portable Font Resource (PFR) format, use the

\<link> element by setting the **rel** attribute to **fontdef** and the **src** attribute equal to the URL where the font definition file resides. The **\<link>** element must be found within the **\<head>** of the document. An example of how this element would be used is shown here:

```
<!DOCTYPE HTML PUBLIC "-//W3C//DTD HTML 4.01 Transitional//EN">
<html>
<head>
<title>Netscape Font Demo</title>
<link rel="fontdef"
src="http://www.htmlref.com/examples/chapter06/fonts/
customfonts.pfr">
</head>
<body>
<font face="newfont">
   Content rendered in the font "newfont" which is part of the pfr
   file.
</font>
</body>
</html>
```

Note that there might be many fonts in the same font definition file. There is no limit to how many fonts can be used on a page. Once the font is accessed, it is used just as if it were installed on a user's system. Two attributes available under Netscape 4.0 are useful when dealing with dynamic fonts. The first extension to the **\<font>** element is **point-size**, which can be set to the point size of the font. The other extension to **\<font>** is the **weight** attribute, which can be set to a value between **100** and **900** in increments of **100**. The value of the **weight** attribute determines the weight or "boldness" of the font. A value of **100** is the lightest weight, whereas **900** indicates to make the font as bold as it can be. If the **\<b>** element is used, the **weight** attribute is equivalent to **900**. If dynamic fonts are to be used, it is more likely that style sheets will be the preferred way to interact with them, rather than these proprietary extensions. The only obstacle to using dynamic fonts is that the .pfr file describing the font must be created. Otherwise, they are no more troublesome than attempting to guess the font on the end user's system or rasterizing the font into a GIF image.

Note   *One drawback to the Netscape approach to dynamic fonts is that it might cause screen flashing in many versions of Netscape. This can be disorienting for the user. At the time of writing this edition—after three years—this problem still has not been fixed and could account for why so few sites have adopted dynamic fonts.*

Microsoft's Dynamic Fonts

Microsoft also provides a way to embed fonts in a Web page. To include a font, you must first build the page using the **<font>** element, or style sheet rules that set fonts, as discussed in Chapter 10. When creating your page, don't worry about whether or not the end user has the font installed; it will be downloaded. Next, use Microsoft's Web Embedding Fonts Tool available at www.microsoft.com/typography to analyze the font usage on the page. The program should create an .eot file that contains the embedded fonts. The font use information then will be added to the page in the form of CSS (Cascading Style Sheets) style rules, as shown here:

```
<!DOCTYPE HTML PUBLIC "-//W3C//DTD HTML 4.01 Transitional//EN">
<html>
<head>
<title>Microsoft Font Test</title>
<style type="text/css">
<!--

  @font-face {
     font-family: Ransom;
     font-style:  normal;
     font-weight: normal;
     src:
url(http://www.htmlref.com/examples/chapter06/fonts/ransom.eot);
  }
-->
</style>
</head>
<body>
<font face="ransom" size="6">Example Ransom Note Font</font>
</body>
</html>
```

A possible rendering of font embedding is shown in Figure 6-9.

Like the Netscape approach, you first must create a font file and reference it from the file that uses the font. It might be useful to define a fonts directory within your Web site to store font files, similar to storing image files for site use.

The use of the **@font-face** acts as a pseudo-element that allows you to bring any number of fonts into a page. The form of the font embedding supported by Microsoft conforms to the initial W3C specification for font embedding. Again for more information on embedded fonts under Internet Explorer, and links to font file creation tools like WEFT, see the Microsoft Typography site (www.microsoft.com/typography).

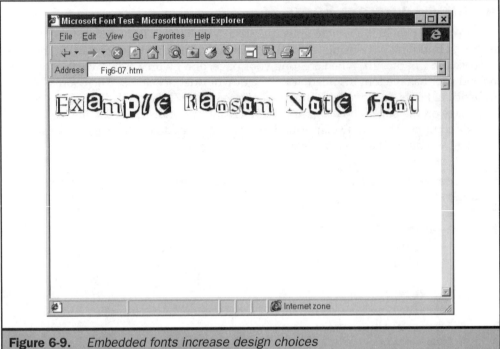

Figure 6-9.   *Embedded fonts increase design choices*

Note   *It is possible to provide links to both Microsoft and Netscape font technology within the same page. This really adds only one line or a few style rules as the rest of the document would continue to use the same* **<font face="">** *statements. TrueDoc technology also supports an ActiveX control to allow Internet Explorer users to view their style of embedded fonts. Given the extra download involved, the double font statement approach is preferred.*

Colors in HTML

HTML 4.0 supports color settings for text as well as for the background of the document, or even individual table cells. With style sheets we will see that it also is possible to set both foreground and background color at any time. There are 16 widely known color names defined in HTML 4. These names and their associated HEX RGB values are shown in Table 6-2.

To set a particular section of text yellow simply surround the content with **<font color="yellow">** and **</font>**. Of course there are many colors names beyond the simple ones in Table 6-2, some of which seem to have been invented by the browser vendors;

Black (#000000)	Green (#008000)
Silver (#C0C0C0)	Lime (#00FF00)
Gray (#808080)	Olive (#808000)
White (#FFFFFF)	Yellow (#FFFF00)
Maroon (#800000)	Navy (#000080)
Red (#FF0000)	Blue (#0000FF)
Purple (#800080)	Teal (#008080)
Fuchsia (#FF00FF)	Aqua (#00FFFF)

Table 6-2.   *Common HTML 4.0 Color Names and HEX Values*

these are listed in Appendix E. The problem with using browser vendor–defined colors is that they don't always do what they are supposed to do. Even worse, you can invent your own colors. Try setting the following and viewing it under Netscape and Microsoft Internet Explorer:

```
<body bgcolor="html color names are troublesome">
```

This color name is totally invalid, but it still results in a shade of green that is very distinct in each browser. It is possible to make up colors like "chilidog brown" or "stale beer yellow," but this is no more recommended than using the Netscape-defined color of "dodgerblue." Using hex color values is the preferred way of setting colors because many non-standard color names are not be supported correctly across browsers.

Consider that a computer displays color using a combination of red, green, and blue. We call this additive color process RGB color. The easiest way to think of RGB color is as a set of three dials that control the amount of red, green, and blue mixed into the final color. Because of the way computers calculate things the dials range from 0–255 in decimal or 00 to FF if we count in hexadecimal like a Computer Scientist. So a color specified by 0, 255, 0 or equivalently 00, FF, 00, would be equivalent to the green dial turned all the way up and the other dials turned off. This would be a pure green. Equivalently FF,00,00 would be pure red. Finally 00,00,FF would be pure blue. Obviously all dials off at 00,00,00 would be the absence of color or simply black, whereas all dials on at FF,FF,FF would be white. In HTML we set these hex values using a pound sign and each of the equivalent RR, GG, and BB values are run together; for example, we could use the hex value **#FFFF00** for the **color** attribute instead of the word yellow.

Rather than becoming an expert at hexadecimal it is easy to use an editor to pick a color or to see Appendix E, which explains the various colors available under HTML. A color reference can be found online at http://www.htmlref.com/Reference/AppE/colorchart.htm.

Document-wide Color Attributes for <body>

The **<body>** element has numerous attributes that can be used to affect the display of content in the body of the document including setting the background color, the color of text, and the color of links. One of the most commonly used **<body>** element attributes, **bgcolor** defines the document's background color. This was a distinct improvement over the default gray (or white under Macintosh) of Mosaic, although it and the other **<body>** attributes have led to a multitude of design sins. Employed wisely, they can enhance a page's appearance; misused, they have been known to induce migraines. Hexadecimal RGB values and color names can be used with **bgcolor** and the four attributes to follow. To create a white background, the attribute could be set to **<body bgcolor="#FFFFFF">** (hexadecimal) or simply **<body bgcolor="white">**.

The **text** attribute of the **<body>** element defines the color of text in the entire document. The attribute takes a color in the form of either a hex code or color name. So **<body bgcolor="white" text="green">** would create a white page with green text.

Note that the text color can be overridden in the text by applying the **<font>** element to selected text with its **color** attribute, as discussed earlier in the chapter.

Aside from the body text, it also is possible to define the colors of links by setting the **<body>** element attributes: **link**, **alink**, and **vlink**.

The attribute **link** defines the color of unvisited links in a document. For example, if you've set your background color to black, it might be more useful to use a light link color instead of the standard blue. **alink** defines the color of the link as it is being clicked. This often happens too quickly to be noticed, but can create a flash effect, if desired. For a more subdued Web experience, it might be better to set the **alink** attribute to match either the **link** attribute or the next one, **vlink**. The **vlink** attribute defines the color of a link after it has been visited, which under many user agents is purple. Many authors wish to set the value of the **vlink** attribute to red, which makes sense given standard color interpretation. So using the last attributes, creating a white page with green text, red links, and fuschia-colored visited links could be accomplished using the code presented here:

```
<!DOCTYPE HTML PUBLIC "-//W3C//DTD HTML 4.01 Transitional//EN">
<html>
<head>
<title>Colors</title>
</head>
<body bgcolor="#FFFFFF" text="#008000" link="#FF0000"
```

```
        vlink="#FF00FF" alink="#FF0000">

... Content to color ...

</body>
</html>
```

Users should be forewarned not to choose link colors that might confuse their viewers. For example, reversing link colors so that visited links are blue and unvisited links are red could confuse a user. While it is unlikely that a page author would do such a thing, it has been seen more than once—particularly in situations where the look and feel is the driving force behind the site. Other common problems with link color changes include the idea of setting all link values to blue with the belief that users will revisit sections thinking they haven't been there before. While this might make sense from a marketing standpoint, the frustration factor due to the lost navigation cues might override any potential benefit from extra visits. As the last example showed, setting all the links colors to red could have a similar effect of encouraging the user to think they have seen the site already.

Page authors also must be extremely careful when setting text and background colors so that readability is preserved. Page designers often are tempted to use light colors on light backgrounds or dark colors on dark backgrounds. For example, a gray text on a black background might look cool, but will it look cool on every person's monitor? If the gamma value of some other person's monitor is much different from your monitor, it will be unreadable. White and black always make a good pairing and red certainly is useful. The best combination, in terms of contrast, actually is yellow and black, but imagine the headache from reading a page that looks like a road sign. Despite the high contrast, designers should be careful of white text on a black background when font sizes are very small, particularly on poor-resolution monitors.

> **Note** *Gamma is a term used to describe the relationship between the input and output for a particular image device. Different monitors have inherently different gamma settings. As a result, the same image on two different monitors might appear significantly different. Whereas the gamma of a monitor cannot be changed by the user, monitor settings such as contrast, brightness, and color can be adjusted.*

Background Images

Aside from setting background colors, you also can change the appearance of a Web page by setting a background image using the **background** attribute of the **<body>** element. The value of **background** should be the URL for a GIF or JPEG file, usually one in the image directory of the Web site in question; for example, **<body background="images/tile.gif">**.

PRESENTATION AND LAYOUT

The value could just as easily include a complete URL to access an image at another site, but this would be a rather unwieldy approach to the task at hand. Images accessed in this fashion repeat, or *tile,* in the background of a Web page. This can make or break a Web page design. Imagine someone using the **background** attribute to place a 200×300 pixel JPEG of a favorite dog on his or her home page. The dog's image would repeat, both vertically and horizontally, in the background of the page. This would make the dog's owner very happy—and make the page very difficult to read. Figure 6-10 shows an example of a bothersome repeating background.

In general, complex background images tend to be a poor design decision. Taking the subtle approach can backfire as well. Some users attempt to create a light background such as a texture or watermark thinking that, like paper, it will create a classy effect. The problem with this is that under many monitors, the image might be difficult to make out at all, or the texture might even slightly blur the text on top of it. Just like setting background colors, the most important consideration is the degree of contrast. Always attempt to keep the foreground and background at a high level of

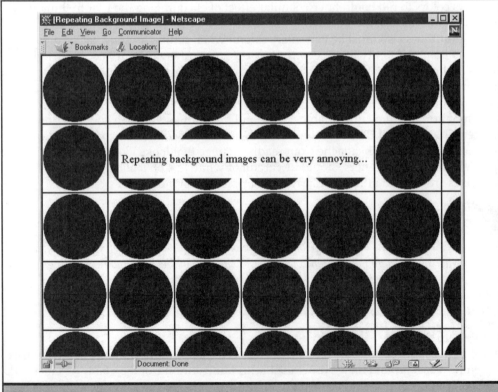

Figure 6-10.   *Repeating background image*

contrast so that users can read the information. What good is an impressive layout if nobody can read it?

If a background is desired, image manipulation programs such as Photoshop can be used to create seamless background tiles that are more pleasing to the eye and show no seam. Figure 6-11 demonstrates the idea of a repeating background tile.

Background images, or tiles, also can be used to create other effects. A single GIF 5 pixels high and 1,600 pixels wide could be used to create a useful page layout. The first 200 horizontal pixels of the GIF could be black, and the rest could be white. Assuming 1,600 pixels as the maximum width of a browser, this tile would repeat only vertically, thus creating the illusion of a two-tone background. This has become a very common concept on the Web. Many sites use the left-hand color for navigation buttons, while the remaining area is used for text, as shown in Figure 6-12. However, to guarantee that content appears on top of the appropriate section of the background image you might be forced to use tables. Make sure to read the next chapter thoroughly before trying this style of page design.

Be very careful when segmenting the screen using a background tile. For example, many people are tempted to create page layout with vertical sectioning, as shown in Figure 6-13.

PRESENTATION AND LAYOUT

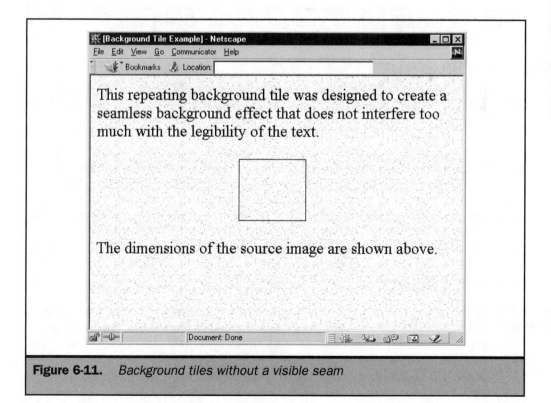

Figure 6-11.   *Background tiles without a visible seam*

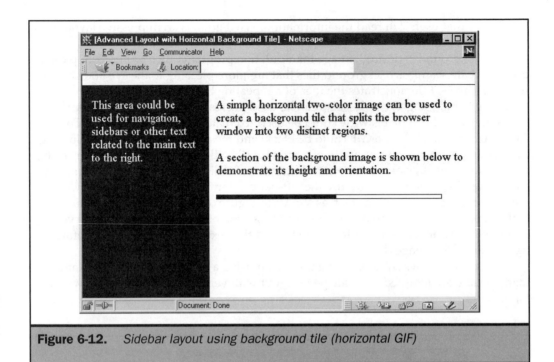

Figure 6-12.   *Sidebar layout using background tile (horizontal GIF)*

However, there is a problem with this layout. Won't the black bar repeat? Quite possibly, because the length of the content is hard to determine. Viewers might find the black bar repeating over and over with content being lost on top. A solution might be to make the background tile very tall. However, this not only increases file size, but also begs the question of how tall is enough? Because content can vary from page to page and increase or decrease over time, determining the width is next to impossible. It would appear that the same problem would occur with sidebar style tiles. This generally is not the case given that pages generally do not scroll left to right, and monitor sizes tend to not exceed 1,600 pixels. In either case, the problem of background tile repeats is solved with style sheets as they provide a way to set the direction and frequency of a tile's repeat pattern. This is discussed further in Chapter 10. There are a few HTML-specific solutions to these and other background layout problems, which are touched on briefly here.

Note   *Another problem with background tiles is that some designers try to minimize file size and download time. For example, a designer can make the background images a single pixel tall; this might cause screen painting problems since the background will have to be tiled as many times as the screen is high in pixels. With a slow video card this might produce an annoying sweeping effect. To avoid the background painting problem, consider balancing physical file size and download size. So a background image can be*

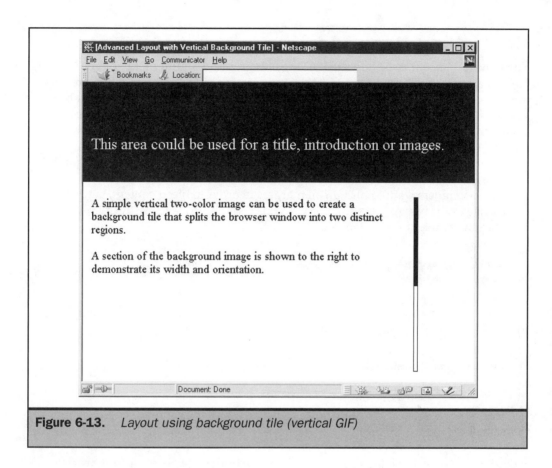

Figure 6-13.   *Layout using background tile (vertical GIF)*

five pixels or taller, depending on how many colors are used. If colors are kept to a minimum, there is no harm in making the image 20 or 30 pixels high.

Internet Explorer Background Attributes

Internet Explorer supports a few special attributes for the **<body>** element that might solve background image and layout problems without resorting to style sheets. The **bgproperties** attribute offers a solution to the problem of scrolling background images. At present, however, it is supported only by Internet Explorer 3.0 and beyond. The **<body>** element's attribute and value **bgproperties="fixed'** will, under Internet Explorer, allow text and images to scroll while the background image accessed with the **background** attribute remains in place. Think of this as a watermark-like effect. It is possible to imitate this action using style sheets as well.

Controlling Page Margins

The **<body>** element also allows the setting of margins; both Internet Explorer 4 and Netscape 4 have a different approach to setting margins. Under Internet Explorer there are two **<body>** attributes that affect margins: **leftmargin** and **topmargin**. Each is set with a pixel value. For example, **leftmargin="25"** will create a margin of 25 pixels between the left edge of the browser window and its content; **topmargin="15"** will create a 15-pixel margin between the top of the browser window and its content, as well as at the bottom if the content extends that far. Under Netscape use **marginheight** and **marginwidth**.

Many designers want to turn off all margins in order to bleed content, particularly to the edge of the browser screen. In HTML this could be done using the following modification to the **<body>** element:

```
<body topmargin="0" leftmargin="0" marginheight="0"
marginwidth="0">
```

Of course this approach to layout will be alleviated with style sheets. A simple rule in the **<style>** block found in the **<head>** of a document like so:

```
<style type="text/css">
<!--
   body     {margin: 0px; }
-->
</style>
```

would do the same trick and will eventually work under all CSS compliant browsers. Of course both could be used just to be sure the margins are removed.

 *Microsoft Internet Explorer also supports the use of **bottommargin** as well as **rightmargin** attributes for the **<body>** element. See Appendix A for more information on these and other Internet Explorer proprietary changes.*

Although many of the elements and attributes discussed in the last few sections are useful to control the layout, color, and background of a page, many of them are browser specific or are deprecated under HTML 4 and XHTML. The goal should be to eventually provide this function solely with style sheets. However, until the problems with style sheets are worked out and browsers are upgraded for backward compatibility as shown by the previous example it might be required to use both layout forms for another year or two.

Summary

Although HTML does not provide a great deal of support for layout, it really wasn't meant to. While it is easy to say that people shouldn't use HTML to lay out pages, the fact of the matter is that they wanted, and needed, to do so. At the time there was no other possibility. Designers desperately want pixel-level layout control of Web pages and support for fonts. The need for improved page design gave rise to the occasional abuse of HTML elements, "cheats" like the invisible pixel GIF trick, and the rise of proprietary elements such as **<spacer>**. Despite the improvement in layout capabilities, fonts are still an open issue in HTML; but with some assumptions regarding the use of downloadable font technology, font use is becoming a reality on the Web. The next chapter will present tables that make it possible to create fairly precise layouts using HTML. However, later chapters will reveal that many of the problems raised in this chapter continue with tables, and will only diminish as style sheets continue to become more prevalent.

PRESENTATION AND
LAYOUT

The
Complete
Reference

Chapter 7

Layout with Tables

The **<table>** element and its associated elements have become one of the most commonly used means of creating Web page layouts. Although positioning through style sheets (see Chapter 10) should provide more precise layout capacities, browser support is inconsistent, and the issue of backward compatibility remains a concern. For better or worse, this leaves the table approach to page layout as the only one likely to work across multiple browsers, especially when taking older browsers into consideration. Tables are not limited to layout, however, as the later portions of this chapter discuss.

Introduction to Tables

A table represents information in a tabular way, like a spreadsheet: distributed across a grid of rows and columns. In printed documents, tables commonly serve a subordinate function, illustrating some point described by an accompanying text. Tables still perform this illustrative function in HTML documents. Because HTML does not offer the same layout capacities available to print designers, Web-based tables also have become a common way to create document layout and design. But unlike printed tables, HTML tables can contain information that is *dynamic*, or interactive, such as the results of a database query. To address this use, the databinding feature allows an HTML table template to be directly connected with a database source. A table is dynamically generated using the template and the results of a particular database query. Taken together, these capabilities make tables one of HTML's most useful and sophisticated resources.

Simple Tables

In its simplest form, a table places information inside the cells formed by dividing a rectangle into rows and columns. Most cells contain data; some cells, usually on the table's top or side, contain headings. HTML represents a basic table using four elements. In HTML a table, **<table>** … **</table>**, contains one or more rows, **<tr>** … **</tr>**. Each row contains cells holding a heading, **<th>** … **</th>**, or data, **<td>** … **</td>**. The following code example illustrates a basic table. Note that the only attribute used in this example is **border**, which is used to specify a 1-pixel border so it is clear what the table looks like. The rendering for the simple table under various browsers is shown in Figure 7-1.

```
<!DOCTYPE HTML PUBLIC "-//W3C//DTD HTML 4.01 Transitional//EN">
<html>
<head>
<title>Simple Table Example</title>
</head>
<body>
```

```
<table border="1">
<caption>Basic Fruit Comparison Chart</caption>
    <tr>
        <th>Fruit</th>
        <th>Color</th>
    </tr>
    <tr>
        <td>Apple</td>
        <td>Red</td>
    </tr>
    <tr>
        <td>Avocado</td>
        <td>Green</td>
    </tr>
    <tr>
        <td>Watermelon</td>
        <td>Pink</td>
    </tr>
</table>
</body>
</html>
```

This simple table example shows the use of the most basic table elements: headings, rows, and data cells.

Again, a table is made up of rows enclosed within **<tr>** . . . **</tr>**. The number of rows in the table is determined by the number of occurrences of the **<tr>** element. What about columns? Generally, the number of columns in a table is determined by the maximum number of data cells indicated by **<td>** . . . **</td>**, or headings indicated by **<th>** . . . **</th>** within the table. It might be useful to hint to the browser at the number of columns in the table by setting the **cols** attribute, introduced by Internet Explorer 4, for the **<table>** element equal to the number of columns in the table (for example, **<table border="1" cols="2">**, as in the last example).

The headings for the table are set using the **<th>** element. Generally, the browser renders the style of headings differently, usually centering the contents of the heading and placing the text in bold style. The actual cells of the table are indicated by the **<td>** element. Both the **<td>** and **<th>** elements can enclose an arbitrary amount of data of just about any type. In the previous example, a full paragraph of text could be enclosed in a table cell along with an image, lists, and links. Last, the table might have a caption enclosed within **<caption>** . . . **</caption>**, whose contents generally are rendered above or below the table indicating what the table contains.

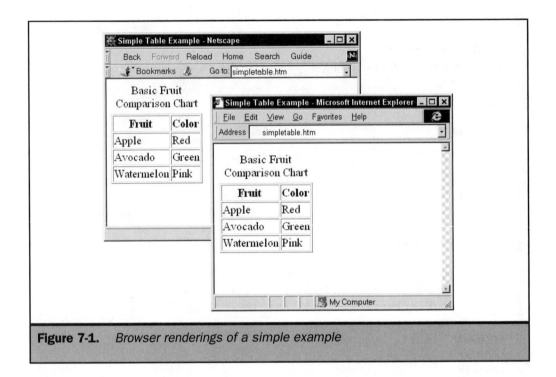

Figure 7-1.   *Browser renderings of a simple example*

Technically speaking, the closing tags for the **<tr>**, **<th>**, and **<td>** tags are optional under the HTML specification. Although this might make for cleaner-looking code in your HTML documents, HTML writers are still encouraged to use the closing tags, as well as indentation. This will ensure that table cells and rows are clearly defined, particularly for nested tables. It also will help to avoid problems with versions of Netscape that often "break" tables that don't use closing tags for these elements. And because XHTML—which requires closing tags for all non-empty elements—promises to become the standard in the near future, there is one more reason to always use closing tags.

The rowspan and colspan Attributes

Whereas the preceding example shows that it is possible to create a simple table with a simple structure, what about when the table cells need to be larger or smaller? The following HTML code creates tables that are somewhat more complicated. By adding the **rowspan** and **colspan** attributes to the table elements, it is possible to create data cells that span a given number of rows or columns. The rendering of this code appears in Figure 7-2.

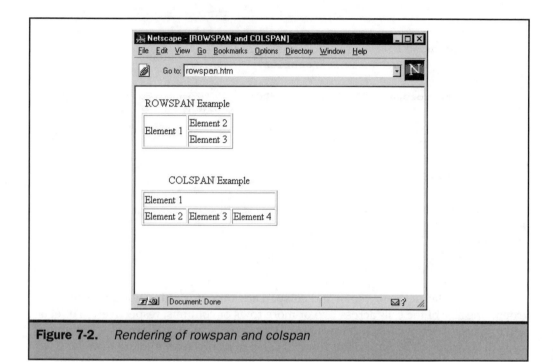

Figure 7-2.   *Rendering of rowspan and colspan*

```
<!DOCTYPE HTML PUBLIC "-//W3C//DTD HTML 4.01 Transitional//EN">
<html>
<head>
<title>Rowspan and Colspan Example</title>
</head>
<body>

<table border="1">
  <caption>ROWSPAN Example</caption>
   <tr>
       <td rowspan="2">Element 1</td>
       <td>Element 2</td>
   </tr>
   <tr>
       <td>Element 3</td>
   </tr>
  </table>

<br><br>
```

```
<table border="1">
  <caption>COLSPAN Example</caption>
    <tr>
       <td colspan="3">Element 1</td>
    </tr>
    <tr>
       <td>Element 2</td>
       <td>Element 3</td>
       <td>Element 4</td>
    </tr>
</table>

</body>
</html>
```

The basic idea of the **rowspan** and **colspan** attributes for **<td>** and **<th>** is to extend the size of the cells across two or more rows or columns, respectively. To set a cell to span three rows, use **<td rowspan="3">**; to set a heading to span two columns, use **<th colspan="2">**. Setting the value of **colspan** or **rowspan** to more than the number of columns or rows in the table should not extend the size of the table. Be aware, however, that some browsers require precise use of these span attributes. Consider the following code:

```
<table border="1" cellspacing="0" width="120">
<tr>
    <td>1</td>
    <td>2</td>
    <td rowspan="2">3</td>
</tr>

<tr>
    <td>4</td>
    <td>5</td>
    <td>6</td>
</tr>
</table>
```

Most browsers will render this code something like this:

The reason is quite simple: The last data cell in the second row should have been removed to account for the rowspan in cell 3 of the first row, like this:

```
<table border="1" cellspacing="0" width="120">
<tr>
    <td>1</td>
    <td>2</td>
    <td rowspan="2">3</td>
</tr>

<tr>
    <td>4</td>
    <td>5</td>
</tr>
</table>
```

The rendering of the correct code then would work properly:

Aside from being able to span rows and columns, the **<table>** element, and its enclosed elements **<td>**, **<th>**, and **<caption>**, support a variety of attributes for alignment, sizing, and layout. The following example shows a more complex kind of table:

```
<!doctype html public "-//w3c//dtd html 4.0 transitional//en">
<html>
<head>
<title>Complex Table Example</title>
</head>
<body>

<p>Notice how the text of a paragraph
```

```
<table align="left" border="1" width="300">
<caption align="bottom">The Super Widget</caption>
   <tr>
      <td rowspan="2"><img src="widget.gif" alt="super widget"
         width="100" height="120"></td>
      <th bgcolor="lightgreen">Specifications</th>
   </tr>
   <tr>
      <td>
         <ul>
            <li>Diameter: 10 cm
            <li>Composition: Kryptonite
            <li>Color: Green
         </ul>
      </td>
   </tr>
</table>
can flow around a table just as it would any other
embedded object form. Notice how the text of a paragraph
can flow around a table just as it would any other
embedded object form. Notice how the text of a paragraph
can flow around a table just as it would any other
embedded object form.</p>

</body>
</html>
```

This example shows that it is possible to place any form of content in a cell, as well as control the individual size of the cells and the table itself. The logical step is to control page layout by creating a grid with the **<table>** element.

Tables for Layout

Tables can be a very important tool for HTML page layout. The foundation of graphic design is the ability to spatially arrange visual elements in relation to each other. Tables can be used to define a layout grid for just this purpose. Prior to the advent of style sheets supporting positioning (see Chapter 10), tables were the only reliable way to accomplish this. They remain the most commonly used technique for Web layout.

The key to using a table in order to create a precise page grid is the use of the **width** attribute. The **width** attribute for the **<table>** element specifies the width of a table in pixels, or as a percentage value such as 80 percent. It also is possible to set the individual pixel widths of each cell within the table, using a **width** attribute for the **<td>** or **<th>** element. Imagine trying to create a 400-pixel column of text down the page with a buffer of 50 pixels on the left and 100 pixels on the right. With older HTML, this would be literally impossible without making the text a giant image. With a table, it is easy, as shown by the markup code here:

```
<!DOCTYPE HTML PUBLIC "-//W3C//DTD HTML 4.01 Transitional//EN">
<html>
<head>
<title>Table Layout</title>
</head>
<body>
  <table border="0">
   <tr>
      <td width="50"> </td>
      <td width="400">
       <h1 align="center">Layout is here!</h1>
          <hr>
    <p>This is a very simple layout that would
      have been nearly impossible to do without tables.</p>
      </td>
      <td width="100"> </td>
   </tr>
  </table>
</body>
</html>
```

In the preceding code, the **border** value is set to zero. This attribute isn't necessary; if the browser does not see a **border** attribute in the **<table>** element, it won't draw a border. It is better practice to keep the attribute in, but set to zero so the border can be turned on and off to check to see what is going on with a particular layout. When creating empty table cells, it is a good idea to put a nonbreaking space (** **) into the cell so it doesn't collapse vertically.

Tables also can be used to provide more precise layout in relation to a background. One popular design concept employs a vertical strip of colored background on the left of the page, which contains navigation controls; the rest of the document contains the main text. Without tables, it is difficult to keep body content flowing over the background image. An example of the HTML markup code to create a two-column design that works on top of a 100-pixel–wide color background is shown here:

```
<!DOCTYPE HTML PUBLIC "-//W3C//DTD HTML 4.01 Transitional//EN">
<html>
<head>
<title>Table Layout with Background</title>
</head>

<body background="yellowtile.gif">

<table width="550">
  <tr>
    <td width="100">
<a href="about.htm">About</a><br><br>
<a href="products.htm">Products</a><br><br>
<a href="staff.htm">Staff</a><br><br>
<a href="contact.htm">Contact</a><br><br>
    </td>
    <td width="450">
  <h1 align="center">Welcome to Demo Company, Inc.</h1>
  <hr>
<p>This text is positioned over a white background;
the navigation links are over a colored background.
This layout combines a table with a background images.
</p>
    </td>
  </tr>
</table>
</body>
</html>
```

The rendering of this layout appears in Figure 7-3. Note how the foreground content (the <body> content) is aligned over the **background** image. Another way to achieve such effects is to set the **bgcolor** attribute for the table cells. **bgcolor** was introduced in Netscape Navigator 3 and also is supported in Internet Explorer. Background shading also can be controlled using style sheets, as discussed in Chapter 10. Although such techniques would appear to help get rid of the headaches of aligning foreground and background elements, there is an issue of backward compatibility.

In HTML documents, tables have many nontraditional uses for graphic design and layout. These extend beyond creating grids; even single-cell tables can be put to many uses. As a simple example, consider using a table to define a pastel-colored "sticky" note. These can be inserted throughout HTML documents to draw attention to important ideas. An example HTML fragment to insert a single-cell, colored table is shown here:

```
<table align="left" bgcolor="#ffffcc" cellpadding="20" hspace="15"
    vspace="15">
<tr>
   <td>This is an important point!</td>
</tr>
</table>
```

Notice that this example contains only a single data item—certainly unusual for a conventional table. It also demonstrates two more **<table>** attributes. The **bgcolor** attribute sets the background color for a table using either a standard color name or hexadecimal RGB value. The given value indicates a light pastel yellow. The **cellpadding** attribute sets the distance in pixels between a table cell's outer border and the point at which content begins. Aside from "sticky" notes and other forms of colored tables to draw out information, there are various uses for single-cell tables. When combined with width, this might just be a good way to constrain the text within a page.

Figure 7-3.   *Rendering of foreground/background layout*

Background Colors

As already mentioned in this chapter, table elements also can be assigned background colors using the **bgcolor** attribute. The **bgcolor** attribute is valid for **<table>**, **<tr>**, **<th>**, and **<td>**.

```
<table border="1" cellspacing="0" cellpadding="8" bgcolor="green">
<tr>
<th bgcolor="lightblue">a</th>
<th bgcolor="lightblue">a</th>
<th bgcolor="lightblue">a</th>
</tr>

<tr bgcolor="orange">
<td>b</td>
<td>b</td>
<td>b</td>
</tr>

<tr>
<td bgcolor="red">c</td>
<td bgcolor="white">c</td>
<td bgcolor="blue">c</td>
</tr>

<tr>
<td> </td>
<td> </td>
<td> </td>
</tr>
</table>
```

In this code, the header cells (**th**) in the first row will have a light blue background; all three cells (**td**) in the second row will have an orange background as defined for the entire row (**tr**). The three cells in the third row will have different background colors as defined by the **bgcolor** attribute for each **<td>** tag. The cells in the last row, which have no background color defined for themselves or their row, will default to the green background color defined in the **<table>** tag, as shown in Figure 7-4.

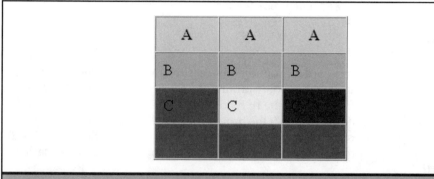

Figure 7-4. *bgcolor applied to different table elements*

Note that the **cellspacing** attribute for **<table>**, which sets how many pixels of space are included between table cells, is set to zero; if it is set to a higher value, the background color will display in the areas between cells in Internet Explorer and Opera browsers.

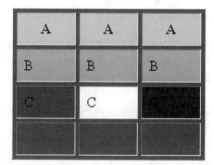

Don't forget that if the **cellspacing** attribute is not included, most browsers will render the table with several pixels of cell spacing by default. Be sure to set it to "0" to prevent inadvertent display of spacing.

Some grouping elements associated with tables such as **<thead>** and **<tfoot>**, as defined in the HTML 4.0 spec, also accept **bgcolor**, but so far only IE 4 and higher support this use of the attribute.

Border Colors

Additional proprietary attributes also have been defined for table elements. Internet Explorer 4 and higher defines a **bordercolor** attribute for **table**. Under IE 4 and higher, the following code

```
<table bordercolor="#ff0000" border="1">
<tr><td>. . . content . . .</td></tr>
</table>
```

will render a table with a red border around all the entire table and its cells. Netscape 4 and higher might render a red outline only around the four outer sides of the table, but the effect is completely different from the IE rendering. Under Netscape, if the border is set to a higher pixel value such as "5", the browser also will render a shading effect. Under IE 4 and up, **bordercolor** also can be applied to rows (**tr**), headers (**th**), and cells (**td**).

IE 4 and higher also provide two more border color attributes: **bordercolordark** and **bordercolorlight**.

```
<table bordercolorlight="#ff0000" bordercolordark="#0000ff"
       border="4">
<tr><td>...content...</td></tr>
</table>
```

Under IE 4 and higher, this will render a two-tone outer border for the table in which the top and left outer borders are blue, and the lower and right outer borders are red. It will have no effect in Netscape. Experiment with the elements and attributes under different browsers to understand and control display variations between browsers.

Browser variations can cause quite a bit of frustration when it comes to table borders, but there's a simple workaround using nested tables that can be used to create a crossbrowser version of the Microsoft approach.

```
<table cellspacing="0" cellpadding="0" border="0" width="200">
<tr>
<td bgcolor="#000000">
<!-- begin nested table -->

<table cellspacing="1" cellpadding="3" border="0" width="200">
<tr>
    <td bgcolor="#FFFFFF" width="100">Cell 1</td>
    <td bgcolor="#FFFFFF" width="100">Cell 2</td>
</tr>

<tr>
    <td bgcolor="#FFFFFF" width="100">Cell 3</td>
    <td bgcolor="#FFFFFF" width="100">Cell 4</td>
</tr>
</table>
```

```
<!-- end nested table -->
</td></tr></table>
```

The outer table employs a single table cell with its **bgcolor** set to black. The cells in the nested table have their **bgcolor** set to white. The **cellspacing** for the nested table is set to 1, allowing the black background of the outer table to show through in the spaces between the cells:

Cell 1	Cell 2
Cell 3	Cell 4

This will work for Netscape browsers as far back as Netscape 3. Still, some care must be taken in using this approach. The two tables must be the same width, or the border effect could be uneven.

Background Images in Tables

Using the **background** attribute developed by Microsoft, it is also possible to apply background images to tables and table elements. Defining a table with the code

```
<table width="220" border="1" cellpadding="0" cellspacing="0"
       background="smalltabletile.gif">
.... other table elements...
</table>
```

would place a repeating background tile behind the table, as shown here:

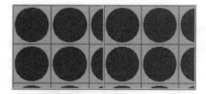

Internet Explorer   **Netscape**

The table on the left, displayed in Internet Explorer, renders the tile in a repeating background behind the entire table. The table on the right, displayed in Netscape, applies the background to each separate table cell. This is a radical cross-browser split that makes this approach impractical.

The same attribute can be applied to table rows (**<tr>**), but this will not display in Internet Explorer; and Netscape, as earlier, applies the tile to each cell in the row, not the row as a whole.

The only practical way to use backgrounds with tables is with table cells, as in this code:

```
<table width="220" border="1" cellpadding="0" cellspacing="0">
<tr>
<td width="110" background="bigtabletile.gif"> <td>
<td width="110" background="smalltabletile.gif"> </td>
</tr>
</table>
```

As you can see here,

this doesn't look too great. Using the **height** attribute in the table cell with the large title, and adjusting the **width** attribute, to make the cell match the dimensions of the tile like this:

```
<table width="220" border="0" cellpadding="0" cellspacing="0">
<tr>
<td background="bigtabletile.gif" height="100" width="100"
align="center"><b>hello!</b></td>
<td width="120" background="smalltabletile.gif"> </td>
</tr>
</table>
```

will produce the following renderings in Internet Explorer 5 and Netscape 4, whereas older browsers such as Netscape 3 will not support the background image at all.

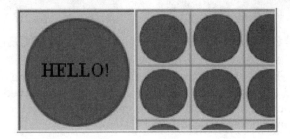

Although this can be used for some nice effects, it is somewhat unwieldy, particularly if the user has the font settings set high.

Advanced Layout Using Tables

Creating more sophisticated layouts with tables can be relatively simple. The following code example shows how a table can be used to create a two-column layout with text and an image. Text in the code example has been truncated to preserve space. The **colspan** attribute is used to create table cells (**<td>**) that contain headlines and subheaders that run across the width of the entire table. The **cellpadding** attribute for **<table>** is set to **10** to prevent the text in the columns from running too close together. The rendering of this code is shown in Figure 7-5.

```
<!DOCTYPE HTML PUBLIC "-//W3C//DTD HTML 4.01 Transitional//EN">
<html>
<head>
<title>2-Column Document Layout with Table</title>
</head>
<body>

<table cellspacing="0" cellpadding="10" border="1" width="550">
<tr>
    <td colspan="2" align="center">
        <font face="arial black, helvetica, sans-serif" size="+2">
        FEZ: IMPERIAL JEWEL OF MOROCCO</font></td>
</tr>

<tr>
    <td width="50%" valign="middle">
        <font face="arial, helvetica, sans-serif" size="+1">
        <b>Beyond the Bou Jeloud Gate....</b></font></td>
    <td width="50%" align="center">
  <img src="boujeloud002.jpg" width="240" height="185" border="0">
    </td>
</tr>
```

```
<tr>
    <td colspan="2" align="center">
    <font face="Arial, Helvetica, Sans-serif">
    <b><i>Luckily, a major UNESCO restoration project is
          now underway...</i></b></font></td>
</tr>

<tr>
    <td width="50%" valign="top">Part of the problem....</td>
    <td width="50%" valign="top">Major landmarks....</td>
</tr>
</table>

</body>
</html>
```

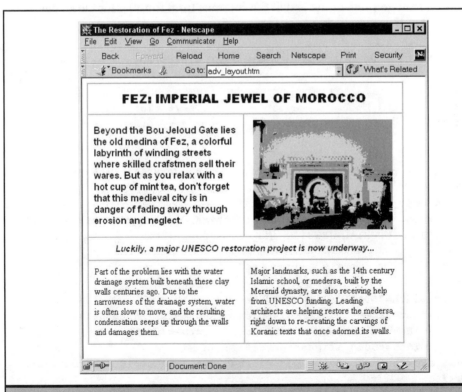

Figure 7-5. *Rendering of a two-column document layout*

It also is possible to apply tables to layout in a more complicated fashion. Layouts combining text and images can be created using large graphics that incorporate text, but this approach produces pages that are slow to download. The code example that follows shows a more complicated layout that breaks up an image and reassembles it like a jigsaw puzzle, using a table as an invisible "frame" to hold it in place. Note that anchors have not been applied to the graphic links in this code (widgets.gif, etc.) to simplify the code example.

```html
<!DOCTYPE HTML PUBLIC "-//W3C//DTD HTML 4.01 Transitional//EN">
<html>
<head>
<title>Demo Company - Early Home Page Concept</title>
</head>
<body>

<table border="0" cellpadding="0" cellspacing="0" width="570">
<tr>
<td>
<img src="roof.gif" border="0" height="45" width="124">
</td>

<td colspan="4">
<img src="logo.gif" border="0" height="45" width="446">
</td>
</tr>

<tr>
<td valign="top" rowspan="7" width="124">
<img src="building.gif" border="0" height="248" width="124">
</td>

<td rowspan="7" valign="top" width="185">
<img src="headline.gif" border="0" height="45" width="185">
And now, thanks to our merger with Massive Industries, we are now
the world's largest manufacturer of Gadgets&#153; and other
useless products.
<br><br>
To learn more about our products or our growing monopoly,
click on any of the links to the right.</td>

<td rowspan="3" width="68" valign="top">
<img src="curve.gif" border="0" height="108" width="68">
```

```
</td>

<td colspan="2" width="193" valign="top">
<img src="blank.gif" border="0" height="35" width="193">
</td>
</tr>

<tr>
<td colspan="2" width="193" valign="top">
<img src="widgets.gif" border="0" height="35" width="193">
</td>
</tr>

<tr>
<td colspan="2" width="193" valign="top">
<img src="gadgets.gif" border="0" height="38" width="193">
</td>
</tr>

<tr>
<td colspan="2" rowspan="4" width="136" valign="top">
<img src="gear.gif" border="0" height="140" width="136">
</td>

<td valign="top" width="125">
<img src="sales.gif" border="0" height="29" width="125">
</td>
</tr>

<tr>
<td valign="top" width="125">
<img src="about.gif" border="0" height="36" width="125">
</td>
</tr>

<tr>
<td valign="top" width="125">
<img src="history.gif" border="0" height="35" width="125">
</td>
```

```
</tr>

<tr>
<td valign="top" width="125">
<img src="map.gif" border="0" height="40" width="125">
</td>
</tr>

<tr>
<td colspan="2" width="309"> </td>
<td width="68"> </td>
<td width="68"> </td>

<td valign="top" width="125">
<img src="lowcurve.gif" border="0" height="31" width="125">
</td>
</tr>
</table>

</body>
</html>
```

When creating a layout like this, it is very important to set the **cellpadding** and **cellspacing** attributes to **0**. Table cell widths should correspond to the width of the image inside the cell, and the width of the table should be the sum of the cells in a table row. It also is important to include the **height** and **width** attributes of the images used. Figure 7-6 shows a browser rendering of this layout, with an overlay to show where the image is broken up.

While the images in the preceding example are all GIFs, JPEGs could also be used. "Photographic" areas of an image should be saved as JPEGs while areas with limited color, such as simple text, should be saved as GIFs. By saving each area in the appropriate format, it is possible to reduce the overall file size and optimize performance. (This is discussed in more detail in Chapter 5.)

Getting too Complicated with Table Layouts

Macromedia's Fireworks program allows designers to create a single image layout design beginning with a file such as a Photoshop (.psd) document, and then "slice" up the image to create an HTML layout using a table and pieces of the image converted into GIF and/or JPEG files, as appropriate. (For more information, visit www.macromedia.com/software/fireworks/.) This program also will create "shim" images to maintain cell widths and heights throughout the table. Although this is a

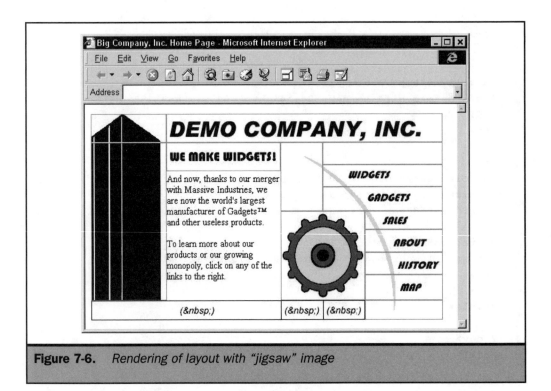

Figure 7-6. Rendering of layout with "jigsaw" image

very convenient tool, it often produces overly complicated tables, laden with wildly varying **colspan** and **rowspan** attributes, as suggested by the following grid:

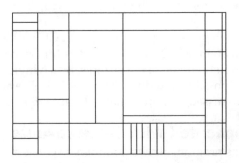

Some designers also might generate similar table layouts on their own. Whether using a tool such as Fireworks or building such layouts by hand, it is useful to step back and consider a simpler approach. Consider a basic layout like this:

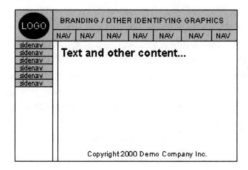

Although it certainly would be possible to create a single table to hold all of the graphic and text elements of this design, it might be simpler to think of the layout as a layer cake, as shown here:

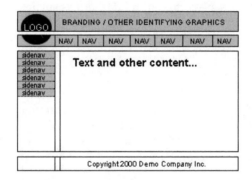

The row featuring the navigation buttons could be one table, and the part of the layout featuring the side navigation could be another one. Whereas the copyright information at the bottom could be included in a cell with the **colspan** attribute, it too could be split off into its own table, simply for the logical reason of keeping different parts of the page separate. As long as the tables are all the same width, each has column widths that add up properly to the overall table width and do not have **
** tags or any other elements between them, they should stack up perfectly.

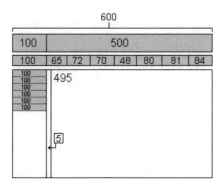

Keeping Table Code Organized with Comments

Even if you keep your table layouts relatively simple according to your own lights, if you're working in a professional setting odds are good that someone else will have to alter or update your code at some point. You might even have to come back to work on your own code at a later date, only to realize that you can't recall half of what you did the first time around! It is good coding practice to comment your code—*any* HTML code—but it is especially useful when working with table layouts. At the very least, it is handy to indicate the beginning and end of any table.

```
<!-- begin top nav table -->
   ... table elements ...
<!-- end top nav table -->
```

If you are nesting tables, be certain to mark them as such.

```
<!-- begin nested table 1 -->
   ... table elements ...
<!-- end nested table 1 -->
```

This can be applied to any extent you desire, from comments noting the start of new table rows to even commenting the purpose of a table cell. As long as your comments are meaningful, it won't hurt to add a few kilobytes to your document size in the interests of good markup practice.

Table Tips

Here a few useful rules of thumb to use when creating layouts with tables.

- Always use these three basic attributes with the **<table>** element: **border**, **cellpadding** and **cellspacing**. Even if you don't want any of these things, set them to zero; **border** is useful for checking your work, and browsers generally throw in a little bit of unwanted **cellpadding** and **cellspacing** if those attributes are not present.

- Always use the closing tags for every element; this will prevent browser display problems and maintain XHTML compatibility as well.

- Make certain that column widths, as defined by **<th>** or **<td>** cells, add up to the overall defined width of the table. Faulty addition has ruined more than a few seemingly perfect tables.

- Don't forget that use of the **colspan** or **rowspan** attributes in one row will require the removal of some table cells in other rows in the table.

- Crossbrowser support of the background attribute is inconsistent with most table elements; it can be used safely enough with the **<td>** element but should *not* be used with **<table>** or **<tr>**.

- Certain Microsoft-created attributes, such as **bordercolor**, **bordercolordark**, and **bordercolorlight**, are not suitable for cross-browser usage. Avoid them unless designing for an IE-only environment such as an intranet.

- Try to simplify layouts; Don't go crazy with excessive **rowspan** and **colspan** usage when you can stack tables much more simply. It might help to visualize the layout as a layer cake, with a separate table as each layer.

- Always comment your code so that it will make sense to you later.

Tables in HTML 4

So far, the discussion of tables has mentioned five elements: **<table>**, **<caption>**, **<tr>**, **<th>**, and **<td>**. These are the most commonly used elements. HTML 4 introduces several new elements that provide increased control over table formatting: **<col>**, **<colgroup>**, **<thead>**, **<tfoot>**, and **<tbody>**. An HTML table as defined by the HTML 4 specification has the following structure:

- An opening **<table>** element.

- An optional caption specified by **<caption>** . . . **</caption>**.

- One or more groups of rows. These might consist of a header section specified by **<thead>**, a footer section specified by **<tfoot>**, and a body section specified by **<tbody>**. Although all these elements are optional, the table must contain at least a series of rows specified by **<tr>**. The rows themselves must contain at least one header or data cell, specified by **<th>** and **<td>**, respectively.

- One or more groups of columns specified by **<colgroup>** with individual columns within the group indicated by **<col>**.

- A closing **</table>** element.

The main difference between HTML 4 tables and the more basic table form is that rows and columns can be grouped together. The advantage to grouping is that it conveys structural information about the table that might be useful for rendering the table more quickly or keeping it together when displaying on the screen. For example, specifying the **<thead>** or **<tfoot>** might allow a consistent header or footer to be used across larger tables when they span many screens (or sheets of paper when printed). The use of these elements is mandatory when working with dynamically populated tables that incorporate databinding as introduced by Microsoft and discussed later in this chapter.

The following example explains the use of the new HTML 4 table elements.

```
<!DOCTYPE HTML PUBLIC "-//W3C//DTD HTML 4.0 Transitional//EN">
<html>
<head>
<title>HTML 4.0 Tables</title>
</head>
<body>
<table border="1" frame="box" rules="groups">
<caption>Fun with Food</caption>
<colgroup>
    <col>
</colgroup>
<colgroup>
    <col align="center">
    <col align="char" char=".">
</colgroup>
<thead>
<tr>
    <th bgcolor="yellow">Fruit</th>
    <th bgcolor="yellow">Color</th>
    <th bgcolor="yellow">Cost per pound</th>
</tr>
</thead>
<tbody>
<tr>
    <td>Grapes</td>
    <td>Purple</td>
    <td>$1.45</td>
</tr>
<tr>
    <td>Cherries</td>
    <td>Red</td>
    <td>$1.99</td>
</tr>
<tr>
    <td>Kiwi</td>
    <td>Brown</td>
    <td>$11.50</td>
</tr>
</tbody>

<tfoot>
<tr>
    <th colspan="3">This has been another fine table example.</th>
```

```
</tr>
</tfoot>
</table>

</body>
</html>
```

The first thing to notice in this code is the use of the **frame** and **rules** attributes for the **<table>** element. the **frame** attribute specifies which sides of the frame that surrounds the table will be visible. In this example, the value is set to **box**, which means that the frame around the outside of the table is on. Other values for this attribute include **above**, **below**, **hsides**, **vsides**, **lhs**, **rhs**, **void**, and **border**. The meaning of all these values is discussed in the table syntax section of Appendix A.

Do not confuse the idea of the **frame** attribute with that of **rules**. The **rules** attribute defines the rules that might appear between the actual cells in the table. In the example, the value of **rules** is set to **groups**; this displays lines between the row or column groupings of the table. The **rules** attribute also takes a value of **none**, **groups**, **rows**, **cols**, and **all**.

The other major difference in the table shown above is the inclusion of the **<thead>** and **<tbody>** elements. **<thead>** contains the rows (**<tr>**), headings (**<th>**), and cells (**<td>**) that make up the head of the table. Beyond organization and the application of styles, the advantage of grouping these items is that it might be possible to repeat the elements over multiple pages (under certain browsers). Imagine printing out a large table and having the headers for the rows appear on every page of the printout. This is what **<thead>** might be able to provide. Similarly, the **<tfoot>** element creates a footer to use in the table, which also might run over multiple pages. Last, the **<tbody>** indicates the body of the table, which contains the rows and columns that make up the inner part of a table. Whereas there should be only one occurrence of **<thead>** and **<tfoot>**, there can be multiple occurrences of **<tbody>**. Multiple bodies in a document might seem confusing, but these elements are more for grouping purposes than anything else. When a table is specified without **<thead>**, **<tfoot>**, or **<tbody>**, it is assumed to have one body by default.

Notice that one of the **col** elements in the example uses the **char** value for **align** in conjunction with the **char** attribute:

```
<col align="char" char=".">
```

This is meant to make the contents of the cells in that column line up with a certain character, in this case a decimal point. The intended effect would be useful for aligning numbers with decimal points.

Fun with Food

Fruit	Color	Cost per pound
Grapes	Purple	$1.45
Cherries	Red	$1.99
Kiwi	Brown	$11.50
This has been another fine table example.		

Unfortunately, this does not seem to work in just any browser:

Fun with Food

Fruit	Color	Cost per pound
Grapes	Purple	$1.45
Cherries	Red	$1.99
Kiwi	Brown	$11.50
This has been another fine table example.		

Although tables are becoming more difficult to code, you can take heart from the variety of tools that can be used to create them. Most HTML editing tools can easily add the elements needed to make tables; Allaire's HomeSite and ColdFusion Studio have excellent table wizards, and DreamWeaver offers good WYSIWYG tools as well. This is good, because the combination of HTML 4's new table elements with various proprietary extensions introduced by Microsoft, Netscape, and WebTV results in a dizzying array of elements, and attributes for the individual table elements.

Microsoft Extensions

Microsoft has added a number of its own extensions to the table-related elements. Some of these, such as **background**, **bordercolor**, **bordercolordark** and **bordercolorlight**, have already been discussed in this chapter. Others not directly associated with table functions include **accesskey** and **tabindex**, applied to the various table elements by Internet Explorer 4 or 5; and **hidefocus**, applied to the table elements by Internet

Explorer 5.5. The **accesskey** attribute allows an accelerator key to be assigned to a table element, whereas **tabindex** allows a table element to be assigned a numerical position in a document's tabbing order. The **hidefocus** attribute allows the focus assigned by a **tabindex** value to be turned off. (For more information, see the appropriate element listings in Appendix A.)

Two more Microsoft extensions, **datapagesize** and **datasrc**, are not associated with design concerns or focus issues, but with databinding. Introduced with Internet Explorer 4, they are discussed in the following section.

Databinding: Tables Generated from a Data Source

Tables often contain row after row of identically formatted data that originates in a database. There are two basic methods to create these data-dependent tables. Neither one is ideal:

- If the table data is relatively static, it is common to build a long table by hand or with a tool, individually coding each data cell.

- If the table data is dynamic, it is common to generate the entire page containing the table using a server-side CGI (Common Gateway Interface) technology.

The first approach is difficult for an HTML author. The second, which does not really qualify as HTML authoring, usually requires programming. *Databinding* is a technology recently introduced by Microsoft to dynamically bind HTML elements to data coming from an external source. Although not technically restricted to HTML tables, it does represent a simpler, more powerful approach for generating large data-dependent tables.

In HTML databinding, a data source that provides information is associated with a data consumer that presents it. The data source is a control with some means to access external information that is embedded in an HTML document using the **<object>** element. This element is further explained in Chapter 15. For now, it will be useful to understand that **<object>** adds a small program to the page that can be used to access an external data source. The document also contains a data consumer, an HTML element that uses special attributes to ask the ActiveX control for data that the element subsequently displays. Data consumers come in two sorts: those that present single data values, and those that present tabular data. Tables fall into the latter category.

Creating an HTML table using databinding is a very simple process. It is necessary to define only one table row. The rest are generated automatically according to the template defined by the first row. Think of each row in a tabular data set as corresponding to a database record, and each column as corresponding to a database field. A template table row is defined in HTML that associates **<td>** or **<th>** elements with field names in the data set. A table will subsequently be generated with one row for each record in the data set, and with cell values filled in from the appropriate record fields. The data source control might support processing capabilities such as sorting or filtering the data set. If so, the table can be dynamically regenerated on the client side in response to updated information from the data source.

For example, a data source might contain a tabular data set for product price information. One field might contain the name of the product; another its price. By default, a table could present this information sorted alphabetically by product name. In response to a button on an HTML page, the data source could sort the data set by price. The table that displays the information would be dynamically regenerated.

Consider a simple databinding example. An external data file contains two or more columns of comma-delimited data. The first line contains the names of the data set fields corresponding to the columns. The following lines contain the actual data for the appropriate fields. A sample external data file called alphabet.txt is shown here.

```
Letter, Thing
A, Apple
B, Boy
C, Cat
D, Dog
E, Elephant
F, Fox
G, Girl
H, Hat
```

To access the data, an HTML document references an object for a data source control and a related table definition. An example of how this would be accomplished is shown here:

```
<!DOCTYPE HTML PUBLIC "-//W3C//DTD HTML 4.0 Transitional//EN">
<html>
<head>
<title>Data Binding Example</title>
</head>
<body>
```

```
<object id="alphabet"
classid="clsid:333C7BC4-460F-11D0-BC04-0080C7055A83">
    <param name="DataURL" value="alphabet.txt">
    <param name="UseHeader" value="True">
</object>

<table datasrc="#alphabet" border="1">
<thead>
    <tr bgcolor="yellow">
        <th>Letter</th>
        <th>Reminder</th>
    </tr></thead>
<tbody>
    <tr align="center">
        <td><span datafld="Letter"></span> </td>
        <td><span datafld="Thing"></span></td>
    </tr>
</tbody>
</table>
</body>
</html>
```

PRESENTATION AND LAYOUT

This HTML code generates a table from the file alphabet.txt in which each table row contains a letter of the alphabet and the name of a thing that can remind the reader of that letter. The rendering of this example under Internet Explorer 4 is shown in Figure 7-7.

Examine a little more closely the pieces needed to make this databinding example work. First, the data source. This example uses the Tabular Data Control (TDC) object: an ActiveX control provided by Microsoft and identified by the lengthy class identifier. This particular control locates and manipulates text data files in a tabular format. Other controls supporting databinding could have been used instead. These can support different data access capabilities such as access to remote relational databases. The Microsoft ActiveX Data Objects control (ADO), however, is a representative example. The TDC supports several parameters of which two are used in this example. The **"DataURL"** parameter tells the TDC the name and location of the data file it is to use. In this case, because only a filename is provided, the TDC looks in the same directory containing the Web page. By default, the TDC treats every line in a data file as data. The **"UseHeader"** parameter tells the TDC that the first line in the data file does not contain data but rather the names of data fields.

As a data consumer, the **<table>** element uses its **datasrc** attribute to connect to a data source. Note in the example how this attribute is set to the name of the **<object>** tag invoking the data source control. The name must be preceded by the # symbol. The

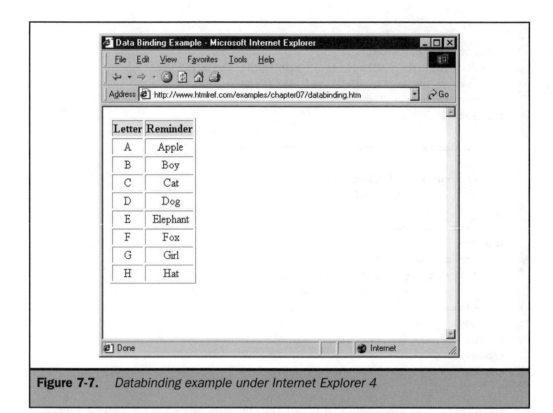

Figure 7-7. Databinding example under Internet Explorer 4

<object> element must declare a name using the **id** attribute in order to be accessed by a data consumer. In summary, the **datasrc** attribute identifies a data source to be used in generating a table.

The next step is to associate cells in the template table row with particular fields in the data set. This is done using the **datafld** attribute of appropriate elements. It contains the name of the field in the data set that its element is to be bound to. If data set–specific names are not defined, fields can be identified using default positional names: "Column1", "Column2", and so fourth. The **<td>** tag, commonly used for cell data, does not support the **datafld** attribute. To bind a field to a table cell, the **<td>** tag needs to contain one of the elements that do support **datafld**. The elements that make the most sense in the context of a table are **<span>**, **<div>**, **<object>**, and **<img>**. The latter two tags illustrate that databinding is not confined to textual data. For example, a column of images can be created by using a tag declaration such as **<img datafld="Picture">** inside a table cell. Note that the usual **src** attribute is not required. Instead, the **datafld** attribute identifies a field inside the data set that contains a valid image filename, such as mypict.gif, and binds the image to that value.

Microsoft provides one additional attribute, **datapagesize**, that can be used to limit the number of records displayed from the datasource document. For example, if the **<table>** element in the preceding example were revised to read

```
<table datasrc="#alphabet" border="1" datapagesize="3">
```

the rendering of the table will display only the first three rows (A, B, and C) of the information in alphabet.txt.

If a table does not explicitly declare header or footer section elements, implicitly all table content is in the body section. In static tables, this usually does not have visual consequences, but it does in tables generated by databinding. All body rows are included in the template for table row generation, not just the rows containing databound fields. To prevent header or footer information from being repeated for every row in the table, it is necessary to enclose it with the **<thead>** or **<tfoot>** element. The **<tbody>** element then can be used to signal the beginning of the template to be databound.

Such a brief example scratches the surface of databinding and merely shows the importance of tables in relation to dynamic data. For more information on databinding, visit Microsoft Web Workshop, at http://msdn.microsoft.com/workshop/, and the Remote Data Servicesite, at http://www.microsoft.com/data/ado/rds/.

Summary

The development of tables was the first step toward effective layout of HTML pages. Tables provide a useful structure in which to place text and images, but they likely will be superseded by positioning with style sheets (discussed in Chapter 10); however, that will have to wait until style sheets are more widely supported by browsers. At that time, tables will continue to be important for use with dynamic data, as discussed in the preceding section. Chapter 8 addresses two more options for page layout—frames and layers—and weighs the pros and cons of both.

PRESENTATION AND LAYOUT

The Complete Reference

Chapter 8

Frames

Tables and the other HTML techniques introduced in the previous chapters provide a significant improvement in Web page layout. Many designers want even more design facilities, including multiple windows. Such expectations aren't unreasonable because these features are common in design programs and computer interfaces. Such power comes at a price, however. Frames seem to provide significant layout flexibility, but when misused, they can confuse users—or even lock them out of a site completely.

Frames

A framed document divides a browser window into multiple panes, or smaller window frames. Each frame can contain a different document. The benefits of this approach are obvious; users can view information in one frame while keeping another frame open for reference instead of moving back and forth between pages. The contents of one frame can be manipulated, or *linked*, to the contents of another. This enables designers to build sophisticated interfaces. For example, one frame can contain links that produce a result in another frame. An example of such an interface is shown in Figure 8-1.

Frames offer many possibilities. They can contain tables of contents, site indexes, and lists of links. Frames offer *fixed-screen navigation*—whereby site navigation buttons stay on screen throughout a visit regardless of the size of the document. The lack of scrolling and the minimization of screen refresh afforded by framed documents can provide great advantages over the single-window approach. On the other hand, framed pages can be difficult to deal with. Frame sites confuse many users because it's not always clear what parts of a page will update when a button is pressed. Furthermore, frames tend to induce other usability problems, such as hiding the current URL, causing printing and bookmarking difficulty, excluding some search engines, and taking up valuable screen real estate with scrollbars and borders.

Regardless of these potential problems, many site designers rushed to develop framed pages as soon as frames were introduced. They removed them just as quickly, however, due to navigational problems and user complaints. Fortunately, today many of the problems associated with frames have been fixed at the browser level, and users have become more comfortable understanding and working with frames. Used properly and in the right situation, frames are important tools in the Web designer's toolbox. Frame-phobic Web designers should consider that frames are no longer considered proprietary browser extensions and are included in the HTML 4 standard.

Overview of Frames

A *frame* is an independent scrolling region, or window, of a Web page. Every Web page can be divided into many individual frames, which can even be nested within other frames. Of course, fixed screen sizes limit how many frames can realistically be used

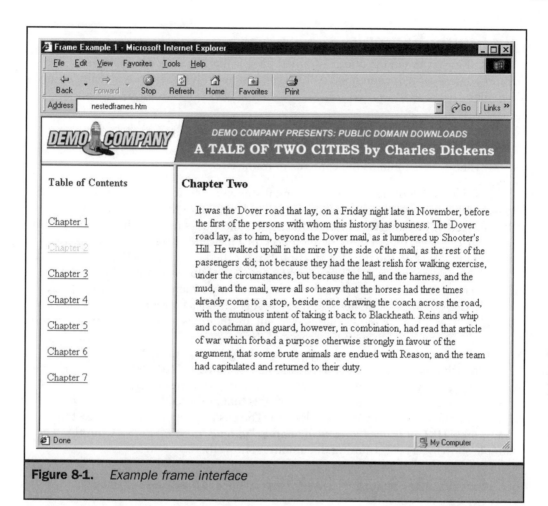

Figure 8-1. *Example frame interface*

simultaneously. Each frame in a window can be separated from the others with a border; in this way, a framed document might resemble a table. However, frames are not a fancy form of tables. Each separate frame might contain a different document, referenced by a unique URL. Because the documents included in a framed region might be much larger than the space available onscreen, each frame might provide a scrollbar or other controls to manipulate the size of the frame. Individual frames usually are named, so that they can be referenced through links or scripting, allowing the contents of one frame to affect the contents of another. This referencing capability is a major difference between tables and frames. Frames provide layout facilities and, potentially, navigation.

Simple Frame Example

The first thing to remember about a framed page is that the screen actually is composed of several documents. To illustrate, a page with two frames actually involves three files:

- The framing document that defines the framing relationship
- The file that contains the contents of frame one
- The file that contains the contents of frame two

Consider the simple two-frame document shown in Figure 8-2. The first frame, on the left, covers about 20 percent of the screen and contains a link contained in a file called links.htm. The larger column on the right, which takes up the other 80 percent of the screen, displays content initially referenced in a file called display.htm. The actual document that sets up the framing relationship is called basicframes.htm.

The framing document (basicframes.htm) has a structure slightly different from a typical HTML file. Specifically, it uses the **<frameset>** element instead of the **<body>** element. The **<frameset>** element defines the set of frames that makes up the document. The major attributes of this element are the **rows** and **cols** attributes. In this case, two columns take up set percentages of the total screen, so the code reads **<frameset cols="20%, 80%">**. Setting up something like **<frameset rows="10%, 80%, 10%">**, which sets up three rows across the screen taking up 10%, 80%, and 10% of the screen respectively, would be just as easy. Within the **<frameset>** element individual **<frame>** tags are used to specify the documents that are placed within the rows or columns defined by the **<frameset>** element. The basic syntax of the **<frame>** tag is **<frame src="*URL of framed document*" name="*unique frame name*">**. A simple example showing a basic framing document is shown here:

```
<!DOCTYPE HTML PUBLIC "-//W3C//DTD HTML 4.01 Frameset//EN">
<html>
<head>
<title>Frame Example 1</title>
</head>
<frameset cols="20%, 80%">
<frame src="links.htm" name="links">
<frame src="display.htm" name="display">
<noframes>
    <body>
    <p>This document uses frames.
     Please follow this link to a
    <a href="noframes.htm">no frames</a>
     version.</p>
```

```
    </body>
</noframes>
</frameset>
</html>
```

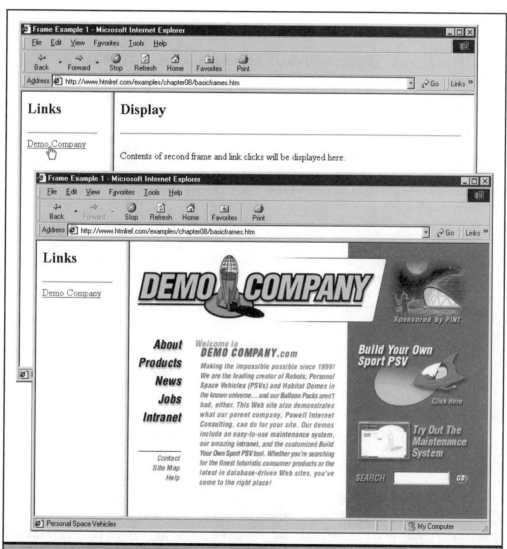

Figure 8-2.   *Simple two-frame example in Internet Explorer*

In the preceding example, the file links.htm would be placed in the frame column comprising 20 percent of the screen, and the file display.htm would be placed in the 80 percent column. Always make sure to consider the order of the **<frame>** elements, as their positions should be relative to the rows or columns defined in the **<frameset>** element. Once the framing document is set up, you then have to populate the individual frames using the **<frame>** elements. The **src** attribute is set to the URL of the document to load in the particular frame. For a complete example, the contents of links.htm and display.htm are presented here:

File: links.htm

```
<!DOCTYPE HTML PUBLIC "-//W3C//DTD HTML 4.01 Transitional//EN">
<html>
<head>
<title>Links</title>
</head>
<body>
<h2>Links</h2>
<hr>
<a href="http://www.democompany.com" target="display">Demo
Company</a>
</body>
</html>
```

File: display.htm

```
<!DOCTYPE HTML PUBLIC "-//W3C//DTD HTML 4.01 Transitional//EN">
<html>
<head>
<title>Display</title>
</head>
<body>
<h2>Display</h2>
<hr>
<p>Contents of second frame and link clicks will be displayed
here.</p>
</body>
</html>
```

Putting all three files in the same directory and loading the framed document (basicframes.htm) into a browser should produce a rendering similar to the one shown in Figure 8-2. (Online, see http://www.htmlref.com/examples/chapter08/basicframes.htm.)

The Use of <noframes>

The **<noframes>** element used in the previous example should contain the HTML and text to be displayed when a browser that doesn't support frames accesses the Web page. The **<noframes>** element should be found only within the **<frameset>** element. Nevertheless, **<noframes>** is often found directly outside the **<frameset>** element. Because of the permissive nature of browsers, this tends to be interpreted correctly. Also, for XHTML compliance the **<noframes>** element should contain a **<body>** element and a correctly formed HTML document within in it; HTML 4 does not require a body tag within **<noframes>**.

The following example provides the links that occur in the Controls frame for browsers that don't support frames:

```
<!DOCTYPE HTML PUBLIC "-//W3C//DTD HTML 4.01 Transitional//EN">
<html>
<head>
<title>Simple Noframes Example</title>
</head>
<frameset cols="20%,80%">
<frame src="links.htm" name="controls">
<frame src="display.htm" name="display">
<noframes>
<body>
<h2>No Frame Navigation</h2>
<hr>
<a href="http://www.yahoo.com">Yahoo</a>
<br>
<a href="http://www.microsoft.com">Microsoft</a>
<br>
<a href="http://www.netscape.com">Netscape</a>
</body>
</noframes>
</frameset>
</html>
```

Most browsers should support frames today. Of course, legacy browsers such as Netscape 1.x generation browsers will not render frames, as shown in Figure 8-3.

Although supporting relatively rare situations of legacy browser use seems more and more pointless, some restricted browsers such as PDA-based browsers or digital cell phone browsers also have problems with frames; so do many search engine indexing spiders. Because of this, **<noframes>** should be used. Whereas the approach of putting a second copy of site content within **<noframes>** makes the site usable across browsers, it results in having to update two copies of the same content. Because

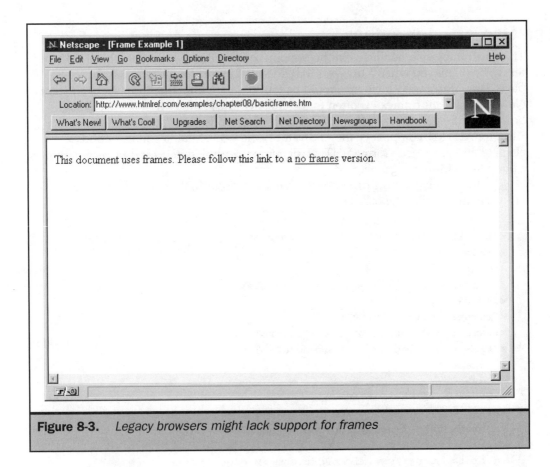

Figure 8-3.   *Legacy browsers might lack support for frames*

of this, many designers simply put a statement in the **<noframes>** element that indicates that the site requires a frame-supporting browser for viewing. This doesn't make the site very accessible, but it does cut down on content duplication.

Frame Targeting

When using frames, you often might find that making the links in one frame target another frame is beneficial. This way, when a user clicks a button or activates a link in one framed document, the requested page loads in another frame. In the simple frame example in the preceding section, you might want have the links in the frame named "controls" target the frame named "display." Link targeting has two steps:

    1. Ensure frame naming by setting the **name** attribute in the **<frame>** element to a unique name.

2. Use the **target** attribute in the **<a>** element to set the target for the anchor. For example, a link such as **<a href="http://www.yahoo.com" target="display">** loads the site specified by the **href** into the window called display, if such a frame exists. If the target specified by the name doesn't exist, the link loads over the window it is in.

You can name your frames anything you like. A simple short word without special characters is the best approach such as "window1", "frame3", "displayregion" or similar value. The specification also encourages the use of the **id** attribute for naming frames; however, practice shows that frame targeting in browsers is still generally accomplished using the **name** attribute and not the **id** attribute, which is used mostly for scripting and style sheet access in modern browsers. For the sake of safety, designers should consider setting both **id** and **name** in a **<frame>** element to the same value. Designers also should be wary of using special characters or spaces in the frame name, as they might cause problems. Some values for the **target** attribute might also have special meanings, and should never be used as a frame name. These values and their meanings are summarized in Table 8-1.

Setting the **target** attribute of the links within a site to **_top** ensures that any frames being used are removed after a link is followed. Regardless of your use of frames, using the **_top** value for the **target** attribute in links in your site might be beneficial. Sites might often frame external links in an attempt to "capture" the user. Because this might limit layout or be undesirable in other ways, site designers often use scripts or simply set target attributes on all site links to **_top** to break out of any enclosing frames.

The **_blank** value for **target** also is useful because it opens another window in which to display the link. The only problem with this action is that the window might tile directly on top of the previous browser window, and the user might not know that multiple windows are open. Using JavaScript, as discussed in Chapter 13, it is possible to size windows that are opened.

The **_parent** value isn't encountered often because it is useful only when frames are nested to a great degree. The **_parent** value enables you to overwrite the parent frame that contains the nested frame without destroying any frames that the parent might be nested within.

Value	Meaning
_blank	Load the page into a new, generally unnamed, window.
_self	Load the page over the current frame.
_parent	Load the link over the parent frame.
_top	Load the link over all the frames in the window.

Table 8-1. *Reserved target Values*

The _self value for **target**, which loads a page over its current frame, duplicates the typical default action for most browsers.

    According to the HTML 4.01 specification, frame names beginning with an underscore are discouraged, because they might be reserved for values such as _top.

The following is an alternative for the file links.htm. This HTML document uses frame targeting with the names defined in the previous simple frame example. Use it in place of the previous links.htm file and load the frameset file to test the target attribute for **<a>** tag. (Online, see http://www.htmlref.com/examples/chapter08/frametargetting.htm, which references this code in the file linktargets.htm.)

```
<!DOCTYPE HTML PUBLIC "-//W3C//DTD HTML 4.01 Transitional//EN">
<head>
<title>Link Targeting</title>
</head>
<body>
<h2 align="center">Test Links</h2>
<hr>
<ul>
<li><a href="http://www.yahoo.com" target="display">
   Yahoo in frame named display</a>
<li><a href="http://www.hotbot.com" target="_blank">
   HotBot in new window</a>
<li><a href="http://www.infoseek.com" target="_self">
   Infoseek in this frame</a>
<li><a href="http://www.excite.com" target="_top">
   Excite over whole window</a>
<li><a href="http://www.google.com" target="_parent">
   Google over the parent window (should be whole window)</a>
<li><a href="http://www.democompany.com" target="mysterywindow">
   Demo Company in a window that hasn't been named</a>
</ul>
</body>
</html>
```

As shown in the example, when referencing a nonexistent window such as "mysterywindow" the browser generally will just create a brand-new window.

As long as names are kept consistent and frame layouts relatively basic, using window targeting is fairly straightforward. However, sloppy coding can lead to a problem where frames keep nesting inside of one another as shown in Figure 8-4; authors are warned to test links in a framed site thoroughly.

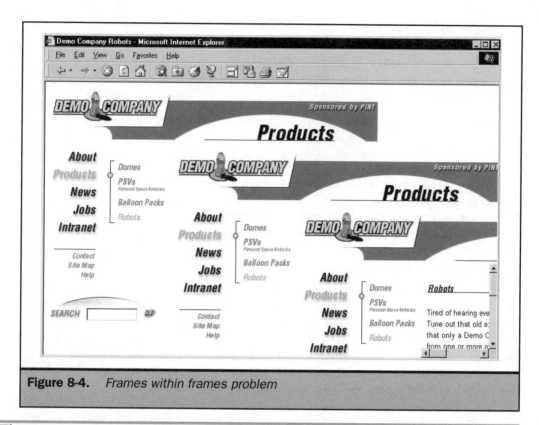

Figure 8-4. *Frames within frames problem*

Frame Layouts

Frames can be used to structure a page in a variety of ways. First consider that it is possible to use not only percentage values for frame sizing, but pixels and wildcard values. The **rows** and **cols** attributes also can be set to pixel values, so that **<frameset cols="200,400">** defines a column 200 pixels wide, followed by a column 400 pixels wide. Of course if the screen is smaller than 600 pixels, this might lead to the contents being clipped, or excessive scrolling being required. If the screen is much larger, there might be a great deal of empty screen space. Because determining the exact size of the screen is difficult, setting these attributes to exact values might be dangerous.

In general, you want to combine absolute pixel sizes with some more flexible measurements such as percentages or wildcards. If you know that the controls frame contains graphic buttons that are 150 pixels wide, consider setting the size of the first frame to 175 pixels to fit the graphic plus some white space. If the frame were any smaller than this size, the graphic would be clipped, so using an absolute pixel value makes sense when you know the size of the contents. But what should the size of the other frame be? To simply take up the rest of the screen with whatever is left over after 175 pixels, use the wildcard character (*) to specify use of the rest of the screen. The code for such a frame set is **<frameset cols="175,*">**. A common design beyond the two-column frame is a three-row, header-footer frameset.

```
<frameset rows="100, *, 50">
<frame src="header.htm" name="header">
<frame src="display.htm" name="display">
<frame src="footer.htm" name="footer">
</frameset>
```

Beyond these simple layouts it is possible to nest framesets together to create complex layouts. Consider the example here:

```
<frameset cols="200, *">
<frame src="links.htm" name="controls">
<frameset rows="100, *">
  <frame src="header.htm" name="header">
  <frame src="display.htm" name="display">
</frameset>
</frameset>
```

This produces a three-frame design with the second column being composed of two rows. An example rendering of such a frame layout is shown in Figure 8-5. (Online, see http://www.htmlref.com/examples/chapter08/nestedframes.htm.)

This sort of layout also can be accomplished by using the **<frame>** elements to reference documents containing additional **<frameset>** elements, although if carried too far this can lead to overly complicated page renderings. Even more complex designs, such as a fixed framed region in the middle of the screen, are possible with nesting. Consider the markup presented here, which could produce a result similar to the one shown in Figure 8-6; it also can be viewed online at http://www.htmlref.com/examples/chapter08/fixedframes.htm.

```
<!DOCTYPE HTML PUBLIC "-//W3C//DTD HTML 4.01 Frameset//EN">
<html>
<head>
<title>Frame Example 3</title>
</head>
<frameset rows="100, *, 100">
<frame src="blue.htm" name="top">
<frameset cols="100,*,100">
<frame src="blue.htm" name="left">
<frame src="center.htm" name="center">
<frame src="blue.htm" name="right">
</frameset>
<frame src="blue.htm" name="bottom">
</frameset>
</html>
```

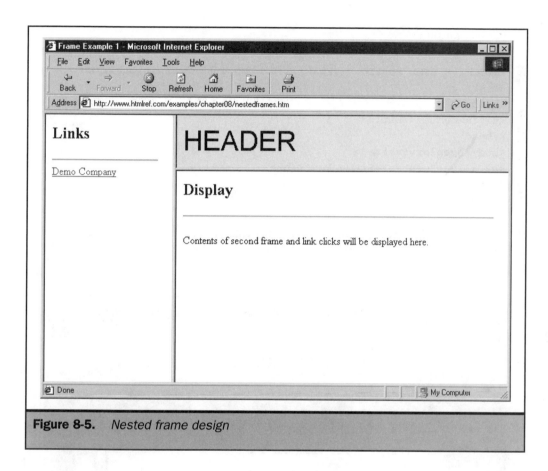

Figure 8-5.   *Nested frame design*

PRESENTATION AND LAYOUT

The corresponding files blue.htm and center.htm are shown here for completeness:
File: blue.htm

```
<!DOCTYPE HTML PUBLIC "-//W3C//DTD HTML 4.01 Transitional//EN">
<html>
<head>
<title>Blue</title>
</head>
<body bgcolor="blue">
<!-- just a blank document -->
</body>
</html>
```

File: center.htm

```
<!DOCTYPE HTML PUBLIC "-//W3C//DTD HTML 4.01 Transitional//EN">
<html>
<head>
<title>Center</title>
</head>
<body bgcolor="white">
<h2 align="center">Frame Fun!</h2>
</body>
</html>
```

The main challenge with complex frame designs such as the previous one is making sure to account for various rendering problems across browsers, such as dealing with scrolling.

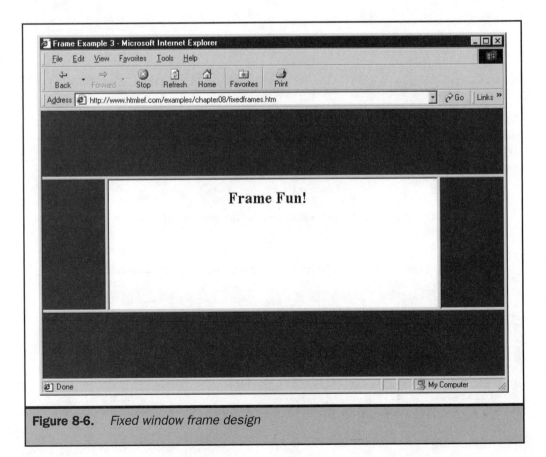

Figure 8-6.   *Fixed window frame design*

First consider removing the frame borders. According to the HTML 4.01 specification, this is best accomplished by setting each individual frame's border using the frameborder attribute. The default value of 1 indicates a frame border should be used while a value of 0 indicates to remove it. So **<frame src="links.htm" name="controls" frameborder="0">** would turn off borders for this particular frame. The problem with the border syntax is that it is not always supported properly, particularly under older browsers such as Netscape 2. Also, most browsers support the frameborder attribute for the **<frameset>** element that should affect all enclosed frames. Of course this isn't part of the specification but is widely supported. Even when you are successful in removing frame borders in all situations you still might have unsightly gaps between frames. Internet Explorer has added a proprietary attribute framespacing to the **<frameset>** element to alleviate this. Just set it to 0 and any gaps should be removed under this browser. The reality of the border settings is that you probably will have to overload the attributes and provide multiple ways of indicating that you do not want them on if you want to cover all browser situations.

If borders are left on you might desire to turn off scrolling or even to indicate that the frame should not be resized. To set scrolling on a frame, use the scrolling attribute; by default the value of this attribute is "Auto," which adds scrollbars as needed. However, setting the value to yes or no will explicitly indicate the presence or lack of scrollbars regardless of the content within the frame. The presence of the noresize attribute indicates that the user cannot resize a frame. The example here shows a frame with scrolling off and no resizing.

```
<frame src="test.htm" name="frame1" border="0" noresize
scrolling="no">
```

Note   *For eventual XHTML compliance, you would have to indicate to close the empty frame element and make special considerations for the value lacking the attribute noresize like so: <frame src="test.htm" name="frame1" id="frame1" border="0" noresize="noresize" scrolling="yes" />*

Always remember that turning off resizing or limiting scrolling could lead to trouble if the user doesn't have a screen that fits the framed content!

The last common attributes to consider for frame layouts are marginheight and marginwidth. Like their use on the **<body>** element under Netscape these attributes are used to control the distance between the frame and its contents. Very often designers will set these values to 0 to achieve the effect of bleeding framed content right to the edge of the frame.

```
<frame src="blue.htm" name="right" marginwidth="0"
marginheight="0">
```

The **<frame>** and **<frameset>** elements take a few other attributes beyond the ones previously discussed and the core attributes **id, class, style,** and **title.** Many browsers—notably Internet Explorer—provide numerous proprietary extensions including the use of transparency and color settings for borders. Interested readers should see Appendix A for complete syntax on these attributes. The next section discusses inline or floating frames which would have made the previously presented nested frame example quite easy.

Floating Frames

Up to this point, all the frames shown have been attached to the sides of the browser (left, right, top, or bottom). Another form of frame, called a *floating frame* (initially introduced by Microsoft), has been incorporated into the HTML 4 standard. The idea of the floating frame is to create an inline framed region, or window, that acts similarly to any other embedded object, insofar as text can be flowed around it. An inline frame is defined by the **<iframe>** element and can occur anywhere within the **<body>** of an HTML document. Compare this to the **<frame>** element that should occur only within the **<frameset>** element; remember that the **<frameset>** element should preclude the body.

The major attributes to set for the **<iframe>** element include **src, height,** and **width.** The **src** is set to the URL of the file to load, while the **height** and **width** are set either to the pixel or percentage value of the screen that the floating frame region should consume. Like an **<img>** element, floating frames should support align attributes for basic positioning within the flow of text. Internet Explorer supports the addition of the **hspace** and **vspace** attributes as well, although the HTML 4.01 specification does not. In general, like most elements, more complex presentation should be handled by CSS rules as discussed in Chapter 10.

Note that, unlike the empty **<frame>** element, the **<iframe>** element comes with a close tag. The tag pair **<iframe>** and **</iframe>** should contain any HTML markup code and text that is supposed to be displayed in browsers that don't support floating frames. A simple example of floating frames is shown here:

```
<!DOCTYPE HTML PUBLIC "-//W3C//DTD HTML 4.01 Transitional//EN">
<html>
<head>
<title>Floating Frame Example</title>
</head>
<body>
<h1 align="center">Floating Frame Example</h1>
<iframe name="iframe1" src="fileone.htm" width="350" height="200"
    align="left">
There would be a floating frame here if your browser supported it.
</iframe>
```

```
<p>This is a simple example of how floating frames are used. Notice
that in many ways the floating frame acts very similar to an inline
image. Floating frames act like embedded objects in many ways.</p>

</body>
</html>
```

The rendering of this example code is shown in Figure 8-7. Note how the Netscape 4.x generation browser does not support the **<iframe>** element, but renders the enclosed text instead, whereas browsers such as Internet Explorer 5.5 and Netscape 6 render the floating frame (see http://www.htmlref.com/examples/chapter08/iframe.htm).

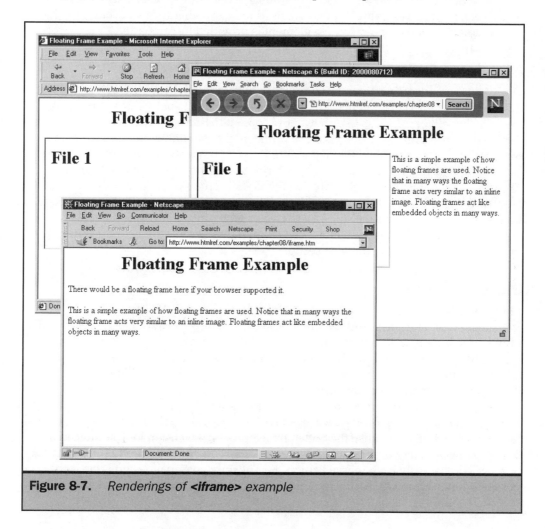

Figure 8-7. *Renderings of <iframe> example*

Like other frames it is possible to target an inline frame using the target attribute of the **<a>** element. Given the previous example a link such as

```
<a href="http://www.democompany.com" target="iframe1">Load in
iframe</a>
```

would have loaded the retrieved file within the inline frame. Unfortunately, a troublesome side effect can occur for those browsers such as Netscape 2.x, 3.x, and 4.x as well as Opera, which support link targeting but not the **<iframe>** element. In this situation the link will still render and open a new window that is the typical result of targeting a nonexistent window.

The syntax for **<iframe>** is strikingly similar to the **<img>** element as well as to other elements, such as **<object>**, that are used to insert other forms of content inline. The complete syntax of the **<iframe>** element is provided in Appendix A.

Using Frames

One of the biggest problems with frames is that they initially were used simply because they existed. Framed documents can provide considerable benefit, but at a price. A potential benefit of frames is that they allow content to be fixed onscreen. As demonstrated in previous examples, one frame might contain navigation, while the other frame contains the actual information. Keeping navigation onscreen provides a convenient way to navigate the body of information. Furthermore, if one frame has fixed navigation, the user might perceive the Web interface to be more responsive, because only part of the screen needs to update between selections. Beyond this benefit frames also allow the designer to present two or more documents simultaneously, which is useful for comparison. However, despite their wonderful benefits frames have their costs, as explained in the next section.

Frame Problems

Many usability experts are extremely critical of frames. Given the current implementation of frames, and the many designers who don't understand the potential drawbacks of framed documents, the statement that "frames can give designers more rope to hang themselves with" has some truth to it. However, browser vendors are addressing many of the problems of frames. With luck, designers will learn to use frames only when they provide added benefit.

The problems with frames are numerous, including design issues, navigation confusion, bookmarking problems, loss of URL context, and printing issues. Designers might not like frames because they often have borders, which can look strange in a design. However, modern frame implementations allow the designer to turn off frame borders, so this really isn't an issue anymore. The only potential design issue is the possibility that a framed document might sacrifice valuable screen real estate because of scrollbars, which could pose trouble for people with lower-resolution monitors. The only way to get around this problem is to limit the number of frames used on a page.

Navigation confusion is still a big issue with frames. Under Netscape 2, the first browser to implement frames, the browser Back button didn't go back in the frame history, but instead went back in the page history. Today this isn't so much of a problem, but it should be considered that using frames makes the navigation model much more difficult to predict. In fact, does the user really know what will happen when a link is clicked? Some framesets are highly predictable, while others seem almost random. Unless the framing is kept very simple, determining which frames will change when a link is clicked might not be obvious to users. In some sites, numerous frames are updated simultaneously, which might cause users to lose their sense of navigation. Even worse, if users want to bookmark the current page, they actually have to bookmark the top-level entry frame rather than the deeper level to which they have progressed. Fortunately Internet Explorer has fixed most frame bookmarking problems, but Netscape and other browser users might find bookmarking framed content difficult. Even if users are somehow able to bookmark the actual frame content, they could lose any navigation needed to navigate the site upon return.

Additional navigational problems include loss of context, because the URL of the document, as displayed in the addressbar of the browser, does not change when using frames; this accounts for why bookmarking doesn't work as expected because a bookmark just records a document's URL. Not letting the users see URLs can lead to trouble as some people use URLs as a way to orient themselves at a site; frames give up this clue to location.

Before the release of Internet Explorer 4, printing frames was difficult. Although the contents of individual frames could be printed, printing an entire document consisting of many frames generally was impossible. The newer versions of the Microsoft browser allow complete frame printing, but page authors should understand that content might be clipped.

Search engines and more limited browsers often find framed layouts troublesome and might not be able to travel to deeper pages in a site, particularly if there is not a **<noframes>** element. Site designers should thoroughly consider this limitation before rushing to use frames, particularly when similar layout effects might be achieved using style sheets without such problems.

While none of the problems with frames are insurmountable, designers should approach the technology with caution, and not just use it to show off their technical prowess. Readers looking for more details should reference Chapter 5 of *Web Design: The Complete Reference* (007212297-8), as it provides many techniques for dynamic frame building, bookmarking fixes, and frame busting.

Summary

Web page layout using HTML tags is not appropriate, but until the rise of CSS, frames often were used as both navigational and presentational elements. Frames often are used as a layout tool, and while the **<frame>** element can afford great power in making sophisticated layouts, it comes with a price. Navigational confusion, printing mishaps, and design problems can all result from misuse of frames. However, when frames are used properly (for example, to provide a fixed table of contents or navigation aid), they are a valuable addition to the page designer's arsenal. Because of their power and popularity, frames finally are included in the HTML specification, so you shouldn't have to worry about their future use. Although frames can be used to create impressive and dynamic layouts, similar effects can be achieved using standardized technology—particularly style sheets, which are discussed in Chapter 10.

Chapter 9

HTML and Multimedia

285

One of the innovations that led to the development of the modern Web was the Mosaic browser's introduction of images in 1993—but this was just the first step toward the dream of a multimedia Web. These days, the Web can bring a variety of media forms—including sound, video, and animation—right to your browser or desktop. The last several years have seen a number of changes in this area of the Web, particularly where music distribution is concerned. This chapter looks at some of the latest, most popular technologies for Web multimedia, and how to include them in Web pages.

Audio

Few things are as persuasive as sound. Just try watching television with the volume muted; it's not terribly interesting. Sound is a vital element of true multimedia Web pages—but how should sound be used? What Web audio technology is appropriate for the job? Simply adding a MIDI file to a site to provide continuous background sound may turn your page into the online equivalent of an in-store electronic organ demonstration. Audio support on the Web has seen a lot of change in the past few years, and the emphasis has shifted greatly from playing music in Web pages to using external applications and standalone devices such as MP3 players, and independent, browser-enabled programs such as RealPlayer and RealJukebox. This section begins with a quick survey of sound and compression basics, reviews some older formats and approaches such as MIDI, and concludes with a look at MP3's impact on the download-and-play approach and the current state of streaming audio represented by RealAudio. URLs in the text provide pointers to sites where you can learn more about these technologies

Digital Sound Basics

Digital sound is measured by the frequency of *sampling*, or how many times the sound is digitized during a specific time period. Sampling frequencies are specified in Kilohertz (KHz), which indicate the sound sampling rate per second. CD-quality sound is approximately 44.1KHz, or 44,100 samples every second. For stereo, two channels are required, each at 8 bits; at 16 bits per sample, that yields 705,600 bits of data for each second of CD-quality sound. In theory, the bits of data on a CD could be delivered over the Internet, creating high-quality music at the end user's demand. In reality, transmitting this amount of data would take nearly half a T1 network's bandwidth. Obviously, this type of sustained guaranteed bandwidth is not available to the average Web user.

Another approach is to lower the sampling rate when creating digital sound for Web delivery. A sampling rate of 8KHz in mono might produce acceptable playback results for simple applications, such as speech, particularly considering that playback hardware often consists of a combination of a simple sound card and a small speaker. Low-quality audio requires a mere 64,000 bits of data per second, but the end user still has to wait to download the sound. For modem users, even in the best of conditions, each second of low-quality sound takes a few seconds to be delivered, making continuous sound unrealistic.

Audio File Formats and Compression

Like graphics files, audio files can be compressed to reduce the amount of data being sent. The software on the serving side compresses the data, which is decompressed and played back on the receiving end. The compression/decompression software is known together as a *codec*. Just like image formats, audio compression methods are either lossy or lossless. *Lossy* data compression doesn't perfectly represent what was compressed, but is close enough, given the size savings. Because *lossless* compression techniques guarantee that what goes in one end comes out the other, most techniques can't compress files to any significant degree. Compression always involves a tradeoff between sound quality and file size; larger file sizes mean longer download times.

Downloading and Playing Audio

Early approaches to delivering sound via the Internet followed the "download and play" model, using formats such as WAV (waveform) files and AU (Sparc-audio, or u-law, format). In this scenario, users must download sounds completely before they can play them. This takes up valuable hard drive space, even if a user wants to hear only the first few seconds of a file. Sounds must be degraded significantly in this situation, which might not be acceptable for content that requires flawless playback. Even at very low sampling rates, these sounds must be fairly short to spare impatient users the agony of prolonged download times. Download time can be reduced by creating smaller audio files, which only accentuates the drawbacks of this method.

Various older formats, such as AU and AIFF, are still in use on the Web, but are becoming less commonplace. One format that remains somewhat popular for this purpose is MIDI (Musical Instrument Digital Interface), which is often used with the Microsoft-specific **<bgsound>** element discussed later in this chapter in the section "Audio Inclusion Basics." Netscape's LiveAudio technology once could be used to create a similar effect in conjunction with the **<embed>** element, but LiveAudio now seems to have been dropped from more recent versions of Netscape and lacked cross-browser viability in any case. Most importantly, MIDI is not actually a digitized audio format, but represents notes and other information so that music can be synthesized. It can be a powerful tool for musicians when used with synthesizers and other electronic instruments, but MIDI files played back via PC sound cards often sound like cheap, synthesized music, which is more a reflection of the playback hardware than the protocol itself. Table 9-1 shows some of the older formats that might still be encountered on the Web.

While many of the file formats listed in Table 9-1 may linger on the Web for quite some time to come, MP3 (MPEG level 3) is really the only choice for high-quality,

File Format	Description
WAV	Waveform (or simply *wave*) files are the most common sound format on Windows platforms. WAVs can also be played on Macs and other systems with player software.
AU	Sparc-audio, or u-law format, is one of the oldest Internet sound formats. A player for nearly every platform is available.
AIFF	Audio Interchange File Format is very common on Macs. Widely used in multimedia applications, it is not very common on the Web.
MIDI	Musical Instrument Digital Interface format is not a digitized audio format. It represents notes and other information so that music can be synthesized. MIDI is well-supported and files are very small, but it is useful only for certain applications because its reproduction quality is often limited by PC playback hardware.

Table 9-1.   *Older Internet Sound Formats*

sampled audio playback. Not surprisingly, MP3 is the most popular form of audio file on the Web today.

MP3

MP3 is one of the formats for audio and video developed by MPEG (Moving Picture Experts Group) for transmission over the Web. MPEG Level 3 is an audio format that generally compresses CD-quality sound by a factor of about 10–12 times, using techniques that were designed to take human audio perception into account, in order to minimize inaudible or unimportant frequencies and optimize the rest. Thus, a typical MP3 file (named for the format's file extension .mp3) of an average-length song weighs in at about 3 Mb, as opposed to the more than 30 Mb required for that same song on a compact disc.

In the last couple of years, this format has really taken off. The reason is simple: It provides high-quality audio that is not just suited for use on the Web, but in the real world as well, thanks to the increased availability of affordable CD copying devices, or burners. Music tracks from CDs can be converted to MP3 files, uploaded and downloaded across the Web, decompressed into CD-quality files, and burned to compact disc by anyone with a computer, a CD burner, and the right software. The grass-roots surge in MP3's popularity has, of course, generated considerable controversy. Regardless of the legal take on the various MP3-related battles, one thing is certain: The format has a very broad user base and will be around for quite some time.

Audio Inclusion Basics

Including download and play audio samples such as MP3 files in a Web page is simply a matter of using the anchor tag **<a>** to link to it. For example,

```
<a href="thememusic.mp3">Demo Company Theme Music</a><br>
<a href="theme.midi">Theme Music 2</a><br>
<a href="robotsound.wav">Robots in Action</a><br>
```

Assuming that users have the appropriate playback hardware and software when they click the link, the sound should be downloaded and then played. Of course if they don't have the appropriate software, nothing may happen either.

> **Note**   *There may be a problem that a Web server is not set up properly to deliver the associated sound files. If files play properly locally but seem to be downloaded as text or always prompt as an unknown type, you might have a problem with your Web server.*

Even when everything is set up properly, it is a very good idea to let users know what they are getting into by indicating the file size, file type, and the fact that the object is a music file. For example,

```
<a href="robotsound.wav"><img src="speaker.gif" height="10" width="10"
border="0">Robots in Action</a> [wav format / 10k]
```

might look something like this:

🔊<u>Robots in Action</u> [wav format / 10k]

Rather than link to an external sound file, you might desire to embed a sound file directly within a page. There are a variety of ways to do this, the easiest probably being Microsoft's proprietary **<bgsound>** element.

Microsoft's <bgsound>

Microsoft Internet Explorer 2 and later supports WAV and MIDI files with the **<bgsound>** element, which plays a sound in the background after it is loaded. The user has no control over the volume or the playback of the sound, which may be annoying. The element takes an **src** attribute that is set to the URL of the sound file to play. A **loop** attribute, which can be set to an integer value indicating how many times the sound should play, is also available. The **loop** attribute can also be set to the value **infinite** to keep playing over and over. A simple example to play a sound called test.wav two times under Internet Explorer could be written as **<bgsound src="test.wav" loop="2">**. As an empty element there is no close tag. While it could be written to be XHTML compliant as **<bgsound src="test.wav" loop="2" />**, the value of doing so is limited considering this a completely Internet Explorer proprietary element.

RealAudio

Download and play formats like MP3 and even WAV are popular because they allow the transfer of high-quality audio files across the Internet—but they also require the user to wait. However, there is a strong desire, both among content creators and end users, to use the Web as a broadcast medium. The key to Webcasting is something called *streaming*. The most popular means of streaming audio is the RealAudio format developed by RealNetworks (www.realnetworks.com), which allows for the transmission of audio programming at a number of different speeds—and even at multiple speeds depending on the end-user's requirements. But before going into what can be done with RealAudio, it might be useful to take a closer look at streaming itself.

Streaming

What is streaming? First of all, consider that a 28.8Kbps modem user receives approximately 2K of data per second. If one second of sound could be represented in 2K, and the data could get to the end user at a rate of 2K every second, the data would effectively *stream*, or play in real time. Streaming seems to make a whole lot of sense. Why wait for an hour-long speech to download before playing when you care only about the current second of data being listened to? Streamed data doesn't take up hard drive space, and it opens up random access to any position in an audio file. However, streaming audio has a few potential serious drawbacks. First, to compress audio far enough for streaming, you have to sacrifice a certain degree of sound quality. Second, the Internet protocols themselves do not readily support the requirements of streaming.

Because the Internet is frequently subject to bursts and traffic delays, there are a couple of key points to remember. The TCP/IP protocols used on the Internet were designed for robustness and scalability. The Internet is a packet-switched network that breaks up data into little chunks and sends them separately, to be reassembled at the other end. Because these packets may be lost along their journey or arrive out of order, the *Transmission Control Protocol* (TCP) guarantees the integrity of the data. This way, many users can share a fixed circuit that allows for economies of scale. However, packet-switched networks have one serious problem: they can't guarantee delivery time without special modifications. This makes streamed audio, video, and other "real time" applications on packet-switched networks very difficult.

Packet-switched networks can be augmented with protocols such as *Real Time Streaming Protocol* (RTSP), which help improve delivery likelihood by buffering, spreading data out over multiple packets, or eventually even making a bandwidth reservation, when needed. While these protocols can improve real-time data delivery, they do introduce changes to the way the Web is used. For example, if true bandwidth reservation is introduced, it raises the question of how to limit reservations because a user would always want maximum bandwidth. Some experts argue that once these protocols are in place, fee structures based on bandwidth will become commonplace. For the moment, this is pure speculation, but something to consider when thinking about building a bandwidth-intensive application using multimedia.

Today the most common solution to real-time data on the Internet is to make a dangerous assumption—you hope the end user has the end-to-end bandwidth to receive the file in real time. If audio compression can get one second of data to fit within those ranges, real-time data can be served to 28.8Kbps users—when the assumption holds. When the assumption doesn't hold, a glitch called a *drop-out* occurs in the audio stream. If too much drop-out occurs, the user turns off the audio stream.

One way to avoid drop-out is to *buffer* data. This process gives you a head start by preloading a certain amount of data into a buffer, so that rough spots can be overcome. An initial buffering delay of 10 or 15 seconds is acceptable for long audio clips; buffering short sounds is counterproductive. Many Internet audio solutions use a combination of intensive compression, buffering, and some level of bandwidth assumption to achieve streaming. More complex audio solutions use servers to control the process. Both approaches to streaming audio have their pros and cons. Even so, with the increased availability of high-speed Internet access through cable and DSL, streaming audio promises to remain a viable means of audio delivery for quite some time.

Enter RealNetworks

The first—and still the most popular—approach to streaming audio was developed by RealNetworks. RealAudio uses a special server to send continuous audio data to a browser helper application, Netscape plug-in, ActiveX control, or RealNetworks' own freestanding RealPlayer (in Version 8 at the time of this writing). With players available for all major platforms, RealAudio is the most common streaming audio format on the Internet. Putting data in RealAudio format is fairly easy if the files exist in WAV or other common audio formats. Simply use the RealAudio production tools, which can be downloaded from RealNetworks, and the data is ready to publish. But despite RealAudio's wide support, it has certain drawbacks, which mostly revolve around the use of a special server.

Streaming servers can provide a higher degree of control. For example, they can limit or control the number of audio streams delivered and allow for easy access to specified points in an audio stream. With simpler "serverless" audio-streaming solutions, the virtual Fast Forward button provided by random access is sacrificed. Some sophisticated servers could potentially upgrade data quality as bandwidth becomes available. Less complex systems give the same quality of data regardless of the end-to-end access speed. Server-based systems are expensive and require computing resources beyond the basic Web server. RealAudio-based streaming audio servers have a per-stream cost for high-end sites that keeps some users from adopting this solution. Fortunately, entry-level RealAudio systems with a few streams are still free or very inexpensive, and RealAudio can also be streamed directly off an ordinary Web server, within certain limitations. Already, many organizations are using the RealAudio platform, which is a testament to the quality of the system.

RealAudio Basics

The first step in producing RealAudio content for the Web is to convert your existing audio files into RealAudio format, which is easy to do with the RealProducer program.

> **Note** *At the time of this writing a free version of RealProducer was available for download from www.realnetworks.com/products/.*

The second step is to link to the RealAudio content from a Web page. This is done using the **<a>** tag, but there is an intermediate step: You do not link directly to the .rm file created with a program like RealProducer but to a text file ending in the extension .ram:

```
<a href="http://www.democompany.com/audio/robotdrone.ram">
Hear our happy robots drone!</a>
```

This simple text file only needs to contain the URL of the .rm file you want to play:

```
http://www.democompany.com/audio/robotdrone.rm
```

Assuming that the user has RealPlayer installed on the system being used, this will cause the RealPlayer program to pop open and begin playing the .rm file, as shown in Figure 9-1. RealAudio content can be played off any ordinary Web server, but content developers planning to reach a wide audience would be advised to look into the various RealServer packages available, which offer various levels of multiple stream support.

More complicated audio presentations that play a sequence of audio clips can be created by linking the .ram file to another file written in *Synchronized Media Integration Language* (SMIL), which should have the file extension .smil. SMIL can also be used to integrate video, text and animations with your audio presentation. SMIL is discussed in Chapter 17.

Embedding RealAudio

RealAudio can also be embedded in a Web page using the **<object>** or **<embed>** elements. To use the **<embed>** element, use a code fragment like this:

```
<embed src="http://www.democompany.com/audio/robotdrone.rpm"
       nojava="true" height="100" width="250" autostart="false">
```

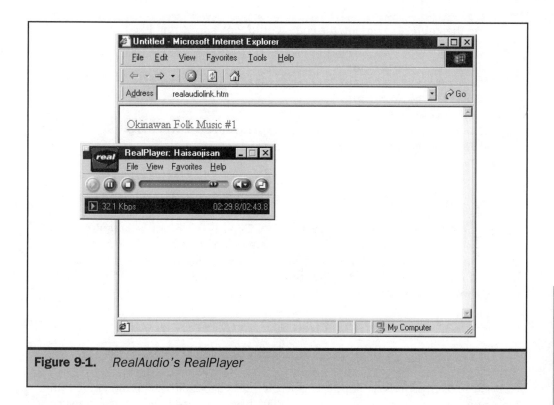

Figure 9-1.   *RealAudio's RealPlayer*

Note that the file referenced ends in the extension .rpm, not .ram. This is the file type used in place of a .ram file when embedding RealPlayer in a Web browser. The .rpm file itself is just like the .ram file; it contains nothing more than the URL for the .rm file, but tells the browser to display the player inside the browser window rather than spawning the RealPlayer application in its own window, shown here in Netscape 6.

The **autostart** attribute determines whether the audio clip plays as soon as the page is loaded; if it is set to **autostart="true"**, the clip will start right away. When it is set to **autostart="false"** or omitted entirely, the audio clip will not start until the user clicks the Play button.

To use the **<object>** element, the code would look something like this:

```
<object id="robotdrone"
 classid="clsid:CFCDAA03-8BE4-11cf-B84B-0020AFBBCCFA"
 width="75" height="30">
<param name="src"
 value="http://www.democompany.com/audio/robotdrone.rpm">
<param name="controls" value="PlayButton">
</object>
```

Again, the file referenced is an .rpm file. The id value can be set to any allowed value; however, the value shown for the **classid** attribute should always be **clsid:CFCDAA03-8BE4-11cf-B84B-0020AFBBCCFA**, as this identifies the RealAudio plugin. The first parameter defined by a **<param>** element is named **src** and has a **value** of the URL of the .rpm file. The second **<param>** tag sets what controls are displayed. In this case it takes the **PlayButton** value, which displays a Play and a Pause button, shown here in Internet Explorer 5.5.

Because of crossbrowser support issues, it might be sensible to avoid embedding RealAudio, and to simply rely on the RealPlayer program itself, which many users already are comfortable using.

It is not really within the scope of this book to go into any great detail about RealAudio, but this should give you a brief glimpse of what can be done with this technology. For more specific information about how to use RealAudio technology, please see the RealNetwork's Web site.

WindowsMedia Audio

Needless to say, Microsoft has its own version of streaming media in the marketplace. After long consideration, they even went and named it WindowsMedia (windowsmedia.com/). WindowsMedia supports the Microsoft-proprietary format known as Advanced Streaming Format (.asf). WAV files and MP3 files can be converted to this format using a tool named Windows Media Encoder. The technique for linking to an .asf file is similar to that used with RealMedia. In this case, simply link to a text file that ends with the extension .asx.

```
<a href="robotdrone.asx">Hear our happy robots drone!</a>
```

The format of the .asx file should be like this:

```
<ASX version="3">
   <Entry>
     <ref href="robotdrone.asf" />
   </Entry>
</ASX>
```

Clicking the link to the .asx file causes the WindowsMedia Player to open and play the audio file. It is important to note that Microsoft's latest player, WindowsMedia Player 7, has a few drawbacks. Notably, it is only available for Windows 98 and Windows 2000; users running the older Windows 95, or the more robust Windows NT (which is very common in the workplace) are advised not to install it on their systems. (An earlier version of the player is available for Macintosh.) WindowsMedia Player also plays these other audio file formats:

- WAV
- MIDI
- AU
- AIFF
- MP3
- WindowsMedia Audio (.wma)

WindowsMedia Player can be used as CD-playing software. It also plays video files, which is discussed in greater depth in the next section, "Video."

Video

The "holy grail" of Internet multimedia is high-quality, 30-frames-per-second real-time video. The use of video on Web pages has expanded considerably in the past few years, with online movie trailers becoming commonplace along with streaming clips on major news sites like www.cnn.com. However, providing video clips on the Internet is no small feat when you consider the amount of data being transferred.

Digital video is measured by the number of frames per second of video and by the size and resolution of these frames. The total size requirement for video is huge, particularly if you want NTSC (TV quality) video. A 640x480 image with 24 bits of data representation for color and a frame rate of 30 frames per second takes up a staggering 27 megabits per second—and that's without sound. Add CD-quality audio—705,600 bits of data for each second of data—and the file size increases proportionately. In theory, the bits of data necessary to deliver TV-quality video could be transmitted over the

Internet, creating the long-sought-after interactive TV. In the real world, transmitting this amount of data generally isn't feasible, even after compression.

Like audio files, video files can be compressed to reduce the amount of data being sent. Because of the degree of compression required by video, most video codecs use a lossy approach that involves a trade-off between picture/sound quality and file size, with larger file sizes obviously resulting in longer download times.

As with audio, simple online video delivery follow the download-and-play model, whereby users must download video clips completely before they can play them. Table 9-2 lists the most common downloadable video formats likely to be encountered on the Web.

The file format usually determines which compression technique is used. However, some file formats, such as QuickTime, allow different codecs to be selected. In some ways, this makes QuickTime the most flexible video format. Like audio, choosing a particular video format is often considering the needs of the audience as well as the need for streaming or downloading the content.

Video Inclusion Basics

Including download and play video samples such as an AVI file in a Web page is simply a matter of using the anchor tag **<a>** to link to it. For example,

```
<a href="movie.avi">Demo Company History</a><br>
```

Video Format	Description
AVI	Audio Video Interleave; the Video for Windows file format for digital video and audio is very common and easy to specify. The file size of AVI is significant.
QuickTime	The file extension MOV indicates the use of Apple's QuickTime format. Probably the most common digital video format, it continues its popularity on the Internet;. QuickTime has a strong following in the multimedia development community. Various codecs and technology enhancements make QuickTime a strong digital video solution that may work in conjunction with MPEG.
MPEG	Motion Picture Experts Group video format is generally considered the standard format for digital video. Although compression and image quality of MPEG files are impressive, this format can be expensive and difficult to work with.

Table 9-2.   *Common Internet Video Formats*

Like audio, if the user has the appropriate playback hardware and software when they click the link, the video should be downloaded and then played. Of course if they don't have the appropriate software nothing will happen either.

Like audio, indicating that the file to be viewed is a video is a very good idea.

```
<a href="movie.avi"><img src="tv.gif" height="10" width="10">Robots
in Action</a> [AVI format / 1200k]
```

The next section shows a simple way to include an AVI file under Internet Explorer.

Using the <img> Element with the dynsrc Attribute under Internet Explorer

The **dynsrc** attribute for the **<img>** element originated in Internet Explorer 2 and allowed AVI files to be played within a Web page. Although the syntax is currently maintained for backward compatibility, using the **<object>** or **<embed>** elements is preferable. Originally the **dynsrc** attribute supported only AVI files, but testing shows that any ActiveMovie-supported data can be included with this syntax. The basic attributes for **<img>** are all valid; however, the following additions are also available:

■ The **dynsrc** attribute should be set to the URL, either relative or absolute, of the content to play.

```
dynsrc="URL of active content"
```

■ If the **controls** attribute is present, controls are presented below the content, if possible. The attribute does not need a value.

```
controls
```

■ The **loop** attribute is used to set the number of times to loop the included content. When set to a positive integer, the content loops the specified number of times. When set to **-1** or the keyword **infinite**, the content loops continuously.

```
loop="value"
```

■ This attribute to the **<img>** element is used with **dynsrc** to specify how the content should be played. Setting the value to **fileopen** plays the content as soon as the data file has finished opening. Setting the value equal to **mouseover** delays playing the content until the mouse is positioned over it. The default action for active content is **fileopen**.

```
start="fileopen | mouseover"
```

An example of using the **dynsrc** attribute with the image element for an AVI movie is shown here. Figure 9-2 shows the rendering of the example under Internet Explorer 4.

```
<!DOCTYPE HTML PUBLIC "-//W3C//DTD HTML 4.01 Transitional//EN">
<html>
<head>
<title>DYNSRC Viewed Under Internet Explorer</title>
</head>

<body>

<font size="4">
This example shows use of the DYNSRC element, with the CONTROL
attribute, as viewed in an Internet Explorer browser.</font>

<img src="critter.gif" dynsrc="critter.avi" controls align="left"
    vspace="20">

</body>
</html>
```

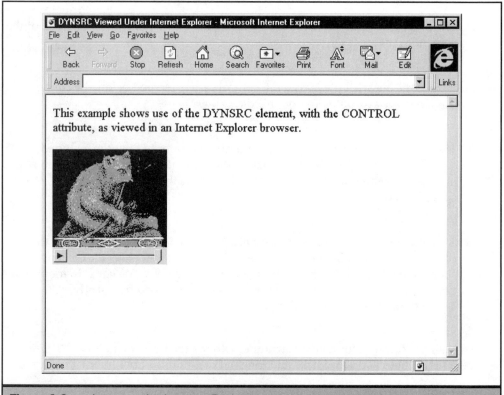

Figure 9-2.   *dynsrc under Internet Explorer*

In terms of browser support, it is difficult to come up with a best bet for simple Web video. Netscape 3 and Internet Explorer both support AVI in their Windows incarnations, but Macintosh users don't even get a consolation prize. For QuickTime, Internet Explorer, and Netscape for Windows users without QuickTime installed on their operating systems are left out in the cold. AVI apparently might be less of a problem, but the size and synchronization quality of AVI video files makes the format far from ideal. In some sense, you probably should stick with a video format such as RealVideo, given its wide acceptance and streaming approach. However, a brief presentation of QuickTime support under HTML is presented here to give you the flavor of how download-and-play video can be included in a page.

QuickTime

The QuickTime format, currently in version 4 and soon to be released in 5, was designed by Apple to provide the framework for the synchronization of time-based data in a variety of formats, including video, sound, MIDI, and even text. Although it was developed by Apple, it is now supported on PC platforms as well. An interesting aspect of QuickTime is that it can work with different video compression codecs, such as Cinepack, Indeo, MPEG, and even exotic fractal compression codecs. By itself, QuickTime with standard Cinepack encoding lacks the small file size of MPEG or proprietary video files, but the quality of QuickTime files is high. Creating or editing QuickTime files is relatively easy using tools such as the popular Adobe Premiere package.

Note   *Windows users are required to install QuickTime services for their operating system.*

The basic HTML syntax for the **<embed>** statement for the QuickTime plug-in is shown here:

```
<embed src="URL of QuickTime object"
       align="top | bottom | center | baseline | left |
              right | texttop | middle | absmiddle | absbottom"
       autoplay="true | false"
       cache="true | false"
       controller="true | false"
       height="pixels or percentage"
       hidden
       href="URL of page to load"
       hspace="pixels"
       loop="true | false | palindrome"
       playeveryframe="true | false"
       pluginspage="URL of page with plug-in information"
       scale="tofit | aspect | number"
```

```
target="valid frame name"
volume="0 - 100"
vspace="pixels"
width="pixels or percentage">
```

The following lists and describes the key attributes in the preceding syntax:

- **src**   Required, and should be set to the URL of a valid QuickTime file.

- **align**   Acts like the same attribute for the **<img>** element and accepts the same values.

- **autoplay**   May be set to **true** or **false** (default); indicates whether the movie should be played as soon as possible.

- **cache**   May be set to **true** or **false**. A **cache** value of **true** causes the browser to treat the information just like other information and keep it in a local disk cache, so that it does not need to be downloaded again. When set to **false**, the movie must be downloaded again.

- **controller**   May be set to **true** or **false**; determines whether the movie controller is visible. The controller provides standard stop, play, pause, rewind, frame selection, and volume controls. The controller is 24-pixels high, so the **height** value should be set to account for this. By default, the value of **controller** is set to **true**.

- **height**   Set like the **width** attribute, with a pixel value or percentage. The value specifies the **height** of the object and is cropped or expanded in the same method as **width**. For example, if a supplied height is greater than the movie's height, the movie is centered within this height. If the value is smaller, the object is cropped. Avoid values of **0** or **1** for the **height** attribute, because it may cause unpredictable results. Be aware that controls for the movie are 24-pixels high, which must be added to the **height** value for the object to display properly.

- **hidden**   Takes no parameters and its presence determines whether the movie should be visible. By default, the **hidden** value is **off**. In most cases this is not an appropriate attribute to use. However, if a sound-only movie is being inserted, this can provide a background sound-like function, assuming that **autoplay** has been set to **true**.

- **href**   Indicates the URL of a page to load when the movie is clicked. The meaning of this attribute is somewhat troublesome if the **controller** attribute is set to **false**. The problem revolves around the click having two meanings: one to start the movie and the other to go to the page. Page authors should either use the autoplay feature or provide controls when using this attribute.

- **hspace**   Sets the horizontal pixel buffer for the plug-in and acts the same way as the **hspace** attribute for the **<img>** element.

■ **loop**   Indicates whether the movie should play in a looped fashion. Setting the attribute to **true** loops the movie until the user stops it. The default value is **false**. When the **loop** value is set to **palindrome**, the movie loops back and forth. Setting this value produces interesting effects with movies, and even reverses the soundtrack.

■ **playeveryframe**   May be set to either **true** or **false**. When set to **true**, instructs the plug-in to play every frame, even if it requires the movie to play at a slower rate. In some sense, this is appropriate in case the processor drops frames that may be valuable. Setting this value to **true** is not advisable for movies with audio tracks; it has the side-effect of turning off the sound.

■ **pluginspage**   Sets the URL of the page that contains information about the required plug-in and how it can be downloaded and installed, if it is not currently installed. This feature is supported by Netscape; it is also documented to work under Internet Explorer. Be careful when using this attribute. It generally should be set to http://quicktime.apple.com, unless special instructions are included beyond standard QuickTime information.

■ **scale**   Takes a value of **tofit**, **aspect**, or a number corresponding to the desired scaling factor, such as **1.5**. The default **scale** value is **1**, which is a normally scaled movie. Setting the attribute to **aspect** scales the movie to fit the bounding box set by the **height** and **width** attributes. A value of **tofit** scales the movie to fit the **height** and **width** attribute, with no regard to aspect ratio. Be careful when scaling movies, because it may degrade the playback performance and image quality.

■ **target**   Used in conjunction with the **href** attribute to set the name of a frame into which to load the page indicated by the **href** attribute. The normal reserved frame names, such as _blank, as well as explicitly named frames are available as valid targets. More information on frames can be found in Chapter 8.

■ **volume**   May be set to a value from **0–100**. The higher the value, the louder the audio track on the QuickTime movie. A value of **0** effectively mutes the soundtrack, whereas **100** sets the volume at the maximum level. If the attribute is not set, the default is **100**. This is a newer attribute and will not be supported under older versions of the QuickTime plug-in.

■ **vspace**   Set to the number of vertical pixels to buffer between the embedded object and surrounding content. Used in the same way as the corresponding attribute for the **<img>** element.

■ **width**   Set to a pixel value or percentage. Be aware that the plug-in may not necessarily stretch the video image to take up the space. As mentioned previously, setting the **scale** attribute to **aspect** scales the movie to fit the bounding box set by the **height** and **width** attributes. If the value supplied for the object width is smaller than the object's true width, it is cropped to fit the dimensions provided. The **width** value must be set, unless the **hidden** attribute is used. Be careful when using small widths, such as 0 and 1 pixels, because this can cause problems.

The following example illustrates only the most basic use of the QuickTime plug-in, a rendering of which is shown in Figure 9-3:

```
<!DOCTYPE HTML PUBLIC "-//W3C//DTD HTML 4.01 Transitional//EN">
<html>
<title>QuickTime Support Under Netscape</title>

<body>

<font size="4">This example shows a frame from a promotional
clip for QuickTime, as viewed in a Netscape browser.</font>

<embed src="quicktime.mov" width="180" height="178"
       autoplay="true" align="left" hspace="12" vspace="20">

</body>
</html>
```

Figure 9-3.   *QuickTime support under Netscape*

Interested readers are directed to Apple's QuickTime site (http://www.apple.com/quicktime/) for more information about using QuickTime video on the Web.

Other Video Choices

The two other video choices beyond QuickTime that are very commonly used online include RealVideo and WindowsMedia. The syntax of these technologies is everchanging and generally videos are viewed in secondary windows rather than directly within a Web page, but a brief mention of the two technologies is made here.

RealVideo

RealVideo is RealNetwork's approach to streaming video. Like RealAudio, RealVideo can be viewed with RealPlayer. The RealProducer program can be used to process a number of digital video formats, including AVI, QuickTime, and MPEG, and converting them to RealVideo files, which, like RealAudio, end with the extension .rm. In fact, the process is much the same as for RealAudio. The video file is accessed by linking to a .ram file (or an .rpm file for embedded video), which in turn calls up the .rm file, or an .smil file that pulls together various sources to create a multimedia presentation. The basic syntax is discussed earlier in this chapter in the section "RealAudio;" for more about SMIL, see Chapter 17. Extensive documentation can be found at the RealNetworks Web site.

WindowsMedia Video

Microsoft's media technology has taken a number of forms, including ActiveMovie, but their latest effort is WindowsMedia, whose audio applications are discussed earlier in this chapter. WindowsMedia Player provides services for the playback of multimedia streams from local files or network-based servers. Specifically, WindowsMedia Player allows playback of video and audio content, compressed in various formats. WindowsMedia Player supports the following video formats:

- AVI
- MPEG
- Video on Demand (VOD)
- MP3
- QuickTime files (.aiff, .mov)
- WindowsMedia Video (.wmv)
- Advanced Streaming Format (.asf)

The last two formats listed here are proprietary Microsoft file formats. Advanced Streaming Format, already mentioned in the audio section, can be linked from a Web page by using an intermediary text file ending with the extension .asx (see the section "WindowsMedia Audio" earlier in this chapter for the appropriate syntax). Again, for more information on using WindowsMedia, see http://msdn.microsoft.com/workshop/imedia/windowsmedia/abc.asp.

Animation

Sometimes full-blown video is a little overboard, in fact just a little animation can spice up a Web page a great deal. Animation on the Web is used for many things: active logos, animated icons, demonstrations, and short cartoons. There are a variety of animation technologies available to Web designers. Some of the most common animation approaches include animated GIFs, Flash and Shockwave, and DHTML animations. Other animation possibilities also exist. Most notably, Java-based animations and older animation techniques such as server push are still possible, but the field has narrowed significantly. Very few older or proprietary animation formats are actually worth exploring, but a few of the browser-specific forms of animation like Microsoft's **<marquee>** tag live on.

Text Animation with <marquee>

One approach to adding new support for multimedia is to add new elements and build in support to the browser for the object. This approach used to be very popular with browser vendors and is partially responsible for the proliferation of browser-specific tags. **<marquee>** is one example of a multimedia-like tag that is fairly common on the Web. Although **<marquee>** isn't an embedded binary object, it tends to act like one in its support for **hspace**, **vspace**, **height**, and **width** attributes. In the proprietary HTML extension wars, Microsoft is the culprit for introducing the dreaded **<marquee>** element, which is certainly as annoying as **<blink>**. Thanks to **<marquee>**, HTML authors now can create messages that scroll and slide across a viewer's screen in a variety of different ways. Like Netscape's **<blink>** element, **<marquee>** degrades fairly well and can be used by HTML authors who understand the ramifications of using such proprietary tags. However, the bottom line is that, in good conscience, authors shouldn't recommend more than very occasional use of the **<marquee>** element.

Internet Explorer, as well as WebTV, supports the **<marquee>** element. The element requires a closing **</marquee>** tag. The text included between the tags is transformed into a scrolling ticker tape, similar to the one found at Times Square. A very simple continuous marquee could be set with the following HTML fragment:

```
<marquee>
Welcome to Demo Company, Inc. -- the biggest fake company in the
world!
</marquee>
```

Under Internet Explorer and other browsers that support the **<marquee>** element, the enclosed text scrolls repeatedly from right to left. Under browsers that don't support **<marquee>**, the text is displayed simply as plain text.

The following is a more complex example that illustrates some of the more common attributes supported by **<marquee>**; the rendering is shown Figure 9-4:

```
<!DOCTYPE HTML PUBLIC "-//W3C//DTD HTML 4.01 Transitional//EN">
<html>
<head>
<title>Marquee Example</title>
</head>
<body>
<div align="center">
<marquee bgcolor="yellow"
         behavior="alternate"
         direction="right"
         loop="6"
         scrollamount="1"
         scrolldelay="40"
         title="Silly tags aren't just for Netscape anymore."
         width="80%">

   Welcome to Demo Company, the biggest fake company of them all!
</marquee>
</div>
</body>
</html>
```

Changing the attributes in this example will adjust the presentation of the marquee. For example, the **behavior** attribute may be set to **alternate**, **scroll**, or **slide**. This attribute determines how the scrolling text behaves. By default, a marquee scrolls text from right to left, unless the **direction** is set. The scrolled text, if it is looped, must first disappear before reappearing on the other side. When the attribute is set to **alternate**, the text bounces across the scroll region. When the attribute is set to **slide**, the text slides into position, based on direction, and stays put once onscreen.

The **direction** attribute is used to set the direction in which the scrolled text moves. The allowed values for this attribute are **down**, **left**, **right**, and **up**.

The **loop** attribute is used to set the number of times that the message loops in the scroll region. By default, unless the **behavior** is set to **slide**, a marquee scrolls forever. The value of the **loop** attribute should be a positive integer.

Setting **scrollamount** to a particular number of pixels allows the smoothness of the scroll to be controlled. The value of the **scrollamount** attribute is set to the number of

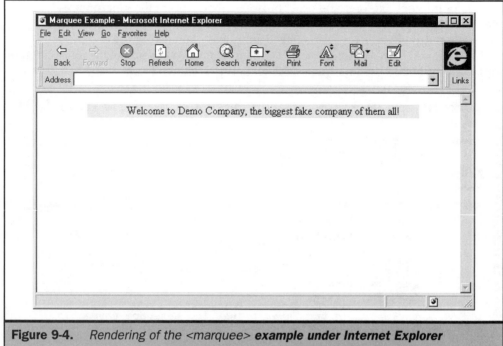

Figure 9-4.   Rendering of the <marquee> **example under Internet Explorer**

pixels between each drawing of the scrolled message in the display area. The larger the value in pixels, the jerkier the scroll.

The **scrolldelay** attribute is used to set the number of milliseconds between each rendering of the scrolled message. A higher value for this attribute slows the scrolling. A reasonable value for this attribute is **50** or greater. Lower values for **scrolldelay** tend to produce marquees that are very difficult to read.

Lastly, because the **<marquee>** element represents a rectangular region, just like an image (or, for that matter, any binary included object), it has attributes such as **align**, **hspace**, **vspace**, **height**, and **width**.

Appendix A provides a complete discussion of the **<marquee>** element and its numerous attributes. Although the **<marquee>** element is certainly interesting, as a simple form of animated text, it doesn't hold a candle to simple animation forms like an animated GIF.

Animated GIFs

Animated GIFs are the simplest form of animation and are supported natively by most browsers. Looping and minimal timing information can be set in an animated GIF, but complex animation is beyond this format's capabilities.

The GIF89a format also supports animation. This works by stacking GIF after GIF in a manner similar to a flip book to create the animation. The animation extension also allows timing and looping information to be added to the image. Animated GIFs are one of the most popular ways to add simple animation to a Web page because nearly every browser supports them. Browsers that do not support the animated GIF format generally display the first frame of the animation in its place. Including a GIF animation is simply just a manner of referencing it like a normal image as shown here:

```
<img src="animation.gif" width="100" height="100" border="0"
    alt="DemoCompany">
```

Even though with animated GIFs plug-ins or other browser facilities are not required, authors should not rush out to use animation on their pages. Excessive animations can be distracting for the user and are often inefficient to download. Because the animation is basically image after image, the file size is the total of all the images within the animation combined and can result in a much larger image than the user is willing to wait for. Thus, it is very important to make sure that every frame of the animation is compressed as much as possible. One approach to combat file bloat is to optimize the image by replacing only the moving parts of an individual animation frame; for more about this subject, see Chapter 5.

Flash

Macromedia Flash (www.macromedia.com/flash) is the leading format for sophisticated Web-based animations. Flash files are very compact. The key to Flash's small size is the fact that it is vector-based. Anyone who has worked with Photoshop, Illustrator, or another vector-based graphics program such as Freehand knows what this means. While Photoshop produces images like GIF and JPEG that are essentially comprised of a mosaic of pixels, vector-based images use mathematically defined curves (Bezier curves, to get technical) to define images. Computers read this mathematical information and create the image on the monitor screen. A 100x100 pixel square with a 2-pixel red border would be defined mathematically, not by a collection of colored dots. If a Web browser could process images in this fashion, it would be feasible to scale images effectively on the Web. By changing the part of the equation—defining the height and width of the square—the browser could increase its size without impacting any other aspect of the image, thus removing the distortion problems you get if you resize a GIF or JPEG using HTML. Unfortunately, most browsers do not support this image type yet, though, a format called *Scalable Vector Graphics* (SVG) hopes to someday be natively supported by browsers and Microsoft already supports a simple format called *Vector Markup Language* (VML) in Internet Explorer. However, for the most part designers are still dependent upon plug-ins to display vector-based formats.

Flash is primarily used to create animations. This requires the Flash plug-in, but the end result is worth it. A Flash animation (file extension .swf) is superior to an animated GIF in several ways. It can contain a great deal more information than a GIF, allowing more sophisticated and complex effects. The image is scalable and can expand or contract to fit a relative display region, thus becoming larger on top-of-the-line monitors, yet scale down to fit reasonably comfortably within low-end displays. The crowning advantage is that .swf files can be smaller in kilobyte size than a comparable GIF animation—particularly in larger, more detailed images. If you view the animation at http://www.democompany.com/splashpage.cfm, you can right-click the image (on a PC) or CTRL-click (on a Mac), and then select a dialog that will let you zoom in and examine its details.

After you assemble the animation and save it as a SWF file, it's fairy simple to reference it from a Web page. To reference a Flash file, you can use the **<embed>** syntax. For example,

```
<embed src="test.swf"
       swLiveConnect="false"
       width="320" height="240"
       quality="autohigh" bgcolor="#ffffff"
       type="application/x-shockwave-flash"
        pluginspage="http://www.macromedia.com/shockwave/download/
                     index.cgi?P1_Prod_Version=ShockwaveFlash">

<noembed>
   <img src="test.gif" height="250" width="320">
</noembed>
</embed>
```

Note the use of the **<noembed>** element to provide an alternative file in case Flash is not supported, such as an animated GIF file.

You also can use the **<object>** syntax to reference an ActiveX control, as follows:

```
<object classid="clsid:D27CDB6E-AE6D-11cf-96B8-444553540000"

codebase="http://download.macromedia.com/pub/shockwave/cabs/flash/
swflash.cab#version=4,0,2,0" width="400" height="250">

<param name="movie" value="test.swf">
<param name="quality" value="high">

   <img src="test.gif" width="320" height="240">
```

```
</object>
```

Lastly you could combine all the formats together to deal with all possible situations as shown here:

```
<object classid="clsid:D27CDB6E-AE6D-11cf-96B8-444553540000"

codebase="http://download.macromedia.com/pub/shockwave/cabs/flash/
swflash.cab#version=4,0,2,0" width="400" height="250">

<param name=movie value="test.swf">
<param name="quality" value="high">

<embed src="test.swf" quality="high"
       pluginspage="http://www.macromedia.com/shockwave/download/
index.cgi?P1_Prod_Version=ShockwaveFlash"
       type="application/x-shockwave-flash" width="400"
height="250">

<noembed>
  <img src="test.gif" height="250" width="320">
</noembed>

</embed>

</object>
```

Given the complexity of the syntax for including Flash files in a document, it is best to let the Flash tool generate the base HTML and modify it or to use a Macromedia program like Dreamweaver to insert the file.

PDF Format

While so far this chapter has focused on dynamic multimedia such as sound, video, and animation, there is one more aspect of Web multimedia worth considering: print. It has long been difficult to get a Web page to print out exactly the way it appears onscreen. Improved browser support of CSS promises greater control in this department, as discussed in Chapter 10, but the simple truth of the matter remains that Web pages do not offer the range of layout control available in a print-oriented program like Quark, or even Microsoft Word. And while it is possible to view Word documents in a Web browser, their file size makes them a poor choice for online viewing. Fortunately, Adobe's Acrobat technology offers a viable approach to the online distribution of electronic documentation.

Originally proposed to help implement the mythical ideal of the "paperless office," Acrobat has matured into a product with uses both on and off the Web. Adobe Acrobat provides the capability to deliver an electronic document to an end user without requiring the reader to have the authoring environment to open the file. Visually, Acrobat preserves the exact look and feel of the document, both onscreen and in print. For design-oriented Web publishers, Acrobat provides a highly motivating alternative to HTML that easily surpasses HTML's relatively simplistic and imprecise layout features, as shown in Figure 9-5.

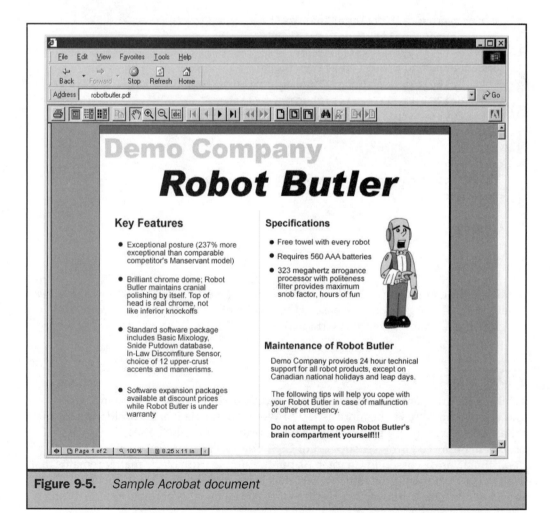

Figure 9-5. *Sample Acrobat document*

Acrobat files are created by using a combination of traditional text authoring tools (word processors and desktop publishing software) and special Acrobat authoring software (Adobe Exchange or Distiller). The files are then saved in a file format aptly named *Portable Document Format* (PDF). PDF files are small, self-contained documents that can be transported in a variety of ways: via diskette, CD-ROM, or network. The end user then reads the files by using special Adobe Acrobat Reader software. Thus, by its very nature, Acrobat reader technology must be cross-platform. Versions of the Acrobat Reader software are currently available for the following operating systems: Microsoft Windows 3.*x*, Windows 95, Windows 98, and Windows NT; Macintosh; Linux; Sun Microsystems' Sun SPARC Solaris and Sun SPARC SunOS; Hewlett-Packard's HP-UX; Silicon Graphic's IRIX; IBM's AIX and OS/2; and Digital's VMS.

Inserting an Acrobat file in a Web page is as simple as linking to the document with the **<a>** element. For example,

```
<a href="document.pdf">Demo Company Data sheet
  (Acrobat PDF Format, 55Kb)</a>
```

If a PDF is used, make sure to let users know what it is with an appropriately named link or PDF icon. It is a good idea to indicate the file size of a linked PDF. The last time the document was modified also might be useful to the user. Lastly, make sure to provide information on where to obtain the Acrobat reader for users who may not have it. All these ideas are illustrated here:

 The 2001 Annual Report is also available as a PDF (Portable Document Format) file which requires the free Acrobat Reader available from Adobe.

For more information about Acrobat and more details on how Acrobat might be included in a Web page, visit Adobe's Web site at www.adobe.com.

Summary

The previous edition of this book suggested that the future of audio on the Internet would be in integration. In a sense, this has proven to be true—but not in the sense expected. The real trend seems to have been toward Web pages that trigger the launch of freestanding programs which can play downloaded files (MP3) or streaming audio (RealAudio), and the development of programs like RealPlayer and WindowsMedia Player that can play a wide variety of file formats. But with the exception of MP3, it remains unrealistic to expect CD quality for Internet-based audio. Where online video is concerned, many of the same developments apply. Embedded QuickTime movie trailers may have become a commonplace promotional tool on the Web, but the emphasis has shifted largely away from video clips in Web pages to clips displayed in RealPlayer and WindowsMedia Player. The rise of vector-based formats like Flash opens the door to more extensive use of animation in Web pages, while animated GIFs still provide a viable, if less powerful, backup where Flash is not supported. For many developers, Flash even seems to offer the layout control so lacking in HTML. Yet do not forgo the use of text for a binary form like Flash, the cost and flexibility of text makes it very compelling. As discussed in the next chapter with the rise of Cascading Style Sheets (CSS), the layout complaints associated with HTML should come to an end.

The Complete Reference

Chapter 10

Style Sheets

HTML is a poor language for page formatting, but this isn't a failing of the technology. As mentioned throughout this book, HTML elements are not supposed to be used to represent layout. Even so, people often use HTML as a visual design environment. They tend to think visually, rather than organizationally, when building Web pages. Why? Well, not very many choices were available in the past. Everybody wanted the same thing—a high degree of control over the layout of their Web pages. Until recently, this control required using tables, HTML tricks, and images for layout, or embedding a binary form, such as Flash, in a page. These solutions generally were unsatisfactory.

A better solution has emerged. Style sheets, in the form of *Cascading Style Sheets* (CSS), finally are available in the major browsers. Style sheets offer what designers have been clamoring for over the years: more control over layout. The main problem with CSS adoption was that older versions of Netscape and Microsoft Internet Explorer fell short in some areas of CSS1 (the first specification) support. Newer versions of the browsers are nearly complete in their support of CSS1, with the happy result that more and more page authors are using style sheets for formatting. Portions of the CSS2 specification also are better supported. Yet even as CSS becomes more commonplace, other issues remain. Large portions of CSS2 remain unsupported, proprietary extensions to style sheets introduced by browser vendors maintain crossbrowser issues, and the World Wide Web Consortium is already making headway with CSS3.

Style Sheet Basics

CSS1 style sheets rely on an underlying markup structure, such as HTML. They are not a replacement for HTML. Without a binding to an element, a style really doesn't mean anything. The purpose of a style sheet is to create a presentation for a particular element or set of elements. Binding an element to a style specification is very simple; it consists of a *selector*—in this case simply the element name—followed by its associated style information—called *rules*—within curly braces. For example, suppose that you want to bind a style rule to the **<h1>** element so that it appears as 28-point text. The following rule would result in the desired display:

```
h1   {font-size: 28pt;}
```

More rules such as setting the color of the **<h1>** to red or the font face to Impact also could be added simply by separating each style property with a semi-colon.

```
h1   {font-size: 28pt;
      color: red;
      font-family: Impact;}
```

Note *The final rule in a list of style properties does not require the semicolon. However, for good measure and easy insertion of future style rules, page authors should always use semicolons between every style property.*

To make the style rule useful, it must be bound to an actual HTML document. There are numerous ways to add style to a document, either using an external style sheet, a document-wide style sheet or using inline styles with the **style** attribute common to most HTML elements. All these methods will be discussed in the next section. For the purpose of this demo we'll use a document-wide style, as defined with the **<style>** element found in the **<head>** element of an HTML document:

```
<!DOCTYPE HTML PUBLIC "-//W3C//DTD HTML 4.01 Transitional//EN">
<html>
<head>
<title>First CSS Example</title>
<style>
  h1    {font-size: 28pt;
         color: red;
         font-family: Impact;}
</style>
</head>
<body>
<h1>New and Improved HTML with Style</h1>
</body>
</html>
```

CSS provides a powerful set of properties for manipulating the look of HTML elements. Notice even with this simple example the rendering difference between a style sheet–capable and non-style-sheet-supporting browser as shown in Figure 10-1.

Adding Style to a Document

Style information can be included in an HTML document in any one of three basic ways:

- Use an outside style sheet, either by importing it or by linking to it.
- Embed a document-wide style in the **<head>** element of the document.
- Provide an inline style exactly where the style needs to be applied.

Each of these style sheet approaches has its own pros and cons, as listed in Table 10-1.

PRESENTATION AND LAYOUT

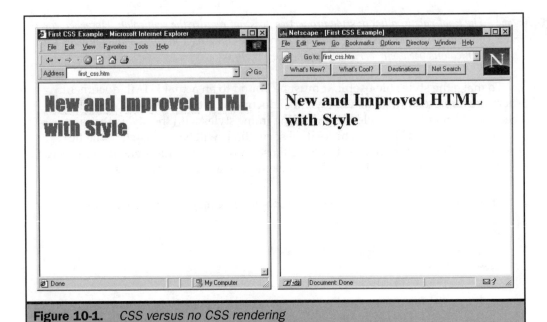

Figure 10-1.   *CSS versus no CSS rendering*

	External Style Sheets	**Document-Wide Style**	**Inline Style**
Pros	*Can set style for many documents with one style sheet	*Can control style easily document by document *No additional download time for style information	*Can control style to a single character instance *Overrides any external or document styles
Cons	*Require extra download time for the style sheet, which might delay page rendering	*Need to reapply style information for other documents	*Need to reapply style information throughout the document and outside documents *Bound too closely to HTML—difficult to update

Table 10-1.   *Comparison of Style Sheet Approaches*

Linking to a Style Sheet

An external style sheet is simply a plain text file containing the style specifications for HTML tags or classes. The common extension indicating that the document provides style sheet information is .css, for Cascading Style Sheets.

 The file extension .jss is used to indicate Netscape's JavaScript Style Sheets (JSSS), which provide the base functions of CSS but in an unusual Netscape-specific fashion. Page designers should avoid the .jss style indicator.

The following CSS1 style rules can be found in a file called sitestyle.css, which defines a style sheet used site wide:

```
body        {font: 10pt;
             font-family: Serif;
             color: black;
             background-color: white;}

h1          {font: 24pt;
             font-family: Sans-Serif;
             color: black;
             text-align: center;}

p           {text-indent: 0.5in;
             margin-left: 50px;
             margin-right: 50px;}

a:link      {color: blue; text-decoration: none;}
a:visited   {color: red; text-decoration: none;}
a:active    {color:red; text-decoration: none;}
a:hover     {color: red; text-decoration: underline;}
```

Note *The pseudo classes, a:link, a:visited, a:active, and a:hover are selectors that are associated with the various states of a link. These selectors are discussed later on in this chapter.*

An HTML file that uses this style sheet could reference it by using the **<link>** tag within the **<head>** element of the document. Recall from Chapter 4 that the **<link>** element isn't exclusive to style sheets and has a variety of possible relationship settings that can be set with the **rel** attribute. The following is an example of how style sheet linking is used:

PRESENTATION AND LAYOUT

```
<!DOCTYPE HTML PUBLIC "-//W3C//DTD HTML 4.01 Transitional//EN">
<html>
<head>
<title>Style Sheet Linking Example</title>
<link rel="stylesheet" href="sitestyle.css" type="text/css">
</head>
<body>
<h1>HTML with Style</h1>
<p>Cascading Style Sheets 1 as defined by the
<a href="http://www.w3.org">W3C</a> provides
powerful page layout facilities.</p>
...Other content affected by style sheet...
</body>
</html>
```

In this example, the relationship for the **<link>** element as indicated by the **rel** attribute is set to be **stylesheet**; then, the **href** attribute is used to indicate the URL of the style sheet to use. In this case, the style sheet resides in the same directory as the referencing file and is known as **sitestyle.css**. However, it would be wise to collect all style sheets in a special styles directory. Of course it also is possible to reference a remote style sheet using a full URL such as http://www.htmlref.com/styles/remotestyle.css. Note that linking to an external style sheet has the same problems as linking to an external object insofar as the object might no longer be available or the speed of acquiring that object could inhibit performance of the page.

The last thing to note in the linked style sheet example is the use of the **type** attribute in the **<link>** element, which is set to the MIME type **"text/css"**. This value indicates that the linked style sheet is a cascading style sheet, but another form of style sheet certainly could be linked. A style sheet type can be defined both inline and document-wide. To avoid having to use the **type** attribute, you might want to set a default style sheet language in the **<head>** element of the document by using the **<meta>** element, as shown here:

```
<meta http-equiv="Content-Style-Type" content="text/css">
```

As it stands, by default, most browsers assume that CSS is being used; the **type** setting might have little effect, regardless of how it is applied.

Embedding and Importing Style Sheets

The second way to include an external style sheet is to embed it. When you embed a style sheet, you write the style rules directly within the HTML document. You could separate the style rules into another file and then import these rules or you could type them directly into the document. Either way involves using the **<style>** element found

within the **<head>** element of an HTML document. You enclose the style rules within
the **<style>** and **</style>** tag pair and place this element within the head section of the
HTML document.

One concern when including style sheets within an HTML document is that not all
browsers understand style information. To avoid problems, comment out the style
information by using an HTML comment, such as **<!-- -->**, so that the style rules aren't
displayed onscreen or misinterpreted by older browsers. A complete example of a
document-wide style sheet, including hiding rules from older browsers, is shown here:

```html
<!DOCTYPE HTML PUBLIC "-//W3C//DTD HTML 4.01 Transitional//EN">
<html>
<head>
<title>Document Wide Style Sheet Example</title>
<style type="text/css">
<!--
body        {font: 10pt;
             font-family: Serif;
             color: black;
             background-color: white;}

h1          {font: 24pt;
             font-family: Sans-Serif;
             color: black;
             text-align: center;}

p           {text-indent: 0.5in;
             margin-left: 50px;
             margin-right: 50px;}

a:link      {color: blue; text-decoration: none;}
a:visited   {color: red; text-decoration: none;}
a:active    {color:red; text-decoration: none;}
a:hover     {color: red; text-decoration: underline;}
-->
</style>
</head>
<body>
<h1>HTML with Style</h1>
<p>Cascading Style Sheets 1 as defined by the
<a href="http://www.w3.org">W3C</a> provides
powerful page layout facilities.</p>
```

```
...Other content affected by style sheet...
</body>
</html>
```

You can have multiple occurrences of the **<style>** element within the head of the document, and you can even import some styles, link to some style rules, and specify some styles directly. Dividing style information into multiple sections and forms might be very useful, but a way must exist to determine which style rules apply. This is the idea of the cascade, which is discussed in more detail later in the chapter.

Another way to use document-wide style rules rather than type the properties directly in the **<style>** element is to import them. The idea is similar to linking. An external style sheet is referenced, but in this case, the reference is similar to a macro expansion inline. The syntax for the rule for importing a style sheet is **@import**, followed by the URL of the style sheet to include, and terminated with a semicolon. This rule must be included within the **<style>** element; it has no meaning outside that element, as compared to the linked style sheet. An example of how to import a style sheets is shown here:

```
<!DOCTYPE HTML PUBLIC "-//W3C//DTD HTML 4.01 Transitional//EN">
<html>
<head>
<title>Imported Style Sheet Example</title>
<style type="text/css">
<!--
@import url(corerules.css);
@import url(linkrules.css);

/* a rule specific to this document */

h1          {font: 24pt;
             font-family: Sans-Serif;
             color: black;
             text-align: center;}
-->
</style>
</head>
<body>
<h1>HTML with Style</h1>
<p>Cascading Style Sheets 1 as defined by the
<a href="http://www.w3.org">W3C</a> provides
powerful page layout facilities.</p>
```

```
. . .Other content affected by style sheet. . .
</body>
</html>
```

Note *The preceding example shows the use of CSS comments as designated by /* and */ which can be used to leave comments about complex or confusing CSS usage.*

In the preceding example the rules for **<body>** and **<p>** were included in the file corestyles.css, whereas the rules effecting the **<a>** element were included via the document linkstyles.css. A special rule for the **<h1>** element, used in this document alone, is placed within the style block to give the reader some sense of how the **@import** feature is used to organize the various parts of a complete style rule. (All **@import** directives should always come before all other style rules.) Although imported style sheets might seem to provide a great advantage for organizing style information, their use currently is limited by the fact that some browsers such as Netscape 4.x do not support this style sheet inclusion form properly. Page designers should stick to the **<link>** form of accessing external style sheets until this form has more support.

Note *Although Netscape 4.x generation browsers released at the time of this writing ignore @import directives they often are used anyway and can be useful when trying to include style rules that Netscape doesn't support properly.*

Using Inline Style

Beyond using a style sheet for the whole document, you can add style information right down to the single element. The simplest way to add style information, but not necessarily the best, is to add style rules to the particular HTML element. Here's how it works: Suppose you want to set one particular **<h1>** tag to render in 48-point, green, Arial font. You could apply that style to all **<h1>** elements, or to a class of them (discussed in the next section), by applying a document-wide style. On the other hand, you could quickly apply the style to only the tag in question using its **style** attribute. Recall that style is one of the core HTML 4 attributes besides **class**, **id**, and **title** that can be used within nearly any HTML element. For example, the following example shows how style rules could be applied to a particular **<h1>** element:

```
<h1 style="font-size: 48pt; font-family: Arial; color: green;">
CSS1 Inline</h1>
```

This sort of style information doesn't need to be hidden from a browser that isn't style sheet–aware, because browsers ignore any attributes that they don't understand.

PRESENTATION AND LAYOUT

Although inline style seems any easy route to using CSS, it does have some significant problems. The main problem is that inline rules are bound very closely to a tag. If you want to affect more than one **<h1>**, as shown in the previous example, you would have to copy-paste the style attribute into every other **<h1>** element. However, for quick and dirty application of rules this might be appropriate.

CSS and HTML Elements

One potential problem with style sheets and HTML is that the default rendering of an HTML element might get in the way. For example, consider applying a style rule to a **<strong>** element like so:

```
<strong style="color: red">I am strong!</strong>
```

Whereas this will put the text contents in red, it also probably will be bold because that is the typical rendering of this HTML element. Designers have to consider these default renderings as rules are added; the nefarious document author can create a potentially confusing use of HTML pretty easily using style sheets as shown here.

```
<!DOCTYPE HTML PUBLIC "-//W3C//DTD HTML 4.01 Transitional//EN">
<html>
<head>
<title>HTML Presentation Override</title>
<style type="text/css">
<!--
    b    {font-style: italic; font-weight: normal;}
-->
</style>
</head>
<body>
<b>What am I?</b>
</body>
</html>
```

<div> and <span> Revisited

When using style sheets and trying to avoid the default rendering of HTML elements document authors will find the use of the **<div>** and **<span>** elements indispensable. Recall from Chapter 3 that the **<div>** element and **<span>** are block and inline elements, respectively, that have no particular rendering. For example, using the **<div>** element to apply a style to a certain section or division of a document is very easy as shown here:

```
<div style="background-color: yellow; font-weight: bold; color:
black;">

<p>Style sheets separate the structure of a document from its
presentation. Dividing layout and presentation has many
theoretical benefits and can provide for flexible documents
that display equally well on large graphically rich systems
and palmtop computers.</p>

<p>This is another paragraph describing the wonderful benefits of
style sheets</p>

</div>
```

However, as a block element **<div>** should induce a return so if you want to provide style information solely for a few words, or even a few letters, the best approach is to use the **<span>** element. For example, notice how **<span>** is used here to call attention to a particular section of text:

```
<p>Calling out <span style="background-color: yellow; font-weight: bold;
color: black;">special sections of text</span> isn't hard with span</p>
```

Creating Style Sheet Rules

As shown in the previous sections, the simplest rules can be applied to all occurrences of a particular element such as **<p>**. For example, consider setting the line spacing for all paragraphs using a rule such as

```
p   {line-height: 150%;}
```

Unfortunately, some of these elements had a default rendering, so often we have to resort to using the elements **<div>** and **<span>** which have no predefined presentation in HTML. Beyond this caveat, designers are free to use style properties with nearly every HTML display element including the **<body>** element itself. For example a rule such as

```
body {background-color: black;}
```

would set the background color of the entire document black. To decrease the amount of typing for setting rules for multiple tags, it is possible to group them with commas. For example, if you want **<h1>**, **<h2>**, and **<h3>** to have the same basic background and color, you could apply the following rule:

```
h1, h2, h3   {background: yellow; color: black}
```

If it turns out that each particular heading should have a different size, you can represent that by adding other rules:

```
h1    {font-size: 200%;}
h2    {font-size: 150%;}
h3    {font-size: 125%;}
```

When the grouping rule and the other rules are encountered, they are combined. The resulting rules create the whole style. Although associating all elements with a certain look is useful, in reality page designers probably will want to create very specific rules that are applied only to certain elements in a document or that can be combined to form more complex rules.

id Rules

Without inline styles, how can a particular style be applied to one occurrence of the **<h1>** element, or to only a few particular **<h1>** elements? The solutions to these problems are the **class** and **id** attributes. As discussed in Chapter 3, you can name a particular tag with the **id** attribute so that it can be made a destination for a link. For example,

```
<h1 id="FirstHeading">Welcome to Demo Company, Inc.</h1>
```

assigns a name of **"FirstHeading"** to the **<h1>** element. One possible use of this as discussed in Chapter 4 is for this item to be linked to like so:

```
<a href="#FirstHeading">Go to Heading 1</a>
```

However, another possible use of the name for an element is to reference it from a style rule. For example, a CSS rule such as

```
#FirstHeading {background-color: green;}
```

would apply a green background to the element with its id attribute set to **FirstHeading**.

The following markup shows how a green background is applied to the **<p>** element with the **id** value of **"SecondParagraph"**, whereas no style is applied to the other paragraph:

```
<!DOCTYPE HTML PUBLIC "-//W3C//DTD HTML 4.01 Transitional//EN">
<html>
<head>
<title>ID Rule Example</title>
<style type="text/css">
<!--
#SecondParagraph    {background-color: green;}
-->
</style>
</head>
<body>
<p>This is the first paragraph.</p>
<p id="SecondParagraph">This is the second paragraph</p>
<p>This is the third paragraph. </p>
</body>
</html>
```

As an HTML 4 core attribute, **id** attribute is common to nearly all HTML elements save a few such as **<html>**, **<head>**, and **<body>**. Page authors need to be very careful to ensure that HTML elements are named uniquely. Do not name two elements the same name using the **id** attribute. If two of the paragraphs have **id="secondparagraph"**, what will happen? In the case of most browsers, both paragraphs should show up green. However, this is such sloppy style that it generally will result in significant errors when eventually scripting is added to the document. If multiple elements should be affected in a similar way, a class rule should be employed instead.

class Rules

The **class** attribute defines the name of the class an element belongs to. **class** values don't have to be unique. Many elements can be members of the same class; in fact, elements don't even have to be of the same type to be in a common class. The idea of using **class** is illustrated here:

```
<!DOCTYPE HTML PUBLIC "-//W3C//DTD HTML 4.01 Transitional//EN">
<html>
<head>
<title>Class Example</title>
<style type="text/css">
```

```
<!--
.veryimportant   {background-color: yellow;}
-->
</style>
</head>

<body>
<h1 class="veryimportant">Example</h1>
<p class="veryimportant">This is the first paragraph.</p>
<p>This is the second paragraph</p>
<p class="veryimportant">This is the third paragraph.</p>
</body>

</html>
```

This example has three elements, each of which has its **class** attribute set to **veryimportant**. According to the style sheet information, all members of the **veryimportant** class, as indicated by the period, have a yellow background color. Writing rules for classes is easy: Simply specify the class name, with a period before it as the selector:

```
.main-item {font-size: 150%;}
```

Other variations on class rules are possible. For example, setting all **<h1>** elements of the class **veryimportant** to have a background color of orange could be written like this:

```
h1.veryimportant {background-color: orange;}
```

Classes can be used to significantly reduce the number of style rules necessary in a document.

Pseudo Classes and Elements

A special pre-defined class grouping, called pseudo-classes, is also used in CSS1 mainly to deal with the states of links. Recall that a hypertext link has three primary states in HTML—unvisited, visited, and active—in which the link text color is blue, purple, and red respectively. In HTML, it is possible to control the color of these link states through the **link**, **vlink**, and **alink** attributes for the **<body>** element. In CSS the presentation of link states is controlled through the pseudo class selectors **a:link**, **a:visited**, and **a:active**. CSS2 also adds **a:hover** for the link state for the browser hovering over and is one of the most commonly supported CSS2 features. The pseudo-class **:focus** also is added by CSS2 and is briefly discussed later in the chapter. An example showing how these link pseudo-class selectors are used is shown here.

```
<!DOCTYPE HTML PUBLIC "-//W3C//DTD HTML 4.0 Transitional//EN">
<html>
<head>
<title>Link Pseudo-Class Example</title>
<style type="text/css">
<!--
a:link       {color: blue; text-decoration: none;}
a:active     {color: red; background-color: #ffffcc;}
a:visited    {color: purple; text-decoration: none;}
a:hover      {color: red; text-decoration: underline;}
-->
</style>
</head>
<body>
<a href="http://www.htmlref.com">HTML: The Complete Reference</a>
</body>
</html>
```

Although the CSS rules associated with the states of a link can be used to change the link's appearance in dramatic ways, designers are encouraged to limit changes to improve usability. Also note that size changes and other significant differences in link presentation might result in undesirable screen repainting.

Another form of selector similar to pseudo-classes in terms of syntax is called a pseudo-element. Under CSS1 two pseudo-elements exist: **:first-letter** and **:first-line**. These selectors are used along with common block-level text elements such as **<p>** to affect the presentation of the first letter or first line of enclosed text. A short example showing their use is presented here:

```
<!DOCTYPE HTML PUBLIC "-//W3C//DTD HTML 4.01 Transitional//EN">
<html>
<head>
<title>First Line and Letter</title>
<style type="text/css">
<!--
p:first-line      {background-color: yellow;}
p:first-letter    {color: red; font-size: 150%;}
-->
</style>
```

```
</head>
<body>
<p>CSS selectors can be used to select elements in a variety
of interesting ways. This is some text to fill up the paragraph.
This is only text to fill up this paragraph. This should be
enough text to make this paragraph.</p>

<p>CSS selectors can be used to select elements in a variety
of interesting ways. This is some text to fill up the paragraph.
This is only text to fill up this paragraph. This should be
enough text to make this paragraph.</p>

</body>
</html>
```

Figure 10-2 shows two renderings of this example to show how the text affected by the rule varies depending on the text flow. Pseudo-classes and elements hint at a much more complex set of CSS rules that are invoked depending on where an element appears in a document.

Contextual Selection

Although the **class** and **id** attributes provide a great deal of flexibility for creating style rules, many other types of rules of equal value exist. For example, it might be useful to specify that all **<strong>** elements that occur within a **<p>** element get treated in a certain way, as compared to the same elements occurring elsewhere within the document. To create such a rule, the concept of *contextual selection* must be used. Contextual selectors are created by showing the order in which the elements must be nested for the rule to be applied. For example, given the rule

```
p strong {background-color: yellow}
```

all occurrences of the **<strong>** element within a **<p>** element to have a yellow background. Other occurrences of **<strong>** might not necessarily have the yellow background, because potential issues of inheritance could creep in.

Inheritance

HTML documents have an implicit structure. They all have an **<html>** element. Within this element lie the **<head>** and **<body>** elements, which can contain the **<title>** and **<p>** elements, respectively. The structure of the document looks somewhat like a

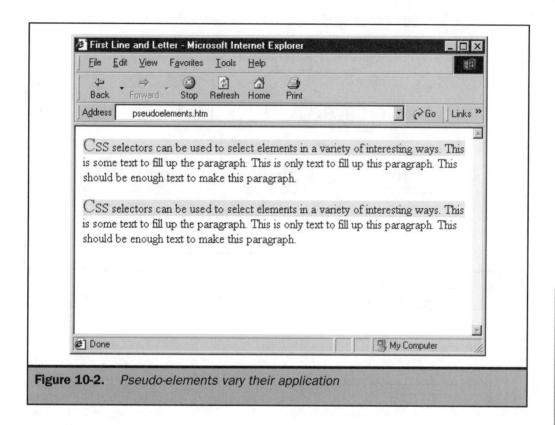

Figure 10-2. *Pseudo-elements vary their application*

family tree. For example, the document shown here would have a parse tree, as shown in Figure 10-3:

```
<!DOCTYPE HTML PUBLIC "-//W3C//DTD HTML 4.01 Transitional//EN">
<html>
<head>
<title>Test File</title>
</head>
<body>
<h1>Test</h1>
<p>This is a <b>Test</b></p>
</body>
</html>
```

In the example parse tree, note how the **<b>** element is enclosed within the **<p>** element, which is in the **<body>**, which is in the **<html>** element. What happens if you set a style rule to the **<p>** element like so?

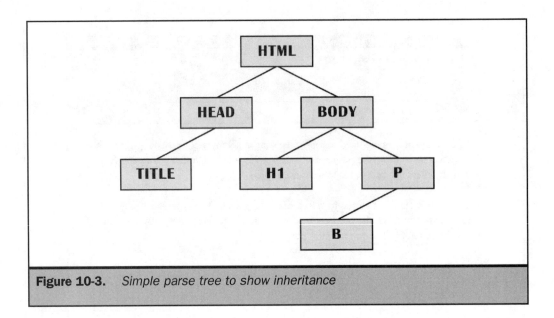

Figure 10-3. *Simple parse tree to show inheritance*

```
p {color: red;}
```

Would the **<b>** tag's contents also be red? The answer is yes because the color is inherited from the parent element. Whereas most elements can inherit the style features of their parents, some style properties do not inherit. For example, consider setting the **border** property of the paragraph like so:

```
p {border: solid;}
```

If the **<b>** element inherited the border, you would expect to see something like this.

This is regular text of the paragraph within a border.

This is bold text and should not be within a border because the bold element does not inherit the border.

Here is a little more paragraph text.

However, this does not happen and the border is limited just to the paragraph itself. As the various CSS properties are introduced later in the chapter important non-inheriting properties will be pointed out. Also Appendix B summarizes all CSS1 properties and clearly indicates whether a property can be inherited.

Assuming that a property does inherit, it is still possible to override the inheritance of a property. For example, consider two rules such as

```
p    {color: red; font-size: 14pt;}
b    {color: yellow;}
```

In this case the color of the text within the **<b>** element would be yellow and in 14 point. Both of the properties were inherited, but the color property was overridden by the color rule for the **<b>** element which is more specific.

The combination of multiple rules with elements inheriting some properties and overriding others is the idea of the *cascade* that CSS is named for. The general idea of the cascade, in effect, is that it provides a system to sort out which rules apply to a document that has many style sheets. For example, a rule for a specific **<p>** element using an **id** attribute is more powerful than a class rule applied to **<p>**, which in turn is more powerful than a rule for the element **<p>** itself. Inline styles set with a style attribute are more important than a document-wide style or linked style. An easy way to think about which rule wins is to think: The more specific the rule the more powerful as well as the closer to the tag the rule the more powerful. There is an actual process to determine the specificity of a particular rule versus another by assigning numeric values to each rule, but if a designer requires such a careful analysis of the style rules to determine an end result, the style sheet is simply too complex.

In the instance that a particular rule should never be overridden by another rule, the **!important** indication should be used. For a rule never to be ignored, insert the indication **!important** just before the semicolon of the rule. For example, to always set all paragraphs to red text you might use

```
p {color: red !important; font-size: 12pt;}
```

Later on you might have a paragraph with an inline style such as

```
<p style="color: green; font-size: 24pt;">
```

In this paragraph the text would still be red due to the inclusion of the **!important** indicator, although it would be larger because that rule was overridden as expected. When using the **!important** indicator make sure to always put it at the end of a rule; otherwise it will be ignored.

Note   *Many older browsers do not support the !important declaration properly, so use it with caution.*

Now that the basics of style sheet rules have been discussed, it is time to turn our attention to the various style sheet properties. Before doing so, the next section shows a brief example using many of the ideas presented in the last few sections.

PRESENTATION AND LAYOUT

Complete Style Sheet Example

The example shown here uses two forms of style: document-wide and inline. The example also illustrates the use of the **class** and **id** attributes and the appropriate use of HTML elements with CSS properties. Most of the properties should make sense, particularly after seeing the rendering. If you don't get it, don't worry; basic CSS properties and examples are covered later in the chapter.

```
<!DOCTYPE HTML PUBLIC "-//W3C//DTD HTML 4.01 Transitional//EN">
<html>
<head>
<title>Simple CSS Example</title>
<style type="text/css">
<!--
body      {background-color: black;}
div.page  {background-color: #FFD040;
            color: black;
            margin: 50px 10px 50px 10px;
            padding: 10px 10px;
            width: 90%;
            height: 90%;}
h1        {font-size: 24pt;
            font-family: Comic Sans Ms, Cursive;
            text-align: center;}
.blackonwhite {color: black; background-color: white;}
.whiteonblack {color: white; background-color: black;}
p            {font-family: Arial, Sans-serif;
              font-size: 16pt;
              line-height: 200%;
              text-align: justify;
              text-indent: 20px;}
.style    {color: blue; font-family: Arial; font-style: oblique;}
.size     {font-size: x-large;}
#letterspace   {letter-spacing: 15pt;}
-->
</style>
</head>
<body>
<div class="page">
<h1><span class="blackonwhite">CSS</span>
    <span class="whiteonblack">Fun</span>
</h1>
```

```
<hr>
<p> With style sheets, you will be able to control the presentation
of Web pages with greater precision. Style sheets can be used to
set everything from <span class="style">font styles</span> and
<span class="size">sizes</span> to <span id="letterspace">letter
spacing</span> and line heights.
</p>

</div>
</body>
</html>
```

Figure 10-4 shows how the preceding CSS example is rendered by Internet Explorer 5, Netscape 6 preview release, Netscape 4.x and Opera 4.x. Notice that the renderings are not exactly the same. Under some older browsers, significant rendering problems might occur. Designers are cautioned to keep compatibility well in mind as they apply style sheets to their pages.

CSS1 Properties

The basic idea of *how* rules are formed in style sheets was discussed earlier in this chapter (refer to "Style Sheet Basics"), but what *are* the various properties that can be set? CSS1 defines more than 50 different properties and values, and the browser vendors are busy inventing new ones all the time. This section covers the standard CSS1 properties as defined by the WC3, which can be found at www.w3.org/TR/REC-CSS1, and should work in all browsers. Although they *should* work, some properties might not work in your browser. Although CSS1 promises a lot more flexibility than HTML, you still have the issues regarding lack of support across browsers and rendering differences. Before turning our attention to the various style properties, it is important to discuss units of measure under CSS1.

CSS Measurements

When you manipulate text and other objects with a style sheet, you often must specify a length or size. CSS1 supports a variety of measurement forms. The CSS1 specification supports traditional English measurements such as inches (**in**) as well metric values in centimeters (**cm**), or millimeters (**mm**). All are demonstrated here with a simple **text-indent** property that can be applied to four **<p>** elements with different **id** attribute values:

```
#para1      {text-indent: 1in;}
#para2      {text-indent: 10mm;}
#para3      {text-indent: 0.5cm;}
#para4      {text-indent: -0.75cm;}
```

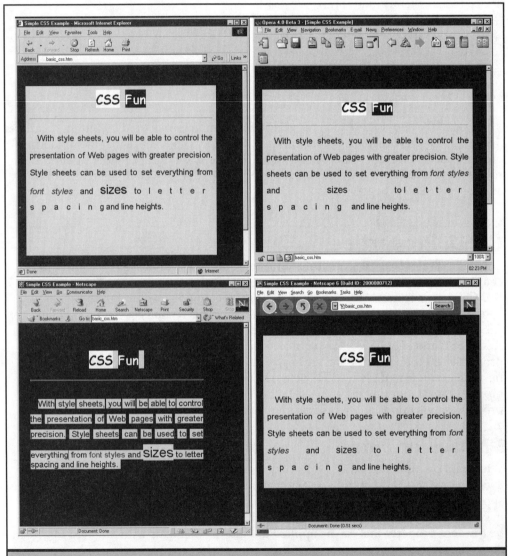

Figure 10-4. Browser renderings of the CSS example

Notice that it is possible to set values in CSS as both positive and negative integer values as well as decimal values. Of course negative values might have somewhat unpredictable results at times.

It also is possible to specify units in publishing length units such as the familiar point size (**pt**) as well as picas (**pc**). For the curious, points relate to inches in that 72 points equals 1 inch, whereas a pica is equivalent to 12 points; thus, there are 6 picas per inch.

```
P.big           {font-size: 64pt;}
.verysmall      {font-size: 6pt;}
#picameasure    {line-height: 2pc;}
```

Interestingly, despite the comfort many designers might have with points as an absolute measurement of text, because of the way point size is calculated onscreen on the Web, 12pt will not be the same between a PC and a Macintosh. It can even vary on the same PC, depending on operating system, browser, and browser version. Because of this, designers looking for supposedly exact measurements might instead opt for pixels (**px**).

```
.bypixel    {font-size: 40px;}
```

Pixels certainly aren't the best measurement form, because you might run into problems depending on the user's screen size. Because of this, many designers opt for relative units like em-height units (**em**), x-height units (**ex**) and percentage values (**%**). The relative units can be difficult for designers to figure out. The **em** unit is equivalent to the size of a given font. So if you assign a font to 12pt, each **"em"** unit would be 12pt, thus 2em would be 24pt. Consider the following markup

```
<div style="font-size: 12pt; text-indent: 1em;">Em example with font-size
at 12pt.</div>
<div style="font-size: 24pt; text-indent: 1em;">Same example with font-size
at 24pt.</div>
```

whose rendering is shown here.

Notice that, in the rendering, the second example is indented roughly twice as far as the first based upon the value of the em unit. Although the value of the em unit might not seem obvious consider that it can be used to adjust all content relative to a base measurement.

Slightly easier to understand compared to em, the x-height measurement (**ex**) is used in typography to describe the height of the lowercase x character in a particular font. When setting font sizes and line spacing, it is important to consider the x-height of the font in use. In fact, even when fonts are the same point size they can be much larger or smaller based upon their x-height, as shown here:

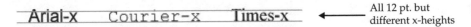

Arial-x   Courier-x   Times-x   ◄—— All 12 pt. but
                                           different x-heights

A simple use of x-height measurements (**ex**) would be to specify the line-height relative to a font's x-height.

```
p {line-height: 2.5ex;}
```

Last, like em, the percentage value can be useful when measuring things in CSS as shown here:

```
b {font-size: 80%;}   /* 80% of the parent element's font */
```

Although page designers who are used to electronic layout tools probably will stick to the measurements most familiar to them, such as points or pixels, the use of relative measurements do make a great deal of sense when trying to create style sheets that work under a variety of conditions.

Note *Many older CSS1 supporting browsers could have problems with relative measurements such as em and ex, as well as negative values for measurements.*

Font Properties

CSS1 provides numerous font-oriented properties to set the family, style, size, and variations of the font used within a Web page. Beyond font properties, you also can combine these rules with rules for color, background, margin, and spacing to create a variety of interesting typographic effects.

font-family

The **font-family** property is used to set the font family that is used to render text. The **font-family** property can be set to a specific font, such as Arial, or to a generic family, such as sans serif. You have to quote any font family names that contain white space, such as **"Britannic Bold"**, and you might have to capitalize font values for a match.

According to the CSS1 specification, the following generic families should be available on all browsers that support CSS1:

- Serif (e.g., Times)
- Sans-serif (e.g., Helvetica)
- Cursive (e.g., Zapf-Chancery)
- Fantasy (e.g., Western)
- Monospace (e.g., Courier)

Like the **<font>** element, when setting the **font-family**, you can provide a prioritized list of names, separated by commas that will be checked in order. Remember to always provide a backup generic font family as defined in CSS1 at the end of the **font-family** list in case the user's browser doesn't support the fonts suggested. To set a document-wide font, use a rule such as the following for the **<body>** element:

```
body    {font-family: customSans, Arial, Helvetica, sans-serif;}
```

Whereas the font-family property allows both specific and generic CSS1 fonts to be specified, the only way to guarantee a font is on a user's system is to use a downloadable font, which is discussed at the conclusion of this chapter.

font-size

The **font-size** property is used to set the relative or physical size of the font used. The value for the property can be a value that is mapped to a physical point size or to a relative word describing the size. Physical point-size values include **xx-small**, **x-small**, **small**, **medium**, **large**, **x-large**, and **xx-large**, or a relative word, such as **larger** or **smaller**. Physical sizes also might include examples, such as **48pt**, **2cm**, or **.25in**. Relative measurements including percentage values, such as **150%**, also are valid for sizing. However, negative percentages or point sizes are not allowed. A few example rules are shown here:

```
p       {font-size: 18pt;}
strong  {font-size: larger;}
.double {font-size: 200%;}
```

One suggestion with the **font-size** property is to avoid setting point sizes, where possible, because users who can't see well might have a hard time adjusting size. On certain monitors, a 10-point font might look fine, but on others, it might be microscopic. If you use exact point size, remember to error in favor of readability and increase size.

font-style

The **font-style** property is used to specify **normal**, **italic**, or **oblique** font style for the font being used. A value of italic should select an italic version of a font, whereas a value of oblique might simply slant the font. In many cases a value of italic or oblique results in the same exact rendering. A value of **normal** produces text that is in the Roman style—straight up and down. A few examples are shown here:

```
h1          {font-style: oblique;}
.firstuse   {font-style: italic;}
em          {font-style: normal;}
```

font-weight

The **font-weight** property selects the weight, or darkness, of the font. Values for the property range from **100–900**, in increments of 100. Keywords also are supported, including **normal**, **bold**, **bolder**, and **lighter**, which are used to set relative weights. Some browsers also might provide keywords such as **extra-light**, **light**, **demi-light**, **medium**, **demi-bold**, **bold**, and **extra-bold**, which correspond to the **100–900** values. A few examples are shown here:

```
.important  {font-weight: bolder;}
h1          {font-weight: 900;}
P.special   {font-weight: extra-bold;}
```

Typically, the value **bold** is the same as **700**, and the **normal** font value is **400**. Note that many browsers have trouble rendering different font weights on screen beyond bold and normal.

font-variant

The **font-variant** property is used to select a variation of the specified (or default) font family. The only current variant supported with this property is **small-caps**, which displays text as small uppercase letters, and **normal**, which displays text in the normal style. (Support is limited to Internet Explorer 5 and better, and Netscape 6.) A simple rule is shown here:

```
em   {font-variant: small-caps;}
```

font

The **font** property provides a concise way to specify all the font properties with one style rule. One attribute that is included within **font** is **line-height**, which specifies the distance between two lines of text. Each font attribute can be indicated on the line, separated by spaces, except for **line-height**, which is used with **font-size** and separated by a slash. You can use as many or as few of the font rules in this shorthand notation as you want. The general form of the font rule is shown here:

```
font: font-style font-variant font-weight font-size/line-height
      font-family
```

The following is an example of using a compact font rule:

```
p {font:italic small-caps 600 18pt/24pt "Arial, Helvetica";}
```

The shorthand notation does not require all the properties, so the next example is just as valid as the complete notation:

```
p    {font: italic 18pt/24pt;}
```

The following is a complete style sheet example that uses all the font rules:

```
<!DOCTYPE HTML PUBLIC "-//W3C//DTD HTML 4.01 Transitional//EN">
<html>
<head>
<title>CSS1 Font Properties Example</title>
<style type="text/css">
<!--
body          {font-size: 14pt;}
.serif        {font-family: serif;}
.sans-serif   {font-family: sans-serif;}
.cursive      {font-family: cursive;}
.fantasy      {font-family: fantasy;}
.comic        {font-family: Comic Sans MS;}
.xx-small     {font-size: xx-small;}
.x-small      {font-size: x-small;}
.small        {font-size: small;}
.medium       {font-size: medium;}
.large        {font-size: large;}
.x-large      {font-size: x-large;}
```

```
.xx-large      {font-size: xx-large;}
.smaller       {font-size: smaller;}
.larger        {font-size: larger;}
.points        {font-size: 18pt;}
.percentage    {font-size: 200%;}
.italic        {font-style: italic;}
.oblique       {font-style: oblique;}
.weight        {font-weight: 900;}
.smallcaps     {font-variant: small-caps;}
-->
</style>
</head>
<body>

<h2>Font Family</h2>
This text is in <span class="serif">Serif.</span><br>
This text is in <span class="sans-serif">Sans-Serif.</span><br>
This text is in <span class="cursive">Cursive.</span><br>
This text is in <span class="fantasy">Fantasy.</span><br>
Actual fonts can be specified like <span class="comic">
Comic Sans MS</span><br>

<h2>Font Sizing</h2>
This is <span class="xx-small">xx-small text.</span><br>
This is <span class="x-small">x-small text.</span><br>
This is <span class="small">small text.</span><br>
This is <span class="medium">medium text.</span><br>
This is <span class="large">large text.</span><br>
This is <span class="x-large">x-large text.</span><br>
This is <span class="xx-large">xx-large text.</span><br>
This is <span class="smaller">smaller text</span> than the rest.
<br>
This is <span class="larger">larger text</span> than the rest.<br>
This is <span class="points">exactly 18 point text.</span><br>
This is <span class="percentage">200% larger text.</span><br>

<h2>Font Style, Weight, and Variant</h2>
This text is <span class="italic">italic.</span><br>
This text is <span class="oblique">oblique.</span><br>
This text is <span class="weight">bold.</span><br>
This text is in <span class="smallcaps">smallcaps.</span><br>
</body>
</html>
```

A rendering of the font example is shown in Figure 10-5. Note that there are rendering differences between browser versions even with this simple example, particularly with named sizes.

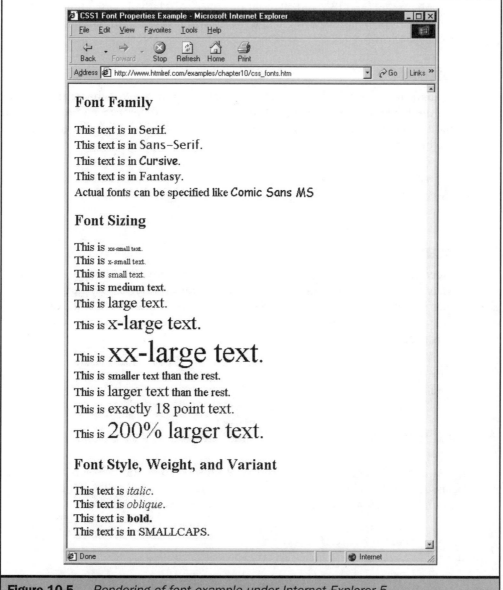

Figure 10-5. *Rendering of font example under Internet Explorer 5*

Text Properties

Text properties are used to affect the presentation, spacing, and layout of text. The basic properties enable the page designer to set text presentation such as decoration, indentation, word spacing, letter spacing, spacing between lines, horizontal and vertical text alignment, and the control of white space. A relatively uncommon CSS text property, **text-transform** allows designers to transform text case and will begin our discussion of these properties.

text-transform

The **text-transform** property determines the capitalization of the text that it affects. The possible values for this property are **capitalize**, **uppercase**, **lowercase**, and **none**, which is the default value. Note that the value **capitalize** might result in capitalizing every word. Here are some possible uses of the **text-transform** property:

```
p          {text-transform: capitalize;}
.upper     {text-transform: uppercase;}
.lower     {text-transform: lower;}
```

text-decoration

The **text-decoration** property is used to define an effect on text. The standard values for this property include **line-through**, **overline**, **underline**, and **none**. The meaning of these values is obvious, except for **overline**, which creates a line above text. Netscape also has added support for the **blink** value. The following examples show possible uses for this property:

```
.struck        {text-decoration: line-through;}
span.special   {text-decoration: blink;}
h1             {text-decoration: overline;}
a              {text-decoration: none;}
#author        {text-decoration: underline;}
```

The **text-decoration** property often is used with the **<a>** element and its associated pseudoclasses, which include a:**link**, **a:active**, **a:visited,** and **a:hover** to change presentation; in particular turning underlining off or on as shown here:

```
a          {text-decoration: none;}
a:hover    {text-decoration: underline;}
```

word-spacing

The **word-spacing** property specifies the amount of space between words. The default value, **normal**, uses the browser's word-spacing default. Designers are free to specify the distance between words in a variety of measurements as previously discussed, including inches (**in**), centimeters (**cm**), millimeters (**mm**), points (**pt**), picas (**pc**), the em (**em**) measurement, and pixels (**px**). A few examples are shown here:

```
body    {word-spacing: 10pt;}
p       {font-size: 18pt; word-spacing: 1em;}
```

 This property is poorly supported in browsers, particularly older CSS1 supporting browsers.

letter-spacing

The **letter-spacing** property specifies the amount of space between letters. The default value, **normal**, uses the browser's letter-spacing default. Like the **word-spacing** property, a variety of measurements can be used to set word spacing, from pixels to em values. A few examples of this property are shown here:

```
p       {letter-spacing: 0.2em;}
body    {letter-spacing: 2px;}
.wide   {letter-spacing: 10pt;}
#Fun    {letter-spacing: 2cm;}
```

vertical-align

The **vertical-align** property controls the vertical positioning of text and images with respect to the baseline currently in effect. The possible values for the **vertical-align** property include **baseline**, **sub**, **super**, **top**, **text-top**, **middle**, **bottom**, **text-bottom**, and percentage values. Compare these values with the **align** attribute for the **<img>** element, as well as alignment options for table cells, and things should begin to make sense. The flexibility of style sheets enables you to set element values on individual characters. When not specified, the default value of **vertical-align** is **baseline**. The following are a few examples:

```
p                {vertical-align: text-top;}
.superscript     {vertical-align: super; font-size: smaller;}
.subscript       {vertical-align: sub; font-size: 75%;}
```

Notice in the preceding example how **vertical-align** can be used with other properties to create an interesting contextual class such as **.superscript**.

Note *According to CSS1 specification the vertical-align property is not inherited by enclosed elements, but testing reveals this not to be the case in most browsers.*

PRESENTATION AND LAYOUT

text-align

The **text-align** property determines how text in a block-level element, such as the **<p>** element, is horizontally aligned. The allowed values for this property are **left** which is the default, **right**, **center**, and **justify**. This property is used only on block level elements such as **<p>** in a similar manner to the **align** attributes from HTML. Be aware that that setting a value of **justify** might not produce an eye-pleasing result when the font is very large as it might obviously show the added spaces. A few examples are shown here:

```
p          {text-align: justify;}
div        {text-align: center;}
.goright   {text-align: right;}
```

text-indent

The **text-indent** property sets the indentation for text in the first line of a block-level element such as **<p>**. Its value can be given either as a length value (**.5cm**, **15px**, **12pt**, and so on) or as a percentage of the width of the block, such as **10%**. The default value for the property is **0**, which indicates no indentation. A few examples of how **text-indent** might be used are shown here:

```
p          {text-indent: 2em;}
p.heavy    {text-indent: 150px;}
```

One interesting effect is the use of negative values to create a hanging indent, wherein the text within the block element expands outside of the block. The following rule creates a paragraph with a yellow background, in which the first line of text starts left of the text:

```
p    {text-indent: -10px; background-color: yellow;}
```

Combining the hanging indent with a large first letter using the pseudo class **:first-letter** for the paragraph element creates an interesting effect.

line-height

The **line-height** property sets the height between lines in a block-level element, such as a paragraph. The basic idea is to set the line spacing, known more appropriately as *leading*. The value of the attribute can be specified as a number of lines (**1.4**), a length (**14pt**), or as a percentage of the line height (**200%**). So, double spacing could be written as

```
p.double    {line-height: 2;}
```

as well as

```
p.double2        {line-height: 200%;}
```

Other examples of using **line-height** are shown here:

```
p                {font-size: 12pt; line-height: 18pt;}
p.carson         {font-size: 24pt; line-height: 6pt;}
```

Notice in the second example how the **line-height** property is much smaller than the **font-size** property. A browser generally should render the text on top of the other text, creating a hard-to-read, but potentially "cool" effect.

white-space

The **white-space** property controls how spaces, tabs, and newline characters are handled in an element. The default value, **normal**, collapses white space characters into a single space and automatically wraps lines, just as normal HTML. When a value of **pre** is used for the property, white-space formatting is preserved, similar to how the **<pre>** element works in HTML. The **nowrap** value prevents lines from wrapping if they exceed the element's content width. This property shows how the **white-space** property would be used to simulate the **<pre>** element:

```
p.pre {white-space:pre;}
```

Note   *The **nowrap** and **pre** values are not well supported in older CSS aware browsers at the time of this writing.*

A complete example showing the HTML and cascading style sheet markup for text properties previously presented is shown here:

```
<!DOCTYPE HTML PUBLIC "-//W3C//DTD HTML 4.01 Transitional//EN">
<html>
<head>
<title>CSS Text Attributes Example</title>
<style type="text/css">
<!--

/* letter and word spacing */
.letterspaced    {letter-spacing: 10pt;}
.wordspaced      {word-spacing: 20px;}
```

```
/* vertical alignment examples */
.sub            {vertical-align: sub;}
.super          {vertical-align: super;}

/* text alignment properties */
.right          {text-align: right;}
.left           {text-align: left;}
.justify        {text-align: justify;}
.center         {text-align: center;}

/* indentation and line-height examples */
p.indent        {text-indent: 20px;
                 line-height: 200%;}

p.negindent     {text-indent: -10px;
                 background-color: yellow;}

#bigchar        {background-color: red;
                 color: white;
                 font-size: 28pt;
                 font-family: Impact;}

p.carson        {font-size: 12pt;
                 font-family: Courier;
                 letter-spacing: 4pt;
                 line-height: 5pt;}

/* text transformation properties */

.uppercase   {text-transform: uppercase;}
.lowercase   {text-transform: lowercase;}
.capitalize  {text-transform: capitalize;}

/* text-decoration properties */
.underline   {text-decoration: underline;}
.blink       {text-decoration: blink;}
.line-through {text-decoration: line-through;}
.overline    {text-decoration: overline;}

/* white space control */
.normal   {white-space: normal;}
.pre      {white-space: pre;}
.nowrap   {white-space: nowrap;}
```

```
-->
</style>
</head>
<body>

<h2>Letter Spacing and Vertical Alignment</h2>

<p>This is a paragraph of text.
<span class="letterspaced">Spacing letters is possible</span>
and so <span class="wordspaced">should  word spacing.
Alas, it not always supported!</span></p>

<p>Vertical alignment can be used to make
<span class="sub">Subscript</span> and
<span class="super">Superscript</span> text, but the
real use of the property is for aligning text next to images.</p>

<h2>Alignment</h2>

<p class="left">Align a paragraph to the left as normal.</p>

<p class="right">Align paragraphs to the right as we did in
HTML</p>

<p class="justify">You can even set the justification of text so
that it is aligned on both the left and the right side.  You need
to be careful with this so that you don't get rivers of white space
running through your paragraphs.</p>

<p class="center">Text can of course also be centered.</span>

<h2>Indentation and Line Height</h2>

<p class="indent">With style sheets it is possible to set
indentation as well as line height. Now double spacing is a
reality. This is just dummy text to show the effects of the
indentation and spacing. This is just dummy text to show the
effects of the indentation and spacing.</p>

<p class="negindent"><span id="bigchar">T</span>his is another
paragraph which has negative indenting. Notice how you can pull
a character outside the paragraph for interesting effects. This
is just dummy text to show the effect of the indent. This is
just dummy text to show the effect of the indent.</p>
```

```
<h2>Surf Gun</h2>

<p class="carson">Don't get carried away with your newfound
powers. You may be tempted to show how cool you can be using
text on top of other text. While this may be good for certain
situations, it may also confuse the viewer.</p>

<h2>Text Transformation</h2>
The next bit of text is transformed <span class="uppercase">to all
uppercase.</span><br> The next bit of text is transformed
<span class="lowercase">to all lowercase.</span><br>
<span class="capitalize">This text is all capitalized. It doesn't
do what you think, does it?</span><br>

<h2>Text Decoration</h2>

This text should <span class="blink">blink under Netscape.</span>
<br><br>
This text should be <span class="underline">underlined.</span>
<br><br>
This text should be <span class="line-through">struck.</span>
<br><br>
This text should be <span class="overline">overline.</span>
<br><br>

<h2>White Space Control</h2>

<p class="normal">This text controls space normally like
  HTML condenses                all spaces and
           returns to a single character</p>

<p class="pre">This paragraph
    preserves any  S  P  E  C  I  A  L   spacing</p>

<p class="nowrap">This paragraph does not wrap at all and
keeps going and going and going and going to the right
until I stop typing.</p>

</body>
</html>
```

The rendering of the text properties example is shown in Figure 10-6.

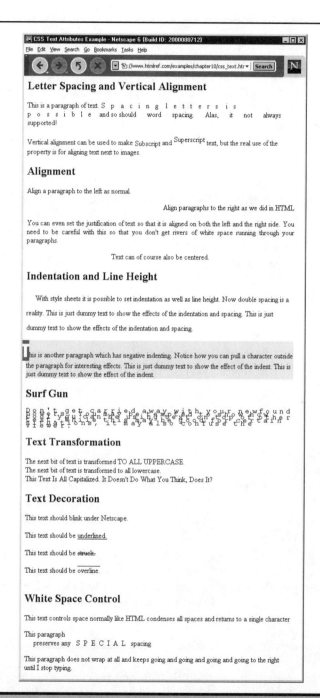

Figure 10-6.   *Rendering of text properties under a preview release of Netscape 6*

List Properties

As discussed in Chapter 3, HTML supports three major forms of lists: ordered lists, unordered lists, and definition lists. HTML also has supported other forms of lists that were more compact or formatted differently, but browser support has been spotty. CSS1 provides some list manipulation, including three style properties that can be set for lists: **list-style-type**, **list-style-image**, and **list-style-position**. A general property, **list-style**, provides a shorthand notation to set all three properties at once.

list-style-type

The items in ordered or unordered lists are labeled with a numeric value or a bullet, depending on the list form. These list labels can be set under CSS1 by using the **list-style-type** property. Six values are appropriate for ordered lists: **decimal**, **lower-roman**, **upper-roman**, **lower-alpha**, and **upper-alpha**. Three values are appropriate for unordered lists: **disc**, **circle**, and **square**. The value **none** prevents a label from displaying. These values are similar to the **type** attribute for the list elements in HTML. Setting the following:

```
ol    {list-style-type: upper-roman;}
```

is equivalent to **<ol type="i">**, whereas the following is equivalent to **<ul type="square">**:

```
ul    {list-style-type: square;}
```

Nested lists can be controlled by using context selection rules. For example, to set an outer order list to uppercase roman numerals, an inner list to lowercase roman numerals, and a further embedded list to lowercase letters, use the following rules:

```
ol           {list-style-type: upper-roman;}
ol ol        {list-style-type: lower-roman;}
ol ol ol     {list-style-type: lower-alpha;}
```

The **list-style-type** property also can be associated with the **<li>** element, but be aware that setting individual list elements to a particular style might require the use of the **id** attribute, or even inline styles.

list-style-image

The **list-style-type** property provides little different functionality from HTML lists, but the **list-style-image** property can assign a graphic image to a list label; this is awkward to do under plain HTML. The value of the property is either the URL of the image to use as a bullet or the keyword **none**. So, to use small flags with your list, create an appropriate graphics file and use a rule such as this:

```
UL    {list-style-image: url("flag.gif")}
```

Notice the use of the keyword url within which you set a URL either absolute or relative to the image to use.

*Although setting the **list-style-image** for an ordered list might be possible, be careful, because the meaning of the list then is lost.*

list-style-position

Display elements in cascading style sheets are treated as existing inside a rectangular box. Unlike other elements, the labels for list items can exist outside and to the left of the list element's box. The **list-style-position** property controls where a list item's label is displayed in relation to the element's box. The values allowed for this property are **inside** or **outside**. The **outside** value is the default. The following example tightens up a list by bringing the bullets inside the box for the list:

```
ul.compact    {list-style-position: inside;}
```

list-style

Like margin, padding, and other shorthand notation, the **list-style** property allows a list's type, image, or position properties all to be set by a single property. The properties can appear in any order and are determined by value. The following is an example of the shorthand notation that sets an unordered list with a bullet image that appears within the list block:

```
ul.special {list-style: inside url("bullet.gif");}
```

A complete example of list properties is shown here, with a rendering in Figure 10-7.

```
<!DOCTYPE HTML PUBLIC "-//W3C//DTD HTML 4.0 Transitional//EN">
<html>
<head>
<title>List Properties Example</title>
<style type="text/css">
<!--
ul    {list-style-image: url("flag.gif");}
```

```
.inside    {list-style-type: upper-roman;
           background-color: yellow;
           list-style-position: inside;}
.outside   {background-color: yellow;
           list-style-position: inside;}
-->
</style>
</head>
<body>
<ul>
    <li>Item a</li>
    <li>Item b</li>
</ul>

<ol class="outside">
    <li>Item a</li>
    <li>Item b</li>
</ol>

<ol class="inside">
    <li>Item a</li>
    <li>Item b</li>
</ol>

</body>
</html>
```

CSS2 provides a wealth of settings beyond this, as well as control over list number. See the section entitled "CSS2 List Changes" for more information on CSS2-based list properties.

Color and Background Properties

CSS1 supports a variety of properties that can be used to control the colors and backgrounds in a document. With style sheets, you can create arbitrary regions with different background colors and images. In the past, such designs were difficult to accomplish without turning to tables or proprietary HTML extensions.

CSS1 style sheets support three basic forms of color specifications:

- **Color names**   The suggested keyword colors supported by browsers are a set of 16 color names taken from the Windows VGA palette. The colors include **Aqua, Black, Blue, Fuchsia, Gray, Green, Lime, Maroon, Navy, Olive, Purple,**

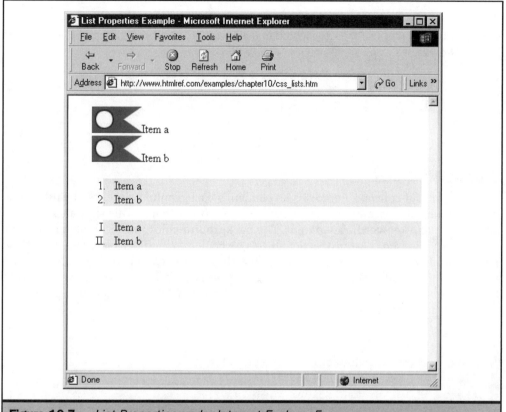

Figure 10-7.   *List Properties under Internet Explorer 5*

Red, **Silver**, **Teal**, **White**, and **Yellow**. These are the same predefined colors from the HTML specification.

- **Hexadecimal values**   Support for the standard, six-digit color form *#RRGGBB* as used with the **<font>** and **<body>** elements. A shortened, three-digit color form, in which R, G, and B are hex digits, also is supported under CSS1. For example, #F00 would represent red. This three-hex color format is an uncommon form of color specification and thus isn't recommended.

- **RGB values**   The RGB format also is specified in the form *rgb (R,G,B)*, whereby the values for R, G, and B range from 0–255. This format should be very familiar to users of Adobe Photoshop. Currently, most browsers don't support the *rgb (R,G,B)* color format, so use it with caution.

color

CSS supports the **color** property, which is used to set the text color. Its use is illustrated in the following examples:

```
body        {color: green;}
h1          {color: #FF0088;}
.fun        {color: #0f0;}
#test       {color: rgb(0,255,0);}
```

background-color

The **background-color** property sets an element's background color. The default value is **none**, which allows any underlying content to show through. This state also is specified by the keyword **transparent**. The **background-color** property often is used in conjunction with the **color** property that sets text color. With block elements, **background-color** colors content and *padding,* the space between an element's contents and its margins. With inline elements, **background-color** colors a box that wraps with the element if it occurs over multiple lines. This property takes colors in the same format as the **color** property. A few example rules are shown here:

```
p           {background-color: yellow;}
body        {background-color: #0000FF;}
.fun        {background-color: #F00;}
#test       {background-color: rgb(0,0,0);}
```

The second example is particularly interesting, because it sets the background color for the entire document.

background-image

The **background-image** property associates a background image with an element. If the image contains transparent regions, underlying content shows through. To prevent this, designers often use the **background-image** property in conjunction with the **background-color** property. The color is rendered beneath the image and provides an opaque background. The **background-image** property requires a URL to select the appropriate image to use as a background. Images that can be used as backgrounds include whatever the browser supports for the **background** attribute of the **<body>** element, typically GIF and JPEG. A few examples are shown here, including some that work in conjunction with the **background-color** property:

```
b          {background-image: url(donut-tile.gif);
            background-color: white;}
body       {background-image: url(funtile.gif);}
.brick     {background-image: url(brick.gif);}
#prison    {background-image: url(bars.gif);}
```

Notice that you can set a background for a small element, such as **<b>**, just as easily as you can for the whole document, by applying the rule to the **<body>** element.

background-repeat

The **background-repeat** property determines how background images tile in cases wherein they are smaller than the canvas space used by their associated elements. The default value is **repeat**, which causes the image to tile in both the horizontal and vertical directions. A value of **repeat-x** for the property limits tiling to the horizontal dimension. The **repeat-y** value behaves similarly for the vertical dimension. The **no-repeat** value prevents the image from tiling.

```
p          {background-image: url(donut-tile.gif);
            background-repeat: repeat-x;}
.tileup    {background-image: url(tile.gif);
            background-repeat: repeat-y;}
body       {background-image: url(tile.gif);
            background-repeat: no-repeat;}
```

Note *By using the **background-repeat** property, you can avoid some of the undesirable tiling effects from HTML-based backgrounds. As discussed in Chapter 6, designers often must resort to making very wide or tall background tiles so that users won't notice the repeat. Because the direction of **repeat** can be controlled, designers can now use much smaller background tiles.*

The second example might present an issue of what happens when the user scrolls the screen: Should the background be fixed or scroll off screen? It turns out that this behavior is specified by the next property, **background-attachment**.

background-attachment

The **background-attachment** property determines whether a background image should scroll as the element content with which it is associated scrolls, or whether the image should stay fixed on the screen while the content scrolls. The default value is **scroll**. The alternate value, **fixed**, can implement a watermark effect, similar to the proprietary attribute **bgproperties** to the **<body>** element that was introduced by Microsoft. An example of how this can be used is shown next.

```
body    {background-image:url(logo.gif);background-attachment:
fixed;}
```

background-position

The **background-position** property specifies how a background image—not a color—is positioned within the canvas space used by its element. There are three ways specify a position:

- The top-left corner of the image can be specified as an absolute distance; usually in pixels.

- The position can be specified as a percentage along the horizontal and vertical dimensions.

- The position can be specified with keywords to describe the horizontal and vertical dimensions. The keywords for the horizontal dimension are **left, center,** and **right**. The keywords for the vertical dimension are **top, center,** and **bottom**. When keywords are used, the default for an unspecified dimension is assumed to be **center**.

The first example shows how to specify the top-left corner of the background by using an absolute distance 10 pixels from the left and 10 pixels from the enclosing element's origin:

```
p  {background-image:url(picture.gif);background-position: 10px
10px;}
```

Remember that this distance is relative to the element and not to the document as a whole, unless, of course, the property is being set for the **<body>** element.

The next example shows how to specify a background image position by using percentage values along the horizontal and vertical dimensions:

```
p   {background-image:url(picture.gif);background-position: 20%
40%;}
```

If you forget to specify one percentage value, the other value is assumed to be **50%**.

Specifying an image position by using keywords is an easy way to do simple placement of an image. When you set a value, the keyword pairs have the following meanings:

Keyword Pair	Horizontal Position	Vertical Position
top left	0%	0%
top center	50%	0%
top right	100%	0%
center left	0%	50%
center center	50%	50%
center right	100%	50%
bottom left	0%	100%
bottom center	50%	100%
bottom right	100%	100%

An example of using keywords to position a background image is shown here:

```
body    {background-image: url(picture.gif);
          background-position: center center;}
```

Note that if only one keyword is set, the second keyword defaults to **center**. Thus, in the preceding example, the keyword **center** was needed only once.

background

The **background** property is a comprehensive property that allows any or all of the specific background properties to be set at once, not unlike the shorthand **font** property. Property order does not matter. Any property not specified uses the default value. A few examples are shown here:

```
p       {background: white url(picture.gif) repeat-y center;}
body    {background: url(tile.jpg) top center fixed;}
.bricks {background: repeat-y top top url(bricks.gif);}
```

A complete example of all the background properties in cascading style sheets is shown here:

```
<!DOCTYPE HTML PUBLIC "-//W3C//DTD HTML 4.01 Transitional//EN">
<html>
<head>
<title>CSS Background Attributes Example</title>
```

```
<style type="text/css">
<!--
body    {background-color: green;}
p       {background: yellow url(flag.gif) repeat-y fixed 100px;}
.red    {background-color: red;}
-->
</style>
</head>
<body>

<p>This is a paragraph of text. The left side will probably be hard to
read because it is on top of an image that repeats along the
y-axis. Notice that the area not covered by the background image is
filled with the background color. <span class="red">Backgrounds anywhere!
</span>
This is more text just to illustrate the idea. This is even more text. This
is more text just to illustrate the idea. This is even more text. This is
more text just to illustrate the idea. This is even more text. This is more
text just to illustrate the idea. This is even more text. This is more text
just to illustrate the idea. This is even more text.</p>
</body>
</html>
```

Notice that multiple background types with a variety of elements can be included.
A similar layout is possible under pure HTML, but the required **<table>** element
would be somewhat complicated. A rendering of the background style sheet example
is shown in Figure 10-8.

Box Properties

Block-level elements, such as the **<p>** element, can be thought of as occupying
rectangular boxes on the screen. Three aspects of these boxes can be controlled with
style properties. The box properties that can be controlled include the following:

- **Margin properties**   Determine the distance between edges of an element's
  box and the edges of adjacent elements.

- **Border properties**   Determine the visual characteristics of a border
  surrounding an element's edges.

- **Padding properties**   Determine the distance inside an element between its
  edges and its actual content.

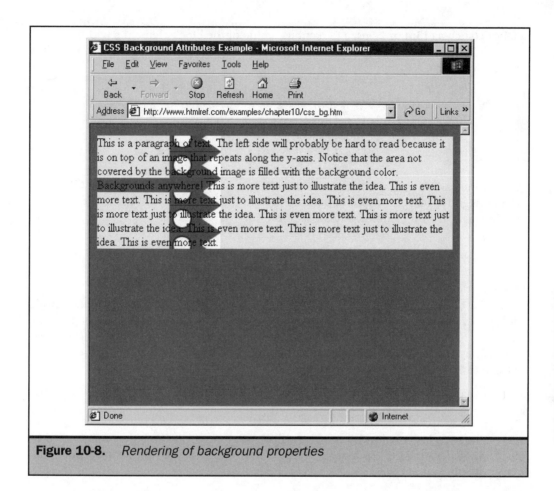

Figure 10-8. *Rendering of background properties*

■ **Height, width, and positioning properties** Determine the size and position of the box that the element creates.

The box properties are equivalent to attributes such as **border**, **height**, and **width** when used with block elements such as **<img>**, but the box properties provide even more power than is available under standard HTML.

Margin Properties

Four margin properties are available to set individually each of an element's four margins. A fifth margin property allows all the margins to be set together. Individual margins for a block element can be set by using **margin-top**, **margin-right**, **margin-bottom**, or **margin-left** properties. The values for the margins should be a length (such as **15pt** or **2em**), a percentage value of the block element's width (such as **20%**), or the value **auto**, which attempts to figure out the appropriate margin automatically:

```
body       {margin-top: 20px; margin-bottom: 20px;
            margin-left: 30px; margin-right: 50px;}
p          {margin-bottom: 20mm;}
div.fun    {margin-left: 1.5cm; margin-right: 1.5cm;}
```

One interesting use of margin properties is to set negative margin values. Of course, negative margins could clip the content of the block element in the browser window, if you aren't careful. Try an example such as

```
p   {margin-left: -2cm; background-color: green;}
```

to get an idea of how negative margins work.

The last few examples show that you can set one or many margins. To make setting multiple margins even easier, a shorthand notation is available that enables page designers to set all the margins at once. Using the **margin** property, one to four values can be assigned to affect the block element margins. If a single value is specified, it is applied to all four margins. For example,

```
p    {margin: 1.5cm;}
```

sets all the margins equal to 1.5 cm. If multiple values are specified, they are applied in clockwise order: first the top margin, followed by (in order) the right, bottom, and left margins. For example,

```
p    {margin: 10px 5px 15px 5px;}
```

sets the top margin to 10 pixels, the right to 5 pixels, the bottom to 15 pixels, and the left to 5 pixels. If only two or three values are specified in the rule, the missing values are determined from the opposite sides. For example,

```
p    {margin: 10px 5px;}
```

sets the top margin to 10 pixels and the right margin to 5 pixels. The opposite sides then are set accordingly, making the bottom margin 10 pixels and the left margin 5 pixels.

A complete example using the margin properties is shown here. Notice that the example uses one negative margin. The background color makes it easier to see the effect.

```
<!DOCTYPE HTML PUBLIC "-//W3C//DTD HTML 4.01 Transitional//EN">
<html>
<head>
<title>CSS Margin Example</title>
<style type="text/css">
<!--
#one      {background-color: yellow;
            margin: 1cm 1cm;}

#two      {background-color: orange;
            margin-top: 1cm;
            margin-bottom: 1cm;
            margin-right: .5cm;
            margin-left: -10px;}

#bigchar  {background-color: red;
             color: white;
             font-size: 28pt;
             font-family: Impact;}
-->
</style>
</head>
<body>

<p id="one">This is a paragraph of text which has
margins set for all sides to 1 cm. This is just dummy
text to show the effects of the margins. This is just
dummy text to show the effects of the margins.</p>

<p id="two"><span id="bigchar">T</span>his is another
paragraph which has negative margins on one side. Be
careful not to clip things with negative margins. This
is just dummy text to show the effect of the margins.
This is just dummy text to show the effect of the margin.</p>

</body>
</html>
```

The rendering of the cascading style sheet margin example under Internet Explorer 5.5 is shown in Figure 10-9.

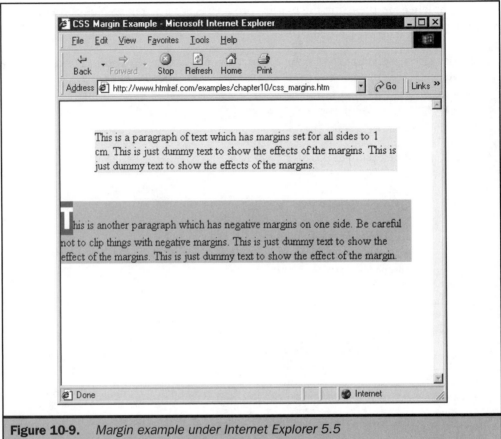

Figure 10-9. *Margin example under Internet Explorer 5.5*

Border Properties

Elements can be completely or partially surrounded by borders placed between their margins and their padding. The border properties control the edges of block elements by setting whether they should have a border, what the borders look like, their width, their color, and so on. Borders are supposed to work with both block-level and inline elements. However, you will not find that border properties are inherited by enclosed elements when used with block elements.

border-style

The **border-style** property is used to set the appearance of the borders. The default value for the property is **none**, which means no border is drawn, regardless of any other setting. The values for **border-style** include

Value	Intended Rendering
dotted	A dotted border
dashed	A dashed-line border
solid	A normal solid-line border
double	A double-line border
groove	An etched border
ridge	An extruded border
inset	An inset border, making an object look like it is set into the page
outset	A beveled border, making an object look raised

A few examples of **border-style** rules are shown here:

```
h1        {border-style: solid;}
p.boxed   {border-style: double;}
.button   {border-style: outset;}
```

The **border-style** property sets the borders for each of the sides of the element. Individual border styles can be controlled with **border-top-style**, **border-bottom-style**, **border-left-style**, and **border-right-style**. The **border-style** property also can act as a shorthand notation and can take up to four values starting from top, right, bottom, and then left. Like the **margin** property, when less than four values are set, the opposite sides are set automatically. To set double borders on the top and bottom, use either of the following rules:

```
p       {border-style: double none;}
p.one   {border-style: double none double none;}
p.two   {border-top-style: double; border-bottom-style: double;
         border-left-style: none; border-right-style: none;}
```

border-width

Numerous properties are used to set the width of borders. Four properties set the width for specific borders: **border-top-width**, **border-right-width**, **border-bottom-width**, and **border-left-width**. Similar to the **border-style** property, the **border-width** property sets all four borders at once and takes from one to four values. Multiple values are applied to borders in a clockwise order: top, right, bottom, left. If only two or three values are used, the missing values are determined from the opposite sides, just as with margins and border styles. Border width can be specified by using the keywords **thin**, **medium**, and **thick** as a value indicating the size of the border, or by using an absolute length measurement such as 10 pixels. The following examples illustrate how border widths can be set:

```
p                {border-style: solid; border-width: 10px;}
p.double         {border-style: double; border-width: thick;}
p.thickandthin   {border-style: solid; border-width: thick thin;}
.fun             {border-style: double none; border-width: thick;}
```

border-color

Borders can be assigned a color by using the **border-color** property. Border colors are specified using either a supported color name or a numeric RGB specification. The **border-color** property sets all four borders and takes from one to four values. Multiple values are applied to borders in a clockwise order: top, right, bottom, left. If only two or three values are used, the missing values are determined from the opposite sides. As with border widths and styles, you can set a color value for each border side individually using **border-top-color**, **border-right-color**, **border-bottom-color**, and **border-left-color**. The following examples illustrate the basic ways to set a border's colors:

```
p        {border-style: solid; border-color: green;}
p.all    {border-style: solid; border-top-color: green;
          border-right-color: #FF0000;
          border-bottom-color: yellow;
          border-left-color: blue;}
```

Border Shorthand

Several border properties allow any combination of width, color, and style information to be set in a single property. The **border-top**, **border-right**, **border-bottom**, and **border-left** properties support this for their respective borders. For example, to set the top border or paragraph elements to be red, double-line style, and 20 pixels thick, use

```
p  {border-top: double 20px red;}
```

The order of the property values to set the style, width, and color might seem arbitrary, but according to the specification, designers probably should set the style, then the width, followed by the color. Multiple properties can be combined in one rule to set the borders differently, as shown in the following example:

```
#RainbowBox {background-color: yellow;
             border-top: solid 20px red;
```

```
            border-right: double 10px blue;
            border-bottom: solid 20px green;
            border-left: dashed 10px orange;}
```

Aside from a shorthand notation for each individual border side, you can use a shorthand notation for all sides by using the **border** property. For example, to set all borders of a paragraph to be red, double-line style, and 20 pixels thick, use

```
p    {border: double 20px red;}
```

Note that it is impossible to set the individual border sides with this shorthand notation. The actual properties to set the various borders must be used, such as **border-top** or, even more specifically, **border-top-style**.

The following brief example shows all the border properties used so far. Notice that both compact and explicit notations are used in the example.

```
<!DOCTYPE HTML PUBLIC "-//W3C//DTD HTML 4.01 Transitional//EN">
<html>
<head>
<title>CSS1 Border Example</title>
<style type="text/css">
<!--
#outer {background-color: orange;
        border-style: solid;
        border-width: 5px;
        padding: 10px 10px;}

#one    {background-color: yellow;
         border-style: double;
         border-width: medium;}

#two    {background-color: yellow;
         border-style: double solid;
         border-color: red green purple blue;
         border-width: thin medium thick .25cm;}
-->
</style>
</head>
<body>
<div id="outer">
```

```
<p id="one">This is a paragraph of text which has a
red double border around it. Notice how the text
creeps up on the edges. Padding values will help you
avoid this problem.</p>

<p id="two">This is another paragraph which has its
borders set in a very bizarre way!</p>

Notice that the paragraph blocks can be within a large
boxed block structure.
</div>
</body>
</html>
```

The rendering of the border property example under Internet Explorer 4 is shown in Figure 10-10.

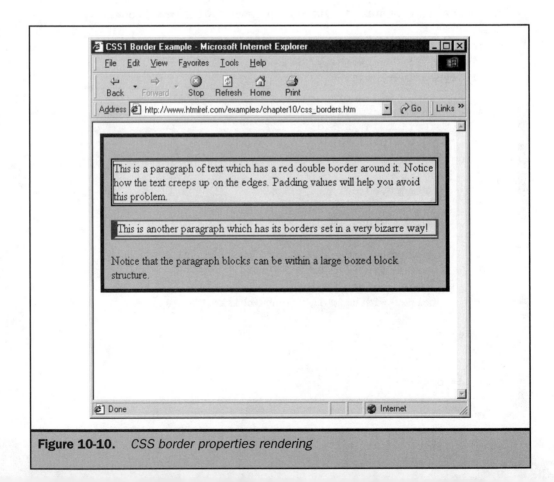

Figure 10-10. *CSS border properties rendering*

Padding Properties

The space between an element's border and its content can be specified by using the padding properties. An element's four padding regions can be set by using the **padding-top**, **padding-right**, **padding-bottom**, and **padding-left** properties. As with borders and margins, you can use a shorthand notation property, called **padding**, to set the padding for all sides at once. This example illustrates some basic uses of padding properties:

```
div {padding-top: 1cm;}
p   {border-style: solid; padding-left: 20mm; padding-right: 50mm;}
```

The shorthand notation property **padding** allows a single property assignment to specify all four padding regions. It can take from one to four values. A single value is applied to all four padding areas. Multiple values are applied to padding regions in a clockwise order: top, right, bottom, left. If only two or three values are used, the missing values are determined from the opposite sides. So,

```
div   {border-style: solid; padding: 1cm;}
```

sets a region with a solid border, but with contents padded 1 cm from the border on all sides.

```
p    {padding: 2mm 4mm;}
```

sets padding on the top and bottom to 2 mm and the right and left to 4 mm for all paragraphs. An example showing padding and borders to help you better understand padding values is shown here:

```
<!DOCTYPE HTML PUBLIC "-//W3C//DTD HTML 4.01 Transitional//EN">
<html>
<head>
<title>CSS1 Padding Example</title>
<style type="text/css">
<!--
#one     {background: yellow;
          border-style: double;
          border-width: medium;
          padding-left: 1cm;
          padding-right: .5cm;}
```

```
#two     {background: yellow;
          border-style: double;
          border-width: medium;
          padding-top: 1cm;
          padding-bottom: 1cm;}

#three   {background: yellow;
          border-style: double;
          border-width: medium;
          padding: 1cm 1cm;
          margin: .5cm 4cm;}
-->
</style>
</head>
<body>
<p id="one">This paragraph of text has padding on the left and
right, but not on the top and bottom.</p>

<p id="two">This paragraph has padding, but this time only on the
top and bottom.</p>

<p id="three">Be careful when using margins. They don't necessarily
apply to the text within the box, but to the box itself.</p>
</body>
</html>
```

The rendering of the padding example is shown in Figure 10-11.

Width and Height

The **width** property sets the width of an element's content region (the width of the area actually filled with content as opposed to its padding, border, or margin). The following example sets a paragraph with a width of 300 pixels:

```
p    {width: 300px;
      padding: 10px;
      border: solid 5px;
      background-color: yellow;
      color: black;}
```

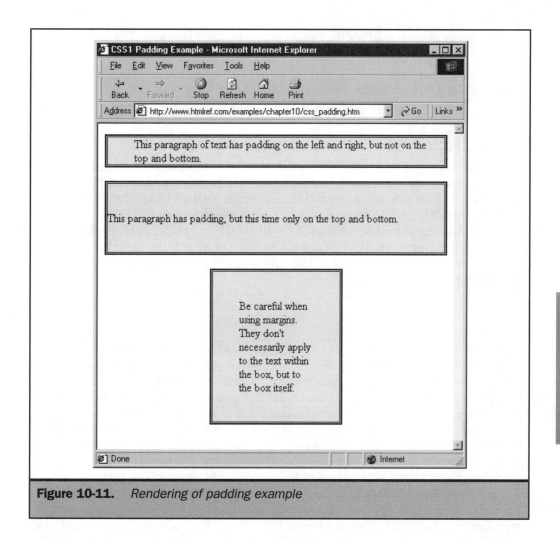

Figure 10-11.   *Rendering of padding example*

You also can use percentage values for the width. With the **width** property, tables apparently aren't necessary under CSS. This is true, but given the current level of support for these style sheets, relying on this feature for layout probably isn't a good idea.

Similar to **width**, the **height** property sets the height of an element's content region. When thinking about elements in Web pages, except images, setting the **height** property might seem unusual. In most cases, it probably is best to leave the **height** property alone, so that the default value, **auto**, is used. The most legitimate use of this property is to set the height for objects such as images. However, when positioning regions of content later on the width and height attributes will become useful. An absolute value or a percentage is supported for the **height** property, just like **width**. The following rules show how these properties might be used:

```
#img1    {height: 100px; width: 200px;}
p        {width: 80%; height: 100px;}
```

float and clear

The **float** property influences the horizontal alignment of elements. It causes them to "float" toward either the left or right margins of their containing element. This is especially useful for placing embedded media objects (such as images and similar support) into a Web page. Similar floating capabilities under vanilla HTML can be found with the **align** attribute settings. As with HTML, the values available for the **float** property include **left**, **right**, or **none**. The value of **none** is the default. To imitate the HTML code **<img id="logo" src="logo.gif" align="right">**, apply a style sheet rule such as this to the element:

```
#logo {float: right;}
```

The preceding example might raise a few questions. How can the **hspace** and **vspace** attributes from HTML be imitated using style sheets? You have a great deal of control over the border, margin, padding, height, and width of any object, so you shouldn't have difficulty achieving the layout that you want. One thing that might not be obvious is how to clear the content that might flow around an object.

The use of floating elements creates the need to position vertically those elements that immediately follow them in an HTML document. Should the content flow continue at the floating element's side or after its bottom? If floating elements are defined on the right and left margins of the page, should content flow continue between them, after the bottom of the left element, the right element, or whichever is larger? The **clear** property allows this to be specified. A value of **left** for the property clears floating objects to the left, a value of **right** clears floating objects to the right, and the **both** value clears whichever is larger. The default value is **none**. Notice that this is extremely similar to the use of the **clear** attribute with the **
** element in HTML. The following code example demonstrates the use of the **clear** and **float** properties in a rather unusual manner. Instead of floating an image, we'll float a paragraph of text to one side of the screen and text around it.

```
<!DOCTYPE HTML PUBLIC "-//W3C//DTD HTML 4.01 Transitional//EN">
<html>
<head>
<title>Object Float and Clear Control under CSS</title>
<style type="text/css">
```

```
<!--
p.aligned-right {border-style: thick;
                 width: 400px;
                 background-color: orange;
                 float:right;}
 .clearright {clear:right;}
-->
</style>
</head>
<body>
<div>This is some dummy text.
<p class="aligned-right">
This is some dummy text. This is some dummy text.
This is some dummy text. This is some dummy text.
This dummy text should stop flowing here.</p>

Here is some more text it should keep going next to the
paragraph for a while. Here is some more text it should
keep going next to the paragraph for a while.

<br class="clearright">
This text should appear after the floating section.
</div>
</body>
</html>
```

The rendering of the image alignment and text flow example is shown in Figure 10-12. The previous section should start to hint at the great deal of control that CSS affords a designer. Perfect pixel-level positioning objects is just a moment away, but before getting to layout nirvana let's see how we can change the very core meaning of an HTML element using CSS.

Display Properties

Cascading style sheets contain several classification properties that determine the display classification of an element. Is it a block-level element or an inline element? The CSS model recognizes three types of displayed elements: block elements, inline elements, and lists. The **display** property allows an element's display type to be changed to one of four values: **block**, **inline**, **list-item**, and **none**. A value of **none** causes an element to not display or use canvas space. This differs from the property setting **visibility**, to be discussed in the next section, which also prevents an element

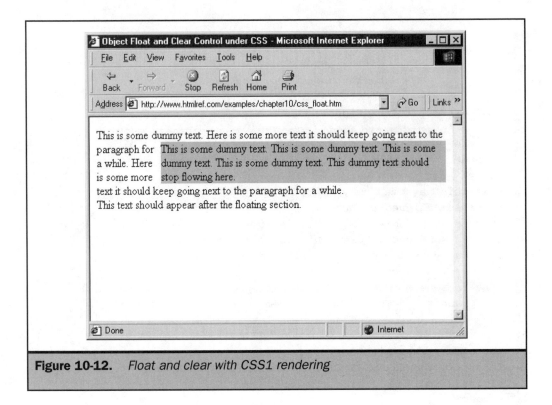

Figure 10-12. *Float and clear with CSS1 rendering*

from displaying, but might reserve canvas space. To turn off a paragraph, try a rule such as the following:

```
p.remove    {display:none;}
```

Aside from turning off elements, the browser should be able to turn a block element (such as a paragraph) into an inline element, thus keeping it from adding a new line. For example, the following would change the form of all paragraphs in the document; overriding the known action if the element is not suggested:

```
p    {display:inline;}
```

Browsers might be able to turn an inline element into a block thus causing a return like so:

```
em    {display:block;}
```

You also can coerce an element to act somewhat like a list by casting it with the display property, as shown here:

```
b    {display: list-item;}
```

In only very few cases, other than setting display to **none**, does overriding the meaning of an HTML element make sense. However, when inventing your own elements using XML as discussed in Chapter 17, this CSS property becomes invaluable. Now, let's finally cover the designer's most coveted capability—positioning of objects.

Positioning with Style Sheets

The W3C finalized the CSS2 specification on May 12, 1998. The complete specification can be viewed online at http://www.w3.org/TR/REC-CSS2/. At the time of this writing only a few important CSS2 features have been implemented by browser vendors, with one major exception: positioning. The rest of this chapter covers positioning in detail, summarizes new, unimplemented features in CSS2, and ends with a discussion of some proprietary style sheet effects introduced by Microsoft.

Positioning originally was developed as a separate specification called CSS-P, which has now been incorporated into the CSS2 specification. Even before finalization of CSS2, the major browsers supported style sheet–based positioning. When combined with elements such as **<div>**, the functionality of Netscape's proprietary **<layer>** element can be achieved with style sheets.

Positioning of Regions

The first property to discuss for layout is the **position** property, which has three values:

- **static**   Places elements according to the natural order in which they occur in a document (the default).

- **absolute**   Defines a coordinate system independent from the usual block and inline element placement common in HTML documents. An element whose position is **absolute** becomes a visual container for any elements enclosed in its content. If the element is repositioned, all the elements defined inside it move with it. If any of those contained elements are assigned coordinates outside of their parent's dimensions, they disappear.

- **relative**   Makes the element's position relative to the its natural position in document flow. This can be confusing, so most designers tend to use absolute values.

- **fixed**   Acts like absolute, but does not allow the object to move off screen. This value allows the designer to peg an object's position similar to using a frame.

- **inherit**   Sets the positioning relative to the enclosing parent.

Generally after you specify how to position the region (**absolute, relative, or fixed**), the actual location of positioned elements should be specified by using their top-left corner. The position generally is set with the **left** and **top** style properties. The coordinate system for positioned elements uses the upper-left corner of the enclosing object as the origin point, 0, 0. Normally the origin should be the upper-left-hand portion of the screen but it might not necessarily be if you consider positioned elements that contain other positioned elements. Values for the x coordinate increase to the right; y values increase going down from a positioned origin. A value such as **10,100** would be 10 units to the right and 100 units down from the origin. Values can be specified as a length in a valid CSS measurement (such as pixels) or as a percentage of the containing object's (parent's) dimension. You might find that elements contain other elements, so 0,0 isn't always the upper-left corner of the browser. Note that it also is possible to set the **bottom** and **right** values for an object, but that not all positioning-aware browsers, notably Netscape 4.x, support these properties; thus it is best to stick to **top** and **left** for describing an object's location.

After you position the region, you might want to set its size. By default, the **height** and **width** of the positioned region are set to fit the enclosed content, but the **height** and **width** properties, as discussed early in the chapter, can be used to specify the region's size.

The following example uses an inline style to set a **<div>** element to be 120 pixels from the left and 50 pixels down from the top-left corner of the browser:

```
<div style="position:absolute;
    left: 120px;  top: 50px;
    height: 100px; width: 150px;
    background-color: yellow">
At last, absolute positioning!
</div>
```

Before you rush off and position elements all over the screen, be aware of the nuances of nested items. For example, look at the following markup. Notice how the position of the second area is relative to the first. If you read the coordinate values numerically, the inner area should be positioned to the left and above where it shows onscreen. Remember, the coordinates are relative to the containing box.

```
<!DOCTYPE HTML PUBLIC "-//W3C//DTD HTML 4.01 Transitional//EN">
<html>
<head>
<title>Positioning Items</title>
<style type="text/css">
<!--
#outer   {position: absolute;
          left: 100px; top: 50px;
```

```
            height: 400px; width: 150px;
            background-color: yellow;}

#inner   {position: absolute;
            left: 75px; top: 50px;
            height: 30px; width: 40px;
            background-color: orange;}

#outer2  {position: absolute;
            left: 90%;
            height: 100px; width: 10%;
            background-color: green;
            color: white;}

#outer3  {position: absolute;
            bottom: 10px; right: 150px;
            height: 100px; width: 100px;
            background-color: purple;
            color: white;}
-->
</style>
</head>
<body>
<div id="outer">
This is the outer part of the nest.

<span id="inner">This is the inner part of the nest.</span>
</div>

<div id="outer2">Way to the far right at the top</div>

<div id="outer3">Using the bottom and right properties</div>

</body>
</html>
```

The rendering of this example is shown in Figure 10-13. Using the fixed value for the position property is fairly similar to the previous positioning example. Consider the following markup:

```
<div style="position: fixed; top: 0px; left: 0px;
background-color: blue; color: yellow;">DemoCompany, Inc.</div>
```

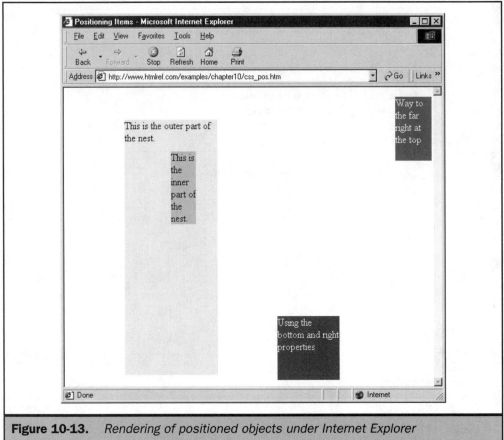

Figure 10-13. *Rendering of positioned objects under Internet Explorer*

In a browser that supported the fixed property this header text would stay in the upper-left corner of the screen regardless of scrolling at all times.

The last value for the **position** property is **relative**. This value is used when we want to position an object relative to its current position in the document flow. This is best illustrated by example; consider the markup here:

```
<p style="background-color: orange;">This is a test of
<span style="position: relative; top: 10px; left: 20px;
background-color: yellow;">relative positioning.</span>
This is only a test.</p>
```

The **<span>** element in this example surrounds text that is dropped down 10 pixels from the top of the paragraph and 20 pixels from the left of the point at which the text normally would fall as shown here.

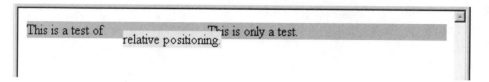

Notice that in this example text overlaps other text, showing that objects can stack on top of one another, and revealing the **z-index** property available to us.

z-index

Absolute and relative positioning allow elements' content to overlap. By default, overlapping elements stack in the order in which they are defined in an HTML document. The most recent elements go on top. This default order can be redefined by using an element's **z-index** property. Absolute- or relative-positioned elements define a **z-index** context for the elements that they contain. The containing element has an index of **0**; the index increases with higher numbers stacked on top of lower numbers. The following example forces all images inside a container to overlap, and uses the top class to position one image on top. Notice how the elements stack in the specified order rather than as defined:

```
<!DOCTYPE HTML PUBLIC "-//W3C//DTD HTML 4.01 Transitional//EN">
<html>
<head>
<title>Z-order Example</title>
<style type="text/css">
<!--
div.one     {position: absolute;
             top: 20px; left: 20px;
             height: 50px; width: 50px;
             color: white;
             background-color: blue;
             z-index: 2;}

div.two     {position: absolute;
             top: 30px; left: 30px;
             height: 25px; width: 100px;
             background-color: orange;
             z-index: 1;}
```

```
div.three   {position: absolute;
             top: 40px; left: 40px;
             height: 25px; width: 25px;
             background-color: yellow;
             z-index: 3;}
-->
</style>
</head>
<body>
<div class="one">This is section one.</div>

<div class="two">This is section two.</div>

<div class="three">This is section three.</div>
</body>
</html>
```

The rendering of this example is shown in Figure 10-14.

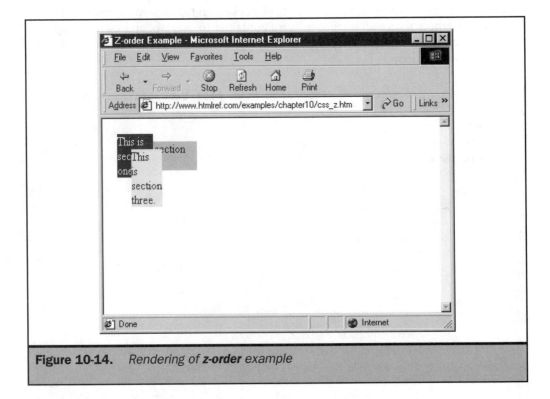

Figure 10-14.   *Rendering of **z-order** example*

It is a good idea not to number z-index values contiguously. Consider using gaps of 5 between layered regions, as this should allow you to later easily insert objects in between.

visibility Property

The **visibility** property determines whether an element is visible. The values for the property are **hidden**, **visible**, or **inherit**. The **inherit** value means that a property inherits its visibility state from the element that contains it. If an element is **hidden**, it still occupies the full canvas space, but is rendered as transparent. This simple example shows how the item is made invisible, but is not removed:

```
<p>This is a <em style="visibility: hidden">test</em> of the
visibility property.
```

The rendering here shows how the word "test" still takes up space, but isn't visible.

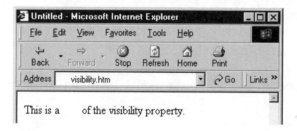

You can of course hide any region, positioned or not. Although the contents might take up canvas space, if you place the object under other objects using the **z-index** the viewer will be none the wiser. When combined with scripting, it is possible to hide and reveal regions easily for an interesting dynamic effect. This effect and others are possible using the powerful combination of HTML, CSS and JavaScript, often dubbed Dynamic HTML, is discussed in Chapter 13.

Content Overflow Properties

This last issue to consider with positioned objects is what to do when the element's content is greater than the space allocated for it. Most browsers allocate space for content, unless size is set explicitly or a clipping region is set. The **overflow** property determines how an element should handle the situation when content doesn't fit. A value of **hidden** for the property clips content to the size defined for the container. The **scroll** value allows content to scroll using a browser-dependent mechanism such as scrollbars. The default value is **none**, which does nothing and might clip the content. The following example, which mimics the functionality of a floating frame, creates a positioned region that allows scrolling if content goes beyond its defined size:

```
<div style="{position:absolute;
            left:20px; top:20px;
            width:100px; height:100px;
            overflow: scroll;}">

This<br>is<br>a<br>case<br>of<br>
lines<br>going<br>outside<br>the<br>box,
which may be clipped.
</div>
```

Try setting the value of the **overflow** property in the preceding example to **hidden** and notice that the content is truncated.

Clipping Regions

Sometimes it might be desirable to clip content. For elements whose position type is **absolute**, a *clipping rectangle* defines the subset of the content rectangle that actually is shown. The property **clip** can be used to set the coordinates of the clipping rectangle that houses the content. The form of the property is

```
clip: rect( top right bottom left)
```

where **top**, **right**, **bottom**, and **left** are the coordinate values that set the clipping region:

```
<div style="position:absolute;
 left:20; top:20;
 width:100; height:100;
 clip: rect(10 90 90 10);">
This<br>is<br>a<br>case<br>of<br>
lines<br>going<br>outside<br>the<br>box,
which may be clipped.
</div>
```

Before closing out this chapter by looking at browser-specific style changes, an overview of the W3C CSS2 specification is important, because it promises even more future possibilities for using style sheets, including expanded media options, discussed in the next section.

CSS2 Feature Summary

This section is not a detailed examination of the CSS2 specification, but rather a summary of some of its new features. The full specification of CSS2 can be found at http://www.w3.org/TR/REC-CSS2/. Keep in mind that only a few of these properties are supported by any browsers, beta or not, at the time of this writing. Designers should be patient, as the major browser vendors are only now beginning to fulfill the promises of CSS1.

CSS2 Selectors

CSS2 provides a much richer set of selectors than CSS1. Most of these selectors can be used to reduce the reliance on id and class attributes instead of relying on the context of an element's use in a document. The first selector is the wildcard selector designated by the asterisk (*). This selector matches any element, so a rule such as

```
* {color: red;}
```

would set the contents of any element red. This wildcard selector is more useful when creating a contextual rule. For example, consider the following rule which says that anytime a **<span>** element is found inside of any element within a **<div>** its background should be made yellow.

```
div * span  {background-color: yellow;}
```

Using the child selector specified by the greater than symbol (>) it is possible in CSS2 to define a rule that matches only elements that are directly enclosed within another element. Consider the rule

```
body > p  {background-color: yellow;}
```

This rule would indicate that only **<p>** elements directly within the **<body>** would have a yellow background. The following example shows the effect of a child selector rule:

```
<!DOCTYPE HTML PUBLIC "-//W3C//DTD HTML 4.01 Transitional//EN">
<html>
<head>
<title>CSS2 Child Selector</title>
<style type="text/css">
<!--
body > p  {background-color: yellow;}
-->
</style>
</head>
```

```
<body>
<div><p>This paragraph is not yellow.</p></div>
<p>While this one is yellow. </p>
</body>
</html>
```

A similar rule called the adjacent-sibling selector is specified using the plus sign (+) and is used to select elements that would be siblings of each other. For example, consider the rule

```
h1 + p {color: red;}
```

this states that all paragraph elements that are directly after an **<h1>** are red as indicated by this markup:

```
<h1>Heading Level 1</h1>
<p>I am red!</p>
<p>I am not!</p>
```

A very interesting new CSS2 selector allows designers to match attributes. For example a rule such as

```
A[href] {background-color: orange;}
```

would match all **<a>** elements that simply have the **href** attribute, whereas a rule such as

```
A[href="http://www.htmlref.com"] {background-color: yellow;}
```

would match only those **<a>** elements that have an **href** value set to the book's support site URL. Under CSS2 it also should be possible to match multiple attribute values or even pieces of the attribute values. However, these examples should be more than enough to show the basics of these new element selectors.

CSS2 Pseudo Classes and Elements

CSS2 also supports a variety of new pseudo-elements, including **:first-child, :focus, :hover,** and **:lang**. The **:first-child** selector is used to find only the first child of a particular element. For example, a rule such as

```
p:firstchild {background-color: green;}
```

will set the background color of the first element within a paragraph green and no other color. The **:focus** pseudo class is used to apply a rule to an element only when that element has focus. Typically form fields can accept keyboard input and thus can gain focus. So to set any text input field to have a yellow background color when it gains focus you would use a rule such as

```
input:focus {background-color: yellow;}
```

The **:hover** pseudo class, as presented earlier, is already well supported and is used primarily to change the appearance of links when the user is hovering over them. For example,

```
A {text-decoration: none;}
A:hover {text-decoration: underline;}
```

However, it is possible to apply this pseudo class to just about any element, so a rule such as

```
p:hover {background-color: yellow;}
```

although producing a potentially annoying effect, is perfectly valid. Last, a few other pseudo-elements including **:before** and **:after** can be used to specify content placed before and after an element respectively. These two selectors might be useful to create special start- and end-of-section indicators. For example,

```
div: before {content: url(sectionstart.gif);}
div: after {content: url(sectionend.gif);}
```

The **content** property, often found with the **before:** and **after:** selectors, can be used to specify images as shown in the preceding code example or to specify regular content; for example,

```
p.warning: before {content: "Warning";}
```

A common use of this pseudo-element might be to include quotation marks so there are built-in values of **open-quote**, **close-quote**, **no-open-quote**, and **no-close-quote**, which can be used to control the insertion of quotation marks in a document as shown by this example:

```
blockquote: before {content: open-quote;}
blockquote: after {content: close-quote;}
```

PRESENTATION AND LAYOUT

Although these final two pseudo-elements sound interesting, testing their functions is difficult because at the time of this writing no browser supports them.

CSS2 Text and Font Improvements

CSS2 introduces a variety of font properties. For example, **font-stretch** is used to stretch or condense a font and takes values of **ultra-condensed**, **extra-condensed**, **condensed**, **semi-condensed**, **normal**, **semi-expanded**, **expanded**, **extra-expanded**, and **ultra-expanded**. The property also can take a relative value of wider or narrower to modify the appearance of text relative to a parent font. A few examples of its use are shown here:

```
.narrow          {font-stretch: narrower;}
#arialstretch    {font-family: Arial; font-stretch: ultra-expanded;}
```

CSS2 also introduces the **font-size-adjust** property. This property is used for scaled fonts to make sure that text takes up the same amount of room regardless of the availability of a particular font or not. The use of this property so far is not supported by any browsers and its exact usage is not well defined.

The last interesting text change made in CSS2 is to support shadows on text using the **text-shadow** property. To specify a shadow for text, you must define the offset of the shadow, both vertical and horizontal, and optionally the blur radius and the color of the shadow. Positive horizontal offsets mean the offset is to the right, and negative values indicate the shadow falls to the left. A positive vertical offsets mean the offset is below, and negative above the text. A simple example setting the shadow for **<h1>** elements is shown here:

```
H1 {color: #CC0000; text-shadow: 0.2em 0.2em blue;}
```

Of course, at the time of the writing no browser yet supports this property. However, readers are warned that the shadows are fast approaching and ready to storm Web page design quicker than a **<blink>** tag. In short: When this property works, please don't abuse it.

CSS2 List Changes

A minor change made by CSS2 is the support of new values for the list-style-type property. Now the property supports a value of **decimal-leading-zero** which creates numbers that are padded with zeros to be equivalent to the largest number in the list. For example when using a value of **decimal-leading-zero** for the **list-style-type** property the first item in a list between 10 and 99 would be 01, in a list from 100–999 would be 001, and so on. Other values include **lower-greek** and **upper-greek**, which count an ordered list in lowercase and uppercase Greek symbols respectively, **lower-latin** and **upper-latin** which are the same as the normal lower and upper alphabetical. A variety of values to indicate foreign language counting systems also are supported under CSS2: **hebrew**, **armenian**, **georgian**, **cjk-ideographic**, **katakana**, **hiragana-iroha**, and **katakana-iroha**.

Automatic Number of Objects

CSS2 returns HTML elements such as lists and headings to their true logical nature with the introduction of automatic numbering. Using the **counter**, **counter-increment**, and **counter-reset** properties you can automatically number sections of an HTML document using a CSS2 rule. For example we could number all **<h1>** elements with a counter using the **:before** pseudo-element like so

```
h1:before {content: "Section" counter(section); counter-increment:
section;}
```

It would be possible to run multiple counters at once to create an outline numbering style and even create lists that count in steps or backward. Again, however, at the time of this writing no browser supports this CSS2 syntax.

Display Property Changes

Under CSS2, the display property supports a variety of values. For example, a display property value of **compact** is used to position enclosed text in the margin of a following block element. A value of **run-in** also is supported for the display property. This should allow a block-level element such as a heading to be run in or combined with the next block-level element. For example, consider the markup here

```
<h1 style="display: run-in">Heading 1</h1>
<p>This paragraph should have the heading run right
   into its first line.</p>
```

which should result in the large **<h1>** text appearing as part of the first line of the paragraph. Last, using display it is possible to set an item as the type marker. A marker indicates that the contents should be treated like a list marker. The position of the marker is now easier to control using the market-offset value and list markers can be anything including numbers, single characters, images, or even large amounts of text. The market value for display is not limited to lists items; it can be used to indicate a market or anything. For example, if you wanted to indicate a particular paragraph as a new piece of text using a GIF image you might use a rule such as

```
#new:before    {display: marker;
                content: url(new.gif);
                marker-offset: 1.5em;}
```

CSS2 also supports a variety of display properties to make content act like a table and to control the display and formatting of tables in general. Once again because no browsers appear to even be close to supporting these values at the time of the writing significant discussion is left for a future edition of this book. Interested readers are directed to the CSS2 specification for further details on the display property.

Media Types

A significant goal of CSS2 is to support other output media forms beyond the computer screen. The CSS2 specification defines numerous media types, listed in Table 10-2. Until browser vendors or developers of other user agents begin to support these media types, these definitions might have no meaning outside of the specification.

Media-Dependent Style Sheets

Under the CSS2 specification, certain style sheet properties are supported only by specific media types. In other cases, more than one media type supports a property, but might call for different values; such as when font-related properties are used for both computer display and for printing, two different media that might require different font styles or sizes. CSS2 provides two main ways to define media types for style sheets. The first method simply uses the HTML language to define the media type. The other method uses either the **@import** rule or the **@media** rule.

Media Type	Definition
all	For use with all devices
aural	For use with speech synthesizers
braille	For use with tactile Braille devices
embossed	For use with Braille printers
handheld	For use with handheld devices
print	For use with printed material and documents viewed onscreen in print preview mode
projection	For use with projected media (direct computer-to-projector presentations), or printing transparencies for projection
screen	For use with color computer screens
tty	For use with low-resolution teletypes, terminals, or other devices with limited display capabilities
tv	For use with television-type devices

Table 10-2.   *Media Types Defined Under CSS2*

The **media** attribute for the **<link>** element is used under CSS2 to provide an indication of which media a linked style sheet should apply to. This attribute enables the page designer to define one style for computer screens, one for print, and perhaps one for personal digital assistants (PDAs). For example, a document could include two links, one for screen and one for print, as shown here:

```
<link rel="stylesheet" href="screenstyle.css" media="screen"
     type="text/css">

<link rel="stylesheet" href="printstyle.css" media="print"
     type="text/css">
```

Multiple values also can be set for the attribute. These should be separated by commas, to show that the style can apply to many media forms; for example, **media="screen,print"**. Currently, the **media** attribute isn't widely understood by browsers.

The **@import** rule has already been discussed in this chapter (refer to "Embedding and Importing Style Sheets"). Defining a media type under CSS2 simply requires the addition of an appropriate media type after defining the URL with the **@import** rule, as shown in this code fragment:

```
@import url("braille.css") braille;
```

The **@media** rule is used to define style rules for multiple media types in a single style sheet. For example, you might want to have a document display in a large sans serif font when viewed on a monitor, but display in a smaller serif font when printed. Multiple media types should be separated by commas, as shown in the following code fragment:

```
<style type="text/css">
<!--
@media screen {body
            {font-family: sans-serif;
             font-size: 18 pt;}
}

@media print {body
            {font-family: serif;
             font-size: 9 pt;}
}
```

PRESENTATION AND
LAYOUT

```
@media screen, print {body
                        {line-height: 150%;}
}
-->
</style>
```

If implemented by a browser or another user agent, this code would cause the body of the document to display in an 18-point sans serif font on a computer monitor, to print out as a 9-point serif font, and to have a line height of 150 percent in both media.

Printer Specific CSS

As shown by the CSS2 specification, in the future style sheets certainly will be extended to support more printing capabilities. Microsoft has already provided the **page-break-before** property and **page-break-after** property under Internet Explorer 4. These properties can be used to set a page break on the printer. By using these properties, you can set the printer to go to a new page before or after a particular element. The default value for either of the properties is **auto**. Other possible values include **always**, **left**, and **right**. Most likely, the value **always** will be used to tell the printer to always insert a page break. Imagine a rule such as this:

```
br.newpage    {page-break-after: always;}
```

Adding this rule would always cause a page break wherever the rule is inserted into a document. Most likely printer-related style sheet changes such as the one presented here will be the first output device-specific aspects of CSS2 to be implemented in browsers.

User Interface Changes

The CSS2 specification also promises more options for user interfaces, allowing page designers to implement various contextual display options for cursors, colors, and fonts, many of which can be set to match the end user's system settings.

cursor

The **cursor** property determines how the cursor displays when passed over the affected element. The **auto** value leaves the display to be determined by the user agent, so the cursor will display according to either the browser default settings or the user settings. The **crosshair** value renders the cursor as a simple cross, whereas **default** displays the system's default cursor (usually an arrow). Various other values listed in the CSS2 specification can indicate that something is a link (**pointer**), that text can be selected (**text**), that something can be resized in various directions (**e-resize**, **ne-resize**, **nw-resize**, **n-resize**, **se-resize**, **sw-resize**, **s-resize**, **w-resize**), or that the user must wait while a program is busy (**wait**).

For example to let the user know he or she will have to wait to access any link on your page you might use a rule such as

```
a    {cursor: wait;}
```

Beyond the built-in cursor forms that are already supported by Internet Explorer, one value, **url**, can be used to reference a cursor source; multiple cursor sources can be listed, as shown in this example from the CSS2 specification:

```
p { cursor : url("mything.cur"), url("second.cur"), text; }
```

As with fonts, the user agent should attempt to render the first cursor listed, try the second one if necessary, and ultimately default to the generic cursor value listed last. No browser supports custom cursors natively, but a variety of tricks are already employed to imitate this CSS2 property.

Integrating Colors with User Preferences

Under CSS2, authors will be able to provide color values that match preexisting settings on the end user's system. This can be particularly useful in providing pages that are set to accommodate a user's visual impairment or other disability. These values can be used with any CSS color properties (**color**, **background-color**, and so on). The CSS2 specification recommends using the mixed-case format of the values shown in Table 10-3, even though they are not, in fact, case-sensitive.

Color Value	Intended Rendering
ActiveBorder	Color of user's active window border setting
ActiveCaption	Color of user's active window caption setting
AppWorkspace	Background color of user's multiple document interface setting
Background	Color of user's desktop background setting
ButtonFace	Face color of user's 3-D display elements setting

Table 10-3. *User Color Preferences Under CSS2*

Color Value	Intended Rendering
ButtonHighlight	Highlight color of user's 3-D display elements setting
ButtonShadow	Shadow color of user's 3-D display elements setting
ButtonText	Color of user's push-button text setting
CaptionText	Color of user's text settings for captions, size box, and scroll bar arrow box
GrayText	Color of user's disabled text setting; if system doesn't display gray, defaults to black
Highlight	Background color of user's control-selected items setting
HighlightText	Text color of user's control-selected items setting
InactiveBorder	Color of user's inactive window border setting
InactiveCaption	Color of user's inactive window caption setting
InactiveCaptionText	Text color of user's inactive caption setting
InfoBackground	Background color of user's tool tip control setting
InfoText	Text color of user's tool tip control setting
Menu	Color of user's menu background setting
MenuText	Text color of user's menus setting
Scrollbar	Color of user's scroll bar setting (gray area)
ThreeDDarkShadow	Dark-shadow color of user's setting for edges of 3-D display elements
ThreeDFace	Face color of user's for 3-D display elements setting
ThreeDHighlight	Highlight color of user's 3-D display elements setting
ThreeDLightShadow	Light-shadow color of user's setting for edges of 3-D display elements
ThreeDShadow	Dark-shadow color of user's setting for 3-D display elements
Window	Background color of user's window setting
WindowFrame	Frame color of user's window setting
WindowText	Text color of user's window setting

Table 10-3. *User Color Preferences Under CSS2* (continued)

The following code fragment shows how these values could be used to make a paragraph display with the same foreground and background colors as the user's system:

```
p { color: WindowText; background-color: Window;}
```

Coordinating Fonts with User Preferences

Under CSS2, designers will have the option of coordinating fonts with the fonts defined by the end user's system. According to specification these system font values can be used only with the shorthand **font** property—*not* with **font-family**. However, browser implementation might be more flexible. Table 10-4 lists these values and their related system font values.

Thus, to make level-three headers in a document display in the same font as a user's system uses to display window status bars, you would use the following code fragment in a style sheet:

```
h3 {font: status-bar;}
```

Outline Properties

Outlines are a new CSS2 feature that resemble borders but take up no additional space, and can be set to a shape different from that of the image, form field, or other element to which they are applied. Outlines are drawn over an item, rather than around it, thus causing no reflow. Outlines can be used dynamically, to indicate what element in a page has focus. Outline properties include **outline-width**, **outline-style**, **outline-color**, and the shorthand property **outline**. Table 10-5 lists the values associated with these properties.

Font Value	System Font Referenced
caption	System font used to caption buttons and other controls
icon	System font used to label icons
menu	System font used for drop-down menus and menu lists
message-box	System font used in dialog boxes
small-caption	System font used for labeling small controls
status-bar	System font used in window status bars

Table 10-4. *Using CSS2 to Match an End-User's System Fonts*

Outline Property	Values Accepted
outline-width	Same values as **border-width**
outline-style	Same values as **border-style**, except **hidden**
outline-color	All color values, including **invert**
outline	Sets all three values

Table 10-5. *CSS2 Outline Properties and Values*

Consider the following rule that would outline paragraph with a dashed line when they are hovered over.

```
p:hover   {outline-style: dashed;}
```

Note that unlike the border property, outlined elements do not draw necessarily as a box. The last major category of CSS2 changes is to support audio renderings of pages and is the most difficult to describe and demonstrate.

CSS2 Aural Improvements

The CSS2 specification contains numerous properties designed to provide aural rendering of Web documents. Although not yet implemented, these properties represent one of the most forward-looking aspects of CSS2, targeted primarily for the sight-impaired, but offering expanded media possibilities for the Web, as well. While the use of a speech-based interface might seem like science fiction, the advances made in both speech synthesis and speech recognition suggest that practical use of this technology is not far away. This is a brief summary of the aural properties defined in CSS2. Again, these properties haven't been implemented, so any references to them in the present tense are based on their definition within the CSS2 specification, not on their actual use.

Basically, aural style sheets allow synthetic speech sources to be associated with paragraphs and other elements. Timing and the spatial relationships between sounds also will be subject to control by style sheets. Presumably, various synthetic voices will function in a way analogous to fonts on a computer screen; different "voices" can be assigned to different elements or classes of elements, or the qualities of any given voice can be altered to suit an element (more emphasis for headers, and so forth).

speech-rate The **speech-rate** property is used to determine the rate of speech. Values include numeric values, **x-slow**, **slow**, **medium**, **fast**, **x-fast**, **faster**, **slower**, and

inherit. Numeric values determine the number of words spoken per minute (wpm). Speeds range from 80 wpm for the value **x-slow**, to 500 wpm for the value **x-fast**. The relative value **faster** increases the speech rate by 40 wpm, while **slower** reduces it by 40 wpm. The default value is **medium**. The value **inherit** also can be used with this property.

voice-family   The **voice-family** property works much like the **font-family** property insofar as it can be set to reference a specific voice "font," generic voice "fonts," or a combination thereof, using a comma-separated list. A sample might look like this:

```
p.voiceone {voice-family: "bill gates", executive, male;}
p.voicetwo {voice-family: "jewel", singer, female;}
```

In this hypothetical example, the first voice name is a specific voice based on a public figure, the second is a specific voice meant to suggest a similar character, and the final voice is a generic voice. According to the CSS2 specification, names can be quoted, and should be quoted if they contain white space. The value **inherit** also can be used with this property.

pitch   The **pitch** property defines the average pitch of a voice. Values include numeric values, which determine the voice's frequency in hertz, as well as **x-low**, **low**, **medium**, **high**, and **inherit**. The default value is **medium**. The values **x-low** through **high** are dependent on the pitch of the voice family in use (as determined by the **voice-family** property). The value **inherit** also can be used with this property.

pitch-range   The **pitch-range** property determines the range of pitch variation of a voice's average pitch, as defined through the **voice-family** and **pitch** properties. Values are either inherited (**inherit**) or defined by a numeric value between 0 and 100. The value 0 produces no pitch variation; 50 approximates normal pitch variation, and **100** produces an exaggerated pitch range. The value **inherit** also be can used with this property.

stress   The **stress** property assigns stress, or peaks, in a voice's intonation. Used in conjunction with **pitch-range**, this might allow the creation of more detailed vocal ranges. The rendering of numeric values might be dependent on the voice's gender and the language spoken. Values are numeric, ranging from **0–100**; the default value is **50**. The value **inherit** also can be used with this property.

richness   The **richness** property determines the richness of a voice. Numeric values range from **0–100**, with a default value of **50**. The higher the number, the more the voice carries. The value **inherit** also can be used with this property.

volume   The **volume** property determines the average volume of a voice. Numeric values range from 0–100. A value of 0 produces the lowest audible volume, and 100 the loudest comfortable volume. Values also can be set to a percentage of the inherited volume. Other values include **silent** (no sound), **x-soft** (equivalent to 0), **soft** (equivalent to 25), **medium** (equivalent to 50), **loud** (equivalent to 75), and **x-loud** (equivalent to 100). The only other value is **inherit**. These values will depend largely on the speech-rendering system used, and on user settings such as speaker volume.

speak   The **speak** property determines whether text is spoken, and how. The value **none** prevents text from being spoken. The default value **normal** renders text in a "normal" speaking voice, as determined by other properties and the user agent. The value **spell-out** causes the user agent to speak text as individual letters, useful when dealing with acronyms. The only other value is **inherit**.

pause-before   The **pause-before** property defines a pause to take place before an element's content is spoken. Values can be expressed as time, measured in seconds (default) or milliseconds (**ms**), or as a percentage. Percentages define pause length in relation to the average length of a word, as determined by the **speech-rate** property. (For a **speech-rate** of **100wpm**, each word takes an average time of 600 milliseconds; a **pause-before** value of **100%** creates a pause of 600 ms, while a value of **50%** creates a pause of 300 ms.) The CSS2 specification recommends the use of relative (percentage) units. This property is not inherited.

pause-after   The **pause-after** property defines a pause to take place before an element's content is spoken. Values can be expressed as time, measured in seconds (default) or milliseconds (**ms**), or as a percentage. Percentages define pause length in relation to the average length of a word, as determined by the **speech-rate** property. (For a **speech-rate** of **100wpm**, each word takes an average time of 600 milliseconds; a **pause-after** value of **100%** creates a pause of 600 ms, and a value of **50%** creates a 300 ms pause.) The CSS2 specification recommends the use of relative (percentage) units. This property is not inherited.

pause   The **pause** property is a shorthand notation for the **pause-before** and **pause-after** properties just discussed. A style rule of

```
p {pause: 12 ms;}
```

creates a 12-second pause before and after rendering an element; a style rule of

```
p {pause: 12 ms 20 ms;}
```

creates a 12-second pause before the element and a 20-second pause after it.

cue-before   The **cue-before** property sets an "audio icon" to be played before an element. One example might be a musical tone at the start of a paragraph, or a voice stating "begin paragraph." In some sense, this might be similar to the page-turning noise that often is used in children's books with an accompanying tape, record, or CD; this would serve as an attention cue for the listener. The value can be set to the URI of an audio file, as shown here:

```
p {cue-before: url("ding.wav");}
```

This would play the sound file ding.wav just before speaking the contents of the paragraph. The value of the property also can be set to **none**. If a URL is used that doesn't reference a viable audio file, the property renders as if the value were **none**. The CSS2 specification recommends that user agents reference a default sound file if the file referenced is not valid. This property is not inherited, but the value can be set to inherit from a parent element.

cue-after   The **cue-after** property sets an "audio icon" to be played after an element. Values are the same as for **cue-before**:

```
p {cue-after: url("ding.wav");}
```

cue   The **cue** property provides shorthand notation for **cue-before** and **cue-after**. A single value sets both properties to the same value; the properties also can be set separately:

```
p {cue: url("ding.wav");}
```

play-during   The **play-during** property allows a background sound (music, sound effects, and such) to play while an element is being rendered. The sound is determined by the URI of an audio file. Additional values include the following:

- **mix**   Causes the sound set by a parent element's **play-during** property to continue playing while the child element is being spoken; otherwise, the sound determined by the child element's **play-during** property plays.

- **repeat**   Causes the sound to repeat if its duration is less than the time needed to render the element's content; if the rendering time of content is shorter than the sound file's duration, the sound is clipped.

- **auto**   Causes the parent element's sound to keep on playing.

- **none**   Terminates the parent element's background sound until the child element is finished rendering, at which time it should resume. The **play-during** property is not inherited unless the value is set to **inherit**.

■ **inherit**   Causes the parent element's background sound to start over for the child element, rather than continue to play as determined by the **mix** and **auto** values.

azimuth   The **azimuth** property determines the horizontal location of a sound. How this renders will depend largely on the user agent and the audio system used with it. Values can be set to specific angles based on the concept of 360-degree surround sound. A value of **0deg** places a sound dead center, as if originating directly in front of the listener. A value of **180deg** places a sound directly behind a listener; **90deg** indicates dead right, while **270deg** or **-90deg** indicates dead left. Named values include **left-side** (270 degrees); **far-left, left, center-left, center** (0 degrees); **center-right, right, far-right,** and **right-side** (90 degrees). The default value is **center**. The relative value **leftward** moves the sound 20 degrees counterclockwise, and **rightward** moves it 20 degrees clockwise. The CSS2 specification notes that these values indicate a desired result, but that how this will work must be determined by user agents. The **azimuth** property is inherited.

elevation   The **elevation** property determines the vertical location of a sound relative to the listener. Angle values range from **90deg** (directly above) to **-90deg** (directly below). A value of **0deg** locates the sound on the same level as the listener. Named values include **above** (90 degrees), **level** (0 degrees), and **below** (-90 degrees). The relative value **higher** adds 10 degrees of elevation, whereas **lower** subtracts 10 degrees. The **elevation** property is inherited.

speak-punctuation   The **speak-punctuation** property gives the option of having punctuation rendered as speech. The value **code** causes punctuation to render as literal speech (in other words, "," is spoken as "comma," "?" as "question mark," and so forth). A value of **none** (default) prevents punctuation from being spoken, presumably to be rendered as it would be in ordinary speech (short and long pause, proper inflection of questions, etc.). The only other value is **inherit**. The **speak-punctuation** property is inherited.

speak-numeral   The **speak-numeral** property provides two options for the rendering of numbers. The value **digits** causes numbers to render as a sequence of digits (**1001** renders as one, zero, zero, one). A value of **continuous** (default) causes numbers to render as complete numbers (**1001** renders as one thousand and one). The only other value is **inherit**. The **speak-numeral** property is inherited.

speak-header   The **speak-header** property provides options for speech rendering of table headers relative to table data. Values include **once, always,** and **inherit**. The value **once** causes the content of a table header to be spoken once before the content of all associated table cells is rendered ("Animal: dog, cat, cow…"). The value **always** causes the table header content to render before each associated table cell is rendered ("Animal: dog; Animal: cat; Animal: cow…"). The **speak-header** property is inherited.

This is just a brief overview of many of the defined aural properties under CSS2. Although the exact syntax is well defined in the CSS2 specification, at the time of this writing, few browsers actually support this technology for testing purposes. Syntax might vary when these style properties are finally implemented.

CSS3: Someday?

Already, significant work is being performed on defining CSS Level 3—despite the fact that no browsers have been implemented that cover CSS2 properly, or even CSS1 for that matter. Readers interested in following the current progress of CSS3 should visit the W3C site's section on CSS (http://www.w3.org/Style/CSS/). A quick perusal of the current activities at the time of this edition's writing indicates that CSS3 will break the CSS specification up into modules so that it can be more easily adapted to suit a variety of situations. CSS3 also promises changes to add support for international languages, including vertically flowing text, more table improvements, better support for print output, support for color correction, downloadable fonts, and integration with other technologies such as Scalable Vector Graphics (SVG), MathML, or SMIL (Synchormized Multimedia Interchange Language). CSS3 also will address the increased integration between HTML, Style Sheets, and scripting languages through ideas like BECSS (Behavioral Extensions to CSS). Although the W3C is aggressively defining the future of the Web, browser vendors have continued to innovate even within the domain of CSS. The next section covers some properties that are implemented by browser vendors, but that may or may not be part of the CSS specification.

Microsoft-Specific Style Sheet Properties Sampler

Browser vendors are already making new additions to cascading style sheets, Microsoft being the most notable extender of the specification. Undoubtedly, these additions are just the beginning of a slew of new proprietary changes introduced into style sheets. For example the **zoom** property can be used to scale content. The **zoom** property takes either a percentage value, a floating point number indicating a magnification scale such as 2.0 for twice as big or 0.5 for half-size or the keyword **normal** indicating an object's normal magnification. A simple example, to zoom objects in a class named "twotimes" use a CSS rule such as

```
.twotimes    {zoom: 200%;}
```

Although setting a zoom property might not make much sense with a static rule, when combined with scripting it can create an interesting possibility of zooming images or text based on response to user events. For example, try this example

```
<p onmouseover="this.style.zoom='200%'"
   onmouseout="this.style.zoom='normal'">
Roll your mouse over me and watch me zoom!</p>
```

under Internet Explorer 5.5 or better to see a possibility of how the **zoom** property can be used.

Another interesting extension supported by Microsoft Internet Explorer 5.5 and higher also is a collection of CSS property extensions that can be used to control the appearance of scrollbars for the entire window as set by a rule on the **<body>** element and for the **<textarea>** element as well. These properties include **scrollbar-3d-light-color**, **scrollbar-arrow-color**, **scrollbar-base-color**, **scrollbar-dark-shadow-color**, **scrollbar-face-color**, **scrollbar-highlight-color,** and **scrollbar-shadow-color**. Each of these properties takes a color value defined in CSS in any form. A simple rule showing how to change your document's scrollbars red is shown here:

```
body {scrollbar-face-color: red;}
```

Aside from cosmetic improvements to screen presentation Microsoft has introduced a variety of style sheet extensions for supporting foreign language display, probably the most interesting being the **writing-mode** property. Using this property it is possible to make text flow up and down. For example, the following markup demonstrates how this property is used:

```
<div style="writing-mode:tb-rl">Up and down text.
<span style="writing-mode:lr-tb; color: red;">Left and
    right.</span>
More up and down.
<span style="writing-mode:lr-tb; color: green;">Back to
    left and right.</span>
</div>
```

This markup produces an interesting layout under Internet Explorer 5.5 or better, as shown here:

Although this is a property extension it would be useful to rendering some languages like Japanese and something similar to this property probably will wind up in CSS3.

There are a variety of other extensions to CSS introduced by Microsoft, most notably multimedia filters that can be used to change the appearance of objects and even control the loading and unloading of pages. The reality is that these properties have bugs and the syntax is not stable, having changed dramatically between releases of the Internet Explorer browsers. Designers are not encouraged to use these properties. For definitive information on the latest style sheet extensions, check Microsoft's developer information for Internet Explorer at http://www.msdn.microsoft.com/workshop/.

Downloadable Fonts

The last requirement for perfect layout control would be the inclusion of dynamic fonts. Although the CSS specifications are still working this out, the browser vendors have gone ahead and provided downloadable fonts since the 4.x releases of the major browsers. As with the font technology discussed in Chapter 6, fonts can be embedded in a Web page by using style sheet syntax. To embed fonts in a Web document under Microsoft Internet Explorer, use the **@font-face** property. This property allows the designer to specify fonts in the document that might not be available on the viewer's system.

To embed a font, first specify the **font-family** property. Then, specify the **src** property and set it equal to the URL of an embedded OpenType file, which should have an .eot extension. When the file is downloaded, it is converted to a TrueType font and then displayed on the screen. By putting a rule such as the following in the style sheet, the font named GhostTown can be used elsewhere on the page by using the **font-family** property:

```
@font-face {font-family:GhostTown;
       src:url(http://www.democompany.com/fonts/ghost.eot);}
```

One big question is, how can a special embedded font file be created? The designer has to run the font through a tool to create the font definition file and then place that file on the Web server. Another potential issue is having to make changes to the Web server so that the file is delivered correctly. See the Microsoft Typography Web site, at http://www.microsoft.com/typography/, for information about font creation tools and other deployment issues.

To embed fonts by the Netscape definition, use the **@fontdef** rule in a style sheet to indicate the downloadable font. You also will need to create an embedded font file for Netscape-based dynamic fonts; in this case, a PFR file. So, to bring in GhostTown, use

```
@fontdef url(http://www.democompany.com/fonts/ghosttown.pfr);
```

or, as discussed in Chapter 6, a **<link>** element could also be used in the **<head>** of the document, as shown here:

```
<link rel="fontdef" src="http://www.democompany.com/fonts/
ghosttown.pfr">
```

These style sheet and HTML font solutions work for Netscape. The Microsoft style of adding an **src** rule for **@font-face** is the proposed solution from the W3C and eventually should be supported by Netscape. More information about Netscape's current font and style sheet syntax, as well as links to dynamic font tools, can be found at http://www.truedoc.com.

Summary

Cascading style sheets provide better control over the look and feel of Web pages. Style sheets aren't just useful for making attractive pages. By dividing structure and style, they make documents simpler and easier to manipulate. Although style sheets provide a great deal of flexibility in creating pages, they are not yet fully implemented in today's browsers. Some inconsistencies exist between implementations. When used carefully, style sheets are a great way to improve the layout of pages without locking into a proprietary solution. Be sure to take advantage of the many resources available at http://www.w3.org/Style/CSS/.

Despite the open nature of style sheets, extensions are already being made by browser vendors, so this open nature of the technology might not be quite what it has been built up to be. Pixel-level layout control and downloadable fonts are almost here, but the innovations don't stop. Why just strive for a print-style layout when fully programmed pages are possible? Chapter 11 starts the transition from static Web pages to programmed pages, beginning with forms.

The Complete Reference

Part IV

Programming and HTML

The Complete Reference

Chapter 11

Basic Interactivity and HTML: Forms

403

One of the Web's most interesting possibilities is the creation of interactive features. Up to this point, the discussion has focused on the Web as a static publishing environment. On the other hand, Web sites also can be thought of as software because users can perform tasks and interact with content in ways that are beyond the capabilities of print. While links provide basic ability for users to make choices, fill-out forms enable users to submit information that can be used to create an interactive environment ranging from an order entry system to a dynamically created Web site. Today forms are commonplace on the Web and mastery over their syntax is required to build a modern Web site.

How Are Forms Used?

There are many uses for forms on the Web. The most common ones include comment response forms, order entry forms, subscription forms, registration forms, and customization forms:

- A comment response generally is used to collect comments from Web site viewers and elicit suggestions for improvement.

- Order entry forms, which now are common on the Web, provide a way for viewers to order goods from online stores. Order entry forms typically require the user to provide an address, credit card number, and other information necessary to facilitate online commerce. (People generally should worry about the interception of credit card numbers if they are sending them to firms they know very little about. There are facilities to encrypt data transmitted between Web browser and server, but users should be very cautious about who is at the other end of the connection. A little common sense can remove much of the fear around sensitive data transmission.)

- Many sites are adopting a subscriber model, particularly those that attempt to generate revenue through direct subscriptions or by selling advertising space.

- Registration forms are used to collect information about a user and often are tied to an authentication system, which limits access to the site.

- Forms often are used to access database-hosted information; for example, looking up information in a catalog. Many e-commerce sites rely on forms and databases to provide order-entry services.

- Some sites allow users to select the look and feel for the site themselves, literally creating a custom site for each visitor. A customization form might allow users to specify what topics they are interested in within an online magazine. When tied to an authentication system, a user accessing the site views a version set according to his or her tastes.

There are many other examples of how forms might be used on the Web. The point here is to illustrate the kind of interactivity provided by forms.

Form Preliminaries

Making forms is easy. Just add the **<form>** element and associated tags for the form fields to the document, as you'll learn more about in the next section. But how can the contents of a form be processed once the user submits the information? After a form is filled in, the specified data is associated with various form field names and sent somewhere (as specified by a URL); generally, a program on a remote Web server will then parse the submitted information and do something with it. The programs that handle the incoming form-submitted data usually are Common Gateway Interface (CGI) programs. They also can utilize various other server-side technologies ranging from server-side scripting solutions such as ColdFusion to complex server modules such as ISAPI programs. A basic overview of how the relationship works is shown in Figure 11-1.

The point here isn't to get into the complications of how to make a CGI or other program handle form-submitted data, just to understand that the form itself is only part of the equation. There still must be some way to make the form do something, but this might not be your responsibility. CGI can get complicated because usually it involves real programming in languages such as C, Java, or Perl. It might be beyond the skill set of the page designer. In many cases it is possible to use off-the-shelf CGI programs.

But why worry about these issues? Does the person who creates the IRS tax form know how the program that calculates taxes works? Why should you worry about how the CGI for the database query form you created is written? This division of labor far too often is missing in Web projects. The people who build the back end of the Web site that the form interacts with probably aren't the best ones to code the form. The person who codes the form isn't necessarily always the best person to write the back-end CGI program. Think about how the form works in the grand scheme of things, but worry most about making your end of the site work. Interested readers should take a look at Chapter 12, which discusses server programming in more depth.

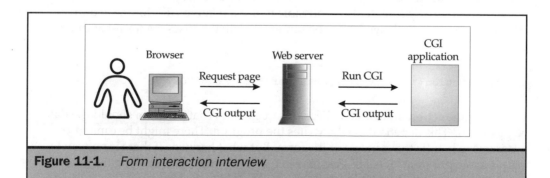

Figure 11-1.   *Form interaction interview*

PROGRAMMING
AND HTML

The <form> Element

A form in HTML is enclosed between the **<form>** and **</form>** tags. The form itself contains regular text, other HTML elements such as tables, and form elements such as check boxes, pull-down menus, and text fields. The W3C specification calls these form elements *controls*. This is somewhat confusing, because Microsoft also refers to ActiveX objects as controls. To avoid confusion, we'll call form elements either "form fields" or "form controls," not just "controls." The form controls are set by a user to indicate the contents of the form. Each form field will be named by setting a value to its **name** attribute. Once the user has finished filling out the form, the contents of each field is related to its name in the form of a name-value pair (e.g. username=Thomas) and generally is submitted to a server-based program such as a CGI script for processing. Completed forms generally are passed to a remote program that handles the data. The contents can even be mailed to a user for further inspection. To make the form work, you must specify two things. First, specify the address of the program that will handle the form contents using **action**. Next, specify the method by which the form data will be passed using the **method** attribute. The **name** attribute also is very important to set a name for the form so it can later be manipulated by a scripting language such as JavaScript. Finally, in some cases you might have to specify how the form will be encoded using the **enctype** attribute.

The action Attribute

How an HTML form is to be handled is set using the **action** attribute for the form element. The **action** attribute usually is set to a URL of the program that will handle the form data. This URL will usually point to a CGI script to decode the form results. For example, the code

```
<form action="http://www.democompany.com/cgi-bin/post-query"
      method="POST">
```

would be for a script called post-query in the cgi-bin directory on the server www.democompany.com. It also is possible to use a relative URL for the **action** attribute if the form is delivered by the same server that houses the form-handling program:

```
<form action="../cgi-bin/post-query" method="POST">
```

Setting the **action** immediately begs this question: What program should the data be passed to? This depends on who writes the program. There might be canned programs to handle the contents of the form. But what happens if there is no way to use a remote program? It is possible to create a "poor man's" form using the mailto

URL. Remember: The **action** attribute is set to a URL. Thus, in some cases a form element such as

```
<form action="mailto:formtest@democompany.com" method="POST"
      enctype="text/plain">
```

will work. It is even possible to use an extended form of mailto URL, which is supported by some browsers such as most versions of Netscape and newer versions of Internet Explorer. For example,

```
<form action="mailto:formtest@democompany.com?
Subject="Comment%20Form%20Result">
```

Note *The %20 is simply the encoding of the space character.*

Although the mailto form seems the best way to do things, not all browsers support this style. There also are potential security issues. Even if the browser supports the mailto style, the data should be passed using the **POST** method. It might be useful to encode the data differently by setting it to use text/plain encoding rather than the default style, which is a cryptic encoding style similar to how URLs look. The next section will discuss the methods and the encoding type.

The method Attribute

It also is necessary to specify how the form will be submitted to the address specified by the **action** attribute. How data will be submitted is handled by the **method** attribute. There are two acceptable values for the **method** attribute: **GET** and **POST**. These are the HTTP methods that a browser uses to "talk" to a server. We'll find out more about that in a moment, as well as in Chapter 12. Note that if the **method** attribute remains unspecified, most browsers should default to the **GET** method. Although much of the following discussion is more applicable to the people writing the programs that handle form data, it is important to understand the basic idea of each method.

Note *When discussing the HTTP methods, we refer to them in uppercase as GET and POST; whereas many HTML attribute values are in lowercase, these should always be in uppercase.*

GET Method

The **GET** method generally is the default method for browsers to submit information. In fact, HTML documents generally are retrieved by requesting a single URL from a Web server using the **GET** method, which is part of the HTTP protocol. When you type a URL such as http://www.democompany.com/staff/thomas.htm into your Web browser, it is translated into a valid HTTP **GET** request like this:

```
GET /staff/thomas.htm HTTP/1.0
```

This request is then sent to the server www.democompany.com. What this request says, essentially, is "Get me the file thomas.htm in the staff directory. I am speaking the 1.0 dialect of HTTP." How does this relate to forms? You really aren't getting a file *per se* when you submit a form, are you? In reality, you are running a program to handle the form data. For example, the **action** value might specify a URL such as http://www.democompany.com/cgi-bin/comment.exe, which is the address of a program that can parse your comment form. So wouldn't the HTTP request be something like the one shown here?

```
GET /cgi-bin/comment.exe HTTP/1.0
```

Almost. You need to pass the form data along with the name of the program to run. To do this, all the information from the form is appended onto the end of the URL being requested. This produces a very long URL with the actual data in it, as shown here:

```
http://www.democompany.com/cgi-bin/comments.exe?
Name=Matthew+Folely&Age=32&Sex=male
```

The **GET** method isn't very secure because the data input appears in the URL. Furthermore, there is a limitation to just how much data can be passed with the **GET** method. It would be impossible to append a 10,000-word essay to the end of a URL, as most browsers limit a URL to several thousand characters. Further problems with **GET** become obvious when dealing with foreign language environments. Would it be possible to deal with Japanese Kanji characters in the URL using the GET method? Probably not. Under the HTML 4.01 specification, the **GET** method has been deprecated. Despite the fact that **GET** is not recommended, it still is the default method when the **method** attribute is not specified.

With all these problems, why use **GET**? First, **GET** is easy to deal with. An example URL like the following should make it obvious that the Name field is set to "Matthew Foley," the Age is "32," and the "Sex" is male:

```
http://www.democompany.com/cgi-bin/
comments.exe?Name=Matthew+Folely&Age=32&Sex=male
```

Form field names are set to values that generally are encoded with plus signs instead of spaces. Non-alphanumeric characters are replaced by "%*nn*" where *nn* is the hexadecimal ASCII code for the character, similar to the URL encoding, as described in Chapter 4. The individual form field values are separated by ampersands. It would be trivial to write a parsing program to recover data out of this form, but it probably is better to use one of the many existing libraries to decode submitted data.

The other method, **POST**, is just as easy, so this is not a motivating reason to use **GET**. Perhaps the best reason to use **GET** is that it comes in the form of a URL, so it can be bookmarked or set as a link. The **GET** method is used well in search engines. When a user submits a query to a search engine, the engine runs the query and then returns page upon page of result. It is possible to bookmark the query results and rerun the query later. It also is possible to create anchors that fire off canned CGI programs. This is particularly useful in certain varieties of dynamic Web sites. For example, the link shown next fires off a CGI program written in the ColdFusion Markup language (CFM) and passes it a value setting—setting the ExecutiveID to 1.

```
<a href="displayexec.cfm?ExecutiveId=1">Joe Somolovich</a>
```

The query is built into the link; when the link is clicked, the CGI program will access the appropriate database of executives and bring up information about Joe Somolovich.

Although the **GET** method is far from perfect, there are certain situations in which it makes a great deal of sense. It is unlikely that **GET** will be truly deprecated for quite some time.

POST Method

In situations where a large amount of information must be passed back, the **POST** method is more appropriate than **GET**. The **POST** method transmits all form input information as a data stream immediately after the requested URL. In other words, once the server has received a request from a form using **POST**, it knows to continue "listening" for the rest of the information. The **GET** method requires only one, because the method comes with the data to use right in the request. The encoding of the form data is handled in the same general way as the **GET** method by default; spaces become plus signs and other characters are encoded in the URL fashion. A sample form might send data that would look like this:

```
Name=Jane+Smith&Age=30&Sex=female
```

Like data transmitted using the **GET** method, the data will still have to be broken up to be used by the handling program. The benefit of using the **POST** method is that a large amount of data can be submitted this way because the form contents are not in the URL. It is even possible to send the contents of files using this method. In the case of the **POST** example, the encoding of the form data is the same as **GET**, although it is possible to change the encoding method using the **enctype** attribute.

Note *One potential downside of the post method is that pages generated by data submitted via post cannot be bookmarked.*

The enctype Attribute

When data is passed from a form to a Web server, it typically is encoded just like a URL. In this encoding, spaces are replaced by the "+" symbol and non-alphanumeric characters are replaced by "*%nn*", where *nn* is the hexadecimal ASCII code for the character. The form of this is described in the special MIME file format *application/x-www-form-urlencoded*. By default, all form data is submitted in this form. It is possible, however, to set the encoding method for form data by setting the **enctype** attribute. When using a mailto URL in the **action** attribute, the encoding type of *text/plain* might be more desirable. The result would look like the example shown here:

```
First Name=Joe
Last Name=Smith
Sex=Male
Submit=Send it
```

Each form field is on a line of its own. Even with this encoding form, non-alphanumeric characters can be encoded in the hexadecimal form.

Another form of encoding also is important: **multipart/form-data**. When passing files back using a form, it is important to designate where each file begins and ends. A value of **multipart/form-data** for the **enctype** is used to indicate this style. In this encoding, spaces and non-alphanumeric characters are preserved; data elements are separated by special delimiter lines. The following file fragment shows the submission of a form with **multipart/form-data** encoding, including the contents of the attached files:

```
Content-type: multipart/form-data;
boundary=---------------------------2988412654262
Content-Length: 5289
---------------------------2988412654262
Content-Disposition: form-data; name="firstname"
Joe
```

```
--------------------------------2988412654262
Content-Disposition: form-data; name="lastname"
Smith
--------------------------------2988412654262
Content-Disposition: form-data; name="myfile";
filename="C:\WINNT\PROFILES\ADMINISTRATOR\DESKTOP\TEST.HTM"
Content-Type: text/html
```
`<html><head><title>`Test File**`</title></head>`**
`<body><h1>`Test File**`</h1></body></html>`**
```
----------------------------------------
8/12/97 4:47:45 PM--SF_NOTIFY_PREPROC_HEADERS
URL=/programs/postit.cfm?
----------------------------------------
8/12/97 4:47:45 PM--SF_NOTIFY_URL_MAP
URL=/programs/postit.cfm
Physical Path=C:\InetPub\wwwroot\programs\postit.cfm
----------------------------------------
```

The name Attribute

Before presenting a simple form, consider the need for the **name** attribute. It often is desirable to check data before it is sent into the Web server. Users find it very frustrating to fill out a form and submit it to a server only to have the server return a page indicating data problems or omissions. Checking data before submission, often termed *form validation,* requires the use of JavaScript, which is discussed in Chapter 13. Key to using JavaScript is making sure to give the form an alphanumeric identifier. The **name** attribute can be set to an alphanumeric value such as "orderform." As with all form elements, you should always be sure to set the **name** attribute for a **`<form>`** element for future manipulation by a scripting language.

There might be some confusion on the use of **name** because the HTML 4.01 specification provides the **id** attribute as a core attribute. However, browsers, including most older versions of Netscape and Microsoft Internet Explorer, depend on the occurrence of **name** to provide access to the form. Page authors looking to use **id** instead should consider setting **name** and **id** to the same value. Practice so far suggests that the **id** attribute is being used primarily for style sheets when a name attribute also exists for an element, as in the case of **`<form>`**.

Simple Form Example

Given that we have a destination for the form contents as specified by the **action** attribute and possibly a **method**, either **GET** or **POST**; and maybe an encoding form, we can write a simple stub example for a form as shown next.

```
<!DOCTYPE HTML PUBLIC "-//W3C//DTD HTML 4.01 Transitional//EN">
<html>
<head>
<title>Form Template</title>
</head>
<body>
<form action="/cgi-bin/post-query.pl" method="POST">
Form fields and standard HTML markup
</form>
</body>
</html>
```

Although this syntax is adequate to build the form framework in most cases, other attributes for the form element might be useful for frame targeting, scripting, and style sheets; these are discussed in Appendix A. Now it is time to cover the various HTML elements needed to create form fields.

Form Field Elements

A form is made up of *fields* or *controls*, as well as the markup necessary to structure the form and control its presentation. The controls are the items filled in or manipulated by the user to indicate the state of the form. Form controls include text fields, password fields, multiple-line text fields, pop-up menus, scrolled lists, radio buttons, check boxes, and buttons. Hidden form controls also are possible. Rather than discuss the syntax of the particular elements, let's first approach learning forms by exploring the form controls, and then the complete syntax for the elements. This discussion covers only basic form controls. Newer form items as represented by **<button>**, **<label>**, **<fieldset>**, and **<legend>** are discussed in the section "New and Emerging Form Elements."

Text Controls

Single-line text entry fields are specified using the **<input>** element and are useful for collecting small bits of data such as a user's name, address, e-mail address, and so on. It also is possible to specify a multiple-line text field using the **<textarea>** element, but for now let's focus on the simplest form of text entry. To set a text entry control, use the **<input>** element and set the **type** attribute equal to **text** as shown here for traditional HTML:

```
<input type="text" name="UserName">
```

In XHTML syntax, because this is an empty element we would write

```
<input type="text" name="UserName" id="UserName">
```

The rest of the discussion will utilize the traditional HTML 4.01 syntax, but all could easily be modified to XHTML.

All form elements should be named by setting the attribute **name** to some unique value. In the previous example, the **name** attribute was set to "UserName" as it was associated with a field that is used to collect a user's name on an order form. Remember to pick a name that makes sense and is unique to the form. The name will be used when the form is submitted, as well as for manipulation by scripting languages.

The last example does not specify the size of the field nor the maximum number of characters that can be entered into the field. By default, unless specified this field generally will be a width of 20 characters, although browsers might not necessarily follow this typical situation. To set the size of the field in characters, use the **size** attribute. For example,

```
<input type="text" name="UserName" size="40">
```

The value of the **size** field for an **<input>** element is the number of characters to be displayed. It is possible for the user to type more characters than this value. The text will just scroll by. If you want to limit the size of the field, you need to set the value of the **maxlength** attribute to the maximum number of characters allowed in the field. The browser will deny the user from typing more than the number of characters specified. Browser feedback might include beeping or might just overstrike the last character. To set a text field that shows 30 characters but has a maximum of 60 characters that can be entered, you can use

```
<input type="text" name="UserName" size="30" maxlength="60">
```

The last attribute that is useful to set with a text entry field is the **value** attribute. With this attribute, you can specify the default text you want to appear in the field when the form is first loaded. For example, in the following code fragment, a value of **"Enter your name here"** is provided as a prompt to the user to fill in the field properly:

```
<input type="text" name="UserName" size="30" maxlength="60"
value="Enter your name here">
```

A very simple example of the basic text field type is shown here:

```
<!DOCTYPE HTML PUBLIC "-//W3C//DTD HTML 4.01 Transitional//EN">
<html>
```

```
<head>
<title>Text Field Example</title>
</head>
<body>
<h1 align="center">Gadget Order Form</h1>
<hr>
<form action="http://www.democompany.com/cgi-bin/post.pl"
    method="POST">
<b>Customer Name:</b>
<input type="text" name="UserName" size="25" maxlength="35">
</form>
</body>
</html>
```

A rendering of the previous example is shown in Figure 11-2.

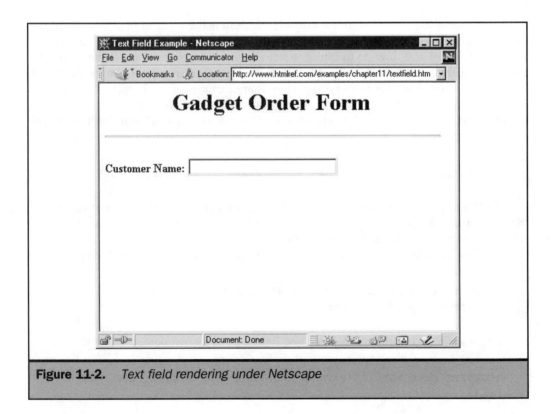

Figure 11-2. *Text field rendering under Netscape*

Password Fields

The password style of form control is the same as the simple text entry field, except that the input to the field is not echoed when typed. In many cases, the browser may render each character as an asterisk or dot to avoid people seeing the password being entered, as shown here:

Not echoing the password onscreen is appropriate. It discourages the idea of "shoulder surfing" in which an unscrupulous user looks on your screen to see what secret data you input. To set a password form control, use the **<input>** element but set the **type** attribute equal to **password**. As with the text entry field, it is possible to specify the size of the field in characters with **size**, and the maximum entry with **maxlength** in characters. In the case of the password control, it probably is wise to limit the length of the field so users don't become confused about how many characters they have entered.

The password form is very similar to the single-line text entry field. However, setting a default value for the password field with the **value** attribute doesn't make much sense because the user can see it by viewing the HTML source of the document. A complete example of the password field's use within the form is shown here:

```
<!DOCTYPE HTML PUBLIC "-//W3C//DTD HTML 4.01 Transitional//EN">
<html>
<head>
<title>Password Field Example</title>
</head>
<body>

<h1 align="center">Gadget Order Form</h1>
<hr>
<form action="http://www.democompany.com/cgi-bin/post.pl"
method="post">
<b>Password:</b>
<input type="password" name="Pass" size="10" maxlength="10">
</form>
```

```
</body>
</html>
```

Make sure to not assume that password fields are secure. The data is not encoded in any special way. Data must be transmitted using an SSL (Secure Sockets Layer) connection as designated by the https communication protocol.

Multiple-Line Text Input

When it is necessary to enter more than one line of text in a form field, the **<input>** element must be abandoned in favor of the **<textarea>** element. Like the text input field, there are similar attributes to control the display size of the data entry area as well as the default value and the name of the control. For example, to set the number of rows in the text entry area, set the **rows** attribute equal to the number of rows desired. To set the number of characters per line, set the **cols** attribute. So, to define a text area of five rows of 80 characters each, use the following:

```
<textarea rows="5" cols="80" name="CommentBox">
</textarea>
```

Because there might be many lines of text within the **<textarea>** element, it is not possible to set the default text for the area using the **value** attribute. Instead, place the default text between the **<textarea>** and **</textarea>** tags:

```
<textarea rows="5" cols="80" name="CommentBox">
Please fill in your comments here.
</textarea>
```

The information enclosed within the **<textarea>** element must be plain text and should not include any HTML markup. In fact, the default text in the **<textarea>** element preserves all the spaces, returns, and other special characters. HTML elements entered within the form control will not be interpreted. A complete example of a multiple-line text field is shown here:

```
<!DOCTYPE HTML PUBLIC "-//W3C//DTD HTML 4.01 Transitional//EN">
<html>
<head>
<title>Textarea Example</title>
</head>
<body>
```

```
<h1 align="center">Gadget Order Form</h1>
<hr>
<form action="http://www.democompany.com/cgi-bin/post.pl"
method="POST">
<b>Comments:</b><br>
<textarea name="Comment" rows="8" cols="40">
</textarea>
</form>
</body>
</html>
```

The rendering of the preceding example is shown in Figure 11-3. When typing in text into a multiline field, wrapping must be considered. By default Internet Explorer will wrap text, but versions 4.0 and previous of Netscape will not. Use the non-standard **wrap** attribute for the **<textarea>** element. The values for this attribute are **off**, **hard**, and **soft**. A value of **off** disables word wrapping in the form control. Any text the user enters is displayed exactly as is, although the user may insert hard returns of his or her

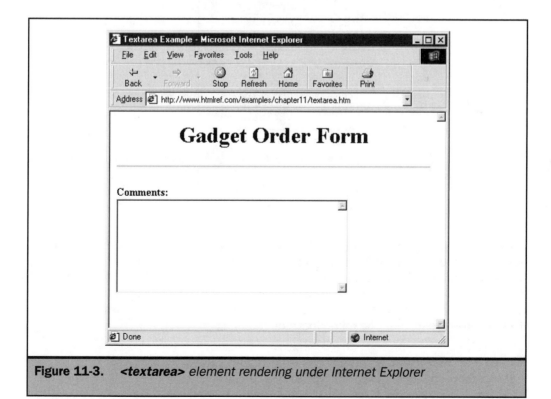

Figure 11-3. *<textarea> element rendering under Internet Explorer*

own. A value of **hard** allows word wrapping, and the actual break points are included when the form is submitted. A value of **soft** allows word wrapping in the form control, but the line breaks are not sent with the form's contents. A value of **soft** is the default in Internet Explorer, but should always be explicitly set to make sure that other browsers such as Netscape wrap text properly.

One interesting omission with **<textarea>** is there is no attribute to limit the amount of content that can be entered into the field. This is a glaring omission from HTML and should be rectified in future versions. For now, consider that JavaScript can be used to limit the contents of a field as users type.

Pull-Down Menus

HTML form controls include pull-down menus. A pull-down menu lets the user select one choice out of many possible choices. One nice aspect of pull-down menus is that all choices do not have to be seen on the screen and normally are hidden. This illustration shows the rendering of a pull-down menu under different browsers:

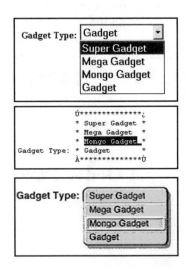

To create a pull-down menu, use the **<select>** element. This element must include both a start and an end tag. It should contain only one or more occurrences of the **<option>** element. The **<option>** elements specify the actual choices on the menu, and do not need a close tag except under XHTML. For good forward compatibility use the close tag anyway. In many ways, the structure of a pull-down menu looks similar to a list structure, as shown in the following code fragment:

```
<select name="GadgetType">
    <option>Super Gadget</option>
```

```
    <option>Mega Gadget</option>
    <option>Mongo Gadget</option>
    <option>Plain Gadget</option>
</select>
```

As shown in the code fragment, like all form controls the **<select>** element has a **name** attribute that is used to set a unique name for the control for purposes of decoding the user selection. It also is possible to set attributes for the **<option>** element. An occurrence of the attribute **selected** in the **<option>** element sets the form control to select this item by default. Generally a browser will choose the first **<option>** in the element as the default if no other element contains the selected attribute. If multiple selected attributes are specified, the result is generally to select the final **<option>** element, but page authors should not assume this result and instead should focus on developing correct markup. Normally, the value submitted when the form is sent is the value enclosed by the **<option>** element. However, it is possible to set the **value** attribute for the element that will be returned instead. A complete example of a simple pull-down menu is shown here:

```
<!DOCTYPE HTML PUBLIC "-//W3C//DTD HTML 4.01 Transitional//EN">
<html>
<head>
<title>Pull-down Menu Example</title>
</head>
<body>
<h1 align="center">Gadget Order Form</h1>

<form action="http://www.democompany.com/cgi-bin/post.pl "
method="POST">
<b>Gadget Type:</b>
<select name="GadgetType">
      <option value="SG-01">Super Gadget</option>
      <option value="MEG-G5">Mega Gadget</option>
      <option value="MO-45">Mongo Gadget</option>
      <option selected>Gadget</option>
</select>
</form>
</body>
</html>
```

<optgroup>

Under HTML 4, a late addition to forms is a special element, **<optgroup>,** that can be used to group option categories. Although this is not well supported by browsers, this element could be rendered in a cascading menu format. This simple example shows how **<optgroup>** might be used:

```
<select name="GadgetType">
    <optgroup label="S* Gadgets">
       <option value="SG-01">Super Gadget</option>
    </optgroup>
    <optgroup label="M* Gadgets">
        <option value="MEG-G5">Mega Gadget</option>
        <option value="MO-45">Mongo Gadget</option>
    </optgroup>
      <option selected>Gadget</option>
</select>
```

An example rendering in a beta release of Netscape 6 (Preview Release 2) shows how this element might eventually be used.

For now, consider that its use is relatively harmless since most browsers will just ignore the element and render the list normally. The complete syntax for this element can be found in Appendix A.

Scrolled Lists

The **<select>** element also might contain the **size** attribute, which is used to specify the number of items showing on the screen at once. The default value for this attribute is 1, which specifies a normal pull-down menu. Setting a positive number creates a list in a window of the specified number of rows, as shown here:

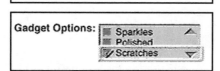

In many cases, scrolled lists act just like pull-down menus. However, if the **<select>** element contains the attribute **multiple**, it becomes possible to select more than one entry. How multiple items are selected depends on the browser, but generally, it requires holding down some modifier key such as CTRL, COMMAND, or SHIFT and selecting the appropriate items with the mouse.

Note *Many novice users have a hard time with the scrolled list control and multiple entries. Depending on your target audience, it might be wise to provide instructions near the control to assist the user.*

Because it is possible to select more than one entry in a scrolled list when the multiple option is applied, it then is possible to use the **selected** attribute multiple times in the enclosed **<option>** elements. A complete example illustrating how the scrolled list is used is shown here:

```
<!DOCTYPE HTML PUBLIC "-//W3C//DTD HTML 4.01 Transitional//EN">
<html>
<head>
<title>Scrolled List Example</title>
</head>
<body>
<h1 align="center">Gadget Order Form</h1>

<form action="http://www.democompany.com/cgi-bin/post.pl"
method="POST">
<b>Gadget Options:</b>
<select name="GadgetOptions" multiple size="3">
```

```
   <option value="Hit with hammer" selected>Bumps</option>
   <option value="Add glitter">Sparkles</option>
   <option value="Buff it">Polished</option>
   <option selected>Scratches</option>
   <option>Shrink wrapped</option>
</select>
</form>
</body>
</html>
```

Check Boxes

With the scrolled list, it is possible to select many items out of a large group of items. Unfortunately, not all the items are presented at once for the user to choose. If there are a few options to select from that are not mutually exclusive, it probably is better to use a group of check boxes that the user can check off. Check boxes are best used to toggle choices on and off. Although it is possible to have multiple numbers of check boxes and let the user select as many as he or she wants, if there are too many it might be difficult to deal with. Don't forget about scrolled lists.

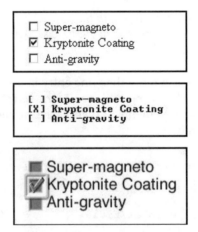

To create a check box, use the **<input>** element and set the **type** attribute equal to **checkbox**. The check box also should be named by setting the **name** attribute. For example, to create a check box asking if a user wants cheese, use some markup like this:

```
Cheese: <input type="checkbox" name="Cheese">
```

Or under XHTML with the self-identifying close tag we would have this:

```
Cheese: <input type="checkbox" name="Cheese" id="Cheese"/>
```

In this example, the label to the left is arbitrary. It could be to the right as well. The label could say "Put cheese on it," but there will be no indication of this label to the receiving program. In this simple example, if the check box is selected, a value of **Cheese=on** will be transmitted to the server. Setting a value for the check box might make more sense. Values to be transmitted instead of the default value can be set with the **value** attribute. The code

```
Cheese: <input type="checkbox" name="Extras" value="Cheese">
```

would send a response such as **Extras=Cheese** to the server. It also is possible to have multiple check box controls with the same name. The code

```
Cheese: <input type="checkbox" name="Extras" value="Cheese">
Pickles: <input type="checkbox" name="Extras" value="Pickles">
```

would send multiple entries such as the following to the server when both extras were selected:

```
Extras=Cheese&Extras=Pickles
```

It is possible to set a check box to be selected by default by using the **checked** attribute within the **<input>** element. The **checked** attribute requires no value. However, under XHTML you would have to use **checked="checked"** to be perfectly correct. A complete example using check box controls is shown here:

```
<!DOCTYPE HTML PUBLIC "-//W3C//DTD HTML 4.01 Transitional//EN">
<html>
<head>
<title>Check Box Example</title>
</head>
<body>
<h1 align="center">Gadget Order Form</h1>
<hr>
<form action="http://www.democompany.com/cgi-bin/post.pl "
method="POST">
<b>Gadget Bonus Options:</b>
<br>
Super-magneto:
<input type="checkbox" name="Bonus" value="Magnetize"><br>
```

```
Kryptonite Coating:
<input type="checkbox" name="Bonus" value="Anti-Superman"
checked><br>
Anti-gravity:
<input type="checkbox" name="Bonus" value="Anti-gravity"><br>
</form>
</body>
</html>
```

Radio Buttons

Radio buttons use a similar notation to check boxes, but only one option may be chosen among many. This is an especially good option for choices that don't make sense when selected together. In this sense, radio buttons are like pull-down menus that allow only one choice. The main difference is that all options are shown at once with radio buttons.

Like check boxes, this form control uses the standard **<input type="">** format. In this case, set **type** equal to **radio**. Setting the **name** field is very important in the case of radio buttons because it groups together controls that share the radio functionality. The radio functionality says that when an item is selected, it deselects the previously pressed item. If the names are different for each radio button, the functionality becomes more like that of a check box, except with a different shape. Possible renderings of the radio button form control are shown here:

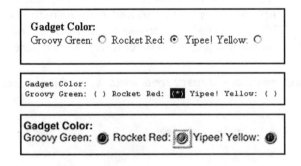

Another important attribute is **value**. It is important to set each individual radio button to a different value entry. Otherwise, it will be impossible to decipher which button was selected. Like check boxes, the occurrence of the **selected** attribute in the **<input>** element will preselect the item. Only one item may be selected as a default out of a radio group. If the **selected** attribute does not occur, the browser typically will not display any items as selected. A complete example using radio buttons is shown here:

```
<!DOCTYPE HTML PUBLIC "-//W3C//DTD HTML 4.01 Transitional//EN">
<html>
<head>
<title>Radio Button Example</title>
</head>
<body>
<h1 align="center">Gadget Order Form</h1>
<hr>
<form action="http://www.democompany.com/cgi-bin/post.pl"
method="POST">
<b>Gadget Color:</b><br>
Groovy Green: <input type="radio" name="Color" value="Green">
Rocket Red: <input type="radio" name="Color" value="Red" checked>
Yipee! Yellow: <input type="radio" name="Color" value="Yellow">
</form>
</body>
</html>
```

Reset and Submit Buttons

Once a form has been filled in, there must be a way to send it on its way, whether it is submitted to a program for processing or simply mailed to an e-mail address. The **<input>** element has two values, **reset** and **submit**, for the **type** attribute; these can create common buttons that are useful for just about any form. Setting the **type** attribute for the **<input>** element to **reset** creates a button that allows the user to clear or set to default all the form controls at once. Setting the **type** attribute for **<input>** to **submit** creates a button that triggers the browser to send the contents of the form to the address specified in the **action** attribute of the **<form>** element. Common renderings of the **submit** and **reset** form buttons are shown here:

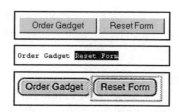

The buttons themselves have two basic attributes: **value** and **name**. The **value** attribute sets both the value of the button when pressed and the wording of the button. The **name** value associates an identifier with the form field. A complete example showing a small form with submit and reset buttons is shown next.

```
<!DOCTYPE HTML PUBLIC "-//W3C//DTD HTML 4.01 Transitional//EN">
<html>
<head>
<title>Complete Form Example</title>
</head>
<body>
<h1 align="center">Gadget Order Form</h1>
<hr>
<form action="http://www.democompany.com/cgi-bin/post.pl"
method="POST"
<b>Customer Name:</b>
<input type="text" name="UserName" size="25" maxlength="35">
<b>Password:</b>
<input type="password" name="Pass" size="10"
maxlength="10"><br><br>
<br><br>
<b>Gadget Type:</b>
<select name="GadgetType">
      <option value="SG-01">Super Gadget</option>
      <option value="MEG-G5">Mega Gadget</option>
      <option value="MO-45">Mongo Gadget</option>
      <option selected>Gadget</option>
</select>
<br><br>
<input type="submit" value="Order Gadget" name="SubmitButton">
<input type="reset" value="Reset Form" name="ResetButton">
</form>
</body>
</html>
```

> **Note** *Under XHTML the syntax of this example would require the various <input> elements, which are mostly empty, to self-close; for example **<input type="reset" value="Reset Form" name="ResetButton" />***

Because the submit and reset buttons cause an action, either form submission or field reset, it would not seem obvious why the **name** field might be useful. Although having multiple reset buttons might not be useful, multiple submit buttons are useful because the value of the button is sent to the address specified in the **<form>** element's **action** attribute. One possible use might be to have three submit buttons: one for add, one for delete, and one for update.

```
<input type="submit" value="Place Order" name="Add">
```

```
<input type="submit" value="Delete Order" name="Delete">
<input type="submit" value="Update Order" name="Update">
<input type="reset"  value="Reset Form" name="ResetButton">
```

When the form is submitted, the value of the button is sent to the form-handling program, which will decide what to do with the submitted data based upon its contents. This use of a submit button hints at a more generalized form of button, which will be discussed in the next section.

Note *If you have two buttons next to each other, it is useful to separate the two with a non-breaking space ( ). Otherwise, the buttons probably will render too closely together. Another approach would be to use a small table around the buttons and provide some cell padding or a blank cell between the buttons.*

Additional <input> Types

There are a few forms of the **<input>** element that have not been discussed. These form elements hint at the potential complexity of using forms. Some of these elements, particularly the file selection form element, are not supported in older browsers.

Hidden Text and Its Uses

The usefulness of this form control is not always obvious to the new user. By setting the **type** attribute of the **<input>** element to a value of **hidden**, it is possible to transmit default or previously specified text that is hidden from the user to the handling program. If there were many versions of the same form all over a Web site, the hidden text could be used to specify where the form came from, as shown here:

```
<input type="hidden" name="SubmittingFormName" value="Form1">
```

Because this field is not shown on the page, it is difficult but not impossible for the user to modify it. Thus, it must have its **value** attribute set. While this last example seems rather contrived, there actually is a very important use for hidden form controls.

Note *There are some problems with relying on hidden values too much. Consider that nefarious users might be able to determine the internal workings of your system or even falsify requests that include control information in the hidden fields. Not to alarm page designers, but do consider that to see hidden form fields all the user has to do is view the page source!*

When filling in forms, there often is an issue of remembering information from one form to the next. Imagine a form in which the user fills in his or her personal information on one page and the ordering information on the next page. How will the

PROGRAMMING AND HTML

two pages be related to each other? This presents the state-loss problem. The protocols of the Web, primarily HTTP, do not support a "memory." In other words, they don't preserve state. One way to get around this is to use hidden text. Imagine that, in the last example, the personal information is passed to the next page by dynamically embedding it in the ordering page as hidden text. Then state has been preserved—or has it? When users are finished ordering, they submit the whole form at once as a complete transaction. This idea of using hidden text to get around the state-loss problem is illustrated in Figure 11-4.

There are other approaches to saving state, including extended path information and cookies.

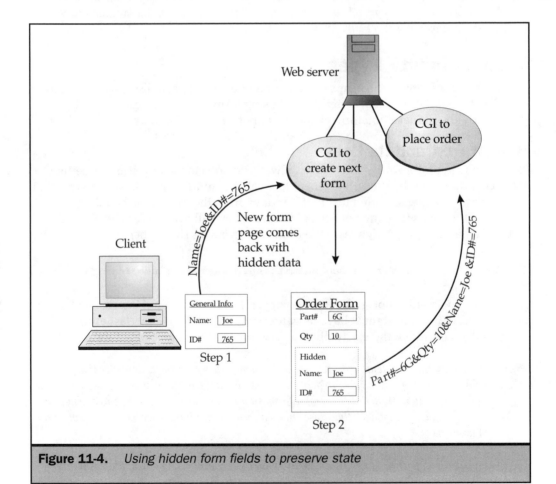

Figure 11-4. *Using hidden form fields to preserve state*

Image Type

One form of the **<input>** element that is somewhat strange is the image type, as specified by setting **type="image"**. This form of **<input>** creates a graphical version of the submit button, which not only submits the form but transmits coordinate information about where the user clicked in the image. The image is specified by the **src** attribute. Many of the attributes used for the **<img>** element might be valid for this form of **<input>** as well. The specification defines **alt** and **align**. Other attributes such as **border**, **hspace**, or **vspace** may or may not be supported by browsers. Like all other forms of **<input>**, the **name** attribute is a very important part of how the coordinate information is transmitted. The example use of **<input>** shown next could be used to insert a map of the United States, allowing users to click on the regional office where they want to submit their order forms.

```
<input type="image" src="usamap.gif" name="Sales" alt="Sales Region Map">
```

When clicked, the form values would be submitted along with two extra values, **Sales.x** and **Sales.y**. **Sales.x** and **Sales.y** would be set equal to the x and y coordinates of where the image was clicked. The x and y coordinates are relative to the image with an origin in the upper left-hand corner of the image. You might notice a similarity to image maps. Indeed, much of the functionality of this form control could be imitated with a client-side image map in conjunction with some scripting code. A future extension to this form of the **<input>** element would be to make it less server-side dependent, possibly even allowing the page author to set a map name to decode coordinates or set function. Except for specialized needs, page designers probably should look to provide the functionality of the image form control in some other way.

File Form Control

A recent addition to the **<input>** element that now is part of the HTML 4 specification is the possibility of setting the **type** attribute to **file**. This form control is used for file uploading. The field generally consists of a text entry box for a filename that can be manipulated with the **size** and **maxlength** attributes, as well as a button immediately to the right of the field, which usually is labeled "Browse." Pressing the "Browse" button enables the user to browse the local system to find a file to specify for upload. The logistics of how a file is selected depends on the user agent.

Following is an example of the syntax of the file form control, in which the **enctype** value has been set to **multipart/form-data** to allow the file to be attached to the uploaded form:

```
<!DOCTYPE HTML PUBLIC "-//W3C//DTD HTML 4.01 Transitional//EN">
<html>
<head>
<title>File Upload Test</title>
```

```
</head>
<body>
<h1 align="center">File Upload System </h1>
<hr>
<form action="http://www.democompany.com/cgi-bin/upload.pl" method="POST"
           enctype="multipart/form-data">
<b>File Description:</b><br>
<input type="text" name="Description" size="50" maxlength="100">
<br><br>
<b>Specify File to Upload:</b><br>
<input type="file" name="FileName">
<hr>
<input type="submit" value="Send File" name="SubmitButton">
<input type="reset" value="Reset Form" name="ResetButton">
</form>
</body>
</html>
```

A rendering of this example is shown in Figure 11-5.

Although it is possible to set the **size** and **maxlength** values of the **<input type="file">** element, this is not suggested because the path name might be larger than the size specified. (This depends on how the user has set up his or her system.)

HTML 4.0 also specifies the **accept** attribute for the **<input type="file">** element, which can be used to specify a comma-separated list of MIME types that the server receiving the contents of the form will know how to handle properly. Browsers could use this attribute to keep users from uploading files that are unacceptable to a server (for example, executable files). It is not known whether browsers actually pay any attention to this attribute.

Note   *The file form control is not supported by all browsers, particularly older versions.*

Generalized Buttons

One last form of the **<input>** element, hinted at earlier, is the generalized button. By using **<input type="button">**, it is possible to create a button in the style of the submit or reset buttons, but that has no predetermined actions. Inserting something like the following doesn't really do much:

```
<input type="button" value="Press Me!" name="mybutton">
```

If you click the rendering of this button, no action is triggered, and no value will be submitted. So what's the point? By using a scripting language, it is possible to tie an event to the button and create an action. At the end of this chapter, as well as in

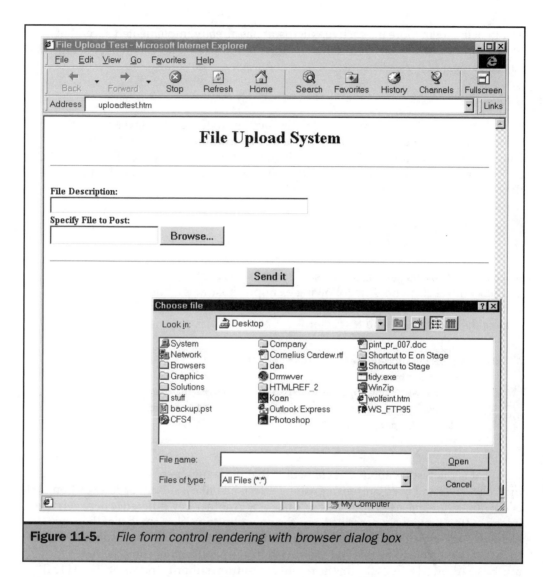

Figure 11-5.   *File form control rendering with browser dialog box*

PROGRAMMING
AND HTML

Chapter 13, you'll see how forms can be tied to scripting languages to create powerful interactive documents.

New and Emerging Form Elements

HTML 4.0 added several form-related tags and attributes beyond those commonly used by HTML authors. These are intended to address limitations in the current forms and to make them more interactive. Microsoft has already implemented several of these proposed extensions in Internet Explorer and the newest version of Netscape also supports most of these elements.

<button>

This element provides a way to add generic buttons to forms. The text enclosed by the tag is the button's label. In its simplest usage, the **<button>** element is functionally equivalent to **<input type="button">**, which is not supported by the official HTML 3.2 definition. In newer browsers like Internet Explorer 4 that support both button forms, the following two statements render identically:

```
<input type="button" value="Press Me">
<button>Press Me</button>
```

The **<button>** usage is more versatile because its content can include most inline and block-level elements. The following example illustrates a button element containing text, an embedded image, and the use of a cascading style sheet rule to change the background and text color.

```
<button name="HomePage" value="Test Button"
        type="button"
        style="background-color:blue; color:yellow">
   <img src="images/logonotext.gif" width="141" height="197">
   <br>Demo Company Home Page
</button>
```

What is interesting about this element is that the browser should render the button in a relief style and even present a pushing effect, just like a submit or reset button, so it is not quite the same as **<input type ="image">**. Another key difference between the image button previously described and the new **<button>** element is that the new element does not submit any coordinate information, nor is it strictly a submit button. In fact, it is possible to tie this style of button to a general action using the **type** attribute. Allowed values for this attribute are **button**, **submit**, and **reset**. The HTML 4.0 documentation suggests that **submit** is the default value.

Note   *It is incorrect to associate an image map with any image enclosed by a **<button>** element.*

Although the **<button>** element seems a more generalized way to deal with images as form buttons, it is not widely supported yet. Older browsers might require an alternative approach.

Labels

Another new form element introduced in HTML 4.0 and supported by advanced browsers is the **<label>** element. One motivation for this tag is to better support speech-based browsers that can read descriptions next to form fields. However, a more common use of the **<label>** element is to associate the labeling text of form controls with the actual controls they describe.

The **<label>** element can be associated with a form control by enclosing it as shown here:

```
<label>First Name:
    <input type="text" name="FirstName" size="20" maxlength="30">
</label>
```

A **<label>** element also can be associated with a control by referring to the control's **id** with the **for** attribute. In this usage, the label does not need to enclose the control. This allows labels to be positioned in tables with their own cells. It is common to use tables to make better-looking forms. Far too often, form elements snake down a page and are not aligned very well. The following code fragment illustrates how the **<label>** element with the **for** attribute would be used.

```
<table>
   <tr>
      <td align="right">
         <label for="CustName">Customer Name:</label>
      <td align="left">
         <input type="text" id="CustName" size="25" maxlength="35">
   </tr>
</table>
```

The **<label>** element also supports the **id**, **class**, **style**, **title**, **lang**, and **dir** attributes as well as numerous event handlers. These are used in the same way as on any other HTML element. In particular consider the use of label within style sheets to set the look of all form labels at once or in a group. The **disabled** and **accesskey** also are supported attributes for this element; these are discussed further later in the chapter in the section on form accessibility enhancements.

<fieldset>

This HTML 4 element groups related form elements analogous to the way the **<div>** element groups general body content. Like that element, **<fieldset>** can be especially useful in conjunction with CSS to apply look or positioning information to a group of form fields at once. The **<fieldset>** element also can have an associated **<legend>**

element to describe the enclosed items. The **<fieldset>** element itself has no special attributes aside from those core attributes common to all elements. However, the **<legend>** element does support the **align** attribute, which can be used to specify where the description will be rendered in relation to the group of form items; its values are **top** (the default value), **bottom**, **left**, or **right**. The example here illustrates how the **<fieldset>** and **<legend>** elements are used:

```
<!DOCTYPE HTML PUBLIC "-//W3C//DTD HTML 4.01 Transitional//EN">
<html>
<head>
<title>Fieldset and Legend Example</title>
</head>
<body>
<form action="http://www.democompany.com/cgi-bin/postquery.pl" method="POST"
      enctype="multipart/form-data">
<fieldset>
<legend>Customer Identification</legend>
<br>
<label>Customer Name:
<input type="text" name="CustomerName" size="25">
</label>
<br><br>
<label>Password:
<input type="password" name="CustomerID" size="8" maxlength="8">
</label>
<br>
</fieldset>
<input type="submit" value="send">
<input type="reset" value="Reset Form" name="ResetButton">
</form>
</body>
</html>
```

The W3C proposal recommends that a **<fieldset>** be enclosed by a box. An example rendering as supported by Internet Explorer is shown in Figure 11-6.

Form Accessibility Enhancements

One of the most important changes made to forms under HTML 4 is the improved support for accessibility. HTML 4 defines the **accesskey** attribute for form fields. Setting the value of the key to a character creates an accelerator key that can activate the form control associated with the element. Generally, the key must be pressed in combination with the CONTROL, ALT, or OPTION key to activate the field. An example of how this attribute might be used is shown in the following code example:

```
<label accesskey="N">Customer <u>N</u>ame:
   <input type="text" name="CustomerName" size="25">
</label>
```

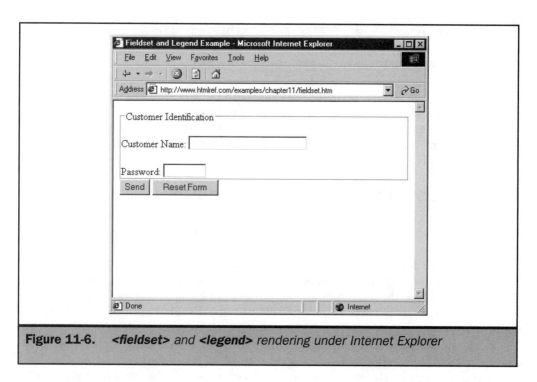

Figure 11-6. *<fieldset>* and *<legend>* rendering under Internet Explorer

Notice how the **<u>** element is used to highlight the letter that will activate the field. This is the common practice to indicate accelerator keys in a Windows GUI. According to the HTML 4.0 specification, browsers should provide their own form of highlighting for an access key, but in practice this isn't very common.

The HTML 4 standard defines the **accesskey** attribute for the **<label>**, **<input>**, **<legend>**, and **<button>** elements, although it leaves off support for **<select>** and **<textarea>**. Microsoft supports this attribute for the **<select>** and **<textarea>** elements. It seems likely that eventually this will be rolled into a future HTML specification.

While the **accesskey** attribute can improve a form by making it more keyboard access–friendly, there are certain letters to avoid because they map to browser functions in the two major browsers, as shown in Table 11-1.

Another accessibility improvement introduced in HTML 4.0 is the use of the **tabindex** attribute for the **<input>**, **<select>**, **<textarea>**, and **<button>** elements. This attribute allows the tab order between fields to be defined. In the Microsoft implementation, elements with **tabindex** values greater than zero are selected in increasing order. Generally, if a browser supports tabbing through form fields it is by the order in which they are defined. However, with the **tabindex** set the tabbing order goes from the lowest positive **tabindex** value to the highest. Any elements with a **tabindex** of 0 are selected in the order they are encountered after the rest of the tabbing controls have been exhausted. Fields with negative **tabindex** values should be left out of the tabbing order. So, in the next fragment, the last field gets selected first, then the first, and then the second field is completely skipped over.

PROGRAMMING AND HTML

```
<input type="text" name="FirstName" tabindex="2">
<input type="text" name="MiddleName" tabindex="-1">
<input type="text" name="LastName" tabindex="1">
```

Be careful when setting the **tabindex** value with radio buttons, as the browser might use arrow keys to move among a group of radio buttons rather than the TAB key.

Page designers are encouraged to set **accesskey** and **tabindex** attributes to their documents immediately; they will have no harmful side effects in older browsers, which will simply ignore them.

Miscellaneous HTML 4.0 Form Attributes

The HTML 4 specification also adds two other attributes to certain form controls: **disabled** and **readonly**. When the **disabled** attribute is present in a form control element, it turns off the field. Disabled elements will not be submitted, nor may they receive any focus from the keyboard or mouse. The browser might also gray out the disabled form. The point of the **disabled** attribute might not be obvious, but imagine being able to disable the form submission button until the appropriate fields had been filled in. Of course, being able to dynamically turn the **disabled** attribute for a form control on or off requires scripting support that not all browsers have.

When the **readonly** attribute is present in a form control element, it prevents the control's value from being changed. A form control set to **readonly** can be selected by the user but cannot be changed. Selection might even include the form control in the tabbing order. Unlike disabled controls, the values of read-only controls are submitted with the form. In some sense, a read-only form control can be thought of as a visible

Key	Mapping	Notes
F	File menu	
E	Edit menu	
C	Communicator menu	Netscape Communicator Only
V	View menu	
G	Go menu	
A	Favorites menu	Internet Explorer Only
H	Help	
LEFT ARROW	Back in history	
RIGHT ARROW	Forward in history	

Table 11-1. *Reserved Browser Key Bindings*

form of **<input type="hidden">**. According to the HTML 4.0 specification, the
readonly attribute is defined for the **<input type="text">**, **<input type="password">**,
and **<textarea>** elements, but some browser vendors might also support the **<select>**
element or even check boxes. Like a disabled form control, read-only controls can be
changed only through the use of a script.

Form Presentation

Up to this point, most of the form elements in the HTML 4.0 specification, as well as those
supported by the major browsers, have been presented. Some special considerations for
the WebTV environment will be considered in a moment. However, let's first turn our
attention to making forms more presentable. Unfortunately, on the Web, little attention
seems to be paid to making logical or even presentable-looking forms. For example, take a
look at the form in Figure 11-7; notice that nothing is grouped or lined up.

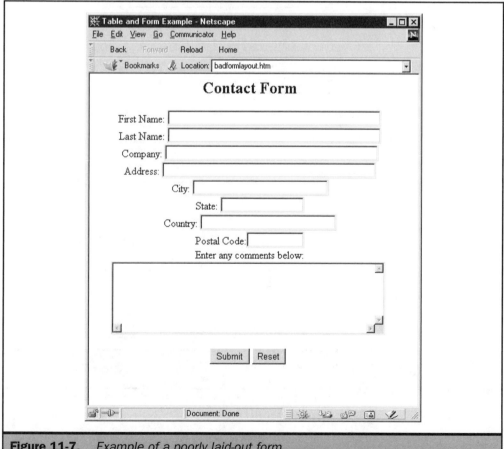

Figure 11-7.   *Example of a poorly laid-out form*

Form designers are reminded that other HTML markup elements can be used within forms, so there is no excuse for having a poorly laid-out form. For example, a form can be vastly improved by using a table as shown in Figure 11-8.

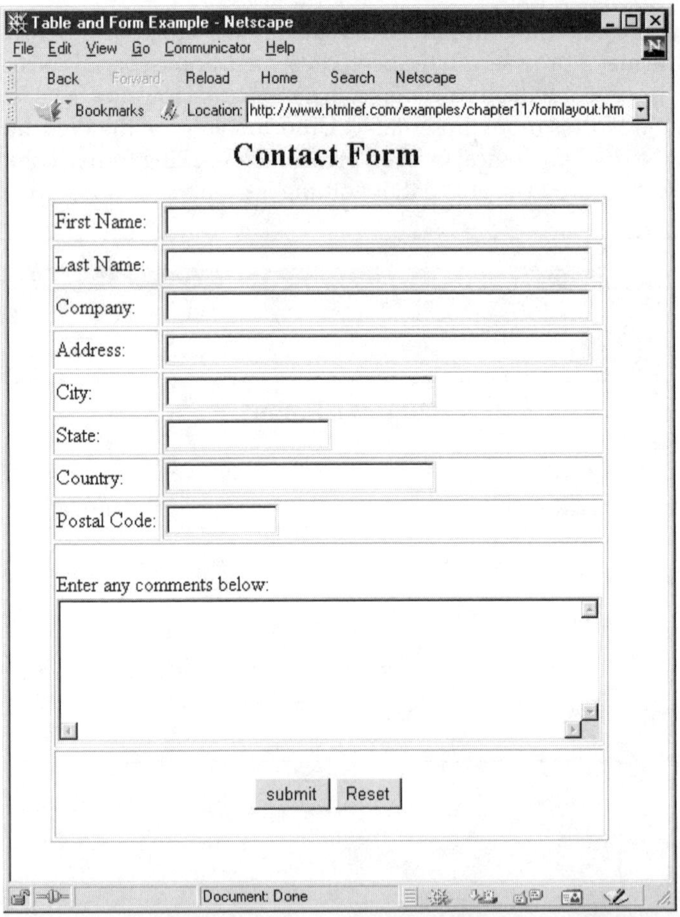

Figure 11-8.   *Form layout improved with a table*

The markup for the form using a table is shown here:

```
<!DOCTYPE HTML PUBLIC "-//W3C//DTD HTML 4.01 Transitional//EN">
<html>
<head>
<title>Table and Form Example</title>
</head>
<body>
<div align="center">
<h2>Contact Form</h2>
<form action="http://www.democompany.com/cgi-bin/postquery.pl"
      method="POST">
<table border="1">
   <tr>
      <td>First Name:</td>
      <td><input name="firstname" size="40"></td>
   </tr>

   <tr>
      <td>Last Name:</td>
      <td><input NAME="lastname" SIZE="40"></td>
   </tr>

   <tr>
      <td>Company:</td>
      <td><input name="company" size="40"></td>
   </tr>

   <tr>
      <td>Address:</td>
      <td><input name="address" size="40"></td>
   </tr>

   <tr>
      <td>City:</td>
      <td><input name="city" size="25"></td>
   </tr>

   <tr>
      <td>State:</td>
      <td><input name="state" size="15"></td>
   </tr>

   <tr>
      <td>Country:</TD>
      <td><input name="country" size="25"></td>
   </tr>
```

```
    <tr>
      <td>Postal Code:</td>
      <td><input name="zip" size="10"></td>
    </tr>

    <tr>
      <td colspan="2"><br>Enter any comments below:<br>
      <textarea name="text" rows="5" cols="50"></textarea></td>
    </tr>

    <tr>
      <td colspan="2" align="center"><br>
        <input type="submit" value="submit"> <input type="reset">
        <br><br>
      </td>
    </tr>
</table>
</form>
</div>
</body>
</html>
```

Tooltips and Form Fields

It also is possible to use the title attribute to give users a hint about how to use a form field. Consider this code:

```
<form>
Phone Number:
<input type=text" size="10" name="phone"
 title="Please enter your phone number here without dashes.">
</form>
```

This is fairly well supported in most recent browsers; the following rendering is in the Netscape 4.7 browser.

Be careful not to put critical information in a tooltip, in case the user has a browser that will not display them. JavaScript can be used in some browsers to simulate a tooltip, or to display similar information in the browser's status bar.

Forms and CSS

Page authors might wonder if it is possible to improve the look and feel of forms using style sheets. Under the HTML 4.0 specification, both the **<form>** element and the form control elements support the **class**, **id**, and **style** attributes to allow access from style sheets. For backward compatibility, particularly with scripting environments, they also support the **name** attribute. Renderings of this code under Internet Explorer 5.5 and Netscape 4.7 are shown in Figure 11-9. As this shows, older versions of the Netscape browser do not render any of the CSS formatting; Netscape 6 (Preview Release 2) renders this in much the same way as Internet Explorer.

```
<form>
    <input type="text" value="but this text is blue"
           style="font-family: Arial; color: blue;
                  font-size: 12px; background: lightblue">
<br><br>

    <input value="Submit" type="Submit" style="color: white;
           background: green; font-weight: bold; font-size: 22px">

</form>
```

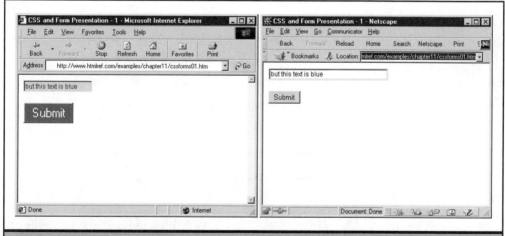

Figure 11-9. *Form presentation enhanced with CSS*

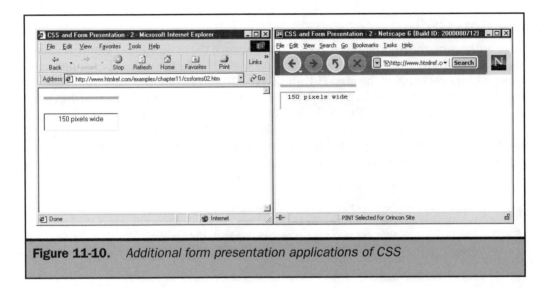

Figure 11-10. *Additional form presentation applications of CSS*

Under Internet Explorer 5.x and Netscape 6, it also is possible to set dimensions for some uses of the **<input>** element. The IE 5.5 rendering of this code is shown in Figure 11-10; the rendering also includes a 150-pixel–wide horizontal rule for reference.

```
<form>

<input type="text" value="150 pixels wide"
        style="width: 150; height: 35px; text-align: center">

</form>
```

As shown here, older versions of Netscape such as 4.7 do not render the CSS formatting.

```
150 pixels wide
```

It is, however, possible to approximate the CSS formatting of the text input field's width using the **size** attribute:

```
<form>

<input type="TEXT" value="150 pixels wide" size="18"
```

```
    style="width: 150; height: 35px; text-align: center">

</form>
```

Here is how this would now look under Netscape 4.7:

```
150 pixels wide
```

Bear in mind that this is just an approximation; user font settings might cause the text input field to increase or decrease in size in older Netscape browsers. And of course, the other CSS properties such as **text-align** and **height** cannot be faked using plain HTML.

Additional uses of CSS with forms might include using style sheet properties to indicate when a field in selected, using the pseudo-element hover:

```
input:focus {background-color: black; color: white}
```

A text field that receives focus will thus render with white text and a black background. A complete example using this CSS property, which also uses a background color to indicate required fields, is shown here; its rendering in Netscape 6 is shown in Figure 11-11.

```
<!doctype html public "-//W3C//DTD HTML 4.01 Transitional//EN">
<html>
<head>

<title>CSS Forms: Focus and Required Fields</title>

<style type="text/css">
<!--
input:focus {background-color: black; color: white}
.required    {background-color: lightblue}
-->
</style>

</head>
```

```
<body bgcolor="#FFFFFF">
<form action="http://www.democompany.com/cgi-bin/postquery.pl"
      method="POST">
<table border="0" cellspacing="5" cellpadding="0">
<tr>
<td><b>First Name * </b></td>
<td>
<input type="text" name="firstname" size="30" maxlength="50"
      class="required">
</td>
</tr>

<tr>
<td><b>Last Name * </b></td>
<td>
<input type="text" name="lastname" size="30" maxlength="50"
      class="required">
</td>
</tr>

<tr>
<td><b>Company * </b></td>
<td>
<input type="text" name="company" size="30" maxlength="50" class=
"required">
</td>
</tr>

<tr>
<td><b>Shoe Size</b></td>
<td>
<input type="text" name="company" size="30" maxlength="50">
</td>
</tr>

<tr>
<td align="center" colspan="2">
<input type="reset" value="Clear">
 
<input type="submit" value="Submit">
</td>
</tr>
```

```
</table>
</form><br><br>
<b>* = Required Field</b>

</body>
</html>
```

Of course under many browsers CSS is poorly supported; for example, the **input:focus** pseudoelement shown in Figure 11-11 only works in Netscape 6, at present. Until these issues are cleared up for commonly used browsers, page authors should carefully explore the use of style sheets with form elements before using them.

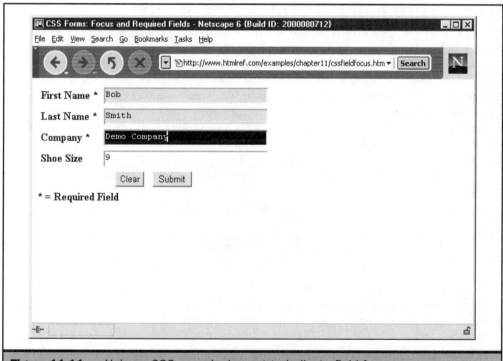

Figure 11-11.   *Using a CSS pseudoelement to indicate field focus*

Special Form Considerations for WebTV

The WebTV browser introduces many attributes to form elements specifically designed to enhance TV-based interaction. This section covers some of these actions. For the latest extensions, visit the WebTV developer's site at http://developer.webtv.net.

While the **<form>** element itself is not modified under WebTV, the **<input>** element has many proprietary extensions. Because it is difficult to fill in forms using the onscreen keyboard, WebTV provides some attributes that can be used to make form input a little easier. Because it might be difficult to see the text onscreen, you can set the background color (**bgcolor**) as well as the cursor color (**cursor**) for individual **<input type="text">** elements. WebTV has introduced many other form extensions. The purpose here is only to illustrate that forms might present issues unique to the viewing environment. This makes extensions worthwhile. However, for the future such presentational controls are better suited to style sheet developments. Perhaps "tv" will become a supported media type for style sheets as defined in CSS2.

Internet Explorer Form Accessibility

The primary proprietary form improvement introduced by Internet Explorer 5 is a feature called AutoComplete. The concept of AutoComplete is to help users to fill out forms by providing a pick list of previously used values for similar form names, or even relating the information in their personal data profile or vCard to form fields. To enable the AutoComplete feature for forms in IE 5, select Internet Options on the Tools menu, select the Content tab, and then click the AutoComplete button. You might also want to fill out your personal information by selecting the My Profile button on the same dialog. Once you have enabled AutoComplete, the browser should provide a pick list for text fields when you either press the down arrow key or the characters you are typing match a previously entered value for a similar field as shown here:

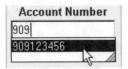

From an HTML perspective, there are a few things that are important to know. First, some people might want to disable AutoComplete. You can set an attribute called **autocomplete** to off in either the **<form>** or the **<input>** tag:

```
<form autocomplete="off"> ... </form>
```

or

```
<input type="password" autocomplete="off" name="secretcodeword">
```

Finally, HTML document authors might want to use the **vcard_name** attribute within the **<input>** tag to suggest to IE 5 to use data from a person's personal profile for basic fields such as name, address, city, state, zip, and so on. For example, to allow someone to automatically fill in form data from their vCard you might have **<input>** tags like this:

```
<input type="text" name="company" vcard_name="vCard.Company">
```

A complete list of vCard values is shown in Table 11-2.

For more information on proprietary features of Internet Explorer such as Autocomplete interested readers should visit http://msdn.microsoft.com.

Forms and Events

As presented here, forms really don't finish the job. It is easy to create a form that asks users for their name and the number of gadgets they want to order. It also is easy to write a CGI program (assuming you're a programmer) that can take submitted form data and do something with it. However, it is not easy to make sure that the submitted data is correct. Why should you let the user enter a quantity of −10 (negative ten) gadgets in the form and submit it when that is obviously wrong? Sure, the CGI could catch this, but it's best to try to catch this at the browser level before submitting the form for processing. This is one of the main reasons for client-side scripting. Of course you'll probably end up having to do both client- as well as server-side validation just to be on the safe side.

vCard.Cellular	vCard.Company	vCard.Department
vCard.DisplayName	vCard.Email	vCard.FirstName
vCard.Gender	vCard.Home.City	vCard.Home.Country
vCard.Home.Fax	vCard.Home.Phone	vCard.Home.State
vCard.Home.StreetAddress	vCard.Home.Zipcode	vCard.Homepage
vCard.JobTitle	vCard.LastName	vCard.MiddleName
vCard.Notes	vCard.Office	vCard.Pager
vCard.Business.City	vCard.Business.Country	vCard.Business.Fax
vCard.Business.Phone	vCard.Business.State	vCard.Business.StreetAddress
vCard.Business.URL	vCard.Business.Zipcode	

Table 11-2.   *vCard attribute values*

Starting with Netscape 2.0 and continuing until today, it has been possible to use a scripting language such as JavaScript to associate scripts with user-generated events in a browser. The way to handle events for a form control is by setting an event handler using an attribute that corresponds to the name of the event. If you want to trigger a script when a button is pressed, you could insert some script code associated with the event attribute, as shown in the following dummy form:

```
<form>
   <input type="button" value="Don't Press Me!"
    onclick="alert('Danger! Danger!');">
</form>
```

Events are added to form controls using attribute declarations such as **onclick**, **onsubmit**, **onreset**, and so on. The number of events has grown significantly and now applies to elements outside forms. In fact, under the concept of "Dynamic HTML" the trend is for every displayed HTML element to have events associated with it. Let's look at a short example of how forms might be validated using a small amount of scripting code and follow with an overview of the form-related events supported in current HTML dialects. Chapter 13 provides more detail on scripting in general.

Already you have learned that one possible use of form events is to validate form data before it is sent. In the following example, a form collects a customer name, a customer identification value, and the quantity of gadgets requested. In this example, all values should be entered and a positive number of gadgets ordered. To perform this check, create a simple validation script that looks at the fields and prompts the user to fix any errors. The validation is triggered by the click of the submit button. If an error is encountered a message is printed and a false value is returned, killing the submission of the form. If all the fields check out, a true value is submitted and the form is sent.

```
<!DOCTYPE HTML PUBLIC "-//W3C//DTD HTML 4.01 Transitional//EN">
<html>
<head>
<title>Basic Form Validation</title>
<script>
<!--
function validate ()
{
    if (document.forms.order.CustomerName.value == "") {
        alert("Please enter your name.")
        return false;
}

    if (document.forms.order.CustomerID.value == "") {
        alert("Please enter your Customer ID.")
        return false;
```

```
        }

        if (document.forms.order.Qty.value <= 0) {
            alert("Please enter a positive number of gadgets.")
            return false;
        }

        return true;
    }
    // -->
    </script>
    </head>
    <body>
    <h1 align="center">Gadget Order Form</h1>
    <hr>
    <form name="order" method="POST"
          action="http://www.democompany.com/cgi-bin/gadgetorder.pl"
          onsubmit="return validate()">
    <b>Customer Name: </b>
    <input type="text" name="CustomerName" id="CustomerName"
           size="25" maxlength="35">
    <br><br>
    <b>Customer ID:</b>
    <input type="password" name="CustomerID"
           id="CustomerID" size="8" maxlength="8">
    <br><br>
    <b>Quantity of Gadgets:</b>
    <input type="text" name="Qty" id="Qty" size="2"
           maxlength="2">

    <input type="submit" value="Order">
    <input type="reset" value="Reset">
    </form>
    </body>
    </html>
```

There are a few things to point out in this example. First, the form has been assigned a name. Giving the form a name allows it to be referred to by name in the validation script. Another thing to notice is the use of the **onsubmit**. The value for this attribute is the name of the JavaScript function, defined elsewhere, that validates the form. The validation function is declared in the document head inside the **<script>**

element. Don't worry if the scripting issues, particularly the events, don't make complete sense. They are covered in great detail in Chapter 13.

Summary

HTML forms provide a basic interface for adding interactivity to a Web site. HTML supports traditional graphical user interface controls such as check boxes, radio buttons, pull-down menus, scrolled lists, multi- and single-line text areas, and buttons. These fields can be used to build a form that can be submitted to a server-side program for processing. While making a rudimentary form isn't terribly difficult, laying out the form often is overlooked. Using tables and improved grouping elements such as **<label>**, **<fieldset>**, and **<legend>** can improve a form dramatically. Other features new to HTML 4.0, such as accelerator keys and tabbing order specification, also can improve how a form might be used. Next generation forms also are in the works under the name Xforms (http://www.w3.org/MarkUp/Forms/), but for now designers should be content with the standard form features offered in HTML. Yet regardless of the markup implementation, even if a nice form can be developed, it is missing the spark that makes it go. The logic of the form needs to be added either by a server-side program, or through a client-side technology such as JavaScript. Until then, forms provide only a simple way to collect information.

The Complete Reference

Chapter 12

Introduction to Server-Side Programming

The last chapter hinted at the move from static Web pages to a more dynamic paradigm. The Web is undergoing a shift from a page-oriented view of the world to a more program-oriented view. Although there is increased focus on the programmed elements of a Web page, this doesn't mean that HTML is going away anytime soon. Knowing how to author well-formed HTML documents could become more important than ever, because XHTML requires it, and technologies such as CSS and JavaScript need a solid, well-formed markup foundation to operate properly. Yet even before the rise of more advanced client-side technologies, HTML has intersected with programming through CGI (Common Gateway Interface) programs. Server-side programs eventually have to produce results in HTML, so server-side computing on the Web often has had an HTML flavor to it—particularly when parsed HTML solutions such as Microsoft's Active Server Pages (ASP) or Allaire's ColdFusion are involved. These technologies blur the lines between HTML and programming, because they appear in the form of special markup tags that include information or perform programming tasks. These topics might not seem to be part of HTML, and are not official in the standards sense, but they do illustrate how programming and HTML interact.

This chapter examines the general concept of the programmed Web site and some of the technologies that can be used on the server side to add interactivity to Web pages. The following chapters will continue the discussion, but with a focus on client-side scripting and programming technologies.

Overview of Client/Server Programming on the Web

When it comes right down to it, the Web is just a form of client/server interaction. Web browsers make requests of Web servers to do some processing, or to return a file that is sent back and displayed in the browser. In this basic printed-page idea of the Web, a Web server acts as a file server that delivers HTML files to a Web browser, as shown in Figure 12-1.

As introduced in the last chapter, thinking about the Web as a static medium is somewhat limiting, and does not take advantage of the potential for interactivity. The most basic form of interactivity on the Web, beyond link selection, is using fill-out forms that are handled by programs, typically CGI applications, running on a Web server. The way a user interacts with a CGI-based Web site is easy to describe. First, the user requests a dynamic page or fills out a form to perform a task, such as ordering a product. The request is sent to the Web server, which runs the CGI program, which then outputs information (generally in HTML) to return to the Web browser. This is shown in Figure 12-2. In this sense, the Web can be used to run programs on a remote server, which then returns a result. When described this way, the Web begins to look more and more like a client/server application environment.

The diagram in Figure 12-2 suggests two questions. First, where should the computing happen? And second, what technology should it use? On the early Web, the browser tended to do very little computing. It was responsible only for rendering pages

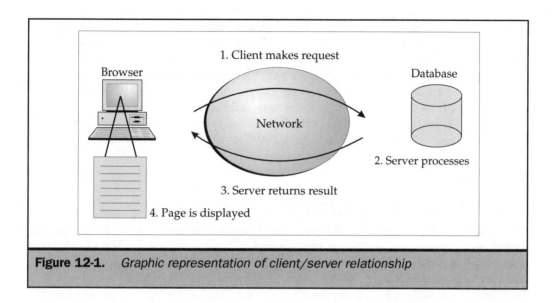

Figure 12-1. *Graphic representation of client/server relationship*

on the screen. Now, with the rise of client-side technologies such as Java, ActiveX, and JavaScript, it is possible to perform a great deal of computation from within the browser. Put all the pressure on the server, and it might bog down, or the user might get frustrated with poor responsiveness. Doing most of the computing on the client side might cause problems with compatibility because it's difficult to know what kinds of clients are out there. Security also could be a problem. The best solution is a mixture: Some things are better suited for the client; some are better suited for the server.

As discussed in Chapter 11, it makes sense to use JavaScript to check the contents of a form before it is submitted to a CGI program, rather than have the CGI program check the data. However, you still would want to check the data at the server side for users who are running older clients or who have turned off client-side scripting. Remember, on the Internet things can go wrong, and users don't always have the best browser with all the right settings. And, of course, you still would want to check whether a malicious user has deliberately sent the CGI bad data. A developer who

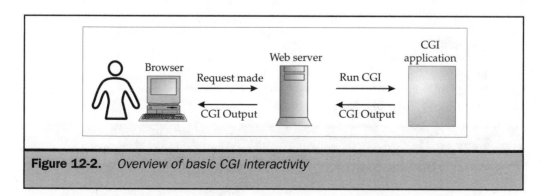

Figure 12-2. *Overview of basic CGI interactivity*

wants to build a Web-based application must choose where to host the logic of the program (client side or server side) and which technology should be used to do it. The decision isn't easy; there are many choices, as listed in Table 12-1.

What's interesting about the numerous technologies available for Web programming is that developers often focus solely on one tool or one side of the equation (client or server) rather than thinking about how the applications they are trying to build will work. This should be avoided at all costs, if possible, to ensure that the correct mix of technologies is used. This chapter will look at the server side of the equation; subsequent chapters will focus on the client side.

Server-Side Programming

When adding interactivity to a Web page, it often makes sense to add all functionality on the server side. There are two basic reasons for doing this. First, the server side is the only part of the equation that can be completely controlled. If we only rely on the browser to render HTML pages, life is simple. If we assume that users have JavaScript, Java, or a particular plug-in, things become less predictable. Given that most modern browsers come with many of these technologies, this might seem unlikely. However,

Client-Side	Server-Side
Helper Programs	CGI programs
Netscape plug-ins	Web Server API programs
	NSAPI programs
	ISAPI programs
	Apache Modules
	Java Servlets
ActiveX Controls	Server-side Scripting
	Server-side Includes (SSI)
	Active Server Pages (ASP)
	ColdFusion (CFM)
	PHP
	Java Server Pages (JSP)
Java Applets	
Client-Side Scritping	
JavaScript	
VBScript	
Dynamic HTML (DHTML)	

Table 12-1. *Web Programming Technology Choices*

the reality is that there are just too many variables and too many bugs. Users often turn off support for Java, JavaScript, or ActiveX due to fear of security breaches. Even when turned on, these technologies often are far from robust. For example, JavaScript comes in numerous flavors, all with their own subtle and not-so-subtle differences, including feature disparity and bugs. It is no wonder we would want to move computation to the server, where these issues are more controllable.

While server-side computing provides safety and control, it relies greatly on server resources. In many Web sites, the server is required to do all the computation, from database access to building dynamic pages. In such a scenario the browser is responsible for only basic page rendering, and simple data collection tasks such as form entry. The downside to such heavy reliance on the server is that it is the critical part of the interactivity. If the server becomes overloaded or the network connection to the server is clogged, the result might be an unresponsive site and a disappointed user. Although control is gained with server-side programming, it is exchanged for speed and scalability.

For now we'll put the theory aside and turn our discussion the various approaches to server-based interactivity and how it intersects with HTML.

Common Gateway Interface (CGI)

Probably the most common way to add interactivity to a Web page is through a CGI program. CGI is a protocol standard that specifies how information can be passed from a Web page through a Web server, to a program, and back from the program to a browser in the proper format. Unfortunately many people confuse the actual program that does a particular task with the CGI protocol. In reality, the program is just a program. It just happens to be a CGI program because it was written to pass information back and forth using the CGI specification. Furthermore, CGI programs can be written in any language the server can execute; whereas Perl most commonly is associated with CGI, there is no reason that C, C++, Pascal, Visual Basic, or even FORTRAN couldn't be used to create a CGI program.

It is possible to create anything, including games, with CGI. Some common CGI applications include

- Form processing
- Database access
- Page Counters
- Custom document generation
- Browser-specific page delivery
- Banner ad serving
- Guest book and authentication
- Threaded discussion
- Games

Later in this section we'll take a look at how such programs can be built from scratch, or even downloaded from various Web sites for little or no cost. For now, treat the inner workings of a CGI program as a black box, and consider in general the various steps that a typical CGI-based program would perform when interacting with a user providing data through a form fill-out.

1. The user submits a form.

2. The form is sent to the server and eventually to the CGI program using the following steps:

   a. The server determines whether the request is a document or program request by examining execution settings and path.

   b. The server locates the program (often in the cgi-bin directory on the server) and determines if the program can be executed.

   c. The server starts the program and prepares the data, and any extra information from the environment, to be sent to the program from the form fields.

   d. The program runs.

   e. The server waits for the program to exit and potentially produce any output (optional), and then passes back any result or error message to the client.

3. The CGI program processes the data and responds to the server.

4. The Web server passes the CGI response back to the client.

> **Note** *Server launching of the program (step 2c) is operating system–dependent and might require starting a new process, which could be slow, thus contributing to CGI's reputation for being slow.*

Understanding how CGI works requires an understanding of how the HTTP protocol works. The only magic behind CGI is knowing how to read data in and write data out to talk to a Web browser. Writing data out is the easiest part. The key to writing data out for Web browsers is understanding the headers so the browser knows what it is getting; namely, MIME types. MIME stands for *Multipurpose Internet Mail Extension*. The MIME content type of a file tells a browser how to process it.

The following example, which shows how a Web browser and a Web server communicate, should help us to better understand exactly what CGI programs do.

You can access a Web server directly by using a telnet program literally to log in to the TCP service port for HTTP. To do this, use a telnet program to access a Web server and set the port number to 80. In UNIX, you might type

```
telnet www.democompany.com 80
```

This also could be performed using Windows 98/NT, which has telnet built into it. Just make sure to set the port value to 80 as shown here.

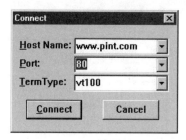

Once connected to the Web server, type in the proper HTTP request. A simple request would be

```
GET / HTTP/1.0
```

Then press ENTER twice to send a blank line, without which the operation won't work.

Once the server processes the request, the result should look something like the listing shown here:

```
HTTP/1.0 200 OK
Date: Monday, 01-January-99 09:00:00 GMT
Server:   NCSA/1.3.1
MIME-version: 1.0
Content-type: text/html
Content-length: 1200

<html>
<head>
<title>Sample HTML Document</title>
</head>

<body>
...content...
</body>
```

If a Web browser were reading this data stream, it would read the **Content-type** line, and then determine what to do with the data. Browsers have a mapping that takes a MIME type and then determines what to do with it. Figure 12-3 shows the mapping file from Netscape Navigator 4.7.

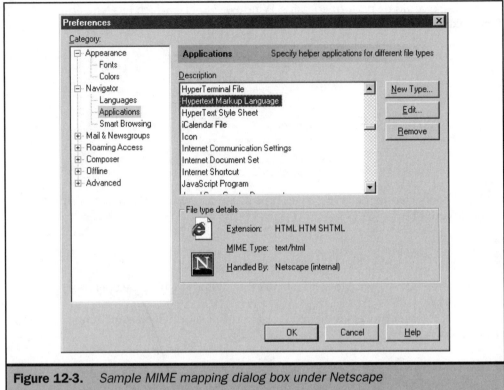

Figure 12-3. *Sample MIME mapping dialog box under Netscape*

Notice in the preceding code that the content type is **text/html**. This has the action of a browser, which would render the HTML within the browser window. Remember that Web servers can serve just about any type of data and pass that data to a plug-in or helper, or query the user to save the file.

CGI Output

Given that you now have seen the manual execution of an HTTP request, what is important to the Web browser? The simple answer is the MIME type and its associated data. In most cases, the pages being delivered are HTML based, so the MIME type should be **text/html** and any HTML you want on your screen. With this idea in mind, it should be easy to write a CGI program that fakes an HTML page. To do this, you need to print out the MIME type indication **Content-type: text/html**, followed by a series of HTML codes. The following small Perl program shows how this might be done; any language, including C, Pascal, or BASIC, could also be used to make such an example:

```
#!/usr/bin/perl
# Note the path to Perl may vary.
#
print "Content-type: text/html\n\n";

print "<html>\n<head><title>First CGI</title></head>\n";

print "<body><h1>\n";
print "Wow! I was created by a CGI program!!";
print "</h1>\n </body>\n</html>";
```

Note   *In the preceding example it is very important to note the two line feeds in the first print statement. The blank line after the content-type line indicates the server is done sending headers. Without the two returns the example will not work.*

If this example were typed and set to run on a Perl-capable Web server, it could be accessed directly by a user to print out the simple page shown in Figure 12-4. To see the program in action, try the URL http://www.htmlref.com/examples/chapter12/firstcgi.pl.

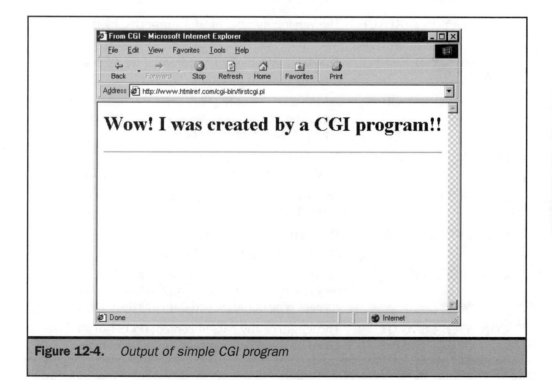

Figure 12-4. *Output of simple CGI program*

In summary: To create a document on the fly, you have to print a group of headers and then print out the appropriate HTML tags that compose the page. How you determine the contents of the page is up to you. the only real magic that makes it CGI is the inclusion of the appropriate MIME type header. This section covers only getting information back from the server, which is just half of the CGI equation. The following section discusses getting information to your program.

Passing Information to a CGI Program: Environment Variables

In order to get information into a CGI program, you generally need to use a form. The CGI program itself actually can read some information from the HTTP request and the local environment. This information can be used in conjunction with form data to understand the environment the program is running. Environment variables actually are very valuable; they can be used to help the CGI program decide what kind of pages to prepare. A list of the most common CGI environment variables is provided in Table 12-2.

Variable Name	Description
GATEWAY_INTERFACE	The version number of CGI supported by the server; for example, CGI/1.1.
SERVER_NAME	The domain name or IP address of the Web server running the CGI program.
SERVER_SOFTWARE	Information about the Web server, typically the name and version number of the software; for example, Netscape-Commerce/1.12.
SERVER_PROTOCOL	The version number of the HTTP protocol being used in the request; for example, HTTP/1.1.
SERVER_PORT	The port on which the Web server is running, typically 80.
REQUEST_METHOD	The method by which the information is being passed, either in **GET** or **POST**.
CONTENT_TYPE	For queries that have attached information, because they use the **POST** or **PUT** method; contains the content type of the passed data in MIME format.
CONTENT_LENGTH	The length of any passed content (**POST** or **PUT**) as given by the client, typically as length in bytes.

Table 12-2. *Common CGI Variables*

Variable Name	Description
PATH_INFO	Any extra path information passed in with the file request. This usually would be associated with the **GET** request.
SCRIPT_NAME	The relative path to the script that is running.
QUERY_STRING	Query information passed to the program.
DOCUMENT_ROOT	The document root of the Web server.
REMOTE_USER	If the server supports user authentication and the script is protected, this variable holds the user name that the user has authenticated.
AUTH_TYPE	This variable is set to the authentication method used to validate the user if the script being run is protected.
REMOTE_IDENT	If the Web server supports RFC 931–based identification, this variable will be set to the remote user name retrieved from the server. This is rarely used.
REMOTE_HOST	The remote host name of the browser passing information to the server; for example, sun1.bigcompany.com.
REMOTE_ADDR	The IP address of the browser making the request.
HTTP_ACCEPT	A list of MIME types the browser can accept.
HTTP_USER_AGENT	A code indicating the type of browser making the request.
HTTP_REFERER	The URL of the linking document (the document that is linked to the CGI being run). If the user typed in the address of the program directly, the **HTTP_REFERER** value will be unset.

Table 12-2.   *Common CGI Variables* (continued)

Figure 12-5 shows the results of a CGI program that prints out the environment information. Try to execute the program at http://www.htmlref.com/examples/chapter12/printenv.cgi to see if the results are different.

Depending on the Web server and browser, there might be other useful environment variables. These include **HTTPS**, which is used to indicate whether Secure Sockets Layer (SSL) security is on; **HTTP_CONNECTION**, which is used to

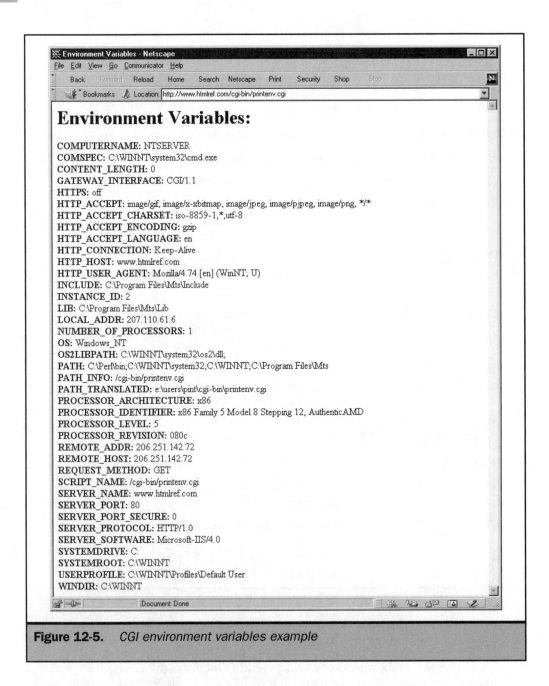

Figure 12-5. CGI environment variables example

indicate to the server to keep a connection open for improved performance; and
HTTP_ACCEPT_LANGUAGE, which is used to indicate what language the server
accepts data in. There are other potential values available, so be certain to check the
Web server programming documentation.

The Perl code for the result in Figure 12-5 is shown here:

```perl
#!/usr/bin/perl

&print_HTTP_header;
&print_head;
&print_body;
&print_tail;

# print the HTTP Content-type header

sub print_HTTP_header {
    print "Content-type: text/html\n\n";
}

#Print the start of the HTML file

sub print_head {
    print <<END;

<html>
<head>
<title>CGI Environment Variables</title>
</head>

<body>
<h1 align="center">Environment Variables</h1>
<hr>
END
}

#Loop through the environment variable

#associative array and print out its values.

sub print_body {
    foreach $variable (sort keys %ENV) {
        print "<b>$variable:</b> $ENV{$variable}<br>\n";
    }

}

#Print the close of the HTML file
```

```
sub print_tail {
        print <<END;
</body>
</html>
END
}
```

Notice that the code is written to make the printing of the appropriate headers, the start of the HTML file, the results, and the close of the file more straightforward. Code libraries, which do much of the work of CGI, are commonly available.

Browser Sensing with CGI

At first glance, the environment variables might not seem very useful. When used properly, however, they are indispensable. One of the most important uses of CGI is to sense the browser being used so that customized pages can be delivered for different browser types. This is often called browser sniffing. Using a sniffing program, it is possible to sense a user's browser type and redirect him or her automatically to another page. This can be done using either a client-side program or a server-side program, although it is recommended to do basic sniffing on the server side first, just in case a user's browser doesn't support client-side programming features such as JavaScript.

Note *To make browser sensing work, the server might have to be configured to run the CGI program automatically. This might require simply putting a file called index.cgi in the root directory or performing some similar renaming. A server configuration also can be modified to first deliver whatever file you like, whether it is being named index or not, and to just give out the file sniffer.htm when the directory is accessed.*

Here is how browser sensing works: The CGI environment variable called **HTTP_USER_AGENT** is read in by the CGI program using a simple call available from a Perl CGI library. Once the value is set, a set of conditions determines which page to send, depending on the browser accessing the page. In the following example (available online at http://www.htmlref.com/examples/chapter12/browsersensing.pl), the file netscapepage.htm is sent if the browser is Netscape. If the browser is Microsoft Internet Explorer, the file mspage.htm is sent. Otherwise, the file page.htm is sent. The is just a basic illustration of how this could be done; this code easily could be modified for any particular version of Netscape or Microsoft, and could be made quite sophisticated.

```
#!/usr/local/bin/perl

#print "Content-type: text/html\n\n";
$agent = $ENV{'HTTP_USER_AGENT'};
```

```
if($agent =~ m/MSIE/i) {
        $file = "mspage.htm";
}
elsif ($agent =~ m/Opera/i || $agent =~ m/WebTV/i ||
$agent =~ m/Tango/i || $agent =~ m/Sextant/i ||
$agent =~ m/Oracle/i || $agent =~ m/OmniWeb/i ||
$agent =~ m/Lynx/i || $agent =~ m/Konqueror/i ||
$agent =~ m/iCab/i || $agent =~ m/FrontPage/i ||
$agent =~ m/Dreamcast/i || $agent =~ m/AOL/i ||
!($agent =~ m/Mozilla/i))
{
        $file = "page.htm";
}
else {
        $file = "netscapepage.htm";
}


print "Location:
http://www.htmlref.com/examples/chapter12/$file\n\n";
```

Using browser sensing, it is possible to avoid having a site entrance page that declares things like "Click here for Netscape" and "Click here for other browsers." Things just work, because the site has browser-aware pages. Of course, one huge problem with this idea is building different browser versions for the same page, and keeping up with all the different types of browsers out there. Products such as BrowserHawk (www.browserhawk.com), used in conjunction with parsed HTML technologies such as ColdFusion or Active Server Pages (discussed later in the chapter), might offer a better solution to rolling your own browser sensing programs.

Passing Information to a CGI Program: Form Data

Forms are a good way to collect user input such as survey results or comments. They also can start database queries or launch programs. Creating HTML forms was discussed in Chapter 11. For a quick refresher on how HTML forms are used, take a look at the following example:

```
<!DOCTYPE HTML PUBLIC "-//W3C//DTD HTML 4.01 Transitional//EN">
<html>
<head>
```

PROGRAMMING AND HTML

```
<title>Meet and Greet</title>
</head>

<body>
<h1 align="center">Welcome to CGI!</h1>
<hr>

<form method="POST"
      action="http://www.htmlref.com/cgi-bin/hello.pl">
<b>What's your name?</b>
<input type="text" name="username" size="25">
<br><br>
<input type="submit" value="Hi I am...">
<input type="reset" value="Reset">
</form>

</body>
</html>
```

If this example is typed and run, or viewed at http://www.htmlref.com/
examples/chapter12/postwelcome.htm, it will greet the user by whatever name he or
she types in. The **<form>** element is the key to this example, because it has an action to
perform (as indicated by the **action** attribute when the form is submitted). The action is
to launch a CGI program indicated by the URL value of the **action** attribute. The
<form> element has another attribute, **method**, which indicates how information will
be passed to the receiving CGI program. There are two basic methods to pass data in
through a form: **GET** and **POST**. To see the preceding example in action using **GET**
instead of **POST**, view http://www.htmlref.com/examples/chapter12/
getwelcome.htm. The **GET** method appends information on the end of the submitting
URL, so the URL accessed through getwelcome.htm might be something like

```
http://www.htmlref.com/cgi-bin/gethello.pl?username=Joe+Smith
```

The data sent will be encoded; the string might have all spaces turned into **+** signs,
and special characters might be encoded as *%nn* hex character values. The various
form element names will be sent to the CGI program as name/value pairs such as
username=Joe separated by ampersands. For example, if the previous example had
other fields in the form named age and sex, you might see a **get** query string like

```
http://www.htmlref.com/cgi-bin/hello.pl?username=Joe+Smith&
age=32&sex=male
```

(The format of URL-encoded data is discussed in Chapter 11.) The problem with the **GET** method is that, besides being ugly, it is limited to the amount of data that can easily be sent in. However, the **GET** method does have two advantages: It is easy to understand and provides the possibility for canned queries that also can be bookmarked, unlike posted data. The more common approach for larger forms is to use the **POST** method, which sends the form data as a separate data stream—in other words, a file—to the server. This data stream consists of many lines, such as **username=Joe%20Smith**, that are the various name value pairs created by the form entry made by the user. Once received by the server-side program, these lines can be parsed for later processing. Given how data is encoded, a skilled programmer easily could determine how to parse data and access the values. The following simple helloworld.pl example (see it in action online by viewing http://www.htmlref.com/examples/chapter12/helloworld.htm) shows how this might be done in a brute force manner that does no error checking, using the same basic HTML as the preceding examples.

```perl
#! /usr/bin/perl

# Print the HTTP headers

print "Content-type: text/html\n";
print "\n";

read (STDIN, $GN_QUERY, $ENV{CONTENT_LENGTH});

# This statement will split data into different fields

@QUERY_LIST = split( /&/, $GN_QUERY);

foreach $item (@QUERY_LIST) {

    # First convert plus signs into spaces

    $item =~ s/\+/ /g;

    # Now convert $nn encoded data to characters

    $item =~ s/%(..)/pack("c",hex($1))/ge;

    # Now put the result into the QueryArray

    $loc=index($item,"=");
```

```
        $param=substr($item, 0, $loc);
        $value=substr($item, $loc+1);
        $QUERY_ARRAY{$param} .= $value;
}

# Now get the users name

$name = "$QUERY_ARRAY{username}";

# Print Return HTML
print "<html><head><title>Hello</title></head>\n<body>\n";
print "<h1>Hello $name. Welcome to CGI!</h1>\n";
print "</body></html>";
```

Note   *The preceding example works only with data passed in when the **POST** method is used. It does not work when the method attribute is set to get.*

Writing CGI Programs

The preceding examples might seem to suggest that writing CGI programs is trivial. This is true if data is only to be read in and written out. In fact, this part of CGI is so mechanical that page designers are discouraged from attempting to parse the data themselves. There are many scripting libraries available for Perl. These include cgic (http://www.boutell.com/cgic/) for ANSI C programs, cgi++ (http://www.webthing.com/ cgiplusplus/) for C++, and CGI.pm (http://stein.cshl.org/WWW/software/CGI/cgi_docs.html) for Perl 5. These libraries, and others available on the Internet, make the reading of environment variables and parsing of encoded form data a simple process.

The difficult part of CGI isn't the input and output of data; it's the logic of the code itself. Given that the CGI program can be written in nearly any language, Web programmers might wonder what language to use. Performance, Web suitability, and string handling are important criteria for selecting a language for CGI authoring. Performance-wise, compiled CGI programs typically will have better performance than interpreted programs written in a scripting language such as Perl. However, it probably is easier to write a simple CGI in a scripting language such as Perl and then use a form of compiled Perl or the mod_perl module to get most of the performance gains of compilation with the ease of a scripting language.

Some programming languages might have better interfaces to Web servers and HTTP than others. For example, Perl has a great number of CGI libraries and operating system facilities readily available. Because much of CGI is about reading and writing text data, ease of string handling also might be a big consideration in selecting the language. The bottom line is that the choice of scripting language mainly depends on the server the script must run on and the programmer's preference. It is even possible to use an old version of FORTRAN or some obscure language to write a CGI program, although it would be easier to pick a language that works well with the Web server and use it to access some other program. CGI lives up to its name as a gateway.

Table 12-3 lists the common languages for CGI coding based on the Web server's operating system. Notice that Perl is common to most of the platforms, due to its ease of use and long-standing use on the Web.

 Note   *Writing CGI programs in a UNIX shell scripting language such as csh, ksh or sh can pose serious security risks and should be avoided if possible.*

Don't rush around getting ready to code your own form handlers. Consider how many other people in the world need to access a database or e-mail a form. Given these common needs, it might be better to borrow or buy a canned CGI solution than to build a new one.

Buying or Borrowing CGI Programs

Most CGI programs are similar to one another. There are many shareware, freeware, and commercial packages available to do most of the common Web tasks. Matt's Script Archive (www.worldwidemart.com/scripts) and the CGI Resource Index (www.cgi-resources.com) are good places to start looking for these. There are many scripts for form parsing, bulletin boards, counters, and countless other things available free of charge on the Internet. There also are compiled commercial CGI programs made to perform a particular task. Site developers are urged to consider the cost of developing custom solutions versus buying canned solutions, particularly when time is an important consideration in building the site.

Server Modules: NSAPI, ISAPI, and Others

One serious problem with CGI programs is their slowness. There are two reasons that CGI programs can be slow. First of all, the launch of the CGI program by the Web

Web Server Operating System	Common CGI Languages
Unix	Perl, C, C++, Java, Shell script languages (csh, ksh, sh), Python
Windows	Visual Basic, C, C++, Perl
Macintosh	AppleScript, Perl, C, C++

Table 12-3.   *Common CGI Language Choices*

server can itself be slow. Then, once launched, the program might run relatively slowly because it is written in an interpreted language such as Perl. Solving the second problem is easy: Simply rewrite the program in a compiled language such as C. Performance should quickly improve. What about the launch problem? One approach would be to pre-launch the main CGI program so that it is running all the time, and have smaller CGI programs launch when needed. Although this would help, the server still would have to communicate with an external program, which might be time consuming. If speed is of the essence, migrating the functionality of the CGI program into the server is required. This would avoid task switching between the Web server and the external CGI program. This is the idea behind a server module, which basically is a program that is written to be a component of a Web server. There are many types of server modules that tend to be associated with a particular server. For example, the Netscape Server Application Programming Interface (NSAPI) and the Internet Server Application Programming Interface (ISAPI) are for Netscape- (now Iplanet) and Microsoft-based Web servers, respectively. Other types of server modules include Apache modules, Java servlets, and various others. Collectively we will refer to these server programs simply as server modules.

In short, server modules are like plug-ins for a server. A program, typically written in C or C++, that conforms to a particular server-module specification, can be plugged into the server to add functionality to the system. Obviously, writing such a solution is much more difficult than writing a simple CGI program. There are other drawbacks as well. For example, a misbehaving server module can bring a whole server down. Developers who write a server module–based solution also might be stuck using a particular server platform, whereas CGI programs generally are portable from server to server. Regardless of their drawbacks, server modules have the advantage of speed and the ability to share data across sessions and users very easily. With this power, many third-party developers have created server extensions to allow fast and easy database access, threaded discussion capability, and many other features. Although most developers are about as likely to write custom server modules as they are to write browser plug-ins, the technology has enabled the creation of server-side parsing technology, which is useful to almost every Web page developer.

Server-Side Scripting

CGI and server modules often are beyond the technical understanding of some Web developers. However, adding interactivity to a site does not always have to be difficult. Another form of server-based programming, generically termed *server-side scripting* or sometimes *parsed HTML*, provides much of the sophistication of general CGI with the ease of HTML. The idea of parsed HTML is simple. First, code a page using standard HTML. Then add special new elements or directives to indicate what to do in particular cases. Imagine if you wanted to print out different HTML headings for

Netscape users, Microsoft Internet Explorer, and other browser users. Using parsed HTML, you might put statements in a parsed HTML language in your file like this:

```
$if browser = Netscape
      <blink>Hey Netscape User!</blink>
$else if browser = IE
      <marquee>Hello Microsoft User!</marquee>
$else
      <h1>Hello User!</h1>
$endif
```

To indicate that the file is a special parsed HTML file, end its name with the extension .parsedhtml. Next, configure the server to parse and execute the special statements you have added to the file. In this case, the server then will output only the HTML, depending on the particular browser being used. This of course is a completely fictitious server-side scripting language but it serves to illustrate how all of them fundamentally work. An overview of server-parsed script solutions is shown in Figure 12-6.

Although server-side scripts are very easy for people to deal with, they can put an excessive load on the server and might be unnecessarily parsed over and over again. The next few sections describe three common parsed HTML technologies used on the Web: server-side includes (SSI), ColdFusion, and Active Server Pages (ASP).

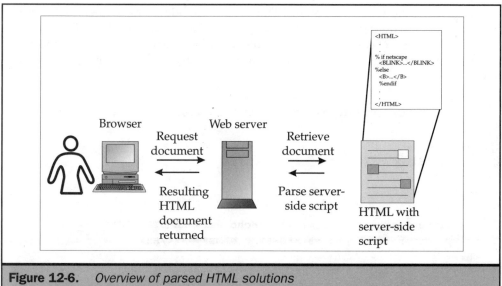

Figure 12-6.   *Overview of parsed HTML solutions*

Server-Side Includes (SSI)

SSIs are the simplest form of parsed HTML. SSIs are short directives you can embed in an HTML document to indicate files to be read and included in the final output. This might be useful if the designer wants to make one file with footer information, such as an address and copyright, and then append it to all pages dynamically. To do this, create a file called footer.htm and then include it dynamically using SSI. The contents of footer.htm might look something like this:

```
<hr noshade>
<center>
<font size="-1">
Copyright 2000, Demo Company<br>
</font></center>
```

To include this file in another file, you would need an SSI directive like this:

```
<!--#include file="footer.htm" -->
```

Notice that this is just a special form of an HTML comment with a command **#include** and a parameter file, which is set to the file you want to include. To indicate to the server that the page contains SSI commands, use the .shtml extension. If the server is properly configured, it should pick up the file and execute it before sending the result. Aside from including external files, SSI also can be used to show the results of programs, including CGI programs. Thus, it can provide a way to query databases and make a page counter, among other things. The simple example that follows (http://www.htmlref.com/examples/chapter12/ssidemo.shtml) shows how the echo SSI command can be used to access the environment variables to which CGI programs have access.

```
<!DOCTYPE HTML PUBLIC "-//W3C//DTD HTML 4.01 Transitional//EN">
<html>
<head>
<title>SSI Demo</title>
</head>
<body>

<h2 align="center">Welcome <!--#echo var="REMOTE_HOST" -->
to my server <!--#echo var="SERVER_NAME" --></H2>
<hr>
```

```
You are using <!--#echo var="HTTP_USER_AGENT" -->.
</body>
</html>
```

One possible result of this example is shown in Figure 12-7. Remember that your result will be different because the page is dynamically generated and must be run from a server with SSI turned on.

The environment variables that are accessible from SSI are similar to those that can be accessed by any CGI program. They also include the variables listed in Table 12-4.

Aside from inserting CGI environment variable values, it also is possible to use SSI to embed the results of a CGI program into an HTML document by using the EXEC CGI command. For example, it would be possible to add a simple page counter to an HTML document by using an SSI command to execute the counter program and display its results in the page. Assuming there is a program called counter.cgi in the

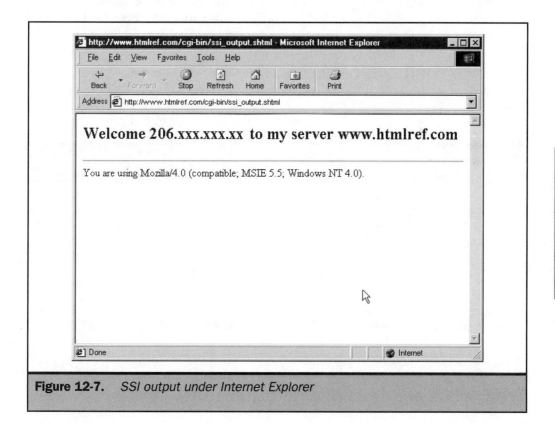

Figure 12-7. *SSI output under Internet Explorer*

Variable Name	Description
DATE_GMT	This value references the current server local date, same as **DATE_LOCAL**, but in Greenwich mean time. This variable is subject to formatting from the CONFIG SSI command.
DATE_LOCAL	The current date, local time zone. Subject to formatting from the CONFIG SSI command.
DOCUMENT_NAME	The variable holds the current filename.
DOCUMENT_URI	The variable contains the virtual path to the current document; for example, /about/democompany/contact.shtml.
LAST_MODIFIED	The last modification date of the current document. This variable is subject to the date formatting set by the CONFIG SSI command.
QUERY_STRING_UNESCAPED	This variable contains the "unescaped" version of any search query (**GET**) sent by the browser. Any special characters are escaped using the \ character.

Table 12-4. *SSI-Available Variables Potentially Outside the CGI Set*

cgi-bin directory on the server, you could use a simple SSI statement like the following to add the page count:

```
<!--#exec cgi="cgi-bin/counter.cgi"-->
```

In general, SSI consists of a special comment form that indicates the SSI command, as well as any parameters to modify the command in the general format, as follows:

```
<!--#command parameter=value-->
```

Following are some of the common SSI commands and their associated parameters.

ECHO

Parameters   VAR

Description   Used to insert the values of special SSI variables and environment variables into the page.

```
<!--#ECHO VAR="REMOTE_HOST"-->
```

INCLUDE

Parameters   FILE, VIRTUAL

Description   Used to insert the contents of a document into the current file. This pathname of the file can be either relative or virtual. Relative files paths are relative to the current directory, whereas virtual file names may access other directories using the ../ directory style or an absolute path.

```
<!--#INCLUDE FILE="footer.htm"-->
<!--#INCLUDE VIRTUAL="../templates/footer.htm"-->
```

FSIZE

Parameters   FILE

Description   Inserts the size of a given file.

```
<!--#FSIZE FILE="index.htm"-->
```

FLASTMOD

Parameters   FILE

Description   Inserts the last modification date of a given file.

```
<!--#FLASTMOD FILE="index.htm"-->
```

EXEC

Parameters   CMD, CGI

PROGRAMMING
AND HTML

Description   Allows you to execute external programs, either an application on the host or a CGI program.

```
<!--#EXEC CMD="/usr/bin/ls"-->
<!--#EXEC CGI="cgi-bin/counter.cgi"-->
```

CONFIG

Parameters

```
ERRMSG= string, SIZEFMT= bytes | abbrev, TIMEFMT= format string
```

Description   Allows you to configure SSI output options for error output, file size output, and data output. The value for the ERRMSG is simply a string value for the error message. The SIZEFMT may be set to bytes or abbrev, while the TIMEFMT can be set to a Unix date format string in the form compatible with the strftime library.

```
<!--#config errmsg="[SSI Statement Failed!]"-->
<!--#CONFIG SIZEFMT="bytes"-->
<!--#CONFIG TIMEFM="%A %b %d %j"-->
```

Depending on the server, there could be more SSI statements, including **ODBC** and **EMAIL**, which are used to access a database and send e-mail, respectively. These commands are the ones most common across most SSI-capable servers.

While SSI looks appealing, it has two potential problems: security and performance. SSI's security problem is mainly due to the EXEC command, which can be used to execute a program on the server. With this command, security breaches are possible. For example, it might be possible to insert a command to launch a remote session. Even if security isn't a big issue, depending on how SSI and the Web server are configured, the executing command could have a great deal of permissions and be able to remove values. Web administrators are advised to limit use of this SSI command.

The other problem with SSI, performance, is typical of any server-parsed scripting solution. Because all SSI files have to be parsed, they can cause a performance hit. If a site has serious performance requirements, parsed HTML solutions might be inappropriate. Fortunately, it is possible to limit parsed HTML or mix it with standard HTML by having only certain files, for example those ending in .shtml, parsed by the server. When used in a limited fashion, SSI can provide powerful features that are within the technical ability of any HTML writer. However, SSI is limited. Page designers might find other server-side scripting solutions, such as ColdFusion or ASP, more appropriate.

ColdFusion

One of the most popular server-parsed HTML solutions is Allaire's ColdFusion (http://www.allaire.com). ColdFusion is a complete Web application development tool that enables developers to create dynamic, database-driven Web site applications with an easy-to-use, server-side markup language similar to HTML. Getting started with ColdFusion requires learning a few new markup tags that look like HTML but make up what is called ColdFusion Markup Language (CFML). Since one of its primary functions is database access, ColdFusion uses the Open Database Connectivity (ODBC) standard to connect to popular database servers such as Microsoft SQL Server, Access, Sybase, Oracle, and others. ColdFusion is not dependent on a particular database or Web server, and it works well on a variety of Windows NT–based servers as well as Solaris and Linux. While ColdFusion is not a W3C-defined standard, it is widely used. It is presented here to illustrate an example of parsed HTML and to show how HTML might be used to interact with a database.

Web applications built with ColdFusion use dynamic pages composed of a mixture of CFML and HTML markup. When the page is requested, the ColdFusion application running on the server preprocesses the page, interacts with a database or other server-side technologies, and returns a dynamically generated HTML page. It probably is better to refer to ColdFusion-enabled pages as templates as the actual page output varies.

Using CFML

The following discusses how to use CFML to select and output data in a dynamic Web page. This section will show how to use a number of CFML tags to query data from a database, take the results of the query, and populate a Web page.

Database Overview

A *database* is a collection of data that is organized in a regular fashion, typically in the form of a table. Imagine you want to create a Web site to post the various job openings in your company. The first thing you need to do is decide what information is relevant: position number, job title, location, brief job description, hiring manager, and posting date. This information could be organized in the form of a database table, called Positions, as shown in Table 12-5.

The example is populated with some simple data, but how can the data be retrieved to be displayed in a Web page automatically?

Selecting the Data

The first step is to define a database query using *Structured Query Language* (SQL). SQL is the language used to retrieve or modify data from the tables in a database. The

Position-Num	JobTitle	Location	Description	Hiring Manager	PostDate
343	Gadget Sales	Austin	This position requires an aggressive sales person to sell gadgets to guys and gals.	M. Spacely	01/20/00
525	Office Manager	San Jose	Responsible for running the entire office single-handedly.	P. Mohta	01/24/00
2585	President	San Diego	Figurehead position requires daily golf games and nightly poker parties.	T. Powell	01/30/00
3950	Grounds-keeper	San Diego	Must like outdoor work and long hours in the sun with no sunscreen.	J. Tam	01/30/00
1275	HTML Hacker	Seattle	Must be able to recite HTML specifications by heart and code HTML by hand. Long hours, low pay.	D. Whitworth	01/27/00
2015	Game Tester	Los Angeles	Must be able to play games all day long; poor posture and junk food diet essential.	J. Daffyd	01/18/00

Table 12-5. *Simple Database Table Called Positions*

language is relatively simple, at least as far as mastering the basics. If you were interested in making a query to the database table called Positions, you would use a SQL statement like

```
SELECT * FROM Positions
```

This query simply says to select all items indicated by the wildcard (*) in the table called Positions. If you want only to list all the positions in Austin, you could qualify the query by adding a **WHERE** modifier, indicating you only want entries for which the location is Austin.

```
SELECT * FROM Positions WHERE Location="Austin"
```

Using the **WHERE** modifier, it is possible to create complex queries. For example, you could query all jobs in Austin, or in Los Angeles, where the position is Game Tester.

```
SELECT *
      FROM Positions
      WHERE ((Location="Austin" OR
            (Location="Los Angeles") AND
            (Position="Game Tester"))
```

This brief discussion should reveal the flavor of SQL. Although the basic language is simple, queries can be more complicated. A full discussion of SQL is well beyond the scope of this book. For the sake of this discussion, only simple queries are used in the examples.

To pull data out of the database, write a SQL query, and then place it within a **<CFQUERY>** element. The following example illustrates the use of **<CFQUERY>**. A select SQL query called **ListJobs**, as specified by the **NAME** attribute, will query a database and retrieve all the records in the Positions table. The syntax for this example is shown here:

```
<CFQUERY NAME="ListJobs"
        DATASOURCE="CompanyDataBase">
              SELECT * FROM Positions
</CFQUERY>
```

Notice that the **DATASOURCE** attribute is set equal to CompanyDataBase, which is the ODBC data source that contains a database called Company, which contains the Positions table from which data is pulled.

> **Note** *Open Database Connectivity (ODBC) is a standardized way to access data from a variety of different databases. ODBC provides a layer of abstraction that protects the developer from having to learn the particulars of a specific database system. To query the Positions table, your server might connect to a simple Microsoft Access database or a powerful Oracle system. To access a database, a developer needs to set up an ODBC data source. This requires that developer to select an ODBC driver, name the data source, and configure any specific settings for the database. A complete discussion of how to set up ODBC drivers and configure data sources can be found in the documentation for ColdFusion.*

Aside from **NAME** and **DATASOURCE**, the **<CFQUERY>** element has a variety of attributes, as described in Table 12-6.

Attribute	Description
NAME	Required. This attribute is used to assign a name to the SQL query. The name is later used in the template to reference the query results.
DATASOURCE	Required. This attribute is used to specify the name of the ODBC data source that will be used to access the database.
MAXROWS	Optional. This attribute is used to specify the maximum number of rows as a positive integer number that should be returned by the query. More output rows beyond this value will be dropped.
USERNAME	Optional. Because many databases have login features, this attribute is used to set the user name to access the data source. This attribute overrides the default settings in the ColdFusion Administrator.
PASSWORD	Optional. This attribute is used to set the password associated for the user name that will access the database. This value overrides the default settings in the ColdFusion Administrator.
TIMEOUT	Optional. This attribute can be set to a time, in milliseconds, for a query to successfully execute. Queries that take longer than this value will fail.
DEBUG	Optional. When present, this attribute turns on the tracing and debugging features for the file.

Table 12-6. *<CFQUERY> Attribute Summary*

Outputting the Data

Using the **<CFOUTPUT>** element, it is possible to display the data retrieved from a previously defined **<CFQUERY>** element. For example, in order to output the query called ListJobs, you would use a code fragment, as shown here:

```
<CFOUPUT QUERY="ListJobs">

        <hr noshade><br>
        Position Number: #PositionNum#<br><br>
        Title: #JobTitle#<br><br>
        Location: #Location#<br><br>
        Description: #Description#

</CFOUPUT>
```

Notice the use of the # symbols throughout this code fragment. These values are used to delimit the areas in which you wish to place the data from the database. For example, **#PositionNum#** will be populated with data from the column **PositionNum**, while **#JobTitle#** will get the values for the **JobTitle** column in the database. Notice also that normal HTML markup can be used within the query.

The primary attribute for the **<CFOUTPUT>** element is **QUERY**, but there are numerous other attributes, as shown in Table 12-7.

By putting both the **<CFQUERY>** and the **<CFOUTPUT>** elements together in a complete CFML template file, which you could call example1.cfm, and putting this on

Attribute	Description
QUERY	Required. This is set to the name of the **<CFQUERY>** that will be used to query the database.
MAXROWS	Optional. This attribute is used to specify the maximum number of rows in the query: a positive integer, which should be displayed.
GROUP	Optional. This attribute is used to group output and is useful for nested reporting.
STARTROW	Optional. This attribute is used to specify an integer row from which to start output; for example, setting this attribute to 5 would start the output with the fifth row returned by the query.

Table 12-7. *<CFOUTPUT> Attribute Summary*

a server that understands ColdFusion, you could create a dynamically generated page. A complete example showing the two primary ColdFusion elements is shown here:

```
<!DOCTYPE HTML PUBLIC "-//W3C//DTD HTML 4.01 Transitional//EN">
<!-- SQL statement to select jobs available from the database-->

<CFQUERY NAME="ListJobs" DATASOURCE="CompanyDataBase">
SELECT * from Positions
</CFQUERY>

<html>
<head>
<title>Demo Company Job Listings</title>
</head>

<body bgcolor="#FFFFFF">
<h2 align="center">Job Listings</h2>
<hr>

<CFOUTPUT QUERY="ListJobs">
<hr noshade><br>
Position Number: #PositionNum#<br><br>
Title: #JobTitle#<br><br>
Location: #Location#<br><br>
Description: #Description#
</CFOUTPUT>
<hr>

<address>
Demo Company, Inc.
</address>

</body>
</html>
```

Figure 12-8 shows a ColdFusion dynamically generated page under Netscape. Note that there are no browser-side requirements for ColdFusion. In other words, this application would work equally well under Internet Explorer, Lynx, WebTV, or any other browser.

Conditional Statements

When creating dynamic pages, things don't always work out as expected. What happens if there are no jobs in the database to print out? Should the user get a blank

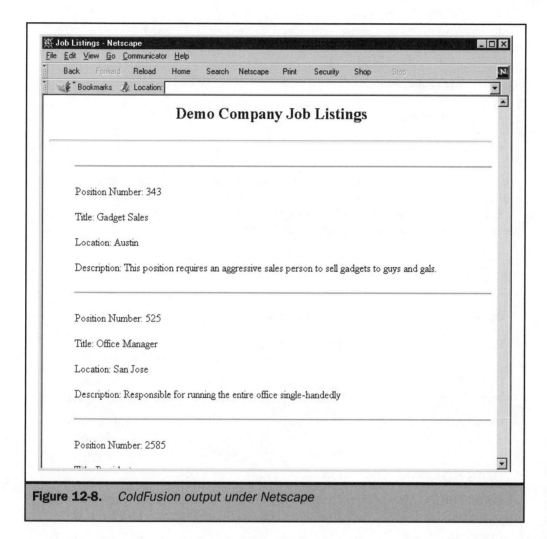

Figure 12-8.   *ColdFusion output under Netscape*

page, or one that says "Sorry, no jobs available?" ColdFusion provides a number of facilities to take care of just such problems. Using the **<CFIF>** element, simple comparison conditions can be added to the page and simple applications can be built. The basic syntax for the **<CFIF>** element is shown here:

```
<CFIF expression>
HTML and CFML tags
<CFELSE>
HTML and CFML tags
</CFIF>
```

An expression is a comparison condition. For example, **IS NOT ""** would be an expression to see if something is not set. So

```
<CFIF ListJobs.PostionNum IS NOT "">

Print the query here.

</CFIF>
```

would do the section "Print the query here" only if the **PostionNum** field were not empty. Note that, as shown in this example, the **<CFELSE>** element is optional.

The expression used in the **<CFIF>** element can be complex and might consist of one or many of the operators shown in Table 12-8.

Operator	Description
IS	Performs a case-insensitive comparison of two values and returns **TRUE** if the values are identical.
IS NOT or **NEQ**	Performs the opposite function of the IS operator, returning **TRUE** only if the values are not equal.
CONTAINS	Performs a check to determine if the value on the left of the operator is contained in the value on the right of the operator and returns **TRUE** if it is.
DOES NOT CONTAIN	Opposite of the **CONTAINS** operator.
GREATER THAN or **GT**	Checks whether the value on the left is greater than the value on the right and returns **TRUE** if it is.
LESS THAN or **LT**	Checks whether the value on the left is less than the value on the right and returns **TRUE** if it is.
GREATER THAN OR EQUAL TO or **GTE**	Checks whether the value on the left is greater than or equal to the value on the right and returns **TRUE** if it is.
LESS THAN OR EQUAL TO or **LTE**	Checks whether the value on the left is less than or equal to the value on the right and returns **TRUE** if it is.

Table 12-8. *<CFIF> Operators Summary*

Using the conditional capabilities provided by the **<CFIF>** element, it is possible to create an improved example that checks whether the table has open positions. If not, it prints out a statement indicating that no jobs are available, as shown here:

```
<!DOCTYPE HTML PUBLIC "-//W3C//DTD HTML 4.01 Transitional//EN">
<!-- SQL statement to select jobs available from the database-->

<CFQUERY NAME="ListJobs" DATASOURCE="CompanyDataBase">
SELECT * FROM Positions
</CFQUERY>

<CFIF ListJobs.PositionNumber IS NOT "">

<html>
<head>
<title>Demo Company Job Listings</title>
</head>

<body>
<h1 align="center">Demo Company Job Listings</H2>
<hr>

<CFOUTPUT QUERY="ListJobs">
   <ul>
      <hr noshade><br>
       Position Number: #PositionNum#<br><br>
       Title: #JobTitle#<br><br>
       Location: #Location#<br><br>
       Description: #Description#
   </ul>
</CFOUPUT>

<hr>
<address>
Demo Company, Inc.
</address>

</body>
</html>

<CFELSE>
   <CFLOCATION URL="nojobs.htm">
</CFIF>
```

The **<CFIF>** statement in this example checks to see if the **PositionNum** field is empty in the database. If the field is not empty, it proceeds to populate the Web page. If the field is empty, it redirects to a page called nojobs.htm, which indicates that there are no positions currently available at the company.

CFML Summary

It should be obvious from the examples presented that ColdFusion can be used to create useful dynamic Web pages. When using conditional operators, as well as other CFML elements that can be used to loop or set variables, it is even possible to create full-fledged applications with ColdFusion. ColdFusion and other HTML-like, server-parsed languages are great, because they are relatively easy to get started with. There are fewer than two dozen CFML elements to learn. Some of these provide very powerful features such as file upload, cookie manipulation, file inclusion, automatic HTML table creation, and mailing. A brief overview of some the CFML elements available in ColdFusion is presented in Table 12-9.

The preceding discussion is just a sample of what ColdFusion can do. It is meant only to illustrate what a server-side HTML language can do. For more detailed information on the syntax of ColdFusion, as well as examples of its use, see the

Element	Description
<CFABORT>	Aborts the processing of the CFML application or template at the specified location.
<CFAPPLICATION>	Defines the CFML application name and activates the client variables.
<CFCOL>	Defines a table column header, including setting width and alignment of the column.
<CFCONTENT>	Defines the content type and the name of the file to be uploaded from the application.
<CFCOOKIE>	Defines and sets a cookie, which can be used to preserve state information.
<CFERROR>	Used to customize HTML error pages.
<CFFILE>	Allows the developer to define file-handling tasks within the CFML application.
<CFHEADER>	Used to generate HTTP headers in the application, which can be useful to avoid having the page cached.
<CFIF>	Creates a conditional expression that is useful for catching error conditions or setting up more output logic.

Table 12-9.   *CFML Language Summary*

Element	Description
<CFINCLUDE>	Used to include a ColdFusion template file in the application. Useful for keeping routines in separate files.
<CFINSERT>	Used to insert records into an ODBC database.
<CFLOCATION>	Opens a ColdFusion template or HTML file. Most often used for redirection of output.
<CFLOOP>	Used to "loop" or repeat a set of instructions or display conditional output.
<CFMAIL>	Used to send SMTP e-mail from the CFML application.
<CFOUTPUT>	Displays the results of a database query as specified by the **<CFQUERY>** element.
<CFPARAM>	Used to assign a parameter an initial value.
<CFQUERY>	Used to pass a SQL statement, typically a query, to an ODBC-connected database.
<CFREPORT>	Used to embed a report from Crystal Reports into the page.
<CFSET>	Used to define a variable within the CFML application that can be accessed later using a **<CFIF>** or similar construct.
<CFTABLE>	Used to build a quick HTML table to hold the output of a query.
<CFUPDATE>	Used to update records in an ODBC data source.

Table 12-9.   *CFML Language Summary* (continued)

ColdFusion Language Reference at Allaire's Web site (http://www.allaire.com). Whereas ColdFusion is somewhat specific to database access, there are other server-side parsed HTML solutions, such as Microsoft's ASP, which might provide more general functionality.

Active Server Pages (ASP)

Microsoft's ASP is a server-side scripting environment primarily for the Microsoft Internet Information Server (IIS) Web server, although third-party vendors such as ChiliSoft (http://www.chilisoft.com) have ported ASP to other Web servers and operating systems. Using ASP, it is possible to combine HTML, scripting code, and server-side ActiveX components to create dynamic Web applications. The ability to write scripts in standard scripting languages such as VBScript, JavaScript, or other scripting languages such as Perl, enables developers to create applications with almost any type of functionality. This makes the ASP approach to server-side scripting very generalized for a broad range of applications. Server-side scripts also can access server-side objects in the form of ActiveX controls for a variety of functions, such as database access through ODBC. Like other parsed HTML solutions, an ASP-enabled page is parsed by the Web server to generate the dynamic HTML that is sent to the Web browser. This means that ASP-enabled pages work equally well on every browser.

Creating ASP Pages

To get started using ASP, the developer needs to have a working knowledge of HTML, as well as knowledge of a scripting language like VBScript or JavaScript. Files created for ASP have an .asp file extension. When an ASP-enabled server sees a file with such an extension, it will execute it before delivering it to the user. For example, the simple VBScript embedded into the file shown here is used to dynamically display the current date on a Web page:

```
<!DOCTYPE HTML PUBLIC "-//W3C//DTD HTML 4.01 Transitional//EN">
<script language="VBScript" runat="Server"></script>
<html>
<head>
<title>ASP Example</title>
</head>
<body>
<h1>Breaking News</h1>

<% = date() %>

<p>Today the stock of a major software company <br>
reached an all time high, making the Demo Company CEO<br>
the world's first and only trillionaire.</p>
</body>
</html>
```

The **<script>** element is used to indicate the primary scripting language being employed. This element also tells the Web server to execute the script code on the server rather than the client with the **runat** attribute. This can be abbreviated as **<%@ LANGUAGE=***<script_language>* **%>**. Notice how the **<% %>** is used to delimit the script code that is run. ASP is a generalized technology. It can be used to do whatever a user dreams up. Because people commonly want to do things on the Web like access a database, it has been enhanced to do this as well.

Database Access in ASP   In the following discussion, ASP will be used to access the Positions database described earlier in the chapter. Although this probably could be done more easily using ColdFusion, the point here is to introduce the idea of object access from ASP. The first step in this example is to create an instance of the database component by adding the following line to an ASP file, which might be named example.asp.

```
<object runat="Server" id="Conn" progid="ADODB.Connection">
</object>
```

or more appropriately, just use a simple statement like

```
<%
Set Conn = Server.CreateObject("ADODB.Connection")
%>
```

This statement creates an instance of a database access object called **Conn** that can be used with a server-side script.

Later, the file will open a connection to the database and execute a SQL command to select job positions and return a set of records. The small code fragment shown next does this. The code is enclosed within <% and %> so that the server knows to execute this rather than display it onscreen.

```
<%
    Conn.Open ODBCPositions
    SQL = "SELECT * FROM Positions"
    SET RS = Conn.Execute(SQL)
    Do While Not RS.EOF
%>
```

The code between the <% %> statements is VBScript, which is interpreted by the Web server when this page is requested. The Do While statement is a standard VBScript looping statement, which is used here to loop through the record set until an end of file (EOF) marker is reached, signifying the end of the records. While looping through each record, the output is displayed in the context of regular HTML code, such as displaying the Job Department field in a table cell:

```
<td>
<% = RS("JobDepartment") %>
</td>
```

Putting this all together in a file called example.asp provides a complete ASP database access example:

```
<!DOCTYPE HTML PUBLIC "-//W3C//DTD HTML 4.01 Transitional//EN">
<%@ LANGUAGE = VBScript %>
<html>
<head>
<title>Job Openings</title>
</head>
<body>
<h2 align="center">Open Positions</h2>
<br><br>
<table width="100%" border="1" cellspacing="0" cellpadding="4">
<tr>
<th>Position Number</th>
<th>Location</th>
<th>Description</th>
<th>Hiring Manager</th>
<th>Data Posted</th>
</tr>

<!--
     Open Database Connection
     Execute SQL query statement
     Set RS variable to store results of query
     Loop through records while still records to process
-->
<%
    Set Conn = Server.CreateObject("ADODB.Connection")
   Conn.Open ODBCPositions
    SQL = "SELECT JobTitle, Location, Description, HiringManager,
PostDate FROM Positions"
    Set RS = Conn.Execute(SQL)
    Do While Not RS.EOF
%>

<!-- Display database fields in table cells -->
<tr>
    <td>
    <% = RS("JobTitle") %>
    </td>
     <td>
    <% = RS("Location") %>
    </td>
    <td>
    <% = RS("Description") %>
```

```
    </td>
    <td>
    <% = RS("Hiring Manager") %>
    </td>
    <td>
    <% = RS("Post Date") %>
    </td>
</tr>

<!-- Move to next record and continue loop -->

<%
    RS.MoveNext
    Loop
%>

</table>
</body>
</html>
```

From this example, you can see the advantages of ASP for generating dynamic pages. The actual data to be displayed is a database that the server can access with an ASP script using a database access object. The dynamically created page is built from a combination of VBScript that uses a small amount of programming and HTML. The result can be served to different browsers without any client-side compatibility problems, because the pages are generated on the server. Although this example shows a more complicated way to access data from a database, it hints at the generalized power of ASP. Active Server Pages are useful for creating applications rather than just dynamic pages. With ASP, it is possible to determine the user's browser, keep track of the user's progress through a set of pages, and manage all the data that is passed back and forth from the user (including cookies and form fields). The key to this power is the server-side objects provided with ASP.

Built-In ASP Objects

What makes ASP so powerful is that the technology includes five built-in objects for global use:

- Application
- Request
- Response
- Server
- Session

The application object is used to share common information within an application. An example would be a page counter. You can store the number of times a page has been accessed and use this object to display it on the page. The application object supports locking as multiple users might be using the Web application at the same time and possibly could corrupt data.

The request object is used to get information from the user, including form data, cookies, or standard HTTP request variables such as browser type (user agent). The request object contains collections of information that can be used in scripts. The request object supports the following collections:

- **ClientCertificate** The values of fields stored in the client certificate that is sent in the HTTP request
- **Cookies** The values of cookies sent in the HTTP request
- **Form** The values of the fields sent from a form submission
- **QueryString** The values of the variables sent in an HTTP query string
- **ServerVariables** HTTP server information, such as server name, type, and version

The response object is used to send information to the user. It could be used to set the type of content to be sent to a browser, such as HTML or Word files; or other formats such as graphics. It also could send and retrieve cookie values to a client to determine user preferences for creating customized pages.

The server object provides access to server methods and properties, including setting how long a script should run and asking for server-side objects, such as database objects.

The session object, one of the most useful objects, is used to store information for a particular user session. This means that information is maintained as the user jumps from page to page, thus preserving state. The basic property for this object sets an ID for the session while the events deal with the start or end of a session.

A generalized language such as VBScript or JavaScript, combined with server-side objects to do common tasks like maintaining user state, makes complex server-side applications possible. Many other technologies such as ColdFusion and PHP take a similar approach. When it comes right down to it, the differences between the various server-scripting languages such as ColdFusion and ASP are somewhat cosmetic. Programmers might find ASP comfortable, whereas skilled HTML authors might find ColdFusion more suitable. The choice of any server-side technology should be a logical process rather than a blind acceptance of a single vendor's solution.

This discussion introduces ASP and is by no means complete. It illustrates a much-generalized method of parsed HTML that utilizes the power of popular scripting languages and access to server-side objects with common and powerful functions, such as database access and session tracking. Complete information on ASP can be found on sites like ASPHole (http://www.asphole.com) and 15 seconds (http://www.15seconds.com) or in the documentation that is included with an IIS Web server.

Summary

Server-side programming is one way to add interactivity to a Web page. CGI is the traditional way to do this. Writing a CGI program isn't difficult if you use libraries, but the price to pay for ease often is speed. Because so many CGI programs are very similar, some are rewritten as faster server-side modules including NSAPI, ISAPI and Apache modules. Although these types of server modules tend to be beyond most developers, it is easy to buy one to solve a common problem such as database access. Some Web servers now support a form of server-side scripting known generically as parsed HTML. Parsed HTML solutions such as SSIs, ColdFusion, and ASP provide an easy way for HTML authors to add functionality to Web pages. While server-side technologies provide a great deal of power for the Web developer, they are only half the picture. It also is possible to add interactivity using a client-side technology such as JavaScript or Java. The subsequent chapters discuss these technologies and their intersection with HTML.

The
Complete
Reference

Chapter 13

Introduction to
JavaScript and DHTML

A dding interactivity to a Web site is not limited to server-side programs. The client side of the Web—the browser—generally can execute code in the form of scripting or embedded programmed objects. For HTML writers, the easiest way to begin adding dynamic aspects to a Web page is through client-side scripting, primarily using JavaScript. This chapter discusses the intersection between scripting and HTML, but does not attempt to teach scripting techniques in depth. The idea of scripting requires the page designer to think more carefully about how the user will interact with the page. If scripting is not used carefully, errors might creep in and cause problems for the viewer.

As it stands now, scripting languages such as JavaScript often are relegated to small embellishments such as the ubiquitous rollover button. However, Dynamic HTML (DHTML) and the Document Object Model (DOM) show how the idea of a page can change forever because of client-side scripting. Beyond these new dynamic features, scripting has an even bigger role to play on a Web page. Whereas HTML can provide the structure, scripting can act as the glue, providing a link between static content and user actions, and between various embedded objects as discussed in the next chapter.

Purpose of Scripting

How do Web scripting languages relate to full-fledged Web programming languages such as Java? In general, scripting languages are used in small doses, for specific tasks. Scripting has a very limited domain in the case of client-side scripting, within a Web page or limited to a browser. Some basic uses of client-side scripting include

- Form validation
- Page embellishment, including rollover buttons and animation
- Dynamic markup generation
- Inter-object communication "glue"

HTML developers tend to be comfortable with scripting languages, because they can simply enter script commands into the HTML file along with the text markup. In fact, some developers simply cut and paste scripts to add scrolling marquees, dialog boxes, and other customized features to their pages. This form of quick embellishment comes at a cost. If testing is not rigorous, serious problems—even crashes—can creep in. With the rise of so many variations of the popular scripting language JavaScript bugs are becoming more common. Hopefully, the rise of ECMAScript, a standardized form of JavaScript, will help solve some of these problems. Beyond compatibility issues, scripting occasionally has some security problems, mostly related to browser implementation bugs. Some more cautious users might even turn off script interpretation in their browsers, potentially causing the page to render improperly. If scripting makes sense for your site, you must choose between JavaScript and VBScript.

JavaScript

The most popular client-side scripting language on the
language developed by Netscape. Microsoft also supp
JScript, a clone language used in Internet Explorer. The
the international standards body *European Computer M*
which announced during the summer of 1997 the approv
as a cross-platform Internet standard for scripting. Bro
the specification, but will still use the commonly recog

JavaScript will seem very familiar to programmers.
somewhat like C or Java with Perl-style regular expres
has basic object-oriented capabilities. JavaScript is not, however, a true object-oriented
programming language, and retains features (such as weak typing) that are common to
simple scripting languages. A simple example of JavaScript code being used to greet
the user is shown here; a rendering of the script in action is shown in Figure 13-1:

```html
<!DOCTYPE HTML PUBLIC "-//W3C//DTD HTML 4.01 Transitional//EN">
<html>
<head>
<title>JavaScript Example</title>
<script language="JavaScript">
<!--
  function greet()
   {
     alert("Hello user! Welcome to JavaScript.");
   }
//-->
</script>
</head>
<body>
<h1 align="center">First JavaScript Example</h1>
<div align="center">
<form>
<input type="button" value="Press Me" onclick="greet()">
</form>
</div>
</body>
</html>
```

This is a simple example of how JavaScript can be included in an HTML file. The
form button triggers the function called **greet()**, which greets the user. The event
handler attribute **onclick** is used to tie the HTML to the JavaScript that is contained in
the head of the document within the **<script>** element. Although this example is very

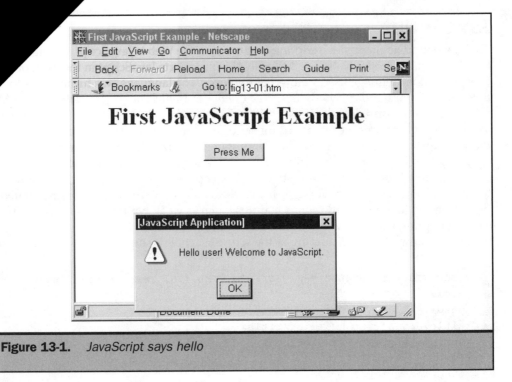

Figure 13-1.   *JavaScript says hello*

easy, remember that it also is a trivial example; this is a real programming language that has many nuances which are discussed later in this chapter.

For more information on JavaScript, visit Netscape's developer site at http://developer.netscape.com/. Information about Microsoft's implementation of JavaScript, called JScript, can be found at http://msdn.microsoft.com/scripting/.

VBScript

Visual Basic Scripting Edition, generally called VBScript, is a subset of the popular Visual Basic language. Because of its Visual Basic heritage, in some ways VBScript is somewhat better defined and seems to have a more stable specification than JavaScript. VBScript is less prevalent than JavaScript on the Internet, largely because VBScript is fully supported in only Internet Explorer 3 and later Microsoft browsers. The language can be used to provide the same functionality as JavaScript, and is just as capable as accessing the various objects that compose a Web page (termed a browser's *Object Model*). Avoid trying to use VBScript as a cross-platform scripting solution. Used in a more controllable environment, such as an intranet, VBScript might just be what the Microsoft-oriented developer needs. When dealing with ActiveX controls (discussed in

Chapter 14), VBScript in fact might provide more functionality. The following is a sample of VBScript to give you a flavor of its syntax; this example has the same functionality as the JavaScript example given previously:

```
<!DOCTYPE HTML PUBLIC "-//W3C//DTD HTML 4.01 Transitional//EN">
<html>
<head>
<title>VBScript Example</title>
<script language="VBScript">
<!--
Sub greet_OnClick
      MsgBox "Hello user! Welcome to VBScript."
End Sub
-->
</script>
</head>
<body>
<h1 align="center">First VBScript Example</h1>
<div align="center">
<form>
<input type="button" value="Press Me" name="greet">
</form>
</div>
</body>
</html>
```

This is a simple example of how VBScript can be included in an HTML file. It produces a rendering similar to the one shown in Figure 13-2.

As in the first example, the form button named "greet" triggers an alert box that greets the user. Notice that rather than using an explicit HTML attribute such as **onclick**, as was used in the JavaScript example, the VBScript example names the subroutine in a certain way to associate it with the button event, in this case **greet_OnClick**.

Other subtle differences in VBScript include the use of the **MsgBox** function to create the alert window, as well as other syntactical differences such as use of parentheses. Readers familiar with Visual Basic should find this example very easy, because this language is just a subset of Visual Basic proper. Unfortunately, as previously mentioned, as a client-side technology VBScript is not very useful outside an intranet. Because it is limited to Internet Explorer, relying on VBScript locks out all Netscape users, which is unacceptable for a public Web site. Because of this, VBScript often is limited to being used within a Microsoft-oriented intranet or on the server side, in the form of Active Server Page code (as discussed in Chapter 12). No further discussion of VBScript occurs during this client-side discussion. However, readers

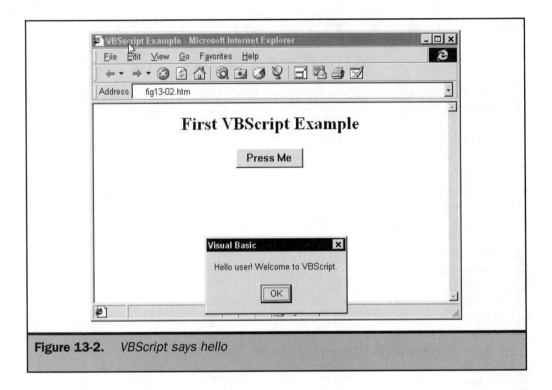

Figure 13-2. *VBScript says hello*

interested in more information about the syntax of VBScript, as well as examples, are encouraged to visit Microsoft's scripting site (http://msdn.microsoft.com/scripting/).

Including Scripts in an HTML Document

As suggested by the introductory examples, the main way to include scripts—written in any language—in a Web page is primarily with the **<script>** element. There actually are five primary ways to include script code into a document:

- Within the **<script>** element
- As a linked file indicated by the **src** attribute of the **<script>** element
- Within an event handler attribute such as **onclick**
- Via the pseudo-URL javascript: referenced by a link
- Through a JavaScript entity

The syntax of each of these approaches is presented in the following sections with simple examples.

The <script> Element

The **<script>** element is used to section off any script included directly within a Web page. Within the element should be script commands; these commands are run through a script interpreter before any results, either plain text or HTML, are returned to the HTML parser for eventual display on the page. For example, consider the short markup and script fragment here that might be found in an HTML document body.

```
<h2>Before the JavaScript</h2>
<script language="JavaScript">
   document.write("Hello world from <b>JavaScript</b>");
</script>
<h2>After the JavaScript</h2>
```

This would produce a heading of text, the short greeting from JavaScript and then the second heading. Notice that the text generated by JavaScript includes the **<b>** element, which then would be interpreted by the browser before final display.

The **<script>** element can occur in either the **<head>** or the **<body>** elements numerous times. Because a document is read from top to bottom, many scripts will be found in the head; these must be read before the page is loaded. Programmers will find scripts in the head of the document useful to declare and initialize variables and set up functions for later use. For example, the following example sets up functions that can be triggered later on in the document:

```
<!DOCTYPE HTML PUBLIC "-//W3C//DTD HTML 4.01 Transitional//EN">
<html>
<head>
<title>JavaScript Example</title>
<script language="JavaScript">
 function greet()
  {
    alert("Hello user! Welcome to JavaScript.");
   }
</script>
</head>
<body>

   ... markup and JavaScript that may eventually trigger script
   found in the head of the document ...

</body>
</html>
```

In this particular example the script in the head is only a function definition. It won't necessarily be executed unless we call it down in the **<body>** of the document. Later on in the page we could have a special script block such as

```
<script>
    greet();
</script>
```

which could invoke the short script defined in the **<head>** of the document. We often characterize the script in the **<head>** as deferred script if it is not executed upon read. The second script is characterized as immediate script because it is executed immediately.

Hiding Script

One potential problem to address when using script markup within a document is what to do when a browser doesn't support scripting. Under traditional HTML, when a browser encounters an element it doesn't support it simply skips it and prints out the contents within the element as plain text. A non-JavaScript-aware browser encountering an example such as

```
<script language="JavaScript">
        alert("I am a script.");
</script>
```

literally would print **alert("I am a script.");** rather than running the script first. In order to avoid this undesirable situation we should attempt to hide the script code from older browsers using comments, in a fashion similar to the technique for hiding style sheets discussed in Chapter 10. An example of commenting on JavaScript is shown here:

```
<script language="JavaScript">
<!--
alert("I am a script.");
//-->
</script>
```

Notice how the HTML comment starts the exclusion of JavaScript, but //--> is used to close the comment. This is because JavaScript interprets lines with // as comments and does not attempt to run a command --> as a command.

Note   *Other scripting languages such as VBScript might have different commenting styles for hiding the script code from older browsers.*

XHTML will allow the inclusion of the **<script>** element, but many of the characters found in a JavaScript, such as > or &, have special meaning and could cause trouble. According to the XHTML specification you also are supposed to hide the contents of the script from the XHTML-enforcing browser using the following technique:

```
<script>
<![CDATA[
   ..script here ..
]]>
</script>
```

Of course this doesn't work in any available browsers, so authors will have to instead use linked scripts in most cases. Also note that the use of comments to hide scripts or style sheets might cause problems for XHTML-compliant browsers.

<noscript>

Like other elements that reference technologies beyond basic HTML, the **<script>** element supports a special element to deal with browsers that don't execute a script. The **<noscript>** element is used to enclose alternative text and markup for browsers that don't interpret a script. Furthermore, users can turn off support for a scripting language in their browsers. The **<noscript>** content renders onscreen, as shown in the following example, if the user has turned off scripting support or is using a browser that doesn't understand JavaScript:

```
<!DOCTYPE HTML PUBLIC "-//W3C//DTD HTML 4.01 Transitional//EN">
<html>
<head>
<title>JavaScript and NOSCRIPT</title>
</head>
<body>
<script language="JavaScript">
<!--
 document.write('JavaScript is on');
//-->
</script>
<noscript>
<b>This page requires JavaScript. Please turn on JavaScript if you
   have it and reload this page!</b>
</noscript>
</body>
</html>
```

It is possible to turn off JavaScript support in a browser rather easily by setting your preferences. This browser modification is performed by users primarily for security reasons, because there are many privacy exploits related to JavaScript usage.

Specifying the Scripting Language

By default, most browsers assume that the script language being used is JavaScript. The **language** attribute can be used to specify other languages including VBScript and many others. The HTML 4.0 specification suggests using the **type** attribute in favor of the **language** attribute. The **type** attribute is used to indicate the MIME type of the script to run; for example, **text/javascript**. However, this indication of scripting dialect is not often used and might not provide the flexibility provided by **language**. For example, consider that not all versions of JavaScript support the same features. The object relied upon by animated buttons wasn't available until JavaScript 1.1; it causes errors in older browsers if it isn't accounted for. The **language** attribute can be used to indicate the version of JavaScript being used. The attribute can be set to "JavaScript1.1" or "JavaScript1.2" rather than simply "JavaScript." Only browsers that understand the particular dialect of JavaScript will execute the enclosed script code. With this idea, you can make a fall-through situation with multiple versions of similar code, as shown here:

```
<script language="JavaScript">
 Traditional JavaScript version
</script>

<script language="JavaScript1.1">
 JavaScript 1.1 version
</script>

<script language="JavaScript1.2">
 JavaScript1.2 version
</script>
```

One caveat to consider with the language attribute is that because a browser will ignore any element with any unknown language, a simple typo such as **<script language="javascipt">** will cause the entire script to be skipped.

Linked Scripts

While it is easy to put scripts directly in a document, it probably is better to separate them out in an external file and link to them, similar to linked style sheets. You can place the script code in a separate file and use the **src** attribute to specify the URL of the script to include. For example,

```
<script src="/scripts/myscript.js"></script>
```

loads a script called myscript.js, specified by the URL for the **src** attribute. The external file would contain only JavaScript and no HTML markup, not even the **<script>** element. For example, using our previous example we would have

```
function greet()
  {
    alert("Hello user! Welcome to JavaScript.");
  }
```

in the file myscript.js.

One major advantage of external scripts is that a browser can cache the script file locally. If the same script code is used over and over again, the files that reference it would require only the simple **<script>** statement and would be able to reuse the cached copy. Considering how much script code is inserted in many pages, this could improve site efficiency. Furthermore, using an included script also keeps HTML, script, and eventual style elements separate.

Although external scripts seem the way to go, they do have problems. Older browser implementations of JavaScript, notably Netscape 2.0 and early versions of Internet Explorer 3.0, do not support external scripts. Care also should be taken when serving scripts. A Web server should map the .js file extension to the appropriate MIME type—in this case, **application/x-javascript**—so that the browser receiving the file knows what to do with it. Older servers, notably IIS 3.0, might require a MIME type that is configured to allow delivery of script files. However, today these problems are becoming less an issue, and linked scripts certainly will be used more commonly.

Script Events and HTML

Script code can also be added to HTML documents through special attributes called *event handlers*. What are events? Events occur as the result of a user action or, potentially, an external event, such as a page loading. Examples of events include a user clicking a button, pressing a key, moving a window, or even simply moving the mouse around the screen. HTML provides a way to bind a script to the occurrence of a particular event, through an *event handler attribute*. This is the name of the event, prefixed by the word "on": for example, **onclick**. The following code shows how the **onclick** event handler attribute is used to bind a script to a button click occurrence:

```
<form>
<input type="button" onclick="alert('This is JavaScript')"
       value="Press Me">
</form>
```

Under HTML 4, event handler attributes can be added to quite a number of HTML elements. For example,

```
<p onclick="alert('Under HTML 4 you can!')">Can you click me?</p>
```

However, so far not all browsers support core events on every HTML element. In reality, it often wouldn't make sense to associated events with some elements. The core event model according to HTML 4 includes **onclick, ondblclick, onkeydown, onkeypress, onkeyup, onmousedown, onmousemove, onmouseout, onmouseover,** and **onmouseup.** These core events are defined for nearly all HTML elements in which the element is displayed onscreen. The specific elements and their events are discussed in Appendix A.

Beyond the core events, certain elements under HTML 4 have their own special events. For example, the **<body>** and **<frameset>** elements have an event for loading and unloading pages, so both elements also have the **onload** and **onunload** event attributes. In the case of the **<frameset>** element, the load and unload events don't fire until all the frames have been loaded or unloaded, respectively. The **<form>** element itself also has two special events that typically are triggered when the user clicks the submit or reset button. These events are **onsubmit** and **onreset.** Of course, with scripting, these events might fire for other reasons. For form text fields set with the **<input>** element, you can catch the focus and blur events with **onfocus** and **onblur.** These events fire when the user accesses the field and moves on to another one. You also can watch for the select event with **onselect,** which is triggered when a user selects some text, as well as the change event (**onchange**), which is triggered when a form field's value changes and loses focus. Table 13-1 summarizes the main events supported by HTML and their associated elements.

Event Attribute	Event Description	Elements Allowed Under HTML 4
onblur	A blur event occurs when a form element loses focus, meaning that the user has entered into another form field either typically, by clicking the mouse on it, or by tabbing to it.	**<a>** **<area>** **<button>** **<input>** **<label>** **<select>** **<textarea>**

Table 13-1. *Events Defined in HTML 4*

Event Attribute	Event Description	Elements Allowed Under HTML 4
onchange	A change event signals both that the form control has lost user focus and that its value has been modified during its last access.	\<input\> \<select\> \<textarea\>
onclick	Indicates that the element has been clicked.	Most elements
ondblclick	Indicates that the element has been double-clicked, which is two consecutive, quick clicks.	Most elements
onfocus	The focus event describes when a form control has received focus, namely that it has been selected for manipulation or data entry.	\<a\> \<area\> \<button\> \<input\> \<label\> \<select\> \<textarea\>
onkeydown	Indicates that a key is being pressed down.	Most elements
onkeypress	Describes the event of a key being pressed and released.	Most elements
onkeyup	Indicates that a key is being released.	Most elements
onload	Indicates the event that occurs when a window or frame finishes loading a document.	\<body\> \<frameset\>
onmousedown	Indicates the press of a mouse button.	Most elements
onmousemove	Indicates that the mouse has moved.	Most elements
onmouseout	Indicates that the mouse has moved away from an element.	Most elements
onmouseover	Indicates that the mouse has moved over an element.	Most elements
onmouseup	Indicates the release of a mouse button.	Most elements

Table 13-1. *Events Defined in HTML 4* (continued)

Event Attribute	Event Description	Elements Allowed Under HTML 4
onreset	Indicates that the form is being reset, possibly by the click of a reset button.	**<form>**
onselect	Indicates the selection of text by the user, typically by highlighting the text.	**<input>** **<textarea>**
onsubmit	Indicates a form submission, generally by clicking a submit button.	**<form>**
onunload	Indicates that the browser is leaving the current document and unloading it from the window or frame.	**<body>** **<frameset>**

Table 13-1.   *Events Defined in HTML 4* (continued)

The following markup illustrates simple use of the HTML 4 event attributes with form elements and links:

```
<!DOCTYPE HTML PUBLIC "-//W3C//DTD HTML 4.01 Transitional//EN">
<html>
<head>
<title>HTML 4.0 Events</title>
</head>
<body onload='alert("Event demo loaded")'
      onunload='alert("Leaving demo")'>

<h1 align="center">HTML 4.0 Events</h1>
<form onreset='alert("Form reset")'
      onsubmit='alert("Form submit");return false;'>

<ul>
<li>onblur: <input type="text" value="Click into field and then leave"
                size="40" onblur='alert("Lost focus")'><br><br></li>

<li>onclick: <input type="button" value="Click Me"
                onclick='alert("Button click")'><br><br></li>

<li>onchange: <input type="text" value="Change this text then leave"
                size="40" onchange='alert("Changed")'><br><br></li>
```

```
<li>ondblclick: <input type="button" value="Double-click Me"
                        ondblclick='alert("Button double-clicked")'>
<br><br></li>

<li>onfocus: <input type="text" value="Click into field"
                     onfocus='alert("Gained focus")'><br><br></li>

<li>onkeydown: <input type="text"
                        value="Press key and release slowly here" size="40"
                        onkeydown='alert("Key down")'><br><br></li>

<li>onkeypress: <input type="text" value="Type here" size="40"
                        onkeypress='alert("Key pressed")'><br><br></li>

<li>onkeyup: <input type="text" value="Type and release" size="40"
                     onkeyup='alert("Key up")'><br><br></li>

<li>onload:    Alert presented on initial document load.<br><br></li>

<li>onmousedown: <input type="button" value="Click and hold"
                        onmousedown='alert("Mouse down")'><br><br></li>

<li>onmousemove: Move mouse over this
<a href=""onmousemove='alert("Mouse moved")'>link</a><br><br></li>

<li>onmouseout: Position
mouse <a href=""onmouseout='alert("Mouse out")'>here</a>
and now leave.<br><br></li>

<li>onmouseover: Position mouse over this
<a href=""onmouseover='alert("Mouse over")'>link</a><br><br></li>

<li>onmouseup: <input type="button" value="Click and release"
                       onmouseup='alert("Mouse up")'><br><br></li>

<li>onreset: <input type="reset" value="Reset Demo"><br><br></li>

<li>onselect: <input type="text" value="Select this text" size="40"
                      onselect='alert("Selected")'><br><br></li>

<li>onsubmit: <input type="submit" value="Test Submit"><br><br>
```

```
<li>onunload: Try to leave document by following this
<a href="http://www.yahoo.com">link</a>.<br><br></li>

</ul>
</form>
</body>
</html>
```

 *You might encounter problems with the **onfocus** demo under some versions of Netscape, because it might not release the focus event. This does not occur under all versions of the browser and, hopefully, will be fixed in the version that you are testing under.*

Whereas HTML 4 specifies numerous events, Netscape and Internet Explorer support many more events. A more detailed discussion of the various events unique to browsers can be found in Appendix A.

The javascript: URL

Most JavaScript-aware browsers introduced the use of a new URL style in the form of **javascript:**, which can be used with links. For example,

```
<a href="javascript:alert('Danger! JavaScript ahead!')">
Click for script</a>
```

creates a link that, when clicked, executes the specified JavaScript code. Although this pseudo-URL form is commonly used in many scripts, it does have a downside in that the link will not function at all when scripting is turned off. Designers should at minimum make sure to include a **<noscript>** element to warn users of this situation or to avoid the use of pseudo-URL script triggers.

JavaScript Entities

A very uncommon way to add JavaScript code to a Web page is with a character entity. (Remember that using **©** would include a copyright symbol.) JavaScript code can be inserted inside of a special entity of the form **&{javascript code};**. The JavaScript code must be included within braces; it can even call functions or perform numerous statements. This entity form can be used only as an attribute value. This style could be used as a form of macro in browsers aware of this form of JavaScript inclusion. Imagine inserting in the head of the document a bunch of identifiers for colors and font style, and then referencing them by name later, as shown in the following example:

```
<!DOCTYPE HTML PUBLIC "-//W3C//DTD HTML 4.01 Transitional//EN">
<html>
<head>
<title>Entity Script</title>
<script language="JavaScript">
<!--
  textColor='green';
//-->
</script>
</head>
<body>
<font color=&{textColor;};>This should be green.</font>
</body>
</html>
```

This example probably would be better handled by a style sheet, but it is presented here solely to show how the entity script style works.

JavaScript Language Overview

Readers familiar with programming should be able to inspect an existing JavaScript program with little trouble. A quick overview of the language to orient a reader familiar with programming is presented here. However, readers new to programming or looking for detailed explanation are encouraged to learn JavaScript from any of the numerous online tutorials or books available, and might want to skip directly to the next section presenting some common JavaScript use.

As a programming language JavaScript itself is not terribly difficult to learn. It shares syntax similarities with C, Perl, and Java and has only a few commands. As a language it has only a few basic types: numbers such as 3, -45, 56.78, strings such as "Hello" and "Thomas Powell," and the Boolean values true and false. The language also supports a few more complex data types such as arrays and objects that should be familiar to anyone who has programmed before.

Variables in JavaScript can be declared at any time. For example,

```
var x = 5;
```

would set a variable named x to an integer value and

```
var today="Wednesday";
```

sets the variable today to the string "Wednesday." As a loosely typed language, it is possible to set variables to other types at any time so a statement such as

```
today = x;
```

is perfectly legal and just changes the value of today to an integer value of 5.

Although loosely typed languages such as JavaScript ease a burden on the programmer for keeping track of what type of data is what variable, they also tend to introduce significant run time errors as a result of sloppy programming.

JavaScript is a case-sensitive language, so invoking the built-in alert method with a call such as **alert('hello');** is okay, whereas **Alert('hello');** is not. Note that most objects, properties, and methods in JavaScript should initially be lowercase with other words in the string capitalized. For example, **alert()** is all lowercase but **document.lastModified** does have the second part of the property initially capitalized. This follows the casing scheme found in many other languages. Remember, JavaScript is case sensitive; HTML is not. Of course, with the rise of XHTML, we will always want to use lowercase in HTML.

Statements in JavaScript are terminated with semicolons (;) or the return character so

```
alert("hi");
alert("there");
```

is equivalent to

```
alert("hi")
alert("there")
```

However, if you remove the return in the second example an error will occur, whereas putting two statements on the same line with semi-colons between such as

```
alert("hi"); alert("there");
```

is perfectly fine.

JavaScript has a simple set of operators including basic arithmetic (+,-, /, *), Boolean comparisons (>, <, >=, <=, !, and = =), string operators, and so on. The actual commands of language include conditional statements using an **if-else** syntax. Consider the following script which alerts the user based on the value of the variable x.

```
x=5;
if (x > 4)
```

```
   alert('Greater than 4');
else
   alert('Less than 4');
```

More complex types of conditions also can be handled using a switch statement, whose syntax is similar to the C programming language.

Loops can be specified with **while**, **for**, or **repeat**.

Consider the short script here that alerts the user three times:

```
x=1;
while (x < 4)
{
 alert(x);
 x++;
}
```

This also could be written as a for loop like so:

```
for (var x = 1; x < 4; x++)
{
     alert(x);
}
```

Like most modern program languages, it is possible to abort a loop or modify the number of loop iterations using the **break** and **continue** statements.

The language also supports the use of functions. For example, you could define a function called 'sayHi' that you use over and over in the document:

```
function sayHi( )
{
 alert('hi');
}
```

This function could be called at any time with a simple call such as **sayHi( )**. Good programming practice suggests that developers try to encapsulate commonly used code in functions. Beyond functions, JavaScript also supports object usage.

The JavaScript language itself is relatively simple for an experienced programmer to learn; however, the key to doing anything terribly useful with the language is figuring out how to access the built-in features of the browser as well as the various pieces of an HTML document. In fact it really is the idea to model an HTML document

**PROGRAMMING
AND HTML**

as a collection of objects, generally dubbed the Document Object Model, that is the key to understanding the potential impact of scripting.

JavaScript and the Document Object Model

Every Web document is made up of a variety of elements such as **<b>**, **<img>**, and **<form>**. Browsers read pages in a regular fashion because they understand the extent of the objects that are possible in a page. A page might be composed of three image elements, two paragraphs, an unordered list, and the text within these elements. The Document Object Model (DOM) describes each document as a collection of individual objects like images, paragraphs, and forms, all the way down to the individual characters. Each particular object can have properties associated with it, typically in the form of HTML attributes. For example, the paragraph element has an alignment attribute that can be set to left, right, or center. In the object model, this attribute is called a *property* of the object. An object can have methods that are associated with it, and events that can occur and affect it. An image tag can have an **onmouseover** event that is triggered when a user places the cursor over the image. A form can have a submit method that can be used to trigger the submission of the form and its contents to a server-based CGI program.

The best way to explain the DOM is by an example. Look at the simple HTML file here:

```
<!DOCTYPE HTML PUBLIC "-//W3C//DTD HTML 4.01 Transitional//EN">
<html>
<head>
<title>Demo Company</title>
</head>
<body bgcolor="white">
<h1 align="center">Demo Company</h1>
<hr>
<p id="para1">This is a paragraph of text.</p>
<ul>
   <li><a href="about.htm">About</a></li>
   <li><a href="products.htm">Products</a></li>
</ul>
</body>
</html>
```

This file could be modeled as a parse tree, as shown in Figure 13-3. The structured breakdown of HTML elements and how they enclose one another should be familiar even from the first chapter of this book.

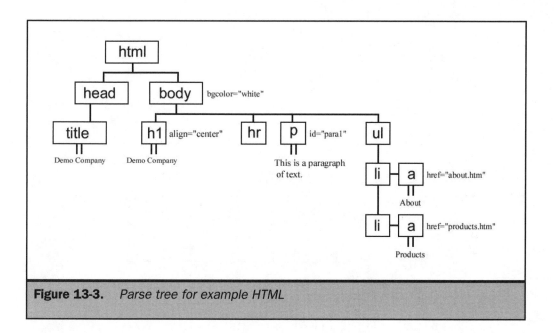

Figure 13-3.   *Parse tree for example HTML*

The concept of the Document Object Model is that there is a rigid structure defined to access the various HTML elements and text items that make up a document using a scripting language. This model starts from the browser window itself. A typical window contains either a document, or a collection of frames (basically windows) which in turn contain documents. Within a document is a collection of HTML elements. Some of these HTML elements, particularly forms, contain even more HTML elements, and some might contain text. The key to accessing the elements in a document is to understand the hierarchy and make sure to name the various elements in the page using either the **id** or the **name** attribute, or for maximum compatibility, both.

Object Models

Since Netscape 2, the browser, window, document, and document contents—forms, images, links, and so on—have been modeled as a collection of objects. As mentioned previously this is generically referred to as an object model or, more precisely, a document object model (DOM). Both of the major browsers support the DOM idea, but each has different naming conventions and a different degree of exposure. For example, under Netscape 3, only particular items—form elements, links, etc.—are accessible for scripting. Figure 13-4 illustrates the object model for Netscape 3 and Internet Explorer 3.

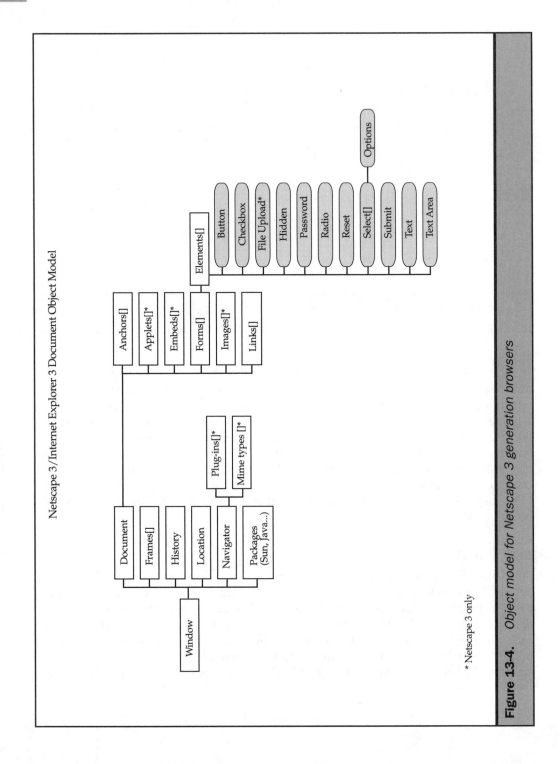

Netscape 3/Internet Explorer 3 Document Object Model

* Netscape 3 only

Figure 13-4. Object model for Netscape 3 generation browsers

Objects in the Netscape 3 object hierarchy provide access to not only page elements such as links, anchors, frames, and forms, but to things such as the browser's name, history, plug-ins, and Java classes associated with the current window.

With the introduction of Netscape 4, more elements, such as the non-standard HTML element layer, became accessible. Under Internet Explorer 4, all page elements are scriptable through the object **document.all**. Figure 13-5 shows an expanded object model. Note that many of the items in this model are available under only one browser or another.

Because of the significant difference in the object models supported by each browser, it can be challenging to write script code that work in both browsers. Fortunately, the W3C is working on standardizing the access to page content. See the section entitled "Dynamic HTML and the Rise of a Standard DOM" for more information on this.

HTML Elements and Scripting Access

HTML elements in a Web page need to be named properly to allow scripting languages to easily read and manipulate them. The basic way to attach a unique identifier to an HTML element under HTML 4 is by using the **id** attribute. The **id** attribute is associated with nearly every element.

The point of the **id** attribute is to bind a unique identifier to the element. To name a particular enclosed bolded piece of text "SuperImportant," you could use the markup shown here:

```
<b id="SuperImportant">This is very important.</b>
```

Naming is very important. Authors are encouraged to adopt a consistent naming style and to avoid using potentially confusing names that include the names of HTML elements themselves. For example, **button** does not make a very good name, and might interfere with scripting language access. To ensure uniqueness in names, you might want to use an underscore in the name; as in, for example, **_myButton**.

Before HTML 4, the **name** attribute often was used to expose items to scripting. For backward compatibility, the **name** attribute is commonly defined for **<a>**, **<applet>**, **<button>**, **<embed>**, **<form>**, **<frame>**, **<iframe>**, **<img>**, **<input>**, **<object>**, **<map>**, **<select>**, and **<textarea>**. Notice that the occurrence of the **name** attribute corresponds closely to the Netscape 3 object model.

> **Note** *Both **<meta>** and **<param>** support attributes called **name**, but these have totally different meanings beyond script access.*

Page developers must be careful to use **name** where necessary to ensure backward compatibility with older browsers. Earlier browsers will not recognize the **id** attribute,

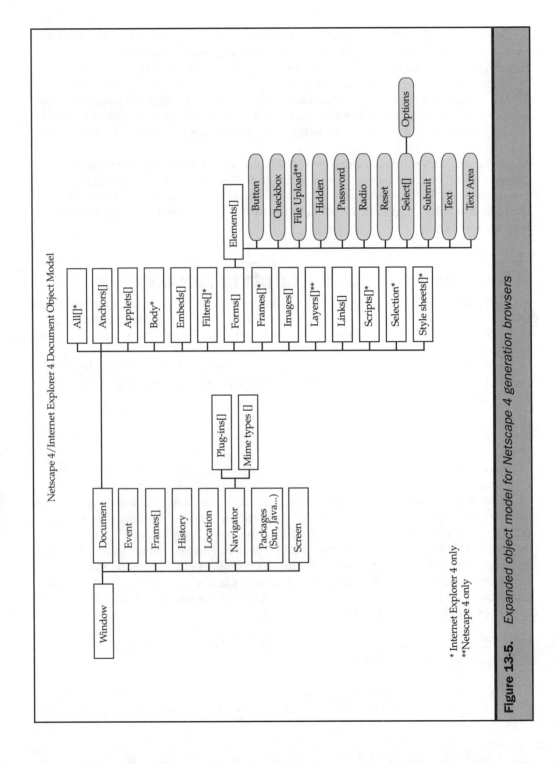

Netscape 4/Internet Explorer 4 Document Object Model

* Internet Explorer 4 only
**Netscape 4 only

Figure 13-5. Expanded object model for Netscape 4 generation browsers

so use **name** as well. For example, **<a name="link1" id="link1">** hopefully would be interpreted both by older script-aware browsers as well as by the latest standards–supporting browser.

> **Note** *There are some statements in standards documentation that suggest that it is not a good idea to set the name and id attributes the same, but practice shows this appears to be the only way to ensure backward browser compatibility.*

When HTML documents are well formed, in the sense that tags are used and named properly, scripting languages such as JavaScript can be used to read and manipulate the various objects in a page. The DOM defines a special set of reserved names that use this notation to allow scripting languages such as JavaScript to refer to entities in the browser and the document, including form elements. The basic notation uses a series of object and property names separated by dots. For example, to access the form defined by

```
<form name="myform" id="myform">
<input type="text" name="username">
</form>
```

with a scripting language, use either **window.document.myform** or simply **document.myform** because the window can be assumed. The field and its value can be accessed in a similar fashion. To access the text field, use **document.myform.username**. To access the actual value of the username field, access the value property using **document.myform.username.value**.

> **Note** *Under Internet Explorer it might be possible to use a shorthand notation such as **myform.username.value** but this will cause problems for older browsers and Netscape, and might not be supported in future standards*

> **Note** *Aside from proper naming, when adding scripting to a page the HTML should always be well formed. Simple things, for example crossed elements such as ****Test****, might cause a problem with a scripting language. This has to do with the manipulation of the text within the elements. Page authors should consider it extremely dangerous to manipulate poorly formed markup with scripts.*

The following example shows how the contents of a form field is accessed and displayed dynamically in an alert window by referencing the fields by name.

```
<!DOCTYPE HTML PUBLIC "-//W3C//DTD HTML 4.01 Transitional//EN">
<html>
<head>
```

```
<title>Meet and Greet</title>
<script language="JavaScript">
<!--
function sayHello()
{
 theirname=document.myform.username.value;
 if (theirname !="")
  alert("Hello "+theirname+"!");
 else
  alert("Don't be shy.");
}
// -->
</script>
</head>
<body>
<form name="myform" id="myform">
<b>What's your name?</b>
<input type="text" name="username" id="username"  size="20"><br><br>
<input type="button" value="Greet" onclick="sayHello()">
</form>
</body>
</html>
```

It also is possible to refer to forms and form elements without assigning them a name using an array notation. Forms can be referred to by a **forms** array with the numbers beginning at 0. Elements within a form can be referred to by an elements array that also begins at 0. The previous example contains only one form and one field, so the syntax **document.forms[0].elements[0].value** is the same as **document.myform.username.value**. Note that it generally is better to name elements than to access them through their position in a page because any additions or movement of the HTML elements within the page could potentially break the script.

Aside from reading the contents of an element with JavaScript, it also is possible, in some cases, to update the contents of certain elements such as form fields. The following example code shows how this might be done:

```
<!DOCTYPE HTML PUBLIC "-//W3C//DTD HTML 4.01 Transitional//EN">
<html>
<head>
<title>Meet and Greet 2</title>
<script language="JavaScript">
```

```
<!--
function sayHello()
{
 theirname = document.myform.username.value;
 if (theirname != "")
  document.myform.response.value="Hello "+theirname+"!";
 else
  document.myform.response.value="Don't be shy.";
}
// -->
</script>
</head>
<body>
<form name="myform" id="myform">
<b>What's your name?</b>
<input type="text" name="username" id="username"  size="20">
<br><br>
<b>Greeting:</b>
<input type="text" name="response" id="response" size="40">
<br><br>
<input type="button" value="Greet" onclick="sayHello()">
</form>
</body>
</html>
```

Note   *You might have noted the use of **name** as well as the **id** in the last examples. Unfortunately, with form elements, browser support is inconsistent with the **id** attribute and might cause errors unless the **name** attribute is used.*

If you look at Figure 13-4 you'll notice that under Netscape 3 and 4, and Internet Explorer 3, only some objects in a page are changeable, notably form elements. Starting with Internet Explorer 4, everything in a page can be modified right down to the very text and markup itself. This is the real idea of Dynamic HTML and is discussed next.

Dynamic HTML and the Rise of a Standard DOM

The previous examples have shown script interaction with HTML elements in the traditional fashion, manipulating form elements. However, with the rise of the 4.x generation of browsers a new concept called Dynamic HTML or DHTML was introduced. DHTML describes the ability to dynamically manipulate the very HTML elements themselves, potentially changing the document's structure in a significant way. However for many, DHTML was more the idea of an HTML page that displayed dynamic characteristics such as movement or the showing or hiding of page content. These sophisticated features were possible through the intersection of HTML, CSS, and JavaScript. So in some sense the idea of DHTML can be summarized in the formula

DHTML = HTML + CSS + JavaScript + Fully Accessible DOM

The only element we have not discussed up to this point in the book is the idea of the "fully accessible DOM." Basically what this says is that it would be possible to manipulate the very contents of a page right down to the elements and even the text of a paragraph element. For example, consider if you had a paragraph in HTML like so:

```
<p id="para1">This is a test</p>
```

There are numerous ways to access this element from JavaScript once it is named. For example, it could be referenced under Internet Explorer 4 or later using a JavaScript identifier such as **window.document.all['para1'], document.all['para1']** or simply **para1**. However, Netscape 4.x generation browsers might not expose this object at all for scripting. Even when Netscape and Internet Explorer expose similar objects for scripting, the syntax is not always the same, which can lead to serious headaches for developers. The W3C has proposed a standard Document Object Model called the DOM that should alleviate many of the incompatibilities and allow for a developer to access the contents of an HTML document in a standard fashion. There will be many levels of the DOM. Level 0 will preserve much of what is considered to be standard JavaScript—that which is supported by Netscape 3—and Level 1 and Level 2 will allow access to HTML elements and style sheets properties. Today we can count on support for DOM Level 1 in Internet Explorer 5 and Netscape 6 browsers.

To access an element using the DOM we use the **getElementById** method and specify the id attribute value of the object we desire to access. For example, we can access the element using **getElementById('para1')**. Once the object is returned we can modify its attributes so **getElementById('para1').align** would access the align attribute the same way IE4 used **para1.align**. The following example, which works under Internet Explorer 5 and Netscape 6 as well as any DOM-compliant browser, illustrates dynamic manipulation of HTML.

```
<!DOCTYPE HTML PUBLIC "-//W3C//DTD HTML 4.01 Transitional//EN">
<html>
<head>
<title>The Dynamic Paragraph</title>
</head>
<body bgcolor="white">
<h1 align="center">The Dynamic Paragraph</h1>
```

```
<hr>
<p id="para1">I am a dynamic paragraph. Watch me dance!</p>
<hr>
<form>
<input type="button" value="Right"
onClick="getElementById('para1').align='right'">
<input type="button" value="Left"
onClick="getElementById('para1').align='left'">
<input type="button" value="Center"
onClick="getElementById('para1').align='center'">
</form>
</body>
</html>
```

In the previous example, every time the user clicks on the spanned text the actual value of the **align** attribute for the **<p>** tag is manipulated. Of course, if you view the source of the page you won't notice anything, but this is basically what is happening.

The DOM allows not only manipulation of the existing tags within a document, but allows you to change the contents of tags or even add new tags dynamically. For example, the following markup shows how data can be added to a page:

```
<!DOCTYPE HTML PUBLIC "-//W3C//DTD HTML 4.01 Transitional//EN">
<html>
<head>
<title>Dynamic Page Demo</title>
<script language="JavaScript">
<!--
function addText()
{
 /* create the string */

 var str = document.testform.newtext.value;
 theString = document.createTextNode(str);

 /* create the <br> element */

 theBreak = document.createElement("BR");

 /* find the  div tag and add the string and <br> */

 theElement = document.getElementById("div1");
```

```
   theElement.appendChild(theString);
   theElement.appendChild(theBreak);
}
//-->
</script>
</head>
<body>
<div id="div1">
  This is some text.
</div>
<hr>
<form name="testform" id="testform">
    New text: <input type="text" name="newtext" id="newtext">
          <input type="button" value="Add" onClick="addText()">
</form>
</body>
</html>
```

| Note |

*Under IE4 it is possible to implement the previous example using the **innerText** and **innerHTML** attributes of an HTML element such as **<div>**. Although this is a much easier way to do things it actually is not part of the DOM standard at the time of this writing and developers should use this with caution.*

The previous example shows that with the DOM it is possible to manipulate the very parse tree of an HTML document. Adding HTML elements, deleting elements, and moving elements around the document all are possible using JavaScipt and the DOM. Now if we combine the ability to interact with CSS properties we can create the interesting effects that many people associate with DHTML.

Script Interaction with Style Sheets

Microsoft Internet Explorer 4 was the first browser to demonstrate how style sheets could be manipulated using scripting language. The following markup fragment shows how events can be tied with style changes to make text that changes color or even size in response to a mouse event:

```
<span onmouseover="this.style.color='#FF0000'"
      onmouseout="this.style.color='#0000FF'"
      onclick="this.style.fontSize='larger'">Click Me!</span>
```

The special scripting keyword **this** is a shortcut reference to the current element, but an **id** attribute could be used just as well, as shown here:

```
<span id="testspan" onmouseover="testspan.style.color='#FF0000'"
      onmouseout="testspan.style.color='#0000FF'"
      onclick="testspan.style.fontSize='larger'">Click Me!</span>
```

Both Netscape and Microsoft support scripting access for style sheets. Of course, the variations between the two browsers are significant. Currently, Microsoft and Netscape differ on how style sheets can be accessed and the degree to which they can be manipulated. For example, under Netscape 4 the only style sheet properties that can be changed after the document has loaded are the absolute positioning properties **left, top, z-index**, and **visibility**. Add in the fact that the standard DOM access is totally different from the way that Microsoft or Netscape tend to reference things in their 4.x generation browsers and you'll soon come to know that writing crossbrowser scripts can be a real chore. However, if you limit yourself to manipulating the position and visibility of objects laid out with a CSS rule you can safely come up with a crossbrowser script that should work in 4.x generation browsers and beyond. A simple example of this is shown here:

```
<!DOCTYPE HTML PUBLIC "-//W3C//DTD HTML 4.01 Transitional//EN">
<html>
<head>
<title>Cross Browser Layer Visibility / Placement Routines</title>
<script language="JavaScript">
<!--
/* test for objects */
(document.layers) ? layerobject=true : layerobject=false;
(document.all) ? allobject = true: allobject = false;
(document.getElementById) ? dom = true : dom = false;

function changeVisibility(id,action)
{
 switch (action)
 {
  case "show":
     if (layerobject)
         document.layers[''+id+''].visibility = "show";
       else if (allobject)
           document.all[''+id+''].style.visibility = "visible";
       else if (dom)
           document.getElementById(''+id+'').style.visibility = "visible";
     break;
```

```
    case "hide":
      if (layerobject)
              document.layers[''+id+''].visibility = "hide";
          else
              if (allobject)
              document.all[''+id+''].style.visibility = "hidden";
          else if (dom)
              document.getElementById(''+id+'').style.visibility = "hidden";
      break;
   default:return;
  }
 return;
 }


function changePosition(id,x,y)
{
  if (layerobject)
   {
    document.layers[''+id+''].left = x;
    document.layers[''+id+''].top = y;
    }
  else if (allobject)
      {
         document.all[''+id+''].style.left=x;
         document.all[''+id+''].style.top=y;
         }
  else if (dom)
      {
         document.getElementById(''+id+'').style.left=x+"px";
         document.getElementById(''+id+'').style.top=y+"px";
         }

  return;
}

//-->
</script>

<style type="text/css">
<!--
  #test {position:absolute;
         top:20px;
         left:300px;
         background-color: yellow;}
```

```
-->
</style>
</head>
<body>
<div id="test">This is a test division</div>

<form name="testform" id="testform">
<input type="button" value="show"
       onClick="changeVisibility('test','show
<input type="button" value="hide"
       onClick="changeVisibility('test','hide
<br><br>
X: <input type="text" name="xcoord" id="xcoord" size="4" maxlength="4"
value="100">
Y: <input type="text" name="ycoord" id="ycoord" size="4" maxlength="4"
value="100">
<input type="button" value="move"
onClick="changePosition('test',document.testform.xcoord.value,
         document.testform.ycoord.value)">
</form>
</body>
</html>
```

This example can be found online at www.htmlref.com/examples/chapter13/crossbrowser.htm. Also note that many tools and libraries exist for crossbrowser effects and movements, so don't insist on creating your own.

Although the DOM can be complex, what it can do is impressive. Developers can use the object model to find an image on a page and replace it with another image when a user rolls a cursor over it. Such rollovers, or animated buttons, are already common on the Web. In conjunction with scripting, the DOM also can animate a page by moving objects around, set up an expanding tree structure to navigate a site, or create a complex application such as a game or simple database front end. To seasoned JavaScript programmers, many of these ideas might not sound so new. They've been around in a limited form since Netscape 2. However, today the extent to which the page can be manipulated is getting to be nearly limitless. Although browser bugs probably will hamper easy code development for some time, readers are encouraged to approach crossbrowser scripting by following the World Wide Web Consortium's DOM (http://www.w3.org/DOM/) rather than adopting a browser specific object model.

Although this has been only a brief introduction to scripting and the ideas of the DOM, it should reveal that to be a seasoned, competent client-side developer in the future you will be required to know HTML/XHTML, CSS, and JavaScript in a very deep way. Readers are encouraged to learn these technologies in that order as they

...another. Before concluding the chapter, we'll present a few of the useful ...monly found on the Web.

ommon Scripts

This section provides a brief overview of simple, common types of JavaScripts used in Web pages. The scripts here are provided only with modest explanation on their use. However, even JavaScript novices should be able to use them by copying them into their pages with little or no modification. Other copy-paste scripts can be found online at sites such as http://www.webreference.com/js and http://www.dynamicdrive.com.

Last Modification Date

A common use of script is to add small bits of content or HTML to a page dynamically. For example, consider the need to write a last modification date to the bottom of every document in a Web site. Using a short JavaScript at the bottom of a page this could be quite easy as illustrated here:

```
<!DOCTYPE HTML PUBLIC "-//W3C//DTD HTML 4.01 Transitional//EN">
<html>
<head>
<title>Last Modified Example</title>
</head>
<body>
...Page Content here...
<hr>
<div align="center"><small>
&copy; 2000, Demo Company Inc.<br>

<script language="JavaScript">
<!--
  document.write("Document last modified: "+document.lastModified);
//-->
</script>

</small></div>
</body>
</html>
```

Using this script is quite easy: Just take the script element and its contents and copy-paste it where you like in your document, and put HTML elements around it or within the quotes for formatting.

Conditional Markup Inclusion

A common use of JavaScript is to add markup to a page in a conditional fashion. It is possible, using JavaScript, to detect the version of the browser in use and then produce some markup that fits. Consider the following example that produces a page with a **<blink>** tag if Netscape is detected or a **<marquee>** tag if Internet Explorer is in use:

```
<!DOCTYPE HTML PUBLIC "-//W3C//DTD HTML 4.01 Transitional//EN">
<html>
<head>
<title>Browser Detect Example</title>
</head>
<body>
<script language="JavaScript">
<!--
      var useragent=navigator.userAgent.toLowerCase();
      var is_nav=((useragent.indexOf('mozilla')!=-1));
      var is_ie=(useragent.indexOf("msie") != -1);

      if (is_nav && !is_ie)
      document.write("<blink>Netscape should blink</blink>");
   else
      document.write("<marquee>IE loves the marquee</marquee>");
//-->
</script>
<noscript>
      <b>Can't tell what browser you have</b>
</noscript>
</body>
</html>
```

Detection is not limited to a particular browser type, but to individual versions or even the support of a particular technology or plug-in. Readers interested in conditional page generation should consider using a script like the one at http://developer.netscape.com/docs/examples/javascript/browser_type.html or even a server-side tool like BrowserHawk (www.browserhawk.com) rather than rolling their own detection routines.

Pull-down Menu Navigation

A common use of JavaScript is for navigation systems. Designers recently have begun to rely more and more on pull-down menu systems within a site for navigation to frequently accessed areas. The following example shows the use of JavaScript.

```html
<!DOCTYPE HTML PUBLIC "-//W3C//DTD HTML 4.01 Transitional//EN">
<html>
<head>
<title>Select Navigation</title>
<style type="text/css">
<!--
   .nochoice    {color: black;}
   .choice      {color: blue;}
-->
</style>
<script language="JavaScript">
<!--
function redirect(pulldown) {
  newlocation = pulldown[pulldown.selectedIndex].value;
  if (newlocation != "")
   self.location = newlocation;
 }

function resetIfBlank(pulldown){
  possiblenewlocation = pulldown[pulldown.selectedIndex].value;
  if (possiblenewlocation == "")
    pulldown.selectedIndex = 0; /* reset to start */
}
//-->
</script>
</head>
<body>
<form name="navForm">
<b>Favorite Sites:</b>
<select name="menu" id="menu" onChange="resetIfBlank(this)">
<option value="" class="nochoice" selected> Choose your
site</option>
```

```
<option value="" class="nochoice"></option>
<option value="" class="nochoice">Search Sites</option>
<option value="" class="nochoice">------------------------
<option value="http://www.yahoo.com" class="choice">Yahoo!</option>
<option value="http://www.hotbot.com" class="choice">HotBot</option>
<option value="http://www.google.com" class="choice">Google</option>
<option value="" class="nochoice"></option>
<option value="" class="nochoice">Demos</option>
<option value="" class="nochoice">-----------------------</option>
<option value="http://www.democompany.com" class="choice">Demo
      Company</option>
</select>
<input type="button" value="go"
      onclick="redirect(document.navForm.menu)">
</form>
<script>
<!--
  document.navForm.menu.selectedIndex = 0;
//-->
</script>
</body>
</html>
```

Adding more choices to the menu is a matter of simply setting an **<option>** element's **class** to "choice" and its **value** attribute the URL of the document to load. Readers can remove the style sheet and **class** attributes if there is no interest in making choices and labels look different.

Note that this example requires the use of a button press to trigger a page load. However, it is easy enough to modify the script to make the menu trigger as soon as a choice is made. Change the **<select>** element to trigger the redirect function using the **onchange** event handler as shown here:

```
<select name="menu" onchange="redirect(document.navForm.menu)">
```

Readers should note that the use of pull-down navigation with such "hair triggers" does introduce some usability problems.

Rollover Buttons

A common use of JavaScript is for page embellishment. One of the most common embellishments is the inclusion of rollover buttons, a JavaScript feature that has been available since Netscape 3. A *rollover button* is a button that becomes active when the user positions the mouse over it. The button also can have a special activation state when it is pressed. To create a rollover button you first will need at least two, perhaps even three images, to represent each of the button's states—inactive, active, and unavailable. A sample set of rollover images is shown here:

To add this rollover image to the page, simply use the **<img>** tag like another image. The idea is to swap the image out when the mouse passes over the image and switch back to the original image when the mouse leaves the image. By literally swapping the value of the **src** attribute when the mouse is over the image, you can achieve the rollover effect. Assuming you have two images, buttonon.gif and buttonoff.gif, this in essence is what the following script, which should work in nearly any browser, would do:

```
<!DOCTYPE HTML PUBLIC "-//W3C//DTD HTML 4.01 Transitional//EN">
<html>
<head>
<title>Rollover Script</title>
<script language="JavaScript">
<!--
/* check to insure rollovers work */
if (document.images)
{
 /* preload the images */
 buttonoff = new Image();
 buttonoff.src = "buttonoff.gif";
 buttonon = new Image();
 buttonon.src = "buttonon.gif";
}
```

SRC equal to the image
images is the names.
button1.gif, we add
statement:

butto
butt
b

```
/* function to set image to on s
function On(imageName)
{
  if (document.images)
   {
     document[imageName].src = ev
   }
}


/* function to reset image back
function Off(imageName)
{
  if (document.images)
    {
      document[imageName].src = eval(imageName+"off.src");
    }
}
//-->
</script>
</head>
<body>
<h1 align="center">Rollover Fun</h1>
<hr>
<a href="http://www.democompany.com" onMouseover="On('button')"
   onMouseout = "Off('button')">
<img src="buttonoff.gif" name="button" width="90" height="20"
    border="0"></a>
</body>
</html>
```

Let's take a look at how the code works. The first section of the JavaScript checks to make sure the browser supports the images part of the document object model. This capability is required if rollover buttons are to work. If the browser supports this feature, the images are loaded in and assigned names. Once the page is loaded, the user can move the mouse over the image. The link, as indicated by the **<a>** element, has two event handlers: one for the mouse passing over the image (**onmouseover**) and one for the mouse leaving the image (**onmouseout**). These handlers call our defined **On()** and **Off()** JavaScript functions, respectively. The function **On()** simply sets the **src** of the **<img>** element to the name of the image passed to it and appends **on.src**, which changes the image to the on state. The function **Off()** does the opposite by setting the

...ame with **off.src** appended to it. The key to adding more
...or example, if we wanted to add another button called
...the following code to the **<script>** element within the first if

```
1off = new Image();
on1off.src = "button1off.gif";
tton1on = new Image();
buttonon1.src = "button1on.gif";
```

and the following code later on in the document:

```
<a href="URL to load " onmouseover="On('button1')"
    onmouseout = "Off('button1')">
<img src="buttonoff1.gif" name="button1" width="90"
    height="20" border="0"></a>
```

Of course the URL to visit, height, width, and even image name can vary from rollover image to rollover image. Make especially sure to name objects uniquely and consistently and set the name attribute for the **<img>** element properly. Because rollovers are so common on Web sites, there are many sites, such as http://www.webreference.com/js, that offer rollover tutorials. Tools such as Macromedia's Dreamweaver also can create the code instantly when provided with two images.

Form Validation

Form validation, the final example of script usage, probably is the most important use of scripting on the Web. Interestingly enough, it was the original reason JavaScript was introduced. JavaScript form validation is the process of checking the validity of user-supplied data in an HTML form before it is submitted to a server-side program such as a CGI program. By checking data before it is sent to a server, you can avoid a lot of user frustration, and reduce communication time between the Web browser and the server.

Now given, as discussed in previous sections, that it is easy to look at a field's value, suppose that you want to make sure that the user enters something in the field before submitting a form. Checking the contents of the field is fairly easy. Consider the example here, which looks at the contents of a field and makes sure it isn't blank before allowing submission:

```
<!DOCTYPE HTML PUBLIC "-//W3C//DTD HTML 4.01 Transitional//EN">
<html>
```

```
<head>
<title>Simple Form Validation</title>
<script language="JavaScript">
<!--
function validate()
  {
   if (document.myform.username.value == "")
    {
     alert('Please enter your name');
     return false;
    }
   else
    return true;
  }
// -->
</script>
</head>
<body>
<form name="myform" id="myform" action="http://www.democompany.com"
      method="get" onsubmit="return validate()">
<b>Name:</b>
<input type="text" name="username" id="username"
       size="25" maxlength="25">
<br><br>
<input type="submit" value="Submit">
</form>
</body>
</html>
```

In this example, the function **validate()** is called and the contents of the field **username** is checked to see whether it is blank or contains information. If the field is left blank when the user clicks the button, the user is told to complete the field and a false value is returned. Otherwise a return value of true is set and the submission is allowed to continue. The return value is related to the call via the HTML event handler attribute **onsubmit**, which is triggered when the user clicks the submit button. The submission will occur unless the event returns a **false** value. Notice how the validation function **validate()** returns a **true** or **false** value, based upon the user's input. Expanding this example to check more fields is not difficult, as was shown in the larger example at the end of Chapter 11.

Note	*Another approach to form field validation is to catch errors as users move from field to field. By using the **onblur** attribute, you can sense when a user has deselected a field and is trying to select another field. Be careful: Many users might be annoyed by form validation using **onblur**, and it might not even always work because of bugs in JavaScript implementations.*

The previous discussion is meant to serve only as a basic introduction to the concept of form validation. It is easy enough to add more fields to the example and even check for other types of data. However, even if you are an experienced programmer, it is not suggested that you go out and attempt to create your own validation scripts for e-mail addresses, credit card numbers, zip codes, and so on. Many libraries already exist that perform these tasks; these libraries are available from JavaScript archive sites as well as from Netscape's original form validation library, located at the following address: http://developer.netscape.com/docs/examples/javascript/formval/overview.html

Summary

Client-side technologies have their place in a Web site. The evolution of scripting technologies has offloaded some of the processing that traditionally occurred on the server. For example, validating form field entries by using JavaScript or VBScript on the client makes more sense than relegating this processing to the server. Integrating scripts into a Web page comes in two major forms: within the **<script>** element, and as event handlers in the form of HTML attributes. By using simple scripts, you can create simple interface changes such a navigation menus or rollover buttons or even perform useful tasks such as form validation. Although the intersection between HTML and scripting originally was very distinct, the idea of DHTML shows that you can modify the very elements in a page through the Document Object Model. Using this approach to scripting Web pages along with improved page layout facilities, such as style sheets, you can make your pages come alive with interaction and movement. Of course this power comes with a price. Designers must ensure that there HTML is well formed, objects named properly, and the various browser incompatibilities well considered before adding script to a page.

Chapter 14

Client-Side Programming: Plug-ins, ActiveX, and Java

The last chapter discusses how scripts could be added to HTML pages. Scripts can manipulate a variety of form elements and, in the case of Dynamic HTML, the page elements themselves. Scripts also are used to access embedded binary objects. As discussed in Chapter 9, embedded objects can be used to bring new media types, such as sounds and movies, to the Web. They also can be used to add small executable programs to a page. Binary objects come in many forms, including Netscape plug-ins, ActiveX controls and Java applets. Each of these requires special HTML elements. In the future, all included media types will be added with the **<object>** element. Until objects are standardized, however, it is useful to understand each individual technology and how it can intersect with HTML.

Scripting, Programming, and Objects

You might wonder why this chapter is separate from the last one. With both scripts and embedded objects, the interactivity takes place on the client side. What's the difference? Why distinguish between scripting and objects? Remember the point of Web client-side scripting—small bits of interpreted code used to add a bit of functionality to a page or fill the gaps in an application. Scripting is *not* necessarily as complex or general as programming, although it often seems as if it is. Programming is more generalized than scripting; programming enables you to create just about anything that you can imagine, although it tends to be more complex in some sense than scripting. Think about checking the data fields of a form; you need only a few lines of code to make sure the fields are filled. Now consider trying to create something sophisticated, such as a full-blown video game within a Web page. This takes more than a few lines of code, and probably should be programmed in a language such as Java, C/C++, or Visual Basic. In fact building objects is not trivial. It can require significant knowledge of programming. You might be able to string together pre-made objects, generically called *components*, by using HTML and either JavaScript or VBScript. Consequently, for most casual Web page designers, putting together a custom object probably isn't necessary. This chapter discusses each of the object technologies, as well as how such objects can be inserted into a Web page in conjunction with HTML and scripting.

Plug-ins

Plug-ins such as the Flash player, Quicktime player, and others, are small helper programs (components) that run within the context of the browser itself. Plug-ins are primarily a Netscape technology and have been around since Netscape Navigator 2. They are supported by some other browsers, notably Opera (www.operasoftware.com). The **<embed>** element used to reference plug-ins is supported under Internet Explorer, although it does result in the launch of an ActiveX control (a similar Microsoft technology discussed later in the chapter). Although plug-ins can go a long way toward extending the possible capabilities of a browser, the technology does have its drawbacks. Users must locate and download plug-ins, install them, and even restart their browsers. Many users find this rather complicated. Netscape 4.*x* offers some installation relief with somewhat self-installing plug-ins and other features, but plug-ins remain troublesome. To further combat this problem, many of the most commonly requested plug-ins, such as Macromedia's Flash, are being included as a standard feature with Netscape browsers. However, even if installation were not such a problem, plug-ins are not available on every machine; an executable program, or *binary*, must be created for each particular operating system. Because of this machine-specific approach, many plug-ins work only on Windows 98/NT. A decreasing number of plug-ins work on Macintosh or UNIX. Finally, each plug-in installed on a system is a persistent extension to the browser, and takes up memory and disk space.

The benefit of plug-ins is that they can be well integrated into Web pages. They can be included by using the HTML elements **<embed>** or **<object>**. Typically, the **<embed>** syntax is used, but the **<object>** syntax is the preferred method and eventually will supplant **<embed>** completely. In general, the **<embed>** element takes an **src** attribute to specify the URL of the included binary object. The **height** and **width** attributes often are used to indicate the pixel dimensions of the included object, if it is visible. To embed a short Audio Video Interleaved (AVI) format movie called welcome.avi that can be viewed by the video plug-in (generally installed with Netscape 3.*x* and 4.*x* generation browsers), use the following HTML fragment:

```
<embed src="welcome.avi" height="100" width="100">
```

The **<embed>** element displays the plug-in (in this case a movie) as part of the HTML document.

A browser can have many plug-ins installed. To check which plug-ins are installed in Netscape, the user can enter a strange URL, such as **about:plugins**, or look under the browser's Help menu for an entry that reads "About Plug-ins." The browser will show a list of plug-ins that are installed, the associated MIME type that will invoke each plug-in, and information as to whether that plug-in is enabled. Figure 14-1 shows an example of the plug-in information page.

<embed> Syntax

The primary way to load plug-ins for Netscape browsers is to use the HTML element **<embed>**, which is not part of any HTML specification. It would be preferable to use the **<object>** element, which is part of the specification, but **<object>** does not work with those older browsers; only under Microsoft Internet Explorer 3 and above, and Netscape 4 and above. For backward compatibility, you might have to use both forms, as shown later in this chapter. The general syntax of the **<embed>** element can be found in the element reference in Appendix A.

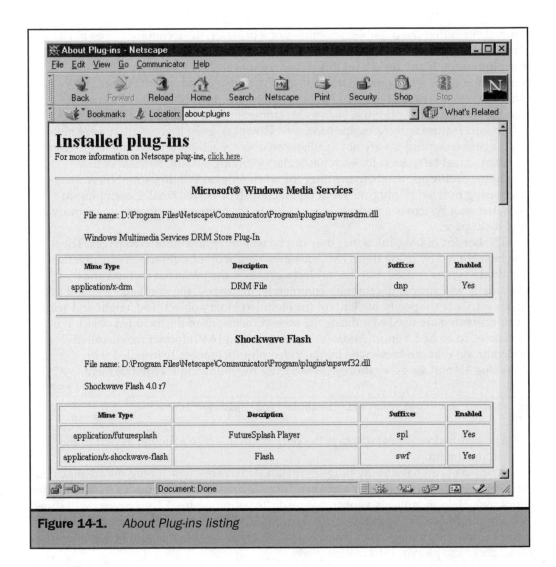

Figure 14-1.   *About Plug-ins listing*

The most important attribute for the **<embed>** element probably is **src**, which is set to the URL of the data object that is to be passed to the plug-in and embedded in the page. The browser generally determines the MIME type of the file—and thus the plug-in to pass the data to—by the filename suffix. For example, a file such as test1.dcr would be mapped to a MIME type of application/x-director and passed to a Shockwave for Director plug-in. In some cases, however, the plug-in to use with a particular **<embed>** tag is not obvious. The plug-in might not need to use a **src** attribute if it reads all of its data at run time or doesn't need any external data.

Because plug-ins are rectangular, embedded objects similar to images, the **<embed>** element has many of the same attributes as the **<img>** element:

- **align**   Use to align the object relative to the page and allow text to flow around the object. To achieve the desired text layout, you might have to use the **
** element with the **clear** attribute.

- **hspace** and **vspace**   Use to set the buffer region, in pixels, between the embedded object and the surrounding text.

- **border**   Use to set a border for the plug-in, in pixels. As with images, setting this attribute to zero might be useful when using the embedded object as a link.

- **height** and **width**   Use to set the vertical and horizontal size of the embedded object, typically in pixels, although you can express them as percentage values. Values for **height** and **width** should always be set, unless the **hidden** attribute is used. Setting the **hidden** attribute to **true** in the **<embed>** element causes the plug-in to be hidden and overrides any **height** and **width** settings, as well as any effect the object might have on layout.

Custom Plug-in Attributes

In addition to the standard attributes for the **<embed>** element, plug-ins might have custom attributes to communicate specialized information between the HTML page and the plug-in code. A movie player plug-in can have a **loop** attribute to indicate how many times to loop the movie. Remember that under HTML, the browser ignores all nonstandard attributes when parsing the HTML. All other attributes are passed to the plug-in, allowing the plug-in to examine the list for any custom attributes that could modify its behavior. Enumerating all the possible custom attributes here is not possible. Each particular plug-in used can have a variety of custom attributes. You should be certain to look at the documentation for whatever plug-in you are going to use.

Attributes for Installation of Plug-ins

Having users figure out themselves which plug-in to install manually isn't the best solution. You can set the **pluginspage** attribute equal to a URL that indicates the instructions for installing the plug-in. This way, if the browser encounters an **<embed>** element that it can't handle, it visits the specified page and provides information on how to download and install the plug-in. Starting with Netscape 4, however, this attribute automatically points to a special Netscape plug-in finder page.

The Netscape 4 browser release also simplifies the plug-in installation process by introducing the JAR Installation Manager (JIM), which is used to install Java Archive files (JARs). JAR files are a collection of files, including plug-ins, which can be automatically downloaded and installed. Set the **pluginurl** attribute for the **<embed>** element to the URL of a JAR file containing the plug-in that is needed. If the user doesn't have the appropriate plug-in already installed, the browser invokes JIM with the specified JAR file and begins the download and installation process. The user has control over this process. The downloaded objects can be signed—a type of authentication—to help users avoid downloading malicious code. Figure 14-2 shows a sample JIM window under Netscape 4.

In Netscape 4 or greater, the **pluginurl** attribute takes precedence over **pluginspage**. However, if neither attribute is used, the Netscape browser should default to a plug-in finder page.

<noembed>

One important aspect of plug-ins is the idea of **<noembed>**. Some browsers don't understand Netscape's plug-in architecture, or even the **<embed>** element. Rather than lock out these browsers from a Web page, the **<noembed>** element enables you to provide some alternative text or marked-up content. In the following short example, an AVI video is embedded in the page. The **<noembed>** element contains an image, which in turn has an alternative text reading set with the **alt** attribute. Note how the

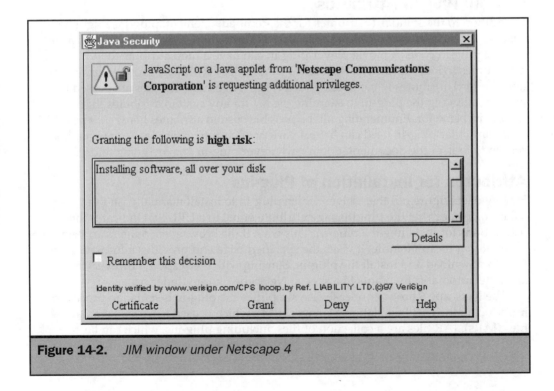

Figure 14-2.   *JIM window under Netscape 4*

example degrades from a very sophisticated setting all the way down to a text-only environment:

```
<embed src="welcome.avi" height="100" width="100">
<noembed>
   <img src="welcome.gif" alt="Welcome to Demo Company, Inc.">
</noembed>
```

One potential problem with the **<noembed>** approach occurs when a browser supports plug-ins but lacks the specific plug-in to deal with the included binary object. In this case, the user is presented with a broken puzzle-piece icon or a similar icon, and then is directed to a page to download the missing plug-in. As discussed previously you should always set the **pluginurl** or **pluginspage** attribute to start the user on the process of getting the plug-in needed to view the content.

<object> Syntax for Plug-ins

Starting with Netscape 4, the **<object>** element can be used to include a variety of object types in a Web page, including Netscape plug-ins. Like the **<embed>** element, the **<object>** element's attributes determine the type of object to include, as well as the type and location of the plug-in. The **<object>** element supports alternative representations, if the browser isn't capable of supporting the object. The **<embed>** element that currently is used for plug-ins does not handle this well, although it does provide the **<noembed>** syntax. The following paragraph discusses the syntax of **<object>** as it relates to the **<embed>** element (a more generalized discussion of the **<object>** element is presented in "ActiveX Controls," later in the chapter):

The primary attribute for **<object>** when referencing plug-ins is **data** which represents the URL of the object's data and is equivalent to the **src** attribute of **<embed>**. Like the **<embed>** element, the **type** attribute represents the MIME type of the object's data. This sometimes can be inferred from the value of the **data** attribute. The **codebase** attribute, which is similar to the **pluginspage** attribute, represents the URL of the plug-in. The **classid** attribute is used to specify the URL to use to install the plug-in, by using the JIM (JAR Installed Manager). If no **classid** attribute is specified and the object can't be handled, the object is ignored, and any nested HTML is displayed. The **id** attribute is used to set the name of the object for scripting. If the browser can't handle the type, or can't determine the type, it can't embed the object. Subsequent HTML is parsed as normal. The following is an example of using Netscape's LiveAudio plug-in under Netscape 4 with the **<object>** syntax:

```
<object data="click.wav" type="audio/wav" height="60" width="144"
       autostart="false">
   <b>Sorry, no LiveAudio installed...</b>
</object>
```

Page authors should avoid referencing plug-ins with the **<object>** element, because compatibility issues with Microsoft Internet Explorer might arise. For the complete syntax of the **<object>** element, refer to the element reference in Appendix A.

Scripting and Plug-ins

Plug-ins can be accessed from a scripting language. Each plug-in in a document can be referenced in Netscape's version of JavaScript as an element of the **embeds[ ]** collection, which is part of the document object as discussed in the previous chapter. Under Netscape you can determine which plug-ins are available in the browser by using the **plugins[ ]** collection, which is part of the navigator object in JavaScript. The following markup displays the plug-ins that are installed in a Netscape browser:

```
<!DOCTYPE HTML PUBLIC "-//W3C//DTD HTML 4.01 Transitional//EN">
<html>
<head>
<title>Print Plug-ins</title>
</head>
<body>
<h2 align="center">Plug-ins Installed</h2>
<hr>
<script language="javascript">
<!--
if (navigator.appName == "Microsoft Internet Explorer")
 document.write("Plug-ins[] collection not supported under IE");
else
 {
   num_plugins = navigator.plugins.length;
   for (count=0; count < num_plugins; count++)
     document.write(navigator.plugins[count].name + "<br>");
 }
//-->
</script>
</body>
</html>
```

Note that this example will not display the plug-ins under Internet Explorer, because that browser doesn't support the same **plugins[ ]** collection. Under Netscape, however, you can use some simple if-then logic to determine which HTML to use if a particular plug-in is loaded in the browser.

Once plug-ins are used in a page they always should be named using the **name** and **id** attributes so they can be accessed easily from JavaScript. For example, the markup

```
<embed src="welcome.avi" name="welcomemovie" id="welcomemovie"
    height="100" width="100">
```

gives this instance of the LiveVideo plug-in the name WelcomeMovie. After the plug-in is named, it can be accessed from JavaScript as **document.welcomemovie**. If it is the second plug-in in the page, it also could be referenced as **document.embeds[1]**. Why not "index 2"? Arrays in JavaScript, which is how collections are implemented, start numbering at zero, so **document.embeds[0]** references the first plug-in, **document.embeds[1]** references the second plug-in, and so on.

After you name an occurrence of a plug-in in a page, you might be able to manipulate the plug-in's actions even after you load the page. Netscape browsers, starting with the 3.x generation, include a technology called *LiveConnect* that enables JavaScript to communicate with Java applets and plug-ins. However, only plug-ins written to support LiveConnect can be manipulated using JavaScript. Fortunately many plug-ins such as Macromedia Flash support LiveConnect. This simple example shows how LiveConnect works by using form buttons to start and stop the playing of a Flash movie in a page using JavaScript:

```
<!DOCTYPE HTML PUBLIC "-//W3C//DTD HTML 4.01 Transitional//EN">
<html>
<head>
<title>Flash JavaScript Control Example</title>
<script>
<!--

var loaded=false;
function playFlash(id)
{
    flashFile = eval("window.document."+id);
    if (!loaded)
      {
       while (!loaded)
          {
           if(flashFile.PercentLoaded() == 100)
             {
              flashFile.Play();
                  loaded = true;
             }
          }
      }
    else
      flashFile.Play();
```

PROGRAMMING AND HTML

```
}

function stopFlash(id)
{
  flashFile = eval("window.document."+id);
  flashFile.StopPlay()
}
//-->
</script>
</head>
<body bgcolor="#FFFFFF">

<h2>Plug-in and JavaScript Interaction</h2>
<embed src="example.swf" quality="high"
pluginspage="http://www.macromedia.com/shockwave/download/
index.cgi?P1_Prod_Version=ShockwaveFlash"
   type="application/x-shockwave-flash" width="400"
   height="250" id="example" name="example"
   swliveconnect="true">

<noembed>
     You need Flash and Netscape for this demo
</noembed>
</embed>
<hr>
<form>
  <input type="button" name="Button1" value="Start Flash"
         onClick="playFlash('example')">
  <input type="button" name="Button2" value="Stop Flash"
         onClick="stopFlash('example')">
</form>
</body>
</html>
```

This example can be viewed in action at www.htmlref.com/examples/chapter14/flash.htm.

> **Note**
>
> *One very important attribute that will ensure that this example works is the* ***swliveconnect="true"****. Without this attribute the demo should not work. Even so, the preceding example is very specific to Netscape. Although it might work under Internet Explorer there is no guarantee of this. Furthermore, the implementation of LiveConnect is buggy and might not work under all versions of Navigator. However, the example still should illustrate the basic concept of script talking to a plug-in.*

Tying together plug-ins by using a scripting language in conjunction with LiveConnect hints at the power of such component models as Netscape's plug-ins. However, Netscape plug-ins often are passed over in favor of ActiveX or Java applets for general programming tasks, and plug-ins often are regulated to handling new media forms as this example just demonstrated.

ActiveX Controls

ActiveX (http://www.microsoft.com/com/tech/activex.asp), which is the Internet portion of the Component Object Model (COM), is Microsoft's component technology for creating small components, or *controls*, within a Web page. ActiveX is intended to distribute these controls via the Internet to add new functionality to browsers such as Internet Explorer. ActiveX controls are more similar to generalized programmed components than plug-ins, because ActiveX controls can reside beyond the browser within container programs such as Microsoft Office. ActiveX controls are similar to Netscape plug-ins insofar as they are persistent and machine specific. Although this makes resource use a problem, installation is not an issue: The components download and install automatically.

Security is a big concern for ActiveX controls. Because these small pieces of code could potentially have full access to a user's system, they could cause serious damage. This capability, combined with automatic installation, creates a serious problem with ActiveX. End users might be quick to click a button to install new functionality, only to accidentally get their hard drives erased. This unlimited functionality of ActiveX controls creates a gaping security hole. To address this problem, Microsoft provides authentication information to indicate who wrote a control, in the form of code signed by a certificate, as shown in Figure 14-3.

Certificates provide only some indication that the control creator is reputable; they do nothing to prevent a control from actually doing something malicious. Safe Web browsing should be practiced by accepting controls only from reputable sources.

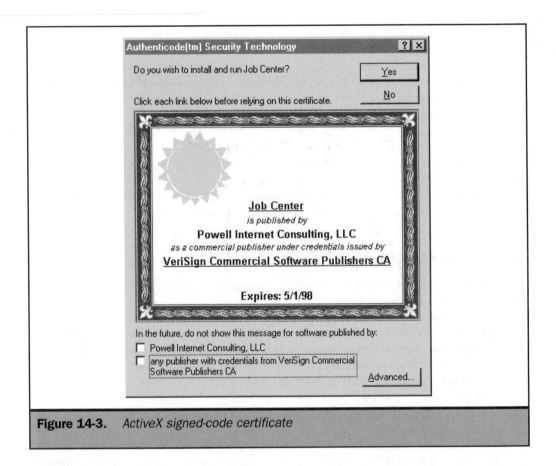

Figure 14-3. ActiveX signed-code certificate

Adding Controls to Web Pages

Adding an ActiveX control to a Web page requires the use of the **<object>** element. The basic form of the **<object>** element for an ActiveX control is as follows:

```
<object classid="CLSID:class-identifier"
        height="pixels"
        width="pixels"
        id="unique identifier">

Parameters and alternative text rendering

</object>
```

classid is the most important attribute for the **<object>** element when you insert ActiveX controls. The value of **classid** identifies the object to include. Each ActiveX control has a class identifier of the form "CLSID: *class-identifier,*" where the value for *class-identifier* is a complex string, such as the following, which uniquely identifies the control:

```
99B42120-6EC7-11CF-A6C7-00AA00A47DD2
```

This is the identifier for the ActiveX label control. The other important attributes for the basic form of **<object>** when used with ActiveX controls include **height** and **width**, which are set to the pixel dimensions of the included control, and **id**, which associates a unique identifier with the control for scripting purposes. Between the **<object>** and **</object>** tags are various **<param>** elements that specify information to pass to the control, and alternative HTML markup that displays in non-ActiveX-aware browsers. The following is a complete example that uses the **<object>** element to insert an ActiveX control into a Web page. The markup shown specifies a simple label control. Figure 14-4 shows the rendering of the control under Internet Explorer 4 and Netscape 4.

```html
<!DOCTYPE HTML PUBLIC "-//W3C//DTD HTML 4.0 Transitional//EN">
<html>
<head>
<title>ActiveX Label Test</title>
</head>
<body>

<h1 align="center">ActiveX Demo</h1>
<hr>

<object classid="CLSID:99B42120-6EC7-11CF-A6C7-00AA00A47DD2"
        id="IeLabel1" height="65" width="325">
  <param name="_ExtentX" value="6879">
  <param name="_ExtentY" value="1376">
  <param name="Caption" value="Hello World">
  <param name="Alignment" value="4">
  <param name="Mode" value="1">
  <param name="ForeColor" value="#FF0000">
  <param name="FontName" value="Arial">
  <param name="FontSize" value="36">
  <b>Hello World for you non-ActiveX users!</b>
</object>
```

```
</body>
</html>
```

After you look at the ActiveX Label Test markup you might have questions about how to determine the **classid** value for the control and the associated **<param>** values that can be set. However, providing a chart for all the controls and their associated identifiers isn't necessary. Many Web page tools, including Microsoft Visual InterDev support the automated insertion of controls into a page, as well as configuration of the various control properties.

Installing ActiveX Controls

As mentioned earlier, the most important attribute in the **<object>** syntax probably is **classid**, which is used to identify the particular object to include. For example, the syntax "CLSID:class-identifier" is for registered ActiveX controls. Generally, however, when the **<OBJECT>** element supports other included items well, **classid** might be set to other forms, such as "java: Blink.class," as discussed later in the chapter when Java applets are presented. Microsoft also allows the use of the **code** attribute for the **<object>** element; **code** is used to set the URL of the Java class file to include.

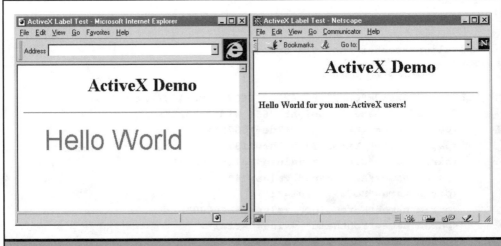

Figure 14-4. Rendering of ActiveX control under Internet Explorer and under Netscape

ActiveX and plug-ins are similar in the sense that both are persistent, platform-specific components. ActiveX controls, however, are easy to download and install. This installation, or running of ActiveX controls, can be described as a series of steps:

- The browser loads an HTML page that references an ActiveX control with the **<object>** element and its associated **classid** attribute.

- The browser checks the system registry to see whether the control specified by the **classid** value is installed; this control takes the form "CLSID: some-id-number."

- If the control is installed, the browser compares the **codebase** version attribute stored in the registry against the **codebase** version attribute in the HTML page. If a newer version is specified in the page, a newer control is needed.

- If the control is not installed or a newer control is needed, the value of the **codebase** attribute is used to determine the location of the control to download. The **codetype** attribute also can be used to set the MIME type of the object to download. Most inclusions of ActiveX controls avoid this, because it tends to default to the MIME type application/octet-stream.

For security reasons, the browser checks to see whether the code is signed, before the download and installation begins. If the code is not signed, the user is warned. If the code is signed, the user is presented with an Authenticode certificate bearing the identity of the author of the control. Based on these criteria, the user can allow or deny the installation of the control on his or her system. If the user accepts the control, it is automatically downloaded, installed, and invoked in the page for its specific function. Finally, the control is stored persistently on the client machine for further invocation. This process can be avoided when the **declare** attribute is present. The **declare** attribute is used to indicate whether the **<object>** is being defined only and not actually instantiated until later **<object>** occurrences, which will start the installation process.

 *The W3C HTML 4 specification also indicates use of the **standby** attribute, which can be used to specify a message to display as the object is being downloaded. This currently is not supported by most browsers.*

Passing Data to ActiveX Controls

Unlike plug-ins, ActiveX controls do not use special element attributes to pass data. Instead, they use a completely different element, called **<param>**, which is enclosed within the **<object>** element. You can pass parameters to the label control by using the **<param>** elements, as shown here:

```
<object classid="CLSID:99B42120-6EC7-11CF-A6C7-00AA00A47DD2"
        id="IeLabel1" height="65" width="325">
```

```
    <param name="Caption" value="Hello World">
    <param name="FontName" value="Arial">
    <param name="FontSize" value="36">
    <b>Hello World for you non-ActiveX users!</b>
</object>
```

In this case, the **Caption** parameter is set to Hello World, the **FontName** parameter is set to Arial, and the **FontSize** parameter is set to 36 points.

ActiveX Controls and Scripting

Similar to plug-ins, you can control ActiveX controls by using a scripting language such as JavaScript or VBScript. One advantage to ActiveX controls is that many pre-made controls with exposed properties are available that can be easily manipulated by a scripting language. Before a control can be modified, however, it must be named by using the **id** attribute. After it is named, scripting code for a particular event can be set for the control so that it can respond to events such as user clicks or mouse movements. The following simple example shows how two ActiveX command buttons can be used to communicate with a label control to change its message:

```
<!DOCTYPE HTML PUBLIC "-//W3C//DTD HTML 4.01 Transitional//EN">
<html>
<head>
<title>ActiveX Scripting Demo</title>
</head>
<body>
<h1 align="center">ActiveX and Scripting</h1>
<hr>

<b>Label:</b>
<object id="Label1" width="200" height="80" align="top"
    classid="CLSID:978C9E23-D4B0-11CE-BF2D-00AA003F40D0">
        <param name="BackColor" value="8454143">
        <param name="Caption" value="I'm a label">
        <param name="Size" value="4233;1212">
        <param name="BorderColor" value="8421504">
        <param name="BorderStyle" value="1">
        <param name="FontHeight" value="200">
        <param name="FontCharSet" value="0">
        <param name="FontPitchAndFamily" value="2">
        <param name="ParagraphAlign" value="3">
    </object>
```

```
<hr>
<script language="JavaScript" for="CommandButton1" event="Click()">
<!--
Label1.Caption = "The button was clicked!"
//-->
</script>

<object id="CommandButton1" width="168" height="52"
    classid="CLSID:D7053240-CE69-11CD-A777-00DD01143C57">
        <param name="ForeColor" value="65535">
        <param name="BackColor" value="10485760">
        <param name="Caption" value="Update Label">
        <param name="Size" value="3577;1101">
        <param name="FontHeight" value="200">
        <param name="FontCharSet" value="0">
        <param name="FontPitchAndFamily" value="2">
        <param name="ParagraphAlign" value="3">
</object>

<script language="JavaScript" for="CommandButton2" event="Click()">
<!--
Label1.Caption = "I'm a label"
//-->
</script>

<object id="CommandButton2" width="168" height="52"
    classid="CLSID:D7053240-CE69-11CD-A777-00DD01143C57">
        <param name="ForeColor" value="65535">
        <param name="BackColor" value="10485760">
        <param name="Caption" value="Reset Label">
        <param name="Size" value="3577;1101">
        <param name="FontHeight" value="200">
        <param name="FontCharSet" value="0">
        <param name="FontPitchAndFamily" value="2">
        <param name="ParagraphAlign" value="3">
</object>
</body>
</html>
```

**PROGRAMMING
AND HTML**

> **Note**
>
> *This example uses JavaScript for event handling, but developers might find that VBScript is preferred to interact with ActiveX controls. Given that ActiveX is such a Microsoft-specific technology the use of VBScript might not be a problem. (This example won't work in anything other than Internet Explorer 3 or better running on a Windows-based system.)*

Using ActiveX Without Programming

Developers can access an abundance of available controls for various purposes. Many repositories of free and commercial ActiveX controls, such as ActiveX.com (http://www.activex.com), are available on the Web. Microsoft also includes a variety of controls with its applications including Internet Explorer. Page designers also can write their own ActiveX controls, although in some cases this might be like reinventing the wheel. Controls can be created using a variety of languages such as Visual Basic, C++, and Java. You also can convert existing Windows programs to controls. The ActiveX model is not limited to client-side controls. It is part of a larger Microsoft development framework that has undergone numerous name changes and at the time of this writing is now known as the .NET platform. Undoubtedly, that might change by the time you read this so for the very latest information on development for the Microsoft platform see http://msdn.microsoft.com.

Java Applets

Whereas both Microsoft's ActiveX and Netscape's plug-ins are platform and browser specific, Sun Microsystems' Java technology (http://java.sun.com) aims to provide a platform-neutral development language allowing programs to be written once and deployed on any machine, browser, or operating system that supports the Java virtual machine (JVM). Java uses small Java programs, called *applets*, that were first introduced by Sun's HotJava browser. Today applets are supported by just about any Web browser, including Netscape Navigation and Microsoft Internet Explorer. Of course the nirvana of perfect cross-platform development never really materialized; Java applets continue to play an important role even in client-side development, particularly within controlled environments such as intranets.

Applets are written in the Java language and compiled to a machine-independent byte-code, which is downloaded automatically to the Java-capable browser and run within the browser environment. But even with a fast processor, the end system might appear to run the byte-code slowly compared to a natively compiled application, because the byte code must be interpreted by the JVM. Even with recent Just-In-Time (JIT) compilers in newer browsers, Java often doesn't deliver performance equal to natively compiled applications. Even if compilation weren't an issue, current Java applets generally aren't persistent; they might have to be downloaded again in the future. Java-enabled browsers act like thin-client applications, because they add code only when they need it. In this sense, the browser doesn't become bloated with added features, but expands and contracts upon use.

Security in Java has been a serious concern from the outset. Because programs are downloaded and run automatically, a malicious program could be downloaded and run without the user being able to stop it. Under the first implementation of the technology, Java applets had little access to resources outside the browser's environment. Within Web pages, applets can't write to local disks or perform other harmful functions. This framework has been referred to as the *Java sandbox*. Developers who want to provide Java functions outside of the sandbox must write Java applications, which run as separate applications from browsers. Other Internet programming technologies (plug-ins and ActiveX) provide little or no safety from damaging programs.

Oddly, Java developers often want to add just these types of insecure features, as well as such powerful features as persistence and inter-object communication. In fact, under new browsers, extended access can be requested for signed Java applets. (A *signed applet* enables users to determine who authored its code, and to accept or reject the applet accordingly.) Java applets can securely request limited disk access, limited disk access and network usage, limited disk read access and unlimited disk write access, and unrestricted access. Users downloading an applet that is requesting any enhanced privileges are presented with a dialog box that outlines the requested access and presents the applet's credentials in the form of its digital signature. The user then can approve or reject the applet's request. If the user doesn't approve the request, the applet can continue to run, but it can't perform the denied actions.

Java code looks very much like C++. The following code fragment shows a simple example of a Java applet:

```
import java.applet.Applet;
import java.awt.Graphics;

public class helloworld extends Applet {

    public void paint(Graphics g)
      {
         g.drawString("Hello World", 50, 25);
      }

}
```

Sending this code through a Java compiler (such as JavaSoft's javac) should produce a class file called helloworld.class, which can be used on a Web page to display the phrase "Hello World." You can use the **<applet>** element to add a Java applet to a Web page. As with the **<embed>** element, you must indicate the object to add. In this case, use the **code** attribute to indicate the URL of the Java class file to load. Because this is an included object, the **height** and **width** attributes should also be set.

ple includes the HelloWorld applet in a Web page. Figure 14-5
of the Java example under Netscape 4 with Java turned on and

```
                PUBLIC "-//W3C//DTD HTML 4.01 Transitional//EN">
<html>
<head>
<title>Java Hello World</title>
</head>
<body>
<h1 align="center">Java Applet Demo</h1>
<hr>
<applet code="helloworld.class"
        height="50" width="175">
<h1>Hello World for you non-Java-aware browsers</h1>
</applet>
</body>
</html>
```

In the preceding code example, between **<applet>** and **</applet>** is an alternative rendering for browsers that don't support Java or the **<applet>** element, or that have Java support disabled.

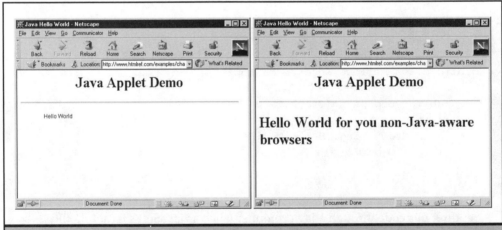

Figure 14-5. *Java example under Netscape 4 with Java turned on and off*

<applet> Syntax

Because Java applets are included objects, just like Netscape plug-ins, the syntax for the **<applet>** element is similar to the **<embed>** element, particularly for things such as alignment and sizing. The general syntax for **<applet>** is shown in the element reference in Appendix A.

The most important attribute for the **<applet>** element probably is **code**, which is set to the URL of the Java class to load into the page. The **codebase** attribute can be set to the URL of the directory that contains the Java classes; otherwise, the current document's URL is used for any relative URLs.

Because Java applets are rectangular, embedded objects similar to images or plug-ins, the **<applet>** element has many of the same attributes as images and plug-ins, including **align**, **height**, **width**, **hspace**, and **vspace**.

The **archive** attribute can be used to include many classes into a single archive file, which then can be downloaded to the local disk. The file specified by the **archive** attribute can be a compressed PKZIP file (.zip) or a Java Archive (.jar), which can be made with a JAR packaging utility. For example,

```
<applet archive="bunchofclasses.zip"
        code="sampleApp.class"
        width="560"
        height="270">
</applet>
```

downloads all the classes in bunchofclasses.zip. After the file is downloaded, the **code** attribute is examined and the archive is checked to see whether sampleApp.class exists there. If not, it is fetched from the network. Because of the expense of fetching many class files by using HTTP, ideally, you should attempt to archive all potentially used classes and send them simultaneously. You also can derive some caching benefit by using the **archive** attribute, because it keeps class files in the user's cache or a temporary directory. According to the HTML 4 specification, the **archive** attribute can take a comma-separated list of archive files, although this actually might not be supported by today's browsers.

Passing Data to Java Applets

Unlike plug-ins, Java applets don't use special attributes to pass data. Instead, like ActiveX control's syntax they use a different element called **<param>**, which is enclosed within the **<applet>** element as the way to pass in information. You could extend the HelloWorld applet to allow the message output to be modified by using **<param>** elements to pass in a message, as shown here:

```
<applet code="helloworld.class"
        width="50" height="175">
<param name="Message" value="Hello World in Java!">

<h1>Hello World for you non-Java-aware browsers</h1>

</applet>
```

The following is the basic HTML 4 syntax for **<PARAM>**; it is the same for Java applets and ActiveX controls:

```
<param name="Object property name"
       value="Value to pass in with object name"
       valuetype="DATA | REF | OBJECT"
       type="MIME Type"
       id="document-wide unique id">
```

The **name** attribute for **<param>** is used to specify the name of the object property that is being set; in the preceding example, the name is "Message." If you are using a pre-made Java applet, the various property names should be specified in the documentation for the applet. The actual value to be assigned to the property is set by the **value** attribute. The **valuetype** attribute specifies the meaning of the **value** attribute. The data passed to an attribute typically takes the form of a string. Setting the **valuetype** attribute to **data** results in the default action. Setting **valuetype** to **ref** indicates that the data assigned to the **value** attribute is a URL that references an external file to load for the attribute. The last value for **valuetype** is **object**, which indicates that **value** is set to the name of an applet or object located somewhere else within the document. The data in the applet or object can be referenced to allow objects to "talk" to each other.

The **<param>** elements for a particular Java applet occur within the **<applet>** tag; a Java applet can have many **<param>** elements. The **<applet>** element also can enclose regular HTML markup that provides an alternative rendering for non-Java-capable browsers. When alternative content is found within the **<applet>** element, the **<param>** elements should be placed before the other content. Note that you also can set the **alt** attribute for the **<applet>** element to provide a short description. Authors should use the text contained within the element as the alternative text, and not the **alt** attribute.

Java Applets and Scripting

Java applets can control scripts in a Web page. Inclusion of the **mayscript** attribute in the **<applet>** element permits the applet to access JavaScript. When dealing with applets retrieved from other sources, you can use the **mayscript** attribute to prevent the applet from accessing JavaScript without the user's knowledge. If an applet attempts to access JavaScript when this attribute has not been specified, a run-time exception should occur.

Probably more interesting for page designers is the fact that scripts can control or even modify Java applets that are embedded in a page. For the applet to be accessed, it should be named using the **name** attribute for the **<applet>** element as well as the **id** attribute. Providing a unique name for the applet allows scripts to access the applet and its public interfaces. The name also can be used by other applets to allow the applets to communicate with each other. JavaScript in Netscape 3 and above, as well as in Internet Explorer 4 and above, allows access to the applets in a page via the **applets[ ]** collection, which is a property of the document object. When an applet is named, it can be accessed through JavaScript as **document.***appletname*, such as **document.myApplet**, or through the array of applets in the document such as **document.applets[0]** or **document.applets["myApplet"]**. If the Java applet has public properties exposed, they can be modified from a script in a Web page. The following simple Java code takes the "Hello World" example from earlier in the chapter and expands it with a **setMessage** method, which can be used to change the message displayed in the applet:

```java
import java.applet.Applet;
import java.awt.Graphics;
public class newhelloworld extends Applet {

    String theMessage;

    public void init()
      {
        theMessage = new String("Hello World");
      }
    public void paint(Graphics g)
      {
         g.drawString(theMessage, 50, 25);
      }
    public void setMessage(String message)
      {
        theMessage = message;
        repaint();
      }
}
```

If this Java code is compiled into a class file, it can be included in a Web page and accessed via JavaScript, as shown next. The following example markup shows how a form could be used to collect data from the user and update the applet in real time.

```
<!DOCTYPE HTML PUBLIC "-//W3C//DTD HTML 4.01 Transitional//EN">
<html>
<head>
<title>Java and Scripting Demo</title>
<script>
<!--
function setMessage()
{
  var message = document.TestForm.NewMessage.value;
  document.NewHello.setMessage(message);
}
//-->
</script>
</head>
<body>
<h1 align="center">Java and Scripting Demo</h1>
<hr>
<applet code="newhelloworld.class"
        name="NewHello"
        height="50" width="175">

<h1>You need Java for this example.</h1>

</applet>

<form name="TestForm">
<input type="text" size="15" maxlength="15" name="NewMessage">
<input type="button" value="Set Message" onclick="setMessage()">
</form>

</body>
</html>
```

Similar to communication between scripts and plug-ins, this script and applet communication initially was dubbed "LiveConnect" by Netscape. Microsoft also supports the same form of applet access under Internet Explorer, so it is unclear whether "LiveConnect" will continue to be the name used to describe using JavaScript to communicate with Java applets. The bottom line is that this technology is not unique to Netscape.

<object> Syntax for Java Applets

The strict HTML 4 specification indicates that the **<applet>** element has been deprecated and that **<object>** should be used instead. However, this has yet to be an issue and although this syntax might be decreed official by the W3C, using **<object>** for Java applets has some serious problems since few browsers support this syntax properly. The following is the most basic HTML 4 syntax for inserting an object, such as a Java applet:

```
<object classid="URL of Object to include"
        height="pixels"
        width="pixels">

Parameters and alternative text

</object>
```

For the complete **<object>** syntax, see the element reference in Appendix A.

Notice that the **classid** attribute is used to specify the URL of the object to include. In the case of Java applets, you should use **java:**. For ActiveX controls, use **clsid:**. To rewrite a simple Java example, use the following code:

```
<object classid="java:Blink.class" width="300" height="100">
 <param name="LBL" value="Java, is, fun, exciting, and new.">
 <param name="speed" value="2">
  This will display in non-Java-aware or non-Java-enabled browsers.
</object>
```

Because of the fragmentation of the Java community, Sun has made some attempts to bring together the syntax of Java applets using a Java plug-in. The specific syntax for this plug-in under Netscape and Internet Explorer includes both **<object>** and **<embed>** forms. Readers interested in this syntax for applet inclusion are directed straight to Sun's Java support site for the latest syntax (http://java.sun.com), because the syntax has changed numerous times.

Using Java Without Programming

The broad functionality of Java can cost both time and money. Java programming assumes that you have a familiarity with an advanced programming language as well as object-oriented design. Web professionals lacking programming skills or budgets can find many free, pre-made applets available for reuse or sale at directories such as Gamelan's Jars.com site (http://www.jars.com). Commercial vendors actively sell a variety of pre-made Java applets, as well as Java components called *JavaBeans,* which can be used to create powerful Web applications.

JavaBeans is a portable, platform-independent component model written in Java. Like other components, such as ActiveX controls, JavaBeans components (called *Beans* for short) are reusable software components that can be strung together to form complex applications. In one sense, Beans are just a special form of applet that are written in such a manner that tools can inspect and manipulate the Beans and the Beans can intercommunicate in a predictable manner. Beans generally are self-contained and persistent. You can analogize components such as Beans as bricks that form larger structures like buildings. In fact some Web development tools provide some basic drag-and-drop programming capabilities by tying together JavaBeans components with JavaScript code.

Cross-Platform Object Syntax Today and Tomorrow

Although the whole point of Java applets is to deal with cross-platform compatibility issues, Microsoft ActiveX controls and Netscape plug-ins are extremely platform- and browser-dependent. Yet whereas this might suggest that using Java applets would be the way to go, in many cases it is more likely that ActiveX controls and Netscape plug-ins can be referenced side-by-side in a Web page before Java applets are even considered. For example, consider the **<object>** syntax, embed syntax and **<noembed>** syntax combined in the following way:

```
<object classid="…" id="object1" name="object1"
      height="100" width="100">
   <param name="sample param" value="sample">
   <!--   other param elements here -->
   <embed src="..." id="plug1" name="plug1" height="100" width="100">
       <noembed>
          Sorry your browser supports neither ActiveX nor plug-ins.
       </noembed>
</object>
```

In this case the ActiveX control is tried first, then the plug-in, and finally the content within the **<noembed>** could be consulted. Other methods might include using JavaScript to detect what browser is being run and then outputting the appropriate HTML syntax; either **<embed>**; **<object>**; referencing an ActiveX control, Java applet, or maybe even some other alternative form. The point is that it is possible with some careful thought to cover all the possible situations and until the syntax and technology for including objects is straightened out, this is the only reasonable approach to handling crossbrowser issues, short of locking out users from a page or falling back to less interactive or less motivating technology.

Although the future of crossbrowser object support sound enticing, it has yet to materialize. For example, according to the HTML 4 specification, **<object>** will be the main way to add any form of object to a Web page, whether it's an image, image map, sound, video, ActiveX control, Java applet, or anything else. This approach seems appropriate, but before rushing out to use **<object>**, understand the ramifications. Even though **<object>** can be used in some browsers, the syntax is not consistent. The **<object>** element is still used mostly to include ActiveX controls in a page. Other meanings are not fully supported, if at all. According to the HTML 4 specification, the **<object>** element can be used to include HTML from another file by using the **data** attribute. Any file included must not introduce elements that would ruin the syntax of the document. For example, including a file that already has a **<head>** and **<body>** element can result in an ill-formed document with multiple **<head>** and **<body>** elements. Imagine specifying a header file called "header.htm" with the contents shown here:

```
<h1 align="center">Demo Company, Inc.</h1>
<hr>
```

This file then could be included in a Web page by using the **<object>** element, like so:

```
<object data="header.htm">
Header not included
</object>
```

This example should pull in the contents of the file header.htm in browsers that support this feature, and display "Header not included" in all others. No major browser appears to support this functionality for the **<object>** element.

Eventually, the **<object>** element will be used in a generalized sense and maybe object technologies will be supported through very simple markup. For now, HTML page authors should carefully use the **<applet>**, **<embed>**, and **<object>** elements to include components and media objects beyond images in pages along with any required scripting to avoid locking users out of viewing your Web page.

Summary

With the inclusion of programmed objects such as ActiveX controls, Java applets, and Netscape plug-ins, Web pages can become complex, living documents. Choosing the appropriate component technology is not very straightforward. Netscape plug-ins are very popular for including media elements such as Flash animations, video, or sound files. Unfortunately, they are platform specific, and largely limited to Netscape browsers, although other browsers such as Opera might support them as well, and Microsoft supports the **<embed>** element syntax to include plug-ins in a page. The preferred solution in the Microsoft world is ActiveX controls. ActiveX controls are just as platform specific as Netscape plug-ins, and have some potential security issues. Solving the cross-platform problem requires complex page scripting or the use of Java applets that provide cross-platform object support, typically at the expense of performance. Either way, the page rendering should degrade gracefully if the user can't support the particular object technology. Eventually, the syntax for all included media will be handled with the **<object>** element; but for now, **<embed>** and **<applet>** should be used within **<object>** to provide backward compatibility for including plug-ins and Java applets in a Web page.

The Complete Reference

Part V

Site Delivery and Management

The
Complete
Reference

Chapter 15

Site Delivery

So far, this book has said nothing about how to deliver Web pages. Even if developers master the creation of Web pages using HTML, they can still fall flat on their faces if they don't pay careful consideration to how they deliver the pages to the user. As far as the viewer of a page is concerned, the Web is one big system. If a page is slow because of a server, the user still views the site in a negative light no matter how correctly implemented the HTML or other technology used might be, and in spite of how compelling the content or inspiring the design. Leaving important site delivery considerations until the very end of Web projects is a surefire way to improve the chances the site will fail.

The Importance of Delivery

Unfortunately, delivery issues often are only contemplated after a Web site has been designed and built. In many cases, the budget for the site doesn't significantly consider delivery costs, and so corners are cut. This is like spending big money to design and print a corporate brochure, only to have it delivered by third-class postal mail because no funds were left after design and printing. The effect of the brochure would be severely diminished by its slow arrival. Delivery of Web sites is even more critical, particularly given the rise of task-oriented Web sites or e-commerce sites, in which any delay can mean the difference between a successful sale and a lost one.

Although designers might admit that users don't like slow sites, they tend to focus only on a few aspects of what makes a site slow. Consider that users will not be able to distinguish which aspect of site delivery is causing a page to load slowly. They are going to view it as a slow site, whether or not the graphics were optimized properly. Too much emphasis on optimizing file size, and not enough attention to servers, network choice, and even the characteristics of the medium itself, is a common mistake made by Web site designers. Consider all the possible reasons a site might be slow, as illustrated in Figure 15-1.

Although there are numerous potential problems to consider when delivering a site, the one inescapable fact is that, eventually, data will have be transferred. Whether you download now or download later, you eventually have to do it. From the user's perspective, how much data is downloaded doesn't really matter; it only matters how responsive the site is. The user only counts the seconds on their watch, not the number of bytes delivered. How much data comes down doesn't matter to the end user. Furthermore, if you are using huge graphics by downloading them during the idle moments, the user certainly won't care.

The bottom line is keeping the user happy. If your design requires a great deal of bandwidth, has many individual requests, or requires real-time delivery, you might have to shelve it. Always respect the medium of the Web. Just as a print designer understands that ink might bleed through paper, the Web designer should understand the nature of the network and servers used to deliver their creations.

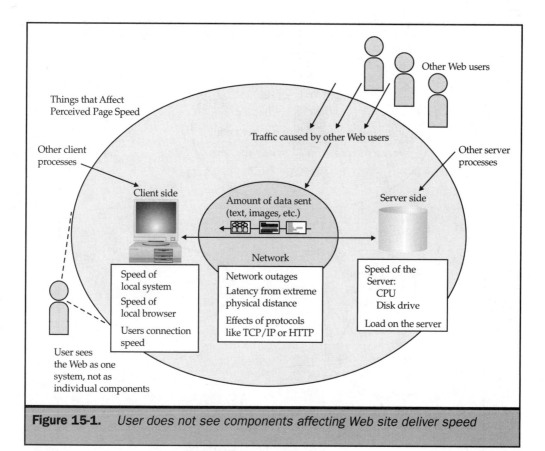

Figure 15-1. *User does not see components affecting Web site deliver speed*

How to Deliver Web Sites

There are two basic choices for publishing your Web site on the public Internet: doing it yourself or outsourcing. Doing it yourself requires having a dedicated connection to the Internet and running your own server, whereas outsourcing involves renting physical space, bandwidth, or services on an existing Web server from an outside vendor.

Running your own Web server and connection to the Internet might seem like the way to go, but it can be quite expensive. A common leased line such as a T1 with Internet services might cost thousands of dollars a year. When factoring in labor, server, facilities, and other expenses, the total cost starts to approach six figures. Often, many of these facilities already are available within the organization and should be used. Yet using someone else's server might be the only choice for people who want to publish Web documents but can't afford a huge fee. Even firms that have capable staffs should consider outsourcing, as it provides many benefits. Figure 15-2 gives a basic overview of the two hosting approaches.

SITE DELIVERY AND
MANAGEMENT

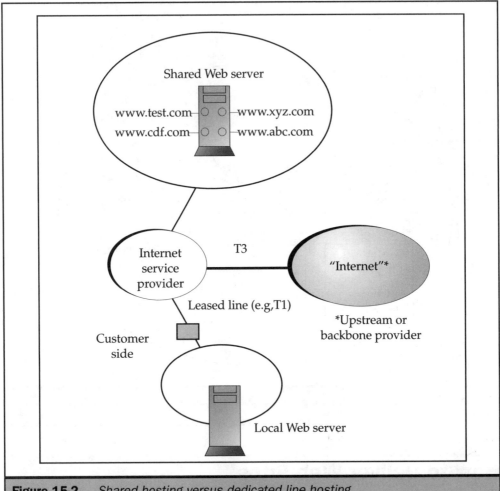

Figure 15-2. *Shared hosting versus dedicated line hosting*

Outsourcing Web Hosting

As Web sites become more critical to the information infrastructure of companies, there is a growing need to provide high-quality, high-availability solutions. For example, a business selling something only online can't afford to have its site go down at all. The serving of a site to an e-business is as critical as power and telephone services would be to a traditional business. This trend might be termed the "utilization" of the Web, as some might consider the health and delivery of their Web site as important as utility.

However, given that the site must be run in a very efficient and reliable manner, firms quickly discover that it is in fact quite expensive for companies to develop in-house the talents and facilities to run a mission-critical Web site. Because of this fact, many firms have decided to outsource their Web facilities. Web server outsourcing comes in many flavors, but many of the differences revolve around two factors. The first differentiating factor is whether you are sharing a machine with other sites. The second is whether or not the machine being used is owned and managed by you or the outsource vendor. Each type of service will be discussed in turn, with special focus on their pros and cons.

Shared Hosting

The most basic form of hosting, shared hosting, can range from free Web space added to other services, or in exchange for advertisement placement, to high-end application service providers (ASPs). At the low end, many Internet service providers will provide a directory on one of their Web servers with a few megabytes of disk space and possibly access to a few shared tools that can be used on your Web site, such as simple form handling scripts, counters, or message boards. Usually, the URL for a site such as this is of the form http://www.isp.net/~enduser or http://www.isp.net/enduser. The hosting service lacks any customization such as your domain name (*yourname*.com), and might impose limits on traffic delivered or programming tools that can be used. The upside to these types of services is that they often are free and might be included in the cost of your Internet connection. There also are many vendors who will provide free Web serving in exchange for personal information for marketing purposes, or if you agree to show banner advertisements they book on your Web site. Whereas these services are appealing to home users or those looking to put up a site for fun, most will prefer other forms of shared hosting.

Shared host services that provide a domain name (www.*yourname*.com), often called a *virtual server*, generally are not free. These services also provide improved development facilities such as your own cgi-bin directory, statistical reports on site traffic, and other useful features, including shopping cart facilities. The costs for virtual server accounts on a shared system usually start around $20 or more per month. However, costs vary greatly and the more bandwidth your site consumes or the more special requests you have, the higher the possible cost—even if the machine is not dedicated to you. In fact, with complex shared hosting services, in which you might have access to content management systems or e-commerce facilities, the cost can literally skyrocket to hundreds or even thousands of dollars per month.

The major downside of shared Web hosting is that it involves using the shared server facilities of a hosting vendor. This means that the site will share Web server resources and bandwidth with other hosted sites. Server responsiveness might be significantly affected because of other hosted Web sites, particularly if those sites become popular. Furthermore, many customers are wary of sharing a server with others, because security often cannot be guaranteed on these shared systems. Despite its drawbacks, shared hosting is very popular—mainly due to price.

Dedicated Hosting

Because of the downside of sharing a server with others—most notably security and control—many people opt to use a dedicated server. Dedicated servers are advantageous because you can customize your server with whatever tools or programs you like and they are not affected by other sites as much. However, the trade-off is cost. Dedicated servers tend to be more expensive.

There are two forms of dedicated server hosting. In the first, the outsource vendor owns and maintains the equipment. This can be called *fully managed* or *dedicated hosting*. In the other, you own and might even be responsible for maintaining your server. This usually is called *co-location*. With co-location, the vendor provides space at its facility, electrical power, a network connection, a certain amount of bandwidth, and very limited system management for your server (such as rebooting it if it crashes or maybe doing tape backups). Co-location generally is cheaper than fully managed services, but for those who don't want to be bothered with the details of Web site delivery, co-location is not as great a deal as it might seem.

Dedicated hosting solutions are very attractive to those who want control, security, and power, but don't want to deal with many of the day-to-day issues of running a Web server. The major downside of these solutions is price. Services-provided top-tier vendors such as Exodus (www.exodus.net) and AboveNet (www.above.net) might run many thousands of dollars per month based on the equipment and bandwidth required as well as any services added, such as security monitoring or sophisticated hosting requirements such as mirroring a site at multiple locations. However, if a business really relies on robust, fast Web site delivery, many of these vendors are a bargain even at what appears to be a high price. Consider the actual cost of maintaining a telephone company–grade equipment room filled with servers connected to numerous Internet providers being monitored twenty-four hours a day, seven days a week by capable system and network administrators, and you'll see that the cost might be well worth it. Consider that some of the largest content, search engine, and e-commerce sites don't run their own servers and you'll see that considering an outside hosting vendor is a good idea.

Companies looking to save money on Web delivery might find outsourcing very attractive, but some flexibility and security might have to be sacrificed. With less experienced hosting companies, this lack of control can be disastrous, resulting in hidden costs or problems with reliability. Those who want more control over their Web services should consider co-location or running their own servers locally. Of course, running your own servers introduces the potential headaches involved with setting up and administering your Web server 24 hours a day, seven days a week. For a large site, this might be a significant amount of work.

 A directory of commercial hosting vendors can be found at http://www.webhostlist.com.

In-House Web Servers

If you decide to run your own Web server it is important to consider how they work. To many people, Web servers seem mystical. In reality, a Web server is just a computer running a piece of software that fulfills HTTP requests made by browsers. In the simplest sense, a Web server is just a file server, and a slow one at times. Consider the operation of a Web server resulting from a user requesting a file, as shown in Figure 15-3. Basically, a user just requests a file and the server either delivers it back or issues some error message, such as the ubiquitous 404 not found message.

However, a Web server isn't just a file server, because it also can run programs and deliver results. In this sense, Web servers also could be considered application servers—if occasionally simple or slow ones.

Web Server Components

A Web server is composed of both hardware and software. The primary operation of a Web server is to copy the many (generally small) files making up a Web page from disk to network as fast as possible for numerous simultaneous users. A secondary mission is to run programs for numerous individuals and deliver their results as fast as possible. Given these requirements, consider the hardware requirements of a Web server shown in Table 15-1.

Beyond getting the best hardware you can afford, it is important to consider that the operating system running on the hardware is going to have a great effect on the speed of the Web server, as well as the server and development software options available. In general, given that Web servers have to deal with multiple requests at once and need a rich set of development options, most developers tend to use either Windows NT or some variant of UNIX, including Linux, for their operating system. Table 15-2 presents the major operating system choices as well as some of the issues in using them for Web serving.

Although Table 15-2 presents a good overview of some of the issues faced when choosing one operating system over another for a Web server, the decision often might be made due to familiarity or personal taste. Whereas one person might argue about the merits of UNIX, introducing a UNIX server into an environment with heavy Macintosh investment would be foolish. The bottom line is to always remember

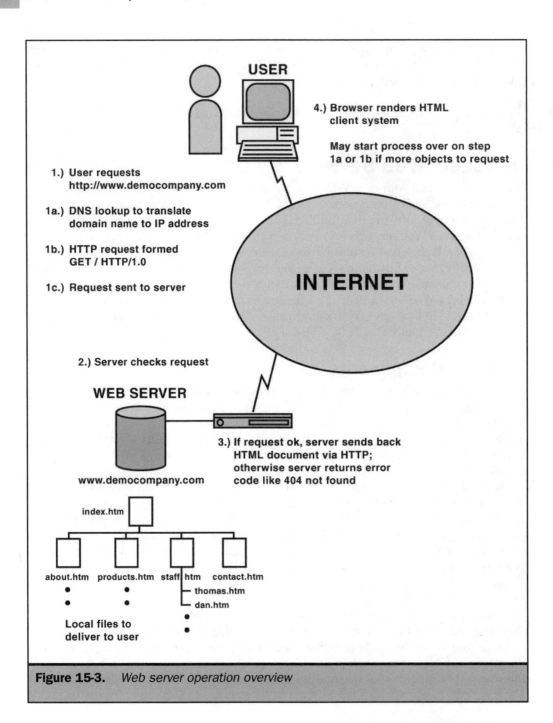

Figure 15-3. *Web server operation overview*

Hardware Component	Considerations
Processor	Although a fast processor seems key to a fast Web server, the reality is that computational requirements of a Web server are limited. Multiple processors might be more useful than a single fast processor when dealing with numerous requests made on a server.
Memory	A Web server might need a large amount of RAM to hold numerous individual processes running CGI programs for users or fulfilling file requests.
Bus	Web data will constantly move from disk to memory to network. Don't limit the data path with a slow bus.
Disk drive	Because a Web server's primary task is delivering files to a user, a high-speed disk drive that is kept optimized is a primary goal. Spend extra on drives with high-speed adapters such as SCSI-3.
Network interface	Once files are retrieved from disk, they are delivered back to the user via the network. Don't limit a server by its network interface card. Consider Fast Ethernet or better. For high-volume servers, multiple network interfaces might be mandatory.
Other	Most other aspects of a Web server have little bearing on the delivery of a site. However, some peripherals such as tape drives or other backup storage facilities are mandatory for site maintenance.

Table 15-1.   *Web Server Hardware Issues*

suitability and total cost over time. A relatively low-traffic site for a school might do well on a Macintosh. A Windows NT system might make a great departmental server in a corporation that favors Windows systems. A Linux system might appeal to a technical-minded individual looking to avoid spending money on hardware and software, and a high-end Sun server running Solaris might be appropriate for a large e-commerce venture. Some sites might find that a server appliance that does not expose operating system issues also might be appropriate if maintenance is a significant concern. The point is always to choose an operating system for a server based on the practicality of performance, development, and long-term maintenance characteristics of the OS.

Operating System	Pros	Cons
UNIX	Tends to run on fast hardware such as UltraSparc and Alpha systems Very flexible development environment High-end applications and servers are available Highly stable	Can be complicated to use and difficult to set up and maintain Labor costs might be high Buy-in costs for hardware and software are relatively high
Windows NT	Runs on both high- and low-end hardware Many servers and development tools available Basic administration is simple	Might require multiple servers for high-volume sites Advanced administration might rival UNIX in difficulty Guaranteeing server stability can be troublesome
Linux	Available on low-end equipment and a variety of hardware platforms Cost is low Many servers and development tools available and most are free	Can be complicated to use and difficult to maintain Lacks volume of commercial software support found with mainstream UNIX systems such as Solaris
Windows 95/98	Easy to run Low equipment costs Inexpensive software	Not a multi-user environment Not as robust as NT or UNIX for server applications Selection of Web software is limited compared to Windows NT or UNIX variants Security concerns can be significant
Macintosh	Easy to run and administer Low equipment costs Inexpensive software	Not a multiuser environment Selection of Web software is limited compared to Windows or UNIX Often not as robust as NT or UNIX for serving

Table 15-2. *Operating Systems and Web Serving Considerations*

Web Server Software

Once hardware and operating system are selected, it is time to consider which Web server package to use. Only a few years ago, there were only two major Web servers available: NCSA's httpd server for UNIX and CERN's httpd server for UNIX, both free servers that required fairly significant knowledge of UNIX and programming to use and develop for. Today, there are dozens of different Web servers—both commercial and freeware—available on a variety of machines. Rather than considering all Web servers in your decision, it might be wise to look at the most common Web servers used. Based on surveys and analysis of reachable servers on the Internet, the following are considered to be some of the most common Web servers used, although their exact market percentage is a topic of hot debate. The major Web servers include

Apache	WebSite
Microsoft's IIS	WebStar
IPlanet servers (formerly Netscape)	Domino

Each of the popular Web servers is discussed next. This should by no means be considered an endorsement of these products, but rather just a synopsis of each product and some of its known characteristics.

 Serverwatch (www.serverwatch.com) provides links and reviews of the most of the popular Web servers available.

Apache

A descendant of NCSA's httpd server, Apache (http://www.apache.org/) probably is the most popular Web server on the Internet, at least as far as public Web sites are concerned. Apache's popularity stems from the fact that it is free and fast. It also is very powerful, supporting features such as HTTP 1.1, extended server-side includes (SSIs), a module architecture similar to NSAPI/ISAPI, and numerous free modules that perform functions such as server-based Perl interpretation. However, Apache is not for everyone. The main issue with Apache is that it isn't a commercial package. Some firms are hesitant to run their mission-critical systems on a user-supported product. However, as with operating systems such as Linux, various third parties offer commercial support for Apache. Another potential limiting factor for Apache is that the system currently is mainly for UNIX. Although there is a port of Apache to Windows 32-bit systems, as well as one for the Macintosh OS X environment, the server is optimized for popular UNIX and Linux variant. The lack of heavy NT support might limit the use of Apache within many Windows-centric enterprises. Probably the most troublesome aspect of Apache for some developers is that it might require modification of configuration files or even compilation to install properly. Of course this might be the upside of Apache as you can literally customize the source code of the server itself! If you like to tinker or desire speed, have a UNIX system, and don't have a lot of money, Apache might just be for you. You'll be in good company: Some of the largest Web sites on the Internet swear by this product.

 For Web trivia buffs, the name "Apache" is derived from the description of the software as a patched version of NCSA. Think "a patchy NCSA server."

Microsoft Internet Information Services

IIS is Microsoft's server for Windows NT (http://www.microsoft.com/iis/). Windows 95/98 also supports a similar but much less powerful version of IIS called the Personal Web Server (PWS). Whereas PWS certainly is popular, of the two, most organizations favor IIS. One very important aspect of IIS is that it is very tightly integrated with the Windows NT environment. In fact, today it is hard to distinguish IIS as a standalone service within Windows 2000. Unfortunately, being so Windows NT–specific also is considered one of the problems with IIS. Because of hardware and clustering issues, IIS hasn't proved quite as scalable as some UNIX-based servers. With new Microsoft clustering technologies and integration with a transaction processor, this scalability problem is likely to change. For an intranet environment—particularly one with heavy Microsoft investment—it is difficult to beat the features offered by IIS—particularly its integration with other Microsoft products such as the SQL Server database. The price for IIS currently is a major positive point for the software—it's freely bundled with the operating system.

iPlanet: Servers Formerly Known as Netscape

iPlanet, the new software concern born of the Sun-Netscape alliance formed after the merger between Netscape and AOL, has a larger number of Web servers (http://www.iplanet.com). These servers continue Netscape's long history of supporting high-end Web and application servers running on most major variants of UNIX (Solaris, SunOS, AIX, HP-UX, Digital UNIX, and IRIX) as well as Windows NT. The servers are well developed, as they represent more than four generations of software releases. The servers also are very developer friendly and powerful, with support for databases and directory services, content management, HTTP 1.1, and a variety of other features. If you are in a cross-platform or UNIX environment and you are looking for commercial-quality Web serving solutions, you might consider using iPlanet servers.

WebSite

A very easy-to-use Web server for Window 95/98 and Windows NT, O'Reilly's WebSite (http://website.ora.com/) is one of the few robust Web servers available for Windows 95/98. Although some suggest WebSite lacks the performance of Netscape or Microsoft servers running on more powerful systems, WebSite is considered one of the easiest servers to install and administer. Furthermore, the system provides many nice development features such as a special server-parsed languages called iHTML. For intranets or sites that don't need the performance of high-end Windows NT or UNIX systems, WebSite is a great choice.

WebStar

The most popular Web server for the Macintosh was originally based on MacHTTPD. WebStar (http://www.webstar.com/) integrates well with the Macintosh. It supports AppleScript and other Macintosh-specific tools. The system supports UNIX-style CGI programs, a Java virtual machine for server-side Java, and extended SSI, and has solid security features. The performance of WebStar often leaves much to be desired, although it is improving and probably is more than adequate for intranets or small Web sites. Many developers favor running UNIX shells on top of Macintosh to run Apache. The Mac OS X, in fact, also supports Apache.

Lotus Domino

Domino (http://www.lotus.com/domino) is an example of the collision between traditional Web serving and messaging and groupware. Domino runs on Windows NT, variants of UNIX, and even large IBM systems such as AS/400s, and often is used in corporate intranet and extranet environments where workflow and integration with messaging and backend systems might be more important than raw, Web serving performance. Designing Web pages within in the Domino environment can be somewhat restrictive because of the template approach Domino takes. However, it is possible to integrate Domino with other servers, including IIS, to provide raw HTTP facilities.

There are numerous Web server software choices. Remember that different packages will have different performance characteristics. Using the same hardware, one Web server software package might far outperform another. When planning to build a Web server, start either from the hardware and build up, or start from the particular software and build down, picking the best possible hardware. If you make good software and hardware choices, the performance of the site can be significantly improved. Always try to base your choices on usage requirements, such as target number of simultaneous users or requests per minute or second. Once the requirements of the site have been carefully determined, it is possible to best choose how to serve a site.

How Web Servers Work

When it comes to the physical process of publishing documents, the main issues are whether to run your own server or to host elsewhere in conjunction with Web server software and hardware. However, a deeper understanding of how Web servers do their job is important to understanding potential bottlenecks. Recall that in general, all that a Web server does is listen for requests from browsers or, as they are called more generically, *user agents*. Once the server receives a request, typically to deliver a file, it determines whether it should do it. If so, it copies the file from the disk out to the network. In some cases, the user agent might ask the server to execute a program, but the idea is the same: Eventually, some data is transmitted back to the browser for display. This discussion between the user agent, typically a Web browser, and the server takes place using the HTTP protocol.

HTTP

The Hypertext Transfer Protocol (HTTP) is the basic, underlying, application-level protocol used to facilitate the transmission of data to and from a Web server. HTTP provides a simple, fast way to specify the interaction between client and server. The protocol actually defines how a client must ask for data from the server and how the server returns it. HTTP does not specify how the data actually is transferred; this is up to lower-level network protocols such as TCP.

The first version of HTTP, known as version 0.9, was used as early as 1990. HTTP version 1.0 as defined by RFC 1945, is supported by most servers and clients (Web browsers). However, HTTP 1.0 does not properly handle the effects of hierarchical proxies and caching, or provide features to facilitate virtual hosts. More important, HTTP 1.0 has significant performance problems due to the opening and closing of many connections for a single Web page.

The current version, HTTP 1.1, solves many of the past problems of the protocol. It currently is supported by version 4–generation Web browsers as well as servers. There still are many limitations to HTTP, however. It is used increasingly in applications that need more sophisticated features, including distributed authoring, collaboration, multimedia support, and remote procedure calls. Various ideas to extend HTTP have been discussed and a generic Extension Framework for HTTP has been introduced by the W3C. Already some facilities such as client capability detection and privacy negotiation between browser and server have been implemented on top of HTTP, but most of these protocols are still being worked out. For now, HTTP continues to be fairly simple, so this discussion will continue to deal with HTTP 1.0 and 1.1.

The process of a Web browser or other user agent—such as Web spider or Robot—requesting a document from a Web—or more correctly HTTP—server is simple, and has been discussed throughout the book. The overall process was diagrammed in Figure 15-3. In the figure, the user first requests a document from a Web server by specifying the URL of the document desired. During this step, a domain name lookup might occur, which translates a machine name such as www.democompany.com to an underlying IP address such as 206.251.142.3. If the domain name lookup fails, an error message such as "No Such Host" or "The server does not have a DNS entry" will be returned. Certain assumptions, such as the default service port to access for HTTP requests (80), also might be made. This is transparent to the user, who simply uses a URL to access a page. Once the server has been located the browser forms the proper HTTP request and sends the request to the server residing at the address specified by the URL. A typical HTTP request consists of

```
HTTP-Method Identifier HTTP-version
<Optional additional request headers>
```

In this example, the HTTP-Method would be **GET** or **POST**. An identifier might correspond to the file desired (for example, /examples/Chapter15/report.htm), and the HTTP-version indicates the dialect of HTTP being used, such as HTTP/1.0.

If a user requests a document with the URL http://www.htmlref.com/examples/chapter15/report.htm, the browser might generate a request such as the one shown here to retrieve the object from the server:

```
GET /examples/chapter15/report.htm HTTP/1.0
If-Modified-Since: Tuesday, 15-Aug-00 01:39:39 GMT;
Connection: Keep-Alive
User-Agent: Mozilla/4.02 [en] (X11; I; SunOS 5.4 sun4m)
Accept: image/gif, image/x-xbitmap, image/jpeg, image/pjpeg, */*
Accept-Language: en
Accept-Charset: iso-8859-1,*,utf-8
```

People often ask why the complete URL is not shown in the request. It isn't necessary in most cases, except when using a proxy server. The use of a relative URL in the header is adequate. The server knows where it is; it just needs to know what document to get from its own file tree. In the case of using a proxy server, which requests a document on behalf of a browser, a full URL is passed to it that later is made relative by the proxy. Aside from the simple **GET** method, there are various other methods specified in HTTP. Not all are commonly used. Table 15-3 provides a summary of the HTTP 1.1 request methods.

It is interesting to note that two of the methods (**GET** and **POST**) supported by HTTP, are the values of the **<form>** element's **method** attribute. Recall that this attribute indicates the method in which data is passed from the form to the server-side program. In the case of **GET** it is passed through the URL because another page is simply being fetched, as a normal **GET** request would do. In the case of a **POST** value the data of the form is passed behind the scenes to the server program that should return a result page to the browser as well. As shown by the **<form>** element it should become clear that HTML and HTTP do interact in more than a casual way.

Within an HTTP request, there are a variety of optional fields for creating a complete request. The common fields and an example for each are shown in the following sections.

Method	Description
GET	Returns the object specified by the identifier. Notice that it also is one of the values of the **method** attribute for the **<form>** element.
HEAD	Returns information about the object specified by the identifier, such as last modification data, but does not return the actual object
OPTIONS	Returns information about the capabilities supported by a server if no location is specified, or the possible methods that can be applied to the specified object
POST	Sends information to the address indicated by the identifier; generally used to transmit information from a form using the **method="POST"** attribute of the **<form>** element to a server-based CGI program
PUT	Sends data to the server and writes it to the address specified by the identifier overwriting previous content; in basic form, can be used for file upload
DELETE	Removes the file specified by the identifier; generally disallowed
TRACE	Provides diagnostic information by allowing the client to see what is being received on the server

Table 15-3. *Summary of HTTP 1.1 Request Methods*

 The value of this header information should not be understated. With them you can detect things such as the browser being used, the particular types of images supported by the browser, the language of the browser such as French, English, or Japanese, and so on.

Accept: *MIME-type/MIME-subtype*

This field indicates the data types accepted by the browser. An entry of */* indicates anything is accepted; however, it is possible to indicate particular content types such as image/jpeg so the server can make a decision on what to return. This facility could be used to introduce a form of content negotiation so that a browser could be served only data it understands or prefers, although this approach is not widely understood or implemented.

```
Accept: image/gif, image/x-xbitmap, image/jpeg, image/pjpeg, */*
```

Accept-Charset: *charset*

This field indicates the character set that is accepted by the browser, such as ASCII or foreign character encodings.

```
Accept-Charset: iso-8859-1,*,utf-8
```

Accept-Encoding: *encoding-type*

This field instructs the server on what type of encoding the browser understands. Typically this field is used to indicate to the server that compressed data can be handled.

```
Accept-Encoding: x-compress
```

Accept-Language: *language*

This field lists the languages preferred by the browser and could be used by the server to pass back the appropriate language data.

```
Accept-Language: en
```

Authorization: *authorization-scheme authorization-data*

This field typically is used to indicate the userid and encrypted password if the user is returning authorization information.

```
Authorization: user joeblow:testpass
```

 Generally, the password is transmitted unencrypted, thus the need for security protocols such as SSL.

Content-length: *bytes*

This field gives the length in bytes of the message being sent to the server, if any. Remember that the browser can upload or pass data using the **PUT** or **POST** method.

```
Content-length: 1805
```

Content-type: *MIME-type/MIME-subtype*

This field indicates the MIME type of a message being sent to a server, if any. The value of this field would be particularly important in the case of file upload.

SITE DELIVERY AND MANAGEMENT

```
Content-type: text/plain
```

Date: *date-time*

This field indicates the date and time that a request was made in Greenwich Mean Time (GMT). GMT time is mandatory for time consistency, given the worldwide nature of the Web.

```
Date: Thursday, 15-Jan-98 01:39:39 GMT
```

Host

This field indicates the host and port of the server to which the request is being made.

```
Host: www.democompany.com
```

If-Modified-Since: *date-time*

This field indicates file freshness to improve the efficiency of the **GET** method. When used in conjunction with a **GET** request for a particular file, the requested file is checked to see if it has been modified since the time specified in the field. If the file has not been modified, a "not modified" code (304) is sent to the client so a cached version of the document can be used; otherwise, the file is returned normally.

```
If-Modified-Since: Thursday, 15-Jan-98 01:39:39 GMT
```

If-Match: *selector-string*

This field makes a request conditionally only if the items match some selector value passed in. Imagine only using **POST** to add data once it has been moved to a file called olddata.

```
If-Match: "olddata"
```

If-None-Match: *selector-string*

This field does the opposite of If-Match. The method is conditional only if the selector does not match anything. This might be useful for preventing overwrites of existing files.

```
If-None-Match: "newfile"
```

If-Range: *selector*

If a client has a partial copy of an object in its cache and wants to have an up-to-date copy of the entire object there, it could use the Range request header with this conditional If-Range modifier to update the file. Modification selection can take place on time as well.

```
If-Range: Thursday, 15-Jan-98 01:39:39 GMT;
```

If-Unmodified-Since

This field makes a conditional method. If the requested file has not been modified since the specified time, the server should perform the requested method; otherwise, the method should fail.

```
If-Unmodified-Since: Thursday, 15-Jan-98 01:39:39 GMT
```

Max-Forwards: *integer*

This field is used with the **TRACE** method to limit the number of proxies or gateways that can forward the request. This would be useful to determine failures if a request moves through many proxies before reaching the final server.

```
Max-Forwards: 6
```

MIME-version: *version-number*

This field indicates the MIME protocol version, understood by the browser, that the server should use when fulfilling requests.

```
MIME-Version: 1.0
```

Proxy-Authorization: *authorization information*

This field allows the client to identify itself or the user to a proxy that requires authentication.

```
Proxy-Authorization: joeblow: testpass; Realm: All
```

Pragma: *server-directive*

This field passes information to a server; for example, this field can be used to inform a caching proxy server to fetch a fresh copy of a page.

```
Pragma: no-cache
```

Range: *byte-range*

This field requests a particular range of a file such as a certain number of bytes. The example shows a request for the last 500 bytes of a file.

```
Range: bytes=-500
```

Referer: *URL*

This field indicates the URL of the document from which the request originates (in other words, the linking document). This value might be empty if the user has entered the URL directly rather than by following a link.

```
Referer: http://www.democompany.com/reports/index.html
```

User-Agent: *Agent-code*

This field indicates the type of browser making the request.

```
User-Agent: Mozilla/4.0 (compatible; MSIE 5.5; Windows 98)
```

Once again, note that all of these request headers seem very familiar. They constitute the same environment variables that you can access from within a CGI program. Now it should be clear how this information is obtained.

After receiving a request, the Web server attempts to process the request. The result of the request is indicated by a server status line that contains a response code; for example, the ever popular "404 Not Found." The server response status line takes this form:

```
HTTP-version Status-code Reason-String
```

For a successful query, a status line might read as follows:

```
HTTP/1.0   200   OK
```

whereas in case of error the status line might read

```
HTTP/1.0   404   Not Found
```

The status codes for the emerging HTTP 1.1 standard are shown in Table 15-4.

Status-Code	Reason-String	Description
Informational Codes (Process Continues After This)		
100	Continue	An interim response issued by the server that indicates the request is in progress but has not been rejected or accepted. This status code is in support of the persistent connection idea introduced in HTTP 1.1
101	Switching Protocols	Can be returned by the server to indicate that a different protocol should be used to improve communication. This could be used to initiate a real-time protocol.
Success Codes (Request Understood and Accepted)		
200	OK	Indicates the successful completion of a request.
201	Created	Indicates the successful completion of a **PUT** request and the creation of the file specified.
202	Accepted	This code indicates that the request has been accepted for processing, but that the processing has not been completed and the request might or might not actually finish properly.
203	Non-Authoritative Information	Indicates a successful request, except that returned information, particularly meta-information about a document, comes from a third source and is unverifiable.
204	No Content	Indicates a successful request, but there is no new data to send to the client.
205	Reset Content	Indicates that the client should reset the page that sent the request (potentially for more input). This could be used on a form page that needs consistent refreshing, rather than reloading as might be used in a chat system.

Table 15-4.   *HTTP 1.1 Status Codes*

Status-Code	Reason-String	Description
206	Partial Content	Indicates a successful request for a piece of a larger document or set of documents. This response typically is encountered when media is sent out in a particular order, or byte- served, as with streaming Acrobat files.
Redirection Codes (Further Action Necessary to Complete Request)		
300	Multiple Choices	Indicates that there are many possible representations for the requested information, so the client should use the preferred representation, which might be in the form of a closer server or different data format.
301	Moved Permanently	Requested resource has been assigned a new permanent address and any future references to this resource should be done using one of the returned addresses.
302	Moved Temporarily	Requested resource temporarily resides at a different address. For future requests, the original address should still be used.
303	See Other	Indicates that the requested object can be found at a different address and should be retrieved using a **GET** method on that resource.
304	Not Modified	Issued in response to a conditional **GET**; indicates to the agent to use a local copy from cache or similar action as the request object has not changed.
305	Use Proxy	Indicates that the requested resource must be accessed through the proxy given by the URL in the Location field.

Table 15-4.   *HTTP 1.1 Status Codes* (continued)

Status-Code	Reason-String	Description
Client Error Codes (Syntax Error or Other Problem Causing Failure)		
400	Bad Request	Indicates that the request could not be understood by the server due to malformed syntax.
401	Unauthorized	Request requires user authentication. The authorization has failed for some reason, so this code is returned.
402	Payment Required	Obviously in support of commerce, this code is currently not well defined.
403	Forbidden	Request is understood but disallowed and should not be reattempted, compared to the 401 code, which might suggest a reauthentication. A typical response code in response to a query for a directory listing when the latter are disallowed.
404	Not Found	Usually issued in response to a typo by the user or a moved resource, as the server can't find anything that matches the request nor any indication that the requested item has been moved.
405	Method Not Allowed	Issued response to a method request such as **GET**, **POST**, or **PUT** on an object where such a method is not supported. Generally an indication of what methods that are supported will be returned.
406	Not Acceptable	Indicates that the response to the request will not be in one of the content types acceptable by the browser, so why bother doing the request? This is an unlikely response given the */* acceptance issued by most, if not all, browsers.
407	Proxy Authentication Required	Indicates that the proxy server requires some form of authentication to continue. This code is similar to the 401 code.

Table 15-4.   *HTTP 1.1 Status Codes* (continued)

Status-Code	Reason-String	Description
408	Request Time-out	Indicates that the client did not produce or finish a request within the time that the server was prepared to wait.
409	Conflict	The request could not be completed because of a conflict with the requested resource; for example, the file might be locked.
410	Gone	Indicates that the requested object is no longer available at the server and no forwarding address is known. Search engines might want to add remote references to objects that return this value since it is a permanent condition.
411	Length Required	Indicates that the server refuses to accept the request without a defined Content-Length. This might happen when a file is posted without a length.
412	Precondition Failed	Indicates that a precondition given in one or more of the request header fields, such as If-Unmodified-Since, evaluated to false.
413	Request Entity Too Large	Indicates that the server is refusing to return data because the object might be too large or the server might be too loaded to handle the request. The also server might provide information indicating when to try again if possible, but just as well might terminate any open connections.
414	Request-URI Too Large	Indicates that the Uniform Resource Identifier (URI), generally a URL, in the request field is too long for the server to handle. This is unlikely to occur as browsers probably will not allow such transmissions.

Table 15-4. *HTTP 1.1 Status Codes* (continued)

Status-Code	Reason-String	Description
415	Unsupported Media Type	Indicates the server will not perform the request because the media type specified in the message is not supported. This code might be returned when a server receives a file that it is not configured to accept using the **PUT** method.
Server Error Codes (Server Can't Fulfill a Potentially Valid Request)		
500	Internal Server Error	A serious error message indicating that the server encountered an internal error that keeps it from fulfilling the request.
501	Not Implemented	This response is to a request that the server does not support or might be understood but not implemented.
502	Bad Gateway	Indicates that the server acting as a proxy encountered an error from some other gateway and is passing the message along.
503	Service Unavailable	Indicates the server currently is overloaded or is undergoing maintenance. Headers can be sent to indicate when the server will be available.
504	Gateway Time-out	Indicates that the server, when acting as a gateway or proxy, encountered too long a delay from an upstream proxy and decided to time out.
505	HTTP Version not supported	Indicates that the server does not support the HTTP version specified in the request.

Table 15-4.   *HTTP 1.1 Status Codes* (continued)

After the status line, the server responds with information about itself and the data being returned. There are various selected response headers, but the most important indicates the type of data in the form of a MIME-type and subtype that will be returned. Like request headers, many of these codes are optional and depend on the status of the request.

An example server response for the request shown earlier in this chapter (see "HTTP") follows:

```
HTTP/1.1 200 OK
Date: Wed, 20 Sep 2000 18:59:54 GMT
Server: Apache/1.3.12 (Unix)
Last-Modified: Fri, 25 Aug 2000 22:19:12 GMT
Accept-Ranges: bytes
Content-Length: 205
Connection: close
Content-Type: text/html

<html>
<head>
<title>Report 1</title>
</head>

<body>
<h1>Report About Important Things</h1>
<hr>
<p>Here is some information about important things. </p>

</body>
</html>
```

A list of the common server response headers for HTTP 1.1, as well as examples of each, can be found in Table 15-5.

The most important header response field is the Content-type field. The MIME type indicated by this field is a device by which the browser is capable of figuring out what to do with the data being returned.

MIME

MIME (Multipurpose Internet Mail Extensions) was originally developed as an extension to the Internet mail protocol that allows for the communication of multimedia. The basic idea of MIME is transmission of text files with headers that indicate binary data that will follow. Each MIME header is composed of two parts that indicate the data type and subtype in the following format:

```
Content-type: type/subtype
```

Response Header	Description	Example
Age	Shows the sender's estimate of the amount of time since the response was generated at the origin server. Age values are nonnegative decimal integers, representing time in seconds.	Age: 10
Content-encoding	Indicates the encoding the data returned is in.	Content-encoding: x-compress
Content-language	Indicates the language used for the data returned by the server.	Content-language: en
Content-length	Indicates the number of bytes returned by the server.	Content-length: 205
Content-range	Indicates the range of the data being sent back by the server.	Content-range: -500
Content-type	This probably is the most important field and indicates what type of content is being returned by the server in the form of a MIME type.	Content-type: text/html
Expires	Gives the date/time after which the returned data should be considered stale and should not be returned from a cache.	Expires: Thu, 04 Dec 1997 16:00:00 GMT
Last-modified	The Last-Modified response-header field is used to indicate the date the content returned was last modified. This can be used by caches to decide to keep local copies of objects.	Last-modified: Thursday, 01-Aug-96 10:09:00 GMT

Table 15-5. *Common HTTP 1.1 Server Response Headers*

Response Header	Description	Example
Location	Used to redirect the browser to another page. Occasionally scripts will use this method for browser redirection based on capability.	Location: http://www.democompany. com/products/index.htm
Proxy-authenticate	Included with a 407 (Proxy Authentication Required) response. The value of the field consists of a challenge that indicates the authentication scheme and parameters applicable to the proxy for the request.	Proxy-authenticate: GreenDecoderRing: 0124.
Public	Lists the set of methods supported by the server. The purpose of this field strictly is to inform the browser of the capabilities of the server when new or unusual methods are encountered.	Public: **OPTIONS, MGET, MHEAD, GET, HEAD**
Retry-after	Can be used in conjunction with a 503 (Service Unavailable) response to indicate how long the service is expected to be unavailable to the requesting client. The value of this field can be either an HTTP-date or an integer number of seconds after which to retry.	Retry-after: Fri, 31 Dec 1999 23:59:59 GMT Retry-after: 60
Server	Contains information about the Web software used.	Server: Apache/1.3.12 (Unix)

Table 15-5.   *Common HTTP 1.1 Server Response Headers* (continued)

Response Header	Description	Example
Warning	Used to carry additional information about the status of a response that might not be found in the status code.	Warning: 10 Response is stale
WWW-authenticate	Included with a 401 (Unauthorized) response message. The field consists of at least one challenge that indicates the authentication scheme and parameters applicable to the request made by the client.	WWW-authenticate: Magic-Key-Challenge= 555121, DecoderRing= Green

Table 15-5.   *Common HTTP 1.1 Server Response Headers* (continued)

where *type* can be image, audio, text, video, application, multipart, message, or extension-token; and *subtype* gives the specifics of the content. Some samples are listed here:

```
text/html
application/x-director
application/x-pdf
video/quicktime
video/x-msvideo
image/gif
audio/x-wav
```

Beyond these basic headers, you also can include information such as the character-encoding language. For more information about MIME, refer to RFC 1521, available from many sites including http://www.faqs.org/rfcs/, or the list of registered MIME types at ftp://ftp.isi.edu/in-notes/iana/assignments/media-types/.

When a Web server delivers a file, the header information is intercepted by the browser and questioned. The MIME type, as mentioned earlier, is specified by the Content-type server response field. For example, if a browser receives a basic HTML file, the text/html header indicates what to do and typically renders the file in the browser window. To determine what to do with a particular MIME type that has been sent, the browser consults a look-up table mapping MIME types to actions as shown here.

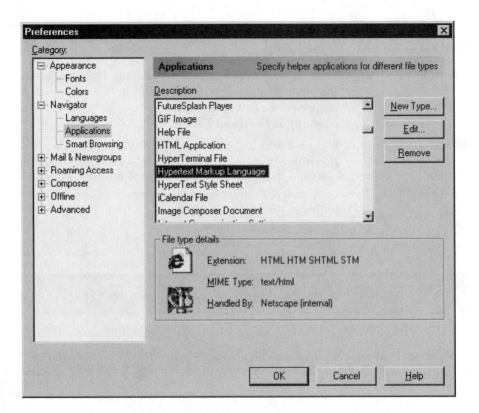

Note *On the server a lookup table that maps file extensions to outgoing MIME type headers exists as well.*

Notice that in the case of the example, the type is text/html and the actual HTML document is passed back after all the headers are finished. The dialog indicates that the browser itself will handle the file internally. Also notice that the browser indicates that it recognizes the file extensions .html, .htm, .stm, and .shtml as HTML files. However, other file extensions seem to appear as normal HTML when they are viewed online. The MIME type is the key to why a file with an extension such as .cfm, .asp, .jsp, and so on is treated as HTML by a Web browser when delivered over a network, but if opened from a local disk drive is not read properly. The reason is that these extensions often are associated with dynamically generated pages that are stamped with the HTML MIME type by the server; when reading off the local drive, the browser relies instead on the file extension such as .htm to determine the contents of a file. If a browser attempts to read a file that it is unsure about, either because of file extension or MIME type, it should respond with a dialog such as the one shown here as Netscape does.

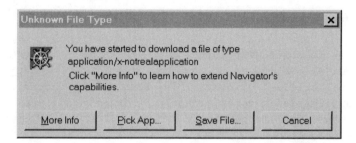

What's very interesting is how Internet Explorer prompts the user to immediately save data if the MIME type is not understood, as shown by this dialog.

What's interesting is that it is very easy to install a relationship between a MIME type and a program to handle the data, yet few people seem to add the relationships to directly deal with any form of data served by a Web server.

Normally, Web pages are delivered properly, so these dialogs are not seen. The browser first would read the HTML being delivered and then retrieve any other objects, such as GIF images, sound files, Flash files, Java applets, etc., that are associated with the page. Each object would result in another request to the server. If the browser encountered something such as

```
<img src="images/logo.gif" height="100" width="200"
alt="Demo Company">
```

it then would form a request like

```
GET /images/logo.gif HTTP/1.1
Connection: Keep-Alive
User-Agent: Mozilla/4.0 (compatible; MSIE 5.01; Windows 98)
Accept: application/x-comet, image/gif, image/x-xbitmap,
        image/jpeg, image/pjpeg, */*
Accept-Language: en-us
```

The server then would respond with a similar answer as before, but this time indicating that a MIME type of image/gif is being returned, followed by the appropriate form of binary data to make up an image as demonstrated here:

```
HTTP/1.1 200 OK
Date: Tue, 18 Jan 2000 04:41:15 GMT
Server: Apache/1.3.4 (Unix)
Last-Modified: Wed, 13 Oct 1999 23:37:38 GMT
Content-Length: 28531
Connection: close
Content-Type: image/gif

GIF87a—  æ÷ÿïÿÿÆï÷òÒÖ÷ïïõñî½Öïïïèñ½ïèóÆçã¿Æçõ½çç÷áß´µçÞï–çÝç½
Þñ¥çß÷´Þï-ÞÞÖä¥Ü÷œÞÖï°Õç"ÞÏ®ŒÞÕï™×÷"ÖÇµŒÖÆ–„ÖÆ-{ÖÅÓsÖ½-½½¥À½œsÎ½
¥¿¹ kÎÎµ¥¬- yµÎ©¨<¥¥¥ ¡–œ>Œ¥Ã{""‡'
X
< ^ŒŒ{„Œ{j ¢„„s, „'}l  {„{s.fT{{s zjq|~¦eUmogKvŠ ]QljZckZoe
PfegccZccRZcRX
… binary file continues …
```

Consider that with the MIME type set properly, it is literally possible to serve any object. Yet page authors often avoid serving custom forms of data beyond HTML or common media types such as GIF, JPEG, or WAV because of unfamiliarity with the MIME-type configuration possibilities on client and server. Probably this is due to how little is said about MIME when discussing Web site development, but how important it is in the discussion between the browser and the server and is the key to making server-side programs work properly as discussed in Chapter 12. In some sense, one can think of the core Web protocols—HTML, HTTP, and MIME—like the world famous three tenors. People only remember the first two, but it takes three to make it work!

The Realities of Publishing and Maintaining a Web Site

Although understanding how Web servers work and the issues in choosing an in-house or outsourced server appears easy enough, it does not hint at the challenges of actually running a Web site. Far too often, Web professionals are quick to start a Web project but slow to continue it. The fun often is in the development of the site, setting the structure, designing the navigation, creating the look and feel, and then coding the page. But what happens next? The site is released to its intended audience, but you can't abandon it now. Web sites need care and feeding. Depending on the site, there might be daily, weekly, or monthly maintenance to perform. Adding new information, checking for broken links, continually testing under new browsers, upgrading HTML or script code to modern standards, running statistics, and performing various server-related activities such as upgrading software or running backups all are vital tasks. The real work of the site comes after it is released. The site was built for some purpose, and now it is time to fulfill it. The next chapter discusses some of these topics and explains how Web publishing truly is an ongoing process.

Summary

Site development should address the need of hosting pages on a Web server. Developers can choose to host sites on servers within companies; obtain the necessary hardware, software, Internet connection, and labor required to do hosting themselves; or elect to outsource hosting to an ISP or Web hosting company. Because of the costs and complications involved in trying to provide sufficient resources to do your own hosting, it often makes sense to outsource. This approach presents the options of renting space on a shared server or the co-location of a dedicated server at a hosting facility. There is more flexibility in running your own server, rather than being at the mercy of what a shared hosting provider makes available. Running your own server requires selection and evaluation of server software and hosting platform as well as consideration of performance requirements. In addition to server and hosting choices, an understanding of how Web servers work using the HTTP and MIME protocols can be useful.

Chapter 16

Site Management

E ven after all the work of building and delivering a Web site, the Web developer's job is not done. Web sites live on and must be maintained to be effective. There are many aspects to Web site maintenance, from adding new content to upgrading a server. This chapter focuses on Web site maintenance issues controlled by or related to HTML. A brief discussion about the potential extent of site maintenance duties will be presented at the end of the chapter.

Meta-Information

Meta-information is simply information about information. Information on the Web often involves many pieces of associated, descriptive information that isn't always explicitly represented in the resource itself. Examples of meta-information include the creator of a document, the document's subject, the publisher, the creation date, and even the title. When used properly, descriptive meta-information has many benefits. It can make information easier to locate by providing search engines with more detailed indexing information, rate information to protect minors from viewing certain content, and a variety of other things. As already discussed, meta-information is related to linking because it helps provide meaning for a document's role in a global or local information space. Meta-information also can provide room for miscellaneous information related to the document. HTML's primary support for meta-information is through the **<meta>** element, which allows authors to add arbitrary forms of metadata.

The name Attribute

A **<meta>** element that uses the **name** attribute is the easiest to understand. The **name** attribute specifies the type of information. The **content** attribute is set to the content of the meta-information itself. For example,

```
<meta name="Favorite Sandwich" content="Turkey and Swiss">
```

defines meta-information indicating the document author's favorite lunch. Although metadata can be inserted into a document and list characteristics limited only by an author's imagination, there are some well-understood values that have meaning for Web search tools such as AltaVista, HotBot, and Infoseek. Many search robots understand the **author**, **description**, and **keywords** values for the **name** attribute. By setting the **name** and **content** attributes, HTML authors can add meta-information to the head of their documents and improve the indexing of their pages by Web search robots. The following code sets the description of a Web page for a fictitious company:

```
<!DOCTYPE HTML PUBLIC "-//W3C//DTD HTML 4.01 Transitional//EN">
<html>
<head>
```

```
<title>Demo Company Home Page</title>
<meta name="author" content="Demo Company, Inc.">
<meta name="description" content="Demo Company, the #1 vendor
     of green gadgets on the Web">
<meta name="keywords" content="Demo Company, green gadgets,
gadgets">
</head>
<body>
. . .Content of the page
</body>
</html>
```

As this example demonstrates, HTML authors can improve the indexing of their pages simply by providing the appropriate keywords in the correct **<meta>** element format and alerting the search robot to the site's existence. This is discussed in more depth later in this chapter in the section entitled "Search Engine Promotion." For now let's turn our attention to the other various uses of the **<meta>** element.

<meta> and http-equiv

The other form of the **<meta>** element uses the **http-equiv** attribute, which directly allows the document author to insert HTTP header information. The browser can access this information during read time. The server also can access it when the document is sent, but this is rare. The **http-equiv** attribute is set to a particular HTTP header type, whereas the **content** value is set to the value associated with the header. For example,

```
<meta http-equiv="Expires" content="Wed, 04 Jun 1998 22:34:07 GMT">
```

placed in the head of a document sets the expiration date to be June 4, 1998. A variety of HTTP headers can be placed in the **<meta>** element. The most useful applications of this form of **<meta>** are cache control, client-pull, and site filtering.

Cache Control

Caching on the Web involves keeping a copy of a page or media item either locally on a user's disk drive or up on a proxy server on the network to avoid fetching a brand new copy from a Web site. This is a very good idea because it avoids redundant network traffic. Consider the value of refetching a page over and over and over again if it is not changing. However good the idea of caching might be, very often browsers or proxy servers too aggressively cache pages. Very often this causes users to inadventertantly view old content. The **<meta>** tag can be used to influence caching by setting expiration dates as well as to provide other cache control information.

There are three **<meta>** tag forms that can be used to control document caching.The first, **Expires**, actually is supposed to specify an expiry date for the Web page. You can set the date for expiration in the past and the browser or proxy should always ask for a new page. For example, as previously shown we placed

```
<meta http-equiv="Expires" content="Wed, 04 Jun 1998 22:34:07 GMT">
```

in the head of a document to set the expiration date to be June 4, 1998. Because this obviously is in the past it should cause the page to expire. However, it's easier just to set the content attribute value to 0 which should indicate an expiration time of "now," and therefore cause the browser to ask for a new version of the page every time.

```
<meta http-equiv="Expires" content="0">
```

Of course you also can set a real time value in GMT format as shown in the previous examples to indicate a page expiration at a future date.

Aside from setting the expiration date, two values for the http-equiv attribute—**Pragma** and **Cache-Control**—are specifically designed to prevent (or control) caching, and should take a value of **no-cache**. So, to prevent your page being cached in most browsers, you should use the following lines:

```
<meta http-equiv="Pragma" content="no-cache">
```

```
<meta http-equiv="Cache-Control" content="no-cache">
```

Client-Pull

Beginning with Netscape, an extension was made that allows a page to be automatically loaded after a certain period of time. This concept is called *client-pull*. For example, you can build an entry page, or *splash page*, that welcomes visitors to a site and then automatically follows with a second page after a certain period of time. The following example **<meta>** element loads a page called "secondpage.htm" 10 seconds after the first page loads:

```
<meta http-equiv="REFRESH" content="10;URL=secondpage.htm">
```

Using the client-pull form of the **<meta>** element is easy. Just set the content equal to the desired number of seconds, followed by a semicolon and the URL (full or relative) of the page to load. Note, however, that not all browsers support this form of meta-refresh so often people add a link to a page that indicates the user should click on the link if a page does not refresh after a certain amount of time.

Note *The client-pull concept often is discussed with a related idea called server-push, which primarily is used to create simple animations. However, server-push animation and other such tricks no longer need to be addressed, because they are more easily accomplished by using animated GIF images or JavaScript.*

The **<meta>** element is very open-ended. The World Wide Web Consortium (W3C) is already developing more sophisticated approaches for representing metadata. The most interesting approach probably is PICS, described next, which provides a standard for site filtering.

Site Filtering with PICS

One major use of meta-information for links and pages is *site filtering*. At its base level, a filter can be used to restrict access to certain files or types of information. As a technology, this sounds rather innocuous, but when extended, site filtering can quickly lead to censorship. Whether filtering information on the Internet is right or wrong is an area of great debate. Obviously, parents and educators are extremely concerned with the availability of pornographic, violent, or other "inappropriate" types of information on the Internet. Deciding what is inappropriate is the key to the censorship problem, because definitions of what should be allowed vary from person to person. Regardless of how "inappropriate" is defined, few people would disagree that information considered inappropriate by just about everyone does exist on the Internet. The perceived extent of this information tends to be directly related to a person's belief system. The W3C has proposed the *Platform for Internet Content Selection*, or PICS (http://www.w3.org/pub/WWW/PICS/), as a way to address the problem of content filtering on the Web.

The idea behind PICS is relatively simple. A rated page or site will include a **<meta>** element within the head of an HTML document. This **<meta>** element indicates the rating of the particular item. A rating service, which can be any group, organization, or company that provides content ratings, assigns the rating. Rating services include independent, nonprofit groups such as the *Recreational Software Advisory Council* (RSAC) (http://www.rsac.org), which already implements a rating system for video games. The rating label used by a particular rating service must be based on a well-defined set of rules that describes the criteria for rating, the scale of values for each aspect of the rating, and a description of the criteria used in setting a value. Usually, the specification of a rating is found in a RAT file that can be accessed by browser or filtering software. Figure 16-1 shows a RAT file for the violence category of RSAC-based (RSACi) PICS ratings. Other categories not shown include sex, nudity, and language.

To add rating information to a site or document, a PICS label in the form of a **<meta>** element must be added to the head of an HTML file. This **<meta>** element must include the URL of the rating service that produced the rating; some information about the rating itself such as its version, submitter, or date of creation; and the rating itself. Many rating services, such as RSACi (the Internet rating system from RSAC),

```
((PICS-version 1.0)
(rating-system "http://www.rsac.org/Ratings/Description/")
(rating-service "http://www.rsac.org/ratingsv01.html")
(name "RSACi")
(description "The Recreational Software Advisory Council
rating service for the Internet. Based on the work of Dr.
Donald F. Roberts of Stanford University, who has studied
the effects of media for nearly 20 years.")

(category
(transmit-as "v")
(name "Violence")
(label
(name "Level 0: No violence")
(description "No aggressive violence; No natural or
accidental violence.")
(value 0) )
(label
```

Figure 16-1.   *RSACi rating system RAT file*

allow free self-rating. Filling out a form and answering a few questions about a site's content are all that is required to generate an RSACi PICS label, as shown in Figure 16-2.

After you complete and submit the questionnaire you will receive an e-mail containing the appropriate meta-information, which then can be placed in the head of your HTML documents. An example of a PICS label using the RSACi rating is shown here:

```
<!DOCTYPE HTML PUBLIC "-//W3C//DTD HTML 4.01 Transitional//EN">
<html>
<head>
<title>PICS Meta Tag Example</title>
<meta http-equiv="PICS-Label"
      content='(PICS-1.1 "http://www.rsac.org/ratingsv01.html"
      l gen true comment "RSACi North America Server"
      by "webmaster@democompany.com" for
"http://www.democompany.com" on
"1997.05.26T13:05-0500" r (n 0 s 0 v 0 l 1))'>
</head>
```

```
<body>

<h1 align="center">Demo Company, Inc.</h1>
<hr>
<p>
There's nothing offensive at this site.
</p>
</body>
</html>
```

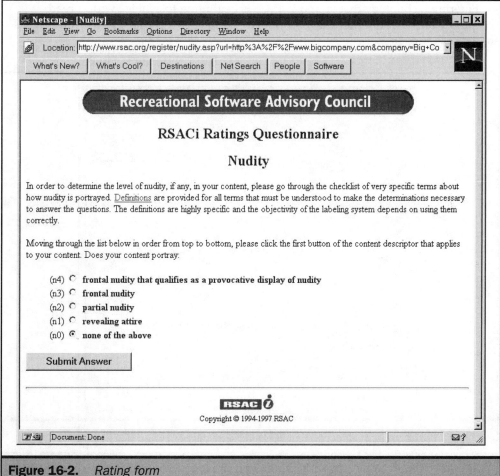

Figure 16-2. *Rating form*

Under the RSACi rating system, information is rated based on nudity, sex, violence, and language, on a five-category scale from 0 to 4. In this case, the rating is for a typical corporate site that generally has little "inappropriate" information concerning sex and violence, but might use slang or jargon that could be misconstrued out of context.

The <meta> element with PICS information must occur within the head of the document; otherwise it will not be recognized. More than one <meta> element may be included within the head, so that multiple rating services can be used simultaneously.

When filtering software reads a file that contains a rating, it determines whether the information should be allowed or denied. Very strict filtering environments might deny all sites that have no rating, so sites with a broad audience are encouraged to use ratings to avoid restricting readership.

Filtering technology that supports PICS is beginning to achieve widespread acceptance and use. Internet Explorer already includes PICS-based rating filtering, as shown in Figure 16-3.

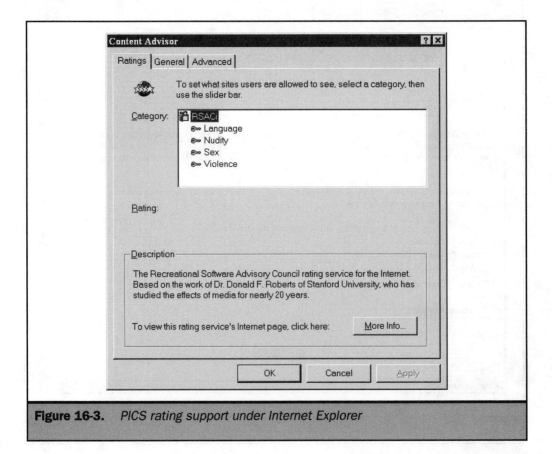

Figure 16-3.   *PICS rating support under Internet Explorer*

Numerous filtering software packages, such as www.surfcontrol.com, are extremely popular both with parents and corporate users trying to limit employee Web abuse. Of course, the technology itself can't cure the problem. Trust in a particular ratings system is a major stumbling block in adoption of the filtering idea. Even when trust is gained, if the rating system seems confusing or arbitrary, its value is lowered. In the "real world," Hollywood's MPAA movie rating system has a single value of G, PG, PG-13, R, or NC-17 for each movie. The assignment of a particular movie rating is based on many factors that often seem arbitrary to casual observers. When considering movies, parents might wonder how scenes of a dinosaur ripping a man to shreds merits a PG or PG-13 rating, whereas the use of certain four-letter words indicates an R rating. Certainly similar situations occur on the Internet. Because of the imprecise nature of ratings, the topic is a loaded one, both off and on the Internet.

Beyond simple content rating, some potential benefits of PICS aren't immediately obvious. With PICS-based environments, employers could limit employee access to Web sites that are used for day-to-day business. The idea of PICS can be extended not just to deny or allow information, but to prefer it. Imagine a filtering service for search engines that could return sites that have a particular quality of content or level of accuracy. In the general sense, labels are important, because they allow documents to move beyond a mere description of where the document *is* to what the document is *about*.

Before moving on to the topic of link management it is a good idea to discuss further the use of the **<meta>** tag for search engine promotion.

Search Engine Promotion

Site owners always want to be number one in search engines. Consider if you are a small travel agent. You probably would love it if people would go to a search engine, type **travel**, and have a link to your site show up as the first one. You'd get a large number of visits for sure. Unfortunately, there probably are a lot of other people who would like to be number one, and being ranked 4,036th isn't going be worth much. In fact, if you are outside the first 20 sites or so returned you probably aren't going to get many clicks at all. Because of this, page authors are always trying to determine how search engines categorize pages, and building their page with keywords in such a way to get a high ranking. In some ways, this idea is similar to how people name their company something like AAA Travel in order to be listed first in the phone book. Unfortunately, consider how many travel agents in the world want their sites to be in the top ten in search engines and you'll see a potential problem. The Web is not as geographically specific as the phone book. Consider if there were a single phone book for the United States. There probably would be dozen of pages filled with companies, all starting with AAA. The Web already has this problem, and that's one of the reasons you get so many results when you run a query for a competitive industry such as discount travel.

The war to be first in the search engine has an obvious final chapter—the rise of pay for position. Consider that the tricks to be at the top of the search engine list have spread rapidly. For common search phrases, it is nearly impossible to stay at the top of the list for long because other sites use the same search engine promotion techniques. Already search engines such as Goto (www.goto.com) are opting to push people who are willing to pay for position to the top of the list. Priority placement also is being made for banner ads triggered to correspond to particular search phrases. Just like with the phone book, naming your company AAA Travel might put you at the top of the line listings, but readers might opt to look at the large display ads. Search engines eventually will adopt the same model. Furthermore, as end users become more sophisticated, they will begin to rely more on directory listings for generic topics and use search engines only for very specific or complex lookups. The eventual outcome of the search engine war will almost certainly be a return to traditional models of information retrieval methods used in other advertising forms in which you pay for audience relevancy and position. For now, page authors should consider the failure to take advantage of search engine positioning tricks to be very foolish, regardless of their long-term viability.

Note *This is by no means a complete discussion of a topic that literally changes on a weekly basis. Readers looking for more up-to-date information are directed to the numerous promotion sites that exist on the Web, especially Search Engine Watch (www.searchenginewatch.com).*

How Search Engines Work

So how do search engines work? First, a large number of pages are gathered from the Web using a process often called *spidering*. Next, the collected pages are indexed to determine what they are about. Finally, a search page is built so that users can enter queries in and see what pages are related to their queries. The best analogy for the process is that the search engine builds as big a haystack as possible, then tries to organize the haystack somehow, and finally lets the user try to find the proverbial needle in the resulting haystack of information by entering a query on a search page. Figure 16-4 shows a basic overview of how search engines work.

Adding to the Engines

Getting a site's pages gathered by a search engine is the first step in making a site findable on the Web. The easiest way to do this is simply to tell search engines that your site exists. Most search engines will allow you to add a URL to be indexed. For example, Lycos allows you to add a site for gathering by using a simple form (http://www.lycos.com/addasite.html). Of course, adding your site to every single search engine could be a tedious task, so many vendors (http://www.submit-it.com) are eager to provide developers with a way to bulk submit to numerous search

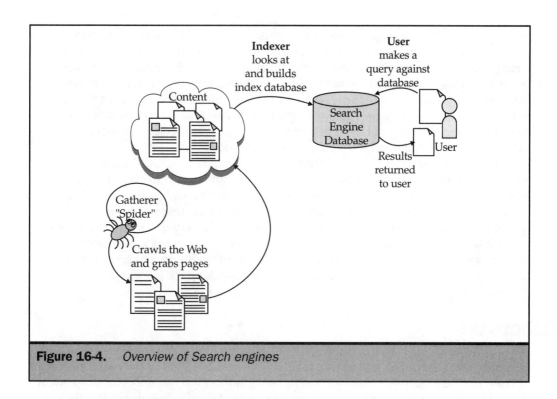

Figure 16-4.   *Overview of Search engines*

engines. Most Web site promotion software, such as WebPosition Gold
(http://www.webposition.com/), also includes automated submission utilities.

A big question is, how many search engines should you submit your site to? Some
people favor adding only a few links to the important top ten engines, especially
Yahoo! Numerous studies, as well as this author's experience, suggest that big search
sites, particularly Yahoo!, account for most search engine referring traffic. However,
some site promotion experts feel this is incorrect, and believe it is best to create as
many links to sites as possible. In fact, a whole class of link sites called "Free For All"
links or FFA sites (not to be confused with anything related to the Future Farmers of
America) have sprung up to service people who believe that "all links should lead to
me" works. The reality is that most of these link services are pretty much worthless
and often generate worthless traffic and spam messages. Further, consider that even if
you do get back links and email, it is mostly from people who are doing the same thing
you're doing—trying to get links.

Robot Exclusion

Before getting too involved with putting yourself in every search engine, consider that
it isn't always a good idea to have a robot index your entire site, regardless of whether

it is your own internal search engine or a public search engine. First consider that some pages, such as programs in your cgi-bin directory, don't need to be indexed. Second, many pages can be transitory, and having them indexed might result in users seeing 404 errors if they enter from a search engine. Last, you might just not want people to enter on every single page—particularly those deep within a site. So-called "deep linking" can be confusing for users entering from public search engines. Consider that because these users start out deep in a site, they are not exposed to the home or entry page information that often is used to orient site visitors.

Probably the most troublesome aspect of search engines and automated site gathering tools such as offline browsers is that they can be used to stage a denial of service attack on a site. The basic idea of most spiders is to read pages and follow pages as fast as they can. Consider if you tell a spider to crawl a single site as fast as it possibly can. All the requests to the crawled server could very quickly overwhelm it, causing the site to be unable to fulfill requests—thus denying services to legitimate site visitors. Fortunately, most people are not malicious in spidering, but understand that it does happen inadvertently when a spider keeps reindexing the same dynamically generated page.

Robots.txt

To deal with limiting robot access, the Robot Exclusion protocol was adopted. The basic idea is to use a special file called robots.txt that should be found in the root directory of a Web site. For example, if a spider was indexing http://www.democompany.com, it would first look for a file at http://www.democompany.com/robots.txt. If it finds a file, it would analyze the file first before proceeding to index the site.

Note *If you have a site such as http://www.bigfakehostingvendor.com/~customer, you will find that many spiders will ignore a robots.txt file with a URL of http://www.bigfakehostingvendor.com/~customer/robots.txt. Unfortunately, you will have to ask the vendor to place an entry for you in their robots.txt file.*

The basic format of the robots.txt file is a listing of the particular spider or user agent you are looking to limit and statements including which directory paths to disallow. For example,

```
User-agent: *
Disallow: /cgi-bin/
Disallow: /temp/
Disallow: /archive/
```

In this case, we have denied access for all robots to the cgi-bin directory, the temp directory, and an archive directory—possibly where we would move files that are very old but still might need to be online. You should be very careful with what you put in your robots.txt. Consider the following file:

```
User-agent: *
Disallow: /cgi-bin/
Disallow: /images/
Disallow: /subscribers-only/
Disallow: /resellers.html
```

In this file, a special subscribers-only and resellers file has been disallowed for indexing. However, you have just let people know this is sensitive. For example, if you have content that is hidden unless someone pays to receive a URL via e-mail, you certainly will not want to list it in the robots.txt file. Just letting people know the file or directory exists is a problem. Consider that malicious visitors actually will look carefully at a robots.txt file to see just what it is you don't want people to see. That's very easy to do; just type in the URL like so: http://www.*companytolookat*.com/robots.txt.

Be aware that the robot exclusion standard assumes that spidering programs will abide by it. A malicious spider will, of course, simply ignore this file, and you might be forced to set up your server to block particular IP addresses or user agents in case someone has decided to attack your site.

Robot Control with <meta>

An alternative method to the robots.txt file that is useful, particularly for those users who have no access to the root directory of their domain, is to use a **<meta>** tag to control indexing. To disallow indexing of a particular page, use a **<meta>** tag such as

```
<meta name="robots" content="noindex">
```

in the **<head>** section of the HTML. You also can instruct a spider to not follow any links coming out of the page:

```
<meta name="robots" content="noindex, nofollow">
```

When using this type of exclusion, just make sure not to confuse the robot with contradictory information such as

```
<meta name="robots" content="index, noindex">
```

or

```
<meta name="robots" content="index, nofollow, follow ">
```

as the spider might either ignore the information entirely or maybe even index anyway. The other downside to the **<meta>** tag approach is that fewer of the public search engines support it than robots.txt.

Optimizing for Search Engines

Optimizing your site for a search engine is not difficult. The first thing to do is to start to think like a search engine—in other words, don't really think at all. Search engines literally look at pages and make educated guesses about what pages are about by following a set of rules to try to understand what the page is about. For example, search engines look for word frequency, **<meta>** tags, and a variety of other things. However, they really can't tell the difference between a page about the Miami Dolphins football team and a dolphin show in Miami. The reason is that search engines generally rely on keyword matching in conjunction with some heuristics such as the placement of words in a page or the number of linking sites. So if a page author knows what a search engine is looking for, it is easy enough to optimize a page for the search engine to rank it highly. The next few sections provide a brief overview of some of the things search engines look for as well as some tricks people have employed to improve their search rankings.

Using <meta> for Search Engines

Many search engines look at the **<meta>** tags for keywords and descriptions of a page's content. A **<meta>** tag such as

```
<meta name="Keywords" content="Butler-1000, Robot butler, Robot butler
specifications, where to buy a robot butler, Metallic Man Servant, Demo
Company, robot, butler">
```

could be used in a Demo Company page about robot butlers. Notice how the content started first with the most specific keywords and phrases and ended with generic keywords. This should play into how most users approach search engines.

Once a search engine looks at the **<meta>** tag, it can rate one site higher than another based upon the frequency of keywords in the **content** attribute. Because of this, some page authors load their **<meta>** tags with redundant keywords:

```
<meta name="Keywords" content=" Robot butler, Robot butler, Robot butler,
"Robot butler, Robot butler, Robot butler, Robot butler, Robot butler,
Robot butler, Robot butler">
```

However, many search engines consider this to be keyword loading and might drop the page from their indexes. If the keyword loading is a little less obvious and combinations of words and phrases are repeated like so,

```
<meta name="Keywords" content="Robot butler, Butler-1000, Metallic
Man Servant, Robot butler, Butler-1000, Metallic Man Servant, Robot
butler, Butler-1000, Metallic Man Servant, Robot butler,
Butler-1000, Metallic Man Servant">
```

the search engine might not consider this improper. An even better approach is to make sure the pattern of repeating words isn't quite as obvious as it varies its order as shown here.

```
<meta name="Keywords" content="Butler-1000, Robot butler, Metallic
Man Servant, Robot butler, Butler-1000, robot, Robot butler,
Democompany, Metallic Man Servant, Butler-1000, robot, butler,
Robot butler, Butler-1000">
```

However, be aware that search engines might still notice the heavy use of certain words or phrases and consider this spamming, potentially reducing the page's ranking or dropping it from the index completely.

Search engines also look at the description value for the **<meta>** tag. For example,

```
<meta name="Description" content="The Demo Company Robot Butler is
the most outstanding metallic man servant on the market. The
Butler-1000 comes complete with multiple personalities and voice
modules including the ever-popular faux-British accent.">
```

would be included on the robot butler page and could be examined by the search engine as well as returned by the search engine on the results page. Because it might be output for the user to see, you should provide some valuable information in the description that will help the user determine whether they want to visit your site. Preferably, keep the description to a sentence or two, and at most three or four sentences.

Titles and File Naming

One important aspect of search engine ranking is making sure your page has a very good title. For example,

```
<title>Robot Butler</title>
```

is a bad title as far as search engine ranking goes. A better title might be

```
<title>Butler-1000: Specification of Demo Company's Robot Butler,
the leading metallic man servant on the market</title>
```

Remember that people also look at page titles, and they are used for bookmarking, so a really long title might be more for search engines than for users.

The name of a file also can be important for search engines. Rather than naming a file "butler.htm", use "butler1000_robot_butler.htm". Consider that if you have a good domain name and directory structure, you can create a URL that almost makes sense. Consider, for example, if we named our server democompany.com as well as www.democompany.com. We might have a URL like this:

```
http://democompany.com/products/robots/butler1000_robot_butler.htm
```

Notice how this almost includes the same information as the title. This provides a secondary benefit of letting the user know where they are, rather than resorting to cryptic URLs such as

```
http://democompany.com/products.exe?prod=robots&mod=butler-1000
```

Relevant Text Content

One of the best ways to get indexed is to have the keywords and phrases actually within the content of the page. Many search engines will look at text within a page, particularly if it is either toward the top of the page or within heading tags such as **<h1>** or **<h2>**. Search engines might also look at the contents of link text. Thus,

```
<a href="specifications.htm">Specifications</a>
```

is not as search engine friendly as

```
<a href="specifications.htm">Robot Butler Specification</a>
```

One problem with the fact that search engines focus on page text is that often page authors create home pages that are primarily graphic. Search engines might have little more to go on than the **<meta>** tag and page title and thus could rank the page lower. Consider first using the **alt** attribute for the **<img>** tag to provide some extra information; for example,

```
<img src="robot.gif" alt="Butler-1000: Demo Company's industry
leading robot butler">
```

Of course, putting the actual text in the page would be better. Some page authors resort to either making text very small or in a color similar to the background—or both—so that users won't see it but search engines hopefully will pick it up. For example,

```
<font size="1" color="white">The Demo Company Butler-1000 is the
best robot butler. The Demo Company Butler-1000 is the best robot
butler. The Demo Company Butler-1000 is the best robot
butler.</font>
```

Be careful with the small or invisible text trick. Many search engines will consider this to be spamming and might drop the page from the search engine.

Links and Entry Points

Another aspect of search engine ranking has to do with the number of links leaving a page as well as the number of pages that link to a page. Landmark pages such as home pages tend to have a lot of outgoing and incoming links. Search engines would prefer to rank landmark pages highly, so it is important that key pages in your site have links to them from nearly every page. Some search engines also favor sites that have many sites pointing to them. Because of this, people are already starting to create sites solely for the purpose of pointing to other sites.

Another approach to improving search engine ranking is to submit many pages in a site, or even off a site to a search engine. All of these entry pages, often called *doorway pages*, point to important content within your site. Unfortunately for many users, doorway pages are more like decoy pages, as they can be loaded with false content to attract the visitor and nearly always eventually deposit the user at page they didn't really want to see. The problem with search engine promotion is that the distance from simple logical keyword loading and various tricks is a short one—particularly if page authors are obsessed with top-ten ranking.

Tricky Business

The tricks employed by search engine specialists are numerous and change all the time. Many ideas are simple add-ons to normal Web design techniques. For example, many page authors rely on invisible pixel shims to force layout. Search engine promoters say, "why not put **alt** attributes on these images to improve things?" Imagine this:

```
<img src="pixel.gif" alt="robot butler robot butler robot butler">
```

all over your page. Then pity the user who pauses on top of one of these invisible pixels only to have a ToolTip pop up screaming about whatever the page is promoting. Spamming pages with invisible text, small text, and multiple images, or just loading the **<meta>** or **<title>** tags, are not the most sophisticated tricks, but they often work.

Other tricks include the infamous "bait and switch," in which a special search engine page is created and then posted to a search engine. Once the ranking is high, the bait page is replaced with a real page built for users. A more complicated version of this could be dubbed "feeding the dogs." In the "feeding the dogs" scenario, you write a program that senses when a search engine hits the site and "feed" the engine the page it wants to see. Like a ravenous dog, it gobbles up the food with no idea it just ate the equivalent of informational pig snouts. As real users hit the site, they aren't served the dog food, but instead get the real site.

Detecting search engines versus regular users isn't terribly difficult because the engines identify themselves and come from consistent IP addresses. In reality, "feeding the dogs" is just a modified form of browser detection. Search engines can do little to combat this approach because they would have to consider eliminating dynamically built pages—which is impossible given their growing importance—or not informing sites that they are search engines while indexing. A few search engines have already begun to provide a link to a page that shows what was indexed so users can determine if they are being shown something different than what a search engine indexed.

The problem with all the search engine promotion business is that it tempts the page author to stop building pages for users and start building them for search engines. This is just another form of designing more for your own needs than for your users. One of the most interesting aspects about search engines is that many large organizations don't rely greatly on them for driving traffic. In fact, for many corporations, unless you type their name in directly, you'll be hard-pressed to find them in a search engine. However, despite what appears to be a major oversight on their part, these sites continue to get huge amounts of traffic. According to studies such as the GVU Internet Survey, people type in URLs directly quite often. How are they finding out about sites? Always remember that search engines aren't the only way to drive traffic. Next we'll discuss a common maintenance task for HTML authors: link management.

Link Maintenance

Even when links are used correctly within a site they eventually will require maintenance as pages are moved around. Commonly, links to external sites will break as other sites move their pages without considering outside linkage. Ferreting out the broken links within a site can be tedious, but doing so should be a top priority. A broken link should be considered a serious problem. Users clicking on a broken link are on the road to nowhere, eventually to receive the now infamous "404 Not Found" message or something similar. Imagine if a menu on a software application triggered a message saying "Sorry, spell check not found." Such oversights would not be tolerated within software and should be considered the same level of problem within a site.

Fortunately, identifying and fixing broken links isn't terribly difficult. Armed with a tool such as LinkBot (www.linkbot.com) or Coast WebMaster (www.coast.com), finding broken links is a simpler matter. However, consider that if you have external links within a site, even constant monitoring isn't going to keep broken links out of the site at all times. To account for the unforeseen broken link, consider installing a custom 404 page. Then put information such as a link to a site map or a method to contact the site's administrator in the custom error page. An example custom 404 page is shown in Figure 16-5.

Note *Installation of a custom 404 error page depends on the server being utilized.*

Redirection Pages

Rather than showing errors many sites prefer to redirect users to new pages. If the content at a URL such as http://www.democompany.com/movedon.htm has moved

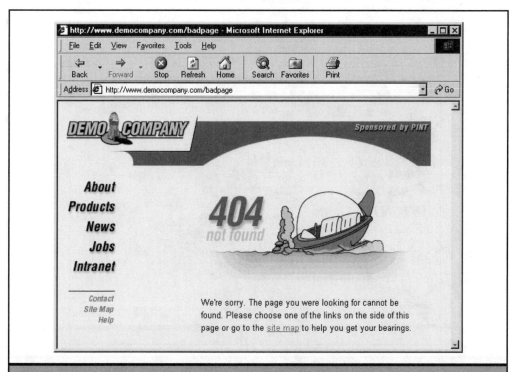

Figure 16-5. *Custom 404 pages can fit with a site design*

SITE DELIVERY AND
MANAGEMENT

to a new location, it is best to install a page that points people to the new page or even quickly redirects them there. The URL previously given will do just that. Some site maintainers prefer to send people directly to the new page whereas others will install a temporary page informing visitors of the page change, like the one shown in Figure 16-6.

Sending people directly to the new page might be seamless, but it does take some control away from the user. For example, if the user requests a particular page on, say robotic dogs, and a redirect takes them to a different page, they will become very frustrated. Always make sure that the new page is related to the moved page.

Maintaining site links can be a great deal of work. Custom error pages and redirection pages can help, but Web managers will have to be ever vigilant in link monitoring. Good Web sites should make sure to watch log files for referring sites. Furthermore, consider visiting a search engine and doing a reverse search. Specifically, search for sites that link to yours and make sure they are up to date on any significant site changes made. Making sure that other sites link to you correctly might be a great

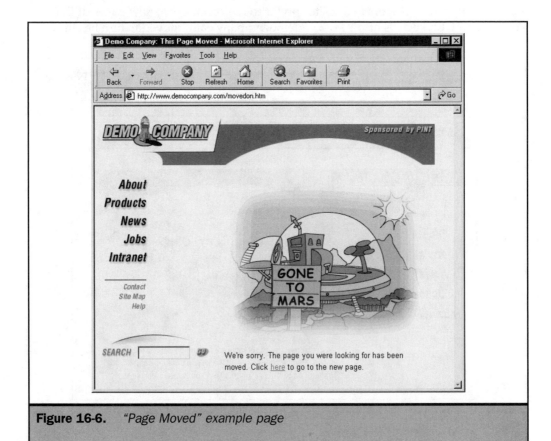

Figure 16-6.   *"Page Moved" example page*

deal of work, but it is all part of being a good Web citizen. The next section presents a brief overview of common site management duties.

Managing Web Sites

Once a Web server is installed and successfully delivering content to users, there are a great number of maintenance tasks that should take place. Servers must be continually monitored for availability, performance, and security. Site content must also be checked for accuracy and freshness as content probably will be continually added and deleted. Functional elements of sites beyond simple links also might have to be maintained as bugs might be discovered or new features required by users. Even the introduction of a new browser might require some modification of site code to handle new features or account for rendering or use problems. Finally, as visitors use the site their usage patterns should be analyzed to determine which sections are being used as well as which are not. Usage analysis can lead to further modification of the site. Given the multitude of tasks involved in Web site maintenance, the line between system, network, and content management blurs fairly often, which can be a problem. Providing 24/7 monitoring of systems, upgrades, usage analysis, testing, and content management of any significantly sized corporate site probably is beyond the means of a single individual—whether they have the title "Web master" or not. Readers are encouraged to focus on acquiring enough skills in individual areas as required. Knowledge of server maintenance and management should not be considered a requirement for authoring content for a Web site. However, HTML document authors probably will be directly involved content management so a more in-depth discussion will be presented here.

Content Management

Maintaining content is just as important as maintaining the server itself. Large sites or those with numerous contributors will quickly degrade if special care is not taken. First, make sure there is a set policy for naming files. For example, consider avoiding using special characters such as underscores (_) in filenames, because it will be difficult for users to notice them in the address line of a browser. Instead of robot_butler.htm, consider robot-butler.htm or just robotbutler.htm. However, be careful with using filenames such as RobotButler.htm or even capitalizing directories. The domain aspect of a URL is not case sensitive and the user might not be consistent in his or her use of case. Also, some servers such as UNIX systems are case sensitive, whereas others such as NT are not, so moving sites between the systems could be troublesome. Always use lowercase to avoid such problems. Shorter extensions generally are better if you just consider the extra characters to type, as well as the fact that some older systems prefer three-character extensions. However, regardless of your take on .htm versus .html, pick one and be consistent.

Consider even limiting filename length, or using consistent naming schemes. For example, some files might include dates in them such as press releases. Consider that pr021299.htm and pr010500.htm could reference press releases on 2/12/1999 and 01/05/2000, respectively.

Make sure to use the same care with directories that you do with files. Pick short, easy-to-type and -spell directories in all lowercase letters that lack special characters. Also, consider using common directory names to hold site assets. Table 16-1 details a few common directory names and their usual contents.

Probably the hardest part of dealing with site content is all the changes that are made. When many people are working on a site, it is easy for conventions to be overlooked and for simple errors to be introduced. To reduce the possibility that content degrades, first carefully limit who can make changes to a site. Second, resist the desire to fix site problems or add content on a moment's notice. It is far better to make

Directory Name	Contents
/cgi-bin	The traditional location for executable programs on a Web server, particularly CGI programs.
/scripts	Contains scripts for the site including JavaScripts, CGI scripts, and server-parsed languages such as Cold Fusion or Active Server pages. Occasionally, the directory might be named after the type of script stored; for example, /js or /javascripts for linked JavaScript files.
/styles or /css	Should contain any linked style sheets used on a site.
/images	Contains all site images, including GIFs, JPEGs, and PNG files.
/video	Contains video assets—primarily nonstreamed video clips.
/audio	Contains audio assets—primarily nonstreamed audio files.
/pdfs	Contains PDF files such as a library of datasheets.
/download or /binaries	A central location for any programs or software distributions that are to be downloaded from the site.

Table 16-1.   *Common Site Directory Names*

regular updates, such as once a day or once a week. This allows backups to be made and provides a stable base to roll back to in case problems are introduced.

If a site is heavily updated, consider employing a content management tool. A simple source code control system can be used. A source code control system will provide an audit trail and rollback facilities, and will force site contributors to check out pages to make changes to them. More powerful content management systems that include easy-to-use, browser-based front ends, including form-based page editing, can be built or purchased. The Demo Company site (www.democompany.com) itself uses such a tool, as shown in Figure 16-7.

Regardless of the methodology used to control the update of a site, one rule cannot be stressed enough: Never work directly on a live site. Consider that users might see your changes as they happen, and even see pages in half-finished form. Furthermore, if

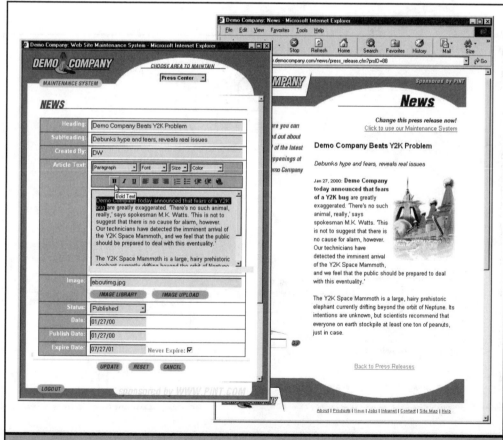

Figure 16-7.   *Demo Company's content management system*

any serious blunder is made, it might be difficult to recover from if the live site is being edited directly.

Rather than working on a live site consider using a three-site architecture as illustrated in Figure 16-8. First, set aside a development server where a copy of the site is kept and major changes and programming features can be added and tested. Second, create a staging server with an exact duplicate of the published site. The staging server is where changes are made and tested. Lastly, a production server should be utilized to actually hold the site being delivered. Changes should only be made on the development or staging site, which is later synchronized with the production server.

As Web sites become more and more important to organizations, the care and feeding of sites and servers certainly will be treated with increased seriousness and procedures and policies will be adopted to ensure that changes are made properly.

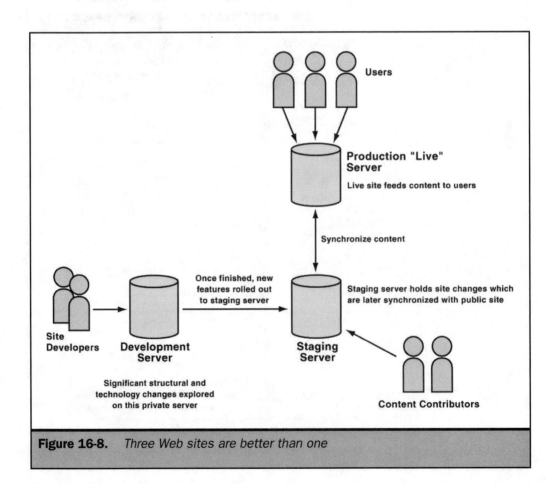

Figure 16-8. *Three Web sites are better than one*

Summary

Building a site is only half the battle; keeping it working and up to date requires constant vigilance. Web developers should make sure their HTML supports maintenance activities by using the **\<meta\>** tag properly and being aware of link usage. However, the maintenance requirements of a site will far exceed correct use of HTML. Monitoring the server, upgrading software, adding content, and analyzing log files can require significant time. In fact, for most sites, maintenance duties might have to be shared among many individuals. As we conclude the book we turn to the future of HTML—XML.

The Complete Reference

Part VI

Advanced Topics

Chapter 17

XML: Beyond HTML

With much fanfare, *Extensible Markup Language* (XML) has emerged rapidly as a new approach to delivering structured data over the Web. Why XML? Simply put, using this Web-efficient adaptation of the *Standard Generalized Markup Language* (SGML), the mother language used to define HTML, will enable authors to define their own elements. Although much of the full XML vision is not widely supported in many currently shipping browsers, and important features have yet to be finalized, the effects of XML already can be felt.

Microsoft, Netscape, and numerous others are furiously working to make XML real, under the aegis of the *World Wide Web Consortium* (W3C). Numerous languages have been developed with XML. Many are already in use, including Microsoft's push-technology *Channel Definition Format* (CDF), the *Wireless Markup Language* (WML) used by many Web enabled cellular phones, *Scalable Vector Graphics* (SVG), *Open Software Description* (OSD) format, and numerous others. But why XML? What's so wrong with HTML? Quite simply, HTML isn't flexible enough to meet the document structuring requirements of specific industries or new viewing environments. In the short term, XML isn't necessarily going to replace HTML—but it might redefine it in the guise of XHTML.

Relationship Between HTML, SGML, and XML

To understand what all the XML excitement is about, you need to understand the connection between HTML, SGML, and XML. XML is defined as an application profile, or restricted form, of SGML that is designed to support the efficient use of SGML documents over the Web. Informally, an *application profile* is a subset of a standard that has been given a little twist to accommodate real-world use. Understanding the twist that XML gives to SGML requires that you understand the strengths and weaknesses of SGML and its most famous application, HTML. However, the goal of XML is not to replace either technology, but to complement and augment them as appropriate.

The first question that needs to be addressed is why XML is even necessary when HTML is already available. Any technology that is used globally by millions and millions of people must be doing something right. As a general-purpose markup technology, HTML meets an extraordinarily broad set of user needs. However, it doesn't fit very well with applications that rely upon specialized information, either as data files or as complex, structured documents. This is particularly true for applications such as automated data interchange, which requires data to be structured in a consistent manner. Imagine trying to format a complex mathematical formula in HTML. The only choices are to make an image out of the formula, embed a special math technology, or use another document-formatting technology such as Adobe's Acrobat.

As you have seen already, by itself, HTML can't realistically accommodate the structuring and formatting needs of documents that require more than paragraphs, sections, and lists. HTML can't deal with more complex, application-specific problems because its elements are fixed; the language contains no provision for extending itself; namely, it has no provision for defining new elements. Although browser vendors used to add new elements all the time, any proposed extension now entails lengthy advocacy before the W3C.

Regardless, adding more element types to HTML doesn't make sense at this point. The language is already large enough. It is meant to be a general-purpose language that is capable of handling a large variety of documents. Thus, HTML needs some mechanism so that its general-purpose framework can be augmented to accommodate specialized content.

SGML seems like a reasonable candidate to increase HTML's flexibility. SGML is a *meta-language*, a language that is used to define other languages. Although HTML is the best-known SGML-defined language, SGML itself has been used successfully to define special document types ranging from aviation maintenance manuals to scholarly texts. SGML can represent very complex information structures, and it scales well to accommodate enormous volumes of information. SGML is extremely complex, however, and wasn't built with today's online applications in mind. The language first appeared in the late 1970s, the golden age of batch processing, and wasn't designed to be used in networked, interactive applications. Without resolving these issues, the full SGML language can't be efficiently used over the Web.

Thus, XML is an attempt to define a subset of SGML that is specifically designed for use in a Web context. As such, it will be influenced by both its SGML parent and by HTML. The exact way that XML will fit into Web documents is still a topic of great debate, but the general role of the language is clear. Initially, it will be used to represent specialized data to augment HTML documents. In fact, it is already being used to do this. For example, Microsoft's Channel Definition Format, which specifies documents for "push" delivery on the Internet, actually is an application of XML. (*Push* is a technology in which data, such as news, is sent to users on a scheduled basis, saving them the trouble of hunting for it on the Web.)

Purpose-specific extensions to Web documents will be the first use of XML, but at some point, XML will be used in its own right to design Web documents. Instead of using traditional SGML-defined HTML we will use a new form of HTML defined with XML called XHTML. Eventually we might even be using XML languages of our own definition directly within a Web browser.

Basic XML

Because XML is a subset of SGML, it should be somewhat familiar, as HTML itself is an application of SGML. However, to support efficient Web usage, XML doesn't allow the use of many SGML constructs that are used to define documents. The eliminated constructs are either infrequently used or add a performance penalty to document parsing. Writing XML sounds like a daunting task, requiring an esoteric knowledge of SGML beyond the capabilities of most HTML authors. Actually, writing simple XML documents is fairly easy. For example, suppose that you have a compelling need to define some elements to represent a fast-food restaurant's combination meals, which contain a burger, drink, and fries. How might you do this in XML? You would simply create a file such as burger.xml that contains the following markup:

```
<?xml version="1.0" encoding="UTF-8" standalone="yes" ?>
<combomeal>
   <burger>
   <name>Tasty Burger</name>
   <bun bread="white">
      <meat />
      <cheese />
      <meat />
   </bun>
   </burger>
   <fries size="large" />
   <drink size="large">
      Cola
   </drink>
</combomeal>
```

A rendering of this example under Internet Explorer 5.5 is shown in Figure 17-1.

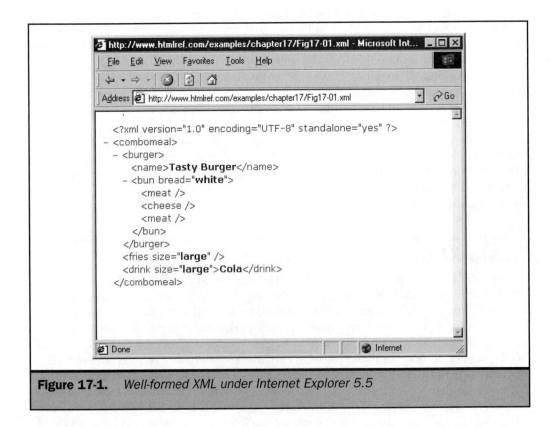

Figure 17-1. *Well-formed XML under Internet Explorer 5.5*

Notice that the browser shows a structural representation of the file, not a screen representation. You'll see how to make this file actually look like something later in the chapter. First, take a look at the document syntax. In many ways, this example "Meal Markup Language" (or MML, if you like) looks similar to HTML—but how do you know to name the element **<combomeal>** instead of **<mealdeal>** or **<lunchspecial>**? You don't need to know, because the decision is completely up to you. Simply choose any element and attribute names that meaningfully represent the domain that you want to model. Does this mean that XML has no rules? It has rules, but they are few, simple, and relate only to syntax:

■ *The document must start with the appropriate XML declaration,* like so:

```
<?xml version="1.0" encoding="UTF-8" standalone="yes" ?>
```

or maybe more simply just

```
<?xml version="1.0" ?>
```

■ *A root element must enclose the entire document.* For example, in the previous example notice how the **<combomeal>** element encloses all other elements. In fact not only must a root element enclose all other elements, the internal elements should close properly.

■ *All elements must be closed.*

```
<burger>Tasty
```

is not allowed under XML, but

```
<burger>Tasty</burger>
```

would be allowed. Even when elements do not contain content they must be closed properly as discussed in the next rule for a valid XML document.

■ *All elements with empty content must be self-identifying, by ending in "/>" instead of the familiar ">."* An empty element is one such as the HTML **
, **<hr>, or **<img>** elements. In XML, these would be represented, respectively, as **
, **<hr />, and **<img src="test.gif" />**.

■ Just like well-written HTML, *all elements must be properly nested.* For example,

```
<outer><inner>ground zero</inner></outer>
```

is correct, whereas this isn't:

```
<outer><inner>ground zero</outer></inner>
```

■ *All attribute values must be quoted.* In HTML, quoting is good authoring practice, but it is required only for values that contain characters other than letters (A–Z, a–z), numbers (0–9), hyphens (-), or periods (.). For example, under XML,

```
<blastoff count="10" ></blastoff>
```

is correct, whereas this isn't:

```
<blastoff count=10></blastoff>
```

- *All elements must be cased consistently.* If you start a new element such as **<BURGER>**, you must close it as **</BURGER>**, not **</burger>**. Later in the document, if the element is in lowercase, you actually are referring to a new element known as **<burger>**. Attribute names also are case sensitive.

- *A valid XML file may not contain certain characters that have reserved meanings.* These include characters such as **&**, which indicates the beginning of a character entity such as **&**, or **<** , which indicates the start of an element name such as **<sunny>**. These characters must be coded as **&** and **<**, respectively, or can occur in a section marked off as character data. In fact under a basic standalone XML document this rule is quite restrictive as only **&**, **<**, **>**, **'**, and **"** would be allowed.

A document constructed according to the previous simple rules is known as a *well-formed document*. Take a look in Figure 17-2 at what happens to a document that doesn't follow the well-formed rules presented here.

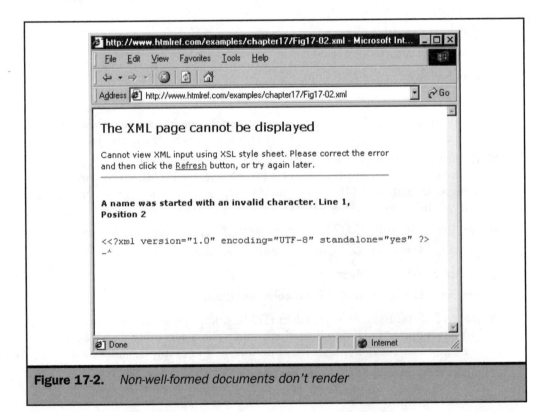

Figure 17-2. *Non-well-formed documents don't render*

SGML purists might find the notion of well-formed-ness eccentric and somewhat troubling. Although SGML itself currently is being revised, traditional SGML has no notion of well-formed documents—documents that are in some sense okay because they conform to some basic syntax guidelines. Instead, conventional SGML uses the notion of *valid* documents—documents that adhere to a formally defined document type definition (DTD). Although this concept also is part of HTML, often it is lost on page authors. For anything beyond casual applications, defining a DTD and validating documents against that definition are real benefits. XML supports both well-formed and valid documents. The well-formed model that just enforces the basic syntax should encourage those not schooled in the intricacies of SGML to begin authoring XML documents, thus making XML as accessible as HTML has been. The valid model is available for applications in which a document's logical structure needs to be verified.

Valid Documents

Most HTML authors are familiar with basic elements and attributes. Now, due to the rising complexity of pages, they are becoming more familiar with the importance of making an HTML document conform to the rules of a DTD such as HTML 4. As noted in the previous paragraph, a document that conforms to a DTD is said to be *valid*. Unlike most HTML authors, SGML authors normally concern themselves with producing valid documents. Many also concern themselves with writing the DTDs that HTML authors usually take for granted. With the appearance of XML, HTML authors can look forward to mastering a new skill: writing DTDs. The following example illustrates how XML might be used to record student grades for a high school class. A definition of the sample language to accomplish this task can be found within the document, although this definition can be kept outside the file as well. The students.xml file shown here includes both the DTD and an occurrence of a document that conforms to the language in the same document:

```
<?xml version="1.0"?>
<!DOCTYPE grades [

<!ENTITY   schoolname "Demo School">
<!ELEMENT grades (school, student+)>
<!ELEMENT school (#PCDATA)>

<!ELEMENT   student (name, level, course+)>
<!ELEMENT   name (#PCDATA)>
<!ELEMENT   level (#PCDATA)>
<!ELEMENT   course (title, grade)>
<!ATTLIST   course type (required | elective) #REQUIRED>

<!ELEMENT   title (#PCDATA)>
```

```
<!ELEMENT  grade (#PCDATA)>

]>
<!-- the document instance -->
<grades>
<school>&schoolname;</school>

<student>
    <name>Paul Thomas</name>
    <level>10</level>

    <course type="required">
      <title>Math</title>
      <grade>C</grade>
    </course>

    <course type="required">
     <title>English</title>
     <grade>D</grade>
    </course>

    <course type="elective">
      <title>Shop</title>
      <grade>B</grade>
    </course>
</student>

<student>
    <name>Jennifer Croft</name>
    <level>12</level>

    <course type="required">
     <title>Math</title>
     <grade>A</grade>
    </course>

    <course type="required">
     <title>English</title>
     <grade>A</grade>
    </course>

    <course type="elective">
      <title>French</title>
```

```
      <grade>B+</grade>
   </course>

   <course type="elective">
      <title>Computer Science</title>
      <grade>A</grade>
   </course>
</student>

</grades>
```

> **Note**   *For more information on reading DTDs, you might want to reference Appendix F.*

We could easily have just written the document itself and put the DTD in an external file using a statement such as

```
<!DOCTYPE grades SYSTEM "grades.dtd">
```

at the top of the document and the various element, attribute and entity definitions in the external file grades.dtd. Regardless of how it is defined and included, the meaning of the defined language is relatively straightforward. A document is enclosed by the **<grades>** element, which in turn contains a single **<school>** element followed by numerous **<student>** elements. Each **<student>** element contains a **<name>** and **<level>**, which contains the student's name and grade level as well as a collection of course elements containing **<title>** and **<grade>** elements.

One interesting aspect of using a DTD with an XML file is that the correctness of the document can be checked. For example, adding non-defined elements or messing up the nesting orders of elements should cause a validating XML parser to reject the document, as shown in Figure 17-3.

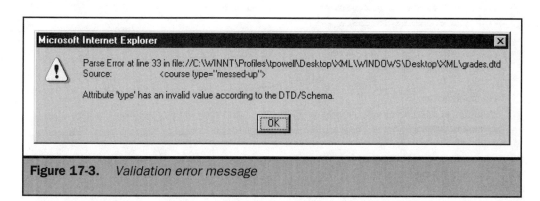

Figure 17-3.   *Validation error message*

Note *At the time of this writing most browser-based parsers don't necessarily validate the document, but just check to make sure the document is well formed. The IE 5.5 browser snapshot was performed using an Internet Explorer extension that validates XML documents.*

Writing a DTD might seem like an awful lot of trouble, but without one, the value of XML is limited. If you can guarantee conformance to the specification, you can start to allow automated parsing and exchange of documents. Writing a DTD is going to be a new experience for most HTML authors, and not everybody will want to write one. Fortunately, although not apparent from the DTD rules in this brief example, XML significantly reduces the complexity of full SGML. However, regardless of how easy or hard it is to write a language definition readers might wonder what to do with an XML document once it is written. The display so far has been less than valuable for most applications.

Displaying XML

As you have already seen, simply including new XML elements in the body of a document can cause problems, because most browsers will want to display the contents of the elements. Of course, no formatting will be applied to raw XML elements, because (unlike HTML) XML elements have no default appearance; they must be assigned one. The most basic way to render XML is to translate it into HTML. All browsers support HTML, at least to some degree, so you can use a server-side program to translate your XML documents to HTML documents at delivery time. You might wonder what benefit this might have, given that HTML doesn't provide the rich structuring that XML does. The most obvious benefit is the abstraction provided. Imagine if you had a press release that you marked up in a simple press-release language. It might look something like the following file, called pressrelease1.xml:

```
<?xml version="1.0"?>
<!DOCTYPE PRESSRELEASE SYSTEM "pressrelease.dtd">
<!-- the document instance -->
<PRESSRELEASE>
<DATE>January 5, 2000</DATE>
<HEADING>Demo Company Releases Super Widget</HEADING>

<RELEASEBODY>
This is a sample press release. This is just some dummy text.
</RELEASEBODY>

<IMG SRC="widget.gif" />
<CONTACT TYPE="PHONE">619-555-1212</CONTACT>
```

```
<CONTACT TYPE="FAX">619-444-1212</CONTACT>
<CONTACT TYPE="EMAIL">info@democompany.com</CONTACT>
</PRESSRELEASE>
```

Assume that all the elements are used appropriately according to the referenced DTD. Obviously, you can't deliver this file as-is, but you could write a server-side program that would take these tags and convert them into HTML fragments to assemble an HTML file to be delivered. Maybe this file would look something like this:

```
<html>
<head>
<title>Demo Company Releases Super Widget</title>
</head>
<body>
<h3 align="right" id="DATE">January 5, 2000</h3>
<h1 align="center" id="HEADING">Demo Company Releases Super Widget</h1>
<hr>

<div id="RELEASEBODY">
<p>This is a sample press release. This is just some dummy text.
<img src="widget.gif" align="right" id="IMG">
</p>
</div>
<hr>

<!--Contact block -->
<address>
E-mail: <a href="mailto: info@democompany.com">info@democompany.com</a><br>
Phone: 619-555-1212<br>
FAX: 619-444-1212<br>
</address>
</body>
</html>
```

You can tell by the use of the **id** attributes and comments how the XML was translated into various chunks of HTML. Although there are numerous ways you might be able to manually convert XML into HTML, XSL (eXtensible Style Language) provides a standard way to perform these transformations.

Note *There is always some confusion about whether we are speaking of XSL transformations known as XSLT or XSL-based formatting. The acronym XSL plain and simply will be used in general to refer to the idea of applying any use of XSL to an XML document.*

Using XSL to Transform XML to HTML

Using XSL we can easily transform and then format an XML document. Various elements and attributes can be matched using XSL and other languages such as HTML then can be output. For example, consider the following simple well-formed XML document called demo.xml:

```
<?xml version="1.0" ?>
<?xml-stylesheet type="text/xsl" href="test.xsl"?>
<example>
  <demo>Look </demo>
  <demo>formatting  </demo>
  <demo> XML </demo>
  <demo>as HTML</demo>
</example>
```

Notice that the second line applies an XSL file called test.xsl to the document. That file will create a simple HTML document and convert each occurrence of the <demo> element to an <h1> element in HTML. The XSL template called test.xsl is shown here:

```
<?xml version='1.0'?>
<xsl:stylesheet xmlns:xsl="http://www.w3.org/TR/WD-xsl">
   <xsl:template match="/">
       <html>
       <head>
       <title>XSL Test</title>
       </head>
       <body>

          <xsl:for-each select="example/demo">
           <h1><xsl:value-of select="."/></h1>
          </xsl:for-each>

       </body>
       </html>

   </xsl:template>
</xsl:stylesheet>
```

Given the previous example we could load the main XML document through an XML- and XSL-aware browser such as Internet Explorer 5.5 and we then would end up with the following HTML once the XSL transformation was applied:

```
<html>
<head>
<title>XSL Test</title>
</head>
<body>
<h1>Look</h1>
<h1>formatting</h1>
<h1>XML</h1>
<h1>as HTML</h1>
</body>
</html>
```

The example transformation under Internet Explorer 5.5 is shown in Figure 17-4.

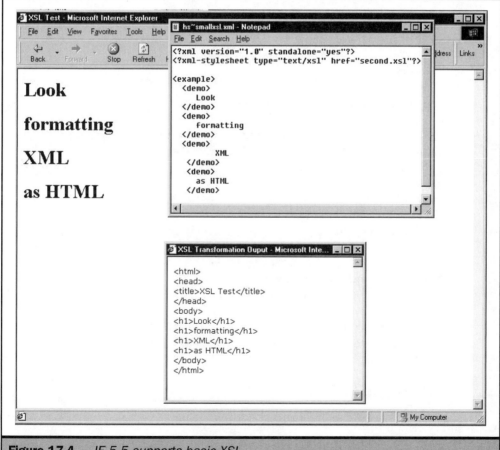

Figure 17-4.   *IE 5.5 supports basic XSL*

Whereas the preceding example is rather contrived, it is possible to create a much more sophisticated example complete with HTML and CSS output. Recall the grades document presented earlier in the chapter. We could use an XSL transformation such as

```xml
<?xml version='1.0'?>
<xsl:stylesheet xmlns:xsl="http://www.w3.org/TR/WD-xsl">

<xsl:template match="/">
<html>
<head>
<title>Class List</title>
<link rel="stylesheet" href="grades.css" />
</head>
<body>

<xsl:for-each select="grades/school">
<h1><xsl:value-of select="."/></h1>
<hr />
</xsl:for-each>

<xsl:for-each select="grades/student">

<div class="studentname"><xsl:value-of select="name"/></div>
<div class="level">Level: <xsl:value-of select="level"/></div>

<table border="1">
   <tr>
       <th>Class Title</th>
       <th>Grade</th>
   </tr>

  <xsl:for-each select="course">

  <tr>
      <td><xsl:value-of select="title"/></td>
      <td><xsl:value-of select="grade"/></td>
  </tr>

  </xsl:for-each>

</table>
<br /><br />
```

```
</xsl:for-each>

</body>
</html>

</xsl:template>
</xsl:stylesheet>
```

When applied to the grades example document using a line such as

```
<?xml-stylesheet type="text/xsl" href="grades.xsl"?>
```

you should get the result shown in Figure 17-5.

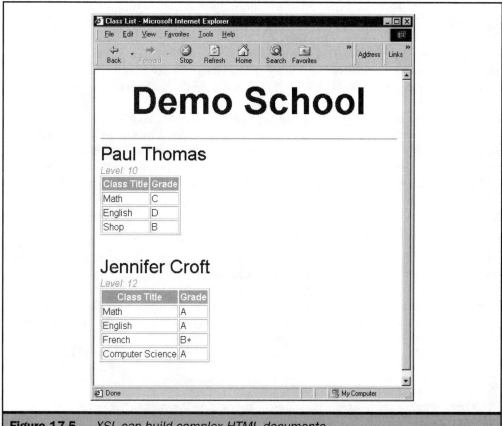

Figure 17-5.   *XSL can build complex HTML documents*

Notice that in the previous example CSS was still required to present the page in an adequate manner as represented by the file grades.css. That file is shown here for the sake of completeness:

```
body            {font-family: Arial;
                 font-size: 12pt;}
h1              {text-align: center;
                 font-size: 48pt;}
th              {text-align: center;
                 background-color:#0099ff;
                 color: white;}
.studentname {font-size: 24pt;}
.level          {color: green;
                 font-style: italic;}
```

Given the necessity to truly separate presentation and structure with HTML using CSS some readers might wonder why we would not format the page just using CSS. The next section will discuss how this can be done. However, even when CSS and XML work properly together there are many instances in which this might make sense. However, consider that the beauty of XSL is that it can be used on the server side to convert XML documents to HTML or HTML and CSS documents for viewing under older browsers.

The previous discussion only begins to touch on the richness of XSL, which provides complex pattern matching and basic programming facilities. Unfortunately, at the time of this new edition's writing, XSL is still not well supported; even the latest browsers have only partial support for this technology. Readers interested in the latest developments in XSL are directed to the W3C Web site (http://www.w3.org/Style/XSL/) as well as Microsoft's XML site (http://msdn.microsoft.com/xml).

Displaying XML Documents Using CSS

The conversion from XML to HTML seems awkward; it would be preferable to deliver a native XML file and display it. By using a *Cascading Style Sheet* (CSS) you should be able to deliver XML documents right to the screen. Note that neither of these technologies is well defined in relation to XML, so these examples might require significant rework to render in your browser. However, both examples should provide the flavor of how native XML can be presented.

The following file is a well-formed XML document representing a small parts catalog:

```
<?xml version="1.0"?>
<?xml-stylesheet href="catalog.css" type="text/css" ?>
<CATALOG>
```

```
<PART>
  <NAME>Super Widget</NAME>
  <DESCRIPTION>
  The Super Widget is the most powerful widget in the world.
</DESCRIPTION>
  <PRICE>$1.95</PRICE>
</PART>

<PART>
  <NAME>Deluxe Widget</NAME>
  <DESCRIPTION>
  The Deluxe Widget is the fanciest widget in the world.
  </DESCRIPTION>
  <PRICE>$2.95</PRICE>
</PART>
</CATALOG>
```

Notice that the second line of the file references a style sheet in the same directory, called catalog.css. The content of this file is shown here:

```
CATALOG       {font-family: Arial; font-size: 14pt;}
PART          {background: orange; display: block}
NAME          {font-size: larger; font-style: italic; display: block}
DESCRIPTION   {text-indent: 10px; display: block;}
PRICE         {color: #009900; text-align: right; font-weight: bold;
               display: block}
```

Notice that the syntax for the style sheet is the same as the syntax discussed for CSS in Chapter 10, except that the element names are the XML elements that were defined in the previous example. One small issue with this approach to formatting XML is that positioning objects with style sheets is difficult, unless you either use positioning rules or assign a display property to the XML element. Notice that the rule **display** assigns a value of **block** to each of the elements. This makes the example XML act like an HTML block element, and thus induces a return in the document. The rendering of this rudimentary example under Internet Explorer 5 is shown in Figure 17-6.

The lack of flow objects in CSS makes properly displaying this XML document very difficult. In some sense, CSS still relies heavily on HTML for basic document structure. It should be obvious that XSL and HTML still play an important role with XML regardless of the eventual support of CSS natively with XML.

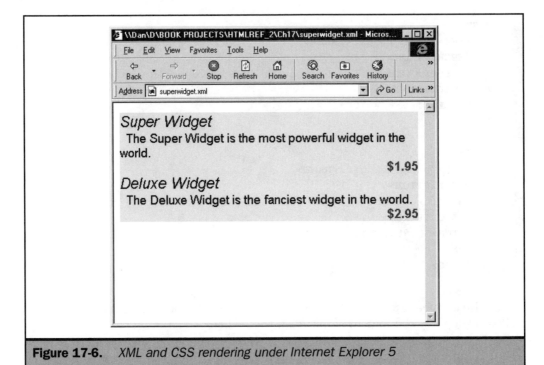

Figure 17-6. *XML and CSS rendering under Internet Explorer 5*

XML Application Languages

What's interesting about XML is how many people do not see that it is the applications built with it, and not the language itself, that is really interesting. The author's opinion is that it probably is not in the best interest of Web designers to invent their own XML-based languages, but rather to use a language written using XML. Even with this approach the Web could spawn thousands of new XML-based languages that many people can't speak. Always remember that the value of knowing a language generally is proportional to the number of people whom you can communicate with by using the language. A short survey of three popular XML languages starting with XHTML (the most important to HTML document authors) is presented here to give readers a flavor to XML-based applications.

XHTML: Rewriting HTML in XML

As you read about XML, you might wonder how this technology is going to affect HTML. In late 1998, the W3C released its first draft of how HTML could be rewritten in light of XML. Code-named Voyager, later to be called XHTML, this form of HTML broke the language into modules and applied all XML rules to HTML elements. By January 2000, XHTML was released as a specification. If adopted by users, XHTML will represent probably the best-known XML language.

Although we have already studied most of the XHTML rules at various points in the book, they are presented together here:

- *An XHTML document must begin with an XML directive* such as

```
<?xml version="1.0"?>
```

- *The second line of a valid XHTML document must reference a valid XHTML DOCTYPE declaration* such as

```
<!DOCTYPE html  PUBLIC "-//W3C//DTD XHTML 1.0 Strict//EN"
"DTD/xhtml1-strict.dtd">
```

```
<!DOCTYPE html PUBLIC "-//W3C//DTD XHTML 1.0 Transitional//EN"
"DTD/xhtml1-transitional.dtd">
```

```
<!DOCTYPE html PUBLIC "-//W3C//DTD XHTML 1.0 Frameset//EN"
"DTD/xhtml1-frameset.dtd">
```

- *The first element in an XHTML document must be <html> and the xmlns attribute must be defined.* An example is shown here:

```
<html xmlns="http://www.w3.org/1999/xhtml" xml:lang="en" lang="en">
```

- *The <title> tag is mandatory in an XHTML document and must be the first tag in the <head>.*

- *All elements must be well formed.* In other words, tags should nest, not cross; so ****Ok**** is ok, but ****Bad**** is not.

- *End tags are always required.* For example, **<p>** must always have a corresponding **</p>**.

- *Empty elements must include a trailing slash.* For example, **
** isn't valid, but **
** is.

- *Attributes must not be minimized.* For example, **<ol compact>** is not allowed, but **<ol compact="compact">** is.

- *Attributes must always be quoted.* So **<img src=bozo.gif alt=bozo />** is not valid but **<img src="bozo.gif" alt="bozo " />** is.

- *All tags and attributes must be lowercase.* So **<hr />** is legal in XHTML whereas **<HR />** is not.

Note *Some older browsers might have problems unless you leave a space between the trailing slash and the > so* **<hr / >** *might be better.*

- *All <img /> elements must have an **alt** attribute.* Always a good idea, but now it is enforced.

- *The <style> element must specify the type attribute.* Generally you will write the element as **<style type="text/css">**.

- *The <script> element must specify the type attribute.* This most likely will be set as **<script type="text/javascript">**.

- *When script or style sheets includes characters such as <, >, [,], or & the data must be either linked externally or contained within* <![CDATA[*and*]]>. So if you had a script like this:

```
<script type="text/javascript">

 var a = [1,2,3,"boom"];
 for (var i=0; i < a.length; i++)
  document.write(a[i]+"<br />");

</script>
```

you would have to write it as

```
<script type="text/javascript">
<![CDATA[
 var a = [1,2,3,"boom"];
 for (var i=0; i < a.length; i++)
  document.write(a[i]+"<br />");
]]>
</script>
```

Of course this is bound to cause a problem under most JavaScript-aware browsers, so resorting to a linked script such as

```
<script src="boomtest.js" type="text/javascript">
</script>
```

would be a better idea.

Given the previously presented rules, a basic XHTML template would look something like this:

```
<?xml version="1.0" ?>
<!DOCTYPE html
    PUBLIC "-//W3C//DTD XHTML 1.0 Transitional//EN"
    "DTD/xhtml1-transitional.dtd">
<html xmlns="http://www.w3.org/1999/xhtml" xml:lang="en" lang="en">
<head>
```

```
<title>Document Title Here</title>
</head>
<body>

Document content here

</body>
</html>
```

Writing XHTML-compliant documents isn't too difficult; consider this more complete HTML document rewritten to conform to XHTML:

```
<?xml version="1.0" ?>
<!DOCTYPE html
     PUBLIC "-//W3C//DTD XHTML 1.0 Transitional//EN"
    "DTD/xhtml1-transitional.dtd">
<html xmlns="http://www.w3.org/1999/xhtml" xml:lang="en" lang="en">
<head>
<title>XHTML Testing, 1..2..3</title>
<script type="text/css">
   h1 {color: red;}
</script>
</head>

<body>
<h1>Welcome to XHTML</h1>
<hr />
<img src="test.gif" alt="must have alt text" />
<p>This is a test of <b><i>XHTML</i></b>. This is only a
test.  <a href="http://www.w3.org/Markup/">Visit the
W3C</a> site for more information on XHTML.</p>

<ul>
   <li>Remember you have to close your tags</li>
   <li>No matter what</li>
</ul>

<hr />

<script type="text/javascript">
```

```
<![CDATA[
var a = [1,2,3,"boom"];
 for (var i=0; i < a.length; i++)
  document.write(a[i]+"<br />");
]]>
</script>

</body>
</html>
```

Note *This example might throw an error under Internet Explorer; instead use a linked script. The point here is simply to illustrate the changes often made to convert HTML to XHTML.*

Using a XHTML validator such as the W3C's online service (http://validator.w3.org) will check the correctness of your XHTML conformance. If everything passes you'll even be encouraged to use a banner such as this on your page:

Although it would seem to be a wonderful idea to include XHTML markup in all documents at once, the reality is that rapid movement to the language will be troublesome if heavy formatting is used in the HTML document or JavaScript is employed. In fact the XHTML specification relies heavily on CSS, which still isn't properly supported by enough browsers at the time of this writing to encourage users to dump HTML-based formatting. Second, linked JavaScripts have problems in many situations and the use of CDATA hiding is just not well supported by even common browsers such as Internet Explorer. Last, if your pages must be viewed under very old browsers XHTML might just not be well liked and serious testing should be performed. Whereas these problems might keep a quick migration to XHTML from happening, most of the formatting and markup rules presented in the book should mean that careful HTML authors are close to XHTML compliance already. For those who need to convert existing documents quickly toward XHTML, consider tools such as HTML Tidy (http://www.w3.org/People/Raggett/tidy/).

Pragmatic readers should note that despite being "official" for nearly one year, XHTML has yet to make major inroads in the Web development community at the time of this edition's writing. This is unfortunate, but does show that just defining a specification is a little different from getting people to use it. Hopefully, readers will understand that the structure provided by XHTML serves as a strong foundation for the future, and will make the extra effort to go from passable HTML documents to fully XHTML-complaint documents. Although XHTML might not have taken off to the degree that many pundits have predicted, other XML-based languages such as the Wireless Markup Language have gained a large following quickly.

Wireless Markup Language (WML)

The *Wireless Markup Language* (WML) defined by the WAP forum (http://www.wapforum.org) is quickly becoming the de facto standard for wireless Web sites. Loosely based on Phone.com's *Handheld Device Markup Language* (HDML), WML aims to be the general-purpose language to present data on devices such as cellular phones. Given that a cellular phone has limited memory, limited network connectivity, a relatively simple user interface that favors content reading and simple selection over data input, and little or no multimedia or programming capabilities, the language is built to be small and speedy. In fact for the sake of speed the entire metaphor of pages that is fundamental to Web sites has been removed from WML and replaced with the idea of a *deck* and *cards*; the idea being that each request to a server fetches an entire deck or document and the deck itself contains individual cards. Further, the deck represents a complete idea or task and the cards represents pieces of the task. This is best illustrated by looking at the generic WML document template, which consists of four elements, **<wml>**, **<head>**, **<template>**, and **<card>**, as shown here:

```
<?xml version="1.0"?>
<!DOCTYPE WML PUBLIC "-//WAPFORUM//DTD WML 1.1//EN"
http://www.wapforum.org/DTD/wml_1.1.xml>
<wml>
    <head>
     head information here
    </head>
    <template>
     template information here
    </template>
    <card>
     card contents
    </card>
     more cards
</wml>
```

Whereas the document is defined by the **<wml>** element, the **<head>** contains supplementary information about the document similar to the **<head>** element in HTML. The **<template>** section, which is optional, contains information that should be applied to multiple cards in the deck. Last, the individual pieces of a deck are defined with the **<card>** element. Within the **<card>** element are the various screen elements defined by WML such as a paragraphs, input fields, tables, images, and so on. Given the standard WML template previously shown the simplest example in WML is presented here:

```
<?xml version="1.0"?>
<!DOCTYPE wml PUBLIC "-//WAPFORUM//DTD WML 1.1//EN"
"http://www.wapforum.org/DTD/wml_1.1.xml">
<wml>
<card id="card1" title="First Deck">
<p>Hello WML World!</p>
</card>
</wml>
```

Using a cell phone simulator such as Phone.com's (http://developer.phone.com) or Nokia's (http://forum.nokia.com) it is possible to view the likely presentation of this document as shown in Figure 17-7.

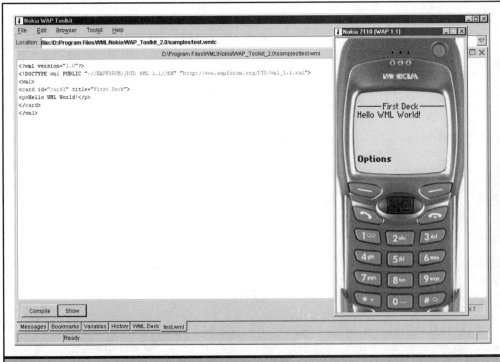

Figure 17-7.   *Hello WML World in Nokia Simulator*

The language itself is relatively simple. Table 17-1 shows all the elements defined under the WML 1.1 specification. Notice the similarity in elements between WML and HTML particularly in text formatting.

Despite its apparent similarities to HTML, WML is very domain specific; consider that many of its elements and attributes are built to reduce network traffic (as in cache control using **<meta>** and deck size reduction using **<template>)**, to improve state management for programming by defining variables with **<setvar>,** and reducing data input using input masks defined with the mask attribute for **<input>**. Compared to XHTML, WML is a better example of how XML can be used to rigorously define a special purpose language in this case for the wireless environment. The next XML application language, SMIL, is even more domain specific.

SMIL

SMIL, or *Synchronized Multimedia Integration Language*, is an XML-based markup language that can be used to combine various media in online presentations. SMIL, as mentioned in the sections of Chapter 9 about streaming audio and video, is predominantly used to create presentations for RealNetwork's RealPlayer. Although there are other Java- and Windows-based applications that can work with SMIL, the examples in this section will focus on the language's use with RealPlayer.

As an XML-based language, SMIL follows the same rules that apply to XHTML as discussed throughout this book. All tags must be lowercase, all attributes must be quoted, and "empty" tags must end with a trailing slash, as shown in this SMIL path to a RealAudio file:

```
http://www.democompany.com/audio/robotdrone.smil
```

Linking to RealAudio or RealVideo file (.rm) with a .ram file was discussed in Chapter 9 (see "RealAudio"). When using SMIL, the SMIL file comes between the .ram file and the .rm file. First, a Web page links to the .ram file using the **<a>** element. The .ram file should contain nothing more than a full or relative path to the .smil file:

```
http://www.democompany.com/audio/robotdrone.smil
```

The SMIL file itself, shown here in its simplest form, uses a syntax very similar to HTML:

```
<smil>
<body>
<audio src="http://www.democompany.com/audio/robotdrone.rm" />
</body>
</smil>
```

Element Category	Sample WML Elements
Deck and card structure	\<wml\> \<card\> \<template\> \<head\>
Head Information	\<access\> \<meta\>
Text Formatting	\<p\> \<br\> \<b\> \<i\> \<u\> \<em\> \<strong\> \<small\> \<big\> \<table\> \<tr\> \<td\>
Links and Anchors	\<a\> \<anchor\>
Images	\<img\>
User Input	\<input\> \<select\> \<option\> \<optgroup\> \<fieldset\>
Variable Control	\<setvar\> \<postfield\>
Timers	\<timer\>
Tasks	\<go\> \<prev\> \<refresh\> \<noop\>
Events	\<do\> \<ontimer\> \<onenterforward\> \<onenterbackward\> \<onpick\> \<onevent\>

Table 17-1. *WML Elements*

The SMIL file, which can end with the extension .smil or .smi, is identified as an SMIL file by the **<smil>** element; the use of the **<body>** element is much the same as it is in HTML. These two elements are mandatory. SMIL also features a **<head>** element, but this is optional. The only other element in the preceding example is the **audio** element, which uses the familiar **src** syntax to link to the .rm file. At this point in the process RealPlayer will open and begin to play the audio file. Of course, adding this extra step just to play one audio file isn't very useful. SMIL's strength lies in its capability to combine multiple files in a variety of media. Consider the following code, which references three different audio files:

```
<smil>
<body>
<audio src="http://www.someotherfakesite.com/fanfare.rm" />
<audio src="http://www.democompany.com/audio/robotdrone.rm" />
<audio src="http://www.democompany.com/audio/robotdrone2.rm" />
</body>
</smil>
```

Upon reading this code, RealPlayer will play each of the three audio files in sequence. Note that the first file, fanfare.rm, is not located at the Demo Company site. SMIL is not limited to files located on the same server any more than HTML hypertext links are limited to one site. But this is just the tip of the SMIL iceberg. It can be used to combine video, audio, text, graphics, Flash, and other formats, and to control the window in which they are displayed. Suppose you want to play a series of still pictures synchronized with audio clips and text descriptions. The following SMIL example defines text and image regions, groups different media files together, defines playback time, and loops the entire presentation. Figure 17-8 shows how part of this presentation would look in RealPlayer.

```
<smil>
<head>
   <meta name="title" content="Singing Robots" />

<layout>
   <root-layout background-color="red" width="200" height="305" />

   <region id="imgregion" top="5" left="5" width="190" height="260"
    background-color="white" />

   <region id="textregion" top="270" left="5" width="190" height="30" />

</layout>
</head>
```

```
<body>

<seq repeat="indefinite">

<par>
    <audio src="http://www.democompany.com/audio/robotdrone.rm" end="7s" />
    <text src="drone01.rt" region="textregion" end="7s" />
    <img src="butler.gif" region="imgregion" end="7s" />
</par>

<par>
    <audio src="http://www.democompany.com/audio/robotoldy.rm" end="7s" />
    <text src="oldies.rt" region="textregion" end="7s" />
    <img src="trainer.gif" region="imgregion" end="7s" />
</par>

<par>
    <audio src="http://www.democompany.com/audio/robotrock.rm" end="7s" />
    <text src="rocking.rt" region="textregion" end="7s" />
    <img src="buddy.gif" region="imgregion" end="7s" />
</par>
</seq>

</body>
</smil>
```

Figure 17-8. Sequence of RealAudio presentation using SMIL

This example uses the **<head>** element which, although optional, can contain other elements that affect the entire document's presentation. There is no **<title>** element in SMIL, but meta tags serve a number of purposes; in this case, the **name** value is set to **"title"**, and the **content** attribute determines the title itself.

The next element in the document head is **<layout>**, which defines how the visual aspects of the presentation are displayed. This formatting actually affects the size of the RealPlayer window when it loads. The **root-layout** element defines the overall visual display area; in this example attributes are used to define height, width and background color.

The **region** attribute is used twice in the head. The **id** attribute assigns a name to the region; and background color, height, and width are defined in a familiar fashion; **top** and **left** define the regions' distance in pixels from the top and left of the root layout area.

In the body of the document, the first element is **<seq>**, which defines a sequence; there can be multiple sequences in a document, but in this case there is only one. The **repeat** attribute is set to **"indefinite"**, which will cause it to repeat endlessly until another document is loaded. It also can take numerical values, which define how many times the sequence will repeat.

The **<seq>** element contains three instances of the **<par>** element. The first **<par>** contains three clips, which will play simultaneously. The first one defines the audio clip:

```
<audio src="http://www.democompany.com/audio/robotdrone.rm" end="7s" />
```

The **end** attribute determines how long the clip will play, in this case seven seconds. It is interesting to note that the **<audio>** tag would not prevent RealPlayer from identifying another file type, if a video file or other format were referenced by mistake.

The next clip references a text file, also lasts seven seconds, and uses the **region** attribute to associate the clip with a named area defined in the **<layout>** element in the document head:

```
<text src="drone01.rt" region="textregion" end="7s" />
```

Finally, the last clip works much in the same way, except that it references an image file:

```
<img src="butler.gif" region="imgregion" end="7s" />
```

The two remaining **<par>** groupings are set up in the same fashion. When loaded in RealPlayer, each audio clip will play for seven seconds, and the image and text file associated with it will display as well. At the end of each **<par>**, the next one will play, and so on. Thanks to the way the **<seq>** element is set, this little slideshow will play over and over again.

One final note: The text regions reference RealText files (.rt), which are written in a simple markup language that allows for fonts and other formatting to be applied to the text region. More about this language, and about SMIL, can be found in the extensive documentation available at the RealNetworks site. This brief look at SMIL can only hint at the possibilities of this language, which supports a wide variety of media, and offers an incredible degree of grouping and sequencing facilities, layering effects, and more. In addition to the RealNetworks site, interested readers can find tutorials at http://www.justsmil.com.

Hopefully this last section has given you a taste of the wide range of XML-based application languages that are possible. Anything from domain-specific languages such as MathML to generic languages such as XHTML can be defined. The possibilities are literally endless, but how will XML actually be used?

Predicting the Future of XML

Predicting the future of XML or its effects on HTML is difficult. One thing is certain: HTML isn't going away in its present form any time soon. Simply too many people are writing HTML documents for it to go away overnight. Furthermore, the definition of HTML as an XML language might not have much effect in the short term. Unfortunately, people just don't seem to follow the rules with HTML; suggesting that all existing documents have to be rewritten in order to render is unlikely. More likely, browsers will contain some sort of compatibility mode to deal with old HTML markup, which will water down the effect of XHTML in the short term by not encouraging enough people to move to it.

So far the uptake of custom XML documents isn't nearly as fast as many of the pundits have suggested. However, it is starting to catch on as has been shown by the new languages such as WML, SMIL, SVG, and so on that are starting to be used on the Web. Within data interchange languages, XML has a particularly strong role to play. The technology is simple to describe, yet provides the power to create data that can be passed between programs or people without loss of meaning. With its structure, XML will enable Web-based automation and improve search engines and a host of motivating e-commerce applications. However, before you get too excited, consider that to achieve the dream of an XML-enabled Web, many diverse groups need to get together and agree on data formats. Just because XML *could* be used to write a special language to be used to automate data interchange in a particular industry doesn't mean that people *will* accept it. Remember that XML is based on SGML, and SGML has promised similar benefits during its history. Getting groups to agree upon a common data format and actually use it isn't always feasible, given the competitive nature of business. Anyone can define his or her own XML-based language. McDonald's could define FFML (Fast Food Markup Language). But does this mean that Burger King will accept it as standard? With people defining languages for their own special needs, the chaos of the Web could multiply into a markup Tower of Babel.

Don't underestimate the simplicity of HTML. It might be ill defined and misused, but it is commonly known and understood. In some sense, HTML is the English of the Web. Unfortunately, this analogy might make many XML languages the equivalent of Esperanto—the supposed well-defined perfect common language. But consider the requirements to move the Web from an HTML-centered approach to an XML-centered one, and you'll see that the widespread adoption of XML is going to take some time.

Summary

This discussion of XML's core syntax and extension only scratches the surface of what remains an emerging technology. The best way to track XML's rapid evolution is to closely monitor the XML activity at the W3C, http://www.w3.org/XML/. The implications of XML are enormous. Just as a metadata definition language, XML has some wonderful uses for extending the Web. Numerous languages such as WML and SMIL show how XML can be used. Other languages certainly are possible, including markup to help search engines more accurately index Web pages. However, eventually, a demand will arise to include XML directly into HTML pages, to augment the functionality of the page, or maybe even replace the page outright.

As it stands, XML is still missing well-defined and well-implemented linking and style definitions. As a middle-ground language, XML attempts to provide much of the power of SGML while keeping the application oriented to the Web and within the easy-to-use spirit of HTML. What XML will eventually bring, if it can be used directly within Web pages, is the power to make data more regular and more specific to particular applications or industries. With improved structure, migrating Web data to and from databases, exchanging documents with other parties, and navigating large collections of documents could get significantly easier.

Like many new hot technologies, XML will go through a "hype phase" that suggests it is good for everything. However, at least in the short term, XML will augment HTML and address its weaknesses rather than replace it outright. Just as Windows relied on DOS and did not quickly supplant it, the market-driven nature of Web technologies in conjunction with the existing heavy investment in HTML-based information probably will spur an XML evolution rather than XML revolution.

Chapter 18

Future Directions

W here HTML is heading isn't always easy to predict. The Web has been rocked by rapid commercialization and the introduction of numerous new technologies. However, the evolution of Web technology is far from finished. Only a few years ago it was hard to imagine the types of multimedia and programmed sites that are common on the Web today. Current trends in structure, presentation, programming, and delivery suggest what might happen to HTML and the Web in the near future.

Untangling the Mess

One of the big problems with Web pages, as discussed throughout this book, is that structural markup, presentation, and business logic—often in the form of script code—is often all jumbled together in one big mess. In many Web pages, HTML is used heavily for formatting, and CSS is added directly to tags using the **style** attribute common to nearly every HTML element. Scripts are placed all over the document, particularly within tags, through the use of event handler attributes such as **onclick** or **onmouseover**. Consider the following markup that works in Internet Explorer:

```
<!DOCTYPE HTML PUBLIC "-//W3C//DTD HTML 4.01 Transitional//EN">
<html>
<head>
<title>Mixed Up</title>
</head>
<body bgcolor="black" text="white">
<p align="center" style="font-size: 18pt; line-height: 200%"
onMouseover="this.style.backgroundColor='orange'"
onmouseout="this.style.backgroundColor='black'">I'm all mixed up!</p>
</body>
</html>
```

In this particular situation, HTML is combined with style sheets and scripting in such a way that it is difficult to update one item without considering the others. Rather than combining this all in one file, it is possible to separate the content out into separate linked files. For example, consider the markup here:

```
<!DOCTYPE HTML PUBLIC "-//W3C//DTD HTML 4.01 Transitional//EN">
<html>
<head>
<title>Not So Mixed Up</title>
<link rel="stylesheet" href="externalstylesheet.css">
</head>
```

```
<body>
<p id="para1">I'm no longer mixed up!</p>
<script src="linkedscript.js"></script>
</body>
</html>
```

In the preceding example, the linked style sheet (externalstylesheet.css) sets the look of the page

```
BODY    {background-color: black;
            color: white;}


#para1          {text-align: center;
                font-size: 18pt;
                line-height: 200%;}
```

whereas the linked script (linkedscript.js) makes the paragraph light up when the user rolls over it.

```
function goOrange()
{
  para1.style.backgroundColor='orange';
}

function goBlack()
{
  para1.style.backgroundColor='black';
}

para1.onmouseover = goOrange;
para1.onmouseout = goBlack;
```

The benefit to this approach is that we have separated all the components out so they can be easily maintained, as well as interchanged between pages. By separating out the components of a Web page, it is much easier to modify complex pages. This is a simple application of modular design as found in complex software systems. The individual components of a Web page will eventually have to be brought together, although individual page elements might have to be stored, sorted, and output based upon various user criteria. Page elements can be changed all the time; thus it is important to carefully manage site assets, typically by using a database. In fact, according to traditional hypertext theory the heart of any hypertext system is a database. Sites with any degree of complexity will find that using a database is mandatory. Figure 18-1 shows a possible relationship between the aspects of a typical Web page.

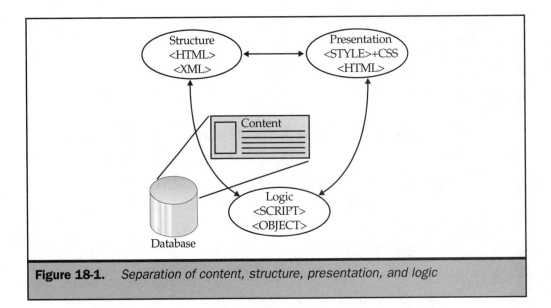

Figure 18-1.   *Separation of content, structure, presentation, and logic*

The benefit of separation of content from its eventual output form cannot be understated. Imagine storing a site's content in a central data repository and then dynamically creating pages for a variety of different output environments based upon user actions. This is possible with a database and good separation of content, structure, presentation styles, and logic, as illustrated in Figure 18-2.

Improving Presentation

Getting pages to look a particular way is one of the chief goals of Web page designers. With the rise of Cascading Style Sheets (CSS), page designers will have the layout features that they have always wanted. Yet at the time of this edition's writing, major browsers still don't support all CSS1 properties properly, despite the fact that widespread CSS1 support has been promised by some industry pundits and browser vendors since the first edition of this book. Even when CSS properties are supported, cross browser support and bugs do nothing but discourage authors from using them. Beyond CSS1, we see CSS2 starting to have some very limited support in the latest browsers. Beyond this, there is the promise of CSS3 as well. Yet despite the frustration and delays, CSS will happen. Whether misused or not, the presentation capabilities of HTML just aren't powerful enough to propel the Web further.

Given the slow uptake of CSS, some have suggested looking elsewhere. Some designers have embraced Macromedia's Flash technology as the solution to the Web's presentation challenge. As tempting as Flash is with its small file sizes, resolution scaling, and increasing browser support, this is simply the wrong direction for the Web

ADVANCED TOPICS

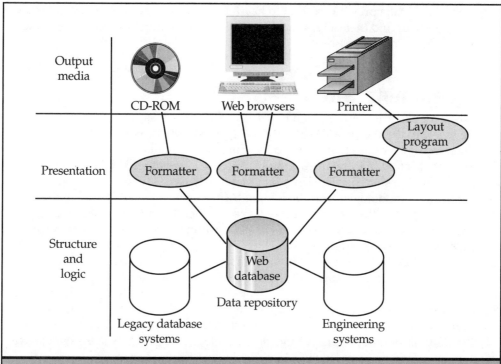

Figure 18-2. *Separation of content, structure, presentation, and logic allows for dynamic pages for a variety of media*

to go. Flash just isn't as flexible as text formats such as HTML/XHTML, not nearly as small file-wise, and not nearly as ubiquitous. Production costs for Flash are much higher than HTML documents, and Flash files can be difficult to change unless they are carefully designed. However, Flash and other multimedia technologies for animation, audio, video, and 3-D environments certainly will be included within more and more Web pages. HTML and CSS will be the host environment for these technologies and, most like the **<object>** element, can serve as the generic way to add new binary forms. Exactly which binary forms will dominate the Web is hard to predict, but it is unlikely that more than two or three formats will be viable in any particular category.

A particularly thorny issue in presentation is what to do about application-specific presentation. The needs of cell phones, PDAs, and other non-computer-based ways to access the Web require a much different approach. Already, PDA-based browsers have begun to support limited forms of HTML, while cell phones have started to support languages similar to HTML, such as HDML and WML, that were designed specifically for the needs of these devices. Designers looking to support presentation for multiple devices from the same content will be forced to take the separation of structure and style presented in the previous section to heart. Otherwise, they will be forced to lock out some users, or find themselves shackled with creating numerous versions of the same content.

Programming Sites

The Web isn't like print. A transition is already underway from a print- and page-oriented view of the Web to a more program-oriented view of Web sites. Think of complex e-commerce sites that allow you to purchase presents online. Simply put—in this form, Web sites are software and should be developed as such. With the rise of complexity in Web sites, particularly those that must be built to scale, rigorous development methodologies must be adopted. The current state of affairs on the Web overemphasizes the look and feel of a site. Back-end work on databases and programming often takes a backseat to visuals. Testing is poorly considered. Sites are often built without solid plans, in a mad rush to get on the Web or outdo the competition. This has to change. To build complex systems, the ideas of software engineering will have to be applied to Web pages; the ad hoc approaches used to date won't work. Principles adopted from Software Engineering, which can be dubbed *Web Site Engineering*, might help curb problems, but there is still a great deal of work left to do in order to develop best practices for Web site development. Don't be fooled: WYSIWYG tools or other Rapid Application Development (RAD) systems won't save the developer facing a complex task. Methodology is required as well.

Beyond a lack of rigor and testing comes the application of the wrong tools for the job. Many Web professionals seem rather religious in their selection of Web technologies. There needs to be more open-mindedness in decisions about Web technologies. There are just too many technologies to settle on one perfect one. Server-side technologies include traditional CGI programs, server-specific APIs such as NSAPI and ISAPI, Java Servlets, and a multitude of server-side scripting solutions such as ColdFusion, ASP, PHP and many others. On the client side there are helpers, plug-ins, Java applets, ActiveX controls, and all varieties of scripting. All these technologies intersect with and potentially manipulate HTML documents. In fact, the symbiotic relationship between HTML and programming facilities is dramatically apparent in the rise of JavaScript and so-called Dynamic HTML (DHTML) using the Document Object Model (DOM).

Choosing which technology to use, and when, can be a challenge. Too much emphasis on the server can slow the site down and keep it from scaling. Placing too much responsibility on the client side also can be problematic, because it is often difficult to ensure that all clients support the technology properly. Because the client is beyond the page designer's control, it might be hard to ensure that things don't go wrong, even with careful design and rigorous testing. There is a balance between what should be done on the client side and what should be done on the server.

The chief problems with programming facilities being added to Web sites include standardization, scalability, and methodology. Web programming technologies such as Java and JavaScript aren't standardized. There also seems to be a growing rift between one browser's idea of Java and another's. Netscape's JavaScript and Microsoft's JScript have major differences despite conformance to the ECMAScript standard. These issues will have to be sorted out by developers if there is to be any hope for a true cross-platform programming environment. Otherwise, it might be necessary to use platform-specific technologies such as ActiveX controls or Netscape plug-ins in conjunction with server-side technologies, regardless of what makes sense in theory.

As more and more users get on the Internet, some programmed sites are going to face a critical problem of scalability. Imagine an airline reservation system on the Web. How is it going to handle tens or hundreds of thousands of people who use it simultaneously to order cheap tickets for the holidays? Numerous sites have failed over the years, from e-commerce sites to auctions to electronic brokerages. The need to build large, robust systems will only increase as electronic commerce continues to develop.

However, many sites simply won't scale. The applications aren't distributed across many servers, and it is difficult to create distributed systems. Many industry pundits like to discuss how programming objects will be flung far over the Internet, and how corporate networks will be served out from various application servers to help solve scalability problems. These objects should help when you think of many application servers distributing ordering objects to airline ticket buyers. In this sense, the Web turns into a giant distribution system. The question arises of how well these objects are going to interact. Even on a single user's computer, the idea of having objects communicate with each other has been less than straightforward. Doing this over a network only makes things worse. The battle for the object world, already in progress, pits a loose alliance of Common Object Request Broker Architecture (CORBA) and Java against Microsoft's Distributed Component Object Model (DCOM). Which of these particular object technologies will dominate the Internet is unclear. One might be popular on intranets, whereas the other might be popular outside the corporation. The true answer might be neither, as XML-based formats provide a way for applications to interact with each other over the Internet.

Solving Web-Wide Problems

Many Web-wide problems intersect HTML every day. Sites are hard to find, difficult to use, and often are delivered painfully slowly. New technologies, standards, and more informed developers are addressing each of these problems.

The Challenge of Search

One major problem involves searching the Web. It is very difficult to find things on the Internet using a search engine. The reason for this problem is obvious if you consider how search engines work. A search engine looks at a Web page and indexes the words it sees there. The engine determines what the page is about based upon a heuristic that combines how many times a particular word occurs, the value of the keywords specified by the **<meta>** elements in the document, and the title of the document. This is terribly imprecise, as anyone who has searched the Web knows. A Web page that contains the word "Intel" might have nothing to do with the Intel Corporation. Typing this word in a search engine could return hundreds of thousands of responses. You should hope to see a site such as www.intel.com listed first, but this doesn't always happen. The robots or spiders that index Web pages really have no idea what they are indexing. They can provide no value to the indexing that a human might. For the search engines to understand the information they are looking at, wouldn't they have to possess artificial intelligence? Yes, if data is unstructured. If structure can be added to data, it is very easy to index information. HTML elements such as **<meta>** and new meta-data formats written in XML should bring such order. However, this actually is more difficult than it sounds. Getting people to agree on the structure of more complex meta-data, the allowable words in the data, and the organizations that will certify the correctness of the meta-data will be very difficult. Until more structure can be added, searching the Web will continue to be difficult.

Improving Accessibility and Usability

Another Web-wide problem is that of accessibility. Accessibility issues come in many forms: an international user dealing with an English-only environment, a visually impaired user dealing with a site that has too much visual emphasis, or a technology-poor user unable to run Netscape to enter the latest and greatest site. The bottom line is that the Web and HTML should not intentionally lock people out. There might be cases where the designers of the site want to limit access based upon their own views, but the technology itself should not be designed to do such a thing.

The first example of accessibility is internationalization. The Web is supposed to be the World Wide Web, but it seems as if a U.S.–centered viewpoint often dominates the landscape. The Web needs to be improved to support other languages' character sets and reading directions. HTML 4 has moved toward a more international approach, but there still is a long way to go. English will probably serve as the dominant language, but Web documents in French, Spanish, German, Japanese, Chinese, Korean, and Russian already are commonplace. Undoubtedly, more languages will be used online. There will need to be facilities to provide friendly help to those with a less-than-perfect mastery of a given language.

Much also can be said about how unfriendly the Web can be for those who have handicaps. Many Web sites completely lock out those users who are sight impaired because such sites provide no meaningful **alt** text and rely heavily on graphics. (You might recall that the **alt** attribute provides alternative text for user agents that do not display images, or for graphical browsers wherein the user has turned image rendering off.) Although the Web will continue to be a medium rich in visuals, the W3C is making sure that many users are not left out of the experience by extending HTML to help make pages more accessible through keyboard, voice, and Braille.

Last, there are those users who, because of limited bandwidth or computing technology, often don't receive the complete picture. HTML does not always degrade gracefully when older or less common browsers view pages. More work, both in standards and development techniques, will be required to keep the Web open to those people who don't always use the latest and greatest gadgets or applications.

Even when the user has the latest and greatest technology, sites can still be difficult to use. Many sites appear not to be built with the user in mind. Heavy downloads, difficult-to-comprehend navigation, restrictive use of technology, and numerous other problems seem to plague even the most popular sites. However, attention is shifting back to the most important element of a Web site visit—the user. Site development is now really starting to focus on users more; this author's *Web Design: The Complete Reference* provides a wealth of information on this subject.

Addressing Delivery

Despite all the problems with usability and accessibility, the biggest gripe with the Web is performance. The Internet is growing at such a wild pace that traffic snarls are an everyday occurrence. Web protocols such as HTTP 1.1, image formats with better compression schemes such as Portable Network Graphics (PNG), and new connection technologies such as DSL and cable modems will help speed the delivery of Web pages in the future. However, the amount of data that users want is quickly increasing. Bandwidth-hungry media forms such as video don't work reliably on the Internet. Delivering reasonable, quality video over today's Web is impossible. Even still images can seem to take an eternity.

Many approaches are being introduced that will help speed the Web experience, including caches, alternative transport protocols, and page-level compression. However, delivery always breaks down because of the idea of point sources. With single Web servers delivering data, eventually there is going to be a bottleneck. Content must be replicated around caches and delivered from mirror sites, or even broadcast. One technique is the use of intelligent hardware devices to balance distribution of pages among different Web servers based on how busy the servers are or which server is closest to the user requesting pages. Always remember that the network is the medium of the Web; its effect is significant. How people access the Web certainly will affect the direction Web design takes.

The Rise of XML

Just as Java seemed to be the savior of the Web a few years back, many predict XML will solve many of the problems that plague today's Web. Some visionaries believe that XML will be the native storage format for documents, potentially even alleviating the need for databases. Some even believe that raw XML will replace HTML as the dominant format on the Web. Other experts believe that in the future everyone will become a markup language creator. Most of these ideas are just plain fanciful.

First consider the idea of data storage in flat XML files rather than a database. If a user wants to search for an item in a particular page in the site, how quickly can it be found? Well, if there are 1,000 pages in no particular order, the best case is that you find something in the first page and the worst case is you have to look through every single page. On average you'll probably have to look through at least half the pages to find what you are looking for. To speed the process you can try sort the pages or provide some form of index. However, this is exactly what a database provides. Databases provide facilities for quickly searching data, maintaining data, providing security, and so on. A flat file system filled with XML files will not provide this benefit. Of course you can go add this functionality but then you start imitating a database. The reality is that databases will absorb XML rather than the other way around.

However, one limitation of databases is that their content cannot easily be shared at times. If you store invoices in your accounting database, it would be nice to automatically ship the invoice to a customer and have it quickly merged into their accounts payable database. Of course, exchanging data between two very different systems might be difficult. The fields on your invoice might not directly match fields in the payment system in name and format. In order to smooth the exchange of data from one system to another a neutral data format could be adopted. XML provides just the tools to define such a language.

Beyond data exchange, XML at its base form might be slow to be adopted for many reasons. First of all, browser rendering of raw XML is not widely supported. Some XML-based languages such as WML, SMIL, and SVG have started to gain acceptance. However, the potential explosion of numerous XML-based languages could be the modern equivalent of the Tower of Babel fragmenting the Web into numerous specialized languages that only small groups of practitioners actually understand. This is already happening to a limited degree on the Web today.

If XML's ultimate promise of allowing anyone to easily create their own language for client-side rendering comes true, the potential for the proliferation of proprietary languages is enormous. Yet will these languages be used widely? It's hard to tell, but the answer is probably not. Many commercial organizations could be hesitant to use languages they did not invent. Imagine that one company in the oil industry creates a language they call SGOML (Standard Gas and Oil Markup Language). Would other firms be willing to adopt it? Maybe. But they might not, out of fear that by using a language they didn't define they might suffer some competitive disadvantage. Firms might prefer instead to wait for a neutral language to be defined and set by a standards body. The bickering between concerned parties when defining an XML language, and the hesitation to use another organization's language, should not be underestimated. Within the SGML community, the human aspect has significantly hampered the use of many languages. Most likely the uptake of XML will be slow, and the main hurdle for adoption will be agreement between users.

While XML-based languages, including XHTML, will become very important in the future, never underestimate the power of traditional HTML itself. It is well known and has a huge installed base of users. Users really are the key to the success of a language. Always remember this fact when considering using a language.

What Is the Future of HTML?

After all this discussion, one might wonder what can be said for sure about the future of HTML. One thing is certain: Page designers won't do things the way they do now. Hacking around in HTML is a throwback to the days of page-setting languages like .troff or LaTeX. With the rise of PostScript and the tools that could output it, document designers stopped editing files directly in most cases. Although older page-setting technologies are still used, and some people even program directly in PostScript, most do not. Using a tool to output PostScript, whether a word processor or a page layout program tool, is the way most designers create documents. As HTML settles down and becomes more standardized, tools that can output pages appropriately certainly will be developed. Right now, with standards and browsers in flux, tool vendors have a nearly impossible time creating such tools. For the moment, HTML designers often have to resort to doing tweaks, if not the whole page, by hand. This won't last long.

XHTML and CSS might finally free the designer from hand edits, but not right away. The rigid structure of XHTML has yet to be rapidly embraced even though it should be. However, if XHTML can gain some ground it should become a lot easier to create machine readable and editable markup. At this point we should be able to focus less on tag syntax and more on document design and content. What does this mean? Simply that sometime in the future—five years, maybe more—HTML hackers will be in about as much demand as typesetting machine operators. With the rise of electronic and improved mechanical printing technologies, the demand for these skills quickly went away. However, HTML as a print formatting language is not the point. The migration to a dynamic, program-like environment already should be clear. Dynamic HTML, databases, and embedded objects all point the way to the Web of tomorrow. Knowledge of HTML will serve as a backbone for accessing these technologies. The benefit of short-term mastery of HTML will be early access to these ideas and a fundamental understanding of how the Web works.

Summary

What is cutting edge today will be trivial tomorrow. The rise of XHTML and properly working Web design tools eventually will make intimate knowledge of HTML obsolete. Many of the ideas and the syntax presented in this book will undoubtedly be passé in a few years. How long it is going to take to move to new technologies such as XHTML, CSS, XML, and so on is anybody's guess. One thing is for sure: It won't happen overnight. There are just too many documents authored in traditional HTML, and the browser vendors have been slow to embrace standardized technology. Authoring HTML correctly today will provide a solid foundation for tomorrow's technologies and allow designers to add sophisticated visual and interactive elements to their sites without fear their site will fail.

The Complete Reference

Appendix A

HTML Element Reference

This appendix provides a complete reference for the HTML 4.01 specification elements and the elements commonly supported by Internet Explorer, Netscape, and WebTV. Some elements presented here might be nonstandard or deprecated, but are included because browser vendors continue to support them or they are still in common use. The HTML 4.01 specification is largely the same as HTML 4.0, but corrects a number of errors in the earlier version. The standard used in this text is the final version of HTML 4.01 as defined on December 24, 1999, and available at http://www.w3.org/TR/html4/.

XHTML Compatibility

One of the World Wide Web Consortium's latest activities is the development of XHTML, which stands for Extensible Hypertext Markup Language. XHTML essentially is a reformulation of HTML 4.01 intended to bring it into compliance with XML and XML-based browsers. Although such user agents are not in common use, the XHTML 1.0 (http://www.w3.org/TR/xhtml1/) specification is designed, among other purposes, to provide a relatively painless transition to XML-compliant HTML coding. Rather than wait until XML-based browsers begin to hit the market, developers are encouraged to implement some simple changes to their HTML coding, changes that will not adversely affect the way their HTML documents are displayed in the current array of HTML 4 based browsers, but will remove the need to reformulate those documents at a later date.

Rules for XHTML Compatibility

To bring new or existing HTML documents into agreement with the XHTML specification, all authors need to do is follow a few simple rules as discussed in Chapter 1. If done properly, these coding practices should be backward-compatible with browsers that are not XHTML-compliant.

Well-Formed Documents Are Now Mandatory

Although this concept is nothing new to conscientious coders, XHTML makes proper nesting of elements mandatory. XHTML-compliant browsers will no longer tolerate poorly nested elements like

```
<p><i><b>How bold it feels to be italic</i></p></b>
```

but will rigorously require properly nested code such as this:

```
<p><i><b>How bold it feels to be italic</b></i></p>
```

All Element and Attribute Names Must Be Lowercased

XHTML is a subset of XML. XML is case-sensitive. HTML to date has not been case-sensitive, leaving coders the choice of using uppercase or lowercase tags; in order for an HTML document to be XHTML-compliant, all elements and attribute names must always be lowercased exclusively. Whereas previous editions of *HTML: The Complete Reference* employed uppercased HTML elements and attributes in order to favor readability, all HTML code in this edition is lowercased (excluding the discussion of Document Type Declarations in Appendix F).

No More Optional End Tags for Non-Empty Elements

To date, HTML specifications and permissive Web browsers have allowed the closing tags for certain elements, such as **<p>** and **<li>**, to be left off. Under XHTML, these closing tags cease to be optional. Wheareas current browsers still allow the omission of these closing tags, future XHTML-compliant browsers will be strict about this. Under XHTML, the following code will no longer be correct:

```
<ul>
    <li>List Item 1
    <li>List Item 1
    <li>List Item 1
 </ul>
```

To be correct under XHTML, this code must be revised as follows:

```
<ul>
    <li>List Item 1</li>
    <li>List Item 1</li>
    <li>List Item 1</li>
 </ul>
```

This change affects the following elements:

<body>	<html>	<td>
<colgroup>	<li>	<tfoot>
<dd>	<option>	<th>
<dt>	<p>	<thead>
<head>	<tbody>	<tr>

Empty Elements Must Be Closed

Under XHTML, *all* elements must be closed, including empty elements such as **
** and **<img>**. The XHTML specification offers two ways to do this. One way is to simply provide a closing tag, like so:

```
<br></br>
```

Because of uncertain browser interpretation of this code, however, the specification recommends the other method, which involves adding a trailing slash in the element tag itself:

```
<br />
```

To ensure compliance with pre-XHTML browsers, be certain to leave a space between the element name (in this case, **br**) and the trailing slash (/). This way, older browsers should simply read the slash as an unknown attribute, and ignore it.

This change affects the following elements:

<area>	<frame>	<link>
<base>	<hr>	<meta>
<basefont>	<img>	<param>
 	<input>	
<col>	<isindex>	

All Attribute Values Must Be Enclosed in Quotes

Although browsers to date have allowed attribute values without quoting—at least when attribute values do not contain any whitespace—XHTML makes quoting mandatory for all attribute values. So wheareas the code

```
<img src="image.gif" width=200 height=20 border=0>
```

might still be valid under most current browsers, to be correct under XHTML it must have all attributes quoted:

```
<img src="image.gif" width="200" height="20" border="0" />
```

All Attributes Must Have Defined Values

To date, certain HTML elements have employed what is called "attribute minimization." One example is the <ul> element, which uses the **compact** attribute. The code

```
<ul compact>
```

actually is shorthand for the code

```
<ul compact="compact">
```

Since the only value defined for **compact** is **compact**, the reason for this minimization is obvious. However, attribute minimization is not allowed under XHTML, which makes

```
<ul compact="compact">
```

the only correct way to implement this code.

XHTML: Other Flavors

The XHTML-based changes discussed so far are based on the XHTML 1.0 specification (http://www.w3.org/TR/xhtml1/), a W3C recommendation issued on January 26, 2000. XHTML 1.0 retains a number of deprecated, presentational elements still present in the HTML specifications.

XHTML 1.1 is a stricter specification that, as defined by the W3C, is "a markup language that is rich in structural functionality, but that relies upon style sheets for presentation." XHTML 1.1's other focus is on modularization of XHTML. The XHTML 1.1 specification can be found online at http://www.w3.org/TR/xhtml11/. A pared-down version of XHTML 1.1, called XHTML Basic (http://www.w3.org/TR/xhtml-basic/), is geared toward mobile applications. For immediate HTML coding purposes, XHTML 1.0 should be sufficient for most developers. Developers interested in the future directions of XHTML are encouraged to read the W3C's working draft "Modularization of XHTML" online at http://www.w3.org/TR/xhtml-modularization/.

Core Attributes Reference

The HTML 4.01 specification provides four main attributes, which are common to nearly all elements and have much the same meaning for all elements. These elements are **class**, **id**, **style**, and **title**.

class

This attribute is used to indicate the class or classes that a particular element belongs to. A class name might be used by a style sheet to associate style rules to multiple elements at once. For example, it might be desirable to associate a special class name called "important" with all elements that should be rendered with a yellow background. Because class values are not unique to a particular element, **<b class="important">** could be used as well as **<p class="important">** in the same document. It also is possible to have multiple values for the **class** attribute separated by white space; **<strong class="important special-font">** would define two classes with the particular **<strong>** element. Currently, most browsers recognize only one class name for this attribute.

id

This attribute specifies a unique alphanumeric identifier to be associated with an element. Naming an element is important to being able to access it with a style sheet, a link, or a scripting language. Names should be unique to a document and should be meaningful, so although **id="x1"** is perfectly valid, **id="Paragraph1"** might be better. Values for the **id** attribute must begin with a letter (A-Z and a-z) and may be followed by any number of letters, digits, hyphens, and periods.

One potential problem with the **id** attribute is that for some elements, particularly form controls and images, the **name** attribute already serves its function. Values for **name** should not collide with values for **id**, as they share the same naming space. For example, the following would not be allowed:

```
<b id="elementX">This is a test.</b>
<img name="elementX" src="image.gif" />
```

There is some uncertainty about what to do to ensure backward compatibility with browsers that understand **name** but not **id**. Some experts suggest that the following is illegal:

```
<img name="image1" id="image1" src="image.gif" />
```

Because **name** and **id** are naming the same item, there should be no problem; the common browsers do not have an issue with such markup. Complex scripting used to deal with two different names for the image, such as

```
<img name="image1name" id="image1id" src="image.gif" />
```

is possible, but might not be necessary.

Page designers are encouraged to pick a naming strategy and use it consistently. Once elements are named, they should be easy to manipulate with a scripting language.

Like the **class** attribute, the **id** attribute also is used by style sheets for accessing a particular element. For example, an element named **Paragraph1** can be referenced by a style rule in a document-wide style using a fragment identifier:

```
#Paragraph1    {color: blue}
```

Once an element is named using **id**, it also is a potential destination for an anchor. In the past an **<a>** element was used to set a destination; now any element can be a destination. For example,

```
<a href="#firstbolditem">Go to first bold element.</a>
<b id="firstbolditem">This is important.</b>
```

style

This attribute specifies an inline style (as opposed to an external style sheet) associated with the element. The style information is used to determine the rendering of the affected element. Because the **style** attribute allows style rules to be used directly with the element, it gives up much of the benefit of style sheets that divide the presentation of an HTML document from its structure. An example of this attribute's use is shown here:

```
<strong style="font-family: Arial;
font-size: 18pt">Important text</strong>
```

title

This attribute supplies advisory text for the element that can be rendered as a tool tip when the mouse is over the element. (Internet Explorer has supported this tool tip display for some time, but Netscape browsers prior to version 6 do not.) A title also might simply provide information that alerts future document maintainers to the meaning of the element and its enclosed content. In some cases, such as the **<a>** element, the **title** attribute can provide additional help in bookmarking. Like the title for the document itself, **title** attribute values as advisory information should be short, yet useful. For example, **<p title="paragraph1">** provides little information of value, whereas **<p title="HTML: The Complete Reference Appendix A Paragraph 10">** provides much more detail. When combined with scripting, it can provide facilities for automatic index generation.

Language Reference

One of the main goals of the HTML 4.01 specification is better support for other languages besides English. The use of other languages in a Web page might require that text direction be changed from left to right or right to left. Furthermore, once supporting non-ASCII languages becomes easier, it might be more common to see documents in mixed languages. Thus, there must be a way to indicate the language in use.

lang

This attribute indicates the language being used for the enclosed content. The language is identified using the ISO standard language abbreviation such as *fr* for French, *en* for English, and so on. RFC 1766 (http://www.ietf.org/rfc/rfc1766.txt?number=1766) describes these codes and their formats.

dir

This attribute sets the text direction as related to the **lang** attribute. The accepted values under the HTML 4.01 specification are **ltr** (left to right) and **rtl** (right to left). It should be possible to override whatever direction a user agent sets by using this attribute with the **<bdo>** element:

```
<bdo dir="rtl">Napoleon never really said "Able was I ere I saw Elba."</bdo>
```

Internet Explorer 5.5 supports **dir** for the **<bdo>** element, but Netscape 6 does not. If used with other block-level elements such as **<p>** and **<div>**, the **dir** attribute might produce right-aligned text, but will not change the actual direction of the text flow.

Events Reference

In preparation for a more dynamic Web, the W3C (World Wide Web Consortium) has defined a set of core events that are associated with nearly every HTML element. Most of these events cover simple user interaction such as the click of a mouse button or a key being pressed. A few elements, such as form controls, have some special events associated with them, signaling that the field has received focus from the user or that the form was submitted. Intrinsic events such as a document loading and unloading also are described. The core events are summarized in Table A-1. Note that in the table, Internet Explorer 4, 5, and 5.5 and Netscape 4, 4.5, and 4.7 are abbreviated to IE4, IE5, IE5.5, N4, N4.5, and N4.7, respectively. Due to the incomplete nature of the Netscape 6 beta (Preview Version 2) available at the time of this edition, Netscape 6 has not been included in this list.

 In Table A-1, *"most display elements" means all elements except <applet>, <base>, <basefont>, <bdo>, <br>, <font>, <frame>, <frameset>, <head>, <html>, <iframe>, <isindex>, <meta>, <param>, <script>, <style>, and <title>.*

This event model is far from complete, and it still is not fully supported by browsers. The event model should be considered a work in progress. It will certainly change as the Document Object Model (DOM) is more carefully defined. More information about the DOM can be found at http://www.w3.org/DOM/.

Event Attribute	Event Description	Allowed Elements Under HTML 4
onblur	Occurs when an element loses focus, meaning that the user has moved focus to another element, typically either by clicking the mouse on it or tabbing to it.	<a>, <area>, <button>, <input>, <label>, <select>, <textarea> Also <applet>, <area>, <div>, <embed>, <hr>, <img>, <marquee>, <object>, <span>, <table>, <td>, <tr> (Internet Explorer 4, 5, 5.5); <body> (IE 4, 5, and 5.5, N 4 –4.7); <frameset>, <ilayer>, <layer> (N 4 –4.7)
onchange	Signals that the form control has lost user focus and its value has been modified during its last access.	<input>, <select>, <textarea>
onclick	Indicates that the element has been clicked.	Most display elements* Also <applet>, <font> (IE 4, 5, 5.5)
ondblclick	Indicates that the element has been double-clicked.	Most display elements* Also <applet>, <font> (IE 4, 5, 5.5)
onfocus	The focus event indicates when an element has received focus; namely it has been selected for manipulation or data entry.	<a>, <area>, <button>, <input>, <label>, <select>, <textarea> Also <applet>, <div>, <embed>, <hr>, <img>, <marquee>, <object>, <span>, <table>, <td>, <tr> (IE 4, 5, 5.5); <body> (N 4 –4.7, IE 4, 5, 5.5); <frameset>, <ilayer>, <layer> (N 4 –4.7)
onkeydown	Indicates that a key is being pressed down with focus on the element.	Most display elements* Also <applet>, <font> (IE 4, 5, 5.5)
onkeypress	Describes the event of a key being pressed and released with focus on the element.	Most display elements* Also <applet>, <font> (IE 4, 5, 5.5)

Table A-1. *Core Events*

Event Attribute	Event Description	Allowed Elements Under HTML 4
onkeyup	Indicates that a key is being released with focus on the element.	Most display elements* Also <applet>, <font> (IE 4, 5, 5.5)
onload	Indicates the event of a window or frame set finishing the loading of a document.	<body>, <frameset> Also <applet>, <embed>, <link>, <script>, <style> (IE 4, 5, 5.5); <ilayer>, <img>, <layer> (N 4–4.7, IE 4, 5, 5.5)
onmousedown	Indicates the press of a mouse button with focus on the element.	Most display elements* Also <applet>, <font> (IE 4, 5, 5.5)
onmousemove	Indicates that the mouse has moved while over the element.	Most display elements* Also <applet> and <font> (IE 4, 5, 5.5)
onmouseout	Indicates that the mouse has moved away from an element.	Most display elements* Also <applet>, <font> (IE 4, 5, 5.5); <ilayer>, <layer> (N 4 –4.7)
onmouseover	Indicates that the mouse has moved over an element.	Most display elements* Also <applet>, <font> (IE 4, 5, 5.5); <ilayer>, <layer> (N 4 –4.7)
onmouseup	Indicates the release of a mouse button with focus on the element.	Most display elements* Also <applet>, <font> (IE 4, 5, 5.5)
onreset	Indicates that the form is being reset, possibly by the press of a reset button.	<form>
onselect	Indicates the selection of text by the user, typically by highlighting the desired text.	<input>, <textarea>
onsubmit	Indicates a form submission, generally by pressing a submit button.	<form>
onunload	Indicates that the browser is leaving the current document and unloading it from the window or frame.	<body>, <frameset>

Table A-1.   *Core Events* (continued)

Extended Events

Browsers might support events other than those defined in the preliminary HTML 4.0 specification. Microsoft in particular has introduced a variety of events to capture more complex mouse actions such as dragging, element events such as the bouncing of **<marquee>** text, and data-binding events signaling the loading of data. (Mouse events might be bound to data in a database.) The events are described in more detail in Table A-2.

Documentation errors might exist. The event model changes rapidly and the browser vendors have not stopped innovating in this area. Events were tested by the author for accuracy, but for an accurate, up-to-date event model for these browsers, visit http://developer.netscape.com or http://msdn.microsoft.com/default.asp.

Event Attribute	Event Description	Associated Elements	Compatibility
onabort	Triggered by the user aborting the image load with a stop button or similar effect.	\<img>	Netscape 3, 4 - 4.7 Internet Explorer 4, 5, 5.5
onafterprint	Fires after user prints document or previews document for printing.	\<body>, \<frameset>	Internet Explorer 5, 5.5
onafterupdate	Fires after the transfer of data from the element to a data provider, namely a data update.	\<applet>, \<body>, \<button>, \<caption>, \<div>, \<embed>, \<img>, \<input>, \<marquee>, \<object>, \<select>, \<table>, \<td>, \<textarea>, \<tr>	Internet Explorer 4, 5, 5.5
onbeforecopy	Fires just before selected content is copied and placed in the user's system clipboard.	\<a>, \<address>, \<area>, \<b>, \<bdo>, \<big>, \<blockquote>, \<caption>, \<center>, \<cite>, \<code>, \<custom>, \<dd>, \<dfn>, \<dir>, \<div>, \<dl>, \<dt>, \<em>, \<fieldset>, \<form>, \<h1> – \<h6>, \<i>, \<img>, \<label>, \<legend>, \<li>, \<listing>, \<menu>, \<nobr>, \<ol>, \<p>, \<plaintext>, \<pre>, \<s>, \<samp>, \<small>, \<span>, \<strike>, \<strong>, \<sub>, \<sup>, \<td>, \<textarea>, \<th>, \<tr>, \<tt>, \<u>, \<ul>	Internet Explorer 5, 5.5

Table A-2. *Extended Event Model*

Event Attribute	Event Description	Associated Elements	Compatibility
onbeforecut	Fires just before selected content is cut from document and added to the system clipboard	<a>, <address>, <applet>, <area>, <b>, <bdo>, <big>, <blockquote>, <body>, <button>, <caption>, <center>, <cite>, <code>, <custom>, <dd>, <dfn>, <dir>, <div>, <dl>, <dt>, <em>, <embed>, <fieldset>, <font>, <form>, <h1> - <h6>, <hr>, <i>, <img>, <input>, <kbd>, <label>, <legend>, <li>, <listing>, <map>, <marquee>, <menu>, <nobr>, <ol>, <p>, <plaintext>, <pre>, <rt>, <ruby>, <s>, <samp>, <select>, <small>, <span>, <strike>, <strong>, <sub>, <sup>, <table>, <tbody>, <td>, <textarea>, <tfoot>, <th>, <thead>, <tr>, <tt>, <u>, <ul>, <var>, <xmp>	Internet Explorer 5, 5.5
onbeforepaste	Fires before the selected content is pasted into document	<a>, <address>, <applet>, <area>, <b>, <bdo>, <big>, <blockquote>, <body>, <button>, <caption>, <center>, <cite>, <code>, <custom>, <dd>, <dfn>, <dir>, <div>, <dl>, <dt>, <em>, <embed>, <fieldset>, <font>, <form>, <h1> – <h6>, <hr>, <i>, <img>, <input >, <kbd>, <label>, <legend>, <li>, <listing>, <map>, <marquee>, <menu>, <nobr>, <ol>, <p>, <plaintext>, <pre>, <rt>, <ruby>, <s>, <samp>, <select>, <small>, <span>, <strike>, <strong>, <sub>, <sup>, <table>, <tbody>, <td>, <textarea>, <tfoot>, <th>, <thead>, <tr>, <tt>, <u>, <ul>, <var>, <xmp>	Internet Explorer 5, 5.5

Table A-2.   *Extended Event Model* (continued)

Event Attribute	Event Description	Associated Elements	Compatibility
onbeforeprint	Fires before user prints document or previews document for printing.	<body>, <frameset>	Internet Explorer 5, 5.5
onbeforeunload	Fires just prior to a document being unloaded from a window.	<body>, <frameset>	Internet Explorer 4, 5, 5.5
onbeforeupdate	Triggered before the transfer of data from the element to the data provider. Might be triggered explicitly or by a loss of focus or a page unload forcing a data update.	<applet>, <body>, <button>, <caption>, <div>, <embed>, <hr>, <img>, <input>, <object>, <select>, <table>, <td>, <textarea>, <tr>	Internet Explorer 4, 5, 5.5
onbounce	Triggered when the bouncing contents of a marquee touch one side or another.	<marquee>	Internet Explorer 4, 5, 5.5
oncopy	Fires on target when selected content is pasted into document	<a>, <address>, <area>, <b>, <bdo>, <big>, <blockquote>, <caption>, <center>, <cite>, <code>, <dd>, <dfn>, <dir>, <div>, <dl>, <dt>, <em>, <fieldset>, <form>, <h1> – <h6>, <hr>, <i>, <img>, <legend>, <li>, <listing>, <menu>, <nobr>, <ol>, <p>, <plaintext>, <pre>, <s>, <samp>, <small>, <span>, <strike>, <strong>, <sub>, <sup>, <td>, <th>, <tr>, <tt>, <u>, <ul>	Internet Explorer 5, 5.5

Table A-2. *Extended Event Model* (continued)

Event Attribute	Event Description	Associated Elements	Compatibility
oncut	Fires when selected content is cut from document and added to system clipboard.	\<a>, \<address>, \<applet>, \<area>, \<b>, \<bdo>, \<big>, \<blockquote>, \<body>, \<button>, \<caption>, \<center>, \<cite>, \<code>, \<dd>, \<dfn>, \<dir>, \<div>, \<dl>, \<dt>, \<em>, \<embed>, \<fieldset>, \<font>, \<form>, \<h1> – \<h6>, \<hr>, \<i>, \<img>, \<input>, \<kbd>, \<label>, \<legend>, \<li>, \<listing>, \<map>, \<marquee>, \<menu>, \<nobr>, \<ol>, \<p>, \<plaintext>, \<pre>, \<rt>, \<ruby>, \<s>, \<samp>, \<select>, \<small>, \<span>, \<strike>, \<strong>, \<sub>, \<sup>, \<table>, \<tbody>, \<td>, \<textarea>, \<tfoot>, \<th>, \<thead>, \<tr>, \<tt>, \<u>, \<ul>, \<var>, \<xmp>	Internet Explorer 5, 5.5
ondataavailable	Fires when data arrives from data sources that transmit information asynchronously.	\<applet>, \<object >	Internet Explorer 4, 5, 5.5
ondatasetchanged	Triggered when the initial data is made available from data source or when the data changes.	\<applet>, \<object>	Internet Explorer 4, 5, 5.5
ondatasetcomplete	Indicates that all the data is available from the data source.	\<applet>, \<object>	Internet Explorer 4, 5, 5.5
ondragdrop	Triggered when the user drags an object onto the browser window to attempt to load it.	\<body>, \<frameset> (window)	Netscape 4 - 4.7

Table A-2.   *Extended Event Model* (continued)

Event Attribute	Event Description	Associated Elements	Compatibility
ondragstart	Fires when the user begins to drag a highlighted selection.	`<a>`, `<acronym>`, `<address>`, `<applet>`, `<area>`, `<b>`, `<big>`, `<blockquote>`, `<body>` (document), `<button>`, `<caption>`, `<center>`, `<cite>`, `<code>`, `<dd>`, `<del>`, `<dfn>`, `<dir>`, `<div>`, `<dl>`, `<dt>`, `<em>`, `<font>`, `<form>`, `<frameset>` (document), `<h1>`, `<h2>`, `<h3>`, `<h4>`, `<h5>`, `<h6>`, `<hr>`, `<i>`, `<img>`, `<input>`, `<bd>`, `<label>`, `<li>`, `<listing>`, `<map>`, `<marquee>`, `<menu>`, `<object>`, `<ol>`, `<option>`, `<p>`, `<plaintext>`, `<pre>`, `<q>`, `<s>`, `<samp>`, `<select>`, `<small>`, `<span>`, `<strike>`, `<strong>`, `<sub>`, `<sup>`, `<table>`, `<tbody>`, `<td>`, `<textarea>`, `<tfoot>`, `<th>`, `<thead>`, `<tr>`, `<tt>`, `<u>`, `<ul>`, `<var>`, `<xmp>`	Internet Explorer 4, 5, 5.5
onerror	Fires when the loading of a document, particularly the execution of a script, causes an error. Used to trap syntax errors.	`<body>`, `<frameset>` (window), `<img>` (`<link>`, `<object>`, `<script>`, `<style>`—IE 4)	Netscape 3, 4 - 4.7 Internet Explorer 4, 5, 5.5
onerrorupdate	Fires if a data transfer has been canceled by the onbeforeupdate event handler.	`<a>`, `<applet>`, `<object>`, `<select>`, `<textarea>`	Internet Explorer 4, 5, 5.5
onfilterchange	Fires when a page filter changes state or finishes.	Nearly all elements	Internet Explorer 4, 5, 5.5
onfinish	Triggered when a looping marquee finishes.	`<marquee>`	Internet Explorer 4, 5, 5.5

Table A-2. *Extended Event Model* (continued)

Event Attribute	Event Description	Associated Elements	Compatibility
onhelp	Triggered when the user presses the F1 key or similar help button in the user agent.	Nearly all elements under Internet Explorer 4 only	Internet Explorer 4, 5, 5.5
onmove	Triggered when the user moves a window.	\<body>, \<frameset>	Netscape 4 - 4.7
onpaste	Fires when selected content is pasted into document.	\<a>, \<address>, \<applet>, \<area>, \<b>, \<bdo>, \<big>, \<blockquote>, \<body>, \<button>, \<caption>, \<center>, \<cite>, \<code>, \<dd>, \<dfn>, \<dir>, \<div>, \<dl>, \<dt>, \<em>, \<embed>, \<fieldset>, \<font>, \<form>, \<h1> – \<h6>, \<hr>, \<i>, \<img>, \<input>, \<kbd>, \<label>, \<legend>, \<li>, \<listing>, \<map>, \<marquee>, \<menu>, \<nobr>, \<ol>, \<p>, \<plaintext>, \<pre>, \<rt>, \<ruby>, \<s>, \<samp>, \<select>, \<small>, \<span>, \<strike>, \<strong>, \<sub>, \<sup>, \<table>, \<tbody>, \<td>, \<textarea>, \<tfoot>, \<th>, \<thead>, \<tr>, \<tt>, \<u>, \<ul>, \<var>, \<xmp>	Internet Explorer 5, 5.5
onreadystatechange	Similar to onload. Fires whenever the ready state for an object has changed.	\<applet>, \<body>, \<embed>, \<frame>, \<frameset>, \<iframe>, \<img>, \<link>, \<object>, \<script>, \<style>	Internet Explorer 4, 5, 5.5
onresize	Triggered whenever an object is resized. Can only be bound to the window under Netscape as set via the \<body> element.	\<applet>, \<body>, \<button>, \<caption>, \<div>, \<embed>, \<frameset>, \<hr>, \<img>, \<marquee>, \<object>, \<select>, \<table>, \<td>, \<textarea>, \<tr>	Netscape 4, 4.5 (supports \<body> only); Internet Explorer 4 - 5.5

Table A-2.   *Extended Event Model* (continued)

Event Attribute	Event Description	Associated Elements	Compatibility
onrowenter	Indicates that a bound data row has changed and new data values are available.	\<applet\>, \<body\>, \<button\>, \<caption\>, \<div\>, \<embed\>, \<hr\>, \<img\>, \<marquee\>, \<object\>, \<select\>, \<table\>, \<td\>, \<textarea\>, \<tr\>	Internet Explorer 4, 5, 5.5
onrowexit	Fires just prior to a bound data source control changing the current row.	\<applet\>, \<body \>, \<button\>, \<caption\>, \<div \>, \<embed\>, \<hr\>, \<img\>, \<marquee\>, \<object\>, \<select\>, \<table\>, \<td\>, \<textarea\>, \<tr\>	Internet Explorer 4, 5, 5.5
onscroll	Fires when a scrolling element is repositioned.	\<body\>, \<div\>, \<fieldset\>, \<img\>, \<marquee\>, \<span\>, \<textarea\>	Internet Explorer 4, 5, 5.5
onselectstart	Fires when the user begins to select information by highlighting.	Nearly all elements	Internet Explorer 4, 5, 5.5
onstart	Fires when a looped marquee begins or starts over.	\<marquee\>	Internet Explorer 4, 5, 5.5

Table A-2. *Extended Event Model* (continued)

HTML Element Reference

This appendix lists all HTML 4 elements, as well as some proprietary elements defined by different browser vendors. The element entries include all or some of the following information:

- **Syntax**   HTML 4.01 syntax for the element, including attributes and event handlers defined by the W3C specification
- **XHTML Syntax**   Notes changes in element syntax that are required for element to be compatible with XHTML 1.0
- **Attributes/Events Defined by Browser**   Additional syntax defined by different browsers
- **Attributes**   Descriptions of all attributes associated with the element
- **Attribute and Event Support**   Browser support of attributes and events
- **Example**   A code example or examples using the element
- **XHTML Example**   Presents an example using XHTML syntax, if that varies from existing HTML syntax for the element under discussion

■ **Compatibility**   The element's general compatibility with HTML/XHTML specifications and browser versions
■ **Notes**   Additional information about the element

Listings of attributes and events defined by browser versions assume that these attributes and events generally remain associated with later versions of that browser; for example, attributes defined by Internet Explorer 4 are valid for Internet Explorer 5 and higher, and attributes defined for Netscape 4 remain valid for Netscape 4.5 and higher, up to Netscape 4.7x.

Although the Netscape 6 browser is planned to be highly compliant with HTML standards, at the time of this edition it is still a work in progress. The latest beta version of the Netscape 6 browser available for this book was Preview Release 2. References in this text to Netscape 6 might not, therefore, reflect element or attribute support as it will be in the final version of the Netscape 6 browser. For this reason, it is unwise to assume that all elements or attributes supported by 4.x generation Netscape browsers will be supported by Netscape 6.

<!-- ... --> (Comment)

This construct is used to include text comments that will not be displayed by the browser.

Syntax

```
<!-- ... -->
```

Attributes
None

Event Handlers
None

Examples

```html
<!-- This is an informational comment that can occur
     anywhere in an HTML document. The next examples
     shows how style sheets and scripts are "commented out" to prevent
     older browsers from misinterpreting the content. -->

<style type="text/css">
<!--
 H1 {color: red; font-size: 40pt;}
-->
</style>

<script>
<!--
document.write("hello world");
// -->
</script>
```

Compatibility

HTML 2, 3.2, 4, 4.01, XHTML 1.0
Internet Explorer 2, 3, 4, 5, 5.5
Netscape 1, 2, 3, 4 –4.7, 6
Opera 4
WebTV

Notes

- Comments often are used to exclude content from older browsers, particularly those that do not understand client-side scripting or style sheets.

- Page developers should be careful when commenting HTML markup. Older browsers may or may not render the enclosed content.

<!DOCTYPE> (Document Type Definition)

This SGML construct specifies the document type definition corresponding to the document.

Syntax

```
<!DOCTYPE "DTD IDENTIFIER">
```

Attributes

None

Event Handlers

None

Examples

```
<!DOCTYPE HTML PUBLIC "-//W3C//DTD HTML 4.01 TRANSITIONAL//EN">

<!DOCTYPE HTML PUBLIC "-//W3C//DTD XHTML 1.0 TRANSITIONAL//EN">
```

Compatibility

HTML 2, 3.2, 4, 4.01, XHTML 1.0
Internet Explorer 2, 3, 4, 5, and 5.5
Netscape 1, 2, 3, 4 –4.7, and 6
Opera 4
WebTV

Notes

- The <!DOCTYPE> element should be used as the first line of all HTML documents. Validation programs might use this construct when determining the correctness of an HTML document. Be certain to use the document type appropriate for the elements used in the document.

■ Because the doctype declaration actually is an SGML statement, the lowercase rule for XHTML compatibility does not apply to **<!DOCTYPE>**.

<a> (Anchor)

This element indicates the portion of the document that is a hyperlink or the named target destination for a hyperlink.

Syntax

```
<a
     accesskey="key"
     charset="character code for language of linked
              resource"
     class="class name(s)"
     coords="comma-separated list of numbers"
     dir="ltr | rtl"
     href="url"
     hreflang="language code"
     id="unique alphanumeric identifier"
     lang="language code"
     name="name of target location"
     rel="comma-separated list of relationship values"
     rev="comma-separated list of relationship values"
     shape="default | circle | poly | rect"
     style="style information"
     tabindex="number"
     target="_blank | frame-name | _parent | _self | _top"
             (transitional)
     title="advisory text"
     type="content type of linked data"
     onblur="script" (transitional)
     onclick="script"
     ondblclick="script">
     onfocus="script"
     onhelp="script"
     onkeydown="script"
     onkeypress="script"
     onkeyup="script"
     onmousedown="script"
     onmousemove="script"
     onmouseout="script"
     onmouseover="script"
     onmouseup="script">

     Linked content

</a>
```

Attributes and Events Defined by Internet Explorer 4

```
datafield="name of column supplying bound data"
datasrc="ID of data source object supplying data"
language="javascript | jscript | vbs | vbscript"
methods="http-method"
ondragstart="script"
onselectstart="script"
```

Attributes and Events Defined by Internet Explorer 5.5

```
contenteditable="false | true | inherit"
hidefocus="true | false"
```

Attributes Defined by WebTV

```
NOCOLOR
SELECTED
```

Attributes

accesskey   This attribute specifies a keyboard navigation accelerator for the element. Pressing ALT or a similar key (depending on the browser and operating system) in association with the specified key selects the anchor element correlated with that key.

charset   This attribute defines the character encoding of the linked resource. The value is a space- and/or comma-delimited list of character sets as defined in RFC 2045. The default value is **ISO-8859-1**.

class   See "Core Attributes Reference," earlier in this appendix.

contenteditable   This proprietary Microsoft attribute allows users to edit content rendered in the Internet Explorer 5.5 browser. Values are **false**, **true**, and **inherit**. A value of **false** will prevent content from being edited by users; **true** will allow editing. The default value, **inherit**, applies the value of the affected element's parent element.

coords   For use with object shapes, this attribute uses a comma-separated list of numbers to define the coordinates of the object on the page.

datafld   This attribute specifies the column name from that data source object that supplies the bound data. This attribute is specific to Microsoft's Data Binding in Internet Explorer 4.

datasrc   This attribute indicates the **id** of the data source object that supplies the data that is bound to this element. This attribute is specific to Microsoft's Data Binding in Internet Explorer 4.

dir   See "Language Reference," earlier in this appendix.

hidefocus   This proprietary element, introduced with Internet Explorer 5.5, hides focus on an element's content. Focus must be applied to the element using the **tabindex** attribute.

href   This is the single required attribute for anchors defining a hypertext source link. It indicates the link target, either a URL or a URL fragment, that is a name preceded by a hash mark (#), which specifies an internal target location within the current document. URLs are not restricted to Web (http)-based documents. URLs might use any protocol supported by the browser. For example, file, ftp, and mailto work in most user agents.

hreflang   This attribute is used to indicate the language of the linked resource. See "Language Reference," earlier in this appendix for information on allowed values.

id   See "Core Attributes Reference," earlier in this appendix.

lang   See "Language Reference," earlier in this appendix.

language   This attribute specifies the language the current script is written in and invokes the proper scripting engine. The default value is **JAVASCRIPT**. **JAVASCRIPT** and **JSCRIPT** represent that the scripting language is written in JavaScript. **VBS** and **VBSCRIPT** represent that the scripting language is written in VBScript. It also might be possible to use extended names, such as **JavaScript1.1**, to hide code from JavaScript-aware browsers that don't conform to a particular version of the language.

methods   The value of this attribute provides information about the functions that might be performed on an object. The values generally are given by the HTTP protocol when it is used, but it might (for similar reasons as for the **title** attribute) be useful to include advisory information in advance in the link. For example, the browser might choose a different rendering of a link as a function of the methods specified; something that is searchable might get a different icon, or an outside link might render with an indication of leaving the current site. This element is not well understood nor supported, even by the defining browser, Internet Explorer 4.

name   This attribute is required in an anchor defining a target location within a page. A value for **name** is similar to a value for the **id** core attribute and should be an alphanumeric identifier unique to the document. Under the HTML 4.01 specification, **id** and **name** both can be used with the **<a>** element as long as they have identical values.

nocolor   Supported only by WebTV, this attribute overrides the **link** color set in the **body** element and prevents the link from changing color.

rel   For anchors containing the **href** attribute, this attribute specifies the relationship of the target object to the link object. The value is a comma-separated list of relationship values. The values and their semantics will be registered by some authority that might have meaning to the document author. The default relationship, if no other is given, is **void**. The **rel** attribute should be used only when the **href** attribute is present.

rev   This attribute specifies a reverse link, the inverse relationship of the **rel** attribute. It is useful for indicating where an object came from, such as the author of a document.

selected   Supported only in WebTV, this attribute selects the anchor with a yellow highlight box.

shape   This attribute is used to define a selectable region for hypertext source links associated with a figure to create an image map. The values for the attribute are **circle**, **default**, **polygon**, and **rect**. The format of the **coords** attribute depends on the value of **shape**. For **circle**, the value is x,y,r where x and y are the pixel coordinates for the center of the circle and r is the radius value in pixels. For **rect**, the **coords** attribute should be x,y,w,h. The x,y values define the upper-left-hand corner of the rectangle, while w and h define the width and height respectively. A value of **polygon** for **shape** requires $x1,y1,x2,y2,...$ values for **coords**. Each of the x,y pairs define a point in the polygon, with successive points being joined by straight lines and the last point joined to the first. The value **default** for **shape** requires that the entire enclosed area, typically an image, be used.

*Today because of browser support it is advisable to use the **usemap** attribute for the **<img>** element and the associated **<map>** element to define hotspots.*

style   See "Core Attributes Reference," earlier in this appendix.

tabindex   This attribute uses a number to identify the object's position in the tabbing order for keyboard navigation using the TAB key.

target   This attribute specifies the target window for a hypertext source link referencing frames. The information linked to it will be displayed in the named window. Frames must be named to be targeted. There are, however, special name values. These include **_blank**, which indicates a new window; **_parent**, which indicates the parent frame set containing the source link; **_self**, which indicates the frame containing the source link; and **_top**, which indicates the full browser window.

title   See "Core Attributes Reference," earlier in this appendix.

type   This attribute specifies the media type in the form of a MIME type for the link target. Generally, this is provided strictly as advisory information; however, in the future a browser might add a small icon for multimedia types. For example, a browser might add a small speaker icon when **type** was set to audio/wav. For a complete list of recognized MIME types, see http://www.w3.org/TR/html4/references.html#ref-MIMETYPES.

Attribute and Event Support

Netscape 4   **href**, **name**, **target**, **onclick**, **onmouseout**, and **onmouseover**. (**class**, **id**, **lang**, and **style** are implied.)

Internet Explorer 4   **accesskey**, **class**, **href**, **id**, **lang**, **name**, **rel**, **rev**, **style**, **target**, **title**, **onblur**, **onclick**, **ondblclick**, **onfocus**, **onhelp**, **onkeydown**, **onkeypress**, **onkeyup**, **onmousedown**, **onmousemove**, **onmouseout**, **onmouseover**, **onmouseup**, and all attributes and events defined by Internet Explorer 4.

Internet Explorer 5.5   Same as IE 4, plus **contenteditable** and **hidefocus**.

WebTV   href, id, name, nocolor, selected, onclick, onmouseout, and onmouseover.

Event Handlers

See "Events Reference," earlier in this appendix.

Examples

```
<!-- anchor linking to external file -->
<a href="http://www.democompany.com/">External Link</a>

<!-- anchor linking to file on local filesystem -->
<a href="file:/c:\html\index.htm">local file link</a>

<!-- anchor invoking anonymous FTP -->
<a href="ftp://ftp.democompany.com/freestuff">Anonymous FTP
link</a>

<!-- anchor invoking FTP with password -->
<a href="ftp://joeuser:secretpassword@democompany.com/path/file">
FTP with password</a>

<!-- anchor invoking mail -->
<a href="mailto:fakeid@democompany.com">Send mail</a>

<!-- anchor used to define target destination within document -->
<a name="jump">Jump target</a>

<!-- anchor linking internally to previous target anchor -->
<a href="#jump">Local jump within document</a>

<!-- anchor linking externally to previous target anchor -->
<a href="http://www.democompany.com/document#jump">
Remote jump within document</a>
```

Compatibility

HTML 2, 3.2, 4, 4.01, and XHTML 1.0
Internet Explorer 2, 3, 4, 5, and 5.5
Netscape 1, 2, 3, 4 –4.7, and 6
Opera 4
WebTV

Notes

- The following are reserved browser key bindings for the two major browsers and should not be used as values to **accesskey: a, c, e, f, g, h, v**, left arrow, and right arrow.
- HTML 3.2 defines only **name, href, rel, rev,** and **title.**

- The **target** attribute is not defined in browsers that do not support frames, such as Netscape 1 generation browsers.

- The **dir** attribute for **<a>** is not yet supported by any browsers.

<abbr> (Abbreviation)

This element allows authors to clearly indicate a sequence of characters that compose an acronym or abbreviation for a word (XML, WWW, and so on). See **<acronym>**, which is similar in use.

Syntax

```
<abbr
    class="class name(s)"
    dir="ltr | rtl"
    id="unique alphanumeric identifier"
    lang="language code"
    style="style information"
    title="advisory text"
    onclick="script"
    ondblclick="script"
    onkeydown="script"
    onkeypress="script"
    onkeyup="script"
    onmousedown="script"
    onmousemove="script"
    onmouseout="script"
    onmouseover="script"
    onmouseup="script">

</abbr>
```

Attributes

class   See "Core Attributes Reference," earlier in this appendix.

dir   See "Language Reference," earlier in this appendix.

id   See "Core Attributes Reference," earlier in this appendix.

lang   See "Language Reference," earlier in this appendix.

style   See "Core Attributes Reference," earlier in this appendix.

title   See "Core Attributes Reference," earlier in this appendix.

Attribute and Event Support

The support in Netscape 6 of attributes and events for this element remain unclear, but Preview Release Version 2 clearly supports the **title** attribute, and displays its contents as a tooltip.

Event Handlers

See "Events Reference," earlier in this appendix.

Examples

```
<abbr title="Dynamic Hypertext Markup Language">DHTML
</abbr>

<abbr lang="fr" title="World Wrestling Federation">WWF
</abbr>
```

Compatibility

HTML 4, 4.01, XHTML 1.0
Netscape 6

Note

- **<abbr>** is a new element that is not defined under HTML 2 or 3.2. At present, only Netscape 6 appears to support the **<abbr>** element. **<acronym>** serves a similar function but is only supported by Internet Explorer 4 and later. Because there is no HTML-oriented presentation for this element so far, it is primarily used in conjunction with style sheets and scripts.

<acronym> (Acronym)

This element allows authors to clearly indicate a sequence of characters that compose an acronym or abbreviation for a word (XML, WWW, and so on).

Syntax

```
<acronym
    class="class name(s)"
    dir="ltr | rtl"
    id="unique alphanumeric identifier"
    lang="language code"
    style="style information"
    title="advisory text"
    onclick="script"
    ondblclick="script"
    onkeydown="script"
    onkeypress="script"
```

```
        onkeyup="script"
        onmousedown="script"
        onmousemove="script"
        onmouseout="script"
        onmouseover="script"
        onmouseup="script">

</acronym>
```

Attributes and Events Defined by Internet Explorer 4

```
        language="javascript | jscript | vbs | vbscript"
        ondragstart="script"
        onhelp="script"
        onselectstart="script"
```

Attributes and Events Defined by Internet Explorer 5.5

```
        accesskey="key"
        contenteditable="false | true | inherit"
        hidefocus="true | false"
        tabindex="number"
```

Attributes

accesskey   This attribute specifies a keyboard navigation accelerator for the element. Pressing ALT or a similar key (depending on the browser and operating system) in association with the specified key selects the anchor element correlated with that key.

class   See "Core Attributes Reference," earlier in this appendix.

contenteditable   This proprietary Microsoft attribute allows users to edit content rendered in the Internet Explorer 5.5 browser. Values are **false**, **true**, and **inherit**. A value of **false** will prevent content from being edited by users; **true** will allow editing. The default value, **inherit**, applies the value of the affected element's parent element.

dir   See "Language Reference," earlier in this appendix.

hidefocus   This proprietary element, introduced with Internet Explorer 5.5, hides focus on an element's content. Focus must be applied to the element using the **tabindex** attribute.

id   See "Core Attributes Reference," earlier in this appendix.

lang   See "Language Reference," earlier in this appendix.

language   This attribute specifies the language the current script is written in and invokes the proper scripting engine. The default value is **javascript**. **Javascript** and **jscript** represent that the script is written in JavaScript. **vbs** and **vbscript** represent that the script is written in VBScript. It may also be possible to use extended names, such as **JavaScript1.1**, to hide code from JavaScript-aware browsers that don't conform to a particular version of the language.

style   See "Core Attributes Reference," earlier in this appendix.

tabindex   This attribute uses a number to identify the object's position in the tabbing order for keyboard navigation using the TAB key. Internet Explorer 5.5 applies this attribute to the **acronym** element; under IE 5.5, this focus can be disabled with the **hidefocus** attribute.

title   See "Core Attributes Reference," earlier in this appendix.

Attribute and Event Support

Internet Explorer 4   All attributes.

Internet Explorer 5.5   All attributes, plus **contenteditable**, **hidefocus**, and **tabindex**.

Netscape 6   Netscape 6's support for attributes and events for this element remain unclear, but Preview Release Version 2 clearly supports the **title** attribute, and displays its contents as a tooltip.

Event Handlers
See "Events Reference," earlier in this appendix.

Examples

```
<acronym title="Extensible Markup Language">XML</acronym>

<acronym lang="fr" title="Soci&eacute;t&eacute; Nationale de Chemins de
Fer">SNCF</acronym>
```

Compatibility
HTML 4, 4.01, XHTML 1.0
Internet Explorer 4, 5, and 5.5
Netscape 6

Note

■ `<acronym>` is a new element that is not defined under HTML 2 or 3.2. Under Internet Explorer 4 and above, the **title** attribute renders as a tool tip that can be used to define the meaning of the acronym.

APPENDIX A

`<address>` (Address)

This element marks up text indicating authorship or ownership of information. It generally occurs at the beginning or end of a document.

Syntax

```
<address
    class="class name(s)"
    dir="ltr | rtl"
    id="unique alphanumeric identifier"
    lang="language code"
    style="style information"
    title="advisory text"
    onclick="script"
    ondblclick="script"
    onkeydown="script"
    onkeypress="script"
    onkeyup="script"
    onmousedown="script"
    onmousemove="script"
    onmouseout="script"
    onmouseover="script"
    onmouseup="script">

</address>
```

Attributes and Events Defined by Internet Explorer 4

```
    language="javascript | jscript | vbs | sbscript"
    ondragstart="script"
    onhelp="script"
    onselectstart="script"
```

Attributes and Events Defined by Internet Explorer 5.5

```
    accesskey="key"
    contenteditable="inherit | false | true"
    hidefocus="true | false"
    tabindex="number"
    unselectable="off | on"
```

Attributes

accesskey   This attribute specifies a keyboard navigation accelerator for the element. Pressing ALT or a similar key (depending on the browser and operating system) in association with the specified key selects the anchor element correlated with that key.

class   See "Core Attributes Reference," earlier in this appendix.

contenteditable   This proprietary Microsoft attribute allows users to edit content rendered in the Internet Explorer 5.5 browser. Values are **false**, **true**, and **inherit**. A value of **false** will prevent content from being edited by users; **true** will allow editing. The default value, **inherit**, applies the value of the affected element's parent element.

dir   See "Language Reference," earlier in this appendix.

hidefocus   This proprietary element, introduced with Internet Explorer 5.5, hides focus on an element's content. Focus must be applied to the element using the **tabindex** attribute.

id   See "Core Attributes Reference," earlier in this appendix.

lang   See "Language Reference," earlier in this appendix.

language   This attribute specifies the language the current script is written in and invokes the proper scripting engine. The default value is **javascript**. **Javascript** and **jscript** represent that the scripting language is written in JavaScript. **Vbs** and **vbscript** represent that the scripting language is written in VBScript. It may also be possible to use extended names, such as **JavaScript1.1**, to hide code from JavaScript-aware browsers that don't conform to a particular version of the language.

style   See "Core Attributes Reference," earlier in this appendix.

tabindex   This attribute uses a number to identify the object's position in the tabbing order for keyboard navigation using the TAB key. Internet Explorer 5.5 applies this attribute to the **address** element; under IE 5.5, this focus can be disabled with the **hidefocus** attribute.

title   See "Core Attributes Reference," earlier in this appendix.

unselectable   This proprietary Microsoft element can be used to prevent content displayed in Internet Explorer 5.5 from being selected. Testing suggests that this might not work consistently. Values are **off** (selection permitted) and **on** (selection not allowed).

Attribute and Event Support

Netscape 4   class, id, lang, and style.

Internet Explorer 4   class, id, lang, language, style, title, onclick, ondblclick, ondragstart, onhelp, onkeydown, onkeypress, onkeyup, onmousedown, onmousemove, onmouseout, onmouseover, onmouseup, and onselectstart.

Internet Explorer 5.5   Adds support for **dir, tabindex**, plus IE 5.5 attributes **contenteditable, hidefocus, tabindex**, and **unselectable**.

WebTV   No attributes

Event Handlers
See "Events Reference," earlier in this appendix.

Example

```
<address>Big Company, Inc.<br>2105 Demo Street<br>
San Diego, CA U.S.A.</address>
```

Compatibility
HTML 2, 3.2, 4, 4.01, and XHTML 1.0
Internet Explorer 2, 3, 4, 5, and 5.5
Netscape 1, 2, 3, 4 –4.7, and 6
Opera 4
WebTV

Note

■ Under HTML 2.0, 3.2, and WebTV there are no attributes for **<address>**.

<applet> (Java Applet)

This element identifies the inclusion of a Java applet. The strict HTML 4.01 definition does not include this element; it has been deprecated in favor of **<object>**.

Syntax (HTML 4.01 Transitional Only)

```
<applet
      align="bottom | left | middle | right | top"
      alt="alternative text"
      archive="URL of archive file"
      class="class name(s)"
      code="URL of Java class file"
      codebase="URL for base referencing"
      height="pixels"
      hspace="pixels"
      id="unique alphanumeric identifier"
      name="unique name for scripting reference"
      object="filename"
      style="style information"
      title="advisory text"
```

```
      vspace="pixels"
      width="pixels">

      <param> elements

      Alternative content

</applet>
```

Attributes and Events Defined by Internet Explorer 4

```
      align="absbottom | absmiddle | baseline | bottom |
            left | middle | right | texttop"
      datafld="name of column supplying bound data"
      datasrc="ID of data source object supplying data"
      src="URL"
      onafterupdate="script"
      onbeforeupdate="script"
      onblur="script"
      onclick="script"
      ondataavailable="script"
      ondatasetchanged="script"
      ondatasetcomplete="script"
      ondblclick="script"
      ondragstart="script"
      onerrorupdate="script"
      onfocus="script"
      onhelp="script"
      onkeydown="script"
      onkeypress="script"
      onkeyup="script"
      onmousedown="script"
      onmousemove="script"
      onmouseout="script"
      onmouseover="script"
      onmouseup="script"
      onreadystatechange="script"
      onresize="script"
      onrowenter="script"
      onrowexit="script"
```

Attributes and Events Defined by Internet Explorer 5.5

```
accesskey="key"
hidefocus="true | false"
tabindex="number"
```

Attributes Defined by Netscape 4

```
align="absbottom | absmiddle | baseline | center | texttop"
mayscript
```

Attributes

accesskey   This attribute specifies a keyboard navigation accelerator for the element. Pressing ALT or a similar key (depending on the browser and operating system) in association with the specified key selects the anchor element correlated with that key.

align   This attribute is used to position the applet on the page relative to content that might flow around it. The HTML 4.01 specification defines values of **bottom**, **left**, **middle**, **right**, and **top**, whereas Microsoft and Netscape also might support **absbottom**, **absmiddle**, **baseline**, **center**, and **texttop**.

alt   This attribute causes a descriptive text alternate to be displayed on browsers that do not support Java. Page designers should also remember that content enclosed within the **<applet>** element may also be rendered as alternative text.

archive   This attribute refers to an archived or compressed version of the applet and its associated class files, which might help reduce download time.

class   See "Core Attributes Reference," earlier in this appendix.

code   This attribute specifies the URL of the applet's class file to be loaded and executed. Applet filenames are identified by a .class filename extension. The URL specified by **code** might be relative to the **codebase** attribute.

codebase   This attribute gives the absolute or relative URL of the directory where applets' .class files referenced by the **code** attribute are stored.

datafld   This attribute, supported by Internet Explorer 4 and higher, specifies the column name from the data source object that supplies the bound data. This attribute might be used to specify the various **<param>** elements passed to the Java applet.

datasrc   Like **datafld**, this attribute is used for data binding under Internet Explorer 4. It indicates the **id** of the data source object that supplies the data that is bound to the **<param>** elements associated with the applet.

height   This attribute specifies the height, in pixels, that the applet needs.

hidefocus   This proprietary element, introduced with Internet Explorer 5.5, hides focus on an element's content. Focus must be applied to the element using the **tabindex** attribute.

hspace   This attribute specifies additional horizontal space, in pixels, to be reserved on either side of the applet.

id   See "Core Attributes Reference," earlier in this appendix.

mayscript   In the Netscape implementation, this attribute allows access to an applet by programs in a scripting language embedded in the document.

name   This attribute assigns a name to the applet so that it can be identified by other resources; particularly scripts.

object   This attribute specifies the URL of a serialized representation of an applet.

src   As defined for Internet Explorer 4 and higher, this attribute specifies a URL for an associated file for the applet. The meaning and use is unclear and not part of the HTML standard.

style   See "Core Attributes Reference," earlier in this appendix.

tabindex   This attribute uses a number to identify the object's position in the tabbing order for keyboard navigation using the TAB key. Internet Explorer 5.5 applies this attribute to the **applet** element; under IE 5.5, this focus can be disabled with the **hidefocus** attribute.

title   See "Core Attributes Reference," earlier in this appendix.

vspace   This attribute specifies additional vertical space, in pixels, to be reserved above and below the applet.

width   This attribute specifies in pixels the width that the applet needs.

Attribute and Event Support

Netscape 4   **align**, **alt**, **archive**, **code**, **codebase**, **hspace**, **mayscript**, **name**, **vspace**, and **width**. (**class**, **id**, and **style** are implied.)

Internet Explorer 4   **alt**, **class**, **code**, **codebase**, **height**, **hspace**, **id**, **name**, **style**, **title**, **vspace**, **width**, and all attributes and events defined by Internet Explorer 4.

Internet Explorer 5.5   Same as IE 4, plus **hidefocus** and **tabindex**.

Event Handlers
None.

Example

```
<applet code="game.class"
        align="left"
        archive="game.zip"
        height="250" width="350">

<param name="difficulty"  value="easy">

<b>Sorry, you need Java to play this game.</b>

</applet>
```

Compatibility

HTML 2, 3.2, 4, 4.01, and XHTML 1.0
Internet Explorer 2, 3, 4, 5, and 5.5
Netscape 1, 2, 3, 4 –4.7, and 6
WebTV

Notes

- The HTML 4.01 specification does not encourage the use of **<applet>** and prefers the use of the **<object>** element. Under the strict definition of HTML 4.01, this element is deprecated.

- The **<applet>** element replaces the original **<app>** element. Parameter values can be passed to applets using the **<param>** element in the applet's content area.

- WebTV's current implementation does not support Java applets.

- Java applets were first supported under Netscape 2–level browsers and Internet Explorer 3–level browsers.

<area> (Image Map Area)

<area> is an empty element used within the content model of the **<p>** element to implement client-side image maps. It defines a hot-spot region on the map and associates it with a hypertext link.

Syntax

```
<area
     accesskey="character"
     alt="alternative text"
     class="class name(s)"
     coords="comma separated list of values"
     dir="ltr | rtl"
```

```
href="url"
id="unique alphanumeric identifier"
lang="language code"
nohref
shape="circle | default | poly | rect"
style="style information"
tabindex="number"
target="_blank | frame-name | _parent | _self |
        _top" (transitional)
title="advisory text"
onblur="script"
onclick="script"
ondblclick="script"
onfocus="script"
onkeydown="script"
onkeypress="script"
onkeyup="script"
onmousedown="script"
onmousemove="script"
onmouseout="script"
onmouseover="script"
onmouseup="script">
```

XHTML Syntax

Because **<area>** is an empty element, a closing forward slash is required before the closing bracket of the tag, as in the following:

```
<area />
```

Attributes and Events Defined by Internet Explorer 4

```
language="javascript | jscript | vbs | vbscipt"
shape="circ | circle | poly | polygon | rect |
        rectangle"
ondragstart="script"
onhelp="script"
onselectstart="script"
```

Attributes and Events Defined by Internet Explorer 5.5

```
hidefocus="true | false"
```

Attributes Defined by Netscape 4

```
name="filename"
shape="circle | default | poly | polygon | rect"
```

Attributes Defined by WebTV

```
notab
```

Attributes

accesskey   This attribute specifies a keyboard navigation accelerator for the element. Pressing ALT or a similar key in association with the specified character selects the form control correlated with that key sequence. Page designers are forewarned to avoid key sequences already bound to browsers.

alt   This attribute contains a text string alternative to display on browsers that cannot display images.

class   See "Core Attributes Reference," earlier in this appendix.

coords   This attribute contains a set of values specifying the coordinates of the hot-spot region. The number and meaning of the values depend upon the value specified for the **shape** attribute. For a **rect** or **rectangle** shape, the **coords** value is two x,y pairs: **left**, **top**, **right**, and **bottom**. For a **circ** or **circle** shape, **coords** value is x,y,r where x,y is a pair specifying the center of the circle and r is a value for the radius. For a **poly** or **polygon** shape, the **coords** value is a set of x,y pairs for each point in the polygon: $x1,y1,x2,y2,x3,y3$, and so on.

dir   See "Language Reference," earlier in this appendix.

hidefocus   This proprietary element, introduced with Internet Explorer 5.5, hides focus on an element's content. Focus must be applied to the element using the **tabindex** attribute.

href   This attribute specifies the hyperlink target for the area. Its value is a valid URL. Either this attribute or the **nohref** attribute must be present in the element.

id   See "Core Attributes Reference," earlier in this appendix.

lang   See "Language Reference," earlier in this appendix.

language   This attribute specifies the language the current script is written in and invokes the proper scripting engine. The default value is **javascript**. **Javascript** and **jscript** represent that the scripting language is written in JavaScript. **vbs** and **vbscript** represent that the scripting language is written in VBScript. It also might be possible to use extended names, such as **JavaScript1.1**, to hide code from JavaScript-aware browsers that don't conform to a particular version of the language.

name   This attribute is used to define a name for the clickable area so that it can be scripted by older browsers.

nohref   This attribute indicates that no hyperlink exists for the associated area. Either this attribute or the **href** attribute must be present in the element.

notab   Supported by WebTV, this attribute keeps the element from appearing in the tabbing order.

shape   This attribute defines the shape of the associated hot spot. HTML 4 defines the values **rect**, which defines a rectangular region; **circle**, which defines a circular region; **poly**, which defines a polygon; and **default**, which indicates the entire region beyond any defined shapes. Many browsers, notably Internet Explorer 4 and higher, support **circ**, **polygon**, and **rectangle** as valid values for **shape**.

style   See "Core Attributes Reference," earlier in this appendix.

tabindex   This attribute represents a numeric value specifying the position of the defined area in the browser tabbing order.

target   This attribute specifies the target window for hyperlink referencing frames. The value is a frame name or one of several special names. A value of **_blank** indicates a new window. A value of **_parent** indicates the parent frame set containing the source link. A value of **_self** indicates the frame containing the source link. A value of **_top** indicates the full browser window.

title   See "Core Attributes Reference," earlier in this appendix.

Attribute and Event Support

Netscape 4   coords, href, nohref, shape, target, onmouseout, and **onmouseover**. (**class**, **id**, **lang**, and **style** are implied but not listed for this element in Netscape documentation.)

Internet Explorer 4   alt, class, coords, href, id, lang, language, nohref, shape, style, **tabindex**, **target**, **title**, all W3C-defined events, and all attributes and events defined by Internet Explorer 4.

Internet Explorer 5.5   Same as IE 4, plus **dir** and **hidefocus**.

WebTV   coords, href, id, name, notab, shape, target, onmouseout, and **onmouseover**.

Event Handlers

See "Events Reference," earlier in this chapter.

Example

```
<map name="primary">
  <area shape="circle" coords="200,250,25" href="another.htm">
```

```
   <area shape="default" nohref>
</map>
```

XHTML Example

```
<map name="primary">
  <area shape="circle" coords="200,250,25" href="another.htm" />
  <area shape="default" nohref-"noref">
</map>
```

Compatibility

HTML 2, 3.2, 4, 4.01, and XHTML 1.0
Internet Explorer 2, 3, 4, 5, and 5.5
Netscape 1, 2, 3, 4–4.7, and 6
Opera 4
WebTV

Notes

■ By the HTML 3.2 and 4.0 specifications, the closing tag **</area>** is forbidden.

■ The XHTML 1.0 specification requires a trailing slash: **<area />**

■ The **id**, **class**, and **style** attributes have the same meaning as the core attributes defined in the HTML 4 specification, but only Netscape and Microsoft define them.

■ Netscape 1–level browsers do not understand the **target** attribute as it relates to frames.

■ HTML 3.2 defines only **alt**, **coords**, **href**, **nohref**, and **shape**.

<audioscope> (Sound Amplitude Display)

This WebTV-specific element displays an audioscope for a sound resource that displays a dynamic, graphical display of a sound's amplitude.

Syntax (Defined by WebTV)

```
<audioscope
    align="absbottom | absmiddle | baseline | bottom |
          left | middle | right | texttop | top"
    border="pixels"
    gain="number"
    height="pixels"
    leftcolor="color name | #RRGGBB"
    leftoffset="number"
    maxlevel="true | false"
    rightcolor="name | #RRGGBB"
```

```
        rightoffset="number"
        width="pixels">
```

Attributes

align   This attribute positions the audioscope object on the page relative to text or other content that might flow around it.

border   This attribute sets the width of the audioscope border in pixels. The default value is **1**.

gain   This attribute takes a numeric value, which is a multiplier for the amplitude display. The default value is **1**.

height   This attribute sets the height of the audioscope in pixels. The default value is **80** pixels.

leftcolor   This attribute sets the color of the line displaying the left audio channel in the audioscope. Values can be given either as named colors or in the numeric *#RRGGBB* format. The default value is **#8ECE10**.

leftoffset   This attribute sets the vertical offset for the display of the left audio channel with positive and negative values relative to the center of the audioscope. The default value is **0**.

maxlevel   This Boolean attribute specifies whether the audioscope should clip sound according to the specified gain. The default value is **false**.

rightcolor   This attribute sets the color of the line displaying the right audio channel in the audioscope. Values can be given either as named colors or in the numeric *#RRGGBB* format. The default value is **#8ECE10**.

rightoffset   This attribute sets the vertical offset for the display of the right audio channel with positive and negative values relative to the center of the audioscope. The default value is **1**.

width   This attribute sets the width of the audioscope in pixels. The default width is **100** pixels.

Attribute and Event Support

WebTV   All attributes

Event Handlers
None

Example

```
<audioscope border="1" height="16" width="240" gain="3"
        maxlevel="false">
```

APPENDIX A

Compatibility

WebTV

Note

- **<audioscope>** is supported only by WebTV. As such it is not subject to the XHTML 1.0 specification, and does not require a trailing slash /.

<b> (Bold)

This element indicates that the enclosed text should be displayed in boldface.

Syntax

```
<b
     class="class name(s)"
     dir="ltr | rtl"
     id="unique alphanumeric identifier"
     lang="language code"
     style="style information"
     title="advisory text"
     onclick="script"
     ondblclick="script"
     onkeydown="script"
     onkeypress="script"
     onkeyup="script"
     onmousedown="script"
     onmousemove="script"
     onmouseout="script"
     onmouseover="script"
     onmouseup="script">

</b>
```

Attributes and Events Defined by Internet Explorer 4

```
     language="javascript | jscript | vbs | vbscript"
     ondragstart="script"
     onhelp="script"
     onselectstart="script"
```

Attributes and Events Defined by Internet Explorer 5.5

```
     accesskey="key"
     contenteditable="false | true | inherit"
```

```
hidefocus="true | false"
tabindex=="n"
```

Attributes

accesskey   This attribute specifies a keyboard navigation accelerator for the element. Pressing ALT or a similar key (depending on the browser and operating system) in association with the specified key selects the anchor element correlated with that key.

class   See "Core Attributes Reference," earlier in this appendix.

contenteditable   This proprietary Microsoft attribute allows users to edit content rendered in the Internet Explorer 5.5 browser. Values are **false**, **true**, and **inherit**. A value of **false** will prevent content from being edited by users; **true** will allow editing. The default value, **inherit**, applies the value of the affected element's parent element.

dir   See "Language Reference," earlier in this appendix.

hidefocus   This proprietary element, introduced with Internet Explorer 5.5, hides focus on an element's content. Focus must be applied to the element using the **tabindex** attribute.

id   See "Core Attributes Reference," earlier in this appendix.

lang   See "Language Reference," earlier in this appendix.

language   This attribute specifies the language the current script is written in and invokes the proper scripting engine. The default value is **javascript**. **Javascript** and **jscript** represent that the scripting language is written in JavaScript. **vbs** and **vbscript** represent that the scripting language is written in VBScript. It also might be possible to use extended names, such as **JavaScript1.1**, to hide code from JavaScript-aware browsers that don't conform to a particular version of the language.

style   See "Core Attributes Reference," earlier in this appendix.

tabindex   This attribute uses a number to identify the object's position in the tabbing order for keyboard navigation using the TAB key. Internet Explorer 5.5 applies this attribute to the **b** element; under IE 5.5, this focus can be disabled with the **hidefocus** attribute.

title   See "Core Attributes Reference," earlier in this appendix.

Attribute and Event Support

Netscape 4   **class**, **id**, **lang**, and **style** are implied but not explicitly listed for this element.

Internet Explorer 4   All W3C-defined attributes and events except **dir**, and attributes and events defined by Internet Explorer 4.

Internet Explorer 5.5   Same as IE 4, plus **contenteditable, dir, hidefocus,** and **tabindex.**

Event Handlers
See "Events Reference," earlier in this appendix.

Example

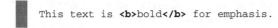

```
This text is <b>bold</b> for emphasis.
```

Compatibility
HTML 2, 3.2, 4, 4.01, and XHTML 1.0
Internet Explorer 2, 3, 4, 5, and 5.5
Netscape 1, 2, 3, 4–4.7, and 6
Opera 4
WebTV

Note

■   HTML 2 and 3.2 do not define any attributes for this element.

<base> (Base URL)
This element specifies the base URL to use for all relative URLs contained within a document. It occurs only in the scope of a **<HEAD>** element.

Syntax

```
<base
    href="url"
    target="_blank | frame-name | _parent | _self | _top" >
```

XHTML Syntax
Because this is an empty element, a closing forward slash is required before the closing bracket on the tag:

```
<base />
```

Syntax Defined by Internet Explorer 5.0/5.5

```
        id="string"
```

Attributes

href   This attribute specifies the base URL to be used throughout the document for relative URL addresses.

target   For documents containing frames, this attribute specifies the default target window for every link that does not have an explicit target reference. Aside from named frames, several special values exist. A value of **_blank** indicates a new window. A value of **_parent** indicates the parent frame set containing the source link. A value of **_self** indicates the frame containing the source link. A value of **_top** indicates the full browser window.

Attribute and Event Support

Netscape 4   href and **target**

Internet Explorer 4   href and **target**

Internet Explorer 5.5   href, id and **target**

WebTV   href and **target**

Event Handlers
None

Examples

```
<base href="http://www.democompany.com/">
<base target="_blank" href="http://www.democompany.com/">
```

XHTML Examples

```
<base href="http://www.democompany.com/" />
<base target="_blank" href="http://www.democompany.com/" />
```

Compatibility
HTML 2, 3.2, 4, 4.01, and XHTML 1.0
Internet Explorer 2, 3, 4, 5, and 5.5
Netscape 1, 2, 3, 4–4.7, and 6
Opera 4
WebTV

Notes

- ■ HTML 2.0 and 3.2 define only the **href** attribute.
- ■ XHTML 1.0 requires a trailing slash: **<base />**

<basefont> (Base Font)

This element establishes a default font size for a document. Font size then can be varied relative to the base font size using the **<font>** element. The **<basefont>** element must be placed near the beginning of the body part of the page.

Syntax (Transitional Only)

```
<basefont
    color="color name | #RRGGBB"
    face="font name(s)"
    id="unique alphanumeric identifier"
    size="1-7 | +/-int">
```

XHTML Syntax

Because this is an empty element, a closing forward slash is required before the closing bracket on the tag:

```
<basefont />
```

Attributes Defined by Internet Explorer 4

```
        class="class name(s)"
        lang="language code"
```

Attributes

class   Internet Explorer 4 documentation indicates that the **class** can be set for the **<basefont>** element; however, this probably is a mistake in the documentation.

color   This attribute sets the text color using either a named color or a color specified in the hexadecimal *#RRGGBB* format.

face   This attribute contains a list of one or more font names. The document text in the default style is rendered in the first font face that the client's browser supports. If no font listed is installed on the local system, the browser typically defaults to the proportional or fixed-width font for that system.

id   See "Core Attributes Reference," earlier in this appendix.

lang   Internet Explorer 4 documentation also mentions use of the **lang** attribute to indicate the language used. Meaning with this element is not well defined.

size This attribute specifies the font size as either a numeric or relative value. Numeric values range from **1** to **7** with **1** being the smallest and **3** the default.

Attribute and Event Support

Netscape 4 **id** (implied) and **size**

Internet Explorer 4 All attributes

WebTV size

Event Handlers
None

Example

```
<basefont color="#FF0000" face="Helvetica" size="+2">
```

XHTML Example

```
<basefont color="#FF0000" face="Helvetica" size="+2" />
```

Compatibility
HTML 2, 3.2, 4, 4.01, and XHTML 1.0
Internet Explorer 2, 3, 4, 5, and 5.5
Netscape 1, 2, 3, 4–4.7
WebTV

Notes

■ HTML 3.2 supports the **<basefont>** element and the **size** attribute. HTML 4.0 transitional specification added support for **color** and **face** as well.

■ The HTML 4.01 strict specification does not support this element.

■ The font sizes indicated by numeric values are browser dependent and not absolute.

■ At the time of this writing, Netscape 6 (Preview Release 2) does not support this element.

■ XHTML 1.0 requires a trailing slash for this element: **<basefont />**

<bdo> (Bidirectional Override)

This element is used to override the current directionality of text.

Syntax

```
<bdo>
     class="class name(s)"
     dir="ltr | rtl"
     id="unique alphanumeric identifier"
     lang="language code"
     style="style information"
     title="advisory text">

</bdo>
```

Attributes and Events Defined by Internet Explorer 5.5

```
     accesskey="key"
     contenteditable="inherit | false | true"
     hidefocus="true | false"
     language="javascript | jscript | vbs | vbscript | xml"
     tabindex="number"
     unselectable="off | on"
```

Attributes

accesskey   This attribute specifies a keyboard navigation accelerator for the element. Pressing ALT or a similar key (depending on the browser and operating system) in association with the specified key selects the anchor element correlated with that key.

class   See "Core Attributes Reference," earlier in this appendix.

contenteditable   This proprietary Microsoft attribute allows users to edit content rendered in the Internet Explorer 5.5 browser. Values are **false**, **true**, and **inherit**. A value of **false** will prevent content from being edited by users; **true** will allow editing. The default value, **inherit**, applies the value of the affected element's parent element.

dir   This attribute is required for the **<bdo>** element. It sets the text direction either to left to right (**ltr**) or right to left (**rtl**).

hidefocus   This proprietary element, introduced with Internet Explorer 5.5, hides focus on an element's content. Focus must be applied to the element using the **tabindex** attribute.

id   See "Core Attributes Reference," earlier in this appendix.

lang   See "Language Reference," earlier in this appendix.

language   This attribute, applied to this element by Internet Explorer 5.5, specifies the language the current script is written in and invokes the proper scripting engine. The default value is **javascript**. **Javascript** and **jscript** represent that the scripting language is written in JavaScript. **vbs** and **vbscript** represent that the scripting language is written in VBScript. It also might be possible to use extended names, such as **JavaScript1.1**, to hide code from JavaScript-aware browsers that don't conform to a particular version of the language.

style   See "Core Attributes Reference," earlier in this appendix.

tabindex   This attribute uses a number to identify the object's position in the tabbing order for keyboard navigation using the TAB key. Internet Explorer 5.5 applies this attribute to the **bdo** element; under IE 5.5, this focus can be disabled with the **hidefocus** attribute.

title   See "Core Attributes Reference," earlier in this appendix.

unselectable   This proprietary Microsoft element can be used to prevent content displayed in Internet Explorer 5.5 from being selected. Testing suggests that this might not work consistently. Values are **off** (selection permitted) and **on** (selection not allowed).

Attribute and Event Support

Internet Explorer 5.5   IE documentation adds support for all attributes, plus **contenteditable**, **hidefocus**, **language**, **tabindex**, and **unselectable**.

Event Handlers
None

Example

```
<!-- Switch text direction -->
<bdo dir="rtl">This text will go right to left if you can
find a browser that supports this element.
</bdo>
```

Compatibility
HTML 4, 4.01, XHTML 1.0
Internet Explorer 5, 5.5

Note

■ Internet Explorer 5 was the first browser to support this element; to date, **<bdo>** is the only element with which the **dir** attribute works.

`<bgsound>` (Background Sound)

This Internet Explorer and WebTV element associates a background sound with a page.

Syntax (Defined by Internet Explorer 4)

```
<bgsound
    balance="number"
    class="class name(s)"
    id="unique alphanumeric identifier"
    lang="language code"
    loop=number
    src="url of sound file"
    title="advisory text"
    volume="number">
```

Attributes

balance   This attribute defines a number between –10,000 and +10,000 that determines how the volume will be divided between the speakers.

class   See "Core Attributes Reference," earlier in this appendix.

id   See "Core Attributes Reference," earlier in this appendix.

lang   See "Language Reference," earlier in this appendix.

loop   This attribute indicates the number of times a sound is to be played and either has a numeric value or the keyword **infinite**.

src   This attribute specifies the URL of the sound file to be played, which must be one of the following types: .wav, .au, or .mid.

title   See "Core Attributes Reference," earlier in this appendix.

volume   This attribute defines a number between -10,000 and 0 that determines the loudness of a page's background sound.

Attribute and Event Support

Internet Explorer 4   All attributes

WebTV   **loop** and **src**.

Event Handlers

None

Examples

```
<bgsound src="sound1.mid">

<bgsound src="sound2.au" loop="infinite">
```

Compatibility

Internet Explorer 2, 3, 4, 5, and 5.5
WebTV

Note

■ Similar functionality can be achieved in Netscape using the **\<embed\>** element to invoke LiveAudio.

\<big\> (Big Font)

This element indicates that the enclosed text should be displayed in a larger font relative to the current font.

Syntax

```
<big
     class="class name(s)"
     dir="ltr | rtl"
     id="unique alphanumeric identifier"
     lang="language code"
     style="style information"
     title="advisory text"
     onclick="script"
     ondblclick="script"
     onkeydown="script"
     onkeypress="script"
     onkeyup="script"
     onmousedown="script"
     onmousemove="script"
     onmouseout="script"
     onmouseover="script"
     onmouseup="script">

</big>
```

Attributes and Events Defined by Internet Explorer 4

```
language="javascript | jscript | vbs | vbsript"
ondragstart="script"
onhelp="script"
onselectstart="script"
```

Attributes and Events Defined by Internet Explorer 5.5

```
accesskey="key"
contenteditable="false | true | inherit"
hidefocus="true | false"
tabindex="number"
```

Attributes

accesskey   This attribute specifies a keyboard navigation accelerator for the element. Pressing ALT or a similar key (depending on the browser and operating system) in association with the specified key selects the anchor element correlated with that key.

class   See "Core Attributes Reference," earlier in this appendix.

contenteditable   This proprietary Microsoft attribute allows users to edit content rendered in the Internet Explorer 5.5 browser. Values are **false**, **true**, and **inherit**. A value of **false** will prevent content from being edited by users; **true** will allow editing. The default value, **inherit**, applies the value of the affected element's parent element.

dir   See "Language Reference," earlier in this appendix.

hidefocus   This proprietary element, introduced with Internet Explorer 5.5, hides focus on an element's content. Focus must be applied to the element using the **tabindex** attribute.

id   See "Core Attributes Reference," earlier in this appendix.

lang   See "Language Reference," earlier in this appendix.

language   This attribute specifies the language the current script is written in and invokes the proper scripting engine. The default value is **javascript**. **Javascript** and **jscript** represent that the scripting language is written in JavaScript. **Vbs** and **vbscript** represent that the scripting language is written in VBScript.

style   See "Core Attributes Reference," earlier in this appendix.

tabindex   This attribute uses a number to identify the object's position in the tabbing order for keyboard navigation using the TAB key. Internet Explorer 5.5 applies this attribute to the **big** element; under IE 5.5, this focus can be disabled with the **hidefocus** attribute.

title   See "Core Attributes Reference," earlier in this appendix.

Attribute and Event Support

Netscape 4   **class**, **id**, **lang**, and **style** are implied.

Internet Explorer 4   All attributes and events except **dir**.

Internet Explorer 5.5   Same as IE 4, plus **contenteditable**, **dir**, **hidefocus**, and **tabindex**.

Event Handlers

See "Events Reference," earlier in this appendix.

Example

```
This text is regular size. <big>This text is larger.</big>
```

Compatibility

HTML 2, 3.2, 4, 4.01, and XHTML 1.0
Internet Explorer 2, 3, 4, 5, and 5.5
Netscape 1, 2, 3, 4 –4.7, and 6
Opera 4
WebTV

Note

■   HTML 3.2 does not support any attributes for this element.

<blackface> (Blackface Font)

This WebTV element renders the enclosed text in a double-weight boldface font. It is used for headings and other terms needing special emphasis.

Syntax

```
<blackface>  Text  </blackface>
```

Attributes

None

Event Handlers

None

Example

```
<blackface>Buy now!</blackface> This offer expires in five
minutes.
```

Compatibility
WebTV

Note

■ This element is supported only by WebTV.

`<blink>` (Blinking Text Display)

This Netscape-specific element causes the enclosed text to flash slowly.

Syntax (Defined by Netscape)

```
<blink
    class="class name(s)"
    id="unique alphanumeric identifier"
    lang="language code"
    style="style information">

</blink>
```

Attributes

class   See "Core Attributes Reference," earlier in this appendix.

id   See "Core Attributes Reference," earlier in this appendix.

lang   See "Language Reference," earlier in this appendix.

style   See "Core Attributes Reference," earlier in this appendix.

Attribute and Event Support

Netscape 4   All attributes

Event Handlers
None

Example

```
<blink>Annoying, isn't it?</blink>
```

Compatibility

Netscape 1, 2, 3, 4–4.7, 6

Note

■ Although not explicitly defined in Netscape documentation, the **class**, **id**, **lang**, and **style** attributes are indicated to be universal to all elements under Netscape 4 and higher, and might have meaning here.

<blockquote> (Block Quote)

This block element indicates that the enclosed text is an extended quotation. Usually this is rendered visually by indentation.

Syntax

```
<blockquote
    cite="url of source information"
    class="class name(s)"
    dir="ltr | rtl"
    id="unique alphanumeric identifier"
    lang="language code"
    style="style information"
    title="advisory text"
    onclick="script"
    ondblclick="script"
    onkeydown="script"
    onkeypress="script"
    onkeyup="script"
    onmousedown="script"
    onmousemove="script"
    onmouseout="script"
    onmouseover="script"
    onmouseup="script">

</blockquote>
```

Attributes and Events Defined by Internet Explorer 4

```
    language="javascript | jscript | vbs | vbscript"
    ondragstart="script"
    onhelp="script"
    onselectstart="script"
```

APPENDIX A

Attributes and Events Defined by Internet Explorer 5.5

```
accesskey="key"
contenteditable="false | true | inherit"
hidefocus="true | false"
tabindex="number"
```

Attributes

accesskey   This attribute specifies a keyboard navigation accelerator for the element. Pressing ALT or a similar key (depending on the browser and operating system) in association with the specified key selects the anchor element correlated with that key.

cite   The value of this attribute should be a URL of the document in which the information cited can be found.

class   See "Core Attributes Reference," earlier in this appendix.

contenteditable   This proprietary Microsoft attribute allows users to edit content rendered in the Internet Explorer 5.5 browser. Values are **false**, **true**, and **inherit**. A value of **false** will prevent content from being edited by users; **true** will allow editing. The default value, **inherit**, applies the value of the affected element's parent element.

dir   See "Language Reference," earlier in this appendix.

hidefocus   This proprietary element, introduced with Internet Explorer 5.5, hides focus on an element's content. Focus must be applied to the element using the **tabindex** attribute.

id   See "Core Attributes Reference," earlier in this appendix.

lang   See "Language Reference," earlier in this appendix.

language   This attribute specifies the language the current script is written in and invokes the proper scripting engine. The default value is **javascript**. **Javascript** and **jscript** represent that the scripting language is written in JavaScript. **Vbs** and **vbscript** represent that the scripting language is written in VBScript.

style   See "Core Attributes Reference," earlier in this appendix.

tabindex   This attribute uses a number to identify the object's position in the tabbing order for keyboard navigation using the TAB key. Internet Explorer 5.5 applies this attribute to the **blockquote** element; under IE 5.5, this focus can be disabled with the **hidefocus** attribute.

title   See "Core Attributes Reference," earlier in this appendix.

Attribute and Event Support

Netscape 4   class, id, lang, and style

Internet Explorer 4   All attributes and events except **cite** and **dir**.

Internet Explorer 5.5   Same as IE 4, plus **contenteditable**, **dir**, **hidefocus**, and **tabindex**.

Event Handlers

See "Events Reference," earlier in this appendix.

Example

```
The following paragraph is taken from our March report:
<blockquote cite="marchreport.htm"> ... text ...
</blockquote>
```

Compatibility

HTML 2, 3.2, 4, 4.01, and XHTML 1.0
Internet Explorer 2, 3, 4, 5, and 5.5
Netscape 1, 2, 3, 4–4.7, and 6
Opera 4
WebTV

Notes

- HTML 2.0 and 3.2 do not support any attributes for this element.
- WebTV only indents the left margin of text enclosed in the **<blockquote>** element.
- Some browsers understand the **<bq>** shorthand notation.

`<body>` (Document Body)

This element encloses a document's displayable content, in contrast to the descriptive and informational content contained in the **<head>** element.

Syntax

```
<body
    alink="color name | #RRGGBB" (transitional)
    background="url of background image" (transitional)
    bgcolor="color name | #RRGGBB" (transitional)
    class="class name(s)"
    dir="ltr | rtl"
    id="unique alphanumeric identifier"
    lang="language code"
```

```
        link="color name | #RRGGBB" (transitional)
        style="style information"
        text="color name | #RRGGBB" (transitional)
        title="advisory text"
        vlink="color name | #RRGGBB" (transitional)
        onclick="script"
        ondblclick="script"
        onkeydown="script"
        onkeypress="script"
        onkeyup="script"
        onload="script"
        onmousedown="script"
        onmousemove="script"
        onmouseout="script"
        onmouseover="script"
        onmouseup="script"
        onunload="script">

</body>
```

XHTML Syntax Notes

Under XHTML 1.0, the closing **</body>** tag no longer can be considered optional.

Attributes and Events Defined by Internet Explorer 4

```
        bgproperties="fixed"
        bottommargin="pixels"
        language="javascript | jscript | vbs | vbscript"
        leftmargin="pixels"
        rightmargin="pixels"
        scroll="no | yes"
        topmargin="pixels"
        onafterupdate="script"
        onbeforeunload="script"
        onbeforeupdate="script"
        ondragstart="script"
        onhelp="script"
        onrowenter="script"
        onrowexit="script"
        onscroll="script"
        onselect="script"
        onselectstart="script"
```

Attributes and Events Defined by Internet Explorer 5.5

```
accesskey="key"
contenteditable="false | true | inherit"
hidefocus="true | false"
tabindex="number"
```

Events Defined by Netscape 4

```
onblur="script"
onfocus="script"
marginheight="pixels"
marginwidth="pixels"
```

Attributes Defined by WebTV

```
credits="url"
instructions="url"
logo="url"
```

Attributes

accesskey   This attribute specifies a keyboard navigation accelerator for the element. Pressing ALT or a similar key (depending on the browser and operating system) in association with the specified key selects the anchor element correlated with that key.

alink   This attribute sets the color for active links within the document. Active links represent the state of a link as it is being pressed. The value of the attribute can be either a browser-dependent named color or a color specified in the hexadecimal #*RRGGBB* format.

background   This attribute contains a URL for an image file, which will be tiled to provide the document background.

bgcolor   This attribute sets the background color for the document. Its value can be either a browser-dependent named color or a color specified using the hexadecimal #*RRGGBB* format.

bgproperties   This attribute, first introduced in Internet Explorer 2, has one value, **fixed**, which causes the background image to act as a fixed watermark and not to scroll.

bottommargin   This attribute specifies the bottom margin for the entire body of the page and overrides the default margin. When set to **0**, the bottom margin is the bottom edge of the window or frame the content is displayed in.

class   See "Core Attributes Reference," earlier in this appendix.

contenteditable   This proprietary Microsoft attribute allows users to edit content rendered in the Internet Explorer 5.5 browser. Values are **false**, **true**, and **inherit**. A value of **false** will prevent content from being edited by users; **true** will allow editing. The default value, **inherit**, applies the value of the affected element's parent element.

credits   In the WebTV implementation, this attribute contains the URL of the document to retrieve when the viewer presses the credits button on the Info Panel.

dir   See "Language Reference," earlier in this appendix.

hidefocus   This proprietary element, introduced with Internet Explorer 5.5, hides focus on an element's content. Focus must be applied to the element using the **tabindex** attribute.

id   See "Core Attributes Reference," earlier in this appendix.

instructions   In the WebTV implementation, this attribute contains the URL of the document to retrieve when the viewer presses the instructions button on the Info Panel.

lang   See "Language Reference," earlier in this appendix.

language   This attribute specifies the language the current script is written in and invokes the proper scripting engine. The default value is **javascript**. **Javascript** and **jscript** represent that the scripting language is written in JavaScript. **Vbs** and **vbscript** represent that the scripting language is written in VBScript.

leftmargin   This Internet Explorer–specific attribute sets the left margin for the page in pixels, overriding the default margin. When set to **0**, the left margin is the left edge of the window or the frame.

link   This attribute sets the color for hyperlinks within the document that have not yet been visited. Its value can be either a browser-dependent named color or a color specified using the hexadecimal #*RRGGBB* format.

logo   In the WebTV implementation, this attribute contains the URL of a 70 × 52–pixel thumbnail image for the page, which is used in the history and bookmarks for WebTV.

marginheight   This Netscape–specific attribute sets the top margin for the document in pixels. If set to **0** or **""**, the top margin will be exactly on the top edge of the window or frame. It is equivalent to combining the Internet Explorer attributes **bottommargin** and **topmargin**.

marginwidth   This Netscape-specific attribute sets the left and right margins for the page in pixels, overriding the default margin. When set to **0** or **""**, the left margin is the left edge of the window or the frame. It is equivalent to combining the Internet Explorer attributes **leftmargin** and **rightmargin**.

rightmargin   This attribute, specific to Internet Explorer, sets the right margin for the page in pixels, overriding the default margin. When set to **0**, the right margin is the right edge of the window or the frame.

scroll   This attribute turns the scrollbars on

style   See "Core Attributes Reference," earl

tabindex   This attribute uses a number to i
keyboard navigation using the TAB key. Inter
element; the entire document will be selected
this focus can be disabled with the **hidefocus**

text   This attribute sets the text color for the
browser-dependent named color or a color sp

title   See "Core Attributes Reference," earlie

topmargin   This Internet Explorer–specific
pixels. If set to **0**, the top margin will be exactl

Attribute and Event Support

Netscape 4   alink, background, bgcolor, link, text, vlink, onblur, onfocus, onload, and onunload. (class, id, lang, and style are implied.)

Internet Explorer 4   All W3C-defined attributes and events except **dir**, all attributes and events defined by Internet Explorer 4, and **onblur** and **onfocus**.

Internet Explorer 5.5   Same as IE 4, plus **contenteditable**, **dir**, **hidefocus**, and **tabindex**.

WebTV   background, bgcolor, credits, instructions, link, logo, text, vlink, onload, and onunload.

Event Handlers
See "Events Reference," earlier in this appendix.

Example

```
<body background="checkered.gif"
      bgcolor="white"
      alink="red"
      link="blue"
      vlink="red"
      text="black"> ... </body>

<!-- myLoadFunction defined in document head in <SCRIPT> element -->
<body onload="myLoadFunction()"> ... </body>
```

Compatibility
HTML 2, 3.2, 4, 4.01, and XHTML 1.0
Internet Explorer 2, 3, 4, 5, and 5.5

732

<bq> (Block Quote)

Netscape 1, 2, 3, 4–4.7, and 6
Opera 4
WebTV

Notes

Whe
ba

defining text colors, it is important to be careful to specify both foreground and background explicitly so that they are not masked out by browser defaults set by the user.

Under the HTML 4.01 strict definition, no color-setting attributes and background attributes are allowed. This includes the **alink**, **background**, **bgcolor**, **link**, **text**, and **vlink** attributes

■ This element must be present in all documents except those declaring a frame set.

■ Under XHTML 1.0, the closing **</body>** tag is mandatory

<bq> (Block Quote)

This obsolete element signifies that the enclosed text is an extended quotation. Although it has been defined in early HTML specifications, currently it is supported only by the WebTV browser as an alias for the **<blockquote>** element.

Syntax (Obsolete)

```
<bq>
</bq>
```

Attributes
None

Event Handlers
None

Example

<bq>The HTML Programmer's Reference says "Don't use this element."**</bq>**

Compatibility
WebTV

Note

■ This element originated in the early days of HTML and is considered obsolete. It should not be used.

 (Line Break)

This empty element forces a line break.

Syntax

```
<br
    class="class name(s)"
    clear="all | left | none | right" (transitional)
    id="unique alphanumeric identifier"
    style="style information"
    title="advisory text">
```

XHTML 1.0 Syntax

Because this is an empty element, a closing forward slash is required before the closing bracket on the tag:

```
<br />
```

Attributes Defined by Internet Explorer 4

```
    language="javascript | jscript | vbs | vbscript"
```

Attributes

class   See "Core Attributes Reference," earlier in this appendix.

clear   This attribute forces the insertion of vertical space so that the tagged text can be positioned with respect to images. A value of **left** clears text that flows around left-aligned images to the next full left margin, a value of **right** clears text that flows around right-aligned images to the next full right margin, and a value of **all** clears text until it can reach both full margins. The default value according to the HTML 4 transitional specification is **none**, but its meaning generally is supported as just introducing a return and nothing more.

id   See "Core Attributes Reference," earlier in this appendix.

language   This attribute specifies the language the current script is written in and invokes the proper scripting engine. The default value is **javascript**. **Javascript** and **jscript** represent that the scripting language is written in JavaScript. **vbs** and **vbscript** represent that the scripting language is written in VBScript.

style   See "Core Attributes Reference," earlier in this appendix.

title   See "Core Attributes Reference," earlier in this appendix.

APPENDIX A

Attribute and Event Support

Netscape 4   clear. (**class**, **id**, and **style** are implied by Netscape documentation.)

Internet Explorer 4   All attributes

WebTV   clear

Event Handlers
None

Examples

This text will be broken here **
**and continued on a new line.

<img src="test.gif" align="right">
This is the image caption.**<br clear="right">**

XHTML Examples

This text will be broken here **
**and continued on a new line.

<img src="test.gif" align="right" />
This is the image caption.**<br clear="right" />**

Compatibility
HTML 2, 3.2, 4, 4.01, and XHTML 1.0
Internet Explorer 2, 3, 4, 5, and 5.5
Netscape 1, 2, 3, 4–4.7, and 6
Opera 4
WebTV

Notes

■ This is an empty element. A closing tag is illegal under all HTML specifications. For
   XHTML compatibility, a closing slash is required: **
**.

■ Under the HTML 4.01 strict specification, the **clear** attribute is not valid. Style sheet rules
   provide the functionality of the **clear** attribute.

<button> (Form Button)

This element defines a nameable region known as a button, which can be used together with
scripts.

Syntax

```
<button
    accesskey="key"
    class="class name(s)"
    dir="ltr | rtl"
    disabled
    id="unique alphanumeric identifier"
    lang="language code"
    name="button name"
    style="style information"
    tabindex="number"
    title="advisory text"
    type="button | reset | submit"
    value="button value"
    onblur="script"
    onclick="script"
    ondblclick="script"
    onfocus="script"
    onkeydown="script"
    onkeypress="script"
    onkeyup="script"
    onmousedown="script"
    onmousemove="script"
    onmouseout="script"
    onmouseover="script"
    onmouseup="script">

</button>
```

Attributes and Events Defined by Internet Explorer 4

```
    datafld="name of column supplying bound data"
    dataformatas="html | text"
    datasrc="id of data source object supplying data"
    language="javascript | jscript | vbs | vbscript"
    onafterupdate="script"
    onbeforeupdate="script"
    ondragstart="script"
    onhelp="script"
    onresize="script"
    onrowenter="script"
    onrowexit="script"
    onselectstart="script"
```

Attributes and Events Defined by Internet Explorer 5.5

```
contenteditable="false | true | inherit"
hidefocus="true | false"
```

Attributes

accesskey   This attribute specifies a keyboard navigation accelerator for the element. Pressing ALT or a similar key in association with the specified key selects the anchor element correlated with that key.

class   See "Core Attributes Reference," earlier in this appendix.

contenteditable   This proprietary Microsoft attribute allows users to edit content rendered in the Internet Explorer 5.5 browser. Values are **false**, **true**, and **inherit**. A value of **false** will prevent content from being edited by users; **true** will allow editing. The default value, **inherit**, applies the value of the affected element's parent element.

datafld   This attribute specifies the column name from the data source object that supplies the bound data that defines the information for the **<button>** element's content.

dataformatas   This attribute indicates whether the bound data is plain text or HTML.

datasrc   This attribute indicates **id** of the data source object that supplies the data that is bound to the **<button>** element.

dir   See "Language Reference," earlier in this appendix.

disabled   This attribute is used to disable the button.

hidefocus   This proprietary element, introduced with Internet Explorer 5.5, hides focus on an element's content. Focus must be applied to the element using the **tabindex** attribute.

id   See "Core Attributes Reference," earlier in this appendix.

lang   See "Language Reference," earlier in this appendix.

language   This attribute specifies the language that the current script associated with the event handlers is written in and invokes the proper scripting engine. The default value is **javascript**. **Javascript** and **jscript** represent that the scripting language is written in JavaScript. **Vbs** and **vbscript** represent that the scripting language is written in VBScript.

name   This attribute is used to define a name for the button so that it can be scripted by older browsers or used to provide a name for submit buttons when there is more than one in a page.

style   See "Core Attributes Reference," earlier in this appendix.

tabindex   This attribute uses a number to identify the object's position in the tabbing order.

title   See "Core Attributes Reference," earlier in this appendix.

type   Defines the type of button. According to the HTML 4.01 specification, by default the button is undefined. Possible values include **button, reset**, and **submit,** which are used to indicate the button is a plain button, reset button, or submit button respectively.

value   Defines the value that is sent to the server when the button is pressed. This might be useful when using multiple **submit** buttons that perform different actions to indicate which button was pressed to the handling CGI program.

Attribute and Event Support

Internet Explorer 4   All attributes and events except **dir, name, tabindex**, and **value**.

Internet Explorer 5.5   All attributes and events, plus **contenteditable, hidefocus**, and **tabindex**.

Event Handlers
See "Events Reference," earlier in this appendix.

Examples

```
<button name="Submit"
        value="Submit"
        type="Submit">Submit Request</button>

<button type="button"
        onclick="doSomething()">Click This Button</button>

<button type="button">
<img src="polkadot.gif" alt="Polkadot"></button>
```

Compatibility
HTML 4
Internet Explorer 4, 5, 4.5
Netscape 6

Notes

- It is illegal to associate an image map with an **<img>** that appears as the contents of a **button** element.

- The HTML 4.01 specification reserves the data-binding attributes **datafld, dataformatas**, and **datasrc** for future use.

<caption> (Figure or Table Caption)

This element is used within both the figure and table elements to define a caption.

Syntax

```
<caption
     align="bottom | left | right | top" (transitional)
     class="class name(s)"
     dir="ltr | rtl"
     id="unique alphanumeric identifier"
     lang="language code"
     style="style information"
     title="advisory text"
     onclick="script"
     ondblclick="script"
     onkeydown="script"
     onkeypress="script"
     onkeyup="script"
     onmousedown="script"
     onmousemove="script"
     onmouseout="script"
     onmouseover="script"
     onmouseup="script">

</caption>
```

Attributes and Events Defined by Internet Explorer 4

```
     language="javascript | jscript | vbs | vbscript"
     valign="bottom | top"
     onafterupdate="script"
     onbeforeupdate="script"
     onblur="script"
     onchange="script"
     ondragstart="script"
     onfocus="script"
     onhelp="script"
     onresize="script"
     onrowenter="script"
     onrowexit="script"
     onselect="script"
     onselectstart="script"
```

Attributes and Events Defined by Internet Explorer 5.5

```
accesskey="key"
contenteditable="false | true | inherit"
hidefocus="true | false"
tabindex="number"
```

Attributes

accesskey   This attribute specifies a keyboard navigation accelerator for the element. Pressing ALT or a similar key (depending on the browser and operating system) in association with the specified key selects the anchor element correlated with that key.

align   This attribute specifies the alignment of the caption. HTML 4 defines **bottom**, **left**, **right**, and **top** as legal values. Internet Explorer and WebTV also support **center**. Because this does not provide the possibility to combine vertical and horizontal alignments, Microsoft has introduced the **valign** attribute for the **<caption>** element.

class   See "Core Attributes Reference," earlier in this appendix.

contenteditable   This proprietary Microsoft attribute allows users to edit content rendered in the Internet Explorer 5.5 browser. Values are **false**, **true**, and **inherit**. A value of **false** will prevent content from being edited by users; **true** will allow editing. The default value, **inherit**, applies the value of the affected element's parent element.

dir   See "Language Reference," earlier in this appendix.

hidefocus   This proprietary element, introduced with Internet Explorer 5.5, hides focus on an element's content. Focus must be applied to the element using the **tabindex** attribute.

id   See "Core Attributes Reference," earlier in this appendix.

lang   See "Language Reference," earlier in this appendix.

language   This attribute specifies the language the current script is written in and invokes the proper scripting engine. The default value is **javascript**. **Javascript** and **jscript** represent that the scripting language is written in JavaScript. **Vbs** and **vbscript** represent that the scripting language is written in VBScript.

style   See "Core Attributes Reference," earlier in this appendix.

tabindex   This attribute uses a number to identify the object's position in the tabbing order for keyboard navigation using the TAB key. Internet Explorer 5.5 applies this attribute to the **caption** element; under IE 5.5, this focus can be disabled with the **hidefocus** attribute.

title   See "Core Attributes Reference," earlier in this appendix.

APPENDIX A

valign   This Internet Explorer–specific attribute specifies whether the table caption appears at the top or bottom.

Attribute and Event Support

Netscape 4   align (**class**, **id**, **lang**, and **style** are implied.)

Internet Explorer 4   All attributes and events except **dir**.

Internet Explorer 5.5   Same as IE 4, plus **contenteditable**, **dir**, **hidefocus**, and **tabindex**.

WebTV   align (center | left | right)

Event Handlers
See "Events Reference," earlier in this appendix.

Example

```
<table>
<caption align="top">Our High-Priced Menu</caption>
    <tr>
        <td>Escargot</td>
        <td>Filet Mignon</td>
        <td>Big Mac</td>
    </tr>
</table>
```

Compatibility
HTML 2, 3.2, 4, 4.01, and XHTML 1.0
Internet Explorer 2, 3, 4, 5, and 5.5
Netscape 1, 2, 3, 4–4.7, and 6
Opera 4
WebTV

Notes

- There should be only one caption per table.
- HTML 3.2 defines only the **align** attribute with values of **bottom** and **top**. No other attributes are defined prior to HTML 4. WebTV adds a **center** value to the **align** attribute.

<center> (Center Alignment)

This element causes the enclosed content to be centered within the margins currently in effect. Margins are either the default page margins or those imposed by overriding elements such as tables.

Syntax (Transitional Only)

```
<center
    class="class name(s)"
    dir="ltr | rtl"
    id="unique alphanumeric identifier"
    lang="language code"
    style="style information"
    title="advisory text"
    onclick="script"
    ondblclick="script"
    onkeydown="script"
    onkeypress="script"
    onkeyup="script"
    onmousedown="script"
    onmousemove="script"
    onmouseout="script"
    onmouseover="script"
    onmouseup="script">

</center>
```

Attributes and Events Defined by Internet Explorer 4

```
    language="javascript | jscript | vbs | vbscript"
    ondragstart="script"
    onhelp="script"
    onselectstart="script"
```

Attributes and Events Defined by Internet Explorer 5.5

```
    accesskey="key"
    contenteditable="false | true | inherit"
    hidefocus="true | false"
    tabindex="number"
```

Attributes

accesskey   This attribute specifies a keyboard navigation accelerator for the element. Pressing ALT or a similar key (depending on the browser and operating system) in association with the specified key selects the anchor element correlated with that key.

class   See "Core Attributes Reference," earlier in this appendix.

contenteditable   This proprietary Microsoft attribute allows users to edit content rendered in the Internet Explorer 5.5 browser. Values are **false**, **true**, and **inherit**. A value of **false** will prevent content from being edited by users; **true** will allow editing. The default value, **inherit**, applies the value of the affected element's parent element.

dir   See "Language Reference," earlier in this appendix.

hidefocus   This proprietary element, introduced with Internet Explorer 5.5, hides focus on an element's content. Focus must be applied to the element using the **tabindex** attribute.

id   See "Core Attributes Reference," earlier in this appendix.

lang   See "Language Reference," earlier in this appendix.

language   This attribute specifies the language the current script is written in and invokes the proper scripting engine. The default value is **javascript**. **Javascript** and **jscript** represent that the scripting language is written in JavaScript. **Vbs** and **vbscript** represent that the scripting language is written in VBScript.

style   See "Core Attributes Reference," earlier in this appendix.

tabindex   This attribute uses a number to identify the object's position in the tabbing order for keyboard navigation using the TAB key. Internet Explorer 5.5 applies this attribute to the **center** element; under IE 5.5, this focus can be disabled with the **hidefocus** attribute.

title   See "Core Attributes Reference," earlier in this appendix.

Attribute and Event Support

Netscape 4   **class**, **id**, **lang**, and **style** are implied.

Internet Explorer 4   All attributes and events except **dir**.

Internet Explorer 5.5   All attributes and events (including **dir**) plus **contenteditable**, **hidefocus**, and **tabindex**.

Event Handlers
See "Events Reference," earlier in this appendix.

Example

```
<center>This is in the center of the page.</center>
```

Compatibility
HTML 3.2 and 4 (transitional)
HTML 2, 3.2, 4, 4.01, and XHTML 1.0
Internet Explorer 2, 3, 4, 5, and 5.5

Netscape 1, 2, 3, 4 –4.7, and 6
Opera 4
WebTV

Notes

■ The **<center>** element defined by the W3C is a shorthand notation for **<div align="center">**. The strict version of HTML 4.01 does not include the **<center>** element.

■ HTML 3.2 does not support any attributes for this element.

<cite> (Citation)

This element indicates a citation from a book or other published source and usually is rendered in italics by a browser.

Syntax

```
<cite
    class="class name(s)"
    dir="ltr | rtl"
    id="unique alphanumeric identifier"
    lang="language code"
    style="style information"
    title="advisory text"
    onclick="script"
    ondblclick="script"
    onkeydown="script"
    onkeypress="script"
    onkeyup="script"
    onmousedown="script"
    onmousemove="script"
    onmouseout="script"
    onmouseover="script"
    onmouseup="script">

</cite>
```

Attributes and Events Defined by Internet Explorer 4

```
    language="javascript | jscript | vbs | vbscript"
    ondragstart="script"
    onhelp="script"
    onselectstart="script"
```

Attributes and Events Defined by Internet Explorer 5.5

```
accesskey="key"
contenteditable="false | true | inherit"
hidefocus="true | false"
tabindex="number"
```

Attributes

accesskey   This attribute specifies a keyboard navigation accelerator for the element. Pressing ALT or a similar key (depending on the browser and operating system) in association with the specified key selects the anchor element correlated with that key.

class   See "Core Attributes Reference," earlier in this appendix.

contenteditable   This proprietary Microsoft attribute allows users to edit content rendered in the Internet Explorer 5.5 browser. Values are **false**, **true**, and **inherit**. A value of **false** will prevent content from being edited by users; **true** will allow editing. The default value, **inherit**, applies the value of the affected element's parent element.

dir   See "Language Reference," earlier in this appendix.

hidefocus   This proprietary element, introduced with Internet Explorer 5.5, hides focus on an element's content. Focus must be applied to the element using the **tabindex** attribute.

id   See "Core Attributes Reference," earlier in this appendix.

lang   See "Language Reference," earlier in this appendix.

language   This attribute specifies the language the current script is written in and invokes the proper scripting engine. The default value is **javascript**. **Javascript** and **jscript** represent that the scripting language is written in JavaScript. **Vbs** and **vbscript** represent that the scripting language is written in VBScript.

style   See "Core Attributes Reference," earlier in this appendix.

tabindex   This attribute uses a number to identify the object's position in the tabbing order for keyboard navigation using the TAB key. Internet Explorer 5.5 applies this attribute to the **cite** element; under IE 5.5, this focus can be disabled with the **hidefocus** attribute.

title   See "Core Attributes Reference," earlier in this appendix.

Attribute and Event Support

Netscape 4   class, id, lang, and style are implied.

Internet Explorer 4   All events and attributes except **dir**.

Internet Explorer 5.5   All events and attributes (including **dir**), plus **contenteditable**, **hidefocus**, and **tabindex**.

Event Handlers

See "Events Reference," earlier in this appendix.

Example

```
This example is taken from <cite>The HTML Programmer's Reference.</cite>
```

Compatibility

HTML 2, 3.2, 4, 4.01, and XHTML 1.0
Internet Explorer 2, 3, 4, 5, and 5.5
Netscape 1, 2, 3, 4–4.7, and 6
Opera 4
WebTV

Note

■ HTML 2 and 3.2 do not indicate any attributes for this element.

<code> (Code Listing)

This element indicates that the enclosed text is source code in a programming language. Usually it is rendered in a monospaced font.

Syntax

```
<code
    class="class name(s)"
    dir="ltr | rtl"
    id="unique alphanumeric identifier"
    lang="language code"
    style="style information"
    title="advisory text"
    onclick="script"
    ondblclick="script"
    onkeydown="script"
    onkeypress="script"
    onkeyup="script"
    onmousedown="script"
    onmousemove="script"
    onmouseout="script"
    onmouseover="script"
    onmouseup="script">
```

```
</code>
```

Attributes and Events Defined by Internet Explorer 4

```
language="javascript | jscript | vbs | vbscript"
ondragstart="script"
onhelp="script"
onselectstart="script"
```

Attributes Defined by Internet Explorer 5.5

```
contenteditable="false | true | inherit"
```

Attributes

class   See "Core Attributes Reference," earlier in this appendix.

contenteditable   This proprietary Microsoft attribute allows users to edit content rendered in the Internet Explorer 5.5 browser. Values are **false**, **true**, and **inherit**. A value of **false** will prevent content from being edited by users; **true** will allow editing. The default value, **inherit**, applies the value of the affected element's parent element.

dir   See "Language Reference," earlier in this appendix.

id   See "Core Attributes Reference," earlier in this appendix.

lang   See "Language Reference," earlier in this appendix.

language   This attribute specifies the language the current script is written in and invokes the proper scripting engine. The default value is **javascript**. **Javascript** and **jscript** represent that the scripting language is written in JavaScript. **Vbs** and **vbscript** represent that the scripting language is written in VBScript.

style   See "Core Attributes Reference," earlier in this appendix.

title   See "Core Attributes Reference," earlier in this appendix.

Attribute and Event Support

Netscape 4   **class**, **id**, **lang**, and **style** are implied.

Internet Explorer 4   All attributes and events except **dir**.

Internet Explorer 5.5   All attributes and events, plus **contenteditable** and **dir**.

Event Handlers

See "Events Reference," earlier in this appendix.

Example

```
To increment a variable called count, use
    <code> count++ </code>
```

Compatibility

HTML 2, 3.2, 4, 4.01, and XHTML 1.0
Internet Explorer 2, 3, 4, 5, and 5.5
Netscape 1, 2, 3, 4 –4.7, and 6
Opera 4
WebTV

Notes

■ This element is best for short code fragments because it does not preserve special indentation.

■ HTML 2.0 and 3.2 do not support any attributes for this element.

`<col>` (Column)

This element defines a column within a table and is used for grouping and alignment purposes. It generally is found within a **`<colgroup>`** element.

Syntax

```
<col
    align="center | char | justify | left | right"
    char="character"
    charoff="number"
    class="class name(s)"
    dir="ltr | rtl"
    id="unique alphanumeric identifier"
    lang="language code"
    span="number"
    style="style information"
    title="advisory text"
    valign="baseline | bottom | middle | top"
    width="column width specification"
    onclick="script"
    ondblclick="script"
    onkeydown="script"
    onkeypress="script"
```

```
onkeyup="script"
onmousedown="script"
onmousemove="script"
onmouseout="script"
onmouseover="script"
onmouseup="script">
```

XHTML Syntax

Because this is an empty element, a closing forward slash is required before the closing bracket on the tag:

```
<col />
```

Syntax Defined by Internet Explorer 5.5

```
bgcolor="color name | #RRGGBB"
```

Attributes

align   This attribute specifies horizontal alignment of a cell's contents.

bgcolor   Applies a background color to all cells in the column (IE 5.5 only).

char   This attribute is used to set the character to align the cells in a column on. Typical values for this include a period (.) when attempting to align numbers or monetary values.

charoff   This attribute is used to indicate the number of characters to offset the column data from the alignment characters specified by the **char** value.

class   See "Core Attributes Reference," earlier in this appendix.

dir   See "Language Reference," earlier in this appendix.

id   See "Core Attributes Reference," earlier in this appendix.

lang   See "Language Reference," earlier in this appendix.

span   When present, this attribute applies the attributes of the <col> element to additional consecutive columns.

style   See "Core Attributes Reference," earlier in this appendix.

title   See "Core Attributes Reference," earlier in this appendix.

valign   This attribute specifies the vertical alignment of the text within the cell. Possible values for this attribute are **baseline**, **bottom**, **middle**, and **top**.

width   This attribute specifies a default width for each column in the current column group. In addition to the standard pixel and percentage values, this attribute might take the special form 0*, which means that the width of each column in the group should be the minimum width necessary to hold the column's contents. Relative widths such as 0.5* also can be used.

Attribute and Event Support

Internet Explorer 4   align (center | left | right), class, id, span, style, title, valign, and width

Internet Explorer 5.5   Adds bgcolor, dir, and lang.

Event Handlers

See "Events Reference," earlier in this appendix.

Example

```
<table border="1" width="400">
<colgroup>
<col align="center" width="150"><col align="right">
</colgroup>

  <td>This column is aligned to the center.</td>
  <td>This one is aligned to the right.</td>
</tr>

<tr><td>!</td><td>?</td></tr>

<tr><td>!</td><td>?</td></tr>
</table>
```

XHTML Example

```
<table border="1" width="400">
<colgroup>
<col align="center" width="150"/><col align="right"/>
</colgroup>

  <td>This column is aligned to the center.</td>
  <td>This one is aligned to the right.</td>
</tr>

<tr><td>!</td><td>?</td></tr>

<tr><td>!</td><td>?</td></tr>
</table>
```

Compatibility

HTML 4, 4.01, XHTML 1.0
Internet Explorer 4, 5, 5.5

Notes

- As an empty element, **<col>** does not require a closing tag.
- Under XHTML 1.0, **<col>** requires a trailing slash: **<col />**
- This element generally appears within a **<colgroup>** element; like that element, it is somewhat of a convenience feature used to set attributes with one or more table columns.

<colgroup> (Column Group)

This element creates an explicit column group to access a group of table columns for scripting or formatting.

Syntax

```
<colgroup
     align="center | char | justify | left | right"
     char="character"
     charoff="number"
     class="class name(s)"
     dir="ltr | rtl"
     id="unique alphanumeric identifier"
     lang="language code"
     span="number"
     style="style information"
     title="advisory text"
     valign="baseline | bottom | middle | top"
     width="column width specification"
     onclick="script"
     ondblclick="script"
     onkeydown="script"
     onkeypress="script"
     onkeyup="script"
     onmousedown="script"
     onmousemove="script"
     onmouseout="script"
     onmouseover="script"
     onmouseup="script">

     <col> elements

</colgroup>
```

XHTML 1.0 Syntax

Under XHTML 1.0, the closing tag **</colgroup>** no longer can be considered optional.

Attributes

align   This attribute specifies horizontal alignment of contents of the cells in the column group. The values of **center**, **left**, and **right** have obvious meanings. A value of **justify** for the attribute should attempt to justify all the column's contents. A value of **char** attempts to align the contents based on the value of the **char** attribute in conjunction with **charoff**.

char   This attribute is used to set the character to align the cells in a column on. Typical values for this include a period (.) when attempting to align numbers or monetary values.

charoff   This attribute is used to indicate the number of characters to offset the column data from the alignment characters specified by the **char** value.

class   See "Core Attributes Reference," earlier in this appendix.

dir   See "Language Reference," earlier in this appendix.

id   See "Core Attributes Reference," earlier in this appendix.

lang   See "Language Reference," earlier in this appendix.

span   When present, this attribute specifies the default number of columns in this group. Browsers should ignore this attribute if the current column group contains one or more **<col>** elements. The default value of this attribute is **1**.

style   See "Core Attributes Reference," earlier in this appendix.

title   See "Core Attributes Reference," earlier in this appendix.

valign   This attribute specifies the vertical alignment of the contents of the cells within the column group.

width   This attribute specifies a default width for each column and its cells in the current column group. In addition to the standard pixel and percentage values, this attribute might take the special form **0***, which means that the width of each column in the group should be the minimum width necessary to hold the column's contents.

Attribute and Event Support

Internet Explorer 4   align (center | left | right), **class, id, span, style, title, valign**, and **width**

Internet Explorer 5.5   align (center | justify | left | right), **class, dir, id, lang, span, style**, and **valign**

APPENDIX A

Event Handlers

See "Events Reference," earlier in this appendix.

Examples

```
<colgroup span="10" align="char" char=":" valign="center">

<colgroup style="background: green">
<col align="left">
<col align="center">
</colgroup>
```

Compatibility

HTML 4, 4.01, XHTML 1.0
Internet Explorer 4, 5, 5.5

Notes

- Each column group defined by a **<colgroup>** can contain zero or more **<col>** elements.
- Under XHTML 1.0, the closing **</colgroup>** tag is mandatory.

<comment> (Comment Information)

This nonstandard element treats enclosed text as nondisplaying comments while processing enclosed HTML. This element should not be used.

Syntax (Defined by Internet Explorer 4)

```
<comment
    id="unique alphanumeric identifier"
    lang="language code"
    title="advisory text">

    Commented information

</comment>
```

Attributes

id   See "Core Attributes Reference," earlier in this appendix.

lang   See "Language Reference," earlier in this appendix.

title   See "Core Attributes Reference," earlier in this appendix.

Attribute and Event Support

Internet Explorer 4   All attributes

Event Handlers
None

Example

```
<comment>This is not the proper way to form
comments.</comment>
```

Compatibility
Internet Explorer 4, 5, and 5.5
WebTV

Notes

- It is better to use the <!--. . .--> element, an alternate comment element that does not process enclosed HTML in all specification-conforming browsers.

- Because the **<comment>** element is not supported by all browsers, commented text done in this fashion will appear in Netscape browsers. Although Internet Explorer still supports this element, IE documentation recommends use of the <!--. . .--> element.

- Although some notes indicate that the **<comment>** element will render HTML included within it, in practice this does not seem to be the case.

<dd> (Definition in a Definition List)

This element indicates the definition of a term within a list of defined terms (**<dt>**) enclosed by a definition list (**<dl>**).

Syntax

```
<dd
    class="class name(s)"
    dir="ltr | rtl"
    id="unique alphanumeric identifier"
    lang="language code"
    style="style information"
    title="advisory text"
    onclick="script"
    ondblclick="script"
    onkeydown="script"
    onkeypress="script"
```

```
        onkeyup="script"
        onmousedown="script"
        onmousemove="script"
        onmouseout="script"
        onmouseover="script"
        onmouseup="script">

</dd>
```

XHTML Syntax

Under XHTML 1.0, the closing tag **</dd>** can no longer be considered optional.

Attributes and Events Defined by Internet Explorer 4

```
    language="javascript | jscript | vbs | vbscript"
    ondragstart="script"
    onhelp="script"
    onselectstart="script"
```

Attributes and Events Defined by Internet Explorer 5.5

```
    accesskey="key"
    contenteditable="false | true | inherit"
    hidefocus="true | false"
    tabindex="number"
```

Attributes

accesskey   This attribute specifies a keyboard navigation accelerator for the element. Pressing ALT or a similar key (depending on the browser and operating system) in association with the specified key selects the anchor element correlated with that key.

class   See "Core Attributes Reference," earlier in this appendix.

contenteditable   This proprietary Microsoft attribute allows users to edit content rendered in the Internet Explorer 5.5 browser. Values are **false**, **true**, and **inherit**. A value of **false** will prevent content from being edited by users; **true** will allow editing. The default value, **inherit**, applies the value of the affected element's parent element.

dir   See "Language Reference," earlier in this appendix.

id   See "Core Attributes Reference," earlier in this appendix.

hidefocus   This proprietary element, introduced with Internet Explorer 5.5, hides focus on an element's content. Focus must be applied to the element using the **tabindex** attribute.

lang   See "Language Reference," earlier in this appendix.

language   This attribute specifies the language the current script is written in and invokes the proper scripting engine. The default value is **javascript**. **Javascript** and **jscript** represent that the scripting language is written in JavaScript. **Vbs** and **vbscript** represent that the scripting language is written in VBScript.

style   See "Core Attributes Reference," earlier in this appendix.

tabindex   This attribute uses a number to identify the object's position in the tabbing order for keyboard navigation using the TAB key. Internet Explorer 5.5 applies this attribute to the **dd** element; under IE 5.5, this focus can be disabled with the **hidefocus** attribute.

title   See "Core Attributes Reference," earlier in this appendix.

Attribute and Event Support

Netscape 4   class, id, lang, and **style**.

Internet Explorer 4   All attributes and events except **dir**.

Internet Explorer 5.5   All attributes and events, plus **contenteditable**, **dir**, **hidefocus**, and tabindex.

Event Handlers
See "Events Reference," earlier in this appendix.

Example

```
<dl>
    <dt>DOG</dt>
        <dd>A domesticated animal that craves attention all the time</dd>
<dt>CAT</dt>
        <dd>An animal that would just as soon ignore you until it
            gets hungry</dd>
</dl>
```

Compatibility
HTML 2, 3.2, 4, 4.01, and XHTML 1.0
Internet Explorer 2, 3, 4, 5, and 5.5
Netscape 1, 2, 3, 4–4.7, and 6
Opera 4
WebTV

Notes

- Under HTML specifications, the closing tag for this element is optional, though encouraged when it will help make the list more understandable.
- Under XHTML 1.0, the closing **</dd>** tag is mandatory
- This element occurs within a list of defined terms enclosed by the **<dl>** element. Typically associated with it is the term it defines, indicated by the **<dl>** element that precedes it.
- HTML 2 and 3.2 define no attributes for this element.

<del> (Deleted Text)

This element is used to indicate that text has been deleted from a document. A browser might render deleted text as strikethrough text.

Syntax

```
<del
     cite="url"
     class="class name(s)"
     datetime="date"
     dir="ltr | rtl"
     id="unique alphanumeric identifier"
     lang="language code"
     style="style information"
     title="advisory text"
     onclick="script"
     ondblclick="script"
     onkeydown="script"
     onkeypress="script"
     onkeyup="script"
     onmousedown="script"
     onmousemove="script"
     onmouseout="script"
     onmouseover="script"
     onmouseup="script"
     onselectstart="script">

</del>
```

Attributes and Events Defined by Internet Explorer 4

```
     language="javascript | jscript | vbs | vbscript"
     ondragstart="script"
     onhelp="script"
```

Attributes Defined by Internet Explorer 5.5

```
accesskey="key"
contenteditable="false | true | inherit"
tabindex="number"
```

Attributes

accesskey Applied to this element under Internet Explorer 5.5 only. This attribute specifies a keyboard navigation accelerator for the element. Pressing ALT or a similar key (depending on the browser and operating system) in association with the specified key selects the anchor element correlated with that key.

cite The value of this attribute is a URL that designates a source document or message that might give a reason that the information was deleted.

class See "Core Attributes Reference," earlier in this appendix.

contenteditable This proprietary Microsoft attribute allows users to edit content rendered in the Internet Explorer 5.5 browser. Values are **false**, **true**, and **inherit**. A value of **false** will prevent content from being edited by users; **true** will allow editing. The default value, **inherit**, applies the value of the affected element's parent element.

datetime This attribute is used to indicate the date and time the deletion was made. The value of the attribute is a date in a special format as defined by ISO 8601. The basic date format is

```
YYYY-MM-DDThh:mm:ssTZD
```

where the following is true:

```
YYYY=four-digit year such as 1999
  MM=two-digit month (01=January, 02=February, and so on.)
  DD=two-digit day of the month (01 through 31)
  hh=two digit hour (00 to 23) (24-hour clock, not AM or PM)
  mm=two digit minute (00 through 59)
  ss=two digit second (00 through 59)
  TZD=time zone designator
```

The time zone designator is either **Z**, which indicates UTC (Universal Time Coordinate, or coordinated universal time format), or **+hh:mm**, which indicates that the time is a local time that is *hh* hours and *mm* minutes ahead of UTC. Alternatively, the format for the time zone designator could be **-hh:mm**, which indicates that the local time is behind UTC. Note that the letter "T" actually appears in the string, all digits must be used, and **00** values for minutes and seconds might be required. An example value for the **datetime** attribute might be **1999-10-6T09:15:00-05:00**, which corresponds to October 6, 1999, 9:15 A.M., U.S. Eastern Standard Time.

dir   See "Language Reference," earlier in this appendix.

id   See "Core Attributes Reference," earlier in this appendix.

lang   See "Language Reference," earlier in this appendix.

language   In the Microsoft implementation, this attribute specifies the scripting language to be used with an associated script bound to the element, typically through an event handler attribute. Possible values might include **javascript**, **jscript**, **vbs**, and **vbscript**. Other values, which include the version of the language used, such as **JavaScript1.1**, also might be possible.

style   See "Core Attributes Reference," earlier in this appendix.

tabindex   This attribute uses a number to identify the object's position in the tabbing order for keyboard navigation using the TAB key. Internet Explorer 5.5 applies this attribute to the **del** element.

title   See "Core Attributes Reference," earlier in this appendix.

Attribute and Event Support

Internet Explorer 4   All attributes and events except **cite**, **datetime**, and **dir**.

Internet Explorer 5.5   Same as IE 4, plus **contenteditable**, **dir**, and **tabindex**.

Event Handlers
See "Events Reference," earlier in this appendix.

Example

```
<del cite="http://www.bigcompany.com/changes/oct97.htm"
    datetime="1998-10-06T09:15:00-05:00">
The penalty clause applies to client lateness as well.
</del>
```

Compatibility
HTML 4, 4.01, XHTML 1.0
Internet Explorer 4, 5, and 5.5
Netscape 6

Notes

■ Browsers can render deleted (**<del>**) text in a different style to show the changes that have been made to the document. Internet Explorer 4 renders the text as strikethrough text. Eventually, a browser could have a way to show a revision history on a document. User agents that do not understand **<del>** or **<ins>** will show the information anyway, so there is no harm in adding information—only in deleting it. Because of the fact that

<del>-enclosed text might show up, it might be wise to comment it out within the element as shown here:

```
<del>
<!-- This is old information. -->
</del>
```

■ The **<del>** element is not supported under the HTML 2.0 and 3.2 specifications.

<dfn> (Defining Instance of a Term)

This element encloses the defining instance of a term. It usually is rendered as bold or bold italic text.

Syntax

```
<dfn
     class="class name(s)"
     dir="ltr | rtl"
     id="unique alphanumeric identifier"
     lang="language code"
     style="style information"
     title="advisory text"
     onclick="script"
     ondblclick="script"
     onkeydown="script"
     onkeypress="script"
     onkeyup="script"
     onmousedown="script"
     onmousemove="script"
     onmouseout="script"
     onmouseover="script"
     onmouseup="script">

</dfn>
```

Attributes and Events Defined by Internet Explorer 4

```
     language="javascript | jscript | vbs | vbscript"
     ondragstart="script"
     onhelp="script"
     onselectstart="script"
```

Attributes and Events Defined by Internet Explorer 5.5

```
accesskey="key"
contenteditable="false | true | inherit"
hidefocus="true | false"
tabindex="number"
```

Attributes

accesskey   This attribute specifies a keyboard navigation accelerator for the element. Pressing ALT or a similar key (depending on the browser and operating system) in association with the specified key selects the anchor element correlated with that key.

class   See "Core Attributes Reference," earlier in this appendix.

contenteditable   This proprietary Microsoft attribute allows users to edit content rendered in the Internet Explorer 5.5 browser. Values are **false**, **true**, and **inherit**. A value of **false** will prevent content from being edited by users; **true** will allow editing. The default value, **inherit**, applies the value of the affected element's parent element.

dir   See "Language Reference," earlier in this appendix.

hidefocus   This proprietary element, introduced with Internet Explorer 5.5, hides focus on

an element's content. Focus must be applied to the element using the **tabindex** attribute.

id   See "Core Attributes Reference," earlier in this appendix.

lang   See "Language Reference," earlier in this appendix.

language   This attribute specifies the language the current script is written in and invokes the proper scripting engine. The default value is **javascript**. **Javascript** and **jscript** represent that the scripting language is written in JavaScript. **Vbs** and **vbscript** represent that the scripting language is written in VBScript.

style   See "Core Attributes Reference," earlier in this appendix.

tabindex   This attribute uses a number to identify the object's position in the tabbing order for keyboard navigation using the TAB key. Internet Explorer 5.5 applies this attribute to the **dfn** element; under IE 5.5, this focus can be disabled with the **hidefocus** attribute.

title   See "Core Attributes Reference," earlier in this appendix.

Attribute and Event Support

Internet Explorer 4   All attributes and events except **dir**.

Internet Explorer 5.5   All attributes and events, plus **accesskey**, **contenteditable**, **hidefocus**, and **tabindex**.

Event Handlers
See "Events Reference," earlier in this appendix.

Example

An **<dfn>**elephant**</dfn>** is too large to make a viable pet for anyone poorer than Bill Gates.

Compatibility
HTML 2, 3.2, 4, and 4.01
Internet Explorer 2, 3, 4, 5, 5.5
Netscape 6
Opera 4
WebTV

Note

- HTML 2 and 3.2 defined no attributes for this element.

<dir> (Directory List)

This element encloses a list of brief, unordered items, such as might occur in a menu or directory. The individual items are indicated by the **<ul>** element. Use of this element is not encouraged, as it is not part of the HTML 4.01 strict specification and provides little extra benefit over the **<ul>** element.

Syntax (Transitional Only)

```
<dir
     class="class name(s)"
     compact
     dir="ltr | rtl"
     id="unique alphanumeric identifier"
     lang="language code"
     style="style information"
     title="advisory text"
     onclick="script"
     ondblclick="script"
     onkeydown="script"
     onkeypress="script"
     onkeyup="script"
     onmousedown="script"
     onmousemove="script"
```

```
            onmouseout="script"
            onmouseover="script"
            onmouseup="script">

    </dir>
```

XHTML Syntax

Due to XHTML 1.0's deprecation of attribute minimization, the **compact** attribute must have a quoted attribute when used:

```
    <dir compact="compact"></dir>
```

Attributes and Events Defined by Internet Explorer 4

```
            language="javascript | jscript | vbs | vbscript"
            ondragstart="script"
            onhelp="script"
            onselectstart="script"
```

Attributes and Events Defined by Internet Explorer 5.5

```
            accesskey="key"
            contenteditable="false | true | inherit"
            hidefocus="true | false"
            tabindex="number"
```

Attributes

accesskey   This attribute specifies a keyboard navigation accelerator for the element. Pressing ALT or a similar key (depending on the browser and operating system) in association with the specified key selects the anchor element correlated with that key.

class   See "Core Attributes Reference," earlier in this appendix.

compact   This attribute reduces the white space between list items.

contenteditable   This proprietary Microsoft attribute allows users to edit content rendered in the Internet Explorer 5.5 browser. Values are **false**, **true**, and **inherit**. A value of **false** will prevent content from being edited by users; **true** will allow editing. The default value, **inherit**, applies the value of the affected element's parent element.

dir   See "Language Reference," earlier in this appendix.

hidefocus This proprietary element, introduced with Internet Explorer 5.5, hides focus on an element's content. Focus must be applied to the element using the **tabindex** attribute.

id See "Core Attributes Reference," earlier in this appendix.

lang See "Language Reference," earlier in this appendix.

language This attribute specifies the language the current script is written in and invokes the proper scripting engine. The default value is **javascript**. **Javascript** and **jscript** represent that the scripting language is written in JavaScript. **Vbs** and **vbscript** represent that the scripting language is written in VBScript.

style See "Core Attributes Reference," earlier in this appendix.

tabindex This attribute uses a number to identify the object's position in the tabbing order for keyboard navigation using the TAB key. Internet Explorer 5.5 applies this attribute to the **dir** element; under IE 5.5, this focus can be disabled with the **hidefocus** attribute.

title See "Core Attributes Reference," earlier in this appendix.

Attribute and Event Support

Netscape 4 **class**, **id**, **lang**, and **style** are explicit.

Internet Explorer 4 All WC3 events and attributes except **compact** and **dir**, all IE 4-defined attributes and events.

Internet Explorer 5.5 All WC3 events and attributes except **compact**, all IE 4- and IE 5.5-defined attributes and events.

WebTV No attributes. (Note: WebTV bolds text enclosed in the **<dir>** element.)

Event Handlers
See "Events Reference," earlier in this appendix.

Example

```
<dir>
  <li>Header Files
  <li>Code Files
  <li>Comment Files
</dir>
```

Compatibility
HTML 2, 3.2, 4 (transitional), and 4.01 (transitional), XHTML 1.0
Internet Explorer 2, 3, 4, 5, and 5.5
Netscape 1, 2, 3, 4–4.7, 6
Opera 4
WebTV

Notes

- Because the **<dir>** element is supposed to be used with short lists, the items in the list should have a maximum width of 20 characters.
- The HTML 4.01 strict specification does not support this element.
- Many browsers will not render the **<dir>** element any differently from the **<ul>** element.
- Many browsers will not render the **compact** list style.
- HTML 2 and 3.2 support only the **compact** attribute.
- For XHTML compatibility, the **compact** attribute must be expanded: **<dir compact="compact">**.

<div> (Division)

This element indicates a block of document content, which should be treated as a logical unit.

Syntax

```
<div
    align="center | justify | left | right"
            (transitional)
    class="class name(s)"
    datafld="name of column supplying bound data"
            (reserved)
    dataformatas="html | text" (reserved)
    datasrc="id of data source object supplying data"
            (reserved)
    dir="ltr | rtl"
    id="unique alphanumeric identifier"
    lang="language code"
    style="style information"
    title="advisory text"
    onclick="script"
    ondblclick="script"
    onkeydown="script"
    onkeypress="script"
    onkeyup="script"
    onmousedown="script"
    onmousemove="script"
    onmouseout="script"
    onmouseover="script"
    onmouseup="script">

</div>
```

Attributes and Events Defined by Internet Explorer 4

```
language="javascript | jscript | vbs | vbscript"
onafterupdate="script"
onbeforeupdate="script"
onblur="script"
ondragstart="script"
onfocus="script"
onhelp="script"
onresize="script"
onrowenter="script"
onrowexit="script"
onscroll="script"
onselectstart="script"
```

Attributes and Events Defined by Internet Explorer 5.5

```
accesskey="key"
contenteditable="false | true | inherit"
hidefocus="true | false"
tabindex="number"
```

Attributes

accesskey   This attribute specifies a keyboard navigation accelerator for the element. Pressing ALT or a similar key (depending on the browser and operating system) in association with the specified key selects the anchor element correlated with that key.

align   This attribute indicates how the tagged text should be horizontally aligned on the page. The default value is **left**. The **justify** value is supported only by the Microsoft implementation.

charset   This attribute defines the character encoding of the linked resource specified by the **HREF** attribute. The value is a space- and/or comma-delimited list of character sets as defined in RFC 2045. The default value is **ISO-8859-1**.

class   See "Core Attributes Reference," earlier in this appendix.

contenteditable   This proprietary Microsoft attribute allows users to edit content rendered in the Internet Explorer 5.5 browser. Values are **false**, **true**, and **inherit**. A value of **false** will prevent content from being edited by users; **true** will allow editing. The default value, **inherit**, applies the value of the affected element's parent element.

datafld   This attribute specifies the column name from the data source object that supplies the bound data.

dataformatas   This attribute indicates if the bound data is plain text or HTML.

APPENDIX A

datasrc   This attribute indicates the **id** of the data source object that supplies the data that is bound to this element.

dir   See "Language Reference," earlier in this appendix.

hidefocus   This proprietary element, introduced with Internet Explorer 5.5, hides focus on an element's content. Focus must be applied to the element using the **tabindex** attribute.

id   See "Core Attributes Reference," earlier in this appendix.

lang   See "Language Reference," earlier in this appendix.

language   This attribute specifies the language the current script is written in and invokes the proper scripting engine. The default value is **javascript**. **Javascript** and **jscript** represent that the scripting language is written in JavaScript. **Vbs** and **vbscript** represent that the scripting language is written in VBScript.

style   See "Core Attributes Reference," earlier in this appendix.

tabindex   This attribute uses a number to identify the object's position in the tabbing order for keyboard navigation using the TAB key. Internet Explorer 5.5 applies this attribute to the **div** element; under IE 5.5, this focus can be disabled with the **hidefocus** attribute.

title   See "Core Attributes Reference," earlier in this appendix.

Attribute and Event Support

Netscape 4   **align, class, id, lang,** and **style**

Internet Explorer 4   All attributes and events except **dir**.

Internet Explorer 5.5   All events and attributes, plus **accesskey, contenteditable, hidefocus,** and **tabindex**.

WebTV   **align (center | left | right)**

Event Handlers
See "Events Reference," earlier in this appendix.

Examples

```
<div align="justify">
All text within this division should be justified in most recent browsers.
</div>

<div class="special" id="div1" style="background: yellow">
Get ready to animate and stylize this.
</div>
```

Compatibility

HTML 3.2, 4, 4.01, XHTML 1.0
Internet Explorer 2, 3, 4, 5, and 5.5
Netscape 2, 3, 4–4.7, and 6
Opera 4
WebTV

Notes

■ Many users are confused by the proper use of the **<div>** element, because all it does is create a block element. It is very useful for binding scripts or styles to an arbitrary section of a document. In this sense, **<div>** complements **<span>**, which is used inline.

■ The HTML 4.01 specification specifies that the **datafld**, **dataformatas**, and **datasrc** attributes are reserved for **<div>** and might be supported in the future. Internet Explorer 4 already supports these reserved attributes.

■ Under the HTML 4.01 strict specification, the **align** attribute is not supported.

■ HTML 3.2 supports only the **align** attribute.

<dl> (Definition List)

This element encloses a list of terms and definition pairs. A common use for this element is to implement a glossary.

Syntax

```
<dl
    class="class name(s)"
    compact
    dir="ltr | rtl"
    id="unique alphanumeric identifier"
    lang="language code"
    style="style information"
    title="advisory text"
    onclick="script"
    ondblclick="script"
    onkeydown="script"
    onkeypress="script"
    onkeyup="script"
    onmousedown="script"
    onmousemove="script"
    onmouseout="script"
    onmouseover="script"
    onmouseup="script">

</dl>
```

XHTML Syntax

Because of XHTML 1.0's deprecation of attribute minimization, the **compact** attribute must have a quoted attribute when used:

```
<dl compact="compact"></dl>
```

Attributes and Events Defined by Internet Explorer 4

```
language="javascript | jscript | vbs | vbscript"
ondragstart="script"
onhelp="script"
onselectstart="script"
```

Attributes and Events Defined by Internet Explorer 5.5

```
accesskey="key"
contenteditable="false | true | inherit"
hidefocus="true | false"
tabindex="number"
```

Attributes

accesskey   This attribute specifies a keyboard navigation accelerator for the element. Pressing ALT or a similar key (depending on the browser and operating system) in association with the specified key selects the anchor element correlated with that key.

class   See "Core Attributes Reference," earlier in this appendix.

compact   This attribute reduces the white space between list items.

contenteditable   This proprietary Microsoft attribute allows users to edit content rendered in the Internet Explorer 5.5 browser. Values are **false**, **true**, and **inherit**. A value of **false** will prevent content from being edited by users; **true** will allow editing. The default value, **inherit**, applies the value of the affected element's parent element.

dir   See "Language Reference," earlier in this appendix.

hidefocus   This proprietary element, introduced with Internet Explorer 5.5, hides focus on an element's content. Focus must be applied to the element using the **tabindex** attribute.

id   See "Core Attributes Reference," earlier in this appendix.

lang   See "Language Reference," earlier in this appendix.

language   This attribute specifies the language the current script is written in and invokes the proper scripting engine. The default value is **javascript**. **Javascript** and **jscript** represent that the scripting language is written in JavaScript. **Vbs** and **vbscript** represent that the scripting language is written in VBScript.

style   See "Core Attributes Reference," earlier in this appendix.

tabindex   This attribute uses a number to identify the object's position in the tabbing order for keyboard navigation using the TAB key. Internet Explorer 5.5 applies this attribute to the **dl** element; under IE 5.5, this focus can be disabled with the **hidefocus** attribute.

title   See "Core Attributes Reference," earlier in this appendix.

Attribute and Event Support

Netscape 4   class, compact, id, lang, and style.

Internet Explorer 4   All attributes and events except **dir**.

Internet Explorer 5.5   All events and attributes, plus **accesskey**, **contenteditable**, **hidefocus**, and **tabindex**.

Event Handlers
See "Events Reference," earlier in this appendix.

Example

```
<dl>
 <dt>Cat
   <dd>A domestic animal that likes fish
 <dt>Skunk
   <dd>A wild animal that needs deodorant
</dl>
```

Compatibility
HTML 2, 3.2, 4, 4.01, XHTML 1.0
Internet Explorer 2, 3, 4, 5, and 5.5
Netscape 1, 2, 3, 4–4.7, 6
Opera 4
WebTV

Notes

■ The items in the list comprise two parts: the term, indicated by the **<dt>** element, and its definition, indicated by the **<dd>** element.

■ Some page designers might use the **<dl>** element or **<ul>** element to help create text indention. Although this is a common practice on the Web, it is not advisable because it confuses the meaning of the element by making it a physical layout device rather than a list.

■ Under the HTML 4.01 strict definition, the **compact** attribute is not allowed.

■ HTML 2 and 3.2 support only the **compact** attribute for this element.

■ For XHTML compatibility, the **compact** attribute must be expanded: **<dl compact="compact"></dl>**.

<dt> (Term in a Definition List)

This element identifies a definition list term in a definition list term-definition pair.

Syntax

```
<dt
      class="class name(s)"
      dir="ltr | rtl"
      id="unique alphanumeric identifier"
      lang="language code"
      style="style information"
      title="advisory text"
      onclick="script"
      ondblclick="script"
      onkeydown="script"
      onkeypress="script"
      onkeyup="script"
      onmousedown="script"
      onmousemove="script"
      onmouseout="script"
      onmouseover="script"
      onmouseup="script">
```

XHTML Syntax

Under XHTML 1.0, the **<dt>** element now requires a closing tag:

```
<dt></dt>
```

Attributes and Events Defined by Internet Explorer 4

```
language="javascript | jscript | vbs | vbscript"
ondragstart="script"
onhelp="script"
onselectstart="script"
```

Attributes and Events Defined by Internet Explorer 5.5

```
accesskey="key"
contenteditable="false | true | inherit"
hidefocus="true | false"
nowrap="true | false"
tabindex="number"
```

Attributes

accesskey   This attribute specifies a keyboard navigation accelerator for the element. Pressing ALT or a similar key (depending on the browser and operating system) in association with the specified key selects the anchor element correlated with that key.

class   See "Core Attributes Reference," earlier in this appendix.

contenteditable   This proprietary Microsoft attribute allows users to edit content rendered in the Internet Explorer 5.5 browser. Values are **false**, **true**, and **inherit**. A value of **false** will prevent content from being edited by users; **true** will allow editing. The default value, **inherit**, applies the value of the affected element's parent element.

dir   See "Language Reference," earlier in this appendix.

hidefocus   This proprietary element, introduced with Internet Explorer 5.5, hides focus on an element's content. Focus must be applied to the element using the **tabindex** attribute.

id   See "Core Attributes Reference," earlier in this appendix.

lang   See "Language Reference," earlier in this appendix.

language   This attribute specifies the language the current script is written in and invokes the proper scripting engine. The default value is **javascript**. **Javascript** and **jscript** represent that the scripting language is written in JavaScript. **Vbs** and **vbscript** represent that the scripting language is written in VBScript.

nowrap   This attribute specifies whether the browser performs wordwrap. A value of **true** means that it will not wrap; a value of **false** means that it can wrap.

style   See "Core Attributes Reference," earlier in this appendix.

tabindex   This attribute uses a number to identify the object's position in the tabbing order for keyboard navigation using the TAB key. Internet Explorer 5.5 applies this attribute to the **dt** element; under IE 5.5, this focus can be disabled with the **hidefocus** attribute.

title   See "Core Attributes Reference," earlier in this appendix.

Attribute and Event Support

Netscape 4   class, id, lang, and **style**.

Internet Explorer 4   All attributes and events except **dir**.

Internet Explorer 5.5   All events and attributes, plus **accesskey**, **contenteditable**, **hidefocus**, **nowrap**, and **tabindex**.

Event Handlers
See "Events Reference," earlier in this appendix.

Example

```
<dl>
   <dt>Rake
     <dd>A garden tool used to gather leaves and rubbish
   <dt>Trowel
     <dd>A small garden tool used to shovel earth
</dl>
```

Compatibility
HTML 2, 3.2, 4, 4.01, XHTML 1.0
Internet Explorer 2, 3, 4, 5, and 6
Netscape 1, 2, 3, 4–4.7, 6
Opera 4
WebTV

Notes

- This element occurs within a list of defined terms enclosed by the **<dl>** element. It generally is used in conjunction with the **<dd>** element, which indicates its definition. However, **<dt>** elements do not require a one-to-one correspondence with **<dd>** elements.

- The close tag for the element is optional but suggested when it will make things more clear, particularly with multiple-line definitions.

- Under XHTML 1.0, the closing **</dt>** tag is mandatory

- HTML 2 and 3.2 support no attributes for this element.

<em> (Emphasis)

This element indicates emphasized text, which many browsers will display as italic text.

Syntax

```
<em
    class="class name(s)"
    dir="ltr | rtl"
    id="unique alphanumeric identifier"
    lang="language code"
    style="style information"
    title="advisory text"
    onclick="script"
    ondblclick="script"
    onkeydown="script"
    onkeypress="script"
    onkeyup="script"
    onmousedown="script"
    onmousemove="script"
    onmouseout="script"
    onmouseover="script"
    onmouseup="script">

</em>
```

Attributes and Events Defined by Internet Explorer 4

```
    language="javascript | jscript | vbs | vbscript"
    ondragstart="script"
    onhelp="script"
    onselectstart="script"
```

Attributes and Events Defined by Internet Explorer 5.5

```
accesskey="key"
contenteditable="false | true | inherit"
hidefocus="true | false"
tabindex="number"
```

Attributes

accesskey   This attribute specifies a keyboard navigation accelerator for the element. Pressing ALT or a similar key (depending on the browser and operating system) in association with the specified key selects the anchor element correlated with that key.

class   See "Core Attributes Reference," earlier in this appendix.

contenteditable   This proprietary Microsoft attribute allows users to edit content rendered in the Internet Explorer 5.5 browser. Values are **false**, **true**, and **inherit**. A value of **false** will prevent content from being edited by users; **true** will allow editing. The default value, **inherit**, applies the value of the affected element's parent element.

dir   See "Language Reference," earlier in this appendix.

hidefocus   This proprietary element, introduced with Internet Explorer 5.5, hides focus on an element's content. Focus must be applied to the element using the **tabindex** attribute.

id   See "Core Attributes Reference," earlier in this appendix.

lang   See "Language Reference," earlier in this appendix.

language   This attribute specifies the language the current script is written in and invokes the proper scripting engine. The default value is **javascript**. **Javascript** and **jscript** represent that the scripting language is written in JavaScript. **VBS** and **VBSCRIPT** represent that the scripting language is written in VBScript.

style   See "Core Attributes Reference," earlier in this appendix.

tabindex   This attribute uses a number to identify the object's position in the tabbing order for keyboard navigation using the TAB key. Internet Explorer 5.5 applies this attribute to the **em** element; under IE 5.5, this focus can be disabled with the **hidefocus** attribute.

title   See "Core Attributes Reference," earlier in this appendix.

Attribute and Event Support

Netscape 4   class, **id**, **lang**, and **style** are implied.

Internet Explorer 4   All attributes and events except **dir**.

Internet Explorer 5.5 All events and attributes, plus **accesskey**, **contenteditable**, **hidefocus**, and **tabindex**.

Event Handlers
See "Events Reference," earlier in this appendix.

Example

```
This is an <em>important point</em> to consider.
```

Compatibility
HTML 2, 3.2, 4, 4.01, XHTML 1.0
Internet Explorer 2, 3, 4, 5, and 5.5
Netscape 1, 2, 3, 4 –4.7, and 6
Opera 4
WebTV

Notes
■ As a logical element, **<em>** is a prime candidate to bind style information to. For example, to define emphasis to mean a larger font size in the Impact font, you might use a CSS rule like the following in a document-wide style sheet:

```
em {font-size: larger; font-family: Impact;}
```

■ HTML 2 and 3.2 support no attributes for this element.

<embed> (Embedded Object)
This widely supported but nonstandard element specifies an object, typically a multimedia element, to be embedded in an HTML document.

Syntax (Defined by Internet Explorer 4)

```
<embed
    align="absbottom | absmiddle | baseline | bottom |
           left | middle | right | texttop | top"
    alt="alternative text"
    class="class name(s)"
    code="filename"
    codebase="url"
    height="pixels"
    hspace="pixels"
    id="unique alphanumeric identifier"
    name="string"
    src="url"
```

APPENDIX A

```
        style="style information"
        title="advisory text"
        vspace="pixels"
        width="pixels">

</embed>
```

Attributes and Events Defined by Internet Explorer 5.5

```
        accesskey="key"
        language="javascript | jscript | vbs | vbscript | xml"
```

Attributes Defined by Netscape 4

```
        border="pixels"
        hidden="true | false"
        palette="background | foreground"
        pluginspage="url"
        type="mime type"
        units="en | pixels"
```

Attributes

accesskey   This attribute specifies a keyboard navigation accelerator for the element. Pressing ALT or a similar key (depending on the browser and operating system) in association with the specified key selects the anchor element correlated with that key.

align   This attribute controls the alignment of adjacent text with respect to the embedded object. The default value is **left**.

alt   This attribute indicates the text to be displayed if the applet cannot be executed.

border   This attribute specifies the size in pixels of the border around the embedded object.

class   See "Core Attributes Reference," earlier in this appendix.

code   This attribute specifies the name of the file containing the compiled Java class if the **<embed>** element is used to include a Java applet. This is a strange alternate form of Java inclusion documented by Microsoft.

codebase   This specifies the base URL for the plug-in or potential applet in the case of the alternative form under Internet Explorer.

height   This attribute sets the height in pixels of the embedded object.

hidden   If this attribute is set to the value **true**, the embedded object is not visible on the page and implicitly has a size of zero.

hspace   This attribute specifies in pixels the size of the left and right margins between the embedded object and surrounding text.

language   This attribute specifies the language the current script is written in and invokes the proper scripting engine. The default value is **javascript**. **javascript** and **jscript** represent that the scripting language is written in JavaScript. **vbs** and **vbscript** represent that the scripting language is written in VBScript. It also might be possible to use extended names, such as **JavaScript1.1**, to hide code from JavaScript-aware browsers that don't conform to a particular version of the language. Internet Explorer adds support for XML as well.

id   See "Core Attributes Reference," earlier in this appendix.

name   This attribute specifies a name for the embedded object, which can be referenced by client-side programs in an embedded scripting language.

palette   This attribute is used only on Windows systems to select the color palette used for the plug-in and might be set to **background** or **foreground**. The default is **background**.

pluginspage   This attribute contains the URL of instructions for installing the plug-in required to render the embedded object.

src   This attribute specifies the URL of source content for the embedded object.

style   See "Core Attributes Reference," earlier in this appendix.

title   See "Core Attributes Reference," earlier in this appendix.

type   This attribute specifies the MIME type of the embedded object. It is used by the browser to determine an appropriate plug-in for rendering the object. It can be used instead of the **src** attribute for plug-ins that have no content or that fetch it dynamically.

units   This Netscape-specific attribute is used to set the units for measurement for the embedded object either in **en** or in the default, **pixels**.

vspace   This attribute specifies in pixels the size of the top and bottom margins between the embedded object and surrounding text.

width   This attribute sets the width in pixels of the embedded object.

Attribute and Event Support

Netscape 4   align (bottom | left | right | top), **height**, **src**, **width**, and all Netscape-defined attributes. (**class**, **id**, **lang**, and **style** are implied.)

Internet Explorer 4   All Microsoft-defined attributes and events.

Internet Explorer 5.5   Same as IE 4, plus **accesskey** and **language**.

WebTV   align (bottom | left | right | top), **border**, **height**, **hidden**, **hspace**, **name**, **src**, **vspace**, and **width**.

Event Handlers
See "Events Reference," earlier in this appendix.

Examples

```
<!-- embed without a close tag -->
<embed src="testmovie.mov" height="150" width="150">
<noembed>
  <img src="testgif.gif" height="150" width="150" alt="Test Image">
</noembed>

<!-- embed with a close tag -->
<embed src="testmovie.mov" height="150" width="150">
<noembed>
  <img src="testgif.gif" height="150" width="150" alt="Test Image">
</noembed>
</embed>
```

Compatibility
Internet Explorer 3, 4, 5, and 5.5
Netscape 2, 3, 4–4.7
WebTV

Notes

- It is unclear whether or not the close tag for **<embed>** is required. Many sites tend not to use it, and documentation is not consistent. Some people claim that a close tag is required and should surround any alternative content in a **<noembed>** element; others do not use a close tag. Because eventually this element should be phased out in favor of **<object>**, this might be a moot issue.

- While WebTV might support the **<embed>** element, it can deal only with media types the equipment knows how to handle, such as Macromedia Flash or certain standard audio files. Other plug-ins cannot be added to the system.

- The **<embed>** element is not favored by the W3C and is not part of any official HTML specification; however, it is very common. The HTML specification says to use the **<object>** element, which can be used in conjunction with the **<embed>** element to provide backward compatibility.

- Embedded objects are multimedia content files of arbitrary type, which are rendered by browser plug-ins. The **type** attribute uses a file's MIME type to determine an appropriate browser plug-in. Any attributes not defined are treated as object-specific parameters and passed through to the embedded object. Consult the plug-in or object documentation to determine these. The standard parameters supported by the Microsoft implementation are **height**, **name**, **palette**, **src**, **units**, and **width**.

`<fieldset>` (Form Field Set)

This element allows form designers to group thematically related controls together.

Syntax

```
<fieldset
    class="class name(s)"
    dir="ltr | rtl"
    id="unique alphanumeric identifier"
    lang="language code"
    style="style information"
    title="advisory text"
    onclick="script"
    ondblclick="script"
    onkeydown="script"
    onkeypress="script"
    onkeyup="script"
    onmousedown="script"
    onmousemove="script"
    onmouseout="script"
    onmouseover="script"
    onmouseup="script">

</fieldset>
```

Attributes and Events Defined by Internet Explorer 4

```
    align="center | left | right"
    language="javascript | jscript | vbs | vbscript"
    onblur="script"
    onchange="script"
    ondragstart="script"
    onfilterchange="script"
    onfocus="script"
    onhelp="script"
    onresize="script"
    onscroll="script"
    onselect="script"
    onselectstart="script"
```

APPENDIX A

Attributes and Events Defined by Internet Explorer 5.5

```
accesskey="key"
contenteditable="false | true | inherit"
hidefocus="true | false"
tabindex="number"
```

Attributes

accesskey   This attribute specifies a keyboard navigation accelerator for the element. Pressing ALT or a similar key (depending on the browser and operating system) in association with the specified key selects the anchor element correlated with that key.

align   Internet Explorer defines the **align** attribute, which sets how the element and its contents are positioned in a table or the window.

class   See "Core Attributes Reference," earlier in this appendix.

contenteditable   This proprietary Microsoft attribute allows users to edit content rendered in the Internet Explorer 5.5 browser. Values are **false**, **true**, and **inherit**. A value of **false** will prevent content from being edited by users; **true** will allow editing. The default value, **inherit**, applies the value of the affected element's parent element.

dir   See "Language Reference," earlier in this appendix.

hidefocus   This proprietary element, introduced with Internet Explorer 5.5, hides focus on an element's content. Focus must be applied to the element using the **tabindex** attribute.

id   See "Core Attributes Reference," earlier in this appendix.

lang   See "Language Reference," earlier in this appendix.

language   This attribute specifies the language the current script is written in and invokes the proper scripting engine. The default value is **javascript**. **Javascript** and **jscript** represent that the scripting language is written in JavaScript. **Vbs** and **vbscript** represent that the scripting language is written in VBScript.

style   See "Core Attributes Reference," earlier in this appendix.

tabindex   This attribute uses a number to identify the object's position in the tabbing order for keyboard navigation using the TAB key. Internet Explorer 5.5 applies this attribute to the **fieldset** element; under IE 5.5, this focus can be disabled with the **hidefocus** attribute.

title   See "Core Attributes Reference," earlier in this appendix.

Attribute and Event Support

Internet Explorer 4   All attributes and events except **dir**.

Internet Explorer 5.5   All events and attributes, plus **accesskey**, **contenteditable**, **hidefocus**, and **tabindex**.

Event Handlers
See "Events Reference," earlier in this appendix.

Example

```
<fieldset>
<legend>Customer Identification</legend>
<br>
<label>Customer Name:
<input type="text" id="CustName" size="25">
</fieldset>
```

Compatibility
HTML 4, 4.01, XHTML 1.0
Internet Explorer 4, 5, and 5.5
Opera 4
Netscape 6

Notes

■ Grouping controls makes it easier for users to understand the purposes of the controls while simultaneously facilitating tabbing navigation for visual user agents and speech navigation for speech-oriented user agents. The proper use of this element makes documents more accessible to people with disabilities.

■ The caption for this element is defined by the **<legend>** element within the **<fieldset>** element.

<fn> (Footnote)
This WebTV-specific element indicates either a reference to a footnote or the footnote itself.

Syntax (Defined by WebTV)

```
<fn
    href="url"
    id="unique alphanumeric identifier">

</fn>
```

APPENDIX A

Attributes

href   This attribute contains a URL that references the footnote. Typically the URL is a fragment in the form of the pound sign (#) followed by the name of the footnote anchor. It indicates that the tagged text is a reference to a footnote.

id   This attribute contains the name of the footnote anchor. It indicates that the tagged text is a footnote.

Attribute and Event Support

WebTV   href and id

Event Handlers
None

Examples

```
This wonderful idea came from <fn href="#smith">Smith.</fn>

<fn id="smith">Smith, Fred, Journal of Really Good Ideas</fn>
```

Compatibility
WebTV

Notes

- Footnotes are implemented as internal links within a document. Use the **href** attribute to indicate a reference to a footnote. Use the **id** attribute to indicate the footnote itself.

- Footnotes are not to be used outside the WebTV environment. They are a leftover of the failed HTML 3 proposal.

<font> (Font Definition)

This element allows specification of the size, color, and font of the text it encloses. Use of this element is not encouraged, as it is not part of the HTML 4.01 strict specification. Style sheets provide a cleaner way of providing the same functionality when they are supported.

Syntax (Transitional Only)

```
<font
    class="class name(s)"
    color="color name | #RRGGBB"
    dir="ltr | rtl"
    face="font name"
```

```
            id="unique alphanumeric identifier"
            lang="language code"
            size="1 to 7 | +1 to +6 | -1 to -6"
            style="style information"
            title="advisory text">

</font>
```

Attributes and Events Defined by Internet Explorer 4

```
            language="javascript | jscript | vbs | vbscript"
            onclick="script"
            ondblclick="script"
            ondragstart="script"
            onhelp="script"
            onkeydown="script"
            onkeypress="script"
            onkeyup="script"
            onmousedown="script"
            onmousemove="script"
            onmouseout="script"
            onmouseover="script"
            onmouseup="script"
            onselectstart="script"
```

Attributes and Events Defined by Internet Explorer 5.5

```
            accesskey="key"
            contenteditable="false | true | inherit"
            hidefocus="true | false"
            tabindex="number"
```

Attributes Defined by Netscape 4

```
            point-size="point size for font"
            weight="100 | 200 | 300 | 400 | 500 | 600 | 700 |
                    800 | 900"
```

Attributes Defined by WebTV

```
            effect="emboss | relief | shadow"
```

Attributes

accesskey   This attribute specifies a keyboard navigation accelerator for the element. Pressing ALT or a similar key (depending on the browser and operating system) in association with the specified key selects the anchor element correlated with that key.

class   See "Core Attributes Reference," earlier in this appendix.

color   This attribute sets the text color using either a browser-dependent named color or a color specified in the hexadecimal *#RRGGBB* format.

contenteditable   This proprietary Microsoft attribute allows users to edit content rendered in the Internet Explorer 5.5 browser. Values are **false**, **true**, and **inherit**. A value of **false** will prevent content from being edited by users; **true** will allow editing. The default value, **inherit**, applies the value of the affected element's parent element.

dir   See "Language Reference," earlier in this appendix.

effect   In the WebTV implementation, this attribute renders the tagged text in a special way. The **relief** value causes the text to appear to be raised off the page. The **emboss** value causes the text to appear embossed into the page.

face   This attribute contains a list of one or more font names separated by commas. The user agent looks through the specified font names and renders the text in the first font that is supported.

hidefocus   This proprietary element, introduced with Internet Explorer 5.5, hides focus on an element's content. Focus must be applied to the element using the **tabindex** attribute.

id   See "Core Attributes Reference," earlier in this appendix.

lang   See "Language Reference," earlier in this appendix.

language   This attribute specifies the language the current script is written in and invokes the proper scripting engine. The default value is **javascript**. **Javascript** and **jscript** represent that the scripting language is written in JavaScript. **Vbs** and **vbscript** represent that the scripting language is written in VBScript.

point-size   This Netscape 4–specific attribute specifies the point size of text and is used with downloadable fonts.

size   This attribute specifies the font size as either a numeric or relative value. Numeric values range from **1** to **7** with **1** being the smallest and **3** the default. The relative values, + and –, increment or decrement the font size relative to the current size. The value for increment or decrement should range only from **+1** to **+ 6** or **–1** to **–6**.

style   See "Core Attributes Reference," earlier in this appendix.

tabindex This attribute uses a number to identify the object's position in the tabbing order for keyboard navigation using the TAB key. Internet Explorer 5.5 applies this attribute to the **font** element; under IE 5.5, this focus can be disabled with the **hidefocus** attribute.

title See "Core Attributes Reference," earlier in this appendix.

transparency WebTV's proprietary **transparency** attribute is used to set the transparency level of the text. A value of **0** indicates the text is opaque; a value of **100** indicates text is fully transparent, allowing the background to show through. The default value for this attribute is **0**.

weight Under Netscape 4, this attribute specifies the weight of the font, with a value of **100** being lightest and **900** being heaviest.

Attribute and Event Support

Netscape 4 **color**, **point-size**, **size**, and **weight**. (**class**, **id**, **lang**, and **style** are implied.)
(At the time of this writing, Netscape 6 did not appear to support **point-size**.)

Internet Explorer 4 All W3C-defined attributes and events except **dir**, and all attributes and events defined by Internet Explorer 4.

Internet Explorer 5.5 All events and attributes, plus **accesskey**, **contenteditable**, **hidefocus**, and **tabindex**.

WebTV **color**, **effect**, **size** and **transparency**

Event Handlers
See "Events Reference," earlier in this appendix.

Example

```
<font color="#FF0000" face="Helvetica, Times Roman" size="+1">
Relatively large red text in Helvetica or Times.
</font>
```

Compatibility
HTML 3.2, 4, 4.01, XHTML 1.0
Internet Explorer 2, 3, 4, 5, and 5.5
Netscape 1.1, 2, 3, 4–4.7, 6
Opera 4
WebTV

Notes

- The default text size for a document can be set using the **size** attribute of the **<basefont>** element.

APPENDIX A

- The HTML 3.2 specification supports only the **color** and **size** attributes for this element.
- The HTML 4.01 transitional specification supports the **class**, **color**, **dir**, **face**, **id**, **lang**, **size**, **style**, and **title** attributes.
- The HTML 4.01 strict specification does not support the **<font>** element at all.

<form> (Form for User Input)

The element defines a fill-in form to contain labels and form controls, such as menus and text entry boxes that might be filled in by a user.

Syntax

```
<form
     accept-charset="list of supported character sets"
     action="url"
     class="class name(s)"
     dir="ltr | rtl"
     enctype="application/x-www-form-urlencoded |
              multipart/form-data | text/plain |
              Media Type as per RFC 2045"
     id="unique alphanumeric identifier"
     lang="language code"
     method="get | post"
     style="style information"
     target="_blank | frame name | _parent | _self |
             _top" (transitional)
     title="advisory text"
     onclick="script"
     ondblclick="script"
     onkeydown="script"
     onkeypress="script"
     onkeyup="script"
     onmousedown="script"
     onmousemove="script"
     onmouseout="script"
     onmouseover="script"
     onmouseup="script"
     onreset="script"
     onsubmit="script">

</form>
```

Attributes and Events Defined by Internet Explorer 4

```
language="javascript | jscript | vbs | vbscript"
```

```
name="string"
ondragstart="script"
onhelp="script"
onselectstart="script"
```

Attributes and Events Defined by Internet Explorer 5.0

```
autocomplete="yes | no"
```

Attributes and Events Defined by Internet Explorer 5.5

```
contenteditable="false | true | inherit"
hidefocus="true | false"
tabindex="number"
```

Attributes

accept-charset   This attribute specifies the list of character encodings for input data that must be accepted by the server processing form. The value is a space- or comma-delimited list of character sets as defined in RFC 2045. The default value for this attribute is the reserved value **unknown**.

action   This attribute contains the URL of the server program, which will process the contents of the form. Some browsers also might support a mailto URL, which can mail the results to the specified address.

autocomplete   This Microsoft proprietary attribute, introduced in Internet Explorer 5.0, will automatically finish filling in information that the user has previously input into an input field, and which has been encrypted and stored by the browser.

class   See "Core Attributes Reference," earlier in this appendix.

contenteditable   This proprietary Microsoft attribute allows users to edit content rendered in the Internet Explorer 5.5 browser. Values are **false, true**, and **inherit**. A value of **false** will prevent content from being edited by users; **true** will allow editing. The default value, **inherit**, applies the value of the affected element's parent element.

dir   See "Language Reference," earlier in this appendix.

enctype   This attribute indicates how form data should be encoded before being sent to the server. The default is **application/x-www-form-urlencoded**. This encoding replaces blank characters in the data with a + and all other nonprinting characters with a % followed by the character's ASCII HEX representation. The multipart/form-data option does not perform character conversion and transfers the information as a compound MIME document. This must be used when using **<input-type="file">**. It also might be possible to use another encoding such as text/plain to avoid any form of hex encoding which might be useful with mailed forms.

hidefocus   This proprietary element, introduced with Internet Explorer 5.5, hides focus on an element's content. Focus must be applied to the element using the **tabindex** attribute.

id   See "Core Attributes Reference," earlier in this appendix.

lang   See "Language Reference," earlier in this appendix.

language   This attribute specifies the language the current script is written in and invokes the proper scripting engine. The default value is **javascript**. **Javascript** and **jscript** represent that the scripting language is written in JavaScript. **Vbs** and **vbscript** represent that the scripting language is written in VBScript.

method   This attribute indicates how form information should be transferred to the server. The **get** option appends data to the URL specified by the **action** attribute. This approach gives the best performance, but imposes a size limitation determined by the command line length supported by the server. The **post** option transfers data using a HTTP post transaction. This approach is more secure and imposes no data size limitation.

name   This attribute specifies a name for the form and can be used by client-side programs to reference form data.

style   See "Core Attributes Reference," earlier in this appendix.

tabindex   This attribute uses a number to identify the object's position in the tabbing order for keyboard navigation using the TAB key. Internet Explorer 5.5 applies this attribute to the **form** element; under IE 5.5, this focus can be disabled with the **hidefocus** attribute.

target   In documents containing frames, this attribute specifies the target frame to display the results of a form submission. In addition to named frames, several special values exist. The **_blank** value indicates a new window. The **_parent** value indicates the parent frame set containing the source link. The **_self** value indicates the frame containing the source link. The **_top** value indicates the full browser window.

title   See "Core Attributes Reference," earlier in this appendix.

Attribute and Event Support

Netscape 4   action, enctype, method, name, target, onreset, and onsubmit. (class, id, lang, and style are implied.)

Internet Explorer 4   All attributes and events except **accept-charset** and **dir**.

Internet Explorer 5.0   All events and attributes except **accept-charset**, plus **autocomplete**.

Internet Explorer 5.5   All events and attributes, plus **autocomplete**, **contenteditable**, **hidefocus**, and **tabindex**.

WebTV   action, method, target, onreset, and onsubmit

Event Handlers
See "Events Reference," earlier in this appendix.

Example

```
<form action="http://www.bigcompany.com/cgi-bin/processit.exe"
method="post" name="testform" onsubmit="validate()">
Enter your comments here:<br>
<textarea name="comments" cols="30" ROWS="8"></textarea>
<br>
<input type="submit">
<input type="reset">
</form>
```

Compatibility
HTML 2, 3.2, 4, 4.01, XHTML 1.0
Internet Explorer 2, 3, 4, 5, and 5.5
Netscape 1, 2, 3, 4–4.7, and 6
WebTV

Notes

■ Form content is defined using the **<button>**, **<input>**, **<select>**, and **<textarea>** elements as well as other HTML formatting and structuring elements. Special grouping elements such as **<fieldset>**, **<label>**, and **<legend>** have been introduced to provide better structuring for forms, but other HTML elements such as **<div>** and **<table>** also can be used to improve form layout.

■ HTML 2 and 3.2 support only the **action**, **enctype**, and **method** attributes for the **<form>** element.

<frame> (Window Region)

This element defines a nameable window region, known as a frame, that can independently display its own content.

Syntax (Transitional Only)

```
<frame
    class="class name(s)"
    frameborder="0 | 1"
    id="unique alphanumeric identifier"
    longdesc="url of description"
    marginheight="pixels"
```

```
marginwidth="pixels"
name="string"
noresize
scrolling="auto | no | yes"
src="url" of frame contents"
style="style information"
title="advisory text">
```

XHTML Syntax

As an empty element, the **<frame>** element must have a trailing slash to be compliant with the XHTML 1.0 specification:

```
<frame />
```

Attributes and Events Defined by Internet Explorer 4

```
bordercolor="color name | #RRGGBB"
datafld="name of column supplying bound data"
datasrc="id of data source object supplying data"
frameborder="no | yes | 0 | 1"
height="pixels"
lang="language code"
language="javascript | jscript | vbs | vbscript"
width="pixels"
onreadystatechange="script"
```

Attributes and Events Defined by Internet Explorer 5.5

```
hidefocus="true | false"
tabindex="number"
```

Attributes Defined by WebTV

```
align="bottom | center | left | right | top"
```

Attributes

bordercolor   This attribute sets the color of the frame's border using either a named color or a color specified in the hexadecimal *#RRGGBB* format.

class   See "Core Attributes Reference," earlier in this appendix.

datafld   This Internet Explorer attribute specifies the column name from the data source object that supplies the bound data.

datasrc   This Internet Explorer attribute indicates the **id** of the data source object that supplies the data that is bound to this element.

frameborder   This attribute determines whether the frame is surrounded by an outlined three-dimensional border. The HTML specification prefers the use of **1** for the frame border on and **0** for off; most browsers also acknowledge the use of **no** and **yes**.

hidefocus   This proprietary element, introduced with Internet Explorer 5.5, hides focus on an element's content. Focus must be applied to the element using the **tabindex** attribute.

id   See "Core Attributes Reference," earlier in this appendix.

lang   See "Language Reference," earlier in this appendix.

language   This attribute specifies the language the current script is written in and invokes the proper scripting engine. The default value is **javascript**. **Javascript** and **jscript** represent that the scripting language is written in JavaScript. **Vbs** and **vbscript** represent that the scripting language is written in VBScript.

longdesc   This attribute specifies a URL of a document that contains a long description of the frame's content. This attribute should be used in conjunction with the **<title>** element.

marginheight   This attribute sets the height in pixels between the frame's contents and its top and bottom borders.

marginwidth   This attribute sets the width in pixels between the frame's contents and its left and right borders.

name   This attribute assigns the frame a name so that it can be the target destination of hyperlinks as well as being a possible candidate for manipulation via a script.

noresize   This attribute overrides the default ability to resize frames and gives the frame a fixed size.

scrolling   This attribute determines if the frame has scroll bars. A **yes** value forces scroll bars, a **no** value prohibits them, and an **auto** value lets the browser decide. When not specified, the default value of **auto** is used. Authors are recommended to leave the value as **auto**. If you turn off scrolling and the contents end up being too large for the frame (due to rendering differences, window size, and so forth), the user will not be able to scroll to see the rest of the contents. If you turn scrolling on and the contents all fit in the frame, the scroll bars will needlessly consume screen space. With the **auto** value, scroll bars appear only when needed.

src   This attribute contains the URL of the contents to be displayed in the frame. If absent, nothing will be loaded in the frame.

style   See "Core Attributes Reference," earlier in this appendix.

APPENDIX A

tabindex   This attribute uses a number to identify the object's position in the tabbing order for keyboard navigation using the TAB key. Internet Explorer 5.5 applies this attribute to the **frame** element; under IE 5.5, this focus can be disabled with the **hidefocus** attribute.

title   See "Core Attributes Reference," earlier in this appendix.

Attribute and Event Support

Netscape 4   bordercolor, frameborder, **marginheight**, **marginwidth**, **name**, **noresize**, scrolling, and src. (**class**, **id**, **lang**, and **style** are implied.)

Internet Explorer 4   All W3C-defined attributes except **longdesc** and **style**, and all attributes and events defined by Internet Explorer 4. (Note: Internet Explorer 4 supports the values **noresize** and **resize**.)

Internet Explorer 5.5   All W3C-defined attributes except **longdesc** and **style**, and all attributes and events defined by Internet Explorer 4, plus **hidefocus**, and **tabindex**.

WebTV   align, frameborder (0 | 1), **marginheight**, **marginwidth**, **name**, and src

Event Handlers
See "Events Reference," earlier in this appendix.

Example

```
<frameset rows="20%,80%">
  <frame src="controls.htm" name="controls" noresize scrolling="no">
  <frame src="content.htm">
</frameset>
```

XHTML Example

```
<frameset rows="20%,80%">
  <frame src="controls.htm" name="controls" noresize scrolling="no" />
  <frame src="content.htm" />
</frameset>
```

Compatibility
HTML 4, 4.01, XHTML 1.0
Internet Explorer 2, 3, 4, 5, and 5.5
Netscape 2, 3, 4–4.7. 6
Opera 4
WebTV

Notes

■ A frame must be declared as part of a frame set as set by the **<frameset>** element, which specifies the frame's relationship to other frames on a page. A frame set occurs in a special HTML document in which the **<frameset>** element replaces the **<body>** element. Another form of frames called *independent frames*, or *floating frames*, also is supported by Microsoft as well as the HTML 4.01 transitional specification. Floating frames can be directly embedded in a document without belonging to a frameset. These are defined with the **<iframe>** element.

■ Many browsers do not support frames and require the use of the **<noframes>** element.

■ Frames introduce potential navigation difficulties; their use should be limited to instances in which they can be shown to help navigation rather than hinder it.

■ XHMTL 1.0 requires a trailing slash for this element: **<frame />**

<frameset> (Frameset Definition)

This element is used to define the organization of a set of independent window regions known as *frames* as defined by the **<frame>** element. This element replaces the **<body>** element in framing documents.

Syntax (Transitional Only)

```
<frameset
    class="class name(s)"
    cols="list of columns"
    id="unique alphanumeric identifier"
    rows="list of rows"
    style="style information"
    title="advisory text"
    onload="script"
    onunload="script">

    <frame> elements and <noframes>

</frameset>
```

Attributes and Events Defined by Internet Explorer 4

```
    border="pixels"
    bordercolor="color name | #RRGGBB"
    frameborder="NO | YES | 0 | 1"
    framespacing="pixels"
    lang="language code"
    language="javascript | jscript | vbs | vbscript"
```

Attributes and Events Defined by Netscape 4

```
border="pixels"
bordercolor="color name | #RRGGBB"
frameborder="no | yes | 0 | 1"
lang="language code"
onblur="script"
onfocus="script"
```

Attributes and Events Defined by Internet Explorer 5.5

```
hidefocus="true | false"
tabindex="number"
```

Attributes Defined by WebTV

```
border="pixels"
frameborder="0 | 1"
```

Attributes

border   This attribute sets the width in pixels of frame borders within the frame set. Setting **border="0"** eliminates all frame borders. This attribute is not defined in the HTML specification but is widely supported.

bordercolor   This attribute sets the color for frame borders within the frame set using either a named color or a color specified in the hexadecimal *#RRGGBB* format.

class   See "Core Attributes Reference," earlier in this appendix.

cols   This attribute contains a comma-delimited list, which specifies the number and size of columns contained within a set of frames. List items indicate columns from left to right. Column size is specified in three formats, which might be mixed. A column can be assigned a fixed width in pixels. It also can be assigned a percentage of the available width, such as 50 percent. Finally, a column can be set to expand to fill the available space by setting the value to *, which acts as a wildcard.

frameborder   This attribute controls whether or not frame borders should be displayed. Netscape supports **no** and **yes** values. Microsoft uses **1** and **0** as well as **no** and **yes**.

framespacing   This attribute indicates the space between frames in pixels.

hidefocus   This proprietary element, introduced with Internet Explorer 5.5, hides focus on an element's content. Focus must be applied to the element using the **tabindex** attribute.

id   See "Core Attributes Reference," earlier in this appendix.

lang   See "Language Reference," earlier in this appendix.

language   This attribute specifies the language the current script is written in and invokes the proper scripting engine. The default value is **javascript**. **Javascript** and **jscript** represent that the scripting language is written in JavaScript. **Vbs** and **vbscript** represent that the scripting language is written in VBScript.

rows   This attribute contains a comma-delimited list, which specifies the number and size of rows contained within a set of frames. The number of entries in the list indicates the number of rows. Row size is specified with the same formats used for columns.

style   See "Core Attributes Reference," earlier in this appendix.

tabindex   This attribute uses a number to identify the object's position in the tabbing order for keyboard navigation using the TAB key. Internet Explorer 5.5 applies this attribute to the **frameset** element; under IE 5.5, this focus can be disabled with the **hidefocus** attribute.

title   See "Core Attributes Reference," earlier in this appendix.

Attribute and Event Support

Netscape 4   border, bordercolor, cols, frameborder, rows, onblur, onfocus, onload, and onunload. (**class**, **id**, **lang**, and **style** are implied.)

Internet Explorer 4   border, bordercolor, class, cols, frameborder, id, lang, language, rows, and title

WebTV   border, cols, frameborder (0 | 1), framespacing, rows, onload, and onunload

Internet Explorer 5.5   All HTML events and attributes except **style**, all IE 4 events and attributes, plus **hidefocus**, and **tabindex**.

Event Handlers
See "Events Reference," earlier in this appendix.

Examples

```
<!-- This example defines a frame set of three columns. The middle column
is 50 pixels wide. The first and last columns fill the remaining space.
The last column takes twice as much space as the first. -->

<frameset cols="*,50,*">
  <frame src="column1.htm">
  <frame src="column2.htm">
<frame src="column3.htm">
```

```
</frameset>

<!-- This example defines a frame set of two columns, one of which is 20%
of the screen, and the other, 80%. -->

<frameset cols="20%, 80%">
  <frame src="controls.htm">
  <frame src="display.htm">
</frameset>

<!-- This example defines two rows, one of which is 10% of the screen,
and the other, whatever space is left. -->

<frameset rows="10%, *">
  <frame src="adbanner.htm" name="ad_frame">
  <frame src="contents.htm" name="content_frame">
</frameset>
```

Compatibility

HTML 4 and 4.01 (frameset), XHTML 1.0
Internet Explorer 2, 3, 4, 5, and 5.5
Netscape 2, 3, 4–4.7, 6
Opera 4
WebTV

Notes

- The **<frameset>** element contains one or more **<frame>** elements, which are used to indicate the framed contents. The **<frameset>** element also might contain a **<noframes>** element whose contents will be displayed on browsers that do not support frames.

- The **<frameset>** element replaces the **<body>** element in a framing document as shown here:

```
<html>
<head>
<title>Collection of Frames</title>
</head>

<frameset cols="*,50,*">
  <frame src="column1.htm" name="col1">
  <frame src="column2.htm" name="col2">
  <frame src="column3.htm" name="col3">
<noframes>
Please visit our <a href"noframes.htm">no frames</a> site.
</frameset>

</html>
```

<h1> Through <h6> (Headings)

These tags implement six levels of document headings; **<h1>** is the most prominent, and **<h6>** is the least prominent.

Syntax

```
<h1
     align="center | justify | left | right"
          (transitional)
     class="class name(s)"
     dir="ltr | rtl"
     id="unique alphanumeric identifier"
     lang="language code"
     style="style information"
     title="advisory text"
     onclick="script"
     ondblclick="script"
     onkeydown="script"
     onkeypress="script"
     onkeyup="script"
     onmousedown="script"
     onmousemove="script"
     onmouseout="script"
     onmouseover="script"
     onmouseup="script">

</h1>
```

Attributes and Events Defined by Internet Explorer 4

```
     language="javascript | jscript | vbs | vbscript"
     ondragstart="script"
     onhelp="script"
     onselectstart="script"
```

Attributes and Events Defined by Internet Explorer 5.5

```
     accesskey="key"
     contenteditable="false | true | inherit"
```

```
hidefocus="true | false"
tabindex="number"
```

Attributes

accesskey   This attribute specifies a keyboard navigation accelerator for the element. Pressing ALT or a similar key (depending on the browser and operating system) in association with the specified key selects the anchor element correlated with that key.

align   This attribute controls the horizontal alignment of the heading with respect to the page. The default value is **left**.

class   See "Core Attributes Reference," earlier in this appendix.

contenteditable   This proprietary Microsoft attribute allows users to edit content rendered in the Internet Explorer 5.5 browser. Values are **false**, **true**, and **inherit**. A value of **false** will prevent content from being edited by users; **true** will allow editing. The default value, **inherit**, applies the value of the affected element's parent element.

dir   See "Language Reference," earlier in this appendix.

hidefocus   This proprietary element, introduced with Internet Explorer 5.5, hides focus on an element's content. Focus must be applied to the element using the **tabindex** attribute.

id   See "Core Attributes Reference," earlier in this appendix.

lang   See "Language Reference," earlier in this appendix.

language   This attribute specifies the language the current script is written in and invokes the proper scripting engine. The default value is **javascript**. **Javascript** and **jscript** represent that the scripting language is written in JavaScript. **Vbs** and **vbscript** represent that the scripting language is written in VBScript.

style   See "Core Attributes Reference," earlier in this appendix.

tabindex   This attribute uses a number to identify the object's position in the tabbing order for keyboard navigation using the TAB key. Internet Explorer 5.5 applies this attribute to the header elements; under IE 5.5, this focus can be disabled with the **hidefocus** attribute.

title   See "Core Attributes Reference," earlier in this appendix.

Attribute and Event Support

Netscape 4   **align**. (**class**, **id**, **lang**, and **style** are implied.)

Internet Explorer 4   All attributes and events except **dir**. (Note: The **justify** value for **align** is not supported.)

Internet Explorer 5.5   All events and attributes, plus **accesskey**, **contenteditable**, **hidefocus**, and **tabindex**.

WebTV   align (center | left | right).

Event Handlers

See "Events Reference," earlier in this appendix.

Example

```
<h1>This is a Major Document Heading</h1>
<h2 align="center=">Second heading, aligned to the center</h2>
<h3 align="right">Third heading, aligned to the right</h3>
<h4>Fourth heading</h4>
<h5 style="font-size: 20pt">Fifth heading with style information</h5>
<h6>The smallest heading</h6>
```

Compatibility

HTML 2, 3.2, 4, 4.01, XHTML 1.o
Internet Explorer 2, 3, 4, 5, and 5.5
Netscape 1, 2, 3, 4–4.7, 6
Opera 4
WebTV

Notes

■ In most implementations, heading numbers correspond inversely with the six font sizes supported by the **<font>** element. For example, **<h1>** corresponds to **<font size="6">**. The default font size is **3**. However, this approach to layout is not encouraged and page designers should consider using styles to set even relative sizes.

■ HTML 3.2 supports only the **align** attribute. HTML 2 does not support any attributes for headings.

■ The strict definition of HTML 4.01 does not include support for the **align** attribute. Style sheets should be used instead.

`<head>` (Document Head)

This element indicates the document head that contains descriptive information about the HTML document as well as other supplementary information such as style rules or scripts.

Syntax

```
<head
    dir="ltr | rtl"
    lang="language code"
```

```
     profile="url">

</head>
```

XHTML Syntax

Under the XHTML 1.0 specification, the **<head>** element no longer can be implied, but must be used in all documents. The closing tag **</head>** also is mandatory.

Attributes and Events Defined by Internet Explorer 4

```
class="class name(s)"
id="unique alphanumeric identifier"
title="advisory text"
```

Attributes

class   See "Core Attributes Reference," earlier in this appendix.

dir   See "Language Reference," earlier in this appendix.

id   See "Core Attributes Reference," earlier in this appendix.

lang   See "Language Reference," earlier in this appendix.

profile   This attribute specifies a URL for a meta-information dictionary. The specified profile should indicate the format of allowed meta-data and the potential meaning of the data.

title   See "Core Attributes Reference," earlier in this appendix.

Attribute and Event Support

Internet Explorer 4   class, id, lang and title

Internet Explorer 5.5   class, id, and lang

Event Handlers
None

Example

```
<head>
<title>Demo Company Home Page</title>
<base href="http://www.democompany.com">
```

```
<meta name="Keywords"content="DemoCompany, SuperWidget">
</head>
```

Compatibility

HTML 2, 3.2, 4, 4.01, XHTML 1.0
Internet Explorer 2, 3, 4, 5, and 5.5
Netscape 1, 2, 3, 4–4.7, 6
Opera 4
WebTV

Notes

■ The **<head>** element must contain a **<title>** element. It also might contain the **<base>**, **<isindex>**, **<link>**, **<meta>**, **<script>**, and **<style>** elements. Internet Explorer 4 supports the inclusion of the **<basefont>** element in the **<head>** element, but **<basefont>** has been deprecated under HTML 4.

■ Under XHTML 1.0, the closing **</head>** tag is mandatory

■ Although the HTML 4.01 specification shows support for the **profile** attribute, no browsers appear to support it.

■ Internet Explorer 4 defines the **<bgsound>** element as another legal element within **<head>**.

■ HTML 2 and 3.2 support no attributes for this element.

<hr> (Horizontal Rule)

This element is used to insert a horizontal rule to visually separate document sections. Rules usually are rendered as a raised or etched line.

Syntax

```
<hr
    align="center | left | right" (transitional)
    class="class name(s)"
    id="unique alphanumeric identifier"
    noshade (transitional)
    size="pixels" (transitional)
    style="style information"
    title="advisory information"
    width="percentage | pixels" (transitional)
    onclick="script"
    ondblclick="script"
    onkeydown="script"
    onkeypress="script"
    onkeyup="script"
```

```
onmousedown="script"
onmousemove="script"
onmouseout="script"
onmouseover="script"
onmouseup="script">
```

XHTML Syntax

As an empy element, **<hr>** requires a trailing slash for XHTML compliance:

```
<hr />
```

Attributes and Events Defined by Internet Explorer 4

```
color="color name | #RRGGBB"
lang="language code"
language="javascript | jscript | vbs | vbscript"
src="url"
onbeforeupdate="script"
onblur="script"
ondragstart="script"
onfocus="script"
onhelp="script"
onresize="script"
onrowenter="script"
onrowexit="script"
onselectstart="script"
```

Attributes and Events Defined by Internet Explorer 5.5

```
accesskey="key"
hidefocus="true | false"
tabindex="number"
```

Attributes Defined by WebTV

```
invertborder
```

Attributes

accesskey   This attribute specifies a keyboard navigation accelerator for the element. Pressing ALT or a similar key (depending on the browser and operating system) in association with the specified key selects the anchor element correlated with that key.

align   This attribute controls the horizontal alignment of the rule with respect to the page. The default value is **left**.

class   See "Core Attributes Reference," earlier in this appendix.

color   This attribute sets the rule color using either a named color or a color specified in the hexadecimal *#RRGGBB* format. This attribute currently is supported only by Internet Explorer.

hidefocus   This proprietary element, introduced with Internet Explorer 5.5, hides focus on an element's content. Focus must be applied to the element using the **tabindex** attribute.

id   See "Core Attributes Reference," earlier in this appendix.

invertborder   This WebTV-specific attribute creates a horizontal rule that appears raised, as opposed to embossed, on the surface of the page.

lang   See "Language Reference," earlier in this appendix.

language   This attribute specifies the language the current script is written in and invokes the proper scripting engine. The default value is **javascript**. **Javascript** and **jscript** represent that the scripting language is written in JavaScript. **Vbs** and **vbscript** represent that the scripting language is written in VBScript.

noshade   This attribute causes the rule to be rendered as a solid bar without shading.

size   This attribute indicates the height in pixels of the rule.

src   This attribute specifies a URL for an associated file.

style   See "Core Attributes Reference," earlier in this appendix.

tabindex   This attribute uses a number to identify the object's position in the tabbing order for keyboard navigation using the TAB key. Internet Explorer 5.5 applies this attribute to the **hr** element; under IE 5.5, this focus can be disabled with the **hidefocus** attribute.

title   See "Core Attributes Reference," earlier in this appendix.

width   This attribute indicates how wide the rule should be, specified either in pixels or as a percent of screen width, such as 80 percent.

Attribute and Event Support

Netscape 4   **align**, **noshade**, **size**, and **width**. (**class**, **id**, and **style** are implied.)

Internet Explorer 4   All attributes and events defined by W3C and Internet Explorer 4.

Internet Explorer 5.5   All attributes and events defined by W3C and Internet Explorer 4, plus **accesskey**, **hidefocus**, and **tabindex**.

WebTV   align, invertborder, noshade, size, and width

Event Handlers

See "Events Reference," earlier in this appendix.

Examples

```
<hr align="left" noshade size="1" width="420">
```

```
<hr align="center" width="100%" size="3" color="#000000">
```

XHTML example

```
<hr align="left" noshade size="1" width="350" />
```

Compatibility

HTML 2, 3.2, 4, 4.01, XHTML 1.0
Internet Explorer 2, 3, 4, 5, ad 5.5
Netscape 1, 2, 3, 4–4.7, 6
Opera 4
WebTV

Notes

- The HTML 4.01 strict specification removes support for the **align**, **noshade**, **size**, and **width** attributes for horizontal rules. These effects are possible using style sheets.

- XHTML 1.0 requires a trailing slash for this element: **<hr />**

<html> (HTML Document)

This element identifies a document as containing HTML-tagged content.

Syntax

```
<html
     dir="ltr | rtl"
     lang="language code"
     version="url" (transitional)>

</html>
```

XHTML Syntax

Under the XHTML 1.0 specification, **<html>** can no longer be implied; **<html>** and the closing tag **</html>** both are mandatory for XHTML compliance.

Attributes Defined by Internet Explorer 4

```
class="class name(s)"
id="unique alphanumeric identifier"
```

Attributes and Events Defined by Internet Explorer 5.0

```
dir="ltr | rtl"
xmlns="namespace"
```

Attributes

class   See "Core Attributes Reference," earlier in this appendix.

dir   See "Language Reference," earlier in this appendix.

lang   See "Language Reference," earlier in this appendix.

version   The **version** attribute is used to set the URL of the location of the document type definition (DTD) that the current document conforms to. This attribute is deprecated under HTML 4.0(1), because this information should be defined by the doctype declaration instead.

xmlns   This attribute declares a namespace for XML-based custom tags in the document.

Attribute and Event Support

Internet Explorer 4   class, id

Internet Explorer 5.0   class, dir, id, and xmlns

Event Handlers
None

Example

```
<!-- Minimal HTML document -->
<html>
<head><title>Minimal Document</title></head>
<body></body>
</html>
```

Compatibility
HTML 4, 4.01, XHTML 1.0
Internet Explorer 4, 5, 5.5
Netscape 4–4.7, 6
Opera 4
WebTV

Notes

- The **<html>** element is the first element in an **<html>** document. Except for comments, the only tags it directly contains are the **<head>** element followed by either a **<body>** element or a **<frameset>** element.

- The **<html>** element and its closing tag **</html>** both are mandatory under XHTML 1.0.

<i> (Italic)

This element indicates that the enclosed text should be displayed in an italic typeface.

Syntax

```
<i
    class="class name(s)"
    dir="ltr | rtl"
    id="unique alphanumeric identifier"
    lang="language code"
    style="style information"
    title="advisory text"
    onclick="script"
    ondblclick="script"
    onkeydown="script"
    onkeypress="script"
    onkeyup="script"
    onmousedown="script"
    onmousemove="script"
    onmouseout="script"
    onmouseover="script"
    onmouseup="script"

</i>
```

Attributes and Events Defined by Internet Explorer 4

```
    language="javascript | jscript | vbs | vbscript"
    ondragstart="script"
    onhelp="script"
    onselectstart="script"
```

Attributes and Events Defined by Internet Explorer 5.5

```
accesskey="key"
contenteditable="false | true | inherit"
hidefocus="true | false"
tabindex="number"
```

Attributes

accesskey   This attribute specifies a keyboard navigation accelerator for the element. Pressing ALT or a similar key (depending on the browser and operating system) in association with the specified key selects the anchor element correlated with that key.

class   See "Core Attributes Reference," earlier in this appendix.

contenteditable   This proprietary Microsoft attribute allows users to edit content rendered in the Internet Explorer 5.5 browser. Values are **false**, **true**, and **inherit**. A value of **false** will prevent content from being edited by users; **true** will allow editing. The default value, **inherit**, applies the value of the affected element's parent element.

dir   See "Language Reference," earlier in this appendix.

hidefocus   This proprietary element, introduced with Internet Explorer 5.5, hides focus on an element's content. Focus must be applied to the element using the **tabindex** attribute.

id   See "Core Attributes Reference," earlier in this appendix.

lang   See "Language Reference," earlier in this appendix.

language   This attribute specifies the language the current script is written in and invokes the proper scripting engine. The default value is **javascript**. **Javascript** and **jscript** represent that the scripting language is written in JavaScript. **Vbs** and **vbscript** represent that the scripting language is written in VBScript.

style   See "Core Attributes Reference," earlier in this appendix.

tabindex   This attribute uses a number to identify the object's position in the tabbing order for keyboard navigation using the TAB key. Internet Explorer 5.5 applies this attribute to the **i** element; under IE 5.5, this focus can be disabled with the **hidefocus** attribute.

title   See "Core Attributes Reference," earlier in this appendix.

Attribute and Event Support

Netscape 4   class, id, lang, and style are implied.

Internet Explorer 4   All attributes and events except **dir**.

Internet Explorer 5.5   All events and attributes, plus **accesskey**, **contenteditable**, **hidefocus**, and **tabindex**.

Event Handlers
See "Events Reference," earlier in this appendix.

Example

```
Here is some <i>italicized</i> text.
```

Compatibility
HTML 4, 4.01, XHTML 1.0
Internet Explorer 4, 5, and 5.5
Netscape 4 –4.7, 6
Opera 4
WebTV

`<iframe>` (Floating Frame)

This element indicates a floating frame, an independently controllable content region that can be embedded in a page.

Syntax (Transitional Only)

```
<iframe
     align="bottom | left | middle | right | top"
     class="class name(s)"
     frameborder="0 | 1"
     height="percentage | pixels"
     id="unique alphanumeric identifier"
     longdesc="url of description"
     marginheight="pixels"
     marginwidth="pixels"
     name="string"
     scrolling="auto | no | yes"
     src="url of frame contents"
     style="style information"
     title="advisory text"
     width="percentage | pixels">

</iframe>
```

Attributes Defined by Internet Explorer 4

```
align="absbottom | absmiddle | baseline | texttop"
border="pixels"
bordercolor="color name | #RRGGBB"
datfld="name of column supplying bound data"
datasrc="id of data source object supplying data"
frameborder="no | yes | 0 | 1"
framespacing="pixels"
hspace="pixels"
lang="language code"
language="javascript | jscript | vbs | vbscript"
noresize="noresize | resize"
vspace="pixels"
```

Attributes and Events Defined by Internet Explorer 5.5

```
hidefocus="true | false"
tabindex="number"
```

Attributes

align   This attribute controls the horizontal alignment of the floating frame with respect to the page. The default is **left**.

border   This attribute specifies the thickness of the border in pixels.

bordercolor   This attribute specifies the color of the border.

class   See "Core Attributes Reference," earlier in this appendix.

datfld   This attribute specifies the column name from the data source object that supplies the bound data.

datasrc   This attribute indicates **id** of the data source object that supplies the data that is bound to this element.

frameborder   This attribute determines whether the frame is surrounded by a border. The HTML 4 specification defines **0** to be off and **1** to be on. The default value is **1**. Internet Explorer also defines the values **no** and **yes**.

framespacing   This attribute creates additional space between the frames.

height   The attribute sets the floating frame's height in pixels.

hidefocus   This proprietary element, introduced with Internet Explorer 5.5, hides focus on an element's content. Focus must be applied to the element using the **tabindex** attribute.

hspace   This attribute specifies margins for the frame.

id   See "Core Attributes Reference," earlier in this appendix.

lang   See "Language Reference," earlier in this appendix.

language   This attribute specifies the language the current script is written in and invokes the proper scripting engine. The default value is **javascript**. **Javascript** and **jscript** represent that the scripting language is written in JavaScript. **Vbs** and **vbscript** represent that the scripting language is written in VBScript.

longdesc   This attribute specifies a URL of a document which contains a long description of the frame's contents. This might be particularly useful as a complement to the **<title>** element.

marginheight   This attribute sets the height in pixels between the floating frame's content and its top and bottom borders.

marginwidth   This attribute sets the width in pixels between the floating frame's content and its left and right borders.

name   This attribute assigns the floating frame a name so that it can be the target destination of hyperlinks.

noresize   When **noresize** is included, the frame cannot be resized by the user.

scrolling   This attribute determines if the frame has scroll bars. A **yes** value forces scroll bars; a **no** value prohibits them.

src   This attribute contains the URL of the content to be displayed in the floating frame. If absent, the frame is blank.

style   See "Core Attributes Reference," earlier in this appendix.

tabindex   This attribute uses a number to identify the object's position in the tabbing order for keyboard navigation using the TAB key. Internet Explorer 5.5 applies this attribute to the **iframe** element; under IE 5.5, this focus can be disabled with the **hidefocus** attribute.

title   See "Core Attributes Reference," earlier in this appendix.

vspace   This attribute specifies margins for the frame.

width   This attribute sets the floating frame's width in pixels.

Attribute and Event Support

Internet Explorer 4   All attributes and events except **longdesc**.

Internet Explorer 5.5 Same as IE 4, plus **hidefocus** and **tabindex**.

Event Handlers

See "Events Reference," earlier in this appendix.

Example

```
<iframe src="http://www.democompany.com" height="150" width="200"
        name="FloatingFrame1">
Sorry, your browser doesn't support inline frames.
</iframe>
```

Compatibility

HTML 4 (transitional)
Internet Explorer 3, 4, 5, and 5.5
Netscape 6

Notes

- A floating frame does not need to be declared by the **<frameset>** element as part of a frame set.
- WebTV and Netscape 4.*x* (4.0 through 4.75) do not support floating frames.
- Under HTML 4.01's strict specification, the **<iframe>** element is not defined. Floating frames can be imitated using the **<div>** element and CSS positioning facilities.

<ilayer> (Inflow Layer)

This Netscape-specific element allows the definition of overlapping content layers that can be positioned, hidden or shown, rendered transparent or opaque, reordered front to back, and nested. An *inflow layer* is a layer with a relative position that appears where it would naturally occur in the document, in contrast to a *general layer*, which might be positioned absolutely regardless of its location in a document. The functionality of layers is available using CSS positioning, and page developers are advised not to use this element.

Syntax (Defined by Netscape 4)

```
<ilayer
    above="layer"
    background="url of image"
    below="layer"
    bgcolor="color name | #RRGGBB"
    class="class name(s)"
    clip="x1, y1, x2, y2"
    height="percentage | pixels"
    id="unique alphanumeric identifier"
```

```
         left="pixels"
         name="string"
         pagex="pixels"
         pagey="pixels"
         src="url of layer contents"
         style="style information"
         top="pixels"
         visibility="hide | inherit | show"
         width="percentage | pixels"
         z-index="number"
         onblur="script"
         onfocus="script"
         onload="script"
         onmouseout="script"
         onmouseover="script">

</ilayer>
```

Attributes

above   This attribute contains the name of the layer to be rendered above the current layer.

background   This attribute contains the URL of a background image for the layer.

below   This attribute contains the name of the layer to be rendered below the current layer.

bgcolor   This attribute specifies a layer's background color. Its value can be either a named color or a color specified in the hexadecimal #*RRGGBB* format.

class   This attribute specifies the class name(s) for access via a style sheet.

clip   This attribute specifies the clipping region or viewable area of the layer. All layer content outside that rectangle will be rendered as transparent. The **clip** rectangle is defined by two x,y pairs: top x, left y, bottom x, and right y. Coordinates are relative to the layer's origin point, **0,0** in its top-left corner.

height   This attribute specifies the height of a layer in pixels or percentage values.

id   See "Core Attributes Reference," earlier in this appendix.

left   This attribute specifies in pixels the horizontal offset of the layer. The offset is relative to its parent layer if it has one or to the left page margin if it does not.

name   This attribute assigns the layer a name that can be referenced by programs in a client-side scripting language. The **id** attribute also can be used.

pagex   This attribute specifies the horizontal position of the layer relative to the browser window.

pagey   This attribute specifies the vertical position of the layer relative to the browser window.

src   This attribute is used to set the URL of a file that contains the content to load into the layer.

style   This attribute specifies an inline style for the layer.

top   This attribute specifies in pixels the top offset of the layer. The offset is relative to its parent layer if it has one or the top page margin if it does not.

visibility   This attribute specifies whether a layer is hidden, shown, or inherits its visibility from the layer that includes it.

width   This attribute specifies a layer's width in pixels.

z-index   This attribute specifies a layer's stacking order relative to other layers. Position is specified with positive integers, with **1** indicating the bottommost layer.

Attribute and Event Support

Netscape 4   All attributes

Event Handlers
None

Example

```
<p>Content comes before.</p>
<ilayer name="background" bgcolor="green">
  <p>Layered information goes here.</p>
</ilayer>
<p>Content comes after.</p>
```

Compatibility
Netscape 4.0–4.7 (Netscape 6 Preview Release 2 did not support this element)

Notes

- This element likely will fall out of fashion because of its lack of cross-browser compatibility. The functionality of **<ilayer>** is possible using the positioning features in CSS. Page developers are discouraged from using this element.

- Applets, plug-ins, and other embedded media forms, generically called *objects,* might be included in a layer; however, they will float to the top of all other layers even if their containing layer is obscured.

<img> (Image)

This element indicates a media object to include in an HTML document. Usually, the object is a graphic image, but some implementations support movies and animations.

Syntax

```
<img
      align="bottom | left | middle | right | top"
            (transitional)
      alt="alternative text"
      border="pixels" (transitional)
      class="class name(s)"
      dir="ltr | rtl"
      height="pixels"
      hspace="pixels" (transitional)
      id="unique alphanumeric identifier"
      ismap
      lang="language code"
      longdesc="url of description file"
      src="url of image"
      style="style information"
      title="advisory text"
      usemap="url of map file"
      vspace="pixels" (transitional)
      width="pixels"
      onclick="script"
      ondblclick="script"
      onkeydown="script"
      onkeypress="script"
      onkeyup="script"
      onmousedown="script"
      onmousemove="script"
      onmouseout="script"
      onmouseover="script"
      onmouseup="script">
```

XHTML Syntax

As an empty element, **<img>** requires a trailing slash for XHTML compliance:

```
<img />
```

Attributes and Events Defined by Internet Explorer 4

```
      align="absbottom | absmiddle | baseline | texttop"
```

```
datafld="name of column supplying bound data"
datasrc="id of data source object supplying data"
dynsrc="url of movie"
language="javascript | jscript | vbs | vbscript"
loop="infinite | number"
lowsrc="url of low-resolution image"
name="unique alphanumeric identifier"
onabort="script"
onafterupdate="script"
onbeforeupdate="script"
onblur="script"
ondragstart="script"
onerror="script"
onfocus="script"
onhelp="script"
onload="script"
onresize="script"
onrowenter="script"
onrowexit="script"
onselectstart="script"
```

Attributes and Events Defined by Internet Explorer 5.5

```
hidefocus="true | false"
tabindex="number"
```

Attributes Defined by Netscape 4

```
align="absbottom | absmiddle | baseline | texttop"
lowsrc="url of low-resolution image"
name="unique alphanumeric identifier"
suppress="true | false"
```

Attributes Defined by WebTV

```
controls
name="unique alphanumeric identifier"
reload="seconds"
selected="x,y pair"
transparency="number (1-100)"
```

Attributes

align   This attribute controls the horizontal alignment of the image with respect to the page. The default value is **left**. Only the Netscape, Internet Explorer 4, and WebTV implementations support the **absbottom, absmiddle, baseline**, and **texttop** values.

alt   This attribute contains a string to display instead of the image for browsers that cannot display images.

border   This attribute indicates the width in pixels of the border surrounding the image.

class   See "Core Attributes Reference," earlier in this appendix.

controls   Under Internet Explorer 3 and WebTV, it is possible to set the controls to show by placing this attribute in the **<img>** element. This attribute does not appear to be supported under Internet Explorer 4, and users are encouraged to use the **<object>** element to embed video for Internet Explorer.

datafld   This attribute specifies the column name from the data source object that supplies the bound data to set the **src** of the **<img>** element.

datasrc   This attribute indicates the **id** of the data source object that supplies the data that is bound to this **<img>** element.

dir   See "Language Reference," earlier in this appendix.

dynsrc   In the Microsoft and WebTV implementations, this attribute indicates the URL of a movie file and is used instead of the **src** attribute.

height   This attribute indicates the height in pixels of the image.

hidefocus   This proprietary element, introduced with Internet Explorer 5.5, hides focus on an element's content. Focus must be applied to the element using the **tabindex** attribute.

hspace   This attribute indicates the horizontal space in pixels between the image and surrounding text.

id   See "Core Attributes Reference," earlier in this appendix.

ismap   This attribute indicates that the image is a server-side image map. User mouse actions over the image are sent to the server for processing.

lang   See "Language Reference," earlier in this appendix.

language   This attribute specifies the language the current script is written in and invokes the proper scripting engine. The default value is **javascript**. **Javascript** and **jscript** represent that the scripting language is written in JavaScript. **Vbs** and **vbscript** represent that the scripting language is written in VBScript.

longdesc   This attribute specifies a URL of a document which contains a long description of the image. This attribute is used as a complement to the **alt** attribute.

loop   In the Microsoft implementation, this attribute is used with the **dynsrc** attribute to cause a movie to loop. Its value is either a numeric loop count or the keyword **infinite**.

lowsrc   In the Netscape implementation, this attribute contains the URL of an image to be initially loaded. Typically, the **lowsrc** image is a low-resolution or black-and-white image that provides a quick preview of the image to follow. Once the primary image is loaded, it replaces the **lowsrc** image.

name   This common attribute is used to bind a name to the image. Older browsers understand the **name** field, and in conjunction with scripting languages it is possible to manipulate images by their defined names to create effects such as "rollover" buttons. The **id** attribute under HTML 4 specifies element identifiers; for backward compatibility, **name** can still be used.

reload   In the WebTV implementation, this attribute indicates in seconds how frequently an image should be reloaded.

selected   In the WebTV implementation, this attribute indicates the initial x,y coordinate location on the image. The cursor is placed at that location when the image is loaded. It requires either the **ismap** or the **usemap** attribute.

src   This attribute indicates the URL of an image file to be displayed.

style   See "Core Attributes Reference," earlier in this appendix.

suppress   This Netscape-specific attribute determines if a placeholder icon will appear during image loading. Values are **true** and **false**. **suppress="true"** will suppress display of the placeholder icon as well as display of any **alt** information until the image is loaded. **suppress="false"** will allow the placeholder icon and any tool tips defined by the **alt** information to display while the image is loading. The default value is **false**. If the browser is set to not load images automatically, the **suppress** attribute is ignored.

tabindex   This attribute uses a number to identify the object's position in the tabbing order for keyboard navigation using the TAB key. Internet Explorer 5.5 applies this attribute to the **img** element; under IE 5.5, this focus can be disabled with the **hidefocus** attribute.

title   See "Core Attributes Reference," earlier in this appendix.

transparency   In the WebTV implementation, this attribute allows the background to show through the image. It takes a numeric argument indicating the degree of transparency, from fully opaque (**0**) to fully transparent (**100**).

usemap   This attribute makes the image support client-side image mapping. Its argument is a URL specifying the map file, which associates image regions with hyperlinks.

vspace   This attribute indicates the vertical space in pixels between the image and surrounding text.

width   This attribute indicates the width in pixels of the image.

Attribute and Event Support

Netscape 4   align, alt, border, space, hspace, ismap, lowsrc, name, src, suppress, usemap, vspace, and width

Internet Explorer 4   All W3C-defined attributes and events except **dir** and **longdesc**, and all attributes and events defined by Internet Explorer 4.

Internet Explorer 5.5   Same as IE 4, plus **dir**, **hidefocus**, and **tabindex**.

WebTV   align, border, height, hspace, id, ismap, name, selected, src, start, transparency, usemap, vspace, width, onabort, onerror, and onload

Event Handlers
See "Events Reference," earlier in this appendix.

Examples

```
<img src="lakers.jpg" lowsrc="lakersbw.jpg" alt="Los Angeles Lakers"
    height="100" width="300">

<img src="hugeimagemap.gif" usemap="#mainmap" border="0" height="200"
    width="200" alt="Image Map Here">

<a href="home.htm"><img src="homebutton.gif" width="50" height="20"
   alt="Link to Home Page"></a>
```

XHTML Examples

```
<img src="mikka.jpg" lowsrc="mikkabw.jpg" alt="Grand Prix Driver"
    height="320" width="150" />
```

Compatibility
HTML 2, 3.2, 4, 4.01, XHTML 1.0
Internet Explorer 2, 3, 4, 5, and 5.5
Netscape 1, 2, 3, 4–4.7, 6
Opera
WebTV

Notes

- Currently no browser appears to support **longdesc**.
- Typically, when you use the **usemap** attribute, the URL is a fragment, such as #map1, rather than a full URL. Some browsers do not support external client-side map files.
- Under the HTML 4 strict definition, the **<img>** element does not support **align**, **border**, **height**, **hspace**, **vspace**, and **width**. The functionality of these attributes should be possible using style sheet rules.
- Whereas the HTML 4 specification reserves data-binding attributes such as **datafld** or **datasrc**, it is not specified for **<img>**, although Internet Explorer provides support for these attributes.
- XHTML 1.0 requires a trailing slash for this element: **<img />**

<input> (Input Form Control)

This element specifies an input control for a form. The type of input is set by the **type** attribute and can be a variety of different types, including single-line text field, multiline text field, password style, check box, radio button, or push button.

Syntax

```
<input
    accept="MIME TYPES"
    accesskey="character"
    align="bottom | left | middle | right | top"
           (transitional)
    alt="text"
    checked
    class="class name(s)"
    dir="ltr | rtl"
    disabled
    id="unique alphanumeric identifier"
    lang="language code"
    maxlength="maximum field size"
    name="field name"
    readonly
    size="field size"
    src="url of image file"
    style="style information"
    tabindex="number"
    title="advisory text"
    type="button | checkbox | file | hidden | image |
          password | radio | reset | submit | text"
    usemap="url of map file"
    value="field value"
    onblur="script"
```

```
onchange="script"
onclick="script"
ondblclick="script"
onfocus="script"
onkeydown="script"
onkeypress="script"
onkeyup="script"
onmousedown="script"
onmousemove="script"
onmouseout="script"
onmouseover="script"
onmouseup="script"
onselect="script">
```

XHTML Syntax

As an empty element, **`<input>`** requires a trailing slash for XHTML compliance:

```
<input />
```

Attributes and Events Defined by Internet Explorer 4

```
align="center"
language="javascript | jscript | vbs | vbscript"
onafterupdate="script"
onbeforeupdate="script"
ondragstart="script"
onhelp="script"
onselectstart="script"
```

Attributes Defined by Internet Explorer 5.5

```
hidefocus="true | false"
```

Attributes Defined by Netscape 4

```
align="absbottom | absmiddle | baseline | texttop"
```

Attributes Defined by WebTV

```
bgcolor="color name | #RRGGBB"
borderimage="url"
```

```
cursor="color name | #RRGGBB"
usestyle
width="pixels"
```

Attributes

accept   This attribute is used to list the MIME types accepted for file uploads when **<input type="file">**.

accesskey   This attribute specifies a keyboard navigation accelerator for the element. Pressing ALT or a similar key in association with the specified character selects the form control correlated with that key sequence. Page designers are forewarned to avoid key sequences already bound to browsers.

align   With image form controls (**type="image"**), this attribute aligns the image with respect to surrounding text. The HTML 4.01 transitional specification defines **bottom, left, middle, right,** and **top** as allowable values. Netscape and Microsoft browsers might also allow the use of attribute values such as **absbottom** or **absmiddle**. Like other presentation-specific aspects of HTML, the **align** attribute is dropped under the strict HTML 4.01 specification.

alt   This attribute is used to display an alternative description of image buttons for text-only browsers. The meaning of **alt** for forms of **<input>** beyond **type="input"** is unclear.

bgcolor   In the WebTV implementation, this attribute specifies the background color of a text form control (**type="text"**). The value of the attribute can be either a named color or a color specified in the hexadecimal *#RRGGBB* format.

borderimage   In the WebTV implementation, this attribute allows specification of a graphical border for **reset, submit,** and **text** controls. Its value is the URL of a .bif (Border Image File) graphics file that specifies the border. Border image files tend to reside in WebTV ROM; the common values are **file://ROM/Border/ButtonBorder2.bif** and **file://ROM/Border/ ButtonBorder3.bif**, although other values might be present under later versions of WebTV.

checked   The **checked** attribute should be used only for check box (**type="checkbox"**) and radio (**type="radio"**) form controls. The presence of this attribute indicates that the control should be displayed in its checked state.

class   See "Core Attributes Reference," earlier in this appendix.

cursor   In the WebTV implementation, this attribute sets the cursor color for a text form control (**type="text"**). The attribute's value is either a named color or a color specified in the hexadecimal *#RRGGBB* format.

dir   See "Language Reference," earlier in this appendix.

disabled   This attribute is used to turn off a form control. Elements will not be submitted, nor will they receive any focus from the keyboard or mouse. Disabled form controls will not be part of the tabbing order. The browser also might gray out the form that is disabled, in order to indicate to the user that the form control is inactive. This attribute requires no value.

hidefocus   This proprietary element, introduced with Internet Explorer 5.5, hides focus on an element's content. Focus must be applied to the element using the **tabindex** attribute.

id   See "Core Attributes Reference," earlier in this appendix.

lang   See "Language Reference," earlier in this appendix.

language   In the Microsoft implementation, this attribute specifies the scripting language to be used with an associated script bound to the element typically through an event handler attribute. Possible values include **javascript**, **jscript**, **vbs** and **vbscript**. Other values that include the version of the language used, such as **JavaScript1.1**, also might be possible.

maxlength   This attribute indicates the maximum content length that can be entered in a text form control (**type="text"**). The maximum number of characters allowed differs from the visible dimension of the form control, which is set with the **size** attribute.

name   This attribute allows a form control to be assigned a name so that it can be referenced by a scripting language. **Name** is supported by older browsers such as Netscape 2 generation browsers, but the W3C encourages the use of the **id** attribute. For compatibility purposes, both might have to be used.

readonly   This attribute prevents the form control's value from being changed. Form controls with this attribute set might receive focus from the user but might not be modified. Because it receives focus, a **readonly** form control will be part of the form's tabbing order. Last, the control's value will be sent on form submission. This attribute can be used only with <input> when **type** is set to **text** or **password**. The attribute also is used with the <textarea> element.

size   This attribute indicates the visible dimension, in characters, of a text form control (**type="text"**). This differs from the maximum length of content, which can be entered in a form control set by the **maxlength** attribute.

src   This attribute is used with image form controls (**type="image"**) to specify the URL of the image file to load.

style   See "Core Attributes Reference," earlier in this appendix.

tabindex   This attribute takes a numeric value that indicates the position of the form control in the tabbing index for the form. Tabbing proceeds from the lowest positive **tabindex** value to the highest. Negative values for **tabindex** will leave the form control out of the tabbing order. When tabbing is not explicitly set, the browser can tab through items in the order they are encountered. Form controls that are disabled due to the presence of the **disabled** attribute will not be part of the tabbing index, although read-only controls will be.

title   See "Core Attributes Reference," earlier in this appendix.

type This attribute specifies the type of the form control. A value of **button** indicates a general-purpose button with no well-defined meaning. However, an action can be associated with the button using an event handler attribute, such as **onclick**. A value of **checkbox** indicates a check box control. Check box form controls have a checked and nonchecked set, but even if these controls are grouped together, they allow a user to select multiple check boxes at once. In contrast, a value of RADIO indicates a radio button control. When grouped, radio buttons allow only one of the many choices to be selected at a given time.

A form control type of **hidden** indicates a field that is not visible to the viewer but is used to store information. A hidden form control often is used to preserve state information between pages. A value of **file** for the **type** attribute indicates a control that allows the viewer to upload a file to a server. The filename can be entered in a displayed field, or a user agent might provide a special browse button allowing the user to locate the file. A value of **image** indicates a graphic image form control that a user can click on to invoke an associated action. (Most browsers allow the use of **img**-associated attributes such as **height**, **width**, **hspace**, **vspace** and **alt** when the **type** value is set to **image**.) A value of **password** for the **type** attribute indicates a password entry field. A password field will not display text entered as it is typed; it might instead show a series of dots. Note that password-entered data is not transferred to the server in any secure fashion. A value of **reset** for the **type** attribute is used to insert a button that resets all controls within a form to their default values. A value of **submit** inserts a special submission button that, when pressed, sends the contents of the form to the location indicated by the **action** attribute of the enclosing **<form>** element. Last, a value of **text** (the default) for the **type** attribute indicates a single-line text input field.

usemap This HTML 4.0 attribute is used to indicate the map file to be associated with an image when the form control is set with **type="image"**. The value of the attribute should be a URL of a map file, but generally will be in the form of a URL fragment referencing a map file within the current file.

usestyle In the WebTV implementation, the presence of this attribute causes control text to be rendered in the default text style for the page. This attribute requires no value.

value This attribute has two different uses, depending on the value for the **type** attribute. With data entry controls (**type="text"** and **type="password"**), this attribute is used to set the default value for the control. When used with check box or radio form controls, this attribute specifies the return value for the control when it is turned on, rather than the default Boolean value submitted.

width This attribute, supported by WebTV and Internet Explorer, is used to set the size of the form control in pixels.

Attribute and Event Support

Netscape 4 name, value, and onclick. (class, id, lang, and style are implied.)

Internet Explorer 4 All W3C-defined attributes and events except **accept** and **usemap**, and all attributes and events defined by Internet Explorer 4. (Note: Internet Explorer 4 supports only the **center**, **left**, and **right** values for the **align** attribute.)

Internet Explorer 4   All W3C-defined attributes and events except **accept**, and **usemap**, and all attributes and events defined by Internet Explorer 4, and adds **hidefocus**. (Note: Internet Explorer 4 supports only the **center**, **left**, and **right** values for the **align** attribute.)

WebTV   align, bgcolor, checked, cursor, id, maxlength, name, size, type, usestyle, value, width, onblur, onchange, onclick, onfocus, and onselect

Event Handlers

See "Events Reference," earlier in this appendix.

Examples

```
<form>
Which is your favorite food?
  <input type="radio" name="favorite" value="Mexican">Mexican
  <input type="radio" name="favorite" value="Russian">Russian
  <input type="radio" name="favorite" value="Japanese">Japanese
  <input type="radio" checked name="favorite" value="Other">Other
<form>


<form>
Enter your name: <input type="text" maxlength="35" size="20"><BR>
Enter your password: <input type="password" maxlength="35" size="20"><br/>
<br/>
  <input type="submit" value="Submit">
  <input type="reset" value="Reset">
</form>
```

XHTML Example

```
<form>
Enter your name: <input type="text" maxlength="35" size="20" /><BR>
Enter your password: <input type="password" maxlength="35" size="20" /><br/>
<br/>
  <input type="submit" value="Submit" />
  <input type="reset" value="Reset" />
</form>
```

Compatibility

HTML 2, 3.2, 4, 4.01, XHTML 1.0
Internet Explorer 2, 3, 4, 5, 5.5
Netscape 1, 2, 3, 4–4.7, 6
Opera 4.0
WebTV

Notes

- The **<input>** element is an empty element and requires no closing tag.
- Some documents suggest the use of **type="textarea"**. Even if this style is supported, it should be avoided in favor of the **<textarea>** element, which is common to all browsers.
- The HTML 2.0 and 3.2 specifications support only the **align**, **checked**, **maxlength**, **name**, **size**, **src**, **type**, and **value** attributes for the **<input>** element.
- The HTML 4.01 specification also reserves the use of the **datafld**, **dataformatas**, and **datasrc** data-binding attributes.
- Under the strict HTML specification, the **align** attribute is not allowed.
- The XHTML 1.0 specification requires the use of a trailing slash: **<input />**

<ins> (Inserted Text)

This element is used to indicate that text has been added to the document.

Syntax

```
<ins
    cite="URL"
    class="class name(s)"
    datetime="date"
    id="unique alphanumeric identifier"
    lang="language code"
    style="style information"
    title="advisory text"
    onclick="script"
    ondblclick="script"
    onkeydown="script"
    onkeypress="script"
    onkeyup="script"
    onmousedown="script"
    onmousemove="script"
    onmouseout="script"
    onmouseover="script"
    onmouseup="script">

</ins>
```

Attributes and Events Defined by Internet Explorer 4

```
    language="javascript | jscript | vbs | vbscript"
    ondragstart="script"
    onhelp="script"
```

Attributes and Events Defined by Internet Explorer 5.5

```
accesskey="key"
contenteditable=" false | true | inherit "
dir="ltr | rtl"
hidefocus="true | false"
tabindex="number"
```

Attributes

accesskey   This attribute specifies a keyboard navigation accelerator for the element. Pressing ALT or a similar key (depending on the browser and operating system) in association with the specified key selects the anchor element correlated with that key.

cite   The value of this attribute is a URL that designates a source document or message for the information inserted. This attribute is intended to point to information explaining why the text was changed.

class   See "Core Attributes Reference," earlier in this appendix.

contenteditable   This proprietary Microsoft attribute allows users to edit content rendered in the Internet Explorer 5.5 browser. Values are **false**, **true**, and **inherit**. A value of **false** will prevent content from being edited by users; **true** will allow editing. The default value, **inherit**, applies the value of the affected element's parent element.

datetime   This attribute is used to indicate the date and time the insertion was made. The value of the attribute is a date in a special format as defined by ISO 8601. The basic date format is

```
yyyy-mm-ddthh:mm:ssTZD
```

where the following is true:

```
yyyy=four-digit year such as 1999
mm=two-digit month (01=January, 02=February, and so on)
dd=two-digit day of the month (01 through 31)
hh=two-digit hour (00 to 23) (24-hour clock not AM or PM)
mm=two-digit minute (00 to 59)
ss=two-digit second (00 to 59)
tzd=time zone designator
```

The time zone designator is either **z**, which indicates UTC (Universal Time Coordinate, or coordinated universal time format), or **+hh:mm**, which indicates that the time is a local time that is *hh* hours and *mm* minutes ahead of UTC. Alternatively, the format for the time zone designator could be **-hh:mm**, which indicates that the local time is behind UTC. Note that the letter "T" actually appears in the string, all digits must be used, and **00** values for minutes and seconds might be required. An example value for the **datetime** attribute might be

1999-10-6T09:15:00-05:00, which corresponds to October 6, 1999, 9:15 A.M., U.S. Eastern Standard Time.

dir See "Language Reference," earlier in this appendix.

hidefocus This proprietary element, introduced with Internet Explorer 5.5, hides focus on an element's content. Focus must be applied to the element using the **tabindex** attribute.

id See "Core Attributes Reference," earlier in this appendix.

lang See "Language Reference," earlier in this appendix.

language In the Microsoft implementation, this attribute specifies the scripting language to be used with an associated script bound to the element, typically through an event handler attribute. Possible values might include **javacript**, **jscript. vbs**, and **vbscript**. Other values that include the version of the language used, such as **JavaScript1.1**, also might be possible.

style See "Core Attributes Reference," earlier in this appendix.

tabindex This attribute uses a number to identify the object's position in the tabbing order for keyboard navigation using the TAB key. Internet Explorer 5.5 applies this attribute to the **ins** element; under IE 5.5, this focus can be disabled with the **hidefocus** attribute.

title See "Core Attributes Reference," earlier in this appendix.

Attribute and Event Support

Internet Explorer 4 All attributes and events except **cite** and **datetime**.

Event Handlers
See "Events Reference," earlier in this appendix.

Example

```
<ins cite="http://www.democompany.com/changes/oct99.htm"
    date="1999-10-06T09:15:00-05:00">
The penalty clause applies to client lateness as well.
</ins>
```

Compatibility
HTML 4, 4.01, XHTML 1.0
Internet Explorer 4, 5, and 5.5
Netscape 6
Opera 4.0

Notes

- Browsers can render inserted (**<ins>**) or deleted (**<del>**) text in a different style to show the changes that have been made to the document. Eventually, a browser could have a way to show a revision history on a document. User agents that do not understand **<del>** or **<ins>** will show the information anyway, so there is no harm in adding information, only in deleting it.

- The **<ins>** element is not supported under the HTML 2 and 3.2 specifications.

<isindex> (Index Prompt)

This element indicates that a document has an associated searchable keyword index. When a browser encounters this element, it inserts a query entry field at that point in the document. The viewer can enter query terms to perform a search. This element is deprecated under the strict HTML 4 specification and should not be used.

Syntax (Transitional Only)

```
<isindex
     class="class name(s)"
     dir="ltr | rtl"
     href="url" (nonstandard but common)
     id="unique alphanumeric identifier"
     lang="language code"
     prompt="string"
     style="style information"
     title="advisory text">
```

XHTML Syntax

As an empty element, **<isindex>** requires a trailing slash for XHTML compliance:

```
<isindex />
```

Attributes Defined by Internet Explorer 4

```
language="javascript | jscript | vbs | vbscript"
```

Attributes and Events Defined by Internet Explorer 5.5

```
accesskey="key"
contenteditable=" false | true | inherit"
hidefocus="true | false"
tabindex="number"
```

Attributes

accesskey   This attribute specifies a keyboard navigation accelerator for the element. Pressing ALT or a similar key (depending on the browser and operating system) in association with the specified key selects the anchor element correlated with that key.

action   This attribute specifies the URL of the query action to be executed when the viewer presses the ENTER key. Although this attribute is not defined under any HTML specification, it is common to many browsers, particularly Internet Explorer 3, which defined it.

class   See "Core Attributes Reference," earlier in this appendix.

contenteditable   This proprietary Microsoft attribute allows users to edit content rendered in the Internet Explorer 5.5 browser. Values are **false**, **true**, and **inherit**. A value of **false** will prevent content from being edited by users; **true** will allow editing. The default value, **inherit**, applies the value of the affected element's parent element.

dir   See "Language Reference," earlier in this appendix.

hidefocus   This proprietary element, introduced with Internet Explorer 5.5, hides focus on an element's content. Focus must be applied to the element using the **tabindex** attribute.

href   The **href** attribute is used with the **<isindex>** element as a way to indicate what the search document is. Another approach is to use the **<base>** element for the document. The HTML 2 documentation suggests that this is a legal approach and browsers appear to support it; however, it is poorly documented at best.

id   See "Core Attributes Reference," earlier in this appendix.

tabindex   This attribute uses a number to identify the object's position in the tabbing order for keyboard navigation using the TAB key. Internet Explorer 5.5 applies this attribute to the **dfn** element; under IE 5.5, this focus can be disabled with the **hidefocus** attribute.

lang   See "Language Reference," earlier in this appendix.

language   In the Microsoft implementation, this attribute specifies the scripting language to be used with an associated script bound to the element, typically through an event handler attribute. Possible values might include **javascript**, **jscript**, **vbs**, and **vbscript**. Other values that include the version of the language used, such as **JavaScript1.1**, also might be possible.

prompt   This attribute allows a custom query prompt to be defined. The default prompt is "This is a searchable index. Enter search keywords." WebTV does not implement this attribute.

style   See "Core Attributes Reference," earlier in this appendix.

title   See "Core Attributes Reference," earlier in this appendix.

Attribute and Event Support

Netscape 4   prompt (**class**, **id**, **lang**, and **style** are implied.)

Internet Explorer 4   class, id, lang, language, prompt, and style

Event Handlers
None

Examples

```
<isindex action="cgi-bin/search" prompt="Enter search terms">

<isindex href="cgi-bin/search" prompt="Keywords:">

<base href="cgi-bin/search">
<isindex prompt="Enter search terms">
```

XHTML Example

```
<isindex action="cgi-bin/search" prompt="Enter search terms" />
```

Compatibility
HTML 2, 3.2, and 4 (transitional), XHTML 1.0 (?)
Internet Explorer 2, 3, 4, 5, 5.5
Netscape 1, 2, 3, 4–4.7
Opera 4.0
WebTV

Notes

- As an empty element, **<isindex>** requires no closing tag under HTML specifications. The XHTML specification, however, requires a trailing slash: **<isindex />**

- The HTML 3.2 specification only allows the **prompt** attribute, whereas HTML 2 expected a text description to accompany the search field.

- Netscape 1.1 originated the use of the **prompt** attribute. WebTV does not support this attribute.

- Originally, the W3C intended this element to be used in a document's header. Browser vendors have relaxed this usage to allow the element in a document's body. Early implementations did not support the **action** attribute and used the **<base>** element or an **href** attribute to specify a search function's URL.

- Older versions of Internet Explorer also support the **action** attribute, which specifies the URL to use for the query rather than relying on the URL set in the **<base>** element.

Internet Explorer 4 does not support the **action**, **dir**, **href**, or **title** attributes. Microsoft documentation suggests using **<input>** instead of this deprecated element.

<kbd> (Keyboard Input)

This element logically indicates text as keyboard input. A browser generally renders text enclosed by this element in a monospaced font.

Syntax

```
<kbd
    class="class name(s)"
    dir="ltr | rtl"
    id="unique alphanumeric identifier"
    lang="language code"
    style="style information"
    title="advisory text"
    onclick="script"
    ondblclick="script"
    onkeydown="script"
    onkeypress="script"
    onkeyup="script"
    onmousedown="script"
    onmousemove="script"
    onmouseout="script"
    onmouseover="script"
    onmouseup="script">

</kbd>
```

Attributes and Events Defined by Internet Explorer 4

```
    language="javascript | jscript | vbs | vbscript"
    ondragstart="script"
    onhelp="script"
    onselectstart="script"
```

Attributes and Events Defined by Internet Explorer 5.5

```
    accesskey="key"
    contenteditable=" false | true | inherit"
    hidefocus="true | false"
    tabindex="number"
```

Attributes

accesskey   This attribute specifies a keyboard navigation accelerator for the element. Pressing ALT or a similar key (depending on the browser and operating system) in association with the specified key selects the anchor element correlated with that key.

class   See "Core Attributes Reference," earlier in this appendix.

contenteditable   This proprietary Microsoft attribute allows users to edit content rendered in the Internet Explorer 5.5 browser. Values are **false**, **true**, and **inherit**. A value of **false** will prevent content from being edited by users; **true** will allow editing. The default value, **inherit**, applies the value of the affected element's parent element.

dir   See "Language Reference," earlier in this appendix.

hidefocus   This proprietary element, introduced with Internet Explorer 5.5, hides focus on an element's content. Focus must be applied to the element using the **tabindex** attribute.

id   See "Core Attributes Reference," earlier in this appendix.

lang   See "Language Reference," earlier in this appendix.

language   In the Microsoft implementation, this attribute specifies the scripting language to be used with an associated script bound to the element, typically through an event handler attribute. Possible values might include **javascript**, **jscript**, **vbs**, and **vbscript**. Other values that include the version of the language used, such as **JavaScript1.1**, also might be possible.

style   See "Core Attributes Reference," earlier in this appendix.

tabindex   This attribute uses a number to identify the object's position in the tabbing order for keyboard navigation using the TAB key. Internet Explorer 5.5 applies this attribute to the **kbd** element; under IE 5.5, this focus can be disabled with the **hidefocus** attribute.

title   See "Core Attributes Reference," earlier in this appendix.

Attribute and Event Support

Netscape 4   **class**, **id**, **lang**, and **style** are implied.

Internet Explorer 4   All attributes and events except **dir**.

Event Handlers
See "Events Reference," earlier in this appendix.

Example

```
Enter the change directory command at the prompt as shown below:<br>
<br>
<kbd>CD .. </kbd>
```

Compatibility

HTML 2, 3.2, 4, and 4.01, XHTML 1.0
Internet Explorer 2, 3, 4, 5, and 5.5
Netscape 1, 2, 3, 4–4.7, 6
Opera 4
WebTV

Note

■ The HTML 2 and 3.2 specifications support no attributes for this element.

<label> (Form Control Label)

This HTML 4 element is used to relate descriptions to form controls.

Syntax

```
<label
    accesskey="key"
    class="class name(s)"
    dir="ltr | rtl"
    for="id of control"
    id="unique alphanumeric identifier"
    lang="language code"
    style="style information"
    title="advisory text"
    onblur="script"
    onclick="script"
    ondblclick="script"
    onfocus="script"
    onkeydown="script"
    onkeypress="script"
    onkeyup="script"
    onmousedown="script"
    onmousemove="script"
    onmouseout="script"
    onmouseover="script"
    onmouseup="script">

</label>
```

Attributes and Events Defined by Internet Explorer 4

```
datafld="column name"
dataformatas="html | text"
datasrc="data source id"
language="javascript | jscript | vbs | vbscript"
ondragstart="script"
onhelp="script"
onselectstart="script"
```

Attributes and Events Defined by Internet Explorer 5.5

```
contenteditable=" false | true | inherit "
hidefocus="true | false"
tabindex="number"
```

Attributes

accesskey   This attribute specifies a keyboard navigation accelerator for the element. Pressing ALT or a similar key in association with the specified key selects the anchor element correlated with that key.

class   See "Core Attributes Reference," earlier in this appendix.

contenteditable   This proprietary Microsoft attribute allows users to edit content rendered in the Internet Explorer 5.5 browser. Values are **false**, **true**, and **inherit**. A value of **false** will prevent content from being edited by users; **true** will allow editing. The default value, **inherit**, applies the value of the affected element's parent element.

datafld   This attribute is used to indicate the column name in the data source that is bound to the content of the **<label>** element.

dataformatas   This attribute indicates whether the bound data is plain text (**text**) or HTML (**html**). The data bound with **<label>** is used to set the content of the label.

datasrc   The value of this attribute is an identifier indicating the data source to pull data from.

dir   See "Language Reference," earlier in this appendix.

for   This attribute specifies the **id** for the form control element the label references. This is optional when the label encloses the form control it is bound to. In many cases, particularly when a table is used to structure the form, the **<label>** element will not be able to enclose the associated form control, so the **for** attribute should be used. This attribute allows more than one label to be associated with the same control by creating multiple references.

hidefocus   This proprietary element, introduced with Internet Explorer 5.5, hides focus on an element's content. Focus must be applied to the element using the **tabindex** attribute.

id   See "Core Attributes Reference," earlier in this appendix.

lang   See "Language Reference," earlier in this appendix.

language   In the Microsoft implementation, this attribute specifies the scripting language to be used with an associated script bound to the element, typically through an event handler attribute. Possible values might include **javascript**, **jscript**, **vbs**, and **vbscript**. Other values that include the version of the language used, such as **JavaScript1.1**, also might be possible.

style   See "Core Attributes Reference," earlier in this appendix.

tabindex   This attribute uses a number to identify the object's position in the tabbing order for keyboard navigation using the TAB key. Internet Explorer 5.5 applies this attribute to the **label** element; under IE 5.5, this focus can be disabled with the **hidefocus** attribute.

title   See "Core Attributes Reference," earlier in this appendix.

Attribute and Event Support

Internet Explorer 4   All W3C-defined attributes and events except **dir**, **onblur**, and **onfocus**, and all attributes and events defined by Internet Explorer 4.

Event Handlers
See "Events Reference," earlier in this appendix.

Examples

```
<form>
    <label id="usernamelabel">Name
    <input type="text" id="username">
    </label>
</form>

<form>
  <table>
    <tr>
      <td><label for="username">Name</label></td>
      <td><input type="text" id="username"></td>
    </tr>
  </table>
</form>
```

Compatibility
HTML 4, 4.01, XHTML 1.0
Internet Explorer 4, 5, and 5.5
Netscape 6
Opera 4.0

Notes

■ To associate a label with another control implicitly, make the control the contents of the **label**. In this case, a **<label>** element might contain only one other control element. The label itself might be positioned before or after the associated control. If it is impossible to enclose the associated form control, the **for** attribute can be used.

■ The HTML 4 specification defines the **onblur** and **onfocus** events for **<label>**. However, Internet Explorer 4 does not document their use.

<layer> (Content Layers)

This Netscape-specific element allows the definition of overlapping content layers that can be exactly positioned, hidden or shown, rendered transparent or opaque, reordered front to back, and nested. The functionality of layers is available using CSS positioning facilities; page developers are advised not to use the **<layer>** element.

Syntax (Defined by Netscape 4)

```
<layer
      abve="layer name"
      background="URL of background image"
      below="layer name"
      bgcolor="color value"
      class="class name(s)"
      clip="clip region coordinates in x1, y1, x2, y2 form"
      height="percentage | pixels"
      id="unique alphanumeric identifier"
      left="pixels"
      name="string"
      pagex="horizontal pixel position of layer"
      pagey="vertical pixel position of layer"
      src="url of layer's contents"
      style="style information"
      title="advisory text"
      top="pixels"
      visibility="hide | inherit | show"
      width="percentage | pixels"
      z-index="number"
      onblur="script"
      onfocus="script"
      onload="script"
      onmouseout="script"
      onmouseover="script">

</layer>
```

Attributes

above   This attribute contains the name of the layer (as set with the **name** attribute) to be rendered directly above the current layer.

background   This attribute contains the URL of a background pattern for the layer. Like backgrounds for the document as a whole, the image might tile.

below   This value of this attribute is the name of the layer to be rendered below the current layer.

bgcolor   This attribute specifies a layer's background color. The attribute's value can be either a named color, such as **red**, or a color specified in the hexadecimal *#RRGGBB* format, such as #FF0000.

class   See "Core Attributes Reference," earlier in this appendix.

clip   This attribute clips a layer's content to a specified rectangle. All layer content outside that rectangle will be rendered transparent. The **clip** rectangle is defined by two *x,y* pairs that correspond to the top *x*, left *y*, bottom *x*, and right *y* coordinate of the rectangle. The coordinates are relative to the layer's origin point, **0,0** in its top-left corner, and might have nothing to do with the pixel coordinates of the screen.

height   This attribute is used to set the height of the layer either in pixels or as a percentage of the screen or region the layer is contained within.

id   See "Core Attributes Reference," earlier in this appendix.

left   This attribute specifies in pixels the left offset of the layer. The offset is relative to its parent layer, if it has one, or to the left browser margin if it does not.

name   This attribute assigns the layer a name that can be referenced by programs in a client-side scripting language. The **id** attribute also can be used.

pagex   This attribute is used to set the horizontal pixel position of the layer relative to the document window rather than any enclosing layer.

pagey   This attribute is used to set the vertical pixel position of the layer relative to the document window rather than any enclosing layer.

src   This attribute specifies the URL that contains the content to include in the layer. Using this attribute with an empty element is a good way to preserve layouts under older browsers.

style   See "Core Attributes Reference," earlier in this appendix.

title   See "Core Attributes Reference," earlier in this appendix.

top   This attribute specifies in pixels the top offset of the layer. The offset is relative to its parent layer if it has one, or the top browser margin if it is not enclosed in another layer.

visibility   This attribute specifies whether a layer is hidden (**hidden**), shown (**show**), or inherits (**inherits**) its visibility from the layer enclosing it.

width   This attribute specifies a layer's width in pixels or as a percentage value of the enclosing layer or browser width.

z-index   This attribute specifies a layer's stacking order relative to other layers. Position is specified with positive integers, with "1" indicating the bottommost layer.

Attribute and Event Support

Netscape 4   All attributes

Event Handlers
See "Events Reference," earlier in this appendix.

Examples

```
<layer name="scene" bgcolor="#00FFFF">
  <layer name="Shaq" left="100" top="100">
    <img src="shaq.gif">
  </layer>
  <layer name="Rodman" left="200" top="100"
         visibility="hidden">
    <img src="pinkhair.gif">
  </layer>
</layer>

<!-- The better way to do layers -->
<layer src="contents.htm" left="20" top="20"
       height="80%" width="80%">
</layer>
```

Compatibility
Netscape 4–4.7

Notes

■   This element likely will fall out of fashion because it lacks cross-browser compatibility. The functionality of **<layer>** is possible using the positioning features in CSS; page developers are discouraged from using the **<layer>** element.

■ Applets, plug-ins, and other embedded media forms, generically called *objects*, can be included in a layer; however, they will float to the top of all other layers even if their containing layer is obscured.

`<legend>` (Field Legend)

This HTML 4 element is used to assign a caption to a set of form fields as defined by the **`<fieldset>`** element.

Syntax

```
<legend
    accesskey="character"
    align="bottom | left | right | top" (transitional)
    class="class name(s)"
    dir="ltr | rtl"
    id="unique alphanumeric identifier"
    lang="language code"
    style="style information"
    title="advisory text"
    onclick="script"
    ondblclick="script"
    onkeydown="script"
    onkeypress="script"
    onkeyup="script"
    onmousedown="script"
    onmousemove="script"
    onmouseout="script"
    onmouseover="script"
    onmouseup="script">

</legend>
```

Attributes and Events Defined by Internet Explorer 4

```
    align="center"
    language="javascript | jscript | vbs | vbscript"
    valign="bottom | top"
    ondragstart="script"
    onhelp="script"
```

Attributes and Events Defined by Internet Explorer 5.5

```
contenteditable=" false | true | inherit"
hidefocus="true | false"
tabindex="number"
```

Attributes

accesskey   This attribute specifies a keyboard navigation accelerator for the element. Pressing ALT or a similar key in association with the specified key selects the form section or the legend itself.

align   This attribute indicates where the legend value should be positioned within the border created by a **<fieldset>** element. The default position for the legend is the upper-left corner. It also is possible to position the legend to the right by setting the attribute to **right**. The specification defines **bottom** and **top** as well. Microsoft defines the use of **center** and also defines another attribute, **valign**, to set the vertical alignment separately. Future support for **valign** is unclear; page designers are encouraged to use only the **align** attribute and to eventually rely on style sheets for legend positioning.

class   See "Core Attributes Reference," earlier in this appendix.

contenteditable   This proprietary Microsoft attribute allows users to edit content rendered in the Internet Explorer 5.5 browser. Values are **false**, **true**, and **inherit**. A value of **false** will prevent content from being edited by users; **true** will allow editing. The default value, **inherit**, applies the value of the affected element's parent element.

dir   See "Language Reference," earlier in this appendix.

hidefocus   This proprietary element, introduced with Internet Explorer 5.5, hides focus on an element's content. Focus must be applied to the element using the **tabindex** attribute.

id   See "Core Attributes Reference," earlier in this appendix.

lang   See "Language Reference," earlier in this appendix.

language   In the Microsoft implementation, this attribute specifies the scripting language to be used with an associated script bound to the element, typically through an event handler attribute. Possible values might include **javascript**, **jscript**, **vbs**, and **vbscript**. Other values that include the version of the language used, such as **JavaScript1.1**, also might be possible.

style   See "Core Attributes Reference," earlier in this appendix.

tabindex   This attribute uses a number to identify the object's position in the tabbing order for keyboard navigation using the TAB key. Internet Explorer 5.5 applies this attribute to the **legend** element; under IE 5.5, this focus can be disabled with the **hidefocus** attribute.

title See "Core Attributes Reference," earlier in this appendix.

valign This Microsoft-specific attribute is used to set whether the legend appears on the **bottom** or the **top** of the border defined by the enclosing **<fieldset>** element. The attribute probably will be dropped, as it is nonstandard.

Attribute and Event Support

Internet Explorer 4 All attributes and events except **accesskey** and **dir**.

Event Handlers

See "Events Reference," earlier in this appendix.

Example

```
<form>
<fieldset>
   <legend align="top">User Information</legend>
   First Name: <input type="text" id="firstname"
   size="20"><br>
   Last Name: <input type="text" id="lastname"
   size="20"><br>
 </fieldset>
</form>
```

Compatibility

HTML 4, 4.01, XHTML 1.0
Internet Explorer 4, 5, and 5.5
Netscape 6
Opera 4.0

Notes

■ The **<legend>** element should occur only within the **<fieldset>** element. There should be only one **<legend>** per **<fieldset>** element.

■ The legend improves accessibility when the **fieldset** is rendered nonvisually.

■ The Microsoft implementation can use the **center** option in the **align** attribute. Microsoft also defines the **valign** attribute for legend positioning. However, the **valign** attribute does not appear to work consistently.

■ WebTV and Netscape do not yet support this element.

<li> (List Item)

This element is used to indicate a list item as contained in an ordered list (**<ol>**), unordered list (**<ul>**), or older list styles such as **<dir>** and **<menu>**.

Syntax

```
<li
    class="class name(s)"
    dir="ltr | rtl"
    id="unique alphanumeric identifier"
    lang="language code"
    style="style information"
    title="advisory text"
    type="circle | disc | square | a | A | i | I | 1"
        (transitional)
    value="number" (transitional)
    onclick="script"
    ondblclick="script"
    onkeydown="script"
    onkeypress="script"
    onkeyup="script"
    onmousedown="script"
    onmousemove="script"
    onmouseout="script"
    onmouseover="script"
    onmouseup="script">
```

XHTML Syntax

Under the XHTML 1.0 specification, the closing tag **</li>** ceases to be optional and must be used with this element:

```
<li></li>
```

Attributes and Events Defined by Internet Explorer 4

```
language="javascript | jscript | vbs | vbscript"
ondragstart="script"
onhelp="script"
onselectstart="script"
```

Attributes and Events Defined by Internet Explorer 5.5

```
accesskey="key"
contenteditable=" false | true | inherit"
hidefocus="true | false"
tabindex="number"
```

Attributes

accesskey   This attribute specifies a keyboard navigation accelerator for the element. Pressing ALT or a similar key (depending on the browser and operating system) in association with the specified key selects the anchor element correlated with that key.

class   See "Core Attributes Reference," earlier in this appendix.

contenteditable   This proprietary Microsoft attribute allows users to edit content rendered in the Internet Explorer 5.5 browser. Values are **false, true**, and **inherit**. A value of **false** will prevent content from being edited by users; **true** will allow editing. The default value, **inherit**, applies the value of the affected element's parent element.

dir   See "Language Reference," earlier in this appendix.

hidefocus   This proprietary element, introduced with Internet Explorer 5.5, hides focus on an element's content. Focus must be applied to the element using the **tabindex** attribute.

id   See "Core Attributes Reference," earlier in this appendix.

lang   See "Language Reference," earlier in this appendix.

language   In the Microsoft implementation, this attribute specifies the scripting language to be used with an associated script bound to the element, typically through an event handler attribute. Possible values might include **javascript, jscript, vbs**, and **vbscript**. Other values that include the version of the language used, such as **JavaScript1.1**, also might be possible.

style   See "Core Attributes Reference," earlier in this appendix.

tabindex   This attribute uses a number to identify the object's position in the tabbing order for keyboard navigation using the TAB key. Internet Explorer 5.5 applies this attribute to the li element; under IE 5.5, this focus can be disabled with the **hidefocus** attribute.

title   See "Core Attributes Reference," earlier in this appendix.

type   This attribute indicates the bullet type used in unordered lists or the numbering type used in ordered lists. For ordered lists, a value of **a** indicates lowercase letters, **A** indicates uppercase letters, **i** indicates lowercase Roman numerals, **I** indicates uppercase Roman numerals, and **1** indicates numbers. For unordered lists, values are used to specify bullet types. Although the browser is free to set bullet styles, a value of **disc** generally specifies a filled circle, a value of **circle** specifies an empty circle, and a value of **b** specifies a filled square. Browsers such as WebTV might include other bullet shapes like triangles.

value   This attribute indicates the current number of items in an ordered list as defined by the <ol> element. Regardless of the value of **type** being used to set Roman numerals or letters, the only allowed value for this attribute is a number. List items that follow will continue numbering from the value set. The **value** attribute has no meaning for unordered lists.

Attribute and Event Support

Netscape 4   class, id, style, lang, type, and value

Internet Explorer 4   All attributes and events except dir

WebTV   type and value

Event Handlers
See "Events Reference," earlier in this appendix.

Examples

```
<ul>
   <li type="circle">First list item is a circle
   <li type="square">Second list item is a square
   <li type="disc">Third list item is a square
</ul>
<ol>
   <li type="i">Roman Numerals
   <li type="a" value="3">Second list item is letter C
   <li type="a">Continue list in lowercase letters
</ol>
```

XHTML Example

```
<ul>
   <li>First list item </li>
   <li>Second list item </li>
   <li>Third list item</li>
</ul>
```

Compatibility
HTML 2, 3.2, 4, 4.01, XHTML 1.0
Internet Explorer 2, 3, 4, 5, and 5.5
Netscape 1, 2, 3, 4–4.7, 6
Opera 4.0
WebTV

Notes

■ Under the strict HTML 4.01 definition, the **<li>** element loses the **type** and **value** attributes, as these functions can be performed with style sheets.

- Whereas bullet styles can be set explicitly, browsers tend to change styles for bullets when **<ul>** lists are nested. However, ordered lists generally do not change style automatically, nor do they support outline style number (1.1, 1.1.1, and so on).

- The closing tag **</li>** is optional under HTML specifications and is not commonly used.

- XHTML 1.0 makes the closing tag **</li>** mandatory.

<link> (Link to External Files or Set Relationships)

This empty element specifies relationships between the current document and other documents. Possible uses for this element include defining a relational framework for navigation and linking the document to a style sheet.

Syntax

```
<link
    charset="charset list from RFC 2045"
    class="class name(s)"
    dir="ltr | rtl"
    href="URL"
    hreflang="language code"
    id="unique alphanumeric identifier"
    lang="language code"
    media="all | aural | braille | print | projection |
          screen | other"
    rel="relationship value"
    rev="relationship value"
    style="style information"
    target="frame name" (transitional)
    title="advisory information"
    type="content type"
    onclick="script"
    ondblclick="script"
    onkeydown="script"
    onkeypress="script"
    onkeyup="script"
    onmousedown="script"
    onmousemove="script"
    onmouseout="script"
    onmouseover="script"
    onmouseup="script">
```

XHTML Syntax

Under the XHTML 1.0 specification, the **<link>** element requires a trailing slash:

```
<link />
```

Attributes Defined by Internet Explorer 4

```
disabled
```

Attributes Defined by Netscape 4

```
src="url"
```

Attributes

charset   This attribute specifies the character set used by the linked document. Allowed values for this attribute are character set names, such as EUC-JP, as defined in RFC 2045.

class   See "Core Attributes Reference," earlier in this appendix.

dir   See "Language Reference," earlier in this appendix.

disabled   This Microsoft-defined attribute is used to disable a link relationship. The presence of the attribute is all that is required to remove a linking relationship. In conjunction with scripting, this attribute could be used to turn on and off various style sheet relationships.

href   This attribute specifies the URL of the linked resource. A URL might be absolute or relative.

hreflang   This attribute is used to indicate the language of the linked resource. See "Language Reference," earlier in this appendix for information on allowed values.

id   See "Core Attributes Reference," earlier in this appendix.

lang   See "Language Reference," earlier in this appendix.

media   This attribute specifies the destination medium for any linked style information, as indicated when the **rel** attribute is set to **stylesheet**. The value of the attribute might be a single media descriptor such as **screen** or a comma-separated list. Possible values for this attribute include **all**, **aural**, **braille**, **print**, **projection**, and **screen**. Other values also might be defined, depending on the browser. Internet Explorer supports **all**, **print**, and **screen** as values for this attribute.

rel   This attribute names a relationship between the linked document and the current document. Possible values for this attribute include **alternate**, **bookmark**, **chapter**, **contents**, **copyright**, **glossary**, **help**, **index**, **next**, **prev**, **section**, **start**, **stylesheet**, and **subsection**. The most common use of this attribute is to specify a link to an external style sheet. The **rel** attribute is set to **stylesheet**, and the **href** attribute is set to the URL of an external style sheet to format the page. WebTV also supports the use of the value **next** for **rel** to preload the next page in a document series.

rev   The value of rev attribute shows the relationship of the current document to the linked document, as defined by the **href** attribute. The attribute thus defines the reverse relationship compared to the value of the **rel** attribute. Values for the **rev** attribute are similar to the possible values for **rel**. They might include **alternate, bookmark, chapter, contents, copyright, glossary, help, index, next, prev, section, start, stylesheet,** and **subsection**.

style   See "Core Attributes Reference," earlier in this appendix.

target   The value of the **target** attribute is used to define the frame or window name that has the defined linking relationship or that will show the rendering of any linked resource.

title   See "Core Attributes Reference," earlier in this appendix.

type   This attribute is used to define the type of the content linked to. The value of the attribute should be a MIME type such as **text/html, text/css,** and so on. The common use of this attribute is to define the type of style sheet linked and the most common current value is **text/css,** which indicates a Cascading Style Sheet format.

Attribute and Event Support

Netscape 4   rel, src, and type. (**class, id, lang,** and **style** are implied.)

Internet Explorer 4   disabled, href, id, media (**all | print | screen**), rel, rev, title, and type

WebTV   href and rel (value="next")

Event Handlers
See "Event Reference," earlier in this appendix.

Examples

```
<link href="products.htm" rel="parent">

<link href="corpstyle.css" rel="stylesheet" type="text/css" media="all">

<link href="nextpagetoload.htm" rel="next">
```

XHTML Example

```
<link href="products.htm" rel="parent" />
```

Compatibility
HTML 2, 3.2, 4, 4.01, XHTML 1.0
Netscape 4–4.7, 6
Internet Explorer 3, 4, 5, and 5.5
WebTV

APPENDIX A

Notes

- As an empty element **<link>** has no closing tag.
- Under XTML 1.0, empty elements such as **<link>** require a trailing slash: **<link />**
- The **<link>** element can occur only in the **<head>** element; there could be multiple occurrences of the element.
- HTML 3.2 defines only the **href**, **rel**, **rev**, and **title** attributes for the **<link>** element.
- HTML 2 defines the **href**, **methods**, **rel**, **rev**, **title**, and **urn** attributes for the **<link>** element. The **methods** and **urn** attributes were later removed from specifications.
- The HTML 4.01 specification defines event handlers for the **<link>** element, but it is unclear how they would be used.

<listing> (Code Listing)

This deprecated element from HTML 2 is used to indicate a code listing; it is no longer part of the HTML standard. Text tends to be rendered in a smaller size within this element. Otherwise, the **<pre>** element should be used instead of **<listing>** to indicate preformatted text.

Syntax (HTML 2; Deprecated)

```
<listing>
</listing>
```

Attributes and Events Defined by Internet Explorer 4

```
class="class name(s)"
id="unique alphanumeric string"
lang="language code"
language="javascript | jscript | vbs | vbscript"
style="style information"
title="advisory text"
onclick="script"
ondblclick="script"
ondragstart="script"
onhelp="script"
onkeydown="script"
onkeypress="script"
onkeyup="script"
onmousedown="script"
onmousemove="script"
onmouseout="script"
onmouseover="script"
onmouseup="script"
onselectstart="script">
```

Attributes and Events Defined by Internet Explorer 5.5

```
accesskey="key"
contenteditable=" false | true | inherit"
dir="ltr | rtl"
hidefocus="true | false"
tabindex="number"
```

Attributes

accesskey   This attribute specifies a keyboard navigation accelerator for the element. Pressing ALT or a similar key (depending on the browser and operating system) in association with the specified key selects the anchor element correlated with that key.

class   See "Core Attributes Reference," earlier in this appendix.

contenteditable   This proprietary Microsoft attribute allows users to edit content rendered in the Internet Explorer 5.5 browser. Values are **false**, **true**, and **inherit**. A value of **false** will prevent content from being edited by users; **true** will allow editing. The default value, **inherit**, applies the value of the affected element's parent element.

dir   See "Language Reference," earlier in this appendix.

hidefocus   This proprietary element, introduced with Internet Explorer 5.5, hides focus on an element's content. Focus must be applied to the element using the **tabindex** attribute.

id   See "Core Attributes Reference," earlier in this appendix.

lang   See "Language Reference," earlier in this appendix.

language   In the Microsoft implementation, this attribute specifies the scripting language to be used with an associated script bound to the element, typically through an event handler attribute. Possible values might include **javascript**, **jscript**, **vbs**, and **vbscript**. Other values that include the version of the language used, such as **JavaScript1.1**, also might be possible.

style   See "Core Attributes Reference," earlier in this appendix.

tabindex   This attribute uses a number to identify the object's position in the tabbing order for keyboard navigation using the TAB key. Internet Explorer 5.5 applies this attribute to the **listing** element; under IE 5.5, this focus can be disabled with the **hidefocus** attribute.

title   See "Core Attributes Reference," earlier in this appendix.

Attribute and Event Support

Internet Explorer 4   All attributes

Event Handlers

See "Events Reference," earlier in this appendix.

Example

```
<listing>
This is a code listing. The preformatted text element &lt;PRE&gt;
should be used instead of this depreciated element.
</listing>
```

Compatibility

HTML 2
Internet Explorer 2, 3, 4, 5, and 5.6
Netscape 1, 2, 3, 4–4.7
Opera 6
WebTV

Notes

- As a deprecated element, this element should not be used. This element is not supported by HTML 4. It is still documented by many browser vendors, however, and does creep into some pages. The **<pre>** element should be used instead of **<listing>**.

- It appears that Netscape and Internet Explorer browsers also make text within **<listing>** one size smaller than normal text, probably because the HTML 2 specification suggested that 132 characters fit to a typical line rather than 80.

- Netscape does not document support for this element, although it is still supported. (Netscape 6 Preview Release 2 did not appear to support this element.)

<map> (Client-Side Image Map)

This element is used to implement client-side image maps. The element is used to define a map to associate locations on an image with a destination URL. Each hot region or hyperlink mapping is defined by an enclosed **<area>** element. A map is bound to a particular image through the use of the **usemap** attribute in the **<img>** element, which is set to the name of the map.

Syntax

```
<map
    class="class name(s)"
    dir="ltr | rtl"
    id="unique alphanumeric identifier"
    lang="language code"
    name="unique alphanumeric identifier"
    style="style information"
    title="advisory text"
```

```
onclick="script"
ondblclick="script"
onkeydown="script"
onkeypress="script"
onkeyup="script"
onmousedown="script"
onmousemove="script"
onmouseout="script"
onmouseover="script"
onmouseup="script">

<area> elements

</map>
```

Events Defined by Internet Explorer 4

```
ondragstart="script"
onhelp="script"
onselectstart="script"
```

Attributes

class   See "Core Attributes Reference," earlier in this appendix.

dir   See "Language Reference," earlier in this appendix.

id   See "Core Attributes Reference," earlier in this appendix.

lang   See "Language Reference," earlier in this appendix.

name   Like **id**, this attribute is used to define a name associated with the element. In the case of the **<map>** element, the **name** attribute is the common way to define the name of the image map to be referenced by the **usemap** attribute within the **<img>** element.

style   See "Core Attributes Reference," earlier in this appendix.

title   See "Core Attributes Reference," earlier in this appendix.

Attribute and Event Support

Netscape 4   **name** (**class**, **id**, **lang**, and **style** are implied.)

Internet Explorer 4   All attributes and events except **dir**.

WebTV   **name**

Event Handlers

See "Events Reference," earlier in this appendix.

Example

```
<map name="mainmap">
    <area shape="circle" coords="200,250,25"
        href="file1.htm">
    <area shape="rectangle" coords="50,50,100,100"
        href="file2.htm#important">
    <area shape="default" nohref>
</map>
```

Compatibility

HTML 3.2, 4, 4.01, XHTML 1.0
Internet Explorer 2, 3, 4, 5, and 5.5
Netscape 1, 2, 3, 4–4.7, 6
Opera
WebTV

Notes

- HTML 3.2 supports only the **name** attribute for the **<map>** element.
- Client-side image maps are not supported under HTML 2. They were first suggested by Spyglass and later incorporated in Netscape and other browsers.

<marquee> (Marquee Display)

This proprietary element specifies a scrolling, sliding, or bouncing text marquee. This is primarily a Microsoft-specific element, although a few other browsers, notably WebTV, support it as well.

Syntax (Defined by Internet Explorer 4)

```
<marquee
    behavior="alternate | scroll | slide"
    bgcolor="color name | #RRGGBB"
    class="class name(s)"
    datafld="column name"
    dataformatas="html | text"
    datasrc="data source id"
    direction="down | left | right | up"
    height="pixels or percentage"
    hspace="pixels"
    id="unique alphanumeric identifier"
```

```
lang="language code"
language="javascript | jscript | vbs | vbscript"
loop="infinite | number"
scrollamount="pixels"
scrolldelay="milliseconds"
style="style information"
title="advisory text"
truespeed
vspace="pixels"
width="pixels or percentage"
onafterupdate="script"
onblur="script"
onbounce="script"
onclick="script"
ondblclick="script"
ondragstart="script"
onfinish="script"
onfocus="script"
onhelp="script"
onkeydown="script"
onkeypress="script"
onkeyup="script"
onmousedown="script"
onmousemove="script"
onmouseout="script"
onmouseover="script"
onmouseup="script"
onresize="script"
onrowenter="script"
onrowexit="script"
onselectstart="script"
onstart="script">

Marquee text

</marquee>
```

Attributes and Events Defined by Internet Explorer 5.0

```
dir="ltr | rtl"
```

Attributes and Events Defined by Internet Explorer 5.5

```
accesskey="key"
contenteditable=" false | true | inherit"
```

```
hidefocus="true | false"
tabindex="number"
```

Attributes Defined by WebTV

```
align="bottom | center | left | right | top"
transparency="number (0-100)"
```

Attributes

accesskey   This attribute specifies a keyboard navigation accelerator for the element. Pressing ALT or a similar key (depending on the browser and operating system) in association with the specified key selects the anchor element correlated with that key.

align   This WebTV-specific attribute is used to indicate how the marquee should be aligned with surrounding text. The alignment values and rendering are similar to other embedded objects such as images. The default value for this attribute under WebTV is **left**. Microsoft Internet Explorer no longer supports this attribute.

behavior   This attribute controls the movement of marquee text across the marquee. The **alternate** option causes text to completely cross the marquee field in one direction and then cross in the opposite direction. A value of **scroll** for the attribute causes text to wrap around and start over again. This is the default value for a marquee. A value of **slide** for this attribute causes text to cross the marquee field and stop when its leading character reaches the opposite side.

bgcolor   This attribute specifies the marquee's background color. The value for the attribute can either be a color name or a color value defined in the hexadecimal #*RRGGBB* format.

class   See "Core Attributes Reference," earlier in this appendix.

contenteditable   This proprietary Microsoft attribute allows users to edit content rendered in the Internet Explorer 5.5 browser. Values are **false**, **true**, and **inherit**. A value of **false** will prevent content from being edited by users; **true** will allow editing. The default value, **inherit**, applies the value of the affected element's parent element.

datafld   This attribute is used to indicate the column name in the data source that is bound to the <**marquee**> element.

dataformatas   This attribute indicates whether the bound data is plain text (**text**) or HTML (**html**). The data bound with <**marquee**> is used to set the message that is scrolled.

datasrc   The value of this attribute is set to an identifier indicating the data source to pull data from. Bound data is used to set the message that is scrolled in the <**marquee**>.

dir   See "Language Reference," earlier in this appendix.

direction   This attribute specifies the direction in which the marquee should scroll. The default is **left**. Other possible values for **direction** include **down, right**, and **up**. WebTV does not support the **down** and **up** values.

height   This attribute specifies the height of the marquee in pixels or as a percentage of the window.

hidefocus   This proprietary element, introduced with Internet Explorer 5.5, hides focus on an element's content. Focus must be applied to the element using the **tabindex** attribute.

hspace   This attribute indicates the horizontal space in pixels between the marquee and surrounding content.

id   See "Core Attributes Reference," earlier in this appendix.

lang   See "Language Reference," earlier in this appendix.

language   In the Microsoft implementation, this attribute specifies the scripting language to be used with an associated script bound to the element, typically through an event handler attribute. Possible values might include **javascript, jscript, vbs**, and **vbscript**. Other values that include the version of the language used, such as **JavaScript1.1**, also might be possible.

loop   This attribute indicates the number of times the marquee content should loop. By default, a marquee loops infinitely unless the **behavior** attribute is set to **slide**. It also is possible to use a value of **infinite** or **−1** to set the text to loop indefinitely.

scrollamount   This attribute specifies the width in pixels between successive displays of the scrolling text in the marquee.

scrolldelay   This attribute specifies the delay in milliseconds between successive displays of the text in the marquee.

style   See "Core Attributes Reference," earlier in this appendix.

tabindex   This attribute uses a number to identify the object's position in the tabbing order for keyboard navigation using the TAB key. Internet Explorer 5.5 applies this attribute to the **marquee** element; under IE 5.5, this focus can be disabled with the **hidefocus** attribute.

title   See "Core Attributes Reference," earlier in this appendix.

transparency   In the WebTV implementation, this attribute specifies the marquee's degree of transparency. Values range from **0** (totally opaque) to **100** (totally transparent). A value of **50** is optimized for fast rendering.

truespeed   When this attribute is present, it indicates that the **scrolldelay** value should be honored for its exact value. If the attribute is not present, any values less than 60 are rounded up to 60 milliseconds.

vspace   This attribute indicates the vertical space in pixels between the marquee and surrounding content.

width   This attribute specifies the width of the marquee in pixels or as a percentage of the enclosing window.

Attribute and Event Support

Internet Explorer 4   All Microsoft-defined attributes and events.

WebTV   align, behavior, bgcolor, direction, **height**, hspace, loop, **scrollamount**, **scrolldelay**, **transparency**, vspace, and **width**. (Note: WebTV supports only the **left** and **right** values for the **direction** attribute.)

Event Handlers

The **<marquee>** element has a few unique events. For example, an event is triggered when the text bounces off one side or another on the marquee. This can be caught with the **onbounce** event handler attribute. When the text first starts scrolling, the start event fires, which can be caught with **onstart**; when the marquee is done, a finish event fires, which can be caught with **onfinish**. The other events are common to HTML 4 elements with Microsoft extensions.

Examples

```
<marquee behavior="alternate">
SPECIAL VALUE !!! This week only !!!
</marquee>

<marquee id="marquee1" bgcolor="red" direction="right" height="30"
        width="80%" hspace="10" vspace="10">
The super scroller scrolls again!!
More fun than a barrel of &lt;BLINK&gt; elements.
</marquee>
```

Compatibility

Internet Explorer 3, 4, 5,and 5.5
WebTV

Note

■ The **<marquee>** element is supported only by Microsoft and WebTV.

<menu> (Menu List)

This element is used to indicate a short list of items that can occur in a menu of choices. Like the ordered and unordered lists, the individual items in the list are indicated by the **<li>** element. Most browsers render the **<menu>** element exactly the same as the unordered list, so there is little reason to use it. Under the HTML 4 strict specification, **<menu>** is no longer supported.

Syntax (Transitional Only)

```
<menu
    class="class name(s)"
    compact
    dir="ltr | rtl"
    id="unique alphanumeric string"
    lang="language code"
    style="style information"
    title="advisory text"
    onclick="script"
    ondblclick="script"
    onkeydown="script"
    onkeypress="script"
    onkeyup="script"
    onmousedown="script"
    onmousemove="script"
    onmouseout="script"
    onmouseover="script"
    onmouseup="script">

</menu>
```

Events Defined by Internet Explorer 4

```
    ondragstart="script"
    onhelp="script"
    onselectstart="script"
```

Attributes and Events Defined by Internet Explorer 5.5

```
    accesskey="key"
    contenteditable=" false | true | inherit"
    hidefocus="true | false"
    tabindex="number"
```

Attributes

accesskey   This attribute specifies a keyboard navigation accelerator for the element. Pressing ALT or a similar key (depending on the browser and operating system) in association with the specified key selects the anchor element correlated with that key.

class   See "Core Attributes Reference," earlier in this appendix.

compact   This attribute indicates that the list should be rendered in a compact style. Few browsers actually change the rendering of the list regardless of the presence of this attribute. The **compact** attribute requires no value.

contenteditable   This proprietary Microsoft attribute allows users to edit content rendered in the Internet Explorer 5.5 browser. Values are **false**, **true**, and **inherit**. A value of **false** will prevent content from being edited by users; **true** will allow editing. The default value, **inherit**, applies the value of the affected element's parent element.

dir   See "Language Reference," earlier in this appendix.

hidefocus   This proprietary element, introduced with Internet Explorer 5.5, hides focus on an element's content. Focus must be applied to the element using the **tabindex** attribute.

id   See "Core Attributes Reference," earlier in this appendix.

lang   See "Language Reference," earlier in this appendix.

style   See "Core Attributes Reference," earlier in this appendix.

tabindex   This attribute uses a number to identify the object's position in the tabbing order for keyboard navigation using the TAB key. Internet Explorer 5.5 applies this attribute to the **menu** element; under IE 5.5, this focus can be disabled with the **hidefocus** attribute.

title   See "Core Attributes Reference," earlier in this appendix.

Attribute and Event Support

Netscape 4   class, **id**, **lang**, and **style**

Internet Explorer 4   All attributes and events except **compact** and **dir**.

Event Handlers
See "Events Reference," earlier in this appendix.

Example

```
<h2>Taco List</h2>
  <menu>
    <li>Fish
    <li>Pork
    <li>Beef
    <li>Chicken
  </menu>
```

Compatibility

HTML 2, 3.2, 4 (transitional), 4.01 (transitional), XHTML 1.0
Internet Explorer 2, 3, 4, 5, and 5.5
Netscape 1, 2, 3, 4–4.7, 6
Opera 4.0
WebTV

Notes

- Under the HTML 4.01 strict specification, this element is not defined. Because most browsers simply render this style of list as an unordered list, using the **<ul>** element instead is preferable.

- Most browsers tend not to support the **compact** attribute.

- The HTML 2.0 and 3.2 specifications support only the **compact** attribute.

<meta> (Meta-Information)

This element specifies general information about a document, which can be used in document indexing. It also allows a document to define fields in the HTTP response header when it is sent from the server. A common use of this element is for *client-pull* page loading, which allows a document to automatically load another document after a specified delay.

Syntax

```
<meta
    content="string"
    dir="ltr | rtl"
    http-equiv="http header string"
    lang="language code"
    name="name of meta-information"
    scheme="scheme type">
```

XHTML Syntax

As an empty element, **<meta>** requires a trailing slash for XHTML 1.0 compatibility:

```
<meta />
```

Attributes Defined by WebTV

```
    url="url"
```

Attributes

CONTENT   This attribute contains the actual meta-information. The form of the actual meta-information varies greatly, depending on the value set for **name**.

dir   This attribute defines the text direction (left to right or right to left) of the content of the <meta> element, as defined by the **content** attribute.

http-equiv   This attribute binds the meta-information in the **content** attribute to an HTTP response header. If this attribute is present, the **name** attribute should not be used. The **http-equiv** attribute often is used to create a document that automatically loads another document after a set time. This is called *client-pull*. An example of a client-pull **<meta>** element is

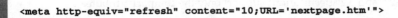
```
<meta http-equiv="refresh" content="10;URL='nextpage.htm'">
```

Note that the **content** attribute contains two values. The first is the number of seconds to wait, and the second is the identifier URL and the URL to load after the specified time.

lang   This attribute is the language code associated with the language used in the **content** attribute.

name   This attribute associates a name with the meta-information contained in the **content** attribute. If present, the **http-equiv** attribute should not be used.

scheme   The scheme attribute is used to indicate the expected format of the value of the **content** attribute. The particular scheme also can be used in conjunction with the meta-data profile as indicated by the **profile** attribute for the **<head>** element.

Attribute and Event Support

Netscape 4   content, http-equiv, and **name**

Internet Explorer 4   All attributes except **dir**.

WebTV   content, http-equiv, and **url**

Event Handlers
None

Examples

```
<!-- Use of the meta element to assist document indexing -->
<meta name="keywords" content="html, scripting"
      scheme="Lycos">

<!-- Use of the meta element to implement client-pull to automatically
```

```
        load a page -->
<meta http-equiv="refresh"
      content="3;URL='http://www.pint.com/'">

<!-- Use of the META element to add rating information -->
<meta http-equiv="PICS-Label" content="(PICS-1.1
                'http://www.rsac.org/ratingsv01.html'
                1 gen true comment 'RSACi North America
                Server' by 'webmaster@bigcompany.com'
                for 'http://www.bigcompany.com' on
                '1999.05.26T13:05-0500'
                r (n 0 s 0 v 0 1 1))">
```

XHTML Example

```
<meta name="keywords" content="html, scripting" />
```

Compatibility

HTML 2, 3.2, 4, 4.01, XHTML 1.0
Internet Explorer 2, 3, 4, 5, and 5.5
Netscape 1.1, 2, 3, 4–4.7, 6
Opera 4.0
WebTV

Notes

- The **<meta>** element can occur only in the **<head>** element. It can be defined multiple times.
- The **<meta>** element is an empty element (as defined in the HTML specifications) and does not have a closing tag nor contain any content.
- Under XTML 1.0, empty elements such as **<meta>** require a trailing slash: **<meta />**
- A common use of the **<meta>** element is to set information for indexing tools such as search engines. The common values for the **name** attribute when performing this function include **author**, **description**, and **keywords**; other attributes also might be possible.
- Along the same line as indexing, meta-information is also used for rating pages.
- The HTML 2.0 and 3.2 specifications define only the **content**, **http-equiv**, and **name** attributes.

<multicol> (Multiple Column Text)

This Netscape-specific element renders the enclosed content in multiple columns. This element should not be used in favor of a table, which is a more standard way to render multiple columns of text across browsers. It is likely that style sheets will provide for multicolumn rendering in the future.

Syntax (Defined by Netscape)

```
<multicol
    class="class name(s)"
    cols="number of columns"
    gutter="pixels"
    id="unique alphanumeric identifier"
    style="style information"
    width="pixels">

</multicol>
```

Attributes

class   See "Core Attributes Reference," earlier in this appendix.

cols   This attribute indicates the number of columns in which to display the text. The browser attempts to fill the columns evenly.

gutter   This attribute indicates the width in pixels between the columns. The default value for this attribute is **10** pixels.

id   See "Core Attributes Reference," earlier in this appendix.

style   See "Core Attributes Reference," earlier in this appendix.

width   This attribute indicates the column width for all columns. The width of each column is set in pixels and is equivalent for all columns in the group. If the attribute is not specified, the width of columns will be determined by taking the available window size, subtracting the number of pixels for the gutter between the columns as specified by the **gutter** attribute, and evenly dividing the result by the number of columns in the group as set by the **cols** attribute.

Attribute and Event Support

Netscape 4   All attributes

Event Handlers
None

Example

```
<multicol cols="3" gutter="20">
Put a long piece of text here....
</multicol>
```

Compatibility

Netscape 3, 4–4.7

Notes

- Do not attempt to use images or other embedded media within a multicolumn layout as defined by **<multicol>**.
- Do not set the number of columns to high or resize the browser window very small, as text will overwrite other lines.

`<nobr>` (No Breaks)

This proprietary element renders enclosed text without line breaks. Break points for where text may wrap can be inserted using the **<wbr>** element.

Syntax

```
<nobr
    class="class name(s)"
    id="unique alphanumeric identifier"
    style="style information"
    title="advisory text">

</nobr>
```

Attributes and Events Defined by Internet Explorer 5.5

```
    contenteditable=" false | true | inherit "
    dir="ltr | rtl"
```

Attributes

class　See "Core Attributes Reference," earlier in this appendix.

contenteditable　This proprietary Microsoft attribute allows users to edit content rendered in the Internet Explorer 5.5 browser. Values are **false**, **true**, and **inherit**. A value of **false** will prevent content from being edited by users; **true** will allow editing. The default value, **inherit**, applies the value of the affected element's parent element.

dir   See "Language Reference," earlier in this appendix.

id   See "Core Attributes Reference," earlier in this appendix.

style   See "Core Attributes Reference," earlier in this appendix.

title   See "Core Attributes Reference," earlier in this appendix.

Attribute and Event Support

Netscape 4   All attributes

Internet Explorer 4   id, style, and title

Event Handlers
None

Examples

```
<nobr>This really long text ... will not be broken.</nobr>

<nobr>With this element it is often important to hint where a line may
be broken using &lt;wbr&gt;.<wbr> This element acts as a soft return.</nobr>
```

Compatibility
Internet Explorer 2, 3, 4, 5, and 5.5
Netscape 1.1, 2, 3, 4–4.7
Opera 4.0
WebTV

Notes

■ While many browsers support this attribute, it is not part of any W3C standard.
■ Netscape 6 Preview Release 2 did not support this element.

<noembed>(No Embedded Media Support)
This Netscape-specific element is used to indicate alternative content to display on browsers that cannot support an embedded media object. It should occur in conjunction with the **<embed>** element.

Syntax

```
<noembed>

    Alternative content here
```

```
</noembed>
```

Attributes

Netscape does not specifically define attributes for this element; however, Netscape documentation suggests that **class**, **id**, **style**, and **title** might be supported for this element.

Event Handlers

None

Example

```
<embed src="trailer.mov" height="150" width="150">
   <noembed>
      <img src="trailer.gif">
      <br>
   Sorry, this browser is not configured to display video.
   </noembed>
</embed>
```

Compatibility

Netscape 2, 3, 4–4.7
WebTV

Note

■ This element will disappear as the **<object>** style of inserting media into a page becomes more common.

<noframes> (No Frame Support Content)

This element is used to indicate alternative content to display on browsers that do not support frames.

Syntax (Transitional Only)

```
<noframes
     class="class name(s)"
     dir="ltr | rtl"
     id="unique alphanumeric identifier"
     lang="language code"
     style="style information"
     title="advisory text"
     onclick="script"
```

```
ondblclick="script"
onkeydown="script"
onkeypress="script"
onkeyup="script"
onmousedown="script"
onmousemove="script"
onmouseout="script"
onmouseover="script"
onmouseup="script">

Alternative content for non-frame-supporting browsers

</noframes>
```

Attributes

class   See "Core Attributes Reference," earlier in this appendix.

dir   See "Language Reference," earlier in this appendix.

id   See "Core Attributes Reference," earlier in this appendix.

lang   See "Language Reference," earlier in this appendix.

style   See "Core Attributes Reference," earlier in this appendix.

title   See "Core Attributes Reference," earlier in this appendix.

Attribute and Event Support

Netscape 4   **class**, **id**, **lang**, and **style** are implied.

Internet Explorer 4   **id**, **style**, and **title**

Event Handlers

It is interesting to note that whereas the **<noframes>** element does support the common events for nearly all HTML 4 elements, their value seems unclear. The only time that content within a **<noframes>** could be rendered is on a browser that does not support frames; however, browsers that do not support frames are unlikely to support an event model or similar features. With clever scripting it might be possible to access framed and nonframed content, but for now the benefit of the events seems unclear. For more information, see "Events Reference," earlier in this appendix.

Example

```
<frameset rows="100,*">
  <frame src="controls.htm">
  <frame src="content.htm">
    <noframes>
    Sorry, this browser does not support frames.
    </noframes>
</frameset>
```

Compatibility

HTML 4 (transitional), 4.01 (transitional), XHTML 1.0
Internet Explorer 2, 3, 4, 5, and 5.5
Netscape 2, 3, 4–4.7 and 6
Opera 4.0
WebTV

Notes

- This element should be used within the scope of the **<frameset>** element.
- The benefit of events and sophisticated attributes such as **style** is unclear for browsers that would use content within **<noframes>**, given that older browsers that don't support frames probably would not support these features.

<noscript> (No Script Support Content)

This element is used to enclose content that should be rendered on browsers that do not support scripting or that have scripting turned off.

Syntax

```
<noscript
    class="class name(s)"
    dir="ltr | rtl"
    id="unique alphanumeric identifier"
    lang="language code"
    style="style information"
    title="advisory text"
    onclick="script"
    ondblclick="script"
    onkeydown="script"
    onkeypress="script"
    onkeyup="script"
    onmousedown="script"
    onmousemove="script"
```

```
      onmouseout="script"
      onmouseover="script"
      onmouseup="script">

      Alternative content for non-script-supporting browsers

</noscript>
```

Attributes

class   See "Core Attributes Reference," earlier in this appendix.

dir   See "Language Reference," earlier in this appendix.

id   See "Core Attributes Reference," earlier in this appendix.

lang   See "Language Reference," earlier in this appendix.

style   See "Core Attributes Reference," earlier in this appendix.

title   See "Core Attributes Reference," earlier in this appendix.

Attribute and Event Support

Netscape 4   class, id, lang, and style are implied.

Internet Explorer 4   id

Event Handlers
As defined in the preliminary specification of HTML 4, the benefits of event handlers are not very obvious, considering that content within the **<noscript>** element assumes the browser does not support scripting, whereas the script handlers themselves are for browsers that support scripting. These are standard events for nearly all HTML 4 elements. For definitions, see "Events Reference," earlier in this appendix.

Example

```
Last Updated:
<script language="javascript">
<!-- document.writeln(document.lastodified); // -->
</script>
<noscript>
1999
</noscript>
```

Compatibility

HTML 4, 4.01, XHTML 1.0
Internet Explorer 3, 4, 5, and 5.5
Netscape 2, 3, 4–4.7
Opera 4.0
WebTV

Notes

- Improved functionality for the **<noscript>** element might come if it is extended to deal with the lack of support for one scripting language or another. Currently, the element is used only to indicate whether any scripting is supported or not.

- It also is useful to comment out scripting information so non–scripting-aware browsers will not read it.

<object> (Embedded Object)

This element specifies an arbitrary object to be included in an HTML document. Initially, this element was used to insert ActiveX controls, but according to the HTML 4.01 specification, an object can be any media object, document, applet, ActiveX control, or even image.

Syntax

```
<object
     align="bottom | left | middle | right | top"
           (transitional)
     archive="url"
     border="percentage | pixels" (transitional)
     class="class name(s)"
     classid="id"
     codebase="URL"
     codetype="MIME Type"
     data="URL of data"
     declare
     dir="ltr | rtl"
     height="percentage | pixels"
     hspace="percentage | pixels" (transitional)
     id="unique alphanumeric identifier"
     lang="language code"
     name="unique alphanumeric name"
     standby="standby text string"
     style="style information"
     tabindex="number"
     title="advisory text"
     type="MIME Type"
     usemap="URL"
```

```
          vspace="percentage | pixels" (transitional)
          width="percentage | pixels"
          onclick="script"
          ondblclick="script"
          onkeydown="script"
          onkeypress="script"
          onkeyup="script"
          onmousedown="script"
          onmousemove="script"
          onmouseout="script"
          onmouseover="script"
          onmouseup="script">

      </object>
```

Attributes and Events Defined by Internet Explorer 4

```
          accesskey="character"
          align="absbottom | absmiddle | baseline | texttop"
          code="url"
          datafld="column name"
          datasrc="id for bound data"
          language="javascript | jscript | vbs | vbscript"
          onafterupdate="script"
          onbeforeupdate="script"
          onblur="script"
          ondragstart="script"
          onfocus="script"
          onhelp="script"
          onreadystatechange="script"
          onresize="script"
          onrowenter="script"
          onrowexit="script"
          onselectstart="script"
```

Attributes and Events Defined by Internet Explorer 5.5

```
          hidefocus="true | false"
```

Attributes

accesskey   This Microsoft attribute specifies a keyboard navigation accelerator for the element. Pressing ALT or a similar key in association with the specified character selects the form control correlated with that key sequence. Page designers are forewarned to avoid key sequences already bound to browsers.

align   This attribute aligns the object with respect to the surrounding text. The default is **left**. The HTML 4.01 specification defines **bottom, middle, right,** and **top** as well. Browsers might provide an even richer set of alignment values. The behavior of alignment for objects is similar to images. Under the strict HTML 4.01 specification, the **<object>** element does not support this attribute.

archive   This attribute contains a URL for the location of an archive file. An archive file typically is used to contain multiple object files to improve the efficiency of access.

border   This attribute specifies the width of the object's borders in pixels or as a percentage.

class   See "Core Attributes Reference," earlier in this appendix.

classid   This attribute contains a URL for an object's implementation. The URL syntax depends upon the object's type. With ActiveX controls, the value of this attribute does not appear to be a URL but something of the form *CLSID: object-id*; for example, **CLSID: 99B42120-6EC7-11CF-A6C7-00AA00A47DD2.**

code   Under the old Microsoft implementation, this attribute contains the URL referencing a Java applet class file. The way to access a Java applet under the HTML 4.01 specification is to use **<object classid="java: classname.class">.** The pseudo-URL *java:* is used to indicate a Java applet. Microsoft Internet Explorer 4 and beyond support this style, so **code** should not be used.

codebase   This attribute contains a URL to use as a relative base to access the object specified by the **classid** attribute.

codetype   This attribute specifies an object's MIME type. Do not confuse this attribute with **type,** which specifies the MIME type of the data the object may use as defined by the **data** attribute.

data   This attribute contains a URL for data required by an object.

datafld   This attribute is used to indicate the column name in the data source that is bound to the **<object>** element.

datasrc   The value of this attribute is set to an identifier indicating the data source to pull data from.

declare   This attribute declares an object without instantiating it. This is useful when the object will be a parameter to another object.

dir   See "Language Reference," earlier in this appendix.

height   This attribute specifies the height of the object in pixels or as a percentage of the enclosing window.

hidefocus   This proprietary element, introduced with Internet Explorer 5.5, hides focus on an element's content. Focus must be applied to the element using the **tabindex** attribute.

hspace   This attribute indicates the horizontal space in pixels or percentages between the object and surrounding content.

id   See "Core Attributes Reference," earlier in this appendix.

lang   See "Language Reference," earlier in this appendix.

language   In the Microsoft implementation, this attribute specifies the scripting language to be used with an associated script bound to the element, typically through an event handler attribute. Possible values might include **javascript**, **jscript**, **vbs**, and **vbscript**. Other values that include the version of the language used, such as **JavaScript1.1**, also might be possible.

name   This attribute under the Microsoft definition defines the name of the control so scripting can access it. The HTML 4.01 specification suggests that it is a name for form submission, but this meaning is unclear and not supported by browsers.

standby   This attribute contains a text message to be displayed while the object is loading.

style   See "Core Attributes Reference," earlier in this appendix.

tabindex   This attribute takes a numeric value indicating the position of the object in the tabbing index for the document. Tabbing proceeds from the lowest positive **tabindex** value to the highest. Negative values for **tabindex** will leave the object out of the tabbing order. When tabbing is not explicitly set, the browser can tab through items in the order they are encountered.

title   See "Core Attributes Reference," earlier in this appendix.

type   This attribute specifies the MIME type for the object's data. This is different from the **codetype**, which is the MIME type of the object and not the data it uses.

usemap   This attribute contains the URL of the image map to be used with the object. Typically, the URL will be a fragment identifier referencing a **<map>** element somewhere else within the file. The presence of this attribute indicates that the type of object being included is an image.

vspace   This attribute indicates the vertical space in pixels or percentages between the object and surrounding text.

width   This attribute specifies the width of the object in pixels or as a percentage of the enclosing window.

Attribute and Event Support

Netscape 4   align, classid, codebase, data, height, type, and width (class, id, lang, and style are implied.)

Internet Explorer 4   align, class, classid, code, codebase, codetype, data, height, id, lang, name, style, tabindex, title, type, width, all W3C-defined events, and all attributes and events defined by Internet Explorer 4.

Internet Explorer 5.5 Same as Internet Explorer 4, plus **hidefocus**.

Event Handlers
See "Events Reference," earlier in this appendix.

Examples

```
<object id="IeLabel1" width="325" height="65"
        classid="CLSID:99B42120-6EC7-11CF-A6C7-00AA00A47DD2">
   <param name="_ExtentX" value="6879">
   <param name ="_ExtentY" value="1376">
   <param name="Caption" value="Hello World">
   <param name="Alignment" value="4">
   <param name="Mode" value="1">
   <param name="ForeColor" value="#FF0000">
   <param name="FontName" value="Arial">
   <param name="Fontize" value="36">
<b>Hello World for non-ActiveX users!</b>
</object>


<object classid="java:Blink.class"
        standby="Here it comes"
        height="100" width="300">
   <param name="lbl"
          value="Java is fun, exciting, and new.">
   <param name="speed" value="2">
This will display in non-Java-aware or -enabled
browsers.
</object>


<object data="pullinthisfile.html">
Data not included!
</object>


<object data ="bigimage.gif" shapes>
   <a href="page1.htm" shape="rect" coords="10,10,40,40">
   Page 1</a>
   <a href="page2.htm" shape="circle" coords="100,90,20 ">
   Page 2</a>
</object>
```

Compatibility
HTML 4, 4.01, XHTML 1.0
Internet Explorer 3, 4, 5, and 5.5
Netscape 4–4.7, 6

Notes

■ Under the strict HTML 4.01 specification the **<object>** element loses most of its presentation attributes, including **align**, **border**, **height**, **hspace**, **vspace**, and **width**. These attributes are replaced by style sheet rules.

■ The HTML 4.01 specification reserves the **datafld**, **dataformatas**, and **datasrc** attributes for future use.

■ Alternative content should be defined within the **<object>** element after the **<param>** elements.

■ The **<object>** element is still mainly used to include binaries in pages. Although the specification defines that it can load in HTML files and create image maps, few, if any, browsers support this.

<ol> (Ordered List)

This element is used to define an ordered or numbered list of items. The numbering style comes in many forms, including letters, Roman numerals, and regular numerals. The individual items within the list are specified by **<li>** elements included with the **<ol>** element.

Syntax

```
<ol
    class="class name(s)"
    compact (transitional)
    dir="ltr | rtl"
    id="unique alphanumeric identifier"
    lang="language code"
    start="number" (transitional)
    style="style information"
    title="advisory text"
    type="a | A | i | I | 1" (transitional)
    onclick="script"
    ondblclick="script"
    onkeydown="script"
    onkeypress="script"
    onkeyup="script"
    onmousedown="script"
    onmousemove="script"
    onmouseout="script"
    onmouseover="script"
    onmouseup="script">

</ol>
```

XHTML Syntax

Because of XHTML 1.0's deprecation of attribute minimization, the **compact** attribute must have a quoted attribute when used:

```
<ol compact="compact"></ol>
```

Attributes and Events Defined by Internet Explorer 4

```
language="javascript | jscript | vbs | vbscript"
ondragstart="script"
onhelp="script"
onselectstart="script"
```

Attributes and Events Defined by Internet Explorer 5.5

```
accesskey="key"
contenteditable="false | true | inherit"
hidefocus="true | false"
tabindex="number"
```

Attributes

accesskey   This attribute specifies a keyboard navigation accelerator for the element. Pressing ALT or a similar key (depending on the browser and operating system) in association with the specified key selects the anchor element correlated with that key.

class   See "Core Attributes Reference," earlier in this appendix.

compact   This attribute indicates that the list should be rendered in a compact style. Few browsers actually change the rendering of the list regardless of the presence of this attribute. The **compact** attribute requires no value.

contenteditable   This proprietary Microsoft attribute allows users to edit content rendered in the Internet Explorer 5.5 browser. Values are **false**, **true**, and **inherit**. A value of **false** will prevent content from being edited by users; **true** will allow editing. The default value, **inherit**, applies the value of the affected element's parent element.

dir   See "Language Reference," earlier in this appendix.

hidefocus   This proprietary element, introduced with Internet Explorer 5.5, hides focus on an element's content. Focus must be applied to the element using the **tabindex** attribute.

id   See "Core Attributes Reference," earlier in this appendix.

lang   See "Language Reference," earlier in this appendix.

language   In the Microsoft implementation, this attribute specifies the scripting language to be used with an associated script bound to the element, typically through an event handler attribute. Possible values might include **javascript**, **jscript**, **vbs**, and **vbscript**. Other values that include the version of the language used, such as **JavaScript1.1**, might also be possible.

start   This attribute is used to indicate the value to start numbering the individual list items from. Although the ordering type of list elements might be Roman numerals such as XXXI or letters, the value of **start** is always represented as number. To start numbering elements from the letter "C," use **<ol type="A" start="3">**.

style   See "Core Attributes Reference," earlier in this appendix.

tabindex   This attribute uses a number to identify the object's position in the tabbing order for keyboard navigation using the TAB key. Internet Explorer 5.5 applies this attribute to the **ol** element; under IE 5.5, this focus can be disabled with the **hidefocus** attribute.

title   See "Core Attributes Reference," earlier in this appendix.

type   This attribute indicates the numbering type: "a" indicates lowercase letters, "A" indicates uppercase letters, "i" indicates lowercase Roman numerals, "I" indicates uppercase Roman numerals, and "1" indicates numbers. Type set in the **<ol>** element is used for the entire list unless a **type** attribute is used within an enclosed **<li>** element.

Attribute and Event Support

Netscape 4   class, id, lang, start, style, and type

Internet Explorer 4   All attributes and events except **dir**.

Internet Explorer 5.5   All attributes and events

WebTV   start and type

Event Handlers
See "Events Reference," earlier in this appendix.

Examples

```
<ol type="1">
    <li>First step
    <li>Second step
    <li>Third step
</ol>

<ol compact type="I" start="30">
    <li>Clause 30
    <li>Clause 31
```

```
    <li>Clause 32
</ol>
```

XHTML Example

```
<ol compact="compact" type="I">
    <li>Clause 1</li>
    <li>Clause 2</li>
    <li>Clause 3</li>
</ol>
```

Compatibility

HTML 2, 3.2, 4, 4.01, XHTML 1.0
Internet Explorer 2, 3, 4, 5, and 5.5
Netscape 1, 2, 3, 4–4.7, 6
Opera 4.0
WebTV

Notes

- Under the strict HTML 4.01 specification, the **<ol>** element no longer supports the **compact**, **start**, and **type** attributes. These aspects of lists can be controlled with style sheet rules.

- Under the XHTML 1.0 specification, the **compact** attribute no longer can be minimized, but must have a quoted attribute value: **<ol compact="compact">...</ol>**

- The HTML 3.2 specification supports only the **compact**, **start**, and **type** attributes. The HTML 2.0 specification supports only the **compact** attribute.

<optgroup> (Option Grouping)

This element specifies a grouping of items in a selection list defined by **<option>** elements so that the menu choices can be presented in a hierarchical menu or similar alternative fashion to improve access through nonvisual browsers.

Syntax

```
<optgroup
    class="class name(s)"
    dir="ltr | rtl"
    disabled
    id="unique alphanumeric identifier"
    label="text description"
    lang="language code"
    style="style information"
```

APPENDIX A

```
        title="advisory text"
        onclick="script"
        ondblclick="script"
        onkeydown="script"
        onkeypress="script"
        onkeyup="script"
        onmousedown="script"
        onmousemove="script"
        onmouseout="script"
        onmouseover="script"
        onmouseup="script">

        <option> elements

</optgroup>
```

Attributes

class   See "Core Attributes Reference," earlier in this appendix.

dir   See "Language Reference," earlier in this appendix.

disabled   Occurrence of this attribute indicates that the enclosed set of options is disabled.

id   See "Core Attributes Reference," earlier in this appendix.

label   This attribute contains a short label that might be more appealing to use when the selection list is rendered as items in a hierarchy.

lang   See "Language Reference," earlier in this appendix.

style   See "Core Attributes Reference," earlier in this appendix.

title   See "Core Attributes Reference," earlier in this appendix.

Attribute and Event Support

Netscape 6   class, disabled, id, label, style, title

Event Handlers
See "Events Reference," earlier in this appendix.

Example

```
Where would you like to go for your vacation?<br>
```

```
<select>
    <option id="ch1" value="China">The Great Wall
  <optgroup label="Mexico">
    <option id="ch2" label="Los Cabos" value="Los Cabos">
     Los Cabos, Mexico
    <option id="ch3" label="Leon" value="Leon">Leon, Mexico
    <option id="ch4" value="MXC">Mexico City
  </optgroup>
    <option id="ch5" value="home" selected>Your backyard
</select>
```

Compatibility

HTML 4, 4.01, XHTML 1.0
Netscape 6

Notes

- This element should occur only within the context of a **<select>** element.
- Netacape 6 Preview Release 2 is the first browser version to present this element in a visually meaningful fashion.

<option> (Option in Selection List)

This element specifies an item in a selection list defined by the **<select>** element.

Syntax

```
<option
    class="class name(s)"
    dir="ltr | rtl"
    disabled
    id="unique alphanumeric identifier"
    label="text description"
    lang="language code"
    selected
    style="style information"
    title="advisory text"
    value="option value"
    onclick="script"
    ondblclick="script"
    onkeydown="script"
    onkeypress="script"
    onkeyup="script"
    onmousedown="script"
    onmousemove="script"
```

```
        onmouseout="script"
        onmouseover="script"
        onmouseup="script">

</option>
```

XHTML Syntax

Under the XHTML 1.0 specification, the closing tag **</option>** ceases to be optional and must be used.

Attributes and Events Defined by Internet Explorer 4

```
        language="javascript | jscript | vbs | vbscript"
        ondragstart="script"
        onselectstart="script"
```

Attributes

class   See "Core Attributes Reference," earlier in this appendix.

dir   See "Language Reference," earlier in this appendix.

disabled   Presence of this attribute indicates that the particular item is not selectable.

id   See "Core Attributes Reference," earlier in this appendix.

label   This attribute contains a short label that might be more appealing to use when the selection list is rendered as a hierarchy due to the presence of an **<optgroup>** element.

lang   See "Language Reference," earlier in this appendix.

language   In the Microsoft implementation, this attribute specifies the scripting language to be used with an associated script bound to the element, typically through an event handler attribute. Possible values might include **javascript**, **jscript**, **vbs**, and **vbscript**. Other values that include the version of the language used, such as **JavaScript1.1**, also might be possible.

selected   This attribute indicates that the associated item is the default selection. If not included, the first item in the selection list is the default. If the **<select>** element enclosing the **<option>** elements has the **multiple** attribute, the **selected** attribute might occur in multiple entries. Otherwise, it should occur in only one entry.

style   See "Core Attributes Reference," earlier in this appendix.

title   See "Core Attributes Reference," earlier in this appendix.

value This attribute indicates the value to include with the form result when the item is selected.

Attribute and Event Support

Netscape 4 selected and **value** (**class, id, lang,** and **style** are implied.)

Internet Explorer 4 class, id, language, selected, value, ondragstart, and onselectstart

WebTV selected and **value**

Event Handlers
See "Events Reference," earlier in this appendix.

Example

```
Where would you like to go for your vacation?<br>
<select>
   <option id="choice1" value="China">The Great Wall
   <option id="choice2" value="Mexico">Los Cabos
   <option id="choice3" value="Home" selected>Your backyard
</select>
```

XHTML Example

```
Sorry, you can't go there. How about one of these vacation spots?
<br/>
<select>
   <option id="choice1" value="Ohio">Cleveland</option>
   <option id="choice2" value="New Jersey">Paramus</option>
   <option id="choice3" value="almost home" selected="selected">
   Your neighbor's overgrown backyard</option>
</select>
```

Compatibility
HTML 2, 3.2. 4, 4.01, XHTML 1.0
Internet Explorer 2, 3, 4, 5, and 5.5
Netscape 1, 2, 3, 4–4.7, 6
Opera 4.0
WebTV

Notes

- Under HTML specifications, the closing tag for **<option>** is optional.
- For XHTML compatibility, the closing tag **</option>** is required.

- This element should occur only within the context of a **<select>** element.
- The HTML 2.0 and 3.2 specifications define only the **selected** and **value** attributes for this element.

<p> (Paragraph)

This element is used to define a paragraph of text. Browsers typically insert a blank line before and after a paragraph of text.

Syntax

```
<p
      align="center | justify | left | right"
            (transitional)
      class="class name(s)"
      dir="ltr | rtl"
      id="unique alphanumeric identifier"
      lang="language code"
      style="style information"
      title="advisory text"
      onclick="script"
      ondblclick="script"
      onkeydown="script"
      onkeypress="script"
      onkeyup="script"
      onmousedown="script"
      onmousemove="script"
      onmouseout="script"
      onmouseover="script"
      onmouseup="script">

</p>
```

XHTML Syntax

Under XHTML 1.0, the **<p>** element requires the closing tag:

```
<p></p>
```

Attributes and Events Defined by Internet Explorer 4

```
      language="javascript | jscript | vbs | vbscript"
      ondragstart="script"
      onhelp="script"
      onselectstart="script"
```

Attributes and Events Defined by Internet Explorer 5.5

```
accesskey="key"
contenteditable="false | true | inherit"
hidefocus="true | false"
tabindex="number"
```

Attributes

accesskey   This attribute specifies a keyboard navigation accelerator for the element. Pressing ALT or a similar key (depending on the browser and operating system) in association with the specified key selects the anchor element correlated with that key.

align   This attribute specifies the alignment of text within a paragraph. The default value is **left**. The transitional specification of HTML 4.01 also defines **center**, **justify**, and **right**. However, under the strict specification of HTML 4.01, text alignment can be handled through a style sheet rule.

class   See "Core Attributes Reference," earlier in this appendix.

contenteditable   This proprietary Microsoft attribute allows users to edit content rendered in the Internet Explorer 5.5 browser. Values are **false**, **true**, and **inherit**. A value of **false** will prevent content from being edited by users; **true** will allow editing. The default value, **inherit**, applies the value of the affected element's parent element.

dir   See "Language Reference," earlier in this appendix.

hidefocus   This proprietary element, introduced with Internet Explorer 5.5, hides focus on an element's content. Focus must be applied to the element using the **tabindex** attribute.

id   See "Core Attributes Reference," earlier in this appendix.

lang   See "Language Reference," earlier in this appendix.

language   In the Microsoft implementation, this attribute specifies the scripting language to be used with an associated script bound to the element, typically through an event handler attribute. Possible values might include **javascript**, **jscript**, **vbs**, and **vbscript**. Other values that include the version of the language used, such as **JavaScript1.1**, also might be possible.

style   See "Core Attributes Reference," earlier in this appendix.

tabindex   This attribute uses a number to identify the object's position in the tabbing order for keyboard navigation using the TAB key. Internet Explorer 5.5 applies this attribute to the **p** element; under IE 5.5, this focus can be disabled with the **hidefocus** attribute.

title   See "Core Attributes Reference," earlier in this appendix.

Attribute and Event Support

Netscape 4   align. (**class**, **id**, **lang**, and **style** are implied.)

Internet Explorer 4   All attributes and events except **dir**. (Note: The **justify** value for **align** is not supported by Internet Explorer 4.)

Internet Explorer 5.0   All attributes and events

WebTV   align (**center** | **left** | **right**)

Event Handlers
See "Events Reference," earlier in this appendix.

Examples

```
<p align="right">A right-aligned paragraph</p>

<p id="Para1" class="defaultParagraph"
    title="Introduction Paragraph">
This is the introductory paragraph for a very long paper about nothing.
</p>
```

Compatibility
HTML 2, 3.2, 4, and 4.01, XHTML 1.0
Internet Explorer 2, 3, 4, 5, and 5.5
Netscape 1, 2, 3, 4–4.7, 6
Opera 4.0
WebTV

Notes

- Under the strict HTML 4.01 specification the **align** attribute is not supported. Alignment of text can be accomplished using style sheets.

- The closing tag for the **<p>** element is optional under the HTML specification.

- Under the XHTML 1.0 specification, the closing tag **</p>** is required for XHTML compatibility.

- As a logical element, empty paragraphs are ignored by browsers, so do not try to use multiple **<p>** elements in a row, like **<p><p><p><p>**, to add blank lines to a Web page. This will not work; use the **
** element instead.

- The HTML 3.2 specification supports only the **align** attribute with values of **center**, **left**, and **right**.

- The HTML 2.0 specification supports no attributes for the **<p>** element.

<param> (Object Parameter)

This element specifies a parameter to pass to an embedded object using the **<object>** or **<applet>** element. This element should occur only within the scope of one of these elements.

Syntax

```
<param
     id="unique alphanumeric identifier"
     name="parameter name"
     type="MIME Type"
     value="parameter value"
     valuetype="data | object | ref">
```

XHTML Syntax

Because **<param>** is an empty element, a closing forward slash is required before the closing bracket of the tag:

```
<param />
```

Attributes Defined by Internet Explorer 4

```
     datafld="column name"
     dataformatas="html | text"
     datasrc="data source id"
```

Attributes

datafld   This Internet Explorer–specific attribute is used to indicate the column name in the data source that is bound to the **<param>** element's value.

dataformatas   This Internet Explorer–specific attribute indicates whether the bound data is plain text (**text**) or HTML (**html**).

datasrc   The value of this attribute is set to an identifier indicating the data source to pull data from. Bound data is used to set the value of the parameters passed to the object or applet with which this **<param>** element is associated.

id   See "Core Attributes Reference," earlier in this appendix.

name   This attribute contains the parameter's name. The name of the parameter depends on the particular object being inserted into the page, and it is assumed that the object knows how to handle the passed data. Do not confuse the **name** attribute with the **name** attribute used for form elements. In the latter case, the **name** attribute does not have a similar meaning as **id**, but rather specifies the name of the data to be passed to an enclosing **<object>** element.

type   When the **valuetype** attribute is set to **ref**, the **type** attribute can be used to indicate the type of the information to be retrieved. Legal values for this attribute are in the form of MIME types such as **text/html**.

value   This attribute contains the parameter's value. The actual contents of this attribute depend on the object and the particular parameter being passed in, as determined by the **name** attribute.

valuetype   This HTML 4–specific attribute specifies the type of the **value** attribute being passed in. Possible values for this attribute include **data**, **object**, and **ref**. A value of **data** specifies that the information passed in through the **value** parameter should be treated just as data. A value of **ref** indicates that the information being passed in is a URL that indicates where the data to use is located. The information is not retrieved, but the URL is passed to the object which then can retrieve the information if necessary. The last value of **object** indicates that the value being passed in is the name of an object as set by its **id** attribute. In practice, the **data** attribute is used by default.

Attribute and Event Support

Netscape 4   **name** and **value** (**id** may be implied.)

Internet Explorer 4   **name**, **datafld**, **dataformatas**, **datasrc**, and **value**

Event Handlers
None

Examples

```
<applet code="plot.class">
   <param name="min" value="5">
   <param name="max" value="30">
   <param name="ticks" value=".5">
   <param name="line-style" value="dotted">
</applet>

<object classid="clsid:D27CDB6E-AE6D-11cf-96B8-444553540000"
        codebase="swflash.cab#version=2,0,0,0"
        height="100" width="100">
   <param id="param1" name="Movie" value="SplashLogo.swf">
   <param id="param2" name="Play" value="True">
</object>
```

Compatibility
HTML 3.2 and 4
Internet Explorer 3, 4, and 5
Netscape 2, 3, 4, and 4.5

Notes

- ■ The closing tag for this element is forbidden.
- ■ The HTML 3.2 specification supports only the **name** and **value** attributes for this element.
- ■ Under XHTML 1.0, empy elements such as **<param>** require a trailing forward slash: **<param />**

<plaintext> (Plain Text)

This deprecated element from the HTML 2.0 specification renders the enclosed text as plain text and forces the browser to ignore any enclosed HTML. Typically, information affected by the **<plaintext>** element is rendered in monospaced font. This element no longer is part of the HTML standard.

Syntax (HTML 2; Deprecated Under HTML 4)

```
<plaintext>
```

Attributes and Events Defined by Internet Explorer 4

```
class="class name(s)"
dir="ltr | rtl"
id="unique alphanumeric identifier"
lang="language code"
language="javascript | jscript | vbs | vbscript"
style="style information"
title="advisory text"
onclick="script"
ondblclick="script"
ondragstart="script"
onhelp="script"
onkeydown="script"
onkeypress="script"
onkeyup="script"
onmousedown="script"
onmousemove="script"
onmouseout="script"
onmouseover="script"
onmouseup="script"
onselectstart="script"
```

Attributes and Events Defined by Internet Explorer 5.5

```
accesskey="key"
contenteditable="false | true | inherit"
hidefocus="true | false"
tabindex="number"
```

Attributes

accesskey   This attribute specifies a keyboard navigation accelerator for the element. Pressing ALT or a similar key (depending on the browser and operating system) in association with the specified key selects the anchor element correlated with that key.

class   See "Core Attributes Reference," earlier in this appendix.

contenteditable   This proprietary Microsoft attribute allows users to edit content rendered in the Internet Explorer 5.5 browser. Values are **false**, **true**, and **inherit**. A value of **false** will prevent content from being edited by users; **true** will allow editing. The default value, **inherit**, applies the value of the affected element's parent element.

dir   See "Language Reference," earlier in this appendix.

hidefocus   This proprietary element, introduced with Internet Explorer 5.5, hides focus on an element's content. Focus must be applied to the element using the **tabindex** attribute.

id   See "Core Attributes Reference," earlier in this appendix.

lang   See "Language Reference," earlier in this appendix.

language   In the Microsoft implementation, this attribute specifies the scripting language to be used with an associated script bound to the element, typically through an event handler attribute. Possible values might include **javascript**, **jscript**, **vbs**, and **vbscript**. Other values that include the version of the language used, such as **JavaScript1.1**, also might be possible.

style   See "Core Attributes Reference," earlier in this appendix.

tabindex   This attribute uses a number to identify the object's position in the tabbing order for keyboard navigation using the TAB key. Internet Explorer 5.5 applies this attribute to the **plaintext** element; under IE 5.5, this focus can be disabled with the **hidefocus** attribute.

title   See "Core Attributes Reference," earlier in this appendix.

Attribute and Event Support

Netscape 4   class, **id**, **lang**, and **style** are implied.

Internet Explorer 4   All attributes and events defined by W3C and Internet Explorer 4.

Internet Explorer 5.5   All attributes and events

Event Handlers
See "Events Reference," earlier in this appendix.

Example

```
<html>
<head><title>Plaintext Example</title></head>
<body>
   The rest of this file is in plain text.
   <plaintext>
   Even though this is supposed to be <b>bold</b>, the tags still show.
   There is no way to turn plain text off once it is on. </plaintext>
   does nothing to help. Even </body> and </html> will show up.
```

Compatibility
HTML 2
Internet Explorer 2, 3, 4, 5, and 5.5
Netscape 1, 2, 3, 4–4.7

Notes

- No closing tag for this element is necessary because the browser will ignore all tags after the starting tag.

- This element should not be used. Plain text information can be indicated by a file type, and information can be inserted in a preformatted fashion using the **<pre>** element.

<pre> (Preformatted Text)

This element is used to indicate that the enclosed text is preformatted, meaning that spaces, returns, tabs, and other formatting characters are preserved. Browsers will, however, acknowledge most HTML elements that are found with the **<pre>** element. Preformatted text generally will be rendered by the browsers in a monospaced font.

Syntax

```
<pre
     class="class name(s)"
     dir="ltr | rtl"
     id="unique alphanumeric value"
     lang="language code"
     style="style information"
     title="advisory text"
     width="number" (transitional)
```

```
            onclick="script"
            ondblclick="script"
            onkeydown="script"
            onkeypress="script"
            onkeyup="script"
            onmousedown="script"
            onmousemove="script"
            onmouseout="script"
            onmouseover="script"
            onmouseup="script">

</pre>
```

Attributes and Events Defined by Internet Explorer 4

```
            language="javascript | jscript | vbs | vbscript"
            ondragstart="script"
            onhelp="script"
            onselectstart="script"
```

Attributes and Events Defined by Internet Explorer 5.5

```
            accesskey="key"
            contenteditable="false | true | inherit"
            hidefocus="true | false"
            tabindex="number"
```

Attributes and Events Defined by Netscape 4

```
            col="columns"
            wrap
```

Attributes

accesskey   This attribute specifies a keyboard navigation accelerator for the element. Pressing ALT or a similar key (depending on the browser and operating system) in association with the specified key selects the anchor element correlated with that key.

class   See "Core Attributes Reference," earlier in this appendix.

contenteditable   This proprietary Microsoft attribute allows users to edit content rendered in the Internet Explorer 5.5 browser. Values are **false**, **true**, and **inherit**. A value of **false** will prevent content from being edited by users; **true** will allow editing. The default value, **inherit**, applies the value of the affected element's parent element.

dir   See "Language Reference," earlier in this appendix.

hidefocus   This proprietary element, introduced with Internet Explorer 5.5, hides focus on an element's content. Focus must be applied to the element using the **tabindex** attribute.

id   See "Core Attributes Reference," earlier in this appendix.

lang   See "Language Reference," earlier in this appendix.

language   In the Microsoft implementation, this attribute specifies the scripting language to be used with an associated script bound to the element, typically through an event handler attribute. Possible values might include **javascript**, **jscript**, **vbs**, and **vbscript**. Other values that include the version of the language used, such as **JavaScript1.1**, also might be possible.

style   See "Core Attributes Reference," earlier in this appendix.

tabindex   This attribute uses a number to identify the object's position in the tabbing order for keyboard navigation using the TAB key. Internet Explorer 5.5 applies this attribute to the **pre** element; under IE 5.5, this focus can be disabled with the **hidefocus** attribute.

title   See "Core Attributes Reference," earlier in this appendix.

width   This attribute should be set to the **width** of the preformatted region. The value of the attribute should be the number of characters to display. In practice, this attribute is not supported and is dropped under the strict HTML 4.01 specification.

Attribute and Event Support

Netscape 4   class, cols, id, lang, style, and **wrap**

Internet Explorer 4   All attributes and events defined by W3C and Internet Explorer 4, except **dir** and **width**.

Internet Explorer 5.5   All attributes and events defined by W3C, Internet Explorer 4, and Internet Explorer 5.5, except **width**.

Event Handlers

See "Events Reference," earlier in this appendix.

Example

```
<pre>
  Within PREFORMATTED text     A L L     formatting IS    PRESERVED
  NO  m    a    t    t    e    r how wild it is. Remember that some
  <b>HTML</b> markup is allowed within the &lt;pre&gt; element.
</pre>
```

APPENDIX A

Compatibility

HTML 2, 3.2, 4, and 4.01, XHTML 1.0
Internet Explorer 2, 3, 4, 5, and 5.5
Netscape 1, 2, 3, 4–4.7, and 6
Opera 4.0
WebTV

Notes

- The HTML 4.01 transitional specification states that the **<applet>**, **<basefont>**, **<big>**, **<font>**, **<img>**, **<object>**, **<small>**, **<sub>**, and **<sup>** elements should not be used within the **<pre>** element. The strict HTML 4 specification states that only the **<big>**, **<img>**, **<object>**, **<small>**, **<sub>**, and **<sup>** elements should not be used within the **<pre>** element. The other excluded elements are missing, as they are deprecated from the strict specification. Although these attributes should not be used, it appears that the two most popular browsers will render them anyway.

- The strict HTML 4.0/4.01 specifications drop support for the **width** attribute, which was not generally supported anyway.

- The HTML 2.0 and 3.2 specifications support only the **width** attribute for **<pre>**.

<q> (Quote)

This element indicates that the enclosed text is a short inline quotation.

Syntax

```
<q
     cite="url of source"
     class="class name(s)"
     dir="ltr | rtl"
     id="unique alphanumeric string"
     lang="language code"
     style="style information"
     title="advisory text"
     onclick="script"
     ondblclick="script"
     onkeydown="script"
     onkeypress="script"
     onkeyup="script"
     onmousedown="script"
     onmousemove="script"
     onmouseout="script"
     onmouseover="script"
     onmouseup="script">

</q>
```

Attributes and Events Defined by Internet Explorer 4

```
language="javascript | jscipt | vbs | vbscript"
ondragstart="script"
onhelp="script"
onselectstart="script"
```

Attributes and Events Defined by Internet Explorer 5.5

```
accesskey="key"
contenteditable="false | true | inherit"
hidefocus="true | false"
tabindex="number"
```

Attributes

accesskey   This attribute specifies a keyboard navigation accelerator for the element. Pressing ALT or a similar key (depending on the browser and operating system) in association with the specified key selects the anchor element correlated with that key.

cite   The value of this attribute is a URL that designates a source document or message for the information quoted. This attribute is intended to point to information explaining the context or the reference for the quote.

class   See "Core Attributes Reference," earlier in this appendix.

contenteditable   This proprietary Microsoft attribute allows users to edit content rendered in the Internet Explorer 5.5 browser. Values are **false**, **true**, and **inherit**. A value of **false** will prevent content from being edited by users; **true** will allow editing. The default value, **inherit**, applies the value of the affected element's parent element.

dir   See "Language Reference," earlier in this appendix.

hidefocus   This proprietary element, introduced with Internet Explorer 5.5, hides focus on an element's content. Focus must be applied to the element using the **tabindex** attribute.

id   See "Core Attributes Reference," earlier in this appendix.

lang   See "Language Reference," earlier in this appendix.

language   In the Microsoft implementation, this attribute specifies the scripting language to be used with an associated script bound to the element, typically through an event handler attribute. Possible values might include **javascript**, **jscript**, **vbs.** and **vbscript**. Other values that include the version of the language used, such as **JavaScript1.1**, also might be possible.

style   See "Core Attributes Reference," earlier in this appendix.

APPENDIX A

tabindex   This attribute uses a number to identify the object's position in the tabbing order for keyboard navigation using the TAB key. Internet Explorer 5.5 applies this attribute to the **q** element; under IE 5.5, this focus can be disabled with the **hidefocus** attribute.

title   See "Core Attributes Reference," earlier in this appendix.

Attribute and Event Support

Internet Explorer 4   All attributes and events defined by the W3C and Internet Explorer 4, except **cite** and **dir**.

Internet Explorer 5.5   All attributes and events, except **cite**.

Event Handlers

See "Events Reference," earlier in this appendix.

Example

```
<q style="color: green">"A few green balls and a rainbow bar will
give you an exciting Web page Christmas Tree!"</q>
```

Compatibility

HTML 4, 4.01, XHTML
Internet Explorer 4, 5, and 5.5
Netscape 6

Notes

■ This element is intended for short quotations that don't require paragraph breaks, as compared to text that would be contained within **<blockquote>**. Microsoft documentation continues to indicate this is a block element, when it is not.

■ Internet Explorer does not make any sort of style change for quotations, but it is possible to apply a style rule.

■ Netscape 6 (Preview Release 2) adds quotes around text enclosed within the **<q>** element.

<rt> (Ruby Text)

This Microsoft-specific proprietary element is used within the **<ruby>** element to create "ruby text," or annotations or pronunciation guides for words and phrases. The base text should be enclosed in the **<ruby>** element; the annotation, enclosed in the **<rt>** element, will appear as smaller text above the base text. This element was introduced with Internet Explorer 5.0.

Syntax Defined by Internet Explorer 5.0

```
<rt
    accesskey="key"
    class="class name(s)"
    dir="ltr | rtl"
    id="unique alphanumeric identifier"
    lang="language code"
    language="javascript | jscript | vbs | vbscript | xml"
    name="string"
    style="style information"
    tabindex="number"
    title="advisory text"
    onfterupdate="script"
    onbeforecut="script"
    onbeforepaste="script"
    onbeforeupdate="script"
    onblur="script"
    onclick="script"
    oncut="script"
    ondblclick="script"
    ondragstart="script"
    onerrorupdate="script"
    onfilterchange="script"
    onfocus="script"
    onhelp="script"
    onkeydown="script"
    onkeypress="script"
    onkeyup="script"
    onmousedown="script"
    onmousemove="script"
    onmouseout="script"
    onmouseover="script"
    onmouseup="script"
    onpaste="script"
    onreadystatechange="script">
... ruby text ..
```

Syntax Defined by Internet Explorer 5.5

```
    contenteditable="false | true | inherit"
    hidefocus="true | false"
```

Attributes

accesskey   This attribute specifies a keyboard navigation accelerator for the element. Pressing ALT or a similar key (depending on the browser and operating system) in association with the specified key selects the anchor element correlated with that key.

class   See "Core Attributes Reference," earlier in this appendix.

contenteditable   This proprietary Microsoft attribute allows users to edit content rendered in the Internet Explorer 5.5 browser. Values are **false**, **true**, and **inherit**. A value of **false** will prevent content from being edited by users; **true** will allow editing. The default value, **inherit**, applies the value of the affected element's parent element.

dir   See "Language Reference," earlier in this appendix.

hidefocus   This proprietary element, introduced with Internet Explorer 5.5, hides focus on an element's content. Focus must be applied to the element using the **tabindex** attribute.

id   See "Core Attributes Reference," earlier in this appendix.

lang   See "Language Reference," earlier in this appendix.

language   This attribute specifies the language the current script is written in and invokes the proper scripting engine. The default value is **javascript**. **Javascript** and **jscript** represent that the scripting language is written in JavaScript. **Vbs** and **vbscript** represent that the scripting language is written in VBScript.

name   Sets a name for the ruby text.

style   See "Core Attributes Reference," earlier in this appendix.

tabindex   This attribute uses a number to identify the object's position in the tabbing order for keyboard navigation using the TAB key. Internet Explorer 5.5 applies this attribute to the **dfn** element; under IE 5.5, this focus can be disabled with the **hidefocus** attribute.

title   See "Core Attributes Reference," earlier in this appendix.

Attribute and Event Support

Internet Explorer 5.0   All attributes and events except **contenteditable** and **hidefocus**.

Internet Explorer 5.5   All attributes and events

Event Handlers
See "Events Reference," earlier in this appendix.

Examples

```
<ruby>Base Text

<rt>Ruby Text

</ruby>
```

Notes

- This element works only in Internet Explorer 5.0 and higher.
- The **<rt>** element must be used within the **<ruby>** element.
- Microsoft defines **<rt>** as an inline element that requires no closing tag; how this might be adapted for XHTML compatibility remains unclear.
- This element should be used only in an Internet Explorer–exclusive environment because other browsers will not interpret it or the **<ruby>** element.

<ruby>

This Microsoft-specific proprietary element is used with the **<rt>** element to create annotations or pronunciation guides for words and phrases. The base text should be enclosed in the **<ruby>** element; the annotation, enclosed in the **<rt>** element, will appear as smaller text above the base text. This element was introduced with Internet Explorer 5.0.

Syntax Defined by Internet Explorer 5.0

```
ruby
    accesskey="key"
    class="class name(s)"
    dir="ltr | rtl"
    id="unique alphanumeric identifier"
    lang="language code"
    language="javascript | jscript | vbs | vbscript | xml"
    name="string"
    style="style information"
    tabindex="number"
    title="advisory text"
    onfterupdate="script"
    onbeforecut="script"
    onbeforepaste="script"
    onbeforeupdate="script"
    onblur="script"
    onclick="script"
    oncut="script"
    ondblclick="script"
```

```
          ondragstart="script"
          onerrorupdate="script"
          onfilterchange="script"
          onfocus="script"
          onhelp="script"
          onkeydown="script"
          onkeypress="script"
          onkeyup="script"
          onmousedown="script"
          onmousemove="script"
          onmouseout="script"
          onmouseover="script"
          onmouseup="script"
          onpaste="script"
          onreadystatechange="script">

... base text ...
<rt>ruby text

</ruby>
```

Syntax Defined by Internet Explorer 5.5

```
          contenteditable="false | true | inherit"
          hidefocus="true | false"
```

Attributes

accesskey   This attribute specifies a keyboard navigation accelerator for the element. Pressing ALT or a similar key (depending on the browser and operating system) in association with the specified key selects the anchor element correlated with that key.

class   See "Core Attributes Reference," earlier in this appendix.

contenteditable   This proprietary Microsoft attribute allows users to edit content rendered in the Internet Explorer 5.5 browser. Values are **false**, **true**, and **inherit**. A value of **false** will prevent content from being edited by users; **true** will allow editing. The default value, **inherit**, applies the value of the affected element's parent element.

dir   See "Language Reference," earlier in this appendix.

hidefocus   This proprietary element, introduced with Internet Explorer 5.5, hides focus on an element's content. Focus must be applied to the element using the **tabindex** attribute.

id   See "Core Attributes Reference," earlier in this appendix.

lang   See "Language Reference," earlier in this appendix.

language   This attribute specifies the language the current script is written in and invokes the proper scripting engine. The default value is **javascript**. **Javascript** and **jscript** represent that the scripting language is written in JavaScript. **Vbs** and **vbscript** represent that the scripting language is written in VBScript.

name   Sets a name for the ruby base text.

style   See "Core Attributes Reference," earlier in this appendix.

tabindex   This attribute uses a number to identify the object's position in the tabbing order for keyboard navigation using the TAB key. Internet Explorer 5.5 applies this attribute to the **dfn** element; under IE 5.5, this focus can be disabled with the **hidefocus** attribute.

title   See "Core Attributes Reference," earlier in this appendix.

Attribute and Event Support

Internet Explorer 5.0   All attributes and events defined by Internet Explorer 5.0.

Internet Explorer 5.5   All attributes and events defined by Internet Explorer 5.0 and 5.5.

Event Handlers
See "Events Reference," earlier in this appendix.

Examples

```
<ruby>This is the base text within the ruby element

<rt>This is the ruby text, which should appear in a smaller font
    above the base text in Internet Explorer 5.0 or higher.

</ruby>
```

Notes

- This element works only in Internet Explorer 5.0 and higher.
- The **<ruby>** element must be used in conjunction with the **<rt>** element; otherwise, it will have no meaning.
- This element should be used only in an Internet Explorer–exclusive environment because other browsers will not interpret it or the **<rt>** element.

<s> (Strikethrough)

This element renders the enclosed text with a line drawn through it.

Syntax (Transitional Only)

```
<s
    class="class name(s)"
    dir="ltr | rtl"
    id="unique alphanumeric identifier"
    lang="language code"
    style="style information"
    title="advisory text"
    onclick="script"
    ondblclick="script"
    onkeydown="script"
    onkeypress="script"
    onkeyup="script"
    onmousedown="script"
    onmousemove="script"
    onmouseout="script"
    onmouseover="script"
    onmouseup="script">

</s>
```

Attributes and Events Defined by Internet Explorer 4

```
    language="javascript | jscript | vbs | vbsscript"
    ondragstart="script"
    onhelp="script"
    onselectstart="script"
```

Attributes and Events Defined by Internet Explorer 5.5

```
    accesskey="key"
    contenteditable="false | true | inherit"
    hidefocus="true | false"
    tabindex="number"
```

Attributes

accesskey   This attribute specifies a keyboard navigation accelerator for the element. Pressing ALT or a similar key (depending on the browser and operating system) in association with the specified key selects the anchor element correlated with that key.

class   See "Core Attributes Reference," earlier in this appendix.

contenteditable   This proprietary Microsoft attribute allows users to edit content rendered in the Internet Explorer 5.5 browser. Values are **false**, **true**, and **inherit**. A value of **false** will prevent content from being edited by users; **true** will allow editing. The default value, **inherit**, applies the value of the affected element's parent element.

dir   See "Language Reference," earlier in this appendix.

hidefocus   This proprietary element, introduced with Internet Explorer 5.5, hides focus on an element's content. Focus must be applied to the element using the **tabindex** attribute.

id   See "Core Attributes Reference," earlier in this appendix.

lang   See "Language Reference," earlier in this appendix.

language   In the Microsoft implementation, this attribute specifies the scripting language to be used with an associated script bound to the element, typically through an event handler attribute. Possible values might include **javascript**, **jscript**, **vbs**, and **vbscript**. Other values that include the version of the language used, such as **JavaScript1.1**, might also be possible.

style   See "Core Attributes Reference," earlier in this appendix.

tabindex   This attribute uses a number to identify the object's position in the tabbing order for keyboard navigation using the TAB key. Internet Explorer 5.5 applies this attribute to the **s** element; under IE 5.5, this focus can be disabled with the **hidefocus** attribute.

title   See "Core Attributes Reference," earlier in this appendix.

Attribute and Event Support

Netscape 4   class, **id**, **lang**, and **style** are implied.

Internet Explorer 4   All attributes and events defined by the W3C and Internet Explorer 4.0, except **dir**.

Internet Explorer 5.5   All attributes and events

Event Handlers
See "Events Reference," earlier in this appendix.

Examples

```
This line contains a <s>misstake</s>.

<s id="strike1"
```

```
    onmouseover="this.style.color='red'"
    onmouseout="this.style.color='black'">Fastball</s>
```

Compatibility

HTML 4 (transitional), 4.01 (transitional), XHTML 1.0
Internet Explorer 2, 3, 4, 5, and 5.5
Netscape 3, 4–4.7, 6
WebTV

Notes

- This element should act the same as the **<strike>** element.
- This HTML 3 element eventually was adopted by Netscape and Microsoft and later was incorporated into the HTML 4 transitional specification.
- This element has been deprecated by the W3C. The strict HTML 4.01 specification does not include the **<s>** element or the **<strike>** element. It is possible to indicate strikethrough text using a style sheet.

<samp> (Sample Text)

This element is used to indicate sample text. Enclosed text generally is rendered in a monospaced font.

Syntax

```
<samp
    class="class name(s)"
    dir="ltr | rtl"
    id="unique alphanumeric string"
    lang="language code"
    style="style information"
    title="advisory text"
    onclick="script"
    ondblclick="script"
    onkeydown="script"
    onkeypress="script"
    onkeyup="script"
    onmousedown="script"
    onmousemove="script"
    onmouseout="script"
    onmouseover="script"
    onmouseup="script">

</samp>
```

Attributes and Events Defined by Internet Explorer 4

```
language="javascript | jscript | vbs | vbscript"
ondragstart="script"
onhelp="script"
onselectstart="script"
```

Attributes and Events Defined by Internet Explorer 5.5

```
accesskey="key"
contenteditable="false | true | inherit"
hidefocus="true | false"
tabindex="number"
```

Attributes

accesskey   This attribute specifies a keyboard navigation accelerator for the element. Pressing ALT or a similar key (depending on the browser and operating system) in association with the specified key selects the anchor element correlated with that key.

class   See "Core Attributes Reference," earlier in this appendix.

contenteditable   This proprietary Microsoft attribute allows users to edit content rendered in the Internet Explorer 5.5 browser. Values are **false**, **true**, and **inherit**. A value of **false** will prevent content from being edited by users; **true** will allow editing. The default value, **inherit**, applies the value of the affected element's parent element.

dir   See "Language Reference," earlier in this appendix.

hidefocus   This proprietary element, introduced with Internet Explorer 5.5, hides focus on an element's content. Focus must be applied to the element using the **tabindex** attribute.

id   See "Core Attributes Reference," earlier in this appendix.

lang   See "Language Reference," earlier in this appendix.

language   In the Microsoft implementation, this attribute specifies the scripting language to be used with an associated script bound to the element, typically through an event handler attribute. Possible values might include **javascript**, **jscript**, **vbs**, and **vbscript**. Other values that include the version of the language used, such as **JavaScript1.1**, also might be possible.

style   See "Core Attributes Reference," earlier in this appendix.

tabindex   This attribute uses a number to identify the object's position in the tabbing order for keyboard navigation using the TAB key. Internet Explorer 5.5 applies this attribute to the **samp** element; under IE 5.5, this focus can be disabled with the **hidefocus** attribute.

title   See "Core Attributes Reference," earlier in this appendix.

Attribute and Event Support

Internet Explorer 4   All attributes and events defined by the W3C and Internet Explorer 4.0, except **dir**.

Internet Explorer 5.5   All attributes and events.

Event Handlers

See "Events Reference," earlier in this appendix.

Example

Use the following salutation in all e-mail messages to the boss:
<samp>Please excuse the interruption, oh exalted manager.**</samp>**

Compatibility

HTML 2, 3.2, 4, and 4.01, XHTML 1.0
Internet Explorer 2, 3, 4, 5, and 5.5
Netscape 1, 2, 3, 4–4.7, 6
Opera 4.0
WebTV

Notes

■ As a logical element, **<samp>** is useful to bind style rules to.

■ The HTML 2.0 and 3.2 specifications supported no attributes for this element.

<script> (Scripting)

This element encloses statements in a scripting language for client-side processing. Scripting statements can either be included inline or loaded from an external file and might be commented out to avoid execution by non–scripting-aware browsers.

Syntax

```
<script
    charset="character set"
    defer
    event="event name" (reserved)
    for="element ID" (reserved)
    language="scripting language name"
    src="url of script code"
    type="mime type">

</script>
```

Attributes Defined by Internet Explorer 4

```
class="class name(s)"
id="unique alphanumeric identifier"
title="advisory text"
```

Attributes

charset   This attribute defines the character encoding of the script. The value is a space-and/or comma-delimited list of character sets as defined in RFC 2045. The default value is **ISO-8859-1**.

class   This Microsoft-defined attribute does not make much sense given that scripting code would not be bound by style sheet rules. Its meaning as defined in the "Core Attributes Reference" in this appendix is unclear within the context of the **<script>** element.

defer   Presence of this attribute indicates that the browser might defer execution of the script enclosed by the **<script>** element. In practice, deferring code might be more dependent on the position of the **<script>** element or the contents. This attribute was added very late to the HTML 4.01 specification and its support is currently minimal.

event   This Microsoft attribute is used to define a particular event that the script should react to. It must be used in conjunction with the **for** attribute. Event names are the same as event handler attributes; for example, **onclick**, **ondblclick**, and so on.

for   The **for** attribute is used to define the name or ID of the element to which an event defined by the **event** attribute is related. For example, **<script event="onclick" for="button1" language="vbscript">** defines a VBScript that will execute when a click event is issued for an element named button1.

id   See "Core Attributes Reference," earlier in this appendix.

language   This attribute specifies the scripting language being used. The Netscape implementation supports JavaScript. The Microsoft implementation supports JScript (a JavaScript clone) as well as VBScript, which can be indicated by either **vbs** or **vbscript**. Other values that include the version of the language used, such as **JavaScript1.1** and **JavaScript1.2**, also might be possible and are useful to exclude browsers from executing script code that is not supported.

src   This attribute specifies the URL of a file containing scripting code. Typically, files containing JavaScript code will have a .js extension, and a server will attach the appropriate MIME type; if not, the **type** attribute might be used to explicitly set the content type of the external script file. The **language** attribute also might be helpful in determining this.

title   See "Core Attributes Reference," earlier in this appendix.

type   This attribute should be set to the MIME type corresponding to the scripting language used. For JavaScript, for example, this would be **text/javascript**. In practice, the **language** attribute is the more common way to indicate which scripting language is in effect.

Attribute and Event Support

Netscape 4   **language** and **src**

Internet Explorer 4   All attributes and events except **charset**.

WebTV   **language** and **src**

Event Handlers

There are no events directly associated with the **<script>** element. However, the Microsoft implementation does allow the **event** attribute to be used to indicate what event a particular script might be associated with.

Examples

```
<script language="JavaScript">
<!-- alert("Hello World !!!"); // -->
</script>

<!-- code in external file -->
<script language="JavaScript1.2" src="superrollover.js">
</script>

<script for ="myButton" event="onclick"
        language="JavaScript">
<!-- alert("I've been clicked!"); // -->
</script>

<form>
    <input type="BUTTON" name="myButton" value="Click me">
</form>
```

Compatibility
HTML 4 and 4.01, XHTML 1.0
Internet Explorer 3, 4, 5, and 5.5
Netscape 2, 3, 4–4.7, 6
Opera 4.0

Notes

■ It is common practice to comment out statements enclosed by the **<script>** element. Without commenting, scripts are displayed as page content by browsers that do not support scripting. The particular comment style might be dependent on the language being used. For example, in JavaScript use

```
<script language="JavaScript">
<!-- Javacript code here // -->
</script>
```

and in VBScript use

```
<script language="vbscript">
<!-- VBScript code here -->
</script>
```

■ The HTML 3.2 specification defined a placeholder **<script>** element, but otherwise the element is new to HTML 4.

■ Refer to the **<noscript>** element reference in this appendix to see how content might be identified for non-scripting-aware browsers.

<select> (Selection List)

This element defines a selection list within a form. Depending on the form of the selection list, the control allows the user to select one or more list options.

Syntax

```
<select
    class="class name(s)"
    dir="ltr | rtl"
    disabled
    id="unique alphanumeric identifier"
    lang="language code"
    multiple
    name="unique alphanumeric name"
    size="number"
    style="style information"
    tabindex="number"
    title="advisory text"
    onblur="script"
    onchange="script"
    onclick="script"
    ondblclick="script"
```

```
            onfocus="script"
            onkeydown="script"
            onkeypress="script"
            onkeyup="script"
            onmousedown="script"
            onmousemove="script"
            onmouseout="script"
            onmouseover="script"
            onmouseup="script">

    <option> elements

</select>
```

Attributes and Events Defined by Internet Explorer 4

```
        accesskey="character"
        align="absbottom | absmiddle | baseline | bottom |
                left | middle | right | texttop | top"
        datafld="column name"
        datasrc="data source ID"
        language="javascript | jscript | vbs | vbscript"
        onafterupdate="script"
        onbeforeupdate="script"
        ondragstart="script"
        onhelp="script"
        onresize="script"
        onrowenter="script"
        onrowexit="script"
        onselectstart="script"
```

Attributes and Events Defined by Internet Explorer 5.5

```
        hidefocus="true | false"
```

Attributes Defined by WebTV

```
        autoactive
        bgcolor="color name | #RRGGBB"
        exclusive
        selcolor="color name | #RRGGBB"
        text="color name | #RRGGBB"
        usestyle
```

Attributes

accesskey This Microsoft attribute specifies a keyboard navigation accelerator for the element. Pressing ALT or a similar key in association with the specified character selects the form control correlated with that key sequence. Page designers are forewarned to avoid key sequences already bound to browsers.

align This Microsoft-specific attribute controls the alignment of the image with respect to the content on the page. The default value is **left**, but other values such as **absbottom**, **absmiddle**, **baseline**, **bottom**, **middle**, **right**, **texttop**, and **top** also might be supported. The meaning of these values should be similar to inserted objects such as images.

auotactive In the WebTV implementation, this attribute causes the selection list control to immediately activate when the user selects it, allowing the user to quickly use the arrow keys to move up and down. Without this attribute, the process is a two-step procedure to select the control and then move around.

bgcolor In the WebTV implementation, this attribute specifies the background color of the selection list. The value for this attribute can be either a named color, such as **red**, or a color specified in the hexadecimal *#RRGGBB* format, such as **#FF0000**.

class See "Core Attributes Reference," earlier in this appendix.

datafld This attribute is used to indicate the column name in the data source that is bound to the options in the **<select>** element.

datasrc The value of this attribute is set to an identifier indicating the data source to pull data from.

dir See "Language Reference," earlier in this appendix.

disabled This attribute is used to turn off a form control. Elements will not be submitted nor can they receive any focus from the keyboard or mouse. Disabled form controls will not be part of the tabbing order. The browser also can gray out the form that is disabled in order to indicate to the user that the form control is inactive. This attribute requires no value.

exclusive In the WebTV implementation, this attribute prevents duplicate entries in the selection list. The attribute requires no value.

hidefocus This proprietary element, introduced with Internet Explorer 5.5, hides focus on an element's content. Focus must be applied to the element using the **tabindex** attribute.

id See "Core Attributes Reference," earlier in this appendix.

lang See "Language Reference," earlier in this appendix.

language In the Microsoft implementation, this attribute specifies the scripting language to be used with an associated script bound to the element, typically through an event handler attribute. Possible values might include **javascript**, **jscript**, **vbs**, and **vbscript**. Other values that include the version of the language used, such as **JavaScript1.1**, also might be possible.

multiple   This attribute allows the selection of multiple items in the selection list. The default is single-item selection.

name   This attribute allows a form control to be assigned a name so that it can be referenced by a scripting language. **Name** is supported by older browsers such as Netscape 2 generation browsers, but the W3C encourages the use of the **id** attribute. For compatibility purposes both might have to be used.

selcolor   In the WebTV implementation, this attribute specifies the background color for selected items. Its value can be either a named color, such as **green**, or a color specified in the hexadecimal #*RRGGBB* format, such as **#00FF00**. The default for this attribute in WebTV is **#EAEAEA**.

size   This attribute sets the number of visible items in the selection list. When the **multiple** attribute is not present, only one entry should show; however, when **multiple** is present, this attribute is useful to set the size of the scrolling list box.

style   See "Core Attributes Reference," earlier in this appendix.

tabindex   This attribute takes a numeric value indicating the position of the form control in the tabbing index for the form. Tabbing proceeds from the lowest positive **tabindex** value to the highest. Negative values for **tabindex** will leave the form control out of the tabbing order. When tabbing is not explicitly set, the browser might tab through items in the order they are encountered. Form controls that are disabled due to the presence of the **disabled** attribute will not be part of the tabbing index, although read-only controls will be.

text   In the WebTV implementation, this attribute specifies the text color for items in the list. Its value can be either a named color, such as **blue**, or a color specified in the hexadecimal #*RRGGBB* format, such as **#0000FF**.

title   See "Core Attributes Reference," earlier in this appendix.

usestyle   This WebTV-specific attribute causes text to be rendered in the style in effect for the page. The attribute requires no value.

Attribute and Event Support

Netscape 4   multiple, name, size, onblur, onchange, and onfocus (class, id, lang, and style are implied.)

Internet Explorer 4   All W3C-defined attributes and events except **dir** and **title**, and all attributes and events defined by Internet Explorer 4.

Internet Explorer 5.0   All W3C-defined attributes and events except **title**, and all attributes and events defined by Internet Explorer 4.

Internet Explorer 5.5   Same as Internet Explorer 5.0, plus **hidefocus**.

WebTV   autoactivate, **bgcolor, multiple, name, selcolor, size, text, usestyle, onblur,** onchange, **onfocus,** and **onclick**

Event Handlers
See "Events Reference," earlier in this appendix.

Examples

```
Choose your favorite colors
<select multiple size="2">
   <option>Red
   <option>Blue
   <option>Green
   <option>Yellow
</select>

Taco Choices
<select name="tacomenu">
   <option value="SuperChicken">Chicken
   <option value="Baja">Fish
   <option value="RX-Needed">Carnitas
</select>
```

Compatibility
HTML 2, 3.2, 4, and 4.01, XHTML 1.0
Internet Explorer 2, 3, 4, 5, and 5.5
Netscape 1, 2, 3, 4–4.7, 6
Opera 4
WebTV

Notes

- The HTML 4.01 specification reserves the attributes **datafld** and **datasrc** for future use.
- The HTML 2.0 and 3.2 specifications define only **multiple, name,** and **size** attributes.

<small> (Small Text)
This element renders the enclosed text one font size smaller than a document's base font size unless it is already set to the smallest size.

Syntax

```
<small
     class="class name(s)"
     dir="ltr | rtl"
     id="unique alphanumeric string"
     lang="language code"
     style="style information"
     title="advisory text"
     onclick="script"
     ondblclick="script"
     onkeydown="script"
     onkeypress="script"
     onkeyup="script"
     onmousedown="script"
     onmousemove="script"
     onmouseout="script"
     onmouseover="script"
     onmouseup="script">

</small>
```

Attributes and Events Defined by Internet Explorer 4

```
language="javascript | jscript | vbs | vbscript"
ondragstart="script"
onhelp="script"
onselectstart="script"
```

Attributes and Events Defined by Internet Explorer 5.5

```
accesskey="key"
contenteditable="false | true | inherit"
hidefocus="true | false"
tabindex="number"
```

Attributes

accesskey   This attribute specifies a keyboard navigation accelerator for the element. Pressing ALT or a similar key (depending on the browser and operating system) in association with the specified key selects the anchor element correlated with that key.

class   See "Core Attributes Reference," earlier in this appendix.

contenteditable   This proprietary Microsoft attribute allows users to edit content rendered in the Internet Explorer 5.5 browser. Values are **false**, **true**, and **inherit**. A value of **false** will prevent content from being edited by users; **true** will allow editing. The default value, **inherit**, applies the value of the affected element's parent element.

dir   See "Language Reference," earlier in this appendix.

hidefocus   This proprietary element, introduced with Internet Explorer 5.5, hides focus on an element's content. Focus must be applied to the element using the **tabindex** attribute.

id   See "Core Attributes Reference," earlier in this appendix.

lang   See "Language Reference," earlier in this appendix.

language   In the Microsoft implementation, this attribute specifies the scripting language to be used with an associated script bound to the element, typically through an event handler attribute. Possible values might include **javascript**, **jscript**, **vbs**, and **vbscript**. Other values that include the version of the language used, such as **JavaScript1.1**, also might be possible.

style   See "Core Attributes Reference," earlier in this appendix.

tabindex   This attribute uses a number to identify the object's position in the tabbing order for keyboard navigation using the TAB key. Internet Explorer 5.5 applies this attribute to the **small** element; under IE 5.5, this focus can be disabled with the **hidefocus** attribute.

title   See "Core Attributes Reference," earlier in this appendix.

Attribute and Event Support

Netscape 4   class, **id**, **lang**, and **style** are implied.

Internet Explorer 4   All attributes and events defined by the W3C and Internet Explorer 4, except **dir**.

Internet Explorer 5.5   All attributes and events

Event Handlers
See "Events Reference," earlier in this appendix.

Examples

```
Here is some <small>small text</small>.

This element can be applied <small><small><small>multiple
times</small></small></small>to make things even smaller.
```

Compatibility

HTML 3.2, 4, and 4, XHTML 1.0
Internet Explorer 2, 3, 4, 5, and 5.5
Netscape 2, 3, 4–4.7, 6
WebTV

Notes

■ The **<small>** element can be used multiple times to decrease the size of text to a greater degree. Using more than six **<small>** elements together doesn't make sense because browsers currently only support relative font sizes from 1 to 7. As style sheets become more common, this element might fall out of favor.

■ The default base font size for a document typically is 3, although it can be changed with the **<basefont>** element.

<spacer> (Extra Space)

This proprietary element specifies an invisible region for pushing content around a page.

Syntax (Defined by Netscape 3)

```
<spacer
    align="absmiddle | absbottom | baseline | bottom |
           left | middle | right | texttop | top"
    height="pixels"
    size="pixels"
    type="block | horizontal | vertical"
    width="pixels">
```

Attributes

align   This attribute specifies the alignment of the spacer with respect to surrounding text. It is used only with spacers with **type="block"**. The default value for the **align** attribute is **bottom**. The meanings of the **align** values are similar to those used with the **<img>** element.

height   This attribute specifies the height of the invisible region in pixels. It is used only with spacers with **type="block"**.

size   Used with **type="block"** and **type="horizontal"** spacers, this attribute sets the spacer's width in pixels. Used with a **type="vertical"** spacer, this attribute is used to set the spacer's height.

type   This attribute indicates the type of invisible region. A **horizontal** spacer adds horizontal space between words and objects. A **vertical** spacer is used to add space between lines. A **block** spacer defines a general-purpose positioning rectangle like an invisible image that text can flow around.

width   This attribute is used only with the **type="block"** spacer and is used to set the width of the region in pixels.

Attribute and Event Support

Netscape 4   All attributes

WebTV   All attributes

Examples

```
A line of text with two <spacer type="horizontal" size="20">words
separated by 20 pixels. Here is a line of text.<br>
<spacer type="vertical" size="50">

Here is another line of text with a large space between the two
lines.<spacer align="left" type="block" height="100" width="100"> This
is a bunch of text that flows around an invisible block region. You
could have easily performed this layout with a table.
```

Compatibility
Netscape 3, 4–4.7, 6
WebTV

Notes

- This element should not be used. If the effect of this element is required and style sheets cannot be used, an invisible pixel trick might be a more appropriate choice. The invisible pixel trick requires a transparent image, which then is resized with the **height** and **width** attributes of the **<img>** element:

  ```
  <img src="pixel.gif" height="100" width="100">
  ```

- This is an empty element; no closing tag is allowed.

<span> (Text Span)

This element typically is used to group inline text so scripting or style rules can be applied to the content. As it has no preset or rendering meaning, this is the most useful inline element for associating style and script with content.

Syntax

```
<span
    class="class name(s)"
```

APPENDIX A

```
            datafld="column name" (reserved)
            dataformatas="html | text" (reserved)
            datasrc="data source id" (reserved)
            dir="ltr | rtl"
            id="unique alphanumeric string"
            lang="language code"
            style="style information"
            title="advisory text"
            onclick="script"
            ondblclick="script"
            onkeydown="script"
            onkeypress="script"
            onkeyup="script"
            onmousedown="script"
            onmousemove="script"
            onmouseout="script"
            onmouseover="script"
            onmouseup="script">

</span>
```

Attributes and Events Defined by Internet Explorer 4

```
    language="javascript | jscript | vbs | vbscript"
    ondragstart="script"
    onhelp="script"
    onselectstart="script"
```

Attributes and Events Defined by Internet Explorer 5.5

```
    accesskey="key"
    contenteditable="false | true | inherit"
    hidefocus="true | false"
    tabindex="number"
```

Attributes

accesskey   This attribute specifies a keyboard navigation accelerator for the element. Pressing ALT or a similar key (depending on the browser and operating system) in association with the specified key selects the anchor element correlated with that key.

class   See "Core Attributes Reference," earlier in this appendix.

contenteditable   This proprietary Microsoft attribute allows users to edit content rendered in the Internet Explorer 5.5 browser. Values are **false**, **true**, and **inherit**. A value of **false** will prevent content from being edited by users; **true** will allow editing. The default value, **inherit**, applies the value of the affected element's parent element.

datafld   This attribute is used to indicate the column name in the data source that is bound to the contents of the **<span>** element.

dataformatas   This attribute indicates whether the bound data is plain text (**text**) or HTML (**html**). The data bound with **<span>** should be used to set the content of the element and might include HTML markup.

datasrc   The value of this attribute is set to an identifier indicating the data source to pull data from.

dir   See "Language Reference," earlier in this appendix.

hidefocus   This proprietary element, introduced with Internet Explorer 5.5, hides focus on an element's content. Focus must be applied to the element using the **tabindex** attribute.

id   See "Core Attributes Reference," earlier in this appendix.

lang   See "Language Reference," earlier in this appendix.

language   In the Microsoft implementation, this attribute specifies the scripting language to be used with an associated script bound to the element, typically through an event handler attribute. Possible values might include **javascript**, **jscript**, **vbs**, and **vbscript**. Other values that include the version of the language used, such as **JavaScript1.1**, also might be possible.

style   See "Core Attributes Reference," earlier in this appendix.

tabindex   This attribute uses a number to identify the object's position in the tabbing order for keyboard navigation using the TAB key. Internet Explorer 5.5 applies this attribute to the **span** element; under IE 5.5, this focus can be disabled with the **hidefocus** attribute.

title   See "Core Attributes Reference," earlier in this appendix.

Attribute and Event Support

Netscape 4   class, id, lang, and style

Internet Explorer 4   All attributes and events defined by the W3C and Internet Explorer 4, except **dir**.

Internet Explorer 5.5   All attributes and events

Event Handlers
See "Events Reference," earlier in this appendix.

APPENDIX A

Examples

```
Here is some <span style="font-size: 14pt; color: purple">very
strange</span> text.

<span id="toggletext"
      onclick="this.style.color='red'"
      ondblclick="this.style.color='black'">
Click and Double Click Me
</span>
```

Compatibility

HTML 4, 4.01, XHTML 1.0
Internet Explorer 3, 4, 5, and 5.5
Netscape 4–4.7, 6

Notes

■ The HTML 4.01 specification reserves the **datafld, dataformatas,** and **datasrc** attributes
for future use. Internet Explorer 4 supports them.

■ Unlike the block level element **<div>,** as an inline element **<span>** does not cause any
line breaks.

<strike> (Strikeout Text)

This element is used to indicate strikethrough text, namely text with a line drawn through it. The
<s> element provides shorthand notation for this element.

Syntax (Transitional Only)

```
<strike
     class="class name(s)"
     dir="ltr | rtl"
     id="unique alphanumeric string"
     lang="language code"
     style="style information"
     title="advisory text"
     onclick="script"
     ondblclick="script"
     onkeydown="script"
     onkeypress="script"
     onkeyup="script"
     onmousedown="script"
     onmousemove="script"
     onmouseout="script"
```

```
        onmouseover="script"
        onmouseup="script">

  </strike>
```

Attributes and Events Defined by Internet Explorer 4

```
        language="javascript | jscript | vbs | vbscript"
        ondragstart="script"
        onhelp="script"
        onselectstart="script"
```

Attributes and Events Defined by Internet Explorer 5.5

```
        accesskey="key"
        contenteditable="false | true | inherit"
        hidefocus="true | false"
        tabindex="number"
```

Attributes

accesskey   This attribute specifies a keyboard navigation accelerator for the element. Pressing ALT or a similar key (depending on the browser and operating system) in association with the specified key selects the anchor element correlated with that key.

class   See "Core Attributes Reference," earlier in this appendix.

contenteditable   This proprietary Microsoft attribute allows users to edit content rendered in the Internet Explorer 5.5 browser. Values are **false**, **true**, and **inherit**. A value of **false** will prevent content from being edited by users; **true** will allow editing. The default value, **inherit**, applies the value of the affected element's parent element.

dir   See "Language Reference," earlier in this appendix.

hidefocus   This proprietary element, introduced with Internet Explorer 5.5, hides focus on an element's content. Focus must be applied to the element using the **tabindex** attribute.

id   See "Core Attributes Reference," earlier in this appendix.

lang   See "Language Reference," earlier in this appendix.

language   In the Microsoft implementation, this attribute specifies the scripting language to be used with an associated script bound to the element, typically through an event handler attribute. Possible values might include **javascript**, **jscript**, **vbs**, and **vbscript**. Other values that include the version of the language used, such as **JavaScript1.1**, also might be possible.

style   See "Core Attributes Reference," earlier in this appendix.

tabindex   This attribute uses a number to identify the object's position in the tabbing order for keyboard navigation using the TAB key. Internet Explorer 5.5 applies this attribute to the **strike** element; under IE 5.5, this focus can be disabled with the **hidefocus** attribute.

title   See "Core Attributes Reference," earlier in this appendix.

Attribute and Event Support

Netscape 4   **class**, **id**, **lang**, and **style** are implied.

Internet Explorer 4   All attributes and events defined by the W3C and Internet Explorer 4, except **dir**.

Internet Explorer 5.5   All attributes and events

Event Handlers
See "Events Reference," earlier in this appendix.

Example

```
This line contains a spelling <strike>misstake</strike> mistake.
```

Compatibility
HTML 3.2, 4 (transitional), and 4.01 (transitional), XHTML 1.0
Internet Explorer 2, 3, 4, 5, and 5.5
Netscape 3, 4–4.7, 6
Opera 4.0
WebTV

Notes

- This element should act the same as the **<s>** element.
- This element has been deprecated by the W3C. The strict HTML 4.01 specification does not include the **<strike>** element nor the **<s>** element. It is possible to indicate strikethrough text using a style sheet.

<strong> (Strong Emphasis)

This element indicates strongly emphasized text. It usually is rendered in a bold typeface, but is a logical element rather than a physical one.

Syntax

```
<strong
    class="class name(s)"
    dir="ltr | rtl"
    id="unique alphanumeric string"
    lang="language code"
    style="style information"
    title="advisory text"
    onclick="script"
    ondblclick="script"
    onkeydown="script"
    onkeypress="script"
    onkeyup="script"
    onmousedown="script"
    onmousemove="script"
    onmouseout="script"
    onmouseover="script"
    onmouseup="script">

</strong>
```

Attributes and Events Defined by Internet Explorer 4

```
language="javascript | jscript | vbs | vbscript"
ondragstart="script"
onhelp="script"
onselectstart="script"
```

Attributes and Events Defined by Internet Explorer 5.5

```
accesskey="key"
contenteditable="false | true | inherit"
hidefocus="true | false"
tabindex="number"
```

Attributes

accesskey   This attribute specifies a keyboard navigation accelerator for the element. Pressing ALT or a similar key (depending on the browser and operating system) in association with the specified key selects the anchor element correlated with that key.

class   See "Core Attributes Reference," earlier in this appendix.

contenteditable   This proprietary Microsoft attribute allows users to edit content rendered in the Internet Explorer 5.5 browser. Values are **false**, **true**, and **inherit**. A value of **false** will prevent content from being edited by users; **true** will allow editing. The default value, **inherit**, applies the value of the affected element's parent element.

dir   See "Language Reference," earlier in this appendix.

hidefocus   This proprietary element, introduced with Internet Explorer 5.5, hides focus on an element's content. Focus must be applied to the element using the **tabindex** attribute.

id   See "Core Attributes Reference," earlier in this appendix.

lang   See "Language Reference," earlier in this appendix.

language   In the Microsoft implementation, this attribute specifies the scripting language to be used with an associated script bound to the element, typically through an event handler attribute. Possible values might include **javascript**, **jscript**, **vbs**, and **vbscript**. Other values that include the version of the language used, such as **JavaScript1.1**, also might be possible.

style   See "Core Attributes Reference," earlier in this appendix.

tabindex   This attribute uses a number to identify the object's position in the tabbing order for keyboard navigation using the TAB key. Internet Explorer 5.5 applies this attribute to the **strong** element; under IE 5.5, this focus can be disabled with the **hidefocus** attribute.

title   See "Core Attributes Reference," earlier in this appendix.

Attribute and Event Support

Netscape 4   class, **id**, **lang**, and **style** are implied.

Internet Explorer 4   All attributes and events defined by the W3C and Internet Explorer 4, except **dir**.

Internet Explorer 5.5   All attributes and events

Event Handlers
See "Events Reference," earlier in this appendix.

Examples

```
It is really <strong>important</strong> to pay attention.

<strong style="font-family: impact; font-size: 28pt">
Important Info
</strong>
```

Compatibility
HTML 2, 3.2, 4, and 4.01, XHTML 1.0
Internet Explorer 2, 3, 4, 5, and 5.5
Netscape 1, 2, 3, 4–4.7, 6
Opera 4.0
WebTV

Notes

- This element generally renders as bold text. As a logical element, however, **<strong>** is useful to bind style rules to.

- As compared to **<b>**, this element does have meaning and voice browsers can state **<strong>** enclosed text in a different voice than text that is enclosed by **<b>**.

<style> (Style Information)

This element is used to surround style sheet rules for a document. This element should be found only in the **<head>** of a document. Style rules within a document's **<body>** element should be set with the style attribute for a particular element.

Syntax

```
<style
     dir="ltr | rtl"
     lang="language code"
     media="all | print | screen | others"
     title="advisory text"
     type="MIME Type">

</style>
```

Attributes Defined by Internet Explorer 4

```
     disabled
```

Attributes

dir   This attribute is used to set the text direction of the title for the style sheet, either left to right (**ltr**) or right to left (**rtl**).

disabled   This Microsoft-defined attribute is used to disable a style sheet. The presence of the attribute is all that is required to disable the style sheet. In conjunction with scripting, this attribute could be used to turn on and off various style sheets in a document.

lang   The value of this attribute is a language code like all other **lang** attributes; however, this attribute defines the language of the **title** attribute rather than the content of the element.

media   This attribute specifies the destination medium for the style information. The value of the attribute can be a single media descriptor like **screen** or a comma-separated list. Possible values for this attribute include **all**, **aural**, **braille**, **print**, **projection**, **screen**, and **tv**. Other values also might be defined, depending on the browser. Internet Explorer supports **all**, **print**, and **screen** as values for this attribute.

title   This attribute associates an informational title with the style sheet.

type   This attribute is used to define the type of style sheet. The value of the attribute should be the MIME type of the style sheet language used. The most common current value for this attribute is **text/css**, which indicates a Cascading Style Sheet format.

Attribute and Event Support

Netscape 4   type

Internet Explorer 4   disabled, media (all | print | screen), title, and type.

Event Handlers
None

Example

```
<html>
<head>
<title>Style Sheet Example</title>
<style type="text/css">
<!--
   body {background: black; color: white;
   font: 12pt Helvetica}
   h1 {color: red; font: 14pt Impact}
-->
</style>
</head>

<body>
<h1>A 14-point red Impact heading on a black
background</h1>
Regular body text, which is 12 point white Helvetica
</body>
</html>
```

Compatibility

HTML 4, 4.01, XHTML 1.0
Netscape 4–4.7, 6
Internet Explorer 3, 4, 5, and 5.5
Opera 4.0

Notes

- Style information also can be specified in external style sheets as defined by the **<link>** element.

- Style information can also be associated with a particular element using the **style** attribute.

- Style rules generally are commented out within the **<style>** element to avoid interpretation by nonconforming browsers.

<sub> (Subscript)

This element renders its content as subscripted text.

Syntax

```
<sub
    class="class name(s)"
    dir="ltr | rtl"
    id="unique alphanumeric string"
    lang="language code"
    style="style information"
    title="advisory text"
    onclick="script"
    ondblclick="script"
    onkeydown="script"
    onkeypress="script"
    onkeyup="script"
    onmousedown="script"
    onmousemove="script"
    onmouseout="script"
    onmouseover="script"
    onmouseup="script">

</sub>
```

Attributes and Events Defined by Internet Explorer 4

```
    language="javascript | jscript | vbs | vbscript"
    ondragstart="script"
```

```
onhelp="script"
onselectstart="script"
```

Attributes and Events Defined by Internet Explorer 5.5

```
accesskey="key"
contenteditable="false | true | inherit"
hidefocus="true | false"
tabindex="number"
```

Attributes

accesskey   This attribute specifies a keyboard navigation accelerator for the element. Pressing ALT or a similar key (depending on the browser and operating system) in association with the specified key selects the anchor element correlated with that key.

class   See "Core Attributes Reference," earlier in this appendix.

contenteditable   This proprietary Microsoft attribute allows users to edit content rendered in the Internet Explorer 5.5 browser. Values are **false**, **true**, and **inherit**. A value of **false** will prevent content from being edited by users; **true** will allow editing. The default value, **inherit**, applies the value of the affected element's parent element.

dir   See "Language Reference," earlier in this appendix.

hidefocus   This proprietary element, introduced with Internet Explorer 5.5, hides focus on an element's content. Focus must be applied to the element using the **tabindex** attribute.

id   See "Core Attributes Reference," earlier in this appendix.

lang   See "Language Reference," earlier in this appendix.

language   In the Microsoft implementation, this attribute specifies the scripting language to be used with an associated script bound to the element, typically through an event handler attribute. Possible values might include **javascript**, **jscript**, **vbs**, and **vbscript**. Other values that include the version of the language used, such as **JavaScript1.1**, also might be possible.

style   See "Core Attributes Reference," earlier in this appendix.

tabindex   This attribute uses a number to identify the object's position in the tabbing order for keyboard navigation using the TAB key. Internet Explorer 5.5 applies this attribute to the **sub** element; under IE 5.5, this focus can be disabled with the **hidefocus** attribute.

title   See "Core Attributes Reference," earlier in this appendix.

Attribute and Event Support

Netscape 4   class, id, lang, and style are implied.

Internet Explorer 4   All attributes and events defined by the W3C and Internet Explorer 4, except dir.

Internet Explorer 5.5   All attributes and events

Event Handlers
See "Events Reference," earlier in this appendix.

Example

```
Here is some <sub>subscripted</sub> text.
```

Compatibility
HTML 3.2, 4, and 4.01, XHTML 1.0
Internet Explorer 2, 3, 4, 5, and 5.5
Netscape 2, 3, 4–4.7, 6
Opera 4.0
WebTV

Note

■ The HTML 3.2 specification supports no attributes for the **<sub>** element.

<sup> (Superscript)
This element renders its content as superscripted text.

Syntax

```
<sup
    class="class name(s)"
    dir="ltr | rtl"
    id="unique alphanumeric string"
    lang="language code"
    style="style information"
    title="advisory text"
    onclick="script"
    ondblclick="script"
    onkeydown="script"
```

```
            onkeypress="script"
            onkeyup="script"
            onmousedown="script"
            onmousemove="script"
            onmouseout="script"
            onmouseover="script"
            onmouseup="script">

</sup>
```

Attributes and Events Defined by Internet Explorer 4

```
        language="javascript | jscript | vbs | vbscript"
        ondragstart="script"
        onhelp="script"
        onselectstart="script"
```

Attributes and Events Defined by Internet Explorer 5.5

```
        accesskey="key"
        contenteditable="false | true | inherit"
        hidefocus="true | false"
        tabindex="number"
```

Attributes

accesskey   This attribute specifies a keyboard navigation accelerator for the element. Pressing ALT or a similar key (depending on the browser and operating system) in association with the specified key selects the anchor element correlated with that key.

class   See "Core Attributes Reference," earlier in this appendix.

contenteditable   This proprietary Microsoft attribute allows users to edit content rendered in the Internet Explorer 5.5 browser. Values are **false**, **true**, and **inherit**. A value of **false** will prevent content from being edited by users; **true** will allow editing. The default value, **inherit**, applies the value of the affected element's parent element.

dir   See "Language Reference," earlier in this appendix.

hidefocus   This proprietary element, introduced with Internet Explorer 5.5, hides focus on an element's content. Focus must be applied to the element using the **tabindex** attribute.

id   See "Core Attributes Reference," earlier in this appendix.

lang   See "Language Reference," earlier in this appendix.

language   In the Microsoft implementation, this attribute specifies the scripting language to be used with an associated script bound to the element, typically through an event handler attribute. Possible values might include **javascript**, **jscript**, **vbs**, and **vbscript**. Other values that include the version of the language used, such as **JavaScript1.1**, also might be possible.

style   See "Core Attributes Reference," earlier in this appendix.

tabindex   This attribute uses a number to identify the object's position in the tabbing order for keyboard navigation using the TAB key. Internet Explorer 5.5 applies this attribute to the **sup** element; under IE 5.5, this focus can be disabled with the **hidefocus** attribute.

title   See "Core Attributes Reference," earlier in this appendix.

Attribute and Event Support

Netscape 4   class, **id**, **lang**, and **style** are implied.

Internet Explorer 4   All attributes and events defined by the W3C and Internet Explorer 4, except **dir**.

Internet Explorer 5.5   All attributes and events.

Event Handlers
See "Events Reference," earlier in this appendix.

Example

```
Here is some <sup>superscripted</sup> text.
```

Compatibility
HTML 3.2, 4, and 4.01, XHTML 1.0
Internet Explorer 2, 3, 4, 5, and 5.5
Netscape 2, 3, 4–4.7, 6
Opera 4.0
WebTV

Note

■ The HTML 3.2 specification defines no attributes for this element.

<table> (Table)

This element is used to define a table. Tables are used to organize data as well as to provide structure for laying out pages.

Syntax

```
<table
     align="center | left | right" (transitional)
     bgcolor="color name | #RRGGBB" (transitional)
     border="pixels"
     cellpadding="pixels"
     cellspacing="pixels"
     class="class name(s)"
     datapagesize="number of records to display"
     dir="ltr | rtl"
     frame="above | below | border | box | hsides |
           lhs | rhs | void | vsides"
     id="unique alphanumeric identifier"
     lang="language code"
     rules="all | cols | groups | none | rows"
     style="style information"
     summary="summary information"
     title="advisory text"
     width="percentage | pixels"
     onclick="script"
     ondblclick="script"
     onkeydown="script"
     onkeypress="script"
     onkeyup="script"
     onmousedown="script"
     onmousemove="script"
     onmouseout="script"
     onmouseover="script"
     onmouseup="script">

</table>
```

Attributes and Events Defined by Internet Explorer 4

```
     background="url"
     bordercolor="color name | #RRGGBB"
     bordercolordark="color name | #RRGGBB"
     bordercolorlight="color name | #RRGGBB"
     cols="number"
     datasrc="data source id"
     height="percentage | pixels"
     language="javascript | jscript | vbs | vbscript"
     onafterupdate="script"
     onbeforeupdate="script"
     onblur="script"
```

```
ondragstart="script"
onfocus="script"
onhelp="script"
onresize="script"
onrowenter="script"
onrowexit="script"
onselectstart="script"
```

Attributes and Events Defined by Internet Explorer 5.5

```
accesskey="key"
hidefocus="true | false"
tabindex="number"
```

Attributes Defined by Netscape 4

```
background="url of image" file
bordercolor="color name | #RRGGBB"
cols="number of columns"
height="pixels"
hspace="pixels"
vspace="pixels"
```

Attributes Defined by WebTV

```
align="bleedleft | bleedright | justify"
background="url of image file"
cellborder="pixels"
gradangle="gradient angle"
gradcolor="color value"
href="url"
hspace="pixels"
name="string"
nowrap
transparency="number (0-100)"
vspace="pixels"
```

Attributes

accesskey This attribute specifies a keyboard navigation accelerator for the element. Pressing ALT or a similar key (depending on the browser and operating system) in association with the specified key selects the anchor element correlated with that key.

align   This attribute specifies the alignment of the table with respect to surrounding text. The HTML 4.01 specification defines **center**, **left**, and **right**. WebTV also defines **bleedleft** and **bleedright**, which cause the table to bleed over the right and left margins of the page, and **justify**, which is used to justify the table within the browser window. Some browsers also might support alignment values, such as **absmiddle**, that are common to block objects.

background   This nonstandard attribute, which is supported by Internet Explorer, Netscape, and WebTV, specifies the URL of a background image for the table. The image is tiled if it is smaller than the table dimensions. Netscape displays the background image in each table cell, rather than behind the complete table like in Internet Explorer.

bgcolor   This attribute specifies a background color for a table. Its value can be either a named color, such as **red**, or a color specified in the hexadecimal *#RRGGBB* format, such as **#FF0000**.

border   This attribute specifies in pixels the width of a table's borders. A value of **0** makes a borderless table, which is useful for graphic layout.

bordercolor   This attribute, supported by Internet Explorer 4 and Netscape 4, is used to set the border color for a table. The attribute should be used only with a positive value for the **border** attribute. The value of the attribute can be either a named color, such as **green**, or a color specified in the hexadecimal *#RRGGBB* format, such as **#00FF00**. Internet Explorer colors the entire table border, including cell borders; Netscape colors only the outer border of the table.

bordercolordark   This Internet Explorer–specific attribute specifies the darker of two border colors used to create a three-dimensional effect for cell borders. It must be used with the **border** attribute set to a positive value. The attribute value can be either a named color, such as **blue**, or a color specified in the hexadecimal *#RRGGBB* format, such as **#00FF00**.

bordercolorlight   This Internet Explorer–specific attribute specifies the lighter of two border colors used to create a three-dimensional effect for cell borders. It must be used with the **border** attribute set to a positive value. The attribute value can be either a named color, such as **red**, or a color specified in the hexadecimal *#RRGGBB* format, such as **#FF0000**.

cellborder   In the WebTV implementation, this attribute sets the width in pixels of the border between table cells. If this value is not present, the default border as specified by the **border** attribute is used.

cellpadding   This attribute sets the width in pixels between the edge of a cell and its content.

cellspacing   This attribute sets the width in pixels between individual cells.

class   See "Core Attributes Reference," earlier in this appendix.

cols   This attribute specifies the number of columns in the table and is used to help quickly calculate the size of the table. This attribute was part of the preliminary specification of HTML 4.0, but was later dropped. A few browsers, notably Netscape 4 and higher, already support it.

< table > (Table)   **933**

datapagesize   The value of this Microsoft-specific attribute is the number of records that can be displayed in the table when data binding is used.

datasrc   The value of this Microsoft-specific attribute is an identifier indicating the data source to pull data from.

dir   See "Language Reference," earlier in this appendix.

frame   This attribute specifies which edges of a table are to display a border frame. A value of **above** indicates only the top edge; **below** indicates only the bottom edge; and **border** and **box** indicate all edges, which is the default when the **border** attribute is a positive integer. A value of **hsides** indicates only the top and bottom edges should be displayed; **lhs** indicates the left-hand edge should be displayed; **rhs** indicates the right-hand edge should be displayed; **vsides** indicates the left and right edges both should be displayed; and **void** indicates no border should be displayed.

gradangle   This WebTV-specific attribute defines the gradient angle for a table, ranging from 90 to -90 degrees. **gradangle="0"** yields a left-to-right gradient, whereas **gradangle="90"** yields a top-to-bottom gradient. The beginning color of the gradient is defined by the **bgcolor** attribute, and the ending color is defined by the **gradcolor** attribute.

gradcolor   This WebTV-specific attribute defines the end color of a table's background gradient, in conjunction with the gradient angle defined by the **gradangle** attribute and the starting color defined by the **bgcolor** attribute.

height   For Netscape 4, this attribute allows the author to specify the height of the table in pixels. Internet Explorer 4 allows both pixels and percentages.

hidefocus   This proprietary element, introduced with Internet Explorer 5.5, hides focus on an element's content. Focus must be applied to the element using the **tabindex** attribute.

href   This WebTV-specific attribute is used to make the entire table function as a hyperlink anchor to the specified URL.

hspace   This Netscape-specified attribute indicates the horizontal space in pixels between the table and surrounding content. This attribute also is supported by WebTV but, oddly, not by Internet Explorer.

id   See "Core Attributes Reference," earlier in this appendix.

lang   See "Language Reference," earlier in this appendix.

language   In the Microsoft implementation, this attribute specifies the scripting language to be used with an associated script bound to the element, typically through an event handler attribute. Possible values might include **javascript**, **jscript**, **vbs**, and **vbscript**. Other values that include the version of the language used, such as **JavaScript1.1**, also might be possible.

name   This WebTV attribute is used to assign the table a unique name. It is synonymous with the **id** attribute.

nowrap   This WebTV-specific attribute keeps table rows from wrapping if they extend beyond the right margin. The attribute requires no value.

rules   This attribute controls the display of dividing rules within a table. A value of **all** specifies dividing rules for rows and columns. A value of **cols** specifies dividing rules for columns only. A value of **groups** specifies horizontal dividing rules between groups of table cells defined by the **<thead>**, **<tbody>**, **<tfoot>**, or **<colgroup>** elements. A value of **rows** specifies dividing rules for rows only. A value of **NONE** indicates no dividing rules and is the default.

style   See "Core Attributes Reference," earlier in this appendix.

summary   This attribute is used to provide a text summary of the table's purpose and structure. This element is used for accessibility, and its presence is important for nonvisual user agents.

tabindex   This attribute uses a number to identify the object's position in the tabbing order for keyboard navigation using the TAB key. Internet Explorer 5.5 applies this attribute to the **table** element; under IE 5.5, this focus can be disabled with the **hidefocus** attribute.

title   See "Core Attributes Reference," earlier in this appendix.

transparency   This WebTV-specific attribute specifies the degree of transparency of the table. Values range from **0** (totally opaque) to **100** (totally transparent). A value of **50** is optimized for fast rendering.

vspace   This Netscape attribute indicates the vertical space in pixels between the table and surrounding content. This attribute also is supported by WebTV but, oddly, not by Internet Explorer.

width   This attribute specifies the width of the table either in pixels or as a percentage value of the enclosing window.

Attribute and Event Support

Netscape 4   align (left | right), bgcolor, border, cellpadding, cellspacing, cols, height, hpace, vspace, and width. (class, id, lang, and style are implied.)

Internet Explorer 4   All W3C-defined attributes and events except **dir** and **summary**, and all attributes and events defined by Internet Explorer 4.

Internet Explorer 5.5   All attributes and events defined by the W3C, Internet Explorer 4, and Internet Explorer 5.5

WebTV   align (bleedleft | bleedright | center | left | right), background, bgcolor, border, cellpadding, cellspacing, gradangle, gradcolor, hspace, id, nowrap, transparency, and width

Event Handlers
See "Events Reference," earlier in this appendix.

<table> (Table) **935**

Examples

```
<table bgcolor="white" border="2">
   <tr>
      <td>Cell 1</td>
      <td>Cell 2</td>
      <td>Cell 3</td>
      <td>Cell 4</td>
   </tr>

   <tr>
      <td>Cell 5</td>
      <td>Cell 6</td>
   </tr>
</table>

<table rules="all" bgcolor="yellow">
<caption>Widgets by Area</caption>
<thead align="center" bgcolor="green" valign="middle">
   <td>This is a Header</td>
</thead>

<tfoot align="right" bgcolor="red" valign="bottom">
   <td>This is part of the footer.</td>
   <td>This is also part of the footer.</td>
</tfoot>

<tbody>
   <tr>
      <td> </td>
      <th>Regular Widget</th>
      <th>Super Widget</th>
   </tr>

   <tr>
      <th>West Coast</th>
      <td>10</td>
      <td>12</td>
   </tr>

   <tr>
      <th>East Coast</th>
      <td>1</td>
      <td>20</td>
   </tr>
</tbody>
</table>
```

Compatibility

HTML 3.2, 4, and 4.01, XHTML 1.0
Internet Explorer 2, 3, 4, 5, and 5.5
Netscape 1.1, 2, 3, 4–4.7, 6
Opera 4.0
WebTV

Notes

- In addition to displaying tabular data, tables are used to support graphic layout and design.

- The HTML 4.01 specification reserves the future use of the **datafld**, **dataformatas**, and **datasrc** attributes for the **<table>** element.

- The HTML 3.2 specification defines only the **align**, **border**, **cellpadding**, **cellspacing**, and **width** attributes for the **<table>** element.

- The **cols** attribute might provide an undesirable result under Netscape, which assumes the size of each column in the table is exactly the same.

<tbody> (Table Body)

This element is used to group the rows within the body of a table so that common alignment and style defaults can easily be set for numerous cells.

Syntax

```
<tbody
        align="center | char | justify | left | right"
        char="character"
        charoff="offset"
        class="class name(s)"
        dir="ltr | rtl"
        id="unique alphanumeric identifier"
        lang="language code"
        style="style information"
        title="advisory text"
        valign="baseline | bottom | middle | top"
        onclick="script"
        ondblclick="script"
        onkeydown="script"
        onkeypress="script"
        onkeyup="script"
        onmousedown="script"
        onmousemove="script"
        onmouseout="script"
        onmouseover="script"
        onmouseup="script">

</tbody>
```

Syntax

Under the XHTML 1.0 specification, the closing tag **</tbody>** no longer can be considered optional.

Attributes and Events Defined by Internet Explorer 4

```
bgcolor="color name | #RRGGBB"
language="javascript | jscript | vbs | vbscript"
valign="center"
ondragstart="script"
onhelp="script"
onselectstart="script"
```

Attributes and Events Defined by Internet Explorer 5.5

```
accesskey="key"
hidefocus="true | false"
tabindex="number"
```

Attributes

accesskey   This attribute specifies a keyboard navigation accelerator for the element. Pressing ALT or a similar key (depending on the browser and operating system) in association with the specified key selects the anchor element correlated with that key.

align   This attribute is used to align the contents of the cells within the **<tbody>** element. Common values are **center**, **justify**, **left**, and **right**. The HTML 4.01 specification also defines a value of **char**. When **align** is set to **char**, the attribute **char** must be present and set to the character to which cells should be aligned. A common use of this approach would be to set cells to align on a decimal point.

bgcolor   This attribute specifies a background color for the cells within the **<tbody>** element. Its value can be either a named color, such as **red**, or a color specified in the hexadecimal *#RRGGBB* format, such as **#FF0000**.

char   This attribute is used to define the character to which element contents are aligned when the **align** attribute is set to the **char** value.

charoff   This attribute contains an offset as a positive or negative integer to align characters as related to the **char** value. A value of **2**, for example, would align characters in a cell two characters to the right of the character defined by the **char** attribute.

class   See "Core Attributes Reference," earlier in this appendix.

dir   See "Language Reference," earlier in this appendix.

hidefocus   This proprietary element, introduced with Internet Explorer 5.5, hides focus on an element's content. Focus must be applied to the element using the **tabindex** attribute.

id   See "Core Attributes Reference," earlier in this appendix.

lang   See "Language Reference," earlier in this appendix.

language   In the Microsoft implementation, this attribute specifies the scripting language to be used with an associated script bound to the element, typically through an event handler attribute. Possible values might include **javascript**, **jscript**, **vbs**, and **vbscript**. Other values that include the version of the language used, such as **JavaScript1.1**, also might be possible.

style   See "Core Attributes Reference," earlier in this appendix.

tabindex   This attribute uses a number to identify the object's position in the tabbing order for keyboard navigation using the TAB key. Internet Explorer 5.5 applies this attribute to the **tbody** element; under IE 5.5, this focus can be disabled with the **hidefocus** attribute.

title   See "Core Attributes Reference," earlier in this appendix.

valign   This attribute is used to set the vertical alignment for the table cells with the **<tbody>** element. HTML 4.01 defines **baseline**, **bottom**, **middle**, and **top**. Internet Explorer replaces **middle** with **center**; the effect should be the same.

Attribute and Event Support

Internet Explorer 4   All W3C-defined attributes and events except **char**, **charoff**, and **dir**. (Note: Internet Explorer 4 does not support the **char** and **justify** values for **align**, nor the **middle** value for **valign**.)

Internet Explorer 5.5   All W3C-defined attributes and events except **char** and **charoff**, and all attributes and events defined by Internet Explorer 4 and 5.5.

Event Handlers
See "Events Reference," earlier in this appendix.

Example

```
<table rule="all" bgcolor="yellow">

<tbody align="center" bgcolor="red" style="bodystyle"
      valign="baseline">
  <tr>
```

```
        <td> </td>
        <th>Regular Widget</th>
        <th>Super Widget</th>
    </tr>

    <tr>
        <th>West Coast</th>
        <td>10</td>
        <td>12</td>
    </tr>

    <tr>
        <th>East Coast</th>
        <td>1</td>
        <td>20</td>
    </tr>
</tbody>
</table>
```

Compatibility

HTML 4, 4.01, XHTML 1.0
Internet Explorer 4, 5, and 5.5
Netscape 6

Notes

■ This element is contained by the **<table>** element and contains one or more table rows as indicated by the **<tr>** element.

■ For XHTML compatibility, the closing **</tbody>** tag must be used with this element.

<td> (Table Data)

This element specifies a data cell in a table. The element should occur within a table row as defined by the **<tr>** element.

Syntax

```
<td
    abbr="abbreviation"
    align="center | justify | left | right"
    axis="group name"
    bgcolor="color name | #RRGGBB" (transitional)
    char="character"
    charoff="offset"
    class="class name"
```

```
    colspan="number"
    dir="ltr | rtl"
     headers="space-separated list of associated header
              cells' id values"
     height="pixels" (transitional)
     id="unique alphanumeric identifier"
     lang="language code"
     nowrap (transitional)
     rowspan="number"
     scope="col | colgroup | row | rowgroup"
     style="style information"
     title="advisory text"
     valign="baseline | bottom | middle | top"
     width="pixels" (transitional)
     onclick="script"
     ondblclick="script"
     onkeydown="script"
     onkeypress="script"
     onkeyup="script"
     onmousedown="script"
     onmousemove="script"
     onmouseout="script"
     onmouseover="script"
     onmouseup="script">

</td>
```

XHTML Syntax

Under the XHTML 1.0 specification, the closing **</td>** tag is mandatory.

Attributes and Events Defined by Internet Explorer 4

```
    background="url of image file"
    bordercolor="color name | #RRGGBB"
    bordercolordark="color name | #RRGGBB"
    bordercolorlight="color name | #RRGGBB"
    language="javascript | jscript | vbs | vbscript"
    valign="center"
    onafterupdate="script"
    onbeforeupdate="script"
    onblur="script"
    ondragstart="script"
    onfocus="script"
    onhelp="script"
    onresize="script"
    onrowenter="script"
```

```
onrowexit="script"
onscroll="script"
onselectstart="script"
```

Attributes and Events Defined by Internet Explorer 5.5

```
accesskey="key"
hidefocus="true | false"
tabindex="number"
```

Attributes Defined by Netscape 4

```
background="url of image file"
bordercolor="color name | #RRGGBB"
```

Attributes Defined by WebTV

```
absheight="pixels"
abswidth="pixels"
background="url of image file"
gradangle="gradient angle"
gradcolor="color"
maxlines="number"
transparency="number (0-100)"
```

Attributes

abbr   The value of this attribute is an abbreviated name for a header cell. This might be useful when attempting to display large tables on small screens.

absheight   This WebTV-specific attribute sets the absolute height of a cell in pixels. Content that does not fit within this height is clipped.

abswidth   This WebTV-specific attribute sets the absolute width of a cell in pixels. Content that does not fit within this width is clipped.

accesskey   This attribute specifies a keyboard navigation accelerator for the element. Pressing ALT or a similar key (depending on the browser and operating system) in association with the specified key selects the anchor element correlated with that key.

align   This attribute is used to align the contents of the cells within the **\<tbody\>** element. Common values are **center**, **justify**, **left**, and **right**.

axis   This attribute is used to provide a name for a group of related headers.

background   This nonstandard attribute, which is supported by Internet Explorer, Netscape and WebTV, specifies the URL of a background image for the table cell. The image is tiled if it is smaller than the cell's dimensions.

bgcolor   This attribute specifies a background color for a table cell. Its value can be either a named color, such as **red**, or a color specified in the hexadecimal #*RRGGBB* format, such as **#FF0000**. (Netscape Navigator often fails to render a cell with a colored background unless a nonbreaking space, at least, is inserted in the cell.)

bordercolor   This attribute, supported by Internet Explorer and Netscape, is used to set the border color for a table cell. The attribute should be used only with a positive value for the **border** attribute. The value of the attribute can be either a named color, such as **green**, or a color specified in the hexadecimal #*RRGGBB* format, such as **#00FF00**.

bordercolordark   This Internet Explorer–specific attribute specifies the darker of two border colors used to create a three-dimensional effect for a cell's borders. It must be used with the **border** attribute set to a positive value. The attribute value can be either a named color, such as **blue**, or a color specified in the hexadecimal #*RRGGBB* format, such as **#00FF00**.

bordercolorlight   This Internet Explorer–specific attribute specifies the lighter of two border colors used to create a three-dimensional effect for a cell's borders. It must be used with the **border** attribute set to a positive value. The attribute value can be either a named color, such as **red**, or a color specified in the hexadecimal #*RRGGBB* format, such as **#FF0000**.

char   This attribute is used to define the character to which element contents are aligned when the **align** attribute is set to the **char** value.

charoff   This attribute contains an offset as a positive or negative integer to align characters as related to the **char** value. A value of **2**, for example, would align characters in a cell two characters to the right of the character defined by the **char** attribute.

class   See "Core Attributes Reference," earlier in this appendix.

colspan   This attribute takes a numeric value that indicates how many columns wide a cell should be. This is useful to create tables with cells of different widths.

dir   See "Language Reference," earlier in this appendix.

gradangle   This WebTV-specific attribute defines the gradient angle for a table cell, ranging from 90 to –90 degrees. **gradangle="0"** yields a left-to-right gradient, while **gradangle="90"** yields a top-to-bottom gradient. The beginning color of the gradient is defined by the **BGCOLOR** attribute, and the ending color is defined by the **gradcolor** attribute.

gradcolor   This WebTV-specific attribute defines the end color of a table cell's background gradient, in conjunction with the gradient angle defined by the **gradangle** attribute and the starting color defined by the **bgcolor** attribute.

headers   This attribute takes a space-separated list of **id** values that correspond to the header cells related to this cell.

height   This attribute indicates the height of the cell in pixels.

hidefocus   This proprietary element, introduced with Internet Explorer 5.5, hides focus on an element's content. Focus must be applied to the element using the **tabindex** attribute.

id   See "Core Attributes Reference," earlier in this appendix.

lang   See "Language Reference," earlier in this appendix.

language   In the Microsoft implementation, this attribute specifies the scripting language to be used with an associated script bound to the element, typically through an event handler attribute. Possible values might include **javascript**, **jscript**, **vbs**, and **vbscript**. Other values that include the version of the language used, such as **JavaScript1.1**, also might be possible.

maxlines   This WebTV-specific attribute takes a numeric argument indicating the maximum number of content lines to display. Content beyond these lines is clipped.

nowrap   This attribute keeps the content within a table cell from automatically wrapping.

rowspan   This attribute takes a numeric value that indicates how many rows high a table cell should span. This attribute is useful in defining tables with cells of different heights.

scope   This attribute specifies the table cells that the current cell provides header information for. A value of **col** indicates that the cell is a header for the the rest of the column below it. A value of **colgroup** indicates that the cell is a header for its current column group. A value of **row** indicates that that the cell contains header information for the rest of the row it is in. A value of **rowgroup** indicates that the cell is a header for its row group. This attribute might be used in place of the **header** attribute and is useful for rendering assistance by nonvisual browsers. This attribute was added very late to the HTML 4 specification so support for this attribute is minimal.

style   See "Core Attributes Reference," earlier in this appendix.

tabindex   This attribute uses a number to identify the object's position in the tabbing order for keyboard navigation using the TAB key. Internet Explorer 5.5 applies this attribute to the **td** element; under IE 5.5, this focus can be disabled with the **hidefocus** attribute.

title   See "Core Attributes Reference," earlier in this appendix.

transparency   This WebTV-specific attribute specifies the degree of transparency of the table cell. Values range from **0** (totally opaque) to **100** (totally transparent). A value of **50** is optimized for fast rendering.

valign   This attribute is used to set the vertical alignment for the table cell. HTML 4 defines **baseline**, **bottom**, **middle**, and **top**. Internet Explorer replaces **middle** with **center**; the effect should be the same.

width   This attribute specifies the width of a cell in pixels.

Attribute and Event Support

Netscape 4   align, background, bgcolor, bordercolor, colspan, height, nowrap, rowspan valign, and width. (class, id, lang, and style are implied.)

Internet Explorer 4   All W3C-defined attributes and events except **abbr, axis, char, charoff, dir, headers,** and **height,** and all attributes and events defined by Internet Explorer 4. (Note: Internet Explorer 4 does not support the **justify** value for **align,** nor the **middle** value for **valign.**)

Internet Explorer 5.5   All W3C-defined attributes and events except **abbr, axis, char, charoff,** and **headers,** and all attributes and events defined by Internet Explorer 4 and 5.5.

WebTV   align (center | left | right), background, bgcolor, colspan, gradangle, gradcolor, height, rowspan, transparency, valign (baseline | bottom | middle | top), and width

Event Handlers

See "Events Reference," earlier in this appendix.

Examples

```
<table>
<tr>
<td align="left" valign="top">
 Put me in the top left corner.
</td>
<td align="right" bgcolor="red" valign="bottom">
Put me in the bottom right corner.
</td>
</tr>
</table>


<table border="1" width="80%">
   <tr>
      <td colspan="3">
      A pretty wide cell
      </td>
      </td>
   <tr>
      <td>Item 2</td>
      <td>Item 3</td>
      <td>Item 4</td>
   </tr>
</table>
```

Compatibility

HTML 3.2, 4, and 4.0, XHTML 1.0
Internet Explorer 2, 3, 4, 5, and 5.5
Netscape 1.1, 2, 3, 4–4.7, 6
Opera 4.0
WebTV

Notes

- Under the XHTML 1.0 specification, the closing **</td>** tag ceases to be optional.
- The HTML 3.2 specification defines only **align**, **colspan**, **height**, **nowrap**, **rowspan**, **valign**, and **width** attributes.
- This element should always be within the **<tr>** element.

<textarea> (Multiline Text Input)

This element specifies a multiline text input field contained within a form.

Syntax

```
<textarea
    accesskey="character"
    class="class name"
    cols="number"
    dir="ltr | rtl"
    disabled
    id="unique alphanumeric identifier"
    lang="language code"
    name="unique alphanumeric identifier"
    readonly
    rows="number"
    style="style information"
    tabindex="number"
    title="advisory text"
    onblur="script"
    onchange="script"
    onclick="script"
    ondblclick="script"
    onfocus="script"
    onkeydown="script"
    onkeypress="script"
    onkeyup="script"
    onmousedown="script"
    onmousemove="script"
    onmouseout="script"
    onmouseover="script"
```

```
          onmouseup="script"
          onselect="script">

</textarea>
```

Attributes and Events Defined by Internet Explorer 4

```
align="absbottom | absmiddle | baseline | bottom |
      left | middle | right | texttop | tcp"
datafld="column name"
datasrc="data source ID"
language="javascript | jscript | vbs | vbscript"
wrap="off | physical | virtual"
onafterupdate="script"
onbeforeupdate="script"
ondragstart="script"
onhelp="script"
onresize="script"
onrowenter="script"
onrowexit="script"
onscroll="script"
onselectstart="script"
onstart="script"
```

Attributes and Events Defined by Internet Explorer 5.5

```
contenteditable="false | true | inherit"
hidefocus="true | false"
```

Attributes Defined by Netscape 4

```
wrap="hard | off | soft"
```

Attributes Defined by WebTV

```
allcaps
autoactivate
autocaps
bgcolor="color name | #RRGGBB"
cursor="color name | #RRGGBB"
growable
nohardbreaks
```

```
nosoftbreaks
numbers
showkeyboard
usestyle
```

Attributes

accesskey   This Microsoft-specific attribute specifies a keyboard navigation accelerator for the element. Pressing ALT or a similar key in association with the specified character selects the form control correlated with that key sequence. Page designers are forewarned to avoid key sequences already bound to browsers.

align   Microsoft defines alignment values for this element. The values for this attribute should behave similarly to any included object or image.

allcaps   This WebTV-specific attribute renders all viewer-entered text in capital letters. This attribute requires no value.

autoactivate   This WebTV-specific attribute causes the text input control to immediately activate. This attribute requires no value.

autocaps   This WebTV-specific attribute renders the first letter of all viewer-entered words in a capital letter. This attribute requires no value.

bgcolor   This WebTV-specific attribute specifies the background color for the text input area. Its value can be either a named color, such as **red**, or a color specified in the hexadecimal *#RRGGBB* format, such as **#FF0000**. The default color for the **<textarea>** element under WebTV is **#EAEAEA**.

class   See "Core Attributes Reference," earlier in this appendix.

cols   This attribute sets the width in characters of the text area. The typical default values for the size of a **<textarea>** element when this attribute is not set is **20** characters.

contenteditable   This proprietary Microsoft attribute allows users to edit content rendered in the Internet Explorer 5.5 browser. Values are **false**, **true**, and **inherit**. A value of **false** will prevent content from being edited by users; **true** will allow editing. The default value, **inherit**, applies the value of the affected element's parent element.

cursor   This WebTV-specific attribute is used to indicate the cursor color for the text input area. Its value can be either a named color, such as **red**, or a color specified in the hexadecimal *#RRGGBB* format, such as **#FF0000**. The default value for the cursor color in the WebTV browser is **darkblue (#3333AA)**.

datafld   This attribute is used to indicate the column name in the data source that is bound to the content enclosed by the **<textarea>** element.

datasrc   The value of this attribute is an identifier indicating the data source to pull data from.

dir   See "Language Reference," earlier in this appendix.

disabled   This attribute is used to turn off a form control. Elements will not be submitted nor can they receive any focus from the keyboard or mouse. Disabled form controls will not be part of the tabbing order. The browser also can gray out the form that is disabled in order to indicate to the user that the form control is inactive. This attribute requires no value.

growable   This WebTV-specific attribute allows the text input area to expand vertically to accommodate extra text entered by the user. This attribute requires no value.

hidefocus   This proprietary element, introduced with Internet Explorer 5.5, hides focus on an element's content. Focus must be applied to the element using the **tabindex** attribute.

id   See "Core Attributes Reference," earlier in this appendix.

lang   See "Language Reference," earlier in this appendix.

language   In the Microsoft implementation, this attribute specifies the scripting language to be used with an associated script bound to the element, typically through an event handler attribute. Possible values might include **javascript**, **jscript**, **vbs**, and **vbscript**. Other values that include the version of the language used, such as **JavaScript1.1**, also might be possible.

name   This attribute allows a form control to be assigned a name so that it can be referenced by a scripting language. **Name** is supported by older browsers, such as Netscape 2 generation browsers, but the W3C encourages the use of the **id** attribute. For compatibility purposes, both attributes might have to be used.

nohardbreaks   This WebTV-specific attribute causes a press of the ENTER key to select the next form element rather than causing a line break in the text input area. The attribute requires no value.

nosoftbreaks   This attribute removes breaks automatically inserted into the text by line wrapping when the form is submitted. The attribute requires no value.

numbers   This WebTV-specific attribute causes the number "1" to be selected in the onscreen keyboard in anticipation of the viewer entering a numeric value.

readonly   This attribute prevents the form control's value from being changed. Form controls with this attribute set might receive focus from the user but might not be modified. Because they receive focus, a **readonly** form control will be part of the form's tabbing order. Finally the control's value will be sent on form submission. The attribute can be used with **<input>** only when **type** is set to **text** or **password**. The attribute also is used with the **<textarea>** element.

rows   This attribute sets the number of rows in the text area. The value of the attribute should be a positive integer.

showkeyboard   In the WebTV implementation, this attribute causes the onscreen keyboard to be displayed when the **<textarea>** element is selected.

style   See "Core Attributes Reference," earlier in this appendix.

tabindex   This attribute takes a numeric value indicating the position of the form control in the tabbing index for the form. Tabbing proceeds from the lowest positive **tabindex** value to the highest. Negative values for **tabindex** will leave the form control out of the tabbing order. When tabbing is not explicitly set, the browser can tab through items in the order they are encountered. Form controls that are disabled due to the presence of the **disabled** attribute will not be part of the tabbing index, although read-only controls will be.

title   See "Core Attributes Reference," earlier in this appendix.

usestyle   This WebTV-specific attribute causes text to be rendered in the style in effect for the page. The attribute requires no value.

wrap   In Netscape and Microsoft browsers, this attribute controls word wrap behavior. A value of **off** for the attribute forces the **<textarea>** not to wrap text, so the viewer must manually enter line breaks. A value of **hard** causes word wrap and includes line breaks in text submitted to the server. A value of **soft** causes word wrap but removes line breaks from text submitted to the server. Internet Explorer supports a value of **physical**, which is equivalent to Netcape's **hard** value, and a value of **virtual**, which is equivalent to Netscape's **soft** value. If the **wrap** attribute is not included, text will still wrap under Internet Explorer, but under Netscape it will scroll horizontally in the text box. It is always a good idea to include the **wrap** attribute.

Attribute and Event Support

Netscape 4   cols, name, rows, wrap (hard I off I soft), onblur, onchange, onfocus, and onselect. (class, id, lang, and style are implied.)

Internet Explorer 4   All W3C-defined events and attributes except **dir**, and all attributes and events defined by Internet Explorer 4.

Internet Explorer 4   All events and attributes defined by the W3C, Internet Explorer 4, and Internet Explorer 5.5.

WebTV   bgcolor, cols, cursor, name, rows, usestyle, onblur, onchange, and onfocus

Event Handlers
See "Events Reference," earlier in this appendix.

Examples

```
<textarea name="CommentBox" cols="40" rows="8">
Default text in field
</textarea>
```

```
<textarea name="comment" rows="10" cols="40" wrap="virtual"
        align="center">
</textarea>
```

Compatibility
HTML 2, 3.2, 4, and 4.01, XHTML 1.0
Internet Explorer 2, 3, 4, 5, and 5.5
Netscape 1, 2, 3, 4–4.7, 6
Opera 4.0
WebTV

Notes

- Any text between the **<textarea>** and **</textarea>** tags is rendered as the default entry for the form control.
- The HTML 2.0 and 3.2 specifications define only the **cols**, **name**, and **rows** attribute for this element.
- The HTML 4.01 specification reserves the **datafld** and **datasrc** attributes for future use with the **<textarea>** element.

<tfoot> (Table Footer)

This element is used to group the rows within the footer of a table so that common alignment and style defaults can easily be set for numerous cells. This element might be particularly useful when setting a common footer for tables that are dynamically generated.

Syntax

```
<tfoot
    align="center | char | justify | left | right"
    bgcolor="color name | #RRGGBB" (transitional)
    char="character"
    charoff="offset"
    class="class name(s)"
    dir="ltr | rtl"
    id="unique alphanumeric identifier"
    lang="language code"
    style="style information"
    title="advisory text"
    valign="baseline | bottom | middle | top"
    onclick="script"
    ondblclick="script"
    onkeydown="script"
    onkeypress="script"
```

```
        onkeyup="script"
        onmousedown="script"
        onmousemove="script"
        onmouseout="script"
        onmouseover="script"
        onmouseup="script">

  </tfoot>
```

XHTML Syntax

Under the XHTML 1.0 specification, the closing **</tfoot>** tag is mandatory.

Attributes and Events Defined by Internet Explorer 4

```
        language="javascript | jscript | vbs | vbscript"
        valign="center"
        ondragstart="script"
        onhelp="script"
        onselectstart="script"
```

Attributes and Events Defined by Internet Explorer 5.5

```
        accesskey="key"
        hidefocus="true | false"
        tabindex="number"
```

Attributes

accesskey   This attribute specifies a keyboard navigation accelerator for the element. Pressing ALT or a similar key (depending on the browser and operating system) in association with the specified key selects the anchor element correlated with that key.

align   This attribute is used to align the contents of the cells within the **<tfoot>** element. Common values are **center**, **justify**, **left**, and **right**. The HTML 4 specification also defines a value of **char**. When **align** is set to **char**, the attribute **char** must be present and set to the character to which cells should be aligned. A common use of this approach would be to set cells to align on a decimal point.

bgcolor   This attribute specifies a background color for the cells within the **<tfoot>** element. Its value can be either a named color, such as **red**, or a color specified in the hexadecimal *#RRGGBB* format, such as **#FF0000**.

char   This attribute is used to define the character to which element contents are aligned when the **align** attribute is set to the **char** value.

charoff   This attribute contains an offset as a positive or negative integer to align characters as related to the **char** value. A value of **2**, for example, would align characters in a cell two characters to the right of the character defined by the **char** attribute.

class   See "Core Attributes Reference," earlier in this appendix.

dir   See "Language Reference," earlier in this appendix.

hidefocus   This proprietary element, introduced with Internet Explorer 5.5, hides focus on an element's content. Focus must be applied to the element using the **tabindex** attribute.

id   See "Core Attributes Reference," earlier in this appendix.

lang   See "Language Reference," earlier in this appendix.

language   In the Microsoft implementation, this attribute specifies the scripting language to be used with an associated script bound to the element, typically through an event handler attribute. Possible values might include **javascript**, **jscript**, **vbs**, and **vbscript**. Other values that include the version of the language used, such as **JavaScript1.1**, also might be possible.

style   See "Core Attributes Reference," earlier in this appendix.

tabindex   This attribute uses a number to identify the object's position in the tabbing order for keyboard navigation using the TAB key. Internet Explorer 5.5 applies this attribute to the **tfoot** element; under IE 5.5, this focus can be disabled with the **hidefocus** attribute.

title   See "Core Attributes Reference," earlier in this appendix.

valign   This attribute is used to set the vertical alignment for the table cells with the **<tfoot>** element. HTML 4 defines **baseline**, **bottom**, **middle**, and **top**. Internet Explorer replaces **middle** with **center**; the effect should be the same.

Attribute and Event Support

Internet Explorer 4   All events and attributes except **char**, **charoff**, and **dir**. (Note: Internet Explorer 4 does not support the **justify** value for the **align** attribute.)

Internet Explorer 5.5   All W3C-defined attributes and events except **char** and **charoff**, and all attributes and events defined by Internet Explorer 4 and 5.5.

Event Handlers
None

Example

```
<table border="1" bgcolor="yellow" width="80%">
<tbody class="tablebody">
```

```
    <tr>
        <td>The contents of the table!</td>
    </tr>
</tbody>

<tfoot align="center" bgcolor="red" class="footer"
        valign="bottom">
    <td>This is part of the footer.</td>
    <td>This is also part of the footer.</td>
</tfoot>
</table>
```

Compatibility

HTML 4, 4.01, XHTML 1.0
Internet Explorer 4, 5, and 5.5
Netscape 6

Notes

- This element is contained only by the **<table>** element and contains table rows as delimited by **<tr>** elements.
- Under the XHTML 1.0 specification, the closing **</tfoot>** tag ceases to be optional.

<th> (Table Header)

This element specifies a header cell in a table. The element should occur within a table row as defined by a **<tr>** element. The main difference between this element and **<td>** is that browsers might render table headers slightly differently.

Syntax

```
<th
    abbr="abbreviation"
    align="center | justify | left | right"
    axis="group name"
    bgcolor="color name | #RRGGBB" (transitional)
    char="character"
    charoff="offset"
    class="class name"
    colspan="number"
    dir="ltr | rtl"
    headers="space-separated list of associated header
            cells' id values"
    height="pixels" (transitional)
    id="unique alphanumeric identifier"
```

```
      lang="language code"
      nowrap (transitional)
      rowspan="number"
      scope="col | colgroup | row | rowgroup"
      style="style information"
      title="advisory text"
      valign="baseline | bottom | middle | top"
      width="pixels" (transitional)
      onclick="script"
      ondblclick="script"
      onkeydown="script"
      onkeypress="script"
      onkeyup="script"
      onmousedown="script"
      onmousemove="script"
      onmouseout="script"
      onmouseover="script"
      onmouseup="script">
</th>
```

XHTML Syntax

Under the XHTML 1.0 specification, the closing **</th>** tag is mandatory.

Attributes and Events Defined by Internet Explorer 4

```
      background="url of image" file
      bordercolor="color name | #RRGGBB"
      bordercolordark="color name | #RRGGBB"
      bordercolorlight="color name | #RRGGBB"
      language="javascript | jscript | vbs | vbscript"
      valign="center"
      ondragstart="script"
      onhelp="script"
      onscroll="script"
      onselectstart="script"
```

Attributes and Events Defined by Internet Explorer 5.5

```
      accesskey="key"
      hidefocus="true | false"
      tabindex="number"
```

Attributes Defined by Netscape 4

```
background="url of image file"
bordercolor="color name | #RRGGBB"
```

Attributes Defined by WebTV

```
absheight="pixels"
abswidth="pixels"
background="url of image" file
gradangle
gradcolor
maxlines="number"
transparency="number (0-100)"
```

Attributes

abbr   The value of this attribute is an abbreviated name for a header cell. This might be useful when attempting to display large tables on small screens.

absheight   This WebTV-specific attribute sets the absolute height of a cell in pixels. Content that does not fit within this height is clipped.

abswidth   This WebTV-specific attribute sets the absolute width of a cell in pixels. Content that does not fit within this width is clipped.

accesskey   This attribute specifies a keyboard navigation accelerator for the element. Pressing ALT or a similar key (depending on the browser and operating system) in association with the specified key selects the anchor element correlated with that key.

align   This attribute is used to align the contents of the cells within the **<tbody>** element. Common values are **center, justify, left**, and **right**.

axis   This attribute is used to provide a name for a group of related headers.

background   This nonstandard attribute, which is supported by Internet Explorer, Netscape and WebTV, specifies the URL of a background image for the table cell. The image is tiled if it is smaller than the cell's dimensions.

bgcolor   This attribute specifies a background color for a table cell. Its value can be either a named color, such as red, or a color specified in the hexadecimal #*RRGGBB* format, such as #FF0000.

bordercolor   This attribute, supported by Internet Explorer and Netscape, is used to set the border color for a table cell. The attribute should be used only with a positive value for the

border attribute. The value of the attribute can be either a named color, such as **green**, or a color specified in the hexadecimal *#RRGGBB* format, such as **#00FF00**.

bordercolordark   This Internet Explorer–specific attribute specifies the darker of two border colors used to create a three-dimensional effect for a cell's borders. It must be used with the **border** attribute set to a positive value. The attribute value can be either a named color, such as **blue**, or a color specified in the hexadecimal *#RRGGBB* format, such as **#00FF00**).

bordercolorlight   This Internet Explorer–specific attribute specifies the lighter of two border colors used to create a three-dimensional effect for a cell's borders. It must be used with the **border** attribute set to a positive value. The attribute value can be either a named color, such as **red**, or a color specified in the hexadecimal *#RRGGBB* format, such as **#FF0000**.

char   This attribute is used to define the character to which element contents are aligned when the **align** attribute is set to the **char** value.

charoff   This attribute contains an offset as a positive or negative integer to align characters as related to the **char** value. A value of **2**, for example, would align characters in a cell two characters to the right of the character defined by the **char** attribute.

class   See "Core Attributes Reference," earlier in this appendix.

colspan   This attribute takes a numeric value that indicates how many columns wide a cell should be. This is useful to create tables with cells of different widths.

dir   See "Language Reference," earlier in this appendix.

gradangle   This WebTV-specific attribute defines the gradient angle for a table header, ranging from 90 to -90 degrees. **gradangle="0"** yields a left-to-right gradient, whereas **gradangle="90"** yields a top-to-bottom gradient. The beginning color of the gradient is defined by the **bgcolor** attribute, and the ending color is defined by the **gradcolor** attribute.

gradcolor   This WebTV-specific attribute defines the end color of a table header's background gradient, in conjunction with the gradient angle defined by the **gradangle** attribute and the starting color defined by the **bgcolor** attribute.

headers   This attribute takes a space-separated list of **id** values that correspond to the header cells related to this cell.

height   This attribute indicates the height in pixels of the header cell.

hidefocus   This proprietary element, introduced with Internet Explorer 5.5, hides focus on an element's content. Focus must be applied to the element using the **tabindex** attribute.

id   See "Core Attributes Reference," earlier in this appendix.

lang   See "Language Reference," earlier in this appendix.

language   In the Microsoft implementation, this attribute specifies the scripting language to be used with an associated script bound to the element, typically through an event handler attribute. Possible values might include **javascript**, **jscript**, **vbs**, and **vbscript**. Other values that include the version of the language used, such as **JavaScript1.1**, also might be possible.

maxlines   This WebTV-specific attribute takes a numeric argument indicating the maximum number of content lines to display. Content beyond these lines is clipped.

nowrap   This attribute keeps the content within a table header cell from automatically wrapping.

rowspan   This attribute takes a numeric value that indicates how many rows high a table cell should span. This attribute is useful in defining tables with cells of different heights.

scope   This attribute specifies the table cells for which the current cell provides header information. A value of **col** indicates that the cell is a header for the the rest of the column below it. A value of **colgroup** indicates that the cell is a header for its current column group. A value of **row** indicates that that the cell contains header information for the rest of the row it is in. A value of **rowgroup** indicates that the cell is a header for its row group. This attribute can be used in place of the **header** attribute and is useful for rendering assistance by nonvisual browsers. This attribute was added very late to the HTML 4.0 specification so support for this attribute is minimal.

style   See "Core Attributes Reference," earlier in this appendix.

tabindex   This attribute uses a number to identify the object's position in the tabbing order for keyboard navigation using the TAB key. Internet Explorer 5.5 applies this attribute to the **th** element; under IE 5.5, this focus can be disabled with the **hidefocus** attribute.

title   See "Core Attributes Reference," earlier in this appendix.

transparency   This WebTV-specific attribute specifies the degree of transparency of the table header. Values range from **0** (totally opaque) to **100** (totally transparent). A value of **50** is optimized for fast rendering.

valign   This attribute is used to set the vertical alignment for the table cell. HTML 4 defines **baseline**, **bottom**, **middle**, and **top**. Internet Explorer further defines **center**, which should act just like **middle**.

width   This attribute specifies the width of a header cell in pixels.

Attribute and Event Support

Netscape 4   **align**, **background**, **bgcolor**, **bordercolor**, **colspan**, **height**, **nowrap**, **rowspan**, **valign**, and **width**. (**class**, **id**, **lang**, and **style** are implied.)

Internet Explorer 4   **align (center | left | right)**, **bgcolor**, **class**, **colspan**, **id**, **lang**, **nowrap**, **rowspan**, **style**, **title**, and **valign (baseline | bottom | top)**, all W3C-defined events, and all attributes and events defined by Internet Explorer 4.

Internet Explorer 5.5   All W3C-defined attributes and events except **abbr**, **axis**, **char** and **charoff**, and all attributes and events defined by Internet Explorer 4 and 5.5.

WebTV   align (center | left | right), bgcolor, colspan, gradangle, gradcolor, nowrap, rowspan, transparency, valign (baseline | bottom, | middle | top), and width

Event Handlers

See "Events Reference," earlier in this appendix.

Examples

```
<table border="1">
   <tr>
      <th>Names</th>
      <th>Apples</th>
      <th>Oranges</th>
   </tr>

   <tr>
      <td>Bobby</td>
      <td>10</td>
      <td>5</td>
   </tr>

   <tr>
      <td>Ruby Sue</td>
      <td>20</td>
      <td>3</td>
   </tr>
</table>
```

Compatibility

HTML 3.2, 4, and 4.01, XHTML 1.0
Internet Explorer 2, 3, 4, 5, and 5.5
Netscape 1.1, 2, 3, 4–4.7, 6
Opera 4.0
WebTV

Notes

- The HTML 3.2 specification defines only **align**, **colspan**, **height**, **nowrap**, **rowspan**, **valign**, and **width** attributes.
- This element should always be within the **<tr>** element.
- Under the XHTML 1.0 specification, the closing **</th>** tag ceases to be optional.

<thead> (Table Header)

This element is used to group the rows within the header of a table so that common alignment and style defaults can easily be set for numerous cells. This element might be particularly useful when setting a common head for tables that are dynamically generated.

Syntax

```
<thead
    align="center | char | justify | left | right"
    char="character"
    charoff="offset"
    class="class name(s)"
    dir="ltr | rtl"
    id="unique alphanumeric identifier"
    lang="language code"
    style="style information"
    title="advisory text"
    valign="baseline | bottom | middle | top"
    onclick="script"
    ondblclick="script"
    onkeydown="script"
    onkeypress="script"
    onkeyup="script"
    onmousedown="script"
    onmousemove="script"
    onmouseout="script"
    onmouseover="script"
    onmouseup="script">

</thead>
```

XHTML Syntax

Under the XHTML 1.0 specification, the closing **</thead>** tag is mandatory.

Attributes and Events Defined by Internet Explorer 4

```
    bgcolor="color name | #RRGGBB"
    language="javascript | jscript | vbs | vbscript"
    valign="center"
    ondragstart="script"
    onhelp="script"
    onselectstart="script"
```

APPENDIX A

Attributes and Events Defined by Internet Explorer 5.5

```
accesskey="key"
hidefocus="true | false"
tabindex="number"
```

Attributes

accesskey   This attribute specifies a keyboard navigation accelerator for the element. Pressing ALT or a similar key (depending on the browser and operating system) in association with the specified key selects the anchor element correlated with that key.

align   This attribute is used to align the contents of the cells within the **<thead>** element. Common values are **center**, **justify**, **left**, and **right**. The HTML 4 specification also defines a value of **char**. When **align** is set to **char**, the attribute **char** must be present and set to the character to which cells should be aligned. A common use of this approach would be to set cells to align on a decimal point.

bgcolor   This attribute specifies a background color for the cells within the **<thead>** element. Its value can be either a named color, such as **red**, or a color specified in the hexadecimal *#RRGGBB* format, such as **#FF0000**.

char   This attribute is used to define the character to which element contents are aligned when the **align** attribute is set to the **char** value.

charoff   This attribute contains an offset as a positive or negative integer to align characters as related to the **char** value. A value of **2**, for example, would align characters in a cell two characters to the right of the character defined by the **char** attribute.

class   See "Core Attributes Reference," earlier in this appendix.

dir   See "Language Reference," earlier in this appendix.

hidefocus   This proprietary element, introduced with Internet Explorer 5.5, hides focus on an element's content. Focus must be applied to the element using the **tabindex** attribute.

id   See "Core Attributes Reference," earlier in this appendix.

lang   See "Language Reference," earlier in this appendix.

language   In the Microsoft implementation, this attribute specifies the scripting language to be used with an associated script bound to the element, typically through an event handler attribute. Possible values might include **javascript**, **jscript**, **vbs**, and **vbscript**. Other values that include the version of the language used, such as **JavaScript1.1**, also might be possible.

style   See "Core Attributes Reference," earlier in this appendix.

tabindex   This attribute uses a number to identify the object's position in the tabbing order for keyboard navigation using the TAB key. Internet Explorer 5.5 applies this attribute to the **thead** element; under IE 5.5, this focus can be disabled with the **hidefocus** attribute.

title   See "Core Attributes Reference," earlier in this appendix.

valign   This attribute is used to set the vertical alignment for the table cells with the **<thead>** element. HTML 4.01 defines **baseline, bottom, middle,** and **top**. Internet Explorer replaces **middle** with **center**; the effect should be the same.

Attribute and Event Support

Internet Explorer 4   All attributes and events except **char, charoff,** and **dir**. (Note: Internet Explorer 4 does not support the **justify** value for the **align** attribute.)

Internet Explorer 5.5   All W3C-defined attributes and events except **char** and **charoff**, and all attributes and events defined by Internet Explorer 4 and 5.5.

Event Handlers
See "Events Reference," earlier in this appendix.

Example

```
<table border="1" bgcolor="yellow" width="80%">
<thead align="center" bgcolor="red" class="footer"
      valign="bottom">
   <td>This is the Important Table Headline</td>
</thead>

<tbody class="tablebody">
   <tr>
      <td>The contents of the table!</td>
   </tr>
</tbody>
</table>
```

Compatibility
HTML 4, 4.01, XHTML 1.0
Internet Explorer 3, 4, 5, and 5.5
Netscape 6

Notes

- This element is contained only by the **<table>** element and contains table rows as delimited by **<tr>** elements.
- Under the XHTML 1.0 specification, the closing **</thead>** tag ceases to be optional.

<title> (Document Title)

This element encloses the title of an HTML document. It must occur within a document's **<head>** element and must be present in all valid documents. Meaningful titles are very important because they are used for bookmarking a page and might be used by search engines attempting to index the document.

Syntax

```
<title
    dir="ltr | rtl"
    lang="language code">

</title>
```

Attributes Defined by Internet Explorer 4

```
        id="unique alphanumeric identifier"
        title="advisory text"
```

Attributes

dir   See "Language Reference," earlier in this appendix.

id   See "Core Attributes Reference," earlier in this appendix.

lang   See "Language Reference," earlier in this appendix.

title   See "Core Attributes Reference," earlier in this appendix.

Attribute and Event Support

Internet Explorer 4   id and title

Event Handlers

None

Example

```
<head><title>Demo Company: Products: Super Widget</title></head>
```

Compatibility

HTML 2, 3.2, 4, and 4.01
Internet Explorer 2, 3, 4, 5, and 5.5
Netscape 1, 2, 3, 4–4.7, 6
Opera 4.0
WebTV

Notes

- Meaningful names should provide information about the document. A poor title would be something like "My Home Page," whereas a better title would be "Joe Smith Home."

- Older versions of Netscape allowed for multiple occurrences of the **<title>** element. When multiple **<title>** elements were encountered, they could be used to simulate an animated title bar. This was a bug with the Netscape browser, however, and the effect of multiple **<title>** elements no longer works.

- Browsers can be extremely sensitive with the **<title>** element. If the title element is malformed or not closed, the page might not even render in the browser.

- The HTML 2.0 and 3.2 specifications define no attributes for the **<title>** element.

<tr> (Table Row)

This element specifies a row in a table. The individual cells of the row are defined by the **<th>** and **<td>** elements.

Syntax

```
<tr
     align="center | justify | left | right"
     bgcolor="color name | #RRGGBB" (transitional)
     char="character"
     charoff="offset"
     class="class name(s)"
     dir="ltr | rtl"
     id="unique alphanumeric identifier"
     lang="language code"
     style="style information"
     title="advisory text"
     valign="baseline | bottom | middle | top"
     onclick="script"
     ondblclick="script"
     onkeydown="script"
     onkeypress="script"
     onkeyup="script"
     onmousedown="script"
     onmousemove="script"
     onmouseout="script"
     onmouseover="script"
     onmouseup="script">

</tr>
```

XHTML Syntax

Under the XHTML 1.0 specification, the closing **</tr>** tag is mandatory.

Attributes and Events Defined by Internet Explorer 4

```
bordercolor="color name | #RRGGBB"
bordercolordark="color name | #RRGGBB"
bordercolorlight="color name | #RRGGBB"
language="javascript | javascript | vbs | vbscript"
valign="center"
onafterupdate="script"
onbeforeupdate="script"
onblur="script"
ondragstart="script"
onfocus="script"
onhelp="script"
onresize="script"
onrowenter="script"
onrowexit="script"
onselectstart="script
```

Attributes and Events Defined by Internet Explorer 5.5

```
accesskey="key"
hidefocus="true | false"
tabindex="number"
```

Attributes Defined by WebTV

```
nowrap
transparency="number (0-100)"
```

Attributes

accesskey   This attribute specifies a keyboard navigation accelerator for the element. Pressing ALT or a similar key (depending on the browser and operating system) in association with the specified key selects the anchor element correlated with that key.

align   This attribute is used to align the contents of the cells within the **<thead>** element. Common values are **center**, **justify**, **left**, and **right**.

bgcolor   This attribute specifies a background color for all the cells in a row. Its value can be either a named color, such as **red**, or a color specified in the hexadecimal *#RRGGBB* format, such as **#FF0000**.

bordercolor   This attribute, supported by Internet Explorer and Netscape, is used to set the border color for table cells in the row. The attribute should be used only with a positive value for the **border** attribute. The value of the attribute can be either a named color, such as **green**, or a color specified in the hexadecimal *#RRGGBB* format, such as **#00FF00**.

bordercolordark   This Internet Explorer–specific attribute specifies the darker of two border colors used to create a three-dimensional effect for the cell's borders. It must be used with the **border** attribute set to a positive value. The attribute value can be either a named color, such as **blue**, or a color specified in the hexadecimal *#RRGGBB* format, such as **#00FF00**.

bordercolorlight   This Internet Explorer-specific attribute specifies the lighter of two border colors used to create a three-dimensional effect for a cell's borders. It must be used with the **border** attribute set to a positive value. The attribute value can be either a named color, such as **red**, or a color specified in the hexadecimal *#RRGGBB* format, such as **#FF0000**.

char   This attribute is used to define the character to which element contents are aligned when the **align** attribute is set to the **char** value.

charoff   This attribute contains an offset as a positive or negative integer to align characters as related to the **char** value. A value of **2**, for example, would align characters in a cell two characters to the right of the character defined by the **char** attribute.

class   See "Core Attributes Reference," earlier in this appendix.

dir   See "Language Reference," earlier in this appendix.

hidefocus   This proprietary element, introduced with Internet Explorer 5.5, hides focus on an element's content. Focus must be applied to the element using the **tabindex** attribute.

id   See "Core Attributes Reference," earlier in this appendix.

lang   See "Language Reference," earlier in this appendix.

language   In the Microsoft implementation, this attribute specifies the scripting language to be used with an associated script bound to the element, typically through an event handler attribute. Possible values might include **javascript**, **jscript**, **vbs**, and **vbscript**. Other values that include the version of the language used, such as **JavaScript1.1**, also might be possible.

nowrap   This WebTV-specific attribute keeps table rows from wrapping if they extend beyond the right margin.

style   See "Core Attributes Reference," earlier in this appendix.

tabindex   This attribute uses a number to identify the object's position in the tabbing order for keyboard navigation using the TAB key. Internet Explorer 5.5 applies this attribute to the **tr** element; under IE 5.5, this focus can be disabled with the **hidefocus** attribute.

title   See "Core Attributes Reference," earlier in this appendix.

transparency   This WebTV-specific attribute specifies the degree of transparency of the table. Values range from **0** (totally opaque) to **100** (totally transparent). A value of **50** is optimized for fast rendering.

valign   This attribute is used to set the vertical alignment for the table cells with the **\<tr>** element. HTML 4.01 defines **baseline, bottom, middle,** and **top.** Internet Explorer replaces **middle** with **center;** the effect should be the same.

Attribute and Event Support

Netscape 4   align, bgcolor, and **valign.** (**class, id, lang,** and **style** are implied.)

Internet Explorer 4   align (center | left | right), bgcolor, id, lang, style, title, and **valign** (**baseline | bottom | top),** all W3C-defined events, and all attributes and events defined by Internet Explorer 4.

Internet Explorer 5.5   align (center | left | right | justify), bgcolor, id, lang, style, title, and valign (baseline | bottom | top | middle), all W3C-defined events, and all attributes and events defined by Internet Explorer 4 and 5.5.

WebTV   align (center | left | right), bgcolor, nowrap, transparency, and **valign** (baseline | bottom | middle | top)

Event Handlers
See "Events Reference," earlier in this appendix.

Example

```
<table width="300" border="1">
   <tr bgcolor="red" align="center" valign="middle">
      <td>3</td>
      <td>5.6</td>
      <td>7.9</td>
   </tr>
</table>
```

Compatibility
HTML 3.2, 4, and 4.01, XHTML 1.0
Internet Explorer 2, 3, 4, 5, and 5.5
Netscape 1.1, 2, 3, 4–4.7, 6
Opera 4.0
WebTV

Notes

■ This element is contained by the **\<table>, \<thead>, \<tbody>,** and **\<tfoot>** elements. It contains the **\<th>** and **\<td>** elements.

- The HTML 3.2 specification defines only the **align** and **valign** attributes for this element.
- Under the XHTML 1.0 specification, the closing **</tr>** tag ceases to be optional.

<tt> (Teletype Text)

This element is used to indicate that text should be rendered in a monospaced font similar to teletype text.

Syntax

```
<tt
    class="class name(s)"
    dir="ltr | rtl"
    id="unique alphanumeric identifier"
    lang="language code"
    style="style information"
    title="advisory text"
    onclick="script"
    ondblclick="script"
    onkeydown="script"
    onkeypress="script"
    onkeyup="script"
    onmousedown="script"
    onmousemove="script"
    onmouseout="script"
    onmouseover="script"
    onmouseup="script">

</tt>
```

Attributes and Events Defined by Internet Explorer 4

```
    language="javascript | jscript | vbs | vbscript"
    ondragstart="script"
    onhelp="script"
    onselectstart="script"
```

Attributes and Events Defined by Internet Explorer 5.5

```
    accesskey="key"
    contenteditable="false | true | inherit"
    hidefocus="true | false"
    tabindex="number"
```

Attributes

accesskey   This attribute specifies a keyboard navigation accelerator for the element. Pressing ALT or a similar key (depending on the browser and operating system) in association with the specified key selects the anchor element correlated with that key.

class   See "Core Attributes Reference," earlier in this appendix.

contenteditable   This proprietary Microsoft attribute allows users to edit content rendered in the Internet Explorer 5.5 browser. Values are **false**, **true**, and **inherit**. A value of **false** will prevent content from being edited by users; **true** will allow editing. The default value, **inherit**, applies the value of the affected element's parent element.

dir   See "Language Reference," earlier in this appendix.

hidefocus   This proprietary element, introduced with Internet Explorer 5.5, hides focus on an element's content. Focus must be applied to the element using the **tabindex** attribute.

id   See "Core Attributes Reference," earlier in this appendix.

lang   See "Language Reference," earlier in this appendix.

language   In the Microsoft implementation, this attribute specifies the scripting language to be used with an associated script bound to the element, typically through an event handler attribute. Possible values might include **javascript**, **jscript**, **vbs**, and **vbscript**. Other values that include the version of the language used, such as **JavaScript1.1**, also might be possible.

style   See "Core Attributes Reference," earlier in this appendix.

tabindex   This attribute uses a number to identify the object's position in the tabbing order for keyboard navigation using the TAB key. Internet Explorer 5.5 applies this attribute to the **tt** element; under IE 5.5, this focus can be disabled with the **hidefocus** attribute.

title   See "Core Attributes Reference," earlier in this appendix.

Attribute and Event Support

Netscape 4   class, id, lang, and style are implied.

Internet Explorer 4   All attributes and events defined by the W3C and Internet Explorer 4, except **dir**.

Internet Explorer 5.5   All attributes and events

Event Handlers
See "Events Reference," earlier in this appendix.

Example

```
Here is some <tt>monospaced text</tt>.
```

Compatibility
HTML 2, 3.2, 4, and 4.01, XHTML 1.0
Internet Explorer 2, 3, 4, 5, and 5.5
Netscape 1, 2, 3, 4–4.7, 6
Opera 4.0
WebTV

<u> (Underline)
This element is used to indicate that the enclosed text should be displayed underlined.

Syntax (Transitional Only)

```
<u
    class="class name(s)"
    dir="ltr | rtl"
    id="unique alphanumeric string"
    lang="language code"
    style="style information"
    title="advisory text"
    onclick="script"
    ondblclick="script"
    onkeydown="script"
    onkeypress="script"
    onkeyup="script"
    onmousedown="script"
    onmousemove="script"
    onmouseout="script"
    onmouseover="script"
    onmouseup="script">

</u>
```

Attributes and Events Defined by Internet Explorer 4

```
    language="javascript | jscript | vbs | vbscript"
    ondragstart="script"
    onhelp="script"
    onselectstart="script"
```

Attributes and Events Defined by Internet Explorer 5.5

```
accesskey="key"
contenteditable="false | true | inherit"
hidefocus="true | false"
tabindex="number"
```

Attributes

accesskey   This attribute specifies a keyboard navigation accelerator for the element. Pressing ALT or a similar key (depending on the browser and operating system) in association with the specified key selects the anchor element correlated with that key.

class   See "Core Attributes Reference," earlier in this appendix.

contenteditable   This proprietary Microsoft attribute allows users to edit content rendered in the Internet Explorer 5.5 browser. Values are **false**, **true**, and **inherit**. A value of **false** will prevent content from being edited by users; **true** will allow editing. The default value, **inherit**, applies the value of the affected element's parent element.

dir   See "Language Reference," earlier in this appendix.

hidefocus   This proprietary element, introduced with Internet Explorer 5.5, hides focus on an element's content. Focus must be applied to the element using the **tabindex** attribute.

id   See "Core Attributes Reference," earlier in this appendix.

lang   See "Language Reference," earlier in this appendix.

language   In the Microsoft implementation, this attribute specifies the scripting language to be used with an associated script bound to the element, typically through an event handler attribute. Possible values might include **javascript**, **jscript**, **vbs**, and **vbscript**. Other values that include the version of the language used, such as **JavaScript1.1**, also might be possible.

style   See "Core Attributes Reference," earlier in this appendix.

tabindex   This attribute uses a number to identify the object's position in the tabbing order for keyboard navigation using the TAB key. Internet Explorer 5.5 applies this attribute to the **u** element; under IE 5.5, this focus can be disabled with the **hidefocus** attribute.

title   See "Core Attributes Reference," earlier in this appendix.

Attribute and Event Support

Netscape 4   **class**, **id**, **lang**, and **style** are implied.

Internet Explorer 4   All attributes and events defined by the W3C and Internet Explorer 4, except **dir**.

Internet Explorer 4   All attributes and events

Event Handlers
See "Events Reference," earlier in this appendix.

Examples

```
Here is some <u>underlined text</u>.

Be careful with <u>underlined</u> text; it looks like
<a href="http://www.yahoo.com/">links</a>.
```

Compatibility
HTML 3.2, 4 (transitional), 4.01 (transitional), XHTML 1.0
Internet Explorer 2, 3, 4, 5, and 5.5
Netscape 3, 4–4.7, 6
Opera 4.0
WebTV

Notes

■ This element has been deprecated by the W3C. Under the strict HTML 4.01 specification, the **<u>** element is not defined. The capabilities of this element are possible using style sheets.

■ Underlining text can be problematic because it looks similar to a link, especially in a black-and-white environment.

<ul> (Unordered List)

This element is used to indicate an unordered list, namely a collection of items that do not have a numerical ordering. The individual items in the list are defined by the **<li>** element, which is the only allowed element within **<ul>**.

Syntax

```
<ul
    class="class name(s)"
    compact (transitional)
    dir="ltr | rtl"
    id="unique alphanumeric identifier"
    lang="language code"
    style="style information"
```

```
      title="advisory text"
      type="circle | disc | square" (transitional)
      onclick="script"
      ondblclick="script"
      onkeydown="script"
      onkeypress="script"
      onkeyup="script"
      onmousedown="script"
      onmousemove="script"
      onmouseout="script"
      onmouseover="script"
      onmouseup="script">

      List items specified by <li> elements

</ul>
```

XHTML Syntax

Due to XHTML 1.0's deprecation of attribute minimization, the **compact** attribute must have a
quoted attribute when used:

```
<ul compact="compact"></ul>
```

Attributes and Events Defined by Internet Explorer 4

```
      language="javascript | jscript | vbs | vbscript"
      ondragstart="script"
      onhelp="script"
      onselectstart="script"
```

Attributes and Events Defined by Internet Explorer 5.5

```
      accesskey="key"
      contenteditable="false | true | inherit"
      hidefocus="true | false"
      tabindex="number"
```

Attributes

accesskey   This attribute specifies a keyboard navigation accelerator for the element. Pressing
ALT or a similar key (depending on the browser and operating system) in association with the
specified key selects the anchor element correlated with that key.

class   See "Core Attributes Reference," earlier in this appendix.

compact   This attribute indicates that the list should be rendered in a compact style. Few browsers actually change the rendering of the list regardless of the presence of this attribute. The **compact** attribute requires no value.

contenteditable   This proprietary Microsoft attribute allows users to edit content rendered in the Internet Explorer 5.5 browser. Values are **false**, **true**, and **inherit**. A value of **false** will prevent content from being edited by users; **true** will allow editing. The default value, **inherit**, applies the value of the affected element's parent element.

dir   See "Language Reference," earlier in this appendix.

hidefocus   This proprietary element, introduced with Internet Explorer 5.5, hides focus on an element's content. Focus must be applied to the element using the **tabindex** attribute.

id   See "Core Attributes Reference," earlier in this appendix.

lang   See "Language Reference," earlier in this appendix.

language   In the Microsoft implementation, this attribute specifies the scripting language to be used with an associated script bound to the element, typically through an event handler attribute. Possible values might include **javascript**, **jscript**, **vbs**, and **vbscript**. Other values that include the version of the language used, such as **JavaScript1.1**, also might be possible.

style   See "Core Attributes Reference," earlier in this appendix.

tabindex   This attribute uses a number to identify the object's position in the tabbing order for keyboard navigation using the TAB key. Internet Explorer 5.5 applies this attribute to the **ul** element; under IE 5.5, this focus can be disabled with the **hidefocus** attribute.

title   See "Core Attributes Reference," earlier in this appendix.

type   The **type** attribute is used to set the bullet style for the list. The values defined under HTML 3.2 and the transitional version of HTML 4.0/4.01 are **circle**, **disc**, and **square**. A user agent might decide to use a different bullet depending on the nesting level of the list unless the **type** attribute is used. The WebTV interface also supports a triangle bullet. The **type** attribute is dropped under the strict version of HTML 4.0 because style sheets can provide richer bullet control.

Attribute and Event Support

Netscape 4   class, id, lang, style, and type

Internet Explorer 4   All attributes and events defined by the W3C and Internet Explorer 4 except **compact** and **dir**.

Internet Explorer 4   All attributes and events

WebTV   type

Event Handlers

See "Events Reference," earlier in this appendix.

Examples

```
<ul compact title="Sushi Short List" type="circle">
    <li>Maguro
    <li>Ebi
    <li>Hamachi
</ul>


<!-- Common but bad example -->
<ul>Indenting using lists should not be used, though it is common.
Many Web editors generate code laden with nonbreaking spaces and
unordered lists.</ul>
```

Compatibility

HTML 2, 3.2, 4, and 4.01, XHTML 1.0
Internet Explorer 2, 3, 4, 5, and 5.5
Netscape 1, 2, 3, 4–4.7, 6
Opera 4.0
WebTV

Notes

- HTML 2.0 supports only the **compact** attribute.
- The HTML 3.2 specification supports **compact** and **type**.
- Under the strict HTML 4.01 specification, the **<ul>** element does not support the **compact** attribute or the **type** attribute. Both of these attributes can be safely replaced with style rules.
- Many Web page designers and page development tools use the **<ul>** element to indent text. Be aware that the only element that should occur within a **<ul>** element is **<li>**, according to HTML standards, so such HTML markup does not conform to standards. However, this common practice is likely to continue.

<var> (Variable)

This element is used to indicate a variable. Variables are identifiers that occur in a programming language or a mathematical expression. The element is logical, although enclosed text often is rendered in italics.

Syntax

```
<var
    class="class name(s)"
```

```
dir="ltr | rtl"
id="unique alphanumeric value"
lang="language code"
style="style information"
title="advisory text"
onclick="script"
ondblclick="script"
onkeydown="script"
onkeypress="script"
onkeyup="script"
onmousedown="script"
onmousemove="script"
onmouseout="script"
onmouseover="script"
onmouseup="script">
```

```
</var>
```

Attributes and Events Defined by Internet Explorer 4

```
language="javascript | jscript | vbs | vbscript"
ondragstart="script"
onhelp="script"
onselectstart="script"
```

Attributes and Events Defined by Internet Explorer 5.5

```
accesskey="key"
contenteditable="false | true | inherit"
hidefocus="true | false"
tabindex="number"
```

Attributes

accesskey   This attribute specifies a keyboard navigation accelerator for the element. Pressing ALT or a similar key (depending on the browser and operating system) in association with the specified key selects the anchor element correlated with that key.

class   See "Core Attributes Reference," earlier in this appendix.

contenteditable   This proprietary Microsoft attribute allows users to edit content rendered in the Internet Explorer 5.5 browser. Values are **false, true**, and **inherit**. A value of **false** will prevent content from being edited by users; **true** will allow editing. The default value, **inherit**, applies the value of the affected element's parent element.

dir   See "Language Reference," earlier in this appendix.

hidefocus   This proprietary element, introduced with Internet Explorer 5.5, hides focus on an element's content. Focus must be applied to the element using the **tabindex** attribute.

id   See "Core Attributes Reference," earlier in this appendix.

lang   See "Language Reference," earlier in this appendix.

language   In the Microsoft implementation, this attribute specifies the scripting language to be used with an associated script bound to the element, typically through an event handler attribute. Possible values might include **javascript**, **jscript**, **vbs**, and **vbscript**. Other values that include the version of the language used, such as **JavaScript1.1**, also might be possible.

style   See "Core Attributes Reference," earlier in this appendix.

tabindex   This attribute uses a number to identify the object's position in the tabbing order for keyboard navigation using the TAB key. Internet Explorer 5.5 applies this attribute to the **var** element; under IE 5.5, this focus can be disabled with the **hidefocus** attribute.

title   See "Core Attributes Reference," earlier in this appendix.

Attribute and Event Support

Netscape 4   class, **id**, **lang**, and **style** are implied.

Internet Explorer 4   All attributes and events defined by the W3C and Internet Explorer 4, except **dir**.

Internet Explorer 5.5   All attributes and events

Event Handlers
See "Events Reference," earlier in this appendix.

Example

    Assign the value 5 to the variable **<var>**x**</var>**.

Compatibility
HTML 2, 3.2, 4, and 4.01, XHTML 1.0
Internet Explorer 2, 3, 4, 5, and 5.5
Netscape 1, 2, 3, 4–4.7, 6
Opera 4.0
WebTV

Notes

- As a logical element, **<var>** is a perfect candidate for style sheet binding.
- The HTML 2.0 and 3.2 specifications support no attributes for this element.

<wbr> (Word Break)

This nonstandard element is used to indicate a place where a line break can occur if necessary. This element is used in conjunction with the **<nobr>** element, which is used to keep text from wrapping. When used this way, **<wbr>** can be thought of as a soft line break in comparison to the **
** element. This element is common to both Netscape and Microsoft implementations, though it is not part of any HTML standard.

Syntax

```
<wbr
    class="class name(s)"
    id="unique alphanumeric value"
    language="javascript | jscript | vbs | vbscript"
    style="style information"
    title="advisory text">
```

Attributes

class   See "Core Attributes Reference," earlier in this appendix.

id   See "Core Attributes Reference," earlier in this appendix.

language   In the Microsoft implementation, this attribute specifies the scripting language to be used with an associated script bound to the element, typically through an event handler attribute. Possible values might include **javascript**, **jscript**, **vbs**, and **vbscript**. Other values that include the version of the language used, such as **JavaScript1.1**, also might be possible.

style   See "Core Attributes Reference," earlier in this appendix.

title   See "Core Attributes Reference," earlier in this appendix.

Attribute and Event Support

Netscape 4   **class**, **id**, **style**, and **title** are implied.

Internet Explorer 4   All attributes

Event Handlers

See "Events Reference," earlier in this appendix.

Example

```
<nobr>A line break can occur here<wbr>but not elsewhere, even if the line is
really long.</nobr>
```

Compatibility

Internet Explorer 2, 3, 4, 5, and 5.5
Netscape 1.1, 2, 3, 4–4.7

Notes

- This element was introduced in Netscape 1.1.
- This is an empty element, so no closing tag is required.

<xml> (XML Data Island)

This proprietary element introduced by Microsoft can be used to embed islands of xml
(Extensible Markup Language) data into HTML documents; this will work only under Internet
Explorer 5.0 or later. The **<xml>** element can be used to reference outside data sources using the
src attribute, or surround XML data in the HTML document itself.

Syntax Defined by Internet Explorer 5.0

```
<xml
    id="unique alphanumeric value"
    ns="url of xml namespace"
    prefix="xml prefix"
    src="url of xml data file"
    ondataavailable="script"
    ondatasetchanged="script"
    ondatasetcomplete="script"
    onreadystatechange="script"
    onrowenter="script"
    onrowexit="script">

. . . embedded xml code . . .

</xml>
```

Attributes

id   See "Core Attributes Reference," earlier in this appendix.

ns   This attribute references the URL of an xml namespace.

prefix   This attribute references the URL of an XML namespace prefix in conjunction with the **ns** attribute.

src   This attribute references an external xml data file.

Event Handlers

ondataavailable   See "Extended Events," earlier in this appendix.

ondatasetchanged   See "Extended Events," earlier in this appendix.

ondatasetcomplete   See "Extended Events," earlier in this appendix.

onreadystatechange   See "Extended Events," earlier in this appendix.

onrowenter   See "Extended Events," earlier in this appendix.

onrowexit   See "Extended Events," earlier in this appendix.

Attribute and Event Support

Internet Explorer 5   id, src, ondataavailable, ondatasetchanged, ondatasetcomplete, onreadystatechange, onrowenter, onrowexit

Examples

```
<!-- This code embeds xml data directly into a document.
     All code between the xml tags is not HTML, but a
     hypothetical example of xml. -->

<xml id="tasty">
   <combomeal>
      <burger>
       <name>Tasty Burger</name>
         <bun bread="white">
            <meat />
            <cheese />
            <meat />
         </bun>
      </burger>
      <fries size="large" />
      <drink size="large" flavor="Cola" />
   </combomeal>
</xml>

<!-- This code fragment uses the src attribute to reference an
     external file containing xml data. -->
```

```
<xml src="combomeal.xml"></xml>
```

Compatibility

Internet Explorer 5

Notes

- Support of the **<xml>** element currently is exclusive to Internet Explorer 5.0 and later.
- For a more detailed discussion of this element, refer to "Embedding XML into HTML Documents" in Chapter 17.

<xmp> (Example)

This deprecated element indicates that the enclosed text is an example. Example text generally is rendered in a monospaced font, and the spaces, tabs, and returns are preserved, as with the **<pre>** element. As the **<xmp>** element is no longer standard, the **<pre>** or **<samp>** elements should be used instead.

Syntax Defined by HTML 2; Deprecated Under HTML 4

```
<xmp>
</xmp>
```

Attributes and Events Defined by Internet Explorer 4

```
class="class name(s)"
id="unique alphanumeric value"
lang="language code"
language="javascript | jscript | vbs | vbscript"
style="style information"
title="advisory text"
onclick="script"
ondblclick="script"
ondragstart="script"
onhelp="script"
onkeydown="script"
onkeypress="script"
onkeyup="script"
onmousedown="script"
onmousemove="script"
onmouseout="script"
onmouseover="script"
```

<xmp> (Example)   *981*

```
        onmouseup="script"
        onselectstart="script"
```

Attributes and Events Defined by Internet Explorer 5.5

```
        accesskey="key"
        contenteditable="false | true | inherit"
        hidefocus="true | false"
        tabindex="number"
```

Attributes

accesskey   This attribute specifies a keyboard navigation accelerator for the element. Pressing ALT or a similar key (depending on the browser and operating system) in association with the specified key selects the anchor element correlated with that key.

class   See "Core Attributes Reference," earlier in this appendix.

contenteditable   This proprietary Microsoft attribute allows users to edit content rendered in the Internet Explorer 5.5 browser. Values are **false**, **true**, and **inherit**. A value of **false** will prevent content from being edited by users; **true** will allow editing. The default value, **inherit**, applies the value of the affected element's parent element.

hidefocus   This proprietary element, introduced with Internet Explorer 5.5, hides focus on an element's content. Focus must be applied to the element using the **tabindex** attribute.

id   See "Core Attributes Reference," earlier in this appendix.

lang   See "Language Reference," earlier in this appendix.

language   In the Microsoft implementation, this attribute specifies the scripting language to be used with an associated script bound to the element, typically through an event handler attribute. Possible values might include **javascript**, **jscript**, **vbs**, and **vbscript**. Other values that include the version of the language used, such as **JavaScript1.1**, also might be possible.

style   See "Core Attributes Reference," earlier in this appendix.

tabindex   This attribute uses a number to identify the object's position in the tabbing order for keyboard navigation using the TAB key. Internet Explorer 5.5 applies this attribute to the **xmp** element; under IE 5.5, this focus can be disabled with the **hidefocus** attribute.

title   See "Core Attributes Reference," earlier in this appendix.

Attribute and Event Support

Netscape 4   class, id, style, and title

Internet Explorer 4   All attributes defined by the W3C and Internet Explorer 4.

Internet Explorer 5.5   All attributes

Event Handlers

See "Events Reference," earlier in this appendix.

Example

```
<xmp>This is a large block of text used as an example. Note that returns
as well as    S P A C E S are preserved.</xmp>
```

Compatibility

HTML 2
Internet Explorer 2, 3, 4, and 5
Netscape 1, 2, 3, 4–4.7
Opera 4.0
WebTV

Notes

- This element is very old, although it continues to be documented. It was first deprecated under HTML 3.2 and continues to be unsupported under HTML 4.0.

- Page designers should not use this element. Internet Explorer documentation supports this element but recommends use of **<pre>** or **<samp>** instead.

The
Complete
Reference

Appendix B

Style Sheet Reference

C ascading style sheets, covered in Chapter 10, offer a powerful new tool for Web page layout. When used properly, style sheets also separate style from document structure, as was originally intended for HTML. Most of the style properties defined by the Cascading Style Sheets 1 (CSS1) specification are supported by major browsers, including Internet Explorer 3, 4, 5, and 5.5, and Netscape Navigator 4, and 4.5–4.7. This appendix provides a concise look at style sheet rules, a listing of commonly supported CSS1 style properties and their values, and their current compatibility with the major browsers. Testing on a beta version of Netscape 6 (Preview Release 2) suggests that the final version of Netscape 6 will support a wider range of style sheet properties. A brief listing of new properties available in Cascading Style Sheets 2 (CSS2) will be followed by a review of CSS2 positioning properties, which are largely supported by the most recent browser versions. For a more detailed discussion of the CSS2 specification, see Chapter 10. A quick look at Microsoft extensions to CSS and a section about CSS measurements and color values round out this appendix.

Style Sheet Terms

This section defines some basic terms used when working with style sheets.

Embedded Styles

Document-wide styles can be embedded in a document's **<head>** element using the **<style>** element. Note that styles should be commented out to avoid interpretation by non-style-aware browsers.

Example

```
<head>
<style type="text/css">
<!--
p  {font-size: 14pt; font-face: Times; color: blue;
    background-color: yellow;}
em {font-size: 16pt; color: green;}
-->
</style>
<title> ... </title></head>
```

Browser Support
Internet Explorer 3, 4, 5, and 5.5
Netscape 4, 4.5–4.7, 6

Inline Styles

Styles can be applied directly to elements in the body of a document. Rather than set document-wide values for the **<h1>** element, it is possible to set the style for an individual header, as shown here:

Example

```
<h1 style="font-size: 48pt; font-family: Arial;
          color: green;">CSS1 Test</h1>
```

An **<h1>** header elsewhere in the document could be assigned a completely different style.

Browser Support
Internet Explorer 3, 4, 5, and 5.5
Netscape 4, 4.5–4.7, 6

Linked Styles

Style can be contained in an external style sheet linked to a document or a set of documents (see Chapter 10), as shown in the following example. Linked information should be placed inside the **<head>** element.

Example

```
<link rel="stylesheet" type="text/css" href="newstyle.css">
```

Browser Support
Internet Explorer 3, 4, 5, and 5.5
Netscape 4, 4.5–4.7, 6

Imported Styles

Styles can be imported from an external file and expanded in place, similar to a macro. Importing can be used to include multiple style sheets. An imported style is defined with the **<style>** element and the **type** attribute, followed by the URL for the style sheet, as shown here:

Example

```
<head>
<style type="text/css">
@import url(newstyle.css)
</style>
<title> . . . </title></head>
```

Browser Support
Internet Explorer 5
Future versions of Netscape (not available in Netscape 6 Preview Release 2)

Selectors

A selector is an HTML element, identifier, or class name associated with a style rule. In the following examples, **p** and **div** are the selectors.

Examples

```
p {font-size: 12pt;}

div {font-family: Courier;}
```

Browser Support

Internet Explorer 3, 4, 5, and 5.5
Netscape 4, 4.5–4.7, 6

Class Selectors

Multiple classes can be defined for individual elements (selectors). To create a class selector, attach a class name to a selector; separate the selector from the class name with a period. Repeat this with the same selector, but give it a different name.

Example

```
p.one {font-face: Arial; font-size: 12pt;}
p.two {font-face: Verdana; font-size: 14pt;}
```

There are now two different paragraph styles to choose from. Use the **class** attribute with the **<p>** element to distinguish between them in the body of the document.

Example

```
<p class="one">This is paragraph style one.</p>
<p class="two">This is paragraph style two.</p>
```

It is also possible to create standalone class selectors by omitting element names.

Example

```
.one {font-face: Arial; font-size: 12pt;}
.two {font-face: Verdana; font-size: 14pt;}

<p class="one">This is paragraph style one.</p>
<p class="two">This is paragraph style two.</p>
<h1 class="two">This header will also be style two.</h1>
```

Browser Support

Internet Explorer 3, 4, 5, and 5.5
Netscape 4, 4.5–4.7, 6

Contextual Selectors

Contextual selectors define the display of elements within other specific elements. In the following example, **\<strong>** text within a **\<div>** element displays as green; however, **\<strong>** text outside the context of the **\<div>** element is not affected by this style. Note that the contextual selectors **div** and **strong** are separated by white space, not by commas. Another way to say this is that a **\<strong>** element with a **\<div>** ancestor will match this style.

Example

```
div strong {color: green;}
```

Browser Support

Internet Explorer 3, 4, 5, and 5.5
Netscape 4, 4.5–4.7, 6

ID Selectors

Styles can be assigned independent of elements by creating ID selectors. Create an ID selector by creating a name preceded by the character # and following it with the style to be associated with that ID.

Example

```
#style43 {font-size: 6pt; font-face: Verdana; font-variant: small-caps;}
```

In the body of the document, use the **id** attribute to assign the style to an element or elements.

Example

```
<p id="style43">This text is hard to read.</p>
<h1 id="style43">So is the text in this header.</h1>
```

Note   *ID must be unique. Each value must appear only once in a given document.*

Browser Support

Internet Explorer 3, 4, 5, and 5.5
Netscape 4, 4.5–4.7, 6

Rules

Style rules determine the styles to be associated with a selector. Style rules are enclosed within braces. A rule must include a property (**font-face**, in the following example) and a value (the font name **Impact**, in the following example).

Example

```
p {font-face: Impact;}
```

Multiple rules can be included within a single style specification, but they must be separated by semicolons. The last semicolon is optional.

Example

```
p {font-face: Impact; font-size: 12pt; line-height: 16pt;}
```

Browser Support

Internet Explorer 3, 4, 5, and 5.5
Netscape 4, 4.5–4.7, 6

Grouping

Selectors and declarations can be grouped together so that all the selectors are associated with a particular rule. Note that the listed selectors are separated by commas.

Example

```
p, div, span {background-color: yellow; font-face: Arial;
              color: black; font-size: 14pt;}
```

Browser Support

Internet Explorer 3, 4, 5, and 5.5
Netscape 4, 4.5–4.7, 6

Inheritance

In most cases, elements contained within another element inherit the property values specified for the parent element, unless those properties are defined differently for the nested elements. In the following example, the **<p>** element retains the background color and font color defined for the **<body>** element; only the font face changes.

Example

```
body {background-color: blue; font-face: Courier; color: white;}
p    {font-face: Arial;}
```

Browser Support
Internet Explorer 3, 4, 5, and 5.5
Netscape 4, 4.5–4.7, 6

Pseudo-Classes

Elements can be assigned pseudo-classes to affect their display. There are three pseudo-classes:
A:active, **A:link**, and **A:visited**.

a:active

This property specifies how the text in active links will display.

Example

```
a:active {text-decoration: none;}
```

Browser Support
Internet Explorer 5 and 5.5
Netscape 6

a:link

This property specifies how text in unvisited links will display.

Example

```
a:link {text-decoration: underline;}
```

Browser Support
Internet Explorer 3, 4, 5, and 5
Netscape 4 and 4.5–4.7, 6

a:visited

This property specifies how text in visited links will display.

Example

```
a:visited {text-decoration: line-through;}
```

Browser Support
Internet Explorer 4, 5, and 5
Netscape 4 and 4.5–4.7, 6

Pseudo-Elements

This section discusses *pseudo-elements*, which affect typographical items, such as the first line of a paragraph, rather than *structural elements*, such as the paragraph (**<p>**) itself.

first-letter

This property specifies how the first letter of text in a block-level element will display.

Example

```
p:first-letter {font-face: Arial Black; font-size: 25pt;}
```

Browser Support
Internet Explorer 5.5
Netscape 6

first-line

This property specifies how the first line of text in a block-level element will display.

Example

```
p:first-line {font-face: Arial Black; font-size: 150%;
              font-weight: bold;}
```

Browser Support
Internet Explorer 5.5
Netscape 6

Miscellaneous

This section discusses some miscellaneous terms associated with style sheets.

/* comments */

Comments can be placed within style sheets. HTML comment syntax (**<!— comment —>**) does not apply. Style sheets use the comment syntax used in C programming (**/*comment*/**).

Example

```
p<style type="text/css">
p {font-face: Courier; font-size: 14pt; font-weight: bold;
   background-color: yellow;}
/*This style sheet was created at Demo Company, Inc.
All rights reserved.*/
</style>
```

Browser Support

Internet Explorer 3, 4, 5, and 5.6
Netscape 4 and 4.5–4.7, 6

!important

This property specifies that a style takes precedence over any different, conflicting styles. A style specified as important by an author takes precedence over a rule set by an end user.

Example

```
.header {font-family: "Times New Roman";}
.code   {font-family: "Courier";}
.body   {font-family: "Times New Roman, Courier";}
```

Browser Support

Internet Explorer 5 and 5.5
Netscape 6

Fonts

The font properties are **font-family**, **font-size**, **font-style**, **font-weight**, **font-variant**, **text-transform**, **text-decoration**, and **font**. The **font** property can be used as a shorthand notation of font values.

Example

```
p.one{font-family: Arial, sans-serif; font-size: 18pt;
      font-style: italic; font-variant: normal; font-weight: bold;
      text-decoration: underline; text-transform: capitalize;}
```

font-family

This property sets the font face for text. It is equivalent to the **face** attribute of the **<font>** element.

Example

```
{font-family: "Arial, Helvetica, sans-serif";}
```

Fonts are read in descending order and must be separated by commas. In the preceding example, Arial is the primary font and will be displayed by browsers and systems with that font. If Arial is not available, Helvetica will be displayed. The final option, the generic font name **sans-serif**, will be used when no other listed font is available.

Browser Support

Internet Explorer 3, 4, 5, and 5.5
Netscape 4 and 4.5–4.7, 6

Name Values

These values define a specific font family or families.

Examples

```
{font-family: "Times New Roman";}

{font-family: "Courier";}

{font-family: "Times New Roman, Courier";}
```

Browser Support

Internet Explorer 3, 4, 5, and 5.5
Netscape 4 and 4.5–4.7, 6

Generic Font Names

These values can be used to set a final option in a list of fonts, generally to the default generic font on a user's system. For example, **serif** defaults to Courier on many systems. There are five generic font names currently available: **serif**, **sans-serif**, **cursive**, **fantasy**, and **monospace**.

serif

This value specifies a default serif font.

Examples

```
p {font-family: "serif";}

p {font-family: "Times New Roman, serif";}
```

Browser Support
Internet Explorer 3 (Windows only), 4, 5, and 5.5
Netscape 4 and 4.5–4.7, 6

sans-serif
This value specifies a default sans-serif font.

Examples

```
p {font-family: sans-serif;}

p {font-family: "Arial, sans-serif";}
```

Browser Support
Internet Explorer 3 (Windows only), 4, 5, and 5.5
Netscape 4 and 4.5–4.7, 6

cursive
This value specifies a default cursive font.

Example

```
p {font-family: cursive;}
```

Browser Support
Internet Explorer 3 (Windows only), 4, 5, and 5.5
Netscape 6

fantasy
This value specifies a default fantasy font.

Example

```
p {font-family: fantasy;}
```

APPENDIX B

Browser Support

Internet Explorer 3 (Windows only), 4, 5, and 5.5
Future versions of Netscape (support under Netscape 6 is unclear)

monospace

This value specifies a default monospace font.

Example

```
p {font-family: monospace;}
```

Browser Support

Internet Explorer 3, 4, 5, and 5.5
Netscape 4 and 4.5–4.7, 6

font-size

This property sets the font size of text. Options include exact sizes (point, pixel, or other values), absolute sizes, relative sizes, and percentages.

Example

```
p {font-face: Arial; font-size: 18pt;}
```

Browser Support

Internet Explorer 3, 4, 5, and 5.5
Netscape 4, 4.5–4.7, 6

Exact Font Size Values

These values set the font size to an exact size in points (pt) or pixels (px).

Examples

```
p {font-size: 12pt;}

p {font-size: 30px;}
```

Browser Support

Internet Explorer 3, 4, 5, and 5.5
Netscape 4, 4.5–4.7, 6

Absolute Font Size Values

These values set the font size to an absolute size. There are seven possible sizes: **xx-small**, **x-small**, **small**, **medium**, **large**, **x-large**, and **xx-large**.

Example

```
p {font-size: xx-small;}
```

Browser Support

Internet Explorer 3, 4, 5, and 5.5
Netscape 4, 4.5–4.7, 6

xx-small

The value sets the font size to the smallest absolute font size, which is usually equivalent to one point size smaller than the HTML code **<font size="1">**.

Example

```
p {font-size: xx-small;}
```

Browser Support

Internet Explorer 3, 4, 5, and 5.5
Netscape 4, 4.5–4.7, 6

x-small

The value sets the font size to the second smallest absolute font size, which is equivalent to the HTML code **<font size="1">**.

Example

```
p {font-size: x-small;}
```

Browser Support

Internet Explorer 3, 4, 5, and 5.5
Netscape 4, 4.5–4.7, 6

small

This value sets the font size to the third smallest absolute font size, which is equivalent to the HTML code **<font size="2">**.

Example

```
p {font-size: small;}
```

Browser Support
Internet Explorer 3, 4, 5, and 5.5
Netscape 4, 4.5–4.7, 6

medium
The value sets the font size to the middle absolute font size, which is equivalent to the HTML code **<font size="3">**.

Example

```
p {font-size: medium;}
```

Browser Support
Internet Explorer 3, 4, 5, and 5.5
Netscape 4, 4.5–4.7, 6

large
The value sets the font size to the third-largest absolute font size, which is equivalent to the HTML code **<font size="4">**.

Example

```
p {font-size: large;}
```

Browser Support
Internet Explorer 3, 4, 5, and 5.5
Netscape 4, 4.5–4.7, 6

x-large
The value sets the font size to the second-largest absolute font size, which is equivalent to the HTML code **<font size="5">**.

Example

```
p {font-size: x-large;}
```

Browser Support
Internet Explorer 3, 4, 5, and 5.5
Netscape 4, 4.5–4.7, 6

xx-large
The value sets the font size to the largest absolute font size, which is generally equivalent to the HTML code **<font size="6">**.

Example

```
p {font-size: xx-large;}
```

Browser Support
Internet Explorer 3, 4, 5, and 5.5
Netscape 4, 4.5–4.7, 6

Percentage Font Size Values
These values set the font size to a percentage of the primary font size of a section or document. For example, if the font size for the **<body>** element were set to 12 points, and font size for a **<p>** element inside the body were set to 200 percent, the text inside the **<p>** element would display in 24-point type. This could be cleared on inheritance.

Example

```
p {font-size: 75%;}
```

Browser Support
Internet Explorer 3 (incomplete), 4, 5, and 5.5
Netscape 4, 4.5–4.7, 6

Relative Font Size Values
These values define the font size relative to the primary font size of a document or section.

smaller
This value sets the font size one point smaller than the primary font size of a section or document. It is equivalent to the HTML code **<font size="-1">**.

Example

```
p {font-size: smaller;}
```

APPENDIX B

Browser Support
Internet Explorer 4, 5, and 5.5
Netscape 4, 4.5–4.7, 6

larger
This value sets the font size to one point larger than the primary font size of a section or document. It is equivalent to the HTML code **<font size="+1">**.

Example

```
p {font-size: larger;}
```

Browser Support
Internet Explorer 4, 5, and 5.5
Netscape 4, 4.5–4.7, 6

font-style

This property sets the style of a font to normal, oblique, or italic. This can also be done by using a specific font (for example, Times New Roman Italic). It also allows control of style across font families.

Examples

```
p {font-style: normal;}
```

```
p {font-style: oblique;}
```

```
p {font-style: italic;}
```

Browser Support
Internet Explorer 3 (incomplete), 4, 5, and 5.5
Netscape 4, 4.5–4.7, 6

normal
This value sets the style of a font to Roman.

Example

```
p {font-style: normal;}
```

Browser Support
Internet Explorer 4, 5, and 5.5
Netscape 4, 4.5–4.7, 6

italic

This value sets the style of a font to italic.

Example

```
p {font-style: normal;}
```

Browser Support

Internet Explorer 4, 5, and 5.5
Netscape 4, 4.5–4.7, 6

oblique

This value sets the style of a font to oblique.

Example

```
p {font-style: oblique;}
```

Browser Support

Internet Explorer 4, 5, and 5.5
Netscape 4, 4.5–4.7, 6

font-weight

This property sets the weight, or relative boldness, of a font. Values can be set with named values (**normal**, **bold**, **bolder**, or **lighter**) or with numbered values (**100–900**).

Examples

```
p {font-weight: bold;}

p {font-weight: 300;}
```

Browser Support

Internet Explorer 3 (incomplete), 4, 5, and 5.5
Netscape 4, 4.5–4.7 (incomplete), 6

normal

This value sets the weight of the font to normal.

Example

```
p {font-weight: normal;}
```

Browser Support
Internet Explorer 4, 5, and 5.5
Netscape 4, 4.5–4.7, 6

bold
This value sets the weight of the font to bold.

Example

```
p {font-weight: bold;}
```

Browser Support
Internet Explorer 4, 5, and 5.5
Netscape 4, 4.5–4.7, 6

bolder
This value sets the weight of the font to one that is bolder than set by the **bold** value.

Example

```
p {font-weight: bolder;}
```

Browser Support
Internet Explorer 4, 5, and 5.5

lighter
This value sets the weight of the font to one that is lighter than set by the **normal** value.

Example

```
p {font-weight: lighter;}
```

Browser Support
Internet Explorer 4, 5, and 5.5

100–900

These values set the weight of the font from lightest (**100**) to boldest (**900**) in increments of 100. In practice, under Internet Explorer 4 and Netscape 4, the values **100–500** display as normal text; **600–900** displays as bold. Browser support for other values is inconsistent at best.

Example

```
.strong {font-weight: 600;}
```

Browser Support

Internet Explorer 4, 5, 5.5 (Windows only, incomplete)
Netscape 4 and 4.5–4.7 (incomplete for Macs), 6

font-variant

This property sets a variation of the specified or default font family. Values currently supported are **normal** and **small-caps**.

Example

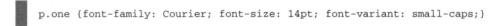

```
p.one {font-family: Courier; font-size: 14pt; font-variant: small-caps;}
```

Browser Support

Internet Explorer 4, 5, and 5.5
Netscape 6

normal

This value, which is the default, or "off" value for this property, sets the display to the font's normal appearance.

Example

```
.normal {font-family: Arial; font-size: 12pt; font-variant: normal;}
```

Browser Support

Internet Explorer 4, 5, and 5.5
Netscape 6

small-caps

This value sets text to all small capitals.

Example

```
p.smallcaps {font-family: Times New Roman; font-size: 20pt;
  font-variant: small-caps;}
```

Browser Support

Internet Explorer 4, 5, and 5.5
Netscape 6

text-transform

This property transforms the case of the affected text. Possible values are **capitalize**, **uppercase**, **lowercase**, and **none**.

Example

```
.caps {text-transform: capitalize;}
```

Browser Support

Internet Explorer 4, 5, and 5.5
Netscape 4 (incomplete for Macs), 4.5–4.7, and 6

capitalize

This value capitalizes the initial letter of each word in the affected text.

Example

```
.caps {font-family: Times New Roman; font-size: 20pt;
     text-transform: capitalize;}
```

Browser Support

Internet Explorer 4, 5, and 5.5
Netscape 4, 4.5–4.7, and 6

uppercase

This value capitalizes all the letters of each word in the affected text.

Example

```
.allcaps {font-family: Helvetica; font-size: 10pt; text-transform: uppercase;}
```

Browser Support

Internet Explorer 4, 5, and 5.5
Netscape 4, 4.5–4.7, and 6

lowercase

This value sets the letters of each word in the affected text to lowercase.

Example

```
.lowercase {font-family: Verdana; font-size: 14pt; text-transform: lowercase;}
```

Browser Support

Internet Explorer 4, 5, and 5.5
Netscape 4, 4.5–4.7, and 6

none

This value leaves text unaffected or overrides another established value.

Example

```
p {font-family: Arial; font-size: 12pt; text-transform: none;}
```

Browser Support

Internet Explorer 4, 5, and 5.5
Netscape 4, 4.5–4.7, and 6

text-decoration

This property defines specific text effects. Possible values are **blink**, **line-through**, **overline**, **underline**, and **none**.

Example

```
p.line {text-decoration: underline;}
```

This property is often used with the **<a>** element and its associated pseudo-classes (**a:active**, **a:link**, and **a:visited**). The following example draws a line through visited links in a page.

Example

```
a:visited {text-decoration: line-through;}
```

Browser Support

Internet Explorer 3 (incomplete), 4, 5, and 5.5
Netscape 4, 4.5–4.7 (incomplete), 6

blink

This value causes text to blink.

Example

```
.blinktext {text-decoration: blink;}
```

Browser Support

Netscape 4, 4.5–4.7, and 6

line-through

This value draws a line through text.

Example

```
.strike {text-decoration: line-through;}
```

Browser Support

Internet Explorer 3, 4, 5, and 5.5
Netscape 4, 4.5–4.7, and 6

overline

This value draws a line over text.

Example

```
.oline {text-decoration: overline;}
```

Browser Support

Internet Explorer 4, 5, and 5.5
Netscape 6

underline

This value draws a line under text.

Example

```
.uline {text-decoration: underline;}
```

Browser Support
Internet Explorer 3, 4, 5, and 5.5
Netscape 4, 4.5–4.7, and 6

none
This value displays plain text. It can be used with **A:active**, **A:link**, and **A:visited** to turn off underlining of links.

Example

```
.nodecor {text-decoration: none;}
```

Browser Support
Internet Explorer 3, 4, 5, and 5.5
Netscape 4, 4.5–4.7, and 6

font

This property provides a shorthand way to specify all font properties with one style rule. Properties are **font-family**, **font-size/line-height**, **font-style**, **font-weight**, and **font-variant**. It is not necessary to include all properties. The **line-height** property is discussed in the following section, "Text." Lists of variant fonts should be separated by commas; font names consisting of more than one word should be placed in quotes.

Example

```
p {font: normal small-caps bold 12pt/18pt "Times New Roman", Courier, serif;}
```

Browser Support
Internet Explorer 3 (incomplete), 4, 5, and 5.5
Netscape 4 (incomplete for Macs), 4.5–4.7, 6

Text
This section discusses style properties that affect text-level elements.

word-spacing

This property sets the spacing between words. Values can be set in inches (**in**), centimeters (**cm**), millimeters (**mm**), points (**pt**), picas (**pc**), em spaces (**em**), or pixels (**px**); or to the default value **normal**. Negative values are possible with this property.

APPENDIX B

Examples

```
p.spaced {font-family: Arial; font-size: 16pt; word-spacing: 3pt;}

p.normal {font-family: Helvetica; font-size: 12pt; word-spacing: normal;}
```

Browser Support

Netscape 6

normal

This value, which is the default for this property, sets word spacing to the browser's setting.

Example

```
p {font-family: Arial; font-size: 10pt; word-spacing: normal;}
```

Browser Support

Netscape 6

letter-spacing

This property sets the amount of spacing between letters. Values can be set in various units (negative values are permitted) or to the default value **normal**.

Example

```
p.spaced {font-family: Arial; font-size: 14pt; letter-spacing: 2pt;}
```

Browser Support

Internet Explorer 4, 5, and 5.5
Netscape 6

Unit Values

These values set letter spacing to a certain number of units in inches (**in**), centimeters (**cm**), millimeters (**mm**), points (**pt**), picas, (**pc**), em spaces (**em**), or pixels (**px**).

Example

```
p.spaced {font-family: Arial; font-size: 14pt; letter-spacing: 2pt;}
```

Browser Support

Internet Explorer 4, 5, and 5.5
Netscape 6

normal

This value sets letter spacing to the browser's default setting.

Example

```
p {font-family: Arial; font-size: 14pt; letter-spacing: normal;}
```

Browser Support

Internet Explorer 4, 5, and 5.5
Netscape 6

line-height

This property sets the height (leading) between lines of text in a block-level element such as a paragraph. Values can be specified as a number of lines, a number of units (pixels, points, and so on), or a percentage of the font size. This property is generally used in conjunction with the **font-size** property.

Examples

```
.dblspace {font-family: Arial; font-size: 14pt; line-height: 2;}

.leading {font-family: Arial; font-size: 14pt; line-height: 16pt;}

p {font-family: Arial; font-size: 14pt; line-height: normal;}

.leading {font-family: Arial; font-size: 14pt; line-height: 125%;}
```

Browser Support

Internet Explorer 3, 4, 5, and 5.5
Netscape 4, 4.5–4.7, 6

text-align

This property sets the horizontal alignment of block-level text elements. Values are **left**, **right**, **center**, and **justify**. The default value is **left**. This property is similar to the **align** attribute available with HTML block-level elements such as **<p>**.

Browser Support

Internet Explorer 3 (incomplete), 4, 5 (Windows only; incomplete), 5.5
Netscape 4, 4.5–4.7, 6

left

This value sets the horizontal alignment of text in block-level elements to the left.

Example

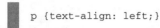
```
p {text-align: left;}
```

Browser Support

Internet Explorer 3, 4, 5, and 5.5
Netscape 4, 4.5–4.7, 6

right

This value sets the horizontal alignment of text in block-level elements to the right.

Example

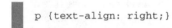
```
p {text-align: right;}
```

Browser Support

Internet Explorer 3, 4, 5, and 5.5
Netscape 4, 4.5–4.7, 6

center

This value sets the horizontal alignment of text in block-level elements to the center.

Example

```
p {text-align: center;}
```

Browser Support

Internet Explorer 3, 4, 5, and 5.5
Netscape 4, 4.5–4.7, 6

justify

This value sets the horizontal alignment of text in block-level elements flush to the left and right.

Example

```
p {text-align: justify;}
```

Browser Support

Internet Explorer 5 and 5.5
Netscape 4, 4.5–4.7, 6

vertical-align

This property sets the vertical positioning of text and images with respect to the baseline setting. Possible values are **baseline**, **sub**, **super**, **top**, **text-top**, **middle**, **bottom**, and **text-bottom**. Percentages can also be given as values. The default value is **baseline**.

Example

```
p {vertical-align: top;}
```

Browser Support
Internet Explorer 4 and 5 (incomplete), 5.5
Netscape 6

baseline
This value, which is the default for this property, aligns text or images to the baseline setting.

Example

```
p {vertical-align: baseline;}
```

Browser Support
Internet Explorer 5.5
Netscape 6

sub
This value positions text or images as a subscript of the baseline setting.

Example

```
p {vertical-align: sub;}
```

Browser Support
Internet Explorer 4, 5, and 5.5
Netscape 6

super
This value positions text or images as a superscript of the baseline setting.

Example

```
p {vertical-align: super;}
```

Browser Support
Internet Explorer 4, 5, and 5.5
Netscape 6

top
This value aligns the top of text or images with the top of the tallest element, relative to the baseline.

Example

```
p {vertical-align: top;}
```

Browser Support
Internet Explorer 5.5
Netscape 6

text-top
This value aligns the top of text or images with the top of the font in the containing element.

Example

```
p {vertical-align: text-top;}
```

Browser Support
Internet Explorer 5.5
Netscape 6

middle
This value aligns the middle of text or images to the middle of the x-height of the containing element.

Example

```
p {vertical-align: middle;}
```

Browser Support
Internet Explorer 5.5
Netscape 6

bottom
This value aligns the bottom of text or images with the bottom of the lowest element, relative to the baseline.

Example

```
p {vertical-align: bottom;}
```

Browser Support
Internet Explorer 5.5
Netscape 6

text-bottom
This value aligns the bottom of text or images with the bottom of the font in the containing element.

Example

```
p {vertical-align: text-bottom;}
```

Browser Support
Internet Explorer 5.5
Netscape 6

text-indent
This property indents the text in the first line of a block-level element. Values can be defined as length values (**.5cm**, **15px**, **12pt**, and so on) or as a percentage of the width of the block element. The default value is **0**, which indicates no indentation.

Examples

```
{text-indent: 5pt;}

{text-indent: 15%;}
```

Browser Support
Internet Explorer 3, 4, 5, and 5.5
Netscape 4, 4.5–4.7, 6

Colors and Backgrounds
This section discusses the style properties that affect backgrounds and various concerns associated with backgrounds, such as color, images, and scrolling, as well as the property that affects the color of text.

color

This property sets the color of text. Values can be specified as color names, hex values in three- or six-digit format, or red-green-blue (RGB) values (numbers or percentages). For browser support of color values, see the section "Style Sheet Color Values," later in this appendix.

Examples

```
{color: yellow;}

{color: #FFFF00;}

{color: #FF0;}

{color: rgb(255,255,0);}

{color: rgb(100%,100%,0%);}
```

Browser Support

Internet Explorer 3, 4, 5, and 5.5
Netscape 4, 4.5–4.7, 6

background-color

This property sets an element's background color. It is often used in conjunction with the **color** property, which sets text color (see the discussion of the **color** property under "color," later in this appendix). Used with block elements, this property colors content and padding but not margins. The default value, **transparent**, allows any underlying content to show through. See "Style Sheet Color Values," later in this appendix, for browser support of color values.

Examples

```
{background-color: #00CCFF;}

{background-color: orange;}

{background-color: rgb(255, 0, 255;}
```

Browser Support

Internet Explorer 4, 5, and 5.5
Netscape 4, 4.5–4.7, 6

transparent

The value, which is the default for this property, sets the background color to allow any underlying content to show through, as it does when used with the **background** property.

Example

```
{background-color: transparent;}
```

Browser Support
Internet Explorer 4, 5, and 5.5
Netscape 4, 4.5–4.7, 6

background-image

This property associates a background image with an element. Underlying content shows through transparent regions in the source image. The background image requires a URL (complete or relative) to link it to the source image. The default value is **none**.

Browser Support
Internet Explorer 4, 5, and 5.5
Netscape 4, 4.5–4.7, 6

Background Image URL Values
These values provide a URL link to a source image for the background image using the same syntax as the **background** property.

Example

```
{background-image: url(yellowpattern.gif);}
```

Browser Support
Internet Explorer 4, 5, and 5.5
Netscape 4, 4.5–4.7, 6

none
This value, which is the default for this property, sets the background so that it doesn't display an image (any underlying content shows through).

Example

```
{background-image: none;}
```

Browser Support
Internet Explorer 4, 5, and 5.5
Netscape 4, 4.5–4.7, 6

background-repeat

This value determines how background images tile when they are smaller than the canvas space used by their associated elements. It is used in conjunction with the **background-image** property. Possible values are **repeat, repeat-x, repeat-y,** and **no-repeat**.

Browser Support
Internet Explorer 4, 5, and 5.5
Netscape 4, 4.5–4.7, 6

repeat
This value, which is the default for this property, sets the background image to repeat horizontally and vertically.

Example

```
{background-image: url(yellowpattern.gif) background-repeat: repeat;}
```

Browser Support
Internet Explorer 4, 5, and 5.5
Netscape 4, 4.5–4.7, 6

repeat-x
This value sets the background image to repeat horizontally only.

Example

```
{background-image: url(yellowpattern.gif); background-repeat: repeat-x;}
```

Browser Support
Internet Explorer 4, 5, and 5.5
Netscape 4, 4.5–4.7, 6

repeat-y
This value sets the background image to repeat vertically only.

Example

```
{background-image: url(yellowpattern.gif); background-repeat: repeat-y;}
```

Browser Support
Internet Explorer 4, 5, and 5.5
Netscape 4, 4.5–4.7, and 6

no-repeat

This value prevents the background image from repeating.

Example

```
{background-image: url(yellowpattern.gif);
 background-repeat: no-repeat;}
```

Browser Support

Internet Explorer 4, 5, and 5.5
Netscape 4, 4.5–4.7, and 6

background-attachment

This property sets the background image to scroll or not to scroll with its associated element's content. The default value is **scroll**. The alternate value, **fixed**, is intended to create a watermark effect similar to the proprietary attribute, **bgproperties**, of the **<body>** element introduced by Microsoft.

Example

```
{background-image: url(yellowpattern.gif);
 background-attachment: scroll;}
```

Browser Support

Internet Explorer 4, 5, and 5.5
Netscape 6

scroll

This value, the default for this property, sets the background image to scroll with associated content, such as text.

Example

```
{background-image: url(yellowpattern.gif);
 background-attachment: scroll;}
```

Browser Support

Internet Explorer 4, 5, and 5.5
Netscape 6

fixed

This value sets the background image to remain static while associated content, such as text, scrolls.

Example

```
{background-image: url(yellowpattern.gif);
 background-attachment: fixed;}
```

Browser Support
Internet Explorer 4, 5, and 5.5
Netscape 6

background-position

This property determines how a background image is positioned within the canvas space used by its associated element. The position of the image's upper-left corner can be specified as an absolute distance in pixels. It can also be specified as a percentage along the horizontal and vertical dimensions. Finally, the position can be specified as named values that describe the horizontal and vertical dimensions. The named values for the horizontal axis are **center**, **left**, and **right**; those for the vertical axis are **top**, **center**, and **bottom**. The default value for an unspecified dimension is assumed to be **center**.

Examples

```
{background-image: url(yellowpattern.gif);
 background-position: 50px 100px;}
```

```
{background-image: url(yellowpattern.gif);
 background-position: 10% 45%;}
```

```
{background-image: url(yellowpattern.gif);
 background-position: top center;}
```

Browser Support
Internet Explorer 4, 5, and 5.5
Netscape 6

Background Position Numeric Values
These values set the position of the background image by specifying a specific pixel position for the upper-left corner of the image.

Example

```
{background-image: url(picture.gif);
 background-position: 10px 10px;}
```

Browser Support

Internet Explorer 4, 5, and 5.5
Netscape 6

Background Position Percentage Values

These values define a background's position as a percentage of its parent element's horizontal and vertical axes.

Example

```
{background-image: url(picture.gif);
 background-position: 20% 40%;}
```

Browser Support

Internet Explorer 4, 5, and 5.5
Netscape 6

Background Position Named Values

These values, which include **top**, **center**, **bottom**, **left**, and **right**, define the position of a background image relative to its parent element.

top

This value sets the position of the background image to the top of its associated element. It can be used in combination with the **center** value or with a horizontal value (**left** or **right**).

Examples

```
{background-image: url(picture.gif);
 background-position: top;}
```

```
{background-image: url(picture.gif);
 background-position: top left;}
```

Browser Support

Internet Explorer 4, 5, and 5.5
Netscape 6

center

This value sets the position of the background image to the center of its associated element. It can be used in combination with a vertical value (**bottom** or **top**).

Examples

```
{background-image: url(picture.gif);
 background-position: center;}

{background-image: url(picture.gif);
 background-position: center bottom;}
```

Browser Support

Internet Explorer 4, 5, and 5.5
Netscape 6

bottom

This value sets the position of the background image to the bottom of its associated element. It can be used in combination with the **center** value or with a horizontal value (**left** or **right**).

Examples

```
{background-image: url(picture.gif);
 background-position: bottom;}

{background-image: url(picture.gif);
 background-position: bottom left;}
```

Browser Support

Internet Explorer 4, 5, and 5.5
Netscape 6

left

This value sets the position of the background image to the left side of its associated element. It can be used in combination with the **center** value or with a vertical value (**bottom** or **top**).

Examples

```
{background-image: url(picture.gif);
 background-position: left;}

{background-image: url(picture.gif);
 background-position: left center;}
```

Browser Support

Internet Explorer 4, 5, and 5.5
Netscape 6

right

This value sets the position of the background image to the right side of its associated element. It can be used in combination with the **center** value or with a vertical value (**bottom** or **top**).

Examples

```
{background-image: url(picture.gif);
 background-position: right;}

{background-image: url(picture.gif);
 background-position: right top;}
```

Browser Support
Internet Explorer 4, 5, and 5.5
Netscape 6

background

This property sets any or all background properties, including images. Properties not specified use their default values. Property order does not matter, and semicolons are not required.

Example

```
{background: white url(picture.gif) repeat-y center;}
```

Browser Support
Internet Explorer 3, 4, 5, and 5.5
Netscape 4, 4.5–4.7 (incomplete), and 6

transparent

This value sets the background color to a transparent setting, which allows any underlying content to show through.

Example

```
{background: transparent;}
```

Browser Support
Internet Explorer 3, 4, 5, and 5.5
Netscape 4, 4.5–4.7, and 6

Background URL Values
These values provide a URL link to a source image to be used as the background image.

Example

```
{background: url(yellowpattern.gif);}
```

Browser Support
Internet Explorer 3, 4, 5, and 5.5
Netscape 4, 4.5–4.7, and 6

none
This value, which is the default for this property, specifies that there will be no background image.

Example

```
{background: none;}
```

Browser Support
Internet Explorer 3, 4, 5, and 5.5
Netscape 4, 4.5–4.7, and 6

repeat
This value sets the background image to repeat horizontally and vertically. If no value is specified, **repeat** is assumed as the default value.

Example

```
{background: url(yellowpattern.gif) repeat;}
```

Browser Support
Internet Explorer 3, 4, 5, and 5.5
Netscape 4, 4.5–4.7, and 6

repeat-x
This value sets the background image to repeat horizontally only.

Example

```
{background: url(yellowpattern.gif) repeat-x;}
```

Browser Support
Internet Explorer 3, 4, 5, and 5.5
Netscape 4, 4.5–4.7, and 6

repeat-y

This value sets the background image to repeat vertically only.

Example

 `{background: url(yellowpattern.gif) repeat-y;}`

Browser Support

Internet Explorer 3, 4, 5, and 5.5
Netscape 4, 4.5–4.7, and 6

no-repeat

This value specifies that the background image does not repeat.

Example

 `{background: url(yellowpattern.gif) no-repeat;}`

Browser Support

Internet Explorer 3, 4, 5, and 5.5
Netscape 4, 4.5–4.7, and 6

scroll

This value specifies that the background image scrolls with its associated content. Under Internet Explorer 3, setting the scroll value does not work; if this value is not specified, however, the background scrolls with its associated content.

Example

 `{background: url(yellowpattern.gif) repeat scroll;}`

Browser Support

Internet Explorer 4, 5, and 5.5
Netscape 6

fixed

This value specifies that the background image remains stationary while its associated content scrolls.

Example

`{background: url(yellowpattern.gif) fixed;}`

Browser Support

Internet Explorer 3, 4, 5, and 5.5
Netscape 6

Background Positioning Percentage Values

These values set the position of the background image as a percentage along the horizontal and vertical dimensions. The first percentage value sets horizontal placement; the second sets vertical placement. If only one value is specified, the vertical placement value defaults to **50%**. Use of these values in a page with no content can lead to problems under Internet Explorer 3. (For example, a value of **bottom** aligns the bottom of the image with the top of the browser window, thus placing it completely out of view. This has been corrected in Internet Explorer 4, which displays the image properly at the bottom of the browser window.) If no values are set, the placement defaults to the upper-left corner of the browser window.

Example

```
{background url(picture.gif) no-repeat 20% 50%;}
```

Browser Support

Internet Explorer 3, 4, 5, and 5.5
Netscape 6

Background Positioning Named Values

These values set the position of the background image. The values **top**, **center**, and **bottom**, assign vertical positions; **center**, **left**, and **right** assign horizontal positions. Values can be combined as common sense suggests. If no values are set, the placement defaults to the upper-left corner of the browser window.

Examples

```
{background: url(picture.gif) no-repeat top center;}

{background: url(picture.gif) no-repeat right bottom;}
```

Browser Support

Internet Explorer 3, 4, 5, and 5.5
Netscape 6

top

This value sets the position of the background image to the top of its associated element. If no other value is set, the top-aligned image defaults to the left.

Example

```
{background url(picture.gif) no-repeat top;}
```

Browser Support
Internet Explorer 3, 4, 5, and 5.5
Netscape 6

center
This value sets the position of the background image to the horizontal center of its associated element. If no other value is set, the center-aligned image defaults to the vertical middle.

Example

```
{background url(picture.gif) no-repeat center;}
```

Browser Support
Internet Explorer 3, 4, 5, and 5.5
Netscape 6

Example

```
{background url(picture.gif) no-repeat middle;}
```

Browser Support
Internet Explorer 3, 4, 5, and 5.5
Netscape 6

bottom
This value sets the position of the background image to the bottom of its associated element. If no other value is set, the bottom-aligned image defaults to the left.

Example

```
{background url(picture.gif) no-repeat bottom;}
```

Browser Support
Internet Explorer 3, 4, 5, and 5.5
Netscape 6

left

This value, which is the default horizontal position for this property, sets the position of the background image to the left of its associated element.

Example

```
{background url(picture.gif) no-repeat left;}
```

Browser Support

Internet Explorer 3, 4, 5, and 5.5
Netscape 6

right

This value sets the position of the background image to the right of its associated element.

Example

```
{background url(picture.gif) no-repeat right;}
```

Browser Support

Internet Explorer 3, 4, 5, and 5.5
Netscape 6

 # Layout

This section discusses style properties that affect the layout of HTML documents.

Margins

Style sheets can be used to set margins around an element with the **margin** property. Margin values can be set to a specific length (**15pt, 2em,** and so on) or to a percentage value of the block element's width. Another value, **auto,** attempts to calculate the margin automatically. The **auto** value is not supported. Four distinct margins can be set separately from one another using the following properties: **margin-top, margin-bottom, margin-right,** and **margin-left**. By itself, **margin** sets a consistent margin on all four sides of the affected element. Margins can be also be set to negative values.

Browser Support

Internet Explorer 3 (Windows only), 4, 5, and 5.5
Netscape 4, 4.5–4.7, 6

margin-top

This property sets an element's top margin.

Example

```
{margin-top: 15pt;}
```

Browser Support
Internet Explorer 3 (Windows only), 4, 5, and 5.5
Netscape 4, 4.5–4.7, 6

margin-bottom
This property sets an element's bottom margin.

Example

```
{margin-bottom: 10pt;}
```

Browser Support
Internet Explorer 3 (Windows only), 4, 5, and 5.5
Netscape 4, 4.5–4.7, 6

margin-right
This property sets an element's right margin.

Example

```
{margin-right: 15pt;}
```

Browser Support
Internet Explorer 3, 4, 5, and 5.5
Netscape 4, 4.5–4.7, 6

margin-left
This property sets an element's left margin.

Example

```
{margin-left: 12pt;}
```

Browser Support
Internet Explorer 3, 4, 5, and 5.5
Netscape 4, 4.5–4.7, 6

margin

This property sets all margins for an element. Up to four values can be defined, in this order: **top**, **right**, **bottom**, and **left**. The value **auto** is not currently supported. A single value defines the same margin for all four sides.

Example

```
{margin: 25pt;}
```

If two values are specified, the first defines the top and bottom margins, while the second defines the left and right margins.

Example

```
{margin: 15pt, 25pt;}
```

If three values are specified, the first defines the top margin, the second defines the left and right margins, and the third defines the bottom margin. Note that the unspecified margin is inferred from the value defined for its opposite side.

Example

```
{margin: 25pt, 50pt, 25pt;}
```

Finally, all four margins can be set to different values if desired (**top**, **right**, **bottom**, and **left**, in that order).

Example

```
{margin: 15pt, 25pt, 50pt, 10pt;}
```

Browser Support

Internet Explorer 3 (incomplete), 4, 5, and 5.5
Netscape 4, 4.5–4.7, 6

Borders

There are five properties for setting the width of borders: **border-top-width**, **border-bottom-width**, **border-right-width**, **border-left-width**, and **border-width**. The first four set the width of specific borders; **border-width** is used to set all four. Values for border widths can be set in numeric measurements or with the named values **thin**, **medium**, or **thick**. Border colors and styles can be set with the properties **border-color** and **border-style**, respectively. The properties **border-top**, **border-bottom**, **border-right**, and **border-left** can be used to set width, style, and color values for different sides of a border; the **border** property sets the width, style, and color of all sides of an element's border.

border-top-width

This property sets the width of an element's top border. Values can be keywords (**thin**, **medium**, or **thick**) and numerical lengths.

Examples

```
{border-top-width: thin;}

{border-top-width: 25px;}
```

Browser Support

Internet Explorer 4, 5, and 5.5
Netscape 4, 4.5–4.7, 6

border-bottom-width

This property sets the width of an element's bottom border. Values can be keywords (**thin**, **medium**, or **thick**) and numerical lengths.

Examples

```
{border-bottom-width: medium;}

{border-bottom-width: 15px;}
```

Browser Support

Internet Explorer 4, 5, and 5.5
Netscape 4, 4.5–4.7, 6

border-right-width

This property sets the width of an element's right border. Values can be keywords (**thin**, **medium**, or **thick**) and numerical lengths.

Examples

```
{border-right-width: thick;}

{border-right-width: 40px;}
```

Browser Support

Internet Explorer 4, 5, and 5.5
Netscape 4, 4.5–4.7, 6

border-left-width

This property sets the width of an element's left border. Values can be keywords (**thin**, **medium**, or **thick**) and numerical lengths.

Examples

```
{border-left-width: thin;}

{border-left-width: 5px;}
```

Browser Support

Internet Explorer 4, 5, and 5.5
Netscape 4, 4.5–4.7, 6

border-width

This property sets the width of an element's complete border. Values can be keywords (**thin**, **medium**, or **thick**) and numerical lengths. The **border-width** property can also be used to specify all four borders individually (e.g., **border-width: 5px 5px 5px 5px;**).

Examples

```
{border-width: medium;}

{border-width: 5px;}
```

Browser Support

Internet Explorer 4, 5, and 5.5
Netscape 4, 4.5–4.7, 6

thin

This property sets the width of an element's border to thin.

Example

```
{border-right-width: thin;}
```

Browser Support

Internet Explorer 4, 5, and 5.5
Netscape 4, 4.5–4.7, 6

thick

This property sets the width of an element's border to thick.

Example

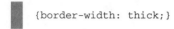

```
{border-width: thick;}
```

Browser Support

Internet Explorer 4, 5, and 5.5
Netscape 4, 4.5–4.7, 6

medium

This property sets the width of an element's border to medium.

Example

```
{border-top-width: medium;}
```

Browser Support

Internet Explorer 4, 5, and 5.5
Netscape 4, 4.5–4.7, 6

border-color

This property defines the color of an element's border. See "Style Sheet Color Values," later in this appendix, for browser support of color values.

Examples

```
{border-color: blue;}

{border-color: #0000EE;}
```

Browser Support

Internet Explorer 4, 5, and 5.5
Netscape 4, 4.5–4.7, 6

border-style

This property defines an element's border style.

Examples

```
{border-style: solid;}
```

   The **border-style** property define the style of up to four different sides of a border, using the values **none**, **dotted**, **dashed**, **solid**, **double**, **groove**, **ridge**, **inset**, and **outset**. These values are listed, in order, for the top, right, bottom, and left sides. Missing values are inferred from the value defined for the opposite side.

```
{border-style: solid, thin, medium, solid;}
```

 Netscape 4 supports only one value for border-style. Use of multiple values will create erratic display under that browser.

Browser Support

Internet Explorer 4, 5, and 5.5
Netscape 4, 4.5–4.7 (incomplete), and 6

none

This value "turns off" the border, even if other border properties have been set.

Example

```
{border-style: none;}
```

Browser Support

Internet Explorer 4, 5, and 5.5
Netscape 4, 4.5–4.7, and 6

dotted

This value defines a dotted border style.

Example

```
{border-style: dotted;}
```

Browser Support

Internet Explorer 5.5
Netscape 6

dashed

This value defines a dashed border style.

Example

```
{border-style: dashed;}
```

Browser Support
Internet Explorer 5.5
Netscape 6

solid
This value, which is the default for this property, sets the border to a solid line. It does not need to be set.

Example

```
{border-style: solid;}
```

Browser Support
Internet Explorer 4, 5, and 5.5
Netscape 4, 4.5–4.7, 6

double
This value sets the border to two solid lines.

Example

```
{border-style: double;}
```

Browser Support
Internet Explorer 4, 5, and 5.5
Netscape 4, 4.5–4.7, 6

groove
This value sets the border to resemble a grooved line.

Example

```
{border-style: grooved;}
```

Browser Support
Internet Explorer 4, 5, and 5.5
Netscape 4, 4.5–4.7, 6

inset
This value sets the border to display a lighter shade of the border color on its right and bottom sides.

Example

 `{border-style: inset;}`

Browser Support

Internet Explorer 4, 5, and 5.5
Netscape 4, 4.5–4.7, 6

outset

This value sets the border to display a lighter shade of the border color on its top and left sides.

Example

 `{border-style: outset;}`

Browser Support

Internet Explorer 4, 5, and 5.5
Netscape 4, 4.5–4.7, 6

ridge

This value sets the border to resemble a raised ridge by reversing the shading of the grooved rendering.

Example

 `{border-style: ridge;}`

Browser Support

Internet Explorer 4, 5, and 5.5
Netscape 4, 4.5–4.7, 6

border-top

This property defines the width, style, and color for the top border of an element.

Example

 `{border-top: thin solid blue;}`

Browser Support

Internet Explorer 4, 5, and 5.5
Netscape 6

border-bottom

This property defines the width, style, and color for the bottom border of an element.

Example

```
{border-bottom: thick double #CCFFCC;}
```

Browser Support

Internet Explorer 4, 5, and 5.5
Netscape 6

border-right

This property defines the width, style, and color for the right border of an element.

Example

```
{border-right: thick solid black;}
```

Browser Support

Internet Explorer 4, 5, and 5.5
Netscape 6

border-left

This property defines the width, style, and color for the left border of an element.

Example

```
{border-left: normal inset green;}
```

Browser Support

Internet Explorer 4, 5, and 5.5
Netscape 6

border

This property defines the width, style, and color for all four sides of an element's border.

Example

```
{border: normal inset green;}
```

Browser Support
Internet Explorer 4, 5, and 5.5
Netscape 6

Padding

The padding properties set the space between an element's border and its content. There are five properties for padding: **padding-top**, **padding-bottom**, **padding-right**, **padding-left**, and **padding**. The **padding** value sets the padding for all four sides; the other four set the padding for specific sides. Values can be specified as specific values (pixels, points, and so on) or as a percentage of the element's overall width. Unlike the **margin** property, the **padding** property cannot take negative values.

padding-top
This property sets the distance between an element's top border and the top of its content.

Example

```
{padding-top: 25px;}
```

Browser Support
Internet Explorer 4, 5, and 5.5
Netscape 4, 4.5–4.7, 6

padding-bottom
This property sets the distance between an element's bottom border and the bottom of its content.

Example

```
{padding-bottom: 15px;}
```

Browser Support
Internet Explorer 4, 5, and 5.5
Netscape 4, 4.5–4.7, 6

padding-right
This property sets the distance between an element's right border and the right side of its content.

Example

```
{padding-right: 5px;}
```

Browser Support
Internet Explorer 4, 5, and 5.5
Netscape 4, 4.5–4.7, 6

padding-left
This property sets the distance between an element's left border and the left side of its content.

Example

```
{padding-left: 25px;}
```

Browser Support
Internet Explorer 4, 5, and 5.5
Netscape 4, 4.5–4.7, 6

padding
This property sets the distance between an element's border and its contents. A single value creates equal padding on all sides.

Example

```
{border-style: solid; padding: 10px;}
```

Up to four values can be used, in the following clockwise order: **top**, **right**, **bottom**, and **left**.

Example

```
{border-style: solid; padding: 10px 20px 10px 50px;}
```

Any missing value defaults to the value defined for the side opposite to it.

Example

```
{border-style: solid; padding: 10px 20px 10px;}
```

Browser Support
Internet Explorer 4, 5, and 5.5
Netscape 4, 4.5–4.7, 6

width
This property sets the width of an element's content region (excluding padding, border, and margin). The next example sets a paragraph with a width of 400 pixels.

Example

```
p {width: 400px; padding: 10px; border: solid 5px;}
```

Percentage values, based on the width of the containing element, can also be used.

Example

```
p {width: 80%; padding: 10px; border: solid 5px;}
```

The **auto** value automatically calculates the width of an element, based on the width of the containing element and the size of the content.

Example

```
p {width: auto; padding: 10px; border: solid 5px;}
```

Browser Support
Internet Explorer 4, 5, and 5.5
Netscape 4, 4.5–4.7, 6

height

This property sets the height of an element's content region (excluding padding, border, and margin). The next example sets a paragraph with a height of 200 pixels.

Example

```
p {height: 200px; padding: 10px; border: solid 5px;}
```

Percentage values, based on the height of the containing element, can also be used.

Example

```
P {height: 80%; padding: 10px; border: solid 5px;}
```

The **auto** value automatically calculates the height of an element, based on the height of the containing element and the size of the content.

Example

```
p {height: auto; padding: 10px; border: solid 5px;}
```

Browser Support
Internet Explorer 5 and 5.5
Netscape 6

float

This property influences the horizontal alignment of an element, making it "float" toward the left or right margin of its containing element. Possible values are **left**, **right**, and **none**.

Example

```
img {float: right;}
```

Browser Support
Internet Explorer 4, 5, and 5.5
Netscape 4, 4.5–4.7, 6

left
This value causes an element to float towards the left margin of its containing element.

Example

```
img {float: left;}
```

Browser Support
Internet Explorer 4, 5, and 5.5
Netscape 4, 4.5–4.7, 6

right
This value causes an element to float towards the right margin of its containing element.

Example

```
img {float: right;}
```

Browser Support
Internet Explorer 4, 5, and 5.5
Netscape 4, 4.5–4.7, 6

none
This value, which is the default for this property, prevents an element from floating.

Example

```
img {float: none;}
```

Browser Support
Internet Explorer 4, 5, and 5.5
Netscape 4, 4.5–4.7, 6

clear

This property specifies the placement of an element in relation to floating objects. Possible values are **left**, **right**, **both**, and **none**.

Example

```
{clear: right;}
```

Browser Support
Internet Explorer 5 and 5.5
Netscape 4 and 4.5–4.7 (incomplete), 6

left

This value clears floating objects to the left of the element.

Example

```
{clear: left;}
```

Browser Support
Internet Explorer 5 and 5.5
Netscape 4 and 4.5–4.7 (incomplete), 6

right

This value clears floating objects to the right of the element.

Example

```
{clear: right;}
```

Browser Support
Internet Explorer 5 and 5.5
Netscape 4 and 4.5–4.7 (incomplete), 6

both

This value clears floating objects to both sides of the element.

Example

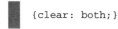
```
{clear: both;}
```

Browser Support

Internet Explorer 5 and 5.5
Netscape 4 and 4.5–4.7 (incomplete), 6

none

This is the default value for this property. Objects around an element will not clear when **clear** is set to none.

Example

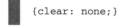
```
{clear: none;}
```

Browser Support

Internet Explorer 5 and 5.5
Netscape 4 and 4.5–4.7 (incomplete), 6

Classification

This section discusses style properties that affect the display type of elements (block-level, inline, and so on) and the display of lists and white space.

display

This property specifies an element's display type. This property can override an element's defined display type. For example, block-level elements can be redefined as inline elements so that extra lines will not be placed between them.

Example

```
p {display: inline;}
```

Browser Support

Internet Explorer 4 and 5 (incomplete)
Netscape 4 and 4.5 (incomplete)

block

This value sets an element to display as a block element.

Example

```
span {display: block;}
```

Browser Support

Internet Explorer 5
Netscape 4 and 4.5

inline

This value sets an element to display as an inline element.

Example

```
p {display: inline;}
```

Browser Support

Internet Explorer 5
Future versions of Netscape

list-item

This value sets an element to display as a list-item element.

Example

```
p {display: list-item;}
```

Browser Support

Netscape 4 and 4.5

none

This value turns off the display of an element. Unlike the **hidden** value of the **visibility** property, **none** does not preserve an element's canvas space.

Example

```
p {display: none;}
```

Browser Support

Internet Explorer 4 and 5
Netscape 4 and 4.5

white-space

This property controls how spaces, tabs, and newline characters are handled in an element. Possible values are **normal**, **pre**, and **nowrap**.

Example

   {white-space: pre;}

Browser Support

Netscape 4 and 4.5 (incomplete)

normal

This value collapses white space characters into single spaces and automatically wraps lines, as in normal HTML.

Example

    {white-space: normal;}

Browser Support

Netscape 4 and 4.5

pre

This value preserves white space formatting, similar to the **<pre>** element in HTML.

Example

    {white-space: pre;}

Browser Support

Netscape 4 and 4.5

nowrap

This value prevents lines from wrapping if they exceed the element's content width.

APPENDIX B

Example

```
{white-space: nowrap;}
```

Browser Support
None currently; likely in future versions of Netscape

list-style-type

This property defines labels for ordered and unordered lists. The value **none** prevents a label from displaying.

Examples

```
OL {list-style-type: upper-roman;}

UL {list-style-type: disc;}
```

Browser Support
Internet Explorer 4 and 5
Netscape 4 and 4.5

none
This value specifies that no label will be displayed for items in ordered or unordered lists.

Examples

```
OL {list-style-type: none;}

UL {list-style-type: none;}
```

Browser Support
Internet Explorer 4 and 5
Netscape 4 and 4.5

Ordered Lists
There are five values for ordered lists: **decimal**, **lower-roman**, **upper-roman**, **lower-alpha**, and **upper-alpha**.

decimal
This value specifies Arabic numerals (1, 2, 3, and so on) for the labeling of items in an ordered list.

Example

```
ol {list-style-type: decimal;}
```

Browser Support
Internet Explorer 4 and 5
Netscape 4 and 4.5

lower-roman
This value specifies lowercase Roman numerals (i, ii, iii, and so on) for the labeling of items in an ordered list.

Example

```
ol {list-style-type: lower-roman;}
```

Browser Support
Internet Explorer 4 and 5
Netscape 4 and 4.5

upper-roman
This value specifies uppercase Roman numerals (I, II, III, and so on) for the labeling of items in an ordered list.

Example

```
ol {list-style-type: upper-roman;}
```

Browser Support
Internet Explorer 4 and 5
Netscape 4 and 4.5

lower-alpha
This value specifies lowercase letters (a, b, c, and so on) for the labeling of items in an ordered list.

Example

```
ol {list-style-type: lower-alpha;}
```

Browser Support
Internet Explorer 4 and 5
Netscape 4 and 4.5

upper-alpha

This value specifies uppercase letters (A, B, C, and so on) for the labeling of items in an ordered list.

Example

```
ol {list-style-type: upper-alpha;}
```

Browser Support

Internet Explorer 4 and 5
Netscape 4 and 4.5

Unordered Lists

There are three values for unordered lists: **disc, circle,** and **square.**

disc

This value specifies a black dot bullet for items in an unordered list.

Example

```
ul {list-style-type: disc;}
```

Browser Support

Internet Explorer 4 and 5
Netscape 4 and 4.5

circle

This value specifies a circular bullet for items in an unordered list.

Example

```
ul {list-style-type: circle;}
```

Browser Support

Internet Explorer 4 and 5
Netscape 4 and 4.5

square

This value specifies a square bullet for items in an unordered list.

Example

```
ul {list-style-type: square;}
```

Browser Support
Internet Explorer 4 and 5
Netscape 4 and 4.5

list-style-image

This property assigns a graphic image to a list label, using the URL of the image. The other value for **list-style-image** other than a URL is **none**.

Example

```
ul {list-style-image: url(ball.gif);}
```

Browser Support
Internet Explorer 4 and 5
Future versions of Netscape

list-style-position

This property specifies whether the labels for an element's list items are positioned inside or outside the "box" defined by the area. By default, labels appear outside the "box."

Example

```
ol {list-style-type: upper-roman; list-style-position: outside;
    background: yellow;}
```

The **inside** value places the bullets inside the "box."

Example

```
ul {list-style-type: square; list-style-position: inside;
    background: yellow;}
```

Browser Support
Internet Explorer 4 and 5

list-style

This property is more concise than the other **list-style** properties. It sets type, image, and position properties for ordered and unordered lists. The properties can appear in any order. The values **inside** and **outside** are not well supported by browsers.

Examples

```
UL {list-style: inside url("bullet.gif");}

UL {list-style: outside square;}

OL {list-style: lower-roman inside;}
```

Browser Support
Internet Explorer 4 and 5

CSS2 Properties

This section discusses new properties in the CSS2 specification (excluding properties carried over from the CSS1 specification). Discussion of some of these properties will be brief due to limited browser support, except for the section "CSS2 Layers and Positioning."

CSS2 Selectors

CSS2 introduces a number of new selectors. These properties use context to determine how styles should be applied to elements, potentially reducing reliance on HTML selectors like **class** and **id**. For more information, see Chapter 10.

* (Wildcard Selector)
This selector matches any element. So, the rule

```
*   {background-color: red;}
```

would apply a red background to all elements in a document.
A more contextualized usage, like this:

```
div * span  {background-color: yellow;}
```

would apply a yellow background to any **<span>** element located within a **<div>** element.
This selector is supported by Internet Explorer 5.5 and Netscape 6.

> (Child Selector)
This selector defines a rule that matches only elements that are directly enclosed within another element, such as a **<p>** element with a document body.

```
body > p  {background-color: yellow;}
```

This selector is supported by Netscape 6.

+ (Adjacent-sibling Selector)

This selector defines a rule that applies a style to the first incidence of an element immediately after the first element.

```
h1 + p {color: red;}
```

Thus, any **\<p\>** element occurring directly after an **\<h1\>** element would be red (the **\<h1\>** itself is not affected by the style rule).

This selector is supported by Netscape 6.

[ ] (Attribute matching selector)

This selector defines a rule that will be applied to an element only if it employs the attribute enclosed in the square brackets.

```
A[href] {background-color: orange;}
```

This can even be taken one step further, and applied only to elements that use a certain attribute with a specific value.

```
A[href="http://www.htmlref.com"] {background-color: orange;}
```

This selector is supported by Netscape 6.

CSS2 Pseudo-Elements

CSS2 introduces a number of new pseudo-elements: **:first-child**, **:focus**, **:hover**, and several more. The following table lists these pseudo-elements, describes their purpose, and notes browser support where applicable. For more information, see Chapter 10.

Pseudo-element	Purpose	Browser support
:first-child	Applies a style to the first child element of an element	None
:focus	Changes the display of an element when the element receives focus (generally, **\<input="text"\>**)	Netscape 6
:hover	Changes the display of an element when a cursor passes over the element	IE 4, 5.0, 5.5 Netscape 6
:lang	Applies style to an element according to what language the element is in	None
:left	Sets page layout rules for a left-hand page when printing	None

Pseudo-element	Purpose	Browser support
:right	Sets page layout rules for a right-hand page when printing	None
:first	Sets page layout rules for the first page in a document when printing	None
:before	Defines content to be placed before an element	None
:after	Defines content to be placed after an element	None
@media	Defines style rules for multiple media types in a single style sheet. See Chapter 10	IE 5.0, 5.5

CSS2 Text and Font Properties

CSS2 introduces several new properties affecting the display of text. To date, they are not supported by any browsers, but are listed here for completeness' sake.

Property	Purpose
font-size-adjust	Allows the x-height of the first font in a font selection list to be maintained for subsequent fonts in the list
font-stretch	Selects face variants from a font family. Values: **ultra-condensed, extra-condensed, condensed, semi-condensed, normal, semi-expanded, expanded, extra-expanded,** and **ultra-expanded**
text-shadow	Applies a shadow effect to text within an element

Printing Styles

CSS2 provides several properties used to define pages for printing purposes, and how those pages should break when printed. For more information, see Chapter 10.

Property	Purpose	Browser Support
page	Defines a type of page where an element should be displayed	Internet Explorer 5.5
page-break-after	Will introduce a page break after an element when printing document	Internet Explorer 4, 5.0, and 5.5
page-break-before	Will introduce a page break before an element when printing document	Internet Explorer 4, 5.0, and 5.5
page-break-inside	Forces or prohibits a printing page break within an element	None

CSS2 Table Properties

CSS2 defines a number of new properties that affect how tables are displayed. There is some browser support for these properties, which is noted in this table.

Property	Purpose	Browser Support
table-layout	Defines if a table layout is fixed or not. Values: **auto** and **fixed**	Internet Explorer 5.0, 5.5
border-collapse	Defines if table cell borders are connected or separate. Values: **separate** and **collapse**	Internet Explorer 5.0, 5.5 Netscape 6
border-spacing	Defines the distance separating adjacent cell borders (numerical values)	Netscape 6
caption-side	Defines position of **<caption>** contents in releation to table. Values: **top**, **bottom**, **left**, and **right**	Netscape 6
empty-cells	Defines if the borders of empty table cells will display. Values: **show**, **hide**, and **inherit**	Netscape 6

CSS2 Border Properties

CSS2 defines a number of additional border properties to be used in conjunction with existing CSS1 border properties (see "Borders," earlier in this appendix). They allow style and color to be defined separately for different sides of an element.

Property	Purpose	Browser Support
border-bottom-color	Defines color for bottom border of elements	Internet Explorer 5.5 Netscape 6
border-bottom-style	Defines style for bottom border of elements	Internet Explorer 5.5 Netscape 6
border-left-color	Defines color for left border of elements	Internet Explorer 5.5 Netscape 6
border-left-style	Defines style for left border of elements	Internet Explorer 5.5 Netscape 6
border-right-color	Defines color for right border of elements	Internet Explorer 5.5 Netscape 6
border-right-style	Defines style for right border of elements	Internet Explorer 5.5 Netscape 6
border-top-color	Defines color for top border of elements	Internet Explorer 5.5 Netscape 6
border-top-style	Defines style for top border of elements	Internet Explorer 5.5 Netscape 6

APPENDIX B

CSS2 Aural Style Properties

CSS2 specifies a number of properties for use with speech-based browsers, which are listed here. No browsers currently support these properties; however, in the future they may be useful for defining how speech enabled browsers will "read" a document, right down to rate of speech, pauses before and after words, and when reading should be cued.

azimuth	cue
cue-after	cue-before
elevation	pause
pause-after	pause-before
pitch	pitch-range
play-during	richness
speak	speak-header
speak-numeral	speak-punctuation
speech-rate	stress
voice-family	volume

For a more complete discussion of aural properties, see Chapter 10.

CSS2 Layers and Positioning

This section discusses style properties that affect layering and positioning of elements. Of all the CSS2 properties, these are the ones with the highest degree of browser support.

position

This property defines how an element is positioned relative to other elements, using the values **static**, **absolute**, and **relative**. The **left, right, top,** and **bottom** properties define the element's precise location, using the affected element's upper-left corner (0,0) as reference. Because elements can contain other elements, 0,0 is not necessarily the upper-left corner of the browser.

Example

```
{position: relative; left: 190px; top: 30px;}
```

Browser Support
Internet Explorer 4, 5, and 5.5
Netscape 6

static

This value, which is the default for this property, places elements according to the natural order in which they occur in a document.

Example

```
{position: static; left: 120px; top: 50px;}
```

Browser Support

Internet Explorer 4, 5, and 5.5
Netscape 6

absolute

This value defines a coordinate system independent from other block and inline element placement. An element whose position is absolute acts as a visual container for any elements enclosed within its content. All elements defined inside it move with it. Contained elements that are assigned coordinates outside their container's dimensions will disappear.

Example

```
{position: absolute; left: 120px; top: 50px;}
```

Browser Support

Internet Explorer 4, 5, and 5.5
Netscape 6

relative

This value positions elements relative to their natural position in document flow.

Example

```
{position: relative; left: 120px; top: 50px;}
```

Browser Support

Internet Explorer 4, 5, and 5.5
Netscape 6

left

This property defines the *x* (horizontal) coordinate for a positioned element, relative to the left side. Values can be specified as lengths (inches, pixels, and so on), as a percentage of the containing object's dimensions, or as **auto**.

Examples

```
{position: absolute; left: 120px; top: 50px;}

{position: absolute; left: 30%; top: 50%;}

{position: absolute; left: auto; top: auto;}
```

Browser Support

Internet Explorer 4, 5, and 5.5
Netscape 4, 4.5–4.7, 6

right

This property defines the x (horizontal) coordinate for a positioned element, relative to the right side. Values can be specified as lengths (inches, pixels, and so on), as a percentage of the containing object's dimensions, or as **auto**.

Examples

```
{position: absolute; right: 120px; top: 50px;}

{position: absolute; right: 30%; top: 50%;}

{position: absolute; right: auto; top: auto;}
```

Browser Support

Internet Explorer 4, 5, and 5.5
Netscape 6

top

This property defines the y (vertical) coordinate for a positioned element, relative to the top. Values can be specified as lengths (inches, pixels, and so on), as a percentage of the containing object's dimensions, or as **auto**, which lets this property function as determined by the browser or as defined by the parent element.

Examples

```
{position: absolute; left: 100px; top: 150px;}

{position: absolute; left: 50%; top: 30%;}

{position: absolute; left: auto; top: auto;}
```

Browser Support
Internet Explorer 4, 5, and 5.5
Netscape 4, 4.5–4.7, 6

bottom
This property defines the *y* (vertical) coordinate for a positioned element, relative to the bottom. Values can be specified as lengths (inches, pixels, and so on), as a percentage of the containing object's dimensions, or as **auto**, which lets this property function as determined by the browser or as defined by the parent element.

Examples

```
{position: absolute; left: 100px; bottom: 150px;}

{position: absolute; left: 50%; bottom: 30%;}

{position: absolute; left: auto; bottom: auto;}
```

Browser Support
Internet Explorer 4, 5, and 5.5
Netscape 6

width
This property defines the width of an element. Values can be specified as lengths (positive values only), percentages (relative to the containing element's width), or **auto**, which defaults to the element's natural width.

Example

```
img {position: absolute; left: 120px; top: 50px; height: 200px;
    width: 400px;}
```

Browser Support
Internet Explorer 4, 5, and 5.5
Netscape 4, 4.5–4.7, 6

height
This property defines the height of an element. Values can be specified as lengths (positive values only), percentages (relative to the containing element's height), or as **auto**, which defaults to the element's natural height.

Example

```
img {position: absolute; left: 120px; top: 50px; height: 100px;
     width: 150px;}
```

Browser Support

Internet Explorer 4, 5, and 5.5
Netscape 6

clip

This property sets the coordinates of the clipping rectangle that houses the content of elements set to a position value of **absolute**. Coordinate values are **top**, **right**, **bottom**, **left**, and **auto**. The **auto** value lets clipping occur as it will.

Example

```
{position: absolute; left: 20; top: 20; width:100; height:100;
 clip: rect(10 90 90 10);}
```

Browser Support

Internet Explorer 5 and 5.5
Netscape 6

overflow

This property determines an element's behavior when its content doesn't fit into the space defined by the element's other properties. Possible values are **clip**, **scroll**, and **none**.

Example

```
{position: absolute; left: 20; top: 20; width: 100; height: 100;
 clip: rect(10 90 90 10); overflow: scroll;}
```

Browser Support

Internet Explorer 5 and 5.5
Netscape 6

clip

This value clips content to the size defined for the container.

Example

```
{position: absolute; left: 20; top: 20; width: 100; height: 100;
  clip: rect(10 90 90 10); overflow: clip;}
```

Browser Support

Internet Explorer 5.5
Netscape 6

scroll

This value allows content to scroll using scroll bars or another browser-dependent mechanism.

Example

```
{position: absolute; left: 20; top: 20; width: 100; height: 100;
  clip: rect(10 90 90 10); overflow: scroll;}
```

Browser Support

Internet Explorer 5 and 5.5
Netscape 6

none

This value does nothing, but can allow clipping of the content.

Example

```
{position: absolute; left: 20; top: 20; width: 100; height: 100;
  clip: rect(10 90 90 10); overflow: none;}
```

Browser Support

Internet Explorer 5 and 5.5
Netscape 6

z-index

This property defines a layering context for elements containing other elements with relative or absolute positioning. By default, overlapping elements stack in the order in which they are defined in an HTML document. This property can override default layering by assigning numeric layering values to an element, with higher numbers layering above lower numbers. The **auto** value tries to determine the z-placement of an element automatically.

Example

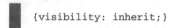

```
{position: absolute; top:20;left:20; height: 50; width: 50;
 background-color: blue; z-index: 2;}
```

Browser Support
Internet Explorer 5 and 5.5
Netscape 4, 4.5–4.7, 6

visibility

This property determines whether or not an element is visible. Possible values are **hidden**, **visible**, and **inherit**.

Example

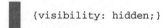

```
{visibility: inherit;}
```

Browser Support
Internet Explorer 4, 5, and 5.5
Netscape 6

hidden

This value specifies that an element is hidden from view. A hidden element still occupies its full canvas space.

Example

```
{visibility: hidden;}
```

Browser Support
Internet Explorer 4, 5, and 5.5
Netscape 6

visible

This value specifies that an element is visible.

Example

```
{visibility: visible;}
```

Browser Support
Internet Explorer 4, 5, and 5.5
Netscape 6

inherit
This value specifies that an element inherits its visibility state from the element that contains it.

Example

```
{visibility: inherit;}
```

Browser Support
Internet Explorer 4, 5, and 5.5
Netscape 6

Additional CSS2 Properties
The following table lists the remaining CSS2 properties with a short description of their intended functions. At this time, none of these properties are supported by any browsers.

Property	Purpose
content	used with **:before** and **:after** pseudo-elements to define URL for actions such a playing audio file, etc.
counter	Designed to aid in automatic numbering of sections in an HTML document. See Chapter 10.
counter-increment	Designed to aid in automatic numbering of sections in an HTML document. See Chapter 10.
counter-reset	Designed to aid in automatic numbering of sections in an HTML document. See Chapter 10.
marker-offset	Defines offset for an element that has been defined as a marker by the display property. See Chapter 10.
marks	Defines if cross marks, crop marks, or both, are rendered just outside a page box edge.
max-height	Defines the maximum height available for an element.
max-width	Defines the maximum width available for an element.
min-height	Defines the minimum height available for an element.
min-width	Defines the minimum width available for an element.
orphans	Defines the minimum number of lines in a paragraph to must be left at the bottom of a page.

Property	Purpose
outline	Shorthand property incorporating values of the three following properties; defines an outline around an element. See Chapter 10.
outline-color	Defines color for an outline around an element. See Chapter 10.
outline-style	Defines style for an outline around an element. See Chapter 10.
outline-width	Defines width for an outline around an element. See Chapter 10.
quotes	Defines style of quotation marks to be used with embedded quotes.
run-in	Allows a block level element to appear in-line with the following block-level element. See Chapter 10.
size	Defines size and orientation for a page box.
unicode-bidi	Defines levels of embedding with regard to Unicode bi-directional algorithm.
widows	Defines the minimum number of lines in a paragraph to must be left at the top of a page.

Microsoft Extensions to CSS

Microsoft has introduced a number of proprietary extensions to CSS, many of which have also been proposed as additions to the CSS specification. The following section provides a quick overview of these, and notes the earliest version of Internet Explorer to support each one. For a more comprehensive overview of these properties, and of Microsoft's CSS support in general, see http://www.msdn.microsoft.com/workshop/author/css/reference/attributes.asp.

background-position-x

This Microsoft-proposed CSS property defines the x-coordinate of the **background-position** property. Introduced in Internet Explorer 4.

Example

```
<body style="background-image: url(picture.gif);
     background-repeat: no-repeat;
     background-position-x: 25%;">
```

background-position-y

This Microsoft-proposed CSS property defines the y-coordinate of the **background-position** property. Introduced in Internet Explorer 4.

Example

```
<body style="background-image: url(picture.gif);
    background-repeat: no-repeat;
    background-position-y: 200px;">
```

behavior

This Microsoft-proposed CSS property is used to define the URL for a script providing DHTML behavior. Introduced in Internet Explorer 5.0.

Example

```
<h1 style="behavior: url(colorchange.js)">What a dynamic header!</h1>
```

filter

This Microsoft-proposed CSS property is used to apply filter effects to associated HTML elements. Introduced in Internet Explorer 4. (See Chapter 10.)

Example

```
<h2 style="filter: Blur(Add = 1, Direction = 90, Strength = 20);
    width: 100%;">This header is all blurry.</h2>
```

ime-mode

This Microsoft-proposed CSS property is used to set the state of an Input Method Editor (IME); for use with Chinese, Japanese, and Korean character sets. Introduced in Internet Explorer 5.0.

Example

```
<textarea style="ime-mode:active"></textarea>
```

layout-grid

This Microsoft-proposed CSS property defines a grid to be used in laying out Japanese or Chinese characters in a Web document. Shorthand property for the following layout grid properties. Introduced in Internet Explorer 5.0.

Example

```
<p style="layout-grid: char line 12px 12px .5in">
    A short text sample.</p>
```

layout-grid-char

This Microsoft-proposed CSS property defines the size of the character grid used for laying out Japanese or Chinese characters in a Web document. Introduced in Internet Explorer 5.0.

Example

```
<p style="layout-grid-char: 50px">
A short text sample.</p>
```

layout-grid-line

This Microsoft-proposed CSS property defines the gridline value used for laying out Japanese or Chinese characters in a Web document. Introduced in Internet Explorer 5.0. Introduced in Internet Explorer 5.0.

Example

```
<p style="layout-grid-line: 100px">
A short text sample<br>
   with line breaks so<br>
   the meaning of this<br>
   property will be obvious.</p>
```

layout-grid-mode

This Microsoft-proposed CSS property defines if the text layout grid uses one or two dimensions. Introduced in Internet Explorer 5.0.

Example

```
<p style="layout-grid-mode: none; layout-grid-line: 100px">
   A short text sample<br>
   with layout-grid-mode<br>
   set to a value of none<br>
   to turn off the grid.</p>
```

layout-grid-type

This Microsoft-proposed CSS property defines the type of grid to be used for laying out Japanese or Chinese characters in a Web document. Introduced in Internet Explorer 5.0.

Example

```
<p style="layout-grid-type: strict; layout-grid-line: 55px">
   A short text sample.</p>
```

line-break

This Microsoft-proposed CSS property defines line-breaking rules for Japanese text. Introduced in Internet Explorer 5.0.

Example

```
p {line-break: normal;}
```

overflow-x

This Microsoft-proposed CSS property defines how content should behave when it exceeds the width of its enclosing element. Introduced in Internet Explorer 4.

Example

```
<p style="overflow-x: scroll; width: 100px">
ABCDEFGHIJKLMNOPQRSTUVWXYZ
</p>
```

overflow-y

This Microsoft-proposed CSS property defines how content should behave when it exceeds the height of its enclosing element. Introduced in Internet Explorer 4.

Example

```
<p style="overflow-y: scroll; height: 25px; width: 50px;
   background-color: lightblue">
ABC<br>
DEF<br>
GHI<br>
JKL<br>
MNO<br>
PQR<br>
STU<br>
VWXYZ
</p>
```

ruby-align

This Microsoft-proposed CSS property defines the alignment of ruby text as defined by the **\<rt\>** element, in relation to base text defined by the **\<ruby\>** element (see entries for **\<ruby\>** and **\<rt\>** in Appendix A). Introduced in Internet Explorer 5.0.

Example

```
<ruby style="ruby-align: right">
This is the base text defined by the ruby element

<rt>This is the ruby text defined by the rt element.
</ruby>
```

ruby-overhang

This Microsoft-proposed CSS property defines the overhang of ruby text as defined by the **\<rt\>** element, in relation to base text defined by the **\<ruby\>** element (see entries for **\<ruby\>** and **\<rt\>** in Appendix A). Introduced in Internet Explorer 5.0.

Example

```
<ruby style="ruby-overhang: auto">
This is the base text defined by the ruby element

<rt>This is the ruby text defined by the rt element
and it's a lot longer than the base text in this example.
A lot longer.</ruby>

This is text outside of the ruby element.
```

ruby-position

This Microsoft-proposed CSS property defines the position of ruby text as defined by the **\<rt\>** element, in relation to base text defined by the **\<ruby\>** element (see entries for **\<ruby\>** and **\<rt\>** in Appendix A). Introduced in Internet Explorer 5.0.

Example

```
<ruby style="ruby-position: inline">
This is the base text defined by the ruby element

<rt>This is the ruby text defined by the rt element but it won't
look that way in IE 5.5 because it has been defined as inline in
relation to the base text.</ruby>
```

scrollbar-3d-light-color

This Microsoft extension to CSS defines a color for the top and left edges of the scroll box in a scrollbar; this and the related scrollbar properties can be applied to the browser window scrollbar when used with the **\<body\>** element, or to other elements when used in conjunction with clipping properties. Introduced in Internet Explorer 5.5.

Example

```
body {scrollbar-3d-light-color: lightblue;}
```

scrollbar-arrow-color

This Microsoft extension to CSS defines a color for the arrows in a scrollbar. Introduced in Internet Explorer 5.5.

Example

```
body {scrollbar-arrow-color: red;}
```

scrollbar-base-color

This Microsoft extension to CSS defines the base color for a scrollbar. Introduced in Internet Explorer 5.5.

Example

```
body {scrollbar-base-color: green;}
```

scrollbar-dark-shadow-color

This Microsoft extension to CSS defines a shadow color for the right and bottom edges of a scrollbar. Introduced in Internet Explorer 5.5.

Example

```
body {scrollbar-darkshadow-color: #0000FF;}
```

scrollbar-face-color

This Microsoft extension to CSS defines a color for the face of a scrollbar. Introduced in Internet Explorer 5.5.

Example

```
body {scrollbar-face-color: #CC00FF;}
```

scrollbar-highlight-color

This Microsoft extension to CSS defines a color for the top and left edges of a scrollbar. Introduced in Internet Explorer 5.5.

Example

```
body {scrollbar-highlight-color: #CCFFFF;}
```

scrollbar-shadow-color

This Microsoft extension to CSS defines a color for the right and bottom edges of a scrollbar. Introduced in Internet Explorer 5.5.

Example

```
body {scrollbar-shadow-color: purple;}
```

text-autospace

This Microsoft-proposed CSS property defines spacing values for text; used when combining different types of characters, such as regular text, ideographic text, and numeric characters. Introduced in Internet Explorer 5.0.

text-justify

This Microsoft-proposed CSS property provides greater control over how justified text should be aligned and spaced. Introduced in Internet Explorer 5.0.

Example

```
<p style="text-align: justify; text-justify: distribute-all-lines;
   width: 250px">
This paragraph is not only justified, but the text-justify property
is set to a value that makes the last line justify as well.
</p>
```

text-kashida-space

This Microsoft-proposed CSS property defines the ration between kashida expansion and white space expansion in justified text (kashida is a typographic effect used with Arabic writing systems). Introduced in Internet Explorer 5.5.

text-underline-position

This Microsoft-proposed CSS property defines the position of underlining set with the text-decoration property. Introduced in Internet Explorer 5.0.

Example

```
<p style="text-decoration: underline;
   text-underline-position: above">
This example uses the text-underline-position property to
place the underlining on top of the text. Why not just set
text-decoration to overline instead?</p>
```

word-break

This Microsoft-proposed CSS property can be used to allow line breaks within words, primarily for use with Asian languages. Introduced in Internet Explorer 5.0.

Example

```
<div style="word-break: break-all; width:50px">
Words can break in this code example. Like this one:
Sesquipedalianism</div>
```

word-wrap

This Microsoft extension to CSS can be set to allow line breaks within words when content exceeds the limits of its containing element. Introduced in Internet Explorer 5.5.

Example

```
<p style="word-wrap: break-word; width: 30px">
Words can break in this code example. Here is another long one:
Transcendentalism</p>
```

writing-mode

This Microsoft-proposed CSS property can be used to set text flow appropriate for European alphabets or East Asian alphabets. Values are **lr-tb** (left-to-right, top-to-bottom) and **tb-rl** (top-to-bottom, right-to-left). Introduced in Internet Explorer 5.5.

Example

```
<p style="writing-mode: tb-rl">
This example will really turn your head if you
view it in Internet Explorer 5.5.</p>
```

zoom

This Microsoft extension to CSS can be used to define a magnification scale for an element. Can be used with scripting to create rollover effects. Introduced in Internet Explorer 5.5.

Example

```
<p onmouseover="this.style.zoom='150%'"
    onmouseout="this.style.zoom='normal'">
    Careful, this text might jump out at you!</p>
```

Style Sheet Measurement Values

This section discusses measurement values used in association with style sheets.

%

This value defines a measurement as a percentage relative to another value.

Example

```
p {font-size: 14pt; line-height: 150%;}
```

Browser Support
Internet Explorer 3, 4, 5, and 5.5
Netscape 4, 4.5–4.7, 6

cm

This value defines a measurement in centimeters.

Example

```
div {margin-bottom: 1cm;}
```

Browser Support
Internet Explorer 3, 4, 5, and 5.5
Netscape 4, 4.5–4.7, 6

em

This value defines a measurement for the height of a font in em spaces.

Example

```
p {letter-spacing: 5em;}
```

Browser Support
Internet Explorer 3 (Mac only), 5 and 5.5
Netscape 4, 4.5–4.7 (incomplete), 6

ex (x-height)

This value defines a measurement relative to a font's x-height. The x-height is determined by the height of the font's lowercase letter *x*.

Example

```
p {font-size: 14pt; line-height: 2ex;}
```

Browser Support
Internet Explorer 3 (Mac only), 5 and 5.5
Netscape 4, 4.5–4.7 (incomplete), 6

in

This value defines a measurement in inches.

Example

```
p {word-spacing: .25in;}
```

Browser Support
Internet Explorer 3, 4, 5, and 5.5
Netscape 4, 4.5–4.7, 6

mm

This value defines a measurement in millimeters.

Example

```
p {word-spacing: 12mm;}
```

Browser Support
Internet Explorer 3, 4, 5, and 5.5
Netscape 4, 4.5–4.7, 6

pc

This value defines a measurement in picas.

Example

```
p {font-size: 10pc;}
```

Browser Support
Internet Explorer 3, 4, 5, and 5.5
Netscape 4, 4.5–4.7, and 6

pt

This value defines a measurement in points.

Example

```
body {font-size: 14pt;}
```

Browser Support
Internet Explorer 3, 4, 5, and 5.5
Netscape 4, 4.5–4.7, 6

px

This value defines a measurement in pixels.

Example

```
p {padding: 15px;}
```

Browser Support
Internet Explorer 3, 4, 5, and 5.5
Netscape 4, 4.5–4.7, 6

Style Sheet Color Values

This section discusses color values used in association with style sheets.

Named Color Values

Color values can be defined using sixteen color names: **aqua**, **black**, **blue**, **fuchsia**, **gray**, **green**, **lime**, **maroon**, **navy**, **olive**, **purple**, **red**, **silver**, **teal**, **white**, and **yellow**. (An extended list of color names has been introduced by Netscape, but it is safer to use the hexadecimal equivalents of those names, which are listed in Appendix E.)

Example

```
body {font-family: Arial; font-size: 12pt; color: red;}
```

Browser Support
Internet Explorer 3, 4, 5, and 5.5
Netscape 4, 4.5–4.7, 6

Six-Digit Hexadecimal Color Values

Color values can be defined using the six-digit hexadecimal color values commonly used on the Web.

Example

```
div {font-family: Courier; font-size: 10pt; color: #00CCFF;}
```

Browser Support
Internet Explorer 3, 4, 5, and 5.5
Netscape 4, 4.5–4.7, 6

Three-Digit Hexadecimal Color Values

Color values can be defined using the three-digit hexadecimal color values, a concise version of the six-digit values just noted.

Example

```
span {font-family: Helvetica; font-size: 14pt; color: #0CF;}
```

Browser Support
Internet Explorer 3, 4, 5, and 5.5
Netscape 4, 4.5–4.7, 6

APPENDIX B

RGB Color Values

Color values can be defined using RGB values. Colors are defined by the letters *rgb,* followed by three numbers between 0 and 255, contained in parentheses and separated by commas, with no spaces between them.

Example

```
p {color: rgb(204,0,51);}
```

Browser Support
Internet Explorer 4, 5, and 5.5
Netscape 4, 4.5–4.7, and 6

RGB Color Values Using Percentages

RGB color values can also be defined using percentages. The format is the same, except that the numbers are replaced by percentage values between **0%** and **100%**.

Example

```
p {color: rgb(75%,10%,50%);}
```

Browser Support
Internet Explorer 4, 5, and 5.5
Netscape 4, 4.5–4.7, and 6

The Complete Reference

Appendix C

Special Characters

This appendix lists the special characters available in standard HTML and HTML 4.0x. Note that browser support of elements in Appendix C is based on testing in the following browser versions: Netscape 1.22, Netscape 2.02, Netscape 3.01, Netscape Communicator 4.0, Netscape Communicator 4.5, Netscape Communicator 4.73, Internet Explorer 3.02, Internet Explorer 4.0, Internet Explorer 5.0, Internet Explorer 5.5, Opera 4.02, and WebTV's browser simulator. Testing also was performed in preview releases of Netscape 6. In the tables in this appendix, the following abbreviations are used for the different Netscape and Internet Explorer versions:

N1 = Netscape 1.22	N6 = Netscape Communicator 6*
N2 = Netscape 2.02	IE3 = Internet Explorer 3.02
N3 = Netscape 3.01	IE4 = Internet Explorer 4.0
N4 = Netscape Communicator 4.0	IE5 = Internet Explorer 5.0
N4.5 = Netscape Communicator 4.5	IE5.5 = Internet Explorer 5.5
N4.7 = Netscape Communicator 4.73	O4 = Opera 4.02

* Netscape 6 support based upon Preview Release 2

"Standard" HTML Character Entities

As discussed throughout the book, Web browsers do not render certain characters if they appear in an HTML document. Some keyboard characters such as < and > have special meanings to HTML because they are part of HTML tags. Other characters such as certain foreign language accent characters and special symbols can be difficult to insert as well. HTML uses a set of character entity codes in order to display these special characters. These codes consist of numbered entities and some, but not all, of these numbered entities have corresponding named entities. For example, the numbered entity Ë produces the character Ë. The named entity Ë produces the same character. Note that the named entity suggests the intended rendering of the character, which provides a handy mnemonic device for dedicated HTML coders. While Ë is widely supported, not all character entities work in all browsers. Theoretically, a browser vendor could even create arbitrary interpretations of these codes. For instance, WebTV has assigned its own unique renderings for the entities numbered 128 and 129. Under the HTML specifications, 128 and 129 are not assigned a character. The codes numbered 32 through 255 (with some gaps) were assigned standard keyboard characters. Some of these codes duplicate characters that Web browsers can already interpret. The entity 5 represents the numeral five, while A represents "A." Character entities become more practical when it is necessary to employ characters used in foreign languages, such as "Œ " or "Å," or special characters such as "¶ ." The following chart lists these "standard" entities and their intended renderings, and identifies which browsers support each.

Named Entity	Browser Support	Numbered Entity	Browser Support	Intended Rendering	Description
		&#32;	N: 1, 2, 3, 4, 4.5, 4.7, 6 IE: 3, 4, 5, 5.5, Opera 4.02, WebTV		Space

Named Entity	Browser Support	Numbered Entity	Browser Support	Intended Rendering	Description
		&#33;	N: 1, 2, 3, 4, 4.5, 4.7, 6 IE: 3, 4, 5, 5.5, Opera 4.02, WebTV	!	Exclamation point
&quot;	N: 1, 2, 3, 4, 4.5, 4.7, 6 IE: 3, 4, 5, 5.5, Opera 4.02, WebTV	&#34;	N: 1, 2, 3, 4, 4.5, 4.7, 6 IE: 3, 4, 5, 5.5, Opera 4.02, WebTV	"	Double quotes
		&#35;	N: 1, 2, 3, 4, 4.5, 4.7, 6 IE: 3, 4, 5, 5.5, Opera 4.02, WebTV	#	Number symbol
		&#36;	N: 1, 2, 3, 4, 4.5, 4.7, 6 IE: 3, 4, 5, 5.5, Opera 4.02, WebTV	$	Dollar symbol
		&#37;	N: 1, 2, 3, 4, 4.5, 4.7, 6 IE: 3, 4, 5, 5.5, Opera 4.02, WebTV	%	Percent symbol
&amp;	N: 1, 2, 3, 4, 4.5, 4.7, 6 IE: 3, 4, 5, 5.5, Opera 4.02, WebTV	&#38;	N: 1, 2, 3, 4, 4.5, 4.7, 6 IE: 3, 4, 5, 5.5, Opera 4.02, WebTV	&	Ampersand
		&#39;	N: 1, 2, 3, 4, 4.5, 4.7, 6 IE: 3, 4, 5, 5.5, Opera 4.02, WebTV	'	Single quote
		&#40;	N: 1, 2, 3, 4, 4.5, 4.7, 6 IE: 3, 4, 5, 5.5, Opera 4.02, WebTV	(	Opening parenthesis
		&#41;	N: 1, 2, 3, 4, 4.5, 4.7, 6 IE: 3, 4, 5, 5.5, Opera 4.02, WebTV	)	Closing parenthesis
		&#42;	N: 1, 2, 3, 4, 4.5, 4.7, 6 IE: 3, 4, 5, 5.5, Opera 4.02, WebTV	*	Asterisk
		&#43;	N: 1, 2, 3, 4, 4.5, 4.7, 6 IE: 3, 4, 5, 5.5, Opera 4.02, WebTV	+	Plus sign

Named Entity	Browser Support	Numbered Entity	Browser Support	Intended Rendering	Description
		&#44;	N: 1, 2, 3, 4, 4.5, 4.7, 6 IE: 3, 4, 5, 5.5, Opera 4.02, WebTV	,	Comma
		&#45;	N: 1, 2, 3, 4, 4.5, 4.7, 6 IE: 3, 4, 5, 5.5, Opera 4.02, WebTV	-	Minus sign (hyphen)
		&#46;	N: 1, 2, 3, 4, 4.5, 4.7, 6 IE: 3, 4, 5, 5.5, Opera 4.02, WebTV	.	Period
		&#47;	N: 1, 2, 3, 4, 4.5, 4.7, 6 IE: 3, 4, 5, 5.5, Opera 4.02, WebTV	/	Slash/virgule/bar
		&#48;	N: 1, 2, 3, 4, 4.5, 4.7, 6 IE: 3, 4, 5, 5.5, Opera 4.02, WebTV	0	Zero
		&#49;	N: 1, 2, 3, 4, 4.5, 4.7, 6 IE: 3, 4, 5, 5.5, Opera 4.02, WebTV	1	One
		&#50;	N: 1, 2, 3, 4, 4.5, 4.7, 6 IE: 3, 4, 5, 5.5, Opera 4.02, WebTV	2	Two
		&#51;	N: 1, 2, 3, 4, 4.5, 4.7, 6 IE: 3, 4, 5, 5.5, Opera 4.02, WebTV	3	Three
		&#52;	N: 1, 2, 3, 4, 4.5, 4.7, 6 IE: 3, 4, 5, 5.5, Opera 4.02, WebTV	4	Four
		&#53;	N: 1, 2, 3, 4, 4.5, 4.7, 6 IE: 3, 4, 5, 5.5, Opera 4.02, WebTV	5	Five
		&#54;	N: 1, 2, 3, 4, 4.5, 4.7, 6 IE: 3, 4, 5, 5.5, Opera 4.02, WebTV	6	Six

Named Entity	Browser Support	Numbered Entity	Browser Support	Intended Rendering	Description
		&#55;	N: 1, 2, 3, 4, 4.5, 4.7, 6 IE: 3, 4, 5, 5.5, Opera 4.02, WebTV	7	Seven
		&#56;	N: 1, 2, 3, 4, 4.5, 4.7, 6 IE: 3, 4, 5, 5.5, Opera 4.02, WebTV	8	Eight
		&#57;	N: 1, 2, 3, 4, 4.5, 4.7, 6 IE: 3, 4, 5, 5.5, Opera 4.02, WebTV	9	Nine
		&#58;	N: 1, 2, 3, 4, 4.5, 4.7, 6 IE: 3, 4, 5, 5.5, Opera 4.02, WebTV	:	Colon
		&#59;	N: 1, 2, 3, 4, 4.5, 4.7, 6 IE: 3, 4, 5, 5.5, Opera 4.02, WebTV	;	Semicolon
&lt;	N: 1, 2, 3, 4, 4.5, 4.7, 6 IE: 3, 4, 5, 5.5, Opera 4.02, WebTV	&#60;	N: 1, 2, 3, 4, 4.5, 4.7, 6 IE: 3, 4, 5, 5.5, Opera 4.02, WebTV	<	Less than symbol
		&#61;	N: 1, 2, 3, 4, 4.5, 4.7, 6 IE: 3, 4, 5, 5.5, Opera 4.02, WebTV	=	Equal sign
&gt;	N: 1, 2, 3, 4, 4.5, 4.7, 6 IE: 3, 4, 5, 5.5, Opera 4.02, WebTV	&#62;	N: 1, 2, 3, 4, 4.5, 4.7, 6 IE: 3, 4, 5, 5.5, Opera 4.02, WebTV	>	Greater than symbol
		&#63;	N: 1, 2, 3, 4, 4.5, 4.7, 6 IE: 3, 4, 5, 5.5, Opera 4.02, WebTV	?	Question mark
		&#64;	N: 1, 2, 3, 4, 4.5, 4.7, 6 IE: 3, 4, 5, 5.5, Opera 4.02, WebTV	@	At symbol
		&#65;	N: 1, 2, 3, 4, 4.5, 4.7, 6 IE: 3, 4, 5, 5.5, Opera 4.02, WebTV	A	

Named Entity	Browser Support	Numbered Entity	Browser Support	Intended Rendering	Description
		&#66;	N: 1, 2, 3, 4, 4.5, 4.7, 6 IE: 3, 4, 5, 5.5, Opera 4.02, WebTV	B	
		&#67;	N: 1, 2, 3, 4, 4.5, 4.7, 6 IE: 3, 4, 5, 5.5, Opera 4.02, WebTV	C	
		&#68;	N: 1, 2, 3, 4, 4.5, 4.7, 6 IE: 3, 4, 5, 5.5, Opera 4.02, WebTV	D	
		&#69;	N: 1, 2, 3, 4, 4.5, 4.7, 6 IE: 3, 4, 5, 5.5, Opera 4.02, WebTV	E	
		&#70;	N: 1, 2, 3, 4, 4.5, 4.7, 6 IE: 3, 4, 5, 5.5, Opera 4.02, WebTV	F	
		&#71;	N: 1, 2, 3, 4, 4.5, 4.7, 6 IE: 3, 4, 5, 5.5, Opera 4.02, WebTV	G	
		&#72;	N: 1, 2, 3, 4, 4.5, 4.7, 6 IE: 3, 4, 5, 5.5, Opera 4.02, WebTV	H	
		&#73;	N: 1, 2, 3, 4, 4.5, 4.7, 6 IE: 3, 4, 5, 5.5, Opera 4.02, WebTV	I	
		&#74;	N: 1, 2, 3, 4, 4.5, 4.7, 6 IE: 3, 4, 5, 5.5, Opera 4.02, WebTV	J	
		&#75;	N: 1, 2, 3, 4, 4.5, 4.7, 6 IE: 3, 4, 5, 5.5, Opera 4.02, WebTV	K	
		&#76;	N: 1, 2, 3, 4, 4.5, 4.7, 6 IE: 3, 4, 5, 5.5, Opera 4.02, WebTV	L	

Named Entity	Browser Support	Numbered Entity	Browser Support	Intended Rendering	Description
		&#77;	N: 1, 2, 3, 4, 4.5, 4.7, 6 IE: 3, 4, 5, 5.5, Opera 4.02, WebTV	M	
		&#78;	N: 1, 2, 3, 4, 4.5, 4.7, 6 IE: 3, 4, 5, 5.5, Opera 4.02, WebTV	N	
		&#79;	N: 1, 2, 3, 4, 4.5, 4.7, 6 IE: 3, 4, 5, 5.5, Opera 4.02, WebTV	O	
		&#80;	N: 1, 2, 3, 4, 4.5, 4.7, 6 IE: 3, 4, 5, 5.5, Opera 4.02, WebTV	P	
		&#81;	N: 1, 2, 3, 4, 4.5, 4.7, 6 IE: 3, 4, 5, 5.5, Opera 4.02, WebTV	Q	
		&#82;	N: 1, 2, 3, 4, 4.5, 4.7, 6 IE: 3, 4, 5, 5.5, Opera 4.02, WebTV	R	
		&#83;	N: 1, 2, 3, 4, 4.5, 4.7, 6 IE: 3, 4, 5, 5.5, Opera 4.02, WebTV	S	
		&#84;	N: 1, 2, 3, 4, 4.5, 4.7, 6 IE: 3, 4, 5, 5.5, Opera 4.02, WebTV	T	
		&#85;	N: 1, 2, 3, 4, 4.5, 4.7, 6 IE: 3, 4, 5, 5.5, Opera 4.02, WebTV	U	
		&#86;	N: 1, 2, 3, 4, 4.5, 4.7, 6 IE: 3, 4, 5, 5.5, Opera 4.02, WebTV	V	
		&#87;	N: 1, 2, 3, 4, 4.5, 4.7, 6 IE: 3, 4, 5, 5.5, Opera 4.02, WebTV	W	

Named Entity	Browser Support	Numbered Entity	Browser Support	Intended Rendering	Description
		&#88;	N: 1, 2, 3, 4, 4.5, 4.7, 6 IE: 3, 4, 5, 5.5, Opera 4.02, WebTV	X	
		&#89;	N: 1, 2, 3, 4, 4.5, 4.7, 6 IE: 3, 4, 5, 5.5, Opera 4.02, WebTV	Y	
		&#90;	N: 1, 2, 3, 4, 4.5, 4.7, 6 IE: 3, 4, 5, 5.5, Opera 4.02, WebTV	Z	
		&#91;	N: 1, 2, 3, 4, 4.5, 4.7, 6 IE: 3, 4, 5, 5.5, Opera 4.02, WebTV	[	Opening bracket
		&#92;	N: 1, 2, 3, 4, 4.5, 4.7, 6 IE: 3, 4, 5, 5.5, Opera 4.02, WebTV	\	Backslash
		&#93;	N: 1, 2, 3, 4, 4.5, 4.7, 6 IE: 3, 4, 5, 5.5, Opera 4.02, WebTV	]	Closing bracket
		&#94;	N: 1, 3, 4, 4.5, 4.7, 6 IE: 3, 4, 5, 5.5, Opera 4.02, WebTV	^	Caret
		&#95;	N: 1, 2, 3, 4, 4.5, 4.7, 6 IE: 3, 4, 5, 5.5, Opera 4.02, WebTV	_	Underscore
		&#96;	N: 1, 2, 3, 4, 4.5, 4.7, 6 IE: 3, 4, 5, 5.5, Opera 4.02, WebTV	`	Grave accent, no letter
		&#97;	N: 1, 2, 3, 4, 4.5, 4.7, 6 IE: 3, 4, 5, 5.5, Opera 4.02, WebTV	a	
		&#98;	N: 1, 2, 3, 4, 4.5, 4.7, 6 IE: 3, 4, 5, 5.5, Opera 4.02, WebTV	b	

Named Entity	Browser Support	Numbered Entity	Browser Support	Intended Rendering	Description
		&#99;	N: 1, 2, 3, 4, 4.5, 4.7, 6 IE: 3, 4, 5, 5.5, Opera 4.02, WebTV	c	
		&#100;	N: 1, 2, 3, 4, 4.5, 4.7, 6 IE: 3, 4, 5, 5.5, Opera 4.02, WebTV	d	
		&#101;	N: 1, 2, 3, 4, 4.5, 4.7, 6 IE: 3, 4, 5, 5.5, Opera 4.02, WebTV	e	
		&#102;	N: 1, 2, 3, 4, 4.5, 4.7, 6 IE: 3, 4, 5, 5.5, Opera 4.02, WebTV	f	
		&#103;	N: 1, 2, 3, 4, 4.5, 4.7, 6 IE: 3, 4, 5, 5.5, Opera 4.02, WebTV	g	
		&#104;	N: 1, 2, 3, 4, 4.5, 4.7, 6 IE: 3, 4, 5, 5.5, Opera 4.02, WebTV	h	
		&#105;	N: 1, 2, 3, 4, 4.5, 4.7, 6 IE: 3, 4, 5, 5.5, Opera 4.02, WebTV	i	
		&#106;	N: 1, 2, 3, 4, 4.5, 4.7, 6 IE: 3, 4, 5, 5.5, Opera 4.02, WebTV	j	
		&#107;	N: 1, 2, 3, 4, 4.5, 4.7, 6 IE: 3, 4, 5, 5.5, Opera 4.02, WebTV	k	
		&#108;	N: 1, 2, 3, 4, 4.5, 4.7, 6 IE: 3, 4, 5, 5.5, Opera 4.02, WebTV	l	
		&#109;	N: 1, 2, 3, 4, 4.5, 4.7, 6 IE: 3, 4, 5, 5.5, Opera 4.02, WebTV	m	

Named Entity	Browser Support	Numbered Entity	Browser Support	Intended Rendering	Description
		&#110;	N: 1, 2, 3, 4, 4.5, 4.7, 6 IE: 3, 4, 5, 5.5, Opera 4.02, WebTV	n	
		&#111;	N: 1, 2, 3, 4, 4.5, 4.7, 6 IE: 3, 4, 5, 5.5, Opera 4.02, WebTV	o	
		&#112;	N: 1, 2, 3, 4, 4.5, 4.7, 6 IE: 3, 4, 5, 5.5, Opera 4.02, WebTV	p	
		&#113;	N: 1, 2, 3, 4, 4.5, 4.7, 6 IE: 3, 4, 5, 5.5, Opera 4.02, WebTV	q	
		&#114;	N: 1, 2, 3, 4, 4.5, 4.7, 6 IE: 3, 4, 5, 5.5, Opera 4.02, WebTV	r	
		&#115;	N: 1, 2, 3, 4, 4.5, 4.7, 6 IE: 3, 4, 5, 5.5, Opera 4.02, WebTV	s	
		&#116;	N: 1, 2, 3, 4, 4.5, 4.7, 6 IE: 3, 4, 5, 5.5, Opera 4.02, WebTV	t	
		&#117;	N: 1, 2, 3, 4, 4.5, 4.7, 6 IE: 3, 4, 5, 5.5, Opera 4.02, WebTV	u	
		&#118;	N: 1, 2, 3, 4, 4.5, 4.7, 6 IE: 3, 4, 5, 5.5, Opera 4.02, WebTV	v	
		&#119;	N: 1, 2, 3, 4, 4.5, 4.7, 6 IE: 3, 4, 5, 5.5, Opera 4.02, WebTV	w	
		&#120;	N: 1, 2, 3, 4, 4.5, 4.7, 6 IE: 3, 4, 5, 5.5, Opera 4.02, WebTV	x	

Named Entity	Browser Support	Numbered Entity	Browser Support	Intended Rendering	Description
		&#121;	N: 1, 2, 3, 4, 4.5, 4.7, 6 IE: 3, 4, 5, 5.5, Opera 4.02, WebTV	y	
		&#122;	N: 1, 2, 3, 4, 4.5, 4.7, 6 IE: 3, 4, 5, 5.5, Opera 4.02, WebTV	z	
		&#123;	N: 1, 2, 3, 4, 4.5, 4.7, 6 IE: 3, 4, 5, 5.5, Opera 4.02, WebTV	{	Opening brace
		|	N: 1, 2, 3, 4, 4.5, 4.7, 6 IE: 3, 4, 5, 5.5, Opera 4.02, WebTV	|	Vertical bar
		&#125;	N: 1, 2, 3, 4, 4.5, 4.7, 6 IE: 3, 4, 5, 5.5, Opera 4.02, WebTV	}	Closing brace
		&#126;	N: 1, 2, 3, 4, 4.5, 4.7, 6 IE: 3, 4, 5, 5.5, Opera 4.02, WebTV	~	Equivalency symbol (tilde)
		&#127;	n/a		No character (Note: In the standard, the values from 127 to 159 are not assigned. Authors are advised not to use them. Many of them only work under Windows or produce different characters on other operating systems or with different default font sets.)
		&#128;	WebTV (nonstandard)*		No character defined

Named Entity	Browser Support	Numbered Entity	Browser Support	Intended Rendering	Description
&trade;	IE: 3, 4, 5, 5.5	&#129;	WebTV (nonstandard) †	™	Trademark symbol (Nonstandard numeric value; use ™ or ™ instead.)
		&#130;	N: 2, 3, 4, 4.5 IE: 3, 4, 5, 5.5, Opera 4.02, WebTV	'	Low-9 quote (nonstandard)
		&#131;	N3, N4, N4.5, 4.7, 6 IE: 3, 4, 5, 5.5, Opera 4.02, WebTV	ƒ	Small "f" with hook (nonstandard)
		&#132;	N: 2, 3, 4, 4.5, 4.7, 6 IE: 3, 4, 5, 5.5, Opera 4.02, WebTV	„	Low-9 double quotes (nonstandard)
		&#133;	N: 2, 3, 4, 4.5, 4.7, 6 IE: 3, 4, 5, 5.5, Opera 4.02, WebTV	…	Ellipsis (nonstandard)
		&#134;	N: 2, 3, 4, 4.5, 4.7, 6 IE: 3, 4, 5, 5.5, Opera 4.02, WebTV	†	Dagger (nonstandard)
		&#135;	N: 2, 3, 4, 4.5, 4.7, 6 IE: 3, 4, 5, 5.5, Opera 4.02, WebTV	‡	Double dagger (nonstandard)
		&#136;	N3, N4, N4.5, 4.7, 6 IE: 3, 4, 5, 5.5, Opera 4.02, WebTV	ˆ	Circumflex accent, no letter (nonstandard)
		&#137;	N: 2, 3, 4, 4.5, 4.7, 6 IE: 3, 4, 5, 5.5, Opera 4.02, WebTV	‰	Per thousand (nonstandard)
		&#138;	N3, N4, N4.5, 4.7, 6 IE: 3, 4, 5, 5.5, Opera 4.02, WebTV	Š	Uppercase S with caron (nonstandard)

Named Entity	Browser Support	Numbered Entity	Browser Support	Intended Rendering	Description
		&#139;	N: 2, 3, 4, 4.5, 4.7, 6 IE: 3, 4, 5, 5.5, Opera 4.02, WebTV	‹	Opening single-angle quote (nonstandard)
		&#140;	N: 3, 4, 4.5, 4.7, 6 IE: 3, 4, 5, 5.5, Opera 4.02, WebTV	Œ	Uppercase "OE" ligature (nonstandard)
		&#141;	None	Ÿ	Uppercase "Y" with umlaut (nonstandard)
		&#142;	n/a		No character
		&#143;	n/a		No character
		&#144;	n/a		No character
		&#145;	N: 1, 2, 3, 4, 4.5, 4.7, 6 IE: 3, 4, 5, 5.5, Opera 4.02, WebTV	`	Opening "smart" single quote (nonstandard)
		&#146;	N: 1, 2, 3, 4, 4.5, 4.7, 6 IE: 3, 4, 5, 5.5, Opera 4.02, WebTV	'	Closing "smart" single quote (nonstandard)
		&#147;	N: 2, 3, 4, 4.5, 4.7, 6 IE: 3, 4, 5, 5.5, Opera 4.02, WebTV	"	Opening "smart" double quote (nonstandard)
		&#148;	N: 2, 3, 4, 4.5, 4.7, 6 IE: 3, 4, 5, 5.5, Opera 4.02, WebTV	"	Closing "smart" double quote (nonstandard)
		&#149;	N: 2, 3, 4, 4.5, 4.7, 6 IE: 3, 4, 5, 5.5, Opera 4.02, WebTV	•	Bullet (nonstandard)
		&#150;	N: 2, 3, 4, 4.5, 4.7, 6 IE: 3, 4, 5, 5.5, Opera 4.02, WebTV	–	En dash (nonstandard)
		&#151;	N: 2, 3, 4, 4.5, 4.7, 6 IE: 3, 4, 5, 5.5, Opera 4.02, WebTV	—	Em dash (nonstandard)

Named Entity	Browser Support	Numbered Entity	Browser Support	Intended Rendering	Description
		&#152;	N3, N4, N4.5, 4.7, 6 IE: 3, 4, 5, 5.5, Opera 4.02, WebTV	~	Tilde (nonstandard)
&trade;	IE: 3, 4, 5, 5.5 N: 2, 3, 4, 4.5, 4.7, 6 O: 4, WebTV	™‡	N: 2, 3, 4, 4.5, 4.7, 6 IE: 3, 4, 5, 5.5, O:4, WebTV	™	Trademark symbol
		&#154;	N3, N4, N4.5, 4.7, 6 IE: 3, 4, 5, 5.5, Opera 4.02, WebTV	š	Lowercase S with caron (nonstandard)
		&#155;	N: 2, 3, 4, 4.5, 4.7, 6 IE: 3, 4, 5, 5.5, Opera 4.02, WebTV	>	Closing single-angle quote (nonstandard)
		&#156;	N3, N4, N4.5, 4.7, 6 IE: 3, 4, 5, 5.5, Opera 4.02, WebTV	œ	Lowercase "oe" ligature (nonstandard)
		&#157;	n/a		No character
		&#158;	n/a		No character
		&#159;	N: 4, 4.5, 4.7, 6 IE:3, 5, 5.5	Ÿ	Uppercase "Y" with umlaut (nonstandard)
	N: 1, 3, 4, 4.5, 4.7, 6 IE: 3, 4, 5, 5.5, O: 4		N: 1, 2, 3, 4, 4.5, 4.7, 6 IE: 3, 4, 5, 5.5		Nonbreaking space
&iexcl;	N3, N4, N4.5, 4.7, 6 IE: 3, 4, 5, 5.5, Opera 4.02, WebTV	&#161;	N: 1, 3, 4, 4.5, 4.7, 6 IE: 3, 4, 5, 5.5, Opera 4.02, WebTV	¡	Inverted exclamation point
&cent;	N3, N4, N4.5, 4.7, 6 IE: 3, 4, 5, 5.5, Opera 4.02, WebTV	&#162;	N: 1, 3, 4, 4.5, 4.7, 6 IE: 3, 4, 5, 5.5, Opera 4.02, WebTV	¢	Cent symbol
&pound;	N3, N4, N4.5, 4.7, 6 IE: 3, 4, 5, 5.5, Opera 4.02, WebTV	&#163;	N: 1, 3, 4, 4.5, 4.7, 6 IE: 3, 4, 5, 5.5, Opera 4.02, WebTV	£	Pound sterling symbol
&curren;	N3, N4, N4.5, 4.7, 6 IE: 3, 4, 5, 5.5, Opera 4.02, WebTV	&#164;	N: 1, 2, 3, 4, 4.5, 4.7, 6 IE: 3, 4, 5, 5.5, Opera 4.02, WebTV	¤	Currency symbol

Named Entity	Browser Support	Numbered Entity	Browser Support	Intended Rendering	Description
&yen;	N3, N4, N4.5, 4.7, 6 IE: 3, 4, 5, 5.5, Opera 4.02, WebTV	&#165;	N: 1, 3, 4, 4.5, 4.7, 6 IE: 3, 4, 5, 5.5, Opera 4.02, WebTV	¥	Japanese Yen
&brvbar;	N3, N4, N4.5, 4.7, 6 IE: 3, 4, 5, 5.5, Opera 4.02, WebTV	&#166;	N: 2, 3, 4, 4.5, 4.7, 6 IE: 3, 4, 5, 5.5, Opera 4.02, WebTV	¦	Broken vertical bar
&sect;	N3, N4, N4.5, 4.7, 6 IE: 3, 4, 5, 5.5, Opera 4.02, WebTV	&#167;	N: 1, 2, 3, 4, 4.5, 4.7, 6 IE: 3, 4, 5, 5.5, Opera 4.02, WebTV	§	Section symbol
&uml;	N3, N4, N4.5, 4.7, 6 IE: 3, 4, 5, 5.5, Opera 4.02, WebTV	&#168;	N: 1, 3, 4, 4.5, 4.7, 6 IE: 3, 4, 5, 5.5, Opera 4.02, WebTV	¨	Umlaut, no letter
&copy;	N: 1, 2, 3, 4, 4.5, 4.7, 6 IE: 3, 4, 5, 5.5, Opera 4.02, WebTV	&#169;	N: 1, 2, 3, 4, 4.5, 4.7, 6 IE: 3, 4, 5, 5.5, Opera 4.02, WebTV	©	Copyright symbol
&ordf;	N3, N4, N4.5, 4.7, 6 IE: 3, 4, 5, 5.5, Opera 4.02, WebTV	&#170;	N: 1, 3, 4, 4.5, 4.7, 6 IE: 3, 4, 5, 5.5, Opera 4.02, WebTV	a	Feminine ordinal indicator
&laquo;	N3, N4, N4.5, 4.7, 6 IE: 3, 4, 5, 5.5, Opera 4.02, WebTV	&#171;	N: 1, 2, 3, 4, 4.5, 4.7, 6 IE: 3, 4, 5, 5.5, Opera 4.02, WebTV	«	Opening double-angle quote
&not;	N3, N4, N4.5, 4.7, 6 IE: 3, 4, 5, 5.5, Opera 4.02, WebTV	&#172;	N: 1, 2, 3, 4, 4.5, 4.7, 6 IE: 3, 4, 5, 5.5, Opera 4.02, WebTV	¬	Logical "not" symbol
&shy;	N3, N4, N4.5, 4.7, 6 IE: 3, 4, 5, 5.5, Opera 4.02, WebTV	&#173;	N: 1, 2, 3, 4, 4.5, 4.7, 6 IE: 3, 4, 5, WebTV	-	Soft hyphen [no display in IE 5.5]
&reg;	N: 1, 2, 3, 4, 4.5, 4.7, 6 IE: 3, 4, 5, 5.5, Opera 4.02, WebTV	&#174;	N: 1, 2, 3, 4, 4.5, 4.7, 6 IE: 3, 4, 5, 5.5, Opera 4.02, WebTV	®	Registration mark
&macr;	N3, N4, N4.5, 4.7, 6 IE: 3, 4, 5, 5.5, Opera 4.02, WebTV	&#175;	N: 1, 3, 4, 4.5, 4.7, 6 IE: 3, 4, 5, 5.5, Opera 4.02, WebTV	¯	Macron

Named Entity	Browser Support	Numbered Entity	Browser Support	Intended Rendering	Description
&deg;	N3, N4, N4.5, 4.7, 6 IE: 3, 4, 5, 5.5, Opera 4.02, WebTV	&#176;	N: 1, 2, 3, 4, 4.5, 4.7, 6 IE: 3, 4, 5, 5.5, Opera 4.02, WebTV	°	Degree symbol
&plusmn;	N3, N4, N4.5, 4.7, 6 IE: 3, 4, 5, 5.5, Opera 4.02, WebTV	&#177;	N: 1, 2, 3, 4, 4.5, 4.7, 6 IE: 3, 4, 5, 5.5, Opera 4.02, WebTV	±	Plus/minus symbol
&sup2;	N3, N4, N4.5, 4.7, 6 IE: 3, 4, 5, 5.5, Opera 4.02, WebTV	&#178;	N: 1, 3, 4, 4.5, 4.7, 6 IE: 3, 4, 5, 5.5, Opera 4.02, WebTV	^{2}	Superscript 2
&sup3;	N3, N4, N4.5, 4.7, 6 IE: 3, 4, 5, 5.5, Opera 4.02, WebTV	&#179;	N: 1, 3, 4, 4.5, 4.7, 6 IE: 3, 4, 5, 5.5, Opera 4.02, WebTV	^{3}	Superscript 3
&acute;	N3, N4, N4.5, 4.7, 6 IE: 3, 4, 5, 5.5, Opera 4.02, WebTV	&#180;	N: 1, 3, 4, 4.5, 4.7, 6 IE: 3, 4, 5, 5.5, Opera 4.02, WebTV	´	Acute accent, no letter
&micro;	N3, N4, N4.5, 4.7, 6 IE: 3, 4, 5, 5.5, Opera 4.02, WebTV	&#181;	N: 1, 2, 3, 4, 4.5, 4.7, 6 IE: 3, 4, 5, 5.5, Opera 4.02, WebTV	µ	Micron
&para;	N3, N4, N4.5, 4.7, 6 IE: 3, 4, 5, 5.5, Opera 4.02, WebTV	&#182;	N: 1, 2, 3, 4, 4.5, 4.7, 6 IE: 3, 4, 5, 5.5, Opera 4.02, WebTV	¶	Paragraph symbol
&middot;	N3, N4, N4.5, 4.7, 6 IE: 3, 4, 5, 5.5, Opera 4.02, WebTV	&#183;	N: 1, 3, 4, 4.5, 4.7, 6 IE: 3, 4, 5, 5.5, Opera 4.02, WebTV	·	Middle dot
&cedil;	N3, N4, N4.5, 4.7, 6 IE: 3, 4, 5, 5.5, Opera 4.02, WebTV	&#184;	N: 1, 3, 4, 4.5, 4.7, 6 IE: 3, 4, 5, 5.5, Opera 4.02, WebTV	¸	Cedilla
&sup1;	N3, N4, N4.5, 4.7, 6 IE: 3, 4, 5, 5.5, Opera 4.02, WebTV	&#185;	N: 1, 3, 4, 4.5, 4.7, 6 IE: 3, 4, 5, 5.5, Opera 4.02, WebTV	^{1}	Superscript 1
&ordm;	N3, N4, N4.5, 4.7, 6 IE: 3, 4, 5, 5.5, Opera 4.02, WebTV	&#186;	N: 1, 3, 4, 4.5, 4.7, 6 IE: 3, 4, 5, 5.5, Opera 4.02, WebTV	º	Masculine ordinal indicator

Named Entity	Browser Support	Numbered Entity	Browser Support	Intended Rendering	Description
&raquo;	N3, N4, N4.5, 4.7, 6 IE: 3, 4, 5, 5.5, Opera 4.02, WebTV	&#187;	N: 1, 2, 3, 4, 4.5, 4.7, 6 IE: 3, 4, 5, 5.5, Opera 4.02, WebTV	»	Closing double-angle quotes
&frac14;	N3, N4, N4.5, 4.7, 6 IE: 3, 4, 5, 5.5, Opera 4.02, WebTV	&#188;	N: 1, 3, 4, 4.5, 4.7, 6 IE: 3, 4, 5, 5.5, Opera 4.02, WebTV	¼	One-quarter fraction
&frac12;	N3, N4, N4.5, 4.7, 6 IE: 3, 4, 5, 5.5, Opera 4.02, WebTV	&#189;	N: 1, 3, 4, 4.5, 4.7, 6 IE: 3, 4, 5, 5.5, Opera 4.02, WebTV	½	One-half fraction
&frac34;	N3, N4, N4.5, 4.7, 6 IE: 3, 4, 5, 5.5, Opera 4.02, WebTV	&#190;	N: 1, 3, 4, 4.5, 4.7, 6 IE: 3, 4, 5, 5.5, Opera 4.02, WebTV	¾	Three-fourths fraction
&iquest;	N3, N4, N4.5, 4.7, 6 IE: 3, 4, 5, 5.5, Opera 4.02, WebTV	&#191;	N: 1, 3, 4, 4.5, 4.7, 6 IE: 3, 4, 5, 5.5, Opera 4.02, WebTV	¿	Inverted question mark
&Agrave;	N: 1, 3, 4, 4.5, 4.7, 6 IE: 3, 4, 5, 5.5, Opera 4.02, WebTV	&#192;	N: 1, 3, 4, 4.5, 4.7, 6 IE: 3, 4, 5, 5.5, Opera 4.02, WebTV	À	Uppercase "A" with grave accent
&Aacute;	N: 1, 3, 4, 4.5, 4.7, 6 IE: 3, 4, 5, 5.5, Opera 4.02, WebTV	&#193;	N: 1, 3, 4, 4.5, 4.7, 6 IE: 3, 4, 5, 5.5, Opera 4.02, WebTV	Á	Uppercase "A" with acute accent
&Acirc;	N: 1, 3, 4, 4.5, 4.7, 6 IE: 3, 4, 5, 5.5, Opera 4.02, WebTV	&#194;	N: 1, 3, 4, 4.5, 4.7, 6 IE: 3, 4, 5, 5.5, Opera 4.02, WebTV	Â	Uppercase "A" with circumflex
&Atilde;	N: 1, 3, 4, 4.5, 4.7, 6 IE: 3, 4, 5, 5.5, Opera 4.02, WebTV	&#195;	N: 1, 3, 4, 4.5, 4.7, 6 IE: 3, 4, 5, 5.5, Opera 4.02, WebTV	Ã	Uppercase "A" with tilde
&Auml;	N: 1, 3, 4, 4.5, 4.7, 6 IE: 3, 4, 5, 5.5, Opera 4.02, WebTV	&#196;	N: 1, 3, 4, 4.5, 4.7, 6 IE: 3, 4, 5, 5.5, Opera 4.02, WebTV	Ä	Uppercase "A" with umlaut
&Aring;	N: 1, 3, 4, 4.5, 4.7, 6 IE: 3, 4, 5, 5.5, Opera 4.02, WebTV	&#197;	N: 1, 3, 4, 4.5, 4.7, 6 IE: 3, 4, 5, 5.5, Opera 4.02, WebTV	Å	Uppercase "A" with ring

Named Entity	Browser Support	Numbered Entity	Browser Support	Intended Rendering	Description
&AElig;	N: 1, 3, 4, 4.5, 4.7, 6 IE: 3, 4, 5, 5.5, Opera 4.02, WebTV	&#198;	N: 1, 3, 4, 4.5, 4.7, 6 IE: 3, 4, 5, 5.5, Opera 4.02, WebTV	Æ	Uppercase "AE" ligature
&Ccedil;	N: 1, 3, 4, 4.5, 4.7, 6 IE: 3, 4, 5, 5.5, Opera 4.02, WebTV	&#199;	N: 1, 3, 4, 4.5, 4.7, 6 IE: 3, 4, 5, 5.5, Opera 4.02, WebTV	Ç	Uppercase "C" with cedilla
&Egrave;	N: 1, 3, 4, 4.5, 4.7, 6 IE: 3, 4, 5, 5.5, Opera 4.02, WebTV	&#200;	N: 1, 3, 4, 4.5, 4.7, 6 IE: 3, 4, 5, 5.5, Opera 4.02, WebTV	È	Uppercase "E" with grave accent
&Eacute;	N: 1, 3, 4, 4.5, 4.7, 6 IE: 3, 4, 5, 5.5, Opera 4.02, WebTV	&#201;	N: 1, 3, 4, 4.5, 4.7, 6 IE: 3, 4, 5, 5.5, Opera 4.02, WebTV	É	Uppercase "E" with acute accent
&Ecirc;	N: 1, 3, 4, 4.5, 4.7, 6 IE: 3, 4, 5, 5.5, Opera 4.02, WebTV	&#202;	N: 1, 3, 4, 4.5, 4.7, 6 IE: 3, 4, 5, 5.5, Opera 4.02, WebTV	Ê	Uppercase "E" with circumflex
&Euml;	N: 1, 3, 4, 4.5, 4.7, 6 IE: 3, 4, 5, 5.5, Opera 4.02, WebTV	&#203;	N: 1, 3, 4, 4.5, 4.7, 6 IE: 3, 4, 5, 5.5, Opera 4.02, WebTV	Ë	Uppercase "E" with umlaut
&Igrave;	N: 1, 3, 4, 4.5, 4.7, 6 IE: 3, 4, 5, 5.5, Opera 4.02, WebTV	&#204;	N: 1, 3, 4, 4.5, 4.7, 6 IE: 3, 4, 5, 5.5, Opera 4.02, WebTV	Ì	Uppercase "I" with grave accent
&Iacute;	N: 1, 3, 4, 4.5, 4.7, 6 IE: 3, 4, 5, 5.5, Opera 4.02, WebTV	&#205;	N: 1, 3, 4, 4.5, 4.7, 6 IE: 3, 4, 5, 5.5, Opera 4.02, WebTV	Í	Uppercase "I" with acute accent
&Icirc;	N: 1, 3, 4, 4.5, 4.7, 6 IE: 3, 4, 5, 5.5, Opera 4.02, WebTV	&#206;	N: 1, 3, 4, 4.5, 4.7, 6 IE: 3, 4, 5, 5.5, Opera 4.02, WebTV	Î	Uppercase "I" with circumflex
&Iuml;	N: 1, 3, 4, 4.5, 4.7, 6 IE: 3, 4, 5, 5.5, Opera 4.02, WebTV	&#207;	N: 1, 3, 4, 4.5, 4.7, 6 IE: 3, 4, 5, 5.5, Opera 4.02, WebTV	Ï	Uppercase "I" with umlaut
&ETH;	N: 1, 3, 4, 4.5, 4.7, 6 IE: 3, 4, 5, 5.5, Opera 4.02, WebTV	&#208;	N: 1, 3, 4, 4.5, 4.7, 6 IE: 3, 4, 5, 5.5, Opera 4.02, WebTV	Ð	Capital "ETH"

Named Entity	Browser Support	Numbered Entity	Browser Support	Intended Rendering	Description
&Ntilde;	N: 1, 3, 4, 4.5, 4.7, 6 IE: 3, 4, 5, 5.5, Opera 4.02, WebTV	&#209;	N: 1, 3, 4, 4.5, 4.7, 6 IE: 3, 4, 5, 5.5, Opera 4.02, WebTV	Ñ	Uppercase "N" with tilde
&Ograve;	N: 1, 3, 4, 4.5, 4.7, 6 IE: 3, 4, 5, 5.5, Opera 4.02, WebTV	&#210;	N: 1, 3, 4, 4.5, 4.7, 6 IE: 3, 4, 5, 5.5, Opera 4.02, WebTV	Ò	Uppercase "O" with grave accent
&Oacute;	N: 1, 3, 4, 4.5, 4.7, 6 IE: 3, 4, 5, 5.5, Opera 4.02, WebTV	&#211;	N: 1, 3, 4, 4.5, 4.7, 6 IE: 3, 4, 5, 5.5, Opera 4.02, WebTV	Ó	Uppercase "O" with acute accent
&Ocirc;	N: 1, 3, 4, 4.5, 4.7, 6 IE: 3, 4, 5, 5.5, Opera 4.02, WebTV	&#212;	N: 1, 3, 4, 4.5, 4.7, 6 IE: 3, 4, 5, 5.5, Opera 4.02, WebTV	Ô	Uppercase "O" with circumflex
&Otilde;	N: 1, 3, 4, 4.5, 4.7, 6 IE: 3, 4, 5, 5.5, Opera 4.02, WebTV	&#213;	N: 1, 3, 4, 4.5, 4.7, 6 IE: 3, 4, 5, 5.5, Opera 4.02, WebTV	Õ	Uppercase "O" with tilde
&Ouml;	N: 1, 3, 4, 4.5, 4.7, 6 IE: 3, 4, 5, 5.5, Opera 4.02, WebTV	&#214;	N: 1, 3, 4, 4.5, 4.7, 6 IE: 3, 4, 5, 5.5, Opera 4.02, WebTV	Ö	Uppercase "O" with umlaut
&times;	N3, N4, N4.5, 4.7, 6 IE: 3, 4, 5, 5.5, Opera 4.02, WebTV	&#215;	N: 1, 3, 4, 4.5, 4.7, 6 IE: 3, 4, 5, 5.5, Opera 4.02, WebTV	×	Multiplication symbol
&Oslash;	N: 1, 3, 4, 4.5, 4.7, 6 IE: 3, 4, 5, 5.5, Opera 4.02, WebTV	&#216;	N: 1, 3, 4, 4.5, 4.7, 6 IE: 3, 4, 5, 5.5, Opera 4.02, WebTV	Ø	Uppercase "O" with slash
&Ugrave;	N: 1, 3, 4, 4.5, 4.7, 6 IE: 3, 4, 5, 5.5, Opera 4.02, WebTV	&#217;	N: 1, 3, 4, 4.5, 4.7, 6 IE: 3, 4, 5, 5.5, Opera 4.02, WebTV	Ù	Uppercase "U" with grave accent
&Uacute;	N: 1, 3, 4, 4.5, 4.7, 6 IE: 3, 4, 5, 5.5, Opera 4.02, WebTV	&#218;	N: 1, 3, 4, 4.5, 4.7, 6 IE: 3, 4, 5, 5.5, Opera 4.02, WebTV	Ú	Uppercase "U" with acute accent
&Ucirc;	N: 1, 3, 4, 4.5, 4.7, 6 IE: 3, 4, 5, 5.5, Opera 4.02, WebTV	&#219;	N: 1, 3, 4, 4.5, 4.7, 6 IE: 3, 4, 5, 5.5, Opera 4.02, WebTV	Û	Uppercase "U" with circumflex accent

Named Entity	Browser Support	Numbered Entity	Browser Support	Intended Rendering	Description
&Uuml;	N: 1, 3, 4, 4.5, 4.7, 6 IE: 3, 4, 5, 5.5, Opera 4.02, WebTV	&#220;	N: 1, 3, 4, 4.5, 4.7, 6 IE: 3, 4, 5, 5.5, Opera 4.02, WebTV	Ü	Uppercase "U" with umlaut
&Yacute;	N: 1, 3, 4, 4.5, 4.7, 6 IE: 3, 4, 5, 5.5, Opera 4.02, WebTV	&#221;	N: 1, 3, 4, 4.5, 4.7, 6 IE: 3, 4, 5, 5.5, Opera 4.02, WebTV	Ý	Uppercase "Y" with acute accent
&THORN;	N: 1, 3, 4, 4.5, 4.7, 6 IE: 3, 4, 5, 5.5, Opera 4.02, WebTV	&#222;	N: 1, 3, 4, 4.5, 4.7, 6 IE: 3, 4, 5, 5.5, Opera 4.02, WebTV	Þ	Capital "thorn"
&szlig;	N: 1, 3, 4, 4.5, 4.7, 6 IE: 3, 4, 5, 5.5, Opera 4.02, WebTV	&#223;	N: 1, 3, 4, 4.5, 4.7, 6 IE: 3, 4, 5, 5.5, Opera 4.02, WebTV	ß	"SZ" ligature
&agrave;	N: 1, 3, 4, 4.5, 4.7, 6 IE: 3, 4, 5, 5.5, Opera 4.02, WebTV	&#224;	N: 1, 3, 4, 4.5, 4.7, 6 IE: 3, 4, 5, 5.5, Opera 4.02, WebTV	à	Lowercase "a" with grave accent
&aacute;	N: 1, 3, 4, 4.5, 4.7, 6 IE: 3, 4, 5, 5.5, Opera 4.02, WebTV	&#225;	N: 1, 3, 4, 4.5, 4.7, 6 IE: 3, 4, 5, 5.5, Opera 4.02, WebTV	á	Lowercase "a" with acute accent
&acirc;	N: 1, 3, 4, 4.5, 4.7, 6 IE: 3, 4, 5, 5.5, Opera 4.02, WebTV	&#226;	N: 1, 3, 4, 4.5, 4.7, 6 IE: 3, 4, 5, 5.5, Opera 4.02, WebTV	â	Lowercase "a" with circumflex
&atilde;	N: 1, 3, 4, 4.5, 4.7, 6 IE: 3, 4, 5, 5.5, Opera 4.02, WebTV	&#227;	N: 1, 3, 4, 4.5, 4.7, 6 IE: 3, 4, 5, 5.5, Opera 4.02, WebTV	ã	Lowercase "a" with tilde
&auml;	N: 1, 3, 4, 4.5, 4.7, 6 IE: 3, 4, 5, 5.5, Opera 4.02, WebTV	&#228;	N: 1, 3, 4, 4.5, 4.7, 6 IE: 3, 4, 5, 5.5, Opera 4.02, WebTV	ä	Lowercase "a" with umlaut
&aring;	N: 1, 3, 4, 4.5, 4.7, 6 IE: 3, 4, 5, 5.5, Opera 4.02, WebTV	&#229;	N: 1, 3, 4, 4.5, 4.7, 6 IE: 3, 4, 5, 5.5, Opera 4.02, WebTV	å	Lowercase "a" with ring
&aelig;	N: 1, 3, 4, 4.5, 4.7, 6 IE: 3, 4, 5, 5.5, Opera 4.02, WebTV	&#230;	N: 1, 3, 4, 4.5, 4.7, 6 IE: 3, 4, 5, 5.5, Opera 4.02, WebTV	æ	Lowercase "ae" ligature

Named Entity	Browser Support	Numbered Entity	Browser Support	Intended Rendering	Description
&ccedil;	N: 1, 3, 4, 4.5, 4.7, 6 IE: 3, 4, 5, 5.5, Opera 4.02, WebTV	&#231;	N: 1, 3, 4, 4.5, 4.7, 6 IE: 3, 4, 5, 5.5, Opera 4.02, WebTV	ç	Lowercase "c" with cedilla
&egrave;	N: 1, 3, 4, 4.5, 4.7, 6 IE: 3, 4, 5, 5.5, Opera 4.02, WebTV	&#232;	N: 1, 3, 4, 4.5, 4.7, 6 IE: 3, 4, 5, 5.5, Opera 4.02, WebTV	è	Lowercase "e" with grave accent
&eacute;	N: 1, 3, 4, 4.5, 4.7, 6 IE: 3, 4, 5, 5.5, Opera 4.02, WebTV	&#233;	N: 1, 3, 4, 4.5, 4.7, 6 IE: 3, 4, 5, 5.5, Opera 4.02, WebTV	é	Lowercase "e" with acute accent
&ecirc;	N: 1, 3, 4, 4.5, 4.7, 6 IE: 3, 4, 5, 5.5, Opera 4.02, WebTV	&#234;	N: 1, 3, 4, 4.5, 4.7, 6 IE: 3, 4, 5, 5.5, Opera 4.02, WebTV	ê	Lowercase "e" with circumflex
&euml;	N: 1, 3, 4, 4.5, 4.7, 6 IE: 3, 4, 5, 5.5, Opera 4.02, WebTV	&#235;	N: 1, 3, 4, 4.5, 4.7, 6 IE: 3, 4, 5, 5.5, Opera 4.02, WebTV	ë	Lowercase "e" with umlaut
&igrave;	N: 1, 3, 4, 4.5, 4.7, 6 IE: 3, 4, 5, 5.5, Opera 4.02, WebTV	&#236;	N: 1, 3, 4, 4.5, 4.7, 6 IE: 3, 4, 5, 5.5, Opera 4.02, WebTV	ì	Lowercase "i" with grave accent
&iacute;	N: 1, 3, 4, 4.5, 4.7, 6 IE: 3, 4, 5, 5.5, Opera 4.02, WebTV	&#237;	N: 1, 3, 4, 4.5, 4.7, 6 IE: 3, 4, 5, 5.5, Opera 4.02, WebTV	í	Lowercase "i" with acute accent
&icirc;	N: 1, 3, 4, 4.5, 4.7, 6 IE: 3, 4, 5, 5.5, Opera 4.02, WebTV	&#238;	N: 1, 3, 4, 4.5, 4.7, 6 IE: 3, 4, 5, 5.5, Opera 4.02, WebTV	î	Lowercase "i" with circumflex
&iuml;	N: 1, 3, 4, 4.5, 4.7, 6 IE: 3, 4, 5, 5.5, Opera 4.02, WebTV	&#239;	N: 1, 3, 4, 4.5, 4.7, 6 IE: 3, 4, 5, 5.5, Opera 4.02, WebTV	ï	Lowercase "i" with umlaut
&eth;	N: 1, 3, 4, 4.5, 4.7, 6 IE: 3, 4, 5, 5.5, Opera 4.02, WebTV	&#240;	N: 1, 3, 4, 4.5, 4.7, 6 IE: 3, 4, 5, 5.5, Opera 4.02, WebTV	ð	Lowercase "eth"
&ntilde;	N: 1, 3, 4, 4.5, 4.7, 6 IE: 3, 4, 5, 5.5, Opera 4.02, WebTV	&#241;	N: 1, 3, 4, 4.5, 4.7, 6 IE: 3, 4, 5, 5.5, Opera 4.02, WebTV	ñ	Lowercase "n" with tilde

APPENDIX C

Named Entity	Browser Support	Numbered Entity	Browser Support	Intended Rendering	Description
&ograve;	N: 1, 3, 4, 4.5, 4.7, 6 IE: 3, 4, 5, 5.5, Opera 4.02, WebTV	&#242;	N: 1, 3, 4, 4.5, 4.7, 6 IE: 3, 4, 5, 5.5, Opera 4.02, WebTV	ò	Lowercase "o" with grave accent
&oacute;	N: 1, 3, 4, 4.5, 4.7, 6 IE: 3, 4, 5, 5.5, Opera 4.02, WebTV	&#243;	N: 1, 3, 4, 4.5, 4.7, 6 IE: 3, 4, 5, 5.5, Opera 4.02, WebTV	ó	Lowercase "o" with acute accent
&ocirc;	N: 1, 3, 4, 4.5, 4.7, 6 IE: 3, 4, 5, 5.5, Opera 4.02, WebTV	&#244;	N: 1, 3, 4, 4.5, 4.7, 6 IE: 3, 4, 5, 5.5, Opera 4.02, WebTV	ô	Lowercase "o" with circumflex accent
&otilde;	N: 1, 3, 4, 4.5, 4.7, 6 IE: 3, 4, 5, 5.5, Opera 4.02, WebTV	&#245;	N: 1, 3, 4, 4.5, 4.7, 6 IE: 3, 4, 5, 5.5, Opera 4.02, WebTV	õ	Lowercase "o" with tilde
&ouml;	N: 1, 3, 4, 4.5, 4.7, 6 IE: 3, 4, 5, 5.5, Opera 4.02, WebTV	&#246;	N: 1, 3, 4, 4.5, 4.7, 6 IE: 3, 4, 5, 5.5, Opera 4.02, WebTV	ö	Lowercase "o" with umlaut
&divide;	N3, N4, N4.5, 4.7, 6 IE: 3, 4, 5, 5.5, Opera 4.02, WebTV	&#247;	N: 1, 3, 4, 4.5, 4.7, 6 IE: 3, 4, 5, 5.5, Opera 4.02, WebTV	÷	Division symbol
&oslash;	N: 1, 3, 4, 4.5, 4.7, 6 IE: 3, 4, 5, 5.5, Opera 4.02, WebTV	&#248;	N: 1, 3, 4, 4.5, 4.7, 6 IE: 3, 4, 5, 5.5, Opera 4.02, WebTV	ø	Lowercase "o" with slash
&ugrave;	N: 1, 3, 4, 4.5, 4.7, 6 IE: 3, 4, 5, 5.5, Opera 4.02, WebTV	&#249;	N: 1, 3, 4, 4.5, 4.7, 6 IE: 3, 4, 5, 5.5, Opera 4.02, WebTV	ù	Lowercase "u" with grave accent
&uacute;	N: 1, 3, 4, 4.5, 4.7, 6 IE: 3, 4, 5, 5.5, Opera 4.02, WebTV	&#250;	N: 1, 3, 4, 4.5, 4.7, 6 IE: 3, 4, 5, 5.5, Opera 4.02, WebTV	ú	Lowercase "u" with acute accent
&ucirc;	N: 1, 3, 4, 4.5, 4.7, 6 IE: 3, 4, 5, 5.5, Opera 4.02, WebTV	&#251;	N: 1, 3, 4, 4.5, 4.7, 6 IE: 3, 4, 5, 5.5, Opera 4.02, WebTV	û	Lowercase "u" with circumflex
&uuml;	N: 1, 3, 4, 4.5, 4.7, 6 IE: 3, 4, 5, 5.5, Opera 4.02, WebTV	&#252;	N: 1, 3, 4, 4.5, 4.7, 6 IE: 3, 4, 5, 5.5, Opera 4.02, WebTV	ü	Lowercase "u" with umlaut

Named Entity	Browser Support	Numbered Entity	Browser Support	Intended Rendering	Description
&yacute;	N: 1, 3, 4, 4.5, 4.7, 6 IE: 3, 4, 5, 5.5, Opera 4.02, WebTV	&#253;	N: 1, 3, 4, 4.5, 4.7, 6 IE: 3, 4, 5, 5.5, Opera 4.02, WebTV	ý	Lowercase "y" with acute accent
&thorn;	N: 1, 3, 4, 4.5, 4.7, 6 IE: 3, 4, 5, 5.5, Opera 4.02, WebTV	&#254;	N: 1, 3, 4, 4.5, 4.7, 6 IE: 3, 4, 5, 5.5, Opera 4.02, WebTV	þ	Lowercase "thorn"
&yuml;	N: 1, 3, 4, 4.5, 4.7, 6 IE: 3, 4, 5, 5.5, Opera 4.02, WebTV	&#255;	N: 1, 3, 4, 4.5, 4.7, 6 IE: 3, 4, 5, 5.5, Opera 4.02, WebTV	ÿ	Lowercase "y" with umlaut

---

* WebTV renders € as a right-pointing arrowhead.
† WebTV renders  as a left-pointing arrowhead.
‡ Support for ™(™) is inconsistent across platforms, although this has improved much in more recent browsers. Designers concerned with backward compatibility might want to consider using a workaround such as **^{<small>TM</small>}**.

HTML 4.0 Character Entities

The HTML 4.0 specification introduced a wide array of new character entities that expand the presentation possibilities of HTML, particularly in the presentation of foreign languages. These include additional Latin characters, the Greek alphabet, special spacing characters, arrows, technical symbols, and various shapes. Some of these entities have yet to be supported by browser vendors. Netscape versions 4.0 through 4.73 support only a few of the extended Latin characters, and some entities that duplicate characters already are available in the "standard" list (32 through 255). Internet Explorer versions 4.0 and higher support many of these entities, including the Greek alphabet and mathematical symbols. Testing in early releases of Netscape 6 shows that Netscape has finally addressed the shortcomings of their earlier browsers.

Latin Extended-A

Named Entity	Browser Support	Numbered Entity	Browser Support	Intended Rendering	Description
&Oelig;	IE: 4, 5, 5.5 N: 6	&#338;	IE: 4, 5, 5.5, N: 4, 4.5, 4.7, 6	Œ	Uppercase ligature "OE"
&oelig;	IE: 4, 5, 5.5 N: 6	&#339;	IE: 4, 5, 5.5, N: 4, 4.5, 4.7, 6	œ	Lowercase ligature "oe"
&Scaron;	IE: 4, 5, 5.5 N: 6	&#352;	IE: 4, 5, 5.5, N: 4, 4.5, 4.7, 6	Š	Uppercase "S" with caron

Named Entity	Browser Support	Numbered Entity	Browser Support	Intended Rendering	Description
&scaron;	IE: 4, 5, 5.5 N: 6	&#353;	IE: 4, 5, 5.5, N: 4, 4.5, 4.7, 6	š	Lowercase "s" with caron
&Yuml;	IE: 4, 5, 5.5 N: 6	&#376;	IE: 4, 5, 5.5, N: 4, 4.5, 4.7, 6	Ÿ	Uppercase "Y" with umlaut

Internet Explorer 5 for Macintosh displays Š, Š, š and š with the caron shifted one space to the left of the "s" or "S" character it should be over.

Latin Extended-B

Named Entity	Browser Support	Numbered Entity	Browser Support	Intended Rendering	Description
&fnof;	IE: 4, 5, 5.5 N: 6	&#402;	IE: 4, 5, 5.5, N:4, 4.5, 4.7, 6	ƒ	Latin small "f" with hook

Spacing Modifier Letters

Named Entity	Browser Support	Numbered Entity	Browser Support	Intended Rendering	Description
&circ;	IE: 4, 5, 5.5 N: 6, O: 4	&#710;	IE: 4, 5, 5.5, N: 4, 4.5, 4.7, 6, O: 4	^	Circumflex accent
&tilde;	IE: 4, 5, 5.5 N: 6, O: 4	&#732;	IE: 4, 5, 5.5, N: 4, 4.5, 4.7, 6, O: 4	~	Small tilde

General Punctuation

Named Entity	Browser Support	Numbered Entity	Browser Support	Intended Rendering	Description
	N: 6		N: 6		En space
	N: 6		N: 6		Em space
	N: 6		N: 6		Thin space
&zwnj;	IE: 4, 5, 5.5	&#8204;	IE: 4, 5, 5.5			Zero width nonjoiner
&zwj;	IE: 4, 5, 5.5	&#8205;	IE: 4, 5, 5.5	Ⴗ	Zero width joiner

Named Entity	Browser Support	Numbered Entity	Browser Support	Intended Rendering	Description
&lrm;	None	&#8206;	None	Unknown	Left-to-right mark
&rlm;	None	&#8207;	None	Unknown	Right-to-left mark
&ndash;	IE: 4, 5, 5.5 N: 6	&#8211;	IE: 4, 5, 5.5, N: 4, 4.5, 4.7, 6	–	En dash
&mdash;	IE: 4, 5, 5.5 N: 6	&#8212;	IE: 4, 5, 5.5, N: 4, 4.5, 4.7, 6	—	Em dash
&lsquo;	IE: 4, 5, 5.5 N: 6	&#8216;	IE: 4, 5, 5.5, N: 4, 4.5, 4.7, 6	'	Left single quotation mark
&rsquo;	IE: 4, 5, 5.5 N: 6	&#8217;	IE: 4, 5, 5.5, N: 4, 4.5, 4.7, 6	'	Right single quotation mark
&sbquo;	IE: 4, 5, 5.5 N: 6	&#8218;	IE: 4, 5, 5.5, N: 4, 4.5, 4.7, 6	‚	Single low-9 quotation mark
&ldquo;	IE: 4, 5, 5.5 N: 6	&#8220;	IE: 4, 5, 5.5, N: 4, 4.5, 4.7, 6	"	Left double quotation mark
&rdquo;	IE: 4, 5, 5.5 N: 6	&#8221;	IE: 4, 5, 5.5, N: 4, 4.5, 4.7, 6	"	Right double quotation mark
&bdquo;	IE: 4, 5, 5.5 N: 6	&#8222;	IE: 4, 5, 5.5, N: 4, 4.5, 4.7, 6	„	Double low-9 quotation mark
&dagger;	IE: 4, 5, 5.5 N: 6	&#8224;	IE: 4, 5, 5.5, N: 4, 4.5, 4.7, 6	†	Dagger
&Dagger;	IE: 4, 5, 5.5 N: 6	&#8225;	IE: 4, 5, 5.5, N: 4, 4.5, 4.7, 6	‡	Double dagger
&bull;	IE: 4, 5, 5.5 N: 6	&#8226;	IE: 4, 5, 5.5, N: 4, 4.5, 4.7, 6	•	Bullet
&hellip;	IE: 4, 5, 5.5 N: 6	&#8230;	IE: 4, 5, 5.5, N: 4, 4.5, 4.7, 6	…	Horizontal ellipsis
&permil;	IE: 4, 5, 5.5 N: 6	&#8240;	IE: 4, 5, 5.5, N: 4, 4.5, 4.7, 6	‰	Per thousand sign
&prime;	IE: 4, 5, 5.5 N: 6	&#8242;	IE: 4, 5, 5.5 N: 6	′	Prime, minutes, or feet
&Prime;	IE: 4, 5, 5.5 N: 6	&#8243;	IE: 4, 5, 5.5 N: 6	″	Double prime, seconds, or inches
&lsaquo;	IE: 4, 5, 5.5 N: 6, O: 4	&#8249;	IE: 4, 5, 5.5, N: 4, 4.5, 4.7, 6, O: 4	‹	Single left-pointing angle quotation mark

Named Entity	Browser Support	Numbered Entity	Browser Support	Intended Rendering	Description
&rsaquo;	IE: 4, 5, 5.5 N: 6, O: 4	&#8250;	IE: 4, 5, 5.5, N: 4, 4.5, 4.7, 6, O: 4	>	Single right-pointing angle quotation mark
&oline;	IE: 4, 5, 5.5 N: 6	&#8254;	IE: 4, 5, 5.5 N: 6	‾	Overline
&frasl;	IE: 4, 5, 5.5 N: 6, O: 4	&#8260;	IE: 4, 5, 5.5 N: 6, O: 4	/	Fraction slash

Greek

Named Entity	Browser Support	Numbered Entity	Browser Support	Intended Rendering	Description
&Alpha;	IE: 4, 5, 5.5 N: 6	&#913;	IE: 4, 5, 5.5 N: 6	A	Greek capital letter alpha
&Beta;	IE: 4, 5, 5.5 N: 6	&#914;	IE: 4, 5, 5.5 N: 6	B	Greek capital letter beta
&Gamma;	IE: 4, 5, 5.5 N: 6	&#915;	IE: 4, 5, 5.5 N: 6	Γ	Greek capital letter gamma
&Delta;	IE: 4, 5, 5.5 N: 6	&#916;	IE: 4, 5, 5.5 N: 6	Δ	Greek capital letter delta
&Epsilon;	IE: 4, 5, 5.5 N: 6	&#917;	IE: 4, 5, 5.5 N: 6	E	Greek capital letter epsilon
&Zeta;	IE: 4, 5, 5.5 N: 6	&#918;	IE: 4, 5, 5.5 N: 6	Z	Greek capital letter zeta
&Eta;	IE: 4, 5, 5.5 N: 6	&#919;	IE: 4, 5, 5.5 N: 6	H	Greek capital letter eta
&Theta;	IE: 4, 5, 5.5 N: 6	&#920;	IE: 4, 5, 5.5 N: 6	Θ	Greek capital letter theta
&Iota;	IE: 4, 5, 5.5 N: 6	&#921;	IE: 4, 5, 5.5 N: 6	I	Greek capital letter iota
&Kappa;	IE: 4, 5, 5.5 N: 6	&#922;	IE: 4, 5, 5.5 N: 6	K	Greek capital letter kappa
&Lambda;	IE: 4, 5, 5.5 N: 6	&#923;	IE: 4, 5, 5.5 N: 6	Λ	Greek capital letter lambda
&Mu;	IE: 4, 5, 5.5 N: 6	&#924;	IE: 4, 5, 5.5 N: 6	M	Greek capital letter mu
&Nu;	IE: 4, 5, 5.5 N: 6	&#925;	IE: 4, 5, 5.5 N: 6	N	Greek capital letter nu

Named Entity	Browser Support	Numbered Entity	Browser Support	Intended Rendering	Description
&Xi;	IE: 4, 5, 5.5 N: 6	&#926;	IE: 4, 5, 5.5 N: 6	Ξ	Greek capital letter xi
&Omicron;	IE: 4, 5, 5.5 N: 6	&#927;	IE: 4, 5, 5.5 N: 6	O	Greek capital letter omicron
&Pi;	IE: 4, 5, 5.5 N: 6	&#928;	IE: 4, 5, 5.5 N: 6	Π	Greek capital letter pi
&Rho;	IE: 4, 5, 5.5 N: 6	&#929;	IE: 4, 5, 5.5 N: 6	P	Greek capital letter rho
&Sigma;	IE: 4, 5, 5.5 N: 6	&#931;	IE: 4, 5, 5.5 N: 6	Σ	Greek capital letter sigma
&Tau;	IE: 4, 5, 5.5 N: 6	&#932;	IE: 4, 5, 5.5 N: 6	T	Greek capital letter tau
&Upsilon;	IE: 4, 5, 5.5 N: 6	&#933;	IE: 4, 5, 5.5 N: 6	Y	Greek capital letter upsilon
&Phi;	IE: 4, 5, 5.5 N: 6	&#934;	IE: 4, 5, 5.5 N: 6	Φ	Greek capital letter phi
&Chi;	IE: 4, 5, 5.5 N: 6	&#935;	IE: 4, 5, 5.5 N: 6	X	Greek capital letter chi
&Psi;	IE: 4, 5, 5.5 N: 6	&#936;	IE: 4, 5, 5.5 N: 6	Ψ	Greek capital letter psi
&Omega;	IE: 4, 5, 5.5 N: 6	&#937;	IE: 4, 5, 5.5 N: 6	Ω	Greek capital letter omega
&alpha;	IE: 4, 5, 5.5 N: 6	&#945;	IE: 4, 5, 5.5 N: 6	α	Greek small letter alpha
&beta;	IE: 4, 5, 5.5 N: 6	&#946;	IE: 4, 5, 5.5 N: 6	β	Greek small letter beta
&gamma;	IE: 4, 5, 5.5 N: 6	&#947;	IE: 4, 5, 5.5 N: 6	γ	Greek small letter gamma
&delta;	IE: 4, 5, 5.5 N: 6	&#948;	IE: 4, 5, 5.5 N: 6	δ	Greek small letter delta
&epsilon;	IE: 4, 5, 5.5 N: 6	&#949;	IE: 4, 5, 5.5 N: 6	ε	Greek small letter epsilon
&zeta;	IE: 4, 5, 5.5 N: 6	&#950;	IE: 4, 5, 5.5 N: 6	ζ	Greek small letter zeta
&eta;	IE: 4, 5, 5.5 N: 6	&#951;	IE: 4, 5, 5.5 N: 6	η	Greek small letter eta
&theta;	IE: 4, 5, 5.5 N: 6	&#952;	IE: 4, 5, 5.5 N: 6	θ	Greek small letter theta
&iota;	IE: 4, 5, 5.5 N: 6	&#953;	IE: 4, 5, 5.5 N: 6	ι	Greek small letter iota

Named Entity	Browser Support	Numbered Entity	Browser Support	Intended Rendering	Description
&kappa;	IE: 4, 5, 5.5 N: 6	&#954;	IE: 4, 5, 5.5 N: 6	κ	Greek small letter kappa
&lambda;	IE: 4, 5, 5.5 N: 6	&#955;	IE: 4, 5, 5.5 N: 6	λ	Greek small letter lambda
&mu;	IE: 4, 5, 5.5 N: 6	&#956;	IE: 4, 5, 5.5 N: 6	μ	Greek small letter mu
&nu;	IE: 4, 5, 5.5 N: 6	&#957;	IE: 4, 5, 5.5 N: 6	ν	Greek small letter nu
&xi;	IE: 4, 5, 5.5 N: 6	&#958;	IE: 4, 5, 5.5 N: 6	ξ	Greek small letter xi
&omicron;	IE: 4, 5, 5.5 N: 6	&#959;	IE: 4, 5, 5.5 N: 6	o	Greek small letter omicron
&pi;	IE: 4, 5, 5.5 N: 6	&#960;	IE: 4, 5, 5.5 N: 6	π	Greek small letter pi
&rho;	IE: 4, 5, 5.5 N: 6	&#961;	IE: 4, 5, 5.5 N: 6	ρ	Greek small letter rho
&sigmaf;	IE: 4, 5, 5.5 N: 6	&#962;	IE: 4, 5, 5.5 N: 6	ς	Greek small letter final sigma
&sigma;	IE: 4, 5, 5.5 N: 6	&#963;	IE: 4, 5, 5.5 N: 6	σ	Greek small letter sigma
&tau;	IE: 4, 5, 5.5 N: 6	&#964;	IE: 4, 5, 5.5 N: 6	τ	Greek small letter tau
&upsilon;	IE: 4, 5, 5.5 N: 6	&#965;	IE: 4, 5, 5.5 N: 6	υ	Greek small letter upsilon
&phi;	IE: 4, 5, 5.5 N: 6	&#966;	IE: 4, 5, 5.5 N: 6	φ	Greek small letter phi
&chi;	IE: 4, 5, 5.5 N: 6	&#967;	IE: 4, 5, 5.5 N: 6	χ	Greek small letter chi
&psi;	IE: 4, 5, 5.5 N: 6	&#968;	IE: 4, 5, 5.5 N: 6	ψ	Greek small letter psi
&omega;	IE: 4, 5, 5.5 N: 6	&#969;	IE: 4, 5, 5.5 N: 6	ω	Greek small letter omega
&thetasym;	IE: 5 (Mac only), N: 6	&#977;	IE: 5 (Mac only), N: 6	ϑ	Greek small letter theta symbol
&upsih;	IE: 5 (Mac only), N: 6	&#978;	IE: 5 (Mac only), N: 6	ϒ	Greek upsilon with hook symbol

Named Entity	Browser Support	Numbered Entity	Browser Support	Intended Rendering	Description
&piv	IE: 5 (Mac only), N: 6	&#982;	IE: 5 (Mac only), N: 6	ϖ	Greek pi symbol

Letter-like Symbols

Named Entity	Browser Support	Numbered Entity	Browser Support	Intended Rendering	Description
&weierp;	N: 6	&#8472;	N: 6	℘	Script capital P, power set
&image;	N: 6	&#8465;	N: 6	ℑ	Blackletter capital I, or imaginary part symbol
&real;	N: 6	&#8476;	N: 6	ℜ	Blackletter capital R, or real part symbol
&trade;	IE: 3, 4, 5, 5.5 N: 6, O: 4	&#8482;	IE: 4, 5, 5.5, N: 4, 4.5, 4.7, 6, O: 4	™	Trademark symbol
&alefsym;	N: 6	&#8501;	N: 6	ℵ	Alef symbol, or first transfinite cardinal

Arrows

Named Entity	Browser Support	Numbered Entity	Browser Support	Intended Rendering	Description
&larr;	IE: 4, 5, 5.5 N: 6	&#8592;	IE: 4, 5, 5.5 N: 6	←	Leftward arrow
&uarr;	IE: 4, 5, 5.5 N: 6	&#8593;	IE: 4, 5, 5.5 N: 6	↑	Upward arrow
&rarr;	IE: 4, 5, 5.5 N: 6	&#8594;	IE: 4, 5, 5.5 N: 6	→	Rightward arrow
&darr;	IE: 4, 5, 5.5 N: 6	&#8595;	IE: 4, 5, 5.5 N: 6	↓	Downward arrow
&harr;	IE: 4, 5, 5.5 N: 6	&#8596;	IE: 4, 5, 5.5 N: 6	↔	Left-right arrow
&crarr;	N: 6	&#8629;	N: 6	↵	Downward arrow with corner leftward

Named Entity	Browser Support	Numbered Entity	Browser Support	Intended Rendering	Description
&lArr;	N: 6	&#8656;	N: 6	⇐	Leftward double arrow
&uArr;	N: 6	&#8657;	N: 6	⇑	Upward double arrow
&rArr;	N: 6	&#8658;	N: 6	⇒	Rightward double arrow
&dArr;	N: 6	&#8659;	N: 6	⇓	Downward double arrow
&hArr;	N: 6	&#8660;	N: 6	⇔	Left-right double arrow

Mathematical Operators

Named Entity	Browser Support	Numbered Entity	Browser Support	Intended Rendering	Description
&forall;	N: 6	&#8704;	N: 6	∀	For all
&part;	IE: 4, 5, 5.5 N: 6	&#8706;	IE: 4, 5, 5.5 N: 6	∂	Partial differential
&exist;	N: 6	&#8707;	N: 6	∃	There exists
&empty;	N: 6	&#8709;	N: 6	∅	Empty set, null set, diameter
&nabla;	N: 6	&#8711;	N: 6	∇	Nabla, or backward difference
&isin;	N: 6	&#8712;	N: 6	∈	Element of
&notin;	N: 6	&#8713;	N: 6	∉	Not an element of
&ni;	N: 6	&#8715;	N: 6	∋	Contains as member
&prod;	IE: 4, 5, 5.5 N: 6	&#8719;	IE: 4, 5, 5.5 N: 6	∏	N-ary product, or product sign
&sum;	IE: 4, 5, 5.5 N: 6	&#8721;	IE: 4, 5, 5.5 N: 6	∑	N-ary summation
&minus;	IE: 4, 5, 5.5 N: 6 O: 4	&#8722;	IE: 4, 5, 5.5 N: 6 O: 4	−	Minus sign
&lowast;	N: 6	&#8727;	N: 6	∗	Asterisk operator
&radic;	IE: 4, 5, 5.5 N: 6	&#8730;	IE: 4, 5, 5.5 N: 6	√	Square root, radical sign
&prop;	N: 6	&#8733;	N: 6	∝	Proportional to

Named Entity	Browser Support	Numbered Entity	Browser Support	Intended Rendering	Description
&infin;	IE: 4, 5, 5.5 N: 6	&#8734;	IE: 4, 5, 5.5 N: 6	∞	Infinity
&ang;	N: 6	&#8736;	N: 6	∠	Angle
&and;	N: 6	&#8869;	N: 6	⊥	Logical and
&or;	N: 6	&#8870;	N: 6	⊢	Logical or
&cap;	IE: 4, 5, 5.5 N: 6	&#8745;	IE: 4, 5, 5.5 N: 6	∩	Intersection, cap
&cup;	N: 6	&#8746;	N: 6	∪	Union, cup
&int;	IE: 4, 5, 5.5 N: 6	&#8747;	IE: 4, 5, 5.5 N: 6	∫	Integral
&there4;	N: 6	&#8756;	N: 6	∴	Therefore
&sim;	N: 6	&#8764;	N: 6	~	Tilde operator
&cong;	N: 6	&#8773;	N: 6	≅	Approximately equal to
&asymp;	IE: 4, 5, 5.5 N: 6	&#8776;	IE: 4, 5, 5.5 N: 6	≈	Almost equal to, asymptotic to
&ne;	IE: 4, 5, 5.5 N: 6	&#8800;	IE: 4, 5, 5.5 N: 6	≠	Not equal to
&equiv;	IE: 4, 5, 5.5 N: 6	&#8801;	IE: 4, 5, 5.5 N: 6	≡	Identical to
&le;	IE: 4, 5, 5.5 N: 6	&#8804;	IE: 4, 5, 5.5 N: 6	≤	Less than or equal to
&ge;	IE: 4, 5, 5.5 N: 6	&#8805;	IE: 4, 5, 5.5 N: 6	≥	Greater than or equal to
&sub;	N: 6	&#8834;	N: 6	⊂	Subset of
&sup;	N: 6	&#8835;	N: 6	⊃	Superset of
&nsub;	N: 6	&#8836;	N: 6	⊄	Not a subset of
&sube;	N: 6	&#8838;	N: 6	⊆	Subset of or equal to
&supe;	N: 6	&#8839;	N: 6	⊇	Superset of or equal to
&oplus;	N: 6	&#8853;	N: 6	⊕	Circled plus, direct sum
&otimes;	N: 6	&#8855;	N: 6	⊗	Circled times, vector product
&perp;	N: 6	&#8869;	N: 6	⊥	Perpendicular
&sdot;	N: 6	&#8901;	N: 6	·	Dot operator

Technical Symbols

Named Entity	Browser Support	Numbered Entity	Browser Support	Intended Rendering	Description
&lceil;	N: 6	&#8968;	N: 6	⌈	Left ceiling
&rceil;	N: 6	&#8969;	N: 6	⌉	Right ceiling
&lfloor;	N: 6	&#8970;	N: 6	⌊	Left floor
&rfloor;	N: 6	&#8971;	N: 6	⌋	Right floor
&lang;	None	&#9001;	None	<	Left-pointing angle bracket
&rang;	None	&#9002;	None	>	Right-pointing angle bracket

Geometric Shapes

Named Entity	Browser Support	Numbered Entity	Browser Support	Intended Rendering	Description
&loz;	IE: 4, 5, 5.5 N: 6	&#9674;	IE: 4, 5, 5.5 N: 6	◊	Lozenge

Miscellaneous Symbols

Named Entity	Browser Support	Numbered Entity	Browser Support	Intended Rendering	Description
&spades;	IE: 4, 5, 5.5 N: 6	&#9824;	IE: 4, 5, 5.5 N: 6	♠	Spade suit
&clubs;	IE: 4, 5, 5.5 N: 6	&#9827;	IE: 4, 5, 5.5 N: 6	♣	Club suit
&hearts;	IE: 4, 5, 5.5 N: 6	&#9829;	IE: 4, 5, 5.5 N: 6	♥	Heart suit
&diams;	IE: 4, 5, 5.5 N: 6	&#9830;	IE: 4, 5, 5.5 N: 6	♦	Diamond suit

The
Complete
Reference

Appendix D

Fonts

This appendix lists fonts commonly available on most systems, as well as those that come with Internet Explorer. While other fonts may be available on users' systems, it is advisable to limit font choices to those most likely to be in use or to provide these as alternative fonts (as discussed in Chapter 6) in case a preferred but uncommon font is not available.

Fonts for Microsoft Platforms and Browsers

The following fonts are available for Microsoft browsers and systems, and they are displayed in Figure D-1.

Font	Systems
Arial	Windows 95, Windows 2000, Windows 3.1x, Windows NT 3.x, 4.0
Arial Black	Internet Explorer 3
Arial Bold	Windows 95, Windows 2000, Windows 3.1x, Windows NT 3.x, 4.0
Arial Italic	Windows 95, Windows 2000, Windows 3.1x, Windows NT 3.x, 4.0
Arial Bold Italic	Windows 95, Windows 2000, Windows 3.1x, Windows NT 3.x, 4.0
Comic Sans MS	Internet Explorer 3, Internet Explorer 4
Comic Sans MS Bold	Internet Explorer 3
Courier New	Windows 95, Windows 2000, Windows 3.1x, Windows NT 3.x, 4.0
Courier New Bold	Windows 95, Windows 2000, Windows 3.1x, Windows NT 3.x, 4.0
Courier New Italic	Windows 95, Windows 2000, Windows 3.1x, Windows NT 3.x, 4.0
Courier New Bold Italic	Windows 95, Windows 2000, Windows 3.1x, Windows NT 3.x, 4.0
Impact	Internet Explorer 3
Lucida Sans Unicode	Windows NT 3.x (except NT 3.0), 4.0
Lucida Console	Windows NT 3.x (except NT 3.0), 4.0
Marlett	Windows 95, Windows 2000
Symbol	Windows 95, Windows 2000, Windows 3.1x, Windows NT 3.x, 4.0
Times New Roman	Windows 95, Windows 2000, Windows 3.1x, Windows NT 3.x
Times New Roman Bold	Windows 95, Windows 2000, Windows 3.1x, Windows NT 3.x, 4.0
Times New Roman Italic	Windows 95, Windows 2000, Windows 3.1x, Windows NT 3.x, 4.0
Times New Roman Bold Italic	Windows 95, Windows 2000, Windows 3.1x, Windows NT 3.x, 4.0
Verdana	Internet Explorer 3, Internet Explorer 4
Verdana Bold	Internet Explorer 3, Internet Explorer 4
Verdana Italic	Internet Explorer 3, Internet Explorer 4
Verdana Bold Italic	Internet Explorer 3, Internet Explorer 4
Webdings	Internet Explorer 4.0
Wingdings	Windows 95, Windows 2000, Windows 3.1x, Windows NT 3.x, 4.0

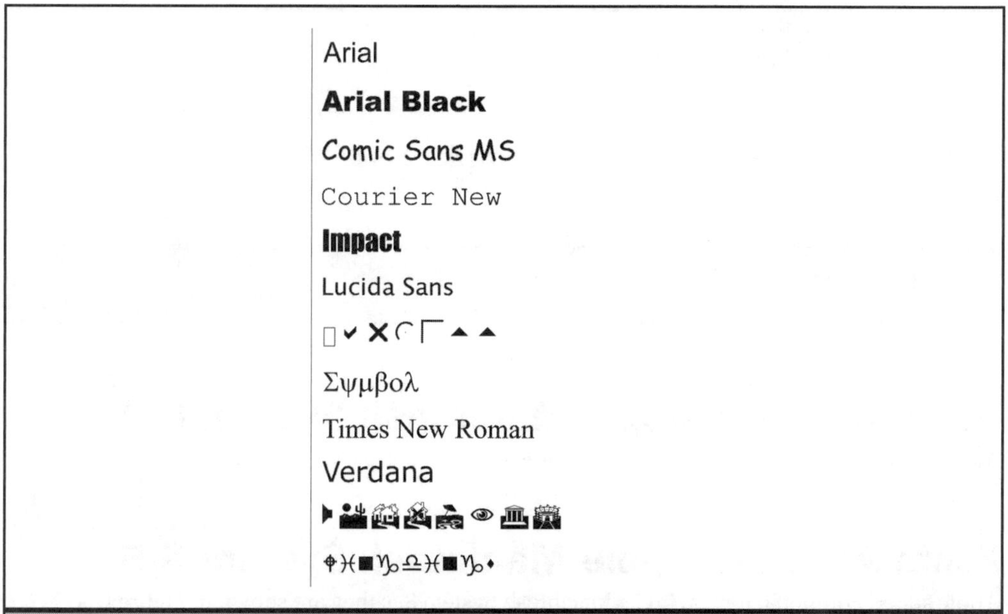

Arial

Arial Black

Comic Sans MS

Courier New

Impact

Lucida Sans

□ ✔ ✗ ⊂ ⌐ ▲ ▲

Σψμβολ

Times New Roman

Verdana

▶ ▦ ▦ ▦ ▦ ◉ ▥ ▦

Φ ⌇ ■ ℣ Ω ⌇ ■ ℣ ◆

Figure D-1.   *Font families available for Microsoft browsers and systems*

Fonts for Apple Macintosh System 7

The fonts for Macintosh System 7 are displayed in Figure D-2.

Chicago

Courier Regular

Geneva

Helvetica

Monaco

New York

Palatino

Σψμβολ

Times

Figure D-2.   *Font families available with Macintosh System 7*

Apple Chancery

Hoefler Text

⚜❀❁❂❃❄❅❆❇ (Hoefler Text Ornaments)

Skia

Figure D-3. *Additional font families available with Macintosh System 8*

Fonts Added to Apple Macintosh System 8.0

Apple added additional fonts with its Macintosh System 8; they are shown in Figure D-3.

Fonts Added to Apple Macintosh System 8.5

Apple added additional fonts with its Macintosh System 8.5; they are shown in Figure D-4

Microsoft Fonts for Macintosh Internet Explorer

Microsoft has made a number of its fonts available with the Macintosh versions of Internet Explorer 4.5 and 5. They are shown in Figure D-5.

Fonts for Unix Systems

The fonts available for Unix systems are displayed in Figure D-6.

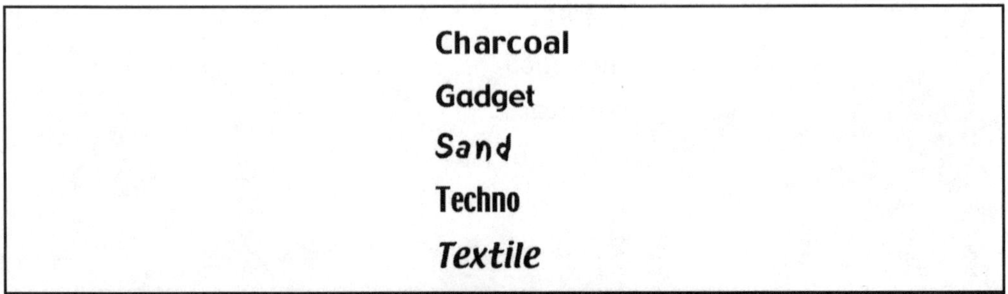

Charcoal

Gadget

Sand

Techno

Textile

Figure D-4. *Additional font families available with Macintosh System 8.5*

Andale Mono

Arial

Arial Black

Comic Sans MS

Courier New

Georgia

Impact

Times New Roman

Trebuchet MS

Verdana

▶🎁 👓 ♥ ①●■ ? (Webdings)

♏♌♎♓■♒♑♦ (Wingdings)

Figure D-5. *Microsoft font families available in IE 4.5 and 5 for the Macintosh*

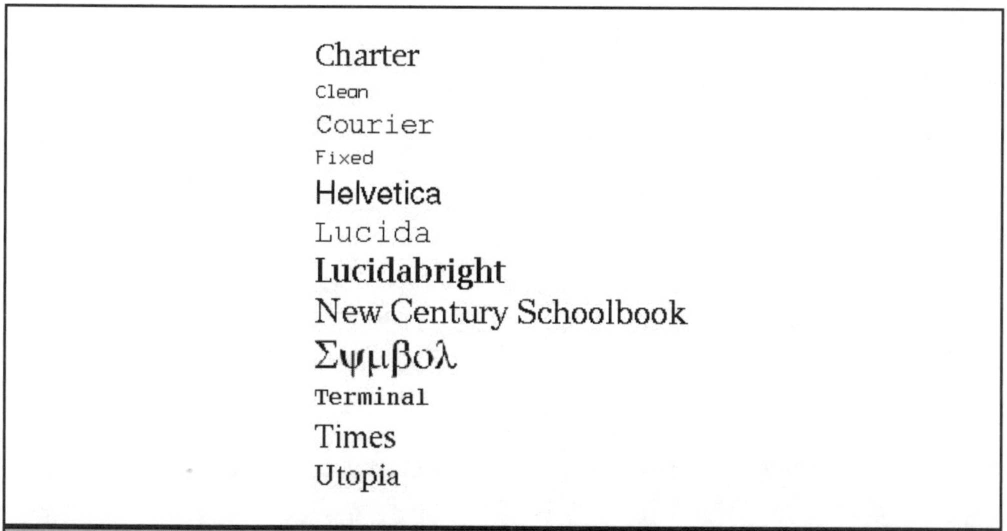

Charter

Clean

Courier

Fixed

Helvetica

Lucida

Lucidabright

New Century Schoolbook

Σψμβολ

Terminal

Times

Utopia

Figure D-6. *Font families available on Unix systems*

The Complete Reference

Appendix E

Color Reference

This appendix provides basic information about the use of colors on the Web, from how to calculate browser-safe colors, adjust unsafe colors, and form hybrid colors, to the use of color names and their numerical equivalents as used in HTML and CSS, and browser support of color names.

Browser-Safe Colors

While 8-bit GIF images support 256 colors, cross-platform issues leave a palette of only 216 colors that are completely safe to use on the Web. This group of Web-safe colors is often called the *browser-safe palette*. Because it is difficult to present this information visually in a black-and-white book, the palette can be viewed online at http://www.htmlref.com/reference/appe/safepalette.htm. Use of other colors beyond this safe set can lead to poor-looking images when viewed under limited color conditions such as 8-bit (256 color) VGA. Selecting a set of colors from the safe color palette and mixing them together in a process called *dithering* will approximate colors outside the safe range. In short, dithering attempts to imitate colors by placing similar colors near them, but generally creates irregularities that render the image unappealing.

The selection of the 216 safe colors is fairly obvious if you consider the additive nature of RGB color. Consider a color to be made up of varying amounts of red, green, or blue that could be set by adjusting an imaginary color dial from the extremes of no color to maximum color saturation. The safe colors suggest six possible intensity settings for each value of red, green or blue. The settings are 0%, 20%, 40%, 60%, 80%, and 100%. A value of 0%, 0%, 0% on the imaginary color dial would be equivalent to black. A value of 100%, 100%, 100% would indicate pure white, while a value of 100%, 0%, 0% is pure red, and so on. The safe colors are those that have an RGB value set only at one of the safe intensity settings. The hex conversions for saturation are shown in Table E-1.

Setting a safe color is simply a matter of selecting a combination of safe hex values. In this case, #9966FF is a safe hex color; #9370DB is not. Most Web design tools like Macromedia Dreamweaver or Allaire HomeSite contain safe color pickers; so do imaging tools like Macromedia Fireworks or recent versions of Adobe PhotoShop. Designers looking for color palettes, including improved color pickers and swatches, should visit http://www.visibone.com/colorlab/.

Color Intensity	Hex Value	Decimal Value
100%	FF	255
80%	CC	204
60%	99	153
40%	66	102
20%	33	51
0%	00	0

Table E-1.   *Color Intensity Conversion Table*

Setting an unsafe color to its nearest safe color is fairly easy—just round each particular red, green, or blue value up or down to the nearest safe value. A complete conversion of hex to decimal values is shown in Table E-2. Safe values are indicated in bold.

00=00	01=01	02=02	03=03	04=04	05=05
06=06	07=07	08=08	09=09	10=0A	11=0B
12=0C	13=0D	14=0E	15=0F	16=10	17=11
18=12	19=13	20=14	21=15	22=16	23=17
24=18	25=19	26=1A	27=1B	28=1C	29=1D
30=1E	31=1F	32=20	33=21	34=22	35=23
36=24	37=25	38=26	39=27	40=28	41=29
42=2A	43=2B	44=2C	45=2D	46=2E	47=2F
48=30	49=31	50=32	**51=33**	52=34	53=35
54=36	55=37	56=38	57=39	58=3A	59=3B
60=3C	61=3D	62=3E	63=3F	64=40	65=41
66=42	67=43	68=44	69=45	70=46	71=47
72=48	73=49	74=4A	75=4B	76=4C	77=4D
78=4E	79=4F	80=50	81=51	82=52	83=53
84=54	85=55	86=56	87=57	88=58	89=59
90=5A	91=5B	92=5C	93=5D	94=5E	95=5F
96=60	97=61	98=62	99=63	100=64	101=65
102=66	103=67	104=68	105=69	106=6A	107=6B
108=6C	109=6D	110=6E	111=6F	112=70	113=71
114=72	115=73	116=74	117=75	118=76	119=77
120=78	121=79	122=7A	123=7B	124=7C	125=7D
126=7E	127=7F	128=80	129=81	130=82	131=83
132=84	133=85	134=86	135=87	136=88	137=89
138=8A	139=8B	140=8C	141=8D	142=8E	143=8F
144=90	145=91	146=92	147=93	148=94	149=95
150=96	151=97	152=98	**153=99**	154=9A	155=9B
156=9C	157=9D	158=9E	159=9F	160=A0	161=A1
162=A2	163=A3	164=A4	165=A5	166=A6	167=A7
168=A8	169=A9	170=AA	171=AB	172=AC	173=AD
174=AE	175=AF	176=B0	177=B1	178=B2	179=B3
180=B4	181=B5	182=B6	183=B7	184=B8	185=B9
186=BA	187=BB	188=BC	189=BD	190=BE	191=BF

Table E-2. _RGB to Hexadecimal Color Conversion Chart_

192=C0	193=C1	194=C2	195=C3	196=C4	197=C5
198=C6	199=C7	200=C8	201=C9	202=CA	203=CB
204=CC	205=CD	206=CE	207=CF	208=D0	209=D1
210=D2	211=D3	212=D4	213=D5	214=D6	215=D7
216=D8	217=D9	218=DA	219=DB	220=DC	221=DD
222=DE	223=DF	224=E0	225=E1	226=E2	227=E3
228=E4	229=E5	230=E6	231=E7	232=E8	233=E9
234=EA	235=EB	236=EC	237=ED	238=EE	239=EF
240=F0	241=F1	242=F2	243=F3	244=F4	245=F5
246=F6	247=F7	248=F8	249=F9	250=FA	251=FB
252=FC	253=FD	254=FE	**255=FF**		

Table E-2.   *RGB to Hexadecimal Color Conversion Chart* (continued)

Although mathematically translating to the closest browser-safe color seems appropriate, it might not look correct to many people. Consider creating a hybrid color by combining multiple safe colors together. This is done simply by creating a checkerboard effect with a GIF image, in which two or more non-dithering colors are placed side by side to give the appearance of a third color. A variety of PhotoShop plug-ins such as Colorsafe (www.boxtopsoft.com) exist for mixing colors.

Color Names and Numerical Equivalents

Table E-3 lists all the color names commonly supported by the major browsers (Netscape 3.0 and better, Internet Explorer 3.0 and better, Opera 4.02, and WebTV). The HTML specification defines sixteen named colors (aqua, black, blue, fuchsia, gray, green, lime, maroon, navy, olive, purple, red, silver, teal, white, and yellow). (Out of these colors, only seven are considered safe in the reproduction sense discussed previously.) Many other color names have been introduced by the browser vendors—particularly Netscape—and are commonly used. Color names are easier to remember than numerical codes, but might cause trouble when viewed under old or uncommon browsers. It is advisable to stick with the hexadecimal approach to colors, as it is generally safer. The corresponding hexadecimal code is shown next to each color name shown in Table E-3, and generally is interchangeable with the corresponding name. Thus, the code **<BODY BGCOLOR="lightsteelblue">** would produce the same result as **<BODY BGCOLOR="#B0C4DE">** under any browser that supported these color names. Identical colors might be reproducible with different names. For example, "magenta" and "fuchsia" are both equivalent to #FF00FF. Regardless of named color support, keep in mind that not all numeric values are completely browser safe either. Although these names and numbers probably won't be an issue for users with high-resolution monitors and higher degrees of color support, don't forget that these users are not the only people on the Web. Browser-safe colors in Table E-3 appear in bold; RGB equivalents are also included.

Note

If designing with the Opera browser in mind, beware that the current version of Opera tested (4.02) supports numerical values well, but has highly inconsistent support of color names. Only 18 color names match their numeric equivalents when viewed in Opera. These are marked with a dagger (†) in the chart. Opera approximates the correct display of most of the remaining color names, but shows such significant variations that, again, the best—and perhaps only—option is to use numeric values exclusively. Finally, there are some color names that Opera does not support at all, or supports in ways radically different from their intended values; these are marked with a double dagger (‡). Hopefully this will be improved with a future release of this browser.

Hexadecimal Code	Name	RGB Equivalent	Notes
#F0F8FF	aliceblue ‡	240,248,255	The name "aliceblue" is not supported by versions of Netscape prior to version 4.0.
#FAEBD7	antiquewhite	250,235,215	
#00FFFF	aqua †	0,255,255	
#7FFFD4	aquamarine	127,255,212	
#F0FFFF	azure	240,255,255	
#F5F5DC	beige	245,245,220	
#FFE4C4	bisque	255,228,196	
#000000	black †	0,0,0	
#FFEBCD	blanchedalmond	255,235,205	
#0000FF	blue †	0, 0,255	
#8A2BE2	blueviolet	138, 43,226	WebTV displays "blueviolet" the same as "blue" (0000EE).
#A52A2A	brown	165, 42, 42	
#DEB887	burlywood ‡	222,184,135	
#5F9EA0	cadetblue	95,158,160	
#7FFF00	chartreuse	127,255, 0	
#D2691E	chocolate	210,105, 30	
#FF7F50	coral	255,127, 80	
#6495ED	cornflowerblue	100,149,237	
#FFF8DC	cornsilk	255,248,220	
#DC143C	crimson ‡	220,20,60	

Table E-3. *Color Names and Their Numerical Equivalents*

Hexadecimal Code	Name	RGB Equivalent	Notes
#00FFFF	cyan †	0,255,255	
#00008B	darkblue ‡	0,0,139	
#008B8B	darkcyan ‡	0,139,139	
#B8860B	darkgoldenrod	184,134, 11	
#A9A9A9	darkgray ‡	169,169,169	
#006400	darkgreen ‡	0,100, 0	
#BDB76B	darkkhaki	189,183,107	
#8B008B	darkmagenta ‡	139, 0,139	
#556B2F	darkolivegreen ‡	85,107, 47	
#FF8C00	darkorange	255,140, 0	
#9932CC	darkorchid ‡	153, 50,204	
#8B0000	darkred	139, 0, 0	
#E9967A	darksalmon	233,150,122	
#8FBC8F	darkseagreen	143,188,143	
#483D8B	darkslateblue ‡	72, 61,139	
#2F4F4F	darkslategray ‡	47, 79, 79	
#00CED1	darkturquoise ‡	0,206,209	
#9400D3	darkviolet	148, 0,211	
#FF1493	deeppink	255, 20,147	
#00BFFF	deepskyblue	0,191,255	
#696969	dimgray ‡	105,105,105	
#1E90FF	dodgerblue	30,144,255	
#B22222	firebrick ‡	178, 34, 34	
#FFFAF0	floralwhite	255,250,240	
#228B22	forestgreen ‡	34,139, 34	
#FF00FF	fuchsia †	255,0,255	
#DCDCDC	gainsboro	220,220,220	
#F8F8FF	ghostwhite	248,248,255	
#FFD700	gold ‡	255,215, 0	

Table E-3.   *Color Names and Their Numerical Equivalents* (continued)

Hexadecimal Code	Name	RGB Equivalent	Notes
#DAA520	goldenrod ‡	218,165, 32	WebTV displays "goldenrod" the same as "gold" (#FFD700).
#808080	gray	127,127,127	
#008000	green †	0,128,0	
#ADFF2F	greenyellow	173,255, 47	WebTV displays "greenyellow" the same as "green" (#008000).
#F0FFF0	honeydew	240,255,240	
#FF69B4	hotpink	255,105,180	
#CD5C5C	indianred ‡	205, 92, 92	
#4B0082	indigo ‡	75,0,130	
#FFFFF0	ivory	255,255,240	
#F0E68C	khaki ‡	240,230,140	
#E6E6FA	lavender	230,230,250	
#FFF0F5	lavenderblush	255,240,245	
#7CFC00	lawngreen	124,252, 0	
#FFFACD	lemonchiffon	255,250,205	
#ADD8E6	lightblue	173,216,230	
#F08080	lightcoral	240,128,128	
#E0FFFF	lightcyan †	224,255,255	
#FAFAD2	lightgoldenrodyellow	250,250,210	
#90EE90	lightgreen ‡	144,238,144	
#D3D3D3	lightgrey ‡	211,211,211	
#FFB6C1	lightpink	255,182,193	
#FFA07A	lightsalmon	255,160,122	
#20B2AA	lightseagreen	32,178,170	
#87CEFA	lightskyblue	135,206,250	
#778899	lightslategray	119,136,153	
#B0C4DE	lightsteelblue ‡	176,196,222	
#FFFFE0	lightyellow	255,255,224	
#00FF00	lime †	0,255,0	

Table E-3. *Color Names and Their Numerical Equivalents* (continued)

Hexadecimal Code	Name	RGB Equivalent	Notes
#32CD32	limegreen ‡	50,205, 50	WebTV displays "limegreen" the same as "lime" (#00FF00).
#FAF0E6	linen	250,240,230	
#FF00FF	magenta †	255, 0,255	
#800000	maroon †	128,0,0	
#66CDAA	mediumaquamarine ‡	102,205,170	
#0000CD	mediumblue ‡	0,0,205	
#BA55D3	mediumorchid ‡	186, 85,211	
#9370DB	mediumpurple	147,112,219	
#3CB371	mediumseagreen ‡	60,179,113	
#7B68EE	mediumslateblue ‡	123,104,238	
#00FA9A	mediumspringgreen ‡	0,250,154	According to the WebTV specification, WebTV supports "mediumspringgreen," but the name display does not match the numerical code display.
#48D1CC	mediumturquoise	72,209,204	
#C71585	mediumvioletred	199, 21,133	
#191970	midnightblue	25, 25,112	
#F5FFFA	mintcream	245,255,250	
#FFE4E1	mistyrose	255,228,225	
#FFE4B5	moccasin	255,228,181	
#FFDEAD	navajowhite	255,222,173	
#000080	navy †	0, 0,128	
#9FAFDF	navyblue ‡	159,175,223	WebTV displays "navyblue" the same as "navy" (#000080).
#FDF5E6	oldlace	253,245,230	
#808000	olive †	128,128,0	
#6B8E23	olivedrab	107,142, 35	WebTV displays "olivedrab" the same as "olive" (#808000).
#FFA500	orange	255,165, 0	
#FF4500	orangered	255, 69, 0	WebTV displays "orangered" the same as "orange" (#FFA500).

Table E-3.   *Color Names and Their Numerical Equivalents* (continued)

Hexadecimal Code	Name	RGB Equivalent	Notes
#DA70D6	orchid	218,112,214	
#EEE8AA	palegoldenrod	238,232,170	
#98FB98	palegreen	152,251,152	
#AFEEEE	paleturquoise	175,238,238	
#DB7093	palevioletred	219,112,147	
#FFEFD5	papayawhip	255,239,213	
#FFDAB9	peachpuff	255,218,185	
#CD853F	peru	205,133, 63	
#FFC0CB	pink	255,192,203	
#DDA0DD	plum	221,160,221	
#B0E0E6	powderblue	176,224,230	
#800080	purple †	128,0,128	
#FF0000	red †	255, 0, 0	
#BC8F8F	rosybrown	188,143,143	
#4169E1	royalblue	65,105,225	
#8B4513	saddlebrown ‡	139,69,19	
#FA8072	salmon ‡	250,128,114	
#F4A460	sandybrown	244,164, 96	
#2E8B57	seagreen	46,139, 87	
#FFF5EE	seashell	255,245,238	
#A0522D	sienna	160, 82, 45	
#C0C0C0	silver †	192,192,192	
#87CEEB	skyblue	135,206,235	
#6A5ACD	slateblue	106, 90,205	
#708090	slategray	112,128,144	
#FFFAFA	snow	255,250,250	
#00FF7F	springgreen	0,255,127	
#4682B4	steelblue	70,130,180	
#D2B48C	tan	210,180,140	
#008080	teal †	0,128,128	

Table E-3.   *Color Names and Their Numerical Equivalents* (continued)

Hexadecimal Code	Name	RGB Equivalent	Notes
#D8BFD8	thistle	216,191,216	
#FF6347	tomato	255, 99, 71	
#40E0D0	turquoise	64,224,208	
#EE82EE	violet	238,130,238	
#F5DEB3	wheat	245,222,179	
#FFFFFF	white †	255,255,255	
#F5F5F5	whitesmoke	245,245,245	
#FFFF00	yellow †	255,255, 0	
#9ACD32	yellowgreen	139,205,50	WebTV displays "yellowgreen" the same as "yellow" (#FFFF00).

Table E-3. *Color Names and Their Numerical Equivalents* (continued)

Note *WebTV supports the color names but displays several colors (noted in the table) differently. General WebTV color support might also vary because of essential differences between computer monitors and television screens.*

Many online color references claim that further color variations can be introduced by adding the numbers 1 through 4 to color names. If this were correct, cadetblue1, cadetblue2, cadetblue3, and cadetblue4 would display as different shades of the same color, with 1 being the lightest and 4 the darkest. Opera seems to support this concept to some degree, but given the inconsistency of that browser's overall color name support and the complete lack of support by the major browsers, there seems little sense in using this approach.

Some online color references also claim that gray supports up to 100 color variations (gray10, gray50, gray90, and so forth). Testing reveals that this does not work under Netscape, Internet Explorer, or WebTV. Opera supports this concept by displaying lighter grays for higher numerical values.

Appendix F

Reading a Document Type Definition

This appendix presents the Document Type Definitions (DTDs) for HTML 4.01. HTML "dialects" are defined using Standard Generalized Markup Language (SGML), a complex language with many nuances. Fortunately, only a small amount of SGML needs to be understood to read the HTML DTDs. Before turning to the DTDs, this appendix examines how to read them.

While the rest of this edition displays HTML elements in lowercase, this appendix does not. The HTML 4.01 specification itself does not specify any casing requirements; this book employs lowercasing to encourage authors to follow XHTML-based coding standards.

Element Type Declarations

Two common types of declarations should be familiar to HTML authors: element type declarations and attribute list declarations. Beyond these, the less familiar declarations for general and parameter entities are not very complicated.

An *element type declaration* defines three characteristics:

- The element type's name, also known as its *generic identifier*
- Whether start and end tags are required, forbidden (end tags on empty elements), or may be omitted
- The element type's *content model*, or what content it can enclose

All element type declarations begin with the keyword **ELEMENT** and have the following form.

```
<!ELEMENT name minimization content_model >
```

The declaration for the HTML 2.0 **
** element type gives a simple example:

```
<!ELEMENT BR - O EMPTY>
```

Tag minimization is declared by two parameters that indicate the start and end tags. These parameters may take one of two values. A hyphen indicates the tag is required. An uppercase "O" indicates it may be omitted. The combination of "O" for the end tag and the content model **EMPTY** means the end tag is forbidden. Thus, the **
** tag requires a start tag but not an end tag. Because the **
** tag does not contain content, its content model is defined by the keyword **EMPTY**.

Most HTML elements enclose content. If a content model is declared, it is enclosed within parentheses and known as a *model group*. The HTML 4.0 declaration for a selection list option gives an example:

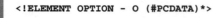
```
<!ELEMENT OPTION - O (#PCDATA)*>
```

Note that the model group contains the keyword **#PCDATA**. This stands for *parsed character data*—character content that contains no element markup but that may contain entity symbols for special characters.

Occurrence Indicators

In the previous example, also note the asterisk appended to the model group. This is an *occurrence indicator*—a special symbol that qualifies the element type or model group to which it is appended, indicating how many times it may occur. There are three occurrence indicators:

- ?   Means optional and at most one occurrence (zero or one occurrence)
- *   Means optional and any number of occurrences (zero or more occurrences)
- +   Means at least one occurrence required (one or more occurrences)

Thus, the content model in the previous declaration says that the **<OPTION>** element may contain any amount of character content, including none.

Content models can also define an element type as containing element content, illustrated by the HTML 2.0 declaration for a definition list (**<DL>**):

```
<!ELEMENT DL -- (DT|DD)+>
```

Logical Connectors

Note that the model group contains **DT** and **DD**, the names of element types that a **<DL>** element may enclose. Note also the vertical bar separating **DT** and **DD**. This is a *logical connector*—a special symbol indicating how the content units it connects relate to each other. There are three logical connectors:

- | Means "or" (one and only one of the connected content units must occur)
- &   Means "and" (all of the connected content units must occur)
- ,   Means "sequence" (the connected content units must occur in the specified order)

Thus, the content model in the previous declaration says that the **<DL>** element must contain either a **<DT>** or **<DD>** element and can contain any additional number of **<DT>** or **<DD>** elements.

Model groups can be nested inside other model groups. Very flexible content models can be declared by combining this with the capability to qualify content units with occurrence indicators and logical operators. The HTML 4.0 declaration for the **<TABLE>** element type illustrates this point:

```
<!ELEMENT TABLE -- (CAPTION?, (COL*|COLGROUP*),
        THEAD?, TFOOT?, TBODY+)>
```

The content model for the **<TABLE>** element type reads as follows:

- Table content begins with zero or one **<CAPTION>** element.
- This must be followed by a content group.
- The content group must contain zero or more **<COL>** elements or zero or more **<COLGROUP>** elements.
- This must be followed by zero or one **<THEAD>** element.
- This must be followed by zero or one **<TFOOT>** element.
- This must be followed by one or more **<TBODY>** elements.

Content Exclusion

Occasionally the need arises to declare that an element type cannot contain certain other element types. This is known as a *content exclusion*. The excluded tags follow the model group, enclosed by parentheses and preceded by the minus sign:

```
(model group) - (excluded tags)
```

Content Inclusion

A *related special need* is the capability to declare that an element type can occur anywhere inside a content model. This is known as a *content inclusion*. The included tags follow the model group, enclosed by parentheses and preceded by the plus sign:

```
(model group) +(included tags)
```

The HTML 4.0 declaration for the **<BODY>** element type illustrates both excluded and included elements:

```
<!ELEMENT BODY O O (%block;) -(BODY) +(INS|DEL)>
```

Why are insertions and deletions used in this declaration? The content inclusion says that the **<INS>** and **<DEL>** elements can occur anywhere in **<BODY>** content. Pragmatically, **<INS>** and **<DEL>** are used to indicate modifications, any inserted or deleted **<BODY>** content. They need to be freed from the normal structural constraints imposed on other **<BODY>** elements.

The content exclusion says that a **<BODY>** element cannot contain another **<BODY>** element. This is necessary because of the curious **"%block"** declaration used in the model group. The leading % character identifies this as a *parameter entity*, essentially a macro symbol that refers to a longer character string declared elsewhere in the DTD. Parameter entities, which commonly occur in HTML DTDs, are discussed shortly (see the section "Parameter Entities"). The **"%block"** entity reference is a shorthand way of referring to all block element types that happen to include **<BODY>**. It is easier to exclude **<BODY>** from the list of block elements than to define a special purpose declaration.

Attribute Declarations

All attribute declarations begin with the keyword **ATTLIST** followed by name of the element type they are associated with. Following this are declarations for one or more individual attributes. Each of these has three parts:

- Attribute's name
- Attribute's value type
- Attribute's default

```
<!ATTLIST  element-type
    name1  type1  default1
    ...
    nameN  typeN  defaultN
>
```

The HTML 4.0 **<BDO>** element type illustrates a small attribute declaration:

```
<!ATTLIST  BDO
    lang  NAME      #IMPLIED
    dir   (ltr|rtl) #REQUIRED
>
```

SGML Keywords

This example declares the **lang** attribute as having values of type **NAME**, an alphabetic string. **NAME** is one of several SGML keywords occurring in HTML declarations to declare an attribute's type:

- **CDATA**   Unparsed character data
- **ID**   A document-wide unique identifier
- **IDREF**   A reference to a document-wide identifier
- **NAME**   An alphabetic character string plus a hyphen and a period
- **NMTOKEN**   An alphanumeric character string plus a hyphen and a period
- **NUMBER**   A character string containing decimal numbers

The **dir** attribute does not declare its type using a keyword. Instead, the type is specified using an enumerated list containing two possible values, **ltr** and **rtl**.

In the example, the attribute's default behavior is specified with a keyword. A default value may be specified using a quoted string.

- **#REQUIRED**   A value must be supplied for the attribute.
- **#IMPLIED**   The attribute is optional.

■ **#FIXED** The attribute has a fixed value that is declared in quotes using an additional parameter. Because the attribute/value pair is assumed to be constant, it does not need to be used in the document instance.

Parameter Entities

An *entity* is essentially a macro that allows a short name to be associated with replacement text. Parameter entities define replacement text used in DTD declarations. Syntactically, a parameter entity is distinguished by using the percent (%) symbol. Its general form is shown here:

```
<!ENTITY % name "replacement text">
```

It is used in DTDs as follows:

```
%name;
```

Parameter entities are a convenient way to define commonly occurring pieces of a DTD so that changes only need to be made in one place. HTML 4.0 uses a parameter entity to define the core attributes common to most elements.

```
<!ENTITY % coreattrs
   "id         ID          #IMPLIED
    class      CDATA       #IMPLIED
    style      CDATA       #IMPLIED
    title      CDATA       #IMPLIED "
  >
```

These attributes could be added to an attribute list declaration as follows:

```
<!ATTLIST some-element  %coreattrs;>
```

In fact, HTML 4.0 also uses the **coreattrs** parameter entity in a different way. Parameter entities can be used inside other parameter entity declarations. The **coreattrs** parameter entity is used with the i18n and events parameter entities to define the expansion text for an aggregate entity called **attrs**.

```
<!ENTITY % attrs "%coreattrs %i18n %events">
```

General Entities

While parameter entities are used to manipulate syntax in DTD declarations, general entities are used to associate symbols with replacement text for use in actual documents. General entities have a versatile syntax. One type is familiar to many HTML authors: the character entity used for special symbols. For example, HTML authors needing to use the ampersand character (&) use the **&** entity. It is declared as follows:

```
<!ENTITY amp CDATA "&#38;">
```

The **ENTITY** keyword without the % character identifies this as a general entity. The name of the entity is **amp**. The entity type is indicated by the **CDATA** keyword, for *character data*. This is followed by the replacement text.

Comments

DTDs contain the type of comments familiar to HTML authors:

```
<!-- this is a comment -->
```

Comments can also be embedded inside HTML SGML declarations for explanatory purposes. Embedded comments are delimited by two dashes, and a single declaration may contain many embedded comments:

```
<!ATTLIST PARAM
   name        CDATA       #REQUIRED -- property name --
   value       CDATA       #IMPLIED  -- property value --
   valuetype (DATA|REF|OBJECT) DATA -- How to interpret value --
   type        CDATA       #IMPLIED  -- Internet media type --
   >
```

Marked Section Declaration

Some HTML DTDs use a special SGML construct to allow them to optionally include or exclude certain declarations from a DTD, such as those supporting deprecated tags. An SGML *marked section declaration* uses keywords to indicate that the content it encloses should be treated in a special way. HTML DTDs use parameter entities to assign the **INCLUDE** and **IGNORE** keywords to marked section declarations. This causes the declarations enclosed by the sections to be included or ignored, respectively.

```
<! [keyword [
affected declarations
]]>
<!ENTITY % HTML.Deprecated "IGNORE">
<! [ %HTML.Deprecated [
affected declarations
]]>
```

The rest of this appendix presents the Document Type Definitions for HTML 4.01, starting with the transitional DTD, which is recommended. This is followed by the strict definition, which removes the presentational elements from HTML. The latest versions of these DTDs can be retrieved from the W3C:

- **Transitional** http://www.w3.org/TR/html4/sgml/loosedtd.html
- **Strict** http://www.w3.org/TR/html4/sgml/dtd.html
- **Frameset** http://www.w3.org/TR/html4/sgml/framesetdtd.html

These DTDs have been found to contain some errors. An updated list of errors can be found at http://www.w3.org/MarkUp/html4-updates/errata. The DTDs for HTML 2.0 (http://www.w3.org/MarkUp/html-spec/html.dtd) and HTML 3.2 (http://www.w3.org/TR/REC-html32#dtd) are also available online.

HTML 4.01 Transitional DTD

```
<!--
    This is the HTML 4.01 Transitional DTD, which includes
    presentation attributes and elements that W3C expects to phase out
    as support for style sheets matures. Authors should use the Strict
    DTD when possible, but may use the Transitional DTD when support
    for presentation attribute and elements is required.

    HTML 4 includes mechanisms for style sheets, scripting,
    embedding objects, improved support for right to left and mixed
    direction text, and enhancements to forms for improved
    accessibility for people with disabilities.

            Draft: $Date: 1999/12/24 23:37:46 $

        Authors:
            Dave Raggett <dsr@w3.org>
            Arnaud Le Hors <lehors@w3.org>
            Ian Jacobs <ij@w3.org>

    Further information about HTML 4.01 is available at:

        http://www.w3.org/TR/1999/REC-html401-19991224

    The HTML 4.01 specification includes additional
    syntactic constraints that cannot be expressed within
    the DTDs.

-->
<!ENTITY % HTML.Version "-//W3C//DTD HTML 4.01 Transitional//EN"
```

```
-- Typical usage:

<!DOCTYPE HTML PUBLIC "-//W3C//DTD HTML 4.01 Transitional//EN"
        "http://www.w3.org/TR/html4/loose.dtd">
<html>
<head>
...
</head>
<body>
...
</body>
</html>

The URI used as a system identifier with the public identifier allows
the user agent to download the DTD and entity sets as needed.

The FPI for the Strict HTML 4.01 DTD is:


    "-//W3C//DTD HTML 4.01//EN"

This version of the strict DTD is:

    http://www.w3.org/TR/1999/REC-html401-19991224/strict.dtd

Authors should use the Strict DTD unless they need the
presentation control for user agents that don''t (adequately)
support style sheets.

If you are writing a document that includes frames, use
the following FPI:

    "-//W3C//DTD HTML 4.01 Frameset//EN"

This version of the frameset DTD is:

    http://www.w3.org/TR/1999/REC-html401-19991224/frameset.dtd

Use the following (relative) URIs to refer to
the DTDs and entity definitions of this specification:

"strict.dtd"
"loose.dtd"
"frameset.dtd"
"HTMLlat1.ent"
"HTMLsymbol.ent"
"HTMLspecial.ent"
-->
```

```
<!--=================== Imported Names ======================================-->
<!-- Feature Switch for frameset documents -->
<!ENTITY % HTML.Frameset "IGNORE">

<!ENTITY % ContentType "CDATA"
    -- media type, as per [RFC2045]
    -->

<!ENTITY % ContentTypes "CDATA"
    -- comma-separated list of media types, as per [RFC2045]
    -->

<!ENTITY % Charset "CDATA"
    -- a character encoding, as per [RFC2045]
    -->

<!ENTITY % Charsets "CDATA"
    -- a space-separated list of character encodings, as per [RFC2045]
    -->

<!ENTITY % LanguageCode "NAME"
    -- a language code, as per [RFC1766]
    -->

<!ENTITY % Character "CDATA"
    -- a single character from [ISO10646]
    -->

<!ENTITY % LinkTypes "CDATA"
    -- space-separated list of link types
    -->

<!ENTITY % MediaDesc "CDATA"
    -- single or comma-separated list of media descriptors
    -->

<!ENTITY % URI "CDATA"
    -- a Uniform Resource Identifier,
       see [URI]
    -->

<!ENTITY % Datetime  "CDATA" -- date and time information. ISO date format -->

!ENTITY % Script "CDATA" -- script expression -->

<!ENTITY % StyleSheet "CDATA" -- style sheet data -->

<!ENTITY % FrameTarget "CDATA" -- render in this frame -->
```

```
<!ENTITY % Text "CDATA">


<!-- Parameter Entities -->

<!ENTITY % head.misc "SCRIPT|STYLE|META|LINK|OBJECT" -- repeatable head
    elements -->

<!ENTITY % heading "H1|H2|H3|H4|H5|H6">

<!ENTITY % list "UL | OL |  DIR | MENU">

<!ENTITY % preformatted "PRE">

<!ENTITY % Color "CDATA" -- a color using sRGB: #RRGGBB as Hex values -->

<!-- There are also 16 widely known color names with their sRGB values:

    Black  = #000000    Green  = #008000
    Silver = #C0C0C0    Lime   = #00FF00
    Gray   = #808080    Olive  = #808000
    White  = #FFFFFF    Yellow = #FFFF00
    Maroon = #800000    Navy   = #000080
    Red    = #FF0000    Blue   = #0000FF
    Purple = #800080    Teal   = #008080
    Fuchsia= #FF00FF    Aqua   = #00FFFF
 -->

<!ENTITY % bodycolors "
  bgcolor        %Color;        #IMPLIED -- document background color --
  text           %Color;        #IMPLIED -- document text color --
  link           %Color;        #IMPLIED -- color of links --
  vlink          %Color;        #IMPLIED -- color of visited links --
  alink          %Color;        #IMPLIED -- color of selected links --
  ">

<!--================ Character mnemonic entities =========================-->

<!ENTITY % HTMLlat1 PUBLIC

   "-//W3C//ENTITIES Latin1//EN//HTML"
   "HTMLlat1.ent">
%HTMLlat1;

<!ENTITY % HTMLsymbol PUBLIC
   "-//W3C//ENTITIES Symbols//EN//HTML"
   "HTMLsymbol.ent">
%HTMLsymbol;
```

```
<!ENTITY % HTMLspecial PUBLIC
   "-//W3C//ENTITIES Special//EN//HTML"
   "HTMLspecial.ent">
%HTMLspecial;
<!--=================== Generic Attributes ===============================-->

<!ENTITY % coreattrs
 "id          ID            #IMPLIED  -- document-wide unique id --
  class       CDATA         #IMPLIED  -- space-separated list of classes --
  style       %StyleSheet;  #IMPLIED  -- associated style info --
  title       %Text;        #IMPLIED  -- advisory title --"
  >

<!ENTITY % i18n
 "lang        %LanguageCode; #IMPLIED  -- language code --
  dir         (ltr|rtl)     #IMPLIED  -- direction for weak/neutral text --"
  >

<!ENTITY % events
 "onclick     %Script;      #IMPLIED  -- a pointer button was clicked --
  ondblclick  %Script;      #IMPLIED  -- a pointer button was double clicked--
  onmousedown %Script;      #IMPLIED  -- a pointer button was pressed down --
  onmouseup   %Script;      #IMPLIED  -- a pointer button was released --
  onmouseover %Script;      #IMPLIED  -- a pointer was moved onto --
  onmousemove %Script;      #IMPLIED  -- a pointer was moved within --
  onmouseout  %Script;      #IMPLIED  -- a pointer was moved away --
  onkeypress  %Script;      #IMPLIED  -- a key was pressed and released --
  onkeydown   %Script;      #IMPLIED  -- a key was pressed down --
  onkeyup     %Script;      #IMPLIED  -- a key was released --"
  >

<!-- Reserved Feature Switch -->
<!ENTITY % HTML.Reserved "IGNORE">

<!-- The following attributes are reserved for possible future use -->
<![ %HTML.Reserved; [
<!ENTITY % reserved
 "datasrc     %URI;         #IMPLIED  -- a single or tabular Data Source --
  datafld     CDATA         #IMPLIED  -- the property or column name --
  dataformatas (plaintext|html) plaintext -- text or html --"
  >
]]>

<!ENTITY % reserved "">

<!ENTITY % attrs "%coreattrs; %i18n; %events;">

<!ENTITY % align "align (left|center|right|justify)  #IMPLIED"
                 -- default is left for ltr paragraphs, right for rtl --
  >
```

```
<!--==================== Text Markup ======================================-->

<!ENTITY % fontstyle
 "TT | I | B | U | S | STRIKE | BIG | SMALL">

<!ENTITY % phrase "EM | STRONG | DFN | CODE |
                  SAMP | KBD | VAR | CITE | ABBR | ACRONYM" >

<!ENTITY % special
   "A | IMG | APPLET | OBJECT | FONT | BASEFONT | BR | SCRIPT |
    MAP | Q | SUB | SUP | SPAN | BDO | IFRAME">

<!ENTITY % formctrl "INPUT | SELECT | TEXTAREA | LABEL | BUTTON">

<!-- %inline; covers inline or "text-level" elements -->
<!ENTITY % inline "#PCDATA | %fontstyle; | %phrase; |
                  %special; | %formctrl;">

<!ELEMENT (%fontstyle;|%phrase;) - - (%inline;)*>
<!ATTLIST (%fontstyle;|%phrase;)
  %attrs;                              -- %coreattrs, %i18n, %events --
  >


<!ELEMENT (SUB|SUP) - - (%inline;)*    -- subscript, superscript -->
<!ATTLIST (SUB|SUP)
  %attrs;                              -- %coreattrs, %i18n, %events --
  >

<!ELEMENT SPAN - - (%inline;)*         -- generic language/style container -->
<!ATTLIST SPAN
  %attrs;                              -- %coreattrs, %i18n, %events --
  %reserved;                   -- reserved for possible future use --
  >


<!ELEMENT BDO - - (%inline;)*          -- I18N BiDi over-ride -->
<!ATTLIST BDO
  %coreattrs;                          -- id, class, style, title --
  lang        %LanguageCode; #IMPLIED  -- language code --
  dir         (ltr|rtl)      #REQUIRED -- directionality --
  >

<!ELEMENT BASEFONT - O EMPTY           -- base font size -->
<!ATTLIST BASEFONT
  id          ID             #IMPLIED  -- document-wide unique id --
  size        CDATA          #REQUIRED -- base font size for FONT elements --
  color       %Color;        #IMPLIED  -- text color --
  face        CDATA          #IMPLIED  -- comma-separated list of font names --
  >
```

```
<!ELEMENT FONT - - (%inline;)*         -- local change to font -->
<!ATTLIST FONT
  %coreattrs;                          -- id, class, style, title --
  %i18n;                     -- lang, dir --
  size          CDATA        #IMPLIED  -- [+|-]nn e.g. size="+1", size="4" --
  color         %Color;      #IMPLIED  -- text color --
  face          CDATA        #IMPLIED  -- comma-separated list of font names --
  >

<!ELEMENT BR - O EMPTY                 -- forced line break -->
<!ATTLIST BR
  %coreattrs;                          -- id, class, style, title --
  clear         (left|all|right|none) none -- control of text flow --
  >


<!--================== HTML content models ==============================-->

<!--
    HTML has two basic content models:

        %inline;     character level elements and text strings
        %block;      block-like elements e.g. paragraphs and lists
-->

<!ENTITY % block
     "P | %heading; | %list; | %preformatted; | DL | DIV | CENTER |
      NOSCRIPT | NOFRAMES | BLOCKQUOTE | FORM | ISINDEX | HR |
      TABLE | FIELDSET | ADDRESS">

<!ENTITY % flow "%block; | %inline;">

<!--================== Document Body ===================================-->

<!ELEMENT BODY O O (%flow;)* +(INS|DEL) -- document body -->
<!ATTLIST BODY
  %attrs;                              -- %coreattrs, %i18n, %events --
  onload        %Script;   #IMPLIED    -- the document has been loaded --
  onunload      %Script;   #IMPLIED    -- the document has been removed --
  background    %URI;      #IMPLIED    -- texture tile for document
                                          background --
  %bodycolors;                         -- bgcolor, text, link, vlink, alink --
  >

<!ELEMENT ADDRESS - - ((%inline;)|P)*  -- information on author -->
<!ATTLIST ADDRESS
  %attrs;                              -- %coreattrs, %i18n, %events --
  >

<!ELEMENT DIV - - (%flow;)*            -- generic language/style container -->
<!ATTLIST DIV
```

```
    %attrs;                               -- %coreattrs, %i18n, %events --
    %align;                               -- align, text alignment --
    %reserved;                            -- reserved for possible future use --
    >

<!ELEMENT CENTER - - (%flow;)*           -- shorthand for DIV align=center -->
<!ATTLIST CENTER
    %attrs;                               -- %coreattrs, %i18n, %events --
    >


<!--================== The Anchor Element =============================-->

<!ENTITY % Shape "(rect|circle|poly|default)">
<!ENTITY % Coords "CDATA" -- comma-separated list of lengths -->

<!ELEMENT A - - (%inline;)* -(A)         -- anchor -->
<!ATTLIST A
    %attrs;                               -- %coreattrs, %i18n, %events --
    charset     %Charset;     #IMPLIED   -- char encoding of linked resource --
    type        %ContentType; #IMPLIED   -- advisory content type --
    name        CDATA         #IMPLIED   -- named link end --
    href        %URI;         #IMPLIED   -- URI for linked resource --
    hreflang    %LanguageCode; #IMPLIED  -- language code --
    target      %FrameTarget; #IMPLIED   -- render in this frame --
    rel         %LinkTypes;   #IMPLIED   -- forward link types --
    rev         %LinkTypes;   #IMPLIED   -- reverse link types --
    accesskey   %Character;   #IMPLIED   -- accessibility key character --
    shape       %Shape;       rect       -- for use with client-side image
                                                     maps --
    coords      %Coords;      #IMPLIED   -- for use with client-side
                                                     image maps --
    tabindex    NUMBER        #IMPLIED   -- position in tabbing order --
    onfocus     %Script;      #IMPLIED   -- the element got the focus --
    onblur      %Script;      #IMPLIED   -- the element lost the focus --
    >

<!--================== Client-side image maps ==========================-->

<!-- These can be placed in the same document or grouped in a
     separate document although this isn't yet widely supported -->

<!ELEMENT MAP - - ((%block;) | AREA)+ -- client-side image map -->
<!ATTLIST MAP
    %attrs;                                -- %coreattrs, %i18n, %events --
    name        CDATA         #REQUIRED   -- for reference by usemap --
    >

<!ELEMENT AREA - O EMPTY                  -- client-side image map area -->
```

```
<!ATTLIST AREA
  %attrs;                                  -- %coreattrs, %i18n, %events --
  shape        %Shape;        rect         -- controls interpretation of coords --
  coords       %Coords;       #IMPLIED     -- comma-separated list of lengths --
  href         %URI;          #IMPLIED     -- URI for linked resource --
  target       %FrameTarget;  #IMPLIED     -- render in this frame --
  nohref       (nohref)       #IMPLIED     -- this region has no action --
  alt          %Text;         #REQUIRED    -- short description --
  tabindex     NUMBER         #IMPLIED     -- position in tabbing order --
  accesskey    %Character;    #IMPLIED     -- accessibility key character --
  onfocus      %Script;       #IMPLIED     -- the element got the focus --
  onblur       %Script;       #IMPLIED     -- the element lost the focus --
  >


<!--================== The LINK Element ================================-->


<!--
  Relationship values can be used in principle:

     a) for document specific toolbars/menus when used
        with the LINK element in document head e.g.
          start, contents, previous, next, index, end, help
     b) to link to a separate style sheet (rel=stylesheet)
     c) to make a link to a script (rel=script)
     d) by stylesheets to control how collections of
        html nodes are rendered into printed documents
     e) to make a link to a printable version of this document
        e.g. a postscript or pdf version (rel=alternate media=print)
-->


<!ELEMENT LINK - O EMPTY                -- a media-independent link -->
<!ATTLIST LINK
  %attrs;                                -- %coreattrs, %i18n, %events --
  charset      %Charset;      #IMPLIED   -- char encoding of linked resource --
  href         %URI;          #IMPLIED   -- URI for linked resource --
  hreflang     %LanguageCode; #IMPLIED   -- language code --
  type         %ContentType;  #IMPLIED   -- advisory content type --
  rel          %LinkTypes;    #IMPLIED   -- forward link types --
  rev          %LinkTypes;    #IMPLIED   -- reverse link types --
  media        %MediaDesc;    #IMPLIED   -- for rendering on these media --
  target       %FrameTarget;  #IMPLIED   -- render in this frame --
  >


<!--==================== Images ========================================-->

<!-- Length defined in strict DTD for cellpadding/cellspacing -->
<!ENTITY % Length "CDATA" -- nn for pixels or nn% for percentage length -->
<!ENTITY % MultiLength "CDATA" -- pixel, percentage, or relative -->
```

```
<![ %HTML.Frameset; [
<!ENTITY % MultiLengths "CDATA" -- comma-separated list of MultiLength -->
]]>


<!ENTITY % Pixels "CDATA" -- integer representing length in pixels -->


<!ENTITY % IAlign "(top|middle|bottom|left|right)" -- center? -->


<!-- To avoid problems with text-only UAs as well as
     to make image content understandable and navigable
     to users of non-visual UAs, you need to provide
     a description with ALT, and avoid server-side image maps -->
<!ELEMENT IMG - O EMPTY                  -- Embedded image -->
<!ATTLIST IMG
  %attrs;                               -- %coreattrs, %i18n, %events --
  src        %URI;        #REQUIRED -- URI of image to embed --
  alt        %Text;       #REQUIRED -- short description --
  longdesc   %URI;        #IMPLIED  -- link to long description
                                       (complements alt) --
  name       CDATA        #IMPLIED  -- name of image for scripting --
  height     %Length;     #IMPLIED  -- override height --
  width      %Length;     #IMPLIED  -- override width --
  usemap     %URI;        #IMPLIED  -- use client-side image map --
  ismap      (ismap)      #IMPLIED  -- use server-side image map --
  align      %IAlign;     #IMPLIED  -- vertical or horizontal alignment --
  border     %Pixels;     #IMPLIED  -- link border width --
  hspace     %Pixels;     #IMPLIED  -- horizontal gutter --
  vspace     %Pixels;     #IMPLIED  -- vertical gutter --
  >


<!-- USEMAP points to a MAP element which may be in this document
     or an external document, although the latter is not widely supported -->



<!--===================== OBJECT =====================================-->
<!--
   OBJECT is used to embed objects as part of HTML pages
   PARAM elements should precede other content. SGML mixed content
   model technicality precludes specifying this formally ...
-->


<!ELEMENT OBJECT - - (PARAM | %flow;)*
  -- generic embedded object -->
<!ATTLIST OBJECT
  %attrs;                               -- %coreattrs, %i18n, %events --
  declare    (declare)    #IMPLIED  -- declare but don't instantiate flag --
  classid    %URI;        #IMPLIED  -- identifies an implementation --
  codebase   %URI;        #IMPLIED  -- base URI for classid, data, archive--
```

```
    data        %URI;           #IMPLIED    -- reference to object's data --
    type        %ContentType;   #IMPLIED    -- content type for data --
    codetype    %ContentType;   #IMPLIED    -- content type for code --
    archive     CDATA           #IMPLIED    -- space-separated list of URIs --
    standby     %Text;          #IMPLIED    -- message to show while loading --
    height      %Length;        #IMPLIED    -- override height --
    width       %Length;        #IMPLIED    -- override width --
    usemap      %URI;           #IMPLIED    -- use client-side image map --
    name        CDATA           #IMPLIED    -- submit as part of form --
    tabindex    NUMBER          #IMPLIED    -- position in tabbing order --
    align       %IAlign;        #IMPLIED    -- vertical or horizontal alignment --
    border      %Pixels;        #IMPLIED    -- link border width --
    hspace      %Pixels;        #IMPLIED    -- horizontal gutter --
    vspace      %Pixels;         #IMPLIED   -- vertical gutter --
    %reserved;                              -- reserved for possible future use --
    >

<!ELEMENT PARAM - O EMPTY               -- named property value -->
<!ATTLIST PARAM
    id          ID              #IMPLIED    -- document-wide unique id --
    name        CDATA           #REQUIRED   -- property name --
    value       CDATA           #IMPLIED    -- property value --
    valuetype   (DATA|REF|OBJECT) DATA      -- How to interpret value --
    type        %ContentType;   #IMPLIED    -- content type for value
                                               when valuetype=ref --
    >


<!--=================== Java APPLET ===================================-->
<!--
  One of code or object attributes must be present.
  Place PARAM elements before other content.
-->
<!ELEMENT APPLET - - (PARAM | %flow;)* -- Java applet -->
<!ATTLIST APPLET
    %coreattrs;                             -- id, class, style, title --
    codebase    %URI;           #IMPLIED    -- optional base URI for applet --
    archive     CDATA           #IMPLIED    -- comma-separated archive list --
    code        CDATA           #IMPLIED    -- applet class file --
    object      CDATA           #IMPLIED    -- serialized applet file --
    alt         %Text;          #IMPLIED    -- short description --
    name        CDATA           #IMPLIED    -- allows applets to find each other --
    width       %Length;        #REQUIRED   -- initial width --
    height      %Length;        #REQUIRED   -- initial height --
    align       %IAlign;        #IMPLIED    -- vertical or horizontal alignment --
    hspace      %Pixels;        #IMPLIED    -- horizontal gutter --
    vspace      %Pixels;        #IMPLIED    -- vertical gutter --
    >
```

```
<!--================== Horizontal Rule ===================================-->

<!ELEMENT HR - O EMPTY -- horizontal rule -->
<!ATTLIST HR
  %attrs;                              -- %coreattrs, %i18n, %events --
  align       (left|center|right) #IMPLIED
  noshade     (noshade)        #IMPLIED
  size        %Pixels;         #IMPLIED
  width       %Length;         #IMPLIED
  >


<!--================== Paragraphs =======================================-->

<!ELEMENT P - O (%inline;)*          -- paragraph -->
<!ATTLIST P
  %attrs;                              -- %coreattrs, %i18n, %events --
  %align;                              -- align, text alignment --
  >


<!--================== Headings =========================================-->

<!--
  There are six levels of headings from H1 (the most important)
  to H6 (the least important).
-->

<!ELEMENT (%heading;)  - - (%inline;)* -- heading -->
<!ATTLIST (%heading;)
  %attrs;                              -- %coreattrs, %i18n, %events --
  %align;                              -- align, text alignment --
  >


<!--================== Preformatted Text ================================-->

<!-- excludes markup for images and changes in font size -->
<!ENTITY % pre.exclusion "IMG|OBJECT|APPLET|BIG|SMALL|SUB|SUP|
                          FONT|BASEFONT">

<!ELEMENT PRE - - (%inline;)* -(%pre.exclusion;) -- preformatted text -->
<!ATTLIST PRE
  %attrs;                              -- %coreattrs, %i18n, %events --
  width       NUMBER           #IMPLIED
  >


<!--==================== Inline Quotes ==================================-->

<!ELEMENT Q - - (%inline;)*          -- short inline quotation -->
<!ATTLIST Q
  %attrs;                              -- %coreattrs, %i18n, %events --
```

```
    cite         %URI;              #IMPLIED  -- URI for source document or msg --
    >


<!--=================== Block-like Quotes ===+==========================-->

<!ELEMENT BLOCKQUOTE - - (%flow;)*      -- long quotation -->
<!ATTLIST BLOCKQUOTE
    %attrs;                              -- %coreattrs, %i18n, %events --
    cite         %URI;              #IMPLIED  -- URI for source document or msg --
    >


<!--=================== Inserted/Deleted Text ============================-->

<!-- INS/DEL are handled by inclusion on BODY -->
<!ELEMENT (INS|DEL) - - (%flow;)*        -- inserted text, deleted text -->
<!ATTLIST (INS|DEL)
    %attrs;                              -- %coreattrs, %i18n, %events --
    cite         %URI;          #IMPLIED  -- info on reason for change --
    datetime     %Datetime;     #IMPLIED  -- date and time of change --
    >


<!--=================== Lists ============================================-->

<!-- definition lists - DT for term, DD for its definition -->

<!ELEMENT DL - - (DT|DD)+             -- definition list -->
<!ATTLIST DL
    %attrs;                           -- %coreattrs, %i18n, %events --
    compact      (compact)      #IMPLIED  -- reduced interitem spacing --
    >


<!ELEMENT DT - O (%inline;)*          -- definition term -->
<!ELEMENT DD - O (%flow;)*            -- definition description -->
<!ATTLIST (DT|DD)
    %attrs;                           -- %coreattrs, %i18n, %events --
    >


<!-- Ordered lists (OL) Numbering style

       1    arabic numbers    1, 2, 3, ...
       a    lower alpha       a, b, c, ...
       A    upper alpha       A, B, C, ...
       i    lower roman       i, ii, iii, ...
       I    upper roman       I, II, III, ...

    The style is applied to the sequence number which by default
    is reset to 1 for the first list item in an ordered list.

    This can't be expressed directly in SGML due to case folding.
```

```
-->

<!ENTITY % OLStyle "CDATA"        -- constrained to: "(1|a|A|i|I)" -->

<!ELEMENT OL - - (LI)+                   -- ordered list -->
<!ATTLIST OL
  %attrs;                                -- %coreattrs, %i18n, %events --
  type          %OLStyle;    #IMPLIED -- numbering style --
  compact       (compact)    #IMPLIED -- reduced interitem spacing --
  start         NUMBER       #IMPLIED -- starting sequence number --
  >


<!-- Unordered Lists (UL) bullet styles -->
<!ENTITY % ULStyle "(disc|square|circle)">

<!ELEMENT UL - - (LI)+                   -- unordered list -->
<!ATTLIST UL
  %attrs;                                -- %coreattrs, %i18n, %events --
  type          %ULStyle;    #IMPLIED -- bullet style --
  compact       (compact)    #IMPLIED -- reduced interitem spacing --
  >


<!ELEMENT (DIR|MENU) - - (LI)+ -(%block;) -- directory list, menu list -->
<!ATTLIST DIR
  %attrs;                                -- %coreattrs, %i18n, %events --
  compact       (compact)    #IMPLIED -- reduced interitem spacing --
  >
<!ATTLIST MENU
  %attrs;                                -- %coreattrs, %i18n, %events --
  compact       (compact)    #IMPLIED -- reduced interitem spacing --
  >


<!ENTITY % LIStyle "CDATA" -- constrained to: "(%ULStyle;|%OLStyle;)" -->

<!ELEMENT LI - O (%flow;)*            -- list item -->
<!ATTLIST LI
  %attrs;                                -- %coreattrs, %i18n, %events --
  type          %LIStyle;    #IMPLIED -- list item style --
  value         NUMBER       #IMPLIED -- reset sequence number --
  >


<!--================ Forms ================================================-->
<!ELEMENT FORM - - (%flow;)* -(FORM)    -- interactive form -->
<!ATTLIST FORM
  %attrs;                                -- %coreattrs, %i18n, %events --
  action        %URI;        #REQUIRED -- server-side form handler --
  method        (GET|POST)   GET       -- HTTP method used to submit
                                           the form--
  enctype       %ContentType; "application/x-www-form-urlencoded"
```

```
   accept       %ContentTypes; #IMPLIED  -- list of MIME types for
                                               file upload --
   name         CDATA          #IMPLIED  -- name of form for scripting --
   onsubmit     %Script;       #IMPLIED  -- the form was submitted --
   onreset      %Script;       #IMPLIED  -- the form was reset --
   target       %FrameTarget;  #IMPLIED  -- render in this frame --
   accept-charset %Charsets;   #IMPLIED  -- list of supported charsets --
   >

<!-- Each label must not contain more than ONE field -->
<!ELEMENT LABEL - - (%inline;)* -(LABEL) -- form field label text -->
<!ATTLIST LABEL
   %attrs;                                -- %coreattrs, %i18n, %events --
   for          IDREF          #IMPLIED  -- matches field ID value --
   accesskey    %Character;    #IMPLIED  -- accessibility key character --
   onfocus      %Script;       #IMPLIED  -- the element got the focus --
   onblur       %Script;       #IMPLIED  -- the element lost the focus --
   >

<!ENTITY % InputType
   "(TEXT | PASSWORD | CHECKBOX |
     RADIO | SUBMIT | RESET |
     FILE | HIDDEN | IMAGE | BUTTON)"
    >

<!-- attribute name required for all but submit and reset -->
<!ELEMENT INPUT - O EMPTY               -- form control -->
<!ATTLIST INPUT
   %attrs;                                -- %coreattrs, %i18n, %events --
   type         %InputType;    TEXT      -- what kind of widget is needed --
   name         CDATA          #IMPLIED  -- submit as part of form --
   value        CDATA          #IMPLIED  -- Specify for radio buttons
                                            and checkboxes --
   checked      (checked)      #IMPLIED  -- for radio buttons and check boxes --
   disabled     (disabled)     #IMPLIED  -- unavailable in this context --
   readonly     (readonly)     #IMPLIED  -- for text and passwd --
   size         CDATA          #IMPLIED  -- specific to each type of field --
   maxlength    NUMBER         #IMPLIED  -- max chars for text fields --
   src          %URI;          #IMPLIED  -- for fields with images --
   alt          CDATA          #IMPLIED  -- short description --
   usemap       %URI;          #IMPLIED  -- use client-side image map --
   ismap        (ismap)        #IMPLIED  -- use server-side image map --
   tabindex     NUMBER         #IMPLIED  -- position in tabbing order --
   accesskey    %Character;    #IMPLIED  -- accessibility key character --
   onfocus      %Script;       #IMPLIED  -- the element got the focus --
   onblur       %Script;       #IMPLIED  -- the element lost the focus --
   onselect     %Script;       #IMPLIED  -- some text was selected --
   onchange     %Script;       #IMPLIED  -- the element value was changed --
   accept       %ContentTypes; #IMPLIED  -- list of MIME types for file upload --
```

```
   align         %IAlign;         #IMPLIED  -- vertical or horizontal alignment --
   %reserved;                               -- reserved for possible future use --
   >


<!ELEMENT SELECT - - (OPTGROUP|OPTION)+ -- option selector -->
<!ATTLIST SELECT
   %attrs;                                  -- %coreattrs, %i18n, %events --
   name          CDATA            #IMPLIED  -- field name --
   size          NUMBER           #IMPLIED  -- rows visible --
   multiple      (multiple)       #IMPLIED  -- default is single selection --
   disabled      (disabled)       #IMPLIED  -- unavailable in this context --
   tabindex      NUMBER           #IMPLIED  -- position in tabbing order --
   onfocus       %Script;         #IMPLIED  -- the element got the focus --
   onblur        %Script;         #IMPLIED  -- the element lost the focus --
   onchange      %Script;         #IMPLIED  -- the element value was changed --
   %reserved;                               -- reserved for possible future use --
   >


<!ELEMENT OPTGROUP - - (OPTION)+ -- option group -->
<!ATTLIST OPTGROUP
   %attrs;                                  -- %coreattrs, %i18n, %events --
   disabled      (disabled)       #IMPLIED  -- unavailable in this context --
   label         %Text;           #REQUIRED -- for use in hierarchical menus --
   >


<!ELEMENT OPTION - O (#PCDATA)          -- selectable choice -->
<!ATTLIST OPTION
   %attrs;                                  -- %coreattrs, %i18n, %events --
   selected      (selected)       #IMPLIED
   disabled      (disabled)       #IMPLIED  -- unavailable in this context --
   label         %Text;           #IMPLIED  -- for use in hierarchical menus --
   value         CDATA            #IMPLIED  -- defaults to element content --
   >


<!ELEMENT TEXTAREA - - (#PCDATA)        -- multi-line text field -->
<!ATTLIST TEXTAREA
   %attrs;                                  -- %coreattrs, %i18n, %events --
   name          CDATA            #IMPLIED
   rows          NUMBER           #REQUIRED
   cols          NUMBER           #REQUIRED
   disabled      (disabled)       #IMPLIED  -- unavailable in this context --
   readonly      (readonly)       #IMPLIED
   tabindex      NUMBER           #IMPLIED  -- position in tabbing order --
   accesskey     %Character;      #IMPLIED  -- accessibility key character --
   onfocus       %Script;         #IMPLIED  -- the element got the focus --
   onblur        %Script;         #IMPLIED  -- the element lost the focus --
   onselect      %Script;         #IMPLIED  -- some text was selected --
   onchange      %Script;         #IMPLIED  -- the element value was changed --
   %reserved;                               -- reserved for possible future use --
```

```
    >

<!--
  #PCDATA is to solve the mixed content problem,
  per specification only whitespace is allowed there!
  -->
<!ELEMENT FIELDSET - - (#PCDATA,LEGEND,(%flow;)*) -- form control group -->
<!ATTLIST FIELDSET
    %attrs;                              -- %coreattrs, %i18n, %events --
    >


<!ELEMENT LEGEND - - (%inline;)*        -- fieldset legend -->
<!ENTITY % LAlign "(top|bottom|left|right)">


<!ATTLIST LEGEND
    %attrs;                              -- %coreattrs, %i18n, %events --
    accesskey    %Character;    #IMPLIED -- accessibility key character --
    align        %LAlign;       #IMPLIED -- relative to fieldset --
    >


<!ELEMENT BUTTON - -
      (%flow;)* -(A|%formctrl;|FORM|ISINDEX|FIELDSET|IFRAME)
      -- push button -->
<!ATTLIST BUTTON
    %attrs;                              -- %coreattrs, %i18n, %events --
    name         CDATA          #IMPLIED
    value        CDATA          #IMPLIED -- sent to server when submitted --
    type         (button|submit|reset) submit -- for use as form button --
    disabled     (disabled)     #IMPLIED -- unavailable in this context --
    tabindex     NUMBER         #IMPLIED -- position in tabbing order --
    accesskey    %Character;    #IMPLIED -- accessibility key character --
    onfocus      %Script;       #IMPLIED -- the element got the focus --
    onblur       %Script;       #IMPLIED -- the element lost the focus --
    %reserved;                           -- reserved for possible future use --
    >


<!--========================= Tables =======================================-->

<!-- IETF HTML table standard, see [RFC1942] -->

<!--
The BORDER attribute sets the thickness of the frame around the
table. The default units are screen pixels.

The FRAME attribute specifies which parts of the frame around
the table should be rendered. The values are not the same as
CALS to avoid a name clash with the VALIGN attribute.

The value "border" is included for backwards compatibility with
```

```
<TABLE BORDER> which yields frame=border and border=implied
For <TABLE BORDER=1> you get border=1 and frame=implied. In this
case, it is appropriate to treat this as frame=border for backward
compatibility with deployed browsers.
-->
<!ENTITY % TFrame "(void|above|below|hsides|lhs|rhs|vsides|box|border)">


<!--
The RULES attribute defines which rules to draw between cells:

 If RULES is absent then assume:
     "none" if BORDER is absent or BORDER=0 otherwise "all"
-->


<!ENTITY % TRules "(none | groups | rows | cols | all)">


<!-- horizontal placement of table relative to document -->
<!ENTITY % TAlign "(left|center|right)">


<!-- horizontal alignment attributes for cell contents -->
<!ENTITY % cellhalign
  "align       (left|center|right|justify|char) #IMPLIED
   char        %Character;    #IMPLIED  -- alignment char, e.g. char=':' --
   charoff     %Length;       #IMPLIED  -- offset for alignment char --"
  >


<!-- vertical alignment attributes for cell contents -->
<!ENTITY % cellvalign
  "valign      (top|middle|bottom|baseline) #IMPLIED"
  >


<!ELEMENT TABLE - -
     (CAPTION?, (COL*|COLGROUP*), THEAD?, TFOOT?, TBODY+)>
<!ELEMENT CAPTION   - - (%inline;)*     -- table caption -->
<!ELEMENT THEAD     - O (TR)+           -- table header -->
<!ELEMENT TFOOT     - O (TR)+           -- table footer -->
<!ELEMENT TBODY     O O (TR)+           -- table body -->
<!ELEMENT COLGROUP - O (COL)*           -- table column group -->
<!ELEMENT COL       - O EMPTY           -- table column -->
<!ELEMENT TR        - O (TH|TD)+        -- table row -->
<!ELEMENT (TH|TD)   - O (%flow;)*            -- table header cell, table data
cell-->


<!ATTLIST TABLE                         -- table element --
  %attrs;                               -- %coreattrs, %i18n, %events --
  summary     %Text;        #IMPLIED  -- purpose/structure for
                                         speech output--
  width       %Length;      #IMPLIED  -- table width --
  border      %Pixels;      #IMPLIED  -- controls frame width
```

```
                                     around table --
   frame       %TFrame;     #IMPLIED -- which parts of frame to render --
   rules       %TRules;     #IMPLIED -- rulings between rows and cols --
   cellspacing %Length;     #IMPLIED -- spacing between cells --
   cellpadding %Length;     #IMPLIED -- spacing within cells --
   align       %TAlign;     #IMPLIED -- table position relative to window --
   bgcolor     %Color;      #IMPLIED -- background color for cells --
   %reserved;                        -- reserved for possible future use --
   datapagesize CDATA       #IMPLIED -- reserved for possible future use --
   >

<!ENTITY % CAlign "(top|bottom|left|right)">

<!ATTLIST CAPTION
   %attrs;                           -- %coreattrs, %i18n, %events --
   align       %CAlign;     #IMPLIED -- relative to table --
   >


<!--
COLGROUP groups a set of COL elements. It allows you to group
several semantically related columns together.
-->
<!ATTLIST COLGROUP
   %attrs;                           -- %coreattrs, %i18n, %events --
   span        NUMBER       1        -- default number of columns in group --
   width       %MultiLength; #IMPLIED -- default width for enclosed COLs --
   %cellhalign;                      -- horizontal alignment in cells --
   %cellvalign;                      -- vertical alignment in cells --
   >


<!--
 COL elements define the alignment properties for cells in
 one or more columns.

 The WIDTH attribute specifies the width of the columns, e.g.

     width=64         width in screen pixels
     width=0.5*       relative width of 0.5

 The SPAN attribute causes the attributes of one
 COL element to apply to more than one column.
-->
<!ATTLIST COL                        -- column groups and properties --
  %attrs;                            -- %coreattrs, %i18n, %events --
  span        NUMBER       1         -- COL attributes affect N columns --
  width       %MultiLength; #IMPLIED -- column width specification --
  %cellhalign;                       -- horizontal alignment in cells --
  %cellvalign;                       -- vertical alignment in cells --
   >
```

```
<!--
    Use THEAD to duplicate headers when breaking table
    across page boundaries, or for static headers when
    TBODY sections are rendered in scrolling panel.

    Use TFOOT to duplicate footers when breaking table
    across page boundaries, or for static footers when
    TBODY sections are rendered in scrolling panel.

    Use multiple TBODY sections when rules are needed
    between groups of table rows.
-->
<!ATTLIST (THEAD|TBODY|TFOOT)           -- table section --
  %attrs;                               -- %coreattrs, %i18n, %events --
  %cellhalign;                          -- horizontal alignment in cells --
  %cellvalign;                          -- vertical alignment in cells --
  >

<!ATTLIST TR                            -- table row --
  %attrs;                               -- %coreattrs, %i18n, %events --
  %cellhalign;                          -- horizontal alignment in cells --
  %cellvalign;                          -- vertical alignment in cells --
  bgcolor     %Color;      #IMPLIED -- background color for row --
  >


<!-- Scope is simpler than headers attribute for common tables -->
<!ENTITY % Scope "(row|col|rowgroup|colgroup)">

<!-- TH is for headers, TD for data, but for cells acting as both use TD -->
<!ATTLIST (TH|TD)                       -- header or data cell --
  %attrs;                               -- %coreattrs, %i18n, %events --
  abbr        %Text;       #IMPLIED -- abbreviation for header cell --
  axis        CDATA        #IMPLIED -- comma-separated list of
                                             related headers--
  headers     IDREFS       #IMPLIED -- list of id's for header cells --
  scope       %Scope;      #IMPLIED -- scope covered by header cells --
  rowspan     NUMBER       1        -- number of rows spanned by cell --
  colspan     NUMBER       1        -- number of cols spanned by cell --
  %cellhalign;                          -- horizontal alignment in cells --
  %cellvalign;                          -- vertical alignment in cells --
  nowrap      (nowrap)     #IMPLIED -- suppress word wrap --
  bgcolor     %Color;      #IMPLIED -- cell background color --
  width       %Length;     #IMPLIED -- width for cell --
  height      %Length;     #IMPLIED -- height for cell --
  >
```

```
<!--==================== Document Frames ====================================-->

<!--
  The content model for HTML documents depends on whether the HEAD is
  followed by a FRAMESET or BODY element. The widespread omission of
  the BODY start tag makes it impractical to define the content model
  without the use of a marked section.
-->

<![ %HTML.Frameset; [
<!ELEMENT FRAMESET - - ((FRAMESET|FRAME)+ & NOFRAMES?) -- window
subdivision-->
<!ATTLIST FRAMESET
  %coreattrs;                          -- id, class, style, title --
  rows        %MultiLengths; #IMPLIED  -- list of lengths,
                                          default: 100% (1 row) --
  cols        %MultiLengths; #IMPLIED  -- list of lengths,
                                          default: 100% (1 col) --
  onload      %Script;       #IMPLIED  -- all the frames have been loaded  --
  onunload    %Script;       #IMPLIED  -- all the frames have been removed --
  >
]]>


<![ %HTML.Frameset; [
<!-- reserved frame names start with "_" otherwise starts with letter -->
<!ELEMENT FRAME - O EMPTY             -- subwindow -->
<!ATTLIST FRAME
  %coreattrs;                          -- id, class, style, title --
  longdesc    %URI;          #IMPLIED  -- link to long description
                                          (complements title) --
  name        CDATA          #IMPLIED  -- name of frame for targetting --
  src         %URI;          #IMPLIED  -- source of frame content --
  frameborder (1|0)          1         -- request frame borders? --
  marginwidth %Pixels;       #IMPLIED  -- margin widths in pixels --
  marginheight %Pixels;      #IMPLIED  -- margin height in pixels --
  noresize    (noresize)     #IMPLIED  -- allow users to resize frames? --
  scrolling   (yes|no|auto)  auto      -- scrollbar or none --
  >
]]>

<!ELEMENT IFRAME - - (%flow;)*        -- inline subwindow -->
<!ATTLIST IFRAME
  %coreattrs;                          -- id, class, style, title --
  longdesc    %URI;          #IMPLIED  -- link to long description
                                          (complements title) --
  name        CDATA          #IMPLIED  -- name of frame for targetting --
  src         %URI;          #IMPLIED  -- source of frame content --
  frameborder (1|0)          1         -- request frame borders? --
  marginwidth %Pixels;       #IMPLIED  -- margin widths in pixels --
```

```
   marginheight %Pixels;       #IMPLIED  -- margin height in pixels --
   scrolling    (yes|no|auto)  auto      -- scrollbar or none --
   align        %IAlign;       #IMPLIED  -- vertical or horizontal alignment --
   height       %Length;       #IMPLIED  -- frame height --
   width        %Length;       #IMPLIED  -- frame width --
   >


<![ %HTML.Frameset; [
<!ENTITY % noframes.content "(BODY) -(NOFRAMES)">
]]>

<!ENTITY % noframes.content "(%flow;)*">

<!ELEMENT NOFRAMES - - %noframes.content;
 -- alternate content container for non frame-based rendering -->
<!ATTLIST NOFRAMES
  %attrs;                             -- %coreattrs, %i18n, %events --
  >


<!--================ Document Head ======================================-->
<!-- %head.misc; defined earlier on as "SCRIPT|STYLE|META|LINK|OBJECT" -->
<!ENTITY % head.content "TITLE & ISINDEX? & BASE?">

<!ELEMENT HEAD O O (%head.content;) +(%head.misc;) -- document head -->
<!ATTLIST HEAD
  %i18n;                              -- lang, dir --
  profile      %URI;       #IMPLIED  -- named dictionary of meta info --
  >

<!-- The TITLE element is not considered part of the flow of text.
      It should be displayed, for example as the page header or
      window title. Exactly one title is required per document.
    -->
<!ELEMENT TITLE - - (#PCDATA) -(%head.misc;) -- document title -->
<!ATTLIST TITLE %i18n>

<!ELEMENT ISINDEX - O EMPTY           -- single line prompt -->
<!ATTLIST ISINDEX
  %coreattrs;                         -- id, class, style, title --
  %i18n;                              -- lang, dir --
  prompt       %Text;      #IMPLIED  -- prompt message -->

<!ELEMENT BASE - O EMPTY              -- document base URI -->
<!ATTLIST BASE
  href         %URI;       #IMPLIED  -- URI that acts as base URI --
  target       %FrameTarget; #IMPLIED  -- render in this frame --
  >


<!ELEMENT META - O EMPTY                 -- generic metainformation -->
```

```
<!ATTLIST META
  %i18n;                                 -- lang, dir, for use with content --
  http-equiv   NAME           #IMPLIED   -- HTTP response header name    --
  name         NAME           #IMPLIED   -- metainformation name --
  content      CDATA          #REQUIRED  -- associated information --
  scheme       CDATA          #IMPLIED   -- select form of content --
  >

<!ELEMENT STYLE - - %StyleSheet         -- style info -->
<!ATTLIST STYLE
  %i18n;                                 -- lang, dir, for use with title --
  type         %ContentType;  #REQUIRED  -- content type of style language --
  media        %MediaDesc;    #IMPLIED   -- designed for use with these media --
  title        %Text;         #IMPLIED   -- advisory title --
  >

<!ELEMENT SCRIPT - - %Script;           -- script statements -->
<!ATTLIST SCRIPT
  charset      %Charset;      #IMPLIED   -- char encoding of linked resource --
  type         %ContentType;  #REQUIRED  -- content type of script language --
  language     CDATA          #IMPLIED   -- predefined script language name --
  src          %URI;          #IMPLIED   -- URI for an external script --
  defer        (defer)        #IMPLIED   -- UA may defer execution of script --
  event        CDATA          #IMPLIED   -- reserved for possible future use --
  for          %URI;          #IMPLIED   -- reserved for possible future use --
  >

<!ELEMENT NOSCRIPT - - (%flow;)*
  -- alternate content container for non script-based rendering -->
<!ATTLIST NOSCRIPT
  %attrs;                                -- %coreattrs, %i18n, %events --
  >

<!--================ Document Structure ====================================-->
<!ENTITY % version "version CDATA #FIXED '%HTML.Version;'">

<![ %HTML.Frameset; [
<!ENTITY % html.content "HEAD, FRAMESET">
]]>

<!ENTITY % html.content "HEAD, BODY">

<!ELEMENT HTML O O (%html.content;)     -- document root element -->
<!ATTLIST HTML
  %i18n;                                 -- lang, dir --
  %version;
  >
```

HTML 4.0 Strict DTD

```
<!--

    This is HTML 4.01 Strict DTD, which excludes the presentation
    attributes and elements that W3C expects to phase out as
    support for style sheets matures. Authors should use the Strict
    DTD when possible, but may use the Transitional DTD when support
    for presentation attribute and elements is required.

    HTML 4 includes mechanisms for style sheets, scripting,
    embedding objects, improved support for right to left and mixed
    direction text, and enhancements to forms for improved
    accessibility for people with disabilities.

        Draft: $Date: 1999/12/24 23:37:46 $

        Authors:
            Dave Raggett <dsr@w3.org>
            Arnaud Le Hors <lehors@w3.org>
            Ian Jacobs <ij@w3.org>

    Further information about HTML 4.01 is available at:

        http://www.w3.org/TR/1999/REC-html401-19991224


    The HTML 4.01 specification includes additional
    syntactic constraints that cannot be expressed within
    the DTDs.

-->
<!--

    Typical usage:

    <!DOCTYPE HTML PUBLIC "-//W3C//DTD HTML 4.01//EN"
            "http://www.w3.org/TR/html4/strict.dtd">
    <html>
    <head>
    ...
    </head>
    <body>
    ...
    </body>
    </html>

    The URI used as a system identifier with the public identifier allows
    the user agent to download the DTD and entity sets as needed.
```

The FPI for the Transitional HTML 4.01 DTD is:

    "-//W3C//DTD HTML 4.01 Transitional//EN"

This version of the transitional DTD is:

    http://www.w3.org/TR/1999/REC-html401-19991224/loose.dtd

If you are writing a document that includes frames, use
the following FPI:

    "-//W3C//DTD HTML 4.01 Frameset//EN"

This version of the frameset DTD is:

    http://www.w3.org/TR/1999/REC-html401-19991224/frameset.dtd

Use the following (relative) URIs to refer to
the DTDs and entity definitions of this specification:

    "strict.dtd"
    "loose.dtd"
    "frameset.dtd"
    "HTMLlat1.ent"
    "HTMLsymbol.ent"
    "HTMLspecial.ent"

-->

```
<!--================== Imported Names =====================================-->
<!-- Feature Switch for frameset documents -->
<!ENTITY % HTML.Frameset "IGNORE">

<!ENTITY % ContentType "CDATA"
    -- media type, as per [RFC2045]
    -->

<!ENTITY % ContentTypes "CDATA"
    -- comma-separated list of media types, as per [RFC2045]
    -->

<!ENTITY % Charset "CDATA"
    -- a character encoding, as per [RFC2045]
    -->

<!ENTITY % Charsets "CDATA"
```

```
        -- a space-separated list of character encodings, as per [RFC2045]
        -->

<!ENTITY % LanguageCode "NAME"
        -- a language code, as per [RFC1766]
        -->

<!ENTITY % Character "CDATA"
        -- a single character from [ISO10646]
        -->

<!ENTITY % LinkTypes "CDATA"
        -- space-separated list of link types
        -->

<!ENTITY % MediaDesc "CDATA"
        -- single or comma-separated list of media descriptors
        -->

<!ENTITY % URI "CDATA"
        -- a Uniform Resource Identifier,
          see [URI]
        -->

<!ENTITY % Datetime "CDATA" -- date and time information. ISO
                               date format -->


<!ENTITY % Script "CDATA" -- script expression -->

<!ENTITY % StyleSheet "CDATA" -- style sheet data -->


<!ENTITY % Text "CDATA">


<!-- Parameter Entities -->

<!ENTITY % head.misc "SCRIPT|STYLE|META|LINK|OBJECT" --
                            repeatable  head elements -->

<!ENTITY % heading "H1|H2|H3|H4|H5|H6">

<!ENTITY % list "UL | OL">

<!ENTITY % preformatted "PRE">
```

```
<!--================= Character mnemonic entities ==========================-->

<!ENTITY % HTMLlat1 PUBLIC
    "-//W3C//ENTITIES Latin1//EN//HTML"
    "HTMLlat1.ent">
%HTMLlat1;

<!ENTITY % HTMLsymbol PUBLIC
    "-//W3C//ENTITIES Symbols//EN//HTML"
    "HTMLsymbol.ent">
%HTMLsymbol;

<!ENTITY % HTMLspecial PUBLIC
    "-//W3C//ENTITIES Special//EN//HTML"
    "HTMLspecial.ent">
%HTMLspecial;
<!--=================== Generic Attributes ============================-->

<!ENTITY % coreattrs
 "id          ID            #IMPLIED  -- document-wide unique id --
  class       CDATA         #IMPLIED  -- space-separated list of classes --
  style       %StyleSheet;  #IMPLIED  -- associated style info --
  title       %Text;        #IMPLIED  -- advisory title --"
  >

<!ENTITY % i18n
 "lang        %LanguageCode; #IMPLIED  -- language code --
  dir         (ltr|rtl)     #IMPLIED  -- direction for weak/neutral text
  --"
  >

<!ENTITY % events
 " onclick     %Script;      #IMPLIED  -- a pointer button was clicked --
   ondblclick  %Script;      #IMPLIED  -- a pointer button was double
                                          clicked--
   onmousedown %Script;      #IMPLIED  -- a pointer button was pressed down --
   onmouseup   %Script;      #IMPLIED  -- a pointer button was released --
   onmouseover %Script;      #IMPLIED  -- a pointer was moved onto --
   onmousemove %Script;      #IMPLIED  -- a pointer was moved within --
   onmouseout  %Script;      #IMPLIED  -- a pointer was moved away --
   onkeypress  %Script;      #IMPLIED  -- a key was pressed and released --
   onkeydown   %Script;      #IMPLIED  -- a key was pressed down --
```

```
  onkeyup      %Script;       #IMPLIED  -- a key was released --"
  >

<!-- Reserved Feature Switch -->
<!ENTITY % HTML.Reserved "IGNORE">

<!-- The following attributes are reserved for possible future use -->
<![ %HTML.Reserved; [
<!ENTITY % reserved
 "datasrc     %URI;          #IMPLIED  -- a single or tabular Data Source --
  datafld    CDATA          #IMPLIED  -- the property or column name --
  dataformatas (plaintext|html) plaintext -- text or html --"
  >
]]>

<!ENTITY % reserved """>

<!ENTITY % attrs "%coreattrs; %i18n; %events;">


<!--==================== Text Markup ========================================-->

<!ENTITY % fontstyle
 "TT | I | B | BIG | SMALL">

<!ENTITY % phrase "EM | STRONG | DFN | CODE |
                   SAMP | KBD | VAR | CITE | ABBR | ACRONYM" >

<!ENTITY % special
   "A | IMG | OBJECT | BR | SCRIPT | MAP | Q | SUB | SUP | SPAN | BDO">

<!ENTITY % formctrl "INPUT | SELECT | TEXTAREA | LABEL | BUTTON">

<!-- %inline; covers inline or "text-level" elements -->
<!ENTITY % inline "#PCDATA | %fontstyle; | %phrase; | %special; |
                  %formctrl;">

<!ELEMENT (%fontstyle;|%phrase;) - - (%inline;)*>
<!ATTLIST (%fontstyle;|%phrase;)
  %attrs;                              -- %coreattrs, %i18n, %events --
  >

<!ELEMENT (SUB|SUP) - - (%inline;)*    -- subscript, superscript -->
<!ATTLIST (SUB|SUP)
  %attrs;                              -- %coreattrs, %i18n, %events --
  >
```

```
<!ELEMENT SPAN - - (%inline;)*          -- generic language/style container -->
<!ATTLIST SPAN
  %attrs;                                -- %coreattrs, %i18n, %events --
  %reserved;                    -- reserved for possible future use --
  >


<!ELEMENT BDO - - (%inline;)*       -- I18N BiDi over-ride -->
<!ATTLIST BDO
  %coreattrs;                          -- id, class, style, title --
  lang        %LanguageCode; #IMPLIED -- language code --
  dir         (ltr|rtl)      #REQUIRED -- directionality --
  >



<!ELEMENT BR - O EMPTY              -- forced line break -->
<!ATTLIST BR
  %coreattrs;                          -- id, class, style, title --
  >


<!--================== HTML content models =============================-->

<!--
    HTML has two basic content models:

        %inline;    character level elements and text strings
        %block;     block-like elements e.g. paragraphs and lists
-->

<!ENTITY % block
    "P | %heading; | %list; | %preformatted; | DL | DIV | NOSCRIPT |
    BLOCKQUOTE | FORM | HR | TABLE | FIELDSET | ADDRESS">

<!ENTITY % flow "%block; | %inline;">

<!--================== Document Body ===================================-->

<!ELEMENT BODY O O (%block;|SCRIPT)+ +(INS|DEL) -- document body -->
<!ATTLIST BODY
  %attrs;                              -- %coreattrs, %i18n, %events --
  onload          %Script;   #IMPLIED -- the document has been loaded --
  onunload        %Script;   #IMPLIED -- the document has been removed --
  >


<!ELEMENT ADDRESS - - (%inline;)* -- information on author -->
<!ATTLIST ADDRESS
  %attrs;                              -- %coreattrs, %i18n, %events --
```

```
  >

<!ELEMENT DIV - - (%flow;)*            -- generic language/style container -->
<!ATTLIST DIV
  %attrs;                              -- %coreattrs, %i18n, %events --
  %reserved;                           -- reserved for possible future use --
  >



<!--================== The Anchor Element ===============================-->

<!ENTITY % Shape "(rect|circle|poly|default)">
<!ENTITY % Coords "CDATA" -- comma-separated list of lengths -->

<!ELEMENT A - - (%inline;)* -(A)       -- anchor -->
<!ATTLIST A
  %attrs;                              -- %coreattrs, %i18n, %events --
  charset     %Charset;      #IMPLIED  -- char encoding of linked resource --
  type        %ContentType;  #IMPLIED  -- advisory content type --
  name        CDATA          #IMPLIED  -- named link end --
  href        %URI;          #IMPLIED  -- URI for linked resource --
  hreflang    %LanguageCode; #IMPLIED  -- language code --
  rel         %LinkTypes;    #IMPLIED  -- forward link types --
  rev         %LinkTypes;    #IMPLIED  -- reverse link types --
  accesskey   %Character;    #IMPLIED  -- accessibility key character --
  shape       %Shape;        rect      -- for use with client-side
                                          image maps --
  coords      %Coords;       #IMPLIED  -- for use with client-side
                                           image maps --
  tabindex    NUMBER         #IMPLIED  -- position in tabbing order --
  onfocus     %Script;       #IMPLIED  -- the element got the focus --
  onblur      %Script;       #IMPLIED  -- the element lost the focus --
  >

<!--================== Client-side image maps ============================-->

<!-- These can be placed in the same document or grouped in a
     separate document although this isn''t yet widely supported -->

<!ELEMENT MAP - - ((%block;) | AREA)+ -- client-side image map -->
<!ATTLIST MAP
  %attrs;                              -- %coreattrs, %i18n, %events --
  name        CDATA          #REQUIRED -- for reference by usemap --
```

```
  >

<!ELEMENT AREA - O EMPTY             -- client-side image map area -->
<!ATTLIST AREA
  %attrs;                              -- %coreattrs, %i18n, %events --
  shape       %Shape;      rect       -- controls interpretation of coords --
  coords      %Coords;     #IMPLIED   -- comma-separated list of lengths --
  href        %URI;        #IMPLIED   -- URI for linked resource --
  nohref      (nohref)     #IMPLIED   -- this region has no action --
  alt         %Text;       #REQUIRED  -- short description --
  tabindex    NUMBER       #IMPLIED   -- position in tabbing order --
  accesskey   %Character;  #IMPLIED   -- accessibility key character --
  onfocus     %Script;     #IMPLIED   -- the element got the focus --
  onblur      %Script;     #IMPLIED   -- the element lost the focus --
  >


<!--=================== The LINK Element =====================================-->


<!--
  Relationship values can be used in principle:

    a) for document specific toolbars/menus when used
       with the LINK element in document head e.g.
         start, contents, previous, next, index, end, help
    b) to link to a separate style sheet (rel=stylesheet)
    c) to make a link to a script (rel=script)
    d) by stylesheets to control how collections of
       html nodes are rendered into printed documents
    e) to make a link to a printable version of this document
       e.g. a postscript or pdf version (rel=alternate media=print)
-->

<!ELEMENT LINK - O EMPTY             -- a media-independent link -->
<!ATTLIST LINK
  %attrs;                              -- %coreattrs, %i18n, %events --
  charset     %Charset;     #IMPLIED   -- char encoding of linked resource --
  href        %URI;         #IMPLIED   -- URI for linked resource --
  hreflang    %LanguageCode; #IMPLIED  -- language code --
  type        %ContentType; #IMPLIED   -- advisory content type --
  rel         %LinkTypes;   #IMPLIED   -- forward link types --
  rev         %LinkTypes;   #IMPLIED   -- reverse link types --
  media       %MediaDesc;   #IMPLIED   -- for rendering on these media --
  >


<!--=================== Images =====================================-->
```

```
<!-- Length defined in strict DTD for cellpadding/cellspacing -->
<!ENTITY % Length "CDATA" -- nn for pixels or nn% for percentage length -->
<!ENTITY % MultiLength "CDATA" -- pixel, percentage, or relative -->

<![ %HTML.Frameset; [
<!ENTITY % MultiLengths "CDATA" -- comma-separated list of MultiLength -->
]]>

<!ENTITY % Pixels "CDATA" -- integer representing length in pixels -->


<!-- To avoid problems with text-only UAs as well as
     to make image content understandable and navigable
     to users of non-visual UAs, you need to provide
     a description with ALT, and avoid server-side image maps -->
<!ELEMENT IMG - O EMPTY                  -- Embedded image -->
<!ATTLIST IMG
  %attrs;                                -- %coreattrs, %i18n, %events --
  src         %URI;         #REQUIRED -- URI of image to embed --
  alt         %Text;        #REQUIRED -- short description --
  longdesc    %URI;         #IMPLIED  -- link to long description
                                         (complements alt) --
  name        CDATA         #IMPLIED  -- name of image for scripting --
  height      %Length;      #IMPLIED  -- override height --
  width       %Length;      #IMPLIED  -- override width --
  usemap      %URI;         #IMPLIED  -- use client-side image map --
  ismap       (ismap)       #IMPLIED  -- use server-side image map --
  >

<!-- USEMAP points to a MAP element which may be in this document
     or an external document, although the latter is not widely supported -->

<!--==================== OBJECT =======================================-->

<!--
  OBJECT is used to embed objects as part of HTML pages
  PARAM elements should precede other content. SGML mixed content
  model technicality precludes specifying this formally ...
-->

<!ELEMENT OBJECT - - (PARAM | %flow;)*
 -- generic embedded object -->
<!ATTLIST OBJECT
  %attrs;                                  -- %coreattrs, %i18n, %events --
  declare     (declare)     #IMPLIED  -- declare but don''t instantiate
flag --
```

```
   classid      %URI;           #IMPLIED  -- identifies an implementation --
   codebase     %URI;           #IMPLIED  -- base URI for classid, data, archive--
   data         %URI;           #IMPLIED  -- reference to object''s data --
   type         %ContentType;   #IMPLIED  -- content type for data --
   codetype     %ContentType;   #IMPLIED  -- content type for code --
   archive      CDATA           #IMPLIED  -- space-separated list of URIs --
   standby      %Text;          #IMPLIED  -- message to show while loading --
   height       %Length;        #IMPLIED  -- override height --
   width        %Length;        #IMPLIED  -- override width --
   usemap       %URI;           #IMPLIED  -- use client-side image map --
   name         CDATA           #IMPLIED  -- submit as part of form --
   tabindex     NUMBER          #IMPLIED  -- position in tabbing order --
   %reserved;                             -- reserved for possible future use --
   >

<!ELEMENT PARAM - O EMPTY           -- named property value -->
<!ATTLIST PARAM
   id           ID              #IMPLIED  -- document-wide unique id --
   name         CDATA           #REQUIRED -- property name --
   value        CDATA           #IMPLIED  -- property value --
   valuetype    (DATA|REF|OBJECT) DATA    -- How to interpret value --
   type         %ContentType;   #IMPLIED  -- content type for value
                                             when valuetype=ref --
   >

<!--================== Horizontal Rule ====================================-->

<!ELEMENT HR - O EMPTY -- horizontal rule -->
<!ATTLIST HR
   %attrs;                              -- %coreattrs, %i18n, %events --
   >

<!--================== Paragraphs =========================================-->

<!ELEMENT P - O (%inline;)*          -- paragraph -->
<!ATTLIST P
   %attrs;                              -- %coreattrs, %i18n, %events --
   >

<!--================== Headings ===========================================-->

<!--
  There are six levels of headings from H1 (the most important)
  to H6 (the least important).
-->
```

```
<!ELEMENT (%heading;)  - - (%inline;)* -- heading -->
<!ATTLIST (%heading;)
  %attrs;                              -- %coreattrs, %i18n, %events --
  >


<!--==================== Preformatted Text ================================-->

<!-- excludes markup for images and changes in font size -->
<!ENTITY % pre.exclusion "IMG|OBJECT|BIG|SMALL|SUB|SUP">

<!ELEMENT PRE - - (%inline;)* -(%pre.exclusion;) -- preformatted text -->
<!ATTLIST PRE
  %attrs;                              -- %coreattrs, %i18n, %events --
  >


<!--==================== Inline Quotes ==================================-->

<!ELEMENT Q - - (%inline;)*           -- short inline quotation -->
<!ATTLIST Q
  %attrs;                              -- %coreattrs, %i18n, %events --
  cite        %URI;         #IMPLIED   -- URI for source document or msg --
  >


<!--================== Block-like Quotes ==============================-->

<!ELEMENT BLOCKQUOTE - - (%block;|SCRIPT)+ -- long quotation -->
<!ATTLIST BLOCKQUOTE
  %attrs;                              -- %coreattrs, %i18n, %events --
  cite        %URI;         #IMPLIED   -- URI for source document or msg --
  >


<!--==================== Inserted/Deleted Text ============================-->


<!-- INS/DEL are handled by inclusion on BODY -->
<!ELEMENT (INS|DEL) - - (%flow;)*       -- inserted text, deleted text -->
<!ATTLIST (INS|DEL)
  %attrs;                              -- %coreattrs, %i18n, %events --
  cite        %URI;         #IMPLIED   -- info on reason for change --
  datetime    %Datetime;    #IMPLIED   -- date and time of change --
  >


<!--==================== Lists ============================================-->

<!-- definition lists - DT for term, DD for its definition -->
```

```
<!ELEMENT DL - - (DT|DD)+              -- definition list -->
<!ATTLIST DL
  %attrs;                             -- %coreattrs, %i18n, %events --
  >


<!ELEMENT DT - O (%inline;)*          -- definition term -->
<!ELEMENT DD - O (%flow;)*            -- definition description -->
<!ATTLIST (DT|DD)
  %attrs;                             -- %coreattrs, %i18n, %events --
  >



<!ELEMENT OL - - (LI)+                -- ordered list -->
<!ATTLIST OL
  %attrs;                             -- %coreattrs, %i18n, %events --
  >


<!-- Unordered Lists (UL) bullet styles -->
<!ELEMENT UL - - (LI)+                -- unordered list -->
<!ATTLIST UL
  %attrs;                             -- %coreattrs, %i18n, %events --
  >



<!ELEMENT LI - O (%flow;)*            -- list item -->
<!ATTLIST LI
  %attrs;                             -- %coreattrs, %i18n, %events --
  >


<!--=============== Forms =============================================-->
<!ELEMENT FORM - - (%block;|SCRIPT)+ -(FORM) -- interactive form -->
<!ATTLIST FORM
  %attrs;                             -- %coreattrs, %i18n, %events --
  action        %URI;          #REQUIRED -- server-side form handler --
  method        (GET|POST)     GET       -- HTTP method used to submit the form--
  enctype       %ContentType;  "application/x-www-form-urlencoded"
  accept        %ContentTypes; #IMPLIED  -- list of MIME types for file upload --
  name          CDATA          #IMPLIED  -- name of form for scripting --
  onsubmit      %Script;       #IMPLIED  -- the form was submitted --
  onreset       %Script;       #IMPLIED  -- the form was reset --
  accept-charset %Charsets;    #IMPLIED  -- list of supported charsets --
  >


<!-- Each label must not contain more than ONE field -->
```

```
<!ELEMENT LABEL - - (%inline;)* -(LABEL) -- form field label text -->
<!ATTLIST LABEL
  %attrs;                             -- %coreattrs, %i18n, %events --
  for           IDREF       #IMPLIED -- matches field ID value --
  accesskey     %Character; #IMPLIED -- accessibility key character --
  onfocus       %Script;    #IMPLIED -- the element got the focus --
  onblur        %Script;    #IMPLIED -- the element lost the focus --
  >

<!ENTITY % InputType
  "(TEXT | PASSWORD | CHECKBOX |
    RADIO | SUBMIT | RESET |
    FILE | HIDDEN | IMAGE | BUTTON)"
   >

<!-- attribute name required for all but submit and reset -->
<!ELEMENT INPUT - O EMPTY            -- form control -->
<!ATTLIST INPUT
  %attrs;                             -- %coreattrs, %i18n, %events --
  type          %InputType; TEXT     -- what kind of widget is needed --
  name          CDATA       #IMPLIED -- submit as part of form --
  value         CDATA       #IMPLIED -- Specify for radio buttons and checkboxes --
  checked       (checked)   #IMPLIED -- for radio buttons and check boxes --
  disabled      (disabled)  #IMPLIED -- unavailable in this context --
  readonly      (readonly)  #IMPLIED -- for text and passwd --
  size          CDATA       #IMPLIED -- specific to each type of field --
  maxlength     NUMBER      #IMPLIED -- max chars for text fields --
  src           %URI;       #IMPLIED -- for fields with images --
  alt           CDATA       #IMPLIED -- short description --

  usemap        %URI;       #IMPLIED -- use client-side image map --
  ismap         (ismap)     #IMPLIED -- use server-side image map --
  tabindex      NUMBER      #IMPLIED -- position in tabbing order --
  accesskey     %Character; #IMPLIED -- accessibility key character --
  onfocus       %Script;    #IMPLIED -- the element got the focus --
  onblur        %Script;    #IMPLIED -- the element lost the focus --
  onselect      %Script;    #IMPLIED -- some text was selected --
  onchange      %Script;    #IMPLIED -- the element value was changed --
  accept        %ContentTypes; #IMPLIED -- list of MIME types for file upload --
  %reserved;                          -- reserved for possible future use --
  >

<!ELEMENT SELECT - - (OPTGROUP|OPTION)+ -- option selector -->
```

```
<!ATTLIST SELECT
  %attrs;                               -- %coreattrs, %i18n, %events --
  name          CDATA       #IMPLIED    -- field name --
  size          NUMBER      #IMPLIED    -- rows visible --
  multiple      (multiple)  #IMPLIED    -- default is single selection --
  disabled      (disabled)  #IMPLIED    -- unavailable in this context --
  tabindex      NUMBER      #IMPLIED    -- position in tabbing order --
  onfocus       %Script;    #IMPLIED    -- the element got the focus --
  onblur        %Script;    #IMPLIED    -- the element lost the focus --
  onchange      %Script;    #IMPLIED    -- the element value was changed --
  %reserved;                            -- reserved for possible future use --
  >

<!ELEMENT OPTGROUP - - (OPTION)+ -- option group -->
<!ATTLIST OPTGROUP
  %attrs;                               -- %coreattrs, %i18n, %events --
  disabled      (disabled)  #IMPLIED    -- unavailable in this context --
  label         %Text;      #REQUIRED   -- for use in hierarchical menus --
  >

<!ELEMENT OPTION - O (#PCDATA)          -- selectable choice -->
<!ATTLIST OPTION
  %attrs;                               -- %coreattrs, %i18n, %events --
  selected      (selected)  #IMPLIED
  disabled      (disabled)  #IMPLIED    -- unavailable in this context --
  label         %Text;      #IMPLIED    -- for use in hierarchical menus --
  value         CDATA       #IMPLIED    -- defaults to element content --
  >

<!ELEMENT TEXTAREA - - (#PCDATA)        -- multi-line text field -->
<!ATTLIST TEXTAREA
  %attrs;                               -- %coreattrs, %i18n, %events --
  name          CDATA       #IMPLIED
  rows          NUMBER      #REQUIRED
  cols          NUMBER      #REQUIRED
  disabled      (disabled)  #IMPLIED    -- unavailable in this context --
  readonly      (readonly)  #IMPLIED
  tabindex      NUMBER      #IMPLIED    -- position in tabbing order --
  accesskey     %Character; #IMPLIED    -- accessibility key character --
  onfocus       %Script;    #IMPLIED    -- the element got the focus --
  onblur        %Script;    #IMPLIED    -- the element lost the focus --
  onselect      %Script;    #IMPLIED    -- some text was selected --
  onchange      %Script;    #IMPLIED    -- the element value was changed --
  %reserved;                            -- reserved for possible future use --
  >
```

```
<!--
  #PCDATA is to solve the mixed content problem,
  per specification only whitespace is allowed there!
  -->
<!ELEMENT FIELDSET - - (#PCDATA,LEGEND,(%flow;)*) -- form control group -->
<!ATTLIST FIELDSET
  %attrs;                            -- %coreattrs, %i18n, %events --
  >


<!ELEMENT LEGEND - - (%inline;)*       -- fieldset legend -->

<!ATTLIST LEGEND
  %attrs;                            -- %coreattrs, %i18n, %events --
  accesskey   %Character;   #IMPLIED -- accessibility key character --
  >


<!ELEMENT BUTTON - -
     (%flow;)* -(A|%formctrl;|FORM|FIELDSET)
     -- push button -->
<!ATTLIST BUTTON
  %attrs;                            -- %coreattrs, %i18n, %events --
  name        CDATA         #IMPLIED
  value       CDATA         #IMPLIED -- sent to server when submitted --
  type        (button|submit|reset) submit -- for use as form button --
  disabled    (disabled)    #IMPLIED -- unavailable in this context --
  tabindex    NUMBER        #IMPLIED -- position in tabbing order --
  accesskey   %Character;   #IMPLIED -- accessibility key character --
  onfocus     %Script;      #IMPLIED -- the element got the focus --
  onblur      %Script;      #IMPLIED -- the element lost the focus --
  %reserved;                         -- reserved for possible future use --
  >


<!--======================= Tables =======================================-->

<!-- IETF HTML table standard, see [RFC1942] -->

<!--
  The BORDER attribute sets the thickness of the frame around the
  table. The default units are screen pixels.

  The FRAME attribute specifies which parts of the frame around
  the table should be rendered. The values are not the same as
  CALS to avoid a name clash with the VALIGN attribute.

  The value "border" is included for backwards compatibility with
```

```
<TABLE BORDER> which yields frame=border and border=implied
For <TABLE BORDER=1> you get border=1 and frame=implied. In this
case, it is appropriate to treat this as frame=border for backward
compatibility with deployed browsers.
-->
<!ENTITY % TFrame "(void|above|below|hsides|lhs|rhs|vsides|box|border)">


<!--
The RULES attribute defines which rules to draw between cells:

 If RULES is absent then assume:
      "none" if BORDER is absent or BORDER=0 otherwise "all"
-->


<!ENTITY % TRules "(none | groups | rows | cols | all)">

<!-- horizontal placement of table relative to document -->
<!ENTITY % TAlign "(left|center|right)">

<!-- horizontal alignment attributes for cell contents -->
<!ENTITY % cellhalign
   "align       (left|center|right|justify|char) #IMPLIED
    char        %Character;      #IMPLIED -- alignment char, e.g. char=':' --
    charoff     %Length;         #IMPLIED -- offset for alignment char --"
   >

<!-- vertical alignment attributes for cell contents -->
<!ENTITY % cellvalign
   "valign      (top|middle|bottom|baseline) #IMPLIED"
   >

<!ELEMENT TABLE - -
      (CAPTION?, (COL*|COLGROUP*), THEAD?, TFOOT?, TBODY+)>
<!ELEMENT CAPTION  - - (%inline;)*      -- table caption -->
<!ELEMENT THEAD    - O (TR)+            -- table header -->
<!ELEMENT TFOOT    - O (TR)+            -- table footer -->
<!ELEMENT TBODY    O O (TR)+            -- table body -->
<!ELEMENT COLGROUP - O (COL)*           -- table column group -->
<!ELEMENT COL      - O EMPTY            -- table column -->
<!ELEMENT TR       - O (TH|TD)+         -- table row -->
<!ELEMENT (TH|TD)  - O (%flow;)*        -- table header cell, table data cell-->

<!ATTLIST TABLE                         -- table element --
  %attrs;                               -- %coreattrs, %i18n, %events --
   summary     %Text;         #IMPLIED -- purpose/structure for speech output--
```

```
  width         %Length;      #IMPLIED  -- table width --
  border        %Pixels;      #IMPLIED  -- controls frame width around table --
  frame         %TFrame;      #IMPLIED  -- which parts of frame to render --
  rules         %TRules;      #IMPLIED  -- rulings between rows and cols --
  cellspacing   %Length;      #IMPLIED  -- spacing between cells --
  cellpadding   %Length;      #IMPLIED  -- spacing within cells --
  %reserved;                            -- reserved for possible future use --
  datapagesize  CDATA         #IMPLIED  -- reserved for possible future use --
  >


<!ATTLIST CAPTION
  %attrs;                               -- %coreattrs, %i18n, %events --
  >


<!--
COLGROUP groups a set of COL elements. It allows you to group
several semantically related columns together.
-->
<!ATTLIST COLGROUP
  %attrs;                               -- %coreattrs, %i18n, %events --
  span          NUMBER        1         -- default number of columns in group --
  width         %MultiLength; #IMPLIED  -- default width for enclosed COLs --
  %cellhalign;                          -- horizontal alignment in cells --
  %cellvalign;                          -- vertical alignment in cells --
  >


<!--
COL elements define the alignment properties for cells in
one or more columns.

The WIDTH attribute specifies the width of the columns, e.g.

    width=64        width in screen pixels
    width=0.5*      relative width of 0.5

The SPAN attribute causes the attributes of one
COL element to apply to more than one column.
-->
<!ATTLIST COL                           -- column groups and properties --
  %attrs;                               -- %coreattrs, %i18n, %events --
  span          NUMBER        1         -- COL attributes affect N columns --
  width         %MultiLength; #IMPLIED  -- column width specification --
```

```
    %cellhalign;                           -- horizontal alignment in cells --
    %cellvalign;                           -- vertical alignment in cells --
    >


<!--
      Use THEAD to duplicate headers when breaking table
      across page boundaries, or for static headers when
      TBODY sections are rendered in scrolling panel.

      Use TFOOT to duplicate footers when breaking table
      across page boundaries, or for static footers when
      TBODY sections are rendered in scrolling panel.

      Use multiple TBODY sections when rules are needed
      between groups of table rows.
-->
<!ATTLIST (THEAD|TBODY|TFOOT)              -- table section --
    %attrs;                                -- %coreattrs, %i18n, %events --
    %cellhalign;                           -- horizontal alignment in cells --
    %cellvalign;                           -- vertical alignment in cells --
    >

<!ATTLIST TR                               -- table row --
    %attrs;                                -- %coreattrs, %i18n, %events --
    %cellhalign;                           -- horizontal alignment in cells --
    %cellvalign;                           -- vertical alignment in cells --
    >


<!-- Scope is simpler than headers attribute for common tables -->
<!ENTITY % Scope "(row|col|rowgroup|colgroup)">

<!-- TH is for headers, TD for data, but for cells acting as both use TD -->
<!ATTLIST (TH|TD)                          -- header or data cell --
    %attrs;                                -- %coreattrs, %i18n, %events --
    abbr        %Text;          #IMPLIED   -- abbreviation for header cell --
    axis        CDATA           #IMPLIED   -- comma-separated list of related
heade
rs--
    headers     IDREFS          #IMPLIED   -- list of id''s for header cells --
    scope       %Scope;         #IMPLIED   -- scope covered by header cells --
    rowspan     NUMBER          1          -- number of rows spanned by cell --
    colspan     NUMBER          1          -- number of cols spanned by cell --
    %cellhalign;                           -- horizontal alignment in cells --
    %cellvalign;                           -- vertical alignment in cells --
    >
```

```
<!--================ Document Head ========================================-->

<!-- %head.misc; defined earlier on as "SCRIPT|STYLE|META|LINK|OBJECT" -->
<!ENTITY % head.content "TITLE & BASE?">

<!ELEMENT HEAD O O (%head.content;) +(%head.misc;) -- document head -->
<!ATTLIST HEAD
  %i18n;                             -- lang, dir --
  profile      %URI;        #IMPLIED -- named dictionary of meta info --
  >

<!-- The TITLE element is not considered part of the flow of text.
       It should be displayed, for example as the page header or
       window title. Exactly one title is required per document.
   -->
<!ELEMENT TITLE - - (#PCDATA) -(%head.misc;) -- document title -->
<!ATTLIST TITLE %i18n>


<!ELEMENT BASE - O EMPTY               -- document base URI -->
<!ATTLIST BASE
  href           %URI;        #REQUIRED -- URI that acts as base URI --
  >

<!ELEMENT META - O EMPTY               -- generic metainformation -->
<!ATTLIST META
  %i18n;                               -- lang, dir, for use with content --
  http-equiv  NAME         #IMPLIED -- HTTP response header name  --
  name        NAME         #IMPLIED -- metainformation name --
  content     CDATA        #REQUIRED -- associated information --
  scheme      CDATA        #IMPLIED -- select form of content --
  >

<!ELEMENT STYLE - - %StyleSheet        -- style info -->
<!ATTLIST STYLE
  %i18n;                               -- lang, dir, for use with title --
  type        %ContentType; #REQUIRED -- content type of style language --
  media       %MediaDesc;   #IMPLIED -- designed for use with these media --
  title       %Text;        #IMPLIED -- advisory title --
  >

<!ELEMENT SCRIPT - - %Script;          -- script statements -->
<!ATTLIST SCRIPT
  charset     %Charset;     #IMPLIED -- char encoding of linked resource --
```

```
    type         %ContentType;   #REQUIRED -- content type of script language --
    src          %URI;           #IMPLIED  -- URI for an external script --
    defer        (defer)         #IMPLIED  -- UA may defer execution of script --
    event        CDATA           #IMPLIED  -- reserved for possible future use --
    for          %URI;           #IMPLIED  -- reserved for possible future use --
    >


<!ELEMENT NOSCRIPT - - (%block;)+
    -- alternate content container for non script-based rendering -->
<!ATTLIST NOSCRIPT
    %attrs;                                 -- %coreattrs, %i18n, %events --
    >


<!--================ Document Structure ====================================-->
<!ENTITY % html.content "HEAD, BODY">


<!ELEMENT HTML O O (%html.content;)     -- document root element -->
<!ATTLIST HTML
    %i18n;                                  -- lang, dir --
    >
```

HTML 4.0 Frameset DTD

```
<!--

    This is the HTML 4.01 Frameset DTD, which should be
    used for documents with frames. This DTD is identical
    to the HTML 4.01 Transitional DTD except for the
    content model of the "HTML" element: in frameset
    documents, the "FRAMESET" element replaces the "BODY"
    element.

        Draft: $Date: 1999/12/24 23:37:46 $

        Authors:
            Dave Raggett <dsr@w3.org>
            Arnaud Le Hors <lehors@w3.org>
            Ian Jacobs <ij@w3.org>

    Further information about HTML 4.01 is available at:

        http://www.w3.org/TR/1999/REC-html401-19991224.
-->
```

```
<!ENTITY % HTML.Version "-//W3C//DTD HTML 4.01 Frameset//EN"
  -- Typical usage:

    <!DOCTYPE HTML PUBLIC "-//W3C//DTD HTML 4.01 Frameset//EN"
            "http://www.w3.org/TR/html4/frameset.dtd">
    <html>
    <head>
    ...
    </head>
    <frameset>
    ...
    </frameset>
    </html>
-->

<!ENTITY % HTML.Frameset "INCLUDE">
<!ENTITY % HTML4.dtd PUBLIC "-//W3C//DTD HTML 4.01 Transitional//EN">
%HTML4.dtd;
```

Index